Vicassan's
PILIPINO-ENGLISH
DICTIONARY
Abridged Edition

ANVIL

MANILA

Vicassan's Pilipino-English Dictionary (Abridged Edition)

Copyright by ARACELI SANTOS, 2006

Published and exclusively distributed by
ANVIL PUBLISHING INC.
8007-B Pioneer St., Brgy. Kapitolyo, Pasig City 1603 Philippines
Sales & Marketing: 637-5141; 637-3621; 747-1622; 747-1624;
marketing@anvilpublishing.com
Fax: 637-6084
URL: www.anvilpublishing.com

Cover design by GERRY BACLAGON

First printing, 2006

ISBN 971-27-1707-0

Printed in the Philippines by
Cacho Hermanos Inc.

SOME OF THE SALIENT FEATURES OF THIS DICTIONARY

I. Entries

(a) Arrangement of Entries

All entries in this Dictionary are listed strictly following the Pilipino alphabetical system. They are all set in large, boldface type.

No run-on entries are given - only main entries - in order to facilitate the location of a word or words, especially by non-Pilipino users. For example, *pag-ibig* is entered under P and not under the root *ibig*. This is particularly helpful to those who cannot readily recognize or trace the roots of even common derivatives.

(b) Syllabication and Pronunciation

All entries are divided into syllables, a new innovation not yet utilized in any Tagalog or Pilipino dictionary at present. This is important to writers, typists, typesetters and linotypists who often make mistakes in dividing words especially at the ends of lines. It is not uncommon, especially to proofreaders, to see such errors committed again and again. AKOMPANYA, for example, is syllabicated *ak-om-pa-nya* instead of *a-kom-pan-ya*.

Stresses and accents are indicated as guides to pronunciation. If an entry has a variant pronunciation, this is also indicated in the syllabication or just following it.

(c) Variants

Where an entry has a variant or variants in spelling, this is usually indicated immediately following the syllabication:

abyerta (ab-yer-ta), var. **abiyerta**, I. *adj.* (Sp. *abierta*) . . .

Variants are also listed as separate entries with or without definitions for the purpose of cross references:

abiyerta (a-bi-yer-ta): var. of **abyerta**, which see.

II. Parts of Speech

All solid and hyphenated entries are provided with part-of-speech labels. Where an entry has two or more parts of speech, these are indicated by Roman numerals, the first following the syllabication or after an indicated variant, if there is any; the second and succeeding parts of speech start separately at the beginning of the following line, preceded with a dash (-) and followed by the corresponding Roman numerals and the part-of-speech labels. See **abyerta**.

All part-of-speech labels appear in abbreviated form and in light italic type.

adj. (adjective)

adv. (adverb)

aux. v. (auxiliary verb)

conj. (conjuction)

interj. (interjection)

n . (noun)

prep. (preposition)

pron. (pronoun)

III. Etymology

The etymologies of Tagalog entries, whether roots or derivatives, have been deliberately omitted, but those of loan words are usually indicated, following the part-of-speech label. See **abyerta**.

A loan-word entry, if spelled in the same way as the original, is usually labelled with the abbreviation of the language from which it is derived: **adelanto** (a-de-lan-to), *n.* (*Sp.*) . . . . ; but if the word is spelled differently, the original spelling is given, together with the language label of origin: **abesedaryo** (a-be-se-dar-yo), *n.* (Sp. *abecedario*) . . . .

To save space, the etymological label is not indicated when a particular entry is a combination of a foreign word and a Tagalog affix or affixes: **abogaduhin** (a-bo-ga-du-hin, *v.*).

IV. Definitions and Numbering of Meanings

Each entry is given a meaning or meanings. If the meanings or meanings of an entry cannot be translated individually with a single English word, or if such a word is not readily available to the author, said meaning or meanings are defined in his own words. See **pasma**.

Meanings are numbered consecutively under any given part of speech in Arabic numerals. Numbering is started anew for each succeeding parts of speech.

V. Synonyms, antonyms, comparisons, etc.

Synonyms, antonyms, comparisons, etc. are indicated (Syn.), (Ant.), (Cf.), etc. respectively, usually following each meaning definition. Where a synonym, antonym, or *confer* is applicable to two or more meanings of a word, it is usually given at the end of the last meaning, with the notation "(for senses 1 and 2, 2-4, 2 and 4, etc.)," or "(for both *n.* and *adj.*)," etc.. as the case may be.

VI. Usage and Illustrative Examples

A usage label usually precedes a given definition. See **aberasyón.**

Slang, colloquialism, provincialism, and the like, are indicated (*Sl.*). (*Colloq.*), (*Prov.*), etc. Likewise, technical, scientific and academic usages are similarly indicated: (*Med.*) for medicine or medical, (*Bot.*) for botany, (*Gram.*) for grammar, (*Ling.*) for linguistics, etc.

Generally, usage illustrative examples are not supplied, except in some instances where the clarification of the shades of meanings of a word has become necessary.

VII. Names of Plants and Animals

Pilipino names of plants and animals, esp. trees and fishes are entered in this Dictionary, usually with their scientific names included parenthetically in the definitions in English.

THE PILIPINO ALPHABET

(Abakada)

The orthographic system used in this Dictionary is the standard spelling based on the Pilipino alphabet, called *Abakada*, as promulgated in the *Balarila ng Wikang Pambansa*, the Pilipino National Language Grammar.

The old Pilipino alphabet is composed of only twenty Romanized letters:

A a	(*as a* in *combat*)	**N n**	(*na*; Sp. *ene*)
B b	(*ba*; Sp. *be*)	**NG ng**	(*nga*)
K k	(*ka*)	**O o**	(*as o* in *solo*)
D d	(*da*; Sp. *de*)	**P p**	(*pa*; Sp. *pe*)
E e	(*as e* in *best*)	**R r**	(*ra*; Sp. *ere*)
G g	(*ga*; Sp. *he*)	**S s**	(*sa*; Sp. *ese*)
H h	(*ha*; Sp. *atse*)	**T t**	(*ta*; Sp. *te*)
I i	(*as i* in *hit*)	**U u**	(*as u* in *buffalo*)
L l	(*la*; Sp. *ele*)	**W w**	(*wa*)
M m	(*ma*; Sp. *eme*)	**Y y**	(*ya*)

The revised Pilipino alphabet has 28 letters: A, B, C, D, E, F, G, H, I, J, K, L, M, N, Ñ, NG, O, P, Q, R, S, T, U, V, W, X, Y, Z. This dictionary, however, features the old Pilipino alphabet.

PARTS OF SPEECH

And Related Terms in Pilipino

gitlapì	*(gitl.)*	infix
hulapì	*(hulp.)*	suffix
pandamdám	*(pdm.)*	interjection
pandiwà	*(pd.)*	verb
panlapì	*(panl.)*	affix
pantukoy	*(pt.)*	article
pang-abay	*(pa.)*	adverb
pang-angkóp	*(pkp.)*	ligature
pangatníg	*(ptg.)*	conjunction
panghalíp	*(ph.)*	pronoun
pangngalan	*(png.)*	noun
pang-ukol	*(pkl.)*	preposition
pang-ugnáy	*(pugn.)*	connective
pang-urì	*(pu.)*	adjective
salitáng-ugát	*(s.u.)*	root word
unlapì	*(unl.)*	prefix

ABBREVIATIONS USED IN THIS DICTIONARY

Acc. (Accounting)
adj. (adjective)
adv. (adverb)
Aeron. (Aeronautics)
Agri. (Agriculture)
Alg. (Algebra)
Am. (American)
AmSp. (American Spanish)
Anat. (Anatomy)
Ant. (Antonym)
Anthrop. (Anthropology)
Ar. (Arabic)
Arch. (Architecture)
Arith. (Arithmetic)
art. (article)
AS (Anglo-Saxon)
Astrol. (Astrology; astrological)
Astron. (Astronomy)
Aug. (August)
aux. v. (auxiliary verb)
Bact. (Bacteriology)
Bats. (Batangas)
Bib. (Bible; Biblical)
Bik. (Bikol)
Biochem. (Biochemistry)
Bis. (Bisayan)
Bot. (Botany)
Brit. (British)
Cap. (Capital)
Carp. (Carpentry)
Cau. (Caucasian)
Cf. (Compare)
Ch. (Chinese)
Chem. (Chemistry)
Colloq. (Colloquial)
Comm. (Commercial)
conj. (conjunction)
contr. (Contraction; contracted)
Crust. (Crustacean)
cu. (cubic)
Dat. (Dative)
Dent. (Dentistry)

deriv. (derivative)
Dial. (Dialect)
Eccles. (Ecclesiastical)
Ecol. (Ecology)
Econ. (Economics)
Educ. (Education)
e.g. (for example)
Elec. (Electricity)
Eng. (English)
Engr. (Engineering)
Entom. (Entomology)
esp. (especially)
etc. (etcetera)
Ethnol. (Ethnology)
Etym. (Etymology)
Ex. (Example)
fem. (feminine)
Fig. (Figurative)
Fr. (French)
fr. (from)
ft. (feet)
fut. (future)
fut. t. (future tense)
gal. (gallon)
Gen. (General)
Geog. (Geography; geographical)
Geol. (Geology; geological)
Geom. (Geometry)
Ger. (German)
Goth. (Gothic)
Gov't. (Government)
Gr. (Greek)
Gram. (Grammar)
Gym. (Gymnastics)
Heb. (Hebrew)
Her. (Heraldry)
Hlg. (Hiligaynon)
Hort. (Horticulture)
Iban. (Ibanag)
Ichth. (Ichthyology;
     ichthyological)
Id. (Idiom)

Idiom. (Idiomatic)
IE. (Indo-European)
i.e. (that is)
If. (Ifugao)
Ilk. (Ilocano)
Ilok. (Ilokano)
in. (inch; inches)
incl. (including)
Indo. (Indonesia)
Inf. (Infix)
Infin. (Infinitive)
Intr. (Intransitive)
Interj. (Interjection)
irreg. (irregular)
It. (Italian)
Ivt. Ivatan)
Jan. (January)
Jap. (Japanese)
Jav. (Javanese)
Lab. (Laboratory)
Lang. (Language)
Lat. (Latin)
lb. (pound)
Ling. (Linguistics)
Lit. (Literature)
Mal. (Malay)
Mar. (Maranaw)
Masc. (Masculine)
Math. (Mathematics)
ME. (Middle English)
Mech. (Mechanics)
Med. (Medicine)
Meta. (Metallurgical)
Meteor. (Meteorology;
        meteorological)
Mex. (Mexican)
Mex.-Sp. (Mexican-Spanish)
Mgd. (Magindanaw)
mi. (mile)
Mil. (Military)
min. (minute)
Mus. (Music)
Myth. (Mythology; mythological)
n. (noun)
Naut. (Nautical)
Neut. (Neuter)

Nom. (Nominative)
Num. (Numbers)
Obs. (Obsolete)
Obstet. (Obstetrics)
Oct. (October)
Orig. (Original)
Oesteol. (Oesteological)
O.T. (Old Testament)
OTag. (Old Tagalog)
oz. (ounce)
p. (page)
part. (participle)
pass. (passive)
pers. (person)
Pharm. (Pharmaceutical)
Phil. (Philippines)
Philos. (Philosopy)
Phonet. (Phonetics)
Photog. (Photography)
phr. (phrase)
Phys. Ed. (Physical Education)
Physiol. (Physiology; physiological)
physiological)
Pil. (Pilipino)
Pl. (Plural)
Poet. (Poetic)
Poss. (Possessive)
pp. (pages)
p.p. (past participle)
Pref. (Prefix)
Prep. (Preposition)
pres. (present)
Print. (Printing)
Prob. (Probably)
Pron. (Pronoun)
Prov. (Provincialism)
Psychol. (Psychology;
          psychological)
pt.; p.t. (past tense)
qt. (quart; quarts)
q.v. (quod vide; which see)
Rad. (Radio)
Ref. (Referring)
Rhet. (Rhetorical)
Rev. (Reverent)
Rom. (Roman)

Russ. (Russian)
Rw. (Rootword)
Sans. (Sanskrit)
sing. (singular)
Sl. (Slang)
s.o. (said of)
Sociol. (Sociology; sociological)
Sp. (Spanish)
sp. (spelling)
specif. (specifically)
sq. (square)
Subj. (Subject; subjunctive)
Suff. (Suffix)
superl. (superlative)
Surg. (Surgical)
Syn. (Synonym; synonyms)
Tab. (Table)
Tag. (Tagalog)
Tech. (Techonology; technological)
Tel. (Telephone)
Theat. (Theatrical)
Theol. (Theology; theological)
Trans. (Transitive)
transla. (translation)
Trig. (Trigonometry)
typo. (typographical)
TV (television)
UN (United Nations)
v. (verb)
v. adj. (verbal adjective)
var. (variant)
Vet. (Veterinary)
vi. (intransitive verb)
v.n. (verbal noun)
vt. (transitive verb)
yd. (yard)
Zool. (Zoology)

A

A, a (pronounced like "a" in *car*), *n*. 1. the
first letter of the *abakada* (Pilipino
alphabet). 2. a type or impression
representing this letter. 3. a symbol for the
first in a group or sequence.

a (ä), *interj*. an exclamation expressing
delight, regret, disgust, surprise, etc., in
accordance with the manner of utterance,
more or less equivalent to "ah" or "oh."

áandáp-andáp (áan-dáp + an-dáp), *adj*. 1.
flickering; burning or shining unsteadily,
as the flame of a candle about to die out.
Syn. *pakuráp-kuráp, paandáp-andáp*. 2.
dying; hovering between life and death.
Syn. *naghihingalô, nagdidiliryo*. 3. almost
used up, consumed or exhausted, referring
to supply or stock of food, etc. Syn. *halos
ubós na; mauubos na*.

abá (a-bá), I. *interj*. 1. an exclamation
expressive of surprise, wonder, admiration,
disgust, etc., more or less similar to "oh."
Cf. *Nakú*! 2. Hail!, as in *Abá Mariang Ina
ng Diyós!* Hail! Mary Mother of God!
—II. *n*. 1. act of greeting or calling the
name or attention of someone, as in
meeting in the street. Cf. *batì, pagbatì*. 2. a
reminding or calling the attention of
someone about something. Syn. *inó, pag-
inó; banggít, pagbanggít*.

abâ (a-bâ), *adj*. 1. poor; indigent; needy;
destitute. Syn. *dukhâ, marálitâ, hiráp,
mahirap*. 2. humble; lowly; ordinary. Syn.
karaniwan, pangkaraniwan. 3. oppressed;
abused; maltreated. Syn. *apí, inápí, apí-
apíhan*. 4. unfortunate. Syn. *kaawá-awà,
waláng-kapalaran, waláng-suwerte*. 5. mean;
vulgar; despicable. Syn. *hamak*.

abaká (a-ba-ká, I. *n*. (Mex.-Sp. *abaca*) 1. the
abaca plant. 2. the fibers of this plant
known commercially as "Manila hemp."
—II. *adj*. abaca; of or made of abaca, as in
lubid na abaká, abaca rope.

abakada (a-ba-ka-da), *n*. the Pilipino
alphabet, derived from letters *a, b, k*, and
d (pronounced *ä, bä, kä*, and *dä*,
respectively). Syn. *alpabeto, abesedaryo*.

abaín (abaín,) *v*. 1. to despise. Syn. *hamakin*.

2. to oppress; maltreat. Syn. *apihín*.

abala (a-ba-la), *n*. 1. delay; a delaying or being
delayed. Syn. *atraso, pagkaatraso*. 2. that
which causes delay or impediment. Syn.
sagabal. 3. bother; disturbance or
interruption. Syn. *istorbo*. 4. act of causing
delay, disturbance, or interruption. Syn.
pag-atraso, pag-abala. 5. occupation;
preoccupation. Syn. *trabaho, gawain*. 6.
(*Colloq*.) act of borrowing something from
someone. Syn. *hirám, paghirám*

abalá (a-ba-lá), *adj*. 1. delayed; late; behind
in time or schedule. Syn. *atrasado, huli*. 2.
busy; occupied; preoccupied. Syn.
matrabaho, magawain; maraming trabaho. 3.
interrupted; disturbed; bothered. Syn. *di-
makatrabaho*.

abaloryo (a-ba-lor-yo), *n*. (Sp. *abalorio*) 1.
glass bead. Syn. *manik*. 2. any kind of bead
work.

abandoná (a-ban-do-ná), *n*. (Sp. *v*.
abandonar) an abandoning or being
abandoned.

abaniko (a-ba-ni-ko), *n*. (Sp. *abanico*) 1.
folding fan. Syn. *pamaypay*. 2. (*Bot*.) a kind
of ornamental plant called 'black berry-lily'
(*Ixia chinensis* Linn.). Cf. *palmá, palmera*.

abante (a-ban-te), 1. *n*. (*Sp*.) 1. act of moving
or going forward; advance. Syn. *sulong,
lakad, tulóy*. 2. advantage (in score); a point
or points in excess of the opponent's score.
Syn. *lamáng, kalamangan; higít, kahigtán*. 2.
progress; development; advance. Syn.
unlád, pag-unlád; progreso. 4. sufficiency, as
of supply or stock, up to a certain period
of time. Syn. *kahustuhán, kasapatán*. ·
—II. *adj*. 1. leading or ahead (in score,
votes, etc.); in favor; winning. Syn. *lamáng,
nakalálamáng* 2. sufficient or enough to last
up to a certain period of time. Syn. *sapát,
kasya, husto, bastante*. 3. forward (opposed
to backward). Syn. *pasulóng*.
—III *v*. (*imper*.) forward; advance; go or
move ahead. Syn. *sulong, sige, lakad*.
—IV. *interj*. Advance! Forward!

abáng (a-báng), *n*. 1. act of waiting or
watching for a person or thing to appear
or pass by. Cf. *bantáy, pagbabantáy; hintáy,
paghihintáy*. 2. act of waiting for an
opportune time to strike, as in boxing. 3.

act of waylaying; a lying in wait. Syn. *abat,
pag-abat.* 4. act or manner of setting up a
trap or snare. Cf. *taan, pagtataan.* 5. a trap
or snare placed or set up strategically. 6. a
person or persons waiting or lying in wait
for someone or something. Syn. *tanod,
bantáy, guwardiyá.*

abasto (a-bas-to), *n.* (*Sp.*) 1. baggage. Syn.
*bagahe, karga, kargada, kargamento, dalá-
dalahan.* 2. supplies; provisions. Cf. *baon.*

abatan (a-ba-tan), *v.* 1. to ambush; waylay.
Syn. *harangin, tambangán.* 2. to intercept
in the way. Syn. *abangán.* 3. to keep watch
or be in the alert for. Syn. *alistuhán,
bantayán.*

abay (a-bay), *n.* 1. best man; groomsman.
Also *abay sa kasál.* 2. maid of honor;
bridesmaid. Syn. *dama* 3. consort. Syn.
konsorte. 4. escort; bodyguard. Syn. *tanod,
bantáy, guwardiyá.* 5. (*Colloq.*) pal; friend;
partner or companion. Syn. *katoto, bigan,
kaibigan.*

abayan (a-ba-yan), *v.* 1. to act or serve as a
best man for; be a maid of honor for. 2. to
act as a consort for. Syn. *konsortihán.*

abenida (a-be-ni-da), *n.* (*Sp. avenida*) a wide,
busy street; avenue. Cf. *kalye, kalsada.*

abentura (a-ben-tu-ra), *n.* (*Sp. aventura*) a
daring feat; adventure. Cf. *sápalarán,
pagkikipagsápalarán.*

abér (a-bér), I. *interj.* (Sp. *haber*) Let's see!
Go ahead! *Abér gawin mo ang gusto mo!*
Go ahead, do what you like. Syn. *Hala!
Sige!*
—II. *adv.* okay; all right.

abería (a-be-rí-a), var. **aberiya, aberyá,** *n.* (Sp.
averia) 1. mechanical defect or trouble.
Syn. *sirá, depekto.* 2. hitch; problem;
obstacle. Syn. *súliranán, problema.* 3. mental
disorder. Syn. *sirà ng isip, pag-kasirá-sirá.*

abilidád (a-bi-li-dád), *n.* (*Sp.*) 1. ability;
capacity for good work. Syn. *kakayahán.*
2. cunningness; tricky ingenuity. Syn.
katusuhan. 3. talent. Syn. *talino,
katalinuhan.*

abiso (a-bi-so), *n.* (Sp. *aviso*) 1. an informing;
notification. Syn. *pagbabalitá.* 2. notice;
announcement. Syn. *paunawà, patalastás,
balità, pahayag.* 3. warning; signal. Syn.
babalà. 4. sign; hint. Syn. *tandâ,*

palátandaan; hiwatig, pahiwatig; senyas.

ábitó (á-bi-tó), *n.* (Sp. *hábito*) cassock of a
priest or clergyman; habit. Cf. *damít,
kasuután.*

abitsuwelas (a-bit-su-we-las), *n.* (Sp.
habichuela) kidney bean.

abiyadór (a-bi-ya-dór), var. **abyadór,** *n.* (Sp.
aviador) aviator; airman; pilot; flier. Syn.
piloto, manlilipad.

abla (a-bla; a-blá), *n.* (Sp. *habla*) idle talk;
babble; senseless chatter. Syn. *daldál, satsát.*

abnormál (ab-nor-mál), *adj.* (*Sp.; Eng.*) not
typical; abnormal; not usual; irregular. Syn.
di-karaniwan; di-normál.

abó (a-bó), I. *n.* 1. ash; ashes. Syn. *titis, abók.*
2. thin dust. Syn. *alikabók.* 3. powder. Syn.
pulbós. 4. ash-like color; gray. Also *kulay-
abó.*
—II. *adj.* 1. reduced to ashes. Syn. *tupók,
sunóg na sunóg.* 2. pulverized. 3. gray; ash-
colored.

abók (a-bók), *n.* 1. dust. Syn. *alikabók.* 2.
ashes; cinders. Syn. *abó, titis.* 3. powder.
Syn. *pulbós.*

abokado (a-bo-ka-do), var. **abukado,** *n.* (Eng.
avocado; Mex.-Sp. *avogato*) 1. alligator
pear; avocado fruit. 2. the tree that bears
this fruit.

abóg (a-bóg), *n.* 1. hollow noise, as that
caused by a heavy object that fell on the
board floor. Cf. *kalabóg, kabóg.* 2. (*Colloq.*)
word, notice, or warning; usually used in
the negative: *waláng abóg,* without notice
or warning.

abogado (a-bo-ga-do), var. **abugado,** *n.* (*Sp.*)
lawyer; attorney. Syn. *mánananggól.*

abono (a-bo-no), *n.* (*Sp.*) 1. soil fertilizer. Syn.
patabâ (sa lupà). 2. act of advancing or
reimbursing money for another. Syn.
pagpapaluwál. 3'. amount of money paid or
reimbursed by someone for another. Syn.
paluwál. 4. money used to replace a loss or
shortage from a fund or capital. Syn. *palít,
kapalít.*

aborsiyón (a-bor-si-yón), var. **abursiyón,** *n.*
(Eng.) 1. deliberate abortion. Syn.
pagpapalaglág, pagpapaagas. 2. miscarriage.
Syn. *agas, pagkahulog, pagkalaglág.*

abot (a-bot), I. *adj.* 1. overtaken or can be
overtaken. 2. occurring continuously;

without letup; without interruption; continuous. Syn. *waláng-patíd, waláng-tigíl, tulúy-tulóy.* 3. having arrived on time, as for a certain occasion. Syn. *di-hulí.* 4. with or having each side or end touching each other, said of two things. Syn. *dikít, magkadikít; hugpóng, magkahugpóng.* 5. caught in the act of; caught red-handed. Syn. *huli sa akto; tutóp.*
—II. *n.* 1. act of overtaking or being overtaken. 2. a coming or arriving on time for an occasion. 3. continuous arrival of persons or things. 4. state or condition of having each side or end (of two things) touching each other. 5. state or fact of being caught red-handed. Syn. *huli, pagkahuli (sa akto).*

abót (a-bót), I. *adj.* 1. within one's reach; can be reached, referring to an object or to a distant place. Syn. *datíng, naratíng, maráratíng.* 2. with or having a range or length sufficient to reach a certain point or distance. 3. within the reach of one's hand. 4. sufficient or enough to meet the need up to a certain limit of time. Syn. *kasya, husto, sapát.* 5. that can be attained; attainable; within the reach of one's understanding or comprehension. Syn. *unawá, náuunawaan.*
—II. *n.* 1. act of handing over a thing to another. Cf. *bigáy, pagbigáy.* 2. act of receiving or accepting something with the hand. Cf. *tanggáp, pagtanggáp.* 3. act of getting something from its place by extending the hand. Syn. *dukwáng, pagdukwáng.* 4. extent of one's reach. 5. place or places a person has reached or able to reach. 6. mental capacity; educational attainment; extent of one's knowledge. Syn. *alam, nalalaman; pinag-aralan, napag-aralan; edukasyón.*

abot-agaw (a-bot + a-gaw), *adj.* 1. dying; hovering between life and death. Syn. *naghihingalô, nagdidiliryo.* 2. almost exhausted or used up, referring to supply or stock of food, etc. Syn. *abot-dilî.*

abot-kisáp (a-bot + ki-sáp), I. *adj.* winking continuously, referring to the eyes. Syn. *abot-kuráp.*
—II. *n.* rapid or continuous winking (of

the eyes).

abót-siko (a-bót + si-ko), I. *adj. & adv.* with the elbows held together tightly at the back.
—II. *n.* state or manner in which the elbows of a person are held together tightly at the back.

abót-sigáw (a-bót + si-gáw), *adj.* within the reach of one's shout; within shouting distance. Syn. *abot-hiyáw.*

abót-tanáw (a-bót + ta-náw), I. *adj.* within a distance visible to the eyes; can be seen from a far distance.
—II. *n.* 1. the farthest distance that the eyes can see. Syn. *abót-tingín.* 2. horizon.

abra (a-bra), *n. (Sp.)* 1. ravine. Syn. *bangín.* 2. (A-) name of a province in the Ilocos Region.

abrasadór (a-bra-sa-dór), *n. (Sp.)* leg pillow. Syn. *dantayan.*

abrasete (a-bra-se-te), *n. (Sp.)* act or manner of walking together arm-in-arm or with arms interlocked.

abrelata (a-bre-la-ta), var. **abrilata**, *n.* (Sp. *abrelatas*) can opener. Cf. *pambukás.*

Abríl (A-bríl), *n. (Sp.)* April, the fourth month of the year.

absolusyón (ab-so-lus-yón), var. **absulusyon**, *n.* (Sp. *absolución*) 1. a freeing from guilt; absolution, Syn. *pagpapapawaláng-sala.* 2. remission of sin; absolution. Syn. *pagpapatawad-kasalanan, kapatawaráng-kasalanan.*

abstinénsiyá (abs-ti-nén-si-yá), *n.* (Sp. *abstinencia*) abstinence; abstention. Syn. *pangingilin, pag-aayuno, kulasyón.*

absuwelto (ab-su-wel-to), I. *adj.* (Sp. *absuelto*) acquitted or absolved from guilt or charge. Syn. *pinawaláng-sala.*
—II. *n.* acquittal. Syn. *pagpapapawaláng-sala*

abuabo (a-bu-a-bo), var. **abu-abo**, *n.* mist; haze; drizzle. Syn. *Abong.*

abubot (a-bu-bot), var. **abobot**, *n.* 1. knick knacks; baubles; gewgaw; trinkets. 2. paraphernalia; personal belongings. Syn. *pansariling mga kagamitán.*

abúg-abóg (abúg + a-bóg), *n. (Colloq.)* noise, word, notice, or warning; usually used in the negative, as in *waláng abúg-abóg,* without any word or warning. See **abóg.**

abuloy (a-bu-loy), I. *n.* 1. act of contributing something to a person or for a cause. Syn. *pag-aabuloy.* Cf. *tulong, pagtulong.* 2. something given as a contribution. Syn. *kontribusyón, tulong, ambág.*
—II. *adj.* referring to something given as contribution.

abundante (a-bun-dan-te), *adj.* (*Sp.*) abundant; plentiful. Syn. *saganà, masaganà, nanánaganà.*

aburidó (a-bu-ri-dó), *adj.* (*Sp. aburido*) very much worried, disgusted, annoyed, etc.; feeling desperate or hopeless. Syn. *guló ang isip; di-mápalagáy.*

abuso (a-bu-so), *n.* (*Sp.*) 1. mistreatment; maltreatment. Syn. *pagmamalupít, kalupitán.* 2. ill use or wrong use, as of one's authority. Syn. *pagmamalabís, kalabisán.* 3. a bad, unjust, or corrupt custom or practice. Syn. *masamáng gawà o gawain.* 4. forcible abuse of a woman; rape. Syn. *gahasà, paggahasà, panggagahasà.* 5. deception. Syn. *pagtataksil, kataksilán; paglililo, kaliluhan.*

ábutan (á-bu-tan). I. *adj.* payable on delivery; payable in cash upon receipt of the goods. Syn. *káliwaan.*
—II. *n.* act or manner of handling over something to each other or to one another personally. Cf. *bígayan.*

abutín (a-bu-tín), *v.* 1. to get or accept with the hand what is being given personally. Cf. *tanggapín.* 2. to get (something) by extending one's hand. Cf. *dukwangín, kunin.*

abyerta (ab-yer-ta), var. **abiyerta**, I. *adj.* (*Sp. abierta*) open; not closed. Syn. *bukás, nakabukás.*
—II. *n.* a man's open coat, usually worn with a shirt and tie. Cf. *sarada.*

akáb (a-káb), *adj.* tight-fitting; tightly set or adjusted. Syn. *hakáb, lapat, kagát.*

akademya (a-ka-dem-ya), *n.* (*Sp. academia*) 1. place of higher learning; academy. Cf. *instituto, surián, koléhiyó, unibersidád.* 2. association. Syn. *samahán, kapisanan, asosiyasyón.*

akagin (a-ka-gin), *v.* to invite (someone) personally to go to a certain place or to do a certain kind of work. Syn. *yakagin, yayain.*

akalà (a-ka-là), *n.* 1. belief. Syn. *paniwalà, paniniwalà.* 2. presumption; surmise; assumption. Syn. *palagáy, pala-palagáy.* 3. idea; concept; notion; thinking. Syn. *kurò, kuru-kurò.* 4. estimate; calculation. Syn. *taya, kalkulá.* 5. intention; purpose; desire. Syn. *hangád, hángarin; layon, láyunin.*

akap (a-kap), I. *n.* 1. tight embrace or hug; close hold within one's arms. Syn. *yapós, yakap.* 2. attachment or fastening, as of a brace or support against a post, wall, or the like. Cf. *sapì, tapal.* 3. a person or thing being held tightly in one's arms.
—II. *adj.* held tightly in one's arms; tightly embraced.

akasya (a-kas-ya), *n.* (*Sp.; Eng.*) acacia.

akay (a-kay), I. *n.* 1. act of guiding or leading a person by holding the hand. 2. guidance; training. Syn. *pagpatnubay, pamamatnubay; pagsanay, pagsasanay.* 3. a person being trained, guided, or led by another 4. act of taking care of the young by the mother hen. 5. the young of a hen or bird being cared for at a time. Also *akayán.*
—II. *adj.* 1. referring to a person being guided or led by the hand by someone. 2. under the protection or care of someone; being taken care of by someone.

akbáy (ak-báy), I. *n.* 1. act or manner of putting one's arm over the shoulders of another. 2. the position of an arm placed over the shoulders of another.
—II. *adj.* 1. standing or walking together with each arm placed over each other's shoulders, referring to two persons. 2. with or having one's arm placed over the shoulders of another.

akdâ (akdâ), *n.* 1. act of writing or composing a literary piece or musical composition. Syn *kathâ, pag-kathâ.* 2. any literary work or composition; anything composed or written by an author. Syn. *kathâ.*

akdáng-buhay (ak-dáng + bu-hay), *n.* novel. Syn. *nóbela, katháng-buhay (kathambuhay).*

akdáng-gurò (ak-dáng + gu-rò), *n.* masterpiece. Syn. *obra maestra; likhánggurò.*

akdáng-sining (ak-dáng + si-ning), *n.* any literary work of art.

akibat (a-ki-bat), I. *n.* 1. act of carrying a thing

on a shoulder, allowing it to hang across the body (diagonally) down to the opposite side. See sakbát. 2. anything carried in this manner. 3. something incumbent upon a person, as a duty or responsibility. Syn. *dálahin, pabigát, pásanin.*
—II. *adj.* 1. referring to something carried on one's shoulder across the body (diagonally) down to the opposite side. 2. incumbent on or upon (someone), referring to a duty or responsibility. Syn. *ságutin, kaakibát.*

akin (a-kin), n. *pron.* 2. *(poss.)* my; mine. *Akin iyán:* That's mine. *Aking aklát iyán:* That's my book. 2. I; me. *Aking ginawâ iyán:* I made (did) that. *Ibigáy mo sa akin ang aklát na iyán:* Give me that book.

akít (a-kít), *adj.* 1. attracted, as by charm; charmed; captivated. Syn. *bighanî, nabighanì, nahalina,* 2. persuaded; induced. Syn. *hikayát, nahikayat.*

aklás (ak-lás), n. act of declaring a strike or walkout. Syn. *welga.*

aklát (ak-lát), n. 1. book; any printed matter or manuscript in bound form. Syn. *libró.* 2. printing and binding into book form.

aklatan (ak-la-tan), n. 1. library. Syn. *libreriya, biblióteká.* 2. book store. Syn. *aklát-tindahan.* 3. book-binding shop; bindery. Syn. *pábalatang-aklát.*

aklát-dasalan (ak-lát + da-sa-lan), n. prayer book.

aklát-pampáaralán (ak-lát + pam-pá-a-ra-lán), n. 1. school book. 2. textbook.

aklát-talaan (ak-lát + ta-la-an), n. 1. record book; registry book. 2. notebook. Syn. *kuwaderno*

aklát-tuusán (aklát+ tu-u-sán), n. accounting book; journal.

akmâ (ak-mâ), I. *adj.* 1. proper; fit; appropriate; suited. Syn. *angkóp, náaangkóp; bagay, nábabagay.* 2. right; correct. Syn. *tamà, tumpak.* 3. well-fitted; well-adjusted. Syn. *lapat, hakab.*
—II. *adv.* in the act of. Syn. *anyô; nasa akto ng.*
—III. n. 1. act or manner of fitting something into another. 2. fact or condition of being fit or proper. 3. threat, as of a hand about to strike. Syn. *ambâ, yambâ, astâ.*

akó (a-kó), *pron.* 1. I. *Walâ akóng pera:* I have no money. 2. me. *Bigyán mo ako ng isáng manggá:* Give me a mango.

akò (a-kò), n. guarantee or promise to assume the obligations or duties of another. Syn. *garantiyá, sagót.*

aksayá (ak-sa-yá), I. *adj.* 1. wasteful; extravagant. Syn. *bulagsák, mapagtapon, mapag-aksayá.* 2. wasted; not properly used or spent. Syn. *patapón, nasayang, aksayado.*
—II. n. 1. a wasting or being wasted. Syn. *sayang, pagsayang, pagkasayang.* 2. useless or profitless spending or consuming; squandering, as of money, time, etc. Syn. *lustáy, paglustáy, pagkalustáy.* 3. gradual loss, decrease, or destruction by use, wear, decay, etc. Syn. *sayang, pagkasayang.*

aksesorya (ak-se-sor-ya), n. (Sp. *accesoria*) apartment house. Syn. *posesyón, bahay-páupahán.*

aksidente (ak-si-den-te), n. (Sp. *accidente*) 1. accident. Syn. *sakunâ.* 2. chance happening. Syn. *di-sinásadyáng pangyayari; pagkakataón.*

akta (ak-ta), n. (Sp. *acta*) 1. minutes of a meeting, etc. Syn. *katitikan.* 2. record, as of proceedings in court. Syn. *talâ, talaan.*

aktibidád (ak-ti-bi-dád), n. (Sp. *actividád*) activity; function. Syn. *gawain.*

aktibo (ak-ti-bo), *adj.* (Sp. *activo*) 1. active; full of energy. Syn. *masiglá.* 2. (Gram.) active; transitive. Syn. *tahás, táhasan, palipát.* 3. of current validity; still enforced. Syn. *umíiral, buháy.* 4. in good standing, as members of an organization.

akto (ak-to), n. (Sp. *acto*) 1. act or manner of acting; action. Syn. *kilos, galáw.* 2. act; actual act, as in *náhuli sa akto,* caught in the act. Syn. *paggawâ, pagsasagawâ.* 3. a division in a play or drama; act. Syn. *yugtô.*

aktuwál (ak-tu-wál), *adj.* (Sp.; Eng.) 1. actual; real; true. Syn. *tunay, totoó, talagá* 2. existing at the present time. Syn. *umíiral, pangkasalukuyan.*

akuin (a-ku-in), *v.* to assume the responsibilities or duties of (another). Syn. *sagutín, panagután, garantiyahán.*

akumulá (a-ku-mu-lá), n. (Sp. *acumular*) an accumulating or being accumulated; accumulation. Syn. *pagtitipon, pagkatipon;*

pagkamál, pagkakamál.

akurdiyón (a-kur-di-yón), *n.* (*Sp. acordeón*) accordion. Syn. *kurdiyón.*

akusá (a-ku-sá), *n.* (*Sp. acusar*) 1. an accusing or being accused; accusation. Syn. *pagpaparatang.* 2. what a person is accused of. Syn. *paratang, kaparatangán.*

akwaryum (ak-war-yum), var. **akwaryum,** *n.* (*Eng.*) aquarium.

akyát (ak-yát), *n.* 1. act of climbing (a tree). Syn. *adyó* (term usually used in Batangas and Quezon provinces). 2. act of going up a height, esp. a slope or the like. Syn. *ahon, pag-ahon.* 3. act of going upstairs. Syn. *panhík, pagpanhík.* 4. rise or ascent, as of water from a lower place. Syn. *sampa, pagsampa, taás, pagtaás,* 5. promotion; rise in rank or position. Syn. *asenso, pag-asenso, taás, pagtaás.* 6. (*Colloq.*) visit of a lover to his girlfriend's house. Syn. *ligaw, pagligaw.* 6. income or earning, as from business Syn. *kita, tubò.*

ada (a-da), *n.* (*Sp.*) fairy. Cf. *diwatà, nimpa.*

Adán (A-dán), *n.* (*Sp.; Bib.*) name of the first man: Adam.

adelantado (a-de-lan-ta-do), I. *adj.* (*Sp.*) 1. ahead; advanced; fast (s.o. a time piece). Syn. *mabilis.* 2. progressive, as of people or nations. Syn. *progresibo, maunlád.* 3. paid in advance Cf. *bayád na; pagado na.* 4. impudent; brazen. Syn. *pangahás, mapangahás.*

—II. *n.* a title of nobility during the early Spanish regime in the islands.

adhíkâ (ad-hí-kâ), *n.* 1. something one wants to attain; aim; ambition; objective; wish. Syn. *layon, láyunin, hangad, hángarin, pangarap, ambisyón.* 2. zeal; diligence. Syn. *tiyagâ, katiyagaán, pagtitiyagâ; sikap, kasikapan, pagsisikap.* 3. thrift; thriftiness; economy. Syn. *tipíd, katipirán, pagtitipíd.*

adobe (a-do-be), var. **adube,** I. *n.* (*Sp.; Eng.*) 1. sun-dried brick. Cf. *ladrilyo.* 2. adobe stone; quarry stone. Syn. *silyár.*

—II. *adj.* of or made of adobe.

adobo (a-do-bo), var. **adubo,** I. *n.* (*Sp.*) pickled meat with condiments.

—II. *adj.* pickled, referring to meat, etc. Syn. *inadobo, adobado*

adorno (a-dor-no), *n.* (*Sp.*). 1. adornment;

decoration; ornament. Syn. *dekorasyón, palamuti, gayák.* 2. act of putting decorations; dressing with ornaments. Syn. *pagdidekorasyón, pagpapalamuti, paggagayák.*

adwana (ad-wa-na), *n.* (*Sp. aduana*) 1. customhouse. 2. customs; government agency in charge of collecting customs duties. 3. duties or taxes imposed on imports and exports.

adya (ad-ya), *n.* 1. redemption or delivery, as from sin, danger, etc.; salvation. Syn. *pagliligtás.* 2. protection; protective care or help. Cf. *tulong, tangkilik.*

adyenda (ad-yen-da) *n.* (*Eng.*) agenda; list of things to be discussed in a meeting, etc. Cf. *programa, palatuntunan.*

adyos (ad-yos; ad-yós), *n.* & *interj.* (*Sp. adios*) goodbye; farewell. Syn. *paalam, gudbáy.*

aga (a-ga), *n.* 1. a coming or occurring in advance of the usual or appointed time; earliness. Cf. *agap, kaagapan.* 2. time ahead of schedule Cf. *una, kaunahan.*

agád (a-gád), I *adv.* immediately; at once; promptly; right away; quickly. Syn. *pagdaka, kapagdaka; mádalî, mádalian; kagyát, kagyatan.*

—II. *adj.* consumed or finished as fast as being supplied or given.

—III. *n.* 1. act of doing or finishing something as fast as being supplied or given. 2. fact or condition of being consumed or finished as fast as being supplied or given.

agahan (a-ga-han), I. *n.* 1. act of eating breakfast. 2. time of eating breakfast. 3. food eaten for breakfast. Syn. *amusál, almusál* (for all the senses).

—II. *v.* to start early; be early.

agam (a-gam), *n.* 1. doubt; suspicion. Syn. *alinlangan, hinalà.* 2. foreboding; premonition. Syn. *kabá, kutób.* 3. fear; disquiet. Syn. *takot, pagkatakot.*

agap (a-gap), *n.* 1. promptness; punctuality; earliness. Cf. *aga* 2. alertness; watchfulness; readiness. Syn. *kaalistuhán, pagkaalisto.*

agapay (a-ga-pay), var. **agabáy,** *n.* 1. act of escorting or guiding someone on the way. Cf. *subaybáy, pagsubaybáy.* 2. escort; bodyguard. Syn. *guwárdiyá, badigard, talibá, tanod.* 3. a support or reinforcement attached or nailed to a post, etc. Syn. *sapî, alalay*. 4. parallel position of two persons or things. Cf. *tabí, siping*.

agar-agar (a-gar + a-gar), n. (Eng.) gelatinous product made from seaweeds; agar-agar. Cf. *gulaman*.

agas (a-gas), n. (Med.) 1. abortion; miscarriage. Syn. *hulog, pagkahulog; laglág, pagkalaglág.* Syn. *pagdurugô.*

agás-as (a-gás + as); var. of agasás.

agaw (a-gaw), I. n. 1. act of taking away something from another by force; snatching or grabbing something from another. Syn. *daklôt, sunggóp, haklít*. 2. illegal seizure of office, position, function, power, etc.; usurpation. Syn. *kamkám, pagkamkám*. 3. interpolation, as in a conversation. Syn. *sabád, pagsabád, pakikisabád*. 4. (Colloq.) act of saving someone, as from death. Syn. *ligtás, pagliligtás; sagíp, pagsagíp*.
—II. adj. referring to something taken from someone illegally or by force. Syn. *kamkám, kinamkám, inagaw*.

agawán (a-ga-wán), I. n. 1. a struggle for the possession of something; act of snatching away things from each other or from one another. Cf. *sunggaban, daklutan*. 2. rivalry; competition or contest for superiority, power, honor, etc. Cf. *páligsahan, tunggalian, labanán*.
—II. adj. (Colloq.) in keen competition or rivalry with each other, as in beauty. Syn. *nagpapaligsahan*.

agaw-buhay (a-gaw + bu-hay), I. adj. dying; hovering between life and death; moribund. Syn. *naghihingalô, nagdídiliryo, abot-dilì*.
—II. n. state or condition of hovering between life and death. Syn. *paghihingalô, pagdidiliryo, pag-aabot-dilì*.

agaw-dilím (a-gaw + di-lím), n. twilight; dusk. Syn. *takípsilim*.

agaw-liwanag (a-gaw + li-wa-nag), n. dawn; daybreak. Syn. *bukáng-liwaywáy, pamimiták-araw*.

agaw-tulog (a-gaw + tu-log), n. state or condition of being half-asleep.

agham (ag-ham), n. science. Syn. *siyénsiyá*.

aghámbilang (ag-hám-bi-lang), var. **agbilang**,

n. (fr. *aghám*, science + *bilang*, number), mathematics. Syn. *matemátiká*.

aghámbuhay (ag-hám-bu-hay), var. **agbuhay**, n. (fr. *aghám*, science + *buhay*, life) biology. Syn. *biyolohiyá*.

aghámlipunán (ag-hám-li-pu-nán), var. **aglipunan**, n. (fr. *aghám*, science + *lipunán*, society) social science; sociology. Syn. *sosyolóhiyá*.

aghámtao (ag-hám-ta-o), var. **agtao**, n. (fr. *aghám*, science + *tao*, man) anthropology. Syn. *antropolóhiyá*.

aghámwikà (ag-hám-wi-kà) var. **agwíkà**, n. (fr. *aghám*, science + *wikà*, language) linguistics. Syn. *lingguwístiká*.

agimat (a-gi-mat), n. 1. amulet. Syn. *antíng-antíng, galíng, dupil, sapî, mutyâ*. 2. economy; thrift. Syn. *tipid, katipirán*. 3. care; concern. Syn. *ingat, kaingatan, pagkamaingat*.

aginaldo (a-gi-nal-do), n. (Sp. *aguinaldo*) Christmas or New Year gift. Syn. *papaskó*. Cf. *regalo, handóg, alaala, bigáy, kaloób*.

agít-it (a-gít + it): var. of **agitít**.

agiw (a-giw), n. old cobwebs covered with soot and dust.

aglahì (ag-la-hì), n. insult; slight; affront; mockery. Syn. *insulto, tuyâ, uyâm, kutyâ*.

agnás (ag-nás), n. 1. erosion. Syn. *erosyón*. Cf. *tibág, pagkatibág, bagbág, pagkabagbág*. 2. decomposition, as of a decaying matter; slow disintegration. Syn. *lusaw, pagkalusaw; lahoy, paglahoy*.

agnós (ag-nós): var. of **agnós**.

agos (a-gos), n. 1. flow, as of water in a river. Cf. *daloy, takbó*. 2. a long line of slow moving people or things. Syn. *parada, prusisyón*.

Agosto (A-gos-to), n. (Sp.) August, the eighth month of the year.

agpáng (ag-páng), I. adj. 1. proper; appropriate; suitable; fit. Syn. *bagay, nábabagay; angkóp, náaangkóp*. 2. right; correct. Syn. *tamà, tumpák, wastô*. Ant. *malî, lisyâ, lihís*. 3. of the right size; fitted; exact. Syn. *hustô, akmâ, lapat, kamado*. 4. applicable. Syn. *maaarì, magagamit, bagay*. 5. marked by harmony of relation or feelings; harmonious. Syn. *kasundô, magkasundô; bagay, màgkabagay; suwatò*, *magkasuwatò.* 6. adequate; sufficient. Syn. *sapát, husto, kaysa, katamtaman.*

—II. *n.* 1. act or manner of fitting or adjusting a thing into another. Syn. *lapat, paglalapat; kabít, pagkakabít.* 2. state or condition marked by harmony or relation or feelings. Syn. *pagkakásundô, pagkakábagay, pagkakásuwatò.* 3. state or condition of being proper or right.

agrabyado (a-grab-ya-do), var. **agrabiyado,** I. *adj.* (Sp. *agraviado*) 1. aggrieved; adversely affected in respect of legal rights. Syn. *apí,* 2. at a disadvantage. Syn. *daíg.* 3. offended; insulted. Cf. *nasaktán.*

—II. *n.* 1. act of taking advantage of another's weakness, ignorance, etc. Syn. *pagsamantalá, pagsasamantalá, paglamáng.* 2. state or condition of being aggrieved, offended, etc. Syn. *pagkaapí, kaapihán.* 3. fact or condition of being at a disadvantage. Syn. *kadaigán, pagkadaíg.*

agresibo (a-gre-si-bo), *adj.* (Sp. *agresivo*) 1. aggressive; disposed to attack or to start a fight or quarrel with another. Syn. *mapusok.* 2. bold and active; full of enterprise and initiative. Syn. *mapunyagî, mapagpunyagî; masipag.*

agresyón (a-gres-yón), *n.* (Sp. *agresión*) 1. aggression; unprovoked attack or invasion. Syn. *salakay, pagsalakay, pananalakay; lusob, paglusob, panlulusob.* 2. aggressive boldness. Syn. *pusok, kapusukan; lakás ng loob.*

agrikultura (a-gri-kul-tu-ra), *n.* (Sp. *agricultura*) agriculture. Syn. *pagsasaka, pagbubukid.*

agtíng (ag-tíng), *n.* 1. tightness; stress on a material produced by the pull of forces. Syn. *bagtíng, banat, hapit, higpít.* 2. fact or state of strained relations; uneasiness due to mutual hostility; tension. Cf. *lubhâ, kalubhaán; tindí, katindihán.*

aguhilya (a-gu-hil-ya), *n.* (Sp.) hairpin. Syn. *sipit* (*ng buhók*); *panuksók.*

agunyas (a-gun-yas; a-gun-yás), *n.* (Sp.) toll or tolling of bells for the dead. Cf. *ripike, dupikál.*

agwa-bendita (ag-wa + ben-di-ta), *n.* (Sp. *agua bendita*) holy water.

agwadór (ag-wa-dór), *n.* (Sp. *aguadór*) water

carrier. Syn. *mangiigib, tagaigíb; mánanalok-tubig, tagasalok-tubig.*

agwahe (ag-wa-he), *n.* (Sp.) tidal wave.

agwanta (ag-wan-ta), *n.* (Sp. *aguante*) 1. ability to suffer or endure (pain, hardship, misfortune, etc.); endurance. Syn. *tiís, pagtitiís; batá, pagbata, pagbabatá.* 2. patience; fortitude. Syn. *tiyagâ, pagtitiyagâ.*

agwa-oksihenada (ag-wa + ok-si-he-na-da), *n.* (Sp. *agua oxigenada*) hydrogen peroxide.

agwardiyente (ag-war-di-yen-te), *n.* (Sp. *aguardiente*) alcohol; hard liquor. Syn. *alkohól.*

agwát (ag-wát), *n.* 1. distance or space between. Syn. *awáng, pagitan, puwáng, distánsiyá.* 2. the difference, as in status, rank, age, etc. Syn. *pagkakáibá, kaibhán; diperensiyá.* 3. interval, as between two specific times. 4. a keeping away or distance from. Syn. *layô, paglayô; awáng, pag-awáng.* 5. a being ahead or leaving one behind, as in a race. Syn. *pag-una, kaunahan.*

ahà (a-hà), *n.* (*Colloq.*) idea; notion; supposition. Syn. *akalà, hinuhà, palagáy, kurò.*

ahas (a-has), *n.* 1. (*Zool.*) snake; serpent. 2. (*Med.*) a kind of skin disease (eruption). Syn. *kulebra.* 3. (*Fig.*) a person who betrays his friends. Syn. *taksíl, traydór.*

ahedres (a-he-dres; a-he-drés) *n.* (Sp. *ajedres*) the game of chess. Cf. *dama.*

ahénsiyá (a-hén-si-yá), *n.* (Sp. *agencia*). 1. agency; establishment for executing business in behalf of others. 2. pawnshop. Syn. *bahay-sanglaan.*

ahente (a-hente), *n.* (Sp. *agente*) 1. (*Bus.*) middleman; commercial or business agent. Syn. *tagapaglakò, tagalakò; tagapagbilí.* 2. representative; agent. Syn. *kinatawán.*

ahin (a-hin), var. **hain,** *n.* 1. act of preparing or setting the table for someone. 2. the food prepared or set on the table for someone to eat. Cf. *handâ.*

ahit (a-hit), *n.* 1. act or manner of shaving with or as with a razor. Cf. *satsát.* 2. the part of the head, chin, etc. left bare by shaving. 3. tonsure. Syn. *anit.*

ahon (a-hon), *n.* 1. a going upward or a climb, esp. on a slope; ascent. Syn. *akyát, pag-*

akyát; sampá, pagsampá. 2. disembarkation,
as from a ship; landing. Syn. *lunsád*,
paglunsád; babâ, pagbabâ; lapág, paglapág.
3.a trip from the town or city to the barrio,
or from the lowland to the highland. Cf.
luwás, pagluwás. 4. getting out from water,
as after taking a bath in a river. Ant. *lusong,
paglusong.* 5. a return trip from a river or
spring after washing clothes, fishing, etc.
Cf. *uwi, pag-uwî.* 6. removal from fire or
stove, as of something being cooked. Syn.
hangò, paghangò. 7. relief or redemption,
as from sin, debt, misery, etc. Syn. *hangò,
pagkahangò; tubós, pagkatubós.*

ahunan (a-hu-nan), *v.* 1. to use as a landing
place or a point of embarkation, as by an
invading naval force. Syn. *sampahán,
lunsarán.* 2. to bring something from a river
to someone at the bank. Cf. *dalhán, hatirán.*

Ala (A-la), *n.* (Sp. *Alá*) Allah, god in the
Moslem religion.

alá (a-lá), *interj.* (Prov.) an exclamation
expressing negation, or sometimes
agreement, depending on the tenor of
expression.

alâ (a-lâ) : aphaeresis of *walâ*, I. *pron.* none;
nobody; no one; not anyone. *Alâ kundî si
Juán:* none but John.

—II. *adj.* absent; not present; away; did not
attend. Syn. *umalís, di-dumatíng, di-dumaló,
di-pumasok.*

—III. *prep. & pref.* without; -less (used as
a combining form). *Aláng-gawâ,* without
work. *Aláng-saysáy:* useless.

alaala (a-la-a-la), *n.* 1. memory; recollection.
Syn. *gunitâ.* Ant. *limot, pagkalimot.* 2. gift;
present. Syn. *handóg, regalo, bigáy, kaloób.*
3. memorial; memento; token. Syn. *tandâ,
palatandaan; sagisag, tagapágpagunitâ.*

alab (a-lab), *n.* 1. blaze; big flame or fire.
Syn. *ningas, apóy.* 2. ardor; fervor;
enthusiasm. Syn. *siglá, kasiglahán; sigasig,
kasigasigan; sigsá, kasigsahán.* 3. intensity,
as of passion or anger. Syn. *sidhî, kasidhián;
silakbó, kasilakbuhán; sigalbó, kasigalbuhán;
sigabo, kasigabuhan; ngitngít, kangitngitán.*
Ant. *lamíg, hinahon.*

alabastro (a-la-bas-tro), *n.* (Sp.; min.),
alabaster.

alabók (a-la-bók), *n.* 1. (poetic) dust. Syn.

abó, alikabók. 2. soil; earth. Syn. *lupà; dutà*
(Bis.)

alak (a-lak), *n.* 1. wine; liquor. Syn. *bino.* 2.
dry, small pieces of firewood placed
between the spaces of firebrands to make
them burn readily. Cf. *gatong.*

alakbát (a-lak-bát), I. *n.* 1. act or manner of
carrying a load on the shoulder allowing
it to hang on both sides. Syn. *sakbát,
pagsakbát.* 2. anything carried in this
manner. 3. a band, strap, or the like, slung
down from a shoulder, usually crossing the
breast to the opposite lower side of the
body.

—II *adj.* slung down from the shoulder,
referring to something being carried.

alakdán (a-lak-dán), var. **alagdán**, *n.* (corr.
fr. Sp. *alacran*) 1. (Entom.) scorpion. Syn.
pitumbukó. 2. (Astrol.) Scorpio, sign of the
zodiac.

alagà (a-la-gà), I. *n.* 1. act of taking care of a
person, animal, plant, etc. Cf. *kalingà,
pagkalingà; kupkóp, pagkupkóp; ampón, pag-
ampón.* 2. a person, animal, plant, etc.
under the care of someone. 3. caution; care
or carefulness. Syn. *ingat, pag-iingat,
kaingatan.*

—II. *adj.* referring to a person, animal,
plant, etc. under the care of someone.

alagád (a-la-gád), *n.* 1. follower, as of a politial
leader. Syn. *tauhan, tagasunod.* 2. disciple;
apostle. Syn. *apostól, disípuló.* 3. helper;
assistant. Syn. *katulong, kawaní.* 4. priest;
minister. Syn. *Ministro; pari; pastór.* 5.
officer; agent. Syn. *punò, pinunò; ahente,
kinatawán.* 6. member of a religious sect
popularly known as *Alagád ni Kristo.*

alagatâ (a-la-ga-tâ), *n.* 1. a minding or
thinking about, as of one's interest;
concern. Cf. *malasakit.* 2. something that
a person wants to attain; ambition. Syn.
layon, layunin; mithî, mithiin; ambisyón.

alahas (a-la-has), *n.* (Sp. *alhaja*) jewel; jewelry.
Syn. *hiyás.*

alalá (a-la-lá), I. *n.* 1. worry; anxiety. Syn.
balisa, pagkabalisa; bahalà, pagkabahalà. 2.
cause of one's worry or anxiety.

—II. *adj.* worried; anxious. Syn. *balisá, di-
mápalagay, nabábahalà.*

alalahanin (a-la-la-ha-nin), *v.* 1. to remember;

recall to one's mind; think about. Syn. *gunitaín, isipin, isaisip.* 2. to take into consideration. Syn. *isaalang-alang, bigyánghalagá.*

álalahanín (á-la-la-ha-nín), n. 1. worry; cause of worry. Syn. *isipín, gúnitain.* 2. responsibility. Syn. *sagutin, pananagutan, responsibilidád.*

álalaón (á-la-la-ón), conj. 1. (with *ko, niyá, nilá,* etc.) what one means. Alalaón ko: What I mean. 2. (with *bagá*) that is; that is to say; therefore. Syn. *samakatwíd.* 3. (with *sana*) should have; could have; might have; might as well. Syn. *dapat.*

alalay (a-la-lay), n. 1. temporary support, prop, or brace. Cf. *tukod, saló, suhay.* 2. carefulness in doing something; care in holding or carrying something. Syn. *ingat.* 3. a slowing down or control, as in driving a car, eating, drinking, etc. Syn. *dahan, pagdarahan-dahan.*

alam (a-lam), n. 1. knowledge; talent; wisdom. Syn. *talino, katalinuhan; dunong, karunungan.* 2. understanding. Syn. *unawà, pagkaunawà* 3. idea or knowledge about something. Syn. *kabatiran, kaalaman.* 4. involvement; participation. Syn. *kinalaman.*

alám (a-lám), I. adj. 1. known to; informed about. 2. aware of; conscious of or about. Syn. *batíd, nálalaman* (for senses 1 & 2). 3. understood; clear. Cf. *maliwanag.*
—II. n. something one knows about.

alamáng (a-la-máng), n. 1. (*Ichth.*) a species of tiny shrimp. Cf. *aptá.* 2. (*Fig.*) a person or thing regarded as unimportant or insignificant; small fry. Cf. *pipitsugin.*

alamát (a-la-mát), n. 1. folklore; legend. Syn. *kuwentong-bayan; leyenda.* 2. tradition. Syn. *kaugaliáng-bayan, matandáng kaugalián.*

alambre (a-lam-bre), n. (*Sp.*) wire. Syn. *kawad.*

alamíd (a-la-míd), n. wild mountain cat. Cf. *musang.*

alamín (a-la-mín), v. find out; investigate. Syn. *imbestigahán.*

alampáy (a-lam-páy), n. 1. neckerchief; shawl. Cf. *bupanda, papandá.* 2. the manner or position by which a neckerchief or shawl is worn around the neck and shoulders.

alang-alang (a-lang + a-lang), I. n. 1. respect; regard. Syn. *galang, paggalang, pítagan.* 2. consideration; taking into account. Syn. *konsiderasyón, pagsasaalang-alang; pagbibigáy* (Colloq.)
—II. adv. (with *sa*) 1. for the sake of. Syn. *dahil sa.* 2. with due regard or respect to. Syn. *bilang paggalang o pagbibigáy.*

alangán (a-la-ngán), adj. 1. unfit; not proper; improper; not suited. Syn. *di-bagay, di-angkóp.* 2. insufficient; not enough; lacking. Syn. *kulang; di-sapát; kapós.* 3. unworthy. Syn. *di-dapat, di-karapat-dapat.* 4. unbecoming. Syn. *masagwâ; laban sa kagandahang-asal; pangit.* 5. medium size. Syn. *katamtaman ang lakí; maykatamtamang lakí.* 6. uncertain; doubtful; hesitant; reluctant. Syn. *bantulót, nagbabantulot; urong-sulong, nag-uurongsulong.*

álanganin (á-la-nga-nin), I. adj. 1. insufficient; not enough; lacking. Syn. *kulang, di-sapát, kapós.* 2. undecided; uncertain; doubtful. Syn. *alinlangan, nagáalinlangan; duda, nagdúduda; di-tiyák.* 3. hesitant; reluctant. Syn. *bantulót, nagbábantulót; urong-sulong, nag-úurongsulong.*

alapaap (a-la-pa-ap), n. 1. clouds in general. 2. high clouds. Syn. *ulap.* 3. (*Fig.*) doubt; incertitude; indecision. Syn. *alinlangan, duda.*

alarma (a-lar-ma), n. (*Sp.*) 1. alarm; sound of siren as a sign of alarm. Syn. *hudyát, babalâ.* 2. state or condition of being alarmed; fear. Syn. *takot, pagkatakot, pangambá, alalá.*

alat (a-lat), I. n. 1. the taste of salt or sea water; saltiness. 2. (*Fig.*) bad luck; unluckiness. Syn. *malas, kamalasan.* 3. (*Slang*) policeman; police officer. Syn. *pulís, alagád ng batás.*
—II. adj. unlucky. Syn. *malas, minamalas, sinásamâ, waláng-suwerte.*

alatiit (a-la-ti-it; a-la-ti-ít), n. (echoic) squeaking sound as that produced by tight door hinges or poorly adjusted wheels, etc. Cf. *agitít, langitngít, lagitlít.*

alay (a-lay), I. *n.* 1. act of offering a gift or sacrifice. Syn. *handóg, paghahandóg.* 2. gift or present. Syn. *handóg, regalo, alaala.* 3. something given or offered as a sacrifice. Syn. *sákripisyo.*
—II. *adj.* referring to something given or offered as a gift or sacrifice.

albino (al-bi-no), *n.* (*Sp.; Eng.*) a person or animal whose skin, hair, and eyes lack normal coloration; albino. Syn. *anák-araw.*

alboroto (al-bo-ro-to), I. *n.* (*Sp.*) 1. restless agitation or fuss, esp. of a baby or infant; tantrum. Cf. *ligalig, pagliligalíg.* 2. a baby or child given to such fuss or tantrum. 3. disturbance; trouble. Syn. *guló, basag-ulo, ligalig.*
—II. *adj.* given to restless crying or agitation, referring to a child or baby. Syn. *maligalig, íyakin.*

alkalde (al-kal-de), *n.* (Sp. *alcalde*) 1. city mayor. Syn. *punong-lunsód.* 2. town mayor. Cf. *punong-bayan, presidente.*

alkampór (al-kam-pór), *n.* (Sp. *alcanfor*) camphor.

alkansiyá (al-kan-si-yá), *n.* (Sp. *alcancía*) piggy bank; penny bank.

alkilá (al-ki-lá), var. **arkilá**, *n.* (Sp. *alquilar*) 1. act of renting or getting temporary possession or use of something in return for certain payment or amount. Syn. *upa, pag-upa.* 2. the amount charged or paid for the temporary use or possession of something. Syn. *upa, renta.*

alkitrán (al-kit-rán), *n.* (Sp. *alquitrán*) 1. tar; pitch. 2. asphalt. Syn. *aspalto.*

alkohól (al-ko-hól), *n.* (*Sp.; Eng.*) alcohol. Syn. *agwardiyente.*

aldaba (al-da-ba), *n.* (Sp.) 1. latch; door latch. Syn. *trangka, tarugo.* 2. the act or manner of fastening or closing (a door or window) with a latch.

aldabís (al-da-bís), *n.* a back stroke or blow with the hand. Cf. *tabig, sikó.*

ale (a-le), var. **ali**, *n.* 1. aunt. Syn. *tiyá, tiyáng.* Cf. *tiyó, tiyóng.* 2. stepmother. Syn. *ináng-pangumán, tiyahin.* 3. a term of respect in speaking to or of any woman not related to the speaker. Cf. *mamà, mang.*

alegasyón (a-le-gas-yón), *n.* (Sp. *alegación*) 1. an alleging or declaration. Syn. *pahayag,* *pagpapahayag.* 2. (*Law*) an assertion which its maker proposes to support with evidence; allegation. Syn. *paratang.*

alegorya (a-le-gor-ya), *n.* (Sp. *alegoria*), allegory. Syn. *talinghagà, pananalinghagà; tayutay, pananayutay.*

alegro (a-leg-ro), I. *adj.* (Sp. *Mus.*) fast, a direction to the performer.
—II. *n.* (*Mus.*) a fast movement or passage; allegro.

alerto (a-ler-to), *adj.* (*Sp.*) alert; vigilant. Syn. *listo, alisto.*

alí (a-lí), *n.* 1. evil influence; diabolic urge. Syn. *tuksó.* 2. fit or attack, as of intermittent pain. Syn. *sumpóng, atake.*

alibadbád (a-li-bad-bád), *n.* 1. nausea; squeamishness, Cf. *suyà, pagkasuyà.* 2. disgust; loathing.

alibambáng (a-li-bam-báng), var. **alibangbáng**, *n.* 1. (*Bot.*) a small stocky tree (*Bauhinia malabarica* Roxb), the young leaves of which are used in flavoring meat or fish. 2. (*Entom.*) small yellow-winged butterfly usually seen along roadsides. Cf. *aliparó, paruparó.*

alibughâ (a-li-bug-hâ), *adj.* 1. prodigal; recklessly wasteful. Syn. *bulagsák, mapaglustáy, gastador.* 2. irresponsible. Syn. *waláng-bahalà, waláng-pananagutan, pabayâ, halaghág.*

alikabók (a-li-ka-bók), *n.* dust. Cf. *abó, abók.*

aligatâ (a-li-ga-tâ), *n.* 1. thoughtful consideration or attention before acting or doing something; forethought. Syn. *muni-muni, pagmumuni-muni; pag-iisip-isip.* 2. a minding or thinking about, as of one's interest; concern. Syn. *malasakit, pagmamalasakit; intindí, pag-iintindí.* 3. something that a person wants to attain; ambition. Syn. *layon, láyunin; mithî míthiin; ambisyón.* See **alagatâ**.

aligí (a-li-gí), *n.* the hardened fat of crabs, shrimps, etc. Cf. *tabâ.*

aligid (a-li-gid), *n.* 1. act of circling or going around a place. Syn. *ligid, pagligid; ikot, pag-ikot.* 2. a single rounding or circuit, as in a race track; also, the distance covered in one round or circuit. Syn. *ligid, ikot.* 3. a sneaking around. Cf. *libot, pagpapalibut-libot.* 4. surroundings; environment of a place. Syn. *paligid, kapaligirán, paligid-ligid*.

alihan (a-li-han), *v.* 1. to have a fit or attack of. Syn. *sumpungín, atakihin*. 2. to be influenced, as by an evil; have a diabolic urge. Syn. *matuksó*.

alilà (a-li-là), *n.* 1. oppressive or slavish treatment of someone under one's care or responsibility. Syn. *alipin, pag-alipin*. 2. servant; houseboy or housegirl. Syn. *utusán; mutsatso o mutsatsa*.

alilang-kanin (a-li-lang + ka-nin), *n.* a servant who serves his master without pay. Cf. *alipin*.

álilisán (á-li-li-sán), *n.* 1. sugar cane mill. Syn. *trapitse*. 2. time or season for milling sugar cane. Syn. *tag-iló, íluhan, tag-ililisán*.

alimango (a-li-ma-ngo), *n.* 1. (*Ichth.*) a species of crab having hard and dark-colored shell (*Neptunus armatus* M. Edw.). Cf. *alimasag*. 2. (*Astrol.*) Cancer, fourth sign of the Zodiac.

alimasag (a-li-ma-sag), *n.* (*Ichth.*) a species of crab having light-colored shell (*Neptunus gladiator* Fabr.). Cf. *alimango*.

alimbukay (a-lim-bu-kay), *n.* 1. sudden surge of strong disagreeable odor or smell. Syn. *alingasaw*. 2. sudden surge of water, dust, etc. due to strong wind. Syn. *sigabo, silakbó*. 2. nausea; turning inside out of one's stomach. Cf. *duwál*.

alimpungát (a-lim-pu-ngát), *n.* 1. trance-like state of consciousness upon awakening. 2. somnabulation.

alimpuyó (a-lim-pu-yó), var. **alipuyó**, *n.* 1. whirl; whirling movement. Syn. *inog, paginog*. 2. whirlpool; eddy. Syn. *uliuli*. 3. whirlwind. Syn. *ipuipo*. 4. sudden burst, as of anger. Cf. *puyós, silakbó, ngitngít*.

alimuom (a-li-mu-om; a-li-mu-óm), *n.* 1. vapor rising from the ground, esp. after a light rain during a hot day. Syn. *singáw*. 2. idle talk; rumors; gossipy talk. Syn. *sitsít, daldál, kadaldalán; balitang-kutsero*. 3. hard feeling; displeasure or resentment against someone, Syn. *hinanakít, tampó, sama ng loób*.

alimura (a-li-mu-ra; a-li-mu-rà), *n.* insult; humiliating remark. Syn. *dustâ, lait, insulto*.

alín (a-lín), *pron.* which; which one. Cf. *anó*.

alinagnág (a-li-nag-nág), I. *n.* hazy light or glow of flame behind a dark glass or any translucent object. 2. hazy visibility through such an object. Cf. *aninag*.

—II. *adj.* seen or can be seen hazily through (a dark glass or any translucent object). Syn. *aninág, náaaninag*.

alín-alín (a-lín + a-lín), *pron.* (collective pl. of **alín**): which ones. Cf. *anú-anó; sinu-sino*.

alindayag (a-lin-da-yag), *n.* (*Ilok.*) a floating in the air; gliding flight. Syn. *alimpayáw, alindayog, salipawpaw*.

alindóg (a-lin-dóg), *n.* charm; captivating beauty. Syn. *gandá, kagandahan; dilág, karilagán; dikít, kariktán*.

alinlangan (a-lin-la-ngan), I. *n.* doubt; indecision; uncertainty. Syn. *duda, pagdududa, salawahan, pagsasalawahan, bantulot*.

—II. *adj.* undecided; doubtful; uncertain. Syn. *nag-áalinlangan, nagbábabantulót, nagdúduda*.

alinmán (a-lin-mán); also **alín man**, *pron.* either one (of two); whichever. Cf. *anumán, sínumán; kahit sino*.

alinsabáy (a-lin-sa-báy), *adj.* happening or occurring at the same time; belonging to the same period of time; contemporary. Syn, *kapanahón, magkapanahón*.

alinsangan (a-lin-sa-ngan), I. *n.* 1. state or condition of being oppressively hot (s.o. weather); sultriness. Syn. *banás, kabanasán; init, kainitan*. 2. the oppressively hot feeling of persons during the hot season.

—II. *adj.* oppressively hot or warm, referring to the weather. Syn. *mainit, mabanás*.

alinsunod (a-lin-su-nod), *prep.* (with *sa, kay, kiná*, etc.) according to; in accordance with; in conformity with. Syn. *sang-ayon, batay sa*.

alintana (a-lin-ta-na), I. *n.* 1. care; attention; thoughtfulness; concern. Syn. *malasakit, pagmamalasakit*. 2. awareness; consciousness. Syn. *malay, kamalayan*.

—II. *adj.* mindful; having in mind; aware of. Cf. *asikaso, nasa-isip, nalalaman*.

alintanahin (a-lin-ta-na-hin), *v.* to care; think about; be thoughtful about. Syn. *alalahanin, isipin, pagmalasakitan*. 2. to be mindful of; be aware of. Syn. *intindihín,* *asikasuhin.*

alingasaw (a-li-nga-saw), ñ. 1. strong disagreeble odor. Syn. *bahò, sangsáng.* 2. effusion or emanation of strong offensive odor. Cf. *singáw, asngáw.*

alingasngás (a-li-ngas-ngás), n. 1. scandal. Syn. *iskandaló.* 2. disgrace; ignominy. Syn. *kahihiyán, kasiraáng-puri.* 3. scandalous report; malicious gossip. Syn. *paninirang-puri.* 4. disorder; trouble; confusion. Syn. *guló, pagkakaguló; ligalig, kaligaligan.*

alingawngáw (a-li-ngaw-ngáw), n. 1. echo; reverberation. Syn. *alingayngay.* 2. noise; clamor. Syn. *ingay, kaingayan; linggál, kalinggalán.* 3. unconfirmed reports; rumors. Syn. *balí-balita, bulung-bulungan, tsismis.*

alipalà (a-li-pa-là), adv. 1. instantly; at once; abruptly. Syn. *agád, kapagdaka.* 2. hence; therefore. Syn. *kayâ, samakatwíd.* 3. perhaps; maybe. Syn. *kaipalà, marahil, bakâ, bakasakalì.*

alipato (a-li-pa-to), n. high flying embers.

alipin (a-li-pin), I. n. 1. slave. Syn. *busabos.* Cf. *alilà, mutsatsa, mutsatso, utusán.* 2. the act or practice of treating a person like a slave. Syn. *pagbusabos, pag-alipin.*

—II. adj. doing menial work for one's master; working as a slave. Syn. *busabos.*

alipungá (a-li-pu-ngá), n. (Med.) 1. athlete's foot. 2. chilblains.

alipuris (a-li-pu-ris), n. blind follower. Syn. *alipunyâ.* Cf. *tauhan, tagasunód, alagád.*

alipustà (a-li-pus-tâ), I. ñ. insult; slight; humiliation. Syn. *insulto, dustâ, lait, paghamak.*

—II. adj. of low moral character; vile; morally evil or wicked; contemptible; despicable. Syn. *hamak, masamâ, kalait-lait.*

alís (a-lís), I. n. 1. act of leaving or going away; departure. Syn. *lakad, yao, tulak.* 2. time of departure or leaving. 3. act of moving from one place to another. Syn. *lipat, paglipat.* 4. act of removing something from a place. Cf. *kuha, pagkuha.*

alisagâ (a-li-sa-gâ), adj. 1. inconstant; fickle. Syn. *pabagu-bagong-isip, salawahan.* 2. restless. Syn. *balisá, di-mápalagay, di-mápakali.* 3. indolent; idle; lazy. Syn. *tamád, batugan, lakuwatsero.* 4. negligent. Syn. *pabayâ.*

alisagság (a-li-sag-ság), adj. neglectful; negligent. Syn. *pabayâ, waláng-asikaso, alisagâ.*

alisán (a-li-sán), v. 1. to deprive (a person) of something given or bestowed to him. Syn. *bawian.* 2. to get or take away something from. Syn. *kunan.* 3. to deduct a part or portion from. Syn. *bawasan, awasán.* 4. to take away; rid of. 5. to leave or get away from. Syn. *iwan, layasan, layuán.*

alisangsáng (a-li-sang-sáng), n. strong offensive odor. Syn. *alingasaw, asngáw.*

alisín (a-li-sín), v. 1. to remove or take away from. Syn. *kunin.* 2. to remove by cutting. Syn. *putulin.* 3. to remove or take out, as from a stove. Syn. *hanguin.* 4. to stop or avoid, as a vice. Syn. *hintuan, ihinto, iwasan.* 5. to deduct from. Syn. *bawasin, awasín.* 6. to remove or lay off, as from work. Syn. *bawasin.* 7. to remove by erasing; erase. Syn. *burahín.* 8. to remove by scraping. Syn. *katkatín.*

alisto (a-lis-to), adj. 1. alert; active. Syn. *masiglá, aktibo.* 2. always ready; ever ready. Syn. *laging-handâ, laging-nakahandâ; listo.* 3. talented. Syn. *matalino, may-talino.* 4. sharp-minded. Syn. *matalisik.*

álitan (á-li-tan), n. 1. misunderstanding; discord; dispute. 2. cause of such dispute or discord.

alitaptáp (a-li-tap-táp), n. (Entom.) firefly.

aliterasyón (a-li-te-rasyón), n. (Sp. *aliteración*) alliteration.

alitiít (a-li-ti-ít), var. alatiít, n. shrill squeaking sound. Cf. *agitít, langitngít.*

álituntunin (á-li-tun-tu-nin; a-lí-tun-tu-nin), n. 1. rules; guiding principles. Syn. *panuto, tuntunin.* 2. regulation. Syn. *pátakarán.* 3. aim; purpose. Syn. *layon, layunin.*

alíw (a-líw), n. 1. act of consoling or cheering up a person in distress or sorrow. Syn. *alò, pag-alò.* 2. that which gives a person comfort or consolation. 3. pleasure; satisfaction; delight. Syn. *ligaya, kasiyahan, tuwâ.*

aliwalas (a-li-wa-las), I. n. 1. spacious and pleasant condition, as of a place. 2. clear open place. Syn. *waag.* 3. gay or pleasant disposition or appearance, as of a person's

áliwan   **alsa**

face. Syn. *sayá, kasáyahan*.

—II. *adj.* 1. spacious and well-ventilated.
Syn. *maluwáng at presko*. 2. gay or pleasant,
as a person's face. Syn. *masayá*. 3. neat and
orderly. Syn. *malinis at maayos*.

áliwan (á-li-wan), *n.* means of amusement or
diversion; recreation; pastime. Syn.
líbangan.

aliwaswás (a-li-was-wás), I. *n.* 1. anomaly;
scandalous irregularity. Syn. *alingasngás,
katiwalián*. 2. disgrace; dishonor; ignominy.
Syn. *kahihiyán, kasiraáng-puri*. 3. scandalous
story; malicious rumors. Syn. *tsismis,
paninirang-puri*. 4. (*Colloq.*) a capricious
person. Syn. *salawahan*. 5. swindler. Syn.
balasubas, manggagantso.

—II. *adj.* 1. anomalous; shameful;
scandalous. Syn. *nakahihiyá, maalingasngás,
nakasisirang-puri*. 2. capricious; fickle. Syn.
salawahan. 3. given to swindling. Syn.
balasubas.

aliwín (a-li-wín), *v.* to console; comfort; cheer
up. Syn. *libangín, aluin*.

alíw-iw (a-líw, + iw), var. **aliwiw**, *n.* gentle
murmur, as of flowing water in a brook.
Cf. *lagaslás*.

alma (al-ma; al-má), *n.* (*Sp.*) 1. standing or
rising on hind legs, esp. of horses, when in
rage or in bad temper. Cf. *lindíg*. 2. tantrum;
fit of bad temper, as of a child. Syn.
alboroto, sumpóng, ligalig.

almanák (al-ma-nák), *n.* (*Eng.*) almanac;
calendar. Syn. *almanake, kalindaryo*.

almasén (al-ma-sén), var. **almasín**, *n.* (*Sp.
almacén*) department store. Cf. *basár*.

almendras (al-men-dras), *n.* (*Sp. almendra*)
1. almond tree. 2. the fruit of this tree;
almond. Cf. *pili*.

almirante (al-mi-ran-te), *n.* (*Sp.*) admiral (in
the navy).

almirés (al-mi-rés), var. **almirís**, *n.* (*Sp.*) small
brass or stone mortar. Cf. *dikdikan, báyuhan*.

almiról (al-mi-ról), var. **amiról**, *n.* (*Sp.
almidón*) 1. laundry starch. Cf. *gawgáw*. 2.
the act or manner of stiffening clothes with
starch.

almohadón (al-mo-ha-dón), var. **almuhadón**,
n. (*Sp.*) cushion. Syn. *almohada*.

almoneda (al-mo-ne-da), *n.* (*Sp.; Econ.*) 1.
public auction. Cf. *subasta*. 2. bargain sale;

clearance sale. Syn. *baratilyo*.

almoranas (al-mo-ra-nas), var. **almuranas**, *n.*
(*Sp. almorranas*) hemorrhoid or piles. Syn.
magkaalmoranas.

almusál (al-mu-sál), var. **amusál** *n.* (*Sp.
almorzar*) 1. the first meal of the day;
breakfast. 2. breakfast food. 3. time for
breakfast. Syn. *agahan* (for senses 1-3)

alò (a-lò), *n.* 1. act of cheering (a person) up,
as by kind words, etc. 2. kind words used
to cheer up someone. 3. act of calming
down (a crying child) by singing a lullaby,
or by giving milk, toy, sucker, etc.

alók (a-lók), *i.* 1. act of offering something
for sale. 2. a proposal or offer to buy
(something) at a certain price. Syn. *tawad*.
3. the price offered for something. Syn.
tawad.

alog (a-log), *n.* pool of standing water, esp.
in a lowland or field. Syn. *sanaw, sanawan,
tubóg*.

alon (a-lon), *n.* 1. wave caused by wind or
earthquake on the surface of the sea. Cf.
daluyong. 2. a single curl or wave on a
person's hair. Cf. *kulót, unda*.

alpa (al-pa), var. **arpa**, *n.* (*Sp. arpa*) harp.

alpabeto (al-pa-be-to), *n.* (*Sp. alfabeto*)
alphabet. Syn. *abakada, abesedaryo*.

alpahól (al-pa-hól), *n.* (*Sp. ?*) sliced sweet
potatoes (*kamote*), cooked in syrup with
sagó.

alpás (al-pás), I. *adj.* loose; free; not confined;
not in captivity; not tied. Syn. *kawalá, di-
nakakulóng, di-nakatali, di-nakapiít, malayà*.

—II. *n.* fact or state of being free or loose,
referring esp. to animals.

alpilér (al-pi-lér), var. **arpilér**, *n.* (*Sp. alfiler*)
1. the common pin. Syn. *aspilé*. 2. brooch.
Syn. *brotse*.

alpombra (al-pom-bra), *n.* (*Sp. alfombra*)
carpet; rug; floor rug.

alsa (al-sa; al-sá), *n.* (*Sp. alza*) 1. act of lifting
or raising something from its position. Syn.
taás, buhat, angát. 2. rise; a becoming larger
or puffier, as of dough. Syn. *umbók, pag-
umbók; tambók, pagtambók*. 3. revolt;
rebellion; uprising. Syn. *bangon,
pagbabangon; himagsik, paghihimaksík;
rebelyón, rebolusyón*. 4. act of cutting (a
deck of cards). Cf. *angát, pag-angát; buhat,*

pagbuhat. 5. strike, as of workers; walkout. Syn. *welga, pagwewelga; aklás, pag-aaklás, aklasan.* 6. appearance on the surface, as of rashes and other skin eruptions. Syn. *litáw, paglitáw; singáw, pagsingáw.*

alsa-balutan (al-sa + ba-lu-tan), *n.* sudden departure or going away with all one's belongings due to disgust or feeling of being unwanted. Cf. *layas, paglayas.*

alsado (al-sa-do), *adj.* (Sp. *alzado*) 1. referring to something that has been slightly raised or lifted from its former position. Syn. *angát, nakaangát.* 2. referring to a deck of cards that has been cut. Syn. *naalsa na.* 3. light and puffy, referring to dough. Syn. *maumbók, matambók.* 4. embossed, as printed letters. Syn. *nakaumbók; litáw, nakalitaw; ultáw, nakaultáw.*

altapresyón (al-ta-pres-yón), *n.* (Sp. *alta presión*) high blood pressure.

altar (al-tar; al-tár), *n.* (Sp.; Eng.) altar. Syn. *dambanà.*

alugbati (a-lug-ba-ti), *n.* (Hlg.; Sb.) a succulent, herbaceous vine called 'Malabar night shade,' used as substitute for spinach. Syn. *libato.*

alugín (a-lu-gín), *v.* 1. to shake; cause to move back and forth, or from side to side, by or as by shaking. Cf. *ugain.* 2. to cause to be shaken, referring to something in a container. Syn. *kalugín.*

aluin (a-lu-in), *v.* to console or cheer up a lonely person or a crying child with or as with kind words. Syn. *amuin, amú-amuin, payapain, patahanín.*

alulód (a-lu-lód), *n.* a trough or channel along or under an eave or eaves to carry off rain water; gutter. Cf. *kanál, páagusán.*

alulong (a-lu-long), *n.* howling or barking of a dog or dogs, usually during night. Syn. *kahól, káhulan, tahól, táhulan.*

álulusán (álu-lu-sán), *n.* waterway; canal; gutter. Syn. *kanál, alulód, páagusán.*

alumahan (a-lu-ma-han), var. **lumahan**, *n.* (Ichth.) fish known as 'striped mackerel' (*Rastrelliger chrysozonus*).

alumana (a-lu-ma-na), *n.* 1. care; attention. Syn. *malasakit, ingat, pag-iingat.* 2. mindfulness; thoughtfulness. Syn. *asikaso, pag-aasikaso.* 3. notice or minding. Syn.

pansín, puná, inó.

aluminyo (a-lu-min-yo), *n.* (Sp. *aluminio*) aluminum; aluminium.

alumna (a-lum-na), *n.* 1. (Sp.) female student; co-ed. Syn. *kolehiyala.* 2. (Eng.) female graduate from a school, college, or university; alumna.

alumno (a-lum-no); a-lum-nó), *n.* (Sp.) 1. male student: Syn. *mag-aarál.* 2. male graduate from a school, college, or university.

alumpihít (a-lum-pi-hít), *n.* state or condition of being restive; restlessness. Syn. *alumihit, balisa, di-pagkápalagáy.*

alún-alón (a-lún + a-lón), I. *adj.* 1. wavy; with or having undulating curves. Syn. *unda-unda.* 2. curly. Syn. *kulót.*

—II. *n.* 1. waviness; wavy quality or state. 2. undulating curves.

alunignig (a-lu-nig-nig), *n.* 1. faint echo. Syn. *bahagyáng alingawngáw.* 2. faint idea about something heard. Syn. *hiwatig.*

alupihan (a-lu-pi-han), var. **ulupihan**, *n.* (Zool.) centipede.

alwagi (al-wa-gi), var. **anluwagi**, *n.* carpenter, esp. of bamboo structures. Cf. *karpintero.*

alwan (al-wan; al-wán), *n.* 1. ease of doing something. Syn. *dalî, kadalián; gaán, kagaanán.* Ant. *hirap, kahirapan.* 2. comfort; ease. Syn. *ginhawa, kaginhawahan.* 3. enjoyment; satisfaction. Syn. *kasiyahan, saráp, kasarapán.*

alwas (al-was; al-wás), *n.* act of unloading (a vehicle) completely. Cf. *diskarga.* 2. act of unharnessing an animal. Syn. *awás.* 3. act of emptying out a container completely. Cf. *halwat, halukay, halungkát.*

alyado (al-ya-do), I. *n.* (Sp. *aliado*) ally. Syn. *kakampí, kaanib, kapangkát, kasapì, kakupong.*

—II. *adj.* allied. Syn. *magkakampí, magkakakampí; magkakaanib, magkasapì, magkakasapì; magkapanalig, magka-kapanalig.*

alyansa (al-yan-sa), *n.* (Sp. *alianza*) alliance. Syn. *samahán, liga, unyón, kompederasyón.*

alyas (al-yas), *n.* (Sp.; Eng.) an assumed name; alias. Syn. *palayaw, tagurî, banság.*

am (am), *n.* (Ch.) rice broth.

ama (a-ma), *n.* (Sp.) 1. mistress. Syn. *sinyora,*

sinyorita. Cf. *amo, panginoón.* 2. amah; woman caretaker of children. Syn. *yaya, sisiwa.*

amá (a-má), n. 1. father. Syn. *tatay, itáy, dadi, papá.* 2. (*Colloq.*) founder; organizer. Syn. *tagapagtatag, pundadór.* 3. sponsor or author, as of a resolution. Syn. *may-panukalà, ang nagpanukalà.*

amá-amahan (a-má + a-ma-han), n. foster father.

amak (a-mak), n. 1. act of taming an animal; domestication. Syn. *pagpapaamò, pagmanso.* 2. act of befriending a person, as with kind words and good treatment. Syn. *suyò, pagsuyò.* 3. a small hut in the woods, hill, or mountain. Syn. *kubo, dampâ.*

amag (a-mag), n. 1. furry growth caused by fungi; mold. 2. mildew. Syn. *tagulamín, pekas.*

amaín (a-ma-ín), n. 1. the brother of one's father or mother; uncle. Syn. *tiyó, tiyóng, tiyuhin.* 2. stepfather. Syn. *amáng-pangumán.*

amano (a-ma-no), var. **amanos**, adj. (Sp. ?) even; owing and being owed nothing; equally gratified. Syn. *patas, pareho, bawî, impate, tablá, di-nanalo-di-natalo.*

amáng (a-máng), n. 1. boy; young boy. Syn. *totoy, totò, batà.* Cf. *iníng, nenè.* 2. a term for 'father' in some Tagalog regions. Syn. *amá, tatay, tatang.*

amáng-binyág (a-máng + bin-yág), var. **amambinyág,** n. male sponsor at baptism; baptismal godfather. Syn. *amá-sa-binyág, ináamá-sa-binyág.*

amargoso (a-mar-go-so), n. (*Sp.; Bot.*) bitter gourd; balsam apple (*Momordica balsamina*). Syn. *ampalayá.*

amarilyo (a-ma-ril-yo), I. n. (Sp. *amarillo*) 1. a plant with beautiful yellow flowers; marigold. 2. the yellow flowers of this plant. 3. yellow; yellow color. Syn. *diláw.* —II. adj. yellow; of yellow color. Syn. *diláw, madiláw.*

amasona (a-ma-so-na), n. (Sp. *amazona*) a mannish woman; amazon. Syn. *binalaki, tomboy.*

ambâ (am-bâ), n. 1. threatening gesture of the hand. Syn. *yambâ, akmâ, astâ.* 2.

grandfather (in some Tagalog regions). Syn. *lolo, abwelo, abuwelo, apò.*

ambasadór (am-ba-sa-dór; am-bá-sa-dór), n. ambassador. Syn. *embahadór, sugò, kinatawán.*

ambî (am-bî), n. 1. eaves. Syn. *áluluran, balisbís, bálisbisan.* 2. awning. Syn. *sibi, pasibi, medyaagwa.*

ambisyón (am-bis-yón), n. (Sp. *ambición*) ambition. Syn. *pangarap (fig.); adhikâ, adhíkain; layon, láyunin.*

ambón (am-bón), n. light shower or rain; drizzle. Syn. *paták-paták na ulán; ihing-langgám (fig.)*

ambos (am-bos; am-bós), n. (*Sp.*) 1. (*Colloq.*) consolation prize in a sweepstake draw. 2. a small share from something divided among many. Syn. *bahagi, kabahagi.*

ambulánsiyá (am-bu-lán-si-yá), n. (Sp. *abulancia*) ambulance.

amén (a-mén), I. interj. (*Sp.*) amen (in prayers). Syn. *siyanawâ.* —II. n. 1. act of kissing the hands of elders as a sign of respect. Syn. *mano, pagmano, pagmamano.* 2. act of saying 'yes', esp. to everything that another says.

amerikana (a-me-ri-ka-na), n. (Sp. *americana*) 1. man's coat. Cf. *abyerta, sarada.* 2. (A-) female American. Cf. *Amerikano.*

amiba (a-mi-ba): var. of **ameba.**

amiga (a-mi-ga), n. (*Sp.*) lady friend. Syn. *kaibigang babae.* Cf. *amigo.*

amigo (a-mi-go), n. (*Sp.*) friend; male friend. Syn. *kaibigan, katoto.* Cf. *amiga.*

amihan (a-mi-han), n. 1. breeze. Syn. *simoy.* 2. northeast wind. Cf. *habagat, balaklaot.*

amilyar (a-mil-yar), n. (Sp. *amillar*) land tax.

amin (a-min), I. pron. 1. (prepositive) we. *Aming gagawín iyán:* We shall do that. Syn. *namin* (postpositive). 2. (poss., exclusive, prepositive) our; ours. *Amin iyán:* That's ours. Syn. *namin.* Cf. *natin, atin.* —II. n. 1. admission or confession, as of one's guilt. Syn. *pagtatapát.* 2. act of appropriating something not his own. Syn. *angkín, pag-angkín.*

aminá (a-mi-na), v. (imperative) Give it over to me. Hand it over to me. Syn. *akiná.*

amís (a-mís), I. adj. 1. with or having one's wish, desire, or ambition unrealized;

disappointed; unfortunate. Syn. *bigô, nabigô; kapós-palad, kulang-palad, waláng-suwerte.* 2. oppressed; ill-treated. Syn. *apí, inapí, ináapí.*
—II. *n.* state or condition of being oppressed, maltreated, or disappointed.

amnestía (am-nes-tía), var. **amnistía**, *n.* amnesty. Syn. *ganáp na pagpapatawad (sa mga nagkasala sa pámahalaán).*

amnesyá (am-nes-yá), *n.* (*Sp.; Eng.*) amnesia. Cf. *pagkamalimutín.*

amo (a-mo), *n.* (*Sp.*) 1. master. Syn. *panginoón.* 2. boss; chief. Syn. *hepe, punò.* 3. employer. Syn. *ang may-patrabaho.* 4. landlord; owner. Syn. *may-arì.*

amò (a-mò), *n.* 1. fact or state of being domesticated or tame. Syn. *kaamuan, kamansuhán, pagkamansó.* 2. a domesticating or taming, as of an animal; domestication. Syn. *mansó, pagmansó.* 3. docility; kindness. Syn. *baít, kabaitán.* 4. civility; courtesy; politeness. Syn. *galang, kagalangan, pagkamagalang.* 5. befriending by coaxing or supplication. Syn. *suyò, pagsuyò.*

amonya (a-mon-ya), *n.* (*Eng.*) ammonia. Syn. *amonyako.*

among (a-mong), *n.* 1. (*Sl.*) vulgarism for 'priest.' Syn. *pari, padre.* 2. master. Syn. *panginoón.* 3. (*Colloq.*) boss; chief; head. Syn. *punò, hepe.*

amór (a-mór), *n.* (*Sp.*) 1. love. Syn. *pag-ibig, pagmamahál.* 2. esteem; affection. Syn. *gusto, pagkakagusto, paghangà.*

amorseko (a-mor-se-ko), var. **amorsiko**, *n.* (*Sp.*) burry love-grass (*Chrysopogon aciculatus* Retz.)

amortisasyón (a-mor-ti-sas-yón), *n.* (*Sp. amortización*) 1. an amortizing or being amortized. 2. money put aside for amortizing a debt, etc. Cf. *hulog, panghulog.*

amos (a-mos), *n.* dirt on face. Cf. *amol, dungis, dusing, tapíng.*

amot (a-mot), I. *n.* act of obtaining or buying a portion of goods from someone at cost. Cf. *bahagi, ambos.*
—II. *adj.* referring to something obtained or bought from someone at cost price.

amóy (a-móy), *n.* 1. act or manner of sensing the smell of something. Cf. *langháp,* *sangháp, singhót.* 2. smell; odor; any smell, pleasant or unpleasant. 3. bad odor; offensive smell; stench. Syn. *bahò, alingasaw, asngáw.* 4. (*Fig.*) act of finding out something by seçret means.

ampalayá (am-pa-la-yá), *n.* 1. (*Bot.*) balsam apple; bitter gourd (*Momordica balsamina* L.). Syn. *apalyá, amargoso.* 2. (*Fig.*) a very selfish person.

ampát (am-pát), I. *adj.* 1. checked or stopped, as the flow of blood in hemorrhage. Syn. *pigîl, hintô, tigil.* 2. suppressed or checked, as an uprising or rebellion. Syn. *apulâ, sawatâ, sugpò.*
—II. *n.* act of checking, stopping, or suppressing something. Syn. *apulà, pag-apulà; sawatâ, pagsawata; sugpò, pagsugpô.*

ampáw (am-páw), I. *n.* 1. sweetened popped rice or corn. 2. (*Colloq.*) state or condition of being weak, referring to a well person.
—II. *adj.* weak or infirm (s.o. persons).

ampibyan (am-pib-yan), I. *n.* (*Eng.*; *Zool.*) 1. any member of the amphibia; amphibian. 2. an aircraft or tank that can be used either on land or water.
—II. *adj.* 1. of the amphibia. 2. of the amphibious.

ampiteatro (am-pi-te-a-tro), *n.* (*Sp. anfiteatro*) amphitheatre, amphitheater. Syn. *dúlaang-pabilóg.*

ampiyás (am-pi-yás), *n.* 1. the entry of rain through open windows, doors, or the like, due to the force of wind. 2. such rain forced by wind to enter open windows, etc. Syn. *anggí.*

ampón (am-pón), I. *n.* 1. act of adopting (a person, esp. a child) as one's own. Syn. *kalingà, pagkalingà; andukâ, pag-andukâ; kupkóp, pagkupkóp; kandilì, pagkandilì.* 2. an adopted person, esp. a child.
—II. *adj.* adopted, as a child.

ampunan (am-pu-nan), *n.* asylum. Syn. *asilo, bahay-ampunan, kandilihán.*

amputasyón (am-pu-tas-yón), *n.* (*Sp. amputación*) cutting off a limb or limbs by surgery; amputation. Syn. *putol, pagputol.*

amukî (a-mu-kî), *n.* a persuading or being persuaded; persuasion; inducement. Syn. *himok, paghimok; hikayat, paghikayat.*

amuin · **andukâ**

amuin (a-mu-in), *v.* to cheer up or comfort (a person) with kind words. Cf. *suyuin, payapain*.

amutan (a-mu-tan), *v.* to give or sell a portion of one's goods to someone at cost price. Cf. *bahagihan*.

amuyín (a-mu-yín), *v.* to smell; test the odor or scent of by smelling.

anak (a-nak), *n.* kin; relative; relation. Syn. *angkán, lipì, lahì*.

anák (a-nák), *n.* 1. child; offspring; son or daughter. Syn. *suplíng, batà (colloq.)*. 2. an offspring or young of an animal. Cf. *sisiw, inakáy, tutà, guyà, bisiro*. 3. act, manner, or time of giving birth to a child. Syn. *pag-anák, pagsisilang*. 4. (*Colloq.*) result; outcome. Syn. *bunga, resulta*.

anák-anakan (a-nák + a-na-kan), *n.* foster child; foster son or daughter; also, an adopted child. Syn. *ampón; batang ampón*.

anák-araw (a-nák + a-raw), *n.* albino. Syn. *albino*.

anák-dálitâ (a-nák + dá-li-tâ), *adj.* born poor; born of poor parents. Syn. *anák-dukhâ, anák-mahirap, anák-pulubi*.

anakì (a-na-kì), I. *adj.* like; similar to. Syn. *katulad ng, animó (ay), tila, para (ng)*.
—II. *adv.* it seems; it looks like; as if. Syn. *tila mandín; warì bagá; mukhá (ng)*.

anakín (a-na-kín), *v.* 1. to adopt (a child) as one's own. Syn. *ampunín*. 2. to act or stand as sponsor of; be a godfather or godmother of.

anák-pawis (a-nák + pa-wis), I. *n.* the common laborer or worker; the common man. Syn. *manggagawá, trabahadór*.
—II. *adj.* born poor; born of poor parents; poor by birth. Syn. *dukhâ, marálitâ*.

anák sa labás (a-nák + sa + la-bás), *n.* an illegitimate child; bastard. Syn. *anák sa ligaw, anák sa puwera*.

anág-ag (a-nág + ag): var. of **anagág**.

ánagrám (á-na-grám), *n.* (*Eng.*) anagram. Syn. *anagrama*.

anahaw (a-na-haw), I. *n.* (*Bot.*) a species of palm (*Livistona rotundifolia* Mart.), the leaves of which are commonly made into fans, hats, etc.
—II. *adj.* made of anahaw leaves.

análisís (á-na-li-sís), *n.* (*Sp.*) 1. analysis. 2.

(*Gram.*) parsing. Syn. *pagsusuri* (for senses 1 & 2).

análogó (á-na-lo-gó), *adj.* (*Sp.*) analogous. Cf. *kahalintulad, magkahalintulad*.

anán (a-nán), var. **an-an**, *n.* (*Med.*) a kind of skin disease caused by fungus (*Tinea flava*). Cf. *pekas, balat, balikuskós*.

anáng (a-náng; fr. *a-* + *nang*), *adv.* 1. say or said by; as stated by. Syn. *sabi ng*. Cf. *aní, anilá, aniyá, aniyón*, etc. 2. in accordance with; according to; in a way consistent with. Syn. *alinsunod sa; sang-ayon sa*.

anarkismo (a-nar-kis-mo), *n.* (*Sp. anarquismo*) anarchism. Syn. *di-pagkilala sa batas o sa nakatatag sa pámahalaán*.

anás (a-nás), *n.* a low soft tone of the voice (slightly louder than whisper), esp. when telling something to another. Cf. *bulóng*.

anatomiya (a-na-to-mi-ya), var. **anatomyá**, *n.* (*Sp. anatomía*) anatomy.

anay (a-nay), *n.* (*Entom.*) 1. termite; white ant. 2. (*Fig.*) a traitor.

andadór (an-da-dór), *n.* (*Sp.*) a baby walker; gocart.

andamyo (an-dam-yo), *n.* (*Sp. andamio*) 1. work platform; scaffold. 2. gangplank. Syn. *túlayan*.

andante (an-dan-te), I. *adj.* (*Sp.; Mus.*) moderately slow; andante. Syn. *dahan-dahan; marahan nang bahagyâ*.
—II. *n.* a moderately slow movement or passage; andante.

andáp (an-dáp), *n.* flicker, as of a weak candle light about to die out. Syn. *kuráp, kisáp, kutitap*.

andár (an-dár), *n.* (*Sp.*) 1. function or operation, as of a machine. Syn. *takbó, pagtakbó; lakad, paglakad; pag-andár*. 2. progress or operation, as of business. Syn. *progreso, takbó, lakad, unlad*. 3. way or manner of movement or acting. Syn. *kilos, pagkilos; galáw, paggaláw*. 4. start of an activity. Syn. *simulâ; kilos, pagkilos*.

andás (an-dás), *n.* (*Sp.*) 1. stretcher; litter. Syn. *kamilya*. 2. bier, esp. one with horizontal shafts.

andukâ (an-du-kâ), var. **andukhâ**, *n.* 1. care, attention, or protection given to helpless persons, animals, etc. Syn. *arugâ, kandilì,*

tulong, tangkilik, alagà. 2. adoption, as of
an orphan. Syn. *ampón, pag-ampón.* 3.
constant efforts; diligence. Syn. *tiyagâ,
sipag, sikap.*

anekdota (a-nek-do-ta; a-nék-do-tá), *n.* (Sp.
anécdota) short, entertaining account;
anecdote. Cf. *salaysáy, kuwento; istorya.*

anemya (a-nem-ya), *n.* (Sp. *anemia;* Med.)
anemia. Syn. *kakulangan sa dugô.*

anestesya (a-nes-tes-ya), *n.* (Sp. *anestesia;*
Med.) 1. insensibility; anesthesia. Syn.
*kawaláng-pakiramdam;   manhíd,
pamamanhid.* 2. (Colloq.) anything that
produces anesthesia; anesthetic. Syn.
pampamanhíd; gamót-pampamanhíd.

ani (a-ni), *n.* 1. act of harvesting crops. Cf.
gapas, pupól. 2. crop harvested; harvest.
3. outcome or consequence reaped or
obtained from any effort. Syn. *palâ, tubò,
tamó, pakinabang.*

aní (a-ní), *adv.* according to (someone); say
or said (by). Cf. *aniyá, anilá, anikó, aniyón,*
etc.

anib (a-nib), *n.* 1. act of joining as a member
of an organization or union. Syn. *sapì,
pagsapì.* 2. fusion or coalition; union. Syn.
sama, pagsasama; pag-iisá. 3. act of joining
two things together, esp. by having the
sides overlap each other. Syn. *sanib, datig.*

anibersaryo (a-ni-ber-sar-yo), *n.* (Sp.
aniversario) anniversary. Syn. *kaarawán.*

anikó (a-ni-kó), *v.* (Idiom.; fr. *aní* + *ko*) said
I; I say or said. Syn. *sabi ko.* Cf. *anáng,
aní, anilá, aniyá,* etc.

anilá (a-ni-lá), *adv.* (fr. *a* + *nilá*) according
to them; they say or said. Syn. *sabi nilá,
alinsunod sa kanila.* Cf. *anikó, aniyá,
aniyón,* etc.

anim (a-nim), *n. & adj.* six. Syn. *seís, saís.*

animado (a-ni-ma-do), *adj.* (Sp.) 1.
animated; lively. Syn. *masiglá, masayá.* 2.
animate; alive; living; having life. Syn.
buháy, may-buhay.

animál (a-ni-mál), I. *n.* (Sp.) 1. animal;
beast; brute. Syn. *halimaw, hayop.* 2. a
brutish or inhuman person; also, a person
who is sensual. Syn. *taong-halimaw, taong-
makahayop.*

ánimás (á-ni-más), *n.* (Sp.; Eccl.) ringing or
church bells at sunset or at vespers. Cf.

orasyón.

animo (a-ni-mo; a-ni-mó), I. *prep.* (usually
used with *ay* or *'y*) like or similar to
(someone or something); somewhat
resembling (someone or something). Syn.
para ng (parang), katulad ng, kawangis ng.
—II. *adv.* as if. Syn. *mukhang; tila ba.*

ánimó (á-ni-mó) *n.* (Sp.) 1. spirit; soul. Syn.
káluluwá, diwà, ispiritu 2. liveliness;
animation. Syn. *siglá, kasiglahán.* 3.
courage; valor. Syn. *tapang, giting, lakás
ng loob.*

aninag (a-ni-nag), *adj.* slightly visible
through a translucent surface or object.
Syn. *sinág, násisinág; aninaw, náaaninaw.*
—II. *n.* 1. slight visibility through a
translucent object. 2. state or condition
of being translucent, referring to an
object. 3. act of looking closely at
something through a translucent surface
or object.

anináw (a-ni-náw), I. *adj.* seen or can be seen
through a transparent or translucent
object. Cf. *aninag, náaaninag; sinág,
násisinág.*
—II. *n.* 1. clear visibility through a
transparent object. Cf. *aninag, sinág.* 2.
state or condition of being transparent;
transparency. 3. act of looking at
something very closely; minute
examination of something. 4. (Fig.) a
trying to understand; understanding. Syn.
unawà, pag-unawà.

anino (a-ni-no), *n.* 1. shadow. Syn. *lilim.* 2.
image or reflection of something, as on
the surface of water. Cf. *larawan.* 3. trace;
faint suggestion or appearance. Cf. *bakás,
palatandaan.*

aninong gumágaláw (a-ni-nong + gu-má-ga-
láw), *n.* moving or motion picture;
photoplay. Cf. *sine, pelíkulá.*

anís (a-nís), *n.* (Sp.; Bot.) 1. the anise plant.
2. the seed of this plant; aniseed.

anisado (a-ni-sa-do), I. *adj.* (Sp.) anise-
flavored, referring esp. to wine. Syn. *may-
anís, inanisán.*
—II. *n.* a sweet, anise-flavored wine;
anisette. Syn. *alak-anisado.*

anit (a-nit), *n.* 1. scalp; skin on the top and
back of the head. Syn. *balát (ng ulo).* 2.

tonsure. Syn. *panot, panit.* 3. act of shaving the top or crown of the head close to the scalp. Cf. *panot, pagpanot.*

anito (a-ni-to), n. 1. heathen deity or god; idol. Syn. *diyús-diyusan.* 2. superstitious belief or custom. Syn. *pámahiín.* 3. amulet. Syn. *agimat, antíng-antíng, galíng.*

anitó (a-ni-tó), *adv.* (fr. *a* + *nitó*) according to this. Syn. *sabi nitó; alinsunod o sang-ayon dito.* Cf. *aniyón, aniré.*

aniyá (a-ni-yá), *adv.* (fr. *a* + *niyá*) according to him or her; said he or she. Syn. *sabi niyá, alinsunod o sang-ayon sa kanyá.* Cf. *aniyán, aniyón.*

anlaw (an-law; an-láw), I. *n.* washing with clean water as a last process in cleansing; rinse or rinsing. Syn. *banláw.* Cf. *hugas, labá, hináw.*

—II. *adj.* referring to something already rinsed or washed in clean water.

anó (a-nó), I. *interrog. pron.* what. *Anó ang pangalan mo?* What is your name?

—II. *relative pron.* anything that; whatever. *Gawín mo kung ano ang ibig mo.* Do whatever (anything that) you want.

—III. *interj.* an exclamation of surprise, anger, etc., more or less equivalent to "what!" *Anó! Aalís kang mulî?* What! You're leaving again?

anod (a-nod), I. *n.* 1. act or fact of being carried away by the flow or current of water. Cf. *tangáy.* 2. anything being carried away by the flow or current of water; specifically, flotage or flotsam.

—II. *adj.* referring to things carried away by the flow or current of water.

anomaliya (a-no-ma-li-ya), var. **anomalyá**, n. (Sp. *anomalia*) anomaly. Syn. *katiwalián, kaalingasngasán.*

anonas (a-no-nas), n. (Bot.; Sp. *anona*) custard apple tree (*Anona reticulata* Linn.). 2. its fruit called 'bullock's heart' or 'custard apple.'

anotasyón (a-no-tas-yón), n. (Sp. *anotación*) 1. an annotating or being annotated; annotation. 2. critical or explanatory note or notes. Syn. *komentaryo, talábabaan, paliwanag.*

anta (an-ta; an-tá), n. rancid odor or taste; rancidity.

antabay (an-ta-bay), n. act of waiting or slowing down in order to wait (for someone or something). Syn. *hintay, alalay.*

anták (an-ták), n. stinging pain, esp. of wounds or cuts caused by bladed tools. Syn. *kirót, matindíng sakít o hapdî.*

antagonismo (an-ta-go-nis-mo), n. (Sp.) antagonism; ill will. Syn. *galit, pagkagalit, kagalitan.* 2. hostile act; expression of ill will. Syn. *paglaban, pagkalaban.*

antala (an-ta-la), n. 1. delay; a being delayed. Syn. *abala, pagkaabala; bimbín, pagkabimbín; atraso, pagkaatraso.* 2. act of intentionally causing delay. Syn. *pag-abala, pagbimbín, pag-atraso.* 3. a native delicacy made of glutinuous rice, cooked dry in coconut milk with little salt and sugar. Syn. *inangít.* 4. the act or process of cooking this native delicacy.

antandâ (an-tan-dâ) n. (fr. *ang* + *tandâ*) act of making the sign of the cross, as before and after praying.

antártikó (an-tár-ti-kó), I. *adj.* (Sp. *antártico*) of or near the South Pole or the region around it; antarctic.

—II. *n.* the region around the South Pole; antarctic.

antas (an-tas; an-tás), n. 1. social rank, position, or class. Syn. *rango, urì, klase.* 2. any of the stages in an orderly progression; step. Syn. *hakbáng.* 3. (in school curriculum) grade or year. Syn. *grado, baitang, taón.* 4. phase; stage. Syn. *bahagi.* 5. level; step. Syn. *andana, baitang.*

antáy (an-táy), I. *n.* 1. act of waiting for (someone or something). Syn. *hintáy, paghihintáy; antabay, pag-aantabay.* 2. something being expected or awaited. Syn. *ang hiníhintáy o ináantabayanan.*

—II. *interj.* Wait! Syn. *Hintáy!*

antem (an-tem), n. (Eng.) anthem. Syn. *imno, awit.*

antemano (an-te-ma-no), var. **antimano**, *adv.* (Sp.) 1. previously; beforehand; at first. Syn. *sa una pa, noón pa, noón pang una, muna.* 2. at once. Syn. *agád, kaagád pagdaka, kapagdaka.*

antemeridyan (an-te-me-rid-yan), *adj.* (Eng.) antemeridian; before noon. Syn.

antena　　　　　　　　　　　　　　　　**anupá**

bago tumanghalì.

antena (an-te-na), n. (*Sp.*; *Eng.*; *Telev. & Rad.*) antenna; aerial.

anti (an-ti), I. adj. (*Colloq.*; *Eng.*) opposed; against. Syn. *laban, kontra, salungát.* —II. n. 1. a person opposed or against some policy, proposal, etc. Syn. *kalaban, kasalungat, kakontra.* 3. (*Pol.*) a member or members of an opposition party. Syn. *oposisyón.*

antikristo (an-ti-kris-to), adj. (*Sp. anticristo*) antichrist; opposed or against Christ. —II. n. (A- C-) Anti-Christ; enemies of Christ.

antikuwado (an-ti-ku-wa-do), var. **antikwado**, adj. (*Sp. anticuado*) 1. obsolete; outdated. Syn. *lipás na.* 2. antiquated. Syn. *sinauna, sáunahín, makalumà.*

antidót (an-ti-dót), n. (*Eng.*) antidote. Syn. *kontra-lason.*

antigín (an-ti-gín), v. 1. to remind a person about something, esp. a promise or an obligation. Syn. *banggitín, ipaalaala.* 2. to touch, tap, or strike lightly. Cf. *kalabitín, tapikín, hipuin, pintigín.*

antigo (an-ti-go), adj. (*Sp. antiguo*) ancient; old. Syn. *lumà, matandâ, sinauna.*

anting (an-ting), n. amulet; fetish. Syn. *galíng, agimat, sapì.*

antíng-antíng (an-tíng + an-tíng), n. same as **anting**.

antiparas (an-ti-pa-ras), n. (*Sp. antiparras*) 1. binoculars. Syn. *largabista, teleskopyo.* 2. spectacles; goggles. Syn. *salamín (sa matá).*

antipatiya (an-ti-pa-ti-ya), var. **antipatyá**, n. (*Sp. antipatia*) antipathy; dislike; aversion.

antipolo (an-ti-po-lo), n. 1. (*Bot.*) a timber tree belonging to the third group (*Artocarpus* L). 2. the lumber obtained from this tree. 3. (A-) name of a town in Rizal province, Philippines.

antiséptikó (an-ti-sép-ti-kó), adj. & n. (*Sp. antiseptico*) antiseptic; disinfectant.

antisipo (an-ti-si-po), n. (*Sp. anticipo*; *Econ.*) partial advance payment. Syn. *páunáng-bayad; adelanto, deposito.*

antisosyál (an-ti-sos-yál), adj. (*Sp. antisocial*) antisocial; subversive.

antitesis (an-ti-te-sis), n. (*Sp.*; *Rhet.*) antithesis. Cf. *kahidwaán, kasalungatán, kabaligtarán.*

antók (an-tók), n. sleepy feeling; sleepiness; drowsiness. Also, *pag-aantók, kaantukán.*

antolohiya (an-to-lo-hi-ya; an-to-ló-hi-yá), n. (*Sp. antologia*) anthology. Syn. *katipunan, koleksiyón.*

antót (an-tót), n. repulsive odor of urine or stagnant water. Syn. *panghí, bantót, antóng, angót.* Cf. *bahò.*

antropolohiya (an-tro-po-lo-hi-ya; an-tro-po-lo-hi-yá), n. (*Sp. antropologia*) anthropology. Syn. *agham-tao, agtao.*

anú-anó (a-nú + a-nó), pron. 1. plural form of **anó**, used in asking questions about things of different kinds. *Anú-anó ba ang binilí mo?* What are the things you bought? 2. (*Colloq.*) referring to different things. *Kung anú-anó ang sinasabi niyá.* He is talking of different things.

anubá (a-nu-bá), interj. (fr. *anó + ba*) an exclamation expressive of disgust, more or less equivalent to 'Hey!' or 'Why!'

anuhín (a-nu-hín), v. to do something on a person or thing with malice or as a plain joke. Cf. *hipuin, biruin, galawín, pakialamán.*

anulá (a-nu-lá), n. (*Sp. anulár*) an annulling or voiding. Syn. *pagpapawaláng-saysáy, pagpapawaláng-bisà.*

anumán (a-nu-mán), I. pron. 1. whatever; whatsoever (emphatic form). Distinguished from **anó man**. 2. any thing, fact, etc. —II. n. a thing, no matter of what kind; anything. Syn. *kulúb-anó, kahit-anó.*

anunsiyo (a-nún-si-yó; a-nun-si-yó), n. (*Sp. anuncio*) 1. advertisement. Syn. *paanunsiyó.* 2. announcement; notice. Syn. *balità, paunawà, babalâ, pahayag, abiso.* 3. (*Colloq.*) warning; sign. Syn. *babalâ, pahiwatig, palátandaan.*

anupá (a-nu-pá), I. interj. (fr. *anó + pa*) What else! What more! —II. pron. what else; what more. *Anupá ang aking magágawâ?* What else can I do? —III. adv. (used usually in the form **anupa't**) 1. in such a manner; in that way.

Syn. *sa gayón.* 2. hence; therefore; consequently. Syn. *samakatwíd.*

ánuwál (á-nu-wál), var. **ánwal,** I. adj. (*Sp. anual*), annual; yearly; once a year. Syn. *taunan; minsan santaon.*

anuwaryo (a-nu-war-yo), var. **anwaryo,** *n.* (Sp. *anuario*) 1. yearbook; annual. Syn. *táunang-aklát, ánuwál.* 2. yearly report. Syn. *táunáng-ulát.*

anyaya (an-ya-ya), *n.* act of inviting someone; verbal invitation. Syn. *imbità, kumbidá.* Cf. *yayà, yakag.*

anyeho (an-ye-ho), *n.* (Sp. *añejo*) aged wine; year-old wine.

ányo (án-yo), *n.* (Sp. *año*) year. Syn. *taón.*

anyô (an-yô), *n.* 1. shape; form; figure. Syn. *hugis, tabas, pigura, korte.* 2. appearance; looks. Syn. *hitsura, ayos.* 3. state or condition; situation. Syn. *lagáy, kalagayan.* 4. manner of acting; gesture. Syn. *kilos, galáw, astâ,* 5. order; orderly condition. Syn. *ayos, kaayusan.*

anyo-bisyesto (an-yo + bis-yes-to), *n.* (Sp. *año bisiesto*) leap year. Syn. *taóng pares.*

anyonuwebo (an-yo-nu-we-bo), *n.* (Sp. Año Nuevo) New Year. Syn. *Bagong Taón.*

ang (ang), *art.* the. *Note: Ang* is used before common nouns, indefinite pronouns, and proper nouns, except names of persons; it is commonly omitted or not translated at all in some English forms. *Gawín mo ang sinásabi ko sa iyó:* Do what I am telling you.

angal (a-ngal), *n.* 1. loud cry or weeping, as of a child. Syn. *palakat, iyák na malakás.* Cf. *atungal, ungal.* 2. expression of resentment or opposition; complaint. Syn. *reklamo, tutol.*

ang-ang (ang + ang), I. *n.* 1. act or habit of stuttering, characterized by the repetition or prolongation of the sound of *ang,* usually at the start of every sentence. Cf. *at-at.* 2. in cooking food, esp. rice, too long exposure over a low fire, resulting in overdryness of the food. 3. fact or state of being overdried or over-cooked due to long exposure over a low fire, referring esp. to rice. Syn. *tayangtáng.* Cf. *inín (in-in).*

—II. *adj.* 1. with or having the habit of stuttering. Cf. *utál, at-at, gago.* 2. overheated or overtoasted due to long

exposure over a low fire, referring to food, esp. rice. Syn. *tayangtángin, pagáng.*

angás (a-ngás), *n.* 1. arrogant; haughty; boastful. Syn. *hambóg, mayabang, burot (sl.), mahangin (fig.)* 2. given to complaining unnecessarily. Syn. *mareklamo.*

angát (a-ngát), I. *n.* 1. act or manner of lifting or raising a thing slightly from its position. Syn. *alsá, buhat, taás.* 2. fact or condition of being slightly lifted or raised. 3. the extent to which a thing is lifted or raised. 4. a being above another or others in rank, position, standard of living, etc. Cf. *higít, kahigtán; taás, kataasan.*

—II. *adj.* 1. slightly raised or lifted. Cf. *awáng, kawang, alsado.* 2. better or higher in rank, position, etc. Syn. *nakahíhigít, nakatátaás.*

angaw (a-ngaw), I. *n.* 1. (*Ch.*) million. Syn. *sanlibong libo.* 2. (*Colloq.*) an uncountable number of things. Syn. *katakut-takot na dami.*

—II. *adj.* 1. numbering one million. 2. very, very many.

angkák (ang-kák), *n.* a specially treated cereal used for seasoning, particularly for fish and shrimps.

angkán (ang-kán), *n.* 1. family; family lineage; clan. Syn. *pamilya, mag-anak, kaanak.* 2. generation. Syn. *salinlahì, henerasyón.* 3. tribe. Syn. *tribo, lipì, lahì.*

angkás (ang-kás), I. *n.* 1. a ride with someone. 2. act of riding together on horseback or in the same vehicle. Syn. *sunò, pagsunò, pakikisunò.* 3. a person or persons riding or taking a ride with another. Syn. *kasunò, kasakáy.*

—II. *adj.* referring to a person riding with another, or to two persons riding together on a horse or in the same vehicle. Syn. *sunò, magkasunò.*

angkát (ang-kát), I. *n.* act or business of importing goods from foreign countries; importation. Syn. *pag-angkát.* 2. act or manner of obtaining goods (for sale) on consignment basis. Syn. *sakâ, pagsakâ.* 3. goods imported from abroad; imports. 4. goods obtained on consignment basis.

—II. *adj.* 1. imported from abroad, referring

to goods. 2. obtained on consignment basis, referring to local commodities.

aṅgkín (ang-kín), I. n. 1. act of appropriating something for oneself; claiming something as one's own. Cf. *kamkám, pagkamkám*. 2. anything inherent or inborn to someone. Syn. *katangian.*
—II. *adj.* 1. referring to something appropriated or claimed by someone for himself. Syn. *kamkám, kinamkám; inangkín.* 2. inherent or inborn to someone. Syn. *likás, katutubò, sarili.*

aṅgkla (ang-kla), n. (Sp. *ancla*; *Naut.*) 1. anchor. Syn. *angkora, sinipete.* 2. a shallow-water fish corral similar to *ágilá.* Cf. *baklád, bangkulóng.*

aṅgkóp (ang-kóp), I. *adj.* 1. proper; suitable; appropriate; suited. Syn. *bagay, nababagay, kabagay.* 2. fit; qualified. Syn. *dapat, karapat-dapat.* 3. right; correct. Syn. *tamà, tumpák, tugmâ.*
—II. *n.* 1. act or manner of fitting or adjusting something in place properly. 2. state or condition of being proper, right, or appropriate.

anggi (ang-gi; ang-gí), n. 1. entry of rain through an open window door, etc. due to the force of wind. 2. the rain or spatters of rain entering a place through an open window, door, etc. Syn. *ampiyás* (for both meanings).

ángguló (áng-gu-ló), n. (Sp. *ángulo*) 1. angle. Cf. *sulok, panulukan.* 2. aspect, as of a problem; point of view. Cf. *kuru-kurò, palagáy, panináw.*

angháng (ang-háng), var. **hangháng**, n. 1. taste of pepper; pepperiness; pungency to the taste. Cf. *paít, alat.* 2. (*Fig.*) pungency or disagreeableness, as of an expression or criticism. Cf. *sakít, kasakitán.*

anghel (ang-hel; ang-hél), n. (Sp. *angel*) 1. angel. Cf. *kerubín.* 2. (A-) a masculine name. Cf. *Angheló, Anghelá.*

anghelús (ang-he-lús), n. (*Sp.-Lat.*) angelus. Syn. *orasyón, ánimás.*

anghina (ang-hi-na), n. (Sp. *angina*; *Med.*) 1. angina. 2. angina pectoris.

anghít (ang-hít), n. the peculiar offensive odor of armpits, goats, and similar animals. Cf. *anggó, panghî, bahò.*

angí (a-ngí), n. the peculiar odor or smell of burnt rice while being cooked. Syn. *anós, kanós.*

angíl (a-ngíl), *adj.* given to growling or muttering complaints angrily.

angó (a-ngó), n. peculiar odor or smell of some fresh meat, esp. of goats, sheep, or the like. Cf. *anggo.*

angót (a-ngót), n. peculiar odor of spoiled meat; stench peculiar to stagnant water. Cf. *bahò, panghí, bantót.*

aorta (a-or-ta), n. (*Eng.*; *Sp.*) aorta.

apa (a-pa), n. (*Jap.*) 1. thin rolled wafer made of rice flour and brown sugar. Cf. *barkilyós.* 2. a cone-shaped container for ice cream, made of wafer.

apak (a-pak), n. 1. act of stepping on something. Syn. *tapak, yapak, tuntóng.* 2. footstep; footprint. Syn. *bakás-paá.*

apák (apak), *adj.* barefoot; barefooted. Syn. *yapák, tapák.*

apahap (a-pa-hap), n. (*Ichth.*) fish called 'silver sea bass' (*Lates calcarifer*).

apalit (a-pa-lit), n. (*Bot.*) 1. sandalwood tree. 2. (A-) name of a town in the province of Pampanga.

apanas (a-pa-nas), n. (*Entom.*) small, whitish and fast-moving ants that usually infest left-over boiled rice. Cf. *langgám, guyam.*

aparadór (a-pa-ra-dór), n. (*Sp.*) 1. cupboard; sideboard. Syn. *paminggalan.* 2. clothes' cabinet or closet; wardrobe; dresser. Cf. *istante, iskaparate.*

aparato (a-pa-ra-to), n. (*Sp.*) 1. machine; apparatus. Syn. *mákiná.* 2. instrument; tool; device. Syn. *kasangkapan, kagamitán, instrumento.*

aparisyón (a-pa-ris-yón), n. (Sp. *aparición*) 1. apparition; vision. Syn. *pangitain, bisyón.* 2. ghost; phantom; spectre. Syn. *multo, impakto.* 3. figment of the mind; phantasm. Syn. *malikmatà, guni-guní.*

apartmen (a-part-men), var. **apartment**, n. (*Eng.*) 1. a room or suit of rooms to live in; apartment. Syn. *silíd-tírahan o mga silíd-tírahan.* 2. (*Colloq.*) an apartment house. Cf. *posisyón.*

apasyonado (a-pas-yo-na-do), *adj.* (Sp. *apacionado*) passionate; impassioned. Syn. *madamdamin.*

apat (a-pat), n. & adj. four.

apatiya (a-pa-ti-ya), var. **apatyá**, n. (Sp. apatia) 1. lack of emotion or feeling; apathy. Syn. kawaláng-damdamin. 2. lack of interest; indifference. Syn. kawaláng-malasakit, lamíg o kalamigán ng loób, pagkaindiperente.

apaw (apaw), I. n. 1. an overflowing, as of water, cereals, etc. from a container. Syn. awas. 2. flood; inundation; deluge. Syn. bahâ, pagbahâ.
—II. adj. 1. overflowing. Syn. awas, umaawas. 2. flooded; inundated. Syn. bahâ, sanaw.

apdó (ap-dó), n. (Anat.) 1. bile; gall. 2. gall bladder.

apeksiyón (a-pek-si-yón), n. (Sp. afección) 1. warm liking; fond of tender feeling or attachment. Syn. pagmamahál, pag-ibig. 2. a disease; ailment. Syn. karamdaman, sakít.

apektado (a-pek-ta-do), adj. (Sp. afectado) affected; having effect on.

apelá (a-pe-lá), n. (Sp. apelar) in Law, appeal.

apelyido (a-pel-yi-do), n. (Sp. apellido) family name; surname. Syn. ngalang-angkán, pangalang-angkán.

apendisé (a-pen-di-sé), n. (Sp. apendice) appendix; supplementary material at the end of a book. Syn. suplemento.

apendisitis (a-pen-di-si-tis), n. (Sp. apendicitis) 1. (Med.) appendicitis; inflammation of the vermiform appendix. 2. (Anat.) appendix; vermiform appendix.

apí (a-pí), I. adj. 1. maltreated; oppressed; looked down upon. Syn. kaawá-awà, dustâ, abâ. 2. aggrieved; taken advantage of. Syn. pinagsamantalahán, pinagsásamantalahán.
—II. n. 1. act of treating another with injustice; maltreatment. Syn. pagdustâ, pagabâ, pagpapahirap. 2. taking advantage of. Syn. pagsasamantalá, pag-apí. 3. a person or persons who is (are) maltreated, looked down upon, or taken advantage of.

apikultura (a-pi-kul-tu-ra), n. (Sp. apicultura) art of beekeeping; apiculture. Syn. pag-aalagà ng laywán o pukyutan.

apíd (a-píd), n. concubinage; illicit cohabitation. See pakikiapíd.

apidabit (a-pi-da-bit), n. (Eng.) affidavit. Syn. sinumpaáng-pahayag, alusithâ.

apinahin (a-pi-na-hin), v. to tune; put into right tune. Syn. isatono.

apinidád (a-pi-ni-dád), n. (Sp. afinidad) 1, relation by marriage. Syn. relasyón o pagkakamag-anak dahil sa matrimonyo. 2. liking. Syn. hilig, pagkahilig, kahiligan, pagkagusto. 3. likeness; similarity. Syn. pagkakatulad, pagkakahawig. 4. relationship; affinity. Syn. relasyón, pagkakaugnáy, kaugnayan. 5. mutual attraction between a man and a woman. Syn. pag-iibigan, pagmamahalan, pagkakagustuhan.

apirmasyón (a-pir-mas-yón), n. (Sp. afirmación) 1. confirmation; ratification. Syn. patibay, pagpapatibay. 2. declaration; assertion. Syn. pahayag, pagpapahayag. 3. declaration that a thing is true. Syn. patunay, pagpapatunay; patotoó, pagpapatotoó.

apisyón (a-pis-yón), n. (Sp. afición) 1. fondness; inclination. Syn. hilig, kahiligan, pagkamahilig. 2. hobby; avocation. Syn. líbangan, áliwan.

apitong (a-pi-tong), n. (Bot.) 1. a timber tree producing third class lumber (Dipterocarpus grandflorus Blanco). 2. the lumber obtained from this tree.

aplaya (a-pla-ya; ap-la-ya), n. (Sp. playa) beach; sandy shore or seashore. Syn. pasigan, dalampasigan. Cf. baybayin, baybaying-dagat, baybay-dagat, tabing-dagat.

apó (a-pó), n. 1. grandchild; grand-daughter or grandson.

apò (a-pò), n. 1. master. Syn. amo, panginoón. 2. grand old man; grandfather. Syn. lolo, abwelo. 3. boss; chief. Syn. punò, hepe.

apog (a-pog), n. lime.

Apolo (a-po-lo), n. (Sp; Myth.) 1. Apollo, god of the sun. 2. (A-) a masculine name.

aporo (a-po-ro), var. **apuro**, n. (Sp. aforro) dress lining. Syn. tutóp, laining.

apó-sa-sakong (a-pó + sa + sa-kong), n. great great grandchild.

apó-sa-talampakan (a-pó + sa + ta-lam-pa-kan), n. great great great grandchild.

apó-sa-tuhod (a-pó + sa + tu-hod), n. great grandchild.

apostól (a-pos-tól), var. *apostoles*, n. (*Sp.*) apostle. Syn. *alagad*.

apostolado (a-pos-to-la-do), var. **apostulado**, n. (*Sp.*; *Eccl.*) apostolate.

apostólikó (a-ps-tó-li-kó) var. **apostúliko**, *adj.* (Sp. *apostólico*) apostolic.

apóy (a-póy), n. 1. fire; flame. Syn. *ningas, liyág, alab.* 2. conflagration; destructive fire. Syn. *sunog, siláb.* 3. (*Fig.*) intense anger. Syn. *matindíng galit, ngitngít, sikláb ng galit.*

apritada (ap-ri-ta-da), I. n. (*Sp. fritada*) a dish of fish or meat sauteed with tomatoes, green pepper, potatoes, etc. Syn. *pritada.* —II. *adj.* referring to fish or meat sauteed with tomatoes, green pepper, potatoes, etc.

aprobá (a-pro-bá), n. (Sp. *aprobar*) approval. Syn. *patibay, pagpapatibay.*

aproksimasyón (a-prok-si-mas-yón), n. (Sp. *aproximación*) 1. approximation; approach or approaching. Syn. *lapit, paglapit.* 2. close estimate. Syn. *taya, pagtaya.*

aptitúd (ap-ti-túd), n. (*Sp.*) 1. aptitude; fitness. Syn. *kaangkupán, kaumpakán.* 2. ability. Syn. *kakayahán.* 3. natural tendency or inclination. Syn. *hilig, kahiligan, pagkamahilig.*

apuhap (a-pu-hap), n. 1. a groping or feeling about with one's hand, as in finding one's way or looking for something in the dark. Syn. *kapâ, pagkapá-kapâ.* 2. act of looking for searching blindly for something, as in desperation. Syn. *hagilap, paghagilap, paghahagiláp.*

apulà (a-pu-là), n. act of checking or stopping the spread or progress of something undesirable. Syn. *sugpô, pagsugpô; pigil, pagpigil; sawatâ, pagsawatâ; payapâ, pagpayapà.*

apulid (a-pu-lid), n. (*Bot.*) water chestnut.

apunta (a-pun-ta; a-pun-tá), n. (Sp. *apuntar*) 1. aim or aiming at, with or as with a gun. Syn. *puntirya (puntriya), tutok, pagtutok.* 2. sudden attack, as of sickness. Syn. *sumpóng, atake.*

apurá (a-pu-rá), n. (Sp. *apurar*) 1. act of doing or having something done in a hurry. Syn. *dalí-dalì, pagdadalí-dalì, pagmamadalí, pag-aapurá.* 2. act of urging someone to go or work faster.

ápuyán (á-pu-yán), n. 1. hearth; fireplace. Syn. *kakalanan.* 2. stove. Syn. *kalán, pugón, tungkô.* 3. matchbox. Syn. *bahay-posporó; kasapwego.*

apuyán (a-pu-yán), v. 1. to set fire on; to burn. Syn. *sindihán, susuhan.* 2. (*Fig.*) to incite; make angry. Syn. *sulsulán, pagalitin.*

apuyín (a-pu-yín), v. to be or feel very hot, as with fever. Cf. *lagnatín.*

arabál (a-ra-bál), n. (Sp. *arrabal*) suburb. Syn. *suburbiyó, paligid-lunsód.*

Arabé (A-ra-bé), I. n. (*Sp.*) 1. an Arabian citizen. 2. the Arabian language. —II. *adj.* Arabian; Arabic.

aral (a-ral), n. 1. moral lesson; teaching or moral learned from reading (something). Syn. *liksiyón.* Cf. *kabatiran, kaalamán.* 2. advice; admonition; counsel. Syn. *payo.* 3. instruction; education. Syn. *turò.* 4. act of studying; study. Syn. *pag-aaral.*

arál (a-rál), adj. given to studying; studious. Syn. *palaarál.* 2. trained; well-trained. Syn. *sanáy.*

aralán (a-ra-lán), I. n. an apprentice; beginner. Syn. *baguhan, aprendis, aprentís.* —II. *adj.* said of a person who needs teaching or training. Syn. *turuán.*

aralín (a-ra-lín), n. lesson or assignment in class.

aranya (a-ran-ya; a-ran-yá), n. (Sp. *araña*) 1. chandelier. 2. spider. Syn. *gagambá.*

arangkada (a-rang-ka-da), n. (Sp. *arrancada*) sudden start; spurt; burst of speed.

araro (a-ra-ro), n. (Sp. *arado*) 1. plow. Syn. *arado.* 2. act or manner of plowing. Syn. *pag-aararo.*

ararú (a-ra-rú), var. **araró**, n. (*Bot.*) arrowroot (*Marantha arudinacea*).

aras (a-ras), n. (Sp. *arras*) the traditional gift of thirteen pieces of coins given by the bridegroom to his bride.

araw (a-raw), n. 1. sun. 2. day; daytime; distinguished from *gabí.* Syn. *adláw* (Bis., for senses 1 & 2.). 3. day of the week, namely, *Linggó, Lunes, Martes, Miyerkolés, Huwebes, Biyernes, Sábadó.* 4. anniversary. Syn. *anibersaryo.* 5. day of birth; birthday. Syn. *kaarawán, kapanganakan.* 6. date; day of the month. Syn. *petsa.* 7. (*Fig.*) opportunity; chance. Syn. *pagkakataón.* 8.

time; period. Syn. *panahón.*

arawán (a-ra-wán), *adj. & adv.* paid by the day; on a daily basis. See **aráw.**

araw-araw (a-raw + a-raw), *adj. & adv.* daily; every day.

aráw-arawin (a-ráw + a-ra-win), *v.* to do (a thing) every day; repeat doing (a thing) every day.

araw-gabí (a-raw + ga-bí), *adj. & adv.* day and night; all day and night. Cf. *araw-araw, gabí-gabí.*

aráy (a-ráy), var. **arúy,** interj. Ouch!

árbitrá (ár-bit-rá), *n.* (Sp. *arbitrar*) settlement of a dispute by an arbiter. Syn. *hatol, paghatol, husgá, paghusgá.* Cf. *pamamagitan.*

arbol (ar-bol; ar-ból), *n.* (Sp.) 1. a tree; arbor. Syn. *kahoy, punong-kahoy.* 2. a shaft; beam; mast. Cf. *poste; haligi.*

arbolaryo (ar-bo-lar-yo), var. **arbularyo, erbolaryo,** *n.* (Sp. *herbolario*) 1. quack doctor; herb doctor. Syn. *doktór-laway (colloq.), médikóng-taingá (colloq.)* 2. herb collector; herbalist.

arka (ar-ka), *n.* (Sp. *arca*) ark, as in *arka ni Noé,* Noah's ark.

arkada (ar-ka-da), *n.* (Sp. *arcada*) row of arches; arcade.

arkansiya (ar-kan-si-ya; ar-kan-si-yá), var. **alkansiya,** *n.* (Sp. *alcancia*) piggy bank; child's bank.

arkanghel (ar-kang-hel; ar-kang-hél), *n.* (Sp. *arcangel*) 1. archangel. 2. (A-) a masculine name.

arkayko (ar-kay-ko), *adj.* (Sp. *arcaico*) archaic; out-of-date. Syn. *lipás na, di na ginagámit.*

arkeolóhiyá (ar-ke-o-ló-hi-yá), var. **arkeyolóhiyá,** *n.* (Sp. *arquelogía*) archaeology.

arkero (ar-ke-ro), *n.* (Sp. *arquero*) 1. archer. Syn. *mámamanà.* 2. bow maker. Syn. *manggagawang-panà.*

arkipélagó (ar-ki-pé-la-gó), *n.* (*Eng.*) archipelago. Syn. *kapuluan.*

arkitektura (ar-ki-tek-tu-ra), *n.* (Sp. *arquitectura*) architecture.

arko (ar-ko; ar-kó), *n.* (Sp. *arco*) 1. arch. Syn. *balantók.* 2. arc. Cf. *hubog.* 3. bow (for arrows). Syn. *busog.* 4. bow (for violins).

Syn. *panghilis.*

areglado (a-reg-la-do), *adj.* (Sp. *arreglado*) 1. well-arranged; in good order. Syn. *ayós, maayos, nasa-ayos.* 2. well-disciplined; trained. Syn. *disiplinado, sanáy.* 3. okayed; approved. Syn. *aprobado, pinagtibay na.* 4. finished; through. Syn. *ayós na, tapós na.*

areglo (a-reg-lo; a-reg-ló), *n.* (Sp. *arreglo*) 1. an arranging or being arranged; arrangement; putting in order. Syn. *ayos, pag-aayos, pagkakaayos.* 2. repair or repairing. Syn. *kumpuní, pagkukumpuní, pagkakakumpuní,* 3. agreement; compromise. Syn. *kásunduan, pagkakásundô.* 4. amicable settlement, as of a dispute or misunderstanding. Syn. *pag-aaregló, pagsasaayos, pagpapakásundô.*

arena (a-re-na), *n.* field of battle or conflict; arena. Syn. *larangan.*

arendamyento (a-ren-dam-yen-to), var. **arindamyento,** *n.* (Sp. *arrendamiento*) 1. act of renting; lease or leasing. 2. rental.

arestado (a-res-ta-do), *adj.* (Sp. *arestado*) 1. arrested; captured; taken into custody, as by an authority. Syn. *hinuli, inaresto.* 2. stopped or checked. Syn. *sugpò na, pigíl na.*

arestes (a-res-tes), *n.* (Sp. *arete*) earring or earrings. Syn. *hikaw, arilyós.*

argolya (ar-gol-ya), var. **arigolya,** *n.* (Sp. *argolla*) 1. a ring or circular band of metal, as that used to hang curtains. Cf. *singsíng.* 2. iron ring usually used in pair or pairs by acrobats. 3. the acrobatic display or exercises made on a pair of rings suspended on a crossbar or the like.

argumento (ar-gu-men-to), *n.* (Sp.) 1. argument; reasoning. Syn. *katwiran, pangangatwiran.* 2. debate; discussion. Syn. *pagtatalo, debate.*

arì (a-rì), *n.* 1. personal belonging; property or possession. Syn. *arí-arian, pag-aarì, propiyedad.* 2. acceptability. Syn. *pagkamaáarì.* 3. (Colloq.) genital organ. Syn. *pag-aarì, punong-katawán.*

ará (a-rá), var. **iri,** I. *pron.* this; this one. Cf. *itó, heto.*

—II. *interj.* Here! Here it is! Syn. *Itó! Heto!*

arí-arian (a-rí + a-ri-an), *n.* property or

properties; possession or possessions. Syn. *propiyedád, biyenes, kayamanan*.

ariin (a-ri-in), *v.* 1. to consider or claim as one's own. Cf. *angkinín, kanyahín*. 2. to consider or hold as one's property or possession. Cf. *gamitin*. 3. to accept; consider as acceptable. Syn. *tanggapín*. 4. to recognize or accept as one's own. Syn. *kilalanin*.

arina (a-ri-na), var. **harina**, *n.* (Sp. *harina*) 1. wheat flour. Cf. *galapóng* (rice flour). 2. starch. Syn. *gawgaw*.

aringkín (a-ring-kín), var. **aringking**, *n.* 1. sudden or accidental somersaulting; falling head over heels. 2. sudden turning and fall, as of a person suddenly attacked by severe pain.

aristokrasya (a-ris-tok-ras-ya), var. **aristokrásiya**, *n.* (Sp. *aristocracia*) aristocracy; nobility; privileged ruling class. Syn. *mga taong aristókratá o maharlikà*. 2. government by a privileged minority.

aritmétiká (a-rit-mé-ti-ká), *n.* (Sp. *aritméticá*) arithmetic. Syn. *palátuusán*. Cf. *pagtutuós, pagkukuwentá*.

arlekín (ar-le-kín), var. **arlikín**, *n.* (Sp. *arlequín*) harlequin; buffoon. Syn. *bubo, payaso, kómikó, komikero*.

arma (ar-ma), *n.* (*Sp.*) weapon. Syn. *sandata, armas*.

armada (ar-ma-da), *n.* (*Sp.; Eng.*) armada; fleet; navy squadron. Syn. *plota, iskuwadrón*.

armado (ar-ma-do), *adj.* armed; with or having arms; provided with weapon. Syn. *may-armás, may-sandata, sandatahán*.

armamento (ar-ma-men-to), *n.* (*Sp.*) armament.

armas (ar-mas; ar-más), *n.* (*Sp.*) arms; weapon. Syn. *mga sandata*.

armi (ar-mi), *n.* (*Eng.*) army. Syn. *hukbó, hukbóng sandatahán*.

armistisiyo (ar-mis-ti-si-yo), var. **armistisyo**, *n.* (Sp. *armisticio*) armistice.

arnés (ar-nés), var. **arnís**, *n.* (*Sp.*) art of fencing; swordplay. Syn. *eskrima, estokada*.

arnibal (ar-ni-bal), (Corr. fr. Sp. *almibar*) simple thick syrup.

aro (a-ro), *n.* (*Sp. ?*) 1. in cockfighting, act

of putting a cock forward, head to head with another, to incite both before the actual bout. Syn. *ulót, pag-uulót*. 2. act of offering or giving something to someone insistently by pushing it forward to be almost touching the face. Cf. *duldól, pagduduldól*.

aró (a-ró), *interj.* an exclamation, meaning "Is that so!" Syn. *Siyangâ ba! Talagá!*

arók (a-rók), I. *n.* 1. act of sounding the depth, as of water in a river or sea. Syn. *tarók, pagtarók*. 2. understanding or finding out the thoughts, motives, meanings, etc. of. Syn. *unawà, pag-unawà*. —II. *adj.* 1. measurable, referring to the depth of water. 2. already measured or sounded (s.o. the depth of water). 3. understood, referring to someone's motives, etc.

arogante (a-ro-gan-te), *adj.* (Sp. *arrogante*) arrogant; haughty. Syn. *palalò, hambóg, mayabang*.

aroma (a-ro-ma), *n.* 1. (*Eng.*) aroma; fragrance. Syn. *bangó*. 2. (*Sp.*) a spiny shrub called 'cassia flower tree' (*Acacia farnesiana*).

arosbalensiyana (a-ros-ba-len-si-ya-na), var. **arusbalensiyana**, *n.* (Sp. *arroz valenciana*) a rice dish with special condiments.

aroskaldo (a-ros-kal-do), var. **aruskaldo**, *n.* (Sp. *arroz caldo*) rice porridge with chicken and other condiments. Cf. *lugaw, nilugaw*.

arsenál (ar-se-nál), *n.* (*Sp.*) 1. shipyard. 2. munition house; arsenal. 3. storehouse. Syn. *bodega*.

arsobispo (ar-so-bis-po), *n.* (Sp. *arzobispo*) archbishop.

arte (ar-te), *n.* (*Sp.*) 1. art. Syn. *sining*. 2. act or manner of acting, as in a play or drama. Syn. *kilos, galáw, astâ*. 3. mannerism. Syn. *naturál na kilos*.

arterya (ar-ter-ya), var. **arteriya**, *n.* (Sp. *arteria*) artery. Cf. *ugát, bena* (vein).

artesano (ar-te-sa-no), var. **artisano**, *n.* (*Sp.*) artisan; craftsman.

artikulante (ar-ti-ku-lan-te), *adj.* (Sp. *articulante*) 1. talkative; loquacious. Syn. *masalitâ, madaldál, matabíl*. 2. argumentive. Syn. *matutól, mareklamo*.

artíkuló | **asap**

artíkuló (ar-tí-ku-ló), n. (Sp. *artículo*) 1. a newspaper or magazine article. Syn. *lathalà, lathalaín.* 2. (Gram.) article. Syn. *pantukoy.* 3. a section or item in a written document. Syn. *pangkát, seksiyón.* 4. commodity; goods. Syn. *kalakal, mga paninda.* 5. materials. Syn. *sangkáp, panangkáp.*

artilyero (ar-til-ye-ro), n. (Sp. *artillero*) gunner; artilleryman. Syn. *kanyonero, mánganganyón.*

artipisyál (ar-ti-pis-yál), adj. (Sp. *artificial*) artificial; superficial; unnatural or affected. Syn. *gawá-gawâ lamang, pakunwarî, pabalat-bunga, paimbabáw.* 2. man-made, opposed to natural. Syn. *likhâ, gawâ.*

artipisyo (ar-ti-pis-yo), n (Sp. *artificio*) 1. artifice; trickery. 2. skill; craftsmanship. Cf. *husay, kahusayan.*

artista (ar-tis-ta), n. (*Sp.*) artist; actor or actress.

artistikó (ar-tis-ti-kó), adj. (Sp. *artistico*) artistic. Syn. *masining.*

artritis (ar-tri-tis), n. (*Sp.*) arthritis.

artsibo (ar-tsi-bo), n. (Sp. *archivo*) archive. Syn. *sinupan.*

arugâ (a-ru-gâ), I. n. 1. act of taking care of (a person); protecting and rearing up, as of a child. Syn. *alagà, pag-aalagà; andukâ, pag-aandukâ; kandili, pagkandili.* 2. a person taken care of by someone. Syn. *ampón, alagà, kandili.*
—II. adj. referring to a person being taken care of or being adopted by someone. Syn. *alagà, inaalagaan, ampón, inampón.*

aruhan (a-ru-han), v. 1. to put forward (a rooster), head to head with another, to incite it to fight. Syn. *ulután.* 2. to offer or give something (to a person) insistently by shoving it forward to be almost touching the face. Syn. *duldulán.*

arupél (a-ru-pél), n. (Sp. *oropel*) tinsel; brass foil; tinfoil. Syn. *palarâ.*

arúy (a-rúy), *interj.* Ouch! (More intense than **aráy**).

aryá (ar-yá), var. **ariyá** (Sp. *arriar*), I. interj. Go ahead! Go on! Syn. *Sigi! Lakad! Tulóy!*
—II. n. 1. a going ahead, as with one's plan or project. Syn. *patuloy,*

pagpapatuloy. 2. act of letting loose (a rope, string, etc.) up to a certain length or extent. Syn. *tustós, pagtutustós; larga, paglalarga.* 3. act of leading or driving an animal with or as with a tether. Cf. *tabóy, pagtatabóy.* 4. (*Colloq.*) act of hitting or striking someone, with or as with one's fist. Syn. *tira, pagtira; banat, pagbanat.*

aryahán (ar-ya-hán), var. **ariyahán**, v. 1. to release or loosen (a length of rope, or the like) to a certain extent. Syn. *largahán, ilargá.* 2. to go ahead with, as of a plan or project. Syn. *sigihan, tuluyan, ipagpatuloy.* 3. (*Colloq.*) to hit or strike, with or as with one's fist. Syn. *tirahan, banatan.*

asa (a-sa), n. 1. expectation; anticipation Syn. *pag-asa.* 2. a depending or relying on, as for support or sustenance. 3. (*Colloq.*) belief. Syn. *paniwalà, palagáy.*

asado (a-sa-do), I. n. (*Sp.*) a dish of meat roasted with condiments.
—II. adj. roasted with condiments, referring to meat.

asag (a-sag), n. woven bamboo splits placed at the bottom of cooking pots to prevent food from sticking or being burned.

asahár (a-sa-hár), n. (Sp. *azahar*) 1. (Bot.) orange blossom. Syn. *bulaklák ng suhâ.* 2. artificial or natural orange blossoms worn by a bride on the head over the veil.

asal (a-sal), n. manners; behavior. Syn. *ugalì, kaugalián.*

asal-batà (a-sal + ba-tà), n. childish manner or behavior.

asal-hayop (a-sal + ha-yop), n. the quality of being beastly; bestiality. Syn. *ugalinghayop, kahayupan.*

asalto (a-sal-to), n. (*Sp.*) 1. surprise party. Cf. *sorpresa.* 2. assault; attack. Syn. *salakay, daluhong, atake.*

asám (a-sám), n. a longing for; eager wish for something; eager anticipation. Cf. *pananabík.*

asamblea (a-sam-ble-a), var. **asambleya**, n. (*Sp.*) assembly. Syn. *kapulungan, katipunan, pagtitipon.*

asap (a-sap), n. 1. smoke; fume. Syn. *asó, usok.* 2. irritation in the eyes caused by smoke. Cf. *silam.*

asaról (a-sa-ról), n. (Sp. *azadon*) 1. large hoe. Cf. *asada.* 2. act of manner of cultivating soil with a large hoe.

asasinasyon (a-sa-si-nas-yón), var. **asasinesyón,** n. (Eng.) assassination; murder. Syn. *pagpatáy ng tao, asesinato.*

asawa (a-sa-wa), n. 1. spouse; wife or husband. Syn. *kabiyák, kabiyák ng dibdíb, kabiyák ng puso, maybahay* (wife). 2. (*Colloq.*) act of attacking a woman sexually.

asbesto (as-bes-to), n. (Sp.) asbestos.

askád (as-kád), n. acrid taste, as of orange peelings. Cf. *kahat, paklá.*

asendero (a-sen-de-ro), n. (Sp. *hacendero*) plantation owner; big landowner.

Asensiyón (A-sen-si-yón), n. (Sp. *Ascención*) Ascension. Syn. *Pag-akyát (sa Langit).*

asenso (a-sen-so), n. (Sp. *ascenso*) 1. promotion in rank or position. Syn. *pagtaás (ng ranggo o tungkulin), promosyón.*

asento (a-sen-to), n. (Sp. *acento*) 1. the accent mark ('). Syn. *tuldík.* 2. stress on a syllable or word; accent. Syn. *diín.*

asero (a-se-ro), n. (Sp. *asero*) 1. steel. Syn. *patalím.* 2. pen point.

asesinasyón (a-se-si-nas-yón), n. (Sp. *asesinacion*) assassination. Syn. *pagpatáy, pagkakápatáy.*

asesor (a-se-sor; a-se-sór), n. (Sp.) tax appraiser; assessor. Syn. *tasadór, tagatayang-halagá.*

asétikó (a-sé-ti-kó), adj. (Sp. *acetileno*) acetylene.

asetona (a-se-to-na), n. (Sp. *acetona*) acetone.

aseyte (a-sey-te), n. (Sp. *aceite*) oil. Syn. *langís.*

aseytuna (a-sey-tu-na), n. (Sp. *aceituna*) olive fruit. Syn. *oliba.* 2. olive oil.

asikaso (a-si-ka-so), var. **hasikaso,** n. (Sp. *hacer caso*) 1. act of attending to someone or something. Syn. *pag-iintindí.* 2. work or project one is very much involved. Syn. *trabaho, gawain.* 3. diligence; industry. Syn. *sikap, pagsisikap; sipag, kasipagan.*

ásidó (á-si-dó), n. (Sp. *ácido*) acid.

asignasyón (a-sig-nas-yón), n. (Sp. *asignación*) in *Law,* transference of a claim, right, property, etc.; assignation or assignment.

asignatura (a-sig-na-tu-ra), n. (Sp.) academic subject at school. Syn. *paksáng-aralín.*

asilo (a-si-lo), n. (Sp.) asylum; refuge. Syn. *ampunan, bahay-ampunan, ospisyo.*

asim (a-sim), n. 1. the taste of vinegar, unripe mangoes and other green fruits; sourness. 2. acidity. 3. (*Colloq.*) distasteful or unpleasant appearance, as in *asim ng mukhâ,* distasteful appearance of the face.

asimilasyón (a-si-mi-las-yón), n. (Sp. *asimilación*) assimilation. Syn. *lagom, paglagom, pagkakálagom.*

asín (a-sín), n. 1. salt, 2. act or manner of applying salt, esp. to preserve food. Syn. *pag-aasín o pagkakáasín.* 3. (*Colloq.*) the taste of salt in cooked food. Syn. *lasa ng asín, alat.*

asinta (a-sin-ta; a-sin-tá), n. (Sp. *asentar*) 1. act or manner of setting or adjusting something in place or in proper position. Syn. *paglalagáy, paglalapat, pagkakabít.* 2. the fact or state a thing has been set or adjusted in its proper place. Syn. *pagkakálagáy, pagkakálapat, pagkakákabít.* 3. act or manner of aiming a shot at a target. Syn. *puntiryá, pagpuntiryá.*

asiste (a-sis-te), var. **asisti,** n. (Sp. *asister*) 1. attendance or service given, as by a band of musicians at a town fiesta. Cf. *pagdaló.* 2. assistance; help; aid. Syn. *tulong, pagtulong.*

asiwâ (a-si-wâ), I. adj. lacking grace and skill, said of an untrained worker or the like. —II. n. lack of grace and skill in the manner of acting or doing things.

asma (as-ma), n. (Sp.) asthma. Syn. *hikà.*

asno (as-no), n. (Sp.; Zool.) ass; donkey. Cf. *buriko.*

aso (a-so), n. (Zool.) dog.

asó (a-só), n. 1. smoke. Syn. *usok, asap.* 2. vapor; steam. Syn. *singáw.*

asoge (a-so-ge), n. (Sp. *azogue*) mercury; quicksilver. Syn. *merkuryo.*

asonante (a-so-nan-te), adj. & n. (Sp.) assonant. Syn. *katunóg, karima, katugmáng-tunóg.*

asosiyasyón (a-so-si-yas-yón), var.

n. (Sp. asociacion) 1. association;
corporation; company. Syn. *samahán*,
kompanya, *korporasyón*. 2. society;
association. Syn. *kapisanan, samahán*. 3.
(*Sociol.*) society. Syn. *lipunán*. 4. social
contact. Syn. *pakikisama, pakikisalamuhà*,
pakikihalubilo, pakikitalamitam.

asotea (a-so-te-a), var. **asoteya**, n. (Sp.
azotea) a rear open balcony made of stone
or concrete above the first floor.

aspaltado (as-pal-ta-do), adj. (Sp. *asfaltado*)
asphalted; paved with asphalt. Syn.
inaspalto, inaspaltuhan. Cf. *sementado.*

aspáragús (as-pá-ra-gús), n. (Eng.) asparagus.

aspeto (as-pe-to), n. (Sp. *aspeto*) 1. aspect;
countenance; appearance. Syn. *hitsura,
anyô, ayos, lagáy.* 2. (*Gram.*) tense. Syn.
panahón, pánahunan.

aspíksiyá (as-pík-si-yá), n. (Sp. *asfixia*) in
Med., asphyxia; suffocation. Syn. *inís,
pagkainís; uóm, pagkauóm.*

aspilé (as-pi-lé), var. **aspilí** n. (Sp. *alfiler*)
the common pin. Syn. *alpilér.*

aspirasyón (as-pi-ras-yón), n. (Sp. *aspiración*)
1. act of breathing; breath. Syn. *hingá,
paghingá.* 2. an aspiring; strong desire or
ambition. Syn. *hangád, paghahangád.*

aspirín (as-pi-rín), n. (Eng.) aspirin. Syn.
aspirina.

B

B, b (ba; be), n. 1. the second letter of the
abakada (Pilipino alphabet). 2. a type or
impression representing this letter. 3. a
symbol for the second in a group or
sequence.

ba (ba), n. the name and pronunciation of
the letter 'B' in Tagalog or Pilipino, also
called and pronounced *be*.

ba (ba), *intrej.* aphaeresis of **abá**, used to
express surprise, wonder, admiration,
disgust, and the like.

babá (ba-bá), I. n. 1. act of carrying a person
pickaback, esp. a child. Cf. *pasán, kargá.*
2. a person or a child carried in this
manner.
—II. adj. carried pickaback, referring to

a person, esp. a child.

babà (ba-bà), n. 1. (*Anat.*) chin. 2. lack of
regular height; lowness. Syn. *kababaan.* 3.
shortness of stature. Syn. *kapandakán* (s.o.
persons). 4. cheapness, as of price. Syn.
kamurahan. 5. humbleness; humility. Syn.
kapakumbabaán. Ant. *kataasan, kapalaluán.*

babâ (ba-bâ), I. n, 1. a going down from a
height; descent. Syn. *lapág, paglapág.* Ant.
taás, pagtaás. 2. act of going downstairs.
Syn. *panaog, pagpanaog.* Ant. *akyát, pag-
akyát.* 3. a going down or alighting, as from
a vehicle. Syn. *lapág, paglapág; panaog,
pagpanaog; ibís, pag-ibís.* Ant. *sakáy,
pagsakáy.* 4. a lowering or decrease, as of
temperature. Syn. *bawa, pag-babawa;
pagbabâ.*
—II. v. (imperative) Go down; Get down.

babaan (ba-ba-an), v. 1. to lower or make
lower; reduce the height. 2. to reduce or
decrease, as in price. Syn. *ibabâ, bawasan.*
3. to lower or make lower in volume. Syn.
hinaan, pahinain, hiná-hinaán.

babaán (ba-ba-án), v. 1. to bring something
for someone downstairs. Syn. *panaugan;
dalhán sa ibabâ.* 2. to make a landing on;
use for landing, as an airfield. Syn. *lapagán,
lunsarán.*

bábaan (bá-ba-an), n. 1. place for unloading
cargoes or passengers. Syn. *lúnsaran,
lápagan, dískargahan.* 2. place for landing,
as in an airfield. Syn. *lúnsaran, lápagan.*

babad (ba-bad), n. 1. leaving or soaking
something in water or liquid. Cf. *tigmák,
pagtigmák.* 2. prolonged stay in water, as
bathing. Syn. *lunoy, paglulunoy.* 3. (*Fig.*)
the bad habit of a person, esp. a gambler,
of staying in the gambling den beyond
necessary or until all his money is lost or
gone.

babae (ba-ba-e) var. **babai**, I. n. 1. woman;
distinguished from *lalaki*, man. 2. any
woman (married or unmarried). Syn. *ale.*
Cf. *binibini, dalaga.* 3. mistress;
concubine; common-law wife. Syn.
kálunyâ, kerida, kaagulò

babaero (ba-ba-e-ro), I. n. (*Hispanized Tag.*)
a man who seduces women or has one love
affair after another; rake; libertine;
philanderer. Cf. *palikero; bohemyo.*

—II. *adj.* referring to a man who is never satisfied of having only one love affair.

babág (ba-bág), *n.* fight;scuffle; quarrel. Syn. *away, awayán.*

babalâ (ba-ba-lâ), *n.* 1. notice; announcement; proclamation. Syn. *pahayag, paunawà, patalastás.* 2. sign; indication. Syn. *tandâ, palatandaan, sinyál.* 3. warning; signal. Syn. *hudyát, pahiwatig.*

babalík (ba-ba-lík), *adj.* with or having intention to return.

babasagáng-alon (ba-ba-sa-gáng + a-lon), *n.* breakwater. Cf. *dike.*

babasagín (ba-ba-sa-gín), I. *n.* anything easily broken; fragile articles; breakables, like glassware, earthenware, etc.

babasahín (ba-ba-sa-hín), I. *n.* 1. reading matter, like newspapers, magazines, etc. 2. reading lessons.

—II. *adj.* intended or prepared as reading materials.

babaw (ba-baw), *n.* 1. shallowness; lack of normal or required depth. Ant. *lalim, kalaliman.* 2. lack of depth in meaning; superficiality.

babay (ba-bay), *n. & interj. (Eng.; Colloq.)* good-bye; farewell. Syn. *paalam, gudbáy.*

babero (ba-be-ro), *n. (Sp.)* bib; chin cloth. Syn. *sapula, salupil.*

baboy (ba-boy), I. *n. (Zool.)* 1. pig; hog; swine. 2. hog meat; pork. Syn. *karnéng-baboy.* 2. a greedy or filthy person.

—II. *adj.* dirty or filthy, referring to a person. Syn. *babúy-babóy, salaulà.* 2. indecent; vulgar. Syn. *bastós, masagwà.*

babuyin (ba-bu-yin), *v.* 1. to make dirty or indecent. Syn. *salaulain.* 2. to make immoral or vulgar. Syn. *bastusín.* 3. to do or make (a thing) haphazardly. Syn. *daskulín, daskúl-daskulín.*

baka (ba-ka), *n. (Sp. vaca; Zool.)* 1. cow; cattle. 2. cow meat; beef. Syn. *karnéng-baka.*

bakâ (ba-kâ), *adv.* perhaps; maybe; possibly. Syn. *marahil, maaarì, posible.*

bakahán (ba-ka-hán), *n.* 1. cattle ranch. 2. place where cattle are sold by the head.

bakal (ba-kal), *n.* 1. *(Min.)* iron. 2. horseshoe. 3. act or manner of shoeing a horse. Syn. *pagbabakal.*

bakalán (ba-ka-lán), *n.* 1. blacksmith shop; smithy. Syn.*pandayan.* 2. horseshoer shop. 3. place or shop of an scrap iron dealer. 4. iron mine. Syn. *mina o minahán ng bakal.*

bakante (ba-kan-te), I. *n.* (Sp. *vacante*) vacancy. Syn. *puwestong waláng-tao.*

—II. *adj.* vacant; not occupied; unoccupied. Syn. *waláng tao, di-okupado.*

bakás (ba-kás) *n.* 1. impression or mark made by a foot, finger, etc.; specifically, fingerprint, footprint. 2. trace; sign. Syn. *palatandaan.* 3. trail; track. Syn. *landás, daán.*

bakasakalì (ba-ka-sa-ka-lì), *adv.* possibly; perchance.

bakás-dalirì (ba-kás + da-li-rì), *n.* fingerprint. Syn. *taták-dilirì.*

bakás-paá (ba-kás + pa-á), *n.* footprint.

bakasyón (ba-kas-yón), *n.* (Sp. *vacacion*) 1. being on leave or on vacation; vacation. Cf. *pahingá, pamamahingá.* 2. a vacationing for pleasure. Syn. *pagliliwalíw, pagbabakasyón.*

bákasyunan (bakas-yu-nan), *n.* 1. vacation place or resort. Syn. *líwaliwan.*

bakat (ba-kat), *n.* 1. a light impression, cut, or dent on a hard surface. Syn. *ukà, ukit.* 2. a scratch or scar, as on a painted surface. Syn. *galos, gurlís.*

bakawan (ba-ka-wan), *n. (Bot.)* 1. a tree of the mangrove swamps that grows up to 12 meters in height, the hard wood of which are used as firewood or are made into charcoal.

bakbák (bak-bák), I. *adj.* 1. decorticated; removed of the bark or husk. Syn. *tukláp, talóp.* 2. forcibly detached. Syn. *tukláp, baklás, puknát.*

—II. *n.* 1. act of detaching or taking out forcibly; stripping. Syn. *tukláp, pagtukláp; baklás, pagbaklás; puknát, pagpuknát.* 2. the part of a thing where the outer portion or covering has been decorticated or forcibly detached.

bakbakan (bak-ba-kan), *n.* heated debate, quarrel, or fight. Syn. *máinitáng pagtatalo, away, o labanán.*

bakbakín (bak-ba-kín), *v.* to decorticate; strip off; detach forcibly. Syn. *tuklapín, puknatín, baklasín.*

bakit (ba-kit), *adv.* for what reason, cause, or purpose; why.

baklá   **bagay**

baklá (bak-lá), n. 1. alarm; fear caused by a sudden realization of danger. Syn. *sindák, bagabag, tigatig.* 2. worry; anxiety; distress. Syn. *pag-aalaala, di-pagkapalagáy.*

baklâ (bak-lâ) I. n. (*Colloq.*) a womanish man; hermaphrodite, gay, homosexual. Syn. *binabaé.*

baklád (bak-lád), n. general term for several kinds of fish corrals.

baklaran (bak-la-ran), n. corral fishing ground; place where fish corrals are set.

baklás (bak-lás), I. adj. 1. stripped off; forcibly detached. Syn. *tukláp, tikláp, tungkáb.* 2. forced open. Syn. *distrungkado.* 3. scraped off. Syn. *bakbák, nabakbák.*

baklasín (bak-la-sín), v. 1. to detach or strip off forcibly. Syn. *tuklapín, tiklapín, tungkabín, bakbakín.* 2. to open forcibly. Syn. *distrungkahín.*

baklî (bak-lî), I. adj. broken off forcibly, referring to a stick, pencil, branch, pole, etc. Syn. *balî, nabalì.*

bakliín (bak-li-ín), v. to break off forcibly, referring to something that is hard and slender. Syn. *baliin.*

bakod (ba-kod), n. 1. fence. 2. act or manner of setting up a fence around a place. Syn. *pagbabakod o pagkakábakod.*

bakood (ba-ko-od), n. highland; plateau.

bakú-bakô (ba-kú + ba-kô), adj. rough and uneven; bumpy, referring esp. to surface or roads. Cf. *hukáy-hukáy.*

bakulaw (ba-ku-law), n. (*Zool.*) 1. orangutan; gorilla. 2. a name usually given to a person who looks and acts like an orangutan. Cf. *tsonggo.*

bakulod (ba-ku-lod), n. 1. highland. Syn. *kataasán.* 2. small plateau or tableland; mesa. Syn. *talampás.*

bakuna (ba-ku-na), n. (Sp. *vacuna;* Med.) 1. vaccination; injection. 2. vaccine, iniksyon.

bakuran (ba-ku-ran), I. v. to fence; enclose with a fence. Syn. *kulungín ng bakod.*
—II. n. lot enclosed with a fence. Syn. *looban, sulár.*

bakwít[1] (bak-wít), adj. hard of pronunciation, referring to a person. Syn. *garíl.* Cf. *humál, utál.*

bakwít[2] (bak-wít), n. (Eng. *evacuate*) 1. (*Sl.*) evacuation. Syn. *likás, paglikás.* 2. (*Sl.*) evacuee.

bakyâ (bak-yâ), n. (*Ch.*) wooden clog; wooden shoe. Syn. *suwekos.*

badigard (ba-di-gard), n. (*Eng., colloq.*) bodyguard. Cf. *bantáy, tanod, guwardiyá, taliba.*

badyá (bad-yá), n. 1. assertion; declaration; statement. Syn. *sabi, wikà, pahayag.* 2. mimicry; imitation; parody. Syn. *gagád, paggagád, panggagagád.*

badyet (bad-yet), n. (*Eng.*) budget. Syn. *laang-gugulín; apropriyasyón, presupuwesto.*

baga (ba-ga), n. ember; live coal; burning charcoal. Cf. *dupong.*

bagà (ba-gà), n. 1. (*Anat.*) lungs. Syn. *pulmón.* 2. the lungs of animals used for food.

bagabag (ba-ga-bag), n. 1. apprehension; uneasiness; restlessness. Syn. *di-pagkapalagáy, tigatig, balisa, balino.* 2. act of causing trouble or uneasiness to someone. Syn. *pagbalisa, pagligalig.*

bagabundo (ba-ga-bun-do), var. **bagamundo**, n. & adj. (Sp. *vagabundo*) vagabond; vagrant.

bagák (ba-gák), adj. muffled, referring to voice, sound or noise. Cf. *paós, pagás.*

bagahe (ba-ga-he), n. (Sp. *bagaje*) baggage; luggage. Syn. *kargada, kargamento; dalá-dalahan, abasto.*

bagal (ba-gal), n. 1. slowness to act or decide. Syn. *kupad, kakuparan; kuyad, kakuyaran.* 2. slow motion or movement; lack of normal speed. Syn. *hinà, kahinaan.* Ant. *bilís, tulín.*

bagamán (ba-ga-mán), var. **bagamat**, conj. although; though; even though; even if. Syn. *kahiman, káhitna, kalubmán.*

bagansiyá (ba-gan-si-yá), n. (Sp. *vagancia*) 1. truancy. Syn. *paglalakwatsá, pagbubulakból, pag-aansikót.* 2. vagrancy. Syn. *paghahampaslupà, pagbabagabundo.*

bagáng (ba-gáng), n. 1. (*Anat.*) molar tooth. Cf. *pangito, pangil.* 2. compatibility. Syn. *pagkakásundô; suwatò, pagkakasuwatò.*

bagay (ba-gay), I. n. 1 thing; matter. 2. circumstance; happening. Syn. *pangyayari.* 3. (*Colloq.*) example. Syn. *halimbawà.*
—II. adj. 1. fit; suitable; appropriate. Syn. *angkóp, tamà, akmâ, agpáng.* 2. becoming.

Syn. *magandá, nakagágandá, kabagay.*

—III. *prep.* (with *sa*) with regards to; concerning; regarding. Syn. *tungkól sa, hinggíl sa.*

bagbág (bag-bág), I. *n.* 1. act of tilling or breaking up the soil, esp. for the first time. Syn. *bungkál, tibág.* 2. erosion. Syn. *agnás, pagkaagnás; guhò, pagguhò.*

bagkús (bag-kús), *adv.* all the more; even more. Syn. *lalò; lalò pa; lalò na; lubhâ; lubhâ pa.*

baghâ (bag-hâ), *n.* state or condition of being suddenly amazed or surprised. Syn. *gulat, pagkagulat; tigagal, pagkatigagal; pagkabigla.*

bagin (ba-gin), var. **baging**, *n.* 1. vine; any climbing or creeping plant. 2. the long, thin stem of this plant. Cf. *amláy.*

bagitò (ba-gi-tò), I. *n.* an inexperienced person; beginner; novice; greenhorn. Syn. *baguhan.*

—II. *adj.* inexperienced; amateurish. Syn. *walâ pang karanasán; di pa sanáy.*

bago (ba-go), *adj.* 1. new; not yet used; newly made. Syn. *bagong-yarì; di pa nagagamit.* 2. different; not the same. Syn. *ibá, náiibá.* 3. not yet familiar or accustomed; inexperienced. Syn. *baguhan, di-sanay; walá pang karanasán.* 4. fresh; newly harvested, gathered or caught. Syn. *sariwà; bagong-ani, bagong-pitás, bagóng-huli.* 5. strange; unfamiliar; foreign. Syn. *náiibá, nábabago, di pa kilalá.*

—II. *prep.* before; earlier than; prior to. Syn. *una, una pa.*

bagók (ba-gók), *n.* an accidental collision or violent contact of a smaller body against a big one. Cf. *salpók, bunggô, banggâ.*

bagong- (ba-gong-): a combining form, prefixed to roots, meaning 'newly' or 'recently', to form adjectives.

bagong-ani (ba-gong + a-ni), I. *adj.* newly harvested. Cf. *bagong-pitás, bagong-gapas.*

—II. *n.* new harvest.

bagong-buhay (ba-gong + bu-hay), I. *adj.* with or having a new lease of life.

—II. *n.* new life; new lease on life. Also spelled *bagumbuhay.*

bagong-kasál (ba-gong + ka-sál), I. *adj.* newly married.

—II. *n.* newlywed; a recently married person.

bagong-datíng (ba-gong + da-tíng), I. *adj.* just arrived; newly arrived. Syn. *karáratíng lamang.*

—II. *n.* a person who has just arrived; new arrival

bagong-gising (ba-gong + gi-sing), *adj.* just awaken; newly awaken. Syn. *kagígising lamang.*

bagong-huli (ba-gong + hu-li), *adj.* newly caught; hence, fresh, referring to fish. Syn. *sariwà.*

bagong-lutò (ba-gong + lu-tò), *adj.* newly cooked; still hot (from the oven). Syn. *kalúlutò lamang; mainit pa.*

Bagong Taon New Year.

bagong-yarì (ba-gong + ya-rì), *adj.* newly made. Syn. *kayayari.*

bagoong (ba-go-ong; ba-go-óng), *n.* small fish or small shrimps preserved in brine, usually used as sauce.

bagót (ba-gót), I. *n.* 1. impatience; loss or lack of patience; annoyance because of delay. Syn. *iníp, pagkaíníp.* 2. exasperation. Syn. *yamót, pagkayamót.*

bagsák (bag-sák), I. *n.* 1. fall or falling from a height, esp. of something heavy. Cf. *hulog, pagkahulog; lagpák, paglagpák.* 2. failure; downfall. Syn. *bigô, pagkabigô.* 3. heavy pouring, as of rain. Cf. *buhos, pagbuhos.* 4. failing in mark or examination. Syn. *di-pagpasá, lagpák, paglagpák.*

—II. *adj.* 1. fallen; knocked down; knocked out. Syn. *tumbado.* Cf. *tulóg, natulog.* 2. did not pass (an examination). Syn. *di-nakapasá; lagpák, lumagpák.* 3. unsuccessful. Syn. *bigô, nabigô; di-nagtagumpáy.* 4. met defeat; defeated. Syn. *talo, natalo.* 5. bankrupt, as in business. Syn. *tumbado, nagsará sa pangangalugi.*

bagsík (bag-sík), *n.* 1. fierceness; severity; cruelty; ferocity; tyranny; atrocity. Syn. *lupít, kalupitán; bangís, kabangisán.* 2. high potency; strong effect. Syn. *tapang, katapangan.*

bagtás (bag-tás), *n.* 1. act of crossing or going across. Syn. *tawíd, pagtawíd.* 2. a short-cut across a field, river, forest, mountain, etc. Cf. *lágusan; tápatang-daán.*

bagtíng (bag-tíng), *n.* 1. chord for stringed musical instrument. Syn. *kuwerdás.* 2. a rope, wire, or the like tied across an entrance or way to prevent free passage or entry into a place. Cf. *harang, hadláng, balakíd.*

baguhan (ba-gu-han), I. n. beginner; novice; neophyte; amateur. Syn. *aralán, aprendis.* —II. adj. inexperienced; amateurish. Syn *walâ pang karanasán; bagitò.*

baguhin (ba-gu-hin), v. 1. to change the form, arrangement, position, etc. Syn. *ibahín.* 2. to renew; make again. Syn. *gawíng mulî, ulitin.*

bagwís (bag-wís), n. wing feather. Syn. *pakpák* (distinguished from *wing*).

bagyó (bag-yó), n. 1. typhoon; storm; tempest. Cf. *unós, sigwá.* 2. (Colloq.) anything that befalls on someone like a storm.

bahâ (ba-hâ), I. n. 1. flood; inundation; deluge. Syn. *apaw, pag-apaw, pagbahâ.* 2. flood water. Syn. *tubig-bahâ.* 3. any flooded place or area. Syn. *sanaw, danaw.* 3. great flow or outpouring. Syn. *dagsâ, pagdagsâ.*

bahág (ba-hág), n. G-string; loincloth; breechcloth.

bahág-buntót (ba-hág + bun-tót), adj. coward; cowardly; afraid. Syn. *duwág, takót.*

bahagdán (ba-hag-dán), n. per cent; percentage; percentum. Syn. *porsyento, parte, bahagi.*

bahagharì (ba-hag-ha-rì), n. rainbow. Syn. *balangáw.*

bahagi (ba-ha-gi), n. 1. act of dividing (something) into parts or share; apportionment. Syn. *hatì, paghahatì, paghahatí-hatì.* 2. part; portion. Syn. *parte, hatì.* 3. share. Syn. *kaparte, tubò, pakinabang.* 4. piece; slice; cut. Syn. *piraso, hiwà; putol.* 5. section; division. Syn. *seksiyón; hatì; parte.*

bahagyâ (ba-hag-yâ), I. adv. 1. hardly; with difficulty. Syn. *halos hindî; nápakahirap.* 2. barely; scarcely. —II. adj. little; slight: *bahagyáng lagnát,* slight fever. Syn. *kauntì, katitíng.*

bahalà (ba-ha-là), I. n. 1. responsibility; care; custody. Syn. *pananagutan, responsibilidád.* 2. care; carefulness; caution; attention. Syn. *ingat, pag-iingat; intindi, pag-iintindi.* 3. management. Syn. *pamamahalà,*

pangangasiwà, pamamatnugot, maneho, pagmamaneho. 4. apprehension; presentiment. Syn. *bagabag, pangambá, tigatig, kabá.* —II. adj. responsible; answerable; accountable. Syn. *mananagót, may-pananagutan.*

bahaw (ba-haw), n. 1. cooked rice left overnight. Syn. *lamíg, kaning- lamíg.* 2. healing of wounds or cuts. Syn. *pagkatuyô, paghihilom, paggalíng.*

bahay (ba-hay), n. 1.house. Syn. *baláy* (Bis.) 2. home; residence; dwelling. Syn. *táhanan, tírahan.*

bahay- (ba-hay-) : a combining form meaning: (a) place of certain activity: as in *bahay-áliwan, bahay-súgalan;* (b) nest: as in *bahay-langgám,* ant nest; (c) holder or case: as in *bahay-katám.* Syn. *kaha.*

bahay-áliwan (ba-hay + á-li-wan), n. amusement house. Syn. *bahay-líbangan.*

baháy-baháy (ba-háy + ba-háy), adj. & adv. from house to house.

baháy-bahayan (ba-hay + ba-ha-yan), n. toy house; play house.

bahay-batà (ba-hay + ba-tà), n. (Anat.) uterus; womb. Syn. *matrís.*

bahay-katayán (ba-hay + ka-ta-yán), n. slaughter house; abattoir. Syn. *matadero.*

bahay-kubo (ba-hay + ku-bo), n. nipa hut. Syn. *dampâ.*

bahay-gagambá (ba-hay + ga-gam-bá), n. cobweb; spider web. Syn. *sapot.*

bahay-manukan (ba-hay + ma-nu-kan), n. poultry house.

bahay-pukyutan (ba-hay + puk-yu-tan) n. beehive. Syn. *bahay-anilan, bahay-laywán.*

bahid (ba-hid), n. 1. stain; smear. Syn. *mantsa.* 2. soil; spot. Syn. *dungis, batik.* 3. trace; mark left on something. Syn. *bakás.*

bahin (ba-hin), n. sneeze; sneezing. Syn. *hatsíng* (colloq.)

bahò (ba-hò), n. (Sp. *vaho*) bad odor or smell; stench; stink. Syn. *masamáng amóy; bantót, angót.*

baít (ba-ít), n. 1. kindness; helpfulness. Syn. *buti, kabutihan; pagkamatulungín, pagkamaunawaín.* 2. prudence; cautiousness or carefulness in conduct. Syn. *hinahon, kahinahunan.*

baitáng (ba-i-táng), var. **baytáng**, n. 1. any of the steps of a staircase. 2. rung-or crosspiece of a ladder. 3. grade (in the elementary level of education). Syn. *grado*. 4. rank; degree. Syn. *antás, ranggo*.

bala (ba-la), n. (*Sp.*) 1. bullet. Syn. *punlô o punglô*. 2. a crude projectile of stone, etc.; pellet. Cf. *perdigonis*.

balaan (ba-la-an), v. 1. to threaten; make threats against. Syn. *bantaán, pagbantaán; takutin*. 2. to warn; give warning. Syn. *babalaán, paalalahanan*.

balabà (ba-la-bà), n. (*Bot.*) the petiole or stalk of a banana leaf or palm leaf, often mistaken for **palapà**. Cf. *tangkáy*.

balabág (ba-la-bág), n. 1. throw; cast; hurl. Syn. *hagis, itsá, balibág*. 2. in wrestling, a throw or overthrowing.

balabal (ba-la-bal), n. 1. wrap; shawl. 2. mantle; cloak.

balak (ba-lak), n. 1. plan; purpose; intention; intent. Syn. *panukalà, plano, layon, layunin; hangád, hangarin*. 2. project. Syn. *panukalang-gawain; proyekto*.

balakáng (ba-la-káng), n. (*Anat.*) 1. hip. 2. pelvic bone; hip bone.

balakangin (ba-la-ka-ngin), v. to feel pains at the hips.

balakíd (ba-la-kíd), n. 1. obstacle; stumbling block. Syn. *hadláng, sagabal, halang, harang*. 2. act of tripping someone's feet. Cf. *patid, pagpatid*.

balaklaot (ba-lak-la-ot), n. northeast wind; monsoon. Cf. *habagat, amihan, sábalás*.

balakubak (ba-la-ku-bak), n. dandruff.

balakyót (ba-lak-yót), adj. morally base or evil; wicked; vile. Syn. *imbí,lilo, sukáb*.

balae (ba-la-e), var. **balai, balaye, balayi**, n. the appellation or term for the parents of one's son-in-law or daughter-in-law. Syn. *baisán, baysán*.

balagat (ba-la-gat), n. clavicle; collarbone.

balagtás (ba-lag-tás), n. 1. (B-) pseudonym of Francisco Baltazar, Father of Tagalog poetry. 2. going across; crossing. Syn. *tawíd, pagtawíd*. 3. a short-cut way to a certain place.

bálagtasan (bá-lag-ta-san), n. 1. poetic joust or debate. Cf. *debate, pagtatalo*. 2. a direct way across to a place. Syn. *tápatang daán*.

balagwít (ba-lag-wít), l. n. 1. act of carrying a load on the shoulder by balancing it on each end of a pole or lever. Cf. *pasán*. 2. the load carried in this manner.

balahibo (ba-la-hi-bo), n. 1. fine body hairs. 2. soft, fine feathers, as on young birds; down. 3. woolly hair of animals, like sheep, horses, dogs, etc.

balahò (ba-la-hò), n. 1. deep mud; mire; slush; slough. Cf. *putikan, pusalì*. 2. moral degradation. Syn. *samâ, pagsamâ, pagkapasamâ*. 3. a pit trap for games. Cf. *patibóng*.

balam (ba-lam), n. 1. a being delayed; delay. Syn. *antala, pagkaantala; abala, pagkaabala; bimbín, pagkabimbín*. 2. waste of time. Syn. *pag-aaksayá ng oras o panahón*.

balambán (ba-lam-bán), n. 1. (*Bot.*) membranous tissue, serving as a covering or lining. Syn. *balok*. 2. (*Anat.*) membrane. Syn. *lamad*. 3. (*Bot.*) sheath or sheating. Syn. *upak, talukap*.

balanse (ba-lan-se), n. (Sp. *balance*), 1. (*Acct.*) balance; balance sheet. 2. remainder; balance. Syn. *ang nátirá o nálabí*. 3. equilibrium; balance. Syn. *timbang, pagkatimbáng, katimbángán*.

balang (ba-lang) n. (*Entom.*) locust. Cf. *luktón*.

balang-araw (ba-lang + a-raw), adv. someday; at some future day or time. Cf. *sa hináharáp*.

balangáw (ba-la-ngáw), n. rainbow. Syn. *bahaghari*.

balangkás (ba-lang-kás), n. 1. framework. Syn. *pormasyón*. 2. structure. Syn. *kayarian*. 3. plot; outline. Syn. *bangháy*. 4. plan; diagram. Syn. *plano; krukis*.

balaráw (ba-la-ráw), n. a kind of double-bladed knife; dagger. Syn. *daga*. Cf. *punyál, sundáng, lanseta*.

balarilà (ba-la-ri-là), n. 1. grammar. 2. the grammar book of the Pilipino national language. Syn. *gramátiká*.

balasa (ba-la-sa), n. 1. in card games, act of shuffling the cards. Syn. *suksók, pagsusuksók*. 2. the shifting or change of gait or steps of a horse while running. 3. a system or practice of drawing lots by mixing or shuffling the numbers in cards. Cf. *palabunután, pilián*.

balasik

balasik (ba-la-sik), var. **bilasik**, n. ferocity; fierceness. Syn. *lupít, kalupitán; bangís, kabangisán.*

balasubas (ba-la-su-bas), I. n. 1. tightwad; miser. Syn. *kuripot.* 2. swindler. Syn. *mánunubà, manggagantso; estapadór.* 3. one who does not pay his obligation promptly. 4. fermented sap of palms. Syn. *tubâ, basì.*

balasubasin (ba-la-su-ba-sin), v. 1. to swindle, referring to someone. Syn. *subain.* 2. not to pay one's obligation regularly to someone.

balat (ba-lat), n. birthmark. Cf. *pekas.*

balát (ba-lát) I. n. 1. the skin in general. 2. rind or peeling (of fruits, etc.). Syn. *pinagtalupan.* 3. leather; hide. Syn. *katad, kuwero.* 4. bark, as of trees. Cf. *upak, talupak.* 5. cover, as of a book. Syn. *pabalát.* 6. shell, as of eggs. 7. husk, as of coconut. Syn. *bunót.*

balatán (ba-la-tán), v. 1. to cover, as a book. Syn. *pabalatán.* 2. to peel; pare. Syn. *talupan.* 3. to take out the bark; unbark. Sn. *tuklapán ng balát.* 4. to shell; remove the shell or covering from. 5. to skin; remove the skin from. Syn. *alisán ng balát.*

balatbát (ba-lat-bát), n. 1. act of binding or tying something carelessly. Syn. *bidbíd, pagbibibdíd.* 2. a piece of wire, cord, or twine tied around something.

balatkayô (ba-lat-ka-yô), n. 1. disguise; act or practice of disguising; hypocrisy. Syn. *pagkukunwarî.* 2. any device used to conceal one's identity, as a mask, costume, etc. Cf. *maskará.* 3. transformation; transfiguration. Syn. *pagbabagong-anyô.*

balato (ba-la-to), n. 1. act of giving someone a small amount from one's winnings in gambling. Sn. *pagpapabalato, pagbibigáy ng balato.* 2. money given away in good-will by a winning gambler. Syn. *pabalato.*

balát-sibuyas (ba-lát + si-bu-yas), adj. 1. sensitive to criticism, insult, etc.; easily hurt; thin-skinned. Syn. *maramdamin; pikón* (slang). 2. smooth and fine, referring to skin. Syn. *pino at makinis.*

balbás (bal-bás), n. (Sp. +) beard. Cf. *bigote, baáng, bungot, misáy.*

balkón (bal-kón), n. (Sp. *bc.'con*), balcony.

balkonahe (bal-ko-na-he), n. (Sp. *balconaje*)

balikán

veranda; small porch. Syn. *beranda.*

balda (bal-da ; bal-dá), n. 1. (Sp. *baldar*) a crippling or being crippled. Syn. *paglumpó, pagkalumpó.* 2. omission. Syn. *palya, pagpalya; palyo, pagpalyo.* 3. absence; non-attendance. Syn. *liban, pagliban; di-pagdaló; di-pagpasok.*

baldado (bal-da-do), adj. (Sp.) 1. overused. Syn. *gastado, gasgás; gamít na gamít.* 2. crippled; disabled. Syn. *salantâ, lumpo.*

bale (ba-le), I. n. (Sp. *vale*) 1. promisory note. Syn. *resibo ng pagkakautang.* 2. buying on credit. Syn. *pagbilí nang utang; pag-utang.* 3. a request for a partial advance payment of one's salary. 4. (*Colloq.*) value; worth; as in *waláng bale*, without value. Syn. *halagá, importansyá; kuwenta.*

bale-walâ (ba-le + wa-lâ), adj. of no value or worth; worthless; not important. Syn. *waláng-halagá, di-mahalagá.*

balì (ba-lì), n. 1. a break in a bone; fracture. Cf. *pilay (colloq.).* 2. act of breaking an elongated hard object, as pencil, stick, or the like. Syn. *baklî, pagbaklî; pagbalì.* 3. the broken part or portion in an elongated hard object.

balî (ba-lî), adj. 1. fractured, referring to a bone or bones. 2. broken, referring to an elongated hard object. Syn. *baklî, nabalì.*

balibág (ba-li-bág), n. a violent throw with or as with a short piece of wood, etc. Cf. *hagis, bató.*

balí-balità (ba-lí + ba-li-tà), n. rumor. Syn. *bulung-bulungan, tsismis.*

balík (ba-lík), I. n. 1. a going or coming back; return to one's home, country, or place. Syn. *uwî, pag-uwî.* 2. return or giving back of something borrowed or bought. Syn. *saulì, pagsasaulì.* 3. a turning back; retreat. Syn. *urong, pag-urong.* 4. a turning over, as of something being cooked over live coals. Syn. *baligtád, pagbaligtád.* 5. return to the former position; restoration. Syn. *pagbabalík (sa dating lugár o puwesto).* 6. doing again what has been done; repetition. Syn. *ulit, pag-uulit.*

balikán (ba-li-kán), v. 1. to go back for; return for. Syn. *pagbalikán.* 2. to do again; repeat. Syn. *ulitin; gawíng mulî.* 3. to return to; go back to. Syn. *pagbalikán.*

bálikan (bá-li-kan), I. n. 1. a going back and forth trip; round trip. Syn. *paroo't paritong paglalakbáy.* 2. return of goods bought, under certain conditions, a practice or privilege given to buyers in some bazaars or department stores. Syn. *sáulián.* 3. simultaneous return, as of a group of visitors or foreign travelers. Syn. *úwian, pag-uuwian.*

balikat (ba-li-kat), n. 1. shoulder. Cf. *paypáy.* 2. (Fig.) full exertion of efforts, often single-handedly, in performing a task or responsibility. Syn. *pagbalikat; totohanang paggawâ; pangatawang paggawâ.*

bálikatán (bá-li-ka-tán), adj. & adv. with all one's efforts. Syn. *totohanan, pangatawanan.*

baliktád (ba-lik-tád): colloq. var. of **baligtád.**

balikukô (ba-li-ku-kô), adj. 1. with or having a bent or hooked end. Cf. *baluktót, nakabaluktót.* 2. twisted. Syn. *pilipít.* 3. wayward; wrong; twisted, as of reasons etc. Syn. *malî, lisyâ.*

balikungkóng (ba-li-kung-kóng), I. n. a bending or curving upward, as of the sides of drying leaves or the like. Syn. *bingkóng, pagbingkóng.* 2. state or condition of being bent or curved upward, as the sides of dried leaves.

balikwás (ba-lik-wás), n. 1. sudden rise or jump from one's bed, as in fright or hurry. Syn. *bigláng bangon o pagtayô.* 2. uprising; rebellion. 2. Syn. *pagbabangon, pag-aalsá.*

balidasyón (ba-li-das-yón), n. (Sp. *validación*) 1. making or declaring valid; validation. Syn. *pagbibigáy-bisà.* 2. proof; confirmation. Syn. *patotoó, pagpapatotoó; patunay, pagpapatunay.*

balighô (ba-lig-hô), adj. 1. absurd. Syn. *di-kapaní-paniwalà.* 2. ridiculous. Syn. *kakatwâ, kakatawá-tawá.* 3. false; untrue. Syn. *di-totoó; waláng-katotohanan.*

baligtád (ba-lig-tád), var. **baliktád,** I. n. 1. a turning upsidedown; somersault. Syn. *sirko, pagsirko.* 2. a turning over of a hitting to expose the other or reverse side, as in roasting meat over live coals or in frying. Syn. *balík, pagbalík.* 3. reversal or turning back, as from one's stand or opinion. Syn. *talikód, pagtalikód.*

—II. adj. 1. turned upside-down. Syn. *tiwarík, patiwarík, nakatiwarik.* 2. turned inside-out. Syn. *baliktád, binaligtád, nakabaligtád.* 3. reversed; in opposite direction. Syn. *saliwâ, pasaliwâ.*

baligtaran (ba-lig-ta-ran), adj. reversible, as a jacket. Syn. *baligtarin, nabábaligtád.*

balimbíng (ba-lim-bíng), var. **balingbíng,** n. 1. a small tree that bears fleshy fruit with five longitudinal, sharp, angular lobes. 2. the fruit of this tree.

balintatáw (ba-lin-ta-táw), n. pupil of the eye.

balintawák (ba-lin-ta-wák), n. a kind of Filipina wear composed of a *barò* and *saya* and worn with a kerchief and apron to match.

balintóng (ba-lin-tóng), n. 1. somersault; act of toppling over and over. Syn. *sirko, pagsirko.* 2. an accidental fall on one's head. Syn. *tumbalilong.*

balintunà (ba-lin-tu-nà), adj. 1. absurd; unbelievable. Syn. *balighô, tiwalî, di-kapaní-paniwalà.* 2. contrary to fact; unnatural, not real; false. Syn. *di-totoó, di-tunay, waláng-katotohanan.*

balintuwád (ba-lin-tu-wád), n. an accidental fall on one's head; a toppling or being toppled down with the head first. Syn. *tumbalilong, balintóng, tumbalík.*

baling (ba-ling), n. 1. slight turn to one side, as in driving. Syn. *paling, kiling.* 2. turn of the head to see something. Syn. *lingón.* 3. turn of one's attention to another thing. 4. turn of one's body to the opposite direction. Syn. *talikód, pagtalikód.*

balingan (ba-li-ngan), v. to turn one's eyes, head, or attention to, Cf. *lingunín, tingnán.*

balisa (ba-li-sa), n. anxiety; restlessness. Syn. *balino, pagkabalino; ligalig, pagkaligalig; bagabag, pagkabagabag; di-pagkapalagáy.*

balisá (ba-li-sá), adj. worried; restless. Syn. *ligalíg, bagabág, di-mápalagáy.*

balisawsáw (ba-li-saw-sáw), n. (Med.) 1. strangury; slow and painful urination. 2. (Fig.) caprice; whim; freakish notion.

baliskád (ba-lis-kád), I. n. 1. act of turning up the edges or corners, as pages of a book. 2. state or condition of being turned or curled upward partially.

balisóng (ba-li-sóng), n. a kind of fan knife made in the Province of Batangas. Cf.

balità   **banat**

lanseta, daga, balaráw.

balità (ba-li-tà), *n.* 1. news; information; report. Cf. *pangyayari, sabí-sabí.* 2. act of passing over to another or others information or report about something. Syn. *pagbabalità.*

balitaan (ba-li-ta-an), *v.* to give or pass to another or others information or news about something; send a communication to.

bálitaán (bá-li-ta-án), *n.* mutual sending of news or information to each other; mutual exchange of news or information.

bálitaktakan (bá-li-tak-ta-kan), *n.* long heated debate; exchange of angry words between two opposing parties. Syn. *túligsaan, átakihán.*

balitang-balità (ba-li-tang + ba-li-tà), *adj.* widely known; known almost everywhere; very famous. Syn. *bantóg na bantóg; tanyág na tanyág; populár na populár.*

balitaw (ba-li-taw), *n.* (*Bis.*) 1. love song. Syn. *kundiman.* 2. Visayan dance of courtship. Cf. *karinyosa.*

balíw (ba-líw), I. *n.* a mentally deranged person. Syn. *ulól, loko.*

—II. *adj.* demented; crazy; mentally deranged. Syn. *ulól, loko, bangáw, sirâ ang ulo.*

balo (ba-lo), *n.* widow or widower; person whose wife or husband is already dead. Syn. *biyuda o biyudo; bao.*

balón (ba-lón), var. **bal-on**, *n.* 1. water well. Cf. *poso.* 2. excavation or diggings. Syn. *hukay.* 3. a dug-out

balór (ba-lór), *n.* (Sp. *valor*) 1. value; worth. Syn. *halagá.* 2. importance. Syn. *importansyá, kahalagahan.* 3. valor; courage. Syn. *tapang, katapangan; lakás ng loób.*

balot (ba-lot), *n.* 1. act of wrapping something with or as with paper. 2. the way or manner (something) is wrapped. Syn. *pagkakabalot.* 3. paper, etc. used for wrapping; wrapper. Syn. *pambalot.* 4. pack; package. Syn. *pakete, kaha.*

balót (ba-lót), I. *n.* duck's egg that has already developed embryo, considered as a Filipino delicacy when cooked. Cf. *pinoy.*

balota (ba-lo-ta), *n.* (*Sp.*) ballot.

balsa (bal-sa; bal-sá), *n.* (*Sp.*) raft. Cf.

bangkilas.

balták (bal-ták), *n.* sudden strong pull; hard pull with a jerk. Syn. *halták, sinták.*

baltík (bal-tík), *n.* fit of bad temper. Syn. *sumpong.* Cf. *init ng ulo.*

balubatâ (ba-lu-ba-tâ), *adj.* referring to a person who is in his (her) middle age; middle-aged. Syn. *talubatâ.*

baluktót (ba-luk-tót), I. *n.* 1. act of bending or twisting something. Syn. *pagbaluktót, pagkalikukô.* 2. the part of something which has been bent, curved, or twisted. Syn. *balikukô.* 3. twisting or distortion of facts or truth. Syn. *pagbaligtad (sa katotohanan).*

—II. *adj.* bent or twisted, referring to a hard, slender object, like nails, iron bar, and the like. Syn. *balikukô.* 2. distorted. Syn. *malî, lisyâ, di-totoó.*

baludbód (ba-lud-bód), *n.* act or manner of spreading or scattering seeds, grain, salt, refined sugar, or the like, sparingly. Syn. *bulabod, budbod.*

balugbóg (ba-lug-bóg), *n.* 1. highland; any high place in a plain or lowland. Syn. *bakolod, bakoor, gulód.* 2. backbone. Syn. *gulugód.*

balutan (ba-lu-tan), I. *n.* 1. a bundle or pack of something, usually wrapped in cloth or paper. Syn. *pakete.* 2. wrapping material; wrapper. Syn. *pambalot.*

—II. *v.* to provide with a wrapper; put in a wrapper. Cf. *ibalot.*

balwarte (bal-war-te), *n.* (Sp. *baluarte*), 1. sphere of influence. Syn. *sakop; poók o lugár na nasasakupan.* 2. bulwark; bastion; fortified rampart. Syn. *tanggulan, muóg, kutà.*

banaag (ba-na-ag), *n.* 1. glimmer; soft rays; faint light. Syn. *aninag, sinag.* 2. glimpse; faint manifestation. 2. Syn. *anaág, silay.*

banál (ba-nál), *adj.* pious; godly; holy; saintly. Syn. *relihiyoso.*

banál-banalan (ba-nál + ba-na-lan), *n.* pretension of being pious or holy.

banat (ba-nat), *n.* 1. act of attacking or hitting someone. Syn. *gulpí, hampás, tira, birá.* 2. act of pulling or stretching something to make it tight or taut. Cf. *batak, hila, unat, hatak.*

banayad (ba-na-yad), *adj*. 1. moderately slow. Syn. *marahan, dahan-dahan*. 2. (*Gram.*) with or having penultimate stress; level. Syn. *malumay, malumì*. 3. reserved; modest. Syn. *mahinhín*. Ant. *magasláw*.

banda (ban-da), *n*. (*Sp.*) 1. band (of musicians). Cf. *pangkát*. 2. a narrow strip of trimming or decorative band; sash.

bandá (ban-dá), I. *n*. direction. Syn. *dako, gawì*. 2. place. Syn *lugál o lugár*.

bandana (ban-da-na), *n*. (*Eng.*) bandanna; scarf. Syn. *alampáy*. Cf. *bupanda, papanda, panyuleta*.

bandeha (ban-de-ha), *n*. (Sp. *bandeja*) 1. tray; salver. 2. a tray and its contents; trayful 3. panel, as of a wall, door, etc.

bandido (ban-di-do), *n*. (*Sp*.) bandit; outlaw. Syn. *tulisán, manloób, mandarambóng*.

bandilà (ban-di-là), *n*. (Sp. *bandera*?) flag; banner; standard. Syn. *bandera, watawat*.

banidád (ba-ni-dád), *n*. (Sp. *vanidad*) vanity; conceit. Syn. *kahambugán, kapalaluán*.

baníg (ba-níg), *n*. mat, used for floor covering. 2. wrapper, as of pins; paper. Cf. *pilyego, pohas*.

banil (ba-nil), *n*. 1. welt; weal; wale. Syn. *latay*. 2. thick dirt on skin, caused by not taking a bath for a long time. Cf. *libág*. 3. a raised line or streak on the skin caused by an enlarged vein or artery. Syn. *litáw na ugát*.

banlág (ban-lág), *n*. 1. the condition of being slightly cross-eyed. Syn. *bahagyáng pagkaduling*. 2. a slightly squint-eyed person.

banláw (ban-láw), I. *n*. final washing with clean water; rinse or rinsing. Syn. *anláw, pag-aanláw; pagbabanláw*.

—II. *adj*. referring to something already rinsed or washed with clean water.

banlî (ban-lî), *n*. 1. use of boiling water, as in sterilizing something, causing injury or burn to someone or in loosening the skins of fruits, etc.; scalding. 2. a burn or injury caused by boiling water; scald. Cf. *pasò, lapnós*.

bansá (ban-sá), var. **bansâ**, *n*. nation; country. Syn. *nasyón*. Cf. *bayan, sariling-bayan, ináng-bayan*.

banság (ban-ság), I. *n*. 1. nickname. Syn. *palayaw*. 2. an assumed name; alias. Syn. *alyas*. Cf. *tag-urî, tawag*. 3. motto; slogan.

Syn. *salawikaín, kasabihán, bukambibíg*.

bansót (ban-sót), *adj*. 1. stunted in growth. Syn. *puríl , di-lumálakí*. 2. aborted or arrested in development. Syn. *unsiyamî, bigô*.

bantâ (ban-tâ), *n*. 1. a threat or threatening; manace. Syn. *pananakot*. Cf. *balà*. 2. (*Colloq.*) plan or intention. Syn. *balák, plano, hangad, hangarin*. 3. an indication of imminent danger, harm, evil, etc.; menacing sign. Cf. *babalâ, palátandaan*.

bantád (ban-tád), *adj*. 1. wont; used or accustomed to. Syn.*sanáy; nasanay na sa; hiratí; nahirati na sa*. 2. sated; satiated; fed up. Syn. *sawâ; nagsásawà na; suyâ; nasúsuyà*. 3. wearied; bored; tired of. Syn. *yamót; nayáyamot na; pagód; napápagod na*.

bantág (ban-tág), *n*. act of tiring oneself unnecessarily, esp. when one is not yet fully recovered from illness. Syn. *pagpapagód, labis na pagkapagod*. 2. fact or state of being used or accustomed to (something). Syn. *hirati, pagkahirati; sanay, pagkasanay*.

bantás (ban-tás), *n*. (*Gram.*) 1. act or system of using punctuation marks; punctuation. Syn. *pagbabantás*. 2. punctuation mark or marks. Cf. *panandâ*.

bantáy (ban-táy), i. 1. watcher. Syn. *tanod, tagatanod; tagabantáy*. 2. caretaker. Syn. *katiwalà, taga-pag-alagà, tagaalagà*. 3. guard; watchman; sentinel. Syn. *guwardiyá, taliba, sentinela*. 4. a person assigned to wait for someone or something to come or pass by. Syn. *abáng, tagaabáng*.

bantayán (ban-ta-yán), *v*. 1. to watch; guard; keep watch of. Syn. *tanuran, guwardiyahan, talibaan*. 2. to watch and wait for. Syn. *abangán, hintayín*.

bantayog (ban-ta-yog), *n*. monument. Syn. *monumento*.

bantáy-salakay (ban-táy + sa-la-kay), *n*. a confidant or trustee who betrays his boss or master.

bantóg (ban-tóg), *adj*. popular; famous; well-known; renown; illustrious. Syn. *tanyág, populár, balità, kilaláng-kilalá*.

bantót (ban-tót), *n*. 1. disagreeable odor or smell of putrid water; fetidness. Cf. *panghî, palot*. 2. (*Fig.*) irregularities; anomalies. Syn. *bulók, kabulukán* (fig.); *bahò, kabahuan*

bantulót   bangon

(fig.) 3. *(Fig.)* fault; defect. Syn. *pintás, kapintasan; samâ, kasamaán.*

bantulót (ban-tu-lót), *adj.* hesitant; irresolute; indecisive. Syn. *alinlangan, nagáalinlangan; atubilî, nag-áatubilî; urungsulong, nag-úurung-sulong*

banyagà (ban-ya-gà), n. foreigner; alien. Syn. *dayo, dayuhan; estranghero.*

banyera (ban-ye-ra), n. (Sp. *bañera*), 1. washtub; wash basin. Cf. *palanggana, lababo.* 2. bathtub.

banyo (ban-yo), n. (Sp. *baño*) bathroom. Syn. *silíd-páliguán.*

banyós (ban-yós), n. (Sp. *baños*) sponge bath. Syn. *punas.*

banyuhay (ban-yu-hay), n. (coined fr. *bagong anyô ng buhay*) metamorphosis. Syn. *metamórposis.*

bangâ (ba-ngâ), n. medium-sized earthen jar, used esp. as water container. Cf. *palayók, katingán.*

bangán (ba-ngán), n. granary; barn. Syn. *baysa; tambubong.* Cf. *kamalig, tangkíl.*

bangás (ba-ngás), *adj.* seriously wounded or injured on the face. Cf. *baság ang mukhâ.*

bangay (ba-ngay), n. act of starting a fight or quarrel with another (usually in reference to dogs and cats, and sometimes to persons, esp. children.) Syn. *pagbangay, pag-away.*

bangayán (ba-nga-yán), n. noisy quarrel or fight among dogs and cats, or sometimes persons, esp. children. Syn. *awayán.*

bangkâ (bang-kâ), n. 1. native boat. Cf. *lundáy; paráw, batél.* 2. the banker in a gambling game. Syn. *bangkero.*

bangkáy (bang-káy), I. n. corpse; cadaver; remains. Cf. *patáy; labí* (colloq.).
—II. *adj.* dead; lifeless. Syn. *patáy; walâ nang buhay; di na humíhingá.*

bangkero (bang-ke-ro), n. (Sp. *banquero*), 1. boatman. Syn. *mámamangkâ.* Cf. *mánanagwán, tagasagwán, tagagaod.* 2. a person who owns or manages a bank; banker. 3. the capitalist or banker in gambling games. Syn. *bangkâ.*

bangketa (bang-ke-ta), n. (Sp. *banqueta*) sidewallk, esp. one which is slightly raised and cemented. Syn. *daanán ng tao sa tabí ng kalye.*

bangkitò (bang-ki-tò), n. (Sp. *banquito*) 1.

stool. Cf. *bangkilyo.* 2. small bench. Cf. *munting bangko.*

bangko (bang-ko), n. (Sp. *banco; Fin.*) bank.

bangkukang (bang-ku-kang), var. **bakukang**, n. an old ulcerous wound, usually on a person's leg that takes a long time to heal.

banggâ (bang-gâ), n. a colliding, hitting, or bumping against something. Syn. *bundól, salpók, bunggô, umpóg.*

banggaan (bang-ga-an), n. 1. collision, as of two or more bodies. Cf. *salpukan, bungguan, umpugan.* 2. clash or encounter, as of two opposing parties. Syn. *ságupaán, labanán, tunggalian.*

banggít (bang-gít), n. 1. act of mentioning something to another; casual mention of something to someone. Syn. *sabi, pagsasabi.* 2. reference; mention. Syn. *tukoy, pagtukoy, ungkát, pag-ungkát.*

banggitín (bang-gi-tín), v. 1. mention something to; make mention of; say in passing. Syn. *sabihin, tukuyin, ungkatin.* 2. *(Bats.)* to hit by throwing a thing at. Syn. *hagisin, pukulín, batuhín, balibagin.*

bangháy (bang-háy), n. 1. skeleton or framework, as of a house. Syn. *balangkás.* 2. rough draft or outline, as of a speech. Syn. *buradór.* 3. plot or summary, as of a story or drama. Syn. *buód; balangkás.* 4. sketch; design; plan. Syn. *plano.* 5. *(Gram.)* conjugation. Syn. *pagbabangháy.* 6. program, as of studies. Syn. *palátuntunan, pánuntunan.*

bangháy-aralín (bang-háy + a-ra-lín), n. lesson plan.

bangín (ba-ngín), n. abyss; ravine. Syn. *labíng.*

bangís (ba-ngís), n. 1. fierceness; ferocity. Syn. *bagsík, kabagsikán; balasik, kabalasikan; tapang, katapangan.* 2. brutality. Syn. *lupít, kalupitán.*

bangó (ba-ngó), n. sweet smell; fragrance; aroma. Cf. *halimuyak, samyô.*

bangon (ba-ngon), n. 1. rising from sleep or from a lying position. Cf. *tayô, pagtayô; tindíg, pagtindíg.* 2. a rising in revolt; rebellion; uprising. Syn. *alsá, pag-aalsá; himagsík, paghihimagsík, himagsikan; rebelyón.* 3. redemption, as from shame or dishonor. Syn. *tubós, pagkatubós.*

bangungot (ba-ngu-ngot),ˈn. nightmare. Syn. *uúm.* Cf. *pangarap, panaginip.*

baóg (ba-óg), *adj.* sterile; barren, referring esp. to a woman. Syn. *di-nag-áanák; matsora; bingí* (fig.)

baon (ba-on), *n.* 1. supply or provisions brought by a person on a trip. Syn. *daláng pagkain at mga kagamitán.* 2. money allowance given a child in attending classes in school. Syn. *pabaon, gastos.*

bapór (ba-pór), *n.* (Sp. *vapor*) steamboat; steamer; steamship; ship. Syn. *sasakyáng-dagat, barko.*

bapór-de-gera (ba-pór + de + ge-ra), *n.* warship. Syn. *bapór-pandigmâ.*

bará (ba-rá), *n.* (Sp. *varar*) 1. anything that hinders the free flow or passage, as of water in a pipe; clog. Syn. *pasak, barál.* 2. hindrance or obstruction placed across a passage way. Syn. *halang, hadláng, sagabal.* 3. temporary halt or delay, as of traffic, due to certain obstruction or obstacle in the way. Syn. *tigil, pagtigil; hintô, paghintô.* 4. a clog or lump in the throat that usually causes choking. Syn. *hirin, bulón.* 5. (*Colloq.*) verbal opposition; contradiction. Syn. *tutol, pagtutol; kontra, pagkontra; salungát, pagsalungát.*

barabás (ba-ra-bás), *n.* (Sp. *barrabás*) fiend; devil.

barako (ba-ra-ko, *n.* 1. (Sp. *verraco*) 1.domestic boar; male hog, used for breeding. Syn. *bulugan.* 2. any uncastrated, adult, male animal, as a bull. Cf. *toro.* 3. (*Colloq.*) a fearless man; bully. Syn. *tiróng; matapang na lalaki.* 4. rake; philanderer; libertine; Don Juan. Syn. *lalaking babaero o palikero.*

barado (ba-ra-do), *adj.* (Sp. *varado*) 1. clogged; obstructed. Syn. *may-pasak, may-bará.* 2. barred or barricaded; closed. Syn. *sarado, may-halang, may-hadláng.*

baraha (ba-ra-ha), *n.* (Sp. *baraja*) playing card or cards.

barandilya (ba-ran-dil-ya), *n.* (Sp. *barandilla*) 1. railing, esp. of light material. Syn. *gabáy; kinsikinsé.* 2. balustrade.

barangka (ba-rang-ka), *n.* (Sp. *barranca*) ravine; gorge. Syn. *bangín.* 2. act of climbing a very steep rock or precipice. Cf.

akyát, ahon.

barát (ba-rát), I. *adj. (Sp.)* given to habitual haggling or arguing over price or term. Syn. *matawád, palátawád.*
—II. *n.* a person given to haggling over price or term; haggler. Syn. *tao o mámimiling palatawád.*

baratilyo (ba-ra-til-yo), *n.* (Sp. *baratillo*) bargain sale. Syn. *murang pagbibilí; almoneda.*

barberia (bar-be-ria), var **baberiya, barberya,** *n.* barbershop. Syn. *gúpitan, págupitan.*

barkada (bar-ka-da), var. **balkada,** *n.* (Sp.) 1. a group or number of persons going together, as on a trip or picnic. Syn. *magkakasama.* 2. an intimate company or group of friends. Syn. *pangkat, grupo.* 3. a group of individuals joining or sticking together in deeds or foolishness; gang. Syn. *gang, pangkat.*

barko (bar-ko), *n.* (Sp. *barco*) boat; ship. Syn. *sasakyáng-dagat, bapór.*

bardagól (bar-da-gól), I. *adj.* (*Slang*) big-bodied; fat, awkward, and slow-moving.
—II. *n.* giant. Syn. *higante, dambuhalà.*

barena (ba-re-na), *n.* (Sp. *barrena*) 1. auger; auger bit; drill; drill bit. Cf. *tribusón, balibol.* 2. act or manner of boring a hole or holes with an auger or drill.

bareta (ba-re-ta), *n.* (Sp. *barreta*) 1. a long metal bar, used for digging or prying; crowbar. 2. act or manner of digging the ground with an iron bar or crowbar. 3. a small bar, as a soap.

barikada (ba-ri-ka-da), *n.* (Sp. *barricada*) barricade. Cf. *halang, hadláng, harang.*

baríl (ba-ríl), *n.* (Sp.) gun; shotgun. Syn. *eskopeta, rebolber, riple.* 2. act or manner of shooting with a gun. Syn. *pagbaríl.*

bariles (ba-ri-les), var. **barilis,** *n.* (Sp. *barril*) barrel; keg; cask.

barilya (ba-ril-ya), *n.* (Sp. *varilla*) 1. thin rod or stick. Syn. *kabilya.* 2. rib, as of an umbrellla. Syn. *tadyang .*

barnis (bar-nis ; bar-nís), *n.* (Sp. *barniz*) 1. varnish (preparation). 2. the act or manner of applying varnish. Syn. *pagbabarnís.*

barò (ba-rò), *n.* 1. general term for women's dresses. Syn. *bestido.* 2. native dress for the upper part of the body.

baróg (ba-róg), n. in *wrestling*, the act of throwing or forcing an opponent to the ground without striking blows. Cf. *bariga*.

barong Tagalog (ba-rong + Ta-ga-log), n. a native Filipino dress or costume, usually made of embroidered material, like piña cloth, and used by men in special occasions or functions.

bartulina (bar-tu-li-na), n. (Sp.) dungeon. Cf. *bilibid, bílangguan, karsíl.*

barya (bar-ya), var. **bariya**, n. (Sp. *varia*) coins in small denominations; loose change. Syn. *sinsilyo, muláy.*

baryo (bar-yo), n. (Sp. *barrio*) political district or division of a municipality; barrio; district. Syn. *nayon, distrito.*

basa (ba-sa), n. act or manner of reading. Syn. *pagbasa.*

basâ (ba-sâ), adj. wet; saturated with water or liquid; not dry. Ant. *tuyô.*

basag (ba-sag), n. 1. act of breaking things, like glassware, earthenware, and the like. Syn. *pagbasag.* Cf. *durog, pagdurog.* 2. crack in glassware, earthenware, or the like. Cf. *lama, biták, putók.*

baság (ba-ság), I. adj. cracked or broken, referring to glassware, earthenware, or the like. Syn. *may-basag, nabasag.*

basag-ulero (ba-sag + u-le-ro), I. adj. referring to a troublesome or quarrelsome fellow. Syn. *mapangguló, paláawáy.*

   II. n. a person who often makes trouble; quarrelsome fellow; troublemaker.

basag-ulo (ba-sag + u-lo), n. quarrel; altercation; trouble; scuffle. Syn. *away, awayán; babág, babagán; alít, álitan; guló, káguluhan; ligalig; kágalitan.*

basahan[1] (ba-sa-han), v. (fr. *basa*) to read something to someone.

basahan[2] (ba-sa-han), n. 1. a piece of waste cloth, used for dusting, cleaning, etc.; rag. Syn. *tarapo (trapo), pamunas.* 2. old, worn out clothes. Syn. *lumà at siráng damít.*

basal (ba-sal), adj. 1. uncultivated, said of land; hence, fertile. Syn. *matabâ.* 2. chaste; pure. Syn. *dalisay, puro, busilak, malinis.* 3. virgin. Syn. *birhen, birgo, imakulada.* 4. (*Gram.*) abstract; not concrete.

basáng-sisiw (ba-sáng + si-siw), I. adj. 1. referring to a person who looks sickly and

dejected. Syn. *lúlugu-lugó.* 2. said also of a person who has lost his credibility. Syn. *sirâ ang kredito.*

   —II. n. a person who has lost his credibility.

basbás (bas-bás), n. 1. blessing; benediction. Syn. *bendisyón.* 2. absolution. Syn. *patawad, pagpapatawad; absolusyón.*

base (ba-se), n. (Sp.) 1. base; basis. Syn. *batayán, pinagbábatayan; saligán, pinagsásaligan.* 2. base; foundation. Syn. *sálalayán, patungán.* 3. base; station. Syn. *himpilan, istasyón.*

basehán (ba-se-hán), var. **basihán**, n. that which is used as basis. Syn. *batayán, pinagbábatayan; saligán, pinagsásaligan.*

baso (ba-so), n. 1. (Sp. *vaso*) glass; drinking glass. 2. (Sp. *bazo; Anat.*) spleen. Syn. *palí, lapáy.*

basta (bas-ta), adv. (Sp.) just; merely; only; simply. Cf. *lamang.*

basta-bastá (bas-ta + bas-tá), adv. simply; merely; only; just. Cf. *lamang.* See **basta.**

bastardo (bas-tar-do), n. bastard; an illegitimate child. Syn. *anák sa labás; anák sa ligaw; anák sa puwera.*

bastidór (bas-ti-dór), n. (Sp.) 1. stretcher or frame for hand embroidery. Cf. *burdahan.* 2. frame or framework. Syn. *baskagan.*

baston (bas-ton), n. (Sp.) 1. cane; walking stick; staff. Syn. *tungkód.* 2. (*Colloq.*) act of hitting (someone) with a cane. 3. a kind of style of trouser's cut in which the legs gradually narrow at the lower end.

bastós (bas-tós), adj. (Sp. *basto*) 1. vulgar; indecent. Syn. *mahalay, masagwâ.* 2. of poor kind; poorly made; crude or coarse (said esp. of dishes). Syn. *magaspáng; mahinang klase.* 3. impolite; disrespectful; not courteous. Syn. *waláng-galang.*

bastusín (bas-tu-sín), v. 1. to act or behave indecently at someone; say or utter something indecent to. Syn. *magpakita ng kabastusán sa; magsalitâ ng kabastusán sa.* 2. to be impolite to; behave discourteously at. Syn. *magwaláng-galang sa, pagwaláng-galangan.*

basura (ba-su-ra), n. (Sp.) 1. trash; refuse; garbage; rubbish. Syn. *sukal.* Cf. *dumí, kalat.* 2. anything that is already useless or not needed anymore. Syn. *bagay na patapón* *o hindî na kailangan.*

básurahán (bá-su-ra-hán), *n.* 1.garbage can or container. Syn. *lalagyán o tipunán ng basura.* 2. garbage dump or pile. Syn. *tambakan o tapunán ng basura.*

basurero (ba-su-re-ro), *n.* (*Sp.*) garbage collector. Syn. *tagahakot-basura; magbabasurá.*

basyada (bas-ya-da), *n.* (Sp. *vaciada*) act or manner of grinding or sharpening the edges or blades of knives, razors, etc. by machine.

basyadór (bas-ya-dór), *n.* (Sp. *vaciador*) a person whose work is grinding tools in machines; grinder. Syn. *magbabásyadá.*

basyo (bas-yo), var. **basiyo,** I. *adj.* (Sp. *vacio*) empty referring to containers. Syn. *waláng-lamán.*
—II. *n.* empty container, esp. bottle.

bata (ba-ta), *n.* (*Sp.*) 1. a kind of house dress; gown. Syn. *damit-pambahay.* 2. bathrobe. Syn. *bata-de-banyo, batang pampaligò.*

batà (ba-tà), *n.* 1. a young boy or girl; child. 2. son or daughter; someone's child. Syn. *anák.* 3. protege. Syn. *protehido; taong tinátangkilik o itinataguyod.* 4. follower; supporter. Syn. *tagataguyod; tagasunód; tauhan.*

batak (ba-tak), var. **hatak,** *n.* 1. act of pulling (something) towards oneself. Syn. *hila, paghila.* 2. act of hauling (load or cargo), as in a cart. Cf. *hakot, paghakot, paghahakót.*

baták (ba-ták), *adj.* 1. well-stretched; tight; taut. Syn. *unát, banát, mabagtíng, hapít.* 2. (*Colloq.*) trained; well-trained. Syn. *sanáy, bihasá.*

bata-de-banyo (ba-ta + de + bén-yo), *n.* bathrobe.

batalán (ba-ta-lán), *n.* a roofless bamboo structure (platform) built at the rear of a barrio house, usually adjoining the kitchen, for use in bathing, washing, etc.

batás (ba-tás), *n.* 1. law; decree; act. Syn. *ley; layé* (colloq.) 2. jurisprudence. Syn. *deretso, abogasiya.* 3. command or order (*colloq.*). Syn. *utos, kautusán, mando.* 4. doctrine or principle. Syn. *tuntunin, alituntunin, panuntunan.* 5. ordinance; municipal ordinance. Syn. *ordinansa, kautusán.* 6. natural order or tendency. Syn. *kalakarán.*

bátasan (bá-ta-san), *n.* legislature; lawmaking body. Syn. *lehislatura, kongreso.*

bátasang-bayan (bá-ta-sang + ba-yan), *n.* 1. municipal council. Syn. *konseho munisipál.* 2. national lawmaking body. Syn. *bátasang-bansá.*

bátasang-bansá (bá-ta-sang + ban-sá), *n.* national lawmaking body; legislature; congress.

bátasang-lunsód (bá-ta-sang + lung-sód), *n.* city council.

batay (ba-tay), I. *adj.* based or taken (from). Syn. *hangò, salig, kuha.*
—II. *adv.* (with sa) according to; in accordance with. Syn. *alinsunod (sa); sang-ayon (sa).*

batayán (ba-ta-yán), *n.* basis; source. Syn. *saligán, pinagsaligan; base, pinagbasihan; hanguán, pinaghanguan*

bathalà (bat-ha-là), *n.* 1. (B-) God. Syn. *Diyós.* 2. goddess; deity. Syn. *diwatà, diyosa.* 3. false god. Syn. *diyús-diyusan.* 4. a woman much adored or admired. Syn. *paraluman, mutyâ.*

bathalain (bat-ha-la-in), *v.* to adore or admire greatly.

bathaluman (bat-ha-lu-man), *n.* goddess. Syn. *diyosa; diwatà.*

batí (ba-tí), *n.* act or manner of beating or stirring (eggs, milk or cream) in a container. Cf. *kanáw, pagkakanáw.*

batì (ba-tì), *n.* 1. act of greeting someone, as in meeting in the street. Syn. *pagbatì.* 2. expressions of pleasure and good wishes for someone who made success, etc.; congratulations. 3. act of calling the attention of someone about his fault, misdeed, etc. Syn. *puná, pagpuná; pansín, pagpansín; inó, pag-inó.* 4. act of renewing friendship with another with whom one has not been on speaking term for sometime by talking or conversing with him or her again. Syn. *pakikipag-usap na mulî.*

batibot (ba-ti-bot), I. *adj.* 1. small but terrible; small but strong and robust. Syn. *busiksík.* 2. strong; enduring. Syn. *matibay.*
—II. *n.* 1. a kind of strong chair made of small iron bars and provided with a metal sheet seat.

batik (ba-tik), n. 1. a blotch, streak, or spot of color on a surface; mottle; stain; blemish. Syn. *paták, bahid, mantsa.* 2. *(Fig.)* bad image; disgrace; dishonor. Syn. *kahihiyán; kasiraáng-puri.*

batikán (ba-ti-kán), adj. 1. mottled; full of spots, blotches, or streaks. Syn. *batík-batík.* 2. *(Fig.)* well-known; famous. Syn. *bantóg, tanyág.* 3. expert; well-seasoned; well-tried or well-tested. Syn. *dalubhasà, eksperto; sanáy na sanáy.*

batík-batík (ba-tík + ba-tík), adj. not evenly colored; with or having spots or stains all over.

batikos (ba-ti-kos), n. verbal attack; severe criticism in public or through newspapers. Syn. *tuligsâ, atake, kritiká.*

batíd (ba-tíd), adj. 1. with or having information or knowledge about; known to. Syn. *alám, nalalaman.* 2. understood. Syn. *náuunawaan; tantô, natátantô.*

batingáw (ba-ti-ngáw), n. large bell. Syn. *kampanà.*

batingtíng (ba-ting-tíng), n. *(Sp. batintín)* a musical instrument made of metal bar shaped like a triangle.

batis (ba-tis), n. spring; stream; rivulet; brook. Syn. *ilúg-ilugan, saluysóy.*

bató (ba-tó), n. 1. stone; rock. Syn. *piyedra, roka.* 2. act of hitting someone or something with or as with a stone. Syn. *pagbató, paghagis, pagpukól.* 3. a precious stone or gem. Syn. *hiyás na bató.* 4. *(Anat.)* kidney. 5. gallstone; biliary calculus.

batok (ba-tok), n. 1. *(Anat.)* the back of the neck; nape. 2. a strike or hit on the nape, esp. with the hand. Syn. *hampás sa batok.*

batón (ba-tón), n. *(Eng.)* a slender stick used by the conductor of an orchestra, etc.; baton.

batóng-bakal (ba-tóng + ba-kal), var. **batumbakal,** n. 1. iron ore. 2. loadstone

batóng-buháy (ba-tóng + bu-háy), var. **batumbuháy,** n. a kind of hard stone with fine grain usually found on river beds.

batóng-hiyás (ba-tóng + hi-yás), n. precious stone or gem; jewel. Syn. *mamáhaling bató.*

batsilyér (bat-sil-yér), n. *(Sp. bachiller)* in *Educ.,* bachelor's degree.

batubalanì (ba-tu-ba-la-nì), n. 1. magnet;

loadstone. Syn. *magneto.* 2. *(Fig.)* magnetic appeal; charm. Syn. *pang-akit, balanì, bighanì.*

batukan (ba-tu-kan), v. to hit or strike on the nape.

batugan (ba-tu-gan), adj. lazy; indolent. Syn. *tamád; matigás ang katawán (fig.)*

batutà (ba-tu-tà), n. *(Sp.)* 1. policeman's club. Cf. *bambú.* 2. act of hitting a person with this club. Syn. *pagbatutà.*

batyâ (bat-yâ), var. **batiyâ,** n. a round, shallow wooden tub used in washing clothes.

baúl (ba-úl), n. *(Sp.)* clothes chest or trunk. Syn. *kabán.* Cf. *takbá, tampipì.*

bautismo (ba-u-tis-mo), n. *(Sp.)* baptism; christening. Syn. *binyág, pagbibinyág.*

bawal (ba-wal), adj. prohibited; forbidden; not allowed. Syn. *ipinagbábawal, hindî pinápayagan; hindî ipinahíhintulot.*

bawas (ba-was), n. 1. *(Econ.)* discount; amount discounted. Syn. *diskuwento, tawad.* 2. reduction or deduction; taking away a part or portion of. Syn. *pagbabawas.*

bawa't (ba-wa't), var. **bawat,** pron. (fr. *bawà at*) each; every; per.

bawì (ba-wì), n. 1. act of taking again a thing already given to another. Syn. *baoy.* 2. recovery of something one has lost, as money in gambling. 3. retraction, as of one's commitment or promise. 4. return to normal position, as of a flying kite which has sunk deep to one side. Syn. *pananangulì sa dati.*

bawì (ba-wì), adj. 1. recovered or has gotten back what has been lost, esp. in gambling. Syn. *nabawì, nakabawì.* 2. had gotten even with. Syn. *amanos, nakaamanos.*

bayaan (ba-ya-an), v. 1. to let or leave alone. Syn. *huwág pakialamán.* 2. to allow; tolerate. Syn. *kunsintihín, pabayaan.* 3. to neglect. Syn. *huwág gawín; pabayaan, kaligtaán.*

bayad (ba-yad), n. 1. payment for debt, articles bought, etc. 2. installment. Syn. *hulog.* 3. paying or discharge of debt or loan. Syn. *pagbabayad.* 4. salary; wage; compensation. Syn. *suweldo, sahop, upa.* 4. payment given for the use or rent of something. Syn. *renta, upa, arkila.*

bayad-pinsalà (ba-yad + pin-sa-là), n.

payment for damage; indemnity.

bayad-utang (ba-yad + u-tang), n. payment for debt or loan.

bayág (ba-yág), n. 1. testis; testicle. Syn. *itlóg* (colloq.). 2. (*Fig.*) guts; pluck; courage. Usually used in the expression: *waláng bayág*, without guts.

bayan (ba-yan), n. 1. town; municipality. Syn. *munisipyo*. 2. nation; country. Syn. *bansá o bansâ; nasyón*. 3. native land; fatherland; motherland. Syn. *ináng-bayan, sariling-bayan, lupang-tinubuan*. 4. the people; public; citizens. Syn. *públikó, taong-bayan, madlâ; mga mamamayán*.

bayani (ba-ya-ni), 1. n. hero; patriot. Syn. *patriyota; taong makabayan*. 2. the leading man in a play or drama; hero. Syn. *bida; pangunahíng tauhang lalaki*.

bayanihán (bá-ya-ni-hán), n. cooperative endeavor or labor, esp. in a community project. Cf. *pasaknóng, pásaknungan*.

bayáw (ba-yáw), n. brother-in-law. Cf. *hipag, bilás*.

baybáy (bay-báy), 1. n. 1. border; edge; side. Syn. *gilid, tabí*. 2. act of spelling a word. Syn. *pagbaybay*. 3. the way a word is spelled. Syn. *ispeling*. 4. enumeration, as by mentioning one by one. Syn. *pag-iisá-isá*. 5. shore; shoreline. Syn. *baybayin, pampáng*. 6. act of tracing or going along the side of a river, street, etc. Syn. *tuntón, taluntón*.

bayó (ba-yó), 1. n. 1. act of pounding (rice, corn, etc.) with pestle and mortar. Cf. *dikdík*. 2. heavy beating or throbbing, as of the heart. Cf. *kabá*. 3. heavy pounding or hitting, as with the hand or fist. Syn. *bugbóg*. 4. heavy blowing, as wind against something. Syn. *salpók, hampás*.

bayóng (ba-yóng), var. **bay-ong**, n. a large bag or sack made of buri palm leaves. Cf. *asako, kustál, supot*.

bayubay (ba-yu-bay), n. 1. dangling movement, as of a hanging carcass or dead body of a person. Cf. *bitin, layláy, lawít*. 2. (*Fig.*) unnecessary or indefinite delay, as in approving or acting on certain matters of importance. Syn. *bitin, pagkabitin; bimbín, pagkabimbín*.

baywáng (bay-wáng), var. **bayawang**,

bewang, n. 1. (*Anat.*) waist of a person or animal. 2. the part of a garment that covers the waist.

Bb.: abbreviation for *Binibini*: Miss. Cf. *Gng*. (*Ginang*) ; *G*. (*Ginoó*). See *binibini*.

behíkuló (be-hí-ku-ló), n. (Sp. *vehículo*) 1. vehicle. Syn. *sasakyán*. 2. any means of communication. Syn. *páhatiran*.

beinte (be-in-te), var. **vainte, bente**, n. & adj. (Sp. *veinte*) twenty. Syn. *dalawampû*.

belat (be-lat), interj. an exclamation expressive of the speaker's disdainful reaction to what has happened to someone. Syn. *Hirát! Hilat! Buti ngâ!*

belo (be-lo), n. (Sp. *velo*) veil; bridal mantle. Syn. *talukbóng, pindóng, pandóng, kulubáng*.

belyas-artes (bel-yas + ar-tes), n. (Sp. *bellas artes*) fine arts.

benda (ben-da), n. (Sp. *venda*) 1. bandage. Syn. *bendahe*. 2. blindfold. Syn. *piríng*.

bendahán (ben-da-hán), v. to bandage; provide with a bandage. Syn. *bendahihan*.

bendeta (ben-de-ta), n. (Sp.; Eng.) vendetta. Syn. *higantí, benggansa*.

bendisyón (ben-dis-yón), var. **bindisyón**, n. (Sp. *bendición*) blessing; benediction. Syn. *basbás, pagbasbás*.

bendita (ben-di-ta), var. **bindita**, n. (Sp.) 1. consecration, as with holy water. 2. holy water; also *agwa-bendita*.

beneno (be-ne-no), n. (Sp.) 1. poison. Syn. *lason*. 2. venom. Syn. *kamandág*.

benepisyaryo (be-ne-pis-yar-yo), n. (Sp. *beneficiario*) in law, beneficiary. Syn. *tagamana, tagapagmana*. 2. anyone receiving benefit. Syn. *ang nakikinabang*.

benepisyo (be-ne-pis-yo), n. (Sp. *beneficio*) 1. gain; profit. Syn. *tubò, pakinabang*. 2. benefit; advantage. Syn. *buti, kabutihan; bentaha, prubetso*. 3. benefit program or show. Syn. *pabenepisyo*.

benta (ben-ta), n. (Sp. *venta*) 1. collection from the sale of goods; sales. Syn. *pinagbilhán, nápagbilhán*. 2. sale of goods; selling. Syn. *pagbibilí, pagtitindá*.

bentaha (ben-ta-ha), **bintaha**, n. (Sp. *ventaja*) 1. the good thing about something; advantage. Syn. *buti, kabutihan; husay, kahusayan*. 2. advantage, as in games. Syn. *lamáng, kalámangan; higít, kahigtán*.

bengga

bengga (beng-ga), n. (Sp. *vengar*) act of vengeance; revenge. Syn. *higantí, paghihigantí; benggansa.*

benggadór (beng-ga-dór), I. n (Sp. *vengador*) avenger.

benggansa (beng-gan-sa), n. (Sp. *venganza*) revenge; vengeance. Syn. *higantí, paghihigantí.*

benggatibo (beng-ga-ti-bo), adj. (Sp. *vengativo*) vengeful; vindictive. Syn. *mapaghigantí.*

berbatím (ber-ba-tím), adj. & adv. (Sp. *verbatim*) word for word; in exactly the same words; verbatim. Syn. *waláng-labis-waláng-kulang, nang waláng-labis-waláng-kulang.*

berbo (ber-bo), n. (Sp. *verbo*) in Gram. verb. Syn. *pandiwà.*

berde (ber-de) I. n. (Sp. *verde*) green; green color. Syn. *luntí (lungtí), luntian (lungtian).* —II. adj. 1. green. Syn. *maberde; luntian.* 2. (Colloq.) indecent; lewd. Syn. *mahalay, bastós.*

berdugo (ber-du-go), n. (Sp. *verdugo*) executioner (of death sentence); hangman; headsman. Syn. *tagabitay.*

beripikasyón (be-ri-pi-kas-yón), n. (Sp. *verificación*) 1. verification. Syn. *pag-alám, pagsisiyasat.* 2. establishment or confirmation of the truth of a fact or theory. Syn. *pagpapatunay.*

bernákulár (ber-ná-ku-lár), n. & adj. (Eng.) vernacular. Cf. *diyalekto.*

bersíkulo (ber-sí-ku-lo), n. (Sp. *versículo*) in the Bible, a line of verse. Syn. *taludtód.*

bersiyón (ber-si-yón), n. (Sp. *versión*) 1. translation. Syn. *salin, pagkakasalin.* 2. one's particular account or statement about something. Syn. *palagáy, kurò, kuru-kurò.*

berso (ber-so), n. (Sp. *verso*) 1. verse; poem. Syn. *tulâ.* 2. (Bib.) a line of verse. Syn. *taludtód, bersíkuló.*

bertikál (ber-ti-kál), adj. (Sp. *vertical*) vertical. Syn. *patayô, patindíg.*

beses (be-ses), n. (Sp. *vez*) times; number of times; occasion. Syn. *ulit.*

bestida (bes-ti-da), var. **bestido**, n. (Sp. *vestida*) a woman's dress. Cf. *barò.*

bestiyál (bes-ti-yál), adj. (Sp. *bestial*) bestial. Syn. *makahayop; gawáng-hayop; asal-hayop.*

beterano (be-te-ra-no), adj. (Sp. *veterano; masc.*) 1 old experienced, referring esp. to an army man. 2. with or having long experience in some kind of services or position. Syn. *sanay na.*

betún (be-tún), var. **bitún**, n. (Sp.) 1. shoe polish. Syn. *sebo* (colloq.) 2. act or manner of polishing shoes. Syn. *pagbibetún, paglilinis-sapatos, pagsisiyain.*

bibero (bi-be-ro), var. **babero**, n. (Sp. *babero*) bib; chin cloth. Syn. *sapula, salupil.*

bibi (bi-bi), n. (Zool.) 1. a species of duck. Cf. *pato, itik.* 2. a young duck; duckling. Cf. *sisiw.*

bibíg (bi-bíg), n. 1. (Anat.) mouth. Syn. *bungangà.* 2. any opening suggestive of a mouth. Syn. *butas, bungangà.* 3. (Fig.) spokesman; mouthpiece. Cf. *kinatawán, taga-pagsalitâ.*

Bíblia (Bí-bli-a), var. **Bibliyá**, n. (Sp.) Bible. Syn. *Kabán ng Tipán; Banál na Kasulatan.*

bibliograpiya (bi-bli-o-gra-pi-ya), var. **bibliograpyá**, n. (Sp. *bibliografia*) bibliography. Cf. *talasangguniang-aklát.*

bibo (bi-bo), adj. (Sp. *vivo*) alert; active. Syn. *listo, alisto; maliksí, aktibo.*

bikakà (bi-ka-kà), n. 1. act of standing with the legs wide apart. Syn. *kaáng, pagkaáng.* 2. act of forcing the legs wide open. Syn. *bisaklát, pagbisaklát.* 3. the position of the legs placed wide apart. Syn. *kaang, bukakà.*

bikas (bi-kas), n. 1. posture; body figure or form; physique. Syn. *pangangatawán, tindíg, tikas.* 2. attitude; manner of action. Syn. *anyô, hitsura, ayos.* 3. dressiness. Syn. *garà, kagaraan, pagmamagará; kisig, kakisigan, pagmamakisíg.*

bikat (bi-kat), n. 1. scar. Syn. *pilat, peklat.* 2. notch or jag at the side or edge of something. Cf. *bungì, bingaw.*

biktimá (bik-ti-má), n. 1. a person murdered or killed in an accident or the like. Syn. *ang nasawî; ang namatáy o pinatáy.* 2. a person who suffered or was injured in an accident. Syn. *ang napinsalà o napahamak.* 3. a person victimized by someone. Syn. *ang nábiktimá o nálinlang.*

bida (bi-da), n. (Sp. *vida*), 1. act of telling a story or narrating something of interest.

Syn. *pagkukuwento, pagsasalaysay, pag-iistorya.* 2. the principal character in a story or play; hero or heroine. Syn. *pángunahíng tauhan.*

bigás (bi-gás), n. hulled rice grains.

bígasan (bí-ga-san), n. 1. rice mill. Syn. *kiskisan.* 2. place where rice supply comes from. 3. rice container. Syn. *palábigasan, sisidlán ng bigás.*

bigát (big-át), n. 1. weight. Syn. *timbáng.* 2. heaviness; fact or state of being heavy. Syn. *kabigatán.* 3. gravity or seriousness, as of sickness, accusation, etc. Syn. *lubhâ, kalubhaán, selang, kaselangan.* 4. importance; great value. Syn. *halagá, kahalagahan.* 5. hardship to tackle. Syn. *hirap, kahirapan.*

bígatin (bí-ga-tin), n. a person of importance or influence. Syn. *malakíng-tao; maha-lagáng-tao.*

bigáy (bi-gáy), I. n. 1. anything given, esp. for free; gift; present; donation. Syn. *handóg, kaloób, regalo, alaala.* 2. act of giving something to another, esp. gift or donation. Syn. *pagbibigáy, pagkakaloób, paghahandog, pagreregalo.*

bigáy-alám (bi-gáy + a-lám), n. act of notifying someone about something; notification. Syn. *pagbibigáy-alám, pagpapasabi, pagpapabatíd, pagpapabalità.* 2. a notice or information given or sent to someone. Syn. *balità, paunawà, babalâ, abiso.*

bigáy-katwiran (bi-gáy + kat-wi-ran), n. justification; giving reason or excuse; justifying.

bigáy-daán (bi-gáy + da-án), n. 1. act of giving way to someone to pass. Syn. *pagpaparaán.* 2. opportunity or chance allowed someone. Syn. *kaluwagan, pagkakataón.*

bigáy-galang (bi-gáy + ga-lang), n. show or demonstration of respect; respectful greeting, as by taking off one's hat or bowing (the head). Syn. *paggalang, pagpipitagan.*

bigáy-hilig (bi-gáy + hi-lig), I. n. excessive indulging of one's pleasure; indulgence. Syn. *pagsunód sa hilig; pamamalabís, pagpapakalabis, pagpapakalayaw.*

—II. *adj. & adv.* with all one's gusto. Syn. *nang buóng lugód o kasiyahan.*

bigay-todo (bi-gay + to-do), I. n. full exertion of one's effort, know-how or ability. Syn. *ubos-kaya, ubos-lakás.*

—II. *adj.* with all one's efforts, know-how, or ability; to one's utmost ability or capability.

bigkás (big-kás), n. 1. act or manner of pronouncing a letter or word; pronunciation. Syn. *pagbigkás, pagsasatinig.* 2. act or manner of reciting a poem; declamation. Syn. *pagtulâ, pagbigkás ng tulâ.*

bigkís (big-kís), n. 1 abdominal band; girdle. Syn. *paha.* 2. a bundle, as of firewood, sugarcane, or the like, tied together with or as with a rope.

bighanì (big-ha-nì), n. 1. charm; charming quality. Syn. *pang-akit, panghalina.* 2. seduction. Syn. *pag-akit, pagkaakit; paghalina, pagkahalina.*

biglâ (big-lâ), adj. 1. sudden; unexpected. Syn. *di-ináasahan.* 2. abrupt; sudden. Syn. *agád, kaagád; kagyát; daglî.*

biglaan (big-la-an), adv. 1. suddenly; abruptly. Syn. *kaagád, pagdaka.* 2. unexpectedly. Syn. *nang di-ináasahan.*

bigláng-yaman (big-láng + ya-man), adj. referring to a person who has suddenly gotten rich, usually through secret or underhanded manipulations.

bigô (bi-gô), adj. disappointed; unsuccessful; frustrated. Syn. *sawíng-palad, kulang-palad, nabigô; di-nagtagumpáy.*

bigote (bi-go-te), n. (Sp.) mustache; whisker. Syn. *misáy, bungot.*

bigotilyo (bi-go-til-yo), n. 1. thin mustache. 2. (Colloq.) a man having thin mustache.

bigti (big-ti), n. 1. killing by hanging. Cf. *bitay, pagbitay.* 2. killing a person by tying the neck with or as with a rope.

bigtíng (big-tíng), I. n. 1. tongs. Syn. *sipit, panipit.* 2. forceps. Syn. *tiyanì.* 3. pliers. Syn. *plais.*

—II. *adj.* tightly tied, as a knot, binding, etc. Syn. *hapít, hapít na hapít; mahigpít.*

biguin (bi-gu-in), v. to disappoint; frustrate. Syn. *hiyaín; di-pagbigyán.*

bigwás (big-wás), n. 1. a sudden hard blow or strike with or as with the fist. 2. a sudden

bigyán

upward stroke or pull made on a fishing
rod or pole. Syn. *biwás, pagbiwás.*

bigyán (big-yán), *v.* 1. to give (something)
to. Cf. *abután.* 2. to bestow or confer. Syn.
pagkalooban, gawaran. 3. (*Colloq.*) to hit
or stike with or as with the fist; give (one
a blow. Syn. *banatan, tirahin, suntukín.*

bihag (bi-hag), *n.* 1. captive; prisoner. Syn.
bilanggô , preso. 2. capture, as of an enemy
soldier. Cf. *paghuli, pagkaptura.* 3.
attraction, as by charm. Syn. *bighanì,
pagkabighanì; akit, pagkaakit; halina,
pagkahalina.*

bihasa (bi-ha-sa), I. *n.* 1. a being accustomed
or used to a certain condition in a place.
Syn. *sanay, pagkasanay; hirati, pagkahirati.*
2. being trained or experienced to some
kind of work. Syn. *karanasán, kasanayan.*

bihirà (bi-hi-rà), I. *adj.* 1. rare; uncommon.
Syn. *di-karaniwan; di-pangkaraniwan;
pambihirà.* 2. seldom. Syn. *madaláng,
manaká-naká, panaká-naká.*
—II. *adv.* 1. rarely; seldom. 2. scarcely.

bihis (bi-his), *n.* 1. act of dressing or changing
one's clothes. Syn. *pagbibihis.* 2. the dress
or clothing that one is presently wearing.
Syn. *suót, kasuutan; damít.* 3. the way or
manner one is dressed. Cf. *garà, pustura.*

bilád (bi-lád), *adj.* 1. exposed under the sun.
Syn. *nasa arawan.* 2. dried under the sun.
Syn. *tuyô sa araw.* 3. in the open; exposed
for all to see. Syn. *nakabuyangyáng; hatád,
lantád.*

bilang (bi-lang), I. *n.* 1. number. Syn. *numero.*
2. count; number of counts. Cf. *dami.* 3.
act or manner of counting. Syn. *pagbilang,
pagbibiláng.*

biláng (bi-láng), *adj.* counted, referring to a
number of persons or things.

bilanggô (bi-lang-gô), I. *n.* prisoner; captive.
Syn. *preso.*

bilás (bi-lás), *n.* 1. the husband of one's sister-
in-law. Cf. *bayáw.* Cf. *hipag.*

bilasâ (bi-la-sâ), *adj.* putrescent, referring to
fish. Syn. *halpók; di-na-sariwà.*

bilhín (bil-hín), *v.* to buy (a certain thing).
Cf. *bayaran.*

bilí (bi-lí), *n.* 1. act of buying; purchase. Syn.
pagbilí. 2. purchase or buying price; amount
paid for something one bought. Syn.

halagáng ibinayad sa binilí; pagkábilí.

bilíg (bi-líg), *n.* 1. (*Biol.*) embryo. 2. (*Pathol.*)
cataract (in the eye). Syn. *katarata.*

bilin (bi-lin), *n.* 1. an order or requisition for
something. Syn. *pabilí.* 2. errand asked to
be done by someone to a certain place.
Syn. *tungkuling ipinagágawa sa isáng
inuutusan.* 3. instructions or directions
given to someone by one leaving
temporarily for a time. Syn. *tagubilin.*

bilís (bi-lís), *n.* 1. speed; velocity. Syn. *tulin,
katulinan.* 2. swiftness; fastness; quickness;
promptness. Syn. *liksí, kaliksihán; kabilisán.*
Ant. *bagal, kabagalan; kupad, kakuparan.*

bilo (bi-lo), *n.* 1. act of shaping or making
something into a small cylindrical roll.
Syn. *rolyo, pagrolyo, pagrorolyo; lulón,
paglulón, paglululón.* 2. a roll or cylindrical
roll, as of paper, cardboard, etc. Syn. *rolyo,
balumbón, kartutso.* 3. small pack wrapped
in a piece of paper, etc.; packet. Syn. *bilot,
balot, pakete.*

bilog (bi-log), *n.* 1. circle. Syn. *sírkuló; pabilóg
na guhit.* 2. roundness; quality of being
round. Syn. *kabilugan.*

bilyón (bil-yón), *n. & adj.* (Sp. *billion*) a
million millions; billion. Syn. *sanlibong-
angaw.*

bimbín (bim-bín), I. *n.* a delaying;
postponement; withholding. Syn. *abala,
pag-abala; pagpapaliban; pag-antala.*
—II. *adj.* delayed; withheld. Syn. *antalá,
abalá.*

bimpo (bim-po), *n.* (*Ch.*) small face towel.
Syn. *labakara, tuwalyáng-pangmukhâ.*

binatà (bi-na-tà), *n.* bachelor; an unmarried
man; young man. Syn. *baguntao.*

binibini (bi-ni-bi-ni), *n.* 1. young lady;
maiden; unmarried woman. Syn. *dalaga.* 2.
(B-) used before the name of a young lady
or an unmarried woman and abbreviated
Bb.: Miss.

binyág (bin-yág), *n.* 1. (*Eccl.*) baptism. Syn.
bawtismo. 2. act of giving a name or
nickname to. 2. the name or nickname
given to someone. Syn. *tawag, ngalan.*

bingí (bi-ngí), *adj.* 1. hard of hearing; deaf.
Syn. *di-nakakáriníg; mahinà ang tainga.* 2.
(*Fig.*) barren or sterile, referring to a
woman. Syn. *di-nag-áanák, di-magkaanák;*

bingí

bingot   **bisita**

matsura, baog. 3. *(Fig.)* unconcerned;
unaffected; unresponsive.

bingot (bi-ngot), *n.* 1. harelip. Syn. *bungî;*
pilas sa labì. 2. notch or dent, as on the rim
of earthenware and glassware. Syn. *pingas,*
bingas, bingaw.

bingwít (bing-wít), *n.* 1. a fishing gear
composed of a rod, line, hook, and sinker.
Syn. *pamingwít; pansing, pamansíng.* 2. act
or manner of catching fish with a *bingwít.*
Syn. *pamamansing, pamimingwít.* 3. *(Fig.)*
a trick, trap or snare. Syn. *panghuli, panilò.*

birá (bi-rá), *n.* (Sp. *virár*) 1. a hard blow or
strike with or as with the fist. Syn. *tira,*
banat, suntók. 2. act of turning a crank, or
the like. Cf. *pihit, pagpihit; pagbirá.*

biradór (bi-ra-dór), *n.* *(Sp.)* 1. wrench. Syn.
liyabe. 2. screwdriver. Syn. *distornilyador.*

birago (bi-ra-go), *n.* *(Sp.; Eng.)* a strong,
manlike woman; virago; amazon. Syn.
binalaki, amasona.

birang (bi-rang), *n.* a kerchief usually used
as a head covering. Syn. *pindóng,*
talukbóng, kulubóng.

birgo (bir-go), I. *adj.* (Sp. *virgo*) virgin;
chaste; referring to a woman who has not
had sexual experience. Syn. *donselya,*
birhén.
—II. *n.* 1. a woman, esp. a young one who
has not had sexual experience. Syn.
dalaga. 2. (B-) in Astrol., Virgo.

birhen (bir-hen; bir-hén), I. *(Sp. virgen) adj.*
virgin; chaste; virgo. Syn. *donselya, birgo.*
—II. *n.* 1. (B-) the Virgin; Mary, the
Mother of Jesus. 2. a virgin woman. Syn.
donselyang babae; dalaga.

birina (bi-ri-na), *n.* glass shade for candles
or glass covering for images of saints, etc.
Syn. *pantalya, imbudo.*

birò (bi-rò), *n.* 1. act of joking another. Syn.
pagbirò, pagbibirô; pagtudyó, panunudyó;
pagtuksó, panunuksó. 2. a joke; jest. Syn.
tuksó, tudyó, kantiyáw.

birtud (bir-tud), *n.* (Sp. *virtud*) 1. virtue;
quality; property. Syn. *katangian.* 2.
efficacy; effective quality. Syn. *bisà,*
kabisaan. 3. strange power. Syn. *himalâ.*
4. power or capacity. Syn. *lakás,*
kapangyarihan.

birtuoso (bir-tu-o-so), I. *adj.* (Sp. *virtuoso*)

virtuous; righteous. Syn. *tapát, matapát,*
makatwiran, makatarungan.
—II. *n.* (Mus.) virtuoso; person having
great technical skill, esp. in music. Syn.
dalubhasà sa músiká o sa pag-awit.

bisa (bi-sa), *n.* *(Sp.; Eng.)* visa.

bisà (bi-sà), *n.* 1. efficacy; potency. Cf. *husay,*
kahusayan; buti, kabutihan. 2. effectivity.
Syn. *pagkabisà, kabisaan.* 3. result;
outcome. Syn. *bunga, resulta.* 4. force;
effect; influence. Syn. *lakás, puwersa,*
impluwensiyá.

bisaklát (bi-sak-lát), I. *adj.* 1. with the legs
wide apart; astraddle. Syn. *bukakâ, bikakâ.*
2. exposed or scattered in the open. Syn.
kalát, nakakalat; tiwangwáng, naka-
tiwangwáng.
—II. *n.* 1. act of standing or sitting with
the legs far apart. Syn. *bukakà, pagbukakà;*
bikakà, pagbikakà. 2. astride position of the
legs. 3. act of forcing the legs to be opened
wide apart. 4. state or condition of being
exposed or scattered in the open.

bisagra (bi-sag-ra), *n.* *(Sp.)* hinge.

Bisayà (Bi-sa-yà), *n.* 1. the Visayan region
or islands. Cf. *Kabisayaan.* 2. a native of
the Visayan region. Cf. *Ilunggo, Sibuwano,*
Samarinyo, etc. 3. the Visayan language.

biskonde (bis-kon-de), *n.* (Sp. *vizconde*)
viscount.

biskotso (bis-kot-so), var. **biskutso**, *n.* (Sp.
viscocho) hardtack; hard biscuit.

bise (bi-se), *n.* (Sp. *vice*) colloquially;
assistant; deputy. Syn. *pangalawá.*

bisebersa (bi-se-ber-sa), *n.* (Lat. viceversa)
vice versa. Syn. *kabaligtarán.*

bisikleta (bi-sik-le-ta), *n.* (Sp. *bicicleta*)
bicycle.

bisig (bi-sig), *n.* 1. arm; forearm. Syn. braso.
2. *(Fig.)* labor; manpower. Syn. *paggawâ.*

bisiro (bi-si-ro), *n.* (Sp. *becerro*) colt; calf;
foal; filly. Cf. *guyà* (a young carabao).

bisita (bi-si-ta), *n.* (Sp. *visita*) 1. visit; act of
visiting. Syn. *dalaw, pagdalaw.* 2.
professional visit or call. Syn. *subida,*
dalaw. 3. guest; visitor; caller. Syn. *dalaw,*
panauhin. 4. visit or call of a suitor. Syn.
akyát-ligaw; dalaw, pagdalaw; panliligaw. 5.
checking or inspection, as of finished
work of laborers. Syn. *inspeksiyón, pag-*

iinspeksiyón. 6. small barrio chapel. Syn. *kapilya, tuklóng*.

bislád (bis-lad), I. n. 1. act of slicing fish, salting and drying it in the sun. Syn. *pagdaing, pagdadaing*. 2. jerked fish, salted and dried. Syn. *daing, binislád*. —II. *adj*. jerked, salted and dried in the sun, referring to fish. Syn. *dinaing, binislád*.

bísperás (bís-pe-rás), var. **bispirás**, n. (Sp. *víspera*) 1. eve; night before. 2. time or day preceding an important event.

bista (bis-ta), n. (Sp. *vista*) 1. (*Law*) court hearing. Syn. *litis, paglilitis*. 2. view; landscape. Syn. *tánawin*. 3. sight. Syn. *tingín, tanáw*. 4. eyesight. Syn. *paningín, pananáw*. 5. visibility. Cf. *linaw, kalinawan; liwanag, kaliwanagan*.

bistado (bis-ta-do), *adj*. 1. seen; in the open; exposed. Syn. *lantád, hayág, kita*. 2. no longer a secret; already known. Syn. *halatá, hindî na lihim, alám na ng marami*.

bistáy (bis-táy), n. 1. a shallow, circular sieve or sifter made of fine bamboo splits. Syn. *bitháy*. 2. act of sifting grains with this kind of sieve. Syn. *agág, pag-aagág*. 3. careful examination, selection, or search. Syn. *maingat na pagsusurì, pagpilì, paghanap*.

bistek (bis-tek), var. **bisti**, n. (Sp. *bistec*) beefsteak. Cf. *pritong tapa, karne-asada*.

bisto (bis-to), *adj*. (Sp. *visto*) obvious; evident; clear. Syn. *bistado, hayág, di na lihim, alám o nalalaman na ng marami*.

bisugo (bi-su-go), n. (*Ichth*.) a species of edible fish belonging to the class Nemimpteridae (*Nemipterus taeniopterus*).

bisyo (bis-yo), n. (Sp. *vicio*) 1. a bad habit or tendency. Syn. *masamáng pinagkámihasnán, masamáng hilig o ugalì*. 2. fit of bad temper or ill humor; tantrum. Syn. *sumpóng, alboroto*.

bisyón (bis-yón), n. (Sp. *visión*) 1. vision. Syn. *pangitain*. 2. sight. Syn. *paningín*.

biták (bi-ták), n. crack; fissure; crevice. Syn. *putók, biyák, basag*.

bitag (bi-tag), n. 1. act of catching (a person or animal) with or as with a trap. 2. trap; snare. Syn. *silò, patibóng*. 3. trick. Syn. *pakanâ, dayà, lansi*.

bitamina (bi-ta-mi-na; bi-tá-mi-ná), n. (Sp. *vitamina*) vitamin.

bitas (bi-tas), n. 1. a small slit or cut. Syn. *punit, hiwà*. 2. placket; placket hole.

bitáw (bi-táw), n. 1. release of one's hold on something. Syn. *bitíw*. 2. practice fight or bout between two roosters. Syn. *butáw*. 3. the release of game cocks facing each other at the start of the bout.

bitay (bi-tay), n. 1. killing by hanging or electrocution. Syn. *pagbitay*. 2. death penalty; capital punishment. Syn. *parusang kamatayan*.

bitayán (bi-ta-yán), n. gallows; scaffold; place of execution.

bitbít (bit-bít), I. n. 1. act of carrying something with the hand, allowing it to hang or dangle at the side. 2. anything carried in this manner. —II. *adj*. carried or held dangling at the side.

bitin (bi-tin), n. 1. hanging position of anything. Syn. *lawít*. 2. act of hanging or placing a thing in a suspended position. Syn. *pagbibitin, paglalawít*. 3. anything held hanging or dangling in the aid. 4. act or manner of hanging oneself by holding one's hands on something overhead. Syn. *pagbitin*. 4. deliberate act of withholding action on something. Syn. *bimbín, pagbimbín*. 5. a kind of game in which the prizes or rewards, composed of things hung or tied dangling from a square trellis that can be lowered or raised, are grabbed by the contestants in order to get them. Syn. *pabitin*. 6. the prizes or rewards in this kind of game.

bitín (bi-tín), *adj*. 1. awkwardly low, as the waist of pants. Syn. *lawít, mababà*. 2. referring to a constrictor (snake) that hangs itself on branches of trees while waiting for its prey or victim.

bitíw (bi-tíw), n. 1. release of one's hold. Syn. *bitáw*. 2. resignation, as from one's position or job. Syn. *dimití, pagdidimití*.

bitlág (bit-lág), n. 1. handbarrow. Syn. *karetilya*. 2. removable seats, placed crosswise the length of boats or canoes. Cf. *úpuan, bangkitò*.

bitsín (bit-sín), n. (Ch.) a kind of flavoring powder.

bitso (bit-so), n. (Ch.) Chinese doughnut.

Also called *bitsú-bitsó*.

bituka (bi-tu-ka), *n*. (*Anat*.) 1. intestine. Cf.
isaw. 2. (*Colloq*.) stomach. 3. (*Colloq*.)
water hose; garden hose.

bitukang-manók (bi-tu-kang + manók), *n*.
(*literal*) chicken's intestine. 2. (*Colloq*.)
zigzag road. Syn. *daáng palikú-likô*.

bitugo (bi-tu-go), *var*. **bitogo**, *n*. (*Bot*.) a
palm-like tree with stout trunk, called
also pitogo (*Cycas rumphii* Mig.).

bituin (bi-tu-in), *n*. 1. (*Astron*.) star. Syn.
estrelya, talà. 2. leading actor or actress.
Syn. *artista, bidang artista*.

bitún (bi-tún), *var*. **bitón**, *n*. (*Sp. betún*) 1.
shoe polish. Syn. sebo (*colloq*.). 2. act or
manner of polishing shoes.

bitunes (bi-tu-nes), *var*. **bitones**, *n*. (*Sp.
botón*) button.

biyâ (bi-yâ), *n*. (*Ichth*.) the common name
for all species of goby (*Family Gobiidae*).

biyák (bi-yák), **I**. *n*. 1. act of cutting or
splitting (a round or cylindrical object)
in halves. Syn. *baak, pagbaak, pagbiyák*.
Cf. *hatì, paghatì*; 2. fact or condition of
being cut or split in halves. Syn.
pagkakábiyák, pagkakáhatì. 3. crack; split;
crevice. Syn. *biták, putók*: 4. a big slit or
cut made on the stomach, as in surgery.
Syn. *malakíng hiwà*. 5. act of opening a
boil, or the like, by surgery. Syn. *tistís,
pagtistís*.
—II. *adj*. 1. split or cut in halves, said of
round or cylindrical objects. Syn. *baák,
hatî*. 2. with or having a crack. Syn. *may-
biták; may-putók*.

biyahe (bi-ya-he), *n*. (*Sp. viaje*) 1. departure.
Syn. *alís, pag-alís; lakad, paglakad* (*colloq*.)
2. journey; trip; voyage. Syn. *lakbáy,
paglalakbáy*. 3. rout ie trip, as of a bus,
taxi, etc. on a tran ,ortation line. Syn.
pasada.

biyananín (bi-ya-na-nín), *v*. to be the
daughter-in-law or son-in-law of.

biyás (bi-yás), *var*. **biás**, *n*. 1. (*Bot*.)
internode (of bamboos, sugar canes, and
the like). 2. the part of the leg or arm
between the joints. 3. (*Colloq*.) legs or
limb.

biyátikó (bi-yá-ti-kó), *n*. (*Sp. viatico*) the
Eucharist as given to a dying person or to

one in danger of death; viaticum. Syn.
hulíng sakramento.

biyayà (bi-ya-yà), *n*. 1. grace; blessing. Syn.
grasya, palà, pagpapalà. 2. mercy. Syn.
awà, pagkaawà; habág, pagkahabág. 3.
favor; kindness. Syn. *tulong, pabor,
kagandahang-loób*. 4. benefit. Syn.
pakinabang, kapakinabangán.

biyenán (bi-ye-nan), *var*. **biyanán**, *n*. parent-
in-law; mother-in-law or father-in-law.

Biyernes (Bi-yer-nes), *n*. (*Sp. Viernes*)
Friday.

biyokímiká (bi-yo-kí-mi-ká), *var*. **biokímiká**,
n. (*Sp. bioquímica*) biochemistry.

biyoleta (bi-yo-le-ta), *var* **bioleta**, I. *n*. 1. the
violet plant or its flowers. 2. violet color.
Syn. *lila*.
—II. *adj*. violet; of or having violet color.
Syn. *lila, kulay-lila*.

biyukos (bi-yu-kos), *var*. **bayukos**, *n*. 1. act
or manner of crushing or crumpling
(something) into creases or wrinkles, esp.
with one's hand. Syn. *kuyumos, lamukos*.
2. the part or portion of something that
has been crushed or crumpled into creases
or wrinkles.

biyuda (bi-yu-da), I. *n*. (*Sp. viuda*) a woman
who has outlived her husband; widow. Cf.
biyudo, bao, balo.
—II. *adj*. referring to a widow; widowed.

biyudo (bi-yu-do), I. *n*. (*Sp. viudo*) widower.
Syn. *balo, bao*.
—II. *adj*. referring to a man whose wife is
already dead.

blangka (blang-ka), I. *n*. (*Sp. blanca*) 1.
blank space. 2. zero score.
—II. *adj*. 1. not written on, as a piece of
paper. Syn. *waláng-sulat*. 2. not filled up,
referring to a space. 3. scoreless. Syn.
waláng nagawáng puntós. 4. expressionless,
as a face.

blangket (blang-ket), *n*. (*Eng*.) bedsheet,
esp. one made of wool; blanket. Cf. *kumot*.

blater (bla-ter), *n*. (*Eng*.) blotter; blotting
paper. Syn. *sekante o sikante*.

bloke (blo-ke), *n*. (*Sp. bloque*) 1. a big, solid
piece, as of wood, stone, ice, or the like;
block. Cf. *tipák, malakíng piraso*. 2. a city
square; block. 3. bloc; faction. Syn.
pangkát, pangkatin.

blumer (blu-mer), n. (*Eng.*) bloomers.

blusa (blu-sa), n. (*Sp.*) blouse.

boa (bo-a), n. (*Eng.*) a large, non-poisonous snake that crushes its prey; boa. Syn. *sawá*.

bóbedá (bó-be-dá), var. **bóbida**, n. (*Sp. bóveda*) arched roof; dome. Cf. *kúpolá, simboryo.*

bobina (bo-bi-na), n. (*Sp.*) bobbin; spool. Syn. *kidkiran, pulunán, karete.*

bobo (bobo), I. n. (*Sp.*) a simpleton; fool. Syn. *loko.*
  —II. *adj.* stupid, silly, or easily deceived, referring to a man. Syn. *sanô.*

boka (bo-ka), n. (*Sp. boca*) mouth. Syn. *bibíg, bungangà.*

bokabularyo (bo-ka-bu-lar-yo), n. (*Sp. vocabulario*) vocabulary. Syn. *talasalitaan.*

boka-inséndiyó (bo-ka + in-sén-di-yó), n. (*Sp. boca incendio*) water or fire hydrant.

bokál (bo-kál), n. (*Sp. vocal*) 1. provincial board member. Syn. *kagawád ng kapulungan panlalawigan.* 2. (Gram.) vowel. Syn. *patinig.*

bokalisasyón (bo-ka-li-sas-yón), n. (*Sp. vocalización*) vocalization. Syn. *pagsasatining.*

bokasyón (bo-kas-yón), n. (*Sp. vocación*) 1. inclination. Syn. *hilig, pagkahilig.* 2. any trade, profession, or occupation. Syn. *trabaho, gawain, tungkulin, hanapbuhay.*

bokasyunál (bo-kas-yu-nál), adj. (*Sp. vocacional*) vocational.

bokilya (bo-kil-ya), var. **bukulya**, n. (*Sp. boquilla*) 1. mouthpiece of a musical instrument. 2. bridle bit. Syn. *bokado.* 3. ability to speak well. Syn. *bokadura, husay magsalitâ.* 4. socket, as for an electric bulb.

boksing (bok-sing), n. (*Eng.*) professional fight with the fists; boxing; fisticuffs. Cf. *suntukan.*

boksingero (bok-si-nge-ro), var. **boksinero**, n. professional boxer.

boda (bo-da), n. (*Sp.*) wedding. Syn. *kasál.* Cf. *pag-iisáng-dibdíb, baysanan* (*Bats.*), *kasál.*

bódabíl (bó-da-bíl), n. (*Sp. vodevil*) vaudeville.

bodega (bo-de-ga), n. (*Sp.*) 1. storeroom; warehouse. Syn. *pintungan, tinggalan.* 2. (*Colloq.*) in boxing, stomach. Syn. *tiyán.*

bogus (bo-gus), adj. (*Eng.*) not genuine; spurious; counterfeit. Syn. *palsipikado.*

bohemyo (bo-hem-yo), n. & adj. (*Sp. bohemio*) referring to a man who is very fond of women. Syn. *palikero.*

bola (bo-la), n. (*Sp.*) 1. ball, as a basketball, volleyball, or the like. 2. a ball game, as baseball game, volleyball game, etc. Syn. *bóliból, basketból, beisbol.* 3. act or manner of drawing lots or lucky numbers in a lottery. Cf. *bunután, palábunután.* 4. practical joke; jest. Syn. *birô, pagbibirô.* 5. bluff; something said to impress. Syn. *kahambugán, paghahambóg; pasikat, pagpapasikat.* 6. flattery. Syn. *pakunwaring papuri, tuyâ, panunuyâ.*

bola-bola (bo-la + bo-la), var. bola-bola, n. (*Sp.*) fish balls or meat balls. Syn. *almundigás.* Cf. *biló-biló.*

bolada (bo-la-da), n. (*Sp. volada*) 1. flight; short flight. Syn. *buwelo, salida.* 2. bluff; something said to impress. Syn. *bola, pambobola.* 3. frill; ruffle. Syn. *bolante.*

boladór (bo-la-dór), n. (*Sp. volador*) 1. kite (in general). Syn. papagayo (*Bats.*). Cf. *saranggola, guryón, sapisapì.* 2. (Ichth.) flying fish (Family Exocoetidae).

bolero¹ (bo-le-ro), I. n. 1. (*Sp. volero*) bluffer. Syn. *mambobola.*

bolero² (bo-le-ro), n. (*Sp. bolero*) 1. a kind of Spanish dance. 2. the music for this dance. 3. a short, open vest, with or without sleeves; jacket; *bolero.*

bolpen (bol-pen), n. (*Eng.*) ball pen. Cf. *pontempen, pluma, lapis.*

boltahe (bol-ta-he), n. (*Sp. voltaje*) voltage.

bomba (bom-ba), n. (*Sp.*) 1. bomb; bombshell; explosive. Cf. *pasabog, pampasabog.* 2. air or water pump. 3. a kill, as in volleyball. 4. air raid; attack by bombers. 5. fire engine. Syn. *pamatáy-sunog.* 6. verbal attack against someone, as in political speeches. Syn. *tuligsâ, atake, tira.* 7. (*Colloq.*) in show business a scene showing nude figures. 8. (*Colloq.*) water hose; garden hose.

bombástikó (bom-bás-ti-kó), adj. (*Sp. bombástico*) bombastic. Cf. *mabungangà, masalitâ.*

bombero   **braso**

bombero (bom-be-ro), var. **bumbero**, n. (Sp.)
1. fire fighter; fireman. Syn. *mamamatay-
sunog*. 2. bombardier; bomber.

bombilya (bom-bil-ya), var. **bumbilya**, n.
(Sp. *bombilla*) 1. electric light bulb. 2.
lamp chimney. Syn. *imbudo*.

bombo (bom-bo), I. n. (Sp.) 1. a big drum;
bass drum. Syn. *tambol*. 2. act or manner
of playing a bass drum. 3. (*Colloq.*) the
big abdomen of a pregnant woman. Cf.
kabuntísán.
—II. *adj.* (*Colloq.*) pregnant, referring to
a woman. Syn. *buntís*; *malakí ang tiyán*;
kagampán.

bonansa (bo-nan-sa), n. (Eng.) bonanza.
Syn. *kasaganaan, pananaganà*.

bonete (bo-ne-te), var. **bunete**, n. (Sp.) 1.
bonnet. Cf. *gora*. 2. a kind of small bread
shaped like a bonnet; bun. Cf. *pandisàl*,
pandiagwa.

bonito (bo-ni-to), I. n. (Sp.) 1. (*Ichth.*) any
of several salt-water 2. a neat, handsome
lad.
—II. *adj.* pretty; neat. Syn. *guwapo*.

bonus (bo-nus), n. (Eng.) bonus. Cf. *dagdág,
karagdagan*.

bopis (bo-pis), var. **bupes, bupis**, n. (Sp.
bofes) lungs of animals, used for food.

boradór (bo-ra-dór), n. (Sp. *borrador*) 1.
rough draft, as of a written speech, etc. 2.
sketch; outline. Cf. *balangkás*. 3. eraser.
Syn. *pamburá*.

borát (bo-rát), var. **burát**, I. n. 1. (*Slang*)
testicle. Syn. *titì, utin*. 2. act of folding
the foreskin or prepuce of the penis to
expose its head. Syn. *busisì, pagbusisì*.
—II. *adj.* with or having the foreskin
folded, referring to the penis. Syn. *busisî*.

boratsero (bo-rat-se-ro), var. **buratsero**, I.
n. (Sp. *borrachero*) drunkard.
—II. *adj.* given to drinking; habitually
drunk or intoxicated. Syn. *lasengo,
maglalasing*.

borlas (bor-las), var. **burlas**, n. (Sp. *borla*)
ornamental tuft of thread, cords, etc.;
tassel. Syn. *palamuting lamuymóy,
lamuymóy, palamuymóy*.

boses (bo-ses), n. 1. (Sp. voces) voice. Syn.
tinig (*tingig*). 2. (*Colloq.*) right or authority
to express one's opinion.

bosero (bo-se-ro), var. **busero**, n. (Sp.) 1. a
person who gets pleasure from watching
women, esp. their secret parts, whenever
there is a chance. Syn. *máninilip*. 2. diver;
skindiver. Syn. *máninisid*.

boso (bo-so), var. **buso**, n. (Sp. *buzo*) 1. act
of watching or looking, esp. through a
small opening or hole, at something that
excites pleasure. Syn. *silip, pagsilip,
paninilip*. 2. diver; skindiver. Syn. *máninisid*.

bosyò (bos-yò), var. **busyò**, n. (Sp. *bocio*)
goiter.

bota (bo-ta), n. (Sp.) boot.

botánikó (bo-tá-ni-kó), I. n. (Sp. *botánico*)
botanist. Syn. *dalúbhalaman, dalub-
aghalmán*.
—II. *adj.* botanical; *hardin botánikó*,
botanical garden.

botante (bo-tan-te), n. (Sp. *votante*) voter.
Syn. *manghahalal, elektór*.

botasyón (bo-tas-yón), n. (Sp. *votación*) 1.
voting; act of voting. Syn. *pagboto,
paghalál*. 2. election. Syn. *hálalan,
paghahalál*.

bote (bo-te), n. (Sp.) 1. bottle. Cf. *botelya,
garapa*. 2. (*Naut.*) speedboat. 3. (*Naut.*)
lifeboat.

botelya (bo-tel-ya), n. (Sp. *botella*) bottle;
small bottle.

botete (bo-te-te), var. **butete**, I. n. 1. (*Ichth.*)
puffer; globefish. 2. a big-bellied person.
—II. *adj.* with or having a big stomach;
big-bellied, referring to a person. Syn.
malakí ang tiyán, may-malakíng tiyán.

botika (bo-ti-ka), var. **butika**, n. (Sp. *botica*)
drugstore. Syn. *parmasya*.

boto (bo-to), n. (Sp. *voto*) 1. vote. Syn.
halál. 2. act of voting. Syn. *pagboto,
paghalál*. 2. vow. Syn. *panata*. Cf. *pangakò*
(promise).

bototoy (bo-to-toy), var. **butotoy**, n. 1. a
kind of bivalve with somewhat elongated
shells. 2. (*Colloq.*) a small boy. Syn. *totoy*.

boykot (boy-kot), n. (Eng.) boycott. Syn.
boykoteo, boykoteyo.

brandi (bran-di), n. (Eng.) an alcoholic
liquor distilled from wine; brandy. Cf.
tinto.

braso (bra-so), n. (Sp. *brazo*) 1. arm. Syn.
bisig. 2. (*Fig.*) force. Syn. *lakás, puwersa*.

brigada (bri-ga-da), n. (Sp.; mil.) brigade.

brilyante (bril-yan-te), I. n. (Sp. brillante) a kind of precious stone; diamond. Cf. diyamante.

—II. adj. of or made of diamond.

brilyo (bril-yo), n. (Sp. brillo) sparkle; glitter; luster. Syn. kináng, kintáb.

brok (brok), adj. (Eng.; Colloq.) broke; bankrupt. Syn. waláng-walâ (colloq.); baligtád ang bulsa (fig.)

bronse (bron-se), I. n. (Sp. bronce) bronze. Syn. tansô. Cf. tumbaga.

—II. adj. of or made of bronze. Syn. yari sa tansô.

brongkitis (brong-ki-tis), n. (Sp. bronquitis) in Med., bronchitis.

brongkonyumonya (brong-kon-yu-monya), n. (Eng.) broncho-pneumonia.

brotsa (brot-sa), var. **brutsa**, n. (Sp. brocha) 1. paint brush. 2. act of manner of using a paint brush.

bruha (bru-ha), var. **buruha**, n. (Sp. bruja) witch. Syn. mangkukulam na babae; manggagaway na babae. 2. hag; an ugly, repulsive old woman. Syn. hukluban, matandáng hukluban.

bruho (bru-ho), var. **buruho**, n. (Sp. brujo) wizard; sorcerer. Syn. mangkukulam, manggagaway.

brusko (brus-ko), adj. (Sp. brusco) rude; rough in manners. Syn. bastós, waláng-galang, waláng-modo, waláng-pítagan.

brutál (bru-tál), adj. (Sp.) brutal. Syn. malupít, marahás.

brutalidád (bru-ta-li-dád), n. (Sp.) brutality. Syn. lupít, kalupitán; dahás, karahasán.

bruto (bru-to), I. n. (Sp.) brute; brutal or cruel person. Syn. malupít na tao, taong makahayop.

—II. adj. brutish; cruel. Syn. malupít, makahayop.

bruwas (bru-was), var. **bruas**, **broas**, n. (Sp. broa) ladyfinger; lady's finger.

bubô (bu-bô), I. n. 1. a spilling or being spilled; spilt.

—II. adj. referring to something spilled from a container. Syn. ligwák. Cf. tapon, pagkapatapon. 2. that which is spilled; spilt.

—II. adj. refering to something spilled from a container.

bubog (bu-bog), n. crystal; glass. Syn. kristál. 2. a small piece or pieces of broken crystal. Syn. durog na kristal o salamín.

bubóng (bu-bóng), n. 1. roof. Syn. bubungán. 2. act or manner of roofing (a house). Syn. pagbububóng. 3. the manner by which a roof was made. Syn. pagkakábubóng, pagkakapágbubóng.

bubót (bu-bót), I. n. (Bot.) a very small young fruit.

—II. adj. referring to a very small young fruit. Syn. murang-murà.

bubuli (bu-bu-li), n. (Zool.) a species of lizard (Lygosona smaragdinum Less). Syn. bangkaláng.

bubungán (bu-bu-ngán), I. n. roof (of a house). See **bubóng**.

—II. v. to provide or cover with a roof. Syn. atipán.

bubuwanin (bu-bu-wa-nin), adj. lunatic; insane. Syn. sirâ ang ulo, sumpungin, sintu-sintô.

bubuwít (bu-bu-wít), n. (Zool.) 1. a newly born mouse. 2. a species of insect-eating mammalia with numerous sharp teeth (crodicura caerculescens Shaw.).

buká (bu-ká), I. n. 1. fact or condition of being open, unfolded, or stretched out, as the wings of birds, petals of flowers, mouth, etc. Syn. bukás, bukad. 2. act of opening or stretching out, as the wings of birds. Cf. unat, pag-unat, pag-uunat.

—II. adj. open; unfolded; stretched out. Syn. bukás, bukád, unát.

bukakâ (bu-ka-kâ), var. **bikakâ**, adj. with the legs wide apart; astride; astraddle. Cf. kaáng, nakakaáng.

bukadkád (bu-kad-kád), I. adj. 1. fully open, referring esp. to flowers. Syn. bukád na bukád. 2. fully exposed to the view. Syn. buyangyáng, nakabuyangyáng.

—II. v. act of opening or unfolding (one by one) the petals of a flower, pages of a book, etc. Cf. bulatlát, pagbulatlát.

bukadora (bu-ka-do-ra), var. **bokadura**, n. (Sp.) 1. mouthpiece as of a musical instrument. 2. ability to talk well. Syn. husay magsalitâ. 3. bridle bit.

bukál (bu-kál), I. n. 1. spring or source of

water flowing out naturally. Syn. *batis,*
saluysóy. 2. source; origin. 3. eruption, as
of rashes or skin diseases. Syn. *singáw.* 4.
provincial board member. See **bokal,** 1.
—II. *adj.* inherent; inborn; innate;
natural. Syn. *likás, katutubò, naturál.*

bukalkalín (bu-kal-ka-lín), *v.* 1. to dig out
(the soil) by or as by scratching with the
hands. Syn. *kalkalín.* 2. to turn (things)
over and over, as in search of something.
Cf. *halungkatín, halukayin.*

bukambibíg (bu-kam-bi-bíg), var. **bukang-
bibig,** *n.* common or favorite expression;
saying; byword. Syn. *kasabihán, sambít-
sambitin, kawikaán.*

bukana (bu-ka-na), *n.* 1. front; threshold.
Syn. *haráp, harapán; una, unahán.* 2.
mouth or opening, as of a cave. Syn.
bungad, bungangà.

bukangkáng (bu-kang-kang), *adj.* wide
open; hence, exposed fully to the view.
Syn. *buyangyáng, nakabuyangyáng;
tiwangwáng, nakatiwangwáng.*

bukáng-liwaywáy (bu-káng + li-way-wáy),
var. **bukanliwaywáy.** *n.* daybreak; dawn.
Syn. *bukang-liwanag, pamimiták-araw,
pamamanaag-araw.*

bukas (bu-kas), I. *n.* 1. the day after today;
next day; tomorrow. 2. (Fig.) the
prospective or potential condition of a
person or thing; future. Syn. *kinabukasan,
hináharáp.*
—II. *adv.* on or for the day after today;
tomorrow.

bukás (bu-kás), I. *adj.* 1. open; not closed.
Syn. *nakabukás, hindi nakasará.* Ant. *sará,
nakasará, sarado; piníd, nakapiníd.* 2.
without cover. Syn. *waláng-takíp, waláng-
sará.*
—II. *n.* 1. act of opening or beginning, as
of a program. Syn. *simulâ, pagsisimulâ;
umpisá, pag-uumpisá.* 2. act of opening a
door, window, lock, etc. Syn. *pagbubukás.*
3. state or condition of being open. 4. the
extent to which a thing is opened.

bukás-isip (bu-kás + i-sip), I. *n.* open mind;
mind open to new ideas.
—II. *adj.* open-minded; broad-minded.
Syn. *bukáng-isip, maybukás na isip,
maúnawaín.*

—III. *adv.* with an open mind; open-
mindedly.

bukás-loób (bu-kás + lo-ób), I. *adj.*
wholehearted; sincere; earnest; frank.
Syn. *bukás-pusò, bukás-dibdib, matapát.*
—II. *adv.* wholeheartedly; sincerely;
frankly; earnestly.

bukas-makalawá (bú-kas + ma-ka-la-wá),
adv. someday; sometime in the future; at
some future day or time. Syn. *balang-araw.*

bukás-palad (bu-kás + pa-lad), var.
bukáspalad. *adj.* openhanded; generous.
Syn. *mapagbigáy, matulungín, buláng-gugò*
(Fig.).

bukás-pusò (bu-kás + pu-sò), I. *adj.*
openhearted; frank; sincere. Syn. *buóng-
pusò, matapát.*
—II. *adv.* openheartedly; frankly;
sincerely.

bukawe (bu-ka-we; bu-ka-wè), var. **bukawi,**
n. 1. (Bot.) long, scrambling bamboo
common in primary forests at low and
medium altitudes (*Bambusa scandens*
Blume). 2. (B-) a town in the province of
Bulacan.

bukatkát (bu-kat-kát), *n.* act of removing
or taking out things, as from a container
or box, in search for something. Syn.
*bulatlát,   pagbulatbulat;   halukay,
paghalukay.* 2. persistent effort to dig into
the truth about something long forgotten.
Cf. *ungkát, pag-ungkát.*

bukayò (bu-ka-yò), *n.* grated coconut meat
cooked dry with sugar. Also called
bukhayò in some Tagalog provinces.

bukaypato (bu-kay-pa-to), *n.* (Sp. bocay
pato) pliers. Syn. *plais.*

bukbók (buk-bók), *n.* 1. weevil. 2. tooth
decay. Syn. *sirà o pagkabulók ng ngipin.*

bukid (bu-kid), *n.* 1. barrio. Syn. *nayon.* 2.
farm; field. Syn. *lináng, tániman, parang.*

buklát (buk-lát), *n.* 1. act of turning or going
over at random, as over the pages of a
book, magazine, or the like. Cf. *bukás,
pagbubukás.* 2. (Colloq.) an unexpected
mention of something, esp. one that has
long been forgotten. Cf. *banggít,
pagbanggít.*

buklíg (buk-líg), var. **butlíg,** *n.* a small
growth on the skin, like pimple or papule.

Syn. *ligatà, butól.*

buklód (buk-lód), n. 1. a metal or rattan ring, used to reinforce the handle of a knife, chisel, etc., or to hold together the palm ribs of a broom. Syn. *baát, saklâ.* 2. that which unites or binds together individuals or groups; bond. Syn. *bigkís.*

buko (bu-ko), n. 1. bud (of a flower). Syn. *butóng.* 2. young coconut fruit. Syn. *mura* (colloq.), *murang niyóg, niyóg na murà.*

bukó (bu-kó), I. n. 1. node, as of a bamboo, sugar cane, or the like. 2. knuckle or joint in a toe or finger. 3. knot, as in a tree or lumber. 4. act or manner of contradicting or finding fault to disappoint or embarrass another. Syn. *pagbigô, paghadláng, pagkontra.*

—II. adj. disappointed; unsuccessful. Syn. *bigô, nabigô.*

bukód (bu-kód), I. adj. apart; separate; segregated. Syn. *hiwaláy, magkahiwaláy, nakahiwaláy.*

—II. adv. (usually with *sa*) 1. apart from; aside of. 2. moreover; besides.

—II. n. 1. act of living separately, as a newly married couple, from their parents. Cf. *hiwalay, paghiwalay.* 2. act of separating or putting aside something for someone.

bukód-tangì (bu-kód + ta-ngì), var. **bukudtangì**, I. adj. exceptional; outstanding; apart and different from all other. Syn. *náiibá, ibáng-ibá, kaibáng-kaibá.*

—II. adv. only; especially; particularly.

bukol (bu-kol), n. 1. a swelling, as one caused by a blow; bump or lump, as on one's head. Syn. *magâ, pamamagâ, umbók.* 2. boil; tumor. Syn. *pigsa.*

bukóng (bu-kóng), n. bone joint.

buksán (buk-sán), v. 1. to open, as a window, door, draw, etc. Syn. *ibukas.* Ant. *sarhán, isará, ipiníd.* 2. to start or begin, as a program, meeting, or the like. Syn. *simulán, umpisahán.* 3. (Colloq.) to mention or make mention of. Syn. *banggitín.*

buktót (buk-tót), adj. wicked; evil; perverse; depraved. Syn. *buhóng, imbí, taksíl.*

bukungbukong (bu-kung-bu-kong), n. (Anat.) ankle. Syn. *buól.*

Buda (Bu-da), n. (Sp.) Buddha.

budbód (bud-bód). n. 1. act or manner of sprinkling salt, pepper, or the like sparingly on food. Syn. *bulabod, pagbubulabod.* 2. that which is sprinkled sparingly on food, e.g., salt, pepper, etc. 2. act of distributing or giving out things in small amount to many person. Syn. *pamimigáy, pamamahagi, pagrarasyón.* 3. act of scattering seeds or kernels of corn, as in feeding fowls. Cf. *sabog, pagsasabog.*

budhî (bud-hî), n. 1. conscience. Syn. *konsiyénsiyá.* 2.conduct; behavior. Syn. *ugalì, pag-uugalì, kaugalian.* 3. (Colloq.) pity; sorrow for other's suffering. Syn. *awà, pag-kaawà; habág, pagkahabág.*

budin (bu-din), n. (Sp.) pudding. Syn. *puding.*

Budismo (Bu-dis-mo), n. (Sp.) Buddhism.

bugá (bu-gá), n. 1. act of blowing out something from the mouth. Cf. *luwà, pagluluwâ.* 2. puff, as of smoke from a chimney or volcano. 3. a kind of game, in which the cue piece, usually a marble or *kalumbibít* nut, is forced out of the player's mouth by a sudden, hard blow to hit the other marbles or *kalumbibit* nuts called *tayâ.* 4. a kind of medical treatment practised by an erbolaryo or quack doctor, in which some substances or herbs are concocted by chewing them and then spat on the part of the patient's body to be treated. 5. the act or practice of blowing smoke on the face of game cocks to make them brave and their eyes clear.

bugà (bu-gà), n. pumice; pumice stone.

bugál (bu-gál), var. **bug-al**, n. a lump or mass, as of earth; clod. Syn. *kimpál.* Cf. *tipák, piraso.*

bugalwák (bu-gal-wák), n. sudden gush of water from a broken pipe, or of blood from a big cut or severed artery. Syn. *bulwák, sagalwák, alawák.*

bugaw (bu-gaw), n. 1. act of driving away an animal or animals. Syn. *abóy, pag-aabóy; tabóy; pagtatabóy; pagpapaalís, pagpapalayas.* 2. pimp; procurer. Syn. *alkahuweta, alkagwete.*

bugbóg (bug-bóg), I. n. 1. flogging; punishing with repeated blows or beating.

Syn. *gulpí, paggulpí, pagpapahirap sa
pamamagitan ng palò o paggulpí.* 2. bruise,
contusion, or swelling caused by a blow
or beating. Syn. *pasâ, pamamasâ; lamóg,
pagkalamóg.*
—II. *adj.* bruised; badly beaten. Syn.
lamóg, pasâ.

ⱷughán (bug-hán), *v.* 1. to blow or smoke
at, referring esp. to the head or face of a
gamecock. 2. to apply medicine of
concocted herbs by blowing or spitting it
on the part of the patient's body to be
treated.

ⱷugháw (bug-háw), I. *n.* blue; azure. Syn.
asúl, kulay-langit.
—II. *adj.* with or having blue color; blue.

ⱷugnót (bug-nót), I. *n.* exasperation,
irritation, or annoyance caused by or as
by a joke. Syn. *galit, pagkagalit, yamót,
pagkayamót; inís, pagkainís.*
—II. *adj.* angry; irritated; annoyed;
exasperated. Syn. *galít, inís, yamót.*

ⱷugók (bu-gók), I. *adj.* addle or rotten,
referring to an egg or eggs that failed to
hatch. Syn. *bulók, nabugók.*
—II. *n.* an addle or rotten egg, esp. one
that failed to hatch.

ⱷugóy (bu-góy), *n.* a derogatory term for a
small boy. Syn. *buging.*

ⱷugsô (bug-sô), *n.* 1. sudden downpour, as
of rain. Syn. *bigláng buhos.* 2. sudden gush,
as of wind. Syn. *bigláng lakás.* 3. a venting
or foaming out, as of anger or passion.
Syn. *silakbó, sidhî, sasál, tindi.* 4. sudden
abundance, as of goods in the market.
Syn. *saksâ, pagsaksâ; saganà, pananaganà.*
5. coming in great numbers, as of people.
Syn. *dagsâ, pagdagsâ.*

bugtóng (bug-tóng), I. *n.* riddle. Cf.
paláisipán, páhulaán.
—II. *adj.* alone; lone; only one. Syn. *tangì,
natatangì; isà, nag-íisá, kaisá-isá; solo.*

buhaghág (bu-hag-hág), I. *adj.* loose; porous;
not compact; spongy: as in *buhaghág na
lupa,* loose soil. Syn. *muyág.*
—II. *n.* 1. act of making loose, as of soil
by cultivation. 2. state or condition of
being porous or loose, referring to soil or
the like.

ⱷuhangin (bu-ha-ngin), *n.* sand.

buhat[1] (bu-hat), *n.* act or manner of lifting
or raising up something. Syn. *taás,
pagtataás; alsa, pagaalsa; angát, pag-aangát.*
Also *buhát* (in some Tagalog region).

buhat[2] (bu-hat), I. *adj.* (with *sa*) 1.
originated or derived from; taken or based
from. Syn. *kuha o hangò sa, batay sa.* 2.
native of; from (a certain place.) Syn.
tagátubò sa. 3. from; coming from. Syn.
galing, mulâ.
—II. *adv.* since; from: as in *buhat
kahapon,* since yesterday. Syn. *mulâ,
simulâ, magmulâ.*

buhawì (bu-ha-wì), *n.* cyclone; tornado;
whirlwind. Syn. *ipuipo.*

buháy (bu-háy), *adj.* 1. alive; living. Ant.
patáy. 2. prosperous; thriving. Syn.
maunlád, umuunlád. 3. spirited;
animated; lively. Syn. *masiglá, punô ng
siglá.* 4. running; functioning: as in *buháy
pa ang mákiná,* the machine is still
functioning. Syn. *umáandár, tumatakbo.*
5. on; not off: as in *buháy pa ang ilaw,*
the light is still on. 6. clear and vivid: as
in *buhay na kulay,* clear and vivid color.
Syn. *matingkád.*

buhay-alamáng (bu-hay + a-la-máng), I. *n.*
insecure existence; short life.
—II. *adj.* short-lived.

buhay-buhay (bu-hay + bu-hay), *n.* living
condition; livelihood, as in certain places.
Syn. *kabuhayan, pagkabuhay.*

buhayin (bu-ha-yin), *v.* 1. to bring back to
life; revive; resuscitate; resurrect. Syn.
bigyáng mulî ng buhay. 2. to support and
take care of, as of one's children. Syn.
pakanin at alagaan; palakihín. 3. to
reanimate; render or make active. Syn.
pasiglahín, bigyáng-siglá, bigyáng-buhay. 4.
to reintroduce or propose again, as a bill
that has been disapproved previously.
Syn. *ipanukalang mulî.*

buhò (bu-hò), *n.* (Bot.) a species of bamboo.
Cf. *kawayan.*

buhók (bu-hók), *n.* hair. Cf. *balahibo, bulból.*

buhól (bu-hól), *n.* 1. knot formed in a
thread, cord, rope, etc. 2. problem;
difficulty; entanglement; obstacle. Syn.
súliranín, problema, sigalót. 3. a unifying
factor; bond. Syn. *bigkís, buklód.*

buhong (bu-hóng), I. *adj*. 1. cunning;
deceitful; sly. Syn. *tuso, mandaraya,
mapanlinláng*. 2. wicked; bad; evil, sinful.
Syn. *buktót, masamâ*. 3. traitorous;
treacherous. Syn. *taksíl, traidór*.
—II. *n*. 1. villain. Syn. *kontrabida, bilyako*.
2. traitor. Syn. *taksíl, taong taksíl; traidor,
taong traidór*.

buhos (bu-hos), *n*. 1. continuous pouring or
fall, as of rain. Cf. *paták, bagsák*. 2. act of
pouring water on oneself or on somebody,
as in taking a bath. 3. full exertion, as of
one's strength. Syn. *paggamit ng buóng
kaya*. 4. act of pouring water on the head,
as in baptism. Cf. *binyág, pagbibinyág*.

bulâ(bu-lâ), *n*. 1. foam; bubble; suds; lather.
2. foaming saliva caused by disease or
great excitement; froth.

bulaan (bu-la-an), *adj.* not telling the truth;
untruthful; lying. Syn. *sinungaling,
nagsísinungalíng, hindî nagsásabi ng
katotohanan*.

bulabog (bu-la-bog), *n*. 1. act of frightening
and driving away, e.g. a flock of birds from
their roost. Syn. *bubó, pagbubó; bulahaw,
pagbulahaw*. 2. sudden flight, as of a flock
of frightened birds. Syn. *pagkabulabog,
pagkabulahaw*.

bulak (bu-lak), *n*. 1. (Bot.) the cotton plant.
2. cotton wool.

bulák (bu-lák), *n*. 1. boil or boiling, as of
liquid. Syn. *kulô, pagkulô; sulák, pagsulák*.
2. bubble or foam formed on the surface
of boiling liquid. Syn. *bulá, espuma*.

Bulakán (Bu-la-kán), *n*. the name of one of
the Tagalog provinces in the Island of
Luzon.

bulakból (bu-lak-ból), I. *adj*. 1. truant;
wandering. Syn. *galâ, pagalà, lagalág, layás*.
2. idle; lazy. Syn. *tamád, batugan*. 3.
vagabond; jobless. Syn. *bagamundo
(bagabundo), palaboy, hampas-lupà*.
—II. *n*. 1. act of playing truant. Syn.
*lakwatsa, paglalakwatsa; ansikót, pag-
aansikót; pagbubulakból*. 2. a truant. Syn.
lakwatsero, bulakbulero, ansikutero.

bulaklák (bu-lak-lák), *n*. 1. flower; blossom.
2. (Fig.) a beautiful woman. Syn.
magandang dalaga o babae.

bulaklák-dilà (bu-lak-lák + di-là), *n*. words

or expression uttered without seriousness;
hence, a loose talk.

bulag (bu-lag), *n*. 1. loss of sight; blindness;
state of being blind. Syn. *pagkabulag,
kabulagán*. 2. act of causing someone's eye
or eyes to be blind; deliberate blinding of
someone's eye or eyes. Syn. *pagbulag*.

bulagâ (Bu-la-gâ), *interj*. an expression used
in playing with children, usually
accompanied by the sudden uncovering
of one's eyes to make them laugh. Syn.
Wâ!

bulagáw (bu-la-gáw), *adj*. 1. gray-eyed; blue-
eyed. Syn. *matáng-pusá, matáng-bugháw*.
2. (Colloq.) shortsighted. Syn. *malabò ang
matá*.

bulagsák (bu-lag-sák), *adj*. 1. wasteful;
prodigal. Syn. *gastadór, mapag-aksayá,
mapagtapón, mapaglustay*. 2. disorderly or
careless in manner or habit. Syn. *busalsál,
burarâ, pabayâ*.

bulagtâ (bu-lag-tâ), I. *n*. state or condition
of being fallen flat or prostrate. Syn.
timbuwáng, handusáy. 2. act or manner of
lying flat with the face up and the arms
and legs stretched, as by a lazy person.
Syn. *pagbulagtâ, pagtimbuwáng,
paghandusáy*.
—II. *adj*. lying flat with the face up and
the arms and legs stretched; fallen prostrate
as if dead or unconscious. Syn. *nakabulagtâ,
nakahandusáy, nakatimbuwáng*.

bulahaw (bu-la-haw), *n*. act of causing
disturbance or commotion among a
group, as by making too much noise.

bulalakaw (bu-la-la-kaw), *n*. (Astron.)
shooting star; meteor. Syn. *taing bituin
(colloq.)*

bulalas (bu-la-las; bu-la-lás), *n*. 1. a venting
or foaming out, as of passion or anger. Syn.
hiyáw, sigáw. 2. paroxysm; outburst, as of
crying or laughter. Syn. *hagulhól o
halakhák*. 3. exclamation; outcry. Syn.
biglâng hiyáw o sigáw.

bulalô (bu-la-lô), *n*. kneecap; kneepan. Syn.
bayugo (ng tuhod).

búlan (bú-lan), *n*. (Bis.) 1. month. 2. moon.
Syn. *buwán*.

bulâng-gugò (bu-láng + gu-gò), I. *n*. gugo
suds or foam.

—II. *adj.* (*fig.*) openhanded or generous with one's money, esp. in spending for friends. Syn. *galante* (*colloq.*), *bukás-palad.* Ant. *kuripot, maramot.*

bulangláng (bu-lang-lang), *n.* a kind of vegetable stew; pottage.

bulaos (bu-la-ot), *n.* trail or footpath, as in a forest. Syn. *landás.*

bulas (bu-las), *n.* 1. robustness. Syn. *lusóg, kalusugán.* 2. luxuriant growth. Syn. *yabong, kayabungan; labay, kalabayan.* 3. loud reproach or censure. Syn. *bulyáw, hiyáw.*

bulastóg (bu-las-tóg), *adj.* 1. mean; low in dignity; ignoble. Syn. *hamak, imbi.* 2. rash; reckless. Syn. *mapusok, pabiglá-biglâ.* 3. boastful; bluffing. Syn. *hambóg, bulaan, mayabang.*

bulati (bu-la-ti), *n.* 1. earthworm. Syn. *bulating-lupà.* 2. intestinal worm; specifically, ascaris. Syn. *ulyabid, tiwà.*

bulatlát (bu-lat-lát), *n.* minute search or inspection by removing or turning over and over everything in a container or opening every page of a book. Syn. *saliksik, halikwát, halukay, halungkát.*

buláw (bu-láw), **I.** *adj.* golden; of reddish-gold color.
—II. *n.* 1. reddish-gold color, esp. of roosters and young pigs. 2. young suckling pig. Syn. *biík, buwík, kulíg.*

bulay (bu-lay), *n.* meditation; reflection; contemplation. Syn. *nilay, pagninilay-nilay.*

bulba (bul-ba), *n.* (*Sp.*) vulva. Syn. *puki, kikì; belat* (*slang*).

bulból (bul-ból), *n.* pubic hair. Cf. *balahibo, buhók.*

bulkan (bul-kan), *n.* (*Sp. volcan*) volcano.

bulkanisá (bul-ka-ni-sá), *n.* (*Sp. vulcanizar*) a vulcanizing or being vulcanized; vulcanization.

buldog (bul-dog), *n.* (*Eng.*) bulldog. Cf. *aso.*

buldoser (bul-do-ser), *n.* (*Eng.*) bulldozer. Cf. *traktora.*

búlebár (bú-le-bár), *n.* (*Eng.*) boulevard. Cf. *kalye, abenida, lansangan.*

bulgár (bul-gár), *adj.* (*Sp.; Eng.*) 1. vulgar; indecent. Syn. *bastós, mahalay.* 2. coarse; unrefined. Syn. *magaspáng.* 3. lowly;

common. Syn. *hamak, mababang-urì.*

buli (bu-li), *n.* 1. act of polishing or making smooth and shiny, as by rubbing. Syn. *pagpapakinis, pagpapakintáb.* 2. removal of vulgarity or crudity from. 3. the manner by which a thing has been polished or made smooth and shiny. Syn. *pagkakábuli, pagkakápakinis, pagkakápakintáb.*

bulí (bu-lí), *n.* (*Bot.*) buri palm (*Coryppha elata* Toxb.).

bulik (bu-lik), **I.** *adj.* referring to a chicken, esp. a rooster, the feathers of which are speckled with white and black colors.
—II. *n.* a chicken, esp. a rooster, having feathers speckled with white and black colors. Cf. *talisayin, malatubâ, alimbuyugin, hiraw, mayahin,* etc.

bulíd (bu-líd), *n.* precipitate fall from or as from the brink or edge of a high or steep place. Cf. *hulog, pagkahulog; buwál, pagkabuwál.*

bulíg (bu-líg), *n.* (*Ichth.*) medium-sized murrel (*dalág*).

bulihalà (bu-li-ha-là), **I.** *n.* 1. rooster with ashy-colored feathers and black feet. Cf. *talisayin, mayahin, alimbuyugin, bulik,* etc. 2. the ashy color of the feathers of a rooster.
—II. *adj.* with or having ashy-colored feathers, referring to a rooster.

bulilit (bu-li-lit), *n.* 1. fact or condition of being much smaller than the usual size. Syn. *di-pangkaraniwang liít o kaliitan.* 2. a person animal or plant that is much smaller than the usual size of its kind; dwarf.

bulinaw (bu-li-naw), *n.* (*Bis.*) a species of bamboo, known also as *kawayang-kilíng* and *kawayang-tsina* (*Bambusa vulgaris* Schrad.).

buling-buling (bu-ling + bu-ling), var. **bulingbuling**, *n.* the practice or custom of wetting people by throwing water at them during the Feast of St. John the Baptist.

bulislís (bu-lis-lís), **I.** *n.* 1. act or manner of pulling up the lower end of a woman's skirt or dress to expose the lower part of her body. Cf. *lislís, lilís.* 2. fact or condition of having one's skirt or dress pulled or

rolled up, referring esp. to a woman.
—II. *adj.* 1. with or having the lower end
of the skirt or dress pulled or rolled up,
exposing the lower portion of the body,
referring esp. to a woman. 2. pulled or
rolled up, referring to the lower end of a
skirt or dress.

bulitín (bu-li-tín), n. 1. news; report;
bulletin. Syn. *balità, ulat.* 2. newspaper or
magazine. Syn. *páhayagán o lingguhan.* 3.
notice. Syn. *patalastás, paunawà.* 4.
numbered ball or balls, as those used in
drawing lots. Syn. *bulilyo.* 5. (Fig.) secret:
as in *nábisto ang kanyáng bulitín,* his secret
was discovered.

bulo (bu-lo), n. 1. silky down or floss on
leaves, fruits and stems of plants. 2. fine
hairy growth on the wings of butterflies,
on bodies of some worms, and the like.

buló (bu-ló), n. an obsolescent root from
which *kabuluhán* is derived, meaning
importance, value, or worth.

bulô (bu-lô), n. a young cow or carabao. Syn.
guyà, bisiro.

bulók (bu-lók), *adj.* 1. decayed, referring to
things like wood, cloth, paper, etc. Syn.
gatô, gapók. 2. putrid; rotten and foul-
smelling. Syn. *sirâ at mabahò.* 3. morally
corrupt; depraved; wicked. Syn. *masama.*
4. of poor kind; inferior. Syn. *mahinang-
klase; mumurahin.*

bulog (bu-log), n. virility; ability to
procreate or produce young. Cf.
pagkalalaki.

bulól (bu-lól), *adj.* referring to a person who
has defective speech. Syn. *utál, humál.*

bulón (bu-lón), n. anything that blocks up
the throat, causing the person to choke.
Cf. *hirin, luóg.*

bulóng (bu-lóng), n. 1. whisper. Syn. *anas.*
2. incantation. Syn. *orasyón.*

bulos (bu-los), n. 1. extra helping or serving
of food. Syn. *ulit na pagkuha o pagdudulot
ng pagkain.* 2. gust or blow, as of wind. Syn.
hihip. 3. a kind of hand-thrown fish
harpoon. Syn. *salapáng.* Cf. sibát. 4.
continuous flow or pouring, as of water.
Syn. *buhos, agos.*

bulsa (bul-sa), n. (Sp. *bolsa*) 1. pocket. Cf.
lukbutan. 2. bag: as in *bulsa ng yelo,* ice

bag. Cf. *supot.* 3. sac or sacs: as in *bulsa ng
hangin,* air sacs.

bulsa-de-yelo (bul-sa + de + ye-lo), n. ice
bag.

bulsilyo (bul-sil-yo), n. (Sp. bolsillo) 1.
small pocket or bag. Syn. *munting bulsa o
supot.* 2. a small purse; pocketbook. Syn.
pitakà, kartamoneda.

bulto (bul-tò), n. (Sp.) 1. a big pack or
bundle, as of cloth. Syn. *kaha, pakete,
balutan.* 2. a throw or hurl (in wrestling).
Syn. *hagis, itsa.*

bulubók (bu-lu-bók), n. 1. bubbling, as of
boiling water. Syn. *kulô, pagkulô; sulák,
pagsulák.* 2. the bubbling sound produced
by boiling water.

bulúbundukin (bu-lú-bun-du-kin), *adj.*
hilly; mountainous.

bulugan (bu-lu-gan), n. an uncastrated male
hog; boar. Syn. *barakong baboy.*

buluntád (bu-lun-tád), I. *adj.* (Sp. *voluntad*)
voluntary; not forced. Syn. *kusá, kusang-
loób; sa sariling kagustuhan.*
—II. *adv.* voluntarily; of one's own free
will, without compulsion. Syn. *kusà;
kusang-loób; sadyâ, sinadyâ.*

bulúng-búlungan (bu-lúng + bú-lu-ngan),
n. rumor; gossip. Syn. *tsismis.* Cf. *sabí-sabí.*

bulusan (bu-lu-san), I. n. 1. blacksmith
bellow. 2. an open place or field where
wind passes freely. Syn. *alulusan.*
—II. *v.* to give an extra serving (helping)
of food.

bulusok (bu-lu-sok), n. sudden or accidental
sinking, as of a foot or feet in deep water
or mud. Syn. *tibusok.* 2. a stab or thrust
with or as with a spear. Cf. *saksák, urak,
tasak,* ulos. 3. a precipitate dive in the air
or water. Syn. *sisid.*

bulutong (bu-lu-tong), n. 1. (Med.)
smallpox; variola. 2. pitted scars left by
smallpox; pockmarks.

bulwagan (bul-wa-gan), n. 1. a big hall, esp.
one used for big gatherings. 2. a big
entrance to a building.

bulyáw (bul-yáw), n. 1. act of shouting
loudly at (an animal or animals) to drive
away. Syn. *malakás na pagbugaw, pasigáw
na pagpapalayas o pagtatabóy.* 2. rough
rebuke or reproach; loud angry shout at

bumaka   **buntál¹**

someone. Syn. *sigáw, hiyáw; bulas.*

bumaka (bu-ma-ka), v. to campaign against. Syn. *kumalaban, kalabanin.*

bumakay (bu-ma-kay), v. 1. to wait for and get, e.g. a taxi to ride in. Syn. *umabáng, mag-abáng.* 2. to guard; act as a guard. Syn. *gumuwardiyá; bumantáy, magbantáy; tumanod, magtanod.*

bumadyá (bu-mad-yá), v. to imitate what another says or does. Syn. *gumagád.*

bumago (bumago), v. 1. to change, referring to one's place; move from one's place to another. Syn. *lumipat, umibá ng lugár.* 2. to become new; look like new. Syn. *maging bago o magmukháng bago.*

bumaít (bu-ma-ít), v. 1. to become good or kind. Syn. *bumuti.* 2. to become domesticated or tame. Syn. umamò. Ant. *umiláp.*

bumandera (bu-man-de-ra), v. 1. (Colloq.) to show oneself openly. Syn. *lumantád, humantád.* 2. in horse racing to win, Cf. *manguna, manalo.*

bumangó (bu-ma-ngó), v. 1. to become sweet-smelling. Cf. *sumamyó, humalimuyak.* 2. (Fig.) to become well-appreciated or well-esteemed by. Syn. *mápuri, mápabuti sa.*

bumbón (bum-bón), n. branches and twigs placed in a deep portion of a river to attract fish to live and nest there.

bumbóng (bum-bóng), n. 1. a cylindrical container, esp. one made of bamboo. Cf. *takil.* 2. a length of bamboo, used as a container in fetching water, esp. in the provinces.

bumbunan (bum-bu-nan), n. (Anat.) the soft, boneless area in the skull of a child, which is later closed up by the formation of bone; fontanel. Cf. *tuktók.*

bundat (bun-dat), I. adj. having eaten all that one wants; full; glutted. Syn. *busóg na busóg.*
—II. n. fact or condition of being full, referring to a person who has eaten all that he wants.

bundók (bun-dók), 1. mountain. Cf. *gulód, buról.* 2. (Fig.) large pile, heap or mount of. Cf. *tambák, timbón, buntón.*

bundól (bun-dól), n. an accidental or deliberate ramming or driving of into with the end or tip of something heavy and long, as a big pole, log, or post. Syn. *bunggô, tumbók, dunggól.*

buni (bu-ni), n. (Med.) herpes; ringworm; ptyriasis.

bunô (bu-nô), n. 1. wrestling (form of sport). Syn. *suóng* (Bats.) 2. act of wrestling another, as in a fight. Syn. *pagbunô, pagsuóng.*

bunot (bu-not), n. 1. uprooting or pulling up a plant. 2. draw or drawing, as of numbered balls in lottery. Syn. *dukot, pagdukot.* 3. act of pulling out something stuck into a hole, esp. one that is elongated. Cf. *hatak, hila, hugot.* 4. an unsheathing, as of a knife, bolo, spear, etc. from the scabbard. Ant. *salong.*

bunót¹ (bu-nót), I. n. 1. coconut husk. 2. coir; husk fibers, as that used in rope making, etc. 3. the fibrous portion of some nuts or seeds, like that of mangoes. 4. act or manner of polishing floors with a coconut husk. Syn. *pagbubunót.*

bunót² (bu-nót), adj. 1. uprooted, referring to plants, post, etc. 2. drawn out, as a gun, bolo, knife, etc.

bunsô (bun-so; bun-sô), I. n. 1. the youngest child in a family. Cf. *panganay* (the first or oldest child in a family). 2. an endearing term for a pet child in the family, which in most case, is the youngest.
—II. adj. youngest or last, referring to a couple's child.

bunsód (bun-sód), n. 1. front or threshold. Syn. *haráp, harapán.* 2. place at the foot of a staircase. Syn. *punò ng hagdanan.* 3. launching, as of a vessel, candidacy, etc. Syn. *lunsád, paglulunsád.* 4. initiation, as of an activity. Syn. *pagbubukas, inagurasyón.*

bunsóng-anák (bun-sóng + a-nák) n. 1. one's youngest child; pinakabatang anák. 2. (Fig.) the only output or accomplishment that a person has done. Cf. *sulong-anák* (fig.).

buntál¹ (bun-tál), n. 1. blow or knock with the fist. Syn. *suntók.* 2. beating or hitting with a big stick, bludgeon, or club. Syn.

bugbóg, gulpi, hampás.

buntál² (bun-tál), I. n. buri palm fibers, usually made into fine hats, better known as panama hats.
—II. adj, made of *buntál* (buri palm fibers), referring esp. to hats.

buntalà (bun-ta-là), n. (Astron), 1. planet. Syn. *planeta.* 2. comet. Syn. *kometa, taingbituin.*

buntis (bun-tis; bun-tís), I. adj. 1. pregnant, referring to a woman. Syn. *nagdadalángtao* (fig.) 2. (Colloq.) big-bellied. Syn. *malakí ang tiyán, butete* (fig.).
—II. n. 1. a pregnant woman. Syn. *nagdadaláng-tao.* 2. fact or state of being pregnant; pregnancy. Syn. *pagkabuntis, kabuntisán.*

bunto (bun-to; bun-tó), n. 1. a venting out or giving vent to anger or strong emotion. Cf. *sidhî, silakbó, sikláb.* 2. concentration of force or pressure on something. Syn. *tindí, diín, bigát.*

bunton (bun-ton), n. 1. a disorderly pile or heap, as of garbage. Syn. *tambak.* 2. act of dumping something on a place. Syn. *pagbubunton, pagtatambák.* 2. (Colloq.) an undetermined number or amount. Cf. *katirbá.*

buntóng-galit (bun-tóng + ga-lit), n. inner feeling of anger; secret anger. Syn. *lihim na galit.*

buntóng-hiningá (bun-tóng + hi-ni-ngá), var. **buntúng-hiningá**, n. sigh. Syn. *himutók, paghihimutók; hinagpís, paghihinagpís.*

buntot (bun-tot; bun-tót), n. 1. tail. 2. act or manner of following or tailing someone wherever he goes. Syn. *sunód, pagsunúdsunód.* 3. posterior; last part or end, as of a long line of people in a parade. Syn. *hulí, hulihán.* Cf. *dulo, duluhan.* 4. (Fig.), result; outcome. Syn. *bunga* (fig.); *resulta, wakás.* 5. train, as of a dress, skirt, etc. 6. tail feathers of chickens, birds, or the like.

buntót-pagi (bun-tót + pa-gi), var. **buntutpagi**, n. tail of rayfish used as a whip.

bunyág (bun-yág), I. n. revelation or disclosure, as of a secret or an anomaly. Syn. *paghahayág ng lihim, pagsisiwalat.*

—II. adj. no longer secret; known; revealed or disclosed. Syn. *hindi na lihim, hayág, alám na ng maram,; siwalát.*

bunyî (bun-yî), I. n. 1. feeling of great joy, happiness, pride, etc.; exaltation; elation. Syn. *malakíng tuwâ.* 2. hilarious celebration. Syn. *masayáng pagdiriwang.* 3. great honor, distinction, or fame. Syn. *kabantugan, katanyagan.*
—II. adj. illustrious; distinguished. Syn. *bantóg, tanyág, dakilà, marangál.*

bunga (bu-nga), n. (Bot.), 1. fruit. Syn. *bungang-kahoy, prutas.* 2. the betel palm (Areca catechu). 3. the fruit of the betel palm; betel nut. 3. result; outcome; consequence. Syn. *resulta, kinalabasán, epekto, wakás.* 4. gain; benefit; profit. Syn. *pakinabang, kapakinabangán, palà, pamá, tamó.*

bungad (bu-ngad), 1. front; threshold. Syn. *haráp, harapán; una, unahán; bukana.* 2. beginning; start. Syn. *umpisá, simulâ.*

bungál (bu-ngal), adj. toothless. Syn. *waláng ngipin.* Cf. *bungî.*

bungalngál (bu-ngal-ngál), I. adj. 1. given to loud crying. Syn. *íyakín, pálahawín.* 2. given to chattering or babbling. Syn. *masatsát, matabíl, madaldál.* 3 always complaining. Syn. *mareklamo, reklamadór.*
—II. n. a crybaby.

bungantulog (bu-ngan-tu-log; bú-ngan-tulóg), n. 1. daydream; reverie. Syn. *panagimpán.* 2. ambition; dream. Syn. *pangarap* (fig.), ambisyón.

bungangá (bu-nga-ngá), n. 1. (Anat.), gullet (of a large animal). Cf. *bibíg.* 2. entrance or opening, as of a cave. Cf. *bungad.* 3. mouth, as of pots, bottles, etc. Syn. *bibíg.* Cf. *labí* 4. the wide mouth of a river; estuary. Syn. *wawá.* 5. crater (of a volcano). Cf. *butas, bibig.*

bungang-araw (bu-ngang + a-raw), n. prickly heat. Syn. *abang abang.* Cf. *imunimon.*

bungang-kahoy (bu-ngang + ka-hoy), var. **bungangkahoy**, n. fruit (of a tree or a plant). See **bunga**, 1. Syn. *prutas.*

bungangera (bu-nga-nge-ra), I. n. a loquacious or talkative woman. Syn. *daldalera, satsatera.*

—II. *adj.* loquacious or talkative, referring to a woman. Syn. *masatsát, madaldál, mabungangà, masalitâ.*

bungang-isip (bu-ngang + i-sip), *n.* 1. product of the (one's) mind (literal). 2. fiction. Syn. *kathâ, kata-katà.* 3. invention. Syn. *likhâ, imbento.*

bungkal (bung-kal), I. *n.* 1. digging or tilling of soil for planting; cultivation or tillage, esp. by plowing. Syn. *pag-araro o pag-aararo.* 2. act of digging or turning over soil, as with trowel, hoe, or the like. Syn. *hukay, paghukay; dukál, pagdukál, pagdudukál.* 2. a ransacking. Syn. *halukay, paghalukay; halungkát, paghalungkát, paghahalungkát.*

—II. *adj.* 1. tilled or cultivated, as soil. Syn. *araró, inararo.* 2. ransacked, as things in a drawer. Syn. *halukáy, hinalukay; halungkát, hinalungkát.*

bungkós (bung-kós), I. *n.* 1. act or manner of tying together a number of things into a bundle. Syn. *talì, pagtatalì; bigkís, pagbibigkís.* 2. a number of things tied together, as heads of garlic. Syn. *talì, bigkís, tungkós.* 3. act of wrapping things with a piece of cloth or handkerchief by tying the corners together. Cf. *balot, pagbalot, pagbabalot.* 4. a bundle of things, wrapped in a piece of cloth, handkerchief, or the like. Syn. *balot, balutan.*

—II. *adj.* 1. tied together, as heads of garlic. Syn. *binungkós, nakabungkós; tinungkós, nakatungkós.* 2. wrapped together in a piece of cloth, handkerchief, or the like. Syn. *balót, nakabalot.*

bunggabilya (bung-ga-bil-ya), *n.* (Sp. *buganvilla*) bougainvillaea.

búnggaló (búng-ga-ló), *n.* (Eng.) bungalow. Cf. *tsalét.*

bunggô (bung-gô), *n.* 1. act of pushing or knocking a person or thing with or as with one's body. Syn. *banggâ, umpóg, bundól.* 2. accidental bumping or knock of one body against another; collision.

bungì (bu-ngì), *n.* 1. the space left by a missing tooth. 2. dent, nick, or notch, esp. in the edge of a bladed tool. Syn. *bingaw.* 2. harelip. Syn. *bingot.*

bungî (bu-ngî), I. *adj.* 1. with or having a missing tooth or teeth, referring to a person. Cf. *bungáw, bungál.* 2. with or having a nick, dent, or notch, referring esp. to bladed tools. Syn. *bingáw.* 3. with or having a harelip. Syn. *bingót.*

bungisngís (bu-ngis-ngís), I. *n.* 1. a person who has the habit of giggling or laughing most of the time; giggler. 2. giggling or laughing suggestive of foolishness. Syn. *ngisngís, ngisí.*

—II. *adj.* with or having the habit of giggling or laughing most of the time. Syn. *ngisí, palangisí.*

bungô (bu-ngô), *n.* (*Anat.*) skull; bones of the head. Cf. *bao ng ulo.* See **kalansáy.**

bunguan (bu-ngu-an), *n.* (*Ichth.*) smooth-headed sea catfish. (*Arius leiotetocephalus*). Cf. *kandulì.*

bungulan (bu-ngu-lan), *n.* (*Bot.*), 1. a species of banana plant, the fruits of which sometimes reach a length of 20 cm. 2. the fruits of this banana plant. Cf. *sabá, lakatán.*

buô (bu-ô), I. *adj.* 1. whole; entire. Syn. *lahát, lahát-lahát.* 2. complete. Syn. *ganáp, lubós.* 3. intact; sound. Syn. *waláng-sirà, waláng-basag.* 4. united; solid. Syn. *nagkakáisa, magkakaisá.* 5. completed or finished. Syn. *yarî na, tapós na.*

—II. *n.* 1. whole piece 2. act of organizing not a single body. Syn. *tatag, pagtatatag.* 3. unification. Syn. *pag-iisá, pagbubuô.*

buód (bu-ód), *n.* 1. summary. Syn. *lagom.* 2. gist; main idea. Syn. *diwà.* 3. core; central part. Syn. *ubod.* 4. act of summarizing . Syn. *pagbubuód, paglagom.*

buóng (bu-óng) *n.* a combining meaning from whole, full, complete, or entire. See **buo.**

bupanda (bu-pan-da), *n.* (Sp. *bufanda*) lady's muffler; scarf. Syn. *panyuwelo, alampáy.*

bupete (bu-pe-te), *n.* (Sp. *bufete*) law office; lawyer's office. Syn. *tanggapan (upisina) ng abogado.*

burá (bu-rá), I. *n.* (Sp. *borrar*) 1. act or manner of erasing. Syn. *pagburá; pawì, pagpawì; katkát, pagkatkát.* 2. the place on a surface where something was erased; erasure. Syn. *pinagburahán; pawì, pinagpawian; katkát, pinagkatkatán; payì,* *pinagpayian.* 3. vociferous outburst of anger or displeasure. Syn. *takáp, busa.*

—II. *adj.* erased or rubbed out, referring to a word, mark, etc. on a surface. Syn. *pawî, katkát, payî, burado.*

burak (bu-rak), *n.* mire; deep mud; slime; slough. Syn. *pusalî; malalim na putik.*

burado (bu-ra-do), *adj.* erased or rubbed out. Syn. *naburá, napawì, napayì, nakatkát.*

buradór (bu-ra-dór), *n.* (Sp. *borrador*) 1. draft as of a speech; rough draft. 2. eraser. Syn. *pamburá, pampawì, pamayì.*

burarâ (bu-ra-rà), *adj.* slovenly; careless or untidy in appearance, habit, work, etc. Syn. *salaulà, busalsál.*

burda (bur-da), var. **borda**, *n.* (Sp. *bordar*) 1. art or work of ornamenting fabric with needlework; embroidering. Syn. *pagboborda, pagbuburda.* 2. embroidery; ornamental needlework.

burikák (bu-ri-kák), I. *n.* a prostitute; whore; harlot. Syn. *babaing asno.*

burikì (bu-ri-kì), *n.* 1. a small, short metal tube with a tapering pointed tip, used in sampling rice in sacks. 2. the act or manner of sampling rice by stabbing or piercing a sack with a *burikì.*

buriko (bu-ri-ko), var. **boriko**, *n.* (Sp. *borrico*) ass; donkey. Syn. *asno.*

burirì (bu-ri-rì), *n.* excessive care or attention to detail in doing something, often resulting in unnecessary delay. Syn. *kuriri, kutiltíl.*

burlas (bur-las), var. **borlas**, *n.* (Sp. *borla*) ornamental tuft of thread, cords, etc.; tassel. Syn. *palamuting lamuymóy, lamuymóy, palamuymóy.*

burlés (bur-lés), *n.* & *adj.* (Eng.) burlesque.

buro[1] (bu-ro), I. *n.* 1. fish or meat preserved in brine or salt. 2. pickled green fruits. Cf. *atsara.*

—II. *adj.* preserved in salt or brine, referring to fish, meat, or the like. 2. pickled, referring to green fruits, like mangoes.

buro[2] (bu-ro), *n.* (Sp.) bureau (government office under a department). Syn. *kawanihan.*

burok (bu-rok), *n.* 1. chubbiness, as of cheeks. Syn. *bintóg, pamimintóg; umbók,*

kaumbukán. 2. yolk (of egg). Syn. *pulá ng itlóg.*

burol (bu-rol), *n.* a lying in state.

buról (bu-ról), *n.* 1. a hill. Syn. *muntíng bundok* 2. hillock; ant hill. Syn. *punso.* 3. an elevated land in a plain; highland. Syn. *bakulód, gulód.*

burot (bu-rot), *adj.* vainglorious; conceited; swell-headed. Syn. *hambóg, palalò, malakí ang ulo* (fig.)

bursitis (bur-si-tis), *n.* (Eng.) inflammation of a bursa; bursitis. Cf. *pamamagâ ng kasúkasuán.*

buruka (bu-ru-ka), *n.* (Sp.) 1. witch; hag. Syn. *buruha* (*bruha*). 2. an ugly, repulsive old woman.

busá (bu-sá), *n.* 1. continuous popping or bursting sound, as that caused by continuous rapid firing of guns. Cf. *pútukan.* 2. act or manner roasting cereals, Cf. *sangág, pagsasangág.* 3. the characteristic sound produced in roasting corn, rice, or the like. 4. (Colloq.) sudden burst of anger. Cf. *talák.*

busabos (bu-sa-bos), I. *n.* 1. slave; vassal. Syn. *alipin.* 2. act of treating a person like a slave; enslavement. Syn. *pag-alipin, pagbusabos.*

—II. *adj.* 1. doing menial work for one's master; working as a slave. Syn. *alipin.* 2. servile; subservient. Syn. *labis na masunurin.*

busal (bu-sal), *n.* corncob.

busál (bu-sál), *n.* 1. muzzle (for animals). 2. act or manner of putting a muzzle on (an animal). Syn. *pagbubusál.* 3. any restraint to free speech; gag.

busalsál (bu-sal-sál), *adj.* 1. slovenly; untidy; careless in habits, behavior, appearance, or methods of work; slipshod. Syn. *pabayà* (*sa ugalì, katawán, atbp.*), *burarâ.* 2. badly beaten or split open, as the head of chisel handle. Cf. *salsál.*

busangsáng (bu-sang-sáng), *adj.* 1. swollen or distended, as the thick or badly battered lips of a person. Syn. *busarga, namúmusarga.* 2. fully open (s.o. flowers). Syn. *bukadkád.* 3. split open at the end, as the badly beaten head of a chisel handle. Syn. *busalsál,* 2.

busbós (bus-bós), I. n. surgical operation; cutting open, as of a boil, or the like. Syn. *tistís, pagtistís; operá, pag-operá, pag-ooperá.* —II. *adj.* operated on; cut open.

busiksík (bu-sik-sík), *adj.* 1. stocky; thickset; massive stout. Syn. *batibot; maskulado.* 2. compact; tightly pressed. Syn. *siksík, siksík na siksík.*

busilak (bu-si-lak), I. n. immaculate whiteness. Syn. *dalisay na kaputián.* —II. *adj.* 1. immaculate; perfectely clean; very clean. Syn. *napakalinis; malinis na malinis; waláng bahid-dungis.* 2. pure. Syn. *dalisay.*

busilig (bu-si-lig), n. 1. the pupil or ball of the eye. 2. a term used derogatorily in referring to someone's eyes. Syn. *matá.*

busina (bu-si-na), n. (Sp. *bocina*) 1. automobile horn. 2. act of sounding an automobile horn. Syn. *pagbusina.* 3. the sound of this horn.

busisì (bu-si-sì), I. n. 1. act of folding or rolling up the foreskin or prepuce. Syn. *burát, pagburát.* 2. act or manner of doing something in a slow, unconcerned manner. Cf. *kutiltíl.* 3. scrupulous manner; scrupulosity. Syn. *kuririì, kakuririan; gigì, kagigian.* —II. *adj.* 1. requiring slow and careful attention, referring to a certain kind of work. 2. unnecessarily slow in a manner or habit of doing things. Syn. *mabusisì, makuririì.*

buslô (bus-lô), n. 1. a kind of small basket, with or without a covering, used as a container for eggs, fruits, and vegetables, like tomatoes, onions, garlic, etc. 2. a basketball net. 3. act of or attempt in shooting the ball in a basketball game. 3. a successful shot in basketball.

busog (bu-sog), n. bow (for shooting arrows). Syn. *arko* (*ng panà*).

busóg (bu-sóg), *adj.* full; having eaten all that one wants; satisfied with or as with food. Cf. *bundát, sandát.*

busól (bu-sól), n. 1. a small, hard growth felt beneath a surface. Cf. *butól, buklíg, bukol.* 2. doorknob.

busóng (bu-sóng), *adj.* irreverent; disrespectful. Syn. *waláng-galang, waláng-*

pitagan.

busto (bus-to), n. (Sp.) bust; a piece shoulders and upper chest of the human body. Cf. *istatwâ.*

butaka (bu-ta-ka; bu-ta-kà), n. (Sp. *butaca*) orchestra seat.

butangero (bu-ta-nge-ro), n. a tough guy; thug; ruffian. Syn. *matón.*

butas (bu-tas), n. 1. hole (in general). 2. orifice; an opening; mouth or outlet, as of a tube, cavity, etc. 3. eye, as of a needle. 4. pit, esp. of snakes, rats, etc. Syn. *lungga.* 5. act or manner of boring or cutting a hole or holes into. Syn. *pagbutas.*

butás (bu-tás), I. *adj.* 1. with or having a hole; pierced with a hole or holes. Syn. *may butas.* 2. (*Fig.*) no longer virgin, referring to a woman. Cf. *disgrasyada.*

butaw (bu-taw), n. 1. membership fees or dues in an association, club, etc. Cf. *singíl, kontribusyón.* 2. fine for delinquency in payment of one's obligation. Syn. *multa, patong* (*colloq.*)

butáw (bu-táw), n. 1. practice or trial bout in cockfighting. Syn. *bitáw.* 2. the release of game cocks facing each other at the start of the bout. 3. a weaning or being weaned, as of a child. Syn. *pag-awat sa suso.*

buti (bu-ti), n. 1. a being good, kind, or honest. Syn. *baít, kabaitan; husay, kahusayan.* 2. recovery, as from sickness. Syn. *galíng, paggalíng.* 3. improvement, as of life, business, etc. Syn. *unlád, pag-unlád.*

butikî (bu-ti-kî), n. (Zool.) house lizard.

butiktík (bu-tik-tík), *adj.* filled to over capacity; fully loaded. Syn. *punúng-punô; siksík na siksík.*

butíg (bu-tíg), n. wart. Syn. *kulugó.*

butigin (bu-ti-gin), *adj.* full or covered with warts; warty. Syn. *mabutíg, makulugó.*

butil (bu-til), n. 1. a grain or small particle, as of salt, sand, etc. 2. a single seed, grain, or kernel. Syn. *bigì, butó.* 3. collectively, grains; cereals 4. a drop, as of tears. Syn. *paták.* 5. bead, as of a rosary, necklaces, etc. Syn. *abaloryo, manik.*

butingtíng (bu-ting-tíng), I. n. 1. act of doing or making something in a slow, lazy manner. Syn. *kutiltíl, butiltíl.*

—II. *adj*. referring to a person who has the habit of doing things in a slow, lazy manner. Syn. *mabutingtíng, makutiltíl, mabutiltíl, mabusisí.*

butitos (bu-ti-tos), *n.* (Sp.) ladies high-heeled shoes.

butó (bu-tó), *n.* 1. bone. 2. seeds, collectively; grains or cereals. Syn. *butil.* 3. a small seed, as of apple, orange, etc. pip. 4. palm leaf rib. Syn. *tadyáng* 5. skeleton. Syn. *kalansáy.*

butò (bu-tò), *n.* (Bis.) male genital organ; penis. Syn. *utin, titì.* (Note: The original Visayan meaning of this word is *vulva, puki*).

butones (bu-to-nes), var. **botones**, *n.* (Sp. *botón*) button or buttons. Syn. *butón o botón.*

butse (but-se; but-sé), *n.* (Sp. *buche*) 1. crop of fowls; craw. 2. sweetened, mashed sweet potatoes or beans (mongo) wrapped in thin dough and fried in oil. Also called *butsé-butsé.*

butuán (bu-tu-án), *n.* (Bot.) 1. a species of banana plant that bears fruits having many seeds. Syn. *butuhán.* 2. the seedy fruit of this plant.

butyóg (but-yóg), var. **botyog**, *adj.* big-bellied.

buwâ (bu-wâ) *n.* (Med.) prolapsed uterus (*natura mullieris*).

buwág (bu-wág), I. *n.* 1. tearing down; demolition. Syn. *gibâ, paggibâ; wasak, pagwasak.* 2. disbandment; abolition. Syn. *lanság, paglanság; pagbuwág.*

—II. *adj.* 1. demolished. Syn. *gibâ, ginibâ; wasák, winasák.* 2. abolished; disband; dissolve, referring to an organization, establishment, office etc. Syn. *lanság (na), patáy na* (Colloq.).

buwál¹ (bu-wál), I. *n.* 1. fall or falling down, as of standing objects like a tree, post, chair, etc. Syn. *tumba, pagkatumba, pagkabuwál.* 2. act or manner of causing something to be knocked or toppled down. Syn. *pagbubuwál, pagtutumba.* 3. (*Fig.*) state or condition of being bankrupt, referring to a business enterprise. Syn. *pagkatumba, pangangalugi, pagkabangkarote.*

—II. *adj.* 1. fallen down on the ground, said of standing objects. Syn. *tumba, natumba.* 2. bankrupt; put out of business due to bankruptcy. Syn. *bangkarote, nábangkarote.*

buwál² (bu-wál), *n.* (Fr. *uwal*) voile (a kind of fabric).

buwán (bu-wán), *n.* 1. (*Astron*) moon. Syn. *luna.* 2. month. Syn. *bulan* (for both senses).

buwán-buwán (bu-wán + bu-wán), *adj.* & *adv.* monthly; every month; once a month. —II. *n.* (*Ichth.*) a species of ox-eyed herring (Megalops cyprinoides Broussonet).

buwáy (bu-wáy), *n.* 1. shaky state, condition, or position; unsteadiness. 2. insecurity. Syn. *kawaláng-tatág.*

buwaya (bu-wa-ya), I. *n.* (Zool.) 1. crocodile. 2. (*Fig.*) an excessively covetous person. Syn. *taong lubháng masakím* (*mapag-imbót*). —II. *adj.* greedy; avaricious; covetous. Syn. *sakím, mapag-imbót, makamkám, matakaw.*

buwaya-sa-katihan (bu-wa-ya + sa + ka-ti-han), *n.* (*Fig.*) usurer. Syn. *usurero.*

buwelo (bu-we-lo), *n.* (Sp. *vuelo*) 1. sway; swinging movement or motion, as of hands, swing, hammock, pendulum, etc. Syn. *undayon, indayog, tabyón, ugóy.* 2. spurt or swift start, as of a runner in racing. Cf. *pulás.* 3. flare (of a garment). Syn. *bulga.*

buwelta (bu-wel-ta), *n.* 1. act of going or coming back; return to one's home, country, place, etc. Syn. *uwî, pag-uwî; balík; pagbabalík.* 2. return or giving back of something taken, borrowed, bought, etc. Syn. *saulî, pagsasaulî.* 3. a turning back; retreat. Syn. *urong, pag-urong.* 4. turning over; putting a thing up-side-down. Syn. *baligtád, pagbaligtád; bilíng, pagbilíng.* 5. something returned as goods bought from a store. Syn. *sauli.* 6. return or restoration of something to its former position. Syn. *pagbabalík* (*sa dating lugár o puwesto*). 7. doing again what has been done; repetition. Syn. *ulit, pag-uulit, paggawang mulî.* 8. rebound; bouncing. Syn. *talbóg, pagtalbóg.* fold. Syn. *lupî, tupî.*

buwenamano   **ka-**

buwenamano (bu-we-na-ma-no), n. (Sp.
buena mano) 1. first sale of the day. 2. the
first buyer of the day, as in a store.

buwenas (bu-we-nas), I. n. (Sp. *buenas*)
good luck. Syn. *suwerte, magandáng
suwerte (kapalaran)*.
—II. adj. lucky. Syn. *masuwerte, mapalad*.

buweno (bu-we-no), adv. well; very well; all
right as in *Buweno, tayo na*; Well, let's
go.

buwik (bu-wik), n. (Zool) a young pig;
piglet. Syn. *biík, kulíg, buláw*.

buwíg (bu-wíg), n. bunch or cluster of fruit,
as bananas, lanzones, or the like. Cf.
kumpól, langkáy.

buwís (bu-wís), n. 1. tax: compulsory
payment of a percentage of income,
property value, sales price, etc. Cf. *rentas,
amilyaramyento*. 2. share of harvest or crop
sharing contract. Cf. *hurnál*. 3. (*Fig.*)
something given as a sacrifice. Syn.
sakripisyo.

buwisit (bu-wi-sit), I. n. 1. a person or thing
which brings bad luck or misfortune 2.
act of causing annoyance to someone.
Syn. *pagbubuwisit, pambubuwisit*.
—II. adj. unlucky; ill-omened. Syn. *malas,
minámalas, sinásamâ; waláng-suwerte*. 2.
that which cause annoyance; annoying.
Syn. *nakabúbuwisit, nakáyayamót,
nakasúsuyà*.

buwitre (bu-wit-re), n. (Sp. *buitre*) 1.
vulture. 2. a greedy and ruthless person
who preys on others. Syn. *ganid, buwaya
(fig.)*

buyagín (bu-ya-gín), v. to loosen; make
loose, as soil. Syn. *muyagín, buhaghagín*.

buyangyáng (bu-yang-yáng), I. adj. exposed
to the element; in the open. Syn. *hantád,
nakahantád; lantád, nakalantád;
tiwangwáng, nakatiwang-wáng*.
—II. n. 1. fact, state, or condition of being
exposed to the element. 2. act of exposing
(a thing) in the open.

buyo (bu-yo; bu-yò), n. (*Bot.*) 1. a climbing
pepper plant; commonly chewed with
little lime, betel nut, and tobacco. Syn.
ikmo, mamín.

buyó (bu-yó), I. n. 1. a seducing or being
seduced; seduction. Syn. *upat, pang-uupat;*

sulsól, panunulsól. 2. state or condition
of being deeply engrossed or absorbed in
doing something. Syn. *pagkawiling mabuti*.
—II. adj. engrossed or absorbed in
(reading, playing, gambling, etc.). Syn.
wilí, náwiwili.

buyon (bu-yon; bu-yón), n. large, protruding
belly; potbelly; paunch. Syn. *tiyáng
malakí*.

K

K, k (ka), n. 1. the third letter of the *abakada*
(Pilipino alphabet). 2. the type or
impression representing this letter. 3. a
symbol for the third in a group or series.

ka (ka), pron. (postpositive of *ikáw*, used in
familiar talk, in the second person,
singular number, and in the nominative
and objective case) you.

ka (ka), n. a particle used as a term of
respect, place before the names of elders
with whom one is acquainted, and of
distant uncles and aunts. Cf. *Mang o
Mamang, Ale o Aleng, Tiyó o Tiyóng, Tiyá
o Tiyáng*.

ka- pref. 1. meaning fellow or mate; or
sometimes expressed by the prefix co- as
in *kamanggagàwa* (fellow worker or co-
worker), *kamánunulát* (fellow writer),
kaklase (classmate), *kababayan*
(townmate; fellow countryman), *kabaháy*
(housemate), etc. 2. expressing
relationship or membership, as in *kaanib*
(member), *kasapì* (member), *kasama*
(companion), etc. 3. expressing the idea
of an action just performed or done: as in
kaaális (has just gone or left); *kakákain*
(having just eaten), *kasúsulat* (written just
now), etc. 4. expressing the idea of
continuity or repetition, as in *kásasalitâ*
(speaking continuously), *kásusulat*
(writing continuously), etc. 5. expressing
a very little amount or quantity, as in
kákaunti (of very little amount or
quantity), *kákarampót, kákatitíng,
kákapurát* (of a very negligible amount or
quantity), etc.

kaabalahan (ka-a-ba-la-han), n. 1. delay; fact or condition of being delayed. Syn. *kahulihán, pagkahulí.* 2. obstacle; hindrance. Syn. *sagabal.*

—II. *v.* to spend or waste time, for referring to something being done. Syn. *pag-ukulan o pag-aksayahán ng panahón.*

kaabáy (ka-a-báy), I. adj. sleeping or lying beside someone. Cf. *kasiping, katabi.*

—II. n. a person with whom one sleeps or lies in the same bed.

kaakbáy (ka-ak-báy), I. n. a person with whom one stands or walks with an arm over the other's shoulder.

—II. adj. referring to a person with whom one stands or walks with an arm over the other's shoulder. Syn. *kaalakbáy* (for both senses).

kaakit-akit (ka-a-kit + a-kit), adj. attractive. Syn. *kahalí-halina.*

kaakuhán (ka-a-ku-hán), n. egotism; self-conceit. Syn. *pagkamakasarili, egotismo.*

kaagád (ka-a-gád), adv. at once; immediately; promptly. Syn. *madalî, mádalian.*

kaagapay (ka-a-ga-pay), I. adj. standing, walking, or placed side by side with another. Cf. *kasiping, katabí, kasigbáy.*

—II. n. a person standing or walking side by side with another. Syn. *kahanay.*

kaagáw (ka-a-gáw), n. rival; competitor. Syn. *karibál, kalaban.*

kaagulò (ka-a-gulò; ka-a-gu-lô), n. concubine. Syn. *kálunyâ; babae, kerida* (colloq.).

kaalám (ka-a-lám), I. n. an accomplice; co-conspirator; confederate. Syn. *kasabuwát, kasabwát, kasapakát, kainalám, katuón.*

—II. adj. referring to one who joins another or others in a conspiracy.

kaalaman (ka-a-la-man), n. 1. competency; ability; skill. Syn. *kakayahán, husay, kahusayan.* 2. knowledge, understanding. Syn. *kabatiran, pagkaunawâ.*

kaalan (ka-a-lan), n. namesake. Syn. *kapangalan, tukayo, katukayo.*

kaalatan (ka-a-la-tan), n. fact or condition of being salty; saltiness. Syn. *pagkamaalat.*

kaalindugán (ka-a-lin-du-gán), n. state or condition of being charming; gorgeousness. Syn. *karilagán, kariktán, karingalán.*

kaalinsabay (ka-a-lin-sa-bay), adj. & n. referring to a person or thing belonging to the same period of time. Syn. *kasabáy, kapanahón.*

kaalipustaán (ka-a-li-pus-ta-án), n. contemptibleness Syn. *pagkaalipustâ, kahamakan, pagkahamak.*

kaalít (ka-a-lít), I. n. adversary; opponent; antagonist; foe; enemy. Syn. *kaaway, kagalít, katunggalî, kalaban.*

—II. adj. said of an enemy, adversary, etc.

kaaliwán (ka-a-li-wán), I. n. state or condition of being comforted, pleased, or entertained. Syn. *pagkaalíw.*

—II. *v.* to obtain pleasure, entertainment, comfort, or the like. Syn. *kawilihan, pagkawilihan.*

kaalwanán (ka-al-wa-nán), n. 1. comfort of body; enjoyment of comfort. Syn. *ginhawa, kaginhawahan.* 2. ease of doing; easiness. Syn. *kadalián o kagaanáng gawín.*

kaalyado (ka-al-ya-do), I. n. ally. Syn. *kakampí, kapanalig, kapanig.*

—II. adj. referring to a person or persons sharing with another or others in some purpose.

kaamuan (ka-a-mu-an), n. domesticity; tameness. Syn. *pagkamaamó, baít, kabaitán.* Ant. *iláp, kailapán.*

kaanak (ka-a-nak), n. relative; relation. Syn. *kamag-anak, hinlóg.*

kaanib (ka-a-nib), I. n. member; affiliate. Syn. *kasapî, miyembro.*

—II. adj. affiliated.

kaantahán (ka-an-ta-hán), n. rancidity, as of stale fat, butter, and the like. Syn. *pagkamaantá.*

kaantasán (ka-an-ta-san), n. 1. (Gram.) comparative degree. 2. class or grade level to which a thing belongs. Syn. *kaurián.*

kaanu-ano (ka-a-nu + a-nu), n. (Colloq.) relative; relation. Syn. *kamag-anak, kaanak.*

kaapíd (ka-a-píd), n. & adj. referring to a person who has an illicit sex relation with another. Syn. *kaagulô.*

kaapihán (ka-a-pi-hán), n. state or condition of being aggrieved or unjustly treated. Syn. *pagkaapí*.

kaarawán (ka-a-ra-wán), n. 1. birthday. Syn. *kapanganakan, kumpleanyo*. 2. anniversary. Syn. *anibersaryo*. 3. the day or date of a scheduled event. Syn. *araw, petsa*.

kaasalán (ka-a-sa-lán), n. standing custom or habit. Syn. *kaugalián*.

kaawaan (ka-a-wa-an), I. *v.* to pity; have pity or mercy on. Syn. *kahabagán*.
—II. n. pity or mercy for (someone). Syn. *awà, pagkaawà; habág, pagkahabág*.

kaawá-awà (ka-a-wá + a-wà), *adj.* pitiful; deserving pity. Syn. *nakaáawà, kahabághabág*.

kaaway (ka-a-way), n. enemy; foe; adversary. Syn. *kagalít, katunggalí, kalaban, kababág*.

kaaya-aya (ka-a-aya + a-ya), *adj.* delightful; pleasurable; pleasant. Syn. *kalugúd-lugód, kasiyá-siyá*.

kaayusan (ka-a-yu-san), n. 1. order ; orderliness. Syn. *pagkamaayos; kalagayang maayos*. 2. arrangement. Syn. *ayos, pagkakaayos*. 3. condition; situation. Syn. *lagáy, kalagayan*.

kabá (ka-bá), n. 1. premonition; foreboding. Syn. *kutób, hinuhá*. 2. irregular palpitation of the heart. 3. a feeling of fear that something wrong happened or may happen. Syn. *agam-agam, pangambá, bagabag*.

kababaan (ka-ba-ba-an), n. 1. a being low, as of a place; lowness. Syn. *babà, pagkamababà*. 2. lack of regular height, as a person. Syn. *kapandakán*. 3. lowland. Ant. *kataasan*. 4. humbleness; lowliness; humility. Syn. *kababaang-loób*. Ant. *kapalaluán*. 5. cheapness (of price). Syn. *kamurahan*.

kababaang-loób (ka-ba-ba-ang + lo-ób) n. humility. Syn. *kapakumbabaán*. Ant. *kapalaluán*.

kababalaghán (ka-ba-ba-lag-hán), n. wonder; miracle; marvel; prodigy. Syn. *himalá, hiwagà, kahiwagaan, milagro, misteryo*.

kababatá (ka-ba-ba-tá), I. n. 1. one's fellow child. Syn. *kapwá batá*. 2. childhood contemporary. Syn. *kapanahón*.
—II. *adj.* of the same age; having the same

age. Syn. *kasinbatá*. Cf. *kasinggulang, kasintandâ*.

kababawan (ka-ba-ba-wan), n. 1. lack of depth; shallowness. Syn. *pagkamababaw*. Ant. *kalaliman, pagkamalalim*. 2. lack of depth in meaning. Syn. *kawaláng-pondo* (*colloq*). 3. a. shallow place in a body of water; shallow; shoal.

kababayan (ka-ba-ba-yan), I. n. 1. townmate. Cf. *kalalawigan*. 2. fellow countryman; compatriot; fellowman. Syn. *kabansâ*. Cf. *kalahì*.
—II. *adj.* referring to one's townmate or fellow countryman.

kababuyan (ka-ba-bu-yan), n. 1. dirty or insanitary habit of a person. Syn. *kasalaulaan*. 2. indecency; immorality. Syn. *kalaswaán, kahalayan, kabastusán*.

kabaka (ka-ba-ka), n. adversary; opponent. Syn. *kalaban, katunggalí*.

kabakahin (ka-ba-ka-hin), *v.* to oppose; fight against. Syn. *kalabanin, katunggaliín*.

kabaklahán (ka-bak-la-hán), I. n. state or condition of being worried, perplexed, etc.; perplexity. Syn. *pagkabaklá, pagkabahalà*.

kabado (ka-ba-do), *adj.* 1. in doubt; having doubt; doubting; not sure. Syn. *nagáalinlangan, may-alinlangan*. 2. nervous; apprehensive; fearful. Syn. *kinákabahán*.

kabag[1] (ka-bag), n. (Med.) gas pain; flatulence. Syn. *usog*.

kabág[2] (ka-bág), n. (Zool.) a species of fruit bat (*Pteropus edulis* Geoff.).

kabagalan (ka-ba-ga-lan), n. slowness; sluggishness. Syn. *kakuparan, kakuyaran*.

kabagáng (ka-ba-gáng), I. n. a person with whom one is compatible with. Syn. *kasundô, katugmâ*.
—II. *adj.* referring to a person with whom one is compatible with. Syn. *nákakabagáng, nákakasundô*.

kabagay (ka-ba-gay), *adj.* fit or appropriate for. Syn. *bagay, nababagay; katugmá; kaangkóp, naaangkóp*.

kabág-kabág (ka-bág + ka-bág), var. **kabagkabág**, n. (Zool.) a small species of bat, smaller than the ordinary bat.

kabagsikán (ka-bag-si-kán), n. 1. fierceness; ferocity; cruelty. Syn. *lupít, kalupitán;*

kabagután
kabatî

bangís, *kabangisán.* 2. potency; effectiveness. Syn. *bisa, kabisaan; tapang, katapangan* (*fig.*).

kabagután (ka-ba-gu-tán), I. n. state or condition of being greatly annoyed or impatient; exasperation; ennui; impatience. Syn. *yamót, kayamután, pagkayamót; inis, kainisán, pagkainis.*

—II. *v.* to feel greatly annoyed or impatient with. Syn. *kayamután, kainisán.*

kabahán (ka-ba-hán), *v.* 1. to have a premonition about something. Syn. *kutubán, magkakutób, magkahinuhà.* 2. to have a feeling of fear that something wrong happened or may happen. Syn. *magkaagam-agam, mabagabag.*

kabahayan (ka-ba-ha-yan), *v.* to live with (someone) in the same house.

kabaitan (ka-bá-i-tan), n. 1. good conduct or behavior. Syn. *kabutihang ugalì.* 2. kindness; helpfulness. Syn. *pagkamatulungín, pagkamagandáng-loób.* 3. domesticity; docility. Syn. *amò, kaamuan.*

kabalakyután (ka-ba-lak-yu-tán), n. atrocity; brutality. Syn. *lupít, kalupitán, kabuhungán.* 2. immorality; wickedness. Syn. *imoralidád, kasamaán, kabuktután.*

kabalát (ka-ba-lát), I. n. a person belonging to the same race with another. Cf. *kalahì, kalipì.*

—II. adj. 1. referring to a person belonging to the same race with another. 2. with or having the same complexion as another. Syn. *kakulay* (*ng balát*)

kabalbalán (ka-bal-ba-lán), n. I. anomaly; fraudulent irregularity. Syn. *katiwalián, anomalya.* 2. nonsense; foolish behavior or talk. Syn. *kaululán, kalokohan, katarantaduhan.*

kabalighuán (ka-ba-lig-hu-án), n. absurdity. Syn. *kahidwaán, kabalintunaan.*

kabaligtarán (ka-ba-lig-ta-rán), n. the reverse or opposite. Syn. *kabalikán.* 2. the wrong side, as of cloth. Syn. *ilalim.* Ant. *karayagán.*

kabalintunaan (ka-ba-lin-tu-na-an), n. 1. irony; absurdity. Syn. *kabalighuán, kahidwaán.* 2. adversity; calamity; misfortune. Syn. *kasawiáng-palad ; sakunâ.*

kabalyero (ka-bal-ye-ro), n. (Sp. *caballero*)

1. a chivalrous man; gentleman. Syn. *máginoó.* 2. sportsman. 3. knight.

kabán (ka-bán), n. 1. clothes' chest or trunk. Syn. *baúl.* 2. dry measure equivalent ot 75 liters or 25 gantas. Syn. *dalawampú't limáng salóp.* 3. (Colloq.) treasury. Syn. *ingatáng-yaman, tesoreriyá.*

kabanalan (ka-bá-na-lan), n. piousness; godliness; holiness; saintliness. Syn. *pagkabanál, pagkamaka-Diyós.*

kabanata (ka-ba-na-tá), n. 1. chapter, as of a book. 2. part or episode, as of one's life. Syn. *yugtô.*

kabansaán (ka-ban-sa-án), n. nationhood. Syn. *pagkabansá* (*pagkabansâ*).

kabantugan (ka-ban-tu-gan; ka-ban-tu-gán), n. fame; renown; popularity. Syn. *katanyagán.*

kabangisán (ka-ba-ngi-sán) n. ferocity; fierceness. Syn. *kabagsikán, kalupitán.*

kabanguhán (ka-ba-ngu-hán), n. 1. fragrance; sweet smell or odor. Syn. *kasamyuhán, kahalimuyakan.* 2. (Fig.) popularity; height of popularity. Syn. *katanyagán, kabantugán.*

kabaong (ka-ba-ong), n. coffin; casket. Syn. *ataúl.*

kabaratán (ka-ba-ra-tán), n. the characteristic habit of a haggler. Cf. *kakuriputan.*

kabarkada (ka-bar-ka-da), n. gang member; fellow member in gang. Syn. *kagáng, kapangkát, kasama.*

kábarét (ká-ba-rét), n. (Sp. *cabaret*) cabaret. Syn. *salón.*

kabaró (ka-ba-ró), I. n. fellow woman. Syn. *kababae.*

—II. adj. referring to another woman wearing a dress similar to what one is wearing.

kabasí (ka-ba-sí), n. (Ichth.) shortfinned gizzard shad (*Anodontostoma chacunda*).

kabataan (ka-ba-ta-an), n. 1. fact or state of being young; youthfulness; youngness. Cf. *kamusmusán.* 2. young people collectively youth; the young generation. 3. childhood; boyhood or girlhood. Syn. *pagkabatà.*

kabatî (ka-ba-ti), var. **kabatián**, n. & adj. referring to a person who is on speaking terms with another. Cf. *kaibigan*.

kabatiran (ka-ba-ti-ran), n. 1. knowledge or familiarity with a certain fact, etc. Syn. *kaalaman, pagkaalam*. 2. know-how; knowledge of how to do something; technical skill. Syn. *dunong, karunungan*. 3. understanding. Syn. *unawà, pagkaunawà*. 4. information. Syn. *balità, impormasyón*.

kabawasán (ka-ba-wa-sán), n. 1. quantity or amount which when deducted or taken would make something incomplete. Syn. *kakulangán*. 2. loss. Syn. *kawalán, pagkawalâ*.

kabayanan (ka-ba-ya-nan), n. town proper.

kabayanihan (ka-ba-ya-ni-han), n. 1. patriotism; heroism. Syn. *pagkamakabayan*. 2. bravery. Syn. *katapangan*.

kabayarán (ka-ba-ya-rán), n. 1. full amount of payment. Syn. *buóng o kabuuáng bayad*. 2. full compensation.

kabayo (ka-ba-yo), n. (Sp. *caballo*; Mex. *cabaio*) 1. horse. 2. carpenter's horse; sawhorse. Syn. *kabalyete* (sense 1). 3. shaft of an animal-drawn plow. 4. (*Colloq.*) act of riding on the back of a person as if riding on an animal. Syn. *pagkabayo*. 5. (In chess or cards) knight.

kabayong-dagat (ka-ba-yong + da-gat), n. (*Ichth.*) sea horse (*Hippocampus kuda*). Syn. *kabá-kabayuhan*.

kabkáb (kab-káb), I. n. 1. act or manner of scraping something with the teeth, as a dog does on bones or the like. Syn. *ngabngab*. 2. the portion of something scraped off with the teeth.

—II. *adj*. scraped off with the teeth or by biting.

kabesa (ka-be-sa), var. **kabisa**, n. (Sp. *cabeza*) 1. a chieftain or headman during the Spanish regime in the Philippines. Cf. *tinente*. 2. act or manner of memorizing; memorization. Syn. *pagsasaulo*.

kabesera (ka-be-se-ra), var. **kabisera**, n. (Sp. *cabecera*) capital, as of a province or country. Syn. *kapitál*. 2. the head of a dining table. 3. the person sitting at the head of a dining table, usually a principal guest.

kabibi (ka-bi-bi), n. (*Zool.*) 1. a species of sea clam. 2. the empty shell of this clam.

kabí-kabilâ (ka-bí + ka-bi-lâ), *adj*. & adv. (usually with *sa*) on or from all sides; from all directions or every direction.

kabiguán (ka-bi-gu-án), n. failure; disapointment. Syn. *pagkabigô*.

kabiguan (ka-bi-gu-an), I. n. failure; disappointment. Syn. *pagkabigô*.

—II. *v*. to cause or be the cause of one's failure or disappointment. Syn. *ikabigô; magíng dahilán ng pagkabigô*.

kabihasahan (ka-bi-ha-sa-han), I. n. fact or condition of being accustomed or acquainted with. Syn. *kasanayan, pagkasanay; kahiratihan, pagkahirati*.

—II. *v*. to be or become accustomed or acquainted with. Syn. *pagkasanayan, pagkahiratihan*.

kabihasnán (ka-bi-has-nán), n. 1. civilization. Syn. *sibilisasyon*. 2. culture. Syn. *kalinangán, kultura*.

kabilâ (ka-bi-lâ), n. 1. the opposite side, as of a street, river, etc. Syn. *ibayo, tapát, katapát*. 2. the reverse or back side of a thing. Syn. *ilalim, likod*. 3. the thing next or following another. Syn. *kasunód*. 4. the other one, referring to two opposing sides. Syn. *katalo, kalaban*.

—II. *adj*. 1. opposite, as in *kabiláng dako*, opposite side. Syn. *katapát*. 2. next; immediately following, as in *kabiláng kuwarto*, next room. Syn. *kasunód, sumúsunód*. 3. other, as in *kabiláng dulo*, the other end.

—III. *adv*. (usually with *sa*) 1. beyond or over. 2. in spite of.

kábilanin (ká-bi-la-nin), *adj*. inconstant; fickle. Syn. *salawahan*.

kábilín-bilinan (ká-bi-lín + bi-li-nan), n. & *adj*. referring to something that a person wants or requests another to do, get, or accomplish.

kabilugan (ka-bi-lu-gan), n. 1. fact or quality of being round like a ball or like a circle. Syn. *pagkamabilog*. 2. circumference. Syn. *paligid, kaligiran, paikot, palibot*. 3. chubbiness; rotundity; robustness. Syn. *katambukán, kaumbukán, katabaán*. 4.

fullness as of the moon.

kabinataan (ka-bi-na-ta-an), n. 1. fact or state of being a bachelor; bachelorship; bachelorhood. Syn. *pagkabinatà*. 2. group of young men; young men collectively. Cf. *kadalagahan, kaginoohan*.

kabisa (ka-bi-sa), var. **kabesa**, n. (Sp. *cabeza*) 1. chieftain or headman during the Spanish regime in the Philippines. Cf. *tinente*. 2. act or manner of memorizing; memorization. Syn. *pagsasaulo*.

kabisado (ka-bi-sa-do), var. *kabesado*, adj. 1. memorized; learned by heart. Syn. *saulado, memoryado*. 2. accustomed or familiar. Syn. *sanáy, hiratí*. 3. fully aware of; having full knowledge about. Syn. *alám, nalalaman; batíd, nabábatíd*.

kabisera (ka-bi-se-ra), var. **kabesera**, n. (Sp. *cabecera*) 1. capital, as of a province or country. Syn. *kapitál*. 2. head of a dining table. 3. the person sitting at the head of a dining table, usually a principal guest.

kabisî (ka-bi-sî), n.(Ch. ?) Chinese store owner or manager.

kabisote (ka-bi-so-te), I. adj. dullheaded; hence, fond of memorizing. Syn. *mahinà* or *mapuról ang ulo*.
—II. n. (Ornith.) a long-tailed bird, having shrill voice and feeds on insects. Syn. *tarát, pakiskís*. 2. a person fond of memorizing.

kabít (ka-bít), I. n. 1. state or condition of being attached or connected with each other, referring to two things. Syn. *dugtóng, hugpóng, sugpóng*. 2. act or manner of connecting or joining one thing with another. Syn. *pagkakabít, pagkakákabít; pagdurugtóng, pagkakarugtóng; paghuhugpóng, pagkakahugpóng*. 2. (Fig.) a common-law wife; paramour. Syn. *babae* (colloq.), *kálunyâ*.
—II. adj. 1. attached; connected; joined. Syn. *nakakabit, nakahugpóng, nakadugtóng*. 2. joined or connected with each other. Syn. *magkakabít, magkahugpóng*. 3. referring to a woman living with a man as common-law wife. Syn. *kinákasama, binábabae*.

kabít-kabít (ka-bít + ka-bít), adj. joined or connected in a series. Syn. *dugtúng-dugtóng, magkakarugtóng; magkakakabít; hugpúng-hugpóng, magkakahugpóng*. 2. attached or clinging to each other. Syn. *dikít-dikít, magkakarikít; digkít-digkít magkakadigkít*.

kabiyák (ka-bi-yák), I. n. 1. either of the two equal parts of a round or cylindrical object divided in halves; half. Cf. *kalahatì*. 2. either one of a pair (of shoes, slippers, etc.). Syn. *kapares*. 3. (Fig.) the husband or wife. Syn. *asawa*.
—II. adj. 1. referring to either of the two equal parts of a round or cylindrical object divided in halves. Syn. *kalahatì*. 2. referring to either one of a pair.

kable (ka-ble; ka-blé), n. (Sp. *cable*) 1. a large, strong rope or chain; cable. Syn. *malakíng lubid o kadena*. 2. message sent by telegraphic cable; cablegram. Syn. *kablegrama*.

kablegrama (ka-ble-gra-ma). n. (Sp. *cablegrama*) cablegram. Syn. *pahatíd-kable*. Cf. *telegrama, radyograma*.

kabo (ka-bo), n. (Sp. *cabo*) 1. (Mil.) corporal. Syn. *kórporál*. 2. (Colloq.) leader; gang leader. Syn. *punò, kapurál*.

kabóg (ka-bóg), n. loud, hollow sound, as that caused by a heavy falling object. Syn. *kalabóg*.

kabukiran (ka-bu-ki-ran), n. 1. wide field; wide tract of arable land. Cf. *parang, kaparangan*. 2. countryside; rural region.

kabuktután (ka-buk-tu-tán), n. 1. wickedness; perversity. Syn. *kasamaán, kabuhungán, kaimbihán*. 2. treachery. Syn. *kataksilán, katraidurán*.

kabuhayan (ka-bu-ha-yan), n. 1. source or means of living. Syn. *hanapbuhay*. 2. way of life; livelihood. Syn. *pagkabuhay, ikinabubuhay*. 3. properties. Syn. *mga ariarian*.

kabuhungán (ka-bu-hu-ngán), n. 1. wickedness; perversity. Syn. *kasamaán, kaimbihán*, 2. treachery. Syn. *kabuktután, kataksilán, katraidurán*.

kabulaanan (ka-bu-la-a-nan), n. lie; falsehood; untruth. Syn. *kasinungalingan; kawaláng-katotohanan*.

kabulagsakán (ka-bu-lag-sa-kán), n. 1. careless or disorderly manner or character.

Syn. *kabusalsalán, pagkabusalsál, pagkabulagsák.* 2. prodigality; wastefulness. Syn. *kagastadurán, pagkagastadór, pagkamapág-aksayá, pagkamapágtapón.*

kabulastugán (ka-bu-las-tu-gán), n. nonsense; foolishness; mischief. Syn. *kalokohan, kaululán, kapilyuhán.*

kabulukán (ka-bu-lu-kán), n. 1. fact, state, or quality of being rotten; rottenness; decay; putrifaction. Syn. *pagkabulók.* 2. anomaly; corruption; irregularity. Syn. *katiwalián, anomalya.* 3. wickedness. Syn. *samâ, kasamaán.*

kabuluhán (ka-bu-lu-hán), n. 1. importance; worth; value; significance. Syn. *halagá, kahalágahan; saysay, kasaysayan; importansiya.* 2. meaning. Syn. *kahulugan.* 3. purpose. Syn. *layon, layunin.*

kabundukan (ka-bun-du-kan), n. mountain range; mountain region.

kabuntisán (ka-bun-ti-sán), n. state or condition of being pregnant; pregnancy. Syn. *pagkabuntís.*

kabuntót (ka-bun-tót), I. n. 1. a person, animal, or thing that always trails or follows another. Syn. *kasunód, kasunúd-sunód.* 2. anything that comes about as a consequence or outcome of; result or resultant. Syn. *bunga, resulta.*
—II. adj. 1. referring to a person, animal, or thing that always trails or follows another. 2. following as a consequence of.

kabunyián (ka-bun-yi-án), n. 1. eminence; excellency; royalty. Syn. *kadakilaan; kamahalan.* 2. prominence; fame. Syn. *kabantugán, katanyagán.*

kabungguang-balikat (ka-bung-gu-ang + ba-li-kat), n. & adj. referring to a fellow with whom another often mingles or rubs shoulders with. Syn. *kahalúbilo, kahalu-halubilo.*

kabuté (ka-bu-té), var. **kabutí**, n. mushroom.

kabutihan (ka-bu-ti-han), n. 1. a being good or fine; goodness; excellence. Syn. *husay, kahusayan; galíng, kagalingán; inam, kainaman.* 2. kindness; benevolence. Syn. *báít, kabaitán, pagkamatulungín.* 3. advantage; benefit derived from. Syn. *bentahe, pakinabang, kapakinabangán.*

kabuuán (ka-bu-u-án), n. 1. total; sum. Syn. *totál, suma.* 2. completeness; wholeness. Syn. *kakumpletuhan.* 2. entirely; complete collection. Syn. *kalahatán; buóng kuleksiyón.* 4. summary. Syn. *buód, kabuurán.* 5. the complete or finish structure. Syn. *kayarian, kaayusan.*

kabuurán (ka-bu-u-rán), n. 1. central idea; gist. Syn. *diwà.* 2. summary. Syn. *buód.*

kabuwanan (ka-bu-wa-nan; -nán), n. 1. the month in which a pregnant woman is supposed to give birth Syn. *buwán ng panganganak.* 2. maturity month, as of payment of loan, etc. Cf. *takdáng buwán.*

kabuwisitan (ka-bu-wi-si-tan), I. n. 1. state or condition of being annoyed or vexed; annoyance; vexation. Syn. *yamót, pagkayamót, pagkabuwisit.* 2. bad luck; unluckiness. Syn. *kamalasan, pagkamalas; kawaláng-suwerte.*
—II. v. to feel annoyed or vexed about. Syn. *kayamután, ikayamót; kasuyaan, ikasuyà.*

kabuyaw (ka-bu-yaw), n. 1. (Bot.) a small citrus tree (Citrus *hystrix*) that bears fruits having astringent, sour juice which is used for seasoning. 2. the fruit of this tree. 3. (K-) a variant spelling of **Cabuyao**, name of a town in the province of Laguna.

kabyáw (kab-yáw), n. 1. milling of sugar cane. Syn. *alilis; iló, pag-iló, pag-iiló* (Bats.) 2. (Bis.; Bik.) a kind of blanket fish net.

kaka (ka-ka), n. the eldest of one's uncle or aunt. Syn. *tiyó o tiyá, amaín, ale, ditse.*

kakâ (ka-kâ), n. appellation for one's eldest brother, sister, or cousin. Syn. *kuya, manong, ate (até), manang.*

kákabá-kabá (ká-ka-bá + ka-bá), adj. 1. beating or pulsating irregularly, referring to the heart. 2. excitedly nervous.

kakak (ka-kak), n. cackle or cackling of a hen, duck, etc. Cf. *puták.*

kakahuyan (ka-ka-hu-yan), n. 1. forests; woods; woodland. Syn. *kagubatan.* 2. quality or state of being woody or thickly covered with trees. Syn. *pagkamagubat.*

kakaibá (ka-ka-i-bá), adj. 1. unusual. Syn. *di-karaniwan, di-pangkaraniwan,* 2. queer. Syn. *kakatwâ.* 3. strange. Syn. *kataká-taká; bago, nábabago.*

kakampí

kakampí (ka-kam-pí), *n.* 1. ally. Syn. *kaalyado, kaani, kapanig, kapanalig.* 2. teammate. Syn. *kakoponan, kakopong.*

kakampón (ka-kam-pón), *n.* co-member of a gang. Syn. *kagáng, kapangkát, kabarkada.*

kákanâ (ká-ka-nâ), *adj.* referring to a person who is not afraid to fight. Syn. *lalaban, hindî takót lumaban.*

kakanán (ka-ka-nán), I. *n.* 1. dining room. Syn. *silíd-kainan, kumidór.* 2. dish or plate to eat on. Syn. *pinggáng kinákainan.* 3. feeding trough. Syn. *labangán. sabsaban.*

kakanín (ka-ka-nín), I. *n.* 1. eatables; food. Syn. *pagkain.* 2. sweetmeats, tidbits, etc.; delicatessen.
—II. *adj.* eatable; said of anything that can be eaten.

kakaníng-itik (ka-ka-ning + i-tik), *n.* (Fig.) an insignificant person; small fry. Syn. *pipitsugin.*

kakanyahán (ka-kan-ya-hán), *n.* individuality; identity. Syn. *sariling katangian.*

kákanggatâ (ká-kang-gatâ), *n.* 1. thick coconut milk, usually the first juice extracted from nut meat. Syn. *unang gatâ.* 2. the very essence; the most important point; gist. Syn. *diwà, buód, kabuurán, kalamnán.*

kakapurát (ka-ka-pu-rát), *adj.* referring to a very tiny bit, or a very insignificant amount or quantity. Syn. *kapurát; katitíng; kákatitíng; kapurít, kákapurít.*

kákarampót (ká-ka-ram-pót), *adj.* said of a very insignificant amount or quantity. Syn. *kákapurát, kákapurít, kákatitíng.*

kakáw (ka-káw), *n.* (Bot.) 1. the cacao tree. 2. the fruit of this plant, used in the manufacture of cocoa or chocolate.

kakawate (ka-ka-wa-te), var. **kakawati**, *n.* (Bot.), a tree also known as *mádre-kakáw* or *marikakáw (maryakakáw).*

kakayahán (ka-ka-ya-hán), *n.* ability; capability; competence. Syn. *husay, kahusayan.* Cf. *lakás, puwersa.*

kaki (ka-ki), I. *n.* 1. a dull yellowish brown color. Syn. *kulay-kaki.* 2. a heavy cotton cloth of this color; khaki.
—II. *adj.* 1. of or having dull yellowish-brown color. 2. made of khaki cloth, as a

kakulangán

military uniform.

kakilá-kilabot (ka-ki-lá- + ki-la-bot), *adj.* horrible; frightful; terrible; awful. Syn. *nakakíkilabot, nakapangíngilabot; nakatátakot na lubhá.*

kakilala (ka-ki-la-la), I. *n.* a person with whom one is acquainted; acquaintance. Cf. *kaibigan, kabatián.*
—II. *adj.* referring to a person with whom one is acquainted.

kakintalán (ka-kin-ta-lán), *n.* impression; effect produced on one's mind, feeling, etc. Syn. *impresyón.*

kakirihán (ka-ki-ri-hán), *n.* 1. lasciviousness; lustfulness. Syn. *kalibugan.* 2. flirtatiousness. Syn. *kalandián.*

kakisigan (ka-ki-si-gan), *n.* elegance. Syn. *kagaraan, kabikasan.*

kakitirang-isip (ka-ki-ti-rang + i-sip), *n.* narrow-mindedness. Syn. *kahinaang-isip.*

kaklase (kak-la-se), I. *n.* classmate. Syn. *kaeskuwela.*
—II. *adj.* of the same class of kind. Syn. *kaurì.*

kako (ka-ko), var. *'kako, ikako* (fr. wikà ko), *idiom.* I said; as I said; what I sad. Syn. *anikó, sabi ko.*

kakompeténsiyá (ka-kom-pé-ten-si-yá), *n.* competitor; rival. Syn. *karibál.*

kakontra (ka-kon-tra), I. *n.* a person or thing opposed or against another. Syn. *kalaban, katunggalî, kasalungát.*
—II. *adj.* against; in contradiction with; opposing. Syn. *laban, nálalaban; salungát, násasalungát.*

kakontrata (ka-kon-tra-ta), *adj.* & *n.* referring to a party in a contract or agreement. Syn. *katrato.*

kakristiyanuhan (ka-kris-ti-ya-nu-han), *n.* 1. fact or state of being a Christian. Syn. *pagka-Kristiyano.* 2. Christendom; Christianity. Syn. *Sangkakristiyanuhan.*

kakrús (ka-krús), *adj.* referring to a thing that crosses or passes another. Cf. *magkakrús, magkahalang.*

kakulangán (ka-ku-la-ngán) *n.* 1. lack; shortage; insufficiency. Syn. *kakapusán, pagkakapós, pagkukuláng.* 2. need; want. Syn. *pangangailangan.* 3. defect; shortcoming. Syn. *kapintasan, depekto;*

kakulimlimán   **kadkád**

kasiraan (colloq.). 4. error; mistake. Syn. *malî, kamálian, pagkakámalî.*

kakulimlimán (ka-ku-lim-li-mán), *n.* 1. cloudiness, as of the sky. Syn. *kaulapan, pagkamaulap.* 2. dimness, as of light. Syn. *kakulabuán, pagkakulabô.*

kakulitán (ka-ku-li-tán), *n.* obstinacy; stubbornness. Syn. *pagkamakulít; katigasán ng ulo (fig.).*

kakunatan (ka-ku-na-tan), *n.* pliability; flexibility; ductility. Syn. *pagkamakunat.*

kakuparan (ka-ku-pa-ran), *n.* sluggishness; slowness in moving, action, work, etc. Syn. *kakuyaran, kabagalan, kagigian.*

kakuriputan (ka-ku-ri-pu-tan), *n.* stinginess; niggardliness. Syn. *pagkakuripot, labis na katipirán.*

kakuririan (ka-ku-ri-ri-an) *n.* scrupulousness; meticulousness. Syn. *pagkamakuriñ; kabusisian, pagkamabusisì; kakutiltilán, pagkamakutiltíl.*

kakutis (ka-ku-tis), *n.* &. *adj.* refering to a person having similar or the same complexion as another. Syn. *kabalát, kakulay ng balát.*

kakutyâ-kutyâ (ka-kut-yâ + kut-yâ), *adj.* ignominious; shameful; contemptible; despicable. Syn. *kalait-lait, kadustâ-dustâ.*

kakuwanán (ka-ku-wa-nán), *n.* any ludicrous act or behavior; antics. Cf. *kalokohan, katatawanán.*

kada (ka-da), *adj.* (Sp. cada) each; every. Syn. *bawa't (bawat).*

kadakilaan (ka-da-ki-la-an), *n.* 1. greatness; noble character. Syn. *karangalan.* 2. nobility; grandness. Syn. *kamaharlikaan, pagkamaharlikà.*

kadahilanan (ka-da-hi-la-nan; ka-dá-hi-la-nan), *n.* 1. cause; real cause. Syn. *dahilán; sanhî, kasanhián.* 2. motive; purpose. Syn. *motibo, layon, layunin.* 3. basis. Syn. *batayán, saligán.*

kadahupán (ka-da-hu-pán), *n.* 1. lack; shortage. Syn. *kakulangán, pagkukulang; kasalatán, pagsasalát.* 2. poverty. Syn. *karálitaán, kahirapan, karukhaán.*

kadalagahan (ka-da-la-ga-han), *n.* 1. group of young women. Syn. *kabiníbinihan.* Cf. *kabinataan.* 2. maidenhood; young women collectively. Cf. *kababaihan.* 3. state of

virginity. Syn. *kabirguhán, pagkabirgo; kabirhinán, pagkabirhín.*

kadalahiraan (ka-da-la-hi-ra-an), *n.* 1. act, attitude, or behavior of a gossip. Syn. *pagkadalahirà, kadaldalán.* 2. idle talk or rumors about others. Syn. *paninirà, paninirang-puri.*

kadalamhatian (ka-da-lam-ha-ti-an), *n.* grief; affliction; sorrow. Syn. *lungkót, kalungkutan; pighatî, kapighatián.*

kadalangan (ka-da-la-ngan), *n.* 1. infrequency, as of visits, trips, etc. Syn. *pagkamadalang, kabihiraan, pagkabihirà.* 2. state or condition of being sparse or set far apart. Syn. *pagkalayú-layô, pagkaputáputakî.* Ant. *kasinsinán, kalimitan.*

kadalasan. (ka-dá-la-san), I. *n.* 1. frequency. Syn. *kalimitan, pagkamalimit; pagkamadalás.* 2. rapidity; fastness. Syn. *bilís, kabilisán.*
—II. *adv.* 1. often; most of the time. Syn. *malimit, kalimitan; madalás.* 2. usually. Syn. *karaniwan.*

kadaldalán (ka-dal-da-lán), *n.* 1. fact, state, or manner of being loquacious; loquacity. Syn. *katabilán, kasatsatán.* 2. idle talk or rumors about another or others. Syn. *paninirà, paninirang-puri.*

kadalisayan (ka-da-li-sa-yan), *n.* 1. freedom from dirt; cleanness. Syn. *kalinisan.* 2. purity; freedom from any mixture. Syn. *kawaláng-halò, kapuruhan.* 3. sincerity. Syn. *kawagasán, katapatan.*

kadalúbhasaan (ka-da-lúb-ha-sa-an), *n.* 1. fact, state, or quality of being an expert. Syn. *kapahamán, kapantasán.* 2. expertise. Syn. *kahusayan, kagalingán.*

kadamay (ka-da-may), var. **karamay**, I. *n.* 1. a person involved or included in a misfortune, blame, or in an undesirable act. Syn. *kasangkót.* 2. a person who shares in one's misfortune, hardship, etc. Cf. *katulong.*
—II. *adj.* involved, as in a blame or in an undesirable act.

kadang-kadang (ka-dang + ka-dang), *n.* a kind of fatal disease of coconut trees.

kadkád (kad-kád), I. *n.* act or manner of unfolding or spreading out something that is rolled or folded. Syn. *ladlád, paglaladlád.*

2. state or condition of being rolled or spread out. Syn. *bukadkád, ladlád.*

—II. *adj.* unrolled; unfolded; spread out. Syn. *nakaladlád, nakabukadkád.*

kadehaduhan (ka-de-ha-du-han), n. 1. fact, quality, or state of being at a disadvantage. Syn. *kadaigán.* Ant. *kalámangan, kahigtán.* 2. in horse racing or cockfighting, the fact or condition of having the least bets, referring to a horse or game cock. Ant. *kaliyamaduhan, pagkaliyamado.*

kademónyuhán (ka-de-món-yu-hán), n. 1. devilment; wicked behavior. Syn. *kahayupan.* 2. reckless mischief, fun, etc. Syn. *kapilyuhán, katarántaduhan.*

kadena (ka-de-na), n. (Sp. cadena) chain. Syn. *tanikalà.*

kadilawán (ka-di-la-wán), n. state or quality of being yellow. Syn. *pagkadiláw, pagkamadiláw.*

kadugô (ka-du-gô), var. karugô, I. adj. 1. of or having the same type of blood as another. Syn. *katipo ng dugô.* 2. of the same, or belonging to the same race or family. Syn. *kalahì, kalipì.*

—II. n. 1. a person having the same type of blood as another. 2. a person belonging to the same race as another.

kaduhagihan (ka-du-ha-gi-han), n. state or condition of being miserably oppressed. Syn. *kaapihán, kadustaán.*

kadunguán (ka-du-ngu-án), n. 1. bashfulness; shyness; timidity. Syn. *pagkamahiyain.* 2. stupidity; dullness; lack of normal intelligence. Syn. *katangahán; kahangalán; kagunggungán.*

kadustaán (ka-dus-ta-án), n. 1. state of being oppressed. Syn. *kaapihán, pagkakaawá-awà.* 2. contemptibleness; despicableness. Syn. *pagkákakutyâ-kutyâ, pagkákalait-lait.*

kaduwelo (ka-du-we-lo), n. & adj. referring to one's opponent in a duel. Cf. *kalaban, katunggalî.*

kaduweto (ka-du-we-to), n. & adj. referring to a person who sings a duet with another.

kadyós (kad-yós), var. **kagyós**, n. (Bot.) pigeon pea (Cajanus cajan Linn.).

kaedád (ka-e-dád), adj. of or having the same age as another. Syn. *kasing-edád, kasinggulang, kasintandà, kasimbatà.*

kaempliyado (ka-em-pli-ya-do), n. co-employee; officemate.

kaeskuwela (ka-es-ku-we-la), n. schoolmate. Syn. *kaklase, kamag-arál.*

kagabi (ka-ga-bi), adv. last night. Syn. *nang lumipas o nakaraáng gabí.*

kágabihán (ká-ga-bi-hán), adv. the following night; next night. Syn. *kinágabihán, nang sumunód na gabí.*

kagagahan (ka-ga-ga-han), n. (Fem.) stupidity. Syn. *katangahán, katorpihán, katontahán.* Cf. *kagaguhan.*

kagahamanan (ka-ga-ha-man), n. greed; greediness; covetousness. Syn. *kasibaan, kasakimán.*

kagahulan (ka-gá-hu-lan; ka-ga-hu-lán), n. lack of time. Syn. *kakulangán sa (ng) panahón.*

kagalakan (ka-ga-la-kan), n. joy; happiness. Syn. *tuwâ, katuwaan; ligaya, kaligayahan.*

kagalang-galang (ka-ga-lang + ga-la-ng), adj. honorable; respectable. Syn. *kapita-pítagan, honorable.*

kagálingan (ka-gá-li-ngan), n. 1. welfare. Syn. *kabutihan, kapakanán.* 2. the good thing about something; advantage. Syn. *bentahe, kahusayan, kabutihan.*

kagalít (ka-ga-lít), I. n. antagonist; enemy; foe; adversary; opponent in a quarrel. Syn. *kaaway, kalaban, katunggalî.*

—II. *adj.* referring to a person engaged in a quarrel or fight with another.

kagamay (ka-ga-may), adj. suited to one's way or manner of using, referring to an instrument, tool, or the like. Cf. *kasundô.*

kagamitán (ka-ga-mi-tán), n. 1. material. Syn. *sangkap, panangkáp.* 2. use; utility. Syn. *silbí.* Cf. *halagá, kahalagahan; buti, kabutihan.* 3. tool or instrument. Syn. *gamit, kasangkapan.* 4. equipment. Syn. *kasangkapan.*

kagampán (ka-gam-pán), I. n. state of being fully pregnant; full pregnancy. Syn. *kabuntisán.*

—II. *adj.* in a state of full pregnancy, referring to a woman. Syn. *buntís na buntís.*

kagánapan (ka-gá-na-pan), n. 1. realization; fulfillment. Syn. *katúparan.* 2. completeness; thoroughness; perfection.

Syn. *kalubusán, kakumpletuhan, kabuuán.*
3. (Gram.) complement, as in *kagánapan
ng simunò*, subject complement. 4. a
person working with another in the
performance of a certain work or job. Syn.
kagampán, kaganáp.

kagandahan (ka-gan-da-han), n. 1. state or
quality of being beautiful; beauty. Syn.
gandá; rikít, kariktán; dilág, karilagán. Ant.
kapangitan. 2. anything good about
something. Syn. *buti , kabutihan; husay,
kahusayan.*

kagandahang-asal (ka-gan-da-hang + a-sal),
n. good manners. Syn. *kagandahang-ugalì.*

kaganiran (ka-ga-ni-ran), n. (Colloq.)
covetousness. Syn. *kasakimán, katakawan,
kaimbután.*

kaganitán (ka-ga-ni-tán), n. 1. quality of
being tough to masticate, as meat;
toughness. Cf. *kunat, kakunatan; tigás,
katigasán.* 2. fact or state of being tightly
fixed, screwed, or embedded, making it
hard to take out or disengage. Syn. *higpít,
kahigpitán.*

kaganyák-ganyák (ka-gan-yák + gan-yák),
adj. 1. attractive; charming; captivating.
Syn. *kaakit-akit.* 2. convincing. Syn.
kapaní-paniwalà, nakahíhikayat.

kagapukán (ka-ga-pu-kán), n. quality or
state of being decayed or weak due to
decay or infestation of weevils. Syn.
dupók, karupukán, kagatuán.

kagaraan (ka-ga-ra-an), n. 1. quality or state
of being dressy; dressiness. Syn. *bikas,
kabikasan, pagkamagarà.* 2. stateliness;
splendor; elegance; pomposity. Syn. *kisig,
kakisigan.*

kagarapalán (ka-ga-ra-pa-lán), n.
outrageousness; shamelessness. Syn.
kawalánghiyaán.

kagaslawán (ka-gas-la-wán), n. 1. coarseness
or roughness in manners or habit. Syn.
kabastusán. 2. roughness in movement.
Syn. *kalikután, kaharután, kagalawgawán.*

kagaspangán (ka-gas-pa-ngán), n. 1.
roughness or coarseness, as of surface. Syn.
kaaligasgasán. Ant. *kakinisan.* 2. lack of
fineness in texture, as of sand. Ant.
kapinuhan. 3. lack of refinement in
conduct or manners; vulgarity. Syn.

kagaslawán, kabastusán.

kagastusán (ka-gas-tu-sán), n. total amount
of expenses. Syn. *buóng gastós.*

kagát (ka-gát), I. n. 1. bite; act or manner
of biting. Syn. *pagkagát.* Cf. *ukab, pag-
ukab.* 2. the wound or cut caused by a
bite. Cf. *sugat.* 3. sting, as of bees. 4. tight
hold or grip as of a wrench. Cf. *hapit,
higpít.* 5. the act or manner by which a
plane, saw, plowshare, or the like cut on
surface. Syn. *kain, pagkain (colloq.); taláb,
pagtaláb.*
—II. *adj.* 1. tightly or properly fitted, as
of joints. Syn. *hakáb, lapat.* 2. becoming;
fit. Syn. *bagay, kabagay.*

kagatuán (ka-ga-tu-án), n. state or quality
of being weak due to decay, referring to
wood, cloth, etc. Syn. *kagapukan,
karupukán.*

kagaw (ka-gaw), n. (Entom.) itchmite.

kagawad (ka-ga-wad; ka-ga-wád), n. 1.
member, as of a committee. Syn.
miyembro. 2. representative. Syn.
kinatawán. 3. assistant; helper. Syn.
katulong.

kagawarán (ka-ga-wa-rán: ká-ga-wa-rán), n.
department (in the government). Syn.
departamento.

kagaya (ka-ga-ya), *adj.* similar; alike;
identical; analogous. Syn. *katulad, kapalit,
kapareho.*

kagáyakan (ka-gá-ya-kan), n. 1. decoration;
adornment. Syn. *palamuti, dekorasyón.* 2.
attire, as for some special occasion. Syn.
suót, kasuután; damít, pananamít. 3. one
who has a plan or intention to go on a
trip with another or others.

kagayután (ka-ga-yu-tán), n. state or quality
of being rough or coarse to the taste,
referring esp. to cooked tubers.

kagiklá-giklá (ka-gik-lá + gik-lá), *adj.*
surprising. Syn. *kataká-taká, kagulat-gulat,
kamanghá-manghâ.*

kagigian (ka-gi-gi-an), n. act or manner of
being slow in action due to being
meticulous or over-attentive to
unnecessary details. Syn. *kakuririan,
kakutiltilán.*

kagilá-gilalás (ka-gi-lá + gi-la-lás), *adj.*
causing wonder; marvelous; wonderful;

astonishing. Syn. *kagulat-gulat, katakátaká, kamanghá-manghâ.*

kagilasan (ka-gi-la-san), n. 1. elegance. Syn. *kisig, kakisigan; garà, kagaraan; bikas, kabikasan.* 2. galantry. Syn. *kagalantihán, pagkagalante; kaginoohan, pagkamaginoó.*

kagiliran (ka-gi-li-ran), n. 1. horizon. Syn. *abot-tanáw, guhit-tagpuan.* 2. the very edge or brink of a high cliff or precipice. Syn. *bingit.*

kagiliwan (ka-gi-li-wan), I. n. fondness; affection. Syn. *pag-ibig, pagmamahál, paggiliw, paghangà.* 2. happiness. Syn. *katuwaan, kaligayahan.*
—II. v. 1. to be fond of. Syn. *mahalin, ibigin.* 2. to be happy about. Syn. *katuwaan, ikatuwâ.*

kagiliw-giliw (ka-gi-liw + gi-liw), adj. lovely; charming. Syn. *kaibig-ibig, kaakit-akit, mapang-akit.*

kagimbál-gimbál (ka-gim-bál + gim-bál), adj. causing great surprise or horror; shocking. Syn. *kasindák-sindák, kakilákilabot, nakapanlulumó.*

kaginhawahan (ka-gin-ha-wa-han), n. 1. ease of life; comfortable means of living. Syn. *kaluwagán sa buhay.* 2. easiness or facility of doing (something). Syn. *alwán, kaalwanán.*

kaginsá-ginsá (ka-gin-sá + gin-sá), adv. suddenly; unexpectedly; all of a sudden. Syn. *waláng anú-anó, pagdaka, kaagád, nang hindi ináasahan.*

kagintuán (ka-gin-tu-án), n. 1. the quality or kind of gold. Syn. *pagkagintô.* 2. fact or condition of having much gold. Syn. *kasaganaan sa gintô, pagkamagintô.*

kagipitán (ka-gi-pi-tán), n. 1. lack of room or space. Syn. *mádaliang pangangailangan.* 2. difficulty; straits. Syn. *mahigpit na pangangailangan; kahirapan, paghihirap.*

kágisnán (ká-gis-nán), var. **kágisngán**, v. 1. to find or see upon waking up. Syn. *mágisnán, mákita sa paggising.* 2. (Fig.) to learn or experience from the time of birth. Syn. *kámulatán, mátutuhan mulâ sa pagkabatà.*

kagitataan (ka-gi-ta-ta-an), n. fact, quality, or state of being sticky or watery with dirt. Syn. *kalamiraan.*

kagitingan (ka-gi-ti-ngan), n. 1. heroism. Syn. *kabayanihan, pagkabayani.* 2. great courage; bravery. Syn. *tapang, katapangan.* 3. great nature or character; greatness. Syn. *kadakilaan.*

kagitlahán (ka-git-la-hán), I. n. sudden feeling of surprise, fear, or fright; scare caused by something unexpected. Syn. *kabiglaanan, pagkabiglâ.*
—II. v. to cause or be the cause of one's sudden feeling of surprise, fear, or fright. Syn. *kábiglaán, ikabiglâ.*

kagitnâ (ka-git-nâ), n. 1. half of any measure of capacity. Cf. *kalahati.* 2. specifically, a measure of capacity equal to one and a half liters, referring esp. to rice, salt, or the like. Syn. *kalahatíng salóp.*

kagiyá-giyagis (ka-gi-yá + gi-ya-gis), adj. causing uneasiness or restlessness. Syn. *diikápalagáy, nakatítigatig, nakabábalisa.*

kagubatan (ka-gu-ba-tan), n. 1. thick forest; wilderness; jungle. Syn. *kakahuyan.* 2. fact, quality, or state of being thickly forested. Syn. *pagkamagubat.*

kagulanitán (ka-gu-la-ni-tán), n. state or condition of being in tatters. Syn. *pagkapunít-punít, pagkagulanít.* Cf. *panlilimahid.*

kagulangan (ka-gu-la-ngan), n. 1. maturity, as of fruits. Cf. *kahinugán.* Ant. *kamuraan.* 2. state or condition of being old; old age. Syn. *katandaán, pagkamatandâ.* Ant. *kabataan.* 3. (Fig.) the quality, act, or manner of a person who always takes advantage of others who have less experience or knowledge than himself. Syn. *pagkamagulang, pagkamapánlamáng, pagkamapágsamantalá.*

kagulatan (ka-gu-la-tan), I. n. 1. sudden surprise. Syn. *pagkagulat, kabiglaanan; pagkabiglâ; kagitlahanan.* 2. sudden fear or fright. Syn. *takot, katakutan, pagkatakot.*
—II. v. to cause one's fright or fear; be frightened by. Syn. *katakutan, ikatakot.* 2. to be surprised.

kagulat-gulat (ka-gu-lat + gu-lat), adj. 1. surprising; causing surprise. Syn. *katakátaká, nakapagtataka; kagitla-gitla, nakagigitla; nakabibigla.* 2. dreadful; causing fear. Syn. *nakatatakot.*

kagúluhan (ka-gu-lu-han), n. 1. violent disorder or disturbance. Syn. *gulo, pagkakaguló; ligalig, kaligaligan.* 2. state or condition of being disorderly; lack of order. Syn. *kawaláng-ayos.*

kagulumihanan (ka-gu-lu-mi-ha-nan), n. brief, sudden feeling of fear, dread, or apprehension. See gulumihan.

kagunggungán (ka-gung-gu-ngán), n. state or quality of being ignorant; ignorance. Syn. *katangahán, kahangalán, katunggakán.*

kagustuhan (ka-gus-tu-han), n. choice; liking; preference. Syn. *gusto, pagkakagusto; ibig, kaibigán.*

kagusutan (ka-gu-su-tan; ka-gu-su-tán), n. 1. quality or state of being intricate; complexity; intricacy. Syn. *kasalimuutan.* 2. disorder; trouble; confusion. Syn. *guló, kaguluhan.*

kagutuman (ka-gu-tu-man), I. n. fact or state of being hungry; hunger; hungriness. Syn. *pagkagutom, pasal, kapasalan.*
—II. v. 1. to have an eager desire for; crave for. Syn. *kasabikán, panabikán.* 2. to have or feel pity for someone suffering from hunger.

kagyát (kag-yát), I. adv. at once; instantly; immediately. Syn. *agád, kaagád, agád-agád, pagdaka.*
—II. adj. 1. immediate. Syn. *madalî, mádalian.* 2. little; slight. Syn. *bahagyâ, muntî, kauntî.*

kaha (ka-ha), n. (Sp. *caja*) 1. carton or package, as of cigarettes. Syn. *kartón, pakete.* 2. case or box, as of beer, apples, orange, etc. Syn. *kahón.* 3. safe; steel box, cabinet, or chest for keeping money and other valuables. Syn. *kaha de yero.* 4 treasury. Syn. *ingatáng-yaman, kabáng-yaman.* 5. cabinet (of a radio, TV set, etc.). Syn. *bahay* (colloq.). 6. body of a car, carriage, wagon, etc. Syn. *bahay* (colloq.). 7. (Colloq.) body of a person. Syn. *katawán.*

kahabaan (ka-ha-ba-an), n. 1. fact, state, or quality of being long. Syn. *pagkamahabá.* 2. longitudinal length; entire length. Syn. *buóng habà.* 3. long duration (of time). Syn. *tagál, katagalán.*

kahabagan (ka-ha-ba-gan), n. pity; compassion. Syn. *awa, kaawaan, pagkaawà, pagkahabág.*

kahagwayán (ka-hag-wa-yán), n. slenderness of stature; well-proportioned tallness. Cf. *tangkád, katangkarán.*

kahalagahan (ka-ha-la-ga-han), n. importance; value; worth. Syn. *importansiyá, kabuluhán, kasaysayan; kuwenta* (colloq.).

kahalayan (ka-ha-la-yan), n. indecency; obscenity; lewdness. Syn. *kabastusán, kalaswaán.*

kahalí-halina (ka-ha-lí + ha-li-na), adj. charming; fascinating; attractive. Syn. *kaakit-akit, mapang-akit, nakaáakit; nakaháhalina.*

kahalili (ka-ha-li-li), n. 1. replacement. Syn. *kapalit.* 2. substitute; alternate. Syn. *pamalít, panghalili.*

kahalintulad (ka-ha-lin-tu-lad), adj. similar; same as; of the same type. Syn. *katulad, kahalimbawà.*

kahalingán (ka-ha-li-ngán), n. passionate fondness for or about something. Syn. *pagkahaling, kahibangán, pagkahibáng.*

kahalíp (ka-ha-líp), n. 1. replacement. Syn. *kapalít.* 2. substitute; alternate. Syn. *kahalili.*

kahaliparután (ka-ha-li-pa-ru-tán), n. flirtatiousness. Syn. *kakirihán, kalandián, kaalembungán.*

kahalò (ka-ha-lò), n. & adj. referring to something added to a mixture. Syn. *kalahók.*

kahalpukán (ka-hal-pu-kán), n. quality or state of being putrid, referring esp. to fish. Syn. *pagkahalpók, bilasà, kabilasaan, pagkabilasà.*

kahalubilo (ka-ha-lu-bi-lo), n. & adj. referring to a person who mixes or intermingles with others in a crowd or gathering. Syn. *kabungguang-balikat, kahalu-halò.*

kahalumígmigán (ka-ha-lu-míg-mi-gán), n. fact, quality, or state of being humid or damp; humidity. Syn. *kaúmiduhán, pagkamamasámasâ.*

kahamakan (ka-ha-ma-kan), n. state or quality of being lowly. Syn. *kaabaán, pagkaabâ.*

kahambál-hambál (ka-ham-bál + ham-bál), *adj.* 1. pitiful; deserving pity. Syn. *kaawáawà, nakaáawà; kahabág-habág, nakaháhabág.* 2. doleful; dismal; sad. Syn. *malungkót, mapangláw.*

kahambíng (ka-ham-bíng), *adj.* similar; comparable; having similarity with. Syn. *katulad, kahalintulad; kawangis, kahawig.*

kahambugán (ka-ham-bu-gán), *n.* boastfulness; haughtiness. Syn. *paghahambóg, kapalaluán, kayabangan, kataasan* (fig.), *kahanginan* (fig.)

kahamok (ka-ha-mok), *adj. & n.* referring to one who is engaged with another in battle or hand-to-hand fight. Syn. *katunggalî, kapamuók.*

kahanay (ka-ha-nay), I. n. 1. a person in the same row or line with another or others. Syn. *kahilera, kapila.* 2. a fellow who is in the same rank with another. Syn. *karanggo, kaantás.*
—II. *adj.* of or belonging in the same line, row, or rank with another or others.

kahandaán (ka-han-da-án), *n.* fact, state, or condition of being ready or prepared; readiness. Syn. *pagkahandâ.*

kahantarán (ka-han-ta-rán), *n.* fact, quality, or state of being open or exposed to view. Syn. *kalantarán, pagkalantád.*

káhantungán (ká-han-tu-ngán), *v.* to result in; end up with. Syn. *káuwian* (colloq.), *magwakás sa.*

kahangaan (ka-ha-nga-an), *n.* 1. feeling of admiration. Syn. *paghangà.* 2. amazement; astonishment. Syn. *pagtataká.*

kahangá-hangà (ka-ha-ngá + ha-ngà), *adj.* 1. admirable; charming. Syn. *kaakit-akit.* 2. wonderful; marvelous; astonishing; amazing. Syn. *kataká-taká, kamanghámanghâ.*

kahangalán (ka-ha-nga-lán), *n.* 1. stupidity; lack of intelligence. Syn. *katangahán, kagunggungán, katunggakán, kaungasán.* 2. folly; foolishness. Syn. *kalokohán, kaululán, katarantaduhán.*

kahanggán (ka-hang-gán), I. n. 1. neighbor. Syn. *kapitbahay.* 2. a neighboring house. Syn. *kalapít-bahay.* 3. a neighboring piece of land or property having common boundary line with another. Syn. *katabing-lupà* (ari-arian).
—II. *adj.* referring to a person, house, or property belonging in the same neighborhood.

kahapdián (ka-hap-di-án), *n.* fact, quality, or state of being smartingly painful; excruciating painfulness. Syn. *pagkamahapdî.* Cf. *kakirután, pagkamakirót.*

kahapisan (ka-ha-pi-san), I. n. feeling of sorrow, grief, or affliction. Syn. *kalungkutan, kadalamhatian, kapighatián.*
—II. *v.* to feel or have pity for. Syn. *kahabagán, kaawaan.*

kahapis-hapis (ka-ha-pis + ha-pis), *adj.* sorrowful; pitiful. Syn. *kahabág-habág, kaawá-awà.*

kahapon (ka-ha-pon), I. n. 1. yesterday; the day just past; the day before today. 2. (Fig.) a person's past. Syn. *lumipas, pinagdaanan* (colloq.).
—II. adv. on the day before today; on the day just past.
—III. *adj.* of yesterday: as in *kahapon ng umaga*, the morning of yesterday; or yesterday morning.

kahapuan (ka-ha-pu-an), I. n. 1. pant or panting. Syn. *pagkahapò, paghingal, pangangapós ng hiningá.* 2. extreme tiredness. Syn. *labis na kapaguran.*
—II. *v.* (Colloq.) to feel or have pity for someone's extreme tiredness.

káhapunan (ka-ha-pu-nan), I. n. the very afternoon of that day; the following afternoon. Syn. *sumunód na hapon.*
—II. adv. on the afternoon of that day; on the following afternoon. Syn. *nang sumunód na hapon.*

kaharaganán (ka-ha-ra-ga-nán), *n.* rudeness; bad manners. Syn. *kawaláng-galang; kabastusán, kapusungán.*

kaharáp (ka-ha-ráp), *adj.* 1. present; at hand; not absent. Cf. *kasaksí.* 2. located or found in the front of; facing the front of; opposite. Syn. *katapát, nasa tapát.*

kaharapín (ka-ha-ra-pín), *v.* to confront; meet one face to face; face boldly. Syn. *harapín.* 2. to meet boldly; challenge. Syn. *labanan.*

kaharian (ka-ha-ri-an), *n.* 1. kingdom; the

king's domain. Syn. *teritoryo ng harì, ang sakóp ng hari.* 2. the position or rank of a king; kingship. Syn. *pagkaharì.*

kaharusán (ka-ha-ru-sán), *n.* mischievousness; naughtiness. Syn. mischievousness; naughtiness. Syn. *kalikután, kagaslawán, kapilyuhán, kaharután.*

kahatì (ka-ha-tì) *n.* a person who shares one half of something with another. Cf. *kabahagi, kasosyo.*

kahatulán (ka-ha-tu-lán), *n.* 1. decision or sentence by a judge in court. Syn. *senténsiyá.* 2. decision or verdict handed down by or as by a board of judges. Syn. *pasiyá, kapasiyahan.* 3. advice; counsel. Syn. *payo, kapayuhán.* 4. medical advice or prescription by a doctor. Syn. *payong gamót o kagamutan, reseta, preskripsiyón.*

kahawasán (ka-ha-wa-sán), *n.* slenderness, as of body. Syn. *kahagwayán, pagkamahagway; kabalingkinitan, pagkabalingkinitan.*

kahawig (ka-ha-wig), *adj.* similar; having similarity or semblance with another. Syn. *katulad, kawangis, kawangkî, kapara.*

kahayagán (ka-ha-ya-gán), *n.* 1. fact, state, or quality of being open or exposed to the view. Syn. *kalantarán, pagkalantád.* 2. (Fig.) frankness. Syn. *katápatan, kaprangkahán.*

kahayapan (ka-ha-ya-pan), *n.* keenness or sharpness, as of blades, points, language, etc. Syn. *katalimán, katalasan.*

kahayukán (ka-ha-yu-kan), *n.* extreme hunger. Syn. *labis na kagutuman o pagkagutom.*

kahayupán (ka-ha-yu-pan), *n.* 1. animal instinct; bestiality; animality. Syn. *pagkahayop.* 2. brutality; animality. Syn. *pagkahayop.* 3. brutality; inhumanity. Syn. *lupít, kalupitán.* 3. bad joke. Syn. *masamáng birô.*

kahél (ka-hél), *n.* (Bot.) 1. a species of citrus tree (*Citrus aurantium* Linn.), called sweet or sour orange. 2. the fruit of this citrus. Syn. *dalandán.*

kahenyuhán (ka-hen-yu-hán), *n.* great natural capacity or ability; genius. Syn. *likás na kadalúbhasaan.*

kahera (ka-he-ra), *n.* (Sp. cajera) lady cashier. Syn. *kahero* (masc.). Cf. *tesorero; ingat-yaman, tagaingat-yaman.*

kahetilya (ka-he-til-ya), var. **kahitilya,** *n.* (Sp. *cajetilla*) 1. small box. Syn. *kahonsito.* 2. a small pack or package, as of cigarettes. Syn. *maliít na pakete o kaha.*

kahi (ka-hi), *conj.* though; although; in spite of the fact that. Now, the form *kahit* or sometimes kahi't (fr. *kahi* and *at*) is usually preferred. Syn. *bagaman, kalubman.*

kahibangán (ka-hi-ba-ngán), I. *n.* 1. delirium; frenzy. Syn. *kadiliryuhán, pagdidiliryo.* 2. folly; foolishness; craziness. Syn. *kaululán, kahalingán, kalokohan.* —II. *v.* to have a craze for. Syn. *kaululán, kalokohan, kahalingan.*

kahikahusán (ka-hi-ka-hu-sán), *n.* fact, quality, or state of being in dire need; indigence. Syn. *karálitaán, kadukhaán, kahirapan sa buhay.*

kahidwaán (ka-hid-wa-án), *n.* 1. fact, state, or condition of being contrary to fact. Syn. *pagkahidwa, pagka-di-totoó, kawaláng-katotohanan.* 2. anomaly; irregularity. Syn. *anomalya, katiwalián.*

kahig (ka-hig), *n.* 1. backward stroke of the feet or hands in scratching. Syn. *kaykáy.* 2. act or manner of pulling or drawing things on a surface with or as with the hands, as in collecting coins on a table. Cf. *hamig, paghamig.* 3. act or manner of scratching off lightly, esp. tiny objects, like a tiny grain of sand that accidentally gets into one's eye. Syn. *kalahig.* 4. in cockfighting, the act or manner of making the two roosters confront each other by having them scratch their feet on the ground and pick each other's head, preventing them however from getting loose by holding their tail feathers.

kahiging (ka-hi-ging), *adj.* of or having the same tone or tune with another. Syn. *kahimig, katono.*

kahigitán (ka-hi-gi-tán), var. **kahigtán,** *n.* 1. the amount in excess of the actual or required number or quantity. Syn. *labis, sobra.* 2. fact, quality, or state of having excess or surplus. Syn. *kalabisán, kasobrahan.* 3. advantage over another. Syn. *lamáng, kalamangán; bentaha,* *kabentahahan.*

kahigpitán (ka-hig-pi-tán), n. 1. fact, state, or quality of being tight; tightness. Syn. *kaigtingán, kahapitan, kasikipán.* 2. strictness; rigidity. Syn. *kaistriktuhán, pagkaistrikto.* 3. closeness or stiffness, as in contests, games, fights, etc. Syn. *kainitan (colloq.).*

kahigtán (ka-hig-tán), var. **kahigitan**, n. 1. the amount in excess of the actual or required number or quantity. Syn. *labis, kalabisán; sobra, kasobrahán.* 2. fact, quality, or state of having excess or surplus. Syn. *kalabisan, kasobrahán.* 3. advantage over another. Syn. *lamáng, kalamangán; bentaha, kabentahahan.*

kahihiyán (ka-hi-hi-yán), n. shame; disgrace; dishonor. Syn. *pagkápahiyâ.*

kahilaban (ka-hi-la-ban), n. 1. the quality of rice and other grains to swell or expand in volume when cooked. Syn. *pagkamahilab.* 2. the quality of dough to rise well. Syn. *kaalsahán, pagkamaalsá.* 3. painfulness felt in the abdomen due to the movement of the fetus in the womb. Syn. *paghilab ng tiyán.*

kahilakbután (ka-hi-lak-bu-tán), n. feeling of horror or sudden fright. Syn. *kasindakanan, kagulatan, kahintakutan.*

kahilagaan (ka-hi-la-ga-an), n. northern region.

kahilawán (ka-hi-la-wán), n. 1. state or quality of being raw or uncooked, referring to food. Syn. *pagkahiláw, di-pagkalutò.* Ant. *kalutuan, pagkalutò.* 2. state or condition of being still green, immature, or unripe, referring to fruits. Cf. *kamuraan, pagkamurà; kabubután, pagkabubót.* Ant. *kahinugán, pagkahinóg.* 3. (Fig.) lack of sincerity, as in friendship, companionship, etc. Syn. *kawalángkatapatan; kawalán ng sensiridad.*

kahilera (ka-hi-le-ra), n. & adj. referring to a person or thing who or which is in the same row or line with another or others. Syn. *kahanay, kapila, kaliñya.*

kahilian (ka-hi-li-an), I. v. to be or feel envious of (someone). Syn. *kainggitán.*
—II. n. feeling of envy. Syn. *pagkahilì, pananaghilì; inggít, kainggitán, pagkainggít.*

kahiligán (ka-hi-li-gán), n. 1. fact or state of being inclined in position. Syn. *pagkahilíg, pagkatagilíd.* 2. inclination; tendency. Syn. *gusto, kagustuhan; hilig, kinahíhiligan.* 3. propensity; talent. Syn. *talino, kakayahán.*

kahílingan (ka-hí-li-ngan), n. & adj. referring to a person with whom another mutually request each other. Syn. *kapákiusapán, kapámanhikan.* 2. (n.) request; something being requested. Syn. *pakiusap, bagay na ipinakikiusap.*

kahiluhan (ka-hi-lu-han), I. n. state or condition of being dizzy; dizziness. Syn. *kalulaan, pagkalulà; kaliyuhán, pagkaliyó.*
—II. v. to feel dizzy from; cause dizziness to. Syn. *kalulaan, ikalulà; kaliyuhan, ikaliyó.*

kahimagsikán (ka-hi-mag-si-kan), n. warlike nature or character. Syn. *pagkamapánghimagsik, pagkamapánlabán.*

kahimá-himalâ (ka-hi-má + hi-ma-lâ), adj. miraculous; mysterious; marvelous. Syn. *kataká-taká, mahiwagá, kamanghá-manghâ.*

kahiman (ka-hi-man), conj. & adv. even if; even though; although. Syn. *kulubmán, kahitmán, kahì na.*

kahimanawarì (ka-hi-ma-na-wa-rì), var. **kahitmanawarì**, interj. (usually used in form *kahimanawari'y*) may it happen; may God grant; may it become true. Syn. *mangyari nawâ, matupád sana.*

kahimasmasán (ka-hi-mas-ma-sán), n. state or condition of having regained consciousness from a fainting spell. Syn. *pagkakamalay, pagkakamalay-tao.*

kahimasukan (ka-hi-ma-su-kan), n. act, character, or manner of meddling or interfering in others' business. Syn. *pagkamapanghimasok, kapakialamán, pagkamapakialám.*

kahimbingán (ka-him-bi-ngán), n. deep sleep; time or period of one's deep sleep. Syn. *kalaliman ng tulog.*

kahimlayán (ka-him-la-yán), n. fact, state, or condition of being leisurely asleep or at rest.

kahinaan (ka-hi-na-an), n. 1. weakness of body; feebleness; debility; infirmity. Syn. *lambót o tamláy ng katawán, panghihinà* *(ng katawán)*. 3. dullness or slowness of sales, business, or the like. Syn. *tumal, katumalan.* 4. lack of speed; slowness of speed. Syn. *bagal, kabagalan.* 5. sluggishness or slowness in walking, manner of working, etc. Syn. *kupad, kakuparan; kuyad, kakuyaran; sagal, kasagalan.* 6. softness or lowness, as of voice, sound, music, etc. 7. lack of strength to lift heavy load. Syn. *kawaláng-kaya sa pagbuhat.* 8. lack of influence. Syn. *kawaláng-impluwensiyá.* 9. reduced or slackened intensity, as of fever. Syn. *babà, kababaan.* 10. reduced or slackened consumption as of water, electricity, etc. Syn. *tipíd, katipirán.* 11. dullness, as of eyes. Syn. *labò, kalabuan.* 12. lack of ability or capacity for good work; inefficiency. Syn. *kawaláng-kaya, kawaláng-kakayahán.* 13. reduced flow or fall, as of water. Syn. *kakauntián.* 14. dullness, as of mind. Syn. *puról, kapurulán.* 15. weakness due to decay. Syn. *dupok, karupukan.* 16. weakness, as of built or structure. Syn. *hunâ, kahunaán.*

kahiná-hinalà (ka-hi-ná + hi-na-là), *adj.* arousing suspicion. Syn. *nakapaghíhinalà.*

kahiná-hinayang (ka-hi-ná + hi-na-yang), *adj.* regrettable; unfortunate. Syn. *nakapanghíhinayáng, kalungkut-lungkót, nakalúlungkót.*

kahinahunan (ka-hi-na-hu-nan), *n.* 1. serenity or calmness, as of weather. Syn. *kakalmahán, katiwasayán, katahimikan.* 2. calmness of character. Syn. *kababaangloób, kapakumbabaán.* 3. self-control; control of self. Syn. *timpî, katimpián, pagtitimpî.*

kahinaingán (ka-hi-na-i-ngán), *n.* a humble, earnest request; supplication. Syn. *daíng, karaingan; pamanhík, kapamanhikán; hilíng, kahilingan.*

kahinalaan (ka-hi-na-la-an), *n.* 1. suspicion; doubt. Syn. *bintáng, suspetsa, sapantahà, paratang.* 2. feeling of suspicion. Syn. *paghihinalà, pagsasapantahà.*

káhinatnán (ká-hi-nat-nán), *v.* to result in; be the result or outcome of; end up with. Syn. *káuwian, kálabasán.*

kahinayan (ka-hi-na-yan), *n.* moderation in the manner of action, speech, etc. Syn. *kabanayaran, pagkabanayad.*

kahinayangan (ka-hi-na-ya-ngan), I. *n.* feeling of regret for the failure to take advantage of something important or for the loss of something valuable. Syn. *pagkahinayang, panghihinayang.*
—II. *v.* to be regretful about; feel regret about something lost or not taken advantage of. Syn. *panghinayangan.*

kahinhinán (ka-hin-hi-nán), *n.* modesty or decency in action or movement. Syn. *binì, kabinian, kabinihan; yumì, kayumian.*

kahinugán (ka-hi-nu-gán), *n.* fact, quality, or state of being ripe, referring to fruits; ripeness. Syn. *pagkahinóg.*

kahíngahan (ka-hí-nga-han), *n.* & *adj.* referring to someone who mutually confides secrets, problems, etc. with another. Syn. *katápatán ng nilóloób.*

kahinggilán (ka-hing-gi-lán), *n.* 1. what a thing is all about. Syn. *kaukulán, kinalaman.* 2. purpose; object. Syn. layon, layunin.

kahíraman (ka-hí-ra-man), *n.* & *adj.* referring to someone who mutually borrows things from another. Cf. *kautangán.*

kahirapan (ka-hi-ra-pan), *n.* 1. difficulty or hardship in doing or undertaking. Syn. *pagkamahirap gawín o isagawâ.* Ant. *kaalwanán, kadalián.* 2. suffering. Syn. *paghihirap, pagtitiís, pagdudusa.* 3. condition of being poor; poverty. Syn. *karálitaán, pagdarálitâ; karukhaán, pagdurukhâ.* 4. lack; scarcity. Syn. *kakulangán, kasalatán, kakapusán.*

kahiratihan (ka-hi-ra-ti-han), *n.* fact or state of being used or habituated to an act, condition, or manner. Syn. *kasanayan, pagkasanay; kabihasahan, kapamihasnán, pagkabihasa.*

kahista (ka-his-ta), *n.* (Sp. cajista) in printing, type compositor; typesetter; type composer.

kahi't (ka-hi't), *var. kahit* (fr. kahi and at), *conj.* though; although; notwithstanding; in spite of the fact that.

kahita (ka-hi-ta), *n.* (Sp. cajeta) small box.

Syn. *kahetilya o kahitilya.*

kahitikan (ka-hi-ti-kan), n. fact, quality, or state of being fully laden, esp. with fruits, referring to a tree or its branches.

kahitsura (ka-hit-su-ra), *adj.* of or having the same appearance, form, or figure. Syn. *katulad, kapareho, kawangis, kahugis, kaporma, kapigura.*

kahiwagaan (ka-hi-wa-ga-an), n. 1. mystery; something mysterious. Syn. *kababalaghán, himalâ.* 2. fact, nature, or state of being mysterious; mysteriousness. Syn. *kahimalaán, pagkamahimalâ, pagká-katakátaká.*

kahiyaán (ka-hi-ya-án), I. n. 1. state or condition of being ashamed; feeling of shame. Syn. *pagkapahiyâ.* 2. disgrace; shame. Syn. *kahihiyán.*
—II. *v.* to feel shame to; be ashamed of someone. Syn. *mahiyâ o mapahiyâ sa (kay).*

kahiyá-hiyâ (ka-hi-yá + hi-yâ), *adj.* shameful; disgraceful; embarrassing. Syn. *nakahihiyâ, nagbíbigáy-hiyâ.*

kahiyáng (ka-hi-yáng), *adj.* 1. agreeable or suitable to one's health or physical condition, referring to medicine, climate, etc. Syn. *kasundô, nakabubuti.* 2. said of something that gives good luck to someone. Syn. *masuwerte, nagbíbigáy-suwerte.*

kahog (ka-hog), n. haste; hurry. Syn. *pagmamadalî, apurá, pag-aapurá.*

kahól (ka-hól), n. bark or barking of a dog. Syn. *tahól, takín.*

kahón (ka-hón), n. (Sp. cajon) 1. box. 2. case. Syn. *kaha.* 3.drawer (of a table). 4. locker.

kahoy (ka-hoy), I. n. 1. wood in general. 2. lumber; timber; log. 3. timber or logs sawed into beams, boards, etc. Syn. *tablá.* 4. tree. Syn. *punô, punong-kahoy.* 5. (Colloq.) firewood. Syn. *kahoy-panggatong.*
—II. *adj.* of or made of wood or lumber.

kahubarán (ka-hu-ba-rán), n. fact or condition of being without dress from the waist up. Cf. *kahubuán.*

kahubog (ka-hu-bog), *adj.* of or having the same shape or form with another. Syn. *kahugis, kakorte, kaporma.*

kahudyatan (ka-hud-ya-tan), n. & *adj.* referring to someone who mutually exchanges signals with another. Syn. *kasenyasan.*

kahugis (ka-hu-gis), *adj.* of or having the same shape or form as another. Syn. *kakorte, kaporma, kahubog.*

kahugpóng (ka-hug-póng), *adj.* & n. referring to something added or joined to another to make it longer or sometimes wider. Syn. *karugtóng, kasudlóng, kasugpóng.* Cf. *karatig.*

kahulán (ka-hu-lán), *v.* to bark at (someone). Syn. *tahulán.*

kahulihán (ka-hu-li-hán), n. 1. fact or state of being late (in time or schedule); lateness; tardiness. Syn. *pagkahulí, pagkaatraso, kaatrasuhan.* 2. fact or condition of being delayed. Syn. *pagkaabala, kaabalahán.*

káhulí-hulihan (ká-hu-lí + hu-li-han), *adj.* & n. referring to the latest of all or to the farthest end of something.

kahulilip (ka-hu-li-lip), n. equal; peer: used only in *waláng kahulilip*, without equal (peer). Distinguished from *waláng-kahulilip.*

kahulugán (ka-hu-lu-gán), n. 1. meaning, as of a word, expression, act, etc. Syn. *ang ibig sabihin.* 2. significance; importance; value. Syn. *halagá, kahalagahan; saysáy, kasaysayan.* 3. (Colloq.) purpose; aim. Syn. *layon, layunin, hangád.*

kahumalán (ka-hu-ma-lán), n. quality or condition of the voice in speaking with a twang. Syn. *kautalán, kagarilán, kangunguan.*

kahumpakán (ka-hum-pa-kán), n. 1. fact, quality, or state of being hollow or depressed. Syn. *kapipián, kaumpisán.* Ant. *kaumbukán, katambukán.* 2. thinness or lack of flesh, as of a cheek. Syn. *kapayatán.*

kahunaán (ka-hu-na-án), n. the state or quality of being easily broken due to poor workmanship or weakness of materials used. Syn. *kanihaan, karupukan; kadaliang masirâ o mawasak; pagkamasiraín.*

kahuntahín (ka-hun-ta-hín), *v.* to engage one in a conversation; talk with (another) lengthily. Syn. *kausapin o kapulungin (nang mátagalan)*.

kahungkagán (ka-hung-ka-gán), n. 1. quality or state of being hollow or depressed; hollowness. Syn. *kahupyakán, kahumpakán*. 2. fact, quality, or condition of being empty; emptiness. Syn. *kawaláng-lamán*.

kahunghangán (ka-hung-ha-ngán), n. stupidity; lack of common sense. Syn. *katangahan, katorpihán, kamangmangán, katontohán*.

kahupaán (ka-hu-pa-án), n. 1. cessation or reduction in intensity. Syn. *kahulawan, paghulaw*. 2. state or condition of being depressed or reduced in bulkiness or volume, as of swelling, balloon, etc. Syn. *kaimpisán*.

kahusayan (ka-hu-sa-yan), n. 1. advantage or goodness, as of one over the other. Syn. *buti, kabutihan; bentaha, kabentahahan*. 2. expertness; efficiency; skill; excellence. Syn. *kadalubhasaan, kagalingán, kaekspertuhán*. 3. order; orderliness. Syn. *kaayusan, pagkamaayos*.

kahustuhan (ka-hus-tu-han), I. n. 1. sufficiency; adequacy. Syn. *kasapatan*. 2. exact or right size for a person or thing. Syn. *hustóng lakí*. 3. the amount needed or added to complete something. Syn. *kapupunán*. Cf. *karagdagan*. 4. propriety; appropriateness; suitableness. Syn. *katumpakan*.
—II. adj. 1. sufficient; enough; adequate. Syn. *sapát, kasya*. 2. of the right size. Syn. *husto sa lakí*.

kahuyan (ka-hu-yan), n. forest. Syn. *kakahuyan*.

kahuyin (ka-hu-yin), v. 1. to gather, referring to firewood. Syn. *pangahuyin*. 2. to utilize for firewood. Syn. *igatong, gamiting panggatong*. 3. to make (something) by using wood. Syn. *gawin sa kahoy*.

kaibá (ka-i-bá), adj. 1. queer. Syn. *katwâ, kakatwâ*. 2. different; not the same. Syn. *ibá, náiibá; bago* (colloq.). 3. unusual; strange. Syn. *di-karaniwan, di-pangkaraniwan*.

kaibayo (ka-i-ba-yo), adj. referring to something located opposite another, that is, in the other side of a street, canal, river, etc. Syn. *nasa kabiláng ibayo*.

kaibigan (ka-i-bi-gan-), n. friend. Syn. *amigo, amiga, katoto*.

kaíbigan (ka-i-bi-gan) n. one's lover or sweetheart. Syn. *kasintahan, kasuyò*.

kaibigán (ka-i-bi-gán) n. strong desire or wish; craving. Syn. *kagustuhan o kagustuhan; kasabikán, pananabik*.

káibigan (ká-i-bi-gan), n. mutual consent. Syn. *kasunduan, kagustuhan*.

kaibig-ibig (ka-i-big + i-big), adj. 1. lovable; endearing. Syn. *kagiliw-giliw*. 2. lovely; beautiful; pretty. Syn. *magandá, marilág, marikít*. 3. attractive; charming. Syn. *kaakit-akit, kahalí-halina*.

kaibsán (ka-ib-sán), n. relief from hardship, sorrow, pain, etc. Syn. *ginhawa; pagkahangò sa hirap, sakit, lungkót, etc.*

kaibuturan (ka-i-bu-tu-ran), n. 1. state or condition of being deep. Syn. *kalaliman*. 2. bottom; the deepest part or portion. Syn. *kalaliman, kálaliman*. 3. the very center or heart of. Syn. *pusod o pinakapusod*.

kaiklián (ka-ik-li-án), n. 1. state or quality of being short; shortness; lack of length. Syn. *igsî, kaigsián; kakulangán sa habà; utdó, kautduhán*. 2. shortness or briefness of time; brevity. Syn. *dalî, kadalián*.

kaigahán (ka-i-ga-hán), var. **kaighán**, n. dryness due to evaporation. Syn. *pagkaigá*. Cf. *katuyuán, pagkatuyô*.

kaigá-igaya (ka-i-gá + i-ga-ya), adj. 1. pleasant, referring to the weather. Syn. *maaliwalas, magandá*. 2. pleasing; delightful. Syn. *kasiyá-siyá, kalugúd-lugód*.

kaigihan (ka-i-gi-han), n. 1. goodness; advantage. Syn. *buti, kabutihan; inam, kainaman; bentaha*. 2. sufficiency; adequacy. Syn. *katamtaman, kainaman, kasapatan*.

kaignorántihán (ka-ig-no-rán-ti-hán), n. quality, fact, or state of being ignorant; ignorance. Syn. *kamangmangán, katangahán, kahangalán*.

kaigsián (ka-ig-si-án), n. 1. shortness; lack of length. Syn. *kaiklián, kautduhán*. 2. shortness or briefness, as of time, happening, etc. Syn. *dalî, kadalián*.

kaigtingán (ka-ig-ti-ngán), n. 1. tightness, as of bite, tie, knot, etc. Syn. *higpít, kahigpitán*. 2. state of being closely even, as in a contest or game. Syn. *kahigpitán*. 3. tautness. Syn. *kabanatan, kabagtingán*.

kailâ (ka-i-lâ), I. *adj*. unknown; kept secret. Syn. *lihim, di-alám, lingíd, sekreto*.

—II. *n*. act of not telling the truth about something being asked. Syn. *paglilihim, paglilingíd*.

kailaliman (ka-i-la-li-man), n. bottom. Syn. *pusod* (colloq.).

kailán (ka-i-lán), I. adv. when; at what time. *Kailán ka dumating? Anóng oras? Anóng araw?*

—II. pron. which time; what time; when.

kailanán (ka-i-la-nán), n. 1. (Gram.) number, as in *kailanáng pangmarami*, plural number. 2. total count or number. Syn. *dami, bilang, kabuuáng bilang*.

kailanmán (ka-i-lan-mán), adv. & conj. whenever; every time; any time; whatever time. Syn. *anómang oras, kahit anóng oras*.

kailangan (ka-i-la-ngan), I. n. need; necessity; thing wanted or lacking. Syn. *pangangailangan, kakulangán*.

—II. *adj*. 1. necessary; needed; indispensable. Syn. *kinákailangan, mahalagá*. 2. obligatory; required; binding. Syn. *sápilitán*.

—III. *aux. v*. should; ought to. *Kailangan itóng gawín*: This should be done. Syn. *dapat, nárarapat*.

kailangán (ka-i-la-ngán), n. 1. distant, wide, open uninhabited place. Syn. *malayong kaparangan*. 2. state or condition of being isolated or unfrequented, referring to distant place. Syn. *kaliblibán*.

kailapán (ka-i-la-pán), n. 1. wildness, as of an untamed animal; fact or condition of being undomesticated. Syn. *kasimarunán, pagkasimarón*. 2. tendency to elude; elusiveness. Cf. *pagkamatakutín*.

kaimbihán (ka-im-bi-hán), n. meanness; ignobleness. Syn. *kahamakan, karawalna; kababaang-asal, kawaláng-dangál*.

kaimbután (ka-im-bu-tán), n. greediness; covetousness; selfishness. Syn.

kakamkamán, kasakimán.

kaimbulugán (ka-im-bu-lu-gán), n. the quality or facility to soar or fly high in the air.

kaimito (ka-i-mi-to), var. **kaymito**, n. 1. star apple tree (*Chrysophyllum cainito*). 2. the sweet fruit of this tree.

kaimpertinentihán (ka-im-per-ti-nen-ti-hán), n. 1. impertinence; irrelevance. Syn. *kawaláng-kaugnayan*. 2. inapplicableness; inappropriateness. Syn. *di-kaangkupán, pagka-di-karapat-dapat*. 3. insolence. Syn. *kapusungán, kawaláng-pakundangan*.

kaimpisán (ka-im-pi-sán), n. 1. fact, quality, or state of being depressed or deflated. Syn. *kahumpakán, kapipián, kaumpisán*. 2. thinness or lack of flesh, as of one's cheek. Syn. *kapayatan*.

kaimpitán (ka-im-pi-tán), n. 1. lack of full force, referring to voice, sound or the like. Syn. *kahinaan*. 2. fact, quality, or condition of being guttural.

kaimpukán (ka-im-pu-kán), n. act, habit, or practice of saving; thriftiness. Syn. *pagkamaimpók, katipirán, pagkamatipíd*.

kain (ka-in), n. 1. act or manner of eating; consumption of food by eating. Syn. *pagkain*. 2. mealtime. Syn. *oras ng pagkain*. 3. amount of food eaten at a time. 4. action of a plane, saw, plow, etc. on the surface. syn. *kagát, taláb*.

kainahán (ka-i-na-hán), n. 1. mothers collectively. Syn. *mga iná*. 2. state of being a mother; motherhood. Syn. *pagkainá*.

kainaman (ka-i-na-man), I. n. 1. the good thing about something; goodness. Syn. *buti, kabutihan; husay, kahusayan*. 2. sufficiency; adequacy. Syn. *katamtaman, kasapatan*.

—II. *adj*. sufficient; enough; adequate. Syn. *sapát, katatagán, husto*.

kaininán (ka-i-ni-nán) var. **kaininan**, n. state or qualtiy of being fully cooked over a low fire or live coals, referring to rice. Cf. *kalutuan*.

kainipán (ka-i-ni-pán), I. n. state or condition of being bored or weary of long waiting; boredom; ennui. Syn. *pagod o yamót sa paghihintáy, pagkainíp*.

kainisán (ka-i-ni-sán), I. n. state or condition of being disgusted or annoyed; exasperation; disgust; annoyance; vexation. Syn. *yamót, kayamutan, pagkayamót; suya, kasuyaan, pagkasuya.*

kainitan (ka-i-ni-tan), I. n. 1. fact, quality, or state of being hot; hotness; heat. 2. sunny state or quality, as of the weather; sunniness. Syn. *kaarawan.* 3. oppressive warmth of weather; sultriness. Syn. *kaalinsanganan, kabanasán.* 4. anger; ire. Syn. *galit, kagalitan, pagkagalit.* 5. fever; temperature. Syn. *lagnát, kalagnatán.* 6. intensity. Syn. *sidhî, kasidhián.* 7. excitement; enthusiasm. Syn. *siglá, kasiglahán.*
—II. v. (Colloq.) to be the object of one's ire. Syn. *mápag-initan.*

kaintíndihán (ka-in-tín-di-hán), n. nature or quality of one's understanding. Syn. *pagkaintindí, pagkaunawà.*

kainutilan (ka-i-nu-ti-lan), n. uselessness or unserviceableness, referring to a person; inutility. Syn. *kawaláng-silbí.*

kaíng (ka-íng), n. a kind of large basket or hamper made of wickerwork, and usually used for containing fruits, vegetables, and the like. Syn. *tiklís.*

káingatan (ká-i-nga-tan), v. to be very careful about; take utmost care of. Syn. *pakaingatan.*

kaingayan (ka-i-nga-yan), n. fact, state, or quality of being noisy; noisiness. Syn. *pagkamaingay, kalinggalán, pagkamalinggál.*

kainggitán (ka-ing-gi-tán), I. n. feeling of discontent and ill will because of the advantage, good fortune, etc. of another; envy; enviousness. Syn. *pagkainggít, pagkahili, pananaghili.*
—II. v. to envy; feel envious with; regard with envy. Syn. *panaghilian.*

kaingin (ka-i-ngin), n. 1. the practice of clearing a forest by cutting and burning the trees for the purpose of raising crops. Syn. *pagkakaingin.* 2. a forest clearing devoted to crop raising. Cf. *lináng, tániman, saka.*

kaipahán (ka-i-pa-hán), n. quality or state of being chaffy, referring to grains; chaffiness. Syn. *pagkamaipá.*

kairalan (ka-i-ra-lan), n. prevalence; widespread occurrence; Syn. *paglaganap, kalaganapan, pagkalat, paghaharì (colloq.).* 2. common practice. Syn. *kaugalian.* 3. effectivity; date of effectivity Syn. *pag-iral, pagkakabisà.*

kaíringan (ka-í-ri-ngan), n. & adj. referring to someone who is mutually hóstile to another. Syn. *kasámaang-loób.*

kaisahán (ka-i-sa-hán), n. 1. singularity; singleness; oneness. Syn. *pagkaisá, pagkakaisá.* 2. unity; harmony. Syn. *pagkakáisá.* 3. union; association. Syn. *samahán, kapisanan.*

kaisá-isá (ka-i-sá + i-sá), adj. lone; alone; only one; single. Syn. *íisa, nag-iisa; bugtóng; kakabugtóng; kabuto, kakabutó.*

kaisipán (ka-i-si-pán), n. 1. mentality; mental attitude. Syn. *pag-iisip, mentalidád.* 2. understanding; sense of judgment. Syn. *pag-unawà, pang-unawà.* 3. opinion; idea. Syn. *palagáy, kuru-kurò.* 4. talent; ingenuity. Syn. *talino, katalinuhan.* 5. viewpoint; point of view. Syn. *pananáw.*

kaít (ka-ít), n. 1. denial of or refusal to give what is due to someone. Syn. *pagtangging ibigáy ang nauukol.* 2. keeping from having, using, or enjoying; deprivation, as of one's rights. Syn. *pag-aalís ng karapatán.* 3. prohibition. Syn. *pagbabawal.*

kaitaasan (ka-i-ta-a-san), n. 1. the highest point or part of a place; top or summit, as of a mountain. Syn. *taluktók, ituktók.* 2. the sky; firmament. Syn. *langit, kalangitan.*

kaitimán (ka-i-ti-mán), n. fact, quality, or state of being black; blackness. Syn. *pagkamaitím.*

kala (ka-la), n. (Sp. *karey*) tortoise shell.

kalaanan (ka-la-a-nan), n. 1. state of being prepared or ready to help or for service; readiness. Syn. *kahandaan.* 2. the purpose for which something is intended or reserved. Syn. *pinagtátaanan, pinaglálaanan.*

kalabagán (ka-la-ba-gán), n. quality or state of being violative of law, moral standard, etc. Syn. *pagkalabág.*

kalaban (ka-la-ban), I. n. 1. adversary; opponent. Syn. *katunggalî.* 2. enemy. Syn. *kaaway.*

kalabasa

kalakasán

—II. *adj.* 1. referring to one's adversary, opponent, or enemy. 2. against; contrary; opposed. Syn. *laban, nalalaban; kontra, kakontra; masamâ, nakasásamâ.*

kalabasa (ka-la-ba-sa), I. *n.* (Sp. *calabaza*) 1. squash plant. 2. the fleshy fruit of this plant eaten as a vetgetable. 3. (Fig.) failure (in school); a student who failed to pass an examination. Syn. *bagsák, lagpák.*
—II. *adj.* (Fig.) 1. failed; unabled to pass. Syn. *lagpák, lumagpák; bagsák, bumagsák; di-pumasá, di-nakapasá.* 2. disappointed; frustrated. Syn. *bigô, nabigô.*

kálabasán (ká-la-ba-sán), var. *kalabsan, v.* to be the result of. Syn. *káuwian, káhinatnán.*

kalabáw (ka-la-báw), *n.* (Zool.) 1. water buffalo; carabao. Cf. *kalakyán, tamaráw.* 2. a mango fruit bigger than a piko (which see). Syn. *kinalabáw.* 3. a derogatory term for a big, lazy person.

kalabisán (ka-la-bi-sán), I. *n.* 1. excess; surplus. Syn. *labis, sobra.* 2. excessiveness; superfluity. Syn. *kasobrahán.* 3. superabundance. Syn. *labis na kasaganaan.* 4. abuse; abusiveness. Syn. *pagmamalabís.*
—II. *adj.* unnecessary; not needed; needless; superfluous. Syn. *di-kailangan; hindî na kailangan.*

kalabít (ka-la-bít), *n.* 1. a light, quick snapping stroke with the tip of a finger, as in calling someone's attention, etc. 2. act of pressing the trigger of a firearm. 3. act or strumming or plucking the string of a musical instrument.

kalabnawán (ka-lab-na-wán), *n.* thinness of broth, soup, etc. Ant. *kalaputan.*

kalabóg (ka-la-bóg), *n.* (echoic) a loud, heavy fall of something big and heavy. Cf. *kalampág, lagapák.*

kalabós (ka-la-bós), *n.* (Sp.) 1. prisoner. Syn. *preso, bilanggô.* 2. putting in prison; imprisonment. Syn. *pagbibilanggô.*

kalabsaáh (ka-lab-sa-án), *n.* over-softness of the consistency of cooked food, esp. rice. Syn. *labis na lambót.* Ant. *kaligatan, katigasán.*

kalabsakán (ka-lab-sa-kán), *n.* quality, state, or condition of being too soft, as of over-ripe fleshy fruits or overcooked tubers. Cf.

kalabsaán, lábis na kalambután.

kalabuan (ka-la-bu-an), *n.* 1. dimmness, as of light. Syn. *kakulabuán, pagkakulabô.* Ant. *kaliwanangan.* 2. turbidity, as of liquid. Ant. *kalinawan, pagkamalinaw.* 3. ambiguity or obscurity (of meaning). Syn. *kahirapang maunawaán (máintidihán), pagkadi-máunawaan.* 4. uncertainty; lack of assurance. Syn. *kawaláng-katiyakan.* 5. dimness of vision. Syn. *kahirapang makakita, hinà ng matá o paningín.* 6. lack of certain qualities, esp. understanding. Syn. *kahinaan, kakulangán.*

kalabukab (ka-la-bu-kab), *n.* sound produced when an inverted drinking glass, or the like, is suddenly pulled out of water; any similar sound. Cf. *kalabusaw.*

kalabugan (ka-la-bu-gan), *n.* over-softness of cooked food, like tubers, vegetables, meat, etc. due to over-cooking. Cf. *kalabsaan, kalabsakan.*

kálabugan (ká-la-bu-gan), *n.* loud, heavy noises as that caused by two wrestlers struggling on the floor. Syn. *kálampagan.*

kalabusaw (ka-la-bu-saw), *n.* 1. fast and uncontrolled movement of a person's hands and feet in water, as of one learning how to swim. 2. the sound of water thus produced. 3. act of stirring water in a pool or river, as with one's feet or hands to make it muddy or turbid. Syn. *paglabusaw.*

kalakal (ka-la-kal), *n.* 1. merchandise; goods for sale. Syn. *tinda, paninda.* 2. selling and buying of goods; commerce.

kalakarán (ka-la-ka-rán), *n.* 1. common practice or custom. Syn. *ugalì, kaugalián.* 2. the prevailing style or vogue. Syn. *moda, uso.* 3. regulation. Syn. *patákarán, reglamento.*

kalakasán (ka-la-ka-sán), *n.* 1. state or quality of being physically strong. Syn. *kapuwersahán.* 2. state or condition of being physically healthy. Syn. *kalusugán, pagkamalusóg.* 3. state or quality of being fast in motion; speediness; swiftness. Syn. *kabilisán, katulinan.* 4. intensity, as of collision, knock, strike, etc. Syn. *katindihán.* 5. fact or quality of being fast-selling, referring to merchandise or goods. Syn. *kabilihán, pagkamabilí.* 6. quality or state of being powerful; powerfulness; mightiness. Syn. *pagkamakapangyarihan.* 7. efficacy or effectiveness, as of drugs, etc. Syn. *kabisaan, pagkamabisà.* 8. power of influence. Syn. *kaimpluwensiyahán, pagkamaimpluwensiyá.* 9. fact or quality of being loud, as of voice, music, etc. Syn. *katunugán.*

kalakbáy (ka-lak-báy), *n. & adj.* referring to a person or persons traveling with another or others in a trip. Syn. *kasama sa paglalakbáy, kabiyahe.*

kalakihán (ka-la-ki-han), var. **kalakhán.** *n.* 1. bigness; largeness; bulkiness. Syn. *pagkamalakí.* 2. magnitude. Syn. *lawak, kalawakan.* 3. the largest or widest part of something. Cf. *kaluwangán, kalaparan.* 4. state or quality of being extra wide or over-sized. Syn. *kaluwangán, pagkamaluwáng.* 5. (*Fig.*) greatness; nobility. Syn. *kadakilaan, kabantugan, katanyagán.* 6. highness, as of water during tide. Syn. *kataugan; taás o kataasan (ng tubig).*

kalakip (ka-la-kip), I. *adj.* attached; enclosed; included. Syn. *kasama, nakapaloób, kakabít.*

—II. *prep.* with. Syn. *kasama.*

kalakyán (ka-lak-yán), *n.* an adult male carabao in its prime. Cf. *bagong-tao.*

kaladkád (ka-lad-kád), I. *n.* 1. act or manner of walking with the feet being dragged noisily on the floor or ground. Cf. *hilahod; lakad na pahilahód.* 2. act or manner of dragging along something noisily. Syn. *paghila nang pakaladkád, pagkaladkád.* 3. a being dragged along noisily. Syn. *pagkakákaladkád.* 4. something dragged or pulled along the ground noisily.

—II. *adj.* 1. with the feet being dragged noisily on the ground, referring to one's manner of walking. Syn. *pakaladkád.* Cf. *hilahód, pahilahód.* 2. dragged or pulled along noisily on the ground, referring to something.

kalado (ka-la-do), *n.* (*Sp. calado*) 1. openwork, esp. on cloth and metal. 2. (*Arch.*) fretwork.

—II. *adj.* 1. ornamented with open designs, referring to cloth, metal, etc. 2. decorated with frets or interlacing designs.

kalág (ka-lág), I. *n.* 1. act or manner of untying or loosening (a knot or tie). Syn. *pagkalág.* Cf. *kalás, pagkalás.* 2. state or fact of being untied or loosened, referring to a knot or tie. Syn. *pagkakalág.* 3. (*Fig.*) a setting free or being free, as from an obligation.

—II. *adj.* 1. untied; not tied; loosened, referring to a tie or knot. 2. free; loose. Syn. *kawalâ, malayà.*

kalaganapan (ka-la-ga-na-pan), *n.* fact, quality, or state of being widespread. Syn. *pagkamalaganap.*

kalagayan (ka-la-ga-yan), *n.* 1. state; condition; status. Syn. *tayo, katayuan; ayos, kaayusan; situwasyón; kondisyón.* 2. circumstances. Syn. *mga pangyayari.*

kalagkág (ka-lag-kág), *n.* 1. sound or noise produced by something being drawn or dragged along a rugged surface. Syn. *kagulkól, kagalkál.* 2. violent scratching to relieve itching. Syn. *kalkal.*

kalagkitán (ka-lag-ki-tán), *n.* state or quality of being sticky; stickiness. Syn. *pagkamalagkít, kadigkitan, pagkamadigkít.*

kalagdaán (ka-lag-da-án), *n.* 1. provisions; terms and conditions provided for, as in a contract. Syn. *mga tadhanà.* 2. rules and regulations. Syn. *patákarán, tuntunin, pánuntunan.* 3. approval, (as in:) *alinsunod sa kalagdaán ng Kongreso,* according to the approval of Congress. Syn. *pagpapatibay, pagkakapagpatibay.*

kalaghalâ (ka-lag-ha-lâ), var. **kanaghalâ,** *n.* phlegm. Syn. *plema.*

kalagimán (ka-la-gi-mán), I. *n.* 1. horribleness. Syn. *pagkamalagím, pagkákakilá-kilabot, pagkákasindák-sindák.* 2. gloominess. Syn. *kalungkután, pagkamalungkót.*

—II. *v.* to feel horrible about.

kalagitnaan (ka-la-git-na-an), *n.* the very middle or center. Syn. *pinakagitnâ, gitnáng-gitnâ.*

kalaguán (ka-la-gu-án), *n.* 1. luxuriant growth. Syn. *kayabungan, kalabayan, kayamungmungán.* 2. longness, as of hair.

kalaguman   **kalamay²**

Syn. *kalambaan, kahabaan.*

kalaguman (ka-la-gu-man), *n.* 1. totality;
entirety; the whole. Syn. *kabuuán,
kalahatán.* 2. summary. Syn. *buod, kabuuran.*
3. confederation. Syn. *kompederasyon,
kalipunán.* 4. collection; anthology. Syn.
koleksiyón, antolóhiyá, katipunan.

kalagusán (ka-la-gu-sán), *n.* 1. state or
condition of being open or passable from
one end to another, referring to a hole.
Syn. *pagkalampasan.* 2. penetration
beyond the other side, as of bullets, spear,
etc. Syn. *katagusán, kalampasán.*

kalaguyò (ka-la-gu-yò), *n.* 1. one with whom
another has an intimate talk. Syn.
katalamitan, kapanayám, karayama. 2. an
intimate friend; crony. Syn. *matalik na
kaibigan.* 3. concubine. Syn. *babae*
(*colloq.*), *binábabae, kálunyâ, kinákasama;
kabít* (*fig.*).

kalagyô (ka-lag-yô), I. *n.* a person having
the same name as another; namesake.
Syn. *tukayo, katukayo; kangalan,
kapangalan; kasangáy.*
—II. *adj.* of, with, or having the same
name as another.

kalahatán (ka-la-ha-tán), *n.* 1. total; sum.
Syn. *kabuuán, totál, suma.* 2. totality;
entirety; sum total. Syn. *buóng dami.* 3.
entire collection. Syn. *buóng katipunan*
(*koleksiyón*).

kalahatì (ka-la-ha-tì), var. **kalhatì,** *n. & adj.*
half; one half.

kalahì (ka-la-hì), *n. & adj.* 1. referring to a
person of or belonging to the same race
or nationality with another. Syn. *kalipî,
kaangkán.* 2. referring to an animal of the
same breed with another. Syn. *kakasta.*

kalahian (ka-la-hi-an), *n.* 1. lineage;
ancestry; pedigree. Syn. *pinaglahian.* 2.
nationality. Syn. *nasyonalidád,
pagkamámamayán.*

kalahig (ka-la-hig), *n.* 1. act or manner of
collecting things with or as with a rake.
Syn. *kalaykáy, pagkalaykáy.* 2. act or
manner of taking out or dislodging a small
object, as in the eye, by slightly scraping
or scratching it off. Syn. *kahig, pagkahig.*
See **kahig.**

kalahók (ka-la-hók), I. *n.* 1. ingredient in a

mixture. Syn. *halò, kahalò.* 2. participant;
contestant. Syn. *kasali.*
—II. *adj.* 1. included; mixed or combined
with something. Syn. *kasama, kahalò,
nakahalò.* 2. taking part; participating.
Syn. *kasali, kalaban.*

kalait-lait (ka-la-it + la-it), *adj.* deserving
contempt; contemptible. Syn. *kadustá-
dustâ, kasumpá-sumpâ, nápakasamâ.*

kalalaán (ka-la-la-án), *n.* seriousness;
gravity. Syn. *lubhâ, kalubhaán; grabe,
kagrabihan; bigát, kabigatán; selan,
kaselanan.*

kalalakihan (ka-la-la-ki-han), *n.* 1. group of
men. Syn. *mga lalaki.* 2. men collectively.
Syn. *kaginoohan.*

kalaláng (ka-la-láng), *n.* fellow creature.

kalaliman (ka-la-li-man), *n.* 1. state or
quality of being deep; deepness. Syn.
pagkamalalim. 2. profundity, as of
meaning, thought, etc. Syn. *kahirapang
unawain.*

kalaluan (ka-la-lu-an), *n.* 1. fact, state, or
quality of being much better than
another. Syn. *kahigtán, bentaha.* 2.
disdainful pride; haughtiness. Syn.
kapalaluán, kataasan.

kalám (ka-lám), *n.* 1. gurgling sound in the
stomach caused by a slight feeling of
hunger. Cf. *kulô* (*ng sikmurà*). 2. slight
feeling of hunger. Syn. *bahagyáng gutom o
pagkagutom.*

kalamán (ka-la-mán), *n.* (*Fig.*) a person
related to another by birth; blood
relation. Cf. *karugô.*

kalamansî (ka-la-man-sî), *n.* (*Bot.*) 1. a spiny
citrus tree that bears small spherical acidic
fruit, used in seasoning food and for
making juice preparation like lemonade.
2. the fruit of this citrus.

kalamangán (ka-la-ma-ngán), *n.* 1.
advantage over another. Syn. *kahigtán,
bentaha.* 2. the point advantage in score.
Syn. *lamáng, abante.*

kalamay¹ (ka-la-may), *n.* a kind of pastry
made from cornmeal, rice or cassava flour,
or the like, cooked with sugar and
coconut milk.

kalamay² (ka-la-may), *n. & adj.* 1. referring
to someone who attends a night vigil with

another or others. Syn. *kasama sa pagpupuyát*. 2. referring to someone who works overtime with another or others during night. Syn. *katrabaho sa gabí*. 3. (Fig.) resignation of oneself to something unavoidable. Syn. *pagtatalagá sa sarilí, pagtitiís*.

kalambâ (ka-lam-bâ), n. 1. widemouthed earthen jar, used as container for drinking water. Syn. *bangâ*. 2. (K-) name of a town in the province of Laguna where Jose Rizal, Filipino hero and patriot, was born.

kalambingán (ka-lam-bi-ngán), n. 1. caressful show of fondness or affection. Syn. *kakarinyuhán*. 2. melodiousness or sweetness of tone or melody. Cf. *katimyasán*. 3. a child's way or habit of wanting to be caressed or fondled. Syn. *kalamyusán*.

kalambóg (ka-lam-bóg), n. 1. heavy pounding or thumping. Syn. *kalampág, kalabóg*. 2. the hollow or dull sound produced by such heavy pounding or thumping.

kalambatán (ka-lam-bu-tán), n. 1. fact, quality, or state of being soft or tender; tenderness; softness. 2. (*Colloq.*) general debility or weakness (of the body). Syn. *panlalambót, panghihinà*.

kalamkám (ka-lam-kám), n. 1. tickling sensation felt by a person when touched. Syn. *kilitî, galamgám, ligawgáw*. 2. feeling of hunger accompanied by a gurgling sound in the stomach. See **kalám**.

kalamigán (ka-la-mi-gán), n. 1. coldness, as of the weather chilliness. Syn. *gináw, kaginawán*. 2. coolness, as of food, etc. Syn. *pagkamalamíg*. 3. lack of enthusiasm or of interest. Syn. *kawaláng-siglá*. 4. self-control. Syn. *hinahon, kahinahunan*.

kalamiraan (ka-la-mi-ra-an), n. 1. state or condition of being filthily sticky or thick, as of mud. Syn. *kagitataan, panggigitatà*. 2. state or quality of being too soft, due esp. to overhandling, said of pulpy fruits like ripe mangoes, papayas, etc. Cf. *kalamugán*.

kalamlamán (ka-lam-la-mán), n. 1. dimness, as of light. Syn. *kalabuan*. 2. gloominess or dimness, as of the moon, sun, etc. Syn.

kakulimlimán, pagkamakulimlím. 3. languidness, as of the eyes. Syn. *kapungayan, pamumungay*. 4. sadness; melancholy. Syn. *lungkót, kalungkután*. 5. lack of spirit or enthusiasm. Syn. *kawaláng-siglá, kalamigán*.

kalamnán (ka-lam-nán), n. 1. the fleshy part of the body. 2. quality or state of being fleshy or meaty. Syn. *pagkamalamán*. 3. the main or important part; substance. Syn. *buód, kabuurán*. 4. fact, quality, or state of having full of meanings. Syn. *kadiwaan, pagkamadiwà*.

kalampág (ka-lam-pág), n. 1. heavy pounding or knocking. Syn. *kalabóg, kalambóg, kalatóg*. 2. the heavy sound thus produced.

kalampahán (ka-lam-pa-hán), n. 1. extreme weakness and feebleness. Syn. *labis na hinà o lambót ng katawán*. 2. state or condition of being awkwardly unsteady in walking. Cf. *pagkamadulasin*.

kalampasán (ka-lam-pa-sán), n. 1. state or condition of being ahead of another or others. Syn. *kaunahan*. 2. advantage over another or others. Syn. *kahigtán, kalamangán, bentaha*. 3. excessiveness. Syn. *kalabisán, kasobrahán, kamasyaduhan*.

kalamukutan (ka-la-mu-ku-tan), n. quality of being fleshy, referring esp. to fruits, like mangoes. Syn. *pagkamalamukot*.

kalamugán (ka-la-mu-gán), n. 1. fact, quality, or state of being too soft due to rough or over handling, referring esp. to fruits. Syn. *kabulbugán*. 2. state or condition of being badly bruised. Syn. *kapasaán, pagkamalamukot*.

kalamundíng (ka-la-mun-díng), n. a species of citron, better known as *kalamansi*. 2. the fruit of this tree. Syn. *kalamansî*.

kalamyaán (ka-lam-ya-án), n. act or manner of talking like a baby. Cf. *kalambingán*.

kalán (ka-lán), n. 1. a trivet, esp. one made of stone, used in cooking foods direct over the fire. Syn. *tungkô*. 2. stove. Syn. *kusinilya*.

kalandák (ka-lan-dák), n. 1. act of spreading rumors or secret about others. Cf. *paninirà, paninirang-puri*. 2. loud boasting about oneself or one's accomplishments. Cf.

paghahambóg, pagmamapurí, pagmama-galíng, pamamarali.

kalansakán (ka-lan-sa-kán), n. 1. simplicity. Syn. *kapayakán, kasimplihán.* 2. entirety; totality. Syn. *kalahatán, kabuuán.*

kalansahán (ka-lan-sa-hán), n. 1. fishy smell or taste. Cf. *kaangisán.* 2. (*Fig.*) indecency; lewdness. Syn. *kahalayan, kabastusán.*

kalansáy (ka-lan-sáy), n. skeleton. Syn. *mga butó ng patáy.*

kalansíng (ka-lan-síng), n. 1. clink or jingling sound of small pieces of metal, esp. coins. Syn. *tagintíng.* 2. tinkle, as of small bells. Syn. *kulilíng.* 3. act of causing jingling sound, by or as by clinking coins or tinkling a small bell.

kalanták (ka-lan-ták), n. & adj. referring to a person engaged in combat or fight with another. Syn. *kapamuók, katunggalî.*

kalantarì (ka-lan-ta-rì), n. 1. loud boasting about oneself or one's accomplishment, etc. Syn. *kalandák, pagmamarali, paghahambóg.* 2. act of spreading rumors or about other's affairs. Syn. *paninirà, paninirang-puri.*

kalantikán (ka-lan-ti-kán), n. graceful bend or curve, esp. of fingers, eyelashes, hips, etc.

kalantóg (ka-lan-tóg), n. 1. act of causing a thing to clatter by or as by rapping or knocking repeatedly. 2. clattering noise or sound, as that produced by loose or badly adjusted mechanical parts of a machine. Syn. *pagalpál, kagalkál, kalampág.*

kalantungán (ka-lan-tu-ngán), n. 1. state or condition of being disagreeable in odor, esp. of rotten fish or meat. Syn. *kabantután.* Cf. *kabahuan.* 2. the act or habit of a child who wants always to be caressed or fondled. Syn. *kalambingán.*

kalang (ka-lang), n. wedge. Syn. *kalso.*

kalangkáp (ka-lang-káp), I. adj. included; appended; incorporated; attached; enclosed. Syn. *kasama, kalakip.*
—II. n. something included or incorporated with.

kalangitan (ka-la-ngi-tan), n. the entire sky; heavens.

kalap[1] (ka-lap), n. act of cutting down trees

and cutting them into logs; logging. Syn. *pagtutroso.* 2. log; lumber. Syn. *troso.*

kalap[2] (ka-lap), n. 1. recruitment, as of military personnel. 2. enlistment of new members for an association, party, etc. Syn. *pagtatalâ o pagtanggap ng bagong kasapì.*

kalapastanganan (ka-la-pas-ta-nga-nan), n. 1. discourtesy; discourteousness; disrespect; impoliteness. Syn. *kawaláng-galang, kawaláng-pítagan.* 2. irreverence. Syn. *kapusungán.* 3. contempt; disrespect for authority. Syn. *paglapastangan, pagsuwáy.*

kalapati (ka-la-pa-ti), n. (*Ornith.*) dove; domestic pigeon.

kalapì (ka-la-pì), I. n. co-member, as of a political party. Syn. *kapartido, kalapian.* 2. member, as of an association or group. Syn. *kasapì, miyembro.* 3. (*Gram.*) a combining form affixed to a word; affix. Syn. *panlapì.*
—II. adj. 1. said of a member of an association; party, or any group. 2. referring to an affix joined to a word. Syn. *nakalapì.*

kalapin (ka-la-pin), v. 1. to cut down (trees) and saw them into logs. Syn. *trosohin.* 2. to enlist for membership, as in an association. Cf. *isapì.* 3. to recruit into military service. Cf. *papaglingkurìn sa hukbó.*

kalapít (ka-la-pít), adj. near; nearby; close to; close at hand. Syn. *malapit; katabí.*

kalarawan (ka-la-ra-wan), I. n. 1. a fellow companion in a picture. Syn. *kasama sa larawan o retrato.* 2. a person who looks like another. Syn. *kamukhâ.*
—II. adj. similar in feature to someone; having the same feature as another.

kalarô (ka-la-rô), I. n. 1. a person playing with another; playmate. 2. a participant in a game like basketball, baseball, tennis, etc.
—II. adj. 1. referring to a person playing with another. 2. participating in a game, referring to a player. Syn. *naglálarô, nakikipáglarô.*

kalás (ka-lás), I. adj. 1. loose or untied, referring to a tie or knot. Syn. *kalág; hindî nakatalì; hindî nakabuhól.* 2. raveled; unraveled. Syn. *natastás, tastás.* 3. separated or broken, as an engagement.

Syn. *hiwaláy, nagkasirâ*.

kalasag (ka-la-sag), n. 1. shield; armor. Syn. *adarga; pananggá*. 2. coat of arms. Syn. *eskudo*. 3. emblem; symbol. Syn. *sagisag, símboló*. 4. defense or argument against. Syn. *panlaban, pananggól, pananggaláng*.

kalasín (ka-la-sín), v. 1. to untie. Syn. *kalagín*. 2. to unravel. Syn. *tastasín*.

kalasingán (ka-la-si-ngán), n. state or condition of being drunk; inebriety; drunkenness; intoxication. Syn. *pagkalasíng; kalanguán, pagkalangô*.

kalaswaán (ka-las-wa-án), n. obscene words of expression. Syn. *kabastusán*.

kalat (ka-lat), n. 1. things scattered all around. Syn. *mga bagay na nakasabog*. 2. spread, as of diseases, news, or information. Syn. *laganap, paglaganap*. 3. act of distributing things to persons in different places. Syn. *pamimigáy, pamumudmód*. 4. propagation, as of a language. Syn. *pagpapalaganap*. 5. act of scattering things all around. Syn. *sabóg, pagsasabog*. 6. (*Colloq.*) garbage. Syn. *basura*.

kalataán (ka-la-ta-án), n. 1. softness or tenderness, as of meat. Syn. *lambót, kalambután*. 2. lack of firmness; weakness; flabbiness. Syn. *hinà, kahinaan*.

kalatas (ka-la-tas), n. 1. letter; missive. Syn. *sulat, liham*. 2. written message or statement. Syn. *mensahe; nakasulat na pahayag*.

kalaunan (ka-la-u-nan), n. 1. long time; long duration. Syn. *tagál, katagalán*. 2. long delay. Syn. *matagál na atraso*.

kalausán (ka-la-u-sán), n. 1. quality or state of being overripe, referring to fruits. Syn. *labis na kahinugán o pagkahinóg; kalunután*. 2. loss of potency or productivity. Syn. *kalipasán*. 3. dotage. Syn. *pakaulianin*.

kalawakan (ka-la-wa-kan), n. 1. wide expanse, as of land, water, or atmospheric space. 2. fact, state, or condition of being very expansive. Syn. *pagkamalawak*.

kalawang (ka-la-wang), n. rust. Syn. *taengmetál (colloq.)*

kalawkáw (ka-law-káw), n. playful stirring of water or liquid with or as with the hand. Syn. *kawkáw, lawláw*.

kalawigan (ka-la-wi-gan), n. 1. long time; long duration of time; state or condition of being long in time. Syn. *kalaunan, katagalán*. 2. unnecessary delay. Syn. *kaabalahan, pagkaabala, kabalaman, pagkabalam*. 3. fact, quality, or habit of acting very slow. Syn. *kabagalan*.

kalawit (ka-la-wit), n. 1. a pole with a hook; gaff. Syn. *pangalawit, kawit*. 2. hook; anything shaped like a hook. Syn. *kawit, gantso.*

kalayaan (ka-la-ya-an), n. 1. freedom; liberty; independence. Syn. *pagsasarili, kasarinlán; independensyá*. 2. freedom given to act on one's own free will; facility. Syn. *kaluwagan*. 3. libertinage; licentiousness. Syn. *layaw, kalayaan*.

kalaykáy (ka-lay-káy), 1. rake. Syn. *pangalaykáy*. 2. act or manner of gathering or scraping together with a rake. Syn. *pagkalaykáy*. Cf. *kahig, kalahig*.

kalayuan (ka-la-yu-an), n. 1. far distance; remoteness. Syn. *pagkamalayò*. 2. the difference in distance between two points or places in reference from the same starting point. Syn. *higít na layò; kahigtáng layò*.

kalbaryo (ka-bar-yo), n. (Sp. *calvario*) 1. (in the Bible) Calvary: place near Jerusalem where the crucifixion of Jesus took place. 2. (*Fig.*) extreme sacrifice. Syn. *matindíng hirap, dusa, sakit, pagtitiís*.

kalbo (kal-bo), I. adj. (Sp. *calvo*) 1. bald, referring to a person's head. Syn. *panót*. 2. bald-headed, referring to a person.
—II. n. 1. a bald-headed person; baldhead. 2. state or condition of being bald-headed. Syn. *kakalbuhán, pagkakalbo; pagkapanót, kapanután*. 3. act or manner of cutting or shaving the head close to the scalp. Syn. *pagkalbo, pagpanot*.

kalkál (kal-kál), I. n. 1. intense scratching with the fingernails to relieve or of itching. Syn. *matindíng pagkakamót*. 2. act of digging or scraping, esp. by scratching with or as with the hand.

kalkulá (kal-ku-lá), var. *karkulá*, n. (Sp. *calcular*) estimate; calculation. Syn. *taya, pagtaya; tantiyá, pagtantiyá*.

kaldera　　　　　　　　　　　　　　　　**kalingà**

kaldera (kal-de-ra), n. (Sp. *caldera*) 1.
caldron; boiler. 2. steam boiler.

kalendaryo (ka-len-dar-yo), var. **kalindaryo**,
n. (Sp. *calendario*) 1. calendar; almanac.
Syn. *almanake*. 2. schedule. Syn.
palátuntunan, talátakdaan.

kalí (ka-lí), n. rest; quietude; repose;
quietness. Cf. *tigil, hintô*.

kalibingan (ka-li-bi-ngan), n. schedule date
of burial. Syn. *araw ng libíng (paglilibíng)*.

kaliblibán (ka-lib-li-bán), n. 1. state or
condition of being distant and
unfrequented. 2. state or condition of
being heavily loaded, referring to a
vehicle, esp. at the front.

kalibre (ka-li-bre), n. (Sp. *calibre*) 1. caliber,
as of a gun. 2. ability; qualification;
capacity. Syn. *kakayahán*. 3. quality. Syn.
urì, klase.

kalikasan (ka-li-ka-san), n. 1. nature; the
entire physical universe. 2. inborn
character; inherent tendencies of a
person. Syn. *ugalì, kaugalián*.

kalikaw (ka-li-kaw), n. act or manner of
poking and stirring the bottom or inside
of a thing with or as with one's hand. Cf.
halukay, kalawkáw.

kalikot (ka-li-kot), n. act or manner of
rotating a finger, stick, pencil, etc. inside
a small hole to clean it, or make it wider
or deeper. Cf. *dalirot, pagdalirot*.

kalikután (ka-li-ku-tán), n. 1. mischief;
mischievousness; naughtiness. Syn.
kapilyuhán, kaligalingan, kagalugawan. 2.
friskiness; frolicsomeness. Syn. *harót,
kaharután*. 3. restlessness. Syn. *di-
pagkápalagáy, di-pagkápakalí, kawaláng-tigil
(ng katawán)*.

kalidád (ka-li-dád), n. (Sp. *calidad*) quality;
kind. Syn. *urì, klase*.

kaligaligan (ka-li-ga-li-gan), I. n. 1. trouble;
disturbance. Syn. *gulò, kaguluhán*. 2.
worry; distress. Syn. *balisa, kabalisahan,
pagkabalisa; bagabag, kabagabagan,
pagkabagabag*. 3. preoccupation; bother.
Syn. *abala, kaabalahan; gambala,
kagambalaan*. 4. quarrel. Syn. *away,
awayán; basag-ulo*.

kaligasgasán (ka-li-gas-ga-sán), n. fact,
quality, or state of being rough, referring

to a surfaces; roughness. Syn. *kagaspangán*.

kaligayahan (ka-li-ga-ya-han), n. 1.
happiness; cheerfulness; gladness. Syn.
kasayahan, katuwaan, kagalakan. 2.
contentment. Syn. *kasiyahan*.

kaligiran (ka-li-gi-ran), n. environment;
surroundings. Syn. *kapaligirán, palibot*.

kaligrapiya (ka-li-gra-pi-ya), var. **kaligrapya**,
n. (Sp. *caligrapia*) calligraphy. Syn. *sulat-
kamáy; magandáng sulat-kamáy*.

kaligtaán (ka-lig-ta-án), v. 1. to neglect; leave
undone. 2. to forget to include; omit;
disregard. Syn. *kalimutan, kalingatán*.

kaligtasan (ka-lig-tasan), n. safety. 2.
redemption, as from sin. Syn. *katubusan,
pagkatubós*.

kalihim (ka-li-him), n. secretary. Syn.
sekretarya, sekretaryo.

kalimitan (ka-li-mi-tan), n. 1. frequency, as
of visits. Syn. *pagkalimit; kadalasán,
pagkamadalás*. 2. state or condition of
being closely spaced or set; closeness. Syn.
kasinsinan, pagkamasinsín. Ant.
kadalangan, pagkamadalang.

kalimutan (ka-li-mu-tan), v. to forget all
about. Syn. *limutin*.

kalinangán (ka-li-na-ngán), n. 1. state or
condition of being well-cultured. Syn.
pagkabihasa, kabihasahan. 2. culture. Syn.
kultura.

kalinawan (ka-li-na-wan), n. 1. clearness,
as of liquid. Cf. *kalinisan*. Ant. *kalabuan*.
2. clearness or brightness, as of light. Syn.
kaliwanagan. Ant. *kadilimán, kalabuan*. 3.
clearness, as of expression, explanation,
etc. Syn. *kadaliáng máunawaan*. 4.
clearness, as of one's sight. Syn.
*kahusayan o kaliwanagan ng matá
(paningin)*.

kalinisan (ka-li-ni-san), n. 1. quality, state,
or condition of being clean; cleanliness;
neatness. Syn. *pagkamalinis*. 2. neatness,
as of workmanship. Syn. *kakinisan*. 3.
orderliness, as of a room. Syn. *kaayusan*.
4. sanitation. Syn. *sanitasyón*. 5. purity;
lack of impurities. Syn. *kadalisayan*. 6.
sincerity. Syn. *katapatan, pagkamatapát*.

kalingà (ka-li-ngà), n. 1. protective care;
help. Syn. *kandili, pagkakandili; arugâ, pag-
aarugâ; tulong, pagtulong*. 2. patronage;

kalingkingan

protection; support. Syn. *tangkilik*, *pagtangkilik*.

kalingkingan (ka-ling-ki-ngan), n. 1. the small finger. Syn. *maliít na daliri*. 2. the small toe (of a foot). Syn. *maliít na daliri ng paá*.

kalipunán (ka-li-pu-nán), n. 1. group, as of persons. Syn. *pangkát, grupo*. 2. association; society; confederation. 2. Syn. *samahán, kapisanan, asosasyón, pederasyón*.

kaliskis (ka-lis-kis), n. 1. scale: one of the thin, flat, hard covering of the body of some fishes, snakes, etc. 2. scales, collectively. 3. act or manner of scraping off the scales. Syn. *pagkaliskis, pagkakaliskis*. 4. thin layers of skin that look like scales. Syn. *balikuskos*. 5. analysis or evaluation of a rooster's chances of winning bouts as indicated in the arrangement of its scales. Syn. *pagkaliskis*. 6. (Fig.) evaluation or seeing for oneself the beauty of, referring to a woman. Syn. *pagpigura* (colloq.).

kalisód (ka-li-sod), var. **kalisúd**, n. (Sp.) hardship; suffering. Syn. *hirap, paghihirap; dusa, pagdurusa*.

kalistuhán (ka-lis-tu-hán), n. 1. cleverness; quickness of mind. Syn. *katalinuhán; katalasan ng isip; katalisikan*. 2. promptness or quickness to act. Syn. *kaliksihán*.

kalituhán (ka-li-tu-hán), I. n. state or condition of being confused or perflexed. Syn. *kahirahán, katuliruhán; kaguluhán ng isip; katarantahán*.
—II. v. to confused or perflexed by. Syn. *ikalito*.

kaliwâ (ka-li-wâ), I. n. 1. left; left side; left-hand side. 2. in traffic, a turn to the left. Syn. *pagkaliwâ*. 3. in boxing, the left hand; also a blow with the left hand.
—II. adj. left. (Ant.) *kanan*.

kalma (kal-ma), I. n. (Sp. *calma*), 1. state or condition of being calm, still, or serene; stillness; quietness; calmness; serenity. Syn. *katahimikan, kapayapaan*. 2. cessation, as of pain, storm, etc. Syn. *hulaw, paghulaw*. 3. absence of excitement. Syn. *hinahon, kahinahunan*.

kalmado (kal-ma-do), adj. (Sp. *calmado*)

kaltás

calm; quiet. Syn. *tahimik*.

kalmante (kal-man-te), I. adj. soothing; sedative. Syn. *pampakalma*.

kalmót (kal-mót), I. n. 1. harrow. Cf. *sugod*. 2. act or manner of leveling or breaking up the soil of a plowed field by harrowing. Syn. *pagkalmót, pagkakalmót*. Cf. *pagsuyod, pagsusuyod*.

kalmutin (kal-mu-tin), v. to harrow; level or break by harrowing, referring to the soil of a plowed field. Cf. *suyurin*. See **kalmót**.

kalò (ka-lo), n. 1. a big cup; bowl. Syn. *tason, sulyáw, mangkók*. 2. hat. Syn. *sumbrero, sambalilo*.

kalokohan (ka-lo-ko-han), var. **kalukuhan**. n. foolish behavior; foolishness. Syn. *kaululán, katarantaduhan*.

kalóg (ka-log), I. n. 1. act or manner of shaking the content of a container. Syn. *alóg, pag-alóg*. 2. act of causing something to shake. Syn. *yugyóg, pagyugyóg; ugà, pag-ugà*. 3. state or condition of being shaken, referring to the content of a bottle, box, etc. Syn. *alóg, pagkaalóg*.

kalong (ka-long), I. n. 1. act or manner of holding or carrying a person or thing on one's lap. Cf. *kandóng*. 2. a person or thing held or carried on one's lap.

kaloób (ka-lo-ób), I. adj. 1. given to someone as a gift. Syn. *bigay, ibinigay; ipinagkaloób*. 2. by the will of God. Syn. *talaga (ng Diyós)*.

kalooban (ka-lo-o-ban), n. 1. way of thinking. Syn. *kaisipan*. 2. will; choice; disposition; pleasure. Syn. *kagustuhan*. 3. divine will. Syn. *katalagahan*. 4. feeling; sentiment. Syn. *damdamin*.

kalop (ka-lop), n. thin metal lining, cover, or cap, sometimes with embossed designs, used as covering or decoration for handles of daggers, knives, etc. Syn. *kalupkóp*.

kalso (kal-so), n. (Sp. *calzo*) 1. wedge. Syn. *kalsa, kalang*. 2. in printing, quoin. Syn. *kunyas*. 3. overlay; pad or cushion. Syn. *sapín*.

kalsón (kal-són), n. (Sp. calzón), 1. trousers; pants. Syn. *pantalón, salawál*. 2. breeches; short pants. Syn. *korto; kutód*.

kaltás (kal-tás), I. n. 1. act of making a small cut in. Syn. *hiwà, paghiwà*. 2. a small cut made on something. Syn. *hiwà*, *gatlâ*. 3. act of deducting or subtracting a certain amount from. Syn. *bawas*, *pagbawas*. 4. amount deducted; deduction. 5. disallowance or cancellation, as of an item in a proposed budget. Syn. *pag-aalís*; *pagkanselá*. 6. discharge or laying off, as of an employee or employees. Syn. *pagbabawas*.

kalubusán (ka-lu-bu-sán), *n.* fact, quality, or state of being complete; absolute completeness. Syn. *kakumpletuhan*, *kaganapán*.

kalugdán (ka-lug-dán), I. *v.* to be pleased or delighted with Syn. *katuwaán*, *ikatuwâ*; *kagalakán*, *ikagalák*.
—II. *n.* delight; pleasure. Syn. *tuwa*, *katuwaan*, *pagkatuwâ*, *galák*, *kagalakan*, *pagkagalák*.

kalugín (ka-lu-gin), *v.* 1. to shake the content of a container; stir by shaking. Syn. *alugín*. 2. to cause something to move by shaking. Syn. *ugain*.

kalugúd-lugód (ka-lu-gúd + lu-gód), *adj.* delightful; giving pleasure; pleasant; enjoyable. Syn. *kasiyá-siyá*, *nakasisiyá*; *nakalulugód*, *nakatutuwâ*.

kaluguran (ka-lu-gu-ran), *n.* delight; pleasure. Syn. *tuwâ*, *katuwaan*, *kasiyahan*.

kaluluwá (ka-lu-lu-wá), var. **kálulwá**, *n.* 1. the spiritual part of a person; soul. Syn. *espíritu*. 2. vital or essential part, principle, or quality. Syn. *diwà*, *buhay*.

kalumatá (ka-lu-ma-tá), *n.* dark rings around the eyes due to lack of sleep. See ngalumata.

kalumbabà (ka-lum-ba-ba), var. **salumbabà**, *n.* the position of the head with the chin placed on the palm or back of the hand.

kalumbáy-lumbáy (ka-lum-báy + lum-báy), adj. sorrowful; mournful; sad. Syn. *kalungkút-lungkót*, *kapighá-pighatî*.

kalumbibit (ka-lum-bi-bit), var. **kalambibit**, *n.* 1. a prickly woody vine that bears pods having hard, ovoid, gray seeds (*Caesalpinia crista*). 2. the seed of this vine, also called *bayag-kambing*.

kalumpón (ka-lum-pon), *n. & adj.* referring to a person included in a small group or crowd. Syn. *kaumpók*.

kálumpunan (ká-lum-pu-nan), *n.* a small crowd or gathering. Syn. *umpukan*.

kalunduán (ka-lun-du-án), *n.* state or condition of being sagged or bent in the middle due to weight or pressure.

kalung-kalong (ka-long + ka-long), *adj.* carried or held on the lap wherever one goes. Syn. *kandúng-kandóng*.

kalungkután (ka-lung-ku-tán), I. *n.* state or condition of being sad or lonely. Syn. *kalumbayán*, *kapighatián*.
—II. *v.* to feel sad or lonely about. Syn. *ikalungkót*.

kalunggatî (ka-lung-ga-tî), *n. adj.* referring to a person who shares with another in ambition, wishes, purpose, etc. Syn. *kalayunin*, *kahangarin*.

kalupî (ka-lu-pî), *n.* 1. wallet; pocketbook. Syn. *pitakà*, *kartera*, *portamoneda*. 2. portfolio; briefcase. Syn. *portpolyo*.

kaluskós (ka-lus-kós), *n.* rustling sound, as that produced when one walks on dried leaves. Syn. *agasás*, *kagaskás*, *kaguskós*.

kalúsugan (ka-lú-su-gan), *n.* health (in general sense): as in *kagawarán ng kalúsugan*, department of health.

kaluwalhatian (ka-lu-wal-ha-ti-an), *n.* 1. glory; great happiness and prosperity. Syn. *kaligayahan*, *glorya*. 2. paradise. Syn. *paraiso*.

kalyehón (kal-he-yon), *n.* (Sp. *callejon*) an alley or lane, usually between hedges or lines of trees. Cf. *iskinita*.

kalyo (kal-yo), *n.* (Sp. *callo*) callus; corn. Syn. *lipak*.

kama (ka-ma), *n.* (Sp. *cama*), 1. bed; couch. Syn. *katre*, *tihiras*. 2. bedstead. 3. garden plot. 4. (Geool.) layer; stratum. Syn. *saray*.

kamakailán (ka-ma-ka-i-lán), *adv.* sometime ago; a few days ago; recently. Syn. *hindi pa natatagalan (nalalaunan)*.

kamakalawá (ka-ma-ka-la-wá), var. **kamakalwa**, *adv.* two days ago; the day before yesterday. Syn. *nang nakaraang dalawang araw*.

kamada (ka-ma-da), *n.* (Sp. *camada*) 1. a well-arranged pile, as of firewood, sacks of rice, etc. Syn. *talaksán*, *salansán*. 2. flock or herd of animals. Syn. *kawan*, *ganado*. 3. a band or gang, as of or thieves or robbers. Syn.

gang, grupo, pangkát, barkada o barkadahán.
4. brood. Syn. *akayán*. 5. litter. Syn.
magkakapatid na tutà (of dogs);
magkakapatíd na kutíng (of cats), etc.

kamalig (ka-ma-lig), n. 1. storehouse;
warehouse. Syn. *bodega, pintungan*. 2.
barn; granary. Syn. *bangán, baysa*.

kamandág (ka-man-dág), n. 1. venom. Cf.
lason. 2. anything harmful or destructive
to happiness or welfare; poison. Syn. *lason*
(colloq.).

kamanghaán (ka-mang-ha-an), n. feeling of
surprise, wonder, or astonishment. Syn.
pagkámanghâ, pagtatakâ.

kamangmangán (ka-mang-ma-ngán), n. 1.
ignorance; stupidity. Syn. *kahangalán,*
katangahán. 2. lack of education or culture;
illiteracy. Syn. *kawaláng-pinag-aralan*.

kamaó (ka-ma-ó), n. fist. Syn. *kamáy na*
nakakimkím.

kámará (ká-ma-rá), n. (Sp. *cámara*) 1. either
of the two houses of the legislature. 2.
(Photog.) camera.

kamarero (ka-ma-me-ro), n. (Sp. *camamero*)
1. steward. Cf. *serbidór*. 2. chamberlain.

kamatayan (ka-ma-ta-yan), n. 1. death. Syn.
pagkamatáy. 2. anniversary of someone's
death. Syn. *anibersaryo ng pagkamátay*. 3.
(Colloq.) total destruction; annihilation;
end. Syn. *pagkalipol*.

kamkám (kam-kam), n. act of appropriating
(someone's property) for one's own. Syn.
angkín, pag-angkín.

kaminero (ka-mi-ne-ro), n. (Sp. *caminero*)
street sweeper. Syn. *magwawalis-kalye*. Cf.
basurero.

kamino (ka-mi-no), n. (Sp. *camiino*) 1. road;
highway. Syn. *kalye, kalsada (karsada)*,
lansangan.

kamisa (ka-mi-sa), n. (Sp. *camisa*) chemise;
shirt. Cf. *baro*.

kamisadentro (ka-mi-sa-den-tro), n. *(Sp.)*
shirt with cuffs.

kamisatsìna (ka-mi-sa-tsi-na), n. (Sp. *camisa*
de China) a close-necked shirt, with long
sleeves and no collar, esp. for men. Syn.
barong insik (intsîk).

kamisón (ka-mi-són), n. (Sp. *camisón*) 1.
lady's long undershirt; chemise. Cf.
nagwas. 2. nightgown; nightdress.

kamít (ka-mít), n. 1. receiving or recipiency,
as of an award, prize, honor, etc. Syn.
tamó, pagtatamó; tanggáp, pagtanggáp. 2.
benefit received or obtained. Syn. *pala,*
pakinabang.

kampanaryo (kam-pa-nar-yo), n. (Sp.
campanario) belfry; bell tower. Syn. *tore*
(ng kampanà).

kampanilya (kam-pa-nil-ya), n. (Sp.
campanilla) 1. small bell; hand bell. Syn.
kampanita, kuliling. 2. act or manner of
ringing a small bell. Syn. *kuliling,*
pagkuliling. 3. *(Bot.)* yellow bell vine or
its flowers.

kampante (kam-pan-te), adj. (Sp. *campante*)
unconcerned; free from solicitude or
anxiety. Syn. *palagay-loob; walang-bahala*.

kampanya (kam-pan-ya), n. (Sp. *campaña*)
campaign; planned course of action. Syn.
kilusán.

kampáy (kam-páy), n. 1. swing of the arm,
as in walking or throwing a ball. 2. flap
of the wings, as in flying.

kampi (kam-pi; kam-pí) I. n. act of taking
side, as in a quarrel, discussion, and the
like. Syn. *panig, pagpanig*. 2. one who
takes side with another. Syn. *kapanig,*
kakampí.

kampít (kam-pít), n. a small kitchen knife.
Syn. *kutsilyo*.

kamposanto (kam-po-san-to), n. (Sp.
camposanto) cemetery. Syn. *sementeryo,*
libingan.

kamukhà (ka-muk-hà), adj. similar to;
having resemblance to. Syn. *katulad,*
kawangis.

kamunduhán (ka-mun-du-hán), n.
worldliness; earthliness.

kamusmusán (ka-mus-mu-sán), n. 1.
immaturity of age or mind. Syn.
kapaslitan. 2. ignorance; stupidiity. Syn.
katangahan, kahangalan.

kanáw (ka-náw), I. n. 1. act or manner of
stirring or beating a substance into a
liquid. Syn. *batí, pagbabatí*. 2. any
substance stirred or beaten in a liquid or
mixture.

kandalapák (kan-da-la-pák), n. prostitute.
Syn. *puta, burikák, patutot; masamang*
babae; kalapating mababa ang lipad (fig.).

kandili (kan-di-li), n. 1. care; protection.
Syn. *tangkilik, pagtangkilik; kalingà,
pagkalingà; alagà, pag-aalagà; arugà, pag-
aarugâ; ampón, pag-aampón.* 2. a person
under one's care or protection. Syn. *alaga,
ampón, tangkilik.*

kandirít (kan-di-rít), n. act or manner of
walking on one foot by making short
leaps; hopping on one foot. Syn. *takindî.*

kandóng (kan-dóng), I. n. 1. act or manner
of carrying something on the front of one's
skirt or dress. 2. act of holding a person
on one's lap. Syn. *kalong, pagkalong.* 3. a
person or thing carried or held on the lap.
4. act of giving protection or support for
someone. Syn. *tangkilik, pagtangkilik.*

kaniíg (ka-ni-íg), adj. n. referring to a person
or persons with whom one is in private
or intimate conversation. Cf. *katalamitan;
kapanayám.*

kanina (ka-ni-na), var. kangina, adv. a while
ago; sometime ago today.

kanino (ka-ni-no), pron. 1. to whom; for
whom; from whom. 2. whose.

kaningningán (ka-ning-ni-ngán), n. 1.
brilliancy; brightness. Syn.
kaluningningán, kaliwanagan. 2 splendor.
Syn. *dingal, karingalan.*

kanlóng (kan-lóng), I. n. 1. act of taking
cover behind or under something. Syn.
pagkanlóng, panganganlóng. Cf. *tagò,
pagtagò, pagtatagò.* 2. a hidden place. Syn.
tago o liblib na lugar; makubli. 3. shade;
shelter; shady place. Syn. *lilim, lilom.*

kanlungan (kan-lu-ngan), n. 1. shed; shelter.
Syn. *silungán.* 2. place to hide in; hideout.
Syn. *taguan, kublihan.*

kantero (kan-te-ro), n. (Sp. *cantero*)
stonecutter; mason; cement worker.

kantiín (kan-ti-ín), v. to touch, tap, or hit
lightly. Syn. *pintigín; hipuin o tapikín nang
marahan.*

kantiyáw (kan-ti-yáw), n. 1. a joke; banter.
Syn. *birò, tudyó, tuksó.* 2. act of joking or
bantering someone. Syn. *panunuksó o
pagbibirô.* 3. ridicule; words or actions that
make fun of somebody or something. Syn.
tuya, pagtuyâ, panunuyâ.

kangkáng (kang-káng), n. 1. cries of a dog,
esp. when it gets hurt. Cf. *tahól, kahól.* 2.

loud boasting. Syn. *paghahambóg.* 3.
(Colloq.) loud complaint. Syn. *reklamo,
pagrereklamo.* 4. loud discussion, esp.
about something unimportant. Syn.
daldalan, satsatan.

kaón (ka-on), n. 1. act of fetching a person
from a certain place. Syn. *sundô,
pagsundô.* 2. a person or group of persons
sent to fetch someone from a certain
place. Syn. *sundô, tagasundô.*

kapál (ka-pál), n. 1. quality or state of being
thick; thickness. Syn. *kakapalán.* Ant.
nipís, kanipisán. 2. dimension from surface
to surface: distinguish from *length* and
width. 3. density, as of clouds, smoke, dust,
etc. 4. great number; multitude;
numerousness. Syn. *dami, karamihan.* 5.
callousity, as of one's palm. Syn. *kalipakán.*

kapalad (ka-pa-lad), adj. of or having the
same fate, luck or fortune. Syn. *kasuwerte,
katadhanà, kaportuna.*

kapalágayang-loób (ka-pa-lá-ga-yang + loób), n. an intimate; confidant; intimate
or close friend. Syn. *matapát na kaibigan;
katápatang-loób.*

kapalaluán (ka-pa-la-lu-án), n. arrogance;
haughtiness; excessive pride. Syn.
kahambugan; kayabangan, kataasan.

kapalít (ka-pa-łít), n. 1. successor. Syn.
kahalili. 2. substitute. Syn. *panghalili,
pamalít.* 3. something given in exchange
for another. Syn. *palit.*

kapanahón (ka-pa-na-hón), adj. & n.
contemporary. Syn. *kaalinsabáy,
kapanabáy.*

kapanalig (ka-pa-na-lig), I. n.1. friend. Syn.
kaibigan, katoto. 2. follower; disciple. Syn.
alagad, tagasunód. 3. admirer; fan. Syn.
tagahangà. 4. ally. Syn. *kakampí, kaanib,
kapanig.* 5. co-believer. Syn. *kapaniwalà.*
—II. adj. referring to a person who shares
the same faith or belief with another or
others.

kapanayám (ka-pa-na-yám), n. & adj.
referring to a person who is in conference
with someone. Syn. *kainterbiyú.* Cf.
kausap, kaniíg.

kapanig (ka-pa-nig), n. & adj. 1. referring
to a person siding with another in a
dispute, etc. Syn. *kakampi, kaalyado.* 2.

referring to a person belonging to the same group with another or others. Syn. *kagrupo, kapangkat*. 3. said of something located in the same side, section, page, etc. with another or others. Syn. *kahanay, kaseksiyón*.

kapanitik (ka-pa-ni-tik), n. co-writer. Syn. *kamánunulát*.

kapantasán (ka-pan-ta-sán), n. 1. erudation; scholarliness. Syn. *katalisikan, kadalubhasaan, kapahamán*.

kapatás (ka-pa-tás), n. (Sp. *capataz*) foreman; superintendent; overseer. Syn. *katiwalà, tagapamahalà*.

kápatiran (ká-pa-ti-ran), n. fraternity; sorority; brotherhood or sisterhood. Syn. *samahán, kapisanan*.

kapayapaán (ka-pa-ya-pa-án), n. 1. peace; freedom from war. 2. peacefulness; tranquility; quiet; calmness. Syn. *katahimikan, katiwasayán, kapanatagan*.

kapkapán (kap-ka-pán), v. to search a person (for something) by running the hands over his body. Syn. *kapaán, halughugán*.

kapighatián (ka-pig-ha-ti-án), n. profound sorrow; anguish; mental suffering; affliction. Syn. *dusa, pagdurusa; dalamhati, pagdadalamhatì, kadalamhatian*.

kapiling (ka-pi-ling), adj. close to one's side. Syn. *katabí, kalapít, kasiping, kaabáy, kasigbáy*.

kapintasan (ka-pin-ta-san), n. 1. defect; fault; imperfection. Syn. *depekto; sirà, kasiraán*. 2. bad traits or habit. Syn. *masamáng kaugalián*.

kapisan (ka-pi-san), adj. 1. living in the same house with another or others. Syn. *kasama o kasuno sa bahay*. 2. living with a man, as a common-law wife. Syn. *kinakapisan, kinakasama*.

kapritso (ka-prit-so), n. (Sp. *capricho*) caprice; whim; fancy. Syn. *bisyo*.

kapusukán (ka-pu-su-kán), n. impulsiveness; impetuosity. Syn. *karahasán, kabiglaanan*.

kápuwâ (ká-pu-wâ), var. **kapwà**, I. n. fellow being; other persons. Syn. *iba* (colloq.).

kara (ka-ra), n. (Sp. *cara*) 1. the side of a coin bearing the face or head of a person;

head. 2. a kind of gambling game in which two coins are tossed in the air: the tosser wins when the head sides of both coins appear, but loses when the eagle side appears. Also called *kara-kara* or *kara y krus*.

karahasán (ka-ra-ha-sán), n. 1. violence; force. Syn. *lakás, puwersa*. 2. ruthlessness; ferocity; furiousity; cruelty. Syn. *lupít, kalupitán; bangís, kabangisán*. 3. audacity; daringness. Syn. *kapangahasán; lakás ng loób; tapang*.

karaingan (ka-ra-i-ngan), n. 1. complaint. Syn. *reklamo*. 2. request; supplication. Syn. *hinaíng, pakiusap*.

karamay (ka-ra-may), I. n.1. a person implicated or involved in a crime. Syn. *kasangkot*. 2. a person who shares with another or others in sorrow or suffering. Syn. *kadalamhatì*.

karamdaman (ka-ram-da-man), n. 1. sickness; ailment; illness. Syn. *sakit*. 2. confinement in bed. Syn. *pagkakasakit; pagkakaratay (sa banig)*.

karampatan (ka-ram-pa-tan), I. n. 1. appropriateness; propriety. Syn. *kaangkupán, pagkamarapat, katumpakan*. 2. adequacy; sufficiency. Syn. *kainaman, katamtaman, kasapatán*.

karampót (ka-ram-pót), I. n. a pinch, as of salt. Syn. *katitíng, kapiyangót, kapurát*.
—II. adj. of a very small quantity; of a very meager amount or quantity.

karanasán (ka-ra-na-sán), n. experience. Syn. *eksperyénsiyá, pinagdanasan, pinagdaanan*.

karaniwan (ka-ra-ni-wan; ka-ra-ni-wan), I. adj. common; ordinary; usual; customary. Syn. *ordinaryo, pangkaraniwan, palasak*.

karangalan (ka-rá-nga-lán), n. honor; dignity; good name. Syn. *puri, kapurihan; onór*.

karapatán (ka-ra-pa-tán), n. 1. right or rights. Syn. *deretso*. 2. privileges. Syn. *kapakinabangán*.

karatig (ka-ra-tig), adj. with or having a common boundary; adjacent; bordering; neighboring; adjoining; contiguous. Syn. *katabí, kahanggán*.

karga (kar-ga; kar-gá), I. n. (Sp. *carga*) 1.

act of carrying a person or thing on the shoulder or with the arms. Syn. *pasán, pagpasán.* 2. act of loading cargo on an animal or in a vehicle. Syn. *paglululan, pagkakargá, pagsasakáy.* 3. load; cargo; burden; freight. Syn. *kargada, kargamento, bagahe, lulan, dalá.*

kargada (kar-ga-da), n. (Sp. *cargada*) 1. load; cargo; burden, freight. Syn. *kargamento, lulan, bagahe.* 2. load or charge, as bullets for firearms. Syn. *bala, karga.*

kargo (kar-go), n. (Sp. *cargo*) 1. responsibility; obligation; duty. Syn. *ságutin, panangútan; tungkulin.* 2. work; employment. Syn. *trabaho, katungkulan, gáwain.* 3. care; taking charge of. Syn. *pamamahalà, pangangasiwà.*

karibál (ka-ri-bál), n. one's rival or competitor. Syn. *kaagáw, kapangagáw; kalaban.*

karimlán (ka-rim-lán), n. 1. fact, quality, or condition of being dark; darkness; obscurity. Syn. *dilím, pagkamadilím.* 2. (Fig.) ignorance. Syn. *kamangmangán, kaignorantihán.*

karinyo (ka-rin-yo), n. (Sp. *cariño*) 1. affectionate regards. Syn. *pagmamahál, paggiliw.* 2. caress; affectionnate touch or gesture, as a kiss, embrace, etc. Syn. *lambíng, paglalambíng.*

karingalan (ka-ri-nga-lan), n. splendor; exquisite beauty; pomp. Syn. *karilagán, kariktán.*

kariwaraan (ka-ri-wa-ra-an), n. misfortune; calamity; adversity. Syn. *kasawian, kasamaang-palad, kasawiang-palad, kapahamakan, pagkariwarà.*

kariwasaán (ka-ri-wa-sa-an), n. 1. abundance; plentifulness. Syn. *kasaganaan.* 2. state or quality of being well-to-do; wealthiness. Syn. *kayamanan, pagkamayaman.*

karta (kar-ta) n. (Sp. *carta*) 1. charter, as of a city. Syn. *prankisa.* 2. playing card. Syn. *baraha'.* 3. authority; power; privilege. Syn. *awtoridad, kapangyariihan; pribilehiyo, pahintulot.* 4. letter. Syn. *sulat, liham.*

kartél (kar-tél), n. (Sp. *cartel*) 1. placard; poster; handbill. Syn. *kartelón, paskíl, poster.* 2. cartel; trust. Cf. *monopolyo.*

kartero (kar-te-ro), n. (Sp. *cartero*) postman;

mailman; letter carrier. Syn. *tagahatíd-sulat.*

kartilya (kar-til-ya), n. (Sp. *cartilla*) 1. primer; book for beginners. Cf. *katón.* 2. a short treatise or basic instructions. Syn. *pánuntunan', álituntunin, pátakarán.*

kasá (ka-sá), I. n. (Sp. *cazar*) 1. act of cocking or setting the hammer (of a gun) in firing position. Syn. *pagkakasa.* 2. acceptance of a ber or bets in gambling. Syn. *pagtanggap sa pusta.* 3. act of marrying a couple. Syn. *kasál, pagkakasál.* 4. acceptance of a challenge. Syn. *pagtanggáp sa hamon.*
—II. adj. 1. set or cocked, referring to a firearm. Syn. *kasado, nakakasa.* 2. married, referring to a couple. Syn. *kasal.*

kasabihán (ka-sa-bi-hán), I. n. common saying; byword; proverb; maxim. Syn. *sáwikaín, saláwikain; bukambibíg.*
—II. adj. (Colloq.) famous; well-known. Syn. *tanyag, bantog.*

kasál (ka-sál), I. n. 1. marriage; wedding; betrothal. Syn. *pag-aasawa; pagharáp sa dambanà* (fig.); *pagmamahabang-dulang* (fig.). 2. act of solemnizing. 3. status of being married. Syn. *pagkamay-asawa.*

kasali (ka-sa-li), I. n. 1. participant; partaker. Syn. *kalahók.* 2. contestant. Syn. *kalaban; kapáligsahan.*

kasambaháy (ka-sam-ba-háy), I. n. a person with whom one lives under one roof; housemate. Syn. *kabaháy.*

kasanib (ka-sa-nib), I. adj. 1. affiliated, as with an association. Syn. *kasapi, kaanib.* 2. with or having a side overlapping with the side of another. Cf. *kahugpong, kakabít.*

kasanggá (ka-sang-gá), n. & adj. referring to one's teammate in a game or gambling. Syn. *kakopong, kakampí.*

kasarián (ka-sa-ri-án), n. 1. in Gram., gender. 2. sex. Syn. *tauhín* (colloq.).

kasarinlán (ka-sa-rin-lán), 1. independence; liberty; freedom. Syn. *kalayaan, independensiyá, pagsasarilí.* 2. individuality. Syn. *kakanyahán; sarili o angking katangian.*

kasagsagán (ka-sag-sa-gán), n. time or period of maximum activity. Syn. *kasasalán.*

kasaysayan (ka-say-sa-yan), n. 1. history. Syn. *istorya.* 2. story; tale. Syn. *kuwento, salaysáy.* 2. importance; value;

kasero   **katás**

significance; worth. Syn. *saysáy; halagá, kahalagahán; kuwenta* (colloq.).

kasero (ka-se-ro), *n.* (*Masc. Sp. casero*) owner of a boarding house or a rented apartment.

kasi (ka-si), *conj.* 1. because; on account of. Syn. *sapagka't; dahil sa.* 2. due to the fact that. Syn. *mangyari'y; papaano'y.*

kasindák-sindák (ka-sin-dák + sin-dák), *adj.* horrible; frightful. Syn. *nakasisindák, nakatátakot.*

kasinsinan (ka-sin-si-nan), *n.* density or crowdedness, as of plants. Syn. *kasiksikan.* 2. closeness together, as of stitches. Syn. *kalimitan.*

kasiphayuan (ka-sip-ha-yu-an), *n.* frustration; disappointment; failure. Syn. *pagkasiphayò, kabiguán, pagkabigô.*

kasiping (ka-si-ping), *adj.* 1. lying side by side with another; adjacent or close to another. Syn. *katabí, kapiling, kalapít.* 2. lying or sleeping on the same bed with another. Syn. *kaabáy.*

kasosyo (ka-sos-yo), *n.* shareholder in a business partnership. Syn. *kabakas.*

kastigo (kas-ti-go), *n.* (*Sp. castigo*) punishment; castigation; chastisement. Syn. *parusa, pagpaparusa, kapárusahán.*

kasukabán (ka-su-ka-bán), *n.* treachery; treason; perfidy; disloyalty. Syn. *kataksilán, kaliluhan, katraidurán.*

kasukdulán (ka-suk-du-lán), *n.* 1. climax; highest point of interest, excitement, etc. Syn. *rurok, karurukan.* 2. state or condition of being at the very end, as of one's self-control. Cf. *hanggán, hangganan, hanggahan.*

kasuklamán (ka-suk-la-mán), I. *v.* to feel disgusted with; hate. Syn. *kainisán, kasuyaan, kayamután.*

kasulatan (ka-su-la-tan), *n.* 1. document; important records or deeds. Syn. *dokumento.* 2. a written agreement; contract. Syn. *kontrata; nakasulat na kasunduan.* 3. (K-) Scripture.

kasundô (ka-sun-dô), I. *adj.* 1. in good terms with; congenial; suited to one's needs or disposition. Syn. *nákakasundô, nakakabagáng, kabagáng.*

katá (ka-tá), *pron.* you and I; the two of us; we (dual, prepositive); us (dual, postpositive). *Kata'y pupunta roón.* We

shall go there. *Pumunta katá roón.* Let us go there.

kataká-taká (ka-ta-ká + ta-ká), *adj.* strange; marvelous; wonderful; astonishing; mysterious. Syn. *kagulat-gulat, kahangáhangá, kagilá-gilalás.*

katagâ (ka-ta-gâ), *n.* 1. (*Gram.*) particle. 2. (*Colloq.*) word. *Ilán lamang katagá ang kanyáng sinabi.* He said only a few words.

katahimikan (ka-ta-hi-mi-kan), *n.* 1. silence; quietness. Syn. *pagkatahimik, pananahimik, kawaláng-ingay.* 2. tranquility; calmness; peace; peacefulness. Syn. *kapayapaan; kahinahunan.*

katalik (ka-ta-lik), *adj. & n.* referring to a person who is engaged in an intimate conversation with another. Syn. *katalamitam.*

kataló (ka-ta-ló), I. *adj.* 1. said of someone not related by blood to another, hence, can be courted or wooed. Syn. *maliligawan.* 2. said of a gambler who is not exempted, as a loser, from paying the winner, even if he is a relative or a close friend. Syn. *kalaban, magkalaban.*

katangian (ka-ta-ngi-an), *n.* 1. virtue; good quality. Syn. *buti, kabutihan; husay, kahusayan.* 2. trait; characteristic. Syn. *ugali, kaugalian.*

katapát (ka-ta-pát), I. *adj.* 1. opposite in front of (another): *bahay na katapát ng simbahan,* a house opposite the church. 2. equivalent: as in *katapát na halagá,* equivalent value.

katapatán (ka-ta-pa-tán), *n.* 1. sincerity; frankness; honesty. Syn. *pagkamatapát; pagkaprangko, kaprangkuhan.* 2. loyalty; faithfulness. Syn. *pagkamatapát.* Ant. *kaliluhan, kataksilán, katraidurán.* 3. truth; fact. Syn. *katotohanan, pagkatotoo.* 4. directness, as of a way or passage. Syn. *katuwiran, kaderetsuhán.*

katarungan (ka-ta-ru-ngan), *n.* 1. (*Law.*) justice. Syn. *hustisya.* 2. sound reason; rightfulness; validity. Syn. *katwiran, pagkamakatwiran.*

katás (ka-tás), *n.* 1. sap, as of plants. Syn. *dagta.* 2. juice, as of fruits. 3. act or manner of extracting juice by or as by pressing with the fingers. Syn. *pigâ, pagpigâ.* 4.

(Fig.) the main idea; digest; summary; synopsis.

katatagan (ka-ta-ta-gan; ka-ta-ta-gan), I. *n.* 1. state or quality of being stable; stability; firmness. Syn. *tibay, katibayan.*

katauhan (ka-ta-u-han), *n.* 1. human nature; personality. Syn. *pagkatao, personalidad.* 2. reputation. Syn. *reputasyon; pangalan; pagkakilala (sa isáng tao).*

katayuan (ka-ta-yu-an), *n.* 1. state or condition, as of a patient. Syn. *lagáy, kalagayan.* 2. position; situation; place. Syn. *lugal (lugár), puwesto.*

kathâ (kat-hâ), I. *n.* 1. invention; creation. Syn. *imbento, pag-imbento; likhâ, paglikhâ.* 2. literary composition. Syn. *akdâ, akdáng pampánitikán.* 3. musical composition. Syn. *tugtugin, músiká.*

katig (ka-tig), *n.* outriggers of a native boat, usually made of bamboos.

katihan (ka-ti-han), I. *n.* land, as distinguish from water or sea. Syn. *lupa, dalatan.*

katipunero (ka-ti-pu-ne-ro), *n.* a member of the secret revolutionary society called *Katipunan* during the Spanish regime in the Philippines.

katiting (ka-ti-ting), I. *n.* a very little amount; a pinch, as of salt. Syn. *kapurát, kapiyangót.*

katiwalà (ka-ti-wa-là), *n.* an overseer; person in charge; caretaker. Syn. *ingkargado, tagapamahalà.* 2. administrator; supervisor. Syn. *tagapangasiwà, tagapamahalà.* 3. foreman. Syn. *kapatás.*

katiwalián (ka-ti-wa-li-án), *n.* 1. anomaly; irregularity; corruption. Syn. *anomalya; kabulukán* (colloq.) 2. violation. Syn. *paglabág.* 3. absurdity. Syn. *kabalighuán, kabalintunaan.*

katiyakan (ka-ti-ya-kan), *n.* assurance; certainty. Syn. *kasiguruhan.*

katoto (ka-to-to), *n.* 1. intimate friend. Syn. *kaibigan.* 2. follower; co-believer; disciple. Syn. *kapanalig; kapaniwala; tagasunód.*

katotohanan (ka-to-to-ha-nan), *n.* 1. truth; actuality. Ant. *kasinungalingan.* 2. reality; veracity. Syn *katunayan.* 3. proof; evidence. Syn. *katibayan, ebidensyá.*

katumbás (ka-tum-bás), I. *adj.* equal in quantity, force, meaning, etc.; equivalent.

Syn. *kapareho, katapát.*
—II. *n.* something equivalent to another.

katungkulan (ka-tung-ku-lan), *n.* 1. duty; obligation; responsibility. Syn. *tungkulin, sagutin, pananágutan, obligasyón, responsibilidád.* 2. position; occupation; work; profession. Syn. *trabaho, gawain, opisyo, hanapbuhay, empleo.* 3. position, esp. a public one; office. Syn. *tungkulin*

katwiran (kat-wi-ran), *n.* 1. reason; explanation; argument in favor of. Syn. *paliwanag.* 2. cause. Syn. *dahilan; kadahilanan.* 3. justice. Syn. *katarungan.* 4. righteousness; uprightness. Syn. *pagkamakatarungan, pagkamakatwiran.*

kaugalián (ka-u-ga-li-án), *n.* 1 standing habit custom, as in particular place. Syn. *kostubre,* 2. common practice. Syn. *pinagkáugalián, pinagkáhiratihan.*

kaugnayan (ka-ug-na-yan), *n.* 1. relation or connection; relationship. Syn. *pagkakaugnáy; koneksyón.* 2. involvement, as in a criminal case. Syn. *pagkakásangkót.*

kaunlarán (ka-un-la-rán), *n.* fact, state, or quality of being progressive; progress; prosperity; prosperous. Syn. *pagkamaunlád, progreso, kaprogresuhan.*

kawan (ka-wan), *n.* 1. herd, as of sheep, cattle, or the like. Syn. *ganado.* 2. flock, as of birds. Syn. *langkay, pulutóng.* 3. swarm, as of bees. Syn. *kuyog.* 4. school as of fish.

kawaní (ka-wa-ní), I. *n.* 1. helper. Syn. *katulong, katulungín.* 2. employee. Syn. *empliyado, tauhan.*

kawangis (ka-wa-ngis), *adj.* similar or alike to; with or having similarity or resemblance to. Syn. *kawangkî, kamukhâ, nákakamukhâ, nakakahawig.*

kawáy (ka-wáy), *n.* wave or waving of a hand of hands, as in bidding goodbye, or in calling or signalling someone. Cf. *wagaywáy.*

kawikaán (ka-wi-ka-án), *n.* 1. idiom; idiomatic expression. Syn. *idyoma.* 2. proverb; saying; adage; maxim. Syn. *kasabihán, sawikaín.*

kawilihan (ka-wi-li-han), I. *n.* 1. fact, state, or condition of being deeply engrossed in something. Syn. *pagkawili,* 2. deep interest

in doing something. Syn. *kahiligan.*
—II. v. to be or become deeply engrossed
in. Syn. *pagkawilihan.*

kawíng (ka-wíng), n. link of a chain.

kawit (ka-wit), n. 1. a curved or bent metal
or wire serving to catch or hold another
object.

kayas (ka-yas) n. act or manner of shaving
or scraping the sides or edges (of a stick,
or the like) with or as with a knife, to
make it smooth or smaller. Cf. *yasyás,*
tapyás.

kéndeng (kén-deng), var. **kinding**, n. an
intentional, exaggerated movement of the
shoulders and hips, esp. in dancing.

kibkib (kib-kíb), I. n. 1. act of biting and
wearing away something little by little;
gnawing. Cf. *ngatngát, pagngatngát.* 2. the
part of something that has been gnawed.

kibít (ka-bít), n. 1. raising up of the
shoulders, as in expressing doubt,
contempt, indifference, etc.; shrug. Cf.
kilig. 2. a small bite of a fish on the bait
of a fish line. Cf. *kagát, kibkíb.*

kikil (ki-kil), n. 1. a rasping tool for steel,
iron, and other metal; file. 2. act or
manner of using a file, as in making (a
piece of iron, steel, or any metal), clean,
smooth, pointed, or smaller. Syn. *pagkikil.*
3. (Colloq.) extortion. Syn. *pangingikil,*
pangunguwarta.

kikilan (ki-ki-lan), v. 1. to make smaller by
rasping with a file. 2. to get money from
by extorting; extort (money) from. Syn.
kuwartahán.

kilabot (ki-la-bot), I. n. 1. goose flesh. Syn.
pangingilabot. 2. grain or texture, as of
wood, meat, etc. Syn. *hilatsa.* 3. fear;
fright; terrror. Syn. *takot, pagkatakot.* 4. a
person being intensely feared by many;
terror. cf. *matón, butangero.*

kilíg (ki-líg), n. shudder; convulsive tremor
of the body, as in fear or cold. Syn. *katóg,*
kinig, katál.

kiling (ki-ling), n. 1. act of inclining (the
body) to one side from a horizontal
position. Syn. *hilig, paghilig.* 2. act of
turning the head or body to one side. Syn.
paling, pagpaling.

kimkím (kim-kím), I. n. 1. act or manner of

holding something within one's closed
hand. Cf. *kimís, kuyóm.* 2. fact or
condition of being held within one's
closed hand. Cf. *hawak, pagkakahawak.*

kimî (ki-mî), adj. shy; timid; bashful. Syn.
mahiyain, mahihiyain.

kinágawián (ki-ná-ga-wian), adj. & n.
referring to one's habit or way, acquired or
natural. Syn. *kináugalián, pinagkáugalián;*
kinahiratihan, pinagkáhiratihan; pinag-
kasanayan.

kinahinatnán (ki-na-hi-nat-nán), n.
outcome; result; consequence. Syn.
bunga, resulta; kináuwian.

kindát (kin-dát), n. a signal, hint, etc. made
by winking; wink, Cf. *kuráp, kisáp.*

kinis (ki-nis), n. 1. smoothness; fineness, as
of skin. Syn. *kakinisan; pino, kapinuhan.*
2. polish, as of surfaces. Syn. *kintáb,*
kakintabán.

kintáb (kin-táb), n. lustre; brilliance; gloss,
glossiness; polish. Syn. *kakintabán, kináng,*
kakinangán.

kipot (ki-pot), n. 1. state or condition of
being narrow or small, as of a hole, door,
window, room, street, etc.; narrowness.
Syn. *kaliitan; kitid, kakitiran.*

kirót (ki-rót), n. sharp or stinging pain, as
of wounds or cuts. Syn. *anták, hapdî, sakít.*

kisig (ki-sig), n. 1. elegance, esp. in dressing.
Syn. *garà, kagaraan; bikas, kabikasan.* 2.
gallantry. Syn. *gilas, kagilasan.*

kisláp (kis-láp), n. 1 sparkle; twinkle. Syn.
ningníng, luningníng; kináng. 2. polish;
gloss; glossiness. Syn. *kintáb, kakintabán.*

kislót (kis-lót), n. slight movement or quiver
of the muscular tissues or flesh observed
on a newly slaughtered animal. Syn.
kimbót, kibót, kisót.

kitid (ki-tid), n. lack of the required or
standard width; narrowness of surface.
Syn. *kakitiran.*

kitíl (ki-tíl), I. n. 1. act or manner of cutting
off or nipping something that or as with
the fingernails. Cf. *pitás, pagpitás.* 2. act
of killing or taking away someone's life
by or as by cutting the throat. Syn.
pagpatáy; puti o pagputi ng buhay.

klima (kli-ma), n. (Sp. *clima*) climate;
weather. Syn. *panahón.*

kodigó (ko-di-gó), n. (Sp. *código*) 1. code, as of laws and rules. 2. secret message in codes. 3. (*Colloq.*) notes; list of important things to remember, esp. by a student who consults it secretly during an examination.

kolorete (ko-lo-re-te), n. (Sp. *colorete*) rouge. Syn. *pangulay-pisngí.*

konsorte (kon-sor-te), n. (Sp. *consorte*) consort or best man, esp. for a reigning festival queen. Syn. *abay.*

konstitusyón (kons-ti-tus-yón), n. (Sp. *constitución*) 1. constitution; basic law. Syn. *saligáng-batás* (*salimgambatás*). 2. physical condition of the body; physique Syn. *pangangatawán.*

kopa (ko-pa), n. (Sp. *copa*) 1. wine cup; goblet. Cf. *kopita, kalis.*

kopita (ko-pi-ta), n. (Sp. *copita*) small wine cup. Cf. *kopa.*

koponán (ko-po-nán), n. team (of players). Cf. *pangkát.*

kopong (ko-pong), n. 1. an arrangement whereby two or more players agree to be in the same team. 2. teamwork.

koreo (ko-re-o), n. (Sp. *correo*) 1. mail; post. 2. mail service. 3. post office. Syn. *tanggapan ng koreo.*

krimen (kri-men), n. (Sp. *crimen*) crime. Syn. *mabigát na kasalanan o pagkakasala.*

krisis (kri-sis), n. (Sp. *crisis*) 1. critical moment. Syn. *panganib, peligro.* 2. economic or financial crisis. Syn. *pagsasalát o pagdarahop* (*sa kabuhayan*). 3. time of hardship and danger. Syn. *kagipitan; panahón ng kagipitan.*

kristo (kris-to), n. (Sp. *cristo*) 1. (K-) Christ. 2. in cockfighting, a person who acts as an agent of a better or bettors. Syn. *tagapusta.*

kubà (ku-bà), I. n. hunchback; a person with a humped back. Syn. *taong kurkubado.*

kubabaw (ku-ba-baw), n. the act or position taken by a male animal in copulation. Syn. *babá, pagbabá.*

kublí (kub-lí; ku-bli), I. adj. 1. hidden or out of sight, referring esp. to a place. Syn. *tagà, liblíb,* 2. secret; unknown. Syn. *lihim, lingid, sekreto.*

kubót (ku-bót), I. n. 1. wrinkle or small fold; pucker. Syn. *kulubót, kunót.* 2. petty thievery. Syn. *umít, pangungumit; kupit,*

pangungupit.

kuha (ku-ha), I. n. 1. act of getting or obtaining something from a place with or as with one's hand. Cf. *abót, pag-abót; dampót, pag-dampót; pulot, pagpulot.* 2. obtaining or receiving something. Syn. *tamó, pagtatamó; kamít, pagkakamít; tanggáp, pagtanggáp.* 3. act or manner of taking, e.g., a picture of someone. Syn. *pagkuha o pagkakákuha* (*ng larawan*).

kulá (ku-lá), n. 1. bleaching of clothes under the heat of the sun. Syn. *pagkukulá; pagpapaputi ng damit sa pamamagitan ng pagbibilad sa araw.*

kulabô (ku-la-bô), I. adj. 1. hazy; somewhat dark; not clear. Syn. *malabò nang bahagyâ.* 2. slightly faded. Syn. *mapusyáw; kupás nang bahagyá.*

kulam (ku-lam), n. witchcraft; witchery; sorcery. Cf. *gaway, panggagaway.*

kulamos (ku-la-mos), n. 1. act or manner or mashing or scratching someone (angrily) on the face. Cf. *lamas, paglamas.* 2. the scratches on the face caused by this.

kulang (ku-lang), I. adj. 1. lacking; insufficient. Syn. *di-sapàt, kapós.* 2. incomplete. Syn. *may-kulang; di-tapós.* 3. short. Syn. *maiklî; kulang sa habà.*

kulapol (ku-la-pol), n. 1. act of smearing something with paint, oil, or any sticky or dirty matter.

kulasisi (ku-la-si-si), n. (*Colloq.*) mistress; paramour. Syn. *kalunyâ; babae* (colloq.); *patikî; kabít* (colloq.)

kulig (ku-lig), n. (*Zool.*) the young of a pig; suckling pig. Syn. *biík, buwík, buláw.*

kuliglíg (ku-lig-líg), n. (*Entom.*) 1. cricket. Syn. *kerwe* (*keruwé*). Also called *kuligliglupà.* 2. cicada. Syn. *kulilis.*

kulilíng (ku-li-líng), n. 1. a small bell. Syn. *kampanilya, kililíng,* 2. act or manner of causing this bell to sound. Syn. *pagkulilíng, pagkililing.*

kulimbát (ku-lim-bát), I. n. 1. act of stealing. Syn. *nakaw, pagnakaw; umít, pag-umít.* 2. anything stolen. Syn. *bagay na nakaw.*

kulimlím (ku-lim-lím), adj. 1. cloudy; overcast; dark; said of the sky or weather. Syn. *maulap; madilím o nagdídilím* (*ang langit*).

kulô   **kusà**

kulô (ku-lô), I. n. 1. bubbling or setting, as
of boiling liquid or water. Syn. *bulák,
pagbulák; sulák, pagsulák*. 2. bubbling
sound produced by boiling liquid or water.
3. a similar sound that heard in the
stomach when a person is hungry.

kulob (ku-lob), var. kulub, n. 1. the
prevention of heat from escaping from a
container by means of covering it tightly.
Syn. *pagkulob*.

kulóg (ku-lóg), n. 1. thunder. Syn. *kaluglóg*.
2. any sound like thunder. Syn.
dagundóng. 3. (*Colloq.*) a term used to refer
to a person whom one dislikes. Syn.
walanghiyâ (colloq.)

kulóng (ku-lóng), I. adj. 1. imprisoned;
confined or locked up in jail. Syn.
nakakulóng, nakabilanggô. 2. confined in
a cage; caged. Syn. *nakahawla; nasa hawla*.

kulto (kul-to), I. n. (Sp. *culto*) 1. cult; system
of religious worship. Syn. *urì ng
pananampalataya o pagsambà*. 2. religious
worship, ceremony, or service, as in
certain sects. Syn. *pagkukulto*. Cf.
pagmimisa.

kultura (kul-tu-ra), n. (Sp. cultura) 1.
culture. Syn. *kalinangán*. 2. civilization.
Syn. *kabihasnán, sibilisasyón*.

kumós (ku-mós), I. adj. 1. held within one's
palm or closed hand. Syn. *kimkím, kimís;
kuyóm sa kamáy*. 2. crumpled or rumpled
due to having been squeezed with the
hand. Syn. *yukós, yukót, kuyumós*.

kumpáy (kum-páy), n. 1. grass foder. Syn.
damóng pagkain (ng mga hayop); sakate. 2.
act of giving fodder to an animal. Syn.
pagkukumpáy.

kuna (ku-na), n. (Sp. *cuna*) 1. crib. 2. cradle.
Syn. *duyan*.

kunat (ku-nat), n. 1. ductility; pliability;
resiliency; flexibility. Cf. *ganít, gatil*. 2.
(Fig.) stinginess Syn. *kakuriputan; damot,
karamutan*.

kundangan (kun-da-ngan), I. n. respect;
regard; consideration. Syn. *galang,
paggalang; pitagan, pamimitagan*.

kundî (kun-dî), prep. but; except: as in *walâ
na kundî itó*, there is no more but this.
Syn. *liban sa; máliban sa*. Cf. *kung hindî*.

kunót (ku-nót), I. n. 1. plait or fold (in

clothes). Syn. *pleges o pileges; lupî, tupî*. 2.
wrinkle; crease. Syn. *kulubót*.

kunsinti (kun-sin-ti), n. (Sp. *consentir*) act
of allowing a person to do something
wrong, unjustified, or immoral.

kunsumí (kun-su-mí), var. konsumí, n. (Sp.
consumir) 1. act of causing annoyance or
vexation to someone. Syn. *yamót,
pagyamót; suyà, pagsuyà; inís, pag-inís*.

kuntíl (kun-tíl) n. 1. tip or point of
something protruding from a surface. Syn.
dulo, tungkî. 2. any fleshy outgrowth on
the skin. Syn. *buklíg o butlíg*.

kuntil-butil (kun-til + bu-til), n. unnecessary
or unimportant matters or details that
cause delay. Syn. *kakuririan, kiyáw-kiyáw;
kuskús-balungos*.

kunyapit (kun-ya-pit); kun-ya-pít), n. act
or manner of climbing a tree, high wall
or cliff with one's hands and feet with all
one's efforts to prevent oneself from
falling. Syn. *ukyabit*.

kupad (ku-pad), n. slowness or sluggishness
in moving or doing something. Syn. *bagal,
kabagalan; kuyad, kakuyaran; kakuparan*.

kupas (ku-pas), n. 1. discoloration; loss of
the natural hue or color; fading. Syn.
pagkawalâ o pagpusyáw ng kulay. 2.
(*Colloq.*) loss or waning, as of strength,
beauty, popularity, etc. Syn. *lipas, paglipas*.

kupkóp (kup-kóp), I. n. 1. act of keeping
and protecting someone needing help or
care. Syn. *kandili, pagkandili; ampón, pag-
ampón*. 2. act of holding a dear one close
to one's breast. Cf. *yakap, pagyakap*. 3. a
person under one's protective care. Syn.
ampón, kandili.

kupit (ku-pit), I. n. 1. act of filching;
pilferage. Syn. *pagkupit, pangungumít;
nakaw, pagnakaw, pagnanakaw*.

kuráp (ku-ráp), n. 1. blink or wink (of the
eyes). Syn. *kisap*.

kurú-kurò (ku-rú + ku-rò), n. 1. opinion;
what one thinks about something. Syn.
palagáy, palá-palagáy. 2. belief. Syn.
paniwalà, paniniwalà. 3. supposition. Syn.
hckà, haká-hakà. 4. meditation; reflection;
thinking about. Syn. *pagsasaalang-alang;
pagsasaisip*.

kusà (ku-sà), I. n. initiative; volition. Syn.

kusot   **dakíp**

pagkukusà; sariling-paló (fig.)

kusot (ku-sot), *n*. 1. sawdust. Syn. *pinaglagarian*. 2. wood shavings. Syn. *pinagkatamán*.

kusót (ku-sót), I. *n*. 1. act of rubbing or scratching one's eye or eyes with or as with the fingers. Cf. *kuskós, pagkuskós*. 2. act of cleaning clothes with soap and water by rubbing them with the hands. 3. act of rumpling or crumpling something with one's hands. Syn. *yugos, pagyukos; lukot, paglukot*.

kutób (ku-tób), *n*. suspicion; presentiment; foreboding; premonition. Syn. *hinalà, hakà, agam-agam, sapantaha*.

kutyâ (kut-yâ), *n*. mockery; scorn; scoff; derision; ridicule. Syn. *tuyâ, pagtuyâ, panunuyâ; paghamak, panghahamak; libak, paglibák, panlilibak; uyam, pag-uyam, panguuyam; aglahì, pag-aglahì, pang-aaglahì*.

kuwán (ku-wán), *pron*. a word used instead of a person or thing that one cannot immediately express or recall to mind, but may usually be understood.

kuwento (ku-wen-to), *n*. (Sp. *cuento*) 1. story; tale; legend; narrative. Syn. *salaysáy, istorya; bida; katha, maikling kathâ*.

kuwerdas (ku-wer-das; ku-wer-dás), *n*. (Sp. *cuerda*) 1. spring of a watch or clock. 2. string or chord of a musical instrument like guitar, violin, and the like. Syn. *bagting*.

kuwintás (ku-win-tás), *n*. (Sp. *cuentas*) necklace; neck chain of beads, jewels, gold, etc. Syn. *gargantilya*.

kuwitis (ku-wi-tis), *n*. (Sp. *cohete*) skyrocket.

kuyakóy (ku-ya-kóy), *n*. act. or manner of swinging the legs or feet, esp. when seated.

kuyap (ku-yap), *n*. swarming movement, as of tiny ants, worms, etc. Syn. *kutô; kutitap, kuyaw*.

kuyog (ku-yog), *n*. 1. a swarm. Syn. *kawan*. 2. legion; throng; crowd; multitude. Syn. *makapál na tao; karamihan ng tao*. 3. group; gang; company. Syn. *kulumpón, pangkat*.

kuyom (ku-yom), *n*. 1. act or manner of holding something tightly within the palm of the hand. Cf. *kimkím, pagkimkím; kimís, pagkimis*. 2. supression or withholding, as of one's anger, love, etc. Syn. *timpi, pagtimpi*.

D

D, d (da), *n*. 1. the fourth letter of the *abakada* (Pilipino alphabet). 2. the type or impression representing this letter. 3. a symbol for the fourth in a group or series.

daan[1] (da-án), var. **daan** (in some areas), *n*. hundred. Syn. *siyento*.

daan[2] (da-án), var. **daan** (in some areas), *n*. 1. a place or space for passing through. Syn. *lagusan, pasukán, daanán*. 2. a road; street. Syn. *kalye, lansangan*, 3. a regular route or course. Syn. *ruta, daanán*. 4. act of passing through a place. Syn. *pagdaán, pagdaraán*. 5 time of passing through a place. Syn. *oras ng daan o pagdaraán*. 6. a passing away, as of time, event, or happening. Syn. *lipas, paglipas*. 7. a dropping in at someone's place along the way. Syn. *sinsáy, pagsinsáy*. 8. means; way; method. Syn. *paraán, kaparaanán*. 9. chance or opportunity. Syn. *pagkakataón*.

daanin (da-a-nin), var. **daanín**, *v*. to make use of a certain indirect means to attain one's purpose.

daántaon (da-án + taón), var. **dantaón**, *n*. century. Syn. *siglo*.

daáng-bakal (da-áng + ba-kal), var. **daambakal**. *n*. rails; railroad; railway. Syn. *riles*.

dabog (da-bog), *n*. act or manner of showing annoyance or irritation, as by stamping of feet, dropping things, grumbling, etc. Cf. *taráng, darag*.

dakdak[1] (dak-dák), *n*. 1. act of holding someone by the head and pushing it hard against something. Cf. *saksák*. 2. a bumping or collision, as one's face against something Syn. *banggá, salpók*.

dakdak[2] (dak-dák), *n*. (Colloq.) 1. speaking out of turn. Syn. *yakyák, ablá, daldál, satsát*, 2. a person given to such manner. Syn. *daldalero, satsatero; taong madaldál o mayakyák*.

dakilà (da-ki-là), *adj*. great; grand; majestic; magnificent; sublime; glorious; noble, Syn. *marangál, bunyî, mahál, tanyág*.

dakíp (da-kíp), *n*. 1. act or manner of catching, esp. loose animals. Syn. *huli,*

daklót **dagsâ**

paghuli. 2. arrest, as of a criminal by a policeman. Syn. *aresto, pag-aresto; huli; paghuli; pagdakip; kaptura, pagkaptura.*

daklót (dak-lót), *n.* act or manner of seizing something suddenly with the hand; grabbing or snatching. Syn. *sunggáb, dakmá, saklót, daklót.*

dakmâ (dak-mâ), *n.* 1. a sudden seizure or snatch with the hand. Syn. *saklót, daklót, sunggáb.* 2 sudden arrest of someone, as by a police authority. Syn. *bigláng paghuli o pag-aresto.*

dako (da-ko). *n.* 1. place; site; location. Syn. *lugál.* 2. part or portion of a place. Syn. *panig, parte.* 3. direction; way. Syn. *bandá, gawî.*

dakót (da-kót), *n.* a sudden grasp or hold with the grab. Syn. *sunggáb, daklót, dakmâ.* 2. act of taking a big handful of something. Syn. *pagdakót.* 3. a handful; amount or quantity of something taken in one grasp or hold. Syn. *kimís, sangkimís.* 4. act of removing or collecting dust, garbage, etc. with or as with a dustpan.

dadaánin (da-da-á-nin), *n.* a hundred-peso bill. Syn. *sasándaanín.*

dadalawámpuin (da-da-lá-wampu-in), *var.* **dadalwámpuin,** *n.* a twenty-peso bill.

dagâ (da-gâ), *n.* (Zool.) mouse; rat.

dagá-dagaan (da-gá + da-ga-an), *n.* 1. (Anat.) the large muscle in the front of the upper arm; biceps, 2. a toy mouse or rat.

dagán (da-gán), *var.* **dagan** (in some areas), *n.* 1. anything used as weight on something. Syn. *pabigát, pandagán.* 2. act of putting a weight on top of something to press it or to prevent it from being scattered or blown away by the wind. Syn. *pagdaragán; pagpapatong ng pabigát sa ibabaw,* 3. act of lying on or over someone Syn. *patong, pagpatong; kubabaw, pagkubabaw.*

dagasâ (da-ga-sâ), *var.* **ragasa,** I. *n.* rush or haste; careless hurrying. Syn. *pagmamadalî, pagpapadalusdalos.* 2. a sudden, violent noise, as that caused by someone who came in a hurry 3. precipitate fall of something heavy or the noise caused by it. Syn. *lagapák.*

—II. *adj.* recklessly hasty or in hurry. Syn. *padalusdalos; waláng-ingát sa pagmamadalî.*

dagat (da-gat), *n.* 1. a body of salt water smaller than an ocean; sea. 2. bay or gulf. Syn. *baiya, golpo, loók.* 3 (Colloq.) lake; lagoon. Syn. *lanaw, baé.*

dagatan (da-ga-tan), *n.* open sea. Syn. *laot.*

dagat-dagatan (da-gat + da-ga-tan), *n.* 1. a small lake; lagoon, Syn. *baé.* 2. pool; puddle. Syn. *sanaw, lanaw.*

dagdag (dag-dág), I. *n.* 1. something added to another; addition; additional. Syn. *karagdagan, adisyón.* 2. something mixed or added to another. Syn. *halò, kahalò.* 3. increase or promotion in salary. Syn. *aumento (omento).* 4. increase in quantity or number. Syn. *pagdami.* 5. act of adding something to another. Syn. *pagdaragdág, paghalò.* 6. supplement; section added. Syn. *suplemento,* 7. something added to complete a thing. Syn. *kapupunán.*

—II. *adj.* referring to anything added to increase or supplement something.

dagím (da-gím), *n.* dark clouds that portend rain.

dagit (da-git), *n.* 1. act of swooping down and snatching a victim, as by a bird of prey. Syn. *simbád, pagsimbád.* 2. act of seizing and carrying away a woman by force.

dagitab (da-gi-tab), *n.* 1. electricity. Syn. *elektrisidad, kuryente.* 2. spark; glare. Syn. *kisláp.*

daglát (dag-lát), *n.* 1. act of shortening or abbreviating a word, phrase, speech, etc.; abbreviation. Syn. *pagdaglát, pagpapaiklî.* 2. a shortened form of a word, phrase, speech, etc.; abbreviation.

daglî (dag-lî), I. *adv.* 1. at once; immediately; soon, instantaneously. Syn. *agád, kapagdaka; agád-agád.* 2. briefly; quickly; in a short time. Syn. *nang madalî o mádalian; sa maiklíng panahón.*

—II. *n.* a short sketch or play.

dagok (da-gok), *n.* 1. a hard blow or hit with the fist, esp. on the nape or on the upper part of the back. Syn. *batok, pagbatok; sapók o bigwás sa batok o likód.* 2. (Fig.) any sudden calamity or misfortune; shock; blow; setback. Syn. *kasawiáng-palad; kabíguan, pagkabigô.*

dagsâ (dag-sâ), *n.* arrival, inflow, or coming in great quantity or number, as of visitors, goods, etc. Syn. *maramiháng pagdatíng*. 2. great abundance or plentifulness, as of goods in the market. Syn. *saksâ, kasakasaân; pananaganà*.

dagtâ (dag-tâ), *n*. 1 the life-giving juice of plants; sap. Cf. *katas*. 2. resin. Syn. *resina*.

dagubdób (da-gub-dób), *n*. 1. a big blaze or flame. Syn. *lagablab; malakíng liyáb o alab*. 2. the noise made by this.

dagundong (da-gun-dong), *n*. loud rolling sound heard from a very far distance, as that caused by thunder or continuous cannon fire. Syn. *lagunlóng, hugong, kalugkóg*.

dagusdós (da-gus-dós), *n*. 1. downward slide, as one inclined plane. Syn. *dalusdós, dausdós*. 2. the sound produced by a sliding object.

dahak (da-hak), *n*. 1. physical effort to clear the throat of phlegm in order to expectorate it. Cf. *duwál*. 2. the sound coming from the throat in an effort to clear it of phlegm.

dahan (da-han), *n*. 1. act, state, or quality of being slow or moderate in movement or action; slowness; moderation. Syn. *bagal, kabagalan; hina, kahinaan*. 2. softness or lowness, as of voice. Syn. *hina, kahinaan*. 3. carefulness or caution, as in speaking, driving, etc. Syn. *ingat, kaingatan*. 4. control or moderation, as in drinking. Syn. *pigil, pagpipigil*. 5. control, as of one's temper. Syn. *hinahon, kahinahunan*.

dahas (da-has), *n*. 1. force; power; strength. Syn. *lakás, kapangyarihan, puwersa*. 2. violence; brutality; cruelty; ruthlessness; severity. Syn. *lupít, kalupitán; bangis, kabangisán; bagsik, kabagsikán*. 3. daringness; recklessness; audacity. Syn. *kapangahasán; tapang, katapangan; lakás ng loob*.

dahikan (dá-hi-kan), *n*. shipyard. Syn. *baradero, gáwaan ng bapór*.

dahil (da-hil), I. *n*. 1. cause; reason. Syn. *katwiran, sanhî*. 2. purpose; motive. Syn. *layon, layunin*.

—II. *prep*. (usually used with *sa*) because of; due to the fact that; by reason of. Syn. *pagká't, sapagká't*.

dahilíg (da-hi-líg), *n*. 1. slope; the inclined side of a mountain. Syn. *talibís*. 2. any

inclined surface, as of a road, plane, or the like. 3. state or condition of being inclined or sloping, referring esp. to a land area.

dahon (da-hon), *n*. 1. leaf (of a plant or tree). 2. (specific) banana leaf. Syn. *dahon ng saging*. 2. a sheet of paper with a page on each side; leaf, as of a book. Syn. *pohas, pilyego*. 3. the movable frame or paneling of a door or window. Syn. *ohas*.

dahóp (da-hóp), *adj*. 1. needy; very poor; destitute; indigent. Syn. *hikahós, marálitâ, naghihirap*. 2. lacking in; insufficient. Syn. *kapós o kulang sa*.

dahumpaláy (da-hum-pa-láy), *var*. **dahong-palay**, *n*. a species of poisonous green snake that resembles the shape of a rice plant leaf.

daig (da-íg), *adj*. 1. surpassed; excelled. Syn. *nahigtán, nalaluan*. 2. defeated; vanquished; overpowered. Syn. *lupíg, talo, gapî, gahís*.

daigdíg (da-ig-díg), *n*. 1. the earth; world; universe. Syn. *mundo, lupa, sankalupaán*. 2. (*Fig.*) any sphere of human activity; world or field: as in *sa daigdíg ng musiká*, in the world of music. Syn. *larangan*.

daing (da-ing), I. *n*. jerked fish, that is, fish cut or sliced longitudinally on the back, salted and dried in the sun. Cf. *tapa, pindáng, bitad (binitád); bislád, binislád*. 2. the act or method of jerking fish. Syn. *pagdaing, pagdadaing, pagkakádaing*.

—II. *adj*. jerked or sliced, salted, and dried in the sun, referring to fish. Syn. *dinaing*.

daíng (da-íng), *n*. 1 moan; groan; wail; lamentation. Syn. *taghóy, hinagpis, himutok, buntóng-hiningá*. 2 plaint; complaint; grievance. Syn. *reklamo, sakdál, hinakdál*. 3. humble request or petition; supplication. Syn. *pamanhík, pakiusap, samó, luhog*.

daís (da-ís), I. *n*. 1. act of moving closer to another or to one another. Syn. *lapit; paglapit; tabi, pagtabi; piling, pagpiling; siping, pagsiping*. 2. fact or state of being close or near another or to one another.

—II. *adj*. close or near each other. Syn. *magkadaís, magkalapít, magkapiling*.

daít (da-ít), *var*. **daiti**, I. *adj*. in a slight physical contact with; contiguous or touching lightly with. Syn. *diit*.

—II. *n.* 1. a slight physical contact or touch. Syn. *lapat, dikit, kabit, pagdadait, pagdadaiti, pagdidiít*. 2. act of moving close to another so as to be touching lightly. Syn. *pagdait, pagdaiti, pagdiít*.

dalá (da-lá), I. *n.* 1. act of carrying something, as in going anywhere. Syn. *taglay, pagtataglay*. 2. act of delivering something to a certain place. Syn. *hatíd, paghahatid*. 3. provisions brought on a trip. Syn. *baon*. 4. something brought home by a new arrival, esp. gifts for loved ones. Syn. *pasalubong*. 5. act of carrying something, as on one's head, back, or shoulder Syn. *sunong, pagsusunong; pasan, pagpapasan; karga, pagkakarga*. 6. anything carried on one's head, back, or shoulder. Syn. *sunong, pasan, karga*. 7. quantity of goods or things delivered; cargo; load. Syn. *kargamento, lulan*.

—II *adj.* 1. brought or delivered (by). Syn. *hatid, inihatíd*. 2. referring to something that a person carries along with him. Syn. *taglay, tinataglay*. 3. taken or carried away. Syn. *tangay, tinangáy*. 4. (*Colloq.*) brought about by; due to. Syn. *dahil sa, likhâ ng, bunga o resulta ng*.

dalâ (da-lâ), I. *adj.* afraid or scared off by a previous painful or unfortunate experience. Syn. *takót na, ilág na*.

—II. *n.* 1. fact, state, or feeling of being afraid or scared off by a previous painful or unfortunate experience. Syn. *pagkadalâ, kadalaán*. 2. act of causing a person to become afraid or scared beforehand by having him undergo some kind of painful or unfortunate experience that he would not easily forget. Syn. *pagdalá*.

dalág (da-lág), *n.* (*Ichth.*) a species of freshwater mudfish; murrel (*Ophicephalus striatus* Bloch).

dalaga (da-la-ga). I. *n.* a young unmarried woman; maiden. Syn. *binibini, soltera* (old maid). Cf. *binatà*.

—II. *adj.* 1. single or unmarried, referring to a woman. Syn. *wala pang asawa, di pa nag-aasawa*. 2. virgin; chaste; pure. Syn. *donselya, basal, hindi pa nagágalaw, birhín, birgo*.

dalagang-bukid (da-lagang + bukid), var. **dalagambukid**, *n.* 1. (*Ichth.*) a local name given to the various species of fish belonging to the Caesio. 2. a barrio or country maiden.

daláginding (da-lá-gin-ding), *n.* female teenager.

dalagita (da-la-gita), *n.* a young maid (younger than a dalaga). Cf. *binatilyo*.

dalahik (da-la-hik), var. **dalahit**, *n.* 1. intermittent attack of intense coughing. Syn. *ihit ng ubó o pag-uubó*.

dalahikan (da-la-hikan), *n.* 1. isthmus. Syn. *tangway*. 2. wharf for small fishing boats and other sailboats. Syn. *pantalán, daungán (duungán)*. 3. breakwater. Syn. *basagáng-alon*.

dálahin (dá-la-hin), *n.* 1. a thing or things to be delivered. Syn. *bagay o mga bagay na ihahatid*. 2. things that a person usually carries along with him, esp. during trips. Cf. *abubot*. 3. responsibility; duty. Syn. *tungkulin, pananagutan, ságutin*. 4. (*Fig.*) anything that a person has to bear up with. Syn. *pabigát, pásanin*.

dalahirà (da-la-hi-rà), I. *adj.* inclined to gossip; gossipy, referring to a woman. Syn. *madaldál, masatsát, matsismís*.

—II. *n.* a woman who chatters or repeats idle talk and rumors about others; a woman gossip. Syn. *daldalera, tsismosa, satsatera*.

dalamhatì (da-lam-ha-tì), *n.* grief; extreme sorrow or sadness; affliction; distress. Syn. *pighatî, hapis, lumbáy, panimdím*.

dalampasigan (da-lam-pa-si-gan), *n.* 1. seashore; seacoast. Syn. *baybay-dagat, baybayin*. 2. beach. Syn. *aplaya*. 3 both sides of a river Syn. *magkabiláng pampang*.

dalandán (da-lan-dán), *n.* (*Bot.*) a generic term for some species of oranges, the most common is *dalanghita* (*naranghita*), also called *sintores* or *sintunis*.

dalang (da-lang), *n.* 1. infrequency; rarity, as of visits. Syn. *pagkahirà, kabihiraan; kadalangan, pagkamadalang*. 2. slowness, as of the beating of the heart. Syn. *bagal, kabagalan*. 3. fact, state, or condition of being set or placed far apart than is usual. Syn. *pagkalayú-layô, pagkahiwá-hiwaláy*.

dalangin   **dalitâ**

Ant. *kasinsinán, kalimitan.* 4. sparseness
or thinness, as of hair. Syn. *nipís,
kanipisán, kadalangan.* 4. fewness, as of
people attending a meeting, show, etc.
Syn. *kakauntián.* Ant. *dami, karamihan.*

dalangin (da-la-ngin), *n.* 1. act of praying;
prayer. Syn. *dasál, pagdarasál,
pananalangin.* 2. earnest request; entreaty;
supplication. Syn. *samò, pagsamò; hilíng,
kahilingan,* 3. a thing prayed for. Syn.
panalangin, bagay na ipinananalangin.

dalás (da-lás), *n.* 1. frequency; frequent
occurrence. Syn. *limit, kalimitan, kadalasán,*
2. rapidity or swiftness, as the movement
of the feet in running. Syn. *bilís, kabilisán.*

dalaw (da-law), *n.* 1. act of visiting or calling
on someone; visit; visitation. Syn.
pagdalaw, bisita, pagbisita. 2. visitor; guest.
Syn. *bisita, panauhin.* 3. visiting hour or
time. Syn. *oras ng dalaw (pagdalaw); oras
ng bisita o pagbisita.* 4. (by extension) visit
of a suitor. Syn. *akyát o pag-akyat ng ligaw.*
5. a suitor paying a visit to his girl friend.
Syn. *ligaw, manliligaw.*

dalawá (da-la-wá), *colloq.* var. **dalwá**, *n. &
adj.* two. Syn. *dos.*

dalawampû (da-la-wam-pû), var.
dalawampú, *n.* & *adj.* twenty. Syn. *beinte.*

dalawit (da-la-wit), *n.* 1. handspike; lever.
Syn. *panikwát, panikwás, panungkál.* 2.
making mention of something or someone
in passing. Syn. *banggit, pagbanggit.* 3.
implication. Syn. *pagsasangkót,
pagkasangkot, pagkakasangkót.*

dalaydayan (da-lay-da-yan), var. **dalayrayan**,
n. 1. a line, esp. wire, that conducts the
flow of electricity. Syn. *talaytayan, daluyán,
dalanán.* 2. handrail, esp. on each side of
a staircase. Syn. *gabáy, gábayan.* 3. trellis-
like framework used for drying nets,
tobacco leaves, etc. Cf. *bílaran, patuyuan.*
4. a system of pipes, canals, etc. used for
conducting water to a place. Syn.
paagusán, padaluyán.

daldál (dal-dál), *n.* 1. impertinent talk or
conversation; gossip talk. Syn. *satsat,
dakdák, yakyák, ablá.* 2. talkativeness, esp.
of a child. Syn. *kadaldalán, pagkamadaldál.*

daldalero (dal-da-le-ro), *I. n.* (Masc.) a
gossip or gossiper; newsmonger. Syn.

tsismoso, satsatero.
—II *adj.* gossipy; given to gossips, referring
to a man. Syn. *madaldál, masatsát, matsismis.*

dale (da-le), *n.* (Colloq.) speaking out of
turn. Syn. *satsát, daldál, tsismis.* 2. an
unprovoked attack verbal or physical.
Syn. *tira, sabak, banat.*

dalì (da-lì), *n.* 1. (Math.) a unit of measure
equal to 1/12 of a foot; inch. Syn. *pulgada.*
2. a measure based on the breadth of a
finger.

dalî (da-lî), *I. n.* 1 quickness, promptness;
rapidity. Syn. *bilis, kabilisán; kadalian,
tulin, katulinan.* 2. ease or easiness; facility.
Syn. *alwán, kaalwanán; gaán, kagaanán.*
3. shortness of duration, as of a visit, etc.
Syn. *iklî, kaiklián.* Ant. *laon, kalaunan;
tagál, katagalan.*
—II. *interj.* (D-) Quick! Hurry! Syn. *Bilis!
Tulin! Takbó!*

dalirì (da-li-rì), *n.* (Anat.) 1. finger. Cf.
galamáy. 2. anyone of the terminal digits
of a foot; toe. Syn. *galamáy.* 3. the part of
a glove that covers each of the fingers, 4.
(Colloq.) act of mentioning things one by
one, as in trying to point them out in
detail. Syn. *pag-isá-isá.*

dalirot (da-li-rot), *n.* 1. act of poking or
pressing something persistently with or as
with the point of a finger. Cf. *dutdót,
kalikot.* 2. persistent mentioning or
pointing out of something irrelevant. Syn.
mapilit na pag-ungkát.

dalisay (da-li-say), *adj.* 1. pure; not adulterated;
without mixture. Syn. *puro, lantáy, waláng-
halò.* 2. true; sincere; genuine. Syn. *tapát,
matapát, wagás.* 3. pure; immaculate;
without sin. Syn. *banál.* 4. clear; clean;
limpid. Syn. *malinis, malinaw.* 5. distilled;
purified. Syn. *distilada, dinalisay.*

dalisdís (da-lis-dís), *n.* 1. slope or incline,
as of the side of a hill or mountain. Syn.
dahilig, talibis. 2. descent or declivity, as
of a road. Syn. *lusong.*

dalít (da-lít), *n.* 1. psalm; religious hymn.
Syn. *salmo, imno.* 2. dithy-rambical epic
or narrative. Syn. *awit, korido.*

dalitâ (da-li-tâ), *I. n.* 1. poverty; misery;
destitution. Syn. *karalitaán, pamumulubi,
paghihikahós, paghihirap, karukhaán.* 2.

great suffering; torment. Syn. *hírap, dusa, sákit, pagtitiis, pagbabatá.*

—II. adj. destitute; very poor; indigent. Syn. *hiráp, hikahós, dukhâ, dahóp.*

daló (da-ló), n. 1. act of attending a party, meeting, performance, etc.; attendance. Syn. *pagdaló, pagtungo.* 2. response to a call for help; succor. Syn. *saklolo, pagsaklolo; sokoro, pagsokoro.* 3. persons in attendance; guests; visitors. Syn. *mga panauhin o bisita.* 4. a person or persons who responded to a call for help. Syn. *sokoro, saklolo.*

dalók (da-lók), n. pickled green fruits. Syn. *atsara, buro.*

dalos (da-los), n. 1. reckless haste or hurry. Syn. *waláng-ingat na pagmamadalî, pagpapabiglá-biglá.* 2. imprudence; recklessness. Syn. *kawaláng-ingat, kawaláng hinahon.* 3. imprudence; lack of respect. Syn. *kapusungán, kawalánggalang, kabastusán.*

daloy (da-loy), n. 1. ooze; slow flow. Syn. *tagas, pagtagas.* 2. spring, as of water. Syn. *bukál, balong, batis.* 3. leak; leakage. Syn. *tulò, pagtulò.* 4. continuous flow, as of blood in the veins, of electricity in wires, etc. Syn. *talaytáy, dalaydáy, agos, takbò.*

dalúb- (da-lúb) a combining form or prefix (fr. *dalubhasà*), meaning expert or specialist in a certain kind of knowledge or study, esp. in sciences.

dalubhasa (da-lub-ha-sa), I. n. expert, specialist.
—II. adj. well-trained; thoroughly proficient. Syn. *sanay na sanay, eksperto, marunong.*

dálubhasaán (da-lub-ha-sa-an), n. college, as in *dálubhasaán ng edukasyon (pagtuturò);* college of education.

dalubwikà (da-lub-wi-kà), n. linguist; philologist. Syn. *pilologo, lingguwista.*

daluhong (da-lu-hong), n. sudden physical attack or onslaught. Syn. *biglâng lusob o salakay, sugod, pagsugod.*

dalumat (da-lu-mat), n. understanding; comprehension; interpretation; perception; interpretation; perception. Syn. *unawà, pag-unawà, pagkaunawa; intindi, pag-intindi, pagkáintindi.*

dalumog (da-lu-mog), n. a sudden furious attack or onslaught by or as by a number

of persons or crowd. See **dumog.**

dalus-dalos (da-lus + da-los), I. adj. 1. in a hurry; hurried; hasty; done, carried on, etc. in a hurry. Syn. *nagmamadalî, dali-dalî.* 2. careless; without proper study or evaluation. Syn. *padaskúl-daskól, waláng-ingat.*

—II. adv. 1. hastily; hurriedly; in a hasty or hurried manner. Syn. *nang dali-dalî, nang nagmamadalî.* 2. carelessly. Syn. *nang padaskúl-daskol, nang waláng-ingat.*

dalusdós (da-lus-dós), n. 1. slipping downward; downward side. Syn. *dausdos, pagdausdós.* Cf. *dulás, pagkádulás* 2. slope or incline, as of a hill, mountain, etc. Syn. *dalisdis, dahilig.*

dalusong (da-lu-song), n. a sudden attack, as upon an enemy position, esp. from a high place or vintage. Cf. *daluhong, lusob.*

daluyan (da-lu-yan), v. 1. to flow up; ooze from. Syn. *tagasan.* 2 to. be the source, as of a spring of water. Syn. *bukalan, balungan.* 3. to act as a conductor or transmitter, as of electricity. Syn. *talaytayán.*

daluyáng-luhà (da-lu-yáng + lu-hà), n. lachrymal or tear duct.

daluyong (da-lu-yong), n. 1. big waves; surge or well of the sea. Syn. *malalaking alon.* 2. (by extension) calamity; big misfortune. Syn. *kapahamakán.*

dalya (dal-ya), n. (*Bot.;* Sp. *dalia*) the dahlia plant; also, its flower.

dama¹ (da-ma), n. (Sp.) 1. the game of checkers. 2. the checker piece or pieces that can be moved in all directions.

dama² (da-ma), n. (Sp.) maid-of-honor; lady in waiting. Syn. *abay.*

damá (da-má), n. 1. feeling; perception; sense of feeling or touch. Syn. *damdám, pakiramdám.* 2. opinion about something. Syn. *kurò, kuru-kurò, palagáy.*

dama-de-notse (da-ma + de + not-se), n. (Sp. *dama de noche*) 1. an ornamental plant known as "night blooming cestrum" (*Cestrum nocturnum*) that bears numerous slender yellowish-green night-smelling flowers. 2. the flowers of this plant.

damahuwana (da-ma-hu-wa-na), n. (Sp. *damajuana*) demijohn.

damay (da-may), n. 1. act of helping another, esp. in sympathy for his or her

damba   **daniw**

predicament. Syn. *tulong, pagtulong, pagdamay, pakikiramdam; pagsaklolo, pagsukoro, pagdalo.* 2. something given as aid or help; contribution. Syn. *tulong, abuloy, kontribusyón.* 3. a person or persons who responded to help another. Syn. *sukoro, saklolo.* 4. an implicating or being implicated, as in an affair he is not really involved. Syn. *sangkót, pagsasangkót, pagkakasangkot.* 5. condolence; expression of sympathy for the suffering of another. Syn. *pakikiramay, pakikidalamhatì.*

damba (dam-ba; dam-bá), *n.* 1. act or manner of jumping and kicking, esp. of a vicious horse. Syn. *alma, pag-aalmá.* 2. a sudden leap or jump by or as by an animal in attacking a victim.

dámbana (dám-ba-na), *n.* altar; shrine. Syn. *altar, sambahan, dálanginán.*

dambóng (dam-bóng), *n.* 1. act of plundering; pillage, roberry. Syn. *nakaw, pagnanakaw, panloloób.* 2. loot; booty; plunder. Syn. *bagay o mga bagay na nakaw.*

dambuhalà (dam-bu-ha-là), *n.* 1. a big whale. Syn. *malaking balyena.* 2. any huge animal or thing; monster. 3. giant. Syn. *higante.*

damdám (dam-dám), *n.* 1. feeling; sensation. Syn. *pakiramdám, pakiwari.* 2. resentment; ill feeling. Syn. *hinanakit, samâ ng loób.* 3. illness; indisposition. Syn. *karamdaman, bigát ng katawan.* See **damdamin.**

damdamin (dam-da-min), *n.* 1. feeling; sense of feeling. Syn. *pandamá, pakiramdám.* 2. personal opinion or idea about something. Syn. *palagáy, palá-palagáy; kurò, kurú-kurò.* 3. sympathetic feeling; sympathy. Syn. *pakikiramay.* 4. (*Colloq.*) resentment. Syn. *hinanakit, paghihinanakit, samâ ng loob.*

damdamín (dam-da-mín), *v.* 1. to feel offended; resent; take offense. Syn. *isama ng loob, ipaghinanakit.* 2. to feel sorry about. Syn. *ikalungkot.* 3. to feel hurt. Syn. *masaktán.*

dami (da-mi), *n.* 1. quantity or amount; total count or number. Syn. *bilang, buong bilang.* 2. great number or amount. Cf. *kapal, kakapalán, karamihan.*

damít (da-mít), *n.* 1. clothes; clothing; dress. Syn. *pananamit, kasuutan, bihisan, barò, bestido, temo.* 2. cloth; textile. Syn. *tela, kayo.*

damó (da-mó), *n.* 1. grass, esp. those green plants with bladelike leaves that are eaten by grazing animals. Cf. *sakate, kumpáy.* 2. herb, esp. those plants usually used for medicines. Syn. *damóng panggamót.* 3. weed. Syn. *sukal na mga halaman.*

damot (da-mot), *n.* 1. selfishness. Syn. *kasakiman, kakamkamán, karamutan, kaimbután.* 2. stinginess; miserliness. Syn. *kakuriputan, kahidhirán, katipirán.*

dampâ (dam-pâ), *n.* hut; hovel; shanty. Syn. *kubo.* Cf. *barung-barong, kubakób.*

dampî (dam-pî), *n.* 1. act of applying (something) lightly or gently as with a piece of cotton ball, or the like. Cf. *pahid, punas.* 2. a light, gentle touch with or as with a handkerchief, as in drying tears.

dampót (dam-pót), *n.* 1. act of picking up something with the hand. Syn. *pulot, pagpulot.* 2. sudden arrest of someone, as by a policeman. Syn. *biglâng paghuli o pag-aresto.* 3. act of selecting or picking something at random. Syn. *pagkuha o pagpulot nang waláng pili-pilì.*

damuhán (da-mu-hán), *n.* 1. grassland; grazing land. Syn. *parang na pangainán o sugahán ng hayop.* 2. any place covered with grass or weeds. Syn. *lugár na madamó.* 3. lawn.

damuhò (da-mu-hò), *adj.* 1. stupid. Syn. *tangá, hangál, gunggóng.* 2. savage; wild. Syn. *salbahe, waláng-hiyâ.*

damulag (da-mu-lag), *n.* 1. general term for animal or beast. Syn. *hayop.* 2. land monster. Syn. *dambuhalang-kati.* 2. carabao; water buffalo. Syn. *kalabáw, anuwáng.* Cf. *tamaráw.*

danak (da-nak) , *n.* 1. copious spilling or shedding, as of blood. Syn. *malakás na agos o bugalwák ng dugô.* 2. spilth; specifically, blood spilled profusely.

danas (da-nas), *n.* an experiencing; actual living through an event or events. See **karanasán.**

danaw (da-naw), *n.* 1. lagoon; pond. Syn. *dagát-dagatan, lanaw.* 2. a small flooded area. Syn. *sanaw, lawá.*

daniw (da-niw), I. *n.* customary usage; current style or fashion. Syn. *uso, kausuhán; moda; lakad, kalakarán.*

—II. adj. common; normal. Syn. karaniwan, pangkaraniwan.

dansa (dan-sa), n. (Sp. danza) 1. dance. Syn. sayaw. 2. formal dance, ball. Syn. bayle, sáyawan. 3. a slow dance music or tune.

dantaón (dan-ta-ón), var. **daantaón**, n. century. Syn. sigló.

dantáy (dan-táy), n. act or manner of placing or positioning a leg on or over someone or something.

danúm (da-núm), n. (Pamp., Ilok., Pang.) 1. water. Syn. tubig. 2. drinking water. Syn. inumin.

danyos (dan-yos), n. (Sp. daño) damage; harm or injury. Syn. pinsala, kapinsalaán; sirà, kasiraán; perwisyo.

dangál (da-ngál), n. 1. honor; reputation. Syn. puri, onór. 2. dignity; nobility. Syn. kadakilaán, kabunyián.

dangan (da-ngan), I. conj. but. Syn. subali't, datapwá't, ngunit.
—II. adv. were it not for; if not for that. Syn. kung hindi (lamang). See kundangan.
—III. n. 1. respect: Syn. galang, paggalang; pitagan, pagpipitagan, pamimitagan. 3. consideration. Syn. alang-alang, pag-aalang-alang.

dangkál (dang-kál), n. 1. the span or unit of measure from the tip of the thumb to the tip of the middle finger or small finger when stretched. Cf. dapal, damak. 2. act or manner of measuring a length by the span of the stretched thumb and middle finger or small finger. Syn. pagdangkal.

daó (da-ó), I. n. (Bot.) 1. a large timber tree (Dracontomelum dao Blanco), the hard wood of which is commonly used in making luxurious furniture. 2. the hard wood (lumber) of this tree.
—II. adj. made of dao (wood).

daóng (da-óng), n. 1. act of steering a vessel into port; dropping anchor; anchorage. Syn. duóng, pag-duóng. 2. a big boat. Syn. malaking bangkâ o kaskó.

daóp (da-óp), I. n. 1. the position of the hands clasped together, as in praying. 2. the placing of a hand over something to cover or feel it. Syn. duop, pagduop; tuóp, pagtuóp. 3. act of clasping the two hands together. Syn. pagsasalikop ng kamáy. 4. a

merging or joining forces together; coalition. Syn. pagsasanib, pag-iisá.
—II, adj. 1. clasped together, as the hands in praying. Syn. salikop, magkasalikop. 2. joined or merged together. Syn. sanib, magkasanib.

daos (da-os), n. 1. act of holding or carrying on (a meeting, program, game, or the like). Syn. pagsasagawa, pagdaraos. 2. celebration or formal observation, as of a town fiesta. Syn. diwang, pagdiriwang. 3. a coming to an end; completion. Syn. tapos, pagtatapós, pagkatapos.

dapâ (da-pâ), I. n. 1. act of lying down on one's stomach. Syn. pagdapâ, paghigâ nang pataób. 2. a stumbling or falling down with the head or face forward. Syn. sungaba, pagkasungabà; subasob, pagkasubasob. 3. the lying position of a person with the face and stomach under. Syn. pagkakádapâ, pagkákasubasob. 4. (Colloq.) defeat; failure to win. Syn. pagkatalo, pagkagapì.
—II. adj. 1. fallen down on one's face and stomach. Syn. nakadapâ, subasób, nakasubasob. 2. defeated; overpowered. Syn. talo, natalo; gapi, nagapi; bagsak (fig.).

dapâ (da-pâ), n. (Ichth.) 1. flounder (Family Pleuronetidae). 2. a kind of tougue fish (Family Cynoglossidae). 3. a kind of fish known as brill (Family Bothidae).

dapal (da-pal), n. a measure equal to the breadth of the palm or open hand. Syn. damák.

dapat (da-pat), I adj. 1. proper; just; right; fitting; appropriate. Syn. tumpák, tamà. 2. worthy. Syn. bagay, nababagay.
—II. aux. v. must; should; ought. Syn. kailangan.
—III. n. the proper thing, way, or manner; that which is right. Syn. ang nararapat.

dapit¹ (da-pit), n. 1. a religious ceremony in which dead body is brought to the church accompanied by a priest and his acolytes where the corpse is given the last blessing before it is taken to the cemetery for burial. Syn. dapitan. 2. an old practice in some localities, esp. in the provinces, whereby the bride, after the wedding party, is fetched from her home by the groom's relatives to the house of her husband. Syn. *sundo, sunduan, dapitan*.

dapit² (da-pit), prep. toward (towards); near.
Syn. *dako, bandá*.

dapit-hapon (da-pit + ha-pon), I. n. dusk;
twilight; sunset. Syn. *takipsilim*.

—II. adv. late in the afternoon.

daplis (da-plis; da-plis), I. adj. near-missed;
hitting tangentially; merely touching.
Syn. *sapyáw, sumapyáw*.

—II. n. 1. a near-missed hit; a grazing or
being grazed with or as with a bullet. Syn.
tamang daplis (dumaplis). 2. a scratch,
scrape, or superficial wound caused by a
near-missed hit. Syn. *galos, gurlis*.

dapò¹ (da-pò), I. n. 1. act of perching or
alighting on a tree, fence, etc., as what
birds do after a flight. Syn. *hapon,
paghapon*. 2. (*Colloq.*) a person related to
a family by marriage. Syn. *hawa* (*colloq.*)
3. contraction or acquirement, as of a
disease. Syn. *pagkakaroon o pagdapo (ng
karamdaman)*.

—II. adj. related to a family through
marriage.

dapò² (da-pò), n. (*Bot.*) any of several
species of air plants, like orchids.

dapóg (da-póg), n. thick, black smoke from
burning humid firewood. Syn. *makapál at
maitím na usok*.

dapóg (da-póg), n. fire in an open stove in
which firewood is used.

dapugán (da-pu-gán), n. 1. hearth;
fireplace. Syn. *apuyan, dupungán*. 2. open
stove, esp. one using firewood. Syn.
kalán, kakálanan.

dapulak (da-pu-lak), n. aphid; plant louse.

dapyó (dap-yó), n. 1. light current, as of air.
Syn. *marahang ihip; simoy*. 2. light touch
or grazing as in passing. Syn. *sagid*. 3. (*Fig.*)
effective influence, as of civilization. Syn.
impluwensiya, bisa.

dapyós (dap-yós), I. n. 1. a slipping due to
misstep. Syn. *dupilas, pagkádupilas*. 2.
making a mistake; falling into error. Syn.
pagkakámali. 3. a near-missed hit. Syn.
daplis.

—II. adj. near-missed; hitting tangentially
or superficially. Syn. *daplisan*.

darák (da-rák), n. powdered or pulverized
rice bran. Cf. *ipa*.

daragan (da-ra-gan), v. 1. to show someone
one's dislike or disobedience by stamping
the feet and making vocal complaint.
Syn. *tarangan*. Cf. *pagmaktulán*. 2. to talk
to in a rough and domineering manner.
Syn. *hiyawán*.

daráng (da-ráng), I. n. exposure to the heat
of fire, flame, or live coals. Syn. *dandáng,
darandáng*.

—II. adj. exposed to the heat of fire,
flame, or live coals.

dárating (dá-ra-ting), I. adj. coming;
forthcoming.

—II. n. 1. the future. Syn. *hináharap*. 2. a
person or thing expected to arrive.

dasa (da-sa), n. (Sp. *raza*) race; breed; stock;
lineage. Syn. *lahi, lipi, angkán*.

dasál (da-sál), n. (Sp. *rezar*) 1. act or manner
of praying (saying a prayer or prayers).
Syn. *pagdarasál, pananalangin*. 2. form of
words said in praying; prayer. Syn.
panalangin. 3. a thing prayed for. Syn. *ang
panalangin o ipinananalangin*. 4. an earnest
request; entreaty; supplication. Syn.
hinaing, samo, panambitan.

dásalan (dá-sa-lan), n. 1. prayer book. Syn.
aklát-dásalan, aklát ng mga dasál. 2. place
for praying, as the altar, church, or the
like. Syn. *dálanginan, sambahan, simbahan,
panalanginán, altar*. 3. a string of beads for
keeping count in saying the prayers;
rosary. Syn. *kuwintás-dásalan; rosaryo*.

daskól (das-kól), I. adj. 1. done in a hasty
and careless manner. Syn. *madalian,
pawardi-wardi* (*colloq.*). 2. careless, esp. of
workers. Syn. *waláng-ingat, padaskúl-daskól*.

—II. n. act of doing a thing in a hasty
and careless manner. Syn. *madalian at
waláng-ingat na paggawá*.

dasig (da-sig), n. 1. act of moving over so as
to be close or near another, or vice versa.
Syn. *ipod, isod*. 2. act of joining or
attaching something to the side of another
to make it larger or wider. Syn. *datig,
pagdaratig*. 3. part or portion joined or
attached to the side of another. Syn. *datig*.

daster (das-ter), n. (Eng.) 1. a bunch of
feathers or fibers for removing dust from
furniture, etc.; duster. Syn. *plumero,
pamispís-alikabók*. 2. a feminine outer

garment worn to protect the clothes from dust; duster. Cf. *bata*.

datál (da-tál), *n.* (used poetically) arrival; coming. Syn. *datíng, pagdatíng*.

datapwâ (da-tap-wâ), *conj.* but; however. Syn. *ngunì (ngunit, nguni't), subalì (subalit, subali't)*.

datay (da-tay), var. **ratay**, I. *n.* long stay in bed due to illness, infirmity, etc. Syn. *matagal na pagkakasakit o pagkahiga sa baníg.*
—II. *adj.* bedrid; bedridden. Syn. *matagál na may-sakit; nakaratay.*

datdát (dat-dát), *n.* speaking out of turn. Syn. *daldal, satsát.*

dati (da-ti), I. *adj.* 1. former; previous. Syn. *noón, noóng una.* 2. accustomed; used to. Syn. *sanáy, hiratí.* 3. experienced; old. Syn. *beterano, matandâ, sanáy.*
—II. *adv.* formerly; previously; before. Syn. *noon, noóng una.*

datig (da-tig), *n.* 1. the part joined or added to the side of another to make it larger or wider. Syn. *ang idinatig, hugpóng.* 2. the point or line of junction thus made. Syn. *pinagdatigan, pinaghugpungán, hugpungán.* 3. state or condition of being contiguous or adjacent to each other. Syn. *pagkamagkatabi, pagkamagkaratig.*
—II. *adj.* adjoining or adjacent to each other. Syn. *tabi, magkatabi; siping, magkasiping.*

datihan (da-ti-han), I. *n.* an oldtimer; veteran. Syn. *beterano.*
—II. *adj.* 1. accustomed or used to; old; experienced. Syn. *sanáy, hiratí, matandâ na, may-karanasán na.* 2. former; previous; old-time. Syn. *una, noon, noóng una.*

datíng (da-tíng), *n.* 1. arriving at a certain destination. Syn. *sapit, pagsapit; datál, pagdatál.* 2. arrival or coming; return to one's place of origin. Syn. *uwî, pag-uwî; balík, pagbalík, pagbabalík.* 3. periodic occurrence of menses in women. Syn. *pagkakaregla, panaog ng regla o sapanahon.*

datò (da-tò), var. **datu**, *n.* 1. middle finger. Syn. *hinlalatô.* 2. Moslem tribal chief.

datos (da-tos), *n.* (Sp. *dato*) 1. datum or data. 2. evidence or evidences. Syn. *katibayan, ebidensiyá.*

dáungan (dá-u-ngan), var. **daungán**, *n.* 1. landing place for vessels; pier; wharf; port; harbor. Syn. *piyér, pantalán.* 2. simultaneous landing of vessels in a port or harbor. Syn. *pagdadáungan.*

dausdós (da-us-dós), var. **dausdús**, *n.* 1. downward motion or slide, as on an inclined surface or slope. Syn. *dausós, pagdausós.* 2. a sliding, as of a knot that forms a running noose. Syn. *higkót, paghigkót.*

daw (daw), var. **raw**, *adv.* (used idiomatically) it is said; according to information. Syn. *umanó, di-umanó.*

dawagan (da-wa-gan), *n.* a place covered with thick undergrowth of spiny vines.

dawdáw (daw-dáw), *n.* act or manner of dipping one's finger or hand in water or liquid often playfully. Syn. *lawláw, kawkáw, sawsáw.*

dawit (da-wit), *n.* 1. act of implicating someone in certain affairs; mention of someone's name as being involved or implicated in a charge of murder, robbery, etc. Syn. *sangkót, pagsasangkót.* 2. a game of pitting strength by hooking the middle fingers and forcing down the opponent's arm to the surface from where the elbows rest. Syn. *sumping.* Cf. *bunóng-braso.*

dayà (da-yà), *n.* an instance of cheating, fraud; deceit. Syn. *pandaraya; linláng, panlilinláng; lansí, panlalansí; gantsó, panggagantsó.*

dayami (da-ya-mi), *n.* 1. rice straw. Syn. *giniikan (ginikan).* 2. dried rice straw for fodder. Syn. *kumpáy na giniikan.*

dayang (da-yang), *n.* 1. Moslem woman of nobility; Moslem princess. Syn. *prinsesang Moslém.*

dayap (da-yap), *n.* (*Bot.*) 1. a species of lime tree (*Citrus aurantifolia*). 2. the fruit of this tree, known also as *bilulo.*

dayo (da-yo), I. *n.* 1. act of going to a certain place not his own; visit to a place without being invited. Syn. *pagtungo sa ibáng lugár.* Cf. *pangangapit-bahay.* 2. immigration; coming to a foreign country to live there. Syn. *pangingibang-bayan, pandarayuhan.* 3. a foreigner; foreign visitor; alien. Syn. *dayuhan, banyagà.* 6. emigrant or immigrant.

—II. *adj.* not native of a place. Syn. *taga-ibáng bansâ o bayan.*

dayukdók (da-yuk-dók), *adj.* extremely hungry; famished; starved. Syn. *gutóm na gutóm, hayók sa gutom.*

dayuhan (da-yu-han), I. *n.* 1. a stranger in a place. Syn. *taong baguhan sa isáng lugar.* 2. a foreigner; alien; emigrant or immigrant. Syn. *banyaga, estranghero, tagá-ibáng bayan.*

—II. *adj.* alien; foreign; not native of a place.

dayupay (da-yu-pay), I. *adj.* emaciated; abnormally thin; extremely thin. Syn. *payát na payát, napakapayát.*

—II. *n.* state or condition of being emaciated; abnormal thinness. Syn. *labis na kapayatán.* 2. locust that has just laid eggs. Syn. *balang na bagong kapangingitlóg.*

de- prefix (Sp. *de*) meaning wearing, having, using, with, etc., as in: *de-salamín* (wearing eyeglasses), *de-kurbata* (wearing a tie), *de-kuryente* (using electricity), *de-color* (having color); *de-amerikana* (wearing a coat), etc. Syn. *may-; naka-; gumagamit ng.*

debate (de-ba-te), *n.* (Sp.) debate; heated discussion. Syn. *pagtatalo, pagkakatwiranán.*

debit (de-bit), *n.* (Eng.) 1. debt. Syn. *utang, pagkakautang.* 2. (Accounting) debit. Syn. *débitó.*

debosyon (de-bos-yón), *n.* (Sp. *devoción*) 1. devotion; piety; devoutness. Syn. *kabanalan.* 2. religious worship. Syn. *pananampalataya.* 3. religious vow. Syn. *panata.* 4. prayers. Syn. *dasál, panalangin.* 5. loyalty; faithfulness; deep affection. Syn. *katapatan, pagmamahál.*

debosyonaryo (de-bos-yo-nar-yo), *n.* (Sp. *devocionario*) prayer book. Syn. *aklát-dásalan.*

debú (de-bú), var. **dibu**, *n.* (Eng.) debut. Syn. *únang pagharáp sa lipunan.*

debutante (de-bu-tan-te), *n.* (Sp.) a person making debut; debutant or debutante.

dekada (de-ka-da), *n.* (Sp. *decada*) decade; ten years. Syn. *sampúng taon.*

dekálogó (de-ká-lo-gó), *n.* (Sp. *decalogo*) decalog. Syn. *sampúng utos.*

dekano (de-ka-no), *n.* (Sp. *decano*) dean. Cf. *dekana.*

deklamá (dek-la-má), *n.* (Sp. *declamar*) act or manner of reciting (a poem, etc.); declamation. Syn. *bigkas, pagbigkás, pagkakábigkás.*

deklarasyón (dek-la-ras-yón), *n.* (Sp. *declaracion*) 1. act of declaring; announcement. Syn. *pagpapahayag.* 2. a thing declared. Syn. *pahayag.* 3. testimony or statement, as of a witness. Syn. *testimonyo, salaysáy.*

dekorasyón (de-ko-ras-yón), *n.* (Sp. *decoracion*) 1. act of decorating. Syn. *pagpapalamuti, pagdidekorasyon, paggagayak.* 2. ornament; decoration; anything used for decorating. Syn. *adorno, palamuti, gayák.*

dekorum (de-ko-rum), *n.* (Eng.) decorum; propriety; good manners. Syn. *dekoro, kagandahang-asal.*

dede (de-de), *n.* (Colloq.) 1. act of babies in feeding milk from the mother's breast or from a milk bottle. Syn. *suso, pagsuso.* 2. milk feeding time of a baby. Syn. *oras ng pagsuso o pagpapasuso.* 3. baby's bottle of milk; baby's milk. Syn. *gatas, bote ng gatas.* 4. a woman's breast.

dedikasyón (de-di-kas-yón), *n.* (Sp. *dedicacion*) 1. a setting apart for a certain purpose; dedication. Syn. *paglalaan, pagtatalaga, pag-uukol.* 2. an offering. Syn. *alay, handog.* 3. devotion, as to one's love. Syn. *katapatan, pagkamatapat.* 4. dedication to a certain purpose. Syn. *malasakit, pagmamalasakit.*

degradasyón (de-gra-das-yón), *n.* (Sp. *degradacion*) 1. low moral state or condition. Syn. *kawalan, kahamakan, kaimbihan, kasamaán.* 2. lowering in rank. Syn. *pagbaba ng kalagayan, pagsamâ.*

degrí (de-grí), *n.* (Eng.) 1. educational degree. Syn. *títuló.* 2. step. Syn. *baitáng (baytáng), antás.* 3. unit for measuring temperature. Syn. *grado, antás.*

dehado (de-ha-do), var. **dihado**, I. *adj.* (Sp. *dejado*) 1. (in horse racing, cockfighting, etc.) with or having the least number of bettors. Ant. *liyamado.* 2. at a disadvantage. Syn. *daig, agrabiyado.* Ant. *lamang, nakalalamang; higit, nakahihigit; may-bentaha.*

—II. n. 1. state or condition of being at a disadvantage. Syn. *pagkaagrabyado, kaagrabyaduhan; pagkadaig, kadaigan.* 2. a horse, cock, etc. that has the least bets. Ant. *liyamado.*

delantera (de-lan-te-ra), n. (Sp.) front; frontage. Syn. *haráp, harapán, bukana, unahán.*

delata (de + la-ta), I. adj. (Sp. *de lata*) canned; preserved in a can or cans. Syn. *nasa-lata, nakalata.*

—II. n. canned goods.

delegado (de-le-ga-do), n. (Sp.) delegate. Syn. *kinatawán, sugò, representante.*

deliberasyón (de-li-be-ras-yón), n. (Sp. *deliberacion*) 1. careful study or thought. Syn. *masusing pag-aaral o pag-iisip, paglilimì.* 2. discussion. Syn. *diskusyón, pagtatalo, tálakayán.*

delikadesa (de-li-ka-de-sa), var. **dilikadesa**, n. (Sp. *delicadeza*) 1. fastidiousness; choosiness; prudishness. Syn. *selang, kaselanan, pagkamaselang; kadelikaduhan; kapihikanan.* 2. refinement. Syn. *kapuliduhan.*

delikado (de-li-ka-do), var. **dilikado**, adj. (Sp. *delicado*) 1. fastidious; choosy; prudish. Syn. *maselang, pihikan, pilian.* 2. serious; grave. Syn. *malubhâ, lalâ, malalâ.* 3. risky; dangerous. Syn. *mapanganib, piligroso.* 4. arduous; hard. Syn. *mahirap.* 5. important. Syn. *mahalagá.* 6. weak; frail. Syn. *mahinâ.* 7. easily broken; fragile. Syn. *mahinâ, marupók.*

delingkuwénsiyá (de-ling-ku-wen-si-ya), var. **delinkuwénsiyá**, n. (Sp. *delincuencia*) 1. failure to do one's duty. Syn. *pagpapabaya, kapabayaan; pagkukulang o kakulangan sa tungkulin.* 2. deliquency; unlawful behavior; misconduct. Syn. *kasalanan, pagkakasala.*

delingkuwente (de-ling-ku-wen-te), var. *delinkuwente, adj.* delinquent; failing in one's obligation or duty.

deliryo (de-lir-yo), var. **diliryo**, I. n. (Sp. *delirio*) delirium; temporary disorder of the mind. Syn. *hibang, pagkahibang, kahibangán.*

—II. adj. in a state of delirium; delirious. Syn. *nahihibáng.*

delta (del-ta), n. (Eng.) 1. delta (of a river). Syn. *deposito ng lupa at buhangin sa wawa*

ng *ilog.* 2. the fourth letter of the Greek alphabet, corresponding to the letter D in English. Syn. *da* (d).

delusyón (de-lus-yón), n. (Sp. *delusion*) 1. delusion. Syn. *kalinlangán, pagkalinláng.* 2. imagination. Syn. *guní-guní, imahinasyón.*

demanda (de-man-da), n. Law. 1. (Sp) act of filing a case in court. Syn. *habla, paghahablá; sakdál, pagsasakdál.* 2. a case or suit filed in court; complaint in court. Syn. *hablá, sakdál, kaso.*

demensiyá (de-men-si-yá), n. (Sp. *demencia*) dementia; insanity. Syn. *pagkasira ng ulo (isip, bait), pagkaloko, pagkabaliw.*

demokrasya (de-mo-kras-ya), n. (Sp. *democracia*) democracy.

demolisado (de-mo-li-sa-do), adj. (Sp.) demolished; destroyed. Syn. *wasák, winasak, nawasak; gibâ, ginibâ, nagibâ.*

demonyo (de-mon-yo), var. **dimonyo**, n. (Sp. *demonio*) demon; devil. Syn. *diyablo.*

demonstrasyón (de-mons-tras-yón), n. (Sp. *demostracion*) 1. demonstration or showing of some kind of new products, etc. in public. Syn. *pagpapakita, pagtatanghál.* 2. showing, as of one's feeling. Syn. *pagpapakilala, pagpapahayag, pagpapakita.*

denominasyón (de-no-mi-nas-yón), n. (Sp. *denominacion*) 1. religious group; sect. Syn. *sekta.* 2. face value of coins or paper money. Syn. *nakataták na halagá (ng kuwarta).*

denotasyón (de-no-tas-yón), n. (Sp. *denotacion*) 1. denotation; exact meaning. Syn. *tunay o aktuwál na kahulugán.* 2. an indication or sign; denotation. Syn. *tandâ, palátandaan.*

densidád (den-si-dád), n. (Sp.) 1. density or thickness, as of liquid. Syn. *lapot, kalaputan.* 2. closeness; compactness. Syn. *kapál, kakapalán, kasiksikán.*

dentista (den-tis-ta), n. (Sp.) dentist.

denunsiyasyón (de-nun-si-yas-yón), n. (Sp. *denunciacion*) 1. act of denouncing someone to the authorities; denunciation. Syn. *pagsusumbong.* 2. accusation in court. Syn. *demanda, hablá.*

departamento (de-par-ta-men-to), n. (Sp.) department. Syn. *kagawarán.*

depeksiyón (de-pek-si-yón), n. (Sp.

depekto **desareglado**

defeccion) desertion; defection. Syn.
paglayas, pagtalikod, pagtiwalág.

depekto (de-pek-to), n. (Sp. *defecto*) defect;
fault; failure to do the right thing. Syn.
kamalian, pagkukulang, diperensiyá. 2.
imperfection; malfunctioning. Syn. *sirà,
kasiraán.*

depende (de-pen-de), I. *interj.* (*colloq.* Sp.)
It depends!
—II. *adj.* based on; dependent; resting
upon. Syn. *batay, nábabatay.*

dependénsiyá (de-pen-dén-si-yá), n. (Sp.
dependencia) dependence on someone,
esp. for support. Syn. *pagpapakalinga,
pagpapakandili, pagpapaaruga, pag-asa sa
iba.* 2. trust; faith. Syn. *tiwalà, pagtitiwalà.*

depensa (de-pen-sa), n. (Sp. *defensa*) 1. act
of defending. Syn. *pagtatanggól,
pagsasanggaláng.* 2. anything that protects.
Syn. *pananggol, panananggalang.* 3. Mil.
fort; a strong place used for defense. Syn.
tanggulan, kutá, muóg.

depiná (de-pi-ná), n. (Colloq.) definition;
explanation. Syn. *paliwanag,
pagpapaliwanag.*

depinido (de-pi-ni-do), *adj.* (Sp. *definido*) 1.
definite; certain. Syn. *tiyak.* 2. clear. Syn.
maliwanag, malinaw.

depinisyón (de-pi-nis-yón), n. (Sp.
definicion) 1. definition or meaning. Syn.
kahulugan, katuturan. 2. explaining the
nature or meaning of. Syn.
pagpapaliwanag.

depisit (de-pi-sit), n. (Eng.) deficit; shortage.
Syn. *kulang, kakulangán, pagkukulang.*

deplorable (de-plo-ra-ble), *adj.* (Sp.)
deplorable; regrettable. Syn.
nakalúlungkót, nakapágdaramdám.

depormidád (de-por-mi-dád), n. (Sp.
deformidad) 1. deformity; ugliness. Syn.
kapangitan. 2. deformity due to injury.
Syn. *pinsala, kapinsalaan; kasalantaan,
pagkasalantá.*

deporta (de-por-ta), n. (Sp. *deportar*)
deportation; exile; banishment. Syn.
destiyero, pagdidestiyero, pagpapatapon.

depositó (de-po-si-tó), n. (Sp.) 1. deposit;
money deposited in a bank. Syn.
*kuwartáng nakalagak sa bangko, lagak (sa
bangko).* 2. partial advance payment for

something. Syn. *paunáng bayad.* 3.
depository. Syn. *lágakan, taguán,
depositoryo.* 4. warehouse; storehouse. Syn.
bodega, tinggalan, pintungan. 5. sediment.
Syn. *latak, tining.*

depositoryo (de-po-si-tor-yo), n. (Sp.
depositorio) 1. depository; warehouse;
storehouse. Syn. *bodega, tinggalan,
pintungan.* 3. place where things are
entrusted for safekeeping. Syn.
katiwalaán, pantaguán.

depresyón (de-pres-yón), n. (Sp. *depresión*)
1. depression; hollow in the ground. Syn.
lubak. 2. economic depression. Syn.
*pagsasalát, pagdarahóp, paghihirap,
pagdaralitá.* 3. atmospheric depression.
Syn. *namumuóng sama ng panahón.*

deretsahan (de-ret-sa-han), I. *adv.* directly;
openly. Syn. *túwiran, tápatan, háyagan.*
—II. *adj.* direct; frank; open.

deretso (de-ret-so), I. n. (Sp. *derecho*) 1.
something that is due to a person; right
or rights. Syn. *karapatán.* 2. law course or
profession. Syn. *abogasiyá.* 3. justice. Syn.
katarungan. 4. tax; duty. Syn. *buwís, butaw.*
—II. *adj.* 1. direct; straight. Syn. *tuwíd,
túwiran.* 2. continuous. Syn. *tulúy-tulóy,
waláng tigil (hintô).* 3. without curve; straight.
Syn. *matuwíd, waláng baluktót.* 4. set up
vertically; in upright position. Syn. *tuwíd.*
—III. *adv.* 1. directly. Syn. *tuwiran, nang
túwiran.* 2. continuously. Syn. *tulúy-tulóy,
nang tulúy-tulóy.*
—IV. *interj.* Straight ahead! Go ahead!
Syn. *Tuloy! Tuluy-tuloy!*

deribasyón (de-ri-bas-yón), n. (Sp.
derivacion) 1. a deriving or being derived;
derivation. Syn. *paghangò, pagkakahangò.*
2. origin; source. Syn. *pinagmulán,
pinanggalingan.* 3. origin and development
of a word; etymology. Syn. *pamuhatán.* 4.
derivative word. Syn. *salitáng hangò.*

derogatoryo (de-ro-ga-tor-yo), adj. (Sp.
derogatorio) 1. tending to lessen or impair;
detracting. Syn. *mapanirà, nakasisirà.* 2.
tending to belittle. Syn. *mapanghamak,
nanghahamak.*

desareglado (des-a-re-gla-do), *adj.* (Sp.
desarreglado) in disorder; disarranged. Syn.
walâ sa ayos, maguló, magusót.

desastre   **desmayá**

desastre (de-sas-tre), n. (Sp.) disaster; great misfortune. Syn. *sakuná, malakíng kapahamakán o disgrasya.*

desbentaha (des-ben-ta-ha), n. (Sp. *desventaja*) disadvantage. Syn. *kasahulan, kaagrabyaduhan.*

deskanso (des-kan-so), var. **diskanso**, n. (Sp. *descanso*) rest; relief. Syn. *pahingá, pamamahingá.*

deskarga (des-kar-ga), var. **diskarga**, n. (Sp. *descargar*) unloading or being unloaded. Syn. *pag-aawás ng kargamento.*

deskargo (des-kar-go), var. **diskargo**, n. (Sp. *descargo*) apology; excuse. Syn. *paumanhin.*

deskaril (des-ka-ril), var. **diskaril**, n. (Sp. *descarril*) derailment. Syn. *paglinsád o pagkakálinsád sa riles.*

deskompiyansa (des-kom-pi-yan-sa), var. **diskompiyansa**, n. (Sp. *descomfinza*) 1. distrust; lack of trust. Syn. *kawaláng-tiwalà.* 2. suspicion; doubt. Syn. *alinlangan, pag-aalinlangan; duda, pagdududa.*

deskomulgado (des-ko-mul-ga-do), adj. (Sp. *descomulgado*) excommunicated. Syn. *iskomulado, itinakwil o itiniwalag sa Iglesya.*

deskontento (des-kon-ten-to), n. (Sp. *descontento*) 1. discontent; dissatisfaction. Syn. *kawaláng-kasiyahan, pagkawaláng-kasiyahan, pagkadi-nasisiyahán.* 2. displeasure. Syn. *yamót, pagkayamót.*

deskortesiya (des-kor-te-si-ya), n. (Sp. *descortesia*) discourtesy; disrespect. Syn. *kawaláng-galang, kawaláng-pitagan.*

deskripsiyón (des-krip-si-yón), n. (Sp. *descripcion*) 1. description; act, manner, or art of describing. Syn. *paglalarawan sa salitâ o pangungusap.* 2. a statement or a group of words that describe. Syn. *pangungusap o mga salitang naglalarawan.* 3. kind; sort. Syn. *uri, ayos.*

deskubri (des-ku-bri), var. **diskubre**, n. (Sp. *descubrir*) 1. a discovering or being discovered. Syn. *pagtuklás, pagkátuklás, pagkakátuklás.* 2. something discovered; discovery. Syn. *tuklás, bagay na natuklasán.*

deskuwento (des-ku-wen-to), var. **diskuwento**, n. (Sp. *descuento*) discount; rebate; reduction in cost or price. Syn. *bawas, tawad, rebaha.*

desenaryo (de-se-nar-yo), n. (Sp. *decenario*)

ten-year period. Syn. *ikasampung taón.*

desendénsiyá (de-sen-dén-si-yá), n. (Sp. *descendencia*) descent; lineage. Syn. *angkán, lipì, lahì.*

desente (de-sen-te), adj. (Sp. *decente*) 1. decent; modest in behavior. Syn. *mahinhín, di-masagwáng kumilos.* 2. proper. Syn. *maayos, nása-ayos, tumpák.*

desentralisasyón (de-sen-tra-li-sas-yón), n. (Sp. *decentralizacion*) decentralization. Syn. *paghihiwa-hiwálay, pagkakahiwáhiwaláy.*

desesperado (de-ses-pe-ra-do), var. **desperado**, adj. (Sp.) 1. desperate; hopeless. Syn. *walâ nang pag-asa.* 2. losing hope; impatient; ready to run any risk. Syn. *abunidá.*

desgrasya (des-gras-ya), var. **disgrasya**, n. (Sp. *desgracia*) 1. mishap; accident. Syn. *sakunâ, aksidente, kapahamakán.* 2. misfortune; affliction. Syn. *kasawiangpalad; malakíng kabiguan.* 3. disgrace; dishonor. Syn. *kahihiyán; kasiraáng-puri.*

desgrasyada (des-gras-ya-da), var. **disgrasyada**, I. n. (Fem.: Sp. *desgraciada*) a woman who has been abused. Syn. *babaing pinagsamantalahán (ng lalaki).*
—II. adj. abused or dishonored, referring esp. to a virgin woman. Syn. *inabuso, pinagsamantalahán, ginahasà.*

desidido (de-si-di-do), var. **disidido**, adj. decided or determined, as in pursuing one's plan, etc. Syn. *determinado, buô na ang pasiyá.*

desimpekta (des-im-pek-ta), n. (Sp. *desinfectar*) a disinfecting or sterilizing; disinfection.

desinteresado (des-in-te-re-sa-do), adj. (Sp.) disinterested; impartial; unbiased. Syn. *waláng-kinikilingan; waláng pinápanigan.* 2. uninterested; indifferent. Syn. *di-interesado, waláng-hilig, waláng-interes.*

desisyón (de-sis-yón), n. (Sp. *decision*) 1. decision. Syn. *pasiyá, pagpapasiyá, kapasiyahan.* 2. judgement, as by a court. Syn. *hatol, paghatol, kahatulán.*

desmayá (des-ma-yá), var. **dismayá**, n. (Sp. *desmayar*) 1. discouragement; dismay. Syn. *pagkasirà ng loób.* 2. faint; swooning. Syn. *pagkawalá ng malay-tao (ulirat), paghihimatáy.*

desmoralisá

detensiyón

desmoralisá (des-mo-ra-li-sá), var. demoralisa, n. (Sp. desmoralizar) a demoralizing or being demoralized. Syn. pagsirà o pagkasirà ng loob.

desorganisado (des-or-ga-ni-sa-do), var. disorganisado, adj. (Sp. deorganizado) disorganized. Syn. maguló, walá sa ayos, waták-waták.

despalkado (des-pal-ka-do), var. dispalkado, adj. (Sp. desfalcado) 1. embezzled. Syn. nilustáy, nalustáy. 2. bankrupt, referring esp. to business.. Syn. bangkarote, bagsák, tumbado.

despatsa (des-pat-sa), var. dispatsa, n. (Sp. despachar) 1. dispatching; sending out. Syn. pagpapadalá, pagpapahatíd. 2. dismissing or being dismissed. Syn. pagtitiwalág, pagkakátiwalág; pagsisante, pagkakasisante. 3. sale, as of goods. Syn. pagbibilí. 4. selling price. Syn. halagá ng pagbibili. 5. completion, as of a work. Syn. pagtapos.

despatsadór (des-pat-sa-dór), var. dispatsadór, n. (Sp. despachador) 1. a bus, train, taxi, etc., dispatcher. Syn. tagapagpalabás ng mga sasakyán. 2. salesclerk; salesman (in a store). Syn. tindero, magtitindá, tagapagbilí.

despedida (des-pe-di-da), n. (Sp.) farewell; parting; leave-taking. Syn. pamamaalam, pagpapaalam.

despigurasyón (des-pi-gu-ras-yón), n. (Sp. desfiguracion) disfiguration. Syn. pagsira o pagkasira ng hugis (hitsura).

despotismo (des-po-tis-mo), n. (Sp.) 1. despotism; rule or government by a despot; autocracy. Syn. awtokrasya. 2. tyranny. Syn. kalupitan, pagkamápanili.

desproporsiyón (des-pro-por-si-yón), n. (Sp. desproporcion) lack of proportion; disproportion; disparity. Syn. pagkadipareho, pagkatagibang, katangibangán, kawalán ng proporsiyón.

despuwés (des-pu-wés), adv. (Sp. despues) then; later; after; afterwards. Syn. pagkatapos, pagkaraán.

desterado (des-te-ra-do), I. adj. (Sp.) exiled; banished. Syn. itinapon, ipinatapon. –II. n. an outcast; exile. Syn. tapon, taong itinapon.

destilá (des-ti-lá), var. distilá, n. (Sp. destilar) a distilling or being distilled; distallation.

destileriyá (des-ti-le-ri-yá), var. distileriyá, distileryá, n. (Sp. destileria) distillery. Syn. alakán, gáwaan ng alak, pabriká ng alak.

destinasyón (des-ti-nas-yón), var. distinasyón, n. (Sp. destinación) 1. destination; place where someone is bound for. Syn. paróroonán, púpuntahán, patútunguhan. 2. place where a thing is bound for. Syn. pagdádalhán, pagháhatirán. 3. fate; destiny. Syn. kapalaran, suwerte.

destino (des-ti-no), var. distino, n. (Sp.) 1. destiny; fate. Syn. kapalaran, suwerte, tadhanà. 2. assignment; post; job. Syn. trabaho, pinagtátrabahuhan. 3. purpose. Syn. pinag-uukulan, láyunin.

destonilyador (des-tor-nil-ya-dor), n. (Sp. destornillador) screwdriver.

destruksiyón (des-truk-si-yón), n. (Sp. destruccion) 1. act of destroying; destruction. Syn. pagwasak, pagwawasak; paggiba, paggigibâ; pagsirà, paninirà. 2. state or condition of being destroyed. Syn. pagkawasák, kawasakán, pagkasirà, pagkagibâ.

destrungka (des-trung-ka), n. (Sp. destroncar) act or manner of opening a lock forcibly.

desyerto (des-yer-to), var. disyerto, I. n. 1. desert; wilderness. Syn. iláng.
—II. adj. 1. deserted; uninhabited. Syn. ilang, waláng naninirahang tao. 2. (in contests, esp. literary) with or having all the entries disqualified.

detalyado (de-tal-ya-do), adj. (Sp. detalado) made or done in detail; detailed.

detektib (de-tek-tib; de-tek-tíb), n. (Eng.) a secret service man; detective. Syn. sekreta, tiktík.

detenido (de-te-ni-do), var. ditinido, adj. (Sp.) 1. detained; arrested. Syn. hinuli, náhuli; nakakulóng, ikinulóng. 2. delayed. Syn. naatraso, naabala.

detensiyón (de-ten-si-yón), var. ditensiyón, n. (Sp. detención) 1. detention; arrest. Syn. huli, paghuli; aresto, pag-aresto. 2. delay. Syn. abala, pagkaabala; pigil, pagkapigil. 3. a keeping in custody; confinement. Syn. pagkulóng, pagkukulóng, pagkakákulóng.

determinado **dikdík**

determinado (de-ter-mi-na-do), *adj.* (Sp.) 1. determined; resolved. Syn. *handa na o nakatalagá na ang loób; desidido.* 2. definite; specific. Syn. *tiyak.* 3. specified. Syn. *binábanggit, tinutukoy.*

determinasyón (de-ter-mi-nas-yón), *n.* (Sp. *determinacíon*) 1. a deciding; settling beforehand. Syn. *pagpapasiyá.* 2. strong resolution. Syn. *matibay na paghahangád, pagtitika.* 3. strong stand or belief. Syn. *paninindigan, matibay na paniniwalà.*

deteryorasyón (de-ter-yo-ras-yón), *n.* (Sp. *deterioracion*) 1. becoming worse; deterioration. Syn. *lalâ, paglalâ, paglubhâ.* 2. state or condition of being damaged. Syn. *pagkasirà.* 3. a becoming weaker. Syn. *paghinà, paghihinà.*

detonasyón (de-to-nas-yón), *n.* (Sp. *detonación*) 1. loud explosion. Syn. *malakás na putók.* 2. act of causing something to explode. Syn. *pagpapaputók, pagpápasabog, pagpápasambulat.*

di (dì), *adv.* (short for *hindi*) no; not.

di- (di-) a prefix or combining form, meaning: 1. no; not, as in *di-mabuti*, not good. 2. cannot; unable: as in *di-makapunta*, unable to go. 3. as an equivalent to the prefixes un- and in-, as in *di-karaniwan* (uncommon), *di-tiyák* (indefinite), etc.

di-akalain (di + a-ka-la-in), *adj.* 1. unthinkable; unbelievable; inconceivable. Syn. *di-kapaní-paniwalà, di-sukat akalain, di-mahihinagap.* 2. unexpected. Syn. *di-inaasahan.*

di-alám (di + a-lám), *adj.* unknown to; ignorant of. Syn. *di-batíd, waláng-kabátiran.*

dialekto (di-a-lek-to), var. diyalekto, *n.* (Sp. *dialecto*) dialect.

dialogó (di-a-lo-gó), var. diyalogo, *n.* (Sp.) dialog. Syn. *salitaan, usapan, pag-uusap, kombersasyón.*

diamante (di-a-man-te), var. diyamante, *n.* (Sp.) diamond. Syn. *brilyante.*

diametro (di-a-me-tro), var. diyametro, *n.* (Sp.) diameter. Syn. *bantod.* Cf. *lapad, luwáng.*

diarea (di-a-re-a), var. diyarres, diyarya, *n.* (Sp. *diarrea*) diarrhea. Syn. *pagtataé, bululós.*

dibán (di-bán), *n.* (Sp.) a low cushioned sofa; divan. Cf. *sopá.*

dibdíb (dib-díb), *n.* 1. a person's chest. 2. breast (of persons). Syn. *suso.* 3. breast (of fowls). Syn. *pitsó.* 4. (*Fig.*) heart. Syn. *pusò.*

dibdiban (dib-di-ban), *adj.* 1. with one's full efforts. Syn. *pángatawanan.* 2. not joking or trifling; sincere; serious. Syn. *tápat, tápatan.*

dibdibín (dib-di-bín), *v.* 1. to take (to heart) seriously; be deeply serious about. Syn. *totohanín.* 2. to feel hurt about. Syn. *damdamín.*

dibersiyón (di-ber-si-yón), *n.* (Sp. *diversion*) amusement; diversion. Syn. *líbangan, paglilibáng; áliwan, pag-aalíw.*

dibidendo (di-bi-den-do), *n.* (Sp. *dividendo*) 1. in racing, the amount of money that a ticket wins. 2. (*Comm.*) interest on investments or shares of stock; dividend.

dibinidád (di-bi-ni-dád), *n.* (Sp. *divinidad*) divinity. Syn. *kadiyusán, pagkadiyós; kabathalaan, pagkabathalà.*

dibino (di-bi-no), *adj.* (Sp. *divino*) 1. of, by, or from God; divine. 2. holy. Syn. *banál.*

di-birú-birô (di + bi-rú + bi-rô), *adj.* not just a few; very many. Syn. *nápakarami, katakut-takot.*

dibisyón (di-bis-yón), *n.* (Sp. *division*) 1. (Math.), act of dividing numbers; division. Syn. *paghahati o pagbabahagi (ng bilang o número).* 2. partition, as of properties. Syn. *paghahati, pagbabahagi, partisyón.* 3. a division in administrative set-up, usually under a bureau or department. Syn. *sangáy.*

dibórsiyó (di-bór-si-yó), *n.* (Sp. *divorcio*) divorce; annulment of marriage. Syn. *pagpapawaláng-bisà sa kasál.*

dibuho (di-bu-ho), *n.* (Sp. *dibujo*) 1. act or manner of drawing, sketching, or designing. Syn. *pagdodrowing, pagguhit ng larawan, pagdidibuho.* 2. a drawing; sketch. Syn. *drowing, larawang-guhit.* 3. pattern; design. Syn. *disenyo.*

di-kawasà (di + ka-wa-sà), *adv.* right away; at once; immediately.

dikdík (dik-tík), I. n. 1. act of pulverizing something by or as by pounding. Syn.

pagdurog, pagligís, pagpulbós. 2. continuous pounding or beating, as with fist blows. Syn. *abut-abot na suntók o bayó ng suntok.* 3. continuous attack, as with artillery. Syn. *bayó o pagbayó* (*colloq.*).
—II. *adj.* pulverized by or as by pounding. Syn. *duróg na duróg, pulbós na pulbós.*

dike (di-ke), n. (Sp. *dique*) 1. dike; dam. Syn. *saplád, prinsa.* 2. a small dam or dike, as of an irrigated field. Syn. *pilapil.*

dikín (di-kín), var. **gikín**, n. a pot support, usually circular and made of braided rattan or bamboo splits. Cf. *sálalayán, patungán.*

dikít[1] (di-kít), var. **rikit**, n. exquisite beauty; loveliness. Syn. *gandá, kagandahan; dilág, karilagán; alindóg, kaalindugán.*

dikit[2] (di-kit), n. 1. act of starting a fire, esp. for the purpose of cooking. Syn. *pagpaparikít ng apóy.* 2. start of fire; a beginning to burn. Syn. *pag-aapóy, pagdidingas, pag-aaláb.* 3. flame. Syn. *dingas* (*ningas*).

dikit[3] (di-kit), var. **digkit**, I. n. 1. act or manner of pasting something, as with paste or glue. Syn. *pagdidikít, pagkokola.* 2. the quality of paste, glue, etc. to stick on something. Syn. *pagdikit, pagkapit.* 3. the state or condition of being glued or pasted. Syn. *pagkakádikit.* 4. act of getting very close to another. Syn. *paglapit na mabuti.*
—II. *adj.* glued; pasted. Syn. *nakadikit, nakadigkít, nakakola.*

diko (di-ko), n. (Ch.) 1. the second eldest brother. Cf. *kuya, manong, kaka.* 2. the appellation given to the second eldest brother by younger brothers, sisters, and cousins.

diksiyón (dik-si-yón), n. (Sp. *diccion*) manner of speaking; enunciation; diction. Syn. *istilo ng pananalitâ, bigkás, pagbigkás.*

diksiyunaryo (dik-si-yu-nar-yo), n. (Sp. *diccionario*) dictionary. Syn. *talahuluganan, talásalitaan.*

dikta (dik-ta), n. (Sp. dicta) 1. act of dictating something for someone to write. Syn, *pagdidikta, pagbigkás o pagsasalitâ ng mga bagay na ibig ipasulat sa*

kapwà. 2. order; command. Syn. *utos, mando.*

diktadór (dik-ta-dór), n. (Sp. *dictador*) dictator. Cf. *harí-harian.*

dikunó (di-ku-nó), *adv.* it is said. Syn. *umano, di-umano, daw* (*raw*).

didál (di-dál), var. **dedál**, n. (Sp.) thimble.

diés (di-és), var. **diyés**, I. n. & *adj.* (Sp. *diez*) ten. Syn. *sampu.*
—II. n. 1. ten centavos. Syn. *sampúng sentimos.* 2. ten pesos. Syn. *sampúng piso.*

dieta (di-e-ta), var. **diyeta**, I. n. (Sp.) 1. diet; regulated nutrition. Syn. *balansing pagkain.* 2. daily allowance given to certain officials or employees. Syn. *perdiyém.*
—II. *adj.* (*Colloq.*) on diet. Syn. *magdidiyeta.*

diga (di-ga), n. (Sp.) 1. act of expressing one's opinion, etc. Syn. *pagpapahayag ng nilóloób.* 2. idle talk. Syn. *satsat, daldal, tsismis.* 3. an out-of-turn or uncalled for statement. Syn. *di-kailangang pagsasalita, walâ sa lugar na pagsasalitâ.* 4. act of expressing love to a woman. Syn. *paghahandóg ng pag-ibig, pagligaw.*

dighál (dig-hál), var. **digháy**, n. belching; eructation.

digmâ (dig-mâ), n. 1. act of attacking an enemy country with or without war declaration. Syn. *paglusob sa kaaway na bansâ.* 2. fight between or among nations; war. Syn. *giyera.* 3. relentless campaign against something bad, as gambling, criminalities, and the like. Syn. *kampanya laban sa masasamâ.*

dignidád (dig-ni-dád), n. (Sp.) dignity. Syn. *dangál, karangalan.*

di-hasâ (di + ha-sâ), *adj.* untrained. Syn. *di-sanáy.*

diín (di-ín), n. 1. act of pressing something with or as with the hand. Syn. *tiín, pagtingiín, pagdiriín.* 2. downward pressure, as of something heavy placed on another. Syn. *tindí, bigát.* 3. emphasis; stress; importance. Syn. *halagá, pagpapahalagá.* 4. (*Phonetics*) syllabic stress or accent. Syn. *asento.*

diít (di-ít), n. 1. slight contact or touch of one thing against another. Syn. *dait, daiti.*

2. act of touching or pressing something lightly on a surface. Syn. *pagdidiit*, *pagdadait*. 3. a light mark or imprint, as of a finger on the surface of something. Syn. *taták*, *marka*.

dilà (di-là), n. 1. the human tongue. 2. an animal tongue used for food. 3. act of sticking out one's tongue, as in showing dislike or hate for someone. Syn. *pagdila*. 4. act or manner of licking or lapping something with the tongue. Syn. *pagdilà*, *himod*, *paghimod*. 5. the flap under the strap of a shoe. 6. the vibrating piece of the red in a wind instrument. 7. a long, narrow flame.

dilà-dilà (di-là + di-là), var. diladilà, n. a native tongue-shaped cake, made of glutinous rice (*malagkit*) flour and cooked by dropping in boiling water. Syn. *palitáw*.

dilág (di-lág), n. 1. splendor; gorgeousness; lustrous beauty. Syn. *dikit*, *kariktán*; *ganda*, *kagandahan*; *alindóg*, *kaalindugán*. 2. a beautiful woman. Syn. *magandáng paraluman*.

diláng (di-láng), adj. all; every; any. Syn. *lahát*, *bawa't (bawat)*.

dilapidado (di-la-pi-da-do), adj. (Sp.) dilapidated. Syn. *sirá-sirá*, *wasák-wasák*, *gibá-gibá*.

dilát (di-lát), adj. awake; not sleeping. Syn. *gising*, *nakamulat ang mga matá*. 2. wide-opened, referring to an eye or eyes. 3. with or having wide-opened eyes. Syn. *malalakí ang matá*; *may malalaking matá*; *maluluwáng ang matá*. 4. educated; well-informed; civilized. Syn. *edukado*, *may pinag-aralan*, *sibilisado*.

diláw (di-láw), I. adj. with or having yellow color; yellow. Syn. *kulay-amarilyo*.
—II. n. 1. yellow; yellow color. Syn. *amarilyo*, *kulay na amarilyo*. 2. (Bot.) a gingerlike plant, called tumeric, the rhizomes of which are bright yellow, thick, and cylindric (*curcuma longa* Linn.); also, the rhizomes of this plant, which are commonly used as condiment, as ingredient of curry powder, and for coloring food and other materials.

dildil (dil-dil), n. 1. act of holding something with the fingers and pressing it hard into

or against another, as a small cut (piece) of green mango into salt. Cf. *dutdót*, *duldól*. 2. act of insisting something to someone. Syn. *giít*, *paggigiít*.

dilema (di-le-ma), n. (Sp.) dilemma; difficult situation; problem. Syn. *mahirap na kalagayan*, *suliranín*, *problema*.

dilì[1] (di-lì), n. 1. sense of judgement; understanding. Syn. *pag-unawa*, *pagkaunawa*. 2. consciousness. Syn. *malay*, *kamalayan*.

dilì[2] (di-lì), adv. 1. hardly, as in *kumain siyá dilì*, he hardly eats. 2. rarely; seldom, as in *dumalaw siyá dili sa amin*, he rarely visits us. 3. (with *kayâ*) if not; or else.

dilí-dili (di-lí + di-li), var. dilídili, n. 1. meditation; reflection; deep thought; contemplation. Syn. *bulay-bulay*, *pagbubulay-bulay*; *wari-wari*, *pagwawari-wari*. 2. memory. Syn. *alaala*, *gunitâ*.

dilíg (di-lig), I. n. 1. act or manner of watering plants with or as with a sprinkler; sprinkling with water. Syn. *pagdidilig*. 2. (Fig.) attention; care. Syn. *alaga*, *pag-aalaga*.
—II. adj. watered or sprinkled with water, referring to plants, street, etc. Syn. *dinilíg o nadilíg na*.

dilihénsiyá (de-li-hén-si-yá), n. (Sp. *diligencia*) 1. act or ability of finding ways and means to obtain what is badly needed. Syn. *kakayaháng makakuha ng bagay na kailangan*, *abilidád*. 2. anything obtained in this manner.

dilì-hindî (di-lì + hin-dî), adv. of course. *Dinadalaw niya kami, dili-hindi, nguni't napakadalang*. He visits us, of course, but very seldom. Syn. *kung sa bagay*.

dilím (di-lim), n. 1. dark; darkness. 2. (Fig.) obscurity; vagueness. Syn. *labo*, *kalabuan*.

dilis (di-lis) n. (Ichth.) a species of long-jawed anchovy (*Stolephorus commersoni*).

diliwariw (di-li-wa-riw), n. (Bot.) an erect or ascending, slightly branched, smooth shrub, called holly-leaved acanthus (*Acanthus ilicifolius* Linn.).

dilubyo (di-lub-yo), var. delubyo, n. (Sp. *deluvio*) a great flood; deluge. Syn. *gunáw*, *pagkagunáw*, *malaking bahâ*.

di-makaugagà (di + ma-ka-u-ga-ga), adj. unable to rest; with or having too much

di-man   **diperensiyá**

work; very busy. Syn. *napakatrabaho, waláng pahingá sa trabaho.*

di-man (di + man), *adv.* although not; even not. Syn. *kahit hindî, kulúb hindî.*

di-masaláng (di + ma-sa-láng), *adj.* that cannot be touched; intangible. Syn. *di-mahipó, di-masalát.*

dimdím (dim-dím), *n.* (obsolescent) 1. sorrow; sadness; grief. Syn. *lumbay, lungkot, pighati.* 2. ill feeling. Syn. *hinanakit, damdamin, sama ng loob.* 3. misgiving; anxiety. Syn. *pangambá, agam-agam.* See **panimdim.**

dimensiyón (di-men-si-yón), *n.* (Sp. dimension) 1. dimension; measurement. Syn. *sukat.* 2. extent; size. Syn. *lakí, lawak, sakláw.*

diminutibo (di-mi-nu-ti-bo), *adj.* (Sp. *diminutivo*) diminutive; tiny; small. Syn. *maliit, munti, bulilít.*

dimpol (dim-pol), *n.* (Eng.) dimple. Syn. *biloy, turupyâ, puyó sa pisngí.*

din (din), *var.* **rin**, *adv.* also; too; likewise. Syn. *pati, sakâ, man.*

dinamita (di-na-mi-ta), *n.* (Sp.) dynamite. Cf. *pampasabog.*

dinamo (di-na-mo), *n.* (Sp.) dynamo. Cf. *motór.*

dinampól (di-nam-pól), I. *adj.* dyed or colored with *dampól,* a locally made dye obtained esp. from a *sapang* tree.
—II. *n.* cloth colored with *dampól.*

dinasta (di-nas-ta), *n.* (Sp.) dynasty; a ruler, esp. a hereditary ruler. Syn. *harî.*

dindíng (din-ding), *var.* **dingding**, *n.* light partition wall in a house, usually of wood, bamboos, etc. Cf. *tabike.*

dine (di-ne), *var.* **dini, rini, rine**, *adv.* here; at or in this place. Syn. *dito, rito, sa lugar na itó, sa dakong itó.*

dinero (di-ne-ro), *n.* (Sp.) money. Syn. *kuwarta (kuwalta), pera, salapî.*

dinig (di-nig), *var.* **dingig**, I. *n.* 1. perception by the ears; hearing. Syn. *pagkádiníg (pagkarinig).* 2. fact, state, or quality of being heard. Syn. *pagigíng diníg.* 3. hearing, as of a case in court. Syn. *pagdinig (pagdingíg), paglilitis.* 4. act of listening to or hearing (something). Syn. *pakikinig.* 5. acoustics. Syn. *pakiníg, akustiká.*

—II. *adj.* loud enough to be heard; that can be heard; audible. Syn. *nápapakinggán, naririníg.*

diningding (di-ning-ding), *n.* (Ilok.) a dish of fish and vegetables. Cf. *bulanglang, pinakbét.*

dinosauro (di-na-sa-u-ro), *n.* (Zool., Sp.) dinosaur.

dinsulan (din-su-lan), *n.* inkwell. Syn. *tintero.*

dinugán (di-nu-gán), *var.* **dinuguán**, I. *n.* dish of animal entrails and blood, seasoned with vinegar, garlic, salt, etc.
—II. *adj.* cooked or made into *dinuguán.*

dingal (di-ngal), *var.* **ringal**, *n.* 1. splendor; glory. Syn. *luwalhati, kaluwalhatian.* 2. pomp; exquisite beauty. Syn. *dilag, karilagán.*

dingas (di-ngas), *var.* **lingas, ningas**, *n.* 1. start of fire. Syn. *pagdiringas, pagliliyáb.* 2. flame. Syn. *alab, liyáb.*

dinggín (ding-gin), *var.* **dinigín**, *v.* 1. to listen to; hear; pay attention to what one is saying. Syn. *pakinggán.* 2. to hear or conduct a hearing or trial, as of a case in court. Syn. *litisin.* 3. to hear or obey. Syn. *sundín.*

dipá (di-pá), *n.* 1. act of extending the arms fully at the sides. Syn. *pagdipá, pag-uunat ng mga braso sa tagiliran.* 2. the position of the arms stretched fully at the sides. 3. the length equal to the stretch of the arms on both sides.

diperensiyá (di-pe-ren-si-yá), *n.* (Sp. *diferencia*) 1. difference. Syn. *kaibhan, pagkakaibá.* 2. the amount in excess of one number from another. Syn. *higit, kahigtán; labis, kalabisán; sobra, kasobrahán.* 3. the amount one number is less than another. Syn. *kulang, kakulangan.* 4. illness; indisposition. Syn. *karamdaman, sakit, pagkakásakit, kapansanan.* 5. disagreement. Syn. *hidwaan, di-pagkakásundo, sámaan ng loób, kagalitan.* 6. mental aberration. Syn. *sirà (colloq.), sirà ng ulo.* 7. defect; mechanical disorder; imperfection. Syn. *depekto, aberiya, sirà, kasiraan.* 8. problem; matter of difficulty. Syn. *súliranín, problema.* 9. mishap; accident. Syn. *aksidente, sakunâ.* 10. reason; cause. Syn.

dahilán, sanhî. 11. menses; menstruation.
Syn. regla, sapanahón. 12. damage; harm
or injury. Syn. pinsala, kapinsalaán; sira,
kasiraán.

diploma (di-plo-ma), n. (Eng., Sp.) diploma.
Cf. katibayan o sertipiko (ng karangalan,
pagtató s, atb.).

diplomatikó (di-plo-ma-ti-kó), n. (Sp.
diplomático) I. n. diplomat. Syn. diplomatá.
—II. adj. 1. diplomatic; of or having to
do with diplomacy. Syn. ng o ukol sa
diplomasya. 2. skillfull in dealing with
people; tactful. Syn. magaling sa
diplomasya o sa pakikipagkapwa.

dipterya (dip-ter-ya), n. (Sp. difteria)
diphtheria.

diptonggo (dip-tong-go), n. (Sp. diptongo)
diphthong. Syn. kambál-patinig.

diputado (di-pu-ta-do), n. (Sp.) deputy;
representative; delegate; congressman.
Syn. representante, kinatawán, delegado,
kongresista.

dirà (di-rà), var. lira, n. watery discharge
from the eyes that thickens at the corners,
causing them to become red and swollen;
rheum of the eyes.

direksiyón (di-rek-si-yón), n. (Sp. direccion)
1. address; place of residence. Syn. tirahan,
tinitirahan, tahanan. 2. mailing address.
Syn. pahatirang-sulat. 2. the way or course
one may go or point. Syn. dako, banda,
gawî. 3. supervision; management;
administration. Syn. pamamahala,
pangangasiwà, pamamatnugot, maneho,
pagmamaneho, administrasyón. 4.
instruction; guide to follow in doing
something. Syn. panuto, tagubilin. 5. order;
command. Syn. utos, mando, orden. 6.
definite course of destination. Syn.
púpuntahán, patutunguhan, destinasyón.

direkta (di-rek-ta), I. adj. (Sp. directa) direct;
straight. Syn. deretso, tuwíd, túwiran,
tulúy-tulóy.
—II. n. 1. direction; supervision. Syn.
pamamahalá, pangangasiwà; maneho,
pagmamaneho; pamamátnugot. 2. order;
command. Syn. utos, mando.

direktiba (di-rek-ti-ba), n. (Sp. directiva) 1.
general instructions or order; directive.
Syn. utos, kautusan, tagubilin. 2. board of

directors; officers. Syn. patnugutan, lupón
ng mga patnugot, pámunuán.

direktór (di-rek-tór), n. (Sp. director) 1.
director; manager. Syn. tagapamahala,
tagapangasiwà, tagapamátnugot. 2. editór.
Syn. patnugot, editór. 3. music director.
Syn. patnugot.

direktoryo (di-rek-tor-yo), n. (Sp. directorio)
1. a book of directions; also, a list of names
and addresses. Syn. aklat o talaan ng mga
pangalan at tirahan. 2. board of directors;
officers. Syn. patnugután, lupon ng mga
patnugot, pamunuán.

diri (di-ri), n. 1. a feeling of dislike or disgust
for something dirty or foul. Syn. rimarim,
panririmarim; aní, panganganí. 2.
abhorrence; detestation; loathing. Syn.
suya, pagkasuya; suklám, pagkasuklám.

dirihí (di-ri-hí), n. (Sp. dirigir) 1. direction;
supervision. Syn. pangangasiwà,
pamamahalà, pamamátnugot. 2. guidance.
Syn. pamamátnubay. 3. order; command.
Syn. utos, mando.

diskitá (dis-ki-tá), n. (Sp. desquitar) turning
of one's ire or retaliation at someone who
is not the real culprit.

disko (dis-ko), n. (Sp. disco) 1. disk. Cf.
plato. 2. phonograph plate. Syn. plaka (ng
ponógrapó).

diskompiyadó (dis-kom-pi-ya-do), adj. (Sp.
desconfiado) distrustful. Syn. waláng-
tiwalà, di-nagtitiwalà; alinlangan, nag-
áalinlangan; duda, nagdududa, mag-duda.

diskresyón (dis-kres-yón), var. diskrisyon,
n. (Sp. discrecion) 1. discretion;
disposition; good judgement or decision.
Syn. mabuting pagpapasiyá. 2. caution;
prudence. Syn. ingát, pag-iingat.

diskriminasyón (dis-kri-mi-nas-yón), n. (Sp.
discriminacion) discrimination; unequal
dealing. Syn. di-parehong pakikitungo,
pagtatangì.

diskubre (dis-ku-bré), var. diskubri, n. (Sp.
descubrir) a discovering or being
discovered; discovery. Syn. tuklás,
pagtuklás.

diskurso (dis-kur-so), n. (Sp. discurso)
speech; discourse. Syn. talumpatì.

diskusyón (dis-kus-yón), n. (Sp. discusion)
1. discussion; exchange of opinions. Syn.

diskuwalipiká

distinggido

pálitáng-kurò, talakayán. 2. debate. Syn. *pagtatalo, debate.*

diskuwalipiká (dis-ku-wa-li-pi-ká), n. (Sp. *descalificar*) a disqualifying or being disqualified; disqualification. Syn. *pagaalis ng karapatán o pagkaalís ng karapatán.*

diseksiyón (di-sek-si-yón), n. (Sp. *diseccion*) 1. dissection. Syn. *pagpipira-piraso sa katawan upang masusing mabuti.* 2. detailed examination. Syn. *masusing pagsusurì.*

diseminasyón (di-se-mi-nas-yón), n. (Sp. *deseminaccion*) dissemination; propagation. Syn. *pagpapakalat, pagpapalaganap.*

disenyo (di-sen-yo), n. (Sp. *diseño*) design; drawing; sketch; plan. Syn. *dibuho, drowing, plano.*

disertasyón (di-ser-tas-yón), n. (Sp. *disertacion*) formal discussion of a subject; dissertation. Syn. *maanyong pagtalakay.*

disgusto (dis-gus-to), n. (Sp.) 1. disgust; displeasure; disappointment. Syn. *pagkabigô, kabiguán.* 2. vexation. Syn. *yamót, pagkayamót; inís, pagkainís; suyà, pagkasuyà.* 3. quarrel; misunderstanding; disagreement. Syn. *sámaan ng loób, dipagkakáunawaán, alitan, hinanakitan.*

disilabó (di-si-la-bó), I. n. dissyllable; a word of two syllables. Syn. *salitang dadalawahing-pantíg.*

—II. *adj.* dissyllabic; consisting of two syllables. Syn. *dadalawahing-pantíg.*

disimulá (di-si-mu-lá), n. (Sp. *disimular*) 1. toleration; justification. Syn. *pagkukunsinte.* 2. dissimulation; pretense; hypocrisy; deception. Syn. *pagkukunwarî, panlilinlang.*

disimulado (di-si-mu-la-do), *adj.* (Sp.) 1. tolerated; justified. 2. sly; underhanded. Syn. *pakunwarî.*

disín (di-sín), *adv. & conj.* a particle used to express a mild regret, more or less equivalent to the phrases "would have" or "might have:" as in: *Kung nárito ka, disin, nákita mo siya.* If you were here, you would have seen him. Cf. *sana.*

disinteriya (di-sin-te-ri-ya), var. **disinteryá**, n. (Sp. *disenteria*) dysentery. Syn. *iti, pagiiti, daragis.*

disiplina (di-si-pli-na), n. (Sp. *disiplina*) discipline, specifically: 1. (Educ.) branch of knowledge or learning. Syn. *sangáy ng karunungan.* 2. self-training to develop self-control, character, efficiency, etc. Syn. *pagsasanay.* 3. self-control; orderly conduct. Syn. *hinahon, kahinahunan.* 4. submission to authorities. Syn. *paggalang o pagsunód sa nakátataás.* 5. restrictive policy; system of rules. Syn. *pátakaran.* 6. punishment. Syn. *parusa.*

disipuló (di-sí-pu-ló), n. (Sp. discipilo) 1. apostle; disciple. Syn. *apostolés, alagád.* 2. follower, as of a political leader. Syn. *tauhan, alagad, tagasunód.* 4. student; pupil. Syn. *mag-aarál, estudyante, pupiló.*

disiseis (di-si-se-is), *adj. & n.* (Sp.) sixteen. Syn. *labíng-anim.*

disonánsiyá (di-so-nan-si-ya), n. (Sp. *disonancia*) dissonance; disharmony. Syn. *wala sa tono, kawalán sa tono.*

disonante (di-so-nan-te), *adj.* (Sp.) dissonant; harsh in sound; not harmonious. Syn. *walá sa tono, disintonado.*

dispensa (dis-pen-sa), n. (Sp.) excuse. Syn. *paumanhín.*

dispensaryo (dis-pen-sar-yo), n. (Sp. *dispensario*) 1. dispensary; medical clinic. Syn. *klinika.* 2. pharmacy. Syn. *parmasya, botika.*

dispensasyon (dis-pen-sas-yon), n. (Sp. *dispensación*) 1. excuse. Syn. *paumanhín.* 2. official permission; permit. Syn. *pahintulot, kapahintulutan.* 3. distribution; dispensation. Syn. *pamamahagi, pamimigáy, pagkakalat, pagmumudmód.*

dispepsiyá (dis-pep-si-ya), n. (Sp. *dispepsia*) dyspepsia; indigestion. Syn. *di-pagkatunaw ng kinain, indihesyón.*

disposisyón (dis-po-sis-yón), n. (Sp. *disposicion*) disposition; decision. Syn. *pasiyá, pagpapasiyá, kapasiyahan.*

distansiyá (dis-tan-si-yá), n. (Sp. *distancia*) 1. distance; remoteness of a thing from another. Syn. *layò, kalayuan.* 2. distance between two places. Syn. *agwát, pagitan.* 3. difference; disparity. Syn. *pagkakáiba, kaibhán.*

distinggido (dis-ting-gi-do), *adj.* (Sp. *distinguido*) 1. great. Syn. *dakilà.* 2. distinguished; famous; well-known. Syn.

distribusyón   **diyunyor**

bantóg, tanyág, balita, kilalang-kilala. 3.
distinguished from another or others. Syn.
iba, naiibá.

distribusyón (dis-tri-bus-yón), n. (Sp.
distribucion) disribution. Syn. *pamamahagi,
pagkakalat, pamimigay, pagmumudmód.*

distrito (dis-tri-to), n. (Sp.) district. Syn.
purók.

Disyembre (Dis-yem-bre), n. (Sp. *Diciembre)*
December, the last month of the year.

dito (di-to), var. **rito,** *adv.* here; in this place.
Syn. *dini, rini. ditse (dit-se),* n. (Ch.)
appelation for the second eldest sister. Cf.
manang, ate.

ditso (dit-so), n. (Sp. *dicho)* 1. lines of an
actor or actress in a *komedya* play. 2.
(*Colloq.*) a contradiction. Syn. *tatsa.* 3.
short for *diyuditso.*

di-umanó (di + u-ma-nó), *adv.* according to
some (unreliable) information; as said by
someone. Syn. *alinsunod sa balità.*

diwà (di-wà), n. 1. consciousness. Syn.
malay-tao, ulirat. 2. sense; meaning. Syn.
kahulugan. 3. central point; core. Syn.
ubod (fig.) 4. sense; common sense. Syn.
bait, isip, sentido-komun. 5. gist; main idea.
Syn. *buod.* 6. content, as of a speech. Syn.
laman, nilalaman. 7. idea; message. Syn.
mensahe, layunin. 8. soul; spirit. Syn.
kaluluwa (kaluluwà).

diwang (di-wang), also, **pagdiriwang,** n.
celebration; festivity. Syn. *pagdaraos ng
kasayahan, pagsasaya, selebrasyón.*

diwarà (di-wa-ra), var. **riwara,** n. 1.
meticulosity; scrupulosity. Syn. *kakuririan,
pagkakuriri; kabusisian, pagkamabusisi.* 2.
change from good to bad; reverses;
misfortune; damage. Syn. *pagkapinsala,
pagkápahamak, disgrasya, kasawiang-palad.*

diwasà (di-wa-sà), var. **riwasa,** n. abudance,
as of wealth; plentifulness; wealthiness.
Syn. *kayamanan, kasaganaan.* See
kariwasaán.

diwatà (di-wa-tà), n. 1. beautiful, lovely
maiden. Syn. *maganda't kaibig-ibig na
dalaga.* 2. muse. Syn. *musa, paraluman,
lakambini.* 3. fairy. Syn. *ada.* 4. nymph.
Syn. *nimpa.* 5. goddess. Syn. *diyosa,
bathaluman.*

diyabetes (di-ya-be-tes), var. **diabetes,**

diyabetis, n. (Sp., Eng.) diabetes. Syn.
pag-ihi ng matamis.

diyablo (di-yab-lo; di-yab-lo), var. **diablo,**
n. devil; demon. Syn. *demonyo.*

diyakonó (di-ya-ko-nó), n. (Sp. *diacono)*
deacon; clergyman ranking just below a
priest.

diyagnosis (di-yag-no-sis), n. (Sp., Eng.)
diagnosis. Syn. *pagsusuri ng karamdaman.*

diyán (di-yán), var. **riyán,** *adv.* 1. there; in
that place (near the person spoken to).
Cf. *doon, roón.* 2. in that (matter). Syn.
sa ganyán, sa ganyáng bagay.

Diyana (Di-ya-na), var. **Diana,** n. (Sp.
Diana) in Rom. mythol., the goddess of
the moon, of hunting, and of virginity;
Diana.

diyanitór (di-ya-ni-tór), var. **dyánitór,** n.
(Eng.) janitor. Syn. *tagapaglinis.*

diyaryo (di-yar-yo), var. **diario,** I. n. (Sp.
diario) 1. daily newspaper. Syn. *pahayagang
pang-araw-araw.* 2. journal; magazine.
Syn. *magasin.* 3. daily wage. Syn. *sahod sa
isang araw.*

—II. *adj.* daily. Syn. *sa isáng araw, bawa't
araw, araw-araw.*

diyás (di-yás), var. **dyás,** n. (Eng.) jazz.

di-yatà (di-ya-tà), *interj.* Is it true! Really!
Syn. *Siyanga ba! Talaga!* Distinguished
from **di-ya-ta.**

di-yatà (di + ya-tà), *adv.* perhaps not;
possibly not. Syn. *marahil ay hindi,
malamang na hindi.*

diyés (di-yés), var. **diés,** I. n. & *adj.* (Sp. *diez)*
ten. Syn. *sampú*

—II. n. ten centavos. Syn. *sampúng
sentimos.* 2. ten pesos. Syn. *sampúng piso.*

diyeta (di-ye-ta), var. **dieta,** I. n. (Sp.) 1.
regulated or prescribed meal; diet. Syn.
balansing pagkain. 2. per diem; daily
allowance given to a worker. Syn.
perdiyém.

Diyós (Di-yós), var. **Dios,** n. (Sp.) God. Syn.
Bathalà, Maykapál, Lumikhâ.

diyosa (di-yo-sa), var. **diosa,** n. (Sp.) n.
goddess. Cf. *bathaluman, paraluman.*

diyudisto (di-yu-dit-so), n. (Eng.) jujitsu.
See **ditso** (3).

diyudo (di-yu-do), n. (Eng.) judo; jujitsu.

diyunyor (di-yun-yor), n. (Eng.) n. & *adj.*

diyús-diyusan   **donselya**

junior. Syn. *bata, anák*.

diyús-diyusan (di-yús + di-yu-san), n. false god.

do (do), n. (*Mus.*) the first and last note or tone in the diatonic scale.

doble (do-ble), var. **duble**, l. n. 1. double, anything twice as large, as many, or as much. Syn. *ibayong dami o laki*. 2. a fold. Syn. *lupi, tupi, tiklop*. 3. a second ply. Syn. *ikalawang patong or sapin*.

doble-antso (do-ble + an-tso), adj. (Sp. *doble + ancho*) with or having double width, referring to cloth.

doble-kara (do-ble + ka-ra), adj. (Sp. *doble + cara*) double-face; two-faced; deceitful; treacherous. Syn. *may-dalawang mukha, traidór, mapanlinlang, taksil*.

doktór (dok-tór), n. (Sp., Eng.) 1. doctor; physician; doctor of medicine. Syn. *manggagamot*. Cf. *doktora*. 2. a doctorate degree. Syn. *doktorado*.

doktór-laway (dok-tór + la-way), n. a quack doctor. Syn. *erbularyo*.

doktrina (dok-tri-na), n. (Sp. *doctrina*) 1. doctrine; teaching. Syn. *turo, aral*. 2. belief. Syn. *paniwala, paniniwalà*.

dokumento (do-ku-men-to), var. **dukumento**, n. (Sp. *documento*) 1. document; anything printed or written, serving as proof. Syn. *kasulatan; nakasulat na katibayan*. 2. specifically: (a) land title. Syn. *titulo o dokumento ng lupa*. (b) animal registry. Syn. *kasulatan o rehistro ng hayop*.

dogma (dog-ma), n. (Eng., Sp.) 1. dogma; doctrine. Syn. *aral, turo, doktrina*. 2. belief. Syn. *paniwala, paniniwalà*.

dogmátikó (dog-ma-ti-ko), adj. (Sp. *dogmatico*) 1. doctrinal. Syn. *pandoktrina; sa o ukol sa mga aral o turo ng Iglesya*. 2. arrogant in expressing opinions. Syn. *mapagmataas; matigas magsalita, palaló*.

dolar (do-lar), var. **dolyar**, n. (Sp.) dollar, a monetary unit of the United States equal to 100 cents.

domestikahín (do-mes-ti-ka-hin), v. 1. to tame; domesticate. Syn. *paamuin, mansuhin*. 2. to accustom to home life. Syn. *sanayin sa buhay pantahanan*.

doméstikó (do-més-ti-kó), adj. (Sp.*domestico*) 1. tame. Syn. *maamó,*

mabait, manso. 2. of the family. Syn. *ng pamilya, ng mag-anak, pangmag-anak, pampamilya*. 3. of the home. Syn. *ng tahanan, pantahanan*. 4. local; of one's country. Syn. *sa o ng sariling bayan, lokál*.

dominante (do-mi-nan-te), adj. (Sp.) 1. inclined to dominate; domineering. Syn. *mapaniil, mapanupil*. 2. influential. Syn. *nakapangyayari, nakapaghahari*, 3. rising above others. Syn. *nangingibabaw; nakatataas*.

dominikano (do-mi-ni-ka-no), n. & adj. (Sp. *dominicano*) dominican.

dóminó (dó-mi-nó; do-mi-nó), n. (Sp.) 1. the game of dominoes. 2. a chip used in this game. 3. a kind of robe or cloak with wide sleeves, hood, and mask, worn at masquarades. 4. a small black mask for the eyes. Syn. *maliit na maskarang itim para sa matá*.

dominyo (do-min-yo), n. (Sp. *dominio*) domain. Syn. *lupang sakop ng ibáng bansâ*.

Dominggo (Do-ming-go), n. (Sp. *Domingo*) 1. Sunday, the first day of the week. Syn. *Linggo, Dinggo* (*colloq.*). 2. masculine name, the original spelling, *Domingo*, is more preferred.

Dominggo de Ramos, n. Palm Sunday. Syn. *Linggo ng Palaspás*

don (don), n. 1. a Spanish title of respect, used with the given name, as in *Don Juan*. Cf. *Ginoo* (G.), *Máginoó, Senyor*. 2. a distinguished man. Syn. *tanyag na tao, maginoo*. 3. a Spanish nobleman or gentleman.

donasyón (do-nas-yón), n. (Sp. *donacion*) 1. act of donating or giving something, as to charitable institutions. Syn. *pagkakaloob o pagbibigay ng tulong, regalo, etc.* 2. anything donated. Syn. *bagay na ipinagkaloob o ibinigay, abuloy, ambag, handog*.

donat (do-nat), n. (Eng.) doughnut.

donor (do-nor), n. (Eng.) donor; giver. Syn. *ang nagkaloob, donadór, donante*.

donselya (don-sel-ya), l. n. (Sp. *docella*) 1. maid; maiden. Syn. *dalaga*. 2. a woman who has not had sexual intercourse; virgin. Syn. *babaing wala pang karanasán (sa buhay)*.

—II. *adj.* virgin or chaste, referring to a woman. Syn. *wala pang karanasan sa buhay, hindi pa nagagaláw.*

Donya (Don-ya), *n.* (Sp. *Doña*) 1. a Spanish title of respect, used with the given name of the elderly woman. Syn. *Senyora, Ginang (Gng.)* 2. a distinguished Spanish woman. Cf. *Don.*

doón (do-ón), var. **roon**, *adv.* there (far from both the speaker and the one addressed); in that place.

dorado (do-ra-do), var. **durado**, *adj.* 1. gilded; golden. Syn. *ginintuan.* 2. gold-plated. Syn. *lubog sa ginto.*

dormitoryo (dor-mi-tor-yo), *n.* (Sp.) dormitory; boarding house. Syn. *bahay-panuluyan.*

dosena (do-se-na), *n.* (Sp. *docena*) dozen. Syn. *labindalawa.*

dosé-dosena (do-sé + do-se-na), *adj. & adv.* by dozen. Syn. *por dosena.*

dosis (do-sis), *n.* (Sp.) dose (of medicine). Syn. *dami ng gamot na iniinom sa bawat tunggâ.*

dosyentos (dos-yen-tos), var. **dosiyentos**, *n. & adv.* (Sp. *dos cientos*) two hundred. Syn. *dalawang-daán.*

dote (do-te), *n.* (Sp.) dowry. Syn. *bigay-kaya, bilang* (in some areas).

draga (dra-ga), *n.* (Sp.) dredge; dredging machine.

dragón (dra-gon), *n.* (Sp.) dragon; a mythical monster. Cf. *dambuhala.*

dram (dram), *n.* (Eng.) 1. drum; barrel-like container of oil, etc. Cf. *bariles.* 2. (Mus.) drum. Syn. *bombo, tamból.*

drama (dra-ma), *n.* (Eng., Sp.) drama; stage play. Syn. *dulà.*

dramaturgo (dra-ma-tur-go), *n.* (Sp.) dramatist; playwright. Syn. *mandudula, manunulat ng dulà.*

dramer (dra-mer), *n.* (Eng.) drummer. Syn. *tambolero, bombista.*

drástikó (drás-ti-kó), *adj.* (Sp. *drastico*) acting with force or violence; drastic. Syn. *marahás, mahigpit, malupit.*

drenahe (dre-na-he), *n.* (Sp. *drenaje*) drainage. Syn. *páagusan, kanál.*

dril (dril), *n.* (Eng., Sp.) a boring tool or apparatus; drill. Syn. *barena.*

dromedaryo (dro-me-dar-yo), *n.* (Sp. *dromedario*) dromedary; camel trained for fast riding. Syn. *kamelyong sasakyan.*

drowing (dro-wing), *n.* (Eng.) 1. drawing; act of designing. Syn. *pagdidibuho, pagdodrowing.* 2. a design or drawing. Syn. *larawang-guhit.*

dubdób (dub-dób), var. **rubdob**, *n.* 1. big blaze or flame caused by fanning or by adding more fuel. Syn. *lagablab, malaking ningas.* 2. intensity; ardency. Syn. *sidhi, kasidhian.*

dukado (du-ka-do), *n.* (Sp. *ducado*) duchy; dukedom.

dukál (du-kal), I. *n.* 1. act of digging the soil little by little, as with a trowel. Cf. *bungkal, dungkal.* 2. a small hole or depression in the ground, made by scratching or digging little by little, as with a trowel.

—II. *adj.* dug up or loosened with or as with a trowel.

dukdók (duk-dók), I. *n.* act of pounding or crushing something with or as with a small pestle. Syn. *dikdik, bayo.*

duke (du-ke), *n.* (Sp. *duque*) duke.

dukesa (du-ke-sa), *n.* (Sp. *duquesa*) duchess; wife or widow of a duke. Syn. *asawa o biyuda ng duke.*

dukhâ (duk-hâ), I. *adj.* poor; needy; destitute; indigent. Syn. *mahirap, naghihirap; maralita, nagdaralita; pobre*
—II. *n.* an indigent person. Syn. *taong maralitâ.* Cf. *pulubi.*

dukit (du-kit), *n.* 1. act or manner of gouging or digging out something with or as with a finger. Syn. *ukit, pag-ukit.* 2. a small hole, cavity, or depression on a surface, made by gouging. Syn. *ukit.*

dukláy (duk-láy), *n.* act or manner of reaching for something by extending the arms. Syn. *abot, pag-abot; dukwang, pagdukwang.*

dukmô (duk-mô), *n.* the position of the head with the face resting on both arms.

dukot (du-kot), *n.* 1. act of drawing out something, as from one's pocket, from a box, bag, hole, etc. Syn. *bunot, hugot.* 2. act of picking someone's pocket. Syn. *pandurukot.* 3. act of kidnapping someone. Syn. *pagdukot.*

dukwáng (duk-wáng), n. 1. act or manner of reaching for something by leaning the body forward to increase the reach of the hand. Cf. *abot ng kamay*. 2. the distance reached by the hand in this manner. Syn. *layo ng abot ng kamay*.

duda (du-da), I. n. (Sp.) 1. doubt. Syn. *alinlangan, pag-aalinlangan*. 2. apprehension. Syn. *pangambá, kabá*.

duelo (du-e-lo), var. **duwelo**, n. (Sp.) duel. Cf. *labanan, sukatán ng lakas*.

dueto (du-e-to), var. **duweto**, n. (Sp.) 1. duet; composition for two voices or two instruments. Syn. *awit o tugtugin sa dalawahang tinig o para sa dalawang instrumento*. 2. the two performers singing or playing a duet. Syn. *ang magkaduweto o magkasaliw*.

dugô (du-gô), n. 1. blood. 2. menses; menstruation. Syn. *regla, sapanahon*. 3. (Fig.) one's child or offspring. Syn. *anak, supling, laman* (fig.)

dugsóng (dug-sóng), n. 1. act of adding a part to increase the length or width. Syn. *hugpong, paghuhugpong; dugtong, pagdurugtong*. 2. the part added to lengthen or widen. Syn. *hugpong, dugatong, sugpong*. 3. a continuation or addition to something. Syn. *karugtong*.

dugtóng (dug-tóng), n. 1. act of connecting or joining two or more things together to increase the length. Syn. *pagkakabit-kabit*. 2. increasing the length by adding a portion. Syn. *pagpapahaba sa pamamagitan ng pagdurugtong*. 3. annex; extension; addition. Syn. *dugsong, hugpong*. 4. a continuation. Syn. *karugtong*. 5. the point or place of connection. Syn. *pinagdugtungan, pinagsugpungan*.

dugtungan (dug-tu-ngan), I. n. 1. point of connection; joint. Syn. *hugpungan, pinaghugpungan; sugpungan, pinagsugpungan*. 2. a serialized novel, article, etc. written by two or more authors.

duhagí (du-ha-gí), I. adj. 1. maltreated. Syn. *api, ináapi*. 2. looked down upon. Syn. *hináhamak, dinudustá*.

—II. n. state or condition of being maltreated or looked down upon.

duhapang (du-ha-pang), n. 1. act of stretching the body forward in an effort to reach for or seize something. Cf. *dukwáng*. 2. a rushing forward, as in attacking someone with or as with fist blows. Syn. *daluhong, sugod*. 3. the act or practice of an opportunist. Syn. *pagsasamantala, pagkamapagsamantala*. 4. an opportunist. Syn. *taong mapagsamantala*.

duhat (du-hat), n. (Bot.) 1. a smooth tree, known as Java plum or black plum (*Syzygium cumini*). 2. the fruit of this tree, which is oval to elliptic, dark-purple, luscious, fleshy, and edible.

dulà (du-là), n. drama; stage play. Syn. *drama, sarsuwela*.

dúlaan (du-la-an), n. theater. Syn. *teatro*.

dulang (du-lang), n. a kind of low dining table. Syn. *hapág, mababang mesa*.

dúlangan (dú-la-ngan), n. 1. a place where one can acquire knowledge, as school, colleges, universities, and the like. Syn. *paaralan*. 2. place where ores are being mined. Syn. *minahan*.

dulas (du-lás), n. 1. a slipping or sliding, as on a slippery surface. Syn. *dupilas, pagkadupilas*. 2. slipperiness. Syn. *kadulasan, pagkamadulas*. 3. (Colloq.) misstatement. Syn. *maling pangungusap*.

dulayanin (du-la-ya-nin), n. (Otag.) an ancient boat song.

duldól dul-dól), n. 1. act or shoving or thrusting a thing on someone or something. Cf. *dildil, silsil*. 2. act of offering something forcibly to someone, as food by shoving it into the mouth. 3. instigation. Syn. *sulsol, pagsusulsol*.

dulíng (du-líng), I. adj. having cross-eye; cross-eyed. Syn. *salubóng ang matá, haláng ang matá*. Cf. *banlag*.

—II. n. 1. state or condition of being cross-eyed. Syn. *pagkadulíng, kadulingán*. 2. a cross-eyed person. Syn. *taong haláng ang matá*.

dulo (du-lo), n. 1. end; extremity; terminal. Syn. *sukdulan, hangganan*. 2. point; tip. Syn. *tulis*. 3. end; conclusion. Syn. *wakas, katapusan*. 4. result; outcome. Syn. *bunga, resulta, kinalabasan*.

dulóg   **dupleks**

dulóg (du-log), n. 1. appearance before a person in authority to present a complaint or to ask for help. Syn. *pagharap (sa maykapangyarihan)*. 2. act of going to the table in order to eat. Syn. *pagtungo sa mesa upang kumain*. 3. civil marriage, as distinguished from church marriage. Syn. *kasal-huwes*.

dulóng (du-lóng), n. (*Ichth.*) 1. fish called starry goby (*Mirogobius stellatus*). 2. fry of anchovies (*Family Engraulidae*).

dulot (du-lot), n. 1. act of offering or presenting something to someone. Syn. *pagkakaloob, pagbibigay*. 2. act of serving (food) to. Syn. *pagpapakain, pagbibigay ng pagkain*. 3. anything given or offered, as a gift or present. Syn. *handog, regalo, alaala*. 4. number of servings given to someone. Syn. *bulos*.

dulse (dul-se), n. (Sp. *dulce*) sweet conserve; dessert. Syn. *matamis, panghimagas*.

dulsera (dul-se-ra), n. (Sp. *dulcera*) dessert dish or container. Syn. *lalagyan ng matamis*.

duluhan (du-lu-han), I. n. 1. backyard. Syn. *likod-bahay*. 2. end or extremity, as of a road. Syn. *dulo, hangganan*. 3. boundary as between two barrios, towns, etc. Syn. *hangganan*.

dumako (du-ma-ko), v. to go to a certain place or direction. Syn. *gumawi, tumungo*.

Dumagat (Du-ma-gat), n. (*Anthrop.*) a Philippine tribe living along the shores of Quezon Province, bordering the Pacific Ocean.

dumal (du-mal), var. **rumal**, n. degradedness or baseness of one's deeds or character; shamefulness; disgracefulness. Syn. *kahamakan, karawalan, kaimbihan*.

dumalaga (du-ma-la-ga), n. 1. a young hen; pullet. 2. a young cow that has not borne a calf; heifer; also a young mare, or a young female carabao.

dumat (du-mat), n. a being slow or sluggish, as in one's work. Syn. *kuriri, kakuririan; bagal, kabagalan; kupad, kakuparan*.

dumí (du-mí), n. 1. dirt. Syn. *dungis, dusing*. 2. dirtiness. Syn. *kadumihan, kadungisan, kadusingan*. 3. stain. Syn. *mantsa, bahid*. 4. rubbish; refuse. Syn. *basura*. 5. excreta;

dung; fecal matter; droppings. Syn. *tae, ipot*. 6. such impurities, like scum, dregs, etc. Syn. *iskoma, linab, latak*. 7. dirt on the skin of persons. Syn. *libag*.

dumog (du-mog), n. simultaneous attack or assault by or as by many persons. Syn. *tulung-tulong na pagsalakay*. 2. an unruly entry, attendance, buying, etc. by or as by an enthusiastic crowd. Cf. *paguunahan, pagsisiksikan*. 3. act or manner of being deeply engrossed as in work or vice. Syn. *pagkawiling mabuti*.

dunong (du-nong), n. 1. know-how; technical skill. Syn. *alam, kaalaman; batid, kabatiran*. 2. wisdom; talent. Syn. *talino*.

dungaw (du-ngaw), n. act of looking out from a window. Syn. *sungaw*.

dunggil (dung-gil), n. a quick thrust or poke on the nose or mouth. Cf. *dunggól*.

dunggít (dung-git) n. 1. tip or point. Syn. *dulo, tulis*. 2. verbal or written insinuation, usually in the form *parunggit*.

dunggól (dung-gól), n. a short straight blow with or as with the fist; jab. Syn. *dyáb, maikling tuwid na suntok*. 2. a light bump or collision. Syn. *bunggo, bundol, bangga*.

dunghál (dung-hál), n. act of stretching the body forward in an effort to see something beyond an obstacle at a distance. Cf. *dukwang*.

dungis (du-ngis), a. 1. slight dirt on the face. Syn. *amos*. 2. stain, blemish. Syn. *mantsa*. 3. (*Fig.*) moral blemish; dishonor; disgrace. Syn. *batik (fig.), kahihiyan*.

dungô (du-ngô), I. adj. 1. shy; bashful; timid. Syn. *mahiyain*. 2. stupid; dull-headed. Syn. *tanga, hangal, tunggak*. —II. n. a timid or stupid person. Syn. *taong mahiyain o tanga*.

dupikál (du-pi-kál), n. continuous ringing of church bells. Syn. *repike*.

dupilas (du-pi-las), n. 1. an accidental slip or slide. Syn. *di-sinásadyáng pagkapadulas*. 2. slip of the tongue; error or mistake in speaking. Syn. *kamalian o pagkakamalí sa pagsasalita*.

dupleks (du-pleks), I. adj. (Eng.) referring to an apartment house composed of two units.

duplero

—II. *n.* a duplex apartment or house.

duplero (du-ple-ro), *n.* (Sp. duplo) a participant in a *duplo.*

duplikado (du-pli-ka-do), *adj.* (Sp. *duplicado*) duplicated; made in duplicate copies. Syn. *ginawang dalawang kopya, yari sa dalawang kopya (sipi).*

duplo (du-plo), *n.* (Sp.) an old-fashioned game, whereby the participants debate on varied subjects in poetical verses. Cf. *balagtasan.*

dupók (du-pók), var. **rupok,** I. *n.* weakness; fragility; frailty; brittleness. Syn. *huná, kahunaán; hinà, kahinaan.*

—II. *adj.* weak, due to decay. Syn. *gato.*

dupong (du-pong), *n.* a piece of burning firewood; firebrand. Syn. *agipó.*

durâ (du-râ), var. **lura,** *n.* 1. act of spitting. Syn. *pagdura, paglura.* 2. spit; spittle; saliva; sputum. Syn. *laway.*

durian (du-ri-an), var. **dúráyan, duryán,** *n.* (Bot.) 1. a tree that grows up to 20 meters or more in height, cultivated for its highly prized fruit which has the odor of very rank, bad-smelling cheese. 2. the fruit of this tree.

durò (du-rò), *n.* 1. act of pricking something with or as with a pin. Syn. *pagduro, pagtusok, pagturok.* 2. a very small puncture made by a sharp point; prick. Syn. *tusok, turok, tundos.*

duróg (du-róg), *adj.* crushed into pieces or into powder; pulverized. Syn. *pulbos, pinulbos; durug-durog; lugas, nilugas.*

durúg-duróg (du-rúg + du-róg), *adj.* 1. crushed into tiny pieces; pulverized. 2. mangled to pieces. Syn. *luray-luray.*

dúrungawán (du-rú-nga-wán), *n.* 1. window. Syn. *bintana.* 2. any opening where to look out from within. Syn. *sungawan.*

dusa (du-ṣa), *n.* 1. suffering; affliction. Syn. *hirap, sakit, pagtitiis.* 2. sorrow; grief. Syn. *dalamhati, pighati, lungkot.* 3. penance; penitence. Syn. *pagpapakasakit, penitensiya.* 4. punishment. Syn. *parusa.*

dúsdusin (dús-du-sin), *adj.* mangry; with having, or infected with, mange. Syn. *gusgusin, may-dusdos, may-gusgos.*

dusing (du-sing), *n.* 1. dirt, esp. on the face. Syn. *amos, dungis.* 2. dirtiness; shabbiness.

Syn. *dumi, karumihan, kadungisan.*

dustâ (dus-tâ), I. *n.* insult; insulting speech or action. Syn. *pagdusta, pag-alipusta, paghamak, paglait.* 2. ignominy; infamy; shame and dishonor. Syn. *kahihiyan.* 3. miserable condition of livelihood. Syn. *karalitaan, karukhaan.*

—II. *adj.* 1. oppressed; maltreated. Syn. *api, inaapi; alipin, inaalipin.* 2. humiliating; disgraceful; ignominous. Syn. *hamak, nakakahiya.* 3. despicable. Syn. *kalait-lait.*

dutdót (dut-dót), *n.* playful poking with the finger or with something pointed. Syn. *dalutdot, pagdalutdot; sundut-sundot, pagsundut-sundot.*

dutsa (dut-sa), *n.* (Sp. *ducha*) shower bath sprinkler; douche.

duwag (du-wag), *adj.* coward; cowardly. Syn. *takot, matakutin, kobarde, mahina ang loob.*

duwál (du-wál), *n.* a straining, involuntary effort to vomit; act of retching. Syn. *duwák.*

duwelo (du-we-lo), var. **duelo,** *n.* (Sp.) duel.

duyan (du-yan), *n.* hammock; swing; cradle. Syn. *uyayi* (Bats.) Cf. *hamaka, kuna.*

dyab[1] (dyab), var. **diyab,** *n.* (Eng). a short, straight blow; jab. Syn. *suntok na panduggol; dunggol na suntok.*

dyab[2] (dyab), *n.* (Eng.) task; job; duty. Syn. *trabaho, gawain, tungkulin.*

dyak (dyak), var. **diyak,** *n.* (Eng.) 1. in Mech., jack. Syn. *gato.* 2. (in cards) jack. Syn. *sota.*

dyaket (dya-ket), var. **diyaket,** *n.* (Eng.) 1. a short coat, usually with sleeves; jacket. Syn. *tsaketa.* 2. a removable outer covering, as of a book. Syn. *kubyerta.*

dyip (dyip), var. **diyip,** *n.* (Eng.) jeep.

E

E, e (pronounced like "e" in get), *n.* 1. the fifth letter of the *abakada* (Pilipino alphabet). 2. the type of impression representing this letter. 3. a symbol for the fifth in a group or series.

Eba (E-ba), *n.* in the Bible, Eve, Adam's wife.

ebakwesyon (e-bak-wes-yon), n. (Eng.) evacuation.

ebanghelista (e-bang-he-lis-ta), n. (Sp. evangelista) evangelist; preacher of the Gospel. Syn. mangangaral ng Ebanghelyo.

Ebanghelyo (E-bang-hel-yo), n. (Sp. Evangelio) Gospel.

ebaporada (e-ba-po-ra-da), adj. (Sp. evaporada) evaporated, said esp. of milk.

ebaporasyón (e-ba-po-ras-yon), n. (Sp. evaporacion) evaporation. Syn. singaw, pagsingaw, pagpapasingaw.

ebidénsyá (e-bi-dén-si-yá), n. (Sp. evidencia) evidence; proof. Syn. patibay, katibayan; patunay, katunayan.

ebolusyón (e-bo-lus-yón), n. (Sp. evolucion) evolution.

ekes (e-kes), var. ekis, n. (Sp. equis) 1. in the name of the 26th letter of the Spanish alphabet: X. 2. a figure shaped like an X. 3. (Colloq.) a staggering or tottering movement, as of a drunk. Syn. pagpapahapay-hapay, pagpapaese-ese.

eklesiyástikó (e-kle-si-yás-ti-kó), var. eklesyastiko, I. adj. (Sp. eclesiastico) ecclesiastical; of the church or of the clergy. Syn. ng, sa, o ukol sa simbahan o Iglesya.
—II, n. a clergyman or priest. Syn. pari, pastor.

eklipse (e-klip-se), n. (Sp. eclipse) eclipse. Syn. laho, pagpalaho.

eko (e-ko), n. (Sp. eco) echo. Syn. alingawngáw

ekonomiya (e-ko-no-mi-ya), var. ekonomya, n. (Sp. economia) 1. economics. Syn. karunungang pangkabuhayan. 2. economy; thriftiness. Syn. pagtitipid, katipiran.

eksakto (ek-sak-to), adj. (Sp. exacto) 1. exact; accurate; correct; without any error. Syn. tama, tamang-tama; husto, hustung-husto; walang-kamali-mali. 2. complete. Syn. kumpleto, buung-buo, walang-kulang.

eksagonál (ek-sa-go-nal), n. (Sp. hexagono) hexagon.

eksaherasyón (ek-sa-he-ras-yón), n. (Sp. exageracion) exaggeration. Syn. pagpapalabis o kalabisan sa katotohanan.

eksamen (ek-sa-men), var. eksamin, iksamin, n. (Sp. examen) 1. examination; test. Syn. pagsusulit. 2. inspection; looking at closely and carefully. Syn. pagsusuri, pagsisiyasat, 3. physical checkup to determine the sickness of a person.

eksaminado (ek-sa-mi-na-do), adj. (Sp. examinado) 1. said of a person who has passed a qualifying examination; eligible or qualified by virtue of passing a required examination. Syn. pasado, nakapasa, 2. already examined or inspected. Syn. nasuri na.

eksaminadór (ek-sa-mi-na-dór), n. (Sp. examinador) 1. examiner; person who gives tests or examinations. Syn. tagasulit. 2. inspector.

eksklamasyón (eks-kla-mas-yón), var. ekslamasyon. n. (Sp. exclamacion) exclamation. Syn. bulalas.

eksklusibo (eks-klu-si-bo). var. eksklusibo, adj. (Sp. exclusivo) 1. exclusive; not included. Syn. di-kasama, puwera. 2. single; sole; not shared with others. Syn. tangi, sarili.

ekskomulgasyón (eks-ko-mul-gas-yón), var. eskomulgasyon. n. excommunication. Syn. pagtitiwalag o pagkakatiwalag sa Iglesya, ekskomonikasyon.

ekskursiyón (eks-kur-si-yón), var. eskursiyon, iskursiyon, n. (Sp. excursion) excursion; pleasure trip. Syn. pagliliwalíw.

eksema (ek-se-ma), n. (Med.: Sp., Eng.) eczema; a kind of skin disease characterized by inflammation, itching, and the formation of scales.

eksemsiyón (ek-sem-si-yón), var. eksensiyon n. (Eng.) exemption.

eksepsiyón (ek-sep-si-yón), n. (Sp. exception) 1. leaving out; exclusion; exception. Syn. di-pagsasama, paghihiwalay. 2. something considered as an exception. Syn. kataliwasan.

eksibit (ek-si-bit), n. (Eng.) 1. public show or display. Syn. tanghalan, pagtatanghál. 2. things exhibited. Syn. tanghal. 2. (Law) exhibit; evidence presented in court. Syn. ebidensya o katibayang iniharáp sa húkuman.

eksonerahin (ek-so-ne-ra-hin), v. (Sp. exonerar) to exonerate; prove or declare

eksorbitante

innocent. Syn. *pawaláng-sala, pawaláng-kasalanan.*

eksorbitante (ek-sor-bi-tan-te), *adj.* (Sp. *exorbitante*) exorbitant; very excessive. Syn. *masyado, labis-labis, napakamahal, nápakataás.*

ekspektorasyón (eks-pek-to-ras-yón), *n.* (Sp. *expectoracion*) 1. expectoration (of phlegm, mucus, etc.). Syn. *pag-ubó upang lumabás ang dura o plema.* 2. what is expectorated. Syn. *durâ o plema.*

ekspedisyón (eks-pe-dis-yón), var. **espedisyon, ispedisyon,** *n.* (Sp. *expedicion*) expedition; journey for a certain purpose.

eksperimento (eks-pe-ri-men-to), var. **esperimento,** *n.* (Sp. *experimento*) experiment; trial or test to find out something. Syn. *pagsubók.*

eksperto (eks-per-to), var. **esperto,** I. *adj.* with or having great skill. Syn. *dalubhasa, sanay-na-sanay, napakagalíng.*
—II. *n.* an expert. Syn. *espesyalista, taong dalubhasà sa isang gawain.*

eksperyensiyá (eks-per-yen-si-ya), var. **esperyensa,** *n.* (Sp. *experiencia*) experience. Syn. *karanasan.*

ekspirasyón (eks-pi-ras-yon), *n.* (Sp. *experacion*) 1. a breathing out, as of air from the lungs. Syn. *paghinga.* 2. a coming to an end. Syn. *lipas, paglipas, pagwawakas, pagtatapos.* 3. breathing one" last; dying. Syn. *pagkamatáy, pagpanaw, pagsakabilang-buhay, pagyao.*

eksplikasyon (eks-pli-kas-yon), *n.* (Sp. *explicacion*) 1. explaining. Syn. *pagpapaliwanag.* 2. reason. Syn. *katwiran.*

eksplorasyón (eks-plo-ras-yón), var. **esplorasyon,** *n.* (Sp. *exploracion*) 1. an exploring or travelling over unknown place for the purpose of discovery. Syn. *pag-eksplora, pag-galugad.* 2. examination; going over something carefully. Syn. *pagsusuring mabuti; pagsaliksik.*

eksplosibo (eks-plo-si-bo). var. **explosibo,** I. *n.* (Sp. *explosivo*) 1. explosives; dynamite; firecrackers. Syn. *paputok, dinamita, kuwitis, labintadór.*
—II. adj. explosive; tending to' explode. Syn. *sumasabog, pampasabog.*

eksplotasyón (eks-plo-tas-yón), var.

ekstensiyón

explotasyon. *n.* (Sp. *explotacion*) 1. development. Syn. *pagpapaunlad.* 2. exploiting or making unfair use of. Syn. *pagsasamantalá, paglinlang, pagkasangkapan.*

eksportasyón (eks-por-tas-yón), *n.* (Sp. *exportacion*) 1. exporting; exportation. Syn. *pagluluwas (ng kalakal).* 2. goods exported. Syn. *luwas, luwas na kalakal.*

eksposisyón (eks-po-sis-yón), var. **esposisyon,** *n.* public show or exhibition. Syn. *tanghalan, pagtatanghal.* 2. explanation. Syn. *paliwanag, pagpapaliwanag.* 3. (Gram.) literary exposition. Syn. *paglalahad.*

eksprés (eks-pres), var. **esprés,** 1. *n.* (Eng.) 1. a message sent by a special messenger. Syn. *pahatid na madalian.* 2. an express train, bus, truck, etc. Syn. *sasakyáng pangmabilisan.*
—II. *adj.* express; quick. Syn. *mabilisan, pangmabilisan.*

ekspresyón (eks-pres-yón), var. **espresyon,** *n.* (Sp. *exprezion*) 1. word or words used to express something. Syn. *pangungusap, pananalita.* 2. putting into words; expression. Syn. *pagpapahayag.* 3. common saying or expression. Syn. *kasabihan, bukambibig.* 4. indirect showing by voice, look, action, etc. Syn. *pagpapahiwatig.* 5. act of making known. Syn. *pagpapakilala.*

ekspulsiyón (eks-pul-si-yon), var. **espulsiyon,** *n.* (Sp. *expulsion*) expulsion; dismissal. Syn. *pagpapaalis, pagpapalayas, pagtitiwalág.*

ekstemporanyo (eks-tem-po-ran-yo), var. **estemporanyo,** (Sp. *extemporaneo*) *adj.* spoken or done without preparation; extemporaneous. Syn. *bíglaan, di-inihandâ.*

ekstensibo (eks-ten-si-bo), var. **estensibo,** *adj.* (Sp. *extensivo*) extensive; far-reaching. Syn. *masaklaw, malawak.*

ekstensiyón (eks-ten-si-yón), var. **estensiyon,** *n.* (Sp. *extension*). 1. extension or lengthening. Syn. *pagpapahaba.* 2. continuation; act of continuing. Syn. *pagdurugtong, pagpapatuloy.* 3. addition or continuation.

eksterminahin   **editór**

Syn. *dagdag, dugtong, sudlong.* 4. extension
of time. Syn. *palugit.* 5. extent. Syn *lawak,
saklaw.*

eksterminahin (eks-ter-mi-na-hin), v. to
exterminate; destroy completely. Syn.
puksain, lipulin, patayin.

eksteryór (eks-ter-yór), var. **esteryor,** I. n.
1. the outside; exterior. Syn. *labas, dakong
labas.* 2. the rubber casing of a vehicle tire.

ekstorsiyón (eks-tor-siyón), var. **estorsiyon,**
n. (Sp. *extorsion*) extortion. Syn.
panghuhuthot, pangingikil.

ekstra (eks-tra), *colloq.* var. **estra,** I. *adj.*
(Eng., Sp.) 1. extra; additional. Syn.
dagdag, karagdagan. 2. more, larger, or
better than what is normal or usual. Syn.
higit sa karaniwan.
—II. n. 1. an extra worker. Syn. *ekstrang
trabahador.* 2. a special edition or issue,
as of a newspaper. Syn. *ekstrang labas (ng
pahayagan).* 3. an extra actor or player.

ekstrabagansa (eks-tra-ba-gan-sa), var.
estrabagansa, n. (Sp. *extravaganza*) a
literary or dramatic presentation
characterized by loose structure and
fantastic plot; extravaganza.

ekstrabagansiyá (eks-tra-ba-gan-si-ya), var.
estrabagansiya, n. (Sp. *extravagancia*) 1.
extravagance in spending. Syn.
*kabulagsakan,   pagkabulagsak,
kagastaduran,   pagkagastador.*   2.
wastefulness. Syn. *kaaksayahan, pag-
aaksaya,* 3. excessiveness. Syn.
pagmamalabis. 4. lavishness in taste,
manner of dressing, etc. Syn. *rangya,
karangyaan, pagkamarangyâ.*

ekstraksiyón (eks-trak-si-yón), var.
estraksiyon, n. (Sp. *extracion*) extraction.
Syn. *pagpiga, pagkatas.*

ekstrakurikulár (eks-tra-ku-ri-ku-lár), var.
estrakurikular, adj. (Sp. *extracurricular*)
not part of the curriculum; Syn.
*wala sa kurikulum,
labás sa kurso.*

ekstradisyón (eks-tra-dis-yón), var.
estradisyón, n. (Sp. *extradicion*)
extradition. Syn. *pagpapabalik ng isang
bansa sa isang salarin o takas sa sarili nitong
bansâ.*

ekstrahudisyál (eks-tra-hu-dis-yál), var.

estrahudisyal, adj. (Sp. *extrajudicial*)
outside or beyond the jurisdiction of a
court; extrajudicial. Syn. *sa labas ng
hukuman.*

ekstranghero (eks-trang-he-ro), var.
estranghero, I. n. (Sp. *extranjero*) a
foreigner; alien. Syn. *dayuhan, banyagà.*
—II. adj. foreign; alien. Syn. *taga-ibang
bansa, dayuhan.*

ekstraordinaryo (eks-tra-or-di-nar-yo), var.
estraordinaryo, adj. (Sp. *extraordinario*)
1. extraordinary; unusual. Syn. *pam-
bihira, di-karaniwan, di-pangkaraniwan.* 2.
exceptional. Syn. *katangi-tangi.* 3.
remarkable; surprising. Syn. *kahanga-
hanga, kagilá-gilalás, kataka-taká.*

ekstremidad (ekstre-mi-dád), n. (Sp.
extremidad) extremity. Syn. *dulo, sukdulan.*

ekstremo (eks-tre-mo), var. **estremo,** I. n.
(Sp. *extremo*) the greatest that is possible;
extreme limit or degree; uttermost;
extreme state or condition. Syn. *sukdulan,
kasukdulán.*
—II. adj. in or to the greatest degree;
excessive. Syn. *sobra-sobra, labis-labis,
masyado.*

eksuma (ek-su-ma), n. (Sp. *exhumar*)
exhumation; disinterment. Syn. *paghukay
(sa nakalibing na patáy).*

ektarya (ek-tar-ya), n. (Sp. *hectarea*) hectare.

ekuwadór (e-ku-wa-dór), var. **ekwador,** n.
(Sp. *ecuador*) equator.

ekuwasyón (e-ku-was-yón), var. **ekwasyon,**
n. (Sp. *ecuacion*) in Math., equation. Syn.
tumbasan, pagtutumbas.

edád (e-dád), var. **idad,** n. (Sp.) age, Syn.
gulang.

Edén (E-dén), n. (Sp.) 1. in the Bible, Eden;
Paradise. Syn. *Paraiso.* 2. any delightful
place or state; a paradise, Syn. *paraiso.*

edipisyo (e-di-pis-yo), n. (Sp. *edificio*)
edifice; building. Syn. *gusali.*

edisyón (e-dis-yón), n. (Sp. *edicion*) edition;
issue. Syn. *labas, limbag, lathala, isyu.*

editahín (e-di-ta-hín), v. (Sp. *editar*) to edit;
revise and make ready (a manuscript) for
publication. Syn. *ayusin (ang manuskrito)
para sa paglilimbág, editin.*

editór (e-di-tór), n. (Sp.) editor. Cf.
patnugot, direktor.

editoryal

editoryal (e-di-tór-yal; e-di-tor-yál), n. (Sp., Eng.) editorial. Syn. *pangulong-tudling.*

edukado (e-du-ka-do), adj. (Sp. *educado*) educated; well-bred. Syn. *nag-aral, may-pinag-aralan.*

edukadór (e-du-ka-dor), n. (Sp. *educador*) 1. educator; teacher. Syn. *guro, maestró o maestrá, tagapagturo;* 2. an authority on educational problems, theories, and methods. Syn. *dalúbturò.*

edukasyón (e-du-kas-yón), n. (Sp. *educacion*) the process of training or teaching, esp. by formal schooling. Syn. *pagtuturo.* 2. knowledge or ability learned from schooling. Syn. *pinag-aralan, nápag-aralan.*

ee (e-e), interj. an exclamation similar to aa!.

ego (e-go), n. (Eng., Sp.) ego; the self. Syn. *sarili, sariling katauhan.* 2. (Colloq.) egotism; conceit. Syn. *labis na pagpapahalaga sa sarili, pagkamasarili, kaakuhán, pagkamakaakó.*

ehe (e-he), n. (Sp. *eje*) axle; axle-tree.

ehekutibo (e-he-ku-ti-bo), n. & adj. (Sp. *ejecutivo*) executive. Syn. *tagapagpaganap.*

ehém (e-hém), interj. an exclamation similar to ahem.

ehemplo (e-hem-plo), n. (Sp. *ehemplo*) example. Syn. *halimbawà.*

ehersisyo (e-her-sis-yo), colloq. var. ersisyo, n. (Sp. *ejercicio*) 1. exercise; physical exercise. Syn. *pagpapalakas ng katawan, pag-eehersisyo.* 2. practice. Syn *pagsasanay.* 3. performance of one's duties in office. Syn. *pagganap o pagtupad (ng tungkulin).*

elaborasyón (e-la-bo-ras-yón), n. (Sp. *elaboracion*) elaboration. Syn. *pagpapapaliwanag na mabuti.*

elástikó (e-lás-ti-kó), adj. (Sp. *elastico*) 1. elastic, as a rubber band. Syn. *nababanat.* 2. changeable; changing easily. Syn. *nababago, sunud-sunuran, pabagu-bago.*

elebadór (e-le-ba-dór), n. (Sp. *elevador*) 1. elevator. Syn. *asensor, elebetor.* 2. hoist; lift. Syn. *pantaás.*

elebasyón (e-le-bas-yon), n. (Sp. *elevacion*). 1. elevation; a high place. Syn. *kataasan; mataas na lugar.* 2. height (above the earth's surface) Syn. *taas, tayog.* 3. raising; act of elevating. Syn. *pagtataas.* 4. (Arch.)

eliminasyón

front elevation. Syn. *harap, patsada.*

eleksiyón (e-lek-si-yón), n. (Sp. *eleccion*), election. Syn. *halalan, paghahalalan, paghahalál.*

elektibo (e-lek-ti-bo), adj. (Sp. *electivo*) 1. elective; chosen in an election. Syn. *halál, inihahalal.* 2. by choice; not required. Syn. *sagustuhan, disaplitan.*

elektor (e-lek-tor) n. (Sp. *elector*) voter; elector. Syn. *botante, manghahalal.*

elektriká (e-lek-tri-ka), var. elektriko, I. adj. (Sp. *electrica*) electric; electrical. Syn. *pang-elektrisidad, pangkoryente.*

elektrisidád (elek-tri-si-dád), n. (Sp. *electricidad*) electricity. Syn. *dagitab, koryente.*

elektrokusyón (e-lek-tro-kus-yón), n. (Sp. *electrocución*) electrocution. Syn. *pagkákoryente, pagpatáy o pagkamatáy sa koryente.*

elektrón (e-lek-trón), n. (Sp., Eng.) electron.

electroniká (e-lek-tro-niká), n. (Sp. *electronica*) electronics.

elegante (e-le-gan-te), adj. (Sp.) elegant. Syn. *makisig, magarà.*

elehiya (e-le-hi-ya), n. (Sp. *elegia*) elegy.

elementál (e-le-men-tál), n. (Sp.) 1. elemental; fundamental. Syn. *mahalaga, napakahalaga, kailangan.* 2. serving as a foundation. Syn. *saligan, batayán.*

elementarya (e-le-men-tar-ya), adj. (Sp. *elementaria*) elementary; introductory. Syn. *pang-elementarya; pangmababang-baytang.*

elemento (e-le-men-to), n. (Sp.) 1. component; basic part. Syn. *sangkap, bahagi.* 2. natural environment. Syn. *likas na kapaligiran.* 3. forces of nature. Syn. *kalikasan.* 4. (Chem.) subsʈance. Syn. *sustansiyá.*

elepante (e-le-pan-te), n. (Zool., Sp. *elefante*) 1. elephant. Syn. *gaaya.* 2. (Colloq.) a derogatory term for a big, lazy fellow.

elepantiyasis (e-le-pan-tí-ya-sis), n. (Sp. *elefantiasis*) elephantiasis. Syn. *elepansiyá.*

eliminasyón (e-li-mi-nas-yon), n. (Sp. *eliminacion*) elimination; removal. Syn. *pag-alis, pagkaltas.*

elipsis (e-lip-sis), n. (Sp.) in Gram., ellipsis; omission of a word or words but understood in the context. Syn. *pagkaltas o pagkakaltas sa isang salita o mga salita nang hindi nababago ang kahulugan ng pangungusap.*

élisé (é-li-sé), var. élisi n. (*Sp. hélice*) propeller.

elisyón (e-lis-yón), n. (Sp. *elisión*) elision; omission or slurring over of a vowel, syllable, etc. in pronunciation. Syn. *dipagbigkás sa patinig, pantig, atb. sa pagsasalitâ.*

elokuwénsiyá (e-lo-ku-wén-si-yá), n. (Sp. *elocuencia*) eloquence. Syn. *katatasán o kahusayang magsalitâ.*

emansipasyón (e-man-si-pas-yón), n. (Sp. *emancipación*) emancipation; release or setting free from any kind of slavery. Syn. *pagpapalayá, pagliligtás.* 2. a redeeming or being redeemed. Syn. *pagtubós o pagkatubós.*

embahada (em-ba-ha-da), n. (Sp. *embajada*) embassy. Syn. *pásuguán.*

embahadór (em-ba-ha-dór), n. (Sp. *embajador*) ambassador. Cf. *kinatawán, emisaryo, sugò.*

embalsamá (em-bal-sa-má), var. embalsamó, n. (Sp. *embalsamar*) an embalming or being embalmed. Syn. *pag-eembalsamá o pagkaká-embalsamá.*

embarkasyón (em-bar-kas-yón), n. (Sp. *embarcación*) 1. putting aboard a ship. Syn. *paglululan sa bapór.* 2. navigation. Syn. *paglalayág.* 3. investment of money in an enterprise. Syn. *pamumuhunan.*

embargo (em-bar-go), var. imbargo, n. (Sp.) 1. embargo; seizure; attachment. Syn. *ilít, pag-ilít, pag-kakaílit; samsám, pagsamsám, pag-kakásamsám; pag-embargo, pag-kakáembargo.* 2. restriction put on commerce by law. Syn. *pagbabawal, pagpigil.*

embés (em-bés), var. imbés, imbís, adv. (Sp. *en vez*) instead of. Syn. *sa halíp na (ng).*

embornál (em-bor-nal), var. imburnál, n. (Sp.) 1. manhole; sewer opening. 2. sewer line or system.

embudo (em-bu-do), var. imbudo, n. (Sp.) funnel.

embutido (em-bu-ti-do), n. (Sp.) 1. salami; sausage. Syn. *salami.* 2. inlaid work. 3. (Amer.) lace. Syn. *puntás.*

emigrante (e-mi-gran-te), n. (Sp.) emigrant; person who emigrates. Syn. *dayuhan, mándarayuhan, mángingibáng-bayan*

eminente (e-mi-nen-te), adj. (Sp.) 1. eminent; famous. Syn. *tanyág, bantóg.* 2. great; celebrated. Syn. *dakilà, mabunyî.* 3. high in rank. Syn. *mataás.*

emisaryo (e-mi-sar-yo), n. (Sp. *emisario*) emissary; person sent on a mission. Syn. *sugò, kinatawán.*

emosyunál (e-mos-yu-nál), var. emosiyunál, adj. (Sp. *emocional*) 1. emotional; easily excited or moved. Syn. *maramdamin, madalíng magdamdám.* 2. appealing to the emotion. Syn. *nakabábagbág-damdamin, makabagbág-damdamin.*

empake (em-pa-ke), n. (Sp. *empaque*) 1. packing; packaging. Syn. *pag-iimpake, pagpapakete.* 2. the manner something is packed. Syn. *pagkakáimpake.* 3. pack; package. Syn. *bastá, pakete.*

empanada (em-pa-na-da), var. panada, n. (Sp.) meat pie.

empasís (em-pa-sís), n. (Sp. *énfasis*) 1. emphasis; stress. Syn. *dín, pagbibigay-dín.* 2. giving importance; stressing the importance of. Syn. *pagpapahalagá.*

empatso (em-pa-tso), var. impatso, n. (Sp. *empacho*) indigestion. Syn. *indihestiyon; dipagkatunaw ng kinain; pagkasira o kasiraan ng tiyan.*

emperadór (em-pe-ra-dór), n. (Sp.) emperor. Cf. *harí.*

empleado (em-ple-a-do), var. empleyado, n. (Sp.) employee; male employee. Syn. *kawaní, lalaking kawaní.*

empleo (em-ple-o), var. empleyo, n. (Sp.) 1. employment; work; job. Syn. *trabaho, gawain, hanapbuhay.* 2. profession. Syn. *tungkulin.* 3. business. Syn. *negosyo.*

emporyo (em-por-yo), n. (Sp. *emporio*) 1. emporium; trading center; market place. Syn. *pámilihan.* 2. department store; bazaar. Syn. *basár, almasen.*

empresaryo (em-pre-sar-yo), var. impresaryo, n. (Sp. *empresario*) impresario

enkanto (en-kan-to), var. engkanto, n. (Sp.

encanto) 1. enchantment; charm; spell. Syn. *pagkagayuma*. 2. in Philippine folklore, a supernatural being (spirit) who has the power to enchant people.

enkargo (en-kar-go), var. **engkargo**, n. (Sp. *encargo*) 1. charge; trust. Syn. *tiwalà,. pagtitiwalà*. 2. recommendation. Syn. *tagubilin*. 3. assignment. Syn. *tungkulin*.

enkarnasyón (en-kar-nas-yón), var. **engkarnasyon**, n. (Sp. *encarnación*) 1. incarnation; embodiment. Syn. *pagkakatawáng-tao*. 2. type of embodiment of a quality or concept. Syn. *larawan, halimbawà*.

enkuwentro (en-ku-wen-tro), var. **engkuwentro**, n. (Sp. *encuentro*) 1. encounter; meeting. Syn. *pagsasalubong, pagtatagpô, pagkikita*. 2. clash; collision. Syn. *banggaan, pagbabanggâ*. 3. encounter; fight; match. Syn. *labanán, ságupaán*. 4. finding Syn. *pagkátagpô, pagkákita*.

endémikó (en-dé-mi-kó), adj. (Sp. *endémico*) endemic; indigenous. Syn. *likás o katutubò sa isáng lugár*.

endorso (en-dor-so), var. **indorso**, n. (Sp.) endorsement. Syn. *paglilipat; paglilipat-tagubilin*.

enema (e-ne-ma) , n. (Sp., Eng.) 1. enema; injection of liquid into the rectum either as a purgative or medicine. Syn. *paglabatiba, paglalabatiba*. 2. the liquid used in such injection. Syn. *panlabatiba*. 3. the apparatus used for this. Syn. *labatiba, sumpít*.

enerhiyá (e-ner-hi-yá), n. (Sp. *energia*) vigor; energy; force. Syn. *lakás, kakayahán*.

Enero (E-ne-ro), n. (Sp.) January, the first month of the year.

enigma (e-nig-ma), n. (Sp., Eng.) 1. enigma. Syn. *hiwagà, kababalaghán, misteryo*. 2. riddle. Syn. *bugtóng, paláisipán*.

enigmátikó (e-nig-má-ti-kó), adj. (Sp. *enigmático*) enigmatic; perplexing; baffling. Syn. *mahiwagá, kataká-taká*.

enmiyenda (en-mi-yen-da), var. **emiyenda, emyenda**, n. (Sp. *enmienda*) 1. correction; change. Syn. *pagtutuwíd, pagbabago*. 2. amendment. Syn. *susog*.

enormidád (e-nor-mi-dád), n. (Sp.) 1. enormousness. Syn. *labis na laki o kalakhán*. 2. enormity; very wicked crime. Syn. *malakíng kasalanan; kabuhungán*.

ensalada (en-sa-la-da), var. **insalada**, n. (Sp.) salad. Syn. *salad*.

ensaymada (en-say-ma-da), var. **ensemada**, n. (Sp. *ensaimada*) a kind of puff cake.

ensayo (en-sa-yo), var. **insayo**, n. (Sp:) practice; rehearsal; training. Syn. *pagsasanay, pag-iinsayo*.

entablado (en-tab-la-do), var. **intablado**, n. (Sp.) stage; speaker's platform or stand. Syn. *plataporma*.

entendido (en-ten-di-do), var. **entindído, intindido**, adj. (Sp.) 1. experienced; able. Syn. *mahusay, may-kakayahán*. 2. well-informed. Syn. *maraming nalalaman*. 3. understood. Syn. *alám, náuunawaan*.

entero (en-te-ro), adj. (Sp.) entire; whole. Syn. *buô, lahát*.

entonasyón (en-to-nas-yón), n. (Sp. *entonación*) intonation. Syn. *punto o estilo (ng pagsasalitâ)*.

entonses (en-ton-ses), adv. (Sp. *entonces*) 1. then; at that time. Syn. *noón; nang panahóng iyón*. 2. well then; therefore. Syn. *samakatwíd, kung gayón*.

entra (en-tra), n. (Sp.) an uncalled-for entry into the conversation of others. Syn. *sabát, pagsabát, pakikisabát*.

entrada (en-tra-da), n. (Sp.) 1. entrance; entry. Syn. *pasukán, daán sa pagpasok*. 2. act of entering (a place). Syn. *pasok, pagpasok*. 3. admission; admittance. Syn. *pasok, pagpapapasok*. 4. payment for admission. Syn. *bayad o upa sa pagpasok*. 5. total of cash receipts from the sale of admission tickets; gate. Syn. *buóng nápagbilhán ng tiket sa pagpasok*. 6. gate. Syn. *tárangkahan, pultahan*. 7. door. Syn. *pintuan*. 8. beginning; start. Syn. *simulâ, umpisá*. 9. in book-keeping, ledger entry. Syn. *pasok*. 10. in lexicography, work entry; the word being defined. 11. (Colloq.) an uncalled-for entry into the conversation of others. Syn. *sabát, pagsabát, pakikisabát*.

entrega (en-tre-ga), n. (Sp.) 1. delivery; submission; handing over. Syn. *pagbibigáy, pag-aabót, pagsusumité*. 2. remittance, as of money by a bill collector. Syn.

entremetido　　　　　　　　　　　　**eskaparate**

pagpapasok ng kuwaltang nápaningilán. 3. the amount (of money) remitted, as by a bill collector.

entremetido (en-tre-me-ti-do), *n.* (Sp.) meddler or intruder. Syn. *taong pakialamero o mapánghimasok.*

entresuwelo (en-tre-su-we-lo), *var.* **entreswelo,** *n.* (Sp. *entresuelo*) mezzanine.

entusiyástikó (en-tu-si-yás-ti-kó), *var.* **entusyástikó,** *adj.* (Sp. *entusiástico*) 1. enthusiastic. Syn. *masiglá, masigasig.* 2. interested. Syn. *interesado, mahilig, mahiligín.*

enumerasyón (e-nu-me-ras-yón), *n.* (Sp. *enumeración*) enumeration; naming one by one. Syn. *pag-isá-isá.*

engganyo (eng-gan-yo), *var.* **ingganyo,** *n.* (Sp. *engaño*) 1. deceit; fraud. Syn. *linláng, panlilinláng; dayà, pandarayà.* 2. bait *(fig.)*; enticement. Syn. *pain, pagtibóng.*

enggrande (eng-gran-de), *adj. & adv.* (Sp. *en grande*) in a big way or manner. Syn. *malakí, málakihan.*

epektibo (e-pek-ti-bo), *adj.* (Sp. *efectivo*) effective. Syn. *mabisà.*

epekto (e-pek-to), *n.* (Sp. *efecto*) 1. effect; potency. Syn. *bisà.* 2. result. Syn. *bunga, resulta.*

epektos (e-pek-tos), *n.* (Sp. *efectos*) 1. effects; personal property or belongings; assets. Syn. *arí-arian, kagamitán.* 2. goods; merchandise. Syn. *kalakal, mga panindá.*

epiká (é-pi-ká), *n.* (Sp. *épica*) epic poetry.

épikó (é-pi-kó), *adj.* (Sp. *épico*) epic; epical.

epidemya (e-pi-dem-ya), *n.* (Sp. *epidemia*) epidemic. Syn. *salot, peste.*

epiglotis (e-pig-lo-tis), *n.* (Anat., Eng.) epiglottis. Syn. *titigukan.*

epigrama (e-pi-gra-ma), *n.* (Sp.) 1. epigram. Cf. *kawikaán, kasabihán.* 2. any terse, witty, pointed statement. Syn. *patutsada.*

epilépsiyá (e-pi-lép-si-yá), *n.* (Med., Sp. *epilepsia*) epilepsy. Syn. *himatay, paghihimatáy.*

epílogó (e-pí-lo-gó), *n.* (Sp.) epilogue. Syn. *pangwakás na pangungusap.*

episodyo (e-pi-sod-yo), *n.* (Sp. *episodio*) episode; incident. Syn. *insidente, pangyayari.*

epistolaryo (e-pis-to-lar-yo), *n.* (Sp.

epistolario) epistolary; book or collection of letters. Syn. *katipunan o aklát ng mga sulat.*

epísyente (e-pís-yen-te), *adj.* (Sp. *eficiencia*) efficient. Syn. *mahusay magtrabaho.*

époka (é-po-ka), *n.* (Sp. *época*) epoch; period of time; era. Syn. *panahón, kapanahunan.*

erata (e-ra-ta), *n.* (Eng., Sp.) errata; errors in printing. Syn. *mga malî o kamalian sa paglilimbág.*

ereksiyón (e-rek-si-yón), *n.* (Sp. *erección*) 1. (Const.) erection; construction; building. Syn. *pagtatayô, pagtitindig.* 2. in physiology, the hardening of the male sexual organ. Syn. *paninigás, pagtayô.*

eredero (e-re-de-ro), *n.* (Sp. *heredero*) heir. Syn. *tagapagmana.*

erehe (e-re-he), *n.* (Sp. *hereje*) heretic.

ermitanyo (er-mi-tan-yo), *n.* (Sp. *ermitaño*) hermit.

erosyón (e-ros-yón), *n.* (Sp. *erosion*) erosion. Syn. *agnás, pagkaagnás.*

erupsiyon (e-rup-si-yon), *n.* (Sp. *erupción*) 1. eruption, as of a volcano. Syn. *putók o pagputók (ng bulkán).* 2. (Med.) a breaking out in a rash. Syn. *pagsingáw (sa balat)* 3. rash. Syn. *singáw (sa balát)*

eryal (er-yal), *n.* (Eng.) aerial. Syn. *antena.*

eskabetse (es-ka-bet-se), *n.* (Sp. *escabeche*) pickled fish.

eskala (es-ka-la), *var.* **iskala,** *n.* (Sp. *escala*) 1. in Mus., scale. 2. step; degree. Syn. *antás, baitáng.* 3. in Arch. & Engin., proportion; scale. Syn. *proporsiyón.* 4 a turning away from the regular route. Syn. *sinsáy, pagsinsáy; lihís, paglihís.* 5. graduated marks on rules and instruments. 6. stop (in an itinerary).

eskaladór (es-ka-la-dór), *n.* (Sp. *escalador*) 1. escalator. Cf. *hagdanan, elebetor, asensór.* 3. climber. Syn. *mang-aakyát, mang-aadyó.*

eskándaló (es-kán-da-ló), *var.* **iskándaló,** *n.* (Sp. *escándalo*) 1. scandal. Syn. *alingasngás, katiwalián.* 2. commotion. Syn. *pagkakaguló, káguluhan.*

eskaparate (es-ka-pa-ra-te), *n.* (Sp. *escaparate*) 1. showcase or cabinet; glass case. 2. show window.

eskape (es-ka-pe), n. (Sp. *escape*) 1. fast gait of a horse. Syn. *matuling takbó (ng kabayo)*. 2. (Mech.) operation or movement of a clock or watch. Syn. *takbó, lakad, andár*. 3. (Mech.) exhaust (of an automobile). Syn. *tambutso*. 4. escape; flight. Syn. *takas, pagtakas; puga, pagpuga*.

eskápulá (es-ká-pu-lá), n. (Anat., Sp., Eng.) scapula; the shoulder blade. Syn. *paypáy*.

eskapularyo (es-ka-pu-lar-yo), n. (Sp. *escapulario*) scapular; scapulary. Syn. *kalmén*.

eskarlata (es-kar-la-ta), n. 1. scarlet red (color). 2. (Bot.) scarlet rose (plant and flower).

eskayola (es-ka-yo-la), var. iskayola, n. (Sp. *escayola*) plaster of paris.

eskéletón (es-ké-le-tón), n. (Eng.) 1. skeleton. Syn. *kalansáy, eskeleto*. 2. framework. Syn. *balangkás, bangháy*.

eskinita (es-ki-ni-ta), var. iskinita, n. (Sp. *esquinita*) small alley. Syn. *malíit na pasilyo*.

eskiról (es-ki-ról), var. iskiról, n. (Sp. *esquirol*) strike-breaker; scrab.

esklamasyón (es-kla-mas-yón), var. eksklamasyón, n. (Sp. *exclamación*) exclamation. Syn. *bulalas*.

esklusibo (es-klu-si-bo), var. eksklusibo, adj. (Sp. *exclusivo*) 1. exclusive; not included. Syn. *di-kasama, puwera*. 2. single; sole; not shared with others. Syn. *tangì, sarili*.

eskoba (es-ko-ba), var. iskoba, n. (Sp. *escoba*) a big scrubbing brush; large hand brush.

eskolar (es-ko-lar), n. (Sp. *escolar*) 1. a scholarly person. Syn. *taong paláarál*. 2. a student scholar. Syn. *pensiyonadong mag-aarál*. 3. a learned person; one trained in a special branch of learning. Syn. *pahám, pantás*.

eskombro (es-kom-bro), var. iskombro, n. (Sp. *escombro*) crushed stones for use in concrete constructions. Syn. *duróg na bató*.

eskopeta (es-ko-pe-ta), var. iskupeta, n. (Sp. *escopeta*) shotgun; rifle. Syn. *riple*.

Eskórpiyó (Es-kór-pi-yó), n. (Eng.) Scorpio, a southern constellation between Libra and Sagittarius.

eskorpiyón (es-kor-pi-yón), n. (Sp. *escorpion*) scorpion. Syn. *alakdan, pitumbukó*.

eskotada (es-ko-ta-da), var. iskotada, adj. (Sp. *escotada*) with a low, wide neck, referring to some dresses; décolleté. Syn. *mababá at maluwáng ang leeg*.

eskribano (es-kri-ba-no), n. (Sp. *escríbano*) clerk of court; notary. Syn. *notaryo*.

eskrima (es-kri-ma), var. iskrima, n. (corr. from Sp. *esgrima*) fencing; swordplay. Syn. *estokada, arnís*.

eskrimadór (es-kri-ma-dór), n. fencer; swordman. Syn. *estokadór*.

eskritór (es-kri-tór), n. (Sp. *escritor*) writer. Syn. *mánunulat*.

eskritoryo (es-kri-tor-yo), n. (Sp. *escritorio*) office desk; writing desk. Syn. *eskribaniya, mesa*.

Eskritura (Es-kri-tu-ra), n. (Sp. *Escritura*) the Bible; Scripture. Syn. *Bibliya, Banál na Kasulatan*.

eskrutinyo (es-kru-tin-yo), n. (Sp. *escrutinio*) 1. scrutiny; close or careful examination or investigation. Syn. *masusing pagsusuri o pagsisiyasat*. 2. official counting of votes or election returns. Syn. *opisyál na bilangán o pagbilang ng mga boto*.

eskultura (es-kul-tu-ra), n. (Sp. *escultura*) 1. the art of carving or modeling figures; sculpture. Syn. *paglilok, paglililok*. 2. a piece of sculptured work. Syn. *lilok, pigurang nililok*.

eskursiyón (es-kur-si-yón), var. iskursiyón, ekskursiyón, n. (Sp. *excursión*) excursion; pleasure trip or outing. Syn. *pagliliwalíw*.

eskuwadra (es-ku-wa-dra), n. (Sp. *escuadra*) 1. (Mil.) squad. Syn. *eskuwád (iskuwád)*. 2. (Naut.) fleet, as of ships. Syn. *plota*. 3. squadron. Syn. *eskuwadrón*. 4. carpenter's square. Syn. *eskuwala (iskuwala)*.

eskuwala (es-ku-wa-la), var. iskuwala, n. (Sp. *escuala*) 1. T-square; carpenter's square. Syn. *eskuwadra* (4). 2. act of testing the accuracy of a square work by using a T-square. Syn. *pag-eskuwala*.

eskuwalado (es-ku-wa-la-do), var. iskuwalado, adj. 1. made square or at right angle, said of corners. 2. made straight, even, level, etc., referring to surfaces.

eskuwela (es-ku-we-la), var. iskuwela, n.
(Sp. *escuela*) 1. student; pupil; school
child. Syn. *mag-aarál, estudyante; pupilo.*
2. school (institution). Syn. *páaralán,
eskuwelahán, kolehiyó, dàlubhasaán,
unibersidád, pámantasan.*

eskuwelahán (es-ku-we-la-hán), var.
iskuwelahán, n. school; school house or
building. Syn. *páaralan, bahay-páaralán.*

esena (e-se-na), n. (Sp. *escena*) in theat.,
scene. Syn. *tagpô, eksena* (colloq. var.).

esenaryo (e-se-nar-yo), n. (Sp. *escenario*) 1.
stage. Syn. *tanghalan, entablado.* 2. setting;
scenery. Syn. *tagpuan.*

esénsiyá (e-sén-si-yá), n. (Sp. *escencia*) 1.
essence; fundamental nature of
something. Syn. *katangian.* 2. in
philosophy, true substance. Syn. *diwà,
pinakadiwà.* 3. a concentrated extract of
a plant, drug, food, etc. Syn. *sustánsiyá.*
4. perfume. Syn. *pabangó.*

esensiyál (e-sen-si-yál), adj. (Sp. *escencial*)
1. needed; necessary. Syn. *kailangan,
kinákailangan.* 2. important; very
important. Syn. *mahalagá, napakahalagá.*

esmeralda (es-me-ral-da), n. (Sp.) emerald.

esópagó (e-só-pa-gó), n. (Sp. *esófago*)
esophagus; gullet. Syn. *lalamunan.*

espada (es-pa-da), var. ispada, n. (Sp.) 1.
sword. Syn. *sable.* 2. (*Colloq.*)
swordplay. Syn. *espadahán.* 3. in cards,
spade. 4. (*Ichth.*) swordfish. 5. (*Bot.*)
sword plant.

Espanya (Es-pan-ya), n. (Sp. *España*) Spain.

Espanyól (Es-pan-yól), I. n. (Sp. *Español*)
1. the Spanish language. Syn. *wiká o
lengguwaheng Kastilà.* 2. Spaniard; Spanish
citizen. Syn. *Kastilà, mámamayáng Kastilà.*
—II. adj. Spanish.

espasól (es-pa-sól), var. ispasól, n. a kind of
sweetmeat made locally from the flour of
glutinous rice (*malagkít*).

espasyo (es-pas-yo), var. ispasyo, n. (Sp.
espacio) space. Syn. *lugár, puwáng.*

espektákuló (es-pek-tá-ku-ló), n. (Sp.
espectáculo) spectacle; public show or
display. Syn. *palabás, pànoorín.*

espekulasyón (es-pe-ku-las-yón), n. (Sp.
especulación) speculation; taking risk for
future gain. Syn. *pagbabakasakalì,*

pakikipagsápalarán.

espeho (es-pe-ho), n. (Sp. *espejo*) mirror.
Syn. *salamin.*

esperansa (es-pe-ran-sa), n. (Sp. *esperanza*)
hope. Syn. *pag-asa.*

esperma (es-per-ma), n. (Sp.) 1. spermaceti.
2. white candle made from the sperm of a
whale. Cf. *kandilà.* 3. semen; sperm. Syn.
tabòd o tamód.

espésimén (es-pé-si-mén), var. ispésimén, n.
(Sp. *espécimen*) specimen; sample. Syn.
muwestra.

espesípikó (es-pe-sí-pi-kó), I. n. patent
medicine; proprietary medicine. Syn.
gamót na espesípikó.
—II adj. 1. specific; definite. Syn. *tiyák.*
2. prepared or patented, said of some
medicine.

espesyál (es-pes-yál), adj. (Sp. *especial*) 1.
exceptional; more than ordinary. Syn. *di-
pangkaraniwan, di-ordinaryo.* 2. of a
particular kind; distinct from others. Syn.
ibá sa karaniwan, nátatangì, pantangì.

espesyalidád (es-pes-ya-li-dád), n. (Sp.
especialidád) 1. special line of work,
profession, etc.; specialty. Syn.
pinagdalubhasaan. 2. a special or particular
characteristic. Syn. *katangian, náiibáng
katangian.*

espiker (es-pi-ker), var. ispiker, n. (Eng.) 1.
Speaker (in the House of Representatives).
2. the person who is speaking or talking.
Syn. *ang nagsásalitâ.* 3. the person
delivering a speech. Syn. *ang nagtáta-
lumpatì.* 4. orator. Syn. *oradór, mánana-
lumpatî.*

espinghe (es-ping-he), n. (Sp. *esfinge*)
sphinx.

espiritismo (es-pi-ri-tis-mo), n. (Sp.)
spiritism; spiritualism.

espíritú (es-pí-ri-tú), n. (Sp.) 1. spirit; soul.
Syn. *káluluwá.* 2. state of mind. Syn. *diwà,
damdamin.* 3. strong liquor. Syn. *alak.* 4.
efficacy; effectiveness, as of wine. Syn.
bisà.

Espiritu Santo n. Holy Spirit; Holy Ghost.

espiyá (es-pi-yá), var. espiyá, n. (Sp. *espía*)
spy. Syn. *tiktík.*

esplikasyón (es-pli-kas-yón), n. (Sp.
explicación) 1. explication; explanation.

espontanyo

Syn. *paliwanag, pagpapaliwanag.* 2. reason. Syn. *katwiran.*

espontanyo (es-pon-tan-yo), *adj.* (Sp. *espontáneo*) spontaneous. Syn. *kusà, kusang-loób, buluntád.*

espongha (es-pong-ha), *n.* (Sp. *esponja*) 1. sponge. 2. powder puff.

esposa (es-po-sa), *n.* (Sp.) wife; spouse. Syn. *maybahay, asawa, kabiyák, kabiyák ng dibdíb.*

esposo (es-po-so), *n.* (Sp.) husband; spouse. Syn. *banà* (Bis.), *tao* (*colloq.*), *asawa.*

espuma (es-pu-ma), *n.* foam; scum; froth; lather. Syn. *bulâ, halagap.*

estabilidád (es-ta-bi-li-dád), *n.* (Sp.) stability; firmness. Syn. *tatag, katatagan, pagkamatatag; tibay, katibayan, pagkamatibay.*

establesimyento (es-ta-ble-sim-yen-to), *n.* (Sp. *establecimiento*) 1. act of establishing; establishment. Syn. *pagtatatag, pagtatayô, pagpupundár.* 2. business establishment. Syn. *bahay-kalakal, kompanya.*

estadista (es-ta-dis-ta), *n.* (Sp.) statesman.

estadístiká (es-ta-dís-ti-ká), *n.* (Sp. *estadistica*) statistics. Syn. *taláng-bilang o tálaang-bilang.*

estado (es-ta-do), *n.* (Sp.) 1. (*Pol.*) state. 2. nation. Syn. *bansá* (*bansâ*); *nasyon.* 3. condition; situation. Syn. *lagáy, kalagayan; tayô, katayuan; situwasyon.* 4. married state. Syn. *buhay-may-asawa, pagkamay-asawa.* 5 adult stage. Syn. *ganáp o hustóng gulang.* 6. status; rank. Syn. *ranggo.*

estalaktita (es-ta-lak-ti-ta), *n.* (Sp. *estalactita*) stalactite. Syn. *tulong-yungíb, tulong-bató* (*túlumbató*).

estalagmita (es-ta-lag-mi-ta), *n.* (Sp.) stalagmite. Syn. *nakatayóng-túlumbató.*

estambre (es-tam-bre), var. **istambre**, *n.* (Sp.) spun thread, used for weaving or knitting; yarn. Cf. *sinulid.*

estáminá (es-tá-mi-ná), *n.* (Eng.) 1. stamina; vigor; endurance. Syn. *lakás; tibay ng katawán.* 2. stamen.

estampa (es-tam-pa), var. **istampa**, *n.* (Sp.) portrait or image of a saint; religious print. Syn. *larawan ng santo.*

estampita (es-tam-pi-ta), var. **istampita**, *n.*

estimá

(Sp.) a small portrait or print of a saint.

estandarte (es-tan-dar-te), *n.* (Sp.) banner; standard; colors. Syn. *bandera, watawat.*

estante (es-tan-te), var. **istante**, *n.* (Sp.) 1. shelf. Syn. *sálansanan.* 2. bookcase; showcase. Syn. *eskaparate* (*iskaparate*).

estapa (es-ta-pa), var. **istapa**, *n.* (Sp. *estafa*) swindle; fraud. Syn. *panunubá, panansô, panggagantso.*

estasyón (es-tas-yón), var. **istasyón**, *n.* (Sp. *estación*) 1. place for regular stopping or parking of vehicles. Syn. *himpilan, páradahán.* 2. railway station. Syn. *himpilan ng tren.* 3. place of assignment. Syn. *destino.* 4. headquarters; station or main office. Syn. *kuwartél, punong-tanggapan.* 5. (*Eccles.*) devotional church visits.

estátikó (es-tá-ti-kó), *adj.* (Sp. *estático*) not moving; at rest; static. Syn. *nakahintô, walang-kilós, waláng-galáw, nakatigil.*

estátuwa (es-tá-tu-wa), var. **estatwá**, **istátuwá**, *n.* (Sp. *estatua*) 1. statue. Syn. *rebulto.* 2. a monument. Syn. *bantayog, monumento.*

esteno (es-te-no), *n.* (Eng.) used colloquially; stenography.

esterilidád (es-te-ri-li-dád), var. **isterilidád**, *n.* (Sp.) sterility or barrenness (of persons or animals). Syn. *kabaugán.* 2. barrenness or infertility (of land). Syn. *kapayatán.*

esterilisá (es-te-ri-li-sá), var. **isterilisá**, *n.* (Sp. *esterilizar*) a sterilizing or being sterilized. Syn. *pag-isterilisá, pagkakáisterilisá.*

estero (es-te-ro), *n.* inlet canal of a river. Cf. *kanál, bambáng, sapà.*

estetoskop (es-te-tos-kop), var. **istetoskop**, *n.* (Eng.) stethoscope. Syn. *estetoskopyo.*

estigma (es-tig-ma), var. **istigma**, *n.* (Sp.) 1. a small spot or mark; stain. Syn. *mantsa, bahid, batik.* 2. mark of disgrace; stain on one's reputation. Syn. *batik sa karangalan, kahihiyán.*

estilo (es-ti-lo), *n.* (Sp.) 1. style; fashion. Syn. *moda, uso.* 2. style, manner, method, etc. (of speaking, writing, etc.) Syn. *paraán, pamamaraán.* 3. stylus.

estimá (es-ti-má), *n.* (Sp.) 1. esteem; regard. Syn. *pagpapahalagá, paggalang.* 2. act of entertaining or attending to a visitor or visitors. Syn. *pagharáp o pag-aasikaso (sa panauhin)*.

estimulá (es-ti-mu-lá), *n.* (Sp. *estimular*) a stimulating or being stimulated; encouragement. Syn. *pagpapasiglá, pagbibigáy-siglá*.

estipulasyón (es-ti-pu-las-yón), *n.* (Sp. *estipulación*) stipulation; proviso. Syn. *tadhanà, takdâ, kondisyón*.

estokada (es-to-ka-da), var. **istokada.**, *n.* (Sp. *estocada*) the art or act of fencing with foils. Syn. *arnés*.

estómagó (es-tó-ma-gó), *n.* (Sp.) stomach. Syn. *tíyán, síkmurà*.

estopado (es-to-pa-do), var. **estupado**, I. *n.* (Sp. *estofado*) stew; stewed meat.
—II. *adj.* stewed, referring to meat.

estorbo (es-tor-bo), var. **istorbo**, *n.* (Sp.) hindrance; obstacle. Syn. *sagabal, hadláng*. 2. nuisance; disturbance. Syn. *pangguló, pambuwisit*.

estorya (es-tor-ya), var. **istorya**, *n.* (Sp. *historia*) 1. story; tale. Syn. *kuwento*. 2. history. Syn. *kasaysayan*. 3. gossip; rumor. Syn. *tsismís*.

estoryadór (es-tor-ya-dór), var. **istoryadór**, *n.* (Sp. *historiador*) 1. story teller. Syn. *ang nagkúkuwentó o nagsásalaysáy*. 2. story writer. Syn. *kuwentista*. 3. historian. Syn. *mánanalaysáy*.

estranggulasyón (es-trang-gu-las-yón), *n.* (Sp. *estrangulación*) strangulation; choking. Syn. *sakál, pagsakál, pagkakásakál*.

estratéhiya (es-tra-té-hi-ya), *n.* (Sp. *estrategia*) strategy. Syn. *pamamaraán*.

estrelya (es-trel-ya), var. **istrelya**, *n.* (Sp. *estrella*) star. Syn. *bituin, talà*.

estrelyado (es-trel-ya-do), *adj.* (Sp. *estrellado*) fried sunny-side-up, referring to an egg or eggs. Syn. *prito o pinirito (colloq.)*

estribo. (es-tri-bo), *n.* (Sp.) 1. stirrup (of a saddle). 2. running board; footboard (of a passenger vehicle).

estrikto (es-trik-to), var. **istrikto**, *adj.* (Sp. *estricto*) strict, referring esp. to a man. Syn. *mahigpit*.

estropa (es-tro-pa), *n.* (Sp. *estrofa*) a stanza (in poetry). Syn. *saknóng, táludturan*.

estruktura (es-truk-tu-ra), *n.* 1. structure; manner or form a building, monument, bridge, etc. is built. Syn. *kayarián*. 2. framework. Syn. *balangkás*. 3. a building; structure. Syn. *gusalì*.

estudyante (es-tud-yan-te), var. **istudyante**, *n.* (Sp. *estudiante*) student. Syn. *mag-aarál*.

estudyo (es-tud-yo), var. **istudyo**, *n.* (Sp. *estudio*) 1. studio (of a painter, sculptor, photographer, etc.) 2. a radio broadcasting station. Syn. *himpilan ng radyo*.

estúpidó (es-tú-pi-dó), var. **istúpidó**, *adj.* (Sp.) stupid. Syn. *tangà, hangál, gunggóng, gago*.

estupendo (es-tu-pen-do), *adj.* (Sp.) stupendous; marvelous; amazing. Syn. *kahangá-hangà, kagulat-gulat, kataká-taká, kagilá-gilalás*.

estutse (es-tut-se), var. **istutse**, *n.* (Sp. *estuche*) 1. instrument bag or case, esp. for a doctor. 2. jewelry box.

eter (e-ter), *n.* (Sp.) ether.

eternidád (e-ter-ni-dád), *n.* (Sp.) 1. eternity; continuance without end. Syn. *kawaláng-hanggán, kawalang-maliw, kawaláng-katapusán*. 2. future life; life after death. Syn. *kabiláng-buhay*.

etiká (e-ti-ká), *n.* (Sp. *ética*) ethics; principles or science of right conduct. Syn. *tuntunin ng moralidád*.

etiketa (e-ti-ke-ta), *n.* (Sp. *etiqueta*) 1. label; tag. Syn. *tag, label, nakakabit na panandâ*. 2. etiquette; conventional rules for good behavior in a polite society. Syn. *tuntunin ng kabutihang-asal*.

etimolohiya (e-ti-mo-lo-hi-ya), *n.* (Sp. *etimología*) etymology. Syn. *pámuhatán, palapámuhatan, palámuhatán; palámulaan*.

etnikó (et-ni-kó), *adj.* (Sp. *étnico*) ethnic.

etnolohiya (et-no-lo-hi-ya), *n.* (Sp. *etnología*) ethnology. Syn. *palálahian, aghamlahì*.

etséterá (et-sé-te-rá), *adv.* et cetera; and others; and the like; and the rest. Syn. *at ibá pa*.

etyoloyiha (et-yo-lo-yi-ha), *n.* (Sp. *etiología*) etiology.

eukalipto (e-u-ka-lip-to), *n.* (Sp. *eucalipto*) eucalyptus.

eupemismo (e-u-pe-mis-mo), n. (Sp. *eufemismo*) euphemism.

G

G, g (ga), n. 1. the sixth letter of the *abakada* (Pilipino alphabet). 2. the type or impression representing this letter. 3. a symbol for the sixth in a group or series.

G., (abbrev. of *Ginoó*) Mr.; Mister; Sir.

ga- (ga), n. pref., meaning: 1. as big as, as in *gabahay*, as big as a house; *gabundók*, as big as a mountain. Syn. *sinlakí ng, kasinlaki ng*. 2. like or similar to, as in *ganiré*, like this; *ganiyán*, like that. Syn. *katulad, kagaya*.

gaán (ga-án), n. 1. lack of regular weight; lightness. Ant. *bigát*. 2. facility; ease or easiness of doing. Syn. *alwán*. Ant. *hirap*. 3. ease, as of life. Syn. *ginhawa*. 4. lightness, as of sleep. Syn. *babaw*. Ant. *himbing*.

gaanó (ga-a-nó), interrog. pron. 1. how much. Syn. *magkano*. 2. how many. Syn. *ilán*.

gabáy (ga-báy), n. 1. handrail; railing. Syn. *barandilya*. 2. guide; leader. Syn. *giyá, patnubay*. 3. a person who conducts another by the hand. Syn. *tagaakay*.

gabi (ga-bi), n. (Bot.) 1. a species of tuber plant called "taro" (Colocasia esculenta). 2. the tuberous rootstock of the plant, used as staple food in many localities.

gabí (ga-bí), n. night; evening.

gabí-gabí (ga-bí + ga-bí), adv. every night; nightly. Syn. *tuwíng gabí, bawa't gabí*.

gabinete (ga-bi-ne-te), n. (Sp.) a body of official advisers to the chief executive of a nation, usually composed of ministers or department secretaries; cabinet.

gabók (ga-bók), n. 1. dust; fine, dry earth. Syn. *alikabók*. 2. ash. Syn. *abó*.

gabót (ga-bót), adj. uprooted; pulled up by the roots.

gadgád (gad-gád), n. 1. act of grating something into shreds or particles by rubbing or scraping. Syn. *kudkód, kaskás*. 2. state or condition of being grated into shreds or particles.

gaga (ga-ga), I. adj. stupid, referring to a woman. Syn. *tangá, hangál, tonta*. 2. referring to a woman who has difficulty in pronouncing words, or one who stammers o stutters. Syn. *at-at (atát)*. Cf. *utal*.
—II. n. 1. a stupid woman. Syn. *babaing tangá*. 2. a woman stutter. Syn. *babaing at-at kung magsalitá*.

gagá (ga-gá), n. 1. usurpation; unlawful seizure of power, rights, property, etc. for oneself. Syn. *kamkám, pagkamkám, pangangamkám*. 2. act of forcing a woman to submit to sexual act; rape. Syn. *gahasà o paggahasa (sa babae)*.

gaga- (ga-ga-), pref., meaning only as big as; as tiny or fine as.

gagád (ga-gád), I. n. 1. imitation; mimicry; copying. Syn. *paggaya, panggagaya, pagtulad, panunulad*. 2. anything imitated or copied. Syn. *bagay na kinopya o ginaya*.
—II. adj. imitated or copied. Syn. *kinopya, ginaya*.

gagambá (ga-gam-bá), n. (Arach.) spider. Syn. *anlalawá*.

gagap (ga-gap), n. act of trying to hold at anything nervously or desperately. Syn. *hagilap, apuhap*.

gago (ga-go), adj. (Sp.) 1. stupid. Syn. *tangá, hangál, torpe, tonto*. 2. given to stuttering, referring to a man. Syn. *at-at*. Cf. *utál*.

gahák (ga-hák), adj. ripped open forcibly. Syn. *wakwák, wasák*.

gahaman (ga-ha-man), n. greed; greediness; covetousness. Syn. *takaw, katakawan, kasakimán, kakamkamán*.

gahasà (ga-ha-sà), n. 1. act of using force against another. Syn. *paggamit ng dahás o lakás, pagpuwersa, pamumuwersa*. 2. act of forcing a woman to submit to sexual act; raping. Syn. *pagpuwersa sa babae, paggahasà*. 3. impetuousity; violent haste; recklessness. Syn. *kawaláng-ingat, kapusukán, karahasán*.

gahì (ga-hì), n. a small rip or tear, esp. in clothes; snag. Cf. *lamat*.

gahís (ga-hís), I. n. 1. act of overpowering; subjugation by the use of force. or violence. Syn. *lupig, paglupig*. 2. act of raping (a woman). Syn. *paggahasà o*

gahól

galing

pagsasamantalá sa babae.
—II. *adj.* overpowered; beaten; subdued (by force). Syn. *lupìg, talo, natalo.*

gahól (ga-hól), *adj.* under pressure of time; late. Syn. *hulí, atrasado.* 2. in a hurry. Syn. *nagmamadalî, nag-aapurá.*

gala (ga-la), *n.* 1. chevron; insignia or stripes on the arm of a military officer. Syn. *galón.* 2. formal dress.

galà (ga-lù), *n.* 1. act of wandering around different places in a certain locality; perambulation. Syn. *libot, paglibot, paglilibót.* 2. act of travelling in far places. Syn. *lakbay, paglalakbáy.* 3. act of going around aimlessly. Syn. *lakwatsa, paglalakwatsa.* 4. (Bats.) act of wooing or courting a woman. Syn. *ligaw, pagligaw, panliligaw.*

galabók (ga-la-bók), *n.* (Prov.) fine dust or powder. Syn. *pinong pulbos o abó.*

galák (ga-lák), *n.* joy; happiness; gladness. Syn. *tuwâ, ligaya, lugód, saya.*

galamáy (ga-la-máy), *n.* 1. any of the appendages of Arthropods, like shrimps, lobsters, crabs, spiders, etc. Syn. *paá.* 2. any of the fingers of the hand or toes of the foot. Syn. *dalirì.* 3. (by extension) agent or representatives, as of a law enforcing body. Syn. *ahente, kinatawán.* 4. follower; subordinate. Syn. *tauhan.* 5. helper; aid; assistant. Syn. *katulong, kátulungín.*

galante (ga-lan-te), *adj.* (Sp.) 1. gallant; brave; chivalrous. Syn. *matapang.* 2. noble; manly. Syn. *máginoó, dakilà.*

galang (ga-lang), *n.* respect; courtesy; regard. Syn. *pítagan, alang-alang, respeto, pakundangan.*

galáng (ga-láng), *n.* 1. bracelet. Syn. *pulseras.* 2. fetter. Syn. *pataw o kadena sa paá.* 3. manacle; handcuff. Syn. *posas.*

galánggalangán (ga-láng-ga-la-ngán), *n.* wrist. Syn. *pupúlsuhan.*

galapóng (ga-la-póng), *n.* 1. rice flour. Cf. *arina.* 2. act of grinding rice into flour. Syn. *paggalapóng.*

galasgás (ga-las-gás), *n.* 1. roughness of surface. Syn. *ligasgás, gaspáng.* 2. rasp; harsh, grating sound, as that caused when cleaning wood with sandpaper. Syn. *kagaskás.*

galáw (ga-láw), *n.* movement; motion. Syn. *kilos, kibô.* 2. movement, as of inanimate objects. Syn. *ugâ, ugóy, yaníg.* 3 act of touching or removing a thing from its place. Syn. *hipò, paghipò; likót, paglikót.* 4. act of stealing a thing. Syn. *kupit, pagkupit; umít, pag-umít.* 5. (Bats.) act of joking or teasing someone. Syn. *birò, pagbirò, pagbibirò; tuksó, pagtuksó, panunuksó.*

galawgáw (ga-law-gáw), I. *adj.* 1. naughty; mischievous. Syn. *malikót, pilyo.* 2. restlessly moving from place to place; restless. Syn. *pagalà, layás, lagalág.*
—II. *n.* 1. a naughty or mischievous person, esp. a child. Syn. *malikót na batà.* 2. an idle wanderer; vagabond. Syn. *bagamundo, taong palaboy, hampaslupà.*

galaygáy (ga-lay-gáy), I. *n.* a going over from one to another until finished, as in visiting houses along a road. Syn. *gaygáy, paggaygáy.*
—II. *adj.* gone over from one to another, e.g, houses along a road. Syn. *pinuntaháng isá-isá, inisá-isá, ginaygáy.*

galbanisado (gal-ba-ni-sa-do), *adj.* (Sp. *galvanizado*) galvanized, referring esp. to iron roofing; plated with zinc.

galbót (gal-bót), *n.* sudden grabbing and pulling with the hand, as in uprooting plants forcibly. Syn. *gabot, labnót, halbót.*

galeón (ga-le-ón), var. **galyón**, *n.* (Sp. *galleón*) galleon; a large, heavy Spanish ship of the 15th and 16th centuries.

galera (ga-le-ra), *n.* (Sp.) 1. galley (ship); rowboat. 2. (Print.) a tray for holding composed types; galley. 3. an enclosure for cockfighting; cockpit. Syn. *galyera, ruweda.*

galeriya (ga-le-ri-ya), *n.* (Sp. *galeria*) 1. gallery; place or establishment for art exhibitions. Syn. *tanghalang-sining.* 2. (Theat.) balcony.

galgál (gal-gál), *adj.* stupid. Syn. *tangá, hangál, tunggák.*

galing (ga-ling), I. *adj.* (with *sa*) coming or proceeding from. Syn. *nagmulá sa, nagsimulá sa, nag-umpisá sa.*
—II. *adv.* 1. (with *sa*) from or originating from (a place). Syn. *mulá o buhat sa.* 2.

(with *kay*, followed by the name of a person) from; given by. Syn. *bigáy ni*. 3. derived from or base on. Syn. *hangó o batay sa*.

gáling (gá-ling), *n.* 1. recovery from sickness. Syn. *pagbuti ng karamdaman (sakít)*. 2. amulet; fetish. Syn. *mutyá, agimat, antíng-antíng*. 3. invulnerability. Syn. *kabál*. 4. merit; advantage; goodness. Syn. *husay, kahusayan; buti, kabutihan*. 5. skill; ability; expertness; mastery. Syn. *kadalubhasaan, kahusayan, kakayahán*. 6. importance. Syn. *halagá, kahalagahan*. 7. benefit. Syn. *pakinabang, kapakinabangán*. 8. luck; fortune. Syn. *suwerte, kapalaran, portuna*.

galís (ga-lís), *n.* a contagious skin disease caused by parasitic mite; itch; scabies. Cf. *dusdós*.

galit (ga-lit), *n.* 1. anger; ire; resentment. Syn. *samâ ng loób, hinanakít*. 2. indignation; wrath; rancor; hatred. Syn. *poót, pagkapoót; muhì, pagkamuhì*.

galón (ga-lón), *n.* (Sp.) 1. gallon; a unit of liquid measure equal to 4 quarts or 3.78 liters. 2. chevron; insignia or stripes on the arm of a military officer. Syn. *gala*.

galong (ga-long), *n.* earthen jar used as container for drinking water. Cf. *bangâ, kalambâ*.

galos (ga-los), *n.* slight scratch on skin or any surface. Syn. *gurlís, kalmós*.

galukgók (ga-luk-gók), *n.* noise caused by the movement of the stomach when one feels hungry. Syn. *kulô, laguklók, ugók*.

galugad (ga-lu-gad), *n.* act of going from place to place in search of something; extensive search for something missing. Syn. *masusing paghahanáp*.

galunggóng (ga-lung-góng), *n.* (*Ichth.*) a kind of fish known as "round scad" (*Decapterus sp.*)

galyetas (gal-ye-tas), *n.* (Sp. *galleta*) cracker; biscuit. Syn. *biskuwít*.

gamas (ga-mas), *n.* act of weeding a field, esp. a rice field, by using a trowel locally known as *dulós*. Syn. *pag-aalis ng mga damó sa tániman*.

gamay (ga-may), *adj.* suited to one's manner of using (instruments, machines, etc.).

Syn. *kasundó, kagamay*.

gambalà (gam-ba-là), *n.* 1. act of disturbing or troubling someone. Syn. *pagguló, pangguguló*. 2. disturbance; trouble. Syn. *guló, ligalig*. 3. delay; hindrance. Syn. *abala, sagwíl, sagabal*.

gamit (ga-mit), *n.* 1. act or manner of using; a putting to use; application. Syn. *paggamit*. 2. act of using as materials. Syn. *pagkasangkapan*. 3. use; utility; usage. Syn. *kagamitán*. 4. tool; instrument; paraphernalia; utensil. Syn. *kagamitán, kasangkapan*. 5. personal belongings or property. Syn. *arì, pag-aarì*. 6. furniture. Syn. *kasangkapan*. 7. material. Syn. *sangkáp, panangkáp*. 8. extra part, as of machine. 9. supplies, as for schools, offices, etc. Syn. *kagamitán*.

gamít (ga-mít), *adj.* used or worn previously by someone; not new; secondhand. Syn. *segunda-mano, hindî na bago*.

gamos (ga-mos), *n.* scratch marks on the skin. Syn. *galmós, kalmós, kalmót, galos*.

gamót (ga-mót), *n.* 1. act of treating a person of his sickness; treatment. Syn. *paggamót, pagbibigáy ng lunas o kagamutan sa maysakit*. 2. anything used to cure a disease; medicine. Syn. *medisina, panggamót*. 3. cure; remedy. Syn. *lunas*.

gampán (gam-pán), *n.* 1. performance, as of one's duty. Syn. *pagganáp o pagtupád (ng tungkulin), panunungkulan*. 2. keeping one's promise. Syn. *pagtupád o pagsasakatuparan sa pangakò*. 3. act of playing a role in a drama or play. Syn. *pagganáp, paglabás*.

gamugamó (ga-mu-ga-mó), *n.* winged termite that usually flies around a flame or light.

gamusa (ga-mu-sa), I. *n.* (Sp. *gamuza*) chamoise; chamoise skin or leather. —II. *adj.* made of chamoise skin or leather. Syn. *yarì sa gamusa*.

gana¹ (ga-na), *n.* (Sp.) appetite; relish for food or drink. Syn. *saráp ng panlasa sa pagkain, kasíyahan sa pagkain*.

gana² (ga-na), *n.* (Sp.) 1. interest in something; inclination; liking. Syn. *hilig, interés, kagustuhan*. 2. zeal; enthusiasm; diligence. Syn. *siglá, sigasig*.

gana³   **gantimpalà**

gana³ (ga-na), n. (Sp.) 1. salary; wages; earnings; income. Syn. *kita, suweldo, sahod.* 2. remuneration; reward; compensation. Syn. *gantimpagál, bayad, gantimpalá.* 3. gain; profit. Syn. *tubò, pakinabang, ganánsiyá.* 4. interest, as from loans. Syn. *tubò, patubò, interes, patong.*

ganado (ga-na-do), adj. (Sp.) 1. fully interested, enthusiastic, or inclined. Syn. *interesado, mahilig.* 2. animated. Syn. *masiglá, masayá.* 3. with or having full appetite. Syn. *nasásarapáng mabuti, magana.*

ganánsiyá (ga-nán-si-yá), n. (Sp. *ganancia*) 1. gain; profit. Syn. *tubò, pakinabang.* 2. benefit; reward. Syn. *pakinabang, palâ; gantimpalà.*

ganáng (ga-náng), I. adj. what is due or alloted to. Syn. *ukol sa, para sa.*
—II. prep., adv. used chiefly with sa: sa ganáng, meaning "as for' or "in the opinion "of".

ganáp (ga-náp), I. n. 1. fulfillment or performance, as of one's duty. Syn. *panunungkól, panunungkulan, paggampán, pagtupád ng tungkulin.* 2. acting or manner of acting, as in a play. Syn. *pagganáp (sa papél ng tauhan ng dulà).* 3. holding, as of a meeting. Syn. *daos, pagdaraos.* 4. fact or state of being complete; completeness. Syn. *kahustuhán, kakumpletuhan.*
—II. adj. 1. complete; full; exact. Syn. *buô, lubós.* 2. completed; finished. Syn. *tapós.* 3. fulfilled; done. Syn. *nagawâ na, náisagawâ na, natupád na.* 4. perfect; without error. Syn. *waláng-malî, tamanglahát.*
—III. adv. 1. sharp; exactly. Syn. *eksakto, hustúng-husto.* 2. completely. Syn. *lubós, lúbusan.*

ganda (gan-da; gan-dá), n. 1. beauty, as of a woman. Syn. *kagandahan, dilág, karilagán.* 2. splendor. Syn. *dikít, kariktán; dingal (ringal), karingalan.* 3. fineness; excellence; fine quality. Syn. *husáy, kahusayan.* 4. brightness or fineness, as of weather. Syn. *kaaliwalasan, kaliwanagan, kagandahan.*

ganid (ga-nid), I. n. 1. wild animal or beast. Syn. *halimaw.* 2. a selfish or greedy

person. Syn. *taong sakím o matakaw.*
—II. adj. 1. bestial. Syn. *makahayop, ugaling-hayop.* 2. fierce. Syn. *mabangís, malupít.* 3. (of persons) selfish; greedy. Syn. *sakím, matakaw, hidhíd.*

ganiri (ga-ni-ri), adj. & adv. like this; in this manner. Syn. *ganitó, gayarí, katulad nitó, gaya nitó.*

ganit (ga-nit), 1. toughness, as of meat. Syn. *tigás, katigasán; kunat, kakunatan.* Ant. *lambót, kalambután.* 2. state or condition of being tight or hard to pull or rotate. Syn. *higpít, kahigpitán.* 3. tightness or firmness of something imbedded, making it hard to dislodge. Syn. *tibay, katibayan.* 4. (Fig.) stinginess. Syn. *kakuriputan, karamutan, katipirán.*

ganitó (ga-ni-tó), adj. & adv. like this; in this way or manner. Syn. *ganirí, gayarí, katulad nitó, gaya nitó.*

ganiyán (ga-ni-yán), var. **ganyán**, adv. 1. like that (referring to something near the person addressed). Syn. *katulad niyán; gaya niyán.* Cf. *ganoón, gayón.* 2. in the same manner or way as that; in that manner or way. Syn. *sa ganyáng paraán.*

ganoón (ga-no-ón), adv. 1. so; really so; true, as in *Ganoon ba? Is it so?* Syn. *talagá, totoó.* 2. like that; in that way or manner. Syn. *gayón, tulad (gaya) noón.*

gansâ (gan-sâ), n. (Zoo.; Sp. *ganso*) goose; gander (male goose).

gansál (gan-sál), I. adj. 1. odd or uneven, referring to numbers. Syn. *di-pares, mayputál.* 2. extra. Syn. *putál.*
—II. n. 1. an odd number. Syn. *numero o bilang na may putál.* 2. extra; excess from round figures. Syn. *putál.*

ganta (gan-ta), n. (of undetermined orig.) a unit of dry measure, the content of which is equivalent to that of a *salop.* Distinguished from *gatang.*

ganti (gan-ti; gan-tí), n. 1. retaliation; return of evil for evil; revenge; reprisal. Syn. *pagganti, higanti, paghihiganti.* 2. any reciprocal act. Syn. *palít, kapalít, tumbás, katumbás.* 3. answer; response. Syn. *sagót, kasagutan; tugón, katugunan.*

gantimpalà (gan-tim-pa-là), var. **gantingpalà**, n. 1. reward. Syn. *pabuyà, bigáy-*

palà. 2. prize given to a winner in a contest or competition. Syn. *premyo*.

gantsilyo (gan-tsil-yo), var. **gansilyo,** n. (Sp. *ganchillo*) 1. crochet; kind of knitting done with a one-hooked needle. 2. act of making cloth or a piece of clothing by looping together yarn or thread by means of a crochet needle; knitting. Syn. *paggagantsilyo*. 3. one-hooked needle; crochet hook. Syn. *panggantsilyo* (*panggansilyo*).

gantso (gan-tso), var. **ganso,** n. 1. hook. Syn. *kawit, kalawit*. 2. act of picking, getting, or taking (something) with a hook. Syn. *pagkalawit, pagkawit, paggantso*. 3. act of cheating or defrauding someone; swindle. Syn. *panggagantso, panunubà, pandaraya*.

ganyák (gan-yák), n. 1. an inducing or being induced; inducement. Syn. *hikayat, paghikayat, pagkahikayat*. 2. anything used to induce. Syn. *panghikayat*. 3. encouragement; stimulation. Syn. *pagpapasiglá, pagbibigáy-siglá*. 4. anything that gives encouragement. Syn. *pampasiglá*.

gangga- (gang-ga-), *pref.* (pl. of **ga-**) as big as, referring to an unspecified number of things, as in *mga along ganggabahay*, waves as big as houses.

ganggrena (gang-gre-na), var. **kanggrena,** n. (Sp. *gangrena*) gangrene. Syn. *pagkabulók ng alinmáng bahagi ng katawán ng taong buháy*.

gangster (gangs-ter), n. (Eng.) gangster; member of a gang of criminals. Syn. *matón, butangero*.

gaod (ga-od), n. 1. oar; paddle. Syn. *sagwán, panagwán, panggaod*. 2. act or manner of paddling or rowing. Syn. *paggaod, pagsagwán*. 3. oarsman. Syn. *mánanagwán, tagasagwán; manggagaod, tagagaod*.

gaot (ga-ot), n. (Eng.) gout; swelling and severe pain of the joints of the fingers and toes. Syn. *pamamagâ at pagsakít ng mga bukó ng daliri ng kamáy at paá*.

gapak (ga-pak), n. 1. a breaking or being broken off, referring esp. to a big branch of a standing tree. Syn. *pagsapak, pagkasapak; pagbalì, pagkabalì*. 2. the part

of a tree from which a big branch has been broken by force.

gapang (ga-pang), n. 1. act of creeping or crawling; moving along on one's hands and knees. Syn. *paggapang*. 2. a growing along the ground, a wall, or the like, as some plants. 3. (*Fig.*) act of getting or obtaining something by secret maneuvering. Syn. *lihim na paglakad (sa isáng bagay na ibig mátamó)*.

gapas (ga-pas), n. act or manner of cutting grass, harvesting rice, wheat, etc. with a scythe or sickle. Syn. *paggapas*.

gapì (ga-pì), n. 1. act of overpowering an opponent; subjugation. Syn. *lupig, paglupig; supil, pagsupil; talo, pagtalo*. 2. act of breaking off (a small branch) with one's hand. Syn. *balì, pagbalì*.

gapok (ga-pok), n. state or condition of being weak, referring esp. to things like wood, paper, clothes, etc., due to decay or destruction of weevils, termites, etc. Syn. *dupók, karupukán*.

gapos (ga-pos), n. 1. act of tying a person, animal, or thing against a post, etc. Syn. *paggagapos sa poste, atb.* 2. act of tying or binding the hands, arms, and legs with or as with a rope. Syn. *paggapos*. 3. a rope, wire, or the like used for binding or tying a person, animal, or thing to prevent from escaping or moving around. 4. (*Fig.*) anything that restrains or restricts. Syn. *hadláng, sagabal*.

garà (ga-rà), n. 1. dressiness; elegance. Syn. *kisig, kakisigan; kapusturahan, pagkapustura*. 2. splendor; pomposity; stateliness. Syn. *dingal, karingalan; rangyâ, karangyaán*.

garahe (ga-ra-he), n. (Sp. *garahe*) 1. garage; shelter or storage place for an automobile or automobiles; also carport. Syn. *silungán ng awto*. 2. (*Colloq.*) private car or cars for hire, esp. those maintained by business establishments. Cf. *taksi*. 3. act of putting a car into the garage. Syn. *paggarahe, pagkarbam*.

garalgál (ga-ral-gál), n. 1. gargling sound as that produced in the throat when one rinses the mouth with liquid. Syn. *kalâ*. 2. the cranky or husky sound caused by the motion of a loose or poorly adjusted mechanical contrivance. Syn. *kalantóg, kasóg*.

garantisado (ga-ran-ti-sa-do), *adj.* (Sp. *garantizado*) 1. guaranteed. Syn. *may garantiyá*. 2. of proven quality, efficiency, worth, etc. Syn. *tiyák na mahusay*.

garantiya (ga-ran-ti-ya; yá), *n.* (Sp. *garantia*) 1. giving security; guarantee. Syn. *paggarantiyá, pananagót, pag-akò*. 2. guarantee; something given or held as security. Syn. *akò, panagót*.

garapa (ga-ra-pa), *n.* (Sp. *garrafa*) a small bottle or carafe. Syn. *botelya*.

garapál (ga-ra-pál), *adj.* (Sp. *garrafal*) outrageous; monstrous, as in *garapál na kawaláng-hiyáan*, outrageous shamelessness. Syn. *nápakalakí, labis-labis, masyado*.

garapata (ga-ra-pa-ta), *n.* (*Entom.* Sp. *garrapata*) a species of tick, usually found in dogs. Cf. *kutô*.

garapinyera (ga-ra-pin-ye-ra), *n.* (Sp. *garapiñera*) ice cream freezer.

garapón (ga-ra-pón), *n.* (Sp. *garrafón*) 1. a medium-sized wide-mouthed bottle, used usually as container for sweet preserves, sugar, candies, etc. 2. demijohn. Syn. *damahuwana*.

garbansos (gar-ban-sos), var. **garabansos**, **grabansos**, *n.* (Sp. *garbanzo*) chick-pea (the plant or its edible pea).

garbo (gar-bo), *n.* 1. grace; gracefulness; elegance. Syn. *kisig, kakisigan*. 2. dressiness. Syn. *garà, kagaraan*.

garden (gar-den), *n.* (Eng.) ground used for planting vegetables, flowering plants, etc.; garden. Syn. *hardin (hardìn), halamanan (hálamanán)*.

gardenya (gar-den-ya), *n.* (*Bot.*, Sp. *gardenia*) 1. gardenia; a tropical tree shrub which bears white or yellowish flowers with fragrant, waxy petals. 2. the flower of this plant. Syn. *rosál*.

garíl (ga-ríl), *adj.* with or having defective speech or pronunciation. Cf. *utál, humál*.

garing (ga-ring), I. *n.* 1. the hard, white substance forming the tusk of elephants, walruses, etc.; ivory. Syn. *marpil*. 2. ivory color; creamy white (color). Syn. *kulay-*

garing, kulay-gatas.
—II. *adj.* 1. of or made of ivory. Syn. *yarì sa garing*. 2. of or having creamy-white color. Syn. *kulay-garing, kulay-gatas*.

garisón (ga-ri-són), *n.* (Eng.) 1. garrison; military post or station. Syn. *himpilang-militár*. 2. troops stationed in a fort. Syn. *mga tropa o kawal na nakatalagá sa isáng tanggulan*.

garlan (gar-lan), *n.* (Eng.) garland; wreath of flowers generally worn around the neck; lei. Syn. *kuwintás na bulaklák*.

garote (ga-ro-te), *n.* (Sp. *garrote*) 1. a thick stick or club; cudgel. Syn. *batutà, panghataw, pamugbóg*. 2. garrote; strangling apparatus for capital punishment. Syn. *bitayán*.

garter (gar-ter), *n.* (Eng.) an elastic band for holding a stocking in position; garter. Syn. *ligas*.

gas (gas), *n.* (Sp., Eng.) 1. gas; kerosene; petroleum. Syn. *gaás, petrolyo*. 2. gasoline. Syn. *gasolina*.

gasa (ga-sa), *n.* (Sp.) 1. gauze. 2. a black armband worn as a sign of mourning.

gasák (ga-sák), *adj.* rent, ripped, or torn, referring esp. to fabrics. Syn. *punít, sirâ, wasák, wakwák*.

gasket (gas-ket), *n.* (Eng.) gasket; a ring or disk made of cork, rubber, etc. used to make a joint tight against leakage. Syn. *sapatilya*.

gasera (ga-se-ra), *n.* (Sp.) gas lamp; kerosene lamp. Syn. *ilaw na (ilawáng) de-gas*.

gaseta (ga-se-ta), *n.* (Sp. *gazeta*) gazette. Cf. *mágasín, páhayagán, rebista*.

gasgás (gas-gás), I. *adj.* 1. worn-out or made thin by friction or constant use. Syn. *pudpód or manipís na sa kágagamit*. 2. with or having a scratch or scratches.
—II. *n.* 1. state or quality of being worn-out or made thin due to friction or constant use. Syn. *kapudpurán o kanipisán sa kágagamit*. 2. the part or portion of a thing that is worn-out by friction or constant use, or that which has a scratch or scratches on the surface. 3. act of rubbing something against another to make it smooth or thinner.

gasino (ga-si-no), I. *adj.* not much; of little

amount or value. *Gasino na ang kuwartáng itó*. This money is not much.

—II. *adv.* (usually with *waláng-* or *di-*) not so much or so many: *Waláng-gasinong dumaló*, not so many attended.

gasláw (gas-láw), *n.* 1. roughness or coarseness in manner or behavior. Syn. *gaspáng o kagaspangán (ng ugalì)*, *bastós, kabastusán, pagkabastós*. 2. rough acting or movement; restlessness; mischievousness. Syn. *harós, kaharusán; harót, kaharután; likót, kalikután*.

gasó (ga-só), *n.* 1. mischievousness; prankishness. Syn. *likót, kalikután; harót, kaharután; pilyo, kapilyuhán*. 2. roughness in manners or behavior. Syn. *gasláw, kagaslawán; gaspáng or kagaspangán (ng ugalì)*.

gasolina (ga-so-li-na), *n.* (Sp.) gasoline.

gaspáng (gas-páng), *n.* 1. roughness to the touch, as of surfaces that are not well-polished. Syn. *ligasgás, kaligasgasán, kagaspangán*. Ant. *kinis, kakinisan*. 2. coarseness, as of things not well-ground or well-pounded. Syn. *pagkadi-duróg na mabuti*. Ant. *pino, kapinuhan*. 3. coarseness or meanness of conduct or behavior. Syn. *gasláw, kagaslawán; hamak, kahamakan*.

gasta (gas-ta), *n.* (Sp. *gastar*) act or manner of spending money for buying things. Syn. *gugol, paggugol*.

gastado (gas-ta-do), *adj.* (Sp.) 1. worn-out by friction or constant use. Syn. *sirâ na o gasgás na sa kágagamit*. 2. already weak due to overwork. Syn. *inutil na, walâ nang kaya, mahinà na*. 3. already used up or expended, referring to money or any appropriation. Syn. *nagasta na, ubós nang gugulin*.

gastadór (gas-ta-dór), I. *n.* (Sp.) spendthrift; squanderer. Syn. *taong bulagsák o mapaggugól*.

—II. *adj.* given to spending uselessly; extravagant. Syn. *bulagsák. palágugól*.

gastos (gas-tos), *n.* (Sp. *gasto*) 1. act or manner of spending money. Syn. *gasta, paggasta; gugol, paggugol*. 2. expenses. Syn. *gugol o mga nagugol*.

Gat. (Gat.), *n.* title of nobility or of recognized greatness of a man, used before the name of a person during the later part of the Spanish regime in the Philippines. Cf. *Lakán*.

gatâ (ga-tâ), *n.* 1. act or manner of squeezing out the juice of grated coconut meat. Syn. *paggatâ*. 2. the juice squeezed out from coconut meat; coconut milk.

gatang (ga-tang), *n.* chupa, a unit of dry measure for grains, more or less equivalent to 1/8 of a ganta (*salóp*).

gatas (ga-tas), *n.* 1. milk. 2. act or manner of milking (an animal). Syn. *paggatas*.

gatasan (ga-ta-san), *v.* 1. to milk; draw or extract the milk of, referring to an animal. Syn. *kunan ng gatas*. 2. to add milk to; mix with milk. Syn. *lagyán o haluan ng gatas*. 3. (Fig.) to extract money from (someone) by exploitation. Syn. *kikilan (fig.)*

gatid (ga-tid), *n.* tough tissues of meat which is hard to masticate. Syn. *gatil*.

gatil (ga-til), I. *n.* tough meat fibers or tissues. See **gatid.**

—II. *adj.* tough or hard to masticate, referring to tissues or fibers of meat. Syn. *maganít, matigás*.

gatilyo (ga-til-yo), *n.* (Sp. *gatillo*) trigger (of a gun). Syn. *gato, kálabitan (ng baríl)*.

gatlâ (gat-lâ), *n.* 1. a small nick, cut, or notch made on the edge of something. Syn. *gatgát*. 2. act or manner of cutting a nick or small notch on something.

gatláng (gat-láng), *n.* 1. a space between two words in a printed matter.. Syn. *pagitan o puwáng*. 2. (Gram.) a dash (–). Cf. *gitlíng* (hyphen). 3. anyone of the several notches or nicks that indicates doses of medicine in a bottle. Syn. *gatgát*.

gatô (ga-tô), I. *adj.* structurally weak due to decay or long exposure to the elements. Syn. *marupók o mahinà na dahil sa pagkabulók, gapók, bulók*.

—II. *n.* 1. state or condition of being structurally weak due to decay or long exposure to the elements. 2. the part or portion of a thing that is already weak due to decay. Syn. *gapok*.

gatod (ga-tod), I. *n.* 1. quality or habit of being luxuriously or overly dressed. 2. a person, esp. a woman, who overly dresses. 3. lasciviousness; lust. Syn. *kalandián, kakirihán*.

—II. *adj.* 1. given to the habit of being over-dressy. Syn. *labis na posturyosa*. 2. lascivious. Syn. *landî, malandî, kirí, makirí*.

gatól (ga-tól), *n.* 1. an unexpected obstacle or difficulty. Syn. *di-inaasahang sagabal o hadláng*. 2. snag or interruption of a smooth movement or operation. Syn. *untól, pagkáuntól*.

gatong (ga-tong), *n.* 1. fuel, as kerosene, coal, charcoal, firewood, etc. Syn. *panggatong*. 2. act of feeding the fire with fuel. 3. (*Fig.*) instigation. Syn. *sulsól, apuyo*.

gauran (ga-u-ran), *v.* to propel (a boat, canoe, or the like) by means of a paddle. Syn. *sagwanán*.

gawâ (ga-wâ), I. *n.* 1. act of making something; creation; manufacture. Syn. *yarì, pagyarì*. 2. act of working or doing something. Syn. *trabaho, pagtatrabaho*. 3. work; occupation; employment. Syn. *trabaho, empleyo, okupasyón, hanapbuhay; propesyón*. 4. task; duty. Syn. *tungkulin, katungkulan*. 5. a thing done or made by someone; work. Syn. *obra, trabaho*. 6. act or deed. Syn. *kagagawán*. 7. literary work or composition. Syn. *akdá, kathá, obra*.

—II. *adj.* 1. made or manufactured (by). Syn. *yarì, niyarì (ni o ng)*. 2. written or authored by. Syn. *sinulat ni*. 3. created or composed by. Syn. *kathâ o kinathâ ni; akdâ o inakdâ ni*. 4. caused by. Syn. *sanhî o likhâ ng*.

—III. *adv.* because of; due to. Syn. *dahil sa*.

gawák (ga-wák), I. *n.* fact, state, or condition of having a wide rip. Syn. *pagkagawak, pagkawakwák*.

—II. *adj.* with or having a big rip, rent, or crack. Syn. *wasák, wakwák, windáng*.

gawad (ga-wad), *n.* 1. act of bestowing or awarding something to someone. Syn. *pagkakaloób, pagbibigáy*. 2. an award or grant. Syn. *kaloób, handóg*. 2. prize; reward. Syn. *premyo, gantimpalà*. 3. declaration or pronouncement, as of sentence on a convicted person. Syn.

paggagawad o paglalapat.

gáwain (gá-wa-in), *n.* 1. work; duty; job; occupation; employment. Syn. *trabaho, empleyo, hanapbuhay, okupasyón, tungkulin*. 2. conduct; behavior; act. Syn. *ugalì, kaugalián*. 3. deed; act. Syn. *kagagawán*. 4. vice; vicious character. Syn. *bisyo*.

gawáng-kamáy (ga-wáng + ka-máy), *adj.* hand-made. Syn. *yaring-kamáy*.

gawáng-isip (ga-wáng + i-sip), *n.* mental work.

gawáng-tao (ga-wáng + ta-o), *adj.* man-made. Syn. *yaring-tao, likháng-tao*.

gaway (ga-way), *n.* witchcraft; sorcery. Syn. *kulam, pangkukulam*.

gawgáw (gaw-gáw), *n.* cassava or corn starch; laundry starch. Syn. *almiról, almidón*.

gawì (ga-wì), *n.* 1. habit; custom. Syn. *ugalì, kaugalián*. 2. propensity; inclination; tendency. Syn. *hilig, pagkahilig*. 3. direction; the way a person faces or points. Syn. *dako, banda*. 4. way or manner of acting. Syn. *kilos, astà*.

gaya (ga-ya), I. *n.* act of copying or imitating something done or made by someone. Syn. *paggaya, pagtulad, paggagád, pagkopya*.

—II. *adj.* 1. imitated; copied. Syn. *ginaya, kinopya, hinuwád, ginagád*. 2. like; similar to. Syn. *katulad, kagaya, kapareho*.

gayák (ga-yák), I. *n.* 1. ornament; decoration. Syn. *palamuti, adorno, dekorasyón*. 2. act, way, or manner of dressing. Syn. *pagbibihis, pagkakábihis*. 3. a person's attire. Syn. *suót, kasuután; bihis; damít, pananamít*. 4. intention; plan. Syn. *balak, plano, tangkâ*. 5. preparation, as for a trip. Syn. *handâ, paghahandâ*.

–II. *adj.* 1. ready; prepared for. Syn. *nakahandâ, preparado*. 2. with or having a plan to go on a trip. Syn. *may-balak*.

gayarí (ga-ya-rí), *adv.* like this; in this way or manner. Syn. *ganitó, ganirí*.

gayat (ga-yat), *n.* 1. act of cutting or slicing (something) into small, thin pieces with or as with a knife. Syn. *paggayat, paghiwà nang pino at maninipís*. 2. a small, thin piece of something; small slice. Cf. *hiwà, piraso, gilít*.

gaygáy (gay-gáy), I. n. 1. act of going over from one (place) to another until finished, as in visiting a row of houses in a certain place. Syn. *pag-isá-isá*. 2. a going over around a certain place, as in search for something. Syn. *galugad, paggalugad*.
—II. adj. 1. gone over from one to another; visited individually. Syn. *nilibot na isá-isá, ginaygáy*. 2. searched all over, referring to a place. Syn. *galugád, ginalugad*.

gayón (ga-yón), I. pron. something like that (those). Syn. *gaya o katulad niyón*.
—II. adv. 1. in that way or manner. 2. so; in such a manner.

gayót (ga-yót), n. coarseness or roughness to the bite, esp. of tubers. Cf. *kunat, ganít*.

gayuma (ga-yu-ma), n. 1. charming quality; love charm. Syn. *panghalina, pang-akit*. 2. a potion or charm that causes a person to fall in love; philter. Syn. *galíng sa babae*.

gayundín (ga-yun-dín), adv. in the same way or manner; likewise; equally.

gayunmán (ga-yun-mán), I. adv. nevertheless; notwithstanding. 2. however. Syn. *kung sa bagay*.

gera (ge-ra), var. **giyera**, n. (Sp. *guerra*) 1. act of waging a war. Syn. *paggera; paglusob sa kaaway*. 2. an open-armed conflict, between or among nations. Syn. *digmâ, digmaan*.

gerero (ge-re-ro), n. (Sp. *guerrero*) warrior; experienced soldier. Syn. *mandirigmâ, sundalo*

gerilya (ge-ril-ya), var. **girilya**, n. (Sp. *guerrilla*) 1. guerilla warfare. 2. a member of a guerilla band; guerilla fighter. Syn. *gerilyero*.

gibâ (gi-bâ), I. n. 1. act of destroying or wrecking a structure; demolition; destruction. Syn. *paggibâ, pagwasák, pagwalat*. 2. state or condition of being wrecked or totally destroyed. Syn. *pagkagibâ, kagibaán; pagkawasák, kawasakán; pagkawalat, kawalatan*. 3. the remains of a structure that has been destroyed or badly damaged; ruin; wreck. Syn. *guhò*.
—II. adj. demolished; fallen down; destroyed; wrecked; totally damaged. Syn. *wasák, guhô, gupô, walát*.

gibík (gi-bík), n. 1. a cry for help. Syn. *hiyáw na humíhingî ng saklolo, pagpapadaló*. 2. a person or thing that succors; succor. Syn. *saklolo, sukoro*. 3. the help or assistance given or sent in response to one crying for help. Syn. *tulong, sukoro, saklolo*.

gikgík (gik-gík), n. 1. giggle or titter. Syn. *ngisi, ngisngís, hagikhík*. 2. grunting, as of a young pig. Syn. *igík*.

gigì (gi-gì), n. meticulosity. Syn. *kurirì, kakuririan*.

gigil (gi-gil), n. suppressed pleasure or thrill, or sometimes anger, manifested by the gritting of the teeth and tight gripping of the hands. Cf. *ngitngít*.

gihà (gi-hà), n. 1. a small crack or fissure. Syn. *lamat, biták*. 2. groove between lobes or parts of an organ, as in the brain; also the cellular division in fruits like oranges. Syn. *lihà*. 3. grain in wood. Syn. *gisok*.

giho (gi-ho; gi-hò), n. (*Bot.*) 1. a tree that produces lumber of the first group (*Shorea guiso*). 2. the lumber obtained from this tree.

giik (gi-ik), var. **giík**, n. 1. act of threshing rice, esp. with the feet. Syn. *paggiík*. 2. act of crushing something with the feet; trampling. Syn. *yurak, pagyurak; yakyák, pagyakyák; yapáw, pagyapáw*.

giit (gi-it; gi-ít), n. 1. act of taking or maintaining a firm stand; insistence. Syn. *pilit, pagpilit, pagpupumilit*. 2. act of elbowing one's way through the crowd. Syn. *siksík, pagsiksík, pagsusumiksík*.

gilagid (gi-la-gid), n. (*Anat.*) gums of the teeth. Syn. *ngidngíd, gidgíd*.

gilalas (gi-las-las), n. astonishment; bewilderment; amazement. Syn. *taká, pagtataká; manghâ, pagkamanghâ; gulat, pagkagulat*.

gilas (gi-las), n. 1. elegance; refined grace in manners or action. Syn. *kisig, kakisigan*. 2. gallantry. Syn. *kagalantihán, pagkamáginoó, kabalyerosidád*. 3. bravery; gallantry. Syn. *tapang, katapangan; giting, kagitingan*.

gilgíl (gil-gíl), n. act of cutting an object with an instrument pressed hard while being moved to and fro, without raising it, as with a dull knife or saw.

gilik (gi-lik), n. powdery substance covering husks of rice, straws, and blades of some grasses that usually causes irritation or itchiness on the skin. Cf. *bulo*.

gilid (gi-lid), n. border; edge; margin; brink; rim. Syn. *tabí*, *bingit*.

giling (gi-ling), n. 1. act or manner of crushing something into powder by grinding. 2. act of milling rice. Syn. *kiskís*, *pagkiskís*.

gilingan (gi-li-ngan), var. **gilingán**, n. 1. grinder; grinding machine; millstone. Syn. *panggiling*, *molino*. 2. mill; rice mill. Syn. *kiskisan*. 3. rice milling season. Syn. *panahón ng paggiling*.

gilit (gi-lit), I. n. 1. act of cutting, esp. fish, into thin pieces or slices. Cf. *hiwà*, *paghiwà*; *gayat*, *paggayat*. 2. a thin cut or slice, as of meat, fish, etc. Syn. *hiwà*, *gayat*, *tahad*, *katay*, *piraso*. 3. a small cut or nick, as made with a knife. Syn. *gatgát*. 4. a wrinkle-like groove around the neck of some persons. Cf. *gatlâ*. 5. act of cutting an object with a bladed instrument pushed forward and backward without raising it. Syn. *gilgil*, *paggilgíl*. 6. act of killing, e.g. a chicken, by cutting the neck in the manner described above.
—II. *adj.* sliced, as fish sold in the market.

giliw (gi-liw), I. n. 1. love; affection. Syn. *pag-ibig*, *pagmamahál*, *pagsuyô*. 2. darling; sweetheart. Syn. *mahál*, *kasuyò*, *sinta*, *mutyâ*, *liyág*, *kasi*, *kasintahan*. 3. fondness. Syn. *paghangà*, *pagsamba*, *pagtatangì*.
—II. *adj.* beloved; dear. Syn. *mahál*, *minámahál*, *iníibig*, *sinísinta*, *nilíliyág*, *kinákasi*, *minúmutyâ*.

gilyotina (gil-yo-ti-na), n. (Sp. *guillotina*) guillotine. Syn. *garote*, *bibitayán*.

gimbál (gim-bál), I. n. 1. great noise; resounding noise. Syn. *malakás na ingay o pagkakáingayán*. 2. great confusion or disturbance caused by loud sounds or noises. Syn. *malakíng guló o pagkakaguló*. 3. kettledrum.
—II. *adj.* greatly disturbed, as by loud sounds or noises. Syn. *ligalíg na ligalíg*, *gulúng-guló*.

ginang (gi-nang), I. n. (abbrev. Gng.) 1. missus; a wife. Syn. *maybahay*. 2. matron; married woman.
—II. *adj.* married, referring to a woman. Syn. *may-asawa na (kung bagá sa isáng babae)*.

ginaok (gi-na-ok), n. a kind of thick syrup or molasses. Cf. *bagkat*, *inuyat*.

ginataán (gi-na-ta-án), var. **ginatán**, I. n. a kind of native food cooked in or with coconut milk.
—II. *adj.* mixed or cooked with or in coconut milk.

gináw (gi-náw), n. 1. coldness of weather; cold temperature. Syn. *lamíg*, *kalamigán*. 2. cold feeling due to coldness of weather. Syn. *kaligkíg o pangangaligkig sa lamíg*. 3. chill, as from fever. Syn. *ngiki*, *pangingiki*.

ginhawa (gin-ha-wa), I. n. 1. ease of life or living; comfort. Syn. *luwág o alwán ng buhay*. 2. convenience or easiness of doing or making something. Syn. *dalî o alwáng gawín*. 3. prosperity; abundance; freedom from want. Syn. *kasaganaan*, *pananaganà*. 4. consolation; satisfaction. Syn. *alíw*, *kaaliwan*, *kasiyahan*. 5. freedom from pain or suffering. Syn. *kawaláng-hirap*, *kaginhawahan*.
—II. *adj.* 1. easy to do or make. Syn. *maalwán o madalíng gawín*. 2. comfortable (to use). Syn. *kombenyente*; *masaráp gamitin*. 3. prosperous; abundant. Syn. *saganà*, *masaganà*.

giniikan (gi-ni-i-kan), n. rice stalks or straw. Syn. *dayami*.

giniling (gi-ni-ling), I. *adj.* ground or milled. Syn. *gilíng*.
—II. n. ground meat, esp. beef; hamburger.

ginintuán (gi-nin-tu-án), *adj.* 1. golden. Syn. *kulay-gintô*. 2. gilded. Syn. *lubóg sa gintô*, *dorado*, *dinorado*.

gining (gi-ning), n. 1. a teenage girl; young lady. Syn. *dalagita*, *munting binibini*, *dalágindíng*. 2. (G-) Miss. Syn. *Binibini*.

ginoó (gi-no-ó), n. (abbrev. G.) 1. gentleman. Syn. *máginoó*, *kabalyero*. 2. (G-) Sir; Mister (Mr.).

ginsa (gin-sa), *adv.* suddenly; all of a sudden; unexpectedly: now becoming obsolescent, except as a combining form, as in *kaginsá-ginsá* and *di-kaginsá-ginsá*.

gintô   **gitil**

gintô (gin-tô), I. n. 1. gold, a precious metal.
Syn. *oro.* 2. gold coin. Syn. *kuwartáng
gintô.* 3. (*Colloq.*) money. Syn. *salapî,
pera, kuwaltá.* 4. (*Colloq.*) riches; wealth.
Syn. *yaman, kayamanan.* 5. the bright
yellow color of gold. Syn. *kulay-gintô.*
—II. adj. 1. of gold; made of gold. Syn.
yarì sa gintô. 2. (*Colloq.*) very important;
of great value. Syn. *nápakahalagá.*

gipalpál (gi-pal-pál), n. 1. thick slimy dirt
on any surface. 2. state or condition of
being thick with slimy dirt.

gipìt (gi-pìt), I. adj. 1. lacking or wanting
in space, referring to a place. Syn. *makipot,
masikíp.* 2. financially in need; needy;
poor; indigent. Syn. *dukhâ, marálitâ; hiráp,
mahirap, naghíhirap; hikahós, naghíhikayós;
dahóp, nagdárahóp.* 3. unable to move
freely due to lack of space. Syn. *sikî.* 4.
cornered or surrounded, as by enemies.
Syn. *pikót, kubkób.* 5. under time pressure;
pressed for time. Syn. *gahól, kulang sa
panahón.*
—II. n. 1. state or condition of being in
need of wider space. Syn. *kakulangán sa
lugár, kakiputan ng lugar.* 2. fact, state, or
condition of being needy or poor. Syn.
karálitaán, karukhaán, kahirapan. 3. tight
or hard situation. Syn. *mahirap na
kalagayan (katayuan).*

gipos (gi-pos), n. complete exhaustion. Syn.
*lubós na pagod (pagkapagod), pangangapós
ng hiningá sa pagod.*

gipuspós (gi-pus-pós), n. disconsolation; low
spirit. Syn. *lungkót, kalungkutan; lumbáy,
kalumbayan; tamláy o katamlayan ng
katawán.* 2. great trouble or affliction.
Syn. *dalamhatì, pagdadalamhatì.*

giray (gi-ray), n. 1. stagger; reeling or
tottering movement, as of a drunk. Syn.
suray, pagsuray, pag-suray-suray. 2.
dilapidated condition, as of a house about
to fall to pieces.

girì (gi-rì), n. 1. a flirting or an affected
show of gallantry, as by a cock before
copulation. 2. (by extension) courting;
courtship. Syn. *ligaw, pagligaw.*

girimpulá (gi-rim-pu-lá), var. **girimpulád,** n.
weathercock; weather vane. Syn.
patubilíng, banóglawin.

gisá (gi-sá), n. (Sp. *guisar*) act or manner of
sautéing food.

gisantes (gi-san-tes), n. (Sp. *guisantes*) sweet
peas.

gisì (gi-sì), n. 1. a slight trace or mark of
tear or rent in cloth. Syn. *simulâ o
pagsísimulân ng punit.* 2. a slight run or
ravel in something knitted, as in a
stocking. Syn. *nisnís.*

gisíng (gi-síng), I. adj. 1. awake; not asleep.
Syn. *di-natutulog, di-tulóg.* 2. alert; active;
well-informed. Syn. *mulát (fig.), alerto,
listo.*
—II. n. 1. state or condition of being
awake (not asleep). 2. a being educated
or cultured.

gitara (gi-ta-ra), n. (Sp. *guitarra*) guitar.

gitatà (gi-ta-tà), n. 1. wet, sticky dirt. Syn.
lamirà. 2. dirty, sticky condition of a place
or thing. Syn. *panggigitatà, panlalamirà.*

gitaw (gi-taw), 1. appearance, showing up,
or coming out, as from long absence of
hiding. Syn. *sipót, pagsipót; litáw, paglitáw;
pagpapakita.* 2. prominence; rising above
others. Syn. *pangingibabaw.* 3. a rising, as
of the sun, moon, etc. Syn. *silang,
pagsilang; sikat, pagsikat.* 4. a rising or
coming out, as from water. Syn. *ulpót, pag-
ulpót; sulpót, pagsulpót.* 5. a showing up,
as from a window. Syn. *sungaw,
pagsungaw.* 6. a coming out, as from a
house, room, etc. Syn. *labás, paglabás.* 7.
eruption, as of skin diseases. Syn. *singáw,
pagsingáw.*

gitgit (git-git), I. n. 1. act of forcing oneself
into a thick crowd. Syn. *siksík, pagsiksík,
pakikipagsiksikan.* 2. insistence, as of one's
desire or wish. Syn. *giít, paggigiít.* 3. a
small cut or nick made by means of a
bladed instrument. Syn. *gatgát.* 4. act of
making a small cut or nick by pressing
forward and backward a dull bladed
instrument. Syn. *gilgíl, paggilgíl.*
—II. adj. crowded. Syn. *sikíp, siksikan,
gipít.*

gitî (gi-tî), n. first appearance, as of
perspiration or sweat from the pores of the
skin. Syn. *litáw o paglitáw (ng pawis).*

gitil (gi-til), n. tight bite or grip of teeth as
a manifestation of thrill, admiration, or

even controlled anger. Cf. *gigil, panggigigil.*

giting (gi-ting), n. heroic character or
quality; heroism; bravery. Syn. *tapang,*
katapangan. 2. heroic deed. Syn.
kabayanihan, pagkabayani. 3. greatness.
Syn. *kadakilaán.*

gitlá (git-lá), var. **giklá**, n. sudden surprise,
fear, or scare; shock. Syn. *pagkabiglâ,*
kabiglaanan; sindák, pagkasindak; gulat,
pagkagulat. 2. act of causing someone to
be surprised. Syn. *paggulat, pagsindák.*

gitlapì (git-la-pì), n. (Gram.) infix. Cf.
panlapì, unlapì, hulapì.

gitlíng (git-líng), n. (Gram.) hyphen. Syn.
giyón. Cf. *gatláng.*

gitnâ (git-nâ), I. n. middle; center; midst;
midway. Syn. *sentro.*

—II. adj. central, as in *Gitnáng Luson,*
Central Luzon.

giwang (gi-wang), var. **gewang**, n. wobbling
movement, as of a running dilapidated
vehicle. Syn. *gibang, giray.*

giya (gi-ya; gi-yá), n. (Sp. *guía*) 1. act of
guiding. Syn. *paggiyá, pagpatnubay.* 2. a
guide; person who shows the way. Syn.
patnubay. 3. instructions to follow;
guiding principle; pointers. Syn. *tuntunin,*
pánuntunan.

giyagis (gi-ya-gis), n. 1. restlessness;
uneasiness; distress. Syn. *balisa,*
pagkabalisa; di-pagkápalagáy. 2. rubbing
of one body against another. Syn. *kiyakis.*

glab (glab), n. (Eng.) 1. glove. Syn. *guwante*
(guwantes). 2. mitt or glove used in
baseball. 3. boxing glove.

gladyadór (glad-ya-dór), n. (Sp. *gladiador*)
gladiator.

gladyola (glad-yo-la), n. (Bot., Sp. *gladiola*)
gladiolus.

glándulá (glán-du-lá), n. (Sp.) gland. Syn.
kulanì.

glaukoma (gla-u-ko-ma), n. (Med., Sp.,
Eng.) glaucoma.

gliserina (gli-se-ri-na), n. (Sp. *glicerina*)
glycerine.

globo (glo-bo), n. (Sp.) globe; world. Syn.
mundo, daigdíg. 2. balloon. Syn. *lobo.*

glorya (glor-ya), n. (Sp. *gloria*) 1. glory. Syn.
luwalhatì, kaluwalhatian. 2. heaven;
paradise. Syn. *langit, paraiso.* 3. fame;

great honor. Syn. *kabantugan.* 4. blessing;
grace. Syn. *biyayà.*

gloryeta (glor-ye-ta), n. (Sp. *glorieta*)
bandstand; kiosk. Syn. *kiyosko.*

glosaryo (glo-sar-yo), n. (Sp. *glosario*)
glossary. Syn. *taláhuluganan.*

Gng. (Gng.), n. (abbrev. of **Ginang**) Mrs.

gobernador (go-ber-na-dor), n. (*Sp.*)
governor. Syn. *punong-lalawigan.*

gobyerno (gob-yer-no), n. (Sp. *gobierno*) 1.
government; administration. Syn.
pámahalaán, pángasiwaán. 2. act of
governing; administration. Syn.
paggobyerno; pamamahalà o pangangasiwà
sa gobyerno.

golondrina (go-lon-dri-na), n. (Sp.) 1.
swallow, a small, swift flying bird with
long, pointed wings and forked tail. 2. a
kind of kite, shaped like a swallow. Cf.
saranggola.

golp (golp), n. (Eng.) golf.

goma (go-ma), I. n. 1. (Bot.) rubber tree.
2. gum; rubber. Syn. *kola, pangola.* 3.
rubber band. Syn. *lastiko.* 4. rubber
eraser. Syn. *pamburá, gomang pamburá.*
5. rubber tire or tube for vehicles. Syn.
gulông na goma, interyor na goma. 6.
rubber shoes. Syn. *sapatos na goma (de-*
goma).

—II. adj. of or made of rubber. Syn. *yarì*
sa goma.

góndolá (gón-do-lá), n. (*Sp.*) gondola. Cf.
paráw.

gonorea (go-no-re-a), var. **gonorya**, n. (Sp.
gonorrea) gonorrhea. Cf. *sípilís.*

gong (gong), n. (Eng.) gong. Syn. *agong.*

gonggóng (gong-góng), n. (Ichth.) fish called
grunt (*Theraponidae*).

gora (go-ra), n. (Sp. *gorra*) cap; close-fitting
head covering, usually brimless or with
only a front visor. Cf. *bonete, sumbrero.*

gorilya (go-ril-ya), n. (Zool., Sp. *gorila*)
gorilla.

goryón (gor-yón), n. (Sp. *gorrión*) 1. a kind
of small kite. Syn. *saranggola.* 2. sparrow.

gota (go-ta), n. (Sp.) 1. drop (of medicine).
Syn. *paták.* 2. gout. Syn. *pananakít ng mga*
bukó ng dalirì.

gótikó (gó-ti-kó), n. & adj. (Sp. *gótico*)
gothic.

goto (go-to), n. (Ch.?) 1. ox or cow tripe. Syn. *labót, tripa.* 2. rice porridge mixed with tripes. Cf. *lugaw, nilugaw.*

goyò, (go-yo), n. (Colloq.) 1. act of making joke on someone, joke. Syn. *birò, pagbibirô.* 2. anything said or done in making a fool of another. Syn. *panloloko.*

graba (gra-ba), n. (Sp. *grava*) gravel. Syn. *mumuntíng bató, duróg na bató.*

grabado (gra-ba-do), I. n. (Sp.) an engraved wooden block for printing; engraving; cut or plate for printing. Syn. *klitse.* 2. any printed impression made from an engraved surface. Syn. *larawan o dibuhong yarì sa klitse.*
—II. adj. engraved; engraven; cut or etched out. Syn. *ukit, inukit.*

grabadora (gra-ba-do-ra), n. (Sp.) tape recorder.

grabe (gra-be), adj. (Sp. *grave*) grave; serious; that cannot be taken lightly; weighty. Syn. *malubhâ, mabigát, seryoso, lalâ, malalâ.*

grabitasyón (gra-bi-tas-yón), n. (Sp. *gravitación*) gravitation.

gradasyón (gra-das-yón), n. (Sp. *gradacion*) gradation.

grado (gra-do), n. (Sp.) 1. (Educ.) grade (in primary and elementary schools). Syn. *baitang.* 2. grade, rating, or mark received in a subject, test, etc. Syn. *marka, nota.* 3. degree; grade. Syn. *antás.* 4. rank. Syn. *ranggo.* 5. title; degree. Syn. *títuló, digrí.* 6. floor of a building; story. Syn. *palapág, piso, sahíg* (colloq.).

graduwado (gra-du-wa-do), var. **gradwado,** I. adj. (Sp. *graduado*) 1. graduated, as from college. Syn. *nagtapós o nakatapos na ng pag-aaral.* 2. graded; divided into degrees; scaled.
—II. n. a graduate; student graduate. Syn. *nagtapós na mag-aarál.*

graduwál (gra-du-wál), var. **gradwál,** adj. (Sp. *gradual*) 1. gradual; by degrees; little by little. Syn. *atay-atay, untí-untí, banayad.* 2. step by step. Syn. *baí-baitang.*

graduwasyón (gra-du-was-yón), var. **gradwasyón,** n. (Sp. *graduacion*) graduation (from college or school). Syn. *pagtatapós.*

gramátiká (gra-má-ti-ká), n. (Sp. *gramática*) grammar. Syn. *balarilà, gramar.*

gramo (gra-mo), n. (Sp.) gram. Syn. *guhi* (colloq.).

grana (gra-na), n. (Sp.) 1. scarlet dye or color. Cf. *tinà.* 2. act or method of coloring something with this dye or color. Syn. *paggagrana.* Cf. *pagtitinà.*

granada (gra-na-da), n. (Sp.) 1. (Bot.) the pomegranate tree or shrub (*Punica granatum*). 2. the fruit of this tree. 3. (Mil.) grenade; hand grenade.

granate (gra-na-te), n. 1. (Min.) garnet, a hard, glasslike silicate mineral of various colors. 2. deep red; garnet (color).

grande (gran-de), adj. (Sp.) 1. large; big. Syn. *malakí.* 2. great; grand; dignified. Syn. *dakilà, maringál, maharlikà.*

grano (gra-no), n. (Sp.) 1. grain; cereal. Syn. *butil, bigì.* 2. boil. Syn. *pigsá.* 3. pimple. Syn. *tagihawat.*

gránuló (grá-nu-ló), n. (Sp.) 1. granule. Syn. *maliít na butil.* 2. boil. Syn. *pigsá.* 3. pimple. Syn. *tagihawat.*

grapóponó (gra-pó-po-nó), n. (Sp. *grafófono*) phonograph; gramaphone. Syn. *ponógrapó.*

grasa (gra-sa), n. (Sp.) grease, thick, oily substance or lubricant.

grasya (gras-ya), n. (Sp. *gracia*) 1. divine grace; blessing. Syn. *palà, pagpapalà, biyayà.* 2. good fortune. Syn. *suwerte, magandáng suwerte o kapalaran.* 3. (Colloq.) satisfaction. Syn. *kasiyahan.* 4. benefit. Syn. *pakinabang, kapakinabangán, probetso.*

grasyas (gras-yas), n. (Sp. *gracias*) thanks. Syn. *salamat, maraming salamat.*

grasyosa (gras-yo-sa), adj. (Sp. *graciosa*) gracious; pleasant and friendly, referring to a woman. Syn. *magiliw, mabaít, mapagbigáy, mapagmahal, may magandáng kaloobán.*

gratipikasyón (gra-ti-pi-kas-yón), n. (Sp. *gratificacion*) 1. a gratifying. Syn. *pagbibigáy-kasiyahan, pagbibigáy-lugód.* 2. anything that pleases or satisfies. Syn. *lugód, kaluguran, kasiyahan, katuwaan.* 3. reward. Syn. *gantimpalà.* 4. bonus; gratuity; tip. Syn. *gantimpagál; pabuyà.*

gratis   **gulapay**

gratis (gra-tis), *adj.* (Sp.) free of charge; gratis; without cost or charge. Syn. *waláng-bayad, libre, bigáy.*

gratitúd (gra-ti-túd), *n.* (Sp.) gratitude; gratefulness. Syn. *utang na loób, pagkilala ng utang na loób.*

gripo (gri-po), *n.* (Sp. *grifo*) 1. faucet; tap. 2. a water container provided with a faucet. 3. (*Colloq.*) artesian well.

groge (gro-ge), var. **grogi,** *adj.* (Eng.) 1. drunk; intoxicated; tipsy; groggy. Syn. *lasíng, langó.* 2. shaky or dizzy. Syn. *hiló, nahihilo.*

gróserí (gró-se-rí), *n.* (Eng.) grocery. Syn. *tindahan ng mga komestibles, groseriya.*

groto (gro-to), *n.* (Eng.) grotto; cave; cavern. Syn. *kuweba, yungíb.*

grupo (gru-po), *n.* (Sp.) 1. group. Syn. *pangkát, pulutóng.* 2. gang. Syn. *barkada, barkadahán, gang.*

guano (gu-a-no), var. **guwano,** n. (Sp., Eng.) 1. guano; bat's manure. Syn. *taing-kabág.* 2. fertilizer made from this manure.

gubat (gu-bat), n. 1. forest; jungle; woods; woodland. Syn. *kakahuyan, kagubatan.* 2. thick growth of bushes; thicket. Syn. *sukal, kasukalan.*

gukgók (guk-gók), n. 1. grunt of pigs. Syn. *iyák o igík ng baboy.* 2. a similar sound produced in the stomach when one runs after drinking much water.

gugò (gu-gò), n. (*Bot.*) a large woody vine which bears pods containing big, somewhat circular-shaped seeds called *bayugo.* 2. the bark of this vine, the sap of which is squeezed out and used locally as hair shampoo. 3. the sap preparation or the shampoo obtained from the bark of this vine. 4. the act or manner of shampooing the hair with the gugò sap.

gugol (gu-gol), n. 1. act of spending money; use of money for buying things. Syn. *paggugol, gasta, paggasta.* 2. money spent; expenses; expenditure. Syn. *gastos.* 3. act of using one's time, effort, thought, etc. in the pursuit of certain purpose or enterprise. Syn. *pag-uukol o paggamit ng panahón, sikap, isip, atb. sa anó mang bagay.*

guhit (gu-hit), I. n. 1. line or any mark drawn or made on a surface. Syn. *linya.* 2. drawing sketch; design. Syn. *drowing, dibuho, larawang-guhit.* 3. act of making or drawing a line. Syn. *paglilinya, pagguhit ng linya.* 4. act of drawing a picture or any object. Syn. *pagdodrowing, pagdidibuho, pagguhit ng larawan.* 5. (in weighing) tenth of a kilogram; gram, as in *dalawáng guhit na karne,* two grams of meat. 6. (*Colloq.*) extremity. Syn. *hangganan, sukdulan.* 7. (Fig.) fate. Syn. *kapalaran, suwerte, destino, tadhanà.*
—II. adj. (usually with ng or ni) drawn, sketched, or designed by. Syn. *iginuhit o dinibuho ni.*

guhit-kamáy (gu-hit + ka-máy), adj. hand-drawn.

guhit-palad (gu-hit + pa-lad), n. 1. fate. Syn. *suwerte, kapalaran, destino, tadhanà.* 2. line mark or marks on a person's palm.

guhò (gu-hò), n. 1. a caving in; collapse. Syn. *bagsák, pagbagsák, pagkawasak, pagkágibâ.* 2. a building, wall, etc. that has fallen down to pieces; ruins. Syn. *wasak, gibâ.* 3. landslide. Syn. *tibág o pagkatibág (ng lupà).*

gulaman (gu-la-man), n. 1. (*Bot.*) a species of seaweeds from which agar-agar is obtained. 2. agar-agar. 3. a gelatin preparation (food) made from agar-agar.

gulanít (gu-la-nít), adj. 1. tattered, referring to clothes. Syn. *punít-punít, gutáy-gutáy.* 2. in tatters or rags. Syn. *nanlílimahid.*

gulantáng (gu-lan-táng), n. 1. act of causing a person to be suddenly frightened, startled, or shocked. Syn. *gulat, paggulat; gitlá, paggitlá.* 2. state or condition of being suddenly frightened, startled, or shocked. Syn. *pagkágulat, pagkágitlâ, pagkabiglâ.*

gulang (gu-lang), n. 1. age; time of life. Syn. *edád.* 2. maturity; old age. Syn. *kagulangan, kaedarán, katandaán.* 3. cunningness; cleverness in deceit. Syn. *katusuhan, katalinuhan; pagkamapágsamantalá.*

gulapay (gu-la-pay), n. 1. slow body movement due to weakness or tiredness. Syn. *mabagal na kilos dahil sa panghihinà o sa kapaguran.* 2. debility. Syn. *panghihinà,*

panlulupaypáy, panlulumó, o panlalambót
ng *katawán.*

gulat (gu-lat), n. 1. act of causing someone
to be suddenly surprised, frightened, or
shocked. Syn. *gulantang, paggulantang;*
gitlá, paggitlá. 2. state or condition of
being suddenly frightened or shocked.
Syn. *gulantáng, pagkagulantáng; gitlá,*
pagkagitlá. 3. state or condition of being
surprised. Syn. *taká, pagtataká; manghâ,*
pagkamanghâ.

gulay (gu-lay), n. 1. plant grown for food;
raw or green vegetable. Syn. *gulayíng*
halaman o bunga. 2. cooked vegetable.
3. act or manner of preparing or cooking
vegetables for food. Syn. *paggulay,*
paglulutò ng gulay.

gulilat (gu-li-lat), n. sudden feeling of slight
fright, surprise, or excitement. Syn.
bahagyáng takot, pagtataká, o pagkabiglâ.

gulis (gu-lis), n. a very light scratch on a
surface caused by something sharp or
pointed. Syn. *gurlís, galos.*

gulmók (gul-mók), n. state or condition of
being fallen flat on the floor or ground
due to unconsciousness or utter
exhaustion. Syn. *gumon.*

guló (gu-ló), I. n. 1. trouble; fight. Syn.
away, awayán, basag-ulo. 2. civil disorder;
public disturbance; tumult. Syn. *ligalig,*
kaligaligan. 3. a free-for-all; brawl. Syn.
labu-labo. 4. crowded condition, as of a
room; disarray; disorder. Syn. *kawaláng-*
ayos. 5. things scattered all around. Syn.
kalat.

—II. adj. 1. in disarray; in disorder;
disarranged. Syn. *walâ sa ayos, maguló.* 2. in
trouble; in confusion. Syn. *nagkákaguló,*
ligalíg.

gulok (gu-lok), n. bolo; machete. Syn. *iták,*
tabák.

gulód (gu-lód), n. 1. highland. Syn.
kataasan. 2. plateau. Syn. *talampás.* 3.
ridge. Syn. *paltók, buról.* 4. summit; crest.
Syn. *tuktók, taluktok.*

gulong (gu-long), n. rolling motion on a
surface, as of the wheels of a vehicle. Syn.
gilong (Bats.).

gulóng (gu-lóng), n. 1. wheel. Syn. *ruweda.*
2. rubber casing of a tire.

gulpi (gul-pi), var. **golpe**, n. (Sp.) 1. severe
beating. Syn. *bugbóg, pagbugbóg.* 2.
castigation by beating. Syn. *palò, pagpalò.*

gulpi-de-estado (gul-pi + de + es-ta-do), n.
(Sp.) coup d'etat. Syn. *biglâng pagbagsák*
ng *pámahalaán.*

gulpi-de-gulat (gul-pi + de + gu-lat), n. (Sp.)
an impressive show of force or ability at
the start. Cf. *pasikat, pakitang-gilas.*

gulpo (gul-po), var. **golpo**, n. (Sp. *golfo*) gulf;
a large bay. Syn. *malakíng loók.*

gulugód (gu-lu-gód), n. (Anat.) 1.
backbone; spinal column. Syn. *tayudtód.*
2. the back, esp. of an animal. Syn. *likód*
(ng *hayop).*

gulumihan (gu-lu-mi-han), n. brief sudden
feeling of slight fear; dread or
apprehension. Syn. *kabá, hintakot,*
kahintakutan.

gulunggulungan (gu-lung-gu-lu-ngan), n. 1.
Adam's apple. Syn. *tatagukán, lalagukán.*
2. throat. Syn. *lalamunan.*

gulyeriya (gul-ye-ri-ya), var. **gulyerya**, n.
(Sp. *golleria*) a delicacy made of starch,
eggs, sugar, etc. and made crisp by putting
in boiling lard of oil.

gumamela (gu-ma-me-la), n. (Bot.) a much
branched, smooth shrub cultivated for its
flowers and planted as a hedge or fence.
(*Hibiscus rosasinensis Linn.*); the plant is
variously known as hibiscus, China rose,
shoeflower, etc.

gumok (gu-mok), I. n. 1. state or condition
of being bedridden. Syn. *ratay, pagkaratay.*
2. wallow; living in filth and wickedness.
Syn. *gumon, pagkagumon.*

—II. adj. 1. bedridden. Syn. *nakaratay*
(*sa baníg ng karamdaman).* 2. addicted to
(a certain vice, etc.). Syn. *nakagumon* (*sa*
bisyo).

gunagunahin (gu-na-gu-na-hin), v. 1. to
take advantage of an opportunity on hand
before one loses his chance. Syn.
samantalahín agád ang pagkakataón. 2. to
do in a hurry. Syn. *dalí-daliin, madalím.*

gunamgunam (gu-nam-gu-nam), n. 1.
anticipation of something good or
interesting. Syn. *asám, pag-asám.* 2. deep
thought; reflection; meditation. Syn.
nilay-nilay, pagninilay-nilay; bulay-bulay,

pagbubulay-bulay; warì-warì, pagwawarì-warì.

gunaw (gu-naw), n. 1. the end of the world; destruction of all things in this world. Syn. *katapusán ng daigdíg.* 2. a great flood. Syn. *malakíng bahâ.* 3. (G-) the Deluge; the great flood in Noah's time. Syn. *dilubyo, paglubóg sa tubig ng buóng mundo.*

guniguni (gu-ni-gu-ni), n. 1. mind. Syn. *isip.* 2. imagination; fancy. Syn. *hinuhà.*

gunitâ (gu-ni-tâ), n. 1. memory; recollection. Syn. *alaala.* 2. reflection; meditation. Syn. *dili-dili.*

guntíng (gun-tíng), n. 1. scissors. Syn. *panggupít.* 2. a pair of big scissors; shears. 3. act or manner of cutting something with scissors or shears. Syn. *paggupít.*

gunggóng (gung-góng), I. adj. stupid; dull; ignoramus. Syn. *tangá, hangál, ungás, bangág, tunggák.*

—II. n. a stupid person.

gupiling (gu-pi-ling), n. (poetic) a light, short sleep. Syn. *himláy, idlíp, hipíg.*

gupít (gu-pít), I. n. 1. act of cutting something with a pair of scissors or shears. Syn. *pagputol sa pamamagitan ng guntíng, paggupít.* 2. act or manner of cutting someone's hair. Syn. *paggupít (sa buhók).* 3. haircut; style of haircut. Syn. *gapás* (Bats.). 4. act of cutting cloth, etc. with a pair of scissors according to pattern. Syn. *tabas, pagtabas.*

—II. adj. cut or trimmed with a pair of scissors or shears.

gupò (gu-pò), n. 1. collapse; a caving in. Syn. *lugsô, paglugsô; gibâ, pagkagibâ; lagpák, paglagpák.* 2. subjugation; overpowering or being overpowered. Syn. *lupig, paglupig, pagkalupig.* 3. overthrowing or being overthrown. Syn. *pagbabagsák o pagkakábagsák ng kapangyarihan.* 4. state or condition of being bedridden. Syn. *pagkaratay sa baníg ng karamdaman, pagkakasakít nang mabigát.*

gurami (gu-ra-mi), n. (Ichth.) a species of fresh-water fish, black in color and thin of body. (*Trichogaster pectoralis Regan*).

gurlís (gur-lís), n. light scratch or cut made with a pointed tool or instrument on the skin or any surface. Syn. *galos, gulis.*

gurò (gu-ro), var. gurô, n. teacher; instructor; mentor; professor. Syn. *maestra o maestro, tagapagturò, propesór, titser, instruktór.*

gusalì (gu-sa-lì), n. building; edifice. Syn. *edipisyo.*

gusgusin (gus-gu-sin), adj. untidy; slovenly; in rags or in tatters. Syn. *marungis, gulágulanít ang damít.*

gusì (gu-sì), n. (Ch.) 1. large burial jar. 2. a large vase or jar of buried treasure. Cf. *tapayan.*

gusilaw (gu-si-law), n. eyeshade; visor. Syn. *bisera.*

gusót[1] (gu-sót), n. 1. conflict; dispute; disagreement; misunderstanding. Syn. *dipagkakáunawaán, hidwaan, dipagkakásundô, labanán, basag-ulo, away.* 2. trouble; disorder; confusion. Syn. *guló, pagkakaguló, kaguluhán.*

gusót[2] (gu-sót), I. adj. 1. crumpled. Syn. *lukót, yukós, bayukós.* 2. entangled; tangled. Syn. *salimuót, salí-salimuót, salásalabíd.*

—II. n. 1. state or condition of being crumpled or entangled. Syn. *pagkalukot, kalukutan; pagkayukos, kayukusan.* 2. the part that is crumpled or entangled. Syn. *lukot, yukos, bayukos, salabíd, salimuót.* (for senses 1 & 2).

gusto (gus-to), I. n. (Sp.) like or liking; preference. Syn. *ibig, hangád, nais, mithî.*

—II. v. (Colloq.) like; have a preference or liking for. Syn. *ibig, nais (colloq.)*

gutáy (gu-táy), I. n. 1. act of tearing (paper, cloth, etc.) into small fragments or pieces. Syn. *gutgót, paggutgót, pagpupunít-punít.* 2. state or condition of being torn into small pieces or fragments. Syn. *gutgót, pagkagutgót; punít-punít, pagkapunit-punit.*

—II. adj. torn into small pieces or fragments (s.o. paper, cloth, etc.). Syn. *gutgót, punít-punít.*

gutáy-gutáy (gu-táy + gu-táy), I. adj. torn into shreds or into very tiny pieces. Syn. *gutgót na gutgót, duróg na duróg.*

—II. n. 1. act or manner of tearing (something) into shreds or into very tiny pieces. Syn. *paggutgót na mabuti.* 2. state

gutgutín   **habà**

or condition of being torn into shreds or into very tiny pieces. Syn. *pagkagutáy-gutáy, pagkagutgót na mabuti*.

gutgutín (gut-gu-tín), *v.* to tear into pieces or into small fragments. Syn. *gutayín, punít-punitín*.

gutlî (gut-lî), *n.* 1. a light mark or indentation on the skin or any surface, as that made by the pressure of the tip of a fingernail. 2. a small cut or nick, as on the edge of a frame, or the like. Syn. *gatgát, gatlâ*.

gutom (gu-tom), *n.* 1. hunger; desire or need for food. Syn. *kagutuman, pagkagutom; pasal, kapasalan*. 2. a strong desire or craving for. Syn. *sabík, kasabikan, pananabík, malakíng pagkakagusto*.

guwaba (gu-wa-ba), *n.* (Eng.) the guava tree (*Psidium guayava* L.); also, its fruit. Syn. *bayabas*.

guwantes (gu-wan-tes), var. **guantes**, *n.* (Sp.) hand glove or gloves.

guwáng (gu-wáng), I. *n.* 1. a hollow or cavity on a surface; big hole. Syn. *lubák, hukay, butas*. 2. state or condition of being hollow or having nothing inside. Syn. *kahungkagán*.
—II. *adj.* hollow; having nothing inside. Syn. *hungkág, waláng-lamán*.

guwapa (gu-wa-pa), I. *adj.* (Fem., Sp. *guapa*) good-looking; beautiful or pretty, referring to a woman. Syn. *magandá, marilág, kaakít-akit*.
—II. *n.* a beautiful or attractive woman. Syn. *magandáng babae*.

guwapo (gu-wa-po), I. *adj.* (Sp. *guapo*) good-looking; handsome. Syn. *maganda*.
—II. *n.* a handsome man. Syn. *magandáng lalaki*.

guwardado (gu-war-da-do), *adj.* (Sp. *guardado*) guarded; under the watchful eyes of guards. Syn. *may-guwardiyá, nagúguwardiyahán; may-talibà, natátalibaan; may-tanod, natátanuran*.

guwárdiyá (gu-wár-di-yá), *n.* (Sp. *guardia*) 1. act of guarding. Syn. *pagguwárdiyá, pagtanod, pagtatanod, pagbabantáy*. 2. guard; watcher; sentinel; sentry. Syn. *tanod, bantáy, sentinela, talibà*.

guyà (gu-yà), *n.* the young of a cow or carabao; calf. Syn. *bisiro, bulô*.

guyabano (gu-ya-ba-no), var. **guwayabano**, *n.* (Sp. *guayabano*) 1. a small tree that bears edible ovoid fruits covered with scattered, soft, spinelike processes (*Anona muricata* Linn.). 2. the fruit of this tree.

guyam (gu-yam), *n.* in Bats., a generic term for the species of small ants. Syn. *langgám*.

guyod (gu-yod), *n.* 1. a moving in swarm, as of a throng or crowd. Syn. *lisaw, paglisaw, kuyaw, pagkuyaw*. 2. throng or crowd of people. Syn. *katakut-takot na tao; kakapalan (o karamihan) ng tao*. 3. a group of animals of one kind; flock; herd. Syn. *kawan*. 4. thick rope used in hauling. Syn. *malakíng lubid na panghatak*. See **guyuran**.

guyuran (gu-yu-ran), *n.* 1. a pair of big rattan used for hauling logs. 2. a pair of ropes used as tugs or traces for carabaos in pulling plows. Syn. *tirante*.

H

H, h (ha), *n.* 1. the seventh letter of the *abakada* (Pilipino alphabet). 2. the type or impression representing this letter. 3. a symbol for the seventh in a series or sequence.

Ha (Ha), I. *interj.* an exclamatory particle expressive of: a) doubt, surprise, or excitement, meaning: What? What is it? What do you mean? Syn. *Anó? Anó iyón? Anó 'ka mo?* b) inquiry, meaning: Don't you think so? Syn. *Dî ba? Hindî ba?* c) wonder or disbelief, meaning: Is that so? Syn. *Ganoón ba? Siyá ngâ ba?*
—II. *adv.* an interrogative particle, meaning: a) Why? Syn. *Bakit?* b) Do you understand? Syn. *Náuunawaan mo ba?*

habà (ha-bà), *n.* 1. extent from end to end; length. Syn. *sukat mulâ sa dulo't dulo*. 2. extent of time. Syn. *tagál, luwát*. 3. lengthiness. Syn. *kahabaan*. 4. long duration of time. Syn. *katagalán, kaluwatán*.

habâ

habâ (ha-bâ), *adj.* elongate; long and narrow. Syn. *pahabâ, taluhabâ.*

habág (ha-bág), *n.* 1. pity; mercy; compassion; clemency. Syn. *awà, pagkaawà, pagkahabág.* 2. disconsolate feeling of one who has been maltreated, etc. Syn. *pagkaawà sa sarili, samâ ng loób, pagdaramdám.* 3. contemptuous treatment; scorn. Syn. *paglait, pag-alipustâ, paghamak, pag-upasalà, paghabág.*

habagat (ha-ba-gat), *n.* 1. south or southwest wind. Syn. *hanging-timog o hanging-timog-kanluran.* 2. southwest monsoon. Syn. *habagat-lubang.*

habang (ha-bang), I. *conj.* while; in the time that, as in: *Dito ka habang akó'y kumákain.* Stay here while I am eating. Syn. *samantala.*

—II. *adv.* as long as. *Matulog ka habang gusto mo.* Sleep as long as you want. Syn. *hanggáng.*

habang-buhay (ha-bang + bu-hay), I. *n.* lifetime; whole life. Syn. *buóng-buhay.*

—II. *adj.* lasting for a lifetime; lifetime as in *habang-buhay na kasaganaan,* lifetime prosperity.

habang buháy (ha-bang + bu-háy), *adv.* while still alive or living. Syn. *habang nabubuhay.*

habas (ha-bas), *n.* 1. (*Vet. Sci.*) a kind of horse disease characterized by callosity in the mouth. 2. satiety; disgust by having too much. Syn. *kabusugan, kabundatán, sawà, pagsasawà.* 3. prudence; wise thought before acting, usually used in the negative. Syn. *hinahon, kahinahunan; hunos-dilì, paghuhunos-dilì.*

habháb (hab-háb), *n.* 1. act or manner of eating noisily, as that of hungry pigs and dogs. Syn. *sabsáb, pagsabsáb.* 2. act or manner of biting something in the way a toothless person does. Syn. *ngabngáb, pagngabngáb.* 3. violent attack by a quadruped, esp. a dog or pig. Syn. *sibasib.* 4. food for pigs. Syn. *kaning baboy, kakaníng baboy.*

habi (ha-bi), I. *n.* 1. act or method of weaving (cloth). Syn. *paghabi; paggawà ng tela sa pamamagitan ng sinulid.* 2. weave; pattern of weave. Syn. *pagkakahabi.*

habol

—II. *adj.* woven, referring to fabrics. Syn. *hinabi.*

Habì (Ha-bì), *interj.* Get out of the way! Syn. *Tabí! Layô!*

habíd (ha-bíd), *n.* 1. an entangling or being entangled, as of one's foot or feet. Syn. *sabíd, pagkakásabíd; salabíd, pagkásalabíd, pagkakásalabíd.* 2. anything that entangles something, esp. foot or feet. Syn. *sabíd, salabíd.*

habihán (ha-bi-hán), *n.* a machine for weaving thread or yarn into cloth; loom. Syn. *panghabi, mákináng panghabi.*

habilin¹ (ha-bi-lin), *n.* 1. act of leaving or entrusting something to someone for temporary safekeeping. Syn. *pag-iiwan o pagpapatagong pansamantalá ng anumán sa kapwà.* 2. anything (money, property, work, etc.) given or left to someone in trust or for safekeeping. Syn. *anó mang bagay na inihabilin sa kapwà.*

habilin² (ha-bi-lin), *n.* (*Leg.*) a will about the disposition of one's property after his death: as in *hulíng habilin,* last will. Syn. *testamento.*

habilóg (ha-bi-lóg), *adj.* oval; egg-shaped. Syn. *hugis-itlóg, obalado, óbaló.*

habín (ha-bín), *n.* 1. string of a kite, top, yoyo, etc. Syn. *hapín.* 2. in weaving, warp or weft. 3. any kind of thread or yarn. Syn. *sinulid.* 4. the string or thread on which beads or the like are strung. Syn. *tuhugáng pisì o sinulid.* 5. the thread of a needle. Syn. *bungót.*

habitasyón (ha-bis-tas-yón), *n.* 1. an inhabiting; occupancy. Syn. *pagtahán, pananahanan; pagtirá, paninirahan.* 2. place to live in; dwelling; residence; home. Syn. *táhanan, tírahan.*

habitsuwelas (ha-bit-su-we-las), *n.* (Sp. *habichuelas*) a variety of kidney beans.

hablá (ha-blá), *n.* (corrup. fr. Sp. *habla*) 2. act of filing a complaint or accusation in court; litigation. Syn *pagsasakdál, pagdedemanda.* 2. an accusation or complaint filed in court; lawsuit. Syn. *demanda, sakdál.*

hablón (ha-blón), *n.* (Bis.) a kind of specially woven cloth from the Visayas.

habol (ha-bol), *n.* 1. act of running after

another; chasing or pursuing. Syn. *paghabol; hagad, paghagad; tugis, pagtugis.* 2. a person running after someone; chaser; pursuer. Syn. *ang hagad, humahagad, o tagahagad; ang tugis, tumutugis, o tagatugis.* 3. act of hurrying to overtake one who is ahead, as in a race. 4. a person, animal, or anything that one is running after. Syn. *ang hináhabol o tinútugis.* 5. (*Law*) appeal or act of appealing to a higher court. Syn. *apelá, pag-apelá; paghahabol.* 6. object of complaint, esp. in an appeal. Syn. *ang ipinagháhabol o hináhabol.* 7. claim; demand; complaint. Syn. *reklamo, sumbóng.* 8. something added to complete the lack from. Syn. *pahabol, dagdág, karagdagan.* 9. postscript. Syn. *pahabol.*

haból (ha-ból), *adj.* 1. lacking time; under pressure of time; in a hurry for lack of time. Syn. *gipít sa oras (panahón), gahól (sa oras o panahón).* 2. referring to a person, esp. a child, who has the habit of crying if not allowed to go with someone who is leaving. Syn. *paláhabol, mapaghaból.*

habonera (ha-bo-ne-ra), *n.* (Sp. *jabonera*) soap dish or tray. Syn. *lalagyán ng sabón, sábunan.*

habong (ha-bong), *n.* 1. an improvised or temporary shed, esp. one made of grass, leaves, palm trees, cloth, etc. Syn. *kuból.* 2. awning or a temporary roof extension of a house. Syn. *medya-agwa, sibi.*

habulán (ha-bu-lán), *n.* 1. act of chasing or running after someone, as by a number of persons; a chasing incident. Syn. *hagárán.* 2. act of trying to overtake each other, as in a running race. Syn. *unahán, paguunahán.* 3. in a competition, the state or condition of being almost equal. —II. *adj.* with or having almost equal chance of winning. Syn. *halos pareho, waláng itulak-kabigin.*

habyas korpus (hab-yas kor-pus), *n.* Law, habeas corpus. Syn. *utos ng hukuman sa mádaliang paglilitis sa isáng ipiniit upang pagpasiyahán kung náalinsunod sa batás ang pagpigil o pagbibilanggô sa kanyá.*

habyóg (hab-yóg), I. *n.* a bending or swaying up and down (of a branch, pole, or the like) due to stress or pressure of weight. Syn. *bayók, pagbayók.* —II. *adj.* bent or swaying up and down, referring to a pole, branch, or the like, due to stress or pressure of weight. Syn. *bayók, bumábayók; humáhabyóg; habyók, humáhabyók.*

hakà (ha-kà), *n.* 1. idea; opinion. Syn. *palagáy, kurò, kuru-kurò, opinyón, ideyá.* 2. notion; understanding. Syn. *pagkáunawà, pagkáintindí, pagkáhiwatig.* 3. belief. Syn. *paniwalà, paniniwalà.* 4. guess. Syn. *hulà.* 5. suspicion. Syn. *hinalà, paghihinalà.*

hakáb (ha-káb), *adj.* 1. firmly attached or held by vacuumatic action. Syn. *hapít na hapít, dikít na dikít.* 2. tight, tightfitting. Syn. *lapát na lapat, mahigpít.*

haká-hakà (ha-ká + ha-kà), *n.* conjecture; supposition; presumption; guess. Syn. *palá-palagáy, hula-hulà, kuru-kurò.*

hakbáng (hak-báng), *n.* 1. a step or pace in walking. Syn. *lakdáw, hakdáw.* 2. act or manner of walking. Syn. *lakad, paglakad.* 3. measure; step; remedy; means to an end. Syn. *paraán, lunas, remedyo.* 4. decision on what to do. Syn. *pasiyá, pagpapasiyá.*

hákbangan (hák-ba-ngan), *n.* 1. a movable barrier for runners to jump over in a race; hurdle. 2. a low barrier made at the doorway, usually near the stairs, to prevent small children from going out or from falling. Syn. *alabát.* 3. a similar barrier made at the gate of a fence. Syn. *hákdawan, lákdawan.*

hakbót (hak-bót), *n.* sudden pulling or grabbing of something from someone. Syn. *galbót, halbót, saklót.*

hakdáw (hak-dáw), *n.* 1. step or pace in walking or dancing. Syn. *hakbáng, lakdáw.* 2. a stepping across or over (a narrow canal, low barrier or obstacle, etc.) 3. act or manner of walking. Syn. *lakad, paglakad.* 4. measure; step; remedy. Syn. *paraán, lunas, remedyo.*

haklít (hak-lít), *n.* sudden pull or grab with the hand or mouth. Syn. *halták, labnót.*

hakot (ha-kot), *n.* 1. act of transporting, loading, carrying, or delivery of things from one place to another. Syn. *paghahatíd*

o *paglululan ng mga bagay na kailangang
ilipat ng lugár*. 2. a specific number of
loading or delivery; load; haul. Syn. *hila,
hatak*. 3. act of collecting or gathering
things either one by one or in quantity.
Syn. *pagtitipon nang untî-untî o máramihán*.

hadláng (had-láng), n. 1. act of suppressing;
suppression by authority. Syn. *pagsugpô,
pagsawatâ*. 2. act of opposing or
contradicting. Syn. *salungát, pagsalungát;
tutól, pagtutol*. 2. a barrier; hindrance;
obstacle; impediment; bar; obstruction.
Syn. *sagabal, sagwíl, harang, halang*. 3.
prohibition. Syn. *pagbabawal*.

hadyi (had-yi), n. 1. (Eng.) hadji or hajji a
Moslem who has made a pilgrimage to
Mecca. 2. (H-) a title of honor to nobility
among the Moslems. 3. (by extension) a
royalty. Syn. *taong maharlikà*.

hagak (ha-gak; ha-gák), n. the hoarse or
husky sound from the throat of a person
having cold or from one gasping for air.
Cf. *hagok, halák*. 2. a gasping or panting.
Syn. *hingal, paghingal*.

hagakhák (ha-gak-hák), n. coarse or gritty
sound of voice in laughter. Syn. *hagalhál*.
Cf. *halakhák*.

hagad (ha-gad), n. 1. act of running after (a
person, animal, etc.) in order to catch or
drive away. Syn. *paghagad; habol, paghabol;
tugis, pagtugis; pagat, pagpagat*. 2. a person
or persons running after someone; chaser;
pursuer. Syn. *ang habol o humáhabol,
tagahabol; tagatugis*. 3. a person or animal
being chased or pursued. Syn. *ang
hináhabol o tinútugis*. 4. a motorcycle cop.
Syn. *pulís-hagad*.

hagalhál (ha-gal-hál), n. 1. a person
inclined to loud laughing. Syn. *taong
malakás tumawa (magtawá)*. 2. coarse or
gritty sound of loud laughing. Syn.
hagakhák, halakhák.

hagap (ha-gap), n. a vague thought or idea;
conjecture; notion; indefinite opinion or
belief. Syn. *hakà, haká-hakà; palagáy, palá-
palagáy; sapantahà*.

hagarán (ha-ga-rán), n. 1. a chasing or
running after each other, as in children's
games. Syn. *hulihán, paghuhulihán*. 2. a
chasing incident, as by a number of

policemen arresting an escaped convict.
Syn. *habulán, paghahabulán; tugisán,
pagtutugisán*.

hagayháy (ha-gay-háy), n. 1. the soft, low,
murmuring sound of breeze. 2. light
current of air; breeze. Syn. *simoy, paláy-
paláy na hangin*.

hagkán (hag-kán), v. to kiss (someone). Syn.
halikán.

hagkisín (hag-ki-sín), v. 1. to lash or strike
with a whip. Syn. *hagupitín, haplitín*. 2.
to hit or attack with words. Syn. *batikusin,
tuligsaín, atakihin*.

hagdán (hag-dán), n. 1. ladder. 2. stairs;
stairway; staircase. Syn. *hagdanan*. 3. (by
extension) a means for advancement;
stepping stone; instrument for success.
Syn. *kasangkapan (colloq.); batóng-
tungtungan (fig.)*.

hagdán-hagdán (hag-dán + hag-dán), I. n.
a series of rows or arrangement of seats
made behind and above each other; tiers.
Syn. *baí-baitáng o andá-andanang úpuan*.
—II. adj. arranged in tiers. Syn. *baí-
baitáng, andá-andana*.

hagibas (ha-gi-bas; ha-gi-bás), n. act or
manner of hitting someone blindly or
heedlessly as with a long stick or pole. Cf.
hambalos.

hagibís (ha-gi-bís), n. 1. swift or
instantaneous passing or flight; also the
sound produced by this. Syn. *hagunót,
harurót, haginít*.

hagikgik (ha-gik-gik), n. 1. outburst of pent-
up laughter. Syn. *halikhík, hagikhík, alikík*.
2. the sound of such laughter.

hagilap (ha-gi-lap), n. 1. act or manner of
trying to get hold of something near oneself
to be utilized immediately or in an
emergency. Syn. *apuhap, pag-apuhap, pag-
aapuháp*. 2. the movement of a hand or
hands in searching or groping for something
in the dark. Syn. *kapâ, pagkapâ, pagkapá-
kapâ*.

haginít (ha-gi-nít), n. 1. cracking sound, as
of a lash or whip. Syn. *laginít, lagitlít*. 2.
swift or instantaneous passage or flight,
as of bullets, strong wind, or speeding
vehicle. Syn. *hagibís, paghagibís; harurót,
pagharurót*. 3. the hissing or whinning

sound caused by this.

haging (ha-ging), n. 1. a buzzing or hissing sound, as of a swift flying bullet. Syn. *haginít*. 2. swift or instantaneous passing or flight of a bullet, causing a buzzing or hissing sound. Syn. *haginít, paghaginít*.

hagingan (ha-gi-ngan), v. to be almost hit, as by a swift flying bullet. Syn. *haginitán*.

hagíp (ha-gíp), I. n. 1. act of grabbing or snatching (a person or thing) with the hand while passing swiftly by the side. Syn. *saklót, pagsaklót*. 2. sideswiping or hitting along the side in passing, as by a speeding vehicle. Syn. *dagil, pagkadagil; sagì, pagkasagì*. —II. *adj*. referring to a person or thing calculated to be within a distance of being sideswiped or hit along the side, as by a speeding vehicle. Syn. *abót, maáabót*.

hagis (ha-gis), n. 1. act of hitting (a person or thing) with or as with a stone; throwing or casting something at. Syn. *batό, pagbató; pukól, pagpukól; balibág, pagbalibág*. 2. (in baseball) act of pitching a ball to the batter. Syn. *paghagis ng bola sa pumápalò*. 3. (in baseball) the turn of a pitcher to pitch or throw the ball. Syn. *paghagis o pagpukól ng bola*. 4. a being thrown or hurled. Syn. *pagkapahagis, pagkapaitsá*. 5. (also in baseball) the turn of a team to be on field. Syn. *tayâ, pagtayâ*. Ant. *palò, pagpalò*.

hagok (ha-gok), n. snore; sound of snoring. Syn. *harok, hilík*.

hagod (ha-god), n. 1. gentle massage with the hand. Syn. *hagpós, haplós, himas, masahe*. 2. act of pressing clothes superficially with a flat iron. 3. gentle stroke of the brush in painting. 4. act of polishing (paint) with a brush. Syn. *buli o pagbuli sa pamamagitan ng brutsa*.

hagot (ha-got), n. 1. act or manner of stripping abaca or palm fibers. 2. act of pressing out the contents or dirt in the intestines as a means of cleansing them for food. Syn. *hilis, paghilis*.

hagpís (hag-pís), I. n. state or condition of being careworn or haggard. Syn. *hapis, pagkahapis*. —II. *adj*. careworn; haggard. Syn. *hapís*.

hagpos (hag-pos), I. n. 1. fact, state, or condition of being loose or slack, referring to a binding or knot. Syn. *habsô, pagkahabsô; luwág, kaluwagán*. 2. a skipping off from one's hold. Syn. *hulagpós, pagkahulagpós*. —II. *adj*. 1. loosened or slack, referring to a binding or knot. Syn. *habsô, nahabsô; maluwág, lumuwág*. 2. having skipped off from one's hold. Syn. *hulagpós, nakahulagpós*.

haguhap (ha-gu-hap), n. act or manner of groping (for something) in the dark. Syn. *apuhap, pagkapá-kapâ*.

hagulhól (ha-gul-hól), n. sudden loud crying or weeping. Syn. *malakás na iyák o pananangis*.

hagunót (ha-gu-nót), I. n. 1. a swift passage or flight producing a turbulent sound, as of a strong gale, speeding vehicle, etc. Syn. *hagibís, haginít*. 2. the turbulent sound thus produced.

hagunoy (ha-gu-noy), n. 1. (Bot.) a kind of climbing herbaceous vine (*Wedelia biflora*, L. D. C.), the roots and leaves of which are medicinal. 2. (H-) name of a fishing town in the province of Bulakán.

hagupít (ha-gu-pít), n. 1. act of lashing with a whip; whipping or lashing with or as with a belt, stick, etc. Syn. *malakás na palò ng kumpás, sinturón, patpát, etc.* Syn. *haplít*. 2. violent verbal attack or criticism. Syn. *tuligsâ, atake, batikos*.

hagwáy (hag-wáy), n. well-proportioned height or tallness of a person. Cf. *tangkád, katangkarán*.

hain (ha-in), n. var. **hayin**, **ahin**. 1. act of setting or preparing the table for meal. Syn. *paghahain, paghahayin, pag-aahin, paghahandâ ng pagkain sa mesa*. 2. the food prepared or set on the table. Syn. *pagkaing nasa (nakahandâ sa) mesa*. 3. act of offering something as a sacrifice. Syn. *paghahandóg ng sakripisyo*. 4. anything offered as a sacrifice; offering. Syn. *sakripisyo*.

haiskul (ha-is-kul), n. (Eng.) high school. Syn. *mataás na páaralán, páaraláng sekundarya*.

Hal. (Hal.): abbrev. of *halimbawà*, example (Ex.).

Hala (Ha-la; Ha-lá), *interj.* 1. Go ahead! Syn. *Sige! Sulong!* 2. a particle used to express a threat or warning, meaning: Go ahead and suffer the consequences! Syn. *Sige, bahalà ka!*

halaan (ha-la-an; ha-la-án), *n.* mussel: species of edible clam or bivalve belonging to the *Paphias.*

halabíd (ha-la-bíd), *n.* 1. an accidental tripping or entanglement of someone's foot or feet. Syn. *salabíd, pagkásalabíd, pagkáhalabíd.* 2. act of tripping or entangling someone's foot or feet with a rope, wire, vine, or the like. Syn. *pagkasalabíd, paghalabíd.* 3. a rope, wire, vine, or the like that entangled someone's foot or feet. Syn. *salabíd, sabíd, habíd.*

halabós (ha-la-bós), var. **halbós,** I. *n.* 1. act or manner of boiling shrimps in a little amount of water without any ingredient or condiment, except a little amount of salt to taste. 2. shrimps cooked or boiled in this manner.
—II. *adj.* boiled or cooked in a little amount of water with a little salt to taste, referring esp. to shrimps.

halabót (ha-la-bót), var. **halbót,** *n.* a sudden draw, as of a revolver from its scabbard. Syn. *bigláng bunot.* 2. act of drawing or taking out all of the contents in a drawer, box, etc. Syn. *halawát, paghalawát.*

halák (ha-lák), *n.* a gargling or raucous sound in the throat due to cold or catarrh. Syn. *garalgál sa lalamunan.*

halakhák (ha-lak-hák), *n.* loud laughter. Syn. *hagalhál, hagakgák, malakás na tawa o pagtatawá.*

halagá (ha-la-gá), *n.* 1. (*Colloq.*) money; amount of money, as in: *Magkanong halagá ang kailangan mo?* How much money do you need? 2. price; cost or selling price; money value of a thing or merchandise. Syn. *presyo.* 3. worth; value; importance. Syn. *kabuluhan, kahalagahan, importansiyá, kasaysayan.* 4. assessment; money value of a property. Syn. *tasa, tasasyón.*

halagap (ha-la-gap), *n.* 1. act of scooping out the scum or the impurities on the surface of something being boiled. Syn. *sagap, pagsagap.* 2. the thin layer of

impurities on the top or surface of liquid that is being boiled; scum. Syn. *iskoma.*

halaghág (ha-lag-hág), *adj.* 1. careless; negligent. Syn. *waláng-ingat, pabayâ, busalsál, bulagsák.* 2. carefree; easy-going. Syn. *waláng-iniintindí, waláng-pag-iintindí.* 3. wandering; vagrant; vagabond. Syn. *palaboy, layás, lagalág, bagamundo.* 4. idle; indolent; slothful. Syn. *tamád, batugan, lakwatsero, matigás ang katawán, ayaw magtrabaho.*

halál (ha-lál), I. *n.* 1. act of voting for a candidate in an election. Syn. *boto, pagboto.* 2. a vote cast in an election. Syn. *boto.*
—II. *adj.* chosen by voters in an election; elective; elected. Syn. *iniháhalál o inihalál.*

hálalan (há-la-lan), *n.* 1. election; holding of an election. Syn. *paghahálalan, botohán, pagbobotohán.* 2. election time. Syn. *panahón ng hálalan (botohán).*

halaman (ha-la-man), *n.* plant. Syn. *taním.*

halamanan (ha-la-ma-nan; há-la-ma-nán), *n.* garden; orchard; plantation. Syn. *hardín, tániman.*

halang (ha-lang), *n.* 1. anything used as a barrier or obstacle. Syn. *hadláng, harang, balakíd, sagabal, sagwíl.* 2. clog; obstruction. Syn. *bará.* 3. a temporary partition or screen. Syn. *tabing.* 4. something placed between two things to separate them. Syn. *pagitan.* 5. a crosspiece. Syn. *krusada.* 6. prevention. Syn. *hadláng, paghadláng.* 7. (Bats.) act of taking the place of someone temporarily; substitution. Syn. *halili, paghalili.* 8. (Bats.) a substitute; alternate. Syn. *kahalili, kapalít.*

haláng (ha-láng), *adj.* passing, extending, or placed across; traverse; transverse. Syn. *pahaláng, nakahalang.*

halapáw (ha-la-páw), *n.* act or manner of skimming or removing slightly the top layer of a heap, pile, etc. See. *hapáw.*

halas (ha-las), *n.* 1. light itchy scratches on skin caused by sharp blades of grassses. Syn. *makakatíng galos ng dahon.* 2. the hairy or powdery coverings on the leaves of some kind of grasses that cause itchiness on the skin. Syn. *makakatíng bulo ng damó.*

halatâ (ha-la-tâ), n. 1. a noticing or being noticed. Syn. paghalatâ, pagkáhalatâ; pansín, pagpansín, pagkapansín. 2. state or condition of being noticeable or perceptible. Syn. pagkahálatain, pagkapánsinin.

halaw (ha-law), n. 1. act of selecting or picking out what are needed or wanted, as from a book, etc. Syn. pagpilì, pamimilì. 2. a being condensed, adapted, or reproduced, as from a novel or any literary or musical composition. Syn. pagkakáhalaw, pagkakáhangò. 3. any literary or musical adaptation, condensation, or reproduction.

halay (ha-lay), n. 1. act of putting someone to shame; insult; disgracing. Syn. paghiyá, paghamak, pagdustâ, paglapastangan. 2. violation of the purity of; rape. Syn. gahasà, paggahasà. 3. indecency; vulgarity; obscenity. Syn. kabastusán, kalaswaán.

halayá (ha-la-yá), var. haleyá, haleá, n. (Sp. jalea) jelly.

halayháy (ha-lay-háy), I. n. 1. act or manner of arranging things in a row or rows. Syn. paghahalayháy; hanay, paghahanay; hilera, paghihilera. 2. a row, line, or pile of things. Syn. hanay, hilera. 3. enumeration of things. Syn. paglalahad nang isá-isá.
—II. adj. placed or arranged in a row or rows. Syn. nakahanay, nakahilera.

hale (ha-le; ha-lé), I. interj. (H-) an exclamation used in daring someone to do something, meaning Go on! Go Ahead! Syn. Sige!
—II. adv. all right; go ahead. Syn. sige.

haling (ha-ling), n. extreme fondness for or about a person or thing; preoccupation of one's mind or attention to some kind of foolish idea. Syn. kahalingán, kahibangán, humaling.

halinghíng (ha-ling-híng), n. 1. neigh or neighing of a horse. 2. moan or moaning, as of a person suffering great pain. Syn. taghóy, pananaghóy; daíng, pagdaíng.

halíp (ha-líp), n. 1. substitute; alternate. Syn. palít, kapalít. 2. place or stead, chiefly used in the forms sa halip ng, ni or niná, meaning "in place of." 3. act of changing something with another. Syn. palít,

pagpapalít.

haliparót (ha-li-pa-rót), I. adj. flirtatious; libertine; licentious. Syn. kirí, makirí; landî, malandî.

halo (ha-lo), n. pestle (for a mortar). Syn. pambayó. Cf. pandikdík, panligís.

haló (ha-ló), var. heló, n. & interj. hello. Cf. Uy! Kumusta!

halò (ha-lò), n. 1. act of mixing things together, as by stirring. Syn. paghalò, paghahalò. 2. matter or substance added to something to make a mixture. Syn. lahók, bantô, dagdág, sahóg. 3. things mixed tógether; mixture. Syn. timplada.

halos (ha-los), adv. almost; nearly. Syn. kamuntík na.

halpók (hal-pók), I. adj. putrid; putrefying or rotting, referring esp. to fish. Syn. bilasâ, nabúbulók na.
—II. n. state or condition of being putrid, referring esp. to fish. Syn. bilasà, pagkabilasà.

halták (hal-ták), n. a sudden, abrupt pull; jerk with the hand. Syn. balták, pagbalták, paghalták.

halubilo (ha-lu-bi-lo), n. act of mixing or mingling with others in a crowd or group. Syn. pakikihalubilo, pakikihalò sa marami.

halukay (ha-lu-kay), n. 1. act of turning things up and down, as in looking or searching for something in a container. Syn. halungkát, paghalungkát, paghahalungkát. 2. a determined search for something badly needed. Syn. paghahanáp na mabuti, pagsasaliksík. 3. act of mixing things together by stirring or turning them up and down repeatedly. Syn. pahalong mabuti.

halukipkíp (ha-lu-kip-kíp), I. n. 1. act of folding thé arms together across the breast. Syn. paghalukipkíp. 2. the position of the two arms placed or folded together across the breast. Syn. pagkakáhalukipkíp. 3. (Fig.) noninterference; show of indifference or neutrality. Syn. dipakikialám, pagwawaláng-bahalà.
—II. adj. folded together across the breast, referring to a person's arms. Syn. nakahalukipkíp, nakasalikop o magkasalikop sa dibdíb ang mga braso.

ɲalughóg (ha-lug-hóg), I. n. 1. act of searching (a person) for concealed weapons, stolen goods, etc. Syn. *kapkáp, pagkapkáp*. 2. act of ransacking or searching a place carefully for something missing or stolen. Syn. *halukay, paghalukay; halungkát, paghalungkát*.
—II. adj. well-searched or ransacked. Syn. *halukáy, hinalukay; halungkát, hinalungkát*.

ɲalú-halô (ha-lú + ha-lò), I. adj. 1. made up of different things or kinds. Syn. *binúbuô ng ibá't ibáng bagay*. 2. mixed up; disorderly; in disorder. Syn. *maguló, walâ sa ayos*.
—II. n. 1. a mixture of different things. 2. specifically, a kind of refreshment made up of a mixture of beans, corn, jackfruit, banana splits, jelly, sugar, milk with shaved ice or ice cream.

ɲalumigmíg (ha-lu-mig-míg), I. n. state or condition of being damp or humid; humidity; dampness; moistness. Syn. *pagkabasâ-basâ, pagmamasâ-masâ; kahalumigmigán; kaúmiduhán, pagkaúmidó*.
—II. adj. humid; damp; moist. Syn. *úmidó, maúmidó, mahalumigmíg, basâ-basâ*.

ɲalungkát (ha-lung-kát), I. n. 1. act of searching for something among a number of other things in a container or place by turning them over and over. Syn. *halukay, paghalukay; halughóg, paghalughóg*.

ɲamak (ha-mak), I. adj. 2. humble; lowly; of low stature in society. Syn. *abâ, mababà ang urì*. 2. mean; vile. Syn. *masamâ, imbí*. 3. insignificant; of little value or worth.
—II. n. 1. lowly treatment of someone. Syn. *paghamak, pag-abâ, pag-apí*. 2. fact, state, or quality of being lowly or humble. Syn. *kaabaán, pagkaabâ*. 3. state or quality of being mean or vile. Syn. *kasamaán, pagkamasamâ; kaimbihán, pagkaimbi*.

ɲamba (ham-ba), n. (Carp., Sp. *jamba*) a side post for a doorway, window frame, etc.; jamb.

ɲambál (ham-bál), n. 1. sorrow felt for another's suffering or misfortune; pity; compassion. Syn. *awà, pagkaawà; habág, pagkahabág*. 2. melancholy; depressed or dismal feeling. Syn. *lungkót, lumbáy, hapis, lunos, pighatî*. 3. a looking down on. Syn.

paghamak, pagmatá, pag-apí.

hambalang (ham-ba-lang), n. 1. act of flying flat across the way. Syn. *hilatà o paghilatà sa gitnâ*. 2. the position of anything fallen or lying across the way. Syn. *pagkakáhilatà o pagkábulagtâ sa gitnâ*. 3. anything fallen or lying across the way. Syn. *bagay na nakahilatà o nakabulagtâ sa gitnâ*.

hambalos (ham-ba-los), n. act of striking or hitting right and left with something elongated, as a long stick, pole, or a cane. Syn. *hampás sa kaliwá't kanan, hagupít*.

hambing (ham-bing), n. 1. comparison. Syn. *paghahambíng, pagwawangis, pagtutulad, komparasyón*. 2. similarity; analogy; semblance. Syn. *pagkakátulad, pagkakáwangis, pagkakápareho, pagkakáhawig*.

hambo (ham-bo; ham-bó), n. bath or bathing. Syn. *ligò, paligò, paliligò*.

hambóg (ham-bóg), adj. arrogant; boastful; vain. Syn. *palalò, mayabang, mahangin (fig.), malakí ang ulo (fig.)*.

Hamo (Ha-mo), I. v. (colloq. of *hayaan mo*) Let it be that way. Leave it alone that way.
—II. interj. Leave it to me! *Hamo! Akó ang bahalà*. Leave it to me! I'll take care of it.

hamok (ha-mok), n. fierce fighting; hand-to-hand fight. Syn. *mahigpít na labanán, baka, pagbabaka*.

hamóg (ha-móg), n. dew; condensed moisture from the air.

hamon (ha-mon), n. 1. a call to participate in a fight or contest; challenge. Syn. *paghamon, reto, pagreto*. 2. defiance; resistance. Syn. *paglaban, pagsuwáy, pagsalungát, pagtutol*.

hamón (ha-món), n. (Sp. *jamón*) ham; hog's hind leg or the meat from it, salted, dried, and smoked.

hampas (ham-pas; ham-pás), n. 1. a strike or blow with something elongated held by the hand. Syn. *palò, bugbóg, hambalos*. 2. a striking or blowing hard against rocks along a shore. Syn. *salpók, pagsalpók; banggâ, pagbanggâ*. 3. punishment. Syn. *parusa, kaparusahán*.

hampasang-alon (ham-pa-sang + a-lon), n. 1. shore; seashore. Syn. *baybayin, baybaying-dagat, tabíng-dagat*. 2.

breakwater. Syn. *babasagáng-alon*, *pamasag-alon*.

hampás-kalabáw (ham-pás + ka-la-báw), var. hampáskalabáw, n. beating without mercy; strong and merciless beating. Syn. *waláng-awang gulpi (paggulpi)*.

hampás-lupà (ham-pás + lu-pà), var. hampáslupà, n. & adj. vagrant; vagabond; hobo; truant; tramp. Syn. *bagamundo (bagabundo), lagalág, palaboy*.

hampás-tikín (ham-pás + ti-kín), var. hampástikín, adj. said of an afternoon sun that has already inclined to about 45 degrees to the west.

Haná (Ha-ná), interj. 1. Let's go! Let's go on! Syn. *Tayo na!* 2. Go ahead! Go on! Syn. *Sige! Tulóy! Lakad!*

hanap (ha-nap), n. 1. act of searching or looking for someone or something. Syn. *pagtingín o pag-alám kung saán naroroón ang isáng tao o bagay, paghanap, paghahanáp.* 2. the object of search or pursuit. Syn. *tao o bagay na hináhanap.* 3. (*Colloq.*) income; earning. Syn. *kita, sahod, suveldo.*

hanapbuhay (ha-nap-bu-hay), n. means of livelihood; employment; occupation; source of income. Syn. *trabaho, gáwain, opisyo, pinagkakakitaan.*

hanay (ha-nay), n. 1. act of forming together in a line. Syn. *pagpila, paglinya, paghanay.* 2. act or manner of arranging things into a line or row. Syn. *paghihilera, paghahanay.* 3. line; row; file; rank. Syn. *hilera, pila, linya, halayháy.* 4. order; orderly arrangement. Syn. *pagkakásunúd-sunód.* 5. enumeration; naming one by one. Syn. *pagbanggít nang isá-isá; pag-isá-isá.*

handâ[1] (han-dâ), I. n. 1. preparation, as of things to be brought in a trip, etc. Syn. *paghahandâ, preparasyón.* 2. state or condition of being prepared. Syn. *pagkahandâ, pagkapreparado.* 3. a being alert; readiness. Syn. *alisto, pagkaalisto, kaalistuhán.* 4. readiness to help. Syn. *pagkalaán, kalaánán.*

—II. adj. 1. prepared; ready. Syn. *preparado, nagkahandâ, náhahandâ.* 2. alert; on the alert; watchful. Syn. *alisto, nakaalisto, alerto.*

handâ[2] (han-dâ), n. food prepared or serve▪ during a feast or party. Syn. *pagkain par▪ sa mga panauhin.*

handaan (han-da-an), n. 1. dinner party Syn. *káinan, salu-salo.* 2. banquet; forma▪ dinner with speeches. Syn. *pigíng▪ bangkete.*

handóg (han-dóg), n. 1. act of offering o presenting something to someone as a gift Syn. *paghahandóg, pagkakaloób.* 2. a gift present. Syn. *regalo, kaloób, bigáy, alaala▪* 3. offering; sacrifice. Syn. *alay, sakripisy▪* 4. dedication, as of a poem, song, etc. t▪ someone. Syn. *dedikasyón, patungkól, alay*

handusáy (han-du-sáy), I. n. 1. act o manner of lying prostrate or flat on th▪ floor, ground or the like. Syn. *pagbulagtâ* 2. state or condition of being prostrate o▪ fallen flat on the floor, ground, etc. Syn▪ *pagkakábulagtâ, pagkakátimbuwáng.*

—II. adj. prostrate; fallen flat on the floo▪ ground, etc. Syn. *nakahandusáy; bulagtâ▪ nakabulagtâ; timbuwáng, nakatimbuwáng*

Hané (Ha-né), var. Haní, interj. Go ahead Go on! Syn. *Sige! Tulóy! Lakad!* See Haná 2.

hani (ha-ni), n. (Eng.) 1. honey (of bees) Syn. *pulót-pukyutan.* 2. dear; darling. Syn *irog, giliw, mahál.*

hánimún (há-ni-mún), n. (Eng▪ honeymoon. Syn. *pulutgatâ.*

hanip (ha-nip), n. chicken louse or flea. Cf *pulgás, kuto.*

hantád (han-tád), I. n. state or condition o▪ being exposed to view. Syn. *lantád pagkalantád; litáw, pagkalitáw; hayág pagkahayág.*

—II. adj. exposed; in the open. Syn *lantád, nakalantád; litáw, nakalitáw; hayág nakahayág.*

hantík (han-tík), n. (Entom.) a species o▪ black or red big ants that live in trees usually in nests that they make from gree▪ leaves. Cf. *langgám, guyam.*

hantungan (han-tu-ngan), n. 1. destination goal; end. Syn. *hanggá, hanggahan.* 2▪ terminal; stopping place; station. Syn▪ *himpilan, páradahán, hintuan.* 3. boundar▪ line. Syn. *hangganan.* 4. graveyard▪ cemetery. Syn. *líbingan, sementeryo▪*

kamposanto. 5. the ultimate or maximum. Syn. *sukdulan, hanggahan.*

angá (ha-ngá), I. n. 1. admiration; high esteem. Cf. *pagpuri, papuri, mabuting palagáy, pagtatangì.* 2. wonder; amazement; astonishment. Syn. *taká, pagtataká; gilalas, panggigilalas.* 3. awe; reverence; veneration. Syn. *pítagan, pamimítagan; galang, paggalang.* —II. *adj.* 1. filled with admiration or wonder. Syn. *humáhangà, may paghangà, nagpupuri.* 2. awed; filled with awe.

angad (ha-ngad), n. 1. purpose; aim; intention; desire; object. Syn. *layon, layunin; nasà, ninanasà; nais, ninanais; gusto, kagustuhan.* 2. ambition; dream; strong desire to succeed. Syn. *lunggatî, lunggatiin, nilúlunggatî; mithî, mithiin, minímithî; pangarap, pángarapín, pinápangarap; ambisyón.*

angál (ha-ngál), *adj.* 1. stupid; slow-witted; dull. Syn. *tangá, ungás, tunggák, bangág.* 2. idiotic; foolish. Syn. *utú-utô, sirâ ang ulo, medyú-medyó.*

ángarin (há-nga-rin), n. 1. purpose; intention; desire; aim. Syn. *láyunin, kagustuhan, kaibigán.* 2. ambition; dream; strong desire for success. Syn. *pangarap, mithiin, lunggatiin, ambisyón.* See **hangád.**

angga (hang-ga; hang-gá), n. 1. destination; place where a person or thing is bound for. Syn. *patútunguhan, púpuntahán, paróroonán, hanggahan.* 2. termination; end. Syn. *wakás, katapusán.* 3. result; outcome. Syn. *bunga, kinálabasán, kináuwián, resulta.*

anggán (hang-gán), I. *prep.* & *conj.* till; until. See **hanggáng.** —II. n. 1. end. Syn. *wakás, katapusán.* 2. limit. Syn. *takdâ.*

anggánan (hang-ga-nan), n. 1. boundary; border; demarcation line. Syn. *hanggahan.* 2. end, as of a road. Syn. *dulo, duluhan.*

anggáng (hang-gáng), *prep.* & *conj.* (sometimes used with *sa*) until; till.

anggá't (hang-gá't), *prep.* & *conj.* (usually used with the negative *hindî* and *walâ*) unless; if not. Syn. *máliban kung, kung hindî, máliban sa, habang hindî.*

angháng (hang-háng), var. **angháng,** n. 1.

pepperiness; pungent taste, esp. of pepper. Syn. *kahanghangán.* 2. fieriness or pungency, as of words or speech.

hangin (ha-ngin), n. 1. wind; air; breeze. Syn. *simoy, amihan, habagat, balaklaot, sábalás.* 2. (*Fig.*) bragging; pomposity; conceit. Syn. *kahambugán, kayabangan.*

hangláy (hang-láy), n. a somewhat sour or acrid taste of some kind of vegetables, like radish.

hangò (ha-ngò), n. 1. removal from the fire or stove of anything being cooked. Syn. *pag-aahon o pag-aalís ng nilúlutò sa kalán.* 2. unit or quantity of food, esp. cakes, cooked at one time. Syn. *ahon, lutô.* Ant. *salang.* 3. deliverance or relief from poverty, sufferings, or difficulties. Syn. *tubós, pagkatubós; ibís, pagkaibís.* 4. literary adaptation or derivation, as of a plot from a novel. Syn. *halaw, paghalaw.*

hangos (ha-ngos), n. 1. leaving or coming in a hurry. Syn. *pag-alís o pagdatíng na nagmámadalî.* 2. gasp; gasping for breath. Syn. *hingal, paghingal, pangangapos ng hiningá.*

hapág (ha-pág), n. 1. table in general. Syn. *mesa, lamesa.* 2. a low or short-legged table, usually made of bamboo. Syn. *dulang, latok.*

hapáw (ha-páw), n. 1. act or manner of skimming or removing slightly the top layer of a heap, pile, etc. See **halapáw.** 2. act of making a cursory or superficial description, reading, study, etc. of something.

hapay (ha-pay), n. 1. an inclining or leaning to one side. Syn. *hilig, paghilig; kiling, pagkiling.* 2. the inclined or leaning position of a standing pole, post, tree, etc; also the degree of inclination or incline. Syn. *hilig, pagkakáhilig; kiling, pagkakákiling.* 3. bankruptcy or insolvency, as of business. Syn. *pangangalugi, pagkalugi, pagbagsák, paghapay.*

hapdî (hap-dî), n. a smarting or pungent pain or sore, as in the eyes, cut wound when a foreign body, like a vinegar, salt, etc. gets into it. Cf. *kirót, anták.*

hapis (ha-pis), n. grief; sorrow; sadness; affliction; anguish. Syn. *lungkót,* *dalamhatì, lumbày, pighatî.*

hapit (ha-pit), *n.* act of tightening or stretching fully, e.g. a clothes-line, to make it taut. Syn. *banat, pagbanat; bagtíng, pagpapabagtíng.* 2. act of tightening a tie or knot, or the like, as by pulling hard. 3. act of pressing (something) tightly, as between two things, in one's arms, or the like.

haplít (hap-lít), *n.* 1. a lash or lashing with a whip. Syn. *labtík, kagupít.* 2. a sarcastic or bitter remark. Syn. *pánanuyâ or masakit na punâ, pasaríng.* 3. act or manner of eating greedily. Syn. *lamon, paglamon; sabsáb, pagsabsáb.*

haplós (hap-lós), *n.* 1. a light or tender massage with the hand to give comfort or relief to a person suffering from some kind of pain. Syn. *hagpós, paghagpós.* 2. act of removing dirt, drops of water, etc. on the skin by wiping directly with a bare hand. Syn. *pahid o pagpahid ng kamáy.*

hapò (ha-pò), *n.* 1. gasping or panting; breathing with difficulty. Syn. *hingal, paghingal, pangangapós ng hiningá.* 2. exhaustion; extreme fatigue or weariness. Syn. *matindíng pagod o pagkapagod, panghihinà sa pagod.* 3. asthma. Syn. *hikà, asma.*

hapon[1] (ha-pon), *n.* the time from noon to evening; afternoon. Syn. *oras mulâ sa tanghalì hanggáng gabí.*

hapon[2] (ha-pon), *n.* act of alighting, perching, or resting of a bird on a tree, fence, or the like. Syn. *dapò, pagdapò.* 2. roosting of fowls in the late afternoon in order to rest and sleep. Syn. *pamamahingá sa hapunán ng mga manók.*

Hapón (Ha-pón), *n.* (Sp. *Japón*) 1. the Japanese Empire; Japan. 2. a Japanese male citizen; native of Japan. Syn. *mámamayáng Haponés.* See **Haponés.** 3. the language of Japan; Japanese. Syn. *Niponggo.*

Haponés (Ha-po-nés), *n.* (Sp. *Japonés*) 1. Japanese man. See **Hapón.** 2. the language of Japan; Japanese language. Syn. *Niponggo.*

hapunan (ha-pu-nan), *n.* 1. the last meal of the day, eaten in the evening; supper. 2. the food served or eaten for supper.

hapunán (ha-pu-nán), *n.* 1. perch; roosting place for birds and fowls. Syn. *dapuán, páhanunán.* 2. time of roosting of birds and fowls. Syn. *oras ng paghapon ng mga ibon manók.*

harà (ha-rà), *n.* act of placing oneself o something in the middle of the way causing inconvenience for others to pass Syn. *paglagáy sa gitnâ o paglalagáy ng an mang bagay sa gitnâ ng daanán.* 2. a perso or thing lying idle in the middle of a way Syn. *halang, hadláng, sagabal.* 3. (b extension) anything left anywhere. Syr *kalat.*

harabás (ha-ra-bás), *n.* act of usin something recklessly. Syn. *waláng-ingat padaskúl-dakól na paggamit.*

harakirí (ha-ra-ki-rí), *n.* (Jap.) harakir ritual suicide by disembowelment practised by high-ranking Japanes officials to avoid execution or disgrace Syn. *pagpapatiwakál.*

haragán (ha-ra-gán), *adj.* (Corruption fr. Sp. 1. irreverent; disrespectful. Syn. *waláng galang, waláng-pítagan, pusóng lapastangan.* 2. roguish; mischievous. Syn *salbahe, pilyo, saragate.*

harana (ha-ra-na), *n.* (Sp. *jarana*) serenade Syn. *tugtóg o awit ng pananapatan.*

harang (ha-rang), *n.* 1. act of interceptin (a person or thing) on the way to preven passage or entry. Syn. *pagharang.* 2. act c waylaying; holdup; highway robbery. Syn *pangharang, holdap.* 3. act of preventin the passage or approval of. Syn. *hadláng paghadláng.* 4. obstacle; barrier; barricade impediment; bar. Syn. *hadláng, sagaba sagwíl, halang.*

haráp (ha-ráp), *n.* 1. front or forepart. Syn *unahán, delantera.* 2. threshold, as of cave. Syn. *bungad, bukana.* 3. facade; fron of a building. Syn. *patsada.* 4. presence attendance. Syn. *daló, pagdaló.* 5. act o presenting oneself to someone appearance face to face with someone Syn. *pakikipagkita, pagharáp, pakikiharáp* 6. submission, as of papers, reports, etc for discussion or approval. Syn. *sulit pagsusulit.* 7. act of presenting or showing as evidences. Syn. *pagbibigáy o pagpapakita*. 8. act of actual attendance or performance, as of one's duty. Syn. *pagtupád, pagsasakatuparan*. 9. attention given, as to a visitor or guest. Syn. *asikaso, paghahasikaso*. 10. (*Anat.*) human sex organ. Syn. *arì, pag-aarì*.

harayà (ha-ra-yà), var. hirayà, n. (Bis.) imagination. Syn. *imahinasyón, guniguni*.

hardín (har-dín), n. (Sp. *jardin*) garden. Syn. *halamanan o hálamanán*. Cf. *tániman*.

harem (ha-rem), var. harim, n. (Eng.) harem.

harì (ha-rì), n. 1. the supreme ruler of a kingdom; king Cf. *emperadór, sultán, raha, datò*. 2. (*Colloq.*) the champion, as in boxing. Syn. *kampeón (kampiyón)*. 3. (*Colloq.*) ring or gang leader. Cf. *amo, punò*. 4. in card games, a playing card with a picture of a king.

Hárimanawarì (Há-ri-ma-na-wa-rì), *interj.* May God make it so! See Hárinangâ and Hárinawâ.

harina (ha-ri-na), var. arina, n. (Sp. *harina*) flour. Cf. *galapóng* (rice flour).

Hárinangâ (Há-ri-na-ngâ), *interj.* (fr. *harì na ngâ*) May it be so! I wish it to be true. Syn. *Hárinawâ*.

Hárinawâ (Há-ri-na-wâ), *interj.* (fr. *harì nawâ*) May God make it so!

harós (ha-rós), n. mischievousness; prankishness; frolicsomeness. Syn. *harót; kaharután; galawgáw, kagalawgawán; likót, kalikután*.

harpón (har-pón), n. (Eng.) harpoon. Syn. *salapáng, sibát o panibát ng patíng, atb.*

hasà (ha-sà), n. 1. act of sharpening or whetting a bladed tool, as on a whetstone. Syn. *tagís, pagtatagís; lagís, paglalagís*. 2. (*Fig.*) practice or training for experience. Syn. *sanay, pagsasanay*.

hasâ (ha-sâ), adj. 1. sharp; keen, referring to a bladed tool. Syn. *matalas, matalím*. 2. well-trained; well-practised. Syn. *sanáy, sanáy-na-sanáy*.

hasaán (ha-sa-án), n. whetstone; grindstone for knife, and other bladed tools. Syn. *lágisang-bató, tágisang-bató*.

hasahasá (ha-sa-ha-sá), n. (*Ichth.*) an adult short-bodied mackerel (*Rastrelliger*

brachysomus).

hasang (ha-sang), n. (*Ichth.*) gills.

hasík (ha-sík), I. n. 1. act of planting seeds by sowing or scattering them in the cultivated farm. Syn. *sabog o pagsasabog (sa lináng) ng butóng binhî*. 2. act of scattering or spreading abroad, as of fear, discontent, etc. Syn. *kalat, pagkakalat*.
—II. adj. sown; planted or propagated by sowing or scattering the seeds. Syn. *sabog, isinabog*.

hasmín (has-mín), n. (Sp. *jasmín*) 1. jasmine or jasmin, a tropical shrub of the olive family. 2. the fragrant flower of this tropical shrub.

hatak (ha-tak), n. 1. act of pulling (something) with the hand. Syn. *hila o paghila ng kamáy, batak o pagbatak*. 2. act of hauling or towing. Syn. *hila o pagpapahila*. 3. number of hauls made. Syn. *hakot, dami o bilang ng hakot*. 4. (*Colloq.*) exertion of efforts to finish or complete something. Syn. *pagsisikap na matapos o magawâ ang isáng bagay*. 5. act of training or practising. Syn. *sanay, pagsasanay*.

hataw (ha-taw), n. 1. act of beating or thrashing (someone) with something held by the hand. Syn. *hampás, bugbóg, hambalos, palò*. 2. club, cudgel, or anything used to bat or thrash someone. Syn. *bambú, pambugbóg, pamalò, panghampás*.

hatkeik (hat-keik), n. (Eng.) hot cake; griddlecake. Syn. *puto-kawalì*.

hatì (ha-tì), I. n. 1. act of dividing (something) into two equal parts. Syn. *paghati, paghahatí*. 2. act of cutting a thing in the middle or into two equal parts. Syn. *pagbiyák o pagputol sa gitnâ*. 3. the partition or dividing line between two things. Syn. *pagitan*. 4. a part or portion of something. Syn. *bahagi, parte*. 5. act of parting the hair. Syn. *paghahawi o paghahati ng buhók*. 6. the dividing line formed by combing the hair in opposite directions; part (of hair). Syn. *hawì, purka* (in some Tagalog areas).
—II. adj. said of two persons or groups who share equally in something. Syn. *magkahatì*.

hatíd (ha-tíd), I. n. 1. act of accompanying, leading, or escorting someone to a certain place. Syn. *pagsama at pagsubaybáy sa isáng taong papuntá sa isáng lugár.* 2. delivery of something from one place to another. Syn. *dalá, pagdadalá, paghahatíd.* 3. a person accompanied or escorted by someone from one place to another. Syn. *taong sinamahan o inihatíd.* 4. anything delivered from one place to another; delivery.
—II. adj. 1. accompanied or escorted by, referring to a person. Syn. *sinamahan, inihatíd.* 2. brought or delivered. 3. (Colloq.) caused or brought about by. Syn. *likhâ o galing sa.*

háting-daigdíg (há-ting + da-ig-díg), n. hemisphere.

hátinggabí (há-ting-ga-bí), n. midnight; the middle of the night; twelve o'clock at night. Syn. *kalágitnaan ng gabí, ika-12 ng gabí.*

hatol (ha-tol), n. 1. act of giving an advice or counsel. Syn. *payo, pagpapayo.* 2. the advice or counsel given. Syn. *payo, paalaala, pangaral.* 3. act of pronouncing judgment or sentence, as by a judge. Syn. *senténsiyá, pagsenténsiyá.* 4. the judgment or sentence rendered by a judge. Syn. *senténsiyá, kahatulán.* 5. decision of a board of judges, as in a contest. Syn. *pasiyá, kapasiyahán.* 6. medical prescription for an ailment. Syn. *hatol na gamót o lunas; reseta, preskripsiyón.*

hatsét (hat-sét), n. (Slang) 1. act of eating. Syn. *kain, pagkain.* 2. food; meal. Syn. *pagkain.*

hatsing (hat-sing; hat-síng), n. 1. sneeze; act of sneezing. Syn. *bahín, pagbahin.* 2. (echoic) the sound of sneezing.

hawa (ha-wa), I. n. 1. transfer of a disease from one person to another. Syn. *lalin, pagkalalin.* 2. a disease caused by germs through contact, etc.; infection; contagion. Syn. *impeksyón.* 3. stain; discoloration by a foreign substance. Syn. *mantsa, lalin.* 4. a person related to someone's family by marriage.
—II. adj. 1. caused by contamination or infection, referring to a disease. 2.

referring to stain or discoloration caused by a foreign substance or matter. 3. related to one's family by marriage.

hawak (ha-wak), I. n. 1. act or manner of holding something in one's hand. Syn. *pigil, pagpigil; tangan, pagtangan.* 2. act of holding on something to support oneself. Syn. *kapit, pagkapit.* 3. act of holding something, as for defense or protection. Syn. *paghahawak o pagtatangan (ng pananggól).* 4. the way or manner something is held by the hand. Syn. *tangan, pagkakátangan, pagkakáhawak.* 5. anything held by the hand. Syn. *bagay na pigil o tangan ng kamáy.* 6. possession or ownership, as of power, responsibility, etc. Syn. *pagmamay-ari.* 7. act of taking a woman as one's common-law wife. Syn. *pagbabae, pagkálunyâ.*
—II. adj. 1. held by the hand; in one's hand. Syn. *tangan o pigil ng kamay, nasa kamáy.* 2. in one's possession or responsibility. Syn. *nasa ilalim ng pananagutan.*

hawakán (ha-wa-kán), n. 1. handle of a bolo, knife, chisel, and the like. Syn. *puluhan, manggo.* 2. the part of an umbrella, cup, cane, etc. Syn. *tatangnán, manggo.* 3. something to hold on, as a handrail. Syn. *gabáy, kapitán.*

hawan (ha-wan), n. 1. act of clearing a place of shrubs, undergrowths, etc., as by cutting and burning. Syn. *paghahawan.* Cf. *paglilinis.* 2. act of making a place safe or cleared of all obstacles. Syn. *paglipol sa lahát ng mga sagabal o hadláng.* 3. state or condition of being cleared of shrubs, undergrowths, etc., or of all obstacles and obstructions. Cf. *linis, kalinisan.* 4. an open place, esp. one cleared of all obstacles and obstructions. Syn. *taháw o aliwalas na lugál.*

hawás (ha-wás), n. 1. slender shape or build, as of a person's body; well-proportioned height or stature. Syn. *hagwáy, kahagwayán.* Cf. *pagkabalingkinitan, kabalingkinitan.* 2. oval-shaped form or build, esp. of a face. Syn. *pagkataluhabâ, kataluhabaân.*

hawháw (haw-háw), n. act of washing

(clothes) by shaking in water carelessly
or superficially. Cf. *luglóg.*

hawì (ha-wì), *n.* 1. act of pushing aside tall
grasses, weeds, etc. to make an opening
or path along the way. 2. the opening or
path made in this manner through a place
covered with tall grasses, etc. Syn. *bulaos.*
Cf. *landás.* 3. act of shoving away or
pushing aside persons along the way, as
in passing or entering a thick crowd. 4.
act of parting the hair with or as with a
comb. Syn. *hatì o paghahatì sa buhók.* 5.
the part or line formed by combing the
hair in opposite directions. Syn. *hatì (ng
buhok), purka* (in some Tagalog areas). 6.
act of opening (curtains) by pushing or
pulling them to one side. Syn. *pagbubukás.*

hawig (ha-wig), *n.* 1. similarity; semblance;
resemblance; likeness. Syn. *wangis,
pagkakáwangis; tulad, pagkakátulad;
wangkî, pagkakáwangkî.* 2. comparison.
Syn. *hambíng, paghahambíng; tulad,
pagtutulad; paris, pagpaparis.*

hawla (haw-la), *n.* (Sp. *jaula*) 1. cage. Syn.
kulungan ng ibon. 2. (Colloq.) jail; cell.
Syn. *piitán, kulungan, bílangguan.*

hayà (ha-yà), *n.* 1. a threatening gesture of
the hand or of anything held by the hand.
Syn. *ambâ o yambâ (ng kamáy).* 2. a
consenting or toleration of an act. Syn.
*konsente, pagkonsente; bayà, pagpapabayà;
payag, pagpayag.* 3. neglect or
abandonment. Syn. *pabayà, pagpapabayà.*

hayaan (ha-ya-an), *v.* 1. to let or leave one
alone. Syn. *iwanang mag-isá, bayaan,
pabayaan.* 2. to abandon; desert. Syn.
pabayaan, layasan, iwan, talikurán. 3. to
threaten with one's fist or with anything
held by the hand. Syn. *ambaán, yambaán.*

hayag (ha-yag), *n.* 1. act of making
(something) known. Syn. *pagsasabi,
pagtatapát.* 2. revelation. Syn. *bunyág;
pagbubunyág; siwalat, pagsisiwalat.* 3. an
announcing or proclaiming. Syn.
pagpapahayag. 4. an announcement;
proclamation. Syn. *pahayag.*

hayág (ha-yág), I. *adj.* 1. in the open;
exposed to view. Syn. *kita, nakikita;
lantád, nakalantád; litáw, nakalitáw; labás,
nakalabás.* 2. known; not secret; open to

the knowledge of all or most people. Syn.
bunyág, alám na ng lahát o ng marami.
—II. *n.* 1. state or condition of being
already known, as of someone's secret. 2.
any open or exposed place for anyone to
see.

Hayán (Ha-yán), *interj.* There! There it is!
Syn. *Iyán!*

hayap (ha-yap), *n.* 1. sharpness or keenness
of blades or points of tools. Syn. *talím,
katalimán; talas, katalasan.* 2. severeness
or harshness, as of one's language. Syn.
sakít, kasakitán (colloq.)

hayku (hay-ku), *n.* (Jap.) haiku: a Japanese
verse or poem consisting of three lines
with a total of 17 syllables.

Hayo (Ha-yo), *interj.* Go! Go ahead! Syn.
Sige! Lakad! Tulóy! Sulong!

hayók (ha-yók), *adj.* 1. extremely hungry.
Syn. *gutóm na gutóm, pasál na pasál.* 2.
extremely or excessively desirous. Syn.
dayukdók, sabík na sabík. 3. greedy. Syn.
matakaw, sakím, masibà.

hayón[1] (ha-yón), I. *n.* 1. act or ability to
carry on something up to the end or
destination. Syn. *agdón.* 2. the farthest
distance that a person or thing can reach.
Syn. *abót, layong abót o kayang maabót.*
—II. *adj.* able or having the ability to
carry on something up to the end or
destination. Syn *maáagdón, makaáagdón.*

Hayón[2] (Ha-yón), var. **Hayún,** *interj.* There!
Over there! Yonder! Syn. *Iyón!*

hayuma (ha-yu-ma), *n.* 1. act of mending
or repairing fishing nets, thatch roofing,
fish corrals, bamboo fence, and the like.
Syn. *pagkukumpuní o pag-aayos ng sirà (ng
lambát, bubungáng pawid, atb.)* 2. such
repair or mending made. Cf. *hulip, tagpî.*

He (He), *intej.* an exclamation expressive
of surprise, disgust, or scorn.

hebilya (he-bil-ya), *n.* (Sp. *jebilla*) a clasp
on a belt; buckle.

heko (he-ko), *n.* (Ch.) a kind of thick, dark
sauce made from the residue in the process
of *patís* making. See *patís.* Cf. *bagoóng.*

hekságono (hek-sá-go-no), *n.* (Sp. *hexágono*)
hexagon.

hedkuwarter (hed-ku-war-ter), *n.* (Eng.)
headquarters; main office. Syn. *kuwartél*

henerál, punong tanggapan, punong himpilan.

helatina (he-la-ti-na), n. (Sp. *gelatina*) gelatine.

hele (he-le), n. 1. act of making a baby fall asleep by singing a lullaby. 2. a kind of cradlesong; lullaby. Syn. *lúlabáy, awit na pampatulog-batà, oyayi.* 3. same as **helehele.**

helehele (he-le-he-le), var. **hele-hele**, I. n. a pretended dislike. Syn. *kunyarì, pagkukunyarî; kunwarî, pagkukunwarî.* —II. adj. pretending to have no liking for. Syn. *nagkúkunyarî, nagkúkunwarî.*

helikopter (he-li-kop-ter), n. (Eng.) helikopter. Syn. *helikópteró.*

helmet (hel-met), n. (Eng.) helmet. Cf. *bastipól, salukót.*

helo (he-lo; he-ló), var. **haló**, n. & interj. hello; hallow; halloo.

henerál (he-ne-rál), n. (Mil., Sp. *generál*) 1. general. 2. (*Colloq.*) leader or head, as of a gang. Syn. *punò, apò.*

heneralisasyón (he-ne-ra-li-sas-yón), n. (Sp. *generalización*) generalization. Syn. *paglahát, paglalahát; paglansák, paglalansák.*

henerasyón (he-ne-ras-yón), n. (Sp. *generación*) generation. Syn. *salinlahí.*

henerosidád (he-ne-ro-si-dád), n. (Sp. *generosidad*) generosity. Syn. *kagandahangloób, kagandahang-asal, kabutihang-loób, kabutihang-asal, pagkabukáng-palad, kabukaháng-palad.*

henyo (hen-yo), n. (Sp. *genio*) genius; person with great natural power of mind. Syn. *taong may likás na kadalubhasaan, pantás, dalubhasà, pahám.*

heograpiya (he-o-gra-pi-ya), var. **heyograpiya, heograpya**, n. (Sp. *heografía*) geography.

heolóhiyá (he-o-ló-hi-yá), var. **heyolóhiyá**, n. (Sp. *geología*) geology.

heometriya (he-o-me-tri-ya), var. **heyometriya**, n. (Sp. *geometría*) geometry.

Hep (Hep), interj. 1. an exclamation used as an answer to a roll call: Present! Here! Cf. *Náritó po!* 2. an exclamation expressive of warning or signal to prevent danger. Stop! Cf. *Tamà na! Hustó na!*

hepe (he-pe), n. (Sp. *jefe*) 1. chief, as in

hepe ng pulisya, chief of police. Syn. *punò.* 2. the head or boss, as of an office. Syn. *bos, punò.*

herarkiya (he-rar-ki-ya), n. (Sp. *jerarquia*) hierarchy.

herbabuwena (her-ba-bu-we-na), n. var. **yerbabuwena**, n. (Bot., Sp. *yerba-buena*) peppermint; marshmint.

heringgilya (he-ring-gil-ya), n. (Sp. *jeringuilla*) hypodermic syringe. Syn. *panginiksiyón, panturók (ng iniksiyón).*

hero (he-ro), var. **hiro**, n. (Sp. *hierro*) 1. a brand made on a cattle, horses, and other animal as a mark of ownership. Cf. *taták, marka.* 2. the hot iron used for burning a brand on animals; brand. Syn. *panghero (panghiro).* 3. the act or manner of burning a mark of ownership on animals. Syn. *paghihero, pagkakahero.*

heroismo (he-ro-is-mo), n. (Sp.) heroism. Syn. *kabayanihan, pagkabayani, kagitingan.*

herúndiyó (he-rún-di-yó), n. (Sp. *gerundio*) gerund. Syn. *pandiwang makangalan, pangngalang-diwà, pangngalang-makadìwà.*

Hesukristo (He-su-kris-to), n. (Sp. *Jesucristo*) Jesus Christ.

Hesús (He-sús), n. (Sp. *Jesús*) Jesus.

Hesús-Maryá't-Husép (He-sús + Mar-yá't + Hu-sép), interj. an exclamation often ejaculated in sudden surprise, horror, danger, etc. as if to invoke or beg for help from Jesus, Mary, and Joseph.

Heswita (Hes-wi-ta), n. & adj. (Sp. *Jesuita*) Jesuit.

Heto (He-to), var. **eto**, interj. Here! Here it is! Syn. *Iré!*

Hey (Hey), interj. Hey! an exclamation used to attract attention, express surprise, or in asking questions. Cf. *Uy! Abá!*

Hi (Hi; Hî), interj. an ejaculation used in getting a horse, esp. to move faster. Cf. *híya (hiyá).*

hibáng (hi-báng), adj. 1. in a state of delirium; delirious. Syn. *nagdídiliryo.* 2. wildly excited. Syn. *halíng, naháhaling.* 3. crazy. Syn. *ulól, naúulól; loko, nalúloko.*

hibás¹ (hi-bás), I. n. diminution, weakening, or cessation of the intensity of: a) fever. Syn. *babâ, pagbabâ.* b) storm, flood, etc. Syn. *hulaw, paghulaw; hupâ, paghupâ.* c) rain. Syn. *tilà, pagtilà.* d) drunkenness. Syn. *himasmás.*

—II. *adj.* 1. with the fever already gone or diminished. Syn. *mababà na ang lagnát o walâ nang lagnát.* 2. reduced or weakened in intensity, referring to storm. Syn. *huláw na.*

hibás² (hi-bás), *adj.* slanting; oblique; inclined. Syn. *hilíg, nakahilig; hapáy, nakahapay; hiwíd, nakahiwíd.*

hibi (hi-bi), *n.* small shrimps, usually cooked dry.

hibî (hi-bî), *n.* 1. act or manner of pursing the lips, as when a child is about to cry.

hibík (hi-bík), *n.* 1. sob or sobbing; lament; lamentation. Syn. *daíng, pagdaíng; taghóy, pananaghóy.* 2. pleading; appealing; supplication. Syn. *samò, pagsamò; pamanhík, pamamanhík; pakiusap, pakikiusap; hilíng, paghilíng.* 3. a humble, earnest request. Syn. *samò; pakiusap; hiling, kahilingan; pamanhík, kapamanhikán.*

hiblá (hi-blá), *n.* (Sp. *hebra*) 1. fiber. Syn. *himaymáy, hilatsá.* 2. thread. Syn. *sinulid.* 3. a length of thread for a needle. Syn. *bungot.*

hibò (hi-bò), *n.* 1. instigation; seduction. Syn. *sulsól, panunulsól, pagsusulsól; upat, pang-uupat; apoyo, pang-aapoyo.* 2. something that seduces; temptation. Syn. *tukso, tentasyón, sulsól, upat.* 3. bad influence. Syn. *masamáng bunga o epekto.* 4. bait; trick; deceit. Syn. *dayà, panlilinlang, lalag.* 5. stain. Syn. *bahid, mantsa.*

hikà (hi-kà), *n.* (*Med.*) asthma. Syn. *asma, hapò, sakít na hapò.*

hikáb (hi-káb), var. **higáb**, I. *n.* 1. yawn; act of yawning. Syn. *paghikáb, paghigáb.* 2. the sound of yawning.

—II. *adj.* given or inclined to too much yawning.

hikahós (hi-ka-hós), *adj.* 1. not sufficiently supplied. Syn. *kapós, kinákapos; kulang, kinúkulang.* 2. indigent; poor; needy. Syn. *dukhâ; maralitâ, nagdaralitâ; hiráp, mahirap, naghihirap.*

híkan (hí-kan), *n.* & *interj.* an ejaculation used in calling pigs, esp. at feeding time.

hikap (hi-kap), *n.* 1. act of going from place to place; travelling from one place to another. Syn. *libot, paglibot, paglilibót; galâ, paggagalâ; pasyál, pamamasyál.* 2. vagrancy; vagabondage. Syn. *lakuwatsa, paglalakuwatsa, lagalág, paglalagalág.*

hikaw (hi-kaw), *n.* earring. Syn. *arilyos, aretes.*

hikayat (hi-ka-yat), *n.* a persuading or being persuaded; inducement. Syn. *himok, paghimok, pagkahimok; ganyák, pagganyák, pagkaganyák; amukî, pag-amukî, pagkaamukî; akit, pag-akit, pagkaakit.*

hikbí (hik-bí; hik-bî), *n.* 1. sob; act or sound of sobbing. 2. lamentation. Syn. *pánangisán.*

hiklás (hik-lás), I. *n.* act of tearing or ripping apart forcibly. Syn. *pigtás, pagpigtás; bakbák, pagbakbák; tukláp, pagtukláp; pigtál, pagpigtál.*

—II. *adj.* torn or ripped apart forcibly. Syn. *pigtás, bakbák, tukláp, pigtál.*

hiklát (hik-lát) I. *n.* 1. act of forcing a small hole to open widely as by pulling or tearing the sides or edges. Syn. *biklát, pagbiklát.* 2. fact, state, or condition of being forcibly widened, referring to a small hole or opening. Syn. *pagkahiklát, pagkabiklát,* 3. a wide hole or tear made so by tearing or pulling apart forcibly. Syn. *biklát; wakwák, gahak.*

—II. *adj.* forcibly widened as by pulling or tearing apart, referring to a small hole, tear, or any small opening. Syn. *biklát, nabiklát; gahák, nagahak.*

hikwatin (hik-wa-tin), *v.* to raise or lift slightly a side of something with or as with a lever. Syn. *tikwasín nang bahagyâ.*

hidhíd (hid-híd), I. *n.* 1. quality of being very stingy; excessive frugality. Syn. *labis na katipirán o pagtitipíd, kakuriputan.* 2. selfishness. Syn. *kasakimán, kaimbután, labis na karamutan, kasakrihán.*

—II. *adj.* 1. very stingy. Syn. *kuripot, labis na matipíd.* 2. selfish. Syn. *sakím, imbót, sakré, lubháng maramot.*

hidwâ (hid-wâ), *adj.* 1. mistaken; wrong; erroneous; erring. Syn. *malî, lisyâ, hindi tamà, lihís.* 2. anomalous. Syn. *tiwalî, iregulár.* 3. contrary; contradictory;

opposed; against. Syn. *salungát,
kasalungát; laban, kalaban.*

hidwaan (hid-wa-an), n. misunderstanding;
disagreement. Syn. *di-pagkakáunawaán,
di-pagkakásundô, samaan ng loób.*

higâ (hi-gâ), n. 1. act of lying down. Syn.
paghigâ. 2. act of going to bed in order to
sleep. Syn. *tulog, pagtulog.* 3. lying
position of the body. Syn. *pagkakáhigâ.* 4.
time of going to bed. Syn. *pagtulog, oras
ng pagtulog.* 5. lying position of anything
on a horizontal surface. Syn. *bagnà,
pagkakábagnà.*
—II. adj. 1. lying down; fallen down on
one's back. Syn. *nakahigâ.* 2. lying flat on
a surface. Syn. *bulagtá, nakabulagtâ.* 3.
(by extension) sick; bed-ridden. Syn.
may-sakít, nakaratay sa baníg.

hígaan (hí-ga-an), n. 1. bed; any thing or
place to lie down on. 2. simultaneous
going to bed, as of persons living in a
boarding house. Syn. *paghihígaan,
pagtutulugán.* 3. usual time of going to
bed, as of a group of persons. Syn. *oras ng
paghihígaan.*

higad (hi-gad), I. n. 1. the woolly worm or
larvae of certain insects that causes
itchiness on the skin when touched. Syn.
tilas. Cf. *uód.* 2. an artful or sly person.
Syn. *taong suwitik o tuso.* 3. a species of
medicinal plant (*Achyranthes aspera* L.).
—II. adj. artful; sly; cunning. Syn. *suwitik,
tuso, magulang* (fig.), *mapanlamáng.*

higante (hi-gan-te), I. n. (Sp. *gigante*) 1.
giant. 2. anything that is extraordinarily
big. Syn. *anó mang bagay na nápakalakí.*
3. any huge animal. Syn. *dambuhalà.*
—II. adj. of extraordinary size; huge. Syn.
nápakalakí, lubháng malakí.

higantí (hi-gan-tí), n. (fr. *gantí*) revenge;
retaliation; vengeance; vendetta. Syn.
benggansa, paghihigantí.

higing (hi-ging), n. 1. a buzzing or humming
sound, as that of bees, mosquitoes, etc.
Syn. *haging, hugong, huni.* 2. tone or tune;
proper pitch. Syn. *tono, himig.* 3. an air
of melody; piece of music. Syn. *tugtugin.*
4. something heard vaguely and not well-
understood. Syn. *ulinig.* 5. a getting wind
of something secret. Syn. *hiwatig,*

pagkahiwatig.

higit¹ (hi-git), n. 1. act of pulling something
with the hand towards oneself. Syn. *hatak,
paghatak; batak, pagbatak; hila, paghila.* 2.
act of stretching something by pulling.
Syn. *pagpapabagtíng sa pamamagitan ng
paghila.*

higit² (hi-git), I. n. 1. state or quality of
being better than another or others;
advantage. Syn. *lamáng, kalamangán; buti,
kabutihan; bentaha, kabentaha.* 3. excess;
surplus. Syn. *sobra, labis, kalabisán.* 4. the
difference or remainder in dividing things
equally. Syn. *putál.* 5. a surpassing or
getting the better of. Syn. *paghigit,
paglampás, paglamáng.*
—II. adv. 1. (with *sa*) more than. Syn.
sobra o higít sa. 2. (with *na*) better; better
than. Syn. *mas, lalò pa.*

higop (hi-gop), n. 1. act of taking in liquid
by sipping or in small gulps, as from a cup,
spoon, etc. Cf. *sipsíp, hitít, hithít, supsóp.*
2. the amount of liquid taken in at one
time. Cf. *lagók.* 3. a sucking or being
sucked; suction. Syn. *lulón, paglulón,
pagkálulón.*

higpít (hig-pít), n. 1. tightness or firmness,
as of hold, bite, fitting, etc. Syn. *hapit,
igtíng, tibay, sikíp.* 2. strictness or severity;
rigidity. Syn. *kaistriktuhán, kahigpitán.* 3.
stiffness, as in competitions or contests.
Syn. *init, kainitan* (fig.). 4. tightness or
tautness. Syn. *bagtíng, kabagtingán.*

hihip (hi-hip), var. **ihip**, n. 1. act or
manner of blowing air at something from
the mouth. Cf. *bugá.* 2. gust or puff of
wind. Syn. *simoy (ng hangin).* 3.
blowpipe, usually made of a length of
small bamboo or a small iron tube, used
for blowing fire to increase the flame of
firewood in the stove. 4. act of playing a
wind instrument.

hila (hi-la), n. 1. act of pulling or drawing
something towards oneself with or as with
the hand. Syn. *higít, hatak, batak.* 2. act
of towing or hauling; haulage. Syn.
*arastre, remolke, paghatak o paghila ng
kargada.* 3. a dragging or being dragged.
Syn. *kaladkád, pagkaladkád.* 4. the thing
or things being hauled or towed; load.

Syn. *kargada, kargamento*. 5. the number of loads or trips made in hauling or towing something. 6. (*Colloq.*) act of persuading someone to go or join another. Syn. *yayà, pagyayà; kayag, pagkayag; hikayat, paghikayat*.

hilab (hi-lab), n. 1. swelling or bulging, as of grains of rice, corn, etc. in cooking. Syn. *pagâ, pamamagâ; bintóg, pamimintóg*. 2. rise or expansion, as of cake, bread, etc. Syn. *alsa, pag-alsa*. 3. distention or enlargement, as of stomach. Syn. *lakí, paglakí; umbók, pag-umbók; tambók, pagtambók*. 4. spasm; convulsive action causing pain, esp. in the stomach, as in having gas pain. 5. pain in the abdomen caused by the movement of the fetus in the womb.

hilakbót (hi-lak-bót), n. sudden fear or fright. Syn. *biglâng takot o pagkatakot; sindák, pagkasindák; gulat, pagkagulat*.

hilagà (hi-la-gà), n. north. Syn. *norte*.

hilagpós (hi-lag-pós), var. **hulagpós**, I. n. 1. a slipping or breaking loose from the hold of the hand. Syn. *pagkawalâ sa hawak ng kamáy*. 2. a loosening or a being loosened, as binding, knot, etc., due to poor tying. Syn. *pagluwág ng talì o pagkakátalì*.
—II. *adj.* 1. having slipped off or broken loose from the hold of the hand. Syn. *nakawalâ sa pagkakáhawak*. 2. loose or having loosened due to poor tying, referring to a knot or binding. Syn. *maluwág, lumuwág; kalág, nakalág*.

hilagyô (hi-lag-yô), n. 1. spirit. Syn. *diwà, espiritu*. 2. namesake. Syn. *tukayo, katukayo, kapangalan*. 3. relative; blood; relation. Syn. *kaanak, kamag-anak, kaangkán*.

hilahid (hi-la-hid), n. 1. a slight rubbing of one thing against another in passing. Syn. *sagid, pagsagid, pagkasagid*. 2. a slight scratch or scratches on a surface caused in this manner. Syn. *galos, gasgás, gurlís*. 3. a smear, blotch or stain from having been touched with something dirty. Syn. *bahid, mantsa, dungis*.

hilahil (hi-la-hil), n. 1. grief; deep sorrow or sadness. Syn. *hapis; lumbáy, kalumbayan; pighatî, kapighatián; lungkót,*

kalungkutan; dalamhatì, kadalamhatian. 2. suffering; pain; hardship. Syn. *hirap, kahirapan, pagtitiís, sakit, dusa*. 3. distress; anxiety; trouble. Syn. *ligalig, pagkaligalig; guló, kaguluhan; balisa, pagkabalisa; bagabag, pagkabagabag*. 4. vexation; annoyance. Syn. *yamót, pagkayamót; inís, pagkainís*.

hilahód (hi-la-hód), adj. with one's foot or feet being dragged along in walking. Syn. *hila o hiníhila ang paá (mga paá)*. Cf. *piláy, hingkód, humíhingkód*. 2. (Fig.) lacking force or effectivity; lame; not convincing, as in *hilahód na katwiran*, lame excuse. Syn. *mahinà, waláng-bisà, di-kapaní-paniwalà*.

hilam (hi-lam), n. 1. smarting or pungent pain in the eyes due to the penetration of soap foam, lye, or the like. Syn. *silam*. 2. dimness or bleariness of sight due to smoke, tears, etc. Syn. *panlalabò ng matá dahil sa usok, luhà, atb*.

hilamos (hi-la-mos), n. 1. act or manner of washing the face. Cf. *hugas, hináw*. 2. act of smearing the face with something sticky or greasy by applying it with the hand as in washing the face with water. Cf. *pahid, haplós*.

hilantád (hi-lan-tád), I. n. 1. act or manner of lying down in abandon on one's back without any cover. Syn. *hilatà, paghilatà; tihayà, pagtihayà*. 2. the position of a person lying down in abandon on one's back. Syn. *hilatà, pagkakáhilatà; tihayà, pagkakátihayà*. 3. fact, state or condition of being exposed in the open. Syn. *lantád, pagkakálantád*.
—II. adj. 1. lying in abandon on one's back without any cover. Syn. *hilatà, nakahilatà; tihayà, nakatihayà*. 2. exposed in the open. Syn. *lantád, nakalantád*.

hilat (hi-lat), I. n. 1. act or manner of pulling or stretching the sides or edges of a small hole, cut, tear, or rip to make it wider. Syn. *hiklát, paghiklát; biklát, pagbiklát*. 2. act of drawing or pulling down the lower eyelid with the tip of a finger, usually accompanied with the utterance of the word *hilat, hibat,* or *hirat*.
—II. *interj.* an exclamation expressive of

hilatà   **hilod**

one's disgust at someone who has just met
an unfavorable experience, meaning
"That's what you deserve!" Syn. *Mabuti
ngâ sa iyó!* See **hirat**.

hilatà (hi-la-tà), *n.* act or manner of lying
down lazily or in abandon on one's back.
Syn. *paghilatà.* Cf. *bulagtâ, pagbulagtâ;
tihayà, pagtihayà.*

hilatlát (hi-lat-lát), I. *n.* 1. act or manner
of playfully stretching the edges or sides
of a small hole, cut, tear, or rip thus
making it wider. See **hilat**. 2. state or
condition of being pulled or stretched
widely, referring to a hole, cut, tear, or
rip. Syn. *pagkahilát, kahilatlatán.*
—II. *adj.* referring to a hole, cut, rip, or
the like, that has been pulled or stretched
widely. Syn. *hiklát, nahiklát.*

hilatsa (hi-lat-sa), *n.* (Sp. *hilacha*) 1. fiber
(in general). Syn. *himaymáy, hiblá.* 2.
thread ravelled from cloth. Syn. *mulmol,
himulmól, lamuymóy.* 3. grain in wood.
Syn. *gisok.* 4. texture in cloth;
arrangement of threads woven together.
Syn. *habi, pagkakáhabi.*

hiláw (hi-láw), I. *adj.* 1. uncooked; not
cooked; raw, referring to food. Syn. *di-lutò.*
2. unripe or green, referring to fruits. Syn.
di-hinóg, di-pa-hinóg. Cf. *murà, bubót.* 3.
raw; in its natural condition; not yet
changed by art, manufacture, etc, as in
hilaw na mga sangkáp, raw materials.
—II. *n.* state or condition of being: a)
uncooked, referring to food; b) unripe or
green, referring to fruits; and c) raw or in
its natural condition, as of materials.

hilbana (hil-ba-na), *n.* (Sp. *hilván*) 1. act of
sewing (cloth) with long, loose,
temporary stitches; basting. Cf. *tutos,
pagtutos, pagtututos.* 2. loose, temporary
stitches; bastings. Syn. *tahíng
pansamantalá.* Cf. *tutos.*

hilera (hi-le-ra), *n.* (Sp.) row; line; file. Syn.
hanay, pila, linya, halayháy.

hilì (hi-lì), *n.* 1. act of making another feel
envious of what one has by showing or
displaying it proudly. Syn. *pag-inggít,
pagpapainggít.* Cf. *pagpaparangyâ.* 2. a
desire for some advantage or possession
belonging to another; envy. Syn. *panaghilì,*

pananaghilì; inggít, pagkainggít.

hilík (hi-lík), *n.* 1. snore; act or manner of
snoring. Syn. *harok, pagharok; hagok,
paghagok.* 2. the sound of snoring. Syn.
harok, hagok.

hilig[1] (hi-lig), *n.* 1. act of leaning or
inclining against something. Syn. *sandál,
pagsandál; sandíg, pagsandíg.* 2. an
inclining or leaning to one side or
direction. Syn. *kiling, pagkiling; hápay,
paghapay; tagilid, pagtagilid.* 3. the position
of a person or thing leaning against
something. Syn. *sandál, pagkakásandál;
sandíg, pagkakásandíg.* 4. fact, state, or
condition of being inclined to one side
or direction. Syn. *kiling, pagkakákiling;
hapay, pagkakáhapay; tagilid, pagkakátagilid.*
5. degree of inclination, as of a post, tree,
house, etc.

hilig[2] (hi-lig), *n.* 1. natural inclination or
bent; tendency; propensity. Syn. *ugalì,
kaugalian; gusto, kagustuhan; gawì,
kagawian.* 2. vocation; inner call or
summons. Syn. *bokasyón.* 3. special
natural ability; talent. Syn. *talino, likás na
kahusayan.*

hilíng (hi-líng), *n.* 1. act of requesting
(something) from someone. Syn.
pakikiusap, pakikisuyò. 2. request; thing
that is being requested. Syn. *pakiusap,
pakisuyò, pamanhik.* 3. petition;
supplication; earnest request. Syn. *samò,
hinaing, luhog, pagmamakaawà.* 4. petition
in prayer; thing prayed for. Syn. *dasál,
dinádasál; panalangin, ipinananálangin.*

hilis (hi-lis), *n.* 1. act or manner of pressing
out with the fingers the contents of a soft
or flexible tube, intestine, and the like.
Cf. *hagot, paghagot.* 2. a small cut or slice
shaped like a parallelogram, that is, with
two slanting sides. Cf. *hiwà, gilít, gayat.*
3. act of playing a violin by passing or
drawing the bow across the strings. Syn.
pagtugtóg ng biyolín sa pamamagitan ng arko.

hilo (hi-lo), *n.* dizziness; giddiness;
grogginess; vertigo. Syn. *liyó, pagkaliyó;
lulà, pagkalulà; pagkahilo.*

hilod (hi-lod), *n.* act or manner of scrubbing
the body with the hand, towel, small
stone, etc. to remove the dirt on the skin.

Syn. *kuskós o pagkuskós sa katawán upang maalís ang libág.*

hilom (hi-lom), n. 1. cicatrization; healing of a wound with the formation of a scar. Syn. *paggalíng o pagkatuyô ng sugat, pagpipilat, pagpipeklát.* 2. closing up of an opening, as of cracks in the ground. Syn. *tikom, pagtitikom; sará, pagsasará.*

hilóng-talilong (hi-lóng + ta-li-long), n & adj. (Fig.) referring to a person who is very much confused on what to do.

hilot (hi-lot), n. 1. midwife. Syn. *komadrona.* 2. act of massaging a part of the body, as in relieving pain or in restoring a dislocated bone or bones. Syn. *masahe, pagmasahe.*

himà (hi-mà), n. smelly, whitish secretion accumulating in the vaginal sheath.

himakás (hi-ma-kás), n. 1. farewell; last word. Syn. *paalam, pamamaalam.* 2. the last or end. Syn. *wakás, katapusán.*

himagal (hi-ma-gal), n. slight tiredness from work. Syn. *bahagyáng pagod (kapaguran).*

himagas (hi-ma-gas), n. 1. dessert. Also, *panghimagas.* Cf. *matamís.* 2. act of taking dessert. Also, *panghihimagas.*

himagsik (hi-mag-sik), n. 1. a rising in revolt; rebellion; revolution; uprising. Syn. *pagpapabangon, pag-aalsá, rebolusyón.* 2. a rebellious or defiant attitude against someone or something. Syn. *paglaban.*

himagsikan (hi-mag-si-kan), n. 1. rebellion; revolution; uprising; revolt. Syn. *rebelyón, rebolusyón, pagbabangon, pag-aalsá.* See **himagsik.** 2. war; hostilities between or among nations. Syn. *digmâ, digmaan; gera (giyera).*

himalâ (hi-ma-lâ), n. miracle; wonder. Syn. *milagro, kababalaghán, hiwagà, misteryo.*

himalay[1] (hi-ma-lay), n. 1. act of picking or collecting grains left on the field by reapers. Syn. *pamumulot o pagsimót sa naiwan ng mga mag-aaní.* 2. the grains thus gleaned; gleanings. 3. picking or selecting those that are needed. Syn. *pagpilì, pamimilì.*

himalay[2] (hi-ma-lay), n. (fr. *malay*) 1. slight consciousness. Syn. *bahagyáng malay-tao.* 2. slight or vague idea or knowledge about something. Syn. *bahagyáng kabatiran o*

kaalaman, hinuhà.

himangláw (hi-mang-láw), n. a feeling of loneliness. Syn. *bahagyáng pamamangláw o pagkalungkót.*

himas (hi-mas), n. 1. affectionate touch or massage with the hand. Syn. *masuyong hagpós o paghagpús-hagpós.* 2. act of petting a rooster by regularly massaging the body and patting the back, etc., as a part of the training for cockfighting. Syn. *panggas, pagpanggás.*

himasmás (hi-mas-más), n. 1. regaining from the loss of consciousness; recovery from a fainting spell. Syn. *pagkakamalay-tao, pagsasaulî o pagbabalík ng malay-tao.* 2. regain of sobriety or soberness after having been drunk. Syn. *panunumbalik ng hinahon, pagkawalâ ng lasíng.*

himasok (hi-ma-sok). Also *panghimasok,* n. meddling; interference in other's affairs. Syn. *pakikialám.*

himatáy (hi-ma-táy), n. loss of consciousness; fainting spell; swoon; syncope. Syn. *pagkawalâ ng malay-tao.* 2. epilepsy; falling sickness. Syn. *pagkahímatayin.*

himatóng (hi-ma-tóng), var. **himatón,** n. 1. act of showing or pointing the way or direction to a place. Syn. *pagtuturò ng daán o dakong patungo sa isáng lugár.* 2. a hint or information given to someone about something. Syn. *pahiwatig.* 3. act of giving this hint or information. Syn. *pagpapahiwatig.* 4. giving information against someone or about something irregular. Syn. *sumbóng, pagsusumbóng; suplóng, pagsusuplóng.*

himáy (hi-máy), n. 1. act of removing or separating the grains, as of corn from the cobs. Syn. *pag-aalís ng mga butil (ng mais) sa busal.* 2. act of removing the bean seeds from the pods. Syn. *talop, pagtatalop.* 3. act of removing meat from the bones and shredding it into pieces. Syn. *pag-aalís ng karne sa butó at pagpipirá-piraso sa lamán.* 4. act of stringing beans and cutting them into small pieces in preparation for cooking. 5. (Fig.) act of studying, examining, or going over something one by one or in detail. Syn. *masusing pag-aaral* *o pagsusuri.* See. **himaymáy.**

himaymáy (hi-may-máy), *n.* careful or detailed study, examination, or investigation about something. Syn. *masususing (maingat na) pag-aaral o pagsusurì.* See **himáy.**

himbíng (him-bíng), *n.* deep or profound sleep. Syn. *malalim na tulog (pagkákatulóg)*

himig (hi-mig), *n.* 1. (*us.*) melody; tune. Syn. *tono; melodya.* 2. key in music. Syn. *tono.* 3. song; musical composition. Syn. *awit, tugtugin.* 4. intonation of the voice that expresses a particular meaning or feeling; tone (of voice). Syn. *estilo, tunóg.*

himláy (him-láy), *n.* 1. act of lying down for a short rest or sleep. Syn. *paghigâ upáng mamahingâ o matulog na sandalî.* 2. a short, light sleep; nap; doze. Syn. *idlíp, hipíg.*

himlayan (him-la-yan), *n.* place for lying down to rest or sleep. Syn. *hígaan sa pagtulog o pamamahingâ, gaya ng kama.*

himno (him-no), *var.* **imno,** *n.* (Sp.) hymn; anthem. Cf. *awit.*

himok (hi-mok), *n.* a persuading or winning over to one side of a proposition, esp. with kind words. Syn. *amukî, pag-amukî; hikayat, paghikayat; suyò, pagsuyò.*

himod (hi-mod), *n.* act or manner of licking or lapping (something) with the tongue. Cf. *dilà, pagdilà.*

himpapawíd (him-pa-pa-wíd), *n.* the vast space above; sky; firmament. Syn. *káitaasan, papawirín, panganorin, langit.*

himpíl (him-píl), *n.* 1. act of stopping or parking (a vehicle) temporarily in a certain place. Syn. *hintô, paghintô; tigil, pagtigil; parada, pagparada.* 2. state or condition of being parked or left temporarily in a certain place, referring to a vehicle. Syn. *parada, pagkakáparada.*

himpilan (him-pi-lan), *n.* 1. station; place or assignment. Syn. *destino.* 2. station, as of buses. Syn. *istasyón.* 3. parking lot or space. Syn. *páradahán.* 4. station; headquarters; place of work. Syn. *kuwartél, hedkuwarter.*

himulá (hi-mu-lá), *n.* (fr. *pulá*) blush or blushing; reddening, esp. of the face due to shame, confusion, etc. Syn. *pamumulá ng mukhá.*

himulmól (hi-mul-mól), *n.* 1. bits of ravelled thread from cloth or yarn; lint. Syn. *nisnís, mulmól, lamuymóy.* 2. tiny, soft feathers; down. Syn. *pinong balahibo.* 3. act of plucking the feathers of fowls or birds; dressing. Syn. *paghihimulmól, pagaalís ng balahibo (ng manók, atb.)*

himutaan (hi-mu-ta-an), *v.* to remove the gummy secretions from the eyes of someone. Syn. *alisán ng mutà.*

himutî (hi-mutî), *n.* slight fading of color. Syn. *panghihimutî, bahagyáng pangungupas (ng kulay).*

himutmót (hi-mut-mót), *n.* 1. bits of frayed or ravelled thread from cloth or yarn. Syn. *himulmól, nisnís.* 2. act or manner of separating or unravelling cloth, yarn, or any woven fabric into bits of thread or lint. 3. act or manner of doing things in a slow, meticulous manner. Syn. *butingtíng, kutiltíl.*

himutók (hi-mu-tók), *n.* 1. sigh; act or sound of sighing. Syn. *himugtô, buntónghiningá, hinagpís.* 2. outcry of disappointment, resentment, etc.; complaint. Syn. *daíng, hinaíng.*

hin- (hin-), *pref.* var. of **hi-,** used before root words that begin with the consonants *d, l, s,* and *t* which are often omitted for the purpose of euphony. Ex.: *hinampó* (fr. *tampó*), *hinaíng* (fr. *daíng*), *hiniksík* (fr. *siksík*).

-hin (-hin), *suffix* var. of **–in,** used after root words ending in liquid vowels in forming verbs, adjectives, and sometimes adverbs. Ex.: *aminin* (fr. *amin*), *basahin* (fr. *basa*), *kayahin* (fr. *kaya*), *dalahín* (fr. *dalá*).

hinà (hi-nà), *n.* 1. weakness of the body; debility; feebleness. Syn. *lambót o panlalambót ng katawán, lupaypáy, panlulupaypáy.* 2. lack of force or intensity, as of a strike, blow, or the like. Syn. *kawalán ng lakás (puwersa), kawalán ng tindí.* 3. slowness; lack of speed. Syn. *bagal, kabagalan; kupad, kakuparan; dahan, karahanan.* Ant. *tulin, katulinan, bilís.* 4. dullness, as of business. Syn. *tumal, katumalan.* Ant. *kabilihán, pagkamabilí.* 5. softness or lowness, as of sound, voice, etc. Syn. *pagkadi-matunóg, dikatunugán,*

kahinaan ng tunóg. Ant. *tunóg, katunugán.*
6. lack of power or influence. Syn.
kawalán ng impluwensiya o lakás. 7. state
or condition of being easily broken,
damaged, or destroyed; fragility. Syn.
*hunâ, kahunaán, pagkamahunâ; dupók,
karupukán, pagkamarupók.* 8. smallness,
meagerness, or insufficiency, as of one's
income. Syn. *liít, kaliitán.* 9. poorness of
quality. Syn. *babà o kababaan ng urì.* 10.
lack of potency or efficacy, as of medicine.
Syn. *kawaláng-bisà, pagkadimabisà.* 11.
dull-headedness; lack of talent. Syn. *puról
o kapurulán ng ulo.* 12. poorness, as of
sight. Syn. *labò o panlalabò (ng matá).* 13.
lightness, as of rain. Ant. *lakás, kalakasán.*

hinabá-habà (hi-na-bá + ha-bà), *adv.*
(usually used with *sa*) as in *sa hinabá-habà,*
in the long run; ultimately; finally. Syn.
wakás.

hinabáng (hi-na-báng), n. loss of interest in
something; indifference; disin-
terestedness. Syn. *pagkawalâ ng gana,
kawaláng-gana; hinawà, panghihinawà.*

hinakdál (hi-nak-dál), n. 1. complaint;
grievance. Syn. *reklamo, daíng, karaingan.*
2. resentment; displeasure. Syn. *samá ng
loób, hinanakít, pagdaramdám.*

hinagap (hi-na-gap), n. 1. idea; notion;
conjecture; presumption. Syn. *akalà,
hakà, palagáy.* 2. suspicion. Syn. *hinalà,
sapantahà.* 3. belief. Syn. *paniwalà,
paniniwalà.* 4. wishful thinking;
premonition. Syn. *guniguní.*

hinagpís (hi-nag-pís), n. 1. sigh; act or
sound of sighing. Syn. *himutók, buntóng-
hiningá.* 2. complaint; grievance. Syn.
hinakdál, hinaíng, karaingan, reklamo. 3.
resentment; displeasure. Syn. *hinakít,
pagdaramdám, samâ ng loób.*

hinahon (hi-na-hon), n. 1. self-control;
prudence; temperance; calmness of
disposition. Syn. *pagtitimpî; lamíg ng loób.*
2. serenity; calmness. Syn. *katiwasayán,
katahimikan, kapanatagán.*

hinaíng (hi-na-íng), n. 1. supplication;
humble, earnest request; entreaty. Syn.
*pamanhík, pamamanhík; daíng, karaingan;
samò, pagsamò.* 2. complaint; grievance.
Syn. *reklamo, hinakdál.*

hinalà (hi-na-là), n. 1. suspicion. Syn.
*sapantahà, pagsasapantahà; sospetsa,
pagsusospetsa.* 2. imputation; charge of
wrong doing; accusation. Syn. *paratang,
pagpaparatang; bintáng, pagbibintáng.*

hinalinhán (hi-na-lin-hán), I. n. (usually
with *ang*) predecessor. Syn. *ang pinalitán.*
—II. *adj.* relieved or changed. Syn.
pinalitán ng ibá.
—III. *v.* past tense of *halinhán.*

hinamon (hi-na-mon), I. n. (usually with
ang) the person challenged.
—II. *adj.* challenged, referring to
someone.
—III. *v.* past tense of *hamunin.*

hinampo (hi-nam-po; hi-nam-pó), n. a
feeling of resentment or displeasure
towards a friend, a loved one, or a relative.
Syn. *kauntíng hinanakít, pagtatampó, o
samâ ng loób.*

hinanakít (hi-na-na-kít), n. resentment;
displeasure. Syn. *pagdaramdám, samâ ng
loób.*

hinang (hi-nang), n. 1. act of soldering or
welding. Syn. *paghihinang, pagkakabít o
pagtatagpî sa pamamagitan ng paghinang.* 2.
the joint or patch made by soldering or
welding. Syn. *pinaghinangan.* 3. the
manner or quality by which a thing is
soldered or welded. Syn. *pagkakahinang.*
4. (Fig.) bond; anything that binds. Syn.
buklód, bigkís.

hináw (hi-náw), I. n. act or manner of
washing the hands or feet. Syn.
paghuhugas ng kamáy o paá.
—II. *adj.* referring to hands or feet that
have been washed with clean water. Syn.
*hugás o nahugasan na kung bagá sa mga
kamáy o paá.*

hinawà (hi-na-wà), n. 1. loss of interest in
something; indifference; dis-
interestedness. Syn. *hinabáng,
panghihinabáng; pagkawalâ ng gana,
kawaláng gana; sawà, pagsasawà.* 2.
boredom; ennui; displeasure. Syn. *yamót,
pagkayamót; suyà, pagkasuyà.* 3. surfeit or
discomfort resulting from over-indulgence
in food or drink. Syn. *sawà, pagsasawà;
suyà, pagkasuyà.*

hinay (hi-nay), n. moderation in the manner

of talking, movement, or action. Syn.
*hinahon, kahinahunan; banayad,
kabanayaran.*

hinayang (hi-na-yang), n. regret; feeling of
regret or loss for not having done, utilized,
or taken advantage of something. Syn.
panghihínayang. Cf. *pagsisisi, pagdaramdám.*

hindî (hin-dî), I. *adv.* no; not; not at all;
not in any degree. See **dî** and **di-**.
—II. *n.* 1. an answer denoting refusal or
denial; a negative answer; no. 2. negative
vote. Syn. *tutol, kontra.*
—III. *interj.* No! Not at all!

hindík (hin-dík), n. 1. feeling of sudden
fear or fright, usually accompanied by
sudden gasping, as when one sees
something horrible. Cf. *sindák,
pagkasindák.* 2. continuous hard
breathing of a person in agony. Syn. *abut-
abot na paghihirap sa paghingá ng isáng
naghihingalô.*

hindót (hin-dót), I. n. the sexual act
performed by a man on a woman. Syn.
asawa, pag-asawa; kanâ, pagkanâ (fig.).
—II. *interj.* an utterance usually used in
dislike or displeasure against someone.
Syn. *Letse!*

hinebra (hi-ne-bra), n. (Sp. *ginebra*) gin. Cf.
alak.

hinekolóhiyá (hi-ne-ko-ló-hi-yá), n. (Sp.
ginecología) gynecology.

hinete (hi-ne-te), n. (Sp. *jinete*) jockey.

hinhín (hin-hín), n. state or quality of being
modest or decent in one's act or manners.
Syn. *kahinhinán; binì, kábinian; yumì,
kayumian.*

hiniksik (hi-nik-sik), n. act or manner of
picking lice and nits from the head. Cf.
hinguto, paghihinguto.

hiningá (hi-ni-nga), n. (fr. *hingá*) 1. breath;
air drawn into and forced out of the lungs.
2. (*Colloq.*) life. Syn. *buhay.* 3. (*Fig.*)
feeling; sense of feeling. Syn. *damdamin.*

hinlalakí (hin-la-la-kí), n. (*Anat.*) 1. the
thumb; pollex; also, the big toe of the
foot. 2. the part of a glove or mitten
which covers the thumb.

hinlalatò (hin-la-la-tò), n. (*Anat.*) 1.
middle finger. Syn. *panggitnáng dalirì.* 2.
the part of a glove or mitten which covers

the middle finger.

hinlóg (hin-lóg), n. kith and kin; relative;
kindred; kinsfolk. Syn. *kaanak, kamag-
anak.*

hinóg (hi-nóg), I. n. & *adj.* ripe, referring to
fruits, boils, and the like.
—II. n. state or condition of being ripe.
Syn. *kahinugán, pagkahinóg.*

hintakót (hin-ta-kót), *adj.* with or having a
slight fear. Syn. *kinákabahán, balisá,
bagabág.*

hintáy (hin-táy), I. n. 1. act of waiting for
(a person or thing). See **antáy,** var.
hantáy, intáy. Syn. *antabay.* 2. a person
or thing being awaited or expected to
come. Syn. *ang hiníhintáy.*
—II. *interj.* Wait! Wait a minute! Syn.
Teka! Tayka! Sandali lamang!

hintô (hin-tô), I. n. 1. a brief stop, as of a
vehicle. Syn. *tigil, pagtigil; para, pagpara.*
2. a brief or temporary rest, as of a worker.
Syn. *paghingá, pagpapahingá,
pamamahingá.* 3. cessation or stopping as
of rain, storm, etc. Syn. *tilà, pagtilà
(specific for rain); hulaw, paghulaw; tigil,
pagtigil.* 4. a coming to an end; finish;
end. Syn. *wakás, pagwawakás; tapos,
pagtatapós, katapusán.* 5. a temporary stay
or sojourn in a certain place. Syn.
pansamantalang pagtirá o pagtulóy. 6. state
or condition of being at rest, not in
motion, not functioning or working. Syn.
pagkadi-ginágamit (kung bagá sa mákiná).
—II. *adj.* 1. not running or functioning,
as vehicles, machines, and the like. Syn.
*tigil, nakatigil, hindî tumátakbó, hindî
umáandár.* 2. at rest; not working. Syn.
waláng ginágawâ, pahingá, namámahingá.
—III. *interj.* Stop! Halt! Syn. *Tigil! Para!*

hintuturò (hin-tu-tu-rò), n. (*Anat.*)
forefinger; index finger; first finger. Cf.
dalirì.

hinukó (hi-nu-kó), var. **hingukó,** n. act or
manner of cutting fingernails or toenails.
Syn. *paghihinukó, panghihingukó.*

hinuhà (hi-nu-hà), n. 1. inference;
deduction; presumption; supposition.
Syn. *akalà, hulò, palagáy, paniwalà.* 2.
suspicion. Syn. *hinalà, sapantahà.*

hinuhod (hi-nu-hod), n. humble

acquiescence. Syn. *mapágpakumbabáng pagsang-ayon o pagbayag*.

hinulí (hi-nu-lí), n. act or manner of removing or picking dry earwax from the ears. Syn. *hinukí*.

hing- (hing-), pref. var. of **hi-**, used before root words that begin with the vowels or the consonants except *d, l, r, s,* and *t*.

hingá¹ (hi-ngá), n. 1. breathing; respiration. Syn. *paghingá*. 2. air breathed out of the lungs. Syn. *hiningá*. 3. (*Colloq.*) act of giving vent to one's hurt feeling, etc. Syn. *pagsasabi o pagtatapát ng samâ ng loób*.

hingá² (hi-ngá), adj. referring to radish that has lost its freshness. Cf. *lipás, lantá*.

hingal (hi-ngal), n. 1. catching of breath with difficulty; gasping or panting. Syn. *hapò, pagkahapò, paghahaból ng hiningá*. 2. the sound of gasping or panting. Syn. *hagok, hingasing*.

hingalay (hi-nga-lay), n. a short rest, esp. by lying down or taking a short nap. Syn. *sandalíng pamamahingá*.

hingalô (hi-nga-lô), I. n. death pangs; agony; moribund state. Syn. *paghihingalô, pag-aagaw-buhay, pagdidiliryo*.

—II. adj. hovering between life and death; in a moribund state. Syn. *naghíhingalô, nag-áagaw buhay, nagdídiliryo*.

hingán (hi-ngán), var. **hingián**, v. 1. to require or ask (a person) to submit, give, explain something. 2. to request (a person, to give or contribute something). Syn. *pakiusapang magbigáy*.

hinggíl (hing-gíl), I. n. purpose; reason; aim. *Anó ang hinggíl ng pagparito mo?* What is the purpose in coming here? Syn. *layon, layunin, dahilán, pakay, hangád*.

—II. prep. (usually with *sa* or *kay*) about; concerning; regarding; with regards to. Syn. *tungkól sa, bagay sa, ukol sa*.

hingî (hi-ngî), I. n. 1. act of requesting or asking something from someone as help, gift, or present. Syn. *paghingî*. 2. act of requiring or asking (a person) to submit or give something as a requirement for a certain purpose. Syn. *pag-uutos na maghanáp o magbigáy ng bagay na kailangan*. 3. the thing or things asked

for, requested, or required. Syn. *ang hiníhingî*. 4. (*Colloq.*) in Law, demand; requirement. Syn. *ang hiníhingî, kailangan, o kinákailangan*. 5. petition; request. Syn. *hilíng, kahilingan*.

—II. adj. referring to something given to someone for free, or as a gift or present. Syn. *bigáy, regalo, handóg*.

hinguto (hi-ngu-to), n. act or manner of picking lice from the head. Cf. *hiniksik*.

hipag (hi-pag), n. sister-in-law. Syn. *kapatid na babae ng asawa*. Cf. *bayáw* (brother-in-law).

hipnosis (hip-no-sis), n. (Sp.) hypnosis.

hipò (hi-pò), n. 1. touch or touching with the hand. Cf. *salát, pagsalát*. 2. sense of touch; feel. Syn. *damdám, panamdám, pandamdam, damá, pandamá*. 3. the nature of a thing perceived through touch. Syn. *salát*. 4. act of touching someone's private part (organ) maliciously.

hipon (hi-pon), n. shrimp.

hipopotamo (hi-po-po-ta-mo), n. (Sp.) hippopotamus.

hirám (hi-rám), I. n. 1. act of borrowing something from another. Syn. *paghirám*. 2. act of borrowing money from a person, bank, or any lending institution. Syn. *utang, pag-utang, pangungutang*. 3. adoption or borrowing, as of words from one language to another. Syn. *panghihirám*.

—II. adj. 1. borrowed. Syn. *hinirám, utang, inutang* (esp. for money). 3. adopted or borrowed, as of words from one language to another.

hirang (hi-rang), I. n. 1. act of appointing a person to a certain position or office. Syn. *paghirang, pagnonombra*. 2. act of selecting the best or preferred ones from among many others. Syn. *pili, pagpili, pamimili*. 3. sweetheart; darling. Syn. *mahál, irog, mutyâ, sinta*. 4. a person appointed to a position or office. Syn. *ang nombrado o hinirang*. 5. the person or thing selected from among others. Syn. *ang pinili o nápili*.

—II. adj. 1. appointed, as to a certain position or office. Syn. *hinirang, nombrado*. 2. selected; chosen or picked out from among others. Syn. *pilì, pinilì*. 3. beloved; dear to one's heart. Syn. *mahál, minámahál; mutyâ, minúmutyâ; sintá, sinísintá*.

hirap (hi-rap), n. 1. difficulty or hardship, as of a task. Syn. *bigát o kabigatáng gawín*. Ant. *alwán, dalî*. 2. financial difficulty; poverty. Syn. *dálitâ, karálitaán, karukhaán, pagdarahóp, pamumulubi*. 3. suffering; affliction. Syn. *tíisin, pagtitiís; dusa, pagdurusa*. 4. pains or labor in childbirth. Syn. *sakít ng tiyán sa panganganák*.

hiráp (hi-ráp), adj. 1. poor; indigent; destitute; needy. Syn. *dukhâ, marálitâ, mahirap, pobre*. 2. tired; feeling tired. Syn. *pagód, napápagod*. 3. burdened with too much work. Syn *matrabaho, lubháng matrabaho*.

Hirat (Hi-rat), var. **Hilat**, *interj*. an exclamation expressive of disgust at someone who has just suffered an unfavorable experience, meaning "That's what you deserve!" Syn. *Mabuti ngâ sa iyó!*

hirati (hi-ra-ti), n. 1. getting accustomed, habituated, or acquainted with something. Syn. *pagkahirati; sanay, pagkasanay; bihasa, pagkabihasa*. 2. state or condition of being accustomed, habituated, or acquainted about something. Syn. *kahiratihan, kasanayan, kabihasahan*.

hirin (hi-rin), n. obstruction or clog in the throat, usually food or water that one fails to swallow, causing him to choke or have difficulty in breathing. Syn. *bulón, bitalók*. Cf. *bikíg*.

hirís (hi-rís), adj. 1. slanting; oblique; diagonal. Syn. *hilís, pahilís; hilíg, pahilíg*. 2. out of alignment. Syn. *hiwíd, pahiwíd; likô, palikô*.

hiro (hi-ro), var. **hero**, n. (Sp. *hierro*) 1. a brand or mark made on cattle, horses, and other animals as a sign of ownership or registration. Cf. *taták, marka*. 2. the (hot) iron used for burning a brand on animals; brand. Syn. *panghero (panghiro)*. 3. act or manner of burning a brand or mark of ownership or registration on animals with

hot iron. Syn. *paghihiro, pagkakahiro*.

hiro-postál (hi-ro + pos-tál), n. (Sp. *giro postal*) postal money order. Also, *hiro postál*.

hisò (hi-sò), n. act or manner of cleaning the teeth with a toothbrush; brushing of teeth. Syn. *pagsisipilyo ng ngipin, paghihisò, paglilinis ng ngipin sa pamamagitan ng panghisò*.

hità (hi-tà), n. (*Anat.*) 1. thigh. 2. the part of a garment that covers the thigh. 3. the upper part of the hindlegs of an animal.

hitâ (hi-tâ), n. 1. an unsatisfactory result or an unworthy reward obtained from a generous, well-intentioned act. Syn. *palâ, nápalâ*. 2. gain; benefit; advantage. Syn. *pakinabang, nápakinabang, kapakinabangán*.

hitád (hi-tád), 1. adj. coquettish; flirtatious. Syn. *landî, talandî, malandî; kirí, makirí; lantód, malantód*.

—II. n. coquette; flirt. Syn. *babaing landî o kirí*.

hitana (hi-ta-na), n. (Sp. *gitana*) a female gypsy.

hithít (hit-hít), var. **hitít**, n. 1. act of smoking a cigarette or cigar. Syn. *paninigarilyo o pananabako*. 2. act of sipping or sucking in liquid. Syn. *sipsíp, pagsipsíp; higop, paghigop*. 3. absorption, as by sponge, etc. Syn. *pagsipsíp, pagkasipsíp; paghithít, pagkahithít*. 4. inhalation. Syn. *langháp, paglangháp* (through the mouth); *singhót, pagsinghót* (through the nose).

hitík (hi-tík), adj. heavy or fully laden with flowers, fruits, etc., referring to a branch or to a tree itself.

hitò (hi-tò), n. (*Ichth.*) a species of freshwater catfish (*Clarias batrachus Linn.*).

hitsó (hit-só), n. 1. a combination of betel nut, chewing tobacco, and little lime wrapped in a betel plant leaf prepared for chewing. Cf. *buyo, ngangá*. 2. a kind of firecracker, rectangular in shape. Cf. *rebentadór*.

hitsura (hit-su-ra), var. **itsura**, n. (Sp. *hechura*) 1. appearance; shape; figure; form; looks. Syn. *anyô, hugis, korte, ayos*. 2. state or condition. Syn. *lagáy*, *kalagayan; tayô, katayuan.*

hiwà (hi-wà), *n.* 1. act of cutting something with or as with a knife. Syn. *paghiwà.* Cf. *gilit, paggilít.* 2. a slice or cut, as of fish, meat, etc. Syn. *gilít, gayat, atado, putol.* 3. a cut or wound made with or as with a knife. Syn. *sugat ng patalím.*

hiwagà (hi-wa-gà), *n.* mystery. Syn. *misteryo, himalâ, kababalaghán.*

hiwalay (hi-wa-lay), *n.* 1. separation of something from another. Syn. *bukód, pagbubukód.* 2. act of separating oneself from another or others. Syn. *layô, paglayô.* 3. act of resigning as a member of an organization. Syn. *tiwalág, pagtiwalág.* 4. act of living separately from another or others. Syn. *pagsasarilí.* 5. divorce; legal separation. Syn. *dibórsiyó, paghihiwaláy.*

hiwás (hi-was), *adj.* oblique; slanting; inclined. Syn. *hirís, hiwíd, tabingî, tagilíd.*

hiwatig (hi-wa-tig), *n.* 1. hint; slight sign or indication. Syn. *palátandaan.* 2. feeling; sensual feeling. Syn. *damdám, pakiramdám; damá, pandamá.* 3. inkling; vague notion or idea. Syn. *malay, kamalayan.* 4. slight understanding. Syn. *bahagyáng pagkáunawà o pagkáintindi.*

híya (hí-ya), var. **hiyá,** *interj.* an ejaculation used in getting a horse to run faster. See **Hi!.**

hiyâ (hi-yâ), *n.* 1. act of putting (someone) to shame; embarrassing (someone). Syn. *paghiyâ, paglalagáy sa kahihiyán.* 2. shame; feeling of shame or embarrassment. Cf. *kimî, kakimián; umíd, kaumirán.*

hiyád (hi-yád), I. *n.* 1. act or manner of standing with the body arched forward. Syn. *liyád, pagliyád.* 2. the position of the body witht the chest and stomach out. Syn. *liyád, pagkakaliyád, pagkakahiyád.*
—II. *adj.* with the body arched forward; standing with the chest and stomach out. Syn. *liyád, nakaliyád, nakahiyád.*

hiyáng (hi-yáng), I. *n.* 1. agreeableness or suitability to one's health or physical constitution, as of medicine, food, climate, etc. Syn. *pagkahiyáng, kahiyangán.* 2. state or quality of being lucky, as in gambling; good luck. Syn. *suwerte, magandáng suwerte (kapalaran).*

—II. *adj.* 1. suited, agreeable, or compatible, as to one's health, etc. Syn. *angkóp, tamà, bagay, agpáng, mabuti, nakabúbuti.* 2. lucky. Syn. *masuwerte, sinúsuwerte, mapalad, ginágalíng.*

hiyás (hi-yás), *n.* 1. gem; precious stone, esp. one used as a jewel. Syn. *mamáhaling bató.* 2. jewel. Syn. *alahas.* 3. ornament; decoration. Syn. *palamuti, gayák, kagayakan.* 4. a person or thing very precious to someone. Syn. *mutyâ, pinakamámahál, yaman, kayamanan (fig.).*

hiyáw (hi-yáw), *n.* 1. scream; loud cry; yell. Syn. *sigáw, palakat, palahaw.* 2. a loud call. Syn. *malakás na tawag.* 3. a loud cry for help. Syn. *padaló, pagpapadaló.* 4. a loud angry shout. Syn. *bulyaw, sigáw.*

Ho (Ho), *interj.* an ejaculation used in stopping a horse, usually repeated: Ho! Ho! Cf. *La!*

hô (hô), *interj.* an honorific term used: a) as an answer to the call of an elder or a superior, meaning "Yes, Sir" or "Yes, Madám!" Syn. *Pô.* b) as an answer expressing doubt to understand what a superior or elder says. Syn. *Anó pô iyón?*

hokuspokus (ho-kus-po-kus), *n.* (Eng.) hocuspocus: a) meaningless action or words used by conjurers as a trick to draw attention. Syn. *waláng-kahulugáng mga salità o kilos na ginágamit ng mga salamangkero.* b) sleight of hand; legerdemain; magician's trick or trickery. Syn. *salamangka.* c) trickery; deception. Syn. *linláng, panlilinláng; dayà, pandarayà.*

holen (ho-len), var. **holens,** *n.* (prob. fr. Eng. hole in) 1. a little ball of stone, glass, or clay used in a game of marbles. 2. the game of marbles.

homoséksuwál (ho-mo-sék-su-wál), *n. & adj.* homosexual. Syn. *binabaé, baklâ.*

hopyá (hop-yá), *n.* (Ch.) a kind of pastry or cake stuffed with sweetened mashed beans or chopped pork with beans.

hornál (hor-nál), var. **hurnál,** *n.* (Sp. jornal) 1. day-work. Syn. *trabahong arawán.* 2. daily wage. Syn. *kitang (suweldong) arawán.* 3. act of paying something by installment. Syn. *pagbabayad nang hulugán.* 3. the amount of installment itself. Syn. *hulog.*

hotél (ho-tél), *n.* (Eng.) hotel.

hototay (ho-to-tay), *n.* (Ch.) a kind of Cantonese soup of chicken meat, carrots, peas, poached eggs, etc.

Hoy (Hoy), *interj.* an exclamation used as a warning or calling the attention of someone, usually accompanied by tapping or touching him lightly.

hu (hu), *interj.* 1. an exclamation used to scare away animals. Syn. *Su!* 2. an utterance expressive of disgust or impatience, more or less equivalent to "What do I care!"

hubád (hu-bád), I. *n.* 1. act of undressing oneself. Syn. *pag-aalís ng kasuután; paghuhubád.* 2. state or condition of being without clothes from the waist up. Syn. *kawaláng suót na anó mang damít sa dakong itaás ng katawán.*
—II. *adj.* 1. bare of clothes from the waist up; without dress or clothing from the waist up. Syn. *nakahubád; waláng damít sa dakong itaás ng katawán.* 2. (*Fig.*) completely without or devoid of, as in *hubád sa katotohanan,* completely devoid of truth.

hubô (hu-bô), I. *adj.* bare of clothes from the waist down; undressed from the waist down. Syn. *waláng damít mulâ sa baywáng na pababâ.*
—II. *n.* 1. fact, state, or condition of being bare of clothes from the waist down. 2. a person undressed from the waist down.

hubog (hu-bog), *n.* 1. act of forming or shaping (a thing) into a certain form, esp. by bending. Syn. *hugis, paghuhugis; porma, pagpoporma.* 2. act of shaping or bending something in the form of an arc, arch, bow, or curve. Syn. *pagbabalantók, pag-aarkó.* 3. general shape or form. Syn. *hugis, porma, korte.* 4. the shape of an arc, arch, bow, or curve. Syn. *arko, balantók.* 5. (*Fig.*) act or manner of training a person to develop in him a certain character or trait. Syn. *sanay, pagsasanay; turò, pagtuturò.*

hubog-kandilà (hu-bog + kan-di-là), I. *n.* the shape or form like that of a candle.

Syn. *hugis o korte na katulad ng sa kandilà.*
—II. *adj.* shaped like a candle; candle-shaped. Syn. *hugis-kandilà, korteng-kandilà, kahugis o kakorte ng kandilà.*

hubó't-hubád (hu-bó't + hu-bád). Also, **hubó't hubád,** *adj.* with or having no clothes on; completely naked. Syn. *waláng anó mang suót.*

Huk (Huk), *n.* (derived fr. *hukbó,* army) a member of a guerilla organization during the Japanese occupation, popularly known as *Hukbalahap.*

hukag (hu-kag), *n.* 1. a big hollow formation; big cavity. Syn. *maluwáng na ukà o bútas.* 2. hollowness; emptiness. Syn. *hungkág, kahungkagán.*

hukay (hu-kay), *n.* 1. act of digging the ground, as in making a canal, pit, grave, or the like. 2. act of getting out something from the ground by digging, as with a hoe, spade, etc. 3. a hollow, pit, or hole in the ground. 4. a hole or grave in the ground in which to bury a dead body. Cf. *líbingan.* 5. a dug-out shelter. Syn. *taguáng-hukay.*

Hukbalahap (Huk-ba-la-hap), *n.* (fr. *Hukbó ng Bayan Laban sa Hapón,* meaning literally People's Army Against Japan) 1. a guerilla organization organized by the Filipinos during the Japanese occupation. 2. a member of this organization; also called *Huk.*

hukbó (huk-bó), var. **hukbô,** *n.* 1. (*Mil.*) a large organized body of soldiers for a country's land defense; army. 2. a large group of people, as of workers. Syn. *malakíng pangkát.*

hukbóng-karagatan (huk-bóng + ka-ra-ga-tan), *n.* the entire sea force of a nation; navy.

hukbóng-panghimpapawíd (huk-bóng + pang-him-pa-pa-wíd), *n.* air force of the armed forces of a country.

hukbóng-sandatahan (huk-bóng + san-da-ta-han), *n.* armed forces.

hukluban (huk-lu-ban), I. *adj.* decrepit; senile. Syn. *ulianin, matandâ na't malimutín.*
—II. *n.* an old, weak person, esp. a woman.

ʌukóm (hu-kóm), n. 1. (Law) judge. Syn. huwés. 2. justice. Syn. mahistrado. 3. a member of a board appointed to decide in a contest or to settle a dispute. Syn. tagahatol. 4. act of passing final judgment on a sinner. Syn. paggagawad ng parusa.

Hukóm-Tagapamayapà (Hu-kóm + Ta-ga-pa-ma-ya-pà), n. Justice of the Peace. Syn. Huwés de Pas.

ʌukót (hu-kót), adj. bent-backed; bent-bodied; hunchbacked. Syn. kurkubado, bukót.

ʌudas (hu-das), I. n. 1. (H-) Judas Iscariot. 2. a traitor or betrayer. Syn. taong taksíl o mapagkánuló.
—II. adj. disloyal; traitorous; treacherous. Syn. taksíl, mapagkánuló, traidór.

ʌudikatura (hu-di-ka-tu-ra), n. (Sp. judicatura) magistry; judgeship. Syn. pagkahukóm, pagkahuwés, pagkamahistrado.

ʌudo (hu-do), n. (Sp. judo) judo.

ʌudyát (hud-yát), n. 1. act of giving signal or warning. Syn. pagsenyas, pagbababalâ. 2. a signal or warning. Syn. senyas, babalâ. 3. password; watchword. Syn. kontrasenyas.

Hudyó[1] (Hud-yó), var. Hudiyó, n. (Sp. Judío) Jew.

hudyó[2] (hud-yó), I. n. a shameless person. Syn. taong waláng-hiyâ.
—II. adj. shameless, referring to a person. Syn. waláng-hiyâ.

hugadór (hu-ga-dór), n. (Sp. jugador) gambler. Syn. sugaról, mánunugal, magsusugal.

hugas (hu-gas), n. 1. act of washing of cleaning things with clean water, esp. plates, cooking utensils, tableware, and the like. 2. act of washing the hands and feet. Syn. hináw, paghihináw, panghihináw. 3. cleansing or washing of wounds. Syn. langgás, paglalanggás. 4. water used in washing hulled rice, usually used as broth in cooking vegetables, etc., or as feed for pigs. See hugas-bigás.

hugas-bigás (hu-gas + bi-gás), n. washing or liquid which has been used for washing hulled rice, usually used as broth in cooking vegetables, etc., or as feed for pigs.

hugis (hu-gis), n. 1. shape; form. Syn. korte, tabas, porma. 2. figure; appearance; looks. Syn. hitsura, pigura, anyô, ayos. 3. act of shaping something into a certain form, as by cutting or carving, drawing or painting, etc. Syn. pagkokorte, paghuhugis.

hugis- (hu-gis-), pref. used as a combining form; shaped like; having the shape of; also expressed by -shaped, suffixed to a root, as in hugis-bola, ball-shaped. Syn. korteng-, tabas-.

hugnáy (hug-náy), var. sugnáy, n. (Gram.) 1. a combining or being combined, as of related clauses to form a complex sentence. Syn. paghuhugnáy, pagsusugnáy. 2. any of the related clauses in a complex sentence.

hugong (hu-gong), n. a humming sound; drone; buzz. Syn. ugong.

hugos (hu-gos), n. 1. act or manner of lowering down something from a height with or as with a rope. Syn. pagbababâ ng isáng bagay sa pamamagitan ng lubid, kawad, atb. 2. continuous flow; influx or onrush, as of a great number of people. Syn. dagsâ, pagdagsâ; bugsô, pagbugsô.

hugot (hu-got), n. 1. act of drawing or pulling out something, esp. a long one, from or as from a hole. Syn. bunot, pagbunot. 2. a picking or selecting, as from a number of candidates for a certain position. Syn. pilì, pagpilì, pamimilì. 3. act of basing something on another. Syn. batay, pagbabatay; salig, pagsasalig.

hugpóng (hug-póng), n. 1. act or manner of joining or connecting two things together; attachment of one thing to another. Syn. dugtóng, pagdurugtóng; kabít, pagkakakabít. 2. the point of connection or attachment of two things. Syn. hugpungan, pinaghugpungán, pinagkabitán. 3. the part or portion added, joined, or connected to a side or extremity of another to enlarge or lengthen it further. Syn. dugtóng, datig, kabít.

huhô (hu-hô), var. uhô, n. 1. act or manner of emptying a container by pouring out its content. Cf. buhos, pagbubuhos. 2. voluminous flow or outpouring, as of water overflowing from a tank or reservoir. Syn. *awas*, *pag-awas*. 3. a spilling, as of grains, liquid, or water from a hole accidentally made in a container. Syn. *bubô*, *pagkábubô*. 4. (by extension) influx or onrush, as of people. Syn. *dagsâ*, *pagdagsâ*; *bugsô*, *pagbugsô*.

hulà (hu-là), n. 1. act of guessing. Syn. *paghulà*. 2. a guess; conjecture; surmise. Syn. *hakà*, *haka-hakà*; *sapantahà*; *palagáy*, *palá-palagáy*. 3. prediction; prophecy. Syn. *prediksiyón*; *propesiya*.

hulagpós (hu-lag-pós), I. n. 1. escape or breaking loose, as from one's hold. Syn. *kawalâ*. 2. state or condition of having been loosened or disentangled due to faulty tying, referring to a knot or binding. Syn. *habsô*, *pagkahabsô*; *husô*, *pagkahusô*; *kalág*, *pagkakalág*. —II. adj. 1. having escaped or freed, as from one's hold. Syn. *nakawalâ*, *nabitiwan*. 2. loosened or disentangled, referring to a knot or binding. Syn. *habsô*, *nahabsô*; *husô*, *nahusô*; *kalág*, *nakalág*.

hulahula (hu-là-hu-la), n. (Haw.) hula-hula, a native Hawaiian dance performed by women.

hulapì (hu-la-pì), n. (Gram.) 1. suffix. Syn. *supiho*. 2. a suffixing or being suffixed. Syn. *paghuhulapì*, *pagkakahulapì*.

hulas (hu-las), n. 1. a slow melting or liquefaction, as of ice, salt, cubes of sugar, etc. Syn. *lusaw*, *pagkalusaw*; *tunaw*, *pagkatunaw*. 2. ooze or oozing, as of a decaying matter. Syn. *tulas*, *pagtulas*; *tagas*, *pagtagas*; *agnás*, *pag-agnás*, *pagkaagnás*. 3. the slimy substance oozing from a decaying matter. Syn. *lahoy*, *kayat*, *gitatâ*, *tulas*. 4. drops of moisture as on the surface of glass. Syn. *tubíg-tubíg*, *pawis* (*colloq.*) 5. a lowering or diminution of intensity, as of fever. Syn. *hibás*, *paghibás*; *hulaw*, *paghulaw*; *babà*, *pagbabà*; *hignáw*, *paghignáw*.

hulaw (hu-law), n. 1. diminution or cessation, as of rain, storm, and the like. Syn. *hinà*, *paghinà*; *tilâ*, *pagtilâ* (for rain); *hignàw*, *paghignàw*. 2. an abating or lessening, as of: (a) fever, etc. Syn. *hibás*, *paghibás*. (b) anger. Syn. *lubág*, *paglubág*. (c) pain. Syn. *lipas*, *paglipas*.

huli (hu-li), I. n. 1. apprehending or being apprehended; arrest; capture. Syn. *dakíp*, *pagdakíp*. 2. act of catching (animals with or as with a trap. Syn. *silò*, *pagsilò*. 3. a person or persons under arrest. Syn. *ang inaresto o hinuli*. 4. (in fishing) catch the amount of fish caught. —II. adj. 1. caught; apprehended arrested; captured. Syn. *hinuli*, *inaresto* *dinakíp*. 2. caught in the act of. Syn. *tutóp* *nátutóp*.

hulí (hu-lí), I. adj. 1. tardy; late. Syn. *atrasado*, *di-nakaratíng sa oras*, *gahól sa* *panahón*; *walâ nang panahón*. 2. behind left behind, as in a race. Syn. *naiwan sa* *hulihán*. 3. last; final. Syn. *pangwakás* *katapusán*. —II. adv. late; tardily. Syn. *atrasado*, *nang* *atrasado*, *nang walâ sa panahón*. —III. n. 1. state or condition of being late in coming, happening, etc. Syn *atraso*, *pagkaatraso*, *kaatrasuhan*. 2. a person or thing late in coming. Syn. *ang* *náhulí o ang naatraso sa pagdatíng*. 3. the last. Syn. *wakas*, *katapusán*. 4. the position behind; rear; tail end. Syn. *likód* *likurán*, *buntót* (*colloq.*).

hulihán (hu-li-hán), n. the rear or tail end back part. Syn. *likód*, *likurán*; *buntó* (*colloq.*). 2. (of a ship or boat) stern. Syn *popa*. 3. the last part; end. Syn. *wakás* *katapusán*.

hulilip (hu-li-lip), n. an obsolescent root meaning: a) changing someone or something with another; b) a person or thing taking the place of another. Now chiefly used in the form *waláng-kahulilip* meaning incomparable or without equal. Syn. *waláng-katulad*, *waláng-kaparis*, *waláng-kapareho*.

hulím- (hu-lím-), pref. used as a combining form before roots beginning with letters *b* and *p*. See *huling-*.

hulímpatì (hu-lím-pa-tì), var. hulíngpatì, n. in a debate, the last turn of the speaker to defend his side. Syn. *huling* *pangungusap*, *hulíng tindíg*.

hulíng- (hu-líng-), pref. meaning "last." See hulím-.

hulíng paalam (hu-líng + pa-a-lam), var.

hulímpaalam, n. last farewell.

hulíng salitâ (hu-líng + sa-li-tâ), var. **hulíng-katagâ,** n. last word; closing remarks.

hulmá (hul-má), n. (Sp. *horma*) 1. act of shaping or reshaping an object in a mold. Syn. *paghulmá, paghuhulmá; hugis, paghuhugis.* 2. a hollow form used for molding an object into a certain shape; mold or mould. Syn. *molde, moldihan, hulmahan.* 3. the form or shape made in a mold. Syn. *hugis, porma, korte.*

hulmado (hul-ma-do), adj. well-fitted; rightly fitted. Syn. *tamà o tamang-tamà sa sukat, lapat na lapat.*

hulò¹ (hu-lò), n. 1. the source or origin of a river or stream. Syn. *bukál, balong, batis.* 2. the northern part of a town or community. Syn. *ilaya.*

hulò² (hu-lò), n. deduction arrived at through reasoning or rationalization. Syn. *kurò, kuru-kurò, pagkukurò.*

hulog¹ (hu-log), n. 1. fall or falling of something from a height. Syn. *lagpák, paglagpák; bagsák, pagbagsák; laglág, paglaglág.* 2. act of dropping something from a height. Syn. *paghuhulog, pagbabagsák, paglalagpák, paglalaglág.* 3. an accidental fall, as from the side or brink of a cliff or precipice. Syn. *bulíd, pagbulíd, pagkabulíd.*

hulog² (hu-log), n. (Comm.) 1. act of paying a debt or loan by installment. Syn. *paghuhulog, paghuhurnál, pagbabayad nang húlugán.* 2. the amount paid for each installment. Syn. *halagá ng bawa't pagbabayad nang hulugán, hurnál.*

hulog³ (hu-log), n. failure in an examination. Syn. *lagpák, paglagpák; bagsák, pagbagsák; pangangalabasa o pangangamote (fig.).*

Hulyo (Hul-yo), n. (Sp. *Julio*) July, the seventh month of the year.

humá (hu-má), n. response or word as a reaction to a surprising or unexpected comment from someone. Syn. *saliâ, sagót, sabi.*

humal (hu-mal), n. 1. nasal speech sound; defective nasal intonation. Syn. *impít na tunóg ng boses na nagdáraán sa ilóng.* 2. way or manner of speaking with a nasal sound.

humaling (hu-ma-ling), I. n. extreme fondness for something; state or quality of being extremely attracted to someone or something. Syn. *labis na pagkahaling sa isáng tao o bagay, kahibangán.*
—II. v. to cause or be the cause of one's extreme fondness or fascination for. Syn. *makahaling, humibáng, makahibáng.*

humbâ (hum-bâ), n. (Ch.) a kind of highly spiced dish of pork meat.

humigít-kumulang (hu-mi-gít + ku-mulang), adv. more or less; about. Syn. *halos, may mangá.*

humpáy (hum-páy), I. n. 1. cessation; stop; pause. Syn. *hintô, paghintô; tigil, pagtigil.* 2. lull; brief calm. Syn. *tigháw, pagtigháw; hupà, paghupà.*
—II. adj. at a standstill. Syn. *hintô, nakahintô; tigil, nakatigil.*

hunâ (hu-nâ), n. weakness or fragility of structure. Syn. *dupók, karupukán; hinà, kahinaan.* Ant. *tibay, katibayan.*

hunáb (hu-náb), n. 1. vapor rising from the ground. Syn. *alimuóm, singáw.* 2. drops of moisture on surface of glass and other solid objects. Syn. *pawis.*

huni (hu-ni), n. 1. chirp or chirping (of birds); also, song. Syn. *awit.* 2. short, sharp sound made by chicks. Syn. *siyáp.* 3. the croak (of frogs). Syn. *kokak.* 4. act of humming a tune. Syn. *higing.* 5. the whistle of siren. Syn. *tunóg, silbato.*

hunos (hu-nos; hu-nós), n. act or process of shedding the skin, esp. of reptiles and crustaceans; molt or molting. Syn. *paglulunó, pagpapalít ng balát.*

hunos-dilì (hu-nos + di-lì), var. **hunusdilì,** n. 1. self-control; prudence; wise thought before acting. Syn. *hinahon, timpî, pagtitimpî.* 2. contemplation; reflection; meditation. Syn. *dili-dili, pagdidili-dili; nilay, pagninilay-nilay; bulay-bulay, pagbubulay-bulay.*

hunta (hun-ta), n. (Sp. *junta*) 1. board; council. Syn. *konseho, kapulungan.* 2. meeting; session. Syn. *pulong, pagpupulong; sesyón, pagsisesyón; miting, pagmimiting.* 3. long, tiresome conversation. Syn. *mahabang úsapan; daldalan.*

hunyangò

huwád

hunyangò (hun-ya-ngò), n. 1. (Zool.) chameleon. 2. a changeable or fickle person. Syn. *taong waláng sariling baít (isip).*

Hunyo (Hun-yo), n. (Sp. *Junio*) June the sixth month of the year.

hungkág (hung-kág), I. *adj.* 1. hollow; with or having a cavity. Syn. *guwáng, may-guwáng.* 2. empty. Syn. *waláng-lamán.* —II. *n.* 1. a hollow formation or cavity. Syn. *guwáng.* 2. fact, state, or quality of being hollow or empty.

hungkuyan (hung-ku-yan), n. native winnowing mill or apparatus; winnowing bellows. Cf. *bulusan.*

hupâ (hu-pâ), I. *adj.* 1. diminished or decreased in size, as a swelling. Syn. *impís, di na magâ.* 2. abated, as storm or typhoon. Syn. *tigháw, huláw.* 3. subsided or receded, as flood. Syn. *kati.* 4. deflated. Syn. *impis, kupís.* —II. *n.* 1. diminution or decrease of size, as of a swelling. Syn. *impís, pag-impís; pagkawalâ ng pamamagâ.* 2. act or process of subsiding or receding, as of flood. Syn. *kati, pagkati.* 3. a lessening or abating, as of storm or typhoon. Syn. *tigháw, pagtigháw; hulaw, paghulaw; paghupâ.*

hupaw (hu-paw), n. abating or lessening of intensity. Syn. *hulaw, paghulaw; tigháw, pagtigháw.*

hurado (hu-ra-do), I. *adj.* (Sp. *jurado*) sworn in, referring to someone who has taken oath. Syn. *sumumpâ o nakasumpâ na, nakahurá na.* —II. *n.* 1. board of judges in a contest or competition; jury. Syn. *inampalán, lupong tagahatol.* 2. juror; member of a jury. Syn. *tagahatol, kagawád ng lupong tagahatol.*

huramentado (hu-ra-men-ta-do), I. *n.* (Sp. *juramentado*) a person who runs amuck. Syn. *taong haláng ang bituka (fig.).* —II. *adj.* referring to a person who is in a frenzy to kill; amuck. Syn. *haláng ang bituka.*

hurisdiksiyón (hu-ris-dik-si-yón), n. (Sp. *jurisdiccion*) 1. jurisdiction; authority or power in general. Syn. *kapangyarihan, awtoridád.* 2. administration. Syn. *pamamahalà.* 3. territorial range of authority. Syn. *sakláw ng kapangyarihan.*

hurisprudensiyá (hu-ris-pru-den-si-yá), n. (Sp. *jurisprudencia*) 1. jurisprudence; science of law. Syn. *aghám-batás o agbatás.* 2. a system of laws. Syn. *palábatasan.* 3. the legal profession. Syn. *abogasiyá.*

hurno (hur-no; hur-nó), n. (Sp. *horno*) 1. oven. Syn. *pugón.* 2. kiln. 3. furnace. Syn. *tapahan.*

hurunghuróng (hu-rung-hu-róng), n. throng; multitude; crowd. Syn. *makapál na tao, karamihan na tao.*

husay (hu-say), n. 1. act or manner of putting or arranging things in order; arranging. Syn. *ayos, pag-aayos, pagsasaayos.* 2. state or condition of being in order; orderly arrangement. Syn. *kaayusan, pagkamaayos.* 3. skill; expertise. Syn. *galíng, kagalingán; kahusayan; buti, kabutihan.* 4. good quality, esp. of workmanship. Syn. *ganda, kagandahan.* 5. act or manner of settling a dispute or quarrel. Syn. *pag-areglo, pag-aareglo.* 6. kindness; friendliness. Syn. *baít, kabaitán.*

husga (hus-ga; hus-gá), n. (Sp. *jusgar*) 1. act of passing judgment. Syn. *hatol, paghatol.* 2. decision; judgment. Syn. *hatol, kahatulán; pasiyá, kapasiyahan; desisyón.*

husgado (hus-ga-do), n. (Sp. *juzgado*) court of justice; tribunal. Syn. *húkuman.*

husi (hu-si), I. *n.* a kind of fabric woven from the mixture of hemp, pineapple, and silk fibers. —II. *adj.* of or made of *husi.* Syn. *yarì o gawâ sa husi.*

hustisya (hus-tis-ya), n. (Sp. *justicia*) 1. justice. Syn. *katarungan.* 2. law enforcement authority. Syn. *alagád ng batás.*

husto (hus-to; hus-tó), adj. (Sp. *justo*) 1. sufficient; enough. Syn. *sapát, supisyente, kasya.* 2. complete; exact; not lacking. Syn. *kumpleto, buô, waláng-kulang.* 3. fit; of, with, or having the right size for. Syn. *kasukát, tamà sa sukat, kasya.* 4. proper; right; appropriate. Syn. *tamà, tumpák, angkóp.*

huwád (hu-wád), I. *adj.* 1. imitated; copied;

reproduced. Syn. *kopya, kinópya; gaya, ginaya*. 2. counterfeit; fake; not genuine; forged; falsified. Syn. *palsipikado*.
—II. *n.* 1. act of imitating, copying, or reproducing. Syn. *gaya, paggaya; kopya, pagkopya; gagád, paggagád*. 2. falsification; counterfeiting. Syn. *pagpalsipiká, paghuwád, panghuhuwád*. 3. counterfeit; imitation made to deceive. Syn. *bagay na palsipikado o hinuwád*. 4. an impostor. Syn. *taong nagpápanggáp; impostór*.

huwág (hu-wág), I. *auxil. v.* don't; do not. *Huwág kang pumunta roón*. Don't go there.
—II. *interj.* Don't.

húwaran (hú-wa-ran), *n.* 1. model. Syn. *modelo, tularán*. 2. pattern. Syn. *padron*. 3. example. Syn. *halimbawà*.

Huwebes (Hu-we-bes), *n.* (Sp. *Jueves*) Thursday, the fifth day of the week.

Huwebes Santo (Hu-we-bes + San-to), *n.* Holy Thursday; Maundy Thursday.

huwego (hu-we-go), I. *n.* (Sp. *juego*) 1. a game of chance for money; gambling. Syn. *sugál, pagsusugál*. 2. a set, as of dishes, tools, instruments, etc. Syn. *set, terno, buhat*. 3. (*Mech.*) looseness or movement of an attachment, as of a steering wheel. Cf. *luwág, galáw*.
—II. *interj.* Game! (used in announcing the start of a gambling game).

huwés (hu-wés), *n.* (Sp. *juez*) judge. Syn. *hukóm*.

huweteng (hu-we-teng), *n.* (Ch.) a kind of Chinese lottery (gambling game) in which winning numbers, usually a pair, are drawn from a *tambiyolo*.

Huy (Huy), *interj.* an exclamation used in calling the attention of someone, usually accompanied by tapping or touching him lightly. See **Hoy**.

I

I, i (sounded like the "i" in "bit"), *n.* 1. the eighth letter of the *abakada* (Pilipino alphabet). 2. the type or impression representing this letter. 3. a symbol for the eighth in a group or series.

I- (i-), *pref.* used to form verbs meaning: a) to use (something) for, as in *ibilí ang kuwarta*, to use the money for buying (something); b) to do or perform something for (someone), as in *ikuha ng gatas ang batâ*, to get milk for the child; c) to cause something to be done in the manner expressed by the root, as in *ilutò*, to cook; *isuót*, to wear.

ibá (i-bá), I. *n.* another; a different one, as in *Bibigyán kita ng ibá*. I'll give you another.
—II. *adj.* 1. different; not the same. Syn. *náiibá, di-kapareho*. 2. another; some other, as in another Pedro. Syn. *isá pa*. 3. new. Syn. *bago, nababago*.

ibà (i-bà), *n.* 1. (*Bot.*) a small deciduos tree which bears acid fruits that are made into jams or jellies (*Cicca disticha* L.) . 2. (I-) name of a town in the province of Zambales, Philippines.

ibabâ (i-ba-bâ), I. *n.* 1. the place under; the under part; underneath. Syn. *ilalim*. 2. the lower part; floor. Syn. *lapág, sahíg*. 3. ground floor; basement. Syn. *silong*. 4. base or foot, as of a staircase, mountain, etc. Syn. *punò, paanán*. 5. the southern part of a district or town. Syn. *timog*. Cf. *ilaya, hilagà, hulò*.
—II. *v.* 1. to bring downstairs. Syn. *ipanaog*. 2. to put down (a thing) on something. Syn. *ipatong*. 3. to bring down as from a tree. Syn. *ilapàg, dalhin sa ibabâ o sa lupà*. 4. to lower or make lower, referring to the position of something. Syn. *pababain*. 5. to pick or gather, referring to fruits from a tree. Syn. *pitasín, putihin, anihin*. 6. to decrease or make lower, as prices. Syn. *bawasan o babaan (ang presyo)*. 7. to demote, as in rank or position. Syn. *pababain ang ranggo o tungkulin*. 8. to lower or soften the volume of, as one's voice. Syn. *hinaan, ihinà, babaan*.

ibabaw (i-ba-baw), I. *n.* 1. top, as of a table. 2. surface, as of the earth. 3. face, as of fabrics. Syn. *karayagán*. 4. summit; apex or top, as of the head, mountains, or the like. Syn. *tuktók, taluktók, ituktók*. 5. back, as of animal. Syn. *likód, gulugód*. 6.

outward appearance or aspect. Syn.
mukhâ, labás.

—II. *v.* to put on the surface, as of boiling
rice, in order to cook or make hot,
referring to eggs and other foods. Syn.
ipaibabaw, ipatong.

ibá-ibá (i-bá + i-bá), *adj.* 1. of different or
several kinds or nature. Syn. *sarí-sarì,
samut-samot.* 2. several; various; many.
Syn. *marami, di lamang íisá.* 3. not of the
same kind. Syn. *nagkakaibá.*

Ibaloy (I-ba-loy; -lóy), *n.* (*Anthrop.*) 1. a
minority tribe or ethnic group living in
the mountain regions north of Baguio. 2.
the language spoken by this group.

Ibanág (I-ba-nág), *n.* (*Anthrop.*) 1. a large
ethnic group or minority tribe living in
the regions around the provinces of
Isabela, Cagayán, and Nueva Viscaya. 2.
the language spoken by this ethnic group.

ibáng-ibá (i-báng + i-bá), *adj.* very different;
completely changed. Syn. *nápakaibá,
lúbusang nabago, malayung-malayó sa dati.*

ibayo (i-ba-yo), *n.* 1. the other, opposite
side, as of a street, mountain, river, sea,
etc. Syn. *kabilang panig; kabilang pampang*
(specific for rivers, seas and other bodies
of water). 2. anything twice as much, as
many, or as large. Syn. *dobleng dami o laki.*

ibayong-dagat (i-ba-yong + da-gat), *n.*
abroad; foreign land or lands, as in: *Galing
siya sa ibayong-dagat.* He came from
abroad.

ibig (i-big), I. *n.* 1. want; desire; wish; like.
Syn. *gusto, hangad, nasa, nais.* 2. choice;
preference. Syn. *kagustuhan.* 3. objective;
purpose; dream. Syn. *layon, layunin; mithi,
mithiin; adhika, adhikain* 4. darling; loved
one. Syn. *irog, iniirog; mahal, minamahal.*

—II. *v.* to have a liking or desire for; want;
wish. Syn. *gusto, may-gusto; hangad, may-
hangad; nais, may-nais.*

íbigan (í-bi-gan), *n.* act of loving each other;
love for each other. Syn. *mahalan,
pagmamahalan, pag-iíbigan.*

ibís (i-bís), *n.* 1. act of alighting from an
animal or vehicle. Syn. *babâ, pagbabâ;
lunsád, paglunsád.* 2. act of unloading
cargo. Syn. *diskarga, pagdidiskarga.* 3. act
of helping someone in unloading a burden

on the head or shoulders. Ant. *atang, pag-
aatang.* 4. act of unharnishing a work
animal. Syn. *awás, pag-aawás.* 5. relief, as
from hardships, pain, sorrow, etc. Syn.
hangò, pagkahangò.

ibô (i-bô), *n.* (*Prov.*) slight movement or
motion of anything without necessarily
changing position. Syn. *galáw, kilos.*

ibon (i-bon), *n.* 1. (*Zool.*) bird. 2. (*Colloq.*)
a male child's sex organ. Syn. *bebot, titì.*

ibos (i-bos), var. **ibus**, *n.* (*Bot.*) 1. buri palm
three (*Corypha elata Roxb.*). Syn. *bulí.* 2.
stripped buri palm .leaves used as
wrappers of *suman,* better known as
suman sa ibos.

ik (ik), *n.* sudden loud cry of pig, as when
hurt. Syn. *igík.*

ikâ (i-kâ), *n.* slight limp in walking. Syn.
ikód, hingkód, tikód.

ikà (i-kà): aphaeresis of **wikà,** usually written
'ikà and used with ni or ng, meaning "say,
said, or according to." Syn. *aní, sabi ni,
alinsunod sa (kay).*

ika- (i-ka-), *pref.* used to form: a) ordinal
numerals to specify the hour of the day,
equivalent to *alas,* as in *ika-8 ng umaga,* 8
o'clock in the morning. b) ordinal
adjectives: as *ikasampú,* tenth. c) causative
verbs, as in *ikamatáy,* to cause one's death;
ikatuwâ, to cause one's joy.

ikakásal (i-ka-ká-sal; i-ká-ka-sál) *n. & adj.*
betrothed. Syn. *kakásalin.*

ikadalawá (i-ka-da-la-wá). *n. & adj.* second.
Syn. *pangalawá.*

ikadalawampû (i-ka-da-la-wam-pû), *n. &
adj.* twentieth. Syn. *pandalawampû.*

ikaisá (i-ka-i-sá), *n. & adj.* first; also written:
iká-1. Syn. *una, pang-una, ikauna, primero.*

ikalabíng-isá (i-ka-la-bíng + i-sá), *n. & adj.*
eleventh.

ikalawá (i-ka-la-wá), *n. & adj.* second. Syn.
pangalawá.

ikalimá (i-ka-li-má), *n. & adj.* fifth. Syn.
panlimá.

ikalimampû (i-ka-li-mam-pû), *n. & adj.*
fiftieth. Syn. *panlimampû.*

ikam- (i-kam-), var. **ika-**, *pref.* used before
roots that begin with b or p, with the first
syllable reduplicated, meaning: to be the
means, cause, or reason for becoming so,

ikan-   **ideál**

but with more intensity, as in *ikambabasag,* *ikampipilay.*

ikan- (i-kan-), var. of **ikam-,** *pref.* used before roots that begin with **d, l, r, s,** and **t,** in the same manner and meaning of *ikam-.*

ikáng- (i-káng-), *pref.* (var of **ikam-** & **ikan-**) used before roots that begin with a vowel and such consonants other than **b, p, d, l, r, s,** and **t,** as in *ikáng-iiyak,* be the cause of one's crying continuously; *ikáng-uubó,* be the cause of one's continued coughing.

ikapág- (i-ka-pág-), *pref.* to be the reason or cause of, as in *ikapág-antók,* (be the cause of one's sleepiness; *ikapág-away,* be the reason or cause of one's quarrel with someone.

ikapitó (i-ka-pi-tó), *n.* & *adj.* seventh. Syn. *pampitó.*

ikasampû (i-ka-sam-pû), *n.* & *adj.* tenth. Syn. *pansampû.*

ikasandaán (i-ka-san-da-án), *n.* & *adj.* hundredth. Syn. *pang-isandaán.*

ikasanlibo (i-ka-san-li-bo), *n.* & *adj.* thousandth. Syn. *pang-isanlibo.*

ikasiyám (i-ka-si-yám), *n.* & *adj.* ninth. Syn. *pansiyám.*

ikatatló (i-ka-tat-ló), *n.* & *adj.* third. Syn. *pangatló.*

ikáw (i-káw), *pron.* you (singular).

ikay (i-kay), *n.* act or manner of doing something thoroughly, that is, without leaving anything undone.

ikì (i-kì), *n.* a folkloric nocturnal, winged creature with long thread-like tongue, which according to belief, is used for sucking blood from the soles of the feet of women who are in the family way. Cf. *tiktík, mánananggál.*

ikid (i-kid), *n.* 1. act or manner of coiling or winding (rope, thread, twine, wire, or the like) around something, as on a spool. Syn. *pulupot, pagpupulupot; bidbíd, pagbidbíd.* 2. a coil or a series of rings formed by winding into a roll. Syn. *likaw, rolyo,* 3. a single coil (of rope, wire, etc.) wound around something. Syn. *ayikid, pulupot.*

ikinabúbuhay (i-ki-na-bú-bu-hay), I. *adj.* referring to something that sustains life. Syn. *nagbíbigáy-buhay.*

—II. *n.* livelihood; means of living. Syn. *kabuhayan, pagkabuhay.*

ikinagágalak (i-ki-na-gá-galak), *adj.* said of something that causes happiness or joy to someone. Syn. *ikinatútuwa, ikinasásayá, ikinalúlugód.*

ikinahíhiyâ (i-ki-na-hí-hi-yâ), *adj.* referring to something that causes shame to someone. Syn. *ikinapápahiyâ.*

ikinalúlumbáy (i-ki-na-lú-lum-báy), *adj.* referring to something that causes one to feel sad.

ikinalúlungkót (i-ki-na-lú-lung-kót), *adj.* said of something causes one to feel sad about. Syn. *ikinalúlumbáy.*

ikirán (i-ki-rán), *n.* spool. Syn. *karete, pulunán, kidkiran.*

ikit (i-kit), *n.* 1. rotation; continuous circular motion; gyration; turning round and round. Syn. *ikot, inog.* 2. a single round, as in race track. Syn. *ligid.* 3. turn, as of a vehicle wheels. Syn. *gulong, paggulong.*

iklî (ik-lî), *n.* 1. shortness; lack of length. Syn. *igsî, utdó.* 2. shortness or briefness of time. Syn. *dalî, kadalián.*

ikmo (ik-mo; ik-mó), *n.* 1. betel pepper plant (*Piper betel L.*), 2. a leaf or leaves of this plant usually chewed with betel nut, lime, and chewing tobacco. Syn. *mamín.*

ikód (i-kod), I. *n.* slight limp; act or manner of walking with a limp. Syn. *ikâ, tikód, hingkód.*

—II. *adj.* limping; walking with a limp. Syn. *umíikâ, umíikód, tumítikód, humíhingkód.*

ikom (i-kom), *n.* the closing or folding, as of the fingers of a hand, petals of flowers, wings of bird, etc. Syn. *tikom.*

ikot (i-kot), *n.* 1. a turning round and round; rotation; revolution. Syn. *ikit, inog.* 2. a single round, as in a circular race track. Syn. *ligid.*

ideá (i-de-a), var. **ideyá,** *n.* (Sp.) 1. idea; opinion. Syn. *palagáy, opinyón, kuru-kurò.* 2. plan; intention. Syn. *balak, layon, hangád.*

ideál (i-de-ál), var. **ideyál,** I. *n.* (Sp.) 1. a model to be imitated; ideal. Syn. *húwaran, ulirán.* 2. ambition. Syn. *mithî, mithiin, pangarap (fig.), ambisyón.*

—II. adj. 1. worthy of imitation. Syn. ulirán, karapat-dapat pamarisan. 2. right; just as one would wish. Syn. tamang-tamà, bagay na bagay.

idealismo (i-de-a-lis-mo), var. **ideyalismo**, n. (Sp.) idealism. Syn. katapatan sa mabubuting símulain.

ideolóhiyá (i-de-o-ló-hi-yá), var. **ideyolóhiyá**, n. (Sp. ideologia) ideology. Syn. kapaniwalaán, kapanaligán.

idlíp (id-líp), n. a light, short sleep; nap. Syn. hipíg.

idolatriya (i-do-la-tri-ya), n. (Sp. idolatria) idolatry; worship of idols. Syn. pagsamba sa mga diyús-diyusan.

idoló (i-do-ló), n. idol; a person who is loved very much. Syn. taong hináhangaan nang labis.

idyoma (id-yo-ma), n. (Sp. idioma) 1. idiom; idiomatic expression. Syn. kawikaán. 2. language. Syn. wikà, lengguwahe. 3. dialect. Syn. diyalekto, wikaín.

idyosinkrasya (id-yo-sin-kras-ya), n. (Sp. idiosincraciä) idiosyncracy; personal peculiarity. Syn. ugalì, kaugalian.

idyotismo (id-yo-tis-mo), n. (Sp. idiotismo) idiotic action or behavior; ignorance. Syn. katangahán, kahangalán, katulalalaán, kawaláng-muwáng.

igá (i-gá), I. adj. evaporated or dried up due to evaporation, referring to water or liquid in a container or to food due to overcooking. Syn. tuyô na.

—II. n. state or condition of being dried up due to evaporation.

igat (i-gat), n. (Ichth.) fresh-water eel (Anguilla mauritiana).

igkás (ig-kás), I. n. 1. a sudden recoil or springing back, as of released spring. Syn. sikad, iskád. 2. sudden release, as the bow of arrows. 3. a sudden snap or snapping, as of a trap or snare.

—II, adj. released or set off; let loose, as a spring.

igi (i-gi), n. 1. state or quality of being good; goodness. Syn. buti, kabutihan; inam, kainaman. 2. excellence; high quality. Syn. galíng, kagalingán; husay, kahusayan. 3. orderliness. Syn. ayos, kaayusan. 4. recovery, as from sickness. Syn. galíng,

paggalíng, pagbuti ng karamdaman. 5. kindness of someone to another or others. Syn. baít, kabaitán.

igíb (i-gíb), n. act of fetching water from a well or spring, esp. for home use. Syn. salok o pagsalok ng tubig sa balón o sa poso para sa bahay.

igík (i-gík), n. 1. grunt; act of grunting. Syn. pag-igík. 2. the deep, gruff, throaty sound made by a pig; grunt. Syn. iyák ng baboy.

igíg (i-gíg), var. **ig-ig**, n. 1. act of shaking a container to make the contents more compact. Syn. liglíg, alóg. 2. act or manner of sifting granular matter, as grains, sand, and the like through a sieve or strainer. Syn. bistáy, pagbibistáy; agág, pag-aagág. 3. act of shaking a tree or its branches so that the fruits or leaves may fall. Syn. yugyóg, ugóg (ug-og).

igláp (ig-láp), n. a very short moment. Syn. saglít.

iglesya (i-gles-ya), n. (Sp. iglesia) the church, as a society. Syn. simbahan.

ignorá (ig-no-rá), n. (Sp. ignorar) an ignoring or being ignored. Syn. di-pagpansín, pagwaláng-bahalà.

ignoramus (ig-no-ra-mus), n. (Eng.) ignoramus; an ignorant person. Syn. taong waláng-muwáng, taong hangál.

ignoránsiyá (ig-no-rán-si-yá), n. (Sp. ignorancia) 1. ignorance; lack of knowledge or education. Syn. kamangmangán, katangahán, kawaláng-pinag-aralan. 2. unawareness of. Syn. kawaláng-malay, pagkawaláng-malay.

ignorante (ig-no-ran-te), adj. (Sp.) ignorant; uneducated. Syn. mangmáng, waláng-pinag-aralan, hangál. 2. unaware about something. Syn. waláng-malay sa.

igos (i-gos), n. (Bot., Sp. higo) the fir tree or its fruit.

igpáw (ig-páw), n. 1. a leap or jump over an obstacle. Syn. lundág, luksó, talón. 2. a successful attempt in overcoming an obstacle. Syn. tagumpáy, pagtatagumpáy.

igsî (ig-sî), var. **iksî**, n. 1. shortness; lack of sufficient length. Syn. iklî, utdó. 2. shortness or briefness, as of time. Syn. dalî, kadalián.

igtád (ig-tád), var. **iktád**, n. 1. a sudden leap

or jump, as in avoiding a blow. Syn. *lundág, tiiplág.* 2. act of jumping over an obstacle. Syn. *igpáw, talón.*

igtíng (ig-tíng). var. **iktíng,** n. 1. tightness, as of a tie, knot, bite, or the like. Syn. *higpít, hapit.* 2. intensity or seriousness, as of rivalry, misunderstanding, etc. Syn. *tindí, lubhâ.*

iha (i-ha), n. (Sp. *hija*) daughter. Syn. *anák na babae.*

ihaw (i-haw), n. act or manner of cooking or roasting (corn, fish, meat, etc.) directly on an open fire; broiling. Syn. *paglulutò nang túwiran sa baga o apóy, bangí* (Bats.).

ihì (i-hì), n. 1. urine. 2. the act or process of urinating. Syn. *pag-ihì.*

íhing-langgám (í-hing + lang-gám), n. (Fig.) 1. a light drizzle or shower. Syn. *mahinang ambón.* 2. slow drip or dripping, as of water from a faucet with a leak.

ihit (i-hit), n. 1. fit; paroxysm. Syn. *sumpóng, atake.* 2. outburst, as of anger. Syn. *simbuyó, silakbó, sikláb, lakás.* 4. outburst, as of applause, laughter, etc. Syn. *sigabo.*

iho (i-ho), n. (Sp. *hijo*) 1. son; male child. Syn. *anák na lalaki.* Cf.*iha.* 2. a term used by an elder in addressing a boy to express affection or fondess. Syn. *anák.*

iilán (i-i-lán), adj. few; not many; of small number. Syn. *kákauntî, di-marami, madalang.*

iisá (i-i-sá), adj. only one; lone; alone; single. Syn. *solo, nag-íisá, tangì.*

iít (i-ít), n. (in a hide-and-seek game) a shrill signal sounded by the hider to announce that the seeking may already be started. Syn. *irit.*

ilado (i-la-do), adj. (Sp. *helado*) frozen; iced.

ilag (i-lag), n. act or manner of avoiding a blow; dodging. Syn. *iwas.* Cf. *igtád, lundág.* 2. avoidance; keeping away, as from trouble, etc. Syn. *layô, paglayô.*

Ilag (I-lag), interj. Get out of the way! Syn. *Tabí! Layô! Habì!*

ilág (i-lág), adj. careful; cautious; wary. Syn. *ingát, maingat.*

ilalim (i-la-lim), I. n. 1. bottom. Syn. *pusod* (fig.) 2. the space below or underneath something. Syn. *babâ, ibabâ, lapág.*
—II. *v.* to make deep or deeper. Syn.

palalimin.

ilán (i-lán), I. *pron.* 1. some; a certain person or persons not specified or known. Syn. *ang ibá (pa).* 2. a certain indefinite or unspecified number or quantity, etc; a few.
—II. adj. some; few; not many. Syn. *kauntî, kakauntî, di-marami.*
—III. interrog. pron. how many; what is the count. Syn. *gaanó karami.*

ilandáng (i-lan-dáng), n. 1. sudden flight of something accidentally thrown out of place. Syn. *tilapon.* 2. surge, as of water from a fountain. Syn. *tilandóy.*

ilanláng (i-lan-láng), var. **ilangláng,** n. a swift rise or flight into the air; soar. Syn. *sibád na paitaás.*

iláng (i-láng), I. n. 1. desert. Syn. *disyerto.* 2. an isolated, unfrequented place. Syn. *liblíb na poók.* 3. a wide open space or field. Syn. *parang, kaparangan.*
—II. adj. isolated, referring to a place. Syn. *liblíb, malayo't waláng nanínirahan.*

ilang-ilang (i-lang + ilang; i-lang + i-lang), var. **ilangílang, alangilang,** n. (Bot.) 1. a tree that bears greenish fragrant flowers that yield volatile perfume oil (*Canangium odorata*). 2. the fragrant flower of this tree.

iláp (i-láp), n. 1. wildness or indomesticity, as of an animal. Syn. *kasimarunán.* Ant. *amò, kaamuan.* 2. elusiveness; tendency to elude.

ilas (i-las), n. secret escape, as from a watcher or guard. Syn. *talilís, puslít.*

ilaw (i-law), n. 1. light. Syn. *tangláw.* 2. lamp; torch. Syn. *lampará, sulô, gasera, kingke.* 3. (Colloq.) persons carrying lighted candles during a procession.

ilawán (i-la-wán), n. kerosene or oil lamp. Syn. *gasera.*

ilaya (i-la-ya), n. 1. the interior or upper part of a town. Syn. *hulò.* 2. north. Syn. *hilagà, norte.*

ilegál (i-le-gal), adj. (Sp.) illegal; unlawful. Syn. *labág sa batás, di-alinsunod sa batás.*

iletrado (i-le-tra-do), adj. (Sp.) illiterate. Syn. *mangmáng, di-nag-aral, waláng-pinag-aralan, di-marunong bumasa't sumulat.*

ilíg (i-lig), n. 1. act of shaking a container so that the contents would set or be mixed well. Syn. *liglig*. 2. act of waking up a person by shaking him lightly. Syn. *alóg, pag-alóg*. 3. act of shaking the head or body, as in shedding off water, dust, etc. Syn. *pilíg*.

ilíng (i-líng), n. shake off the head as an expression of denial, dislike, or disapproval.

ilit (i-lit; i-lít), n. 1. illegal usurpation or seizure of someone's property. Syn. *kamkám*. 2. confiscation of a mortgaged property for failure to redeem it. Syn. *samsám*.

iliterato (i-li-te-ra-to), adj. (Sp.) illiterate; uneducated. Syn. *iletrado, mangmáng, di-marunong bumasa't sumulat*.

iló (i-lo), n. the act or process of milling sugar cane. Syn. *kabyáw, pagkabyáw*.

Ilokano (I-lo-ka-no), n. 1. A Filipino (male) citizen who is a native of the Ilocos region. 2. the dialect spoken in the Ilocos region.

Iloko (I-lo-ko), n. 1. the Ilocos region. 2. the dialect of the Ilocanos.

ilog (i-log), n. river. Cf. *sapá, batis*.

ilóng (i-lóng), n. nose.

Ilonggót (I-long-gót), n. (Anthrop.) 1. a member of a non-Christian tribe living in the southern Caraballo mountains along the border of the province of Nueva Ecija. 2. the dialect spoken by this tribe.

ilúg-ilugan (i-lúg + i-lu-gan), n. rivulet; brook. Syn. *muntíng ilog, sapà*.

iluminado (i-lu-mi-na-do), adj. (Sp.) well-lighted; illuminated. Syn. *maliwanag, may-ilaw, naîilawan*.

iluminasyón (i-lu-mi-nas-yón), n. (Sp. *iluminacion*) 1. illumination; lighting; lights. Syn. *ilaw, pailaw; tangláw, panangláw*. 2. supplying with lights; making clear with a light or lights. Syn. *pag-ilaw, pagpapailaw*. 3. explanation; making clear by explaining. Syn. *pagpapaliwanag; pagbibigáy-liwanag*.

ilustrado (i-lus-tra-do), adj. (Sp.) 1. learned; educated; cultured. Syn. *idukado, nag-aral, may-pinag-aralan*. 2. provided with illustrations; illustrated. Syn. *may mga larawan, nilarawanan*.

ilustradór (i-lus-tra-dór), n. (Sp.) illustrador; designer. Syn. *tagaguhit-larawan*.

ilustrasyón (i-lus-tras-yón), n. (Sp. *ilustracion*) 1. a graphic or pictorial representation used to explain or decorate something; illustration. Syn. *larawan, larawang-guhit*. 2. an example. Syn. *halimbawà*. 3. act or process of illustrating. Syn. *paglalarawan*.

ilustre (i-lus-tre), adj. (Sp.) illustrious; famous. Syn. *tanyág, bantóg*. 2. distinguished. Syn. *mabunyî, dakilà*.

ilusyón (i-lus-yón), n. (Sp. *ilusion*) illusion. Syn. *guniguní, pangitain*.

imâ (i-mâ), n. (Pamp.) mother. Syn. *iná, nanay, ináy*.

imahen (i-ma-hen; i-ma-hén), n. (Sp. *imagen*) 1. a likeness of something; image. Syn. *larawan*. 2. statue, esp. of a saint. Syn. *istatwa*.

imahinasyón (i-ma-hi-nas-yón), n. (Sp. *imaginacion*) imagination. Syn. *guniguní, hinagap*.

imateryál (i-ma-ter-yál), adj. (Sp. *inmaterial*) immaterial; not important. Syn. *di-mahalagá, di-importante*.

imbák (im-bák), I. n. 1. act or manner of storing goods in large quantity. Syn. *pagtatagò ng maraming kalakal, pag-iimbák, pagtitinggál*. 2. preservation of food, like fruits, fish, meat, etc. by packing or canning. Syn. *pagsasalata*.
—II. adj. stored; put in storage. Syn. *tinggál, nakatinggál*.

imbálido (im-bá-li-do), adj. (Sp. *invalido*) not valid; null and void. Syn. *waláng-bisá, waláng-saysáy*.

imbasyón (im-bas-yón), n. (Sp. *invasion*) invasion. Syn. *pagsalakay, paglusob*.

imbay (im-bay; im-báy), n. 1. trot or gait of a horse in which the legs are lifted in alternating diagonal pairs. Syn. *paso, trote*. 2. jogging gait of a person, at a pace between walk and run. Syn. *yagyág*. 3. the characteristic sway of the hands in walking. Syn. *kampáy*.

imbayog (im-ba-yog), n. swaying or swinging movement of a hanging object; oscillation. Syn. *ugóy, indayon, undayon, tabyón*.

imbensiyón (im-ben-si-yón), n. (Sp. *invencion*) 1. act of inventing. Syn. *pag-*

imbento, paglikhâ. 2. an invention; thing invented. Syn *imbento, bagay na inimbento o nilikhâ.*

imbentaryo (im-ben-tar-yo), n. (Sp. *inventario*) inventory.

imbento (im-ben-to), I. n. (Sp. *invento*) 1. act of inventing; invention. Syn. *imbensyón, pag-imbento, paglikhâ.* 2. something invented; an invention. Syn. *imbensyón, bagay na inimbento.* —II. adj. invented; created. Syn. *likhâ, nilikhâ, inimbento.*

imbentór (im-ben-tór), n. (Sp. *inventor*) person who invents; inventor. Syn. *manlilikhâ.*

imbestidura (im-bes-ti-du-ra), n. (Sp. *investidura*) installation in office with ceremony; investiture. Syn. *pagtatalagá sa tungkulin.*

imbestigá (im-bes-ti-gá), n. (Sp. *investigar*) investigation. Syn. *siyasat, pagsisiyasat.*

imbestigadór (im-bes-ti-ga-dor), n. (Sp. *investigador*) investigator. Syn. *tagsiyasat, tagaimbestigá.*

imbí (im-bí; im-bî), I. adj. mean; ignoble; dishonorable. Syn. *hamak, waláng-hiyâ, waláng-dangál, marawal.* —II. n. traitor; betrayar. Syn. *taksíl, lilo, traidór.*

imbisible (im-bi-si-ble), adj. (Sp. *invisible*) invisible. Syn. *di-kita, di-nákikita.*

imbitasyón (im-bi-tas-yón), n. (Sp. *invitacion*) 1. act of inviting; invitation. Syn. *anyaya, pag-aanyaya; kumbidá, pagkumbidá.* 2. the note or message used in inviting; invitation, Syn. *paanyaya.*

imbót (im-bót), I. n. greed; greediness; covetousness. Syn. *kasakímán, kayamuan, kasibaan, katakawan.* —II. n. & adj. referring to a person who is greedy or too covetous.

imbudo (im-bu-do), n. (Sp. *embudo*) funnel.

imbulóg (im-bu-lóg), n. swift upward glide in the air; soar. Syn. *pagpapaimbulóg; ilangláng, pagpapailanláng; imbuyóg.*

imensidád (i-men-si-dád), n. (Sp. *inmensidad*) 1. immensity; great size. Syn. *kalakhán.* 2. vastness; limitless extent. Syn. *lawak, kalawakan.*

imík (i-mik), n. act of saying something;

utterance of words. Syn. *salitâ, pagsasalitâ.* 2. act of starting conversation with whom one has not been on speaking terms for sometime. Syn. *batî, pagbatî, pakikipagbatî.*

imigrante (i-mi-gran-te), n. (Sp. *inmigrante*) immigrant. Syn. *mandarayuhan.*

imigrasyón (i-mi-gras-yón), n. (Sp. *immigracion*) immigration. Syn. *pandarayuhan.*

imis (i-mis), n. act of cleaning or tidying up a place by keeping things in their proper places. Syn. *ligpít, pagliligpít; ayos, pag-aayos.*

imitado (i-mi-ta-do), adj. (Sp.) imitated; copied; not original. Syn. *kinopya, ginaya, huwád, hinuwád.*

imitadór (i-mi-ta-dor), n. (Sp.) imitator. Syn. *manggagaya, manghuhuwád.*

imitasyón (i-mi-tas-yon), I. n. (Sp. *imitacion*) 1. act of imitating. Syn. *paggaya, pagtulad, paghuwád.* 2. a copy or imitation. Syn. *kopya.* 3. a counterfeit, fake. Syn. *huwád, peke.* —II. adj. counterfeit; forged; not real. Syn. *huwád, hinuwád, palsipikado.*

imno (im-no), n. (Sp. *himno*) hymn. Cf. *awit.*

imorál (i-mo-ral), adj. (Sp. *inmorál*) 1. immoral; morally wrong; wicked. Syn. *masamâ.* 2. lewd; indecent. Syn. *mahalay, masagwâ, malaswâ, salaulà.*

imoralidád (i-mo-ra-li-dád), n. (Sp. *inmoralidád*) immorality; wrong doing; wickedness. Syn. *pagkaimorál, kasamáan.* 2. lewdness; indecency. Syn. *kahalayan, kalaswaán, kasagwaán, kasalaulaan.*

imortál (i-mor-tal), I. adj. (Sp. *inmortal*) 1. living forever; deathless. Syn. *waláng-kamatayan.* 2. everlasting; endless. Syn. *waláng hanggán, waláng-maliw, waláng-katapusán.* —II. n. 1. an immortal being. Syn. *taong waláng-kamatayan.* 2. a person having a lasting name. Syn. *taong mananatiling bantóg sa buóng panahón.*

imortalidád (i-mor-ta-li-dád), n. (Sp. *inmortalidad*) 1. immortality; endless life or existence. Syn. *kawaláng-kamatayan.* 2. fitness to last forever. Syn. *kawaláng-maliw, kawaláng-katapusán, kawaláng-hanggan.* 3. lasting fame. Syn. *kabantugang waláng-hanggán.*

imot (i-mot), n. 1. stinginess; close-
fistedness. Syn. *kakuriputan, karamutan.*
2. frugality; thrift or thriftiness. Syn. *tipíd,
katipirán.*

impakto (im-pak-to), n. (Lat. *en facto*) evil
spirit; ghost; spook; specter. Syn. *multo.*

impabilidád (im-pa-bi-li-dád), n. (Sp.
infabilidad) infallibility; state or quality of
being infallible. Syn. *pagka-di-
magkakamalî.*

impánsiyá (im-pán-si-yá), n. (Sp. *infancia*)
infancy. Syn. *kamusmusán, kasanggulán.*

impánteriya (im-pan-te-ri-ya), var.
impántiryá, n. (Sp. *infantería*) infantry.
Syn. *hukbóng-lakád.*

impeksiyón (im-pek-si-yón), n. (Sp.
infeccion) 1. infection. Syn. *lalin,
pagkalalin; hawa, pagkahawa.* 2. infection
in wounds. Syn. *naknák, pagnanaknák.*

impedimento (im-pe-di-men-to), n. (Sp.)
impediment. Syn. *balakíd, hadláng,
sagabal.*

impenetrable (im-pe-ne-tra-ble), adj. (Sp.)
impenetrable. Syn. *di-mapapasok.*

imperatibo (im-pe-ra-ti-bo), adj. (Sp.
imperativo) 1. in Gram., imperative;
expressing a command. Syn. *pautós.* 2.
urgent necessary. Syn. *kailangan,
kinákailangan.*

imperdible (im-per-di-ble), var. perdible, n.
(Sp. *enferdible*) safety pin. Cf. *aspilé, alpilér.*

imperénsiyá (im-pe-rén-si-yá), n. (Sp.
inferencia), inference. Syn. *hakà, haká-
hakà, hulà, hinuhà.*

impertinente (im-per-ti-nen-te), adj. (Sp.)
1. impertinent; disrespectful. Syn. *waláng-
galang, waláng-pítagan.* 2. rude; insolent.
Syn. *bastós, waláng-hiyâ.* 3. impertinent;
irrelevant. Syn. *waláng-kaugnayan,
waláng-kinalaman.*

imperyalismo (im-per-ya-lis-mo), n. (Sp.
imperialismo) imperialism.

imperyo (im-per-yo), n. (Sp. *imperio*)
empire.

imperyoridád (im-per-yo-ri-dád), n. (Sp.
inferioridad) 1. inferiority; inferior nature
or condition. Syn. *kababaan, kababaang-
urì.* 2. inferiority complex. Syn.
panganganino, pagkasilóng.

impinidád (im-pi-ni-dad), n. (Sp. *infinidad*)

infinity. Syn. *kawaláng-hanggán, kawaláng-
katapusán.*

impinitibo (im-pi-ni-ti-bo), 1. adj. (Sp.
infinitivo) in Gram., infinitive. Syn. *pawatás.*
—II. n. the simple, uninflected form of
the verb, expressing action without
person, number, or tense. Syn. *pandiwang
pawatás.*

impís (im-pís), I. n. state or quality of being
thin, deflated, or sunken, as of a
punctured tire or rubber ball.
—II. adj. deflated; sunken. Syn. *hupyák,
humpák, hipâ, kupís.*

impit (im-pit; im-pít), I. n. 1. act of
controlling the volume or force, as of
one's voice. Syn. *pigil, pagpigil.* 2. act of
withholding action unnecessarily, as in
signing papers. Syn. *bimbín, pagbimbín.*

impiyerno (im-pi-yer-no), n. (Sp. *infierno*)
hell.

implamable (im-pla-ma-ble), adj. (Sp.
inflamable) inflammable. Syn. *madalín,
magliyáb, madalíng magsikláb.*

implamasyón (im-pla-mas-yón), n. (Sp.
inflamación) 1. an inflaming or being
inflamed. Syn. *pagliliyáb, pagsisikláb.* 2.
(Med.) diseased condition of some part
of the body, characterized by redness,
pain, heat, and swelling; inflammation.
Syn. *pamumulá't pamamagâ.*

implasyón (im-plas-yón), n. (Sp. *inflacion*)
1. a swelling caused by air, gas, etc. Syn.
pagbintóg, pamimintóg. 2. act of causing
something to swell by pumping air, gas,
etc. into. Syn. *pagpapabintóg.* 3. inflation
(in currency). Syn. *bigláng pagbabâ ng
halaga ng salapî dahil sa máramihán,
pagpapalabás nitó.*

impleksiyón (im-plek-si-yón), n. (Sp.
infleccion) in Gram., inflection; change in
the form of a verb to show case, number,
gender, etc. Syn. *pagbabagong-anyô ng
pandiwà.*

implikasyón (im-pli-kas-yón), n. (Sp.
implicacion) 1. implication; an implicating
or being implicated. Syn. *pagsasangkót,
pagkakasangkót; pagdaramay, pagka-
káramay; pagdarawit, pagkakárawit.* 2.
indirect suggestion; hint. *pahiwatig,
pagpapahiwatig.*

impluensa (im-plu-en-sa), var. **impluwensa**, n. (Sp. *influenza*) in Med., influenza. Syn. *trangkaso*.

impluho (im-plu-ho), n. (Sp. *influho*) influence. Syn. *impluwénsiyá*.

impó (im-po), n. (Ch.) grandmother. Syn. *lola, lelang, abwela*.

impók (im-pók), n. 1. act of saving (money) for the future. Syn. *pagtitipon o pagtitipíd (para sa hináharáp)*. 2. money saved for the future; savings. Syn. *ang natipon o natipíd para sa hinaharáp*.

impormál (im-por-mal), adj. (Sp. *informál*) informal; not formal. Syn. *di-pormál, waláng-kapormalán, waláng-pormalidád*.

impormante (im-por-man-te), n. (Sp. *informante*) 1. informer; person who informs the authorities of violations of the law. Syn. *batyáw; tagasuplóng, tagapagsuplóng; tagasumbóng, tagapagsumbóng*. 2. spy. Syn. *ispiyá, tiktík*. 3. informant. Syn. *tagabigáy-ulat, kukunáng-ulat, sanggunian*.

impormasyón (im-por-mas-yón), n. (Sp. *informacion*) 1. information; facts. Syn. *kabátiran, kaalaman*. 2. news; account or report about something. Syn. *balità, ulat*.

importadór (im-por-ta-dór), n. (Sp.) importer. Syn. *mang-aangkát-kalakal, tagaangkát-kalakal*.

importante (im-por-tan-te), adj. (Sp. *importante*) 1. important; meaning much. Syn. *mahalagá*. 2. of significance; valuable. Syn. *makabuluhán*.

importasyón (im-por-tas-yon), n. (Sp. *importacíon*) 1. importation; bringing in goods from foreign countries. Syn. *pag-angkát*. 2. goods imported; imports. Syn. *angkát, mga kalakal na angkát*.

imposible (im-po-sib-le), adj. (Sp.) impossible; that cannot be. Syn. *di-máaarì*.

imposisyón (im-po-sis-yón), n. (Sp. *imposicion*) 1. act of putting on a burden, tax, or punishment on someone. Syn. *paglalapat, pagpapataw*. 2. taking advantage of someone. Syn. *pagsasamantalá*. 3. burden. Syn. *pataw, pabigát*. 4. tax. Syn. *buwis*. 5. punishment. Syn. *parusa*.

impostór (im-pos-tór), n. (Sp.; Eng.) 1. impostor; a person who assumes a false name or character. Syn. *taong nagpápanggáp*. 2. a cheat or deceiver. Syn. *manlilinláng, mandarayà*.

imprenta (im-pren-ta), n. (Sp.) 1. act of printing. Syn. *paglilimbág*. 2. printing shop or establishment. Syn. *limbagan, pálimbagan*. 3. printing press. Syn. *makináng panlimbág*.

impresyón (im-pres-yon), n. (Sp. *impressión*) 1. mark or imprint. Syn. *taták, marka*. 2. impression; effect on the mind or senses by some force or influence. Syn. *kintál, kakintalán*.

improbabîlidád (im-pro-ba-bi-li-dád), n. (Sp.) improbability. Syn. *pagka-di-maaaring magkátotoó, pagka-di-maaaring mangyari*.

improbisado (im-pro-bi-sa-do), adj. (Sp. *improvisado*) improvised. Syn. *inihandáng (ginawáng) pansamantalá*.

impulsibo (im-pul-si-bo), adj. (Sp. *impulsivo*) impulsive; acting on impulse or without thinking. Syn. *mapusok, pabiglá-biglà*.

imus (i-mus), n. 1. cape; headland; promontory. Syn. *tangway*. 2. (I-) name of a town in the province of Cavite.

in- (in-), pref. used before roots that begin with vowels to form the past tense of verbs, as in *inalís* (removed), *inukit* (carved), *inaklát* (made into a book), etc.

-in- (-in-), infix used to indicate: a) past tense of verbs in the imperative, as in *ibinilí* (<*ibilí*), *isinama* (<*isama*), *isinaing* (<*isaing*), *isinulat* (<*isulat*), etc.

-in (-in), suffix added to the base words ending in consonants or glottal vowels, the meaning of which is generally dependent upon the meaning of the roots.

iná (i-na), n. mother. Syn. *ináy, nanay, ináng*.

ináamá (i-ná-a-má), n. male sponsor; godfather. Syn. *ninong, padrino*.

ináamag (i-ná-a-mag), adj. full of mold; moldy. Syn. *maamag, punô ng amag*.

ináanák (i-ná-a-nák), n. godchild; godson or goddaughter.

ináapurá (i-ná-a-pu-rá), adj. referring to something that is being rushed. Syn. *minámadalî*.

inakáy

inakáy (i-na-káy), n. the young of birds. Cf. sisiw.

inagaw (i-na-gaw), I. adj. 1. taken by force. Syn. kinuha nang sápilitán. 2. kidnapped. Syn. dinukot.
—II. v. past tense of agawin.

inagurasyon (i-na-gu-ras-yon), n. (Sp. inauguracion) 1. inauguration; installation of a person in office. Syn. pagtatalagá sa tungkulin. 2. opening for public service with a ceremony or celebration. Syn. pasinayà, pagpapasinayà.

inahín (i-na-hín), n. 1. the female of the chicken or domestic fowl; hen. 2. any female animal which is already a mother.

inaín (i-na-ín), n. 1. aunt. Syn. tiyá, tiyahin. 2. stepmother. Syn. ináng-pagumán.

inam (i-nam), n. 1. niceness; prettiness; beauty. Syn. gandá, kagandahan; dikít, kariktán; dilág, karilagán. 2. goodness; kindness; generosity. Syn. buti, kabutihan; baít, kabaitán. 3. neatness; orderliness. Syn. ayos, kaayusan. 4. state or condition of being clear and bright, referring to weather; fineness. Syn. aliwalas, kaaliwalasan; gandá, kagandahan.

inampalan (i-nam-pa-lan; -lán), var. ináng-palán, board of judges in a contest. Syn. lupóng tagahatol, hurado.

ináng (i-náng), n. mother. Syn. ináy, nanay, iná.

ináng- (i-náng-), a combining form. meaning "mother," as in inángbayan, ináng-binyag, etc.

ináng-bayan (i-náng + ba-yan), var. inambayan, n. the country of one's birth; motherland. Syn. bayang-tínubuan.

ináng-binyág (i-náng + bin-yág), var. inambínyág, n. baptismal godmother. Syn. ninang o madrina sa binyág.

ináng-kasál (i-náng + ka-sál), n. godmother at wedding. Syn. ninang o madrina sa kasál.

ináng-kumpíl (i-náng + kum-píl), n. godmother at confirmation. Syn. ninang o madrina sa kumpíl.

ináng-hagdán (i-náng + hag-dán), n. the two side boards of a staircase to which the steps are nailed or mortised. Syn. painá ng hagdán.

inangít (i-na-ngít), n. glutinous rice cooked

inkomparable

in coconut milk with little sugar. Syn antala.

ináng-pangumán (i-náng + pa-ngu-mán) var. inampangumán, n. stepmother. Syn inaín, ale, tiyá, madrasta.

ináng-wikà (i-náng + wi-kà), n. one' native language; mother tongue. Syn sariling wikà, katutubong wikà.

inapó (i-na-pó), n. 1. grandchildren. Syn mga apó. 2. descendant. Syn. pinag apuhán, angkán.

inasnán (i-nas-nán), I. adj. salted; preserve in salt. Syn. binuro.
—II. n. salted meat, fish, or fruits. Syn buro.

inat (i-nat), n. act of stretching one's arm and legs, usually after waking up or afte working to relieve muscular tension.

ináy (i-náy), n. appellation for mother. Syn ináng, iná.

inkapasidád (in-ka-pa-si-dád), n. (Sp incapacidad) 1. lack of ability, power, etc Syn. pagkawaláng-kaya, kawaláng-kaya. 2 disability. Syn. pagkainutil, kainutilan. 3 legal disqualification. Syn. pagkawalá kawalán ng karapatan (alinsunod sa batás)

inkilino (in-ki-li-no), n. (Sp. inquilino) 1 tenant; person paying rent for the use o a house, building, etc. Syn. ang nangúngupahan. 2. tenant in a land holding. Syn. kasamá.

inklinasyón (in-kli-nas-yón), n. (Sp inclinacion) 1. inclination; leaning position. Syn. hilig, pagkakáhilig; kiling pagkakákiling. 2. tendency; preference liking. Syn. hilig, kahiligan, kaibigán kagustuhan. 3. bias; favoring one agains another. Syn. kampi, pagkampi; panig pagpanig.

inkoherente (in-ko-he-ren-te), adj. (Sp incoherente) incoherent; confused. Syn malabò, di-malinaw, di-máunawaan.

inkombenyensiyá (in-kom-ben-yen-si-yá) n. (Sp. inconveniencia) 1. inconvenience bother; obstacle. Syn. abala, kaabalahan sagabal. 2. hardship; difficulty. Syn. hirap kahirapan.

inkomparable (in-kom-pa-ra-ble), adj. (Sp incomparable) incomparable. Syn. waláng katulad, waláng-kaparis, waláng-kawangis.

nkompatible (in-kom-pa-ti-ble), adj. (Sp. *incompatible*) not able to agree. Syn. *magkalaban, di-magkatugmâ, di-magkabagáng, di-magkabagay, di-magkasundô.*

nkompetente (in-kom-pe-ten-te), adj. (Sp. *incompetente*) incompetent; lacking ability or qualification. Syn. *waláng-kaya, waláng-kakayahán.*

nkompleto (in-kom-ple-to), adj. (Sp. *incompleto*) incomplete. Syn. *kulang, di-ganáp, di-kompleto.*

nkomunikado (in-ko-mu-ni-ka-do), adj. (Sp. *incomunicado*) incommunicado; not allowed to communicate. Syn. *di-maaaring makausap o kausapin.*

nkonsistensiyá (in-kon-sis-ten-si-yá), n. (Sp. *inconsistencia*) 1. inconsistency; lack of agreement or harmony. Syn. *salungatan, pagkakásalungatan, di-pagkakáayon, di-pagkakátugunan.* 2. failure to keep to the same belief or principle. Syn. *pagpapábagu-bago, kawaláng-kápanatilihan.*

nkorporada (in-kor-po-ra-da), adj. (Sp. *incorporada*) incorporated; combined; united. Syn. *pinagsama, pinaglakip, pinag-isá.* 2. registered as a corporation. Syn. *nakatalâ biláng korporasyón.*

nkubasyón (in-ku-bas-yón), n. (Sp. *incubacion*) incubation; hatching of eggs. Syn. *pagpapápisa ng itlóg.*

nkurable (in-ku-ra-ble), adj. (Sp. *incurable*) incurable; not curable. Syn. *di na mapagágaling, walá nang lunas.*

ndá (in-dá), n. 1. feeling of pain, tiredness, hardships, etc. Syn. *damdam.* 2. feeling of resentment. Syn. *pagdaramdám.*

ndâ (in-dâ), n. 1. a term of respect, used before the name of an old woman, as in *Indâ Juana.* Cf. *ali.* 2. grandmother. Syn. *lola.*

ndák (in-dák), n. 1. act of dancing. Syn. *sayáw, pagsayáw, pagsasayáw.* 2. movement of the body (in dancing) in accordance to the music. Syn. *galáw ng katawán sa pagsayáw.*

ndáy (in-dáy), n. (Bis.) 1. a small girl or a young woman. Syn. *inéng, nene.* 2. an affectionate address to a young woman. 3. (Fig.) girlfriend; darling. Syn. *kasintahan.*

indayog (in-da-yog), n. 1. rhythm. Syn. *ritmo.* 2. upward swing. Syn. *indayon, undayon, tabyón.*

indayon (in-da-yon), n. swing; swinging movement of a hanging object. Syn. *ugóy, pag-ugóy, undayon, tabyón.*

indelible (in-de-li-ble), adj. (Sp.) indelible. Syn. *di-napápawì, di-nabúburá.*

indemnisasyón (in-dem-ni-sas-yón), n. (Sp. *indemnizaccion*) 1. indemnification; act of paying for the damage done. Syn. *pagbabayad-pinsalà.* 2. a compensation for damage. Syn. *bayad-pinsalà.*

independénsiyá (in-de-pen-dén-si-yá), n. (Sp. *independencia*) independence; freedom (from control). Syn. *layà, kalayaan, paglayà; kasarinlán, pagsasarili.*

indesente (in-de-sen-te), adj. (Sp. *indecente*) indecent. Syn. *mahalay, masagwâ, bastós.*

indibiduwál (in-di-bi-du-wál), var. **indibidwál**, I. n. (Sp. *individual*) individual; a person. Syn. *tao, isáng tao.*
—II. adj. belonging to one person or thing. Syn. *sarili.*

indikatibo (in-di-ka-ti-bo), I. adj. (Sp. *indicativo*) 1. indicative; pointing out. Syn. *nagpápakilala.* 2. (Gram.,) indicative. Syn. *paturól.*
—II. n. (Gram.) 1. the indicative mode. Syn. *panaganong paturól.* 2. a verb in the indicative mood. Syn. *pandiwang nasa panaganong paturól.*

indignasyón (in-dig-nas-yón), n. (Sp. *indignacion*) indignation. Syn. *matindíng galit o pagkagalit.*

indigo (in-di-go), n. (Eng.) indigo; blue dye. Syn. *tinang asúl.*

indihestiyón (in-di-hes-ti-yón), n. (Sp. *indigestion*) indigestion. Syn. *impatso, di-pagkatunaw ng kinain.*

Indio (In-dio), var. **Indiyó**, n. (Sp.) name given by the Spanish colonizers to the natives of the Philippines.

indiperénsiyá (in-di-pe-rén-si-yá), n. (Sp. *indiferencia*) indifference. Syn. *pagwawalang-bahalà, kawaláng-bahalà; pagwawaláng-malasakit, kawalang-malasakit.*

indirekta (in-di-rek-ta), *adj.* (Sp. *indirecta*) indirect. Syn. *di-túwiran.*

indisé (in-di-sé), *n.* (Sp. *indice*) index. Syn. *táluntunan, talátuntunan.*

indispensable (in-dis-pen-sa-ble), *adj.* (Sp.) indispensable; absolutely necessary. Syn. *kailangang-kailangan, di-maiiwasan.*

indolénsiyá (in-do-lén-si-yá), *n.* (Sp. *indolencia*) indolence; laziness. Syn. *katamaran, kabatuganan, katigasán ng katawán (fig.).*

indulhensiyá (in-dul-hen-si-yá), *n.* (Sp. *indulgencia*) 1. too much kindness. Syn. *labis na pagbibigáy o pagpapalayaw, pagkukonsinte.* 2. excessive indulging in one's pleasure. Syn. *pagmamalabís, pagpapakalayaw, pag-aabuso.* 3. (*Eccl.*) indulgence. Syn. *pagpapatawad o kapatawarán ng kasalanan.*

indulto (in-dul-to), *n.* (Sp.) amnesty; pardon. Syn. *patawad, kapatawarán.*

industriyá (in-dus-tri-yá), *n.* (Sp. *industria*) industry; habitual employment. Syn. *gawain, hanapbuhay.*

inéng (i-néng), *var.* **iníng**, *n.* appellation for a young girl. Syn. *nene, indáy.*

inhenyeriya (in-hen-ye-ri-ya), *n.* (Sp. *ingenieria*) engineering; science, profession, or work of an engineer.

inhenyero (in-hen-ye-ro), *n.* (Sp. *ingeniero*) engineer.

inhustisya (in-hus-tis-ya), *n.* (Sp. *injusticia*) injustice. Syn. *kawaláng-katarungan.*

iniksiyón (i-nik-si-yón), *n.* (Sp. *inyeccion*) 1. act or process of injecting. Syn. *pag-iiniksiyón.* 2. the liquid for injection. Syn. *pang-iniksiyón.* 3. the part of the body where the injection was made. Syn. *pinág-iniksiyunán.*

inihaw (i-ni-haw), *adj.* cooked directly on an open fire; broiled. Syn. *iniihaw.*

iníibig (i-ní-i-big), I. *adj.* beloved; dear. Syn. *mahál, minámahál.*
—II. *n.* one's beloved; sweetheart. Syn. *mahál, kasintahan.*

iníiná (i-ní-i-ná), *n.* godmother; female sponsor. Syn. *ninang, madrina.*

inilít (i-ni-lít), I. *adj.* confiscated. Syn. *sinamsám, kinumpiska.*
—II. *v.* past tense of *ilitín.*

inimbák (i-nim-bák), I. *adj.* 1. put in storage; stored. Syn. *ibinodega, itinagò s bodega.* 2. preserved, as by packing o canning. Syn. *preserbado.*
—II. *v.* past tense of *imbakín.*

inín (i-nín), *var.* **in-in**, I. *n.* 1. act or proces of cooking rice by keeping the pot over low fire for sometime until well-cooked 2. state or quality of being well-cooke over a low fire, referring to rice. Syr *kainínán (kaín-inán).* 3. (by extension) ac of delaying action on somethin unnecessarily. Syn. *bimbín, pagbimbín.*
—II. *adj.* fully cooked; well-cooked referring to rice.

i-níp (i-níp), *n.* boredom or tiredness due t long waiting. Syn. *yamót o pagod s matagál na paghihintáy.*

i-nís (i-nís), I. *n.* 1. suffocation asphyxiation. Syn. *pangangapós n paghingá o pagkamatay dahil sa kakulangá o kawalán ng hangin.* 2. annoyance vexation; irritation. Syn. *yamót pagkayamót; suyà, pagkasuyà; galit pagkagalit.*
—II. *adj.* 1. suffocated; asphyxiated. 2 annoyed; irritated.Syn. *yamót, nayáyamó suyâ, nasúsuyà; galít, nagágalit.*

inisyatiba (i-nis-ya-ti-ba), *n.* (Sp. *iniciativa*) initiative. Syn. *kusà, pagkukusà, kakusaan sariling-kilos, sariling-palò (fig.).*

init (i-nit), *n.* 1. heat; hotness. Syn *kainitan.* 2. warmth; sultriness, as o weather. Syn. *banás, alisís, alinsangan.* 3 temperature; fever. Syn. *lagnát; sino (slight fever).* 4. intense activity intensity; excitement. Syn. *siglà kasiglahàn.* 5. ire; anger; wrath. Syn. *galit ngitngít, poót.* 6. sexual desire o excitement. Syn. *libog, kalibugan.* 7. (i animals) rut or estrus. Syn. *kandi pangangandi; landî, paglalandî.*

inó (i-nó), *n.* 1. a taking notice o something. Syn. *pansín, pagkápansín puná, pagkápuná.* 2. act of callin attention to some kind of defect, mistake etc. Syn. *pagpuná, pagpansín.*

inodoro (i-no-do-ro), *n.* (Sp.) water close toilet. Cf. *kubeta, kasilyás, pánabihan pálikuran, kumón.*

inog (i-nog), n. whirling motion; fast rotation or gyration, as of a top. Syn. *ikít, mabilís na ikot.*

i-nóm (i-nóm), n. 1. act of drinking (water, liquid, wine, etc.) Syn. *pag-inóm.* 2. act of taking a dose of medicine.

inosente (i-no-sen-te), adj. (Sp. *inocente*) 1. innocent; free from sin, guilt, or wrong; guiltless. Syn. *waláng-kasalanan.* 2. too young to know evil or sin. Syn. *musmós, waláng-malay.*

inot (i-not; i-nót), n. 1. act or manner of doing something little by little. Syn. *atay, pag-aatay-atay; utáy, pag-uutáy-utáy.* 2. act or manner of moving very slowly. Syn. *dahan, pagdadahan-dahan; hinay, paghihinay-hinay.* 3. slow motion or movement. Syn. *mabagal na kilos.*

inseguridád (in-se-gu-ri-dád), n. (Sp.) insecurity; unsafe condition. Syn. *kawaláng-tatag, kawaláng-katiyakan.*

insenso (in-sen-so), var. insiyenso, n. (Sp. *incienso*) incense. Syn. *kamanyáng, kamangyán.*

insentibo (in-sen-ti-bo), n. (Sp. *incentivo*) incentive. Syn. *pangganyák, panghikayat, pampasiglá, pang-akit.*

inseparable (in-se-pa-ra-ble), adj. (Sp.) inseparable. Syn. *di-mapaghíwaláy.*

insidente (in-si-den-te), n. (Sp. *incidente*) 1. incident; an event or happening. Syn. *pangyayari.* 2. a chance happening. Syn. *pagkakátaón, di-sinásadyáng pangyayari.*

insígniyá (in-síg-ni-yá), n. (Sp.) insignia; emblem; symbol. Syn. *sagisag.*

insineradór (in-si-ne-ra-dór), n. (Sp. *incinerador*) incinerator. Syn. *sunugán, panunog; tupukán, panupok; sígaan, panigâ.*

insinuwasyón (in-si-nu-was-yón), var. insinwasyón, n. (Sp. *insinuacion*) insinuation. Syn. *pahiwatig, pagpapahiwatig; paramdám, pagpaparamdám.*

insístensiyá (in-sís-ten-si-yá), n. (Sp. *insistencia*) insistence. Syn. *paggigiít, pagpipilit, pagpupumilit.*

insisyón (in-sis-yón), n. (Sp. *incision*) in Surg., incision. Syn. *hiwà.*

insiyenso (in-si-yen-so), var. insenso, n. (Sp. *incienso*) incense. Syn. *kamanyáng, kamangyán.*

inso (in-so; in-só), n. (Ch.) appellation for the wife of one's elder brother or male cousins. Syn. *ate, manang.* Cf. *hipag.*

insolente (in-so-len-te), adj. (Sp.) insolent; boldly rude. Syn. *pusóng, waláng-galang, waláng-pítagan.*

insómniyá (in-sóm-ni-yá), n. (Sp.; Eng.) insomnia; inability to sleep. Syn. *dipagkákatulóg, pagka-di-mákatulóg.*

inspeksiyón (ins-pek-si-yón), var. ispeksiyón, n. (Sp. *inspeccion*) inspection. Syn. *pagbibisita, pagsisiyasat.*

inspirado (ins-pi-ra-do), var. ispirado, adj. (Sp.) inspired.

inspirasyón (ins-pi-ras-yón), var. ispirasyón, n. (Sp. *inspiracion*) inspiration; any influence that induces effort to make good showing. Syn. *pampasiglá, pamukaw-siglá.*

instalasyón (ins-ta-las-yón), var. istalasyón, n. (Sp. *instalacion*) 1. installation, as of light or water connections. Syn. *pagkakabít.* 2. installation or induction of a person in office. Syn. *pagtatalagá (sa tungkulin).*

instánsiyá (ins-tán-si-yá), var. istánsiyá, n. (Sp. *instancia*) instance; example. Syn. *halimbawà.*

instigasyón (ins-tǐ-gas-yón), n. (Sp. *instigacion*) instigation. Syn. *panunulsól, pang-uudyók, pang-aapoyo.*

institusyón (ins-ti-tus-yón), n. (Sp. *institucion*) 1. institution; association. Syn. *samahán.* 2. school; college. Syn. *páaralán, koléhiyó.*

instituto (ins-ti-tu-to), n. (Sp.) institute. Syn. *surián, páaralán.*

instruksiyón (ins-truk-si-yón), istruksiyón, n. (Sp. *instruccion*) 1. teaching; instruction. Syn. *turò, pagtuturò.* 2. instruction or directions to follow. Syn. *atas, utos, tagubilin.*

instruktór (ins-truk-tór), n. (Sp. *instructor*) instructor; teacher. Syn. *maestro, gurò, tagapagturò.*

instrumento (ins-tru-men-to), var. istrumento, n. (Sp.) 1. instrument; tool; device. Syn. *kasangkapan, kagamitán.* 2. musical instrument.

insubordinasyón (in-su-bor-di-nas-yón), n. (Sp. *insubordinacion*) 1. insubordination;

resistance to authority; disobedience. Syn. *pagsuwáy o di-pagsunód sa nakatátaás.*

insulto (in-sul-to), n. (Sp.) insult. Syn. *lait, paglait; alipustâ, pag-alipustâ; upasalà, pagupasalà; paghamak.*

insupisyente (in-su-pis-yen-te), adj. (Sp. *insuficiente*) insufficient. Syn. *kulang, disapát, kapós.*

insureksiyón (in-su-rek-si-yón), n. (Sp. *insurreccion*) revolt; rebellion; insurrection. Syn. *rebelyón, pagbabangon, pag-aalsá, himagsík, rebolusyón.*

integrasyón (in-te-gras-yón), n. (Sp. *integracion*) integrating or being integrated; integration. Syn. *pag-iisá, pagsasanib.*

integridad (in-te-gri-dad), n. (Sp.) integrity; honesty; sincerity. Syn. *katapatan, pagkamatapát, sinseridád, kalinisang-budhî.* 2. honor; dignity. Syn. *dangál, karangalan.*

intelihénsiyá (in-te-li-hén-si-yá), n. (Sp. *intelegencia*) intelligence. Syn. *talino, katalinuhan.*

intensiyón (in-ten-si-yón), n. (Sp. *intencion*) 1. intention; purpose. Syn. *layon, láyunin; hangád, hángarin.* 2. plan; design. Syn. *tangkâ, pagtatangkâ, balak.*

interbensiyón (in-ter-ben-si-yón), n. (Sp. *intervención*) intervention. Syn. *pamamagitan, pakikialám.*

interbiyú (in-ter-bi-yú), n. (Eng.) interview. Syn. *panayám, pakikipanayám, pagpapanayám.*

interés (in-te-rés), n. (Sp.) 1. (*Comm.*) interest; money paid for the use of money. Syn. *tubò, patubò, pakinabang.* 2. concern; interest. Syn. *malasakit, pagmamalasakit.* 3. benefit; advantage. Syn. *kapakinabangán, kapakanán, kabutihan.* 4. inclination. Syn. *hilig, kagustuhan, pagkakagustó.*

interesado (in-te-re-sa-do), adj. (Sp.) 1. interested. Syn. *may-interés, may-gusto, nagkákagusto.* 2. prejudiced. Syn. *may-kiníkilingan, may-kinákampihán, may-pinápanigan.*

interesante (in-te-re-san-te), adj. 1. interesting. Syn. *kawili-wili, nakakáwili, nakawíwili.* 2. interested. Syn. *may-interés, interesado; may-gusto, nagkákagusto.*

intermedya (in-ter-med-ya), adj. (Sp. *intermedia*) intermediate. Syn. *panggitnâ.*

intermedyaryo (in-ter-med-yar-yo), n. (Sp. *intermediario*) intermediary. Syn. *tagapamagitan.*

intermisyón (in-ter-mis-yón), n. (Sp. *intermision*) 1. (*Theat*), interlude; intermission. Syn. *intermedyo.* 2. time between periods of activity. Syn. *pahingá, pamamahingá.*

interna (in-ter-na), n. (Sp.) 1. a boarding school female student. 2. a female intern; an assistant resident female doctor in a hospital.

internasyonál (in-ter-nas-yo-nál), adj. (Sp. *internacional*) international. Syn. *pandaigdíg.*

interno (in-ter-no), I. n. (Sp.) 1. (*masc.*) a boarding school student. 2. an intern; a doctor serving as an assistant resident in a hospital.

—II. adj. internal. Syn. *panloób.*

interogasyón (in-te-ro-gas-yón), n. (Sp. *interrogacion*) 1. interrogation; cross-examination. Syn. *pagtatanóng.* 2. a question. Syn. *tanóng, katanungan.*

interpelasyón (in-ter-pe-las-yón), n. (Sp. *interpelacion*) interpellation. Syn. *pagtanóng o pagtatanóng sa nagsásalitâ.*

interperensiyá (in-ter-pe-ren-si-yá), n. (Sp. *interferencia*) interference. Syn. *pakikialám, panghihimasok.*

interpretasyón (in-ter-pre-tas-yón), n. (Sp. *interpretacion*) 1. interpretation; explanation. Syn. *paliwanag, pagpapaliwanag.* 2. giving a meaning to. Syn. *pagpapakahulugán.* 3. the meaning as explained. Syn. *pakahulugán.*

interseksiyón (in-ter-sek-si-yón), n. (Sp. *interseccion*) intersection. Syn. *krosing, pinagkrusán, pinagsalikupan, pinagsangahán.*

interyór (in-ter-yór), I. n. (Sp. *interior*) 1. interior; inside. Syn. *loób, dakong loób.* 2. the inner rubber tube of a tire.

—II. adj. 1. inside; interior; inner; situated within. Syn. *sa loób, nasa loób, panloób.* 3. referring to the affairs within a country; domestic. Syn. *panloób.*

intimidasyón (in-ti-mi-das-yón), n. (Sp. *intimidación*) intimidation. Syn.

pagkatakot, pananakot.

intindí (in-tin-dí), n. (Sp. *entender*) 1. understanding. Syn. *unawà, pag-unawà, pagkaunawà.* 2. something one has to attend to. Syn. *trabaho, gawain.* 3. concern; care; interest. Syn. *malasakit, pagmamalasakit.*

intindido (in-tin-di-do), adj. (Sp. *entendido*) 1. clear; understood. Syn. *maliwanag, náiintindihán.* 2. able; experienced. Syn. *sanáy, may-kakayahán.* 3. well-informed; well-learned. Syn. *matalino, maraming nalalaman.*

intoksikasyón (in-tok-si-kas-yón), n. (Sp. *intoxicación*) 1. a becoming intoxicated or drunk. Syn. *pagkalasíng, pagkalangó.* 2. (Med.) a poisoning or becoming poisoned. Syn. *pagkalason.*

intolerable (in-to-le-ra-ble), adj. (Sp.) intolerable; unbearable. Syn. *di-matiís, di-matagalán, di-mabatá.*

intransitibo (in-tran-si-ti-bo), adj. (Sp. *intransitivo*) in Gram., intransitive, referring to a verb. Syn. *kátawanín.*

intriga (in-tri-ga), n. intrigue; machination; secret or under-handed plot or scheme. Syn. *pakanâ, lihim na pataksíl na pagpapasamâ sa kapwà.*

introduksiyón (in-tro-duk-si-yón), n. (Sp. *introduccion*) 1. act of introducing, as a guest speaker. Syn. *pagpapakilala.* 2. the beginning of a speech, story, etc. Syn. *simulâ, pasimulâ, pambungad, páuná.* 3. preface or foreword, often by someone other than the author. Syn. *páunáng-salitâ.*

intrusyón (in-trus-yón), n. (Sp. *intrusion*) intrusion; interference. Syn. *panghihimasok, pakikialám.*

intuwisyón (in-tu-wis-yón), n. (Sp. *intuicion*) intuition. Syn. *hinuhà, guniguní, kutób ng loób.*

inuman (i-nu-man), n. 1. drinking bout. Syn. *lásingan, paglalásingan.* 2. place for drinking liquors; counter at which alcoholic drinks are served; bar. Syn. *bar.* 3. drinking fountain. 4. drinking glass or cup.

inumin (i-nu-min), n. 1. water for drinking. Syn. *tubig-ínumin.* 2. beverage. Syn.

pamatíd-uhaw. 3. wine; any alcoholic drink. Syn. *alak.*

inunan (i-nu-nan), I. n. (Anat.) placenta. Cf. *bahay-batà.*
—II. v. past tense of *unanin.*

inundasyón (i-nun-das-yón), n. (Sp. *inundacion*) inundation; flood. Syn. *bahâ, pagbahâ.*

inutil (i-nu-til), adj. (Sp.) 1. useless; inutile. Syn. *waláng-silbi, di na magágamit, walâ nang saysáy.* 2. incapacitated; paralyzed. Syn. *lumpo, paralisado.*

inút-inót (i-nút + i-nót), adj. & adv. 1. little by little. Syn. *untí-untí, kaú-kauntî.* 2. slowly. Syn. *dahan-dahan.*

inuyat (i-nu-yat), n. a kind of taffy made by boiling sugar or molasses. Cf. *matamís sa bao, bagkát.*

inyó (in-yó), pron. (pl. of **iyó**) 1. (objective) you, as in: *Ibibigáy ko itó sa inyó.* I'll give this to you. *Sa inyó itó.* This is for you. *Sásama akó sa inyó.* I'll go with you. 2. (possessive) your; yours; as in: *Sa inyó bang bahay itó?* Is this house yours? Is this your house? 3. (honorific, poss., sing.) used in addressing an elder, a stranger, or any respected person; your or yours; as in: *Nasa inyó pô and pasiyá.* The decision is yours. *Pará sa inyó pong anák itó.* This is for your child.

ingat (i-ngat), n. 1. care; close attention. Syn. *alagà, pag-aalagà.* 2. caution; carefulness. Syn. *pag-iingat, kaingatan.* 3. certain quality that a person has. Syn. *katangian.* 4. ownership or possession of something, as of firearms. Syn. *paghahawak, pag-iingat, pagtatagláy.* 5. something that a person keeps as a possession. Syn. *arì, pag-aarì.*

ingatáng-yaman (i-nga-táng + ya-man), n. treasury. Syn. *tesorériya.*

ingat-yaman (i-ngat + ya-man), n. treasurer. Syn. *tesorero.*

ingáw (i-ngáw), n. the characteristic vocal sound made by a cat; mew. Syn. *ngiyáw.*

ingay (i-ngay), n. 1. noise. Syn. *linggál.* 2. confused shouting; clamor. Syn. *híyawan, sígawan.* 3. tumult; uproar. Syn. *guló, pagkaguló.*

ingkáng (ing-káng), *n.* act or manner of walking like a duck. Syn. *lakad na parang bibi, lakad-pato.*

ingkisisyón (ing-ki-sis-yón), *n.* (Sp. *inquisicion*) inquisition. Syn. *pagtatanóng, pagsisiyasat.*

ingkóng (ing-kóng), *n.* (Ch.) an appellation for a grandfather or any old man. Syn. *lolo, lelong.*

inggít (ing-gít), *n.* envy; resentful dislike of another who has something desirable. Syn. *hili, panaghili, pananaghili.*

Ingglatera (Ing-gla-te-ra), *n.* (Sp. *Inglatera*) England.

Ingglés (Ing-glés), var. **Inglés**, *n.* 1. Englishman. 2. the English language.

inggreso (ing-gre-so), *n.* (Sp. *ingreso*) 1. money remitted, as by a bill collector; receipts. Syn. *koleksiyón.* 2. income; revenue. Syn. *kita.* 3. credit entry in a book of account. Syn. *pasok.* 4. installment on credit. Syn. *hulog.* 5. (*Colloq.*) a part or the whole of a husband's salary given to his wife every payday. Cf. *entrega.*

ingil (i-ngil), *n.* growl or snarl, as of dogs. Cf. *ungol, angil.*

ingít (i-ngít), *n.* 1. a low whining cry, as of a baby; whimper or whimpering. Syn. *ungót, pag-ungót.* 2. creaking or grating sound, as that produced by friction. Syn. *langitngít, alatiít, agitít.* 3. a peevish, childish complaint.

ingos (i-ngos), *n.* a facial expression showing dislike, superiority, or arrogance, often accompanied by sudden turning of the head. Cf. *simangot.*

ingrato (in-gra-to), *adj.* (Sp.) 1. ungrateful. Syn. *waláng-utang-na-loób.* 2. disagreeable; unpleasant. Syn. *laban sa kalooban.*

ingusan (i-ngu-san), *v.* to show one's dislike, superior attitude, or arrogance by the sour expression of the face and sudden turning of the head. Cf. *labian, simangutan.*

ingusò (i-ngu-sò), *v.* to point someone or something by protruding out one's lips.

ipá (i-pá), *n.* chaff; husks of grains, esp. rice. Cf. *darák.*

ipa- (i-pa-), verbal prefix, meaning "to cause

something to be done or made by someone," as in *ipagawâ, ipasabi, ipatapos, ipasulat,* etc. Syn. *iutos.*

ipaká- (i-pa-ká-), verbal *prefix,* used to express full efforts in doing something, as in *ipakádiín, ipakálakás,* etc.

ipaki- (i-pa-ki-), *prefix,* used to denote a request to do or perform something, usually expressed by "please" or "kindly," as in: *Ipakibasa mo ngâ itó.* Please read this.

ipakipág- (i-pa-ki-pág-), *prefix,* meaning "to do something for a cause" or "be the cause or reason for one's involvement in:" as in *ipakipaglaban, ipakipagtalo,* etc.

ipag- (i-pag-) *pref.,* 1. to use as a means or an instrument in doing a thing, as in *ipagahit,* to use for shaving. Syn. *gamitin sa.* 2. to do or make something for someone, as in *ipaglutò ng pagkain,* to cook food for someone. 3. to be the cause or reason of, as in *ipaghihinanakít,* to be the cause or reason for one's feeling of resentment. Syn. *maging dahilán ng.*

ipagka- (i-pag-ka-), *pref.,* meaning "to cause or be the cause of," as in *ipagkámalí.*

ipagkáng- (i-pag-káng-), a verbal *pref.,* used before a word with the first syllable reduplicated, meaning "to cause or be the cause of an experience that is less expected to happen," as in *ipagkánggagalit.* Note the *ng* ending of the prefix: it becomes *m* or *n,* depending on the first letter of the word following it.

ipagpa- (i-pag-pa-), a verbal *prefix,* meaning: a) to make use of (something) for a certain purpose, as in: *Walâ siyáng kuwartáng ipagpapagamót sa anák.* He has no money to spend for the treatment of his child. b) to have something done for, as in: *Ipagpagawâ mo siyá ng baháy.* Have a house built for him.

ipagpasá- (i-pag-pa-sá-), verbal *prefix,* meaning "to leave the fate of someone or something to," as in *ipagpasá-Diyós,* to leave the fate (of a person or thing) to God.

ipáng- (i-páng-), a verbal *prefix,* used before words beginning with vowels or with consonants like **k, g, h, m,** and **nga,**

meaning to use for a certain purpose, or as an instrument or tool for doing or making something, as in *ipáng-abay*, *ipánggapos*, *ipángngalan*, etc.

ipil (i-pil), I. *n*. (*Bot*.) 1. a species of tree (*Intsia bijuga*) from which a hard, durable wood is obtained. 2. the lumber or wood obtained from this tree.

—II. *adj*. made from the wood of this tree. Syn. *yarì sa ipil*.

ipil-ipil (i-pil + i-pil), *n*. (*Bot*.) a small tree (*Leucaena glauca* L. Benth) used esp. for firewood.

ipit (i-pit), *n*. 1. act of inserting or pressing something between two things. Syn. *singit, pagsisingit, pag-iipit*. 2. clip; paper clip. Syn. *klip*. 3. hairpin; hair clip. Syn. *aguhilya, sipit*. 4. nippers; pincers; tweezers. Syn. *tiyanì*. 5. clothespin. Syn. *sipit, panipit*.

ipod (i-pod), *n*. act or manner of moving a little over to one side so as to give more space for another sitting beside. Syn. *isod, pag-isod, pag-ipod*.

ipodromo (i-po-dro-mo), *n*. (Sp. *hipodromo*) hippodrome; race track. Syn. *kárerahán*.

ipon (i-pon), *n*. 1. act of gathering or collecting things together in one place. Syn. *tipon, pagtitipon*. 2. act of gathering scattered things, as garbage, as by picking and sweeping and putting them in a heap or pile. 3. such pile or heap (of garbage). Syn. *buntón, tambák*. 4. act of saving for the future. Syn. *tipíd, pagtitipíd; impók, pag-iimpók*. 5. savings; money saved for the future. Syn. *ang inimpók o naimpók*.

ipot (i-pot), *n*. 1. the act or manner of excreting dungs, esp. among birds and fowls. Cf. *tae, pagtae; dumí, pagdumí*. 2. the dungs of birds and fowls; droppings. Syn. *dumí, tae*.

ipuipo (i-pu-i-po), var. **ipoipo**, *n*. whirlwind. Syn. *buhawì*.

ipunán (i-pu-nán), *n*. 1. place for storing; storage. Syn. *imbakan, taguán*. 2. any receptacle or container, as an ash tray, garbage can, or the like. Syn. *lalagyán, tipunán*.

iral (i-ral), *n*. 1. prevalence; widespread occurrence. Syn. *pagkalat, paglaganap, paghaharì* (*fig*.). 2. state or condition of being in effect or operative, as an ordinance or law; effectivity. Syn. *bisà, pagkakabisà*. 3. occurrence or happening. Syn. *pangyayari*. 4. predominance. Syn. *pananaíg, pangingibabaw, paghaharì*.

irap (i-rap), *n*. an angry squint or look. Syn. *sulyáp na pagalít*.

iras (i-ras), *n*. salt making. Syn. *paggawâ ng asín, pag-aasín*.

iregulár (i-re-gu-lár), *adj*. (Sp. *irregular*) 1. irregular; not according to rule, method, usage, etc. Syn. *labág, nálalabág*. 2. anomalous; abnormal. Syn. *tiwalî*. 3. not even. Syn. *bakú-bakô, lubák-lubák, dipantáy*. 4. not in accordance with the law; illegal. Syn. *labág sa batas, ilegál*.

ireguláridád (i-re-gu-lá-ri-dád), *n*. (Sp. *irregularidad*) 1. irregularity; state or condition of being contrary to rule, method, usage, etc. Syn. *kalabagán, pagkalabág*. 2. illegality. Syn. *ilegalidád, kalabagan sa batás*. 3. anomaly. Syn. *katiwalián*. 4. unevenness of surface. Syn. *pagkabakú-bakô, pagkalubák-lubák, dikapantayán*.

iresponsabilidád (i-res-pon-sa-bi-li-dád), *n*. (Sp. *irresponsabilidad*) irresponsibility. Syn. *kawaláng-pananagutan, pagkawaláng-pananagutan*.

iresponsable (i-res-pon-sa-ble), *adj*. (Sp. *irresponsable*) irresponsible. Syn. *waláng-pananagutan, di-mapagtítiwalaan*.

irí[1] (i-rí), var. **iré**, I. *pron*. this (referring to something close or near the speaker). Syn. *itó*.

—II. *interj*. Here! (used to call the attention of someone about something being pointed by the speaker near himself). Syn. *Náritó! Nanditó!*

irí[2] (i-rí), *n*. straining effort exerted in the movement of bowels or in childbirth. Syn. *dagís, pagdagís*.

irigado (i-ri-ga-do), *adj*. (Sp. *irrigado*) in Agri., irrigated. Syn. *may-patubig*.

irigasyón (i-ri-gas-yón), *n*. (Sp. *irrigacion*) 1. (*Med*.) douching; application of a douche, esp. to the vagina. Syn. *paglalabatiba*. 2. irrigation of lands. Syn.

pagpapatubig. 3. irrigated land. Syn. *patubig, tubigan.*

iríng (i-ríng), *n.* a despising; insult; hostile attitude towards another; disdainful attitude against another. Syn. *paghamak, pag-alipustâ.*

irit (i-rit), *n.* 1. act of making a high-pitched, echoic sound as a signal in the game of hide-and-seek. 2. shriek; loud, sharp, shrill sound. Syn. *tilî.*

iritasyón (i-ri-tas-yón), *n.* (Sp. *irritacion*) 1. irritation; anger. Syn. *galit, pagkagalit.* 2. annoyance; impatience. Syn. *yamót, pagkayamot; inís, pagkainís.* 3. skin irritation; itch. Syn. *katí, pangangatí.*

irog (i-rog), *n.* 1. beloved; dear one; darling. Syn. *mahál, sinta, mutyâ, giliw.* 2. strong affection for a dear one; love. Syn. *pagmamahál, pagsinta, pag-ibig.*

ironya (i-ron-ya), *n.* (Sp. *ironía*) 1. irony; something contrary to what would naturally be expected. Syn. *kabalighuán, kabalintunaan.* 2. sarcasm. Syn. *panunuyâ, pang-uuyam.*

isá (i-sá), *n.* & *adj.* one.

isá- (i-sá-), prefix meaning: a) to translate, as one language into another, as in *isá-Ingglés,* to translate into English. b) to put into, as in *isabote,* to put into a bottle; *isaisip,* to put into one's mind. c) to carry out; do; perform, as in *isagawâ, isakatuparan,* etc. d) to make something into, as in *isapelíkulá, isaaklát, isadulà,* etc.

isadiwà (i-sa-di-wà), *v.* 1. to instill in one's mind. Syn. *isaisip, itaním sa isip.* 2. to portray, as in a story. Syn. *ilarawan.*

isadlák (i-sad-lák), *v.* to force into something undesirable, as a misfortune. Syn. *ipahamak.*

isagawâ (i-sa-ga-wâ), *v.* to carry out; execute; put into realization. Syn. *isakatuparan.*

isaglít (i-sag-lít), *v.* to bring or deliver (a thing) in a minute or in a hurry. Syn. *ihatíd na madalî, isagila.*

ísahan (í-sa-han), I. *adj.* (Gram.) one in number; singular. Syn. *pang-isá.*
—II. *adv.* & *adj.* 1. one by one; one at a time; individually. Syn. *isá-isá.* 2. one after another. Syn. *sunúd-sunód.*

isahán (i-sa-hán), *v.* to make or be able to make a point against. Syn. *puntusán, malamangan, lamangan.*

isá-isá (i-sá + i-sá), *adj.* & *adv.* 1. one by one; one at a time; individually. Syn. *ísahan.* 2. one after another. Syn. *sunúd-sunód.*

isá-isahín (i-sá + i-sa-hín), *v.* 1. to do, make, count, see, etc. one by one (individually or one after another). Syn. *sunúd-sunurín.*

isaisantabí (i-sa-i-san-ta-bí), *v.* to put aside; put away. Syn. *iligpít.*

isaloób (i-sa-lo-oób), *v.* to put into one's mind; be reminded of; remember. Syn. *tandáan, alalahanín, itaním sa isip.*

isaulo (i-sa-u-lo), *v.* 1. to memorize; commit to memory. Syn. *memoryahín, sauluhin.* 2. to put into one's head; remember. Syn. *tandáan.*

isaw (i-saw), *n.* 1. intestine. Syn. *bituka.* 2. animal entrails used for food. Syn. *lamanloób.*

isip (i-sip), *n.* 1. thinking; act of thinking about something, as a means, method, or solution to a problem. Syn. *pag-isip, pag-iisíp.* 2. mind; faculty or power of understanding. Syn. *kaisipán.* 3. talent; intelligence; ability of the mind. Syn. *talino, katalinuhan; dunong, karunungan.* 4. idea; notion. Syn. *akalà, hakà.* 5. what one thinks or feels. Syn. *loób, kalooban; damdamin.* 6. opinion. Syn. *palagáy, kurúkurò.* 7. sense; common sense. Syn. *baít, sintido kumón.*

isipan (i-si-pan), *v.* to impute something bad on someone; entertain in one's mind something undesirable about someone. Syn. *pag-isipan, hinalaan, paghinalaan.*

ísipan (í-si-pan), *n.* 1. mind; thought; memory. Syn. *alaala, gunitâ.* 2. mind; faculty or power of thinking. Syn. *kaisipán.* 3. belief. Syn. *paniwalà, paniniwalà, kapaniwalaán.*

isipin (i-si-pin), *v.* 1. to think of or about (something). Syn. *alalahanin, gunitaín.* 2. to study carefully before making a decision. Syn. *pag-aralang mabuti.*

isís (i-sís), var. **is-is,** *n.* (Bot.) a small tree or shrub (*Ficus ulimifolia*), the leaves of which are utilized for polishing wood and for cleaning utensils. 2. the leaves of this tree. 3. the act of polishing wood or cleaning utensils with or as with *isís* leaves.

isla (is-la), n. (Sp.) island. Syn. *pulô.*

isláng (is-láng), n. (Eng.) slang. Syn. *balbál, salitâ o pangungusap na balbál.*

ismagler (is-mag-ler), n. (Eng.) smuggler. Syn. *kontrabandista.*

ismíd (is-míd), n. a mocking or sneering expression usually shown by puckering the lips or mouth. Cf. *libák, panlilibák.*

isod (i-sod), n. act of moving over a little to one side. Syn. *ipod, pag-ipod.*

Ispanya (Is-pan-ya), var. **Espanya,** n. (Sp. *España*) Spain.

ispeling (is-pe-ling), n. (Eng.) 1. act of spelling a word. Syn. *pagbaybáy, pagbabaybáy.* 2. the way a word is spelled; orthography. Syn. *baybáy.*

istadyum (is-tad-yum), n. (Eng.) stadium.

istambáy (is-tam-báy), I. n. (Eng. *standby*) 1. act of spending one's time unprofitably. Syn. *paglalakwatsa, pag-aansikót.* 2. a person who spends his time unprofitably; idler. Syn. *lakwatsero, taong tamád, taong ansikót.* 3. a persistent suitor. Syn. *matiyagáng manliligaw.*
—II. *adj.* 1. unemployed; not busy; idle. Syn. *waláng-trabaho, waláng-hanapbuhay.* 2. not inclined to work; lazy. Syn. *tamád, batugan, matigás ang katawán.* 3. inactive; not being used, as machines. Syn. *dinágamit.*

istorya (is-tor-ya), n. (Sp. *historia*) 1. story; tale. Syn. *kuwento, salaysáy.* 2. history. Syn. *kasaysayan.* 3. rumor; gossip. Syn. *tsismís.*

istoryadór (is-tor-ya-dór), n. (Sp. *historiador*) 1. story teller. Syn. *ang nagkúkuwento o nagsásalaysáy.* 2. story writer. Syn. *kuwentista, mángunguwento.* 3. historian. Syn. *mánanaysáy.*

iswád (is-wád), I. *adj.* 1. referring to a person with or having prominent buttocks or rump. Syn. *tuwád o nakatuwád ang puwít.* 2. with the side or end tilted upward. Syn. *baliskád, nakabaliskád; tiwás, nakatiwás; tikwás, nakatikwás.*
—II. n. 1. act or manner of protruding out one's buttocks or rump. Syn. *pag-*

iswád, pagtuwád. 2. state or condition of being prominent, referring to a person's buttocks or rump.

isyu (is-yu), n. *(Eng.)* 1. issue, as of a magazine, newspaper, etc. Syn. *lathalà, labás, bilang.* 2. issue (in a debate). Syn. *paksáng pinagtátalunan.* 3. subject matter or question being presented, as in an election.

It (It), *interj.* shrill, echoic sound made as a signal in the game of hide-and-seek.

Ita (I-ta), n. *(Anthrop.)* a member of a minority mountain tribe in the Philippines called Negrito.

itaás (i-ta-ás), I. *v.* 1. to raise; lift. Syn. *iangat, angatín.* 2. to raise or increase, as prices. Syn. *mahalán, pamahalín.* 3. to raise or increase the volume; make loud or louder. Syn. *ilakás.* 4. to promote, as an employee. Syn. *iasenso.* 5. to put on top of something. Syn. *ipatong, ipaibabaw.* 6. to pull upward. Syn. *bataking paitaás.* 7. to cause (an airplane) to go higher. Syn. *pataasín.*
—II. n. 1. upstairs. 2. top, as of a hill or mountain. Syn. *tuktók, ituktók, taluktók.* 3. high position, as in *mga taong nasa itaás*, people in high positions. 4. the vast space above. Syn. *papawirín.* 4. heaven. Syn. *langit.*

iták (i-ták), n. bolo; machete. Syn. *gulok, tabák.*

italagá (i-ta-la-gá), *v.* 1. to destine to a certain fate. Syn. *itadhanà.* 2. to assign (an employee) to work in a certain place or office. Syn. *idestino.* 3. to set aside for a certain purpose; make available for. Syn. *ilaán, iukol.* 4. to induct or install into office, as officers of an association. Syn. *papanumpaín sa tungkulin.*

itálikó (i-tá-li-kó), I. *adj.* (Sp. *itálico*) italic.
—II. n. italics; an italic type or print.

Italya (I-tal-ya), n. (Sp. *Italia*) Italy.

itaós (i-ta-ós), *v.* to cause (a thing) to penetrate fully into an object. Syn. *itagós, ilalós.*

itapá (i-ta-pá), *v.* 1. to cure (fish, meat, etc.) by smoking. 2. to make dry by exposing near a fire, as firewood. Syn. *idaráng.*

iti (i-ti), n. (Med.) dysentery. Syn. daragís, disentiryá.

itik (i-tik), n. (Zool.) a species of duck, usually raised for their eggs that are made into balút and penoy. Cf. pato.

itik-itik (i-tik + i-tik), n. a kind of folk dance the movement of which is patterned from the manner a duck moves.

itím (i-tím), n. 1. black (color). 2. (Colloq.) a Negro. 3. black clothes; mourning clothes. Syn. luksâ, damít-panluksâ.

itindíg (i-tin-díg), v. 1. to help a person to stand up. Syn. itayô. 2. to set up or place (a thing) in a standing position. Syn. itirik, itayô. 3. to adjourn, as a meeting or session. Syn. ipinid. 4. to construct; build. Syn. itayô, itirik. 5. (Fig.) to restore, for example, the honor of a woman whom one has abused, by marrying her. Syn. ibangon (ang puri), pakasalán.

itineraryo (i-ti-ne-rar-yo), n. (Sp. itinerario) 1. itinerary; route to be taken in a trip. Syn. ruta o mga dádaanán sa paglalakbáy. 2. plan of a journey. Syn. balak patunguhan sa paglalakbáy.

itlóg (it-lóg), var. **iklóg**, n. 1. egg. 2. act of laying eggs. Syn. pag-itlóg, pangingitlóg. 3. (Colloq.) testicle; testís. Syn. bayág, beklog (colloq.).

itó (i-tó), pron. this. Cf. iré (irí).

itsá (it-sá), n. (Sp. echar) 1. act of throwing away (something). Syn. pagtatapon. 2. act of throwing (a thing) at someone. Syn. hagis, paghagis; pukól, pagpukól. 3. in basketball, act or manner of shooting a ball into the basket. 4. in baseball, act or manner of pitching the ball to the batter. Syn. hagis, paghagis.

ituktók (i-tuk-tók), I. n. top; summit; topmost part, as of a mountain. Syn. taluktók, tugatog, rurok.
—II. v. to use for knocking on a door, table top, etc. Syn. ikatók.

iuna (i-u-na), v. 1. to put or place (a person or thing) at the head of a line; bring or take to the front. Syn. ilagáy sa una o unahán. 2. to do or make (a thing) ahead of another or others. Syn. unahin, gawíng una sa lahát.

iwà (i-wà), n. 1. act of inflicting a wound

with or as with a knife. Cf. saksák, pagsaksák. 2. a deep cut or wound inflicted with or as with a knife. Syn. saksák, sugat ng patalím.

iwan (i-wan), v. 1. to leave (a person or thing) behind. Syn. di-isama, di-dalhín, umalís nang di-dalá o di-kasama. 2. to let alone; abandon; forsake. Syn. bayaan, pabayaan, layasan. 3. to get away from. Syn. lisanin, layuán. 4. to desert or divorce. Syn. hiwalayán. 5. to leave behind, as in a race. Syn. lampasán.

iwanan (i-wa-nan), v. to leave something to someone before going away. Syn. mag-iwan.

iwang (i-wang), n. act of cleaning the anus with or as with toilet paper after moving the bowels. Syn. pagpapahid sa puwít pagkatapos tumae.

iwas (i-was), n. 1. avoidance; keeping away from. Syn. ilag, pag-ilag; layô, paglayô. 2. keeping out of the way to avoid direct collision or hitting something. Syn. lihís, paglihís; ilag, pag-ilag.

iwi (i-wi), n. 1. possession or acquisition, as of talent, beauty, etc. Syn. angkín, pag-aangkín; tagláy, pagtatagláy. 2. anything possessed. Syn. arì, pag-aarì. 3. act of nursing, rearing, or bringing up, as of a child. Syn. alagà, pag-aalagà. 4. the practice in which a person takes care of someone's animal and gets half of the offsprings as his share. 5. the animal taken care of for someone.

iya (i-ya), n. 1. relinquishment, as of one's right in favor of another. Syn. ubayà, pagpapaubayà; parayâ, pagpaparayâ. 2. full enjoyment or satisfaction.

iyák (i-yák), n. 1. cry; act of crying. Syn. pagluhà. 2. cry or bleat of a sheep or goat. Syn. mê, meê. 3. cry of a calf. Syn. ungâ, ungal.

iyán (i-yán), pron. & adj. that (referring to a person or thing being pointed nearer someone than to speaker).

iyáng-iyán (i-yáng + i-yán), adj. & pron. referring to something that cannot be mistaken for the object referred to. Syn. talagáng iyán.

iyó (i-yó), pron. (used prepositively in the

second person singular number) your;
yours.

iyók (i-yók), n. sudden shriek or sharp sound
coming from the partially clogged throat
of fowls. Syn. *siyók*.

iyón (i-yón), pron. & adj. that (referring to
something far both from the speaker and
the person addressed). See *iyán*.

iyúng-iyó (i-yúng + i-yó), pron. definitely
yours.

iyúng-iyón (i-yúng + i-yón), (Id.) no doubt
about it (that); it's really the thing.

L

L, l (la), n. the ninth letter of the *abakada*
(Pilipino alphabet.). 2. the type or
impression representing this letter. 3. a
symbol for the ninth in a group or series.

la¹ (la), n. the sixth note in the musical
scale.

la² (la), n. the name and pronunciation of
the letter L in Pilipino.

La³ (La), interj. an utterance used in
directing an animal, esp. carabao, to stop.
Cf. *Ho!* (for horses). *Han!* (for cows).

laab (la-ab; la-áb), n. brilliant mass of flame;
blaze; spreading flame or fire. Syn. *liyáb*;
alab, malakíng ningas.

laán (la-án), adj. 1. prepared or ready, as for
voluntary service. Syn. *handâ, nákahandâ,
náhahandâ*. 2. in reserve; intended or
reserved for the future or for someone.
Syn. *reserbado, nakareserba, nakalaán,
patagana*.

laáng (la-áng), colloq. var. of **lamang**, adv.
no more than; only; just, as in *isá laáng*,
just one.

laáng-gugulín (la-áng + gu-gu-lín), n. sum
of money set aside for some special
purpose; fund; appropriation; budget.
Syn. *pondo, nakatalagáng-gugulín,
presupuwesto, apropriyasyón*.

laba (la-ba), n. (Eng.) lava; volcanic lava.

labá (la-bá), n. (Sp. *lavar*) 1. act or process
of washing clothes with soap and water.
Syn. *paglalabá*. 2. the quality by which
clothes were washed. Syn. *pagkakálabá*.

lababo (la-ba-bo), n. (Sp. *lavabo*) lavatory;
washstand. Cf. *hugasán, hínawan,
hílamusán*.

labák (la-bák), n. 1. lowland. Syn. *kababaan,
kapatagan*. 2. the lower portion of a river
(in contrast with the origin or source).
Ant. *hulò*.

labakara (la-ba-ka-ra), n. (Sp. *lava cara*)
small face towel. Syn. *bimpo, tuwalyáng
pangmukhâ*.

labada (la-ba-da), n. (Sp. *lavado*) clothes to
be laundered; laundry. Syn. *mga damít na
lábahin*.

labág (la-bág), I. adj. 1. contrary or against
the law; unlawful; illegal; illicit. Syn.
ilegál, laban sa batás. 2. against; contrary
to, as in *labág sa kaloobán*, against one's
will.
—II. n. 1. a breaking or violation, as of a
law; infraction; infringement. Syn.
paglabág. 2. fact, state, or condition of
being illegal or violative of law. Syn.
ilegalidád.

labaha (la-ba-ha), n. (Sp. *navaja*) razor;
shaver. Syn. *labasa, pang-ahit*.

lábahin (la-ba-hin), n. & adj. referring to
dirty clothes for washing or laundry. Syn.
lalabhín.

labahita (la-ba-hi-ta), n. (Sp. *lavajita*) 1.
(Ichth.) blue-lined surgeon fish
(*Acanthurus bleekeri Gunther*). 2. (Colloq.)
a small pocket-knife; penknife. Syn.
munting lanseta (laseta).

laban (la-ban), I. n. 1. fight; quarrel. Syn.
away, awayán, basag-ulo. 2. match;
contest; game. Syn. *larô, páligsahan*. 3. a
going against; opposition. Syn. *tutol,
pagtutol; kontra, pagkontra*. 4. fact or
condition of being against or
contradictory. Syn. *salungát,
pagkasalungát, kasalungatán*.
—II. adj. against; contrary; opposed. Syn.
kontra, salungát, kasalungát.

labanán (la-ba-nán), n. 1. fight; fighting;
conflict. Syn. *away, awayán*. 2. battle; war.
Syn. *digmâ, digmaan, gera*. 3. contest;
game; competition. Syn. *páligsahan*.

labandera (la-ban-de-ra), n. (Sp. *lavandera*)
laundrywoman; washerwoman; laundress.
Syn. *babaing maglalaba*.

lábanós   **labò**

lábanós (lá-ba-nós), var. labanós. (Sp.
rábaho) 1. radish plant. 2. the edible,
pungent rootstock of this plant eaten raw
as a relish or in a salad.

labangán (la-ba-ngán), n. feeding tub or
trough for animals, esp. pigs and horses.
Cf. sabsaban, pákaínán.

labás (la-bás), I. n. 1. outside; area or place
outside a house, building, etc.; outdoors;
out-of-doors. Ant. loób. 2. the outer side
or surface. Syn. ibabaw. 3. dismissal, as of
students from school, or of workers from
their place of work. Syn. uwî, pag-uwî,
úwian. 4. time of dismissal (of students,
workers, etc.). Syn. oras ng úwian o
lábasan. 5. outflow; passing out, as of water
from a faucet. Syn. tulò, bugá. 6. coming
out or issue, as of a magazine. Syn. lathalà,
paglalathalà. 7. discharge, as of blood, pus,
etc. Syn. agos, daloy, agsawa. 8. a coming
out, as from hiding; appearance. Syn.
litáw, paglitáw; sipót, pagsipót. 9. showing
or presentation, as of a play. Syn. tanghál,
pagtatanghál. 10. part or role of an actor,
as in play. Syn. parte, papél (colloq.). 11.
a show or film being presented or shown.
Syn. palabas. 12. schedule of program.
Syn. palatuntunan, programa.

lábasan (lá-ba-san), n. 1. a way out; exit.
Syn. salidá, daáng palabás. 2. simultaneous
exit or going out, as of a number of people
from a showhouse. Syn. paglalabasan, pag-
uuwián. 3. dismissal or time of dismissal,
as of students or workers. Syn. úwian, pag-
uuwián. 4. sudden appearance in great
numbers, as of ants. Syn. lítawán,
paglilítawan.

labás-pasok (la-bás + pa-sok), I. n. act of
going inside and then out again
repeatedly or for several times. Syn. paulit-
ulit na pagpasok at paglabás.

—II. adj. & n. referring to a prisoner who
is repeatedly confined and released from
prison.

labatiba (la-ba-ti-ba), n. 1. the apparatus
used for giving an enema. Syn.
panlabatiba, sumpít, panumpít. 2. the liquid
preparation given as enema; clyster. 3. the
injection of such a liquid. Syn.
paglabatiba, paglalabatiba.

labatoryo (la-ba-tor-yo), n. (Sp. lavatorio)
lavatory. Syn. lababo.

labay (la-bay), n. leafiness; luxuriant
foliage. Syn. yabong, kayabungan;
kadahunan, pagkamadahon.

labì (la-bì), n. 1. either of the two fleshy folds
forming the edges of the mouth; lip. 2.
the edge or projecting rim, as of a pitcher,
drinking glass, cup, and the like. Syn. gilid
ng bibíg. 3. brink or edge, as of a ravine,
etc. Syn. bingit, gilid.

labí (la-bí), n. 1. surplus; overplus; excess.
Syn. sobra, labis. 2. remainder; leftover;
remnant. Syn. tirá. 3. the dead body of a
person; remains. Syn. bangkáy.

labian (la-bi-an), v. to pout at (someone or
something); express one's sullenness or
displeasure by pursing the lips.

labintadór (la-bin-ta-dór), var. labíntadór,
n. (Sp. reventador) firecracker. Syn.
paputók.

labíng- (la-bíng-), pref. used to denote
numbers in excess of 10 to 19. The
variants labim- is used before roots
beginning with b and p, and labin- before
roots beginning with d, l, r, s, or t.

labis (la-bis), I. n. 1. surplus; overplus;
excess. Syn. sobra. 2. remainder; leftover.
Syn. tirá.

—II. adj. excessive; more than enough.
Syn. sobra.

labnák (lab-nák). n. state or quality of being
soft and tasteless, referring esp. to
overcooked tubers. Cf. labsâ.

labnáw (lab-náw), n. thinness, as of liquids.
Ant. lapot.

labnós (lab-nós), I. n. 1. state or condition
of being flayed or excorticated, referring
to skin which is burnt or scalded. Syn.
lapnós. 2. the part of the skin which has
been flayed or decorticated.

—II. adj. flayed or excorticated, said of
skin that has been burnt or scalded.

labnót (lab-nót), I. n. sudden snatch,
grabbing, uprooting, or plucking of grass,
hair, feathers, etc. with or as with the
hand or mouth. Cf. bunot, ganot, gabot.

labò (la-bò), n. 1. turbidity (or water or
liquid). Ant. linaw, kalinawan. 2. dimness,
as of light. Syn. lamlám, kalamlamán; dilím,

labó

lakás

kadilimán. Ant. *liwanag*. 3. dimness, as of eyesight. 4. ambiguity or obscurity, as the meaning of a word. Syn. *kahirapang unawain*. 5. lack of proper inking or coloring, as in print. Syn. *pusyáw o kapusyawán (ng kulay)*. 6. uncertainty; unreliability; doubtfulness. Syn. *kawaláng-katiyakan*. 7. lack of understanding. Syn. *di-pagkauñawá*.

labó (la-bó), n. 1. sponginess, as of earth or soil. Syn. *yabó*. 2. mellowness to the taste, as of some fruits and tubers.

labóg (la-bóg), *adj*. 1. excessively soft or tender due to overcooking. Syn. *masyadong malambót dahil sa labis na pagkalutò*.

labóng (la-bóng), n. 1. the young, tender shoot of bamboo. Syn. *usbóng ng kawayan*. 2. a dish or food made from this shoot.

labór (la-bór), n. (Sp.) 1. intricate, artistic design, as on embroidery work. Cf. *burda*. 2. decorative carving, as on picture frames, cabinets, etc. Syn. *ukit o nakaukit na dekorasyón*. 3. decoration in general. Syn. *palamuti, dekorasyón*.

laboratoryo (la-bo-ra-tor-yo), n. (Sp. *laboratorio*) laboratory. Syn. *esperimentuhan*.

laboy (la-boy), n. a roaming or wandering around; vagrancy; vagabondage. Syn. *paghahampas-lupà, pagbabagamundo*.

labrá (lab-rá), n. (Sp. *labrar*) 1. act of shaping or reducing the size of wood, marble, etc. by hewing or chopping. Cf. *tabtáb, pagtabtáb, pagtatabtáb*. 2. the part or portion of a big piece of wood, etc. cut or shaped by hewing or chopping.

labradór (la-bra-dór), n. (Sp.) woodcutter or stonecutter.

labsâ (lab-sâ), n. over softness and tastelessness of food due to overcooking or being watery, esp. rice. Cf. *labsák*.

labsák (lab-sák), n. extreme softness or stickiness of food due to overcooking, or of fruits due to being overripe.

labulabo (la-bu-la-bo), n. a free-for-all fight; brawl. Syn. *magulóng awayán, suntukan, labanán o bugbugan ng marami*.

labusak (la-bu-sak), n. prodigality; reckless spending; abundant generosity or liberality. Syn. *kabulagsakán,*

pagkamapaglustáy, kagastadurán.

labusaw (la-bu-saw), n. 1. act of stirring (with the feet, hands, etc.) the bottom of a pond or pool, thus making the water muddy or turbid. Syn. *labog*. 2. fickleness; capriciousness.

labuyò (la-bu-yò), n. 1. wild chicken; jungle fowl (*Gallus gallus*). 2. a variety of wild pepper plant or its small, many-seeded, hot fruit. Also called *siling-labuyò*.

lakad (la-kad), I. n. 1. walk; act or manner of walking. Syn. *paglakad, paglalakád*. Cf. *hakbáng, paghakbáng*. 2. departure; act of leaving or going to a certain place. Syn. *alís, pag-alís; yao, pagyao*. 3. mission; errand or purpose in going to a certain place. Syn. *misyón, sadyâ, pakay*. 4. act of approaching someone, as in seeking approval or favorable action on certain matters. 5. trend or progress, as of business, political campaign, etc. Syn. *takbó (fig.), progreso*. 6. running or working condition, as of engine, motor, or machine. Syn. *takbó, andár*.

—II. *interj*. (L-) Go! Go ahead! Syn. *Sige! Tulóy! Alís!*

lakambini (la-kam-bi-ni), n. 1. (*Otag*.) goddess. Syn. *diyosa*. 2. muse. Syn. *musa, diwatà, paraluman*. 3. a Tagalog feminine name.

lakán (la-kán), n. 1. a title of nobility used by the early Filipinos. 2. nobleman; man of noble rank, title, or birth. Syn. *mahál na tao, dakilang tao*. 3. chief or chieftain of a clan or tribe during the pre-Spanish era. Cf. *datú*.

lakán- (la-kán-); prefix, meaning a) chief or chieftain, as in *Lakan-dula*; b) charming and beautiful, hence, source of inspiration, as in *Lakambini*. Note the change of *lakán* to *lakám*.

lakandiwà (la-kan-di-wà), n. poet moderator or judge in a poetical debate or joust.

lakás (la-kás), n. 1. physical strength; vigor. Syn. *puwersa*. 2. power; influence; might. Syn. *kapangyarihan, impluwénsiyá*. 3. healthiness, as of one's body. Syn. *lusog, kalusugán*. 4. loudness, as of voice, music, etc. Syn. *tunóg, katunugán*. 5. efficacy; effectiveness. Syn. *bisà, kabisaan*. 6.

intensity or highness, as of temperature or fever. Syn. *taás, kataasán*. 7. velocity or speed, as of a running vehicle. Syn. *tulin, bilís*. 8. intensity or force, as of blow. Syn. *tindi, katindihán*. 9. durability or endurance, as of one's body. Syn. *tibay, katibayan*. 10. heaviness, as of rain. Syn. *tindí*. 11. fastness, as of sales. Syn. *kabilihán, pagkamabilí*. 12. bigness, as of one's income. Syn. *lakí, kalakihán*. 13. intensity, as of anger. Syn. *sidhî, silakbó, tindí*. 14. (with *ng loób*) daringness; fearlessness. Syn. *tapang, katapangan, kapangahasán*.

lakás-loób (la-kás + lo-ób), I. n. courage; bravery; daringness; fearlessness. Syn. *tapang, katapangan; kawaláng-takot*.
   —II. *adv*. without fear; fearlessly; daringly; bravely; courageously. Syn. *nang waláng-takot, nang buô ang loób*.

lakatán (la-ka-tán), n. (Bot.) 1. a variety of banana plant, the fruit of which, when ripe, are yellowish and sweet. 2. the fruit of this plant.

lakbáy (lak-báy), n. travel; trip; journey. Syn. *biyahe, pagbibiyahe*.

lakdáw (lak-dáw), n. step; movement of feet in walking. Syn. *hakdáw, hakbáng*. 2. a skipping over; omission.

laker (la-ker), n. (Eng.) a chest; small closet or cupboard; locker.

laket (la-ket), n. (Eng.) locket.

lakí (la-kí), n. 1. growth, as of plants. Syn. *tubò, pagtubò*. 2. size; dimension; measure or measurement. Syn. *sukat*. 3. bigness; largeness; bulk, bulkiness. Syn. *kalakihán, pagkamalakí*. 4. vastness; extensiveness. Syn. *lawak, kalawakan*. 5. numerousness; greatness, as of amount. Syn. *dami, karamihan*. 6. bigness, as of one's income. Syn. *lakás* (colloq.). 7. wideness, as of a room. Syn. *luwáng, kaluwangán*. 8. high tide; highness of water level. Syn. *taog, taás (ng tubig)*. 9. (Colloq.) greatness. Syn. *kadakilaan, kabantugan*.

lakip (la-kip), n. inclusion of something, as along with a letter in an envelop. Syn. *sama, pagsasama*. 2. something enclosed, as along a letter in an envelop; enclosure. Syn. *ang kalakip o kasama*.

lakí-sa-layaw (la-kí + sa + la-yaw), *adj*. pampered while still young.

laklák (lak-lák), n. 1. act or manner of drinking or gulping liquids noisily and hurriedly, as a dog does. Cf. *lagók, paglagók*. 2. excessive drinking. Syn. *labis na pag-inóm ng alak*.

lakò (la-kò), 1. n. act of selling merchandise by going from place to place; peddling. Syn. *paglalakò*. 2. things being peddled or sold from place to place. Syn. *ang bagay na inilalakò o ipinagbíbilí ng maglalakô*.
   —II. *adj*. referring to goods being sold by a peddler.

lakre (lak-re), n. (Sp. *lacre*) sealing wax.

laksâ (lak-sâ), n. & *adj*. ten thousand. Syn. *sampúng libo*.

laksante (lak-san-te), n. & *adj*. (Sp. *laxante*) laxative. Syn. *laksatiba, panunaw*. Cf. *purga, pamurga*.

laktáw (lak-táw), n. 1. act or manner of stepping or skipping over (a low barrier). Syn. *hakbáng, paghakbáng*. 2. a skipping over; omission. Syn. *palyo, pagpalyo*. 3. that which is omitted or overlooked.

lakuwatsa (la-ku-wat-sa), var. **lakwatsa**, n. (Sp. *lacuacha*) act of playing truant; truancy. Syn. *bulakból, pagbubulakból*.

ladlád (lad-lád), I. n. 1. an unfolding, unfurling, or unrolling, as of a mat, flag, or the like. Syn. *kadkád, bukadkad*. 2. state or condition of being unfolded, unfurled, or unrolled. 3. act of spreading out something on a surface, as a mat on the floor. Syn. *latag, paglalatag*.
   —II. *adj*. unfolded, unfurled, unrolled, or spread out. Syn. *nakakadkád, nakalatag*.

ladó (la-dó), n. a species of orange plant that bears thick-skinned fruits with juicy, sweet pulp when ripe. 2. the fruit of this plant.

ladrilyo (la-dril-yo), n. (Sp. *ladrillo*) brick; tile. Syn. *tisà*.

lagà (la-gà), n. act of cooking or boiling (meat, eggs, corn, sweet potatoes, etc.) in water.

lagablàb (la-gab-làb), n. 1. burst of flame; big blaze. Syn. *malakíng liyáb*. 2. a big fire; conflagration. Syn. *malakíng sunog*.

lagak¹ (la-gak), n. 1. act of depositing

(money) in a bank. Syn. *deposito o pagdideposito*. 2. money deposited in a bank. Syn. *deposito, kuwaltáng nasa bangko*. 3. act of putting or placing something temporarily on a certain place. Syn. *lagáy o paglalagáy na pansamantalá*. 4. act of leaving something temporarily in the care of someone. Syn. *habilin, paghahabilin*.

agak² (la-gak), n. 1. bail; bond. Syn. *piyansa*. 2. pledge; security. Syn. *garantiyá, prenda*. 2. mortgage. Syn. *sanglâ*.

agalág (la-ga-lág), I. adj. 1. well-traveled. Syn. *libót, mapaglibót, mapaglakbáy*. 2. nomadic; wandering from place to place. Syn. *palaboy, layás, pagalà*.

—II. n. vagrant rover. Syn. *taong layás, taong libót*.

agamák (la-ga-mák), adj. 1. long bedridden. Syn. *matagál na nakaratay sa baníg*. 2. helplessly prostrate. Syn. *handusáy, nakahandusáy; lugmók, nakalugmók*. See **lagmák**.

aganap (la-ga-nap), I. n. fact, state, or condition of being widespread. Syn. *kalaganapan*.

—II. adj. 1. widespread; occurring in many places; covering an extensive territory. Syn. *kalát, kalát na kalát*. 2. very common. Syn. *palasak, karaniwan, uso*.

agapák (la-ga-pak), n. 1. a sudden, heavy fall on the floor or ground, esp. of a big, flat body, causing an abrupt, loud noise. Syn. *malakás na bagsák*. 2. the abrupt, loud noise thus created. Cf. *kalabóg*. 3. (*Fig.*) miserable failure, as in an examination. Syn. *lubós na pagkabigô*.

agarì (la-ga-rì), n. (*Carp.*) 1. saw 2. act or manner of using a saw. Syn. *paglagarì, paglalagarì*.

ágarián (lá-ga-ri-án), n. place where lumber sawing is done; sawmill. Syn. *tistisan ng tablá*.

agas (la-gas), n. 1. a falling off, as of leaves, petals, fruits, etc. Syn. *laglág, panlalaglág*. 2. a falling out, as of hair or feathers. Syn. *lugon, panlulugon*. 3. (*Fig.*) loss, as of lives among a group of soldiers in combat.

agaslás (la-gas-lás), n. 1. swift flow or current of water over the rapids or in a shallow part of a river. Syn. *mabilís na agos ng tubig*. 2. the sound of swift flowing water, as over rapids. Syn. *lagasaw*.

lagaták (la-ga-ták), n. sound produced by the sudden lifting or withdrawal of the tip of the tongue from the palate or upper roof of the mouth; any similar sound. Cf. *palaták*.

lagáy (la-gáy), n. 1. act of putting or placing something on a certain place, as on a table. Syn. *patong, pagpapatong*. 2. act of putting something in a container. Syn. *silíd, pagsisilíd; salin, pagsasalin*. 3. act of depositing (money), as in a bank. Syn. *deposito o pagdedeposito*. 4. the manner by which a thing is placed or set up; position. Syn. *pagkakalagáy, ayos, pagkakaayos*. 5. state or condition. Syn. *kalagayan, kondisyón, katayuan*. 6. place; location; situation. Syn. *lugár, puwesto*. 7. unit of size, as of land; lot; piece. Syn. *lote, piraso*. 8. (*Fig.*) bribe or bribery. Syn. *suhol, pagsusuhol; parating o pagpaparatíng (fig.)*. 9. position. Syn. *tungkulin*. 10. appearance. Syn. *itsura, anyô*. 11. in gambling, bet. Syn. *tayâ, pusta*.

lagkít (lag-kít), n. stickiness; adhesiveness; viscosity. Syn. *kalagkitán, kadigkitán*.

lagdâ (lag-dâ), n. 1. act of signing one's name in a letter, article, document, or the like. Syn. *pagpirma, paglagdâ*. 2. signature. Syn. *pirma*. 3. decision, as of a court. Syn. *pasiyá, kapasiyahan; hatol, kahatulán*. 4. a provision or provisions, as of a law or ordinance. Syn. *tadhanâ*. 5. order, as of a court. Syn. *utos, kautusán*. 6. an imprint or mark, as of a kiss. Syn. *taták, marká*.

lagì (la-gì), I. adv. always; all the time; at all times. Syn. *parati, pirmi*.

—II. n. act of staying more or less permanently in a certain place. Also, *pamamalagì*.

lagím (la-gím), n. (also **lagim**) 1. gloom; profound sorrow or sadness. Syn. *matindíng lungkót o lumbáy; pighatî, pamimighatî*. 2. dread; terror. Syn. *takot, pagkatakot*.

laginít (la-gi-nít), n. 1. noise of the crack or a long whip. Syn. *haginít, lagitík*. 2. the creaking sound as that produced when a tight nut is being unscrewed with a wrench. Syn. *lagitlít*.

laging- (la-ging-), a combining form (fr. *lagì*), meaning "always," as in *laging-handâ*, *laging-tulóg*, etc.

lagitík (la-gi-tík), n. sharp creaking sound, as that of a long whip. Syn. *laginít*, *haginít*.

laglág (lag-lág), I. n. 1. fall, as of fruits from a tree. Syn. *lagpák*, *paglagpák*; *hulog*, *pagkahulog*. 2. act of dropping something from a height. Syn. *paglalagpák*, *paghuhulog*. 3. failure, as in an examination. Syn. *di-pagpasá*; *hulog*, *pagkahulog*; *lagpák*, *pagkalagpák*.
  —II. adj. 1. fallen, referring to fruits, leaves, etc. Syn. *lagpák*. 2. with or having failing grade or grades; unsuccessful, as in an examination. Syn. *hulóg*, *bagsák*, *dipumasá*.

laglág-luksâ (lag-lág + luk-sâ), n. the practice of ending the period of mourning for a dead family member by starting to wear ordinary clothes instead of black ones. Syn. *babang-luksâ*.

lagmák (lag-mák), I. n. state or condition of being helplessly prostrate or bedridden.
  —II. adj. helplessly prostrate or bedridden. Syn. *lugmók*, *nakalugmók*.

lagnát (lag-nát), n. (Med.) fever. Cf. *sinat o saynat* (slight fever).

lagô (la-gô), n. 1. growth, as of plants. Syn. *tubò*, *pagtubò*. 2. luxuriant growth. Syn. *yabong*, *pagyabong*; *lambâ*, *paglambâ*. 3. progress; development or growth, as of business. Syn. *unlád*, *pag-unlád*, *progreso*.

lagók (la-gók), n. 1. act or manner of gulping water or liquid. Cf. *lulón*, *lunók*. 2. the amount of water or liquid gulped at one time.

lagom (la-gom), n. 1. gathering of things together; collection. Syn. *tipon*, *pagtitipon*. 2. a summing up. Syn. *pagbuô*, *pagbubuô*, *pagsasama-sama*. 3. summary; résumé. Syn. *buód*, *kabuurán*. 4. act of summarizing. Syn. *pagbubuód*, *paglalagom*. 5. monopoly. Syn. *monopolyo*.

lagós (la-gós), var. **lag-os**, I. n. 1. act of passing through and through, as though a tunnel. Syn. *lampás*, *paglampás*; *lusót*, *paglusót*. 2. penetration or piercing

through from side to side. Syn. *tagó* *pagtagós*.
  —II. adj. passing or piercing through an through. Syn. *lampás*, *lusót*, *tagós*.

lagót (la-gót), I. n. 1. act of cutting o breaking of a rope, cable, string, or th like. Syn. *patíd*, *pagpatíd*; *putol*, *pagputo* 2. a sudden cut or snap, as of a rope, wir cable, etc. Syn. *patíd*, *pagkapatíd*; *puto pagkaputol*. 3. state or condition of bein cut off, as a rope, cable, wire, etc. sudden stop. Syn. *biglâng hintô pagkápahintô*.
  —II. adj. 1. cut or severed; broke disconnected; snapped off. Syn. *patí putól*. 2. put to a stop. Syn. *hintô*, *inihint*

lagpák (lag-pák), I. n. fall; collapse. Sy *bagsák*, *hulog*. 2. failure, as in a examination. Syn. *di-pagpasá*, *pagkahulo bagsák*, *pagbagsák*. 3. downfall. Syr *pagkabigô*.
  —II. adj. 1. fallen, as fruits from a tree Syn. *bagsák*, *bumagsák*. 2. with or havin a failing grade or grades; unsuccessful, a in an examination. Syn. *di-pumasá*, *d pasado*. *bagsák*, *bumagsák*.

lagpás (lag-pás), I. n. 1. act of going over o beyond a certain point or place. Syn *lampás*, *paglampás*. 2. act of passin through a place without being noticed Syn. *pagdaán o paglampás nang d nápapansín*. 3. penetration or piercing o something from one side to another. Syn *tagós*, *pagtagós*; *lagós*, *paglagós*. 4. surpassing or being surpassed. Syn. *higít paghigít*. 5. success, as in an examination Syn. *pasá*, *pagpasá*. 6. survival or passin through a critical period or situation. Syn *ligtás*, *pagkaligtás*.
  —II. adj. 1. having gone beyond a certai point or place. Syn. *lampás*, *lumampás* 2. having gone beyond the limit. Syn *humigít*, *sumobra*. 3. having penetrate or pierced through and through. Syn *lagós*, *lágusan*; *tagós*, *tágusan*. 4 successful, as in an examination. Syn *pasado*, *pumasá*, *nakapasá*. 5. havin survived or passed through a critica period or situation. Syn. *ligtás*, *walâ-nan panganib*.

guna (la-gu-na), n. (Sp.) 1. lagoon; lake. Syn. *dagatan, lanaw*. 2. (L-) name of a province in Southern Luzon, bounded by the provinces of Rizal, Quezon, and Batangas.

gundî (la-gun-dî), n. (*Bot.*) a trailing shrub with obovate unifoliate leaves, numerous blue flowers and black rounded succulent fruit when ripe (*Vitex obovata Thumb*).

gusan (lá-gu-san), I. n. 1. state or condition of being open from one end to another, as a hole, tunnel, underpass; tunnel. Syn. *tunél*. 3. a direct way or passageway to a place. Syn. *tápatan, daáng tápatan*.

—II. adj. 1. open through and through; passable through and through. 2. pierced or penetrated from one side to the other. Syn. *tagós, tágusan*.

guslós (la-gus-lós), n. fast current of water passing through surface. Syn. *malakás na agos ng tubig*. 2. the sound caused by this fast current of water. Syn. *lagaslás*.

gutók (la-gu-tók), n. short, sharp, snapping sound, as that produced by pulling the joints of fingers. Cf. *lagitík, taguktók*.

guyò (la-gu-yò), n. 1. camaraderie; comradeship. Syn. *pakikipágkaibigan, pagkakáibigan*. 2. intimacy; close friendship or association. Syn. *matalik na pagkakaibigan*. 3. an intimate or illicit sexual relation. Syn. *pagtatalik*.

gwerta (lag-wer-ta), var. **laguwerta**, n. (Sp. *laguerta*) orchard. Syn. *looban o bakuran ng mga halaman o punong namumunga*.

gyô (lag-yô), n. 1. soul; spirit. Syn. *diwà, káluluwá, espíritu*. 2. name; appellation. Syn. *ngalan, pangalan, tagurî, tawag*.

had (la-had), n. 1. act or manner of extending out the arms with the open hands, as what beggars do in asking for alms. Syn. *sahod o pagsasahod ng mga kamáy o palad*. 2. act or manner of showing something by unrolling or unfolding it. Syn. *pagbubukás, paglaladlád*. 3. act of explaining (things) one by one. Syn. *pagpapaliwanag o paghahanay nang isá-isá*.

hát (la-hát), I. adj. all; every one of; including all. Syn. *tanán, madlâ*.

—II. pron. 1. all; everyone; everybody. 2. everything.

lahì (la-hì), n. 1. race; people of the same ancestry. Cf. *lipì*. 2. clan; lineage. Syn. *angkán*. 2. breed; stock. Syn. *kasta*.

lahing kayumanggí: n. brown race.

lahò (la-hò), n. 1. eclipse (of the moon or sun). Syn. *eklipse, paglalahò*. 2. sudden or mysterious disappearance. Syn. *biglâ o mahiwagang pagkawalâ*. 3. loss or disappearance, as of pain, tiredness, etc. Syn. *pagkaparam, pagkapawì*.

lahók (la-hók), n. 1. adding or mixing something with another. Syn. *pagdaragdág o paghahalò*. 2. something added to a mixture. Syn. *halò*. 3. ingredient; food ingredient. Syn. *sahóg, panahóg*. 4. participation, as in a contest. Syn. *sali, pagsali*. 5. a participant or entry, as in a game or contest. Syn. *sali, kasali*.

laib (la-ib), n. act of exposing green leaves, esp. banana leaves, to the heat of embers or fire to wilt or soften them. Cf. *salab, pagsasalab*.

lain (la-in), var. **laing**, n. the stalks and leaves of *gabi* (taro plant), usually eaten as vegetable. Syn. *tangkáy at dahon ng gabi*.

lait (la-it), n. vilification; revilement. Syn. *mura, pagmura, alimurà, pag-alimurà; pagdustâ, pandurustâ*.

lala (la-la), n. act, method, manner, or pattern of interlacing or weaving twigs, leaves, reeds, thin bamboo splits, or the like, as in making baskets, mats, etc. Syn. *paglala, paglalala, pagkakálala*.

lalâ (la-lâ), I. n. becoming or growing serious or aggravated. Syn. *paglubhâ, paglalâ*. 2. aggravation; seriousness; graveness. Syn. *lubhâ, kalubhaán; bigát, kabigatán*.

—II. adj. aggravated; grown serious or grave. Syn. *malalâ, malubhâ, mabigát, seryoso*.

lalaki (la-la-ki), I. n. a male person; man. 2. a male animal or plant.

—II. adj. male; masculine.

lalagaín (la-la-ga-ín) n. & adj. referring to meat intended for stewing.

lalagukan (la-la-gu-kan), n. 1. throat. Syn. *lalamunan*. 2. Adam's apple. Syn. *gulúnggulungan, tatagukan*.

lalagyán (la-lag-yán), n. 1. container; receptacle. Syn. *sisidlán*. 2. place for keeping or depositing things. Syn. *taguán, ligpitan*.

lalamunan (la-la-mu-nan), n. (*Anat.*) throat. Cf. *lalaugan*.

laláng (la-láng), I. n. 1. a creating or being created. Syn. *likhâ, paglikhâ, pagkakalikhâ*. 2. an inventing or being invented. Syn. *imbento, pag-imbento, pagkakáimbento*. 3. an invention or creation. Syn. *imbento, likhâ*. 4. trick; deception; artifice; strategy; stratagem. Syn. *linláng, dayà, pakanâ*.
—II. *adj.* created or invented. Syn. *likhâ, nilikhâ, inimbento*.

lalaugan (la-la-u-gan), n. (*Anat.*) 1. esophagus. 2. throat. Syn. *lalamunan*.

lalawigan (la-la-wi-gan), n. province. Syn. *probínsiyá*.

lalik (la-lik), n. 1. lathe; machine for shaping articles of wood, metal, etc. Syn. *torno, tornohan*. 2. act of shaping wood, metal, etc. on a lathe machine. Syn. *paglalik, paglalalik; pagtorno, pagtuturno*. 3. the manner such articles are shaped. Syn. *pagkakálalik, pagkakátorno*.

lalim (la-lim), n. 1. depth; deepness. Syn. *kalaliman, pagkamalalim*. 2. deepness of thought; profundity.

lalin (la-lin). I. n. 1. transfer of a disease from one person to another; contagion. Syn. *hawa, pagkahawa*. 2. any disase thus transferred; infection. Syn. *hawa, sakit na nákuha sa ibá*. 3. a color or spot resulting from staining or discoloration; stain. Syn. *mantsa, hawa, bahid*. 4. belief, influence, etc. transmitted from one person to another.
—II. *adj.* transferred or gotten from one person to another by direct or indirect contact, referring to diseases. Syn. *hawa, nahawa*. 2. designating a disease caused by infection; infected. 3. referring to stain, spots of dirt or color obtained from discoloration, etc.

lalò (la-lò), n. a. surpassing or exceeding. Syn. *higít, paghigít; lampás; daíg, pagdaíg*.

lalung-lalò (la-lung + la-lò), *adv.* (usually with *na*) more especially or particularly. Syn. *lalò pa*.

lamák (la-mák), n. state or condition of being serious, as illness; seriousness or gravity. Syn. *lubhâ, kalubhaán; lalâ kalalaán; bigát, kabigatán*.

lamad (la-mad), n. (*Anat.*), a membranous sheet or layer in animal or plant tissue that serves as covering or lining membrane. Cf. *bakong*.

lamán (la-mán), n. 1. meat; animal flesh for food. Syn. *karne*. 2. human flesh or tissue; muscle. Syn. *kalamnán*. 3. content, as of a bottle, cup, can, pot, etc. Syn. *an nakalamán o nakasilid*. 4. capacity. Syn *lulan*. 5. any root crop or tuber. See **lamanlupá**. 6. meaning; purport substance. Syn. *diwà, kahulugan*, 7. (*Fig.*) one's child. Syn. *anák*.

lamandagat (la-man-da-gat), var. **lamáng dagat**, n. anything useful obtained from the sea, as seaweeds, fishes, shells, etc.

lamanloob (la-man-lo-ob), var. **lamáng loob**, n. giblets. Syn. *minudénsiyá*.

lamanlupà (la-man-lu-pà), var. **lamáng-lupà** n. 1. any kind of root crop or tuber. 2 gnome. Cf. *nunò o matandâ sa punso*.

lamantiyán (la-man-ti-yán), var. **lamáng tiyán**, n. anything that can be eaten.

lamang (la-mang), I. *adj.* one and no more only. Syn. *tangì*.
—II. *adv.* 1. only; merely. 2. exclusively particularly. Syn. *talagá, sadyâ*.

lamáng (la-máng), I. n. act of taking advantage over another or others. Syn *paglamáng; pagsasamantalá (sa kapwà)*. advantage one has over another or other Syn. *higít, kahigtán; bentaha, kabentahan kalamangán*. 3. point advantage of a player or team over the opponent. Syn. *abant kalámangan*.
—II. *adj.* at an advantage over another or others. Syn. *nakalálamáng, nakahíhigít*. ahead in points or score, said of a player or team. Syn. *abante, nakaáabant nakalálamáng*.

lamáng-isip (la-máng + i-sip), n. something (an idea, belief, etc.) that person entertains in his mind. Syn. *an nasaisip o iníisip*. 2. talent. Syn. *talin dunong, karunungan*.

lamas[1] (la-mas), n. 1. act or manner

mashing or squeezing with the hands. Syn. *lamusak, paglamusak.* Cf. *masa, pagmasa, pagmamasa.* 2. combat; hand-to-hand battle or fight. Syn. *baka, pagbabaka, batalya.*

lamat (la-mat), *n.* a slight crack or fissure on glassware, chinaware, or the like. Syn. *bahagyáng biták, basag, o putók.*

lamay (la-may), *n.* 1. night vigil. Syn. *paglalamay, pagpupuyát.* 2. overtime work at night. Syn. *pagtatrabaho sa gabí.*

lambák (lam-bák), *n.* 1. valley; lowland. 2. plain. Syn. *kapatagan.*

lambanog (lam-ba-nog; lam-ba-nóg), *n.* a kind of native wine, made esp. from palm juice.

lambát (lam-bát), *n.* 1. net in general. 2. a big fishing net. Syn. *pukot, pamukot.* 3. hair net. Syn. *hernet.* 4. trap or snare. Syn. *silò, bitag, patibóng.* 5. act or manner of catching fish, birds, and other animals, with or as with a net.

lambî (lam-bî), *n.* (Anat.) 1. wattle of a bird or fowl. 2. dewlap, as of cattle. 3. double chin; fold of flesh under the chin. 4. any anatomical protrusion, as the ear lobe or earlap. Syn. *tainga* (colloq.).

lambíng (lam-bíng), *n.* 1. show or expression of fondness, love, or tenderness, as by embracing, kissing, etc. Syn. *karinyo.* 2. the characteristic attitude of a child wanting to be caressed or fondled. Syn. *lamyós.* 3. tenderness, melodiousness or sweetness of a tune or air. Syn. *tamís o katamisán* (colloq.).

lambitin (lam-bi-tin), *n.* 1. act of hanging (oneself) on a branch, etc. with hands or feet, as do monkeys, bats, and the like. Cf. *kunyapit, ukyabit.* 2. act of clinging or holding fast, as a child, at someone's neck. 3. state or condition of being pendulous, as fruits hanging on tree branches.

lambóng (lam-bóng), *n.* 1. a woman's veil or scarf worn over the hair and shoulders; mantilla. Syn. *belo, kulubóng, talukbóng, kubóng, pindóng.* 2. anything that screens or hides. Syn. *tabing, takíp.*

lambót (lam-bót), *n.* 1. tenderness or softness, as of meat or anything eaten. Syn. *latâ, kalataán, kalambután.* 2.

pliability; flexibility. Syn. *kadaliáng baluktutín o hubugin.* 3. weakness, as of the body due to sickness or tiredness. Syn. *hinà, panghihinà, kahinaan; lambót, panlalambót, kalambután (ng katawan).* 4. fact, state, or condition of being easily influenced or persuaded. Syn. *pagkamasunurin, pagkasunúd-súnuran, kadaliáng makumbinsi.* 5. softness, as of fruits, due to overripeness or over handling. Syn. *kalamugán, kalunután.*

lamentasyón (la-men-tas-yón), *n.* (Sp. *lamentacion*) lamentation. Syn. *daíng, pagdaíng; taghóy, panaghóy.*

lamesa (la-me-sa), *n.* (Sp. *la mesa*) table. Syn. *hapág, dulang.* See **mesa.**

lameseta (la-me-se-ta), *n.* (Sp. *la meseta*) small table. Syn. *muntíng mesa (lamesa).*

lamikmík (la-mik-mík), *n.* 1. silence; quietness. Syn. *katahimikan, kasilénsiyuhán.* 2. calmness; tranquility; repose. Syn. *kapanatagan, katiwasayán, kapayapaán.*

lamíg (la-míg), *n.* 1. cold or coldness, as of the weather. Syn. *gináw, kaginawán.* 2. cool; coolness. Syn. *kapreskuhán.* 3. lack of enthusiasm; indifference. Syn. *kawaláng-siglá.* 4. (Colloq.) leftover cooked rice. Syn. *bahaw, kaninglamig.*

lamirâ (la-mi-râ), *adj.* 1. syrupy and sticky; viscous; viscid. Syn. *lamuták.* 2. filthily thick and sticky. Syn. *gitatâ, nanggitatà.*

lamirat (la-mi-rat), *n.* act or manner of pressing (a small object) with or as with the tips of the fingers resulting in being made thin or reduced to a pulp. Syn. *lapirat, lapirot.*

lamlám (lam-lám), *n.* 1. gloominess or dimness, as of light, sun, moon, etc. Syn. *kulimlím, kakulimlimán.* 2. languidness, as the expression of the eyes. Syn. *pungay, kapungayan.* 3. sadness; melancholy. Syn. *lungkót, kalungkután.* 4. lack of spirit; coldness or lifelessness. Syn. *tamláy, katamlayán.*

lamók (la-mók), *n.* (Entom.) mosquito.

lamod (la-mod), *n.* soft mucuslike substance, as that found in very young coconut fruits (*buko*). Syn. *lahod.*

lamóg (la-móg), I. *n.* 1. act of beating someone, resulting in bruises or

contusions. Syn. *bugbóg, pagbugbóg.* 2. act
of causing (fruits) to become very soft by
over handling. 3. state or condition of
being bruised or contused. Syn. *bugbóg,
pagkabugbóg; pasâ, pamamasâ, kapasaán.*
—II. *adj.* 1. softened by rough handling,
said of fruits. Syn. *bulbóg, bugbóg.* 2
bruised; contused. Syn. *pasâ, may-pasâ.*

lamon (la-mon), *n.* 1. act of eating
(something) voraciously. Syn. *sabsáb,
pagsabsáb.* 2. destruction or consumption,
as by fire. Syn. *tupok, pagtupok,
pagkatupok.* 3. an engulfing or swallowing,
as by big waves. Syn. *lulón, paglulón;
sakmál, pagsakmál.*

lampa (lam-pa), *n. & adj.* referring to a
person who is unsteady or unsure of
footing. Syn. *dúlasin, madulasin.*

lampará (lam-pa-rá), *n.* (Sp.) 1. lamp, esp.
one with a shade. Syn. *paról.* 2. lamp
shade.

lampas (lam-pas; lam-pás), I. *n.* 1. act of
passing or getting ahead of another or
others, as in a race. Syn. *una, pag-una.*
2. an overreaching; going beyond a
limit. Syn. *labis, paglabis; sobra,
pagsobra.* 3. act of surpassing another or
others, as in accomplishment. Syn. *daíg,
pagdaíg; higít paghigít.* 4. state or
condition of having penetrated
something from one side to the other.
Syn. *lagós, paglagós; lagpás, paglagpás;
lusót, paglusót; tagós, pagtagós.* 5. the
distance one is ahead of another. Syn.
layò o distansiyá ng kaunahan. 6. act of
passing (a checkpoint, or the like)
without being noticed. Syn. *lusót,
paglusót.*
—II. *adj.* 1. excessive; too much. Syn.
labis, sobra, masyado. 2. having penetrated
from one side to the other. Syn. *lagós,
tagós, lusót.*

lampaso (lam-pa-so), *n.* (Sp. *lampazo*) 1.
floor mop. Syn. *panlampaso.* 2. act or
manner of cleaning floors with or as with
a mop. Syn. *paglalampaso.* 3. the way or
manner a floor was mopped. Syn.
pagkakálampaso.

lampín (lam-pín), *n.* diaper; baby's
breechcloth.

lampóng (lam-póng), *n.* the characteristic
cries or mewing of cats in courtship or
mating.

lampot (lam-pot), *n.* 1. state or condition
of being dirty and raggedly dressed. Syn.
limahid, panlilimahid. 2. slovenliness. Syn.
dungis, karungisan, kaburaraan.

lamukos (la-mu-kos), *v.* crushing or
crumpling (something) in one's hands.
Syn. *kuyumos, pagkuyumos.*

lamukot (la-mu-kot), *n.* the soft fleshy part
of a fruit; pulp. Cf. *lamán, kalamnán.*

lamuray (la-mu-ray), *n.* act of mangling
(something) to pieces. Syn. *gutáy,
paggutáy.*

lamurit (la-mu-rit), *n.* act of crushing with
or as with the fingers. Syn. *lapurit, lapirot.*

lamusak (la-mu-sak), *n.* 1. act of squeezing,
crushing, or mashing (something) with
the hands. Syn. *lamutak, paglamutak;
lamas, paglamas.* 2. a miry or watery place.
Cf. *pusalì.*

lamutak (la-mu-tak), *n.* act of squeezing,
crushing, or mashing with the hands. Syn.
lamas, paglamas; lamusak, paglamusak.

lamutmót (la-mut-mót), *n.* loose ends of
unravelled thread or fibers, or of frayed
edges of clothes. Syn. *nisnís.* See
lamuymóy.

lamuymóy (la-muy-móy), *n.* 1. tassel. Syn.
borlas, palamuymoy. 2. loose or hanging
thread or fibers, as in frayed edges of
clothes. See **lamutmót.**

lamuyot (la-mu-yot), *n.* 1. act of squeezing,
crushing, or mashing (something) with
the hands. Syn. *lamas, paglamas; lamusak,
paglamusak.* 2. (by extension) persuasion;
inducement; seduction. Syn. *himok,
paghimok; hikayat, paghikayat.*

lamyâ (lam-yâ), *n.* act or manner of talking
like a baby who wants to be caressed or
fondled. Cf. *lamyós, lambíng.*

lamyós (lam-yós), *n.* caress; show of
affection, fondness, or tenderness to a
loved one. Syn. *lambíng, karinyo.*

lana (la-na), I. *n.* (Sp.) 1. the soft hair or fur
of sheep and some other animals; wool.
2. cloth or garment made of wool.
—II. *adj.* woolen; made of wool. Syn. *yarì
sa lana.*

lanaw   **lantád**

lanaw (la-naw), n. 1. a small lake. Syn. *dagát-dagatan, lawà.* 2. a shallow pool or pond; pool of standing water. Syn. *sanaw.* 3. (L-) name of a province in Mindanao. Also spelled Lanao.

landas (lan-das; lan-dás), n. path; trail; pathway; footpath. Syn. *daán, daanán.* 2. a trail in the mountains or forests. Syn. *bulaos.*

landasin (lan-da-sin), n. 1. something a person uses as his guide or guideline. Syn. *patnubay, panuto.* 2. aim; objective. Syn. *layon, layunin.*

landáy (lan-dáy), n. shallowness, esp. of plates or dishes. Syn. *kalandayán.* Cf. *babaw, kababawan.*

landî[1] (lan-dî), I. n. coquette; flirt. Syn. *babaing kirí o hitád.*
—II adj. coquettish; flirtatious; sensuous. Syn. *kirí, lantód, talandî, hitád.*

landî[2] (lan-dî), n. (Colloq.) act of toying or doing something playfully. Syn. *kalantarì, likót.*

landían (lan-dí-an), n. act of making love with each other just for fun. Syn. *paglalandían, kirihan, pagkikírihan.*

landing (lan-ding), n. (Eng.) 1. act of landing, as of an airplane. Syn. *lapág, paglapág.* 2. act of landing or embarking, as of a ship. Syn. *duóng, pagduóng.* 3. place for landing (for airplanes). Syn. *lápagan, pálapagan.* 4. place for landing or anchorage (for ships). Syn. *daungán, duungán.*

lanolina (la-no-li-na), n. (Sp.) lanolin; lanoline.

lanot (la-not), n. 1. loose ends of fibers worn out or unravelled from the edges of clothes. Syn. *nisnis.* 2. the fibrous tissue in husks of fruits, esp. coconut. Syn. *yanot.*

lansa (lan-sa; lan-sá), n. 1. the characteristic smell of fresh fish. Syn. *amóy-isdâ.* 2. the viscious substance covering the scales or skin of fish. 3. (Fig.) obscenity. Syn. *laswâ, kalaswaán, kabastusán.*

lansak (lan-sak; lan-sák), adj. 1. open; sincere; frank. Syn. *tapát, matapát, prangko, tunay.* 2. in large quantities; by wholesale. Syn. *pákyawan, lánsakan.* 3. including all; without any exception. Syn.

láhatan. 4. (Gram.) collective; collective noun (*pangngalang lansák*). Also *palansák.*

lanság (lan-ság), I. n. 1. act of taking apart part by part; dismantling. Syn. *pagtatanggál-tanggál, paglanság.* 2. abolition; dissolution; disorganization. Syn. *buwág, pagbuwág.* 3. state or condition of being dismantled or separated part by part, as a machine. 4. act of demolishing or wrecking a building, etc. Syn. *gibâ, paggibâ.*
—II. adj. 1. dismantled, as a machine, etc. Syn. *tanggál-tanggál, pinagtanggál-tanggál.* 2. abolished; dissolved; disorganized. Syn. *buwág, binuwág.* 3. demolished; wrecked. Syn. *gibâ, ginibâ; wasák, winasák.*

lansangan (lan-sa-ngan), n. street; road. Syn. *kalye, karsada, daán.*

lanseta (lan-se-ta). var. **laseta**, n. (Sp. *lanceta*) folding knife; pocket knife; penknife. Syn. *kortapluma.*

lansi (lan-si; lan-sí), var. **lanse**, n. (Sp. *lance*) strategem; trick; ruse; artifice; wile; deceit. Syn. *laláng, linláng, dayà, pakanâ.*

lansina (lan-si-na), n. (Bot.) castor oil plant (*Ricinus communis*).

lansones (lan-so-nes), n. (Bot.) 1. a fruit tree cultivated for its delicious fruit particularly in Quezon and Laguna provinces, but grows wild in Mindanao and Basilan. 2. the fruit of this tree which is a great favorite among Filipinos.

lantá (lan-tá), I. n. fact, state, or condition of being withered or faded, as flowers and leaves. Syn. *kalantahán, pagkalantá.* Cf. *luoy, pagkaluoy.*

lanták (lan-ták), n. attack; onslaught; assault. Syn. *atake, banat, tira, salakay, lusob.*

lantakà (lan-ta-kà), n. small brass cannon. Syn. *munting kanyón.*

lantád (lan-tád), I. n. 1. act of showing one's self in public. Syn. *litáw, paglitáw.* 2. state or condition of being in full view or in the open. Syn. *kahayagán, kalantarán.* 3. a place exposed to the full view of all. Syn. *tahaw.* 4. act or manner of being frank or open in one's dealing with others. Syn. *tapát na o katapatan ng pakikitungo.*
—II. adj. 1. in full view; exposed to view;

in the open; uncovered. Syn. *hayág, kita, nákikita*. 2. frank; open; sincere. Syn. *tapát, matapát*.

lantáy (lan-táy), *adj.* 1. pure; unalloyed, referring esp. to gold. Syn. *puro, dalisay*. 2. unadulterated, referring esp. to liquid. Syn. *waláng-halò, wálang-bantô, puro*.

lantík (lan-tík). *n.* graceful bend or curve, as of eyelashes, fingers, hips, etc. Syn. *magandáng hubog*.

lantód (lan-tód). I. *adj.* flirtatious; coquettish. Syn. *hitád, kirí, landî, talandî*. —II. *n.* 1. flirt; coquette. Syn. *babaing landî o kirí*. 2. act of a flirt; flirtation. 2. Syn. *paglalandî, kalandián, kakirihán, kaalimbungán*.

lantóng¹ (lan-tóng), *n.* the disagreeable odor or stench of rotten meat or fish. Syn. *angót, bahò*. 2. the peculiar smell of urine. Syn. *panghí, palot*.

lantóng² (lan-tóng), *n.* act or attitude of wanting to be fondled or caressed, esp. of a child. Syn. *lambíng, paglalambíng*.

lantót (lan-tót), *n.* fetor or stench of long-standing water. Syn. *antót, bantót*.

lantsa (lan-tsa), *n.* (Sp. *lancha*) a large, open motorboat; launch. Cf. *yate*.

lanubo (la-nu-bo), *n.* a long, straight tender branch of a tree, esp. when newly cut and devoid of leaves.

langasngás (la-ngas-ngás), *n.* echoic sound produced when one is chewing sugar cane.

langaw (la-ngaw), *n.* (*Entom.*) fly; housefly. Cf. *bangaw, bangyáw*.

langaylangay (la-ngay-la-ngay), var. **langáylangayan**, *n.* a species of bird known as Asiatic swallow (*Hinrundo juvanica*). Cf. *layánglayang*.

langkâ (lang-kâ), var. **nangka**, *n.* (*Bot.*) 1. jackfruit tree (*Artocarpus integripolia L.*) 2. the fruit of this tree; jackfruit.

langkáp (lang-káp), I. *n.* 1. inclusion; incorporation. Syn. *sama, pagsasama; lakip, paglalakip*. 2. something enclosed; enclosure. Syn. *lakip, kalakip*. —II. *adj.* 1. included; incorporated. Syn. *kasama, kalakip*. 2. enclosed, as in an envelope. Syn. *nakapaloób, kalakip*.

langkapan (lang-ka-pan), *adj.* (*Gram.*) compound; compound sentence. (*langkapang pangungusap*). Syn. *hugnayan, tambalan*.

langkáy (lang-káy), *n.* 1. bunch or cluster, as of fruits. Syn. *kumpól, buwíg*. 2. flock, as of birds. Syn. *kawan*. 3. herd, as of cattle. Syn. *kawan, ganado*. 4. a small group or crowd. Syn. *kulumpón, kalibumbong, lipon, umpukan*.

langgám (lang-gám), *n.* (*Entom.*) ant (in general). Syn. *guyam* (Bats.)

langgás (lang-gás), I. *n.* act of washing a wound or wounds with antiseptic preparatory to dressing. Syn. *hugas o paghuhugas (ng sugat), paglalanggás*.

langgót (lang-gót). *n.* the goat's beard. Syn. *balbás ng kambíng*.

langháp (lang-háp), *n.* 1. breathing in air; inhalation. Syn. *langáp, sangháp*. 2. inhalation of perfume or medicinal vapor. Syn. *singhót, pagsinghót*.

langíb (la-ngíb), *n.* scab; crust formed over a wound during healing. Syn. *talukap ng natútuyô nang sugat*.

langís (la-ngís), *n.* 1. oil. Syn. *aseyte*. 2. (*Colloq.*) servile flattery. Syn. *pagmamapurí, paglalangís, panunuyò*.

langit (la-ngit), *n.* 1. (*Theol.*) heaven; place where God and His angels live. Syn. *kalangitan*. 2. sky. Syn. *himpapawíd, papawirín*. 3. (*Fig.*) paradise; place or condition of great happiness. Syn. *paraiso, glorya; kaluwalhatian*.

langitin (la-ngi-tin), *v.* (*Fig.*) to love very much; idolize. Syn. *pakamahalín, pakaibigin*.

langitngít (la-ngit-ngít), *n.* shrill creaking sound as that produced by rusty hinges. Syn. *agitít, lagitlít*.

langó (la-ngó). I. *n.* 1. state or condition of being drunk. Syn. *kalanguhán, kalasingán*. 2. a drunken person. Syn. *taong lasíng*. —II. *adj.* drunk; intoxicated. Syn. *lasíng, barík*.

langóy (la-ngóy), I. *n.* act or manner of swimming. Syn. *paglangóy*. —II. *adj.* (*Colloq.*) referring to a distance on a body of water that a person can negotiate by swimming. Syn. *kayáng languyín o malangóy*.

laon (la-on), *adj.* 1. long time. Syn. *luwát, kaluwatán; tagál, katagalán.* 2. unnecessary delay. Syn. *abala, kaabalahan, pagkaabala; atraso, kaatrasuhan, pagkaatraso.*

laón (la-ón), *adj.* old, referring esp. to rice of a previous year's harvest or wine of old vintage. Syn. *lumà.*

laós (la-ós), I. *n.* fact, state, or condition of being overripe, no longer productive, obsolescent, or exhausted of productivity or potency.
—II. *adj.* 1. overripe, referring to fruits. Syn. *layót, labis na ang pagkahinóg.* 2. exhausted of potency, as by old age or continued use; no longer productive. Syn. *lipás na, walâ nang bisà.* 3. obsolescent. Syn. *di-na-ginágamit.*

laot (la-ot), *n.* 1. midsea; high seas. Syn. *karagatan, gitnâ ng dagat.* 2. midst; middle. Syn. *gitnâ, kalágitnaan.* 3. (Fig.) tight situation, as in. *Nálagáy siyá sa laot.* He was placed in a tight situation.

lapà (la-pà), *n.* 1. act of butchering (an animal) for food. Syn. *katay, pagkatay, pagpatáy.* 2. act of cutting meat into big lumps or pieces. Syn. *atado, pag-aatado.* 3. a big lump or cut of meat. Syn. *katay, lapáng.* 4. autopsy; necropsy. Syn. *awtópsiyá, pag-aawtópsiyá.*

lapad (la-pad), *n.* 1. width; breadth. Syn. *luwáng.* 2. wideness. Syn. *kalaparan, kaluwangán.* 3. extent. Syn. *lakí, kalakhán.* 4. extensiveness. Syn. *lawak, kalawakan.*

lapág (la-pág), *n.* 1. the space below. Syn. *babâ, ibabâ, ilalim.* 2. any low, horizontal level, as the floor or ground. Syn. *sahíg, lupà.* 3. downstairs; basement floor. Syn. *silong, lupà.* 4. act of putting or placing (a thing) down, as on a table. Syn. *patong, pagpapatong.* 5. act of putting down a thing on the floor, ground, etc. Syn. *babâ, pagbababâ.* 6. a going down, as from the house by way of the stairs. Syn. *panaog, pagpanaog.* 7. alighting or getting down, as from an animal or vehicle. Syn. *lunsád, paglunsád; ibís, pag-ibís.* 8. act of unloading cargo. Syn. *diskarga, pagdiskarga.* 9. act of landing, as of an airplane. Syn. *babâ, pagbabâ.* 10. act of going down a deep place, as a well, or the like. Syn. *lusong,* *paglusong.*

lapáng (la-páng), *n.* 1. act of cutting into big pieces or hunks, referring to meat. Syn. *katayin nang malalakí.* 2. a big piece or hunk of meat. Syn. *katay na malaki.*

lapastangan (la-pas-ta-ngan), I. *adj.* disrespectful; discourteous; irreverent. Syn. *waláng-galang, waláng-pítagan, waláng-pakundangan, pusóng.*
—II. *n.* 1. the act of being disrespectful or discourteous to someone. Syn. *pagwaláng-galang o pagwawaláng-galáng, pagwawaláng-pítagan.* 2. a disrespectful or discourteous person; irreverent individual. Syn. *taong waláng-galang.*

lapat (la-pat), I. *n.* 1. fact or state of being closed properly or tightly, referring to a door, window, drawer, etc. Syn. *maayos na sarâ o pagkasará.* 2. state or condition of being properly fitted or adjusted, as a joint in carpentry. Syn. *maayos na kabít o pagkakakabít; maayos na akmâ o pagkaáakmâ.* 3. state or condition of being close enough to be touching each other edge to edge or surface to surface. Syn. *dikít, pagkakádikít; daít, pagkakádaít.* 4. meting out, as a punishment. Syn. *gawad, paggagawad.* 5. application or giving, as of remedy or medicine. Syn. *pagbibigáy (ng lunas).*
—II. *adj.* 1. properly closed, as a door, window, etc. Syn. *nakasará nang maayos.* 2. well-adjusted; well-fitted. Syn. *akmâ, kamado, mahigpit ang kabít o pagkakákabít.* 3. fit; proper; suitable; suited; appropriate. Syn. *bagay, angkóp, tamà, ayos, agpáng.* 4. close enough to be touching each other. Syn. *dikít, magkadikít.*

lapáy (la-páy), *n.* (Anat.) spleen; milt. Syn. *palî.*

lapì[1] (la-pì), *n.* 1. a thing attached or fastened to another, esp. as a reinforcement or support. Syn. *sapî.* 2. act of joining, as member of an association or party. Syn. *sapì, pagsapì.*

lapì[2] (la-pì), *n.* (Gram.) 1. a letter, syllable, or word added or affixed to a word; affix. Syn. *panlapì.* 2. affixture; affixation. Syn. *paglalapì.*

lapián (la-pi-án), *n.* association; society.

lápidá

Syn. *samahán, kapisanan.*

lápidá (lá-pi-dá), *n.* (Sp.) 1. tombstone; gravestone. 2. stone tablet; memorial tablet.

lapirat (la-pi-rat), *n.* act of pressing or squeezing (something) into or as into a soft, flat mass or pulp; squashing. See **lapirot.**

lapirot (la-pi-rot), *n.* act of crumpling or crashing (a thing) with or as with the tips of the fingers. Syn. *pirot, pagpirot, paglapirot.* See **lapirát.**

lapis (la-pis), *n.* (Sp. *lapiz*) pencil.

lapisák (la-pi-sák), I. *n.* state or condition of being crushed flat into a soft mass. Cf. *lapirát.*

—II. *adj.* crushed flat into a soft mass.

lapisin (la-pi-sin), *v.* to draw or write (something) in pencil. Syn. *drowingin o sulatin sa lapis.*

lapit (la-pit), *n.* act of going or coming near or toward a person or place; approach. Syn. *daís, pagdaís.* 2. act of seeking help by approaching someone. Syn. *paghingî ng tulong.* 3. nearness; closeness; proximity. Syn. *kalapitan.* 4. intimacy; closeness. Syn. *talik, katalikan.*

lapláp (lap-láp), I. *n.* act of flaying or stripping off the skin or hide of (a person or animal) with or as with a knife. Cf. *bakbák, pagbakbák; panit, pagpanit.*

—II. *adj.* flayed or stripped off with or as with a knife, referring to skin or hide. Cf. *bakbák, tukláp, panít.*

lapnís (lap-nís), I. *n.* 1. act of tearing or stripping off the bark of a tree. Syn. *tukláp, pagtukláp; paknít, pagpaknít.* 2. a long strip of bark torn off from a branch or trunk of a tree, sometimes used as material for making ropes.

—II. *adj.* torn or stripped off, referring to skin or tree bark. Syn. *talóp, tukláp, paknít.*

lapnit (lap-nit), *n.* 1. act of pulling, tearing, or detaching forcibly something glued, pasted, etc. Syn. *tukláp, pagtukláp; bakbák, pagbakbák.* 2. state or condition of being torn or detached forcibly. Syn. *tukláp, pagkakátukláp; paknit, pagkakápaknít; bakbák, pagkakábakbák.*

lapot (la-pot), *n.* thickness of liquid; viscosity or viscidity. Ant. *labnáw, kalabnawán.*

lapulapu[1] (la-pu-la-po), var. **lapulapu,** *n.* (Ichth.) grouper fish (Family *Serranidae,* all species).

Lapulapu[2] (La-pu-la-po), *n.* the name of a native chieftain in the Island of Mactan, who, according to history, killed Magellan in an encounter with the natives in 1521.

lapurit (la-pu-rit), *n.* act of crushing or pressing hard with or as with the fingers. Syn. *lapirot, paglapirot.*

larang (la-rang), *n.* wide, open field. Syn. *parang, kaparangan.*

larangan (la-ra-ngan), *n.* 1. field of action (in sports, arts, letters, etc.). 2. area of military operations; battlefield. Syn. *poók ng labanán (digmaan).* 3. battle; war. Syn. *digmaan, labanán.*

larawan (la-ra-wan), *n.* 1. picture; portrait; image; photograph. Syn. *retrato (litrato); imahén, potograpiya.* 2. illustration; drawing, as in a book, magazine, etc. Syn. *ilustrasyón, dibuho, drowing, larawang-guhit.* 3. image or reflection, as in a mirror or clear water. Syn. *repleksiyón, anino.*

larba (lar-ba), *n.* (Eng.) larva. Cf. *uód, ulalò.*

larga (lar-ga; lar-gá), I. *n.* (Sp. *largar;* Colloq.) leaving or departure. Syn. *alís, pag-alís; lakad, paglakad.* 2. a loosening or prolongation, as of the string of a kite in the air. Syn. *tustós, pagtutustós.* 3. a letting loose. Syn. *pagpapakawalâ.*

—II. *interj.* (L-) Go! Go ahead! Syn. *Sige! Lakad! Sulong!*

largabista (lar-ga-bis-ta), *n.* (Sp. *larga vista*) binoculars. Cf. *teleskopyo.*

largo (lar-go), *n.* (Sp.) boys' long pants or trousers. Syn. *mahabang salawál o pantalón ng mga batang lalaki.* Ant. *korto.*

laringhitis (la-ring-hi-tis), *n.* (Med., Sp. *laringitis*) laryngitis. Syn. *pamamagá ng lalamunan.*

larô (la-rô), *n.* 1. act or manner of playing a game. Syn. *paglalarô.* 2. game; play; sports; recreation. Syn. *líbangan, áliwan.* 3. time or schedule of playing a game. Syn. *oras ng larô o paglalarô.* 4. gambling. Syn. *sugál, pagsusugál; huwego, paghuhuwego.* 5. act of holding the attention or interest of a

child, as by playing with him or her. Syn.
libáng, paglibáng. 6. act of doing, making,
or handling (something) playfully; trifling
or toying with. 7. free motion or
movement. Syn. *galáw, kilos.*

laruán (la-ru-án), n. children's toy. Syn.
galawan (Bats.)

lasa (la-sa), n. 1. taste; savor; flavor; relish.
Syn. *namnám, linamnám; lasáp.* 2. a liking.
Syn. *gusto, kagustuhan, pagkakagusto.*

lasak (la-sak), I. n. 1. a rooster with red,
black, and white feathers. Cf. *alimbuyugin,
talisayin, bulik.* 2. the red, black, and white
colors of the feathers of a rooster.
—II. *adj.* with or having feathers of red,
black, and white colors, referring to a
rooster.

lasang- (la-sang-), a combining form
meaning "with or having the taste of" as
in *lasang-isdâ,* having the taste of fish.

lasáp (la-sáp), n. 1. fine or enjoyable taste.
Syn. *saráp, linamnám.* 2. an experiencing
or actual undergoing, as of happiness,
success, failure, hardship, etc. Syn. *danas,
pagdanas, pagdaranas; tikím, pagtikím,
pagkátikím.*

lasaw (la-saw), n. 1. a thawing or melting.
Syn. *tunaw, pagkatunaw; lusaw,
pagkalusaw.* 2. thinness; sparseness. Syn.
dalang, kadalangan. 3. wandering about in
great numbers. Syn. *lisaw.*

lasenggo (la-seng-go), n. & adj. referring to
a person who is always drunk. Syn.
buratsero, maglalasing.

laserasyón (la-se-ras-yon), n. (Sp. *laceracion*)
laceration. Syn. *punit, pagkapunit; laslás,
pagkalaslás.*

lasing (la-sing), I. *adj.* drunk; intoxicated;
inebriated. Syn. *langó, barík.*
—II. n. 1. state or condition of being
drunk, referring to a person. Syn.
kalasingán, kalanguhán. 2. a drunken
person. Syn. *taong lasíng* (*langó*)

laslás (las-lás), I. n. 1. act of slashing or
ripping with or as with a knife. Syn.
*paglaslás; pagwakwák sa pamamagitan ng
lanseta.* 2. state or condition of being
slashed or ripped open with or as with a
knife. Syn. *pagkalaslás, pagkawakwák;
pagkagahak.* 3. a rip or cut made by

slashing with or as with a knife; slash. Syn.
wakwák, gahák.
—II. *adj.* ripped or slashed. Syn. *wakwák,
gahák.*

laso (la-so), I. n. (Sp. *lazo*) 1. ribbon. Syn.
sintás. 2. a bow or bowknot made of
ribbon.
—II. *adj.* made of ribbon. Syn. *yarì sa laso.*

lasô (la-sô), n. burn on the tongue. Syn. *pasò
sa dilà.*

lasóg (la-sóg), I. n. 1. act of breaking (bones)
into pieces. Syn. *durog, pagdurog.* 2. state
or condition of being broken into pieces,
referring esp. to bones. Syn. *pagkadurog,
kadurugan.*
—II. *adj.* broken into pieces, referring esp.
to bones. Syn. *duróg, durúg-duróg.*

lason (la-son), I. n. 1. a poisonous drug or
substance; poison. 2. venom. Syn.
kamandág, veneno. 3. anything harmful or
destructive to one's happiness or welfare.

lástikó (lás-ti-kó), n. (Sp. *elástico*) rubber
band; elastic. Cf. *goma.*

lasunâ (la-su-nâ), n. (Bot.) onion. Syn.
sibuyas.

laswâ (las-wâ), n. a lewd or obscene act or
expression. Syn. *kabastusán, kalaswaán,
kababuyan.*

lata (la-ta), I. n. (Sp.) 1. tin; tin plate. 2.
can used as container for preserved food
like milk, fish, meat, fruits, etc. 3. the
contents of a can; canful, as in *dalawáng
lata ng gatas,* two cans of milk. 3. a can, as
of kerosene. Syn. *balde.*
—II. *adj.* of, or made of, tin (tin plate).
Syn. *yarì sa lata.*

latâ (la-tâ), n. 1. softness or tenderness, as
of meat, etc. Syn. *lambót, kalambután.*
Ant. *tigás, katigasán.* 2. weakness; lack of
firmness; flabbiness. Syn. *hinà, panghihinà,
kahinaan; lambót, panlalambót.*

latak (la-tak), n. 1. dregs; lees; residue;
sediment. Syn. *tining.* 2. (Colloq., Fig.) a
couple's last child. Syn. *katapusáng anák,
bunso.*

latag¹ (la-tag), n. 1. act of spreading or
unrolling a mat, rug, etc. on the floor or
ground. Syn. *paglalatag.* 2. an unrolled or
spread out mat, rug, etc. Syn. *baníg,
alpombra, at ibá pang nakalatag.* 3. act or

manner of paving or laying a surface, as with cement, asphalt, tile, or the like. Syn. *paglalatag*, specifically, *pagsisimento*, *pag-aaspalto*, *pagbabaldosa*. 4. cement, asphalt, tiles, etc. laid on a surface. 5. the manner or state by which a surface has been spread over with a mat, rug, etc., or paved or laid with cement, asphalt, tile, etc. Syn. *pagkakálatag*.

latag (la-tag). *n.* (Fig.) state or condition of being weak and long bedridden. Syn. *ratay, pagkakaratay*.

latang (la-tang), *n.* height of severity; intensity. Syn. *tindí, katindihán; sidhî, kasidhián*.

latay (la-tay), *n.* welt; wale; weal; wheal. Syn. *marka ng palò sa balàt*.

lathalà (lat-ha-là), *n.* 1. a publishing or being published; publication. Syn. *paglalathalá, pagkakálathalá*. 2. an advertisement or announcement in a newspaper or magazine. Syn. *anunsiyó, patalastás*. 3. a published or written article in a newspaper or magazine. Syn. *artikulo*. 4. news; news report in a newspaper. Syn. *balità*.

lathalaín (lat-ha-la-ín), I. *n.* magazine article or articles; feature story or stories. Syn. *artikuló*.
—II. *adj.* referring to written works made ready for publication.

latì (la-tì), *n.* swamp; bog; marsh. Syn. *lusak, putikan, balahò*. Cf. *latian*

latian (la-ti-an). I. *n.* swampland; marshland. (*Latian* comprises a wider area than *latì*).
—II. *adj.* swampy; marshy.

latík (la-tík), *n.* 1. residuum of coconut milk after extracting oil by boiling. 2. sweet preparation made from coconut milk, used as a sauce for *suman-sa-ibos*.

látigó (lá-ti-gó), *n.* (Sp.) 1. a long whip; lash. Syn. *kumpas*. 2. act of whipping or lashing with or as with a whip. Syn. *paglátigó, pagpalò o paghaplít ng látigó o kumpás*.

Latín (La-tín), I. *n.* (Sp.) 1. the Latin language. Syn. *wikang Latín*. 2. a native or inhabitant of Ancient Rome. Syn. *Latino*. 3. (Colloq.) any language not understood or considered Latin by a person.
—II. *adj.* referring to the Latin language or the Latin people.

Latino (La-ti-no), *adj.* & *n.* (Sp.) pertaining to the Latin language or to the Latin countries or its inhabitants.

látitúd (lá-ti-túd), *n.* (Eng.) latitude.

latlát (lat-lát), *n.* (now obsolescent) minute inquiry, examination, or search for something hidden or secret. See **bulatlát**.

latok (la-tok), *n.* a kind of low table, usually crudely made and used in the kitchen, esp. in the barrios. Cf. *dulang, hapág*.

latók (la-tók), I. *adj.* decayed or rotten, referring esp. to wood. Syn. *gapók, gatô*.
—II. *n.* state or condition of being decayed or rotten (s.o. wood). Syn. *gapok, kagapukán; gatô, kagatuán*.

latóy (la-tóy), *n.* 1. taste; savor; usually used in the negative as in *waláng-latóy na pagkain*, tasteless food. Syn. *lasa, saráp, linamnám*. 2. (Colloq.) worth, value, or merit. Syn. *halagà, saysáy, kuwenta* (colloq.).

latundán (la-tun-dán), *n.* (Bot.) a variety of banana plant which bears sweet, tasty fruits. 2. the fruit of this banana plant. Also called *turdán*.

laureado (la-u-re-a-do), var. **lauryado**, *adj.* (Sp.) laureate; *makatang laureado*, poet laureate.

laurél (lau-rél), *n.* (Sp.) 1. (Bot.) laurel; bay tree (*Plumbago indica*). 2. the leaves of this tree used as condiment for some kind of food. 3. a crown of laurel foliage. Syn. *koronang laurél*. 4. (a) fame; honor. Syn. *kabantugán, karangalan, katanyagán*; (b) victory. Syn. *tagumpáy*.

lawà (la-wà), I. *n.* 1. any small flooded area. Syn. *sanaw*. 2. pool; pond; puddle; lagoon; small lake. Syn. *lanaw, dagát-dagatan*.
—II. *adj.* flooded; covered with water. Syn. *sanaw, may-sanaw, lubóg sa tubig*.

lawaan (la-wa-an), *n.* (Bot.) a big tree, better known as *lawán* (*Anisoptera*, all species). 2. the timber of this tree.

lawak (la-wak), *n.* 1. extent; expanse. Syn. *lakí, luwáng, lapad, sakláw*. 2. great extent; extensiveness, as of power or authority. Syn. *kasaklawán*.

lawag (la-wag), n. 1. act of clearing a place of dense growth, as in preparing a clearing for planting crops. Syn. *hawan, paghahawan.* 2 a place cleared of dense growth.

lawanít (là-wa-nít), n. a kind of walling, ceiling, or paneling material, said to be made from coconut husk.

laway (la-way), n. 1. saliva; spit; spittle. Syn. *lurâ (durâ).* 2. the slimy substance covering the skins or scales of some fishes. Syn. *lansá.*

lawig (la-wig), n. 1. long duration of time. Syn. *laon, kalaunan; tagál, katagalán.* 2. long-windedness. Syn. *ligoy, kaliguyan.*

lawin (la-win), n. 1. (*Zool.*) hawk; falcon. 2. (*Ichth.*) flying fish (*Family Exocoetidae,* all species).

lawiswís (la-wis-wís), n. light current of air; gentle wind; breeze. Syn. *simoy.*

lawiswis-kawayan (la-wis-wis + ka-wa-yan), n. the soft hissing sound made by bamboo tops as they swing to and fro in the air.

lawít (la-wít), I. n. 1. state or condition of being suspended or hung, as of things fastened above. Syn. *bitin, pagkakábitin.* 2. the extent by which a thing is hung or suspended from above. Syn. *habà ng pagkakálawít.* 3. act of lowering or rolling down something, as sleeves, to a certain degree. Syn. *layláy, paglayláy.*
   —II. adj. hanging down; suspended from above; sticking out loosely, as a tongue. Syn. *nakabitin, layláy, nakalayláy.*

lawitán (la-wi-tán), v. 1. to hang with something; suspend or hang something on. Syn. *bitinan.* 2. to have something lowered to someone with or as with a rope. Syn. *hugusan.* 3. (by extension) to extend or give, as help. Syn. *gawaran, bigyán, pagkalooban.*

lawláw[1] (law-láw), I. n. act of stirring (water or liquid) playfully with or as with hands. Syn. *kawkáw, pagkawkáw; labusaw, paglabusaw.*
   —II. adj. stirred up, referring to water or liquid, hence, dirty. Syn. *labusáw.*

lawlaw[2] (law-law), I. n. 1. the length, as of the legs of pants. Syn. *habà (ng lawit).* 2.

state or condition of being too long, as the legs of pants. Syn. *habà, kahabaan.*
   —II. adj. unproportionately long or low. Syn. *layláy, nakalayláy; luslós, nakaluslós.*

layà (la-yà), n. 1. freedom; liberty. Syn. *kalayaan, pagsasarilí.* 2. release from imprisonment. Syn. *paglabás sa bílangguan.* 3. ease of movement or performance; facility. Syn. *luwág, kaluwagan.* 4. (*Colloq.*) right; privilege. Syn. *karapatán.*

layák (la-yák), n. 1. fallen, dried leaves that are scattered thickly around a place. Syn. *makapál na tuyóng dahong nagkalat.* 2. rubbish carried and left by flood waters. Syn. *sukal na naiwan ng bahâ.*

layag (la-yag), n. 1. sail (of a boat). 2. trip by sea; voyage. Syn. *lakbáy-dagat, paglalakbáy-dagat, biyahe sa dagat.* 3. (*Colloq.*) delayed or irregular occurrence of the menses. Syn. *pagkaatraso ng dating ng reglá.*

layanglayang (la-yang-la-yang), n. (*Ornith.*) a species of swallow known as oustalet's swiftlet (*Collocalia germani*).

layas[1] (la-yas), n. 1. a running away from home; going away unceremoniously. Syn. *alís o pag-alís nang waláng paalam.* 2. running away with a lover; elopement. Syn. *tanan, pagtatanan.*

Layas[2] (La-yas), *interj.* Go away!

layás (la-yás), adj. 1. fond of travel. Syn. *lagalág, mapaglakbây, libót, mapaglibót.* 2. given to aimless wandering. Syn. *palaboy, palabuy-laboy.*

layaw (la-yaw), n. 1. independence and comfort in one's living. Syn. *alwán, kaalwanán, ginhawa, kaginhawahan.* 2. freedom enjoyed by a child as a result of being pampered by the parents. Syn. *kalayawan, kalayaang masunód ang bawa't ibig.*

layláy (lay-láy), I. n. 1. state or condition of being drooped or hanging loosely. Syn. *lawít, kalawitán; kalaylayán; luylóy, kaluyluyán.* 2. the portion of a thing that is drooping or hanging loosely. Sy. *ang lawit o nakalawit.*
   —II. adj. drooping; hanging loosely or weakly. Syn. *lawít, nakalawít; luylóy, nakaluylóy.*

laylayan (lay-la-yan), n. the lower end of
the hem line of a garment.

layò (la-yò), n. 1. the distance from a point
or place to another. Syn. *distánsiyá*. 2. the
distance between two points or places.
Syn. *agwát, pagitang distansiya*. 3. state or
condition of being far or distant; farness;
remoteness. Syn. *kalayuan, pagkamalayò*.
3. big difference; great difference, as of
the meanings of two words. Syn *lakí ng
kaibhán*.

layô (la-yô), n. 1. state or condition of being
away or far from each other. Syn.
pagkakalayô, pagkakahiwaláy. 2. act of
going away from a person, thing, or place.
Syn. *layas, paglayas; alís, pag-alís*.

layog (la-yog), n. height; highness; loftiness.
Syn. *taás, kataasan; tayog, katayugan*.

layon (la-yon), n. 1. purpose; aim; objective;
intention. Syn. *hangád, hángarín, pakay,
tunguhin*. 2. (*Gram.*) object.

layót (la-yót), I. n. 1. state or condition of
being overripe. Syn. *labis na pagkahinóg,
lunót, kalunután*. 2. an overripe fruit. Syn.
bungang-kahoy na labis ang pagkahinóg.
—II. *adj*. overripe; too ripe. Syn. *lunót;
labis ang pagkahinóg*.

láyunin (lá-yu-nin), n. purpose; object or
objectives; aim; intention. Syn. *hangád,
hángarin, pakay*. See **layon**.

lebadura (le-ba-du-ra), var. **libadura**, n. (Sp.
levadura) leaven; yeast. Syn. *pampaalsa*.

Lekat (Le-kat), *interj*. an exclamation
expressing displeasure or disappointment.
Cf. *Anó ba! Anó ba namán!*

leksikógrapó (lek-si-kó-gra-pó), n. (Sp.
lexicografo) lexicographer. Syn. *ang
gumágawâ o nagháhandâ ng diksiyunaryo*.

léksikón (lék-si-kón), n. (Eng.) 1. lexicon;
dictionary. Syn. *diksiyunaryo,
talahuluganan*. 2. a special vocabulary, as
of science. Syn. *bokabularyo, talasalitaan*.

leksiyón (lek-si-yón), var. **liksiyón**, n. (Sp.
leccion) 1. lesson or assignment for a
student to study. Syn. *aralín*. 2 moral
lesson; sort of experience. Syn. *aral,
kaaralán*.

lektór (lek-tór), n. (Sp. *lector*) 1. reader. Syn.
tagabasa. 2. lecturer. Syn. *tagapanayám*.

lektura (lek-tu-ra), n. (Sp. *lectura*) 1.
reading; act or manner of reading. Syn.
basa, pagbasa. 2. lecture. Syn. *panayám,
komperénsiyá*. 3. reprimand; reproof. Syn.
mura, pagmumurá; sermón, pagsesermón
(*colloq*.)

leég (le-ég), var. **liig**, n. 1. (*Anat*.) neck (of
a person or animal). 2. the part of a
garment that covers or encircles the
neck.

legado (le-ga-do), n. (Sp.) 1. legacy. Syn.
mana, pamana. 2. legate; envoy;
ambassador. Syn. *sugò, kinatawán*.

legál (le-gál), adj. (Sp.) legal. Syn. *ayon o
alinsunod sa batás*.

legasyón (le-gas-yón), n. (Sp. *legacion*)
legation; mission. Syn. *misyón*.

leghorn (leg-horn), n. (Zool.; Eng.) a breed
of small chicken.

lego (le-go), n. (Sp.) 1. layman. Syn.
karaniwang tao. 2. lay brother. Cf. *ermano,
manong*.

lehistadór (le-his-ta-dór), n. (Sp. *legislador*)
legislator. Syn. *mambabatas*.

lehislasyón (le-his-las-yón), n. (Sp.
legislacion) 1. making of laws; legislation.
Syn. *pagbabatás, paggawâ ng mga batás*. 2.
the law or laws made. Syn. *batás o mga
batás*.

lehislatura (le-his-la-tu-ra), n. (Sp.
legislatura) legislature. Syn. *bátasan*.

lehítimó (le-hí-ti-mó), adj. (Sp. *legítimo*) 1.
legitimate. Syn. *taál, katutubò*. 2. genuine.
Syn. *tunay*.

lehiya (le-hi-ya; le-hi-yá), var. **lihiya**, n. (Sp.
legia) lye. Syn. *sosa*.

lehiyón (le-hi-yón), n. (Sp. *legion*) legion;
large group of soldiers; army. Syn. *hukbó*.

lelang (le-lang), n. (Ch.) grandma;
grandmother. Syn. *lola, abwela*.

lelong (le-long), n. (Ch.) grandpa;
grandfather. Syn. *lolo, abwelo*.

lente (len-te), n. (Sp.) 1. lens. 2. a
magnifying glass. 3. flashlight. Syn.
plaslait.

lengguwahe (leng-gu-wa-he), n. (Sp.
lenguaje) language; idiom; speech. Syn.
wikà, salitâ, idyoma.

león (le-ón), var. **li-yón**, n. (Sp.) 1. (Zool.)
lion. 2. (*L-*) a masculine name.

leopardo (le-o-par-do), n. (Sp.) leopard.

leprosaryo (le-pro-sar-yo), n. (Sp. *leprosario*) hospital or colony for lepers; leprosarium. Syn. *págamutan ng mga kétongin (leproso)*, *leprosaryum*.

léprosí (lé-pro-sí), n. (Eng.) leprosy. Syn. *ketong*.

leteng (le-teng), n. (Ch.) cotton twine. Cf. *pisì, talì*.

léteríng (lé-te-ríng), n. (Eng.) 1. act of lettering or making letters or inscribing in or with letters, esp. by printing, drawing, or painting. Syn. *pagleletra*. 2. the manner by which such lettering was done. Syn. *pagkakáletra, pagkakapagletra, pagkakátitik*. 3. the series of letters or inscriptions so made. Syn. *mga titik*.

letra (le-tra), n. (Sp.) 1. character of the alphabet; letter. Syn. *titik (ng abakada)*. 2. the type or impression representing a letter or character of the alphabet. Syn. *tipo*. 3. style of handwriting; penmanship. Syn. *sulat-kamáy, porma ng sulat*. 4. words of a song; lyrics. Syn. *titik*. 5 style or manner by which letters were made by hands. Syn. *pagkakáletra, pagkakápagletra*.

letse (let-se), *interj.* (Sp. *Leche!*) an exclamation of disgust or anger. Cf. *Punyeta!*

letseplán (let-se-plán), n. (Sp. *leche flan*) custard.

letsugas (let-su-gas), n. (Sp. *lechugas*) lettuce.

leukemya (le-u-kem-ya), var. **leyukemya**, n. (Eng.) leukemia.

leukoma (le-u-ko-ma), var. **leyukoma**, n. (Eng.) leucoma. Cf. *bilíg sa matá*.

ley (ley), var. **layí, leyí**, n. (Sp.) law. Syn. *batás*. 2. ordinance. Syn. *ordinansa, kautusán*.

leyenda (le-yen-da), n. (Sp.) legend. Syn. *alamát, kuwentóng-bayan*.

libák (li-bák), n. mockery; derision; ridicule; insult. Syn. *aglahì, uyám, kutyâ, tuyâ, uróy, paghamak*.

libág (li-bág), n. thick dirt of the skin.

liban¹ (li-ban), I. n. 1. absence or non-attendance, as in class, work, etc. Syn. *di-pagpasok, palya, pag-palya*. 2. times or number of times of being absent or away. Syn. *bilang o dami ng di-pagpasok*. 3. a person or persons not present in class, work, etc. Syn. *ang di-pumasok o di-nagsipasok*. 4. postponement. Syn. *pagpapaliban, pagpapaibáng-araw*.
—II. adj. absent; not present; away. Syn. *di-pumasok, palyo, pumalyo, di-dumaló, walâ*.

liban² (li-ban), *prep.* (usually with *sa*) except; unless. Also, *máliban sa*.

libán (li-ban), n. 1. act of passing over an obstacle, as by jumping or climbing. Syn. *ibág, pag-ibág; lundág, paglundág*. 2. act of passing or going across; crossing. Syn. *tawíd, pagtawíd; bagtás, pagbagtás*.

libáng (li-báng), n. 1. an engrossing or being engrossed; absorption, as in reading. Syn. *wili, pagkawili*. 2. an entertaining or being entertained. Syn. *alíw, pag-alíw, pagkaalíw*.

líbangan (lí-ba-ngan), n. hobby; amusement; recreation; entertainment. Syn. *áliwan, dibersiyón*.

libay (li-bay), n. (Zool.), a female deer; doe. Syn. *usáng babae*.

libelo (li-be-lo), n. (Sp.) in Law, libel. Syn. *nakasulat na paninirang-puri*.

liberál (li-be-rál), I. adj. (Sp.) 1. generous; giving freely. Sy. *bukás-palad (fig.)*, *maluwág sa kuwarta*. 2 broad-minded; liberal. Syn. *mapagbigáy, maúnawaín, bukás ang isip, may bukás na isip*. 3. of or belonging to the Liberal Political Party. Syn. *Partido Liberál*.
—II. n. 1. a broad-minded person. Syn. *taong maúnawaín o mapagbigáy*. 2 (L-) name of a political party in the Philippines. 3. a member of this party.

liberasyón (li-be-ras-yón), n. (Sp. *liberación*) 1. liberation; setting free. Syn. *pagpapalayà, pagbibigáy-layà*. 2. a being set free. Syn. *layà, paglayà, pagkakalayà*.

libertád (li-ber-tád), n. (Sp.) liberty; freedom. Syn. *kalayaan*.

libid (li-bid), n. 1. single coil, as of rope, wire, etc., around something. Syn. *ikid, ayikid, pulupot, bidbíd, bilibid*. 2. an encircling or going around a place, as in racing. Syn. *pagligid, pag-ikot*. 3. a single round made around a place. Syn. *ligid, ikot*. 4. act of surrounding or encircling a place, as by enemies. Syn. *pagpaligid,* *pagkubkób.*

líbidó (lí-bi-dó), n. (Eng.) libido; sexual urge
or instinct. Syn. *libog, kalibugan; utog,
kautugan.*

libíng (li-bíng), n. 1. burial; interment;
funeral. Syn. *paglilibíng, pagbabaón sa
bangkáy.* 2. grave; tomb; sepulcher. Syn.
puntód.

líbingan (lí-bi-ngan), n. 1. cemetery;
graveyard. Syn. *sementeryo, kamposanto.*
2. grave; tomb; sepulcher. Syn. *libíng,
puntód.*

libís (li-bís), n. 1. slope, as of a hill or
mountain; hillside. Syn. *dalisdís, gilid ng
bundók.* 2. lowland. Syn. *labák, lambák,
kababaan.*

liblíb (lib-líb), I. adj. hidden, secluded, or
unfrequented, referring to a place. Syn.
tagô, kublí, lingíd.
—II. n. 1 state or condition of being
unfrequented or secluded, referring to a
place. 2. an unknown or unfrequented
place. Syn. *lingid na poók.*

libo (li-bo), n. & adj. thousand. Syn.
sampúng-daán.

libog (li-bog), n. sexual urge; lust; libido;
lasciviousness. Syn. *utog, kautugan,
kalibugan.*

libot (li-bot), n. 1. act of going from place
to place; wandering; roaming about. Syn.
galâ, paggagalâ. 2. act of making rounds,
as doctors do among patients in the
different wards in a hospital. Syn.
pagbibisita. 3. act of making trips to
different places, as tourists do. Syn.
paglalakbáy sa ibá't ibáng lugár. 4. a going
around for pleasure. Syn. *pasyál,
pamamasyál.*

libra¹ (lib-ra; li-brá), n. (Sp.) pound (unit
of weight).

Libra² (Li-bra), n. (Sp.) in Astrol., Libra,
the seventh sign of the zodiac. Syn.
Timbangan.

libré (li-bré), adj. (Sp.) 1. free; gratis;
obtained for free. Syn. *waláng-bayad,
gratis, bigáy.* 2. free of responsibility. Syn.
waláng-págutin, di-manánagót. 3. safe. Syn.
ligtás, waláng-panganib. 4. (Colloq.) free;
vacant; not working. Syn. *waláng-
ginágawâ, malayà, namámahingá.*

librería (li-bre-rí-a), var. **libreriya**, n. (Sp.)
1. bookstore. Syn. *tindahan ng aklát.* 2.
library. Syn. *aklatan, bibliyoteka.*

libreta (lib-re-ta), n. (Sp.) 1. bankbook;
deposit book. 2. notebook. Syn. *aklát-
talaan.*

libreto (lib-re-to), n. (It.) in Mus., libretto.

libró (li-bró), n. (Sp.) 1. book. Syn. *aklat.*
2. Accounting, journal; daybook. 3.
(Colloq.) record book. Syn. *aklát-talaan.*

libtóng (lib-tóng), n. deep hole in a river
bed. 2. a small wen-like growth on skin.
Syn. *butlíg, butól, ligatà.*

libtós (lib-tós), I. n. blister. Syn. *paltós.*
—II. adj. with or having blister. Syn. *may-
paltós.*

libu-libo (li-bu + li-bo), adj. & adv.
thousands upon thousands. Syn.
*nápakarami, lubháng marami, katakut-takot
na dami.*

likas (li-kas; li-kás), n. 1. act of withdrawing
from a place to another for safety;
evacuation. Syn. *pag-alís o pag-aálisan sa
isáng lugár, pagtakas mulâ sa mapanganib
na lugár.* 2. an evacuee or evacuees. Syn.
*tao o mga taong tumakas mulâ sa isáng poók
na mapanganib.*

likás (li-kás), adj. 1. inborn; natural; innate.
Syn. *katutubò, naturál.* 2. copious;
plentiful; abundant; in abundance. Syn.
saganà, manánaganà.

likaw (li-kaw), n. 1. act of winding or coiling
(rope, wire, etc.) into a series of coils or
rolls. Syn. *rolyo, pagrorolyo; ayikid, pag-
aayikid; kidkíd, pagkikidkíd.* 2. a coil or roll,
as of rope, wire, etc. Syn. *likid, rolyo,
kidkíd, ayikid.*

likhâ (lik-hâ), I. n. 1. act of making or
producing something. Syn. *gawâ, paggawâ.*
2. a creating or being created; creation, as
by God. Syn. *laláng, paglaláng.* 3. an
inventing or being invented; invention.
Syn. *imbento, pag-imbento.* 4. a creation by
God. Syn. *laláng, nilaláng.* 5. an invention;
thing invented. Syn. *imbento.* 6. a made-up
story; false statement. Syn. *katakatà.* 7. a
coining or being coined; coinage, as of a
word.
—II. adj. 1. made, produced, or
manufactured by. Syn. *gawâ o yarì ng (ni).*

2. created, as by God. Syn. *laláng, nilaláng*.
3. invented. Syn. *imbento, inimbento*. 4.
coined, referring to a word. 5. made-up, as
a story or statement. Syn. *katakatà, gawá-gawaan*.

likidá (li-ki-dá), n. (Sp. *v. liquidar*) 1.
liquidation or payment of debts;
settlement of accounts. Syn. *pagbabayad
ng mga utang*. 2. getting rid of. Syn. *palipol,
pagpuksâ, pagpatáy*.

likidó (li-ki-dó), I. n. (Sp. *liquido*) liquid.
Syn. *tunáw o lusáw na bagay*. Cf. *tubig*.
—II. *adj*. in the form of liquid; melted.
Syn. *tunáw, lusáw*.

likmo (lik-mo), n. 1. act of sitting down
quietly. Syn. *upô, pag-upô; luklók,
pagluklók*. 2. the way or manner a person
sits. Syn. *upô, pagkakáupô; luklók,
pagkakáluklók*.

likmuan (lik-mu-an), n. 1. place for sitting,
as a chair, sofa, bench, etc. Syn. *upuan,
luklukan*. 2. act of sitting simultaneously,
as of a number of persons. Syn. *pag-
uúpuan, paglulúklukan*.

likô (li-kô), I. n. 1. in walking, running, or
in driving a vehicle, a turn to either side
of the way. Syn. *baling, pagbaling; paling,
pagpaling; pihit, pagpihit*. 2. the place where
a turn or change in direction is made;
curve or bend on a road. Syn. *kurba,
kurbada*. 3. state or condition of being
erroneous or improper, as in the treatment
of one's children. Syn. *kalisyaán,
kahidwaán*.
—II. *adj*. 1. bent; curved. Syn. *baluktót,
kurba, kurbada*. 2. erroneous; improper.
Syn. *lisyâ, hidwâ, malî, lihís*.

likód (li-kód), n. 1. the back (of a person or
animal). Syn. *gulugód*. 2. the back of the
neck. Syn. *batok*. 3. the back of a chair or
couch. Syn. *sandalan*. 4. the part opposite
the front. Syn. *likurán*. 5. the other side
or surface of something fronting someone.
Syn. *kabilâ*. 6. the rear or hinder part of
anything. Syn. *hulí, hulihán; puwít,
puwitán*. 7. the reverse side, as of a cloth.
Syn. *kabaligtarán, ilalim*. Ant. *karayagán,
ibabaw*.

likom (li-kom), n. act of collecting or
gathering things and putting them

together. Syn. *ipon, pag-iipon; tipon,
pagtitipon; ligpít, pagliligpít*. 2. collection,
as of taxes. Syn. *singíl, paniningíl*.

likop (li-kop), n. 1. an encircling or
surrounding, as with a fence. Syn. *kulóng,
pagkulóng; paligid, pagpapaligid*. 2. act of
gathering things together and keeping
them in their proper place. Syn. *likom,
paglikom; ligpít, pagliligpít*.

likót (li-kót), n. 1. overactiveness; excessive
agility. Sy. *labis na siglá (kasiglahán)*. 2.
roughness of manners or movement. Syn.
gasláw, kagaslawán; harót, kaharután. 3.
restlessness; fidgetiness. Syn. *di-
pagkápalagáy, balisa, kabalisahan*. 4.
incessant motion or movement; mobility.
Syn. *kawaláng-tigil; kagalawgwán*. 5. act
of trifling or toying with something
dangerous, prohibited, etc. Syn. *larô,
paglalarô (colloq.)*. 6. act of touching,
moving, or taking something not his own.
Syn. *pakialám, pakikialám*. 7.
mischievousness; naughtiness. Syn.
kapilyuhán, kalikután.

liksí (lik-sí), var. **ligsí**, n. 1. quick movement
or action; quickness of action or
movement; agility; nimbleness. Syn. *bilis
kumilos, kabilisán ng kilos, kaliksihán,
kaligsihán*. 2. promptness. Syn. *agap,
kaagapan, pagkamaagap*. 3. nimbleness of
mind; mental quickness; quick-
wittedness. Syn. *talisik, katalisikan*. 4. (by
extension) efficiency; competency. Syn.
*husay, kahusayan; buti, kabutihan; galíng,
kagalingán*.

liksiyón (lik-si-yón), var. **leksiyón**, n. (Sp.
leccion) 1. lesson or assignment for a
student to study. Syn. *aralín*. 2. moral
lesson; sort of experience. Syn. *aral,
kaaralán*.

likú-likô (likú + likô), *adj*. serpentine;
sinuous; tortuous or winding, said esp. of
roads. Syn. *palikú-likó*.

likurán (li-ku-rán), n. 1. place at the back,
as of a house; backside. Syn. *dakong likód,
kabilâ*. 2. a place to behind or at the rear.
Syn. *hulí, hulihán*. 3. background. Syn.
tánawin sa dakong likód.

lider (li-der), n. (Sp.) 1. leader; head of a
group; labor leader. Syn. *punò, lider-*

manggagawà. 2. perpetrator; one who starts something wrong. Syn. *pasimunò.*

liga (li-ga), n. (Sp.) 1. league; alliance; union. Syn. *unyón, kaisahán.* 2. association. Syn. *samahán, kapisanan.* 3. seasonal athletic competition. Syn. *páligsahan.*

ligalig (li-ga-lig), n. 1. trouble; civil disorder; public disturbance. Syn. *guló, pagkakaguló, basag-ulo, sígalutan.* 2. mental distress; perturbation; worry. Syn. *linggatong, bagabag, tigatig, balisa.* 3. fit of bad temper; tantrum. Syn. *alburuto, pag-aalburuto.* 4. bother; preoccupation. Syn. *abala, kaabalahan, pagkaabala; gambalà, pagkagambalà, kagambalaan.*

ligamento (li-ga-men-to), n. (Sp.) ligament. Syn. *litid.*

ligamgám[1] (li-gam-gám), n. 1. slight worry or perturbation. Syn. *ala-alá, pag-aalaalá; bagabag; bahalà, pagkabahalà.* 2. disquietude; restlessness; anxiety. Syn. *balisa, pagkabalisa, tigatig.* 3. feeling of doubt or suspicion. Syn. *álinlangan, pag-aálinlangan; hinalà, paghihinalà.* 4. feeling of insecurity or fear. Syn. *pangambá, takot, agam-agam.*

ligamgám[2] (li-gam-gám), n. tepidness or lukewarmness, as of water. Syn. *bahagyáng init, pagkamainít-init.*

ligas (li-gas), n. (Sp. *liga*) garter. Syn. *garter.*

ligás (li-gás), n. (Bot.) a small tree reaching a height of 12 meters, the fruit of which is borne in clusters, resembling that of *kasúy*, and the sap is a violent contact poison, causing painful swelling and minute pustules on skin.

ligasgás (li-gas-gás), n. coarseness or roughness of surface. Syn. *aligasgás, gaspáng.*

ligat (li-gat), n. delicious consistency, esp. of cooked rice, tubers, etc. Cf. *kunat, ganít.*

ligaw (li-gaw), n. 1. act of wooing; courtship. Syn. *pangingibig, panunuyò sa dalaga upang máibig.* 2. suitor; wooer. Syn. *mángingibig, manliligaw.*

ligáw (li-gáw), adj. 1. wild or uncultivated, referring to plants. Syn. *tumútubò kahit saán.* 2. stray, as bullets. 3. stray or roaming freely, referring to animals. Syn. *alpás, kawalá, di-nakatalì, di-nakakulóng.* 4. wild or undomesticated, as animals. Syn. *mailáp.* 5. misguided; wrong. Syn. *malî, lisyâ, lihís.*

ligaw-tingín (li-gaw + ti-ngín), n. wooing or courtship expressed in one's meaningful looks. Syn. *pangingibig sa pamamagitan ng makahulugáng tingín.*

ligaya (li-ga-ya), n. 1. happiness; joy; felicity. Syn. *sayá, tuwâ, galák, lugód.* 2. pleasure; satisfaction. Syn. *kasiyahan, alíw, kaaliwán.* 3. (L-) a feminine name.

ligid (li-gid), n. 1. act of circling or going around a place, as in running a circular track. Syn. *pagligid, ikot, pag-ikot.* 2. a surrounding or encircling. Syn. *kulóng, pagkulóng.* 3. a detouring. Syn. *lihís o paglihís ng daán.*

ligís (li-gís), I. n. 1. act or manner of grinding, pounding, or crushing (grains, etc.) into powder; pulverizing. Syn. *pagdurog na mabuti, pagpulbós, pagligí.* 2. state or condition of being pulverized. Syn. *kaligisán, pagkaduróg na mabuti, kapulbusán.*

—II. adj. pulverized; made into powder by grinding, pounding, or crushing. Syn. *duróg na duróg, pulbós, pinulbós.*

liglíg (lig-líg), I. n. 1. act of shaking or a being shaken, as of a container. Syn. *alóg, pag-alóg; tigtíg, pagtigtíg.* 2. the irregular movement or shaking of a vehicle on a rugged road. Syn. *tigtíg, pagkatigtíg; alóg, pagkaalóg.*

—II. adj. shaken; being shaken. Syn. *tigtíg, natítigtíg; alóg, naáalóg.*

ligò (li-gò), n. act of manner of bathing; taking a bath. Syn. *paligò, palíligò; hambo, paghambo.*

ligoy (li-goy), n. wordiness or verbosity in speech or writing; long-windedness (in speech or writing); a beating around the bush. Syn. *kaliguyan, pagkamaligoy.*

ligpít (lig-pít), I. n. 1. act of collecting or gathering things and putting them together in a proper place. Syn. *likom, paglilikom.* 2. act of keeping or putting a thing or things in a safe place for future use. Syn. *tagò, pagtatagò.* 3. act of clearing

(a room, etc.) of things scattered all around. Syn. *imis, pag-iimis.* 4. act of silencing a person by or as by killing him. Syn. *pagpatáy.* 5. (*Colloq.*) retirement, as from work, office, or political activity. Syn. *pahingá, pamamahingá.*
—II. *adj.* 1. gathered and put together in a proper place. Syn. *likóm na.* 2. kept or put into a safe place for future use. Syn. *nakatagò.* 3. cleared of things scattered. Syn. *imís, naimis na.* 4. killed or murdered. Syn. *pinatáy.* 5. retired; resting; in retirement. Syn. *namámahingá, retirado.*

ligtâ (lig-tâ), *n.* 1. an unintentional mistake or omission. Syn. *di-sinásadyáng pagkakámalî o dî pagkapasama ng isáng bagay.* 2. neglect; lack of attention, as to one's duty. Syn. *pagpapabayà o pagpapabayâ.*

ligtás (lig-tás), I. *n.* 1. state or condition of being out of danger (safe); freedom from certain obligation, responsibility, punishment, etc. 2. act of saving someone in danger, or redeeming someone from bondage.
—II. *adj.* 1. free from damage, danger, or injury; safe; Syn. *libre o walâ na sa panganib (peligro).* 2. unharmed; saved. Syn. *di-napinsalà, di-nasaktán, di-naanó.* 3. redeemed, as from bondage. Syn. *tubós, tinubós, hangô na.*

ligwák (lig-wák), *n.* 1. a spilling of water or liquid from a container. Syn. *salwák, pagkásalwák, linggák.* 2. liquid or water spilled on something from a container.

liha (li-ha), *n.* (Sp. *lija*) 1. sandpaper. Syn. *papel de liha.* 2. act or manner of cleaning, smoothing, or polishing a surface with sandpaper. Syn. *pagliha, pagliliha, pagpapapél-de-liha, pagpapapapél-de-liha.* 3. the way a surface has been sandpapered. Syn. *pagkakáliha, pagkakápapél-de-liha.*

lihà (li-hà), *n.* 1. each of the internal segments or sections of a fruit, like orange, lemon, etc. 2. each section or region between the principal lines on the palm of the hand.

liham (li-ham), *n.* 1. a written message; letter; missive. Syn. *sulat.* 2. act of writing or sending a letter or a message, as to a friend. Syn. *sulat, pagsulat, pagliham, pagpapapahatíd ng sulat.*

lihí (li-hí), *n.* 1. conception; conceiving. Syn. *paglilihí.* 2. capricious desire or cravings for something by a conceiving woman.

lihim (li-him), I. *n.* 1. secret; anything known only to a certain person or persons concerned and purposely kept from the knowledge of others. Syn. *sekreto.* 2. mystery. Syn. *hiwagà, kahiwagaan.* 3. act of keeping a secret. Syn. *paglilihim.*
—II. *adj.* 1. secret; kept from the knowledge of others. Syn. *sekreto, waláng nakaáalam na ibá, lingíd (sa ibá).* 2. kept from sight; hidden. Syn. *tagô, nakatagò; kublí, nakakublî.* 3. undercover or secret, as an agent. Syn. *nakabalatkayô.*
—II. *adv.* secretly; in a secret manner. Syn. *palihím, patagô.*

lihís (li-hís), I. *n.* 1. a turning aside from a course, standard, etc.; deviation; deflection. Syn. *iwas, pag-iwas.* 2. act of avoiding something by turning to one side. Syn. *ilag, pag-ilag.* 3. state or condition of being out of alignment. Syn. *sinsáy, pagkasinsáy. pagkawala sa hanay.* 4. state or condition of being incorrect, misleading, or erroneous. Syn. *kalisyaán, kamalián, pagkámalî, di-katumpakán.*
—II. *adj.* 1. turned aside from a course, standard, etc.; deviated; deflected. Syn. *lumihís, sumala.* 2. out of alignment. Syn. *walâ sa linya (hanay).* 3. wrong; incorrect; misleading; erroneous. Syn. *malî, lisyâ, di-tamâ.*

liit (li-it; li-ít), *n.* 1. lack of natural size; littleness; smallness. Syn. *kaliitan (kaliitán), linggít, kalinggitán.* 2. inadequacy or scantiness, as of one's income. Syn. *kakulangán, kakapusán, di-kasapatán.* 3. narrowness or smallness of a hole. Syn. *kipot, kakiputan.* Cf. *sikip, kasikipán.* 4. fineness, as of thread, etc. Syn. *pino, kapinuhan.*

lila (li-la), *n.* (*Bot.*) a lilac plant or its tiny, fragrant flower. Syn. *lilak.* 2. a pale-purple color; lilac (color). Syn. *biyuleta.* 3. (L-) a feminine name.
—II. *adj.* of pale-purple color. Syn.

biyuleta, kulay-biyuleta.

lili (li-li), n. (*Bot.*) the lily plant or its flower.

lilik (li-lik), n. sickle. Syn. *karit.*

lilim (li-lim), n. 1. a shaded place, as one under a tree; shade. Syn. *lilom.* 2. shadow. Syn. *anino.*

lilip (li-lip), n. 1. hand sewing of hem. Syn. *pagtahî sa lupî o tutóp sa pamamagitan ng kamáy, paglilip, paglililip.* 2. the manner a hem was hand-sewn. Syn. *pagkakálilip, pagkakátahî ng kamáy.*

lilís (li-lís), I. n. 1. act of pulling, raising, or rolling up the lower end of sleeves, skirts, or legs of trousers. Syn. *bayakís, pagbayakís; bulislís, pagbulislís; lislís, paglislís.* 2. state or condition of being pulled, raised, or rolled up, referring to sleeve, skirts, legs of trousers, etc. Syn. *pagkakábayakís; pagkakálislís, pagkakábulislís.* 3. that which is pulled, raised, or rolled up.

—II. adj. pulled, raised, or rolled up, referring to the lower end of a sleeve, skirt, or leg of pants. Syn. *nakalislís, bayakís, nakabayakís; bulislís, nakabulislís.*

liliw (li-liw), n. 1. (*Ornith.*) long-legged, colorful bird. 2. (L-) name of a town in the province of Laguna.

lilo (li-lo), I. adj. disloyal; unfaithful; traitorous; treacherous. Syn. *taksíl, sukáb, mapagkánuló, traidór.*

—II. n. traitor; betrayer. Syn. *taong taksil o sukáb, traidór.*

lilok (li-lok), n. 1. act of carving wood or stones into figures as statues, ornaments, etc. Syn. *ukit, pag-uukit.* 2. any piece of sculptured work.

lilom (li-lom), n. 1. shade; a shaded place, as one under a tree. Syn. *lilim.* 2. shadow. Syn. *anino.*

limá (li-má), n. & adj. five. Syn. *singko.*

limahid (li-ma-hid), n. extreme untidiness of clothes and body. Syn. *panlilimahid, panlalapot sa dumí ng damít at katawán.*

limampû (li-mam-pû), n. & adj. fifty. Syn. *singkuwenta.*

limang (li-mang), n. distraction or confusion in counting. Syn. *litó o pagkalitó sa pagbilang.*

limás (li-más), I. n. 1. act of scooping or

bailing out water, as from a boat, well, canal, or the like, with or as with bucket or pail. Cf. *salok, pagsalok.* 2. (by extension) act of ransacking a place and taking all of its contents. Syn. *paghalughóg sa isáng lugál at pagnakaw sa lahát ng lamán doón, pagsimót o pagnakaw sa lahát ng lamán.*

—II. adj. 1. drained or scooped out of water with or as with pail or bucket. Syn. *nalimasán na ng tubig.* 2. ransacked or plundered thoroughly. Syn. *simót o sinimót na lahát ang lamán.*

limatik (li-ma-tik), n. 1. an animal that sucks blood, esp. a leech. Syn. *lintâ.* 2. a person who tries persistently to get all what he can from others; bloodsucker. Syn. *manghuhuthót, lintâ sa katihan (fig.), buwaya (fig.), ganid.*

limayón (li-ma-yón), I. n. act of whiling away one's time uselessly. Syn. *lakwatsa, paglalakwatsa; ansikót, pag-aansikót; bulakból, pagbubulakból.*

—II. adj. given to whiling away one's time uselessly. Syn. *lakwatsero, mapáglakuwatsa; ansikutero, mapág-ansikót; bulakbulero, mapágbulakból.*

limbág (lim-bág), I. n. 1. act of printing. Syn. *paglimbág, paglilimbág; pag-imprenta, pag-iimprenta.* 2. edition or printing, as of a book, as in *ikalawáng limbág,* second edition (printing). Syn. *edisyón, pagkakálimbág.* 3. quality of printing. Syn. *pagkakálimbág, pagkakáimprenta.* 4. act of making letters or inscribing with letters esp. by handprinting, drawing, or painting; lettering. Syn. *pagliletra.*

—II. adj. 1. printed or published. Syn. *imprentado.* 2. inscribed by handprinting, drawing, or painting, referring to letters. Syn. *itinitik, nakatitik.*

limbagan (lim-ba-gan), n. 1. printing shop printing house. Syn. *pálimbagan, imprenta.* 2. printing press or machine. Syn. *imprenta, mákináng panlimbág.*

limbás (lim-bás), n. 1. swift-flying bird o prey. Syn. *ibong máninilà, ibong mandaragit.* 2. a person who preys on or upon others Syn. *taong mapágsamantalá sa kapwà.*

limbo[1] (lim-bo), n. (Eng., Sp.) limbo; abode

after death of unbaptized children and of righteous people who lived before Christ. Syn. *paraiso ng mga musmós at taong mga banál noóng bago isinilang si Hesus.*

limbo² (lim-bo; lim-bó), n. 1. a golden circle or disk of light surrounding the heads of divinities, saints, etc. on medals, pictures, and the like; halo. Syn *sinag sa ulo.* 2. a ring of light around the sun, moon, and other shining body.

limi (li-mi), n. attention; careful observation; a giving heed to something important. Syn. *intindí, pag-intindí; hasikaso, paghasikaso (asikaso, pag-asikaso).*

limì (li-mì), n. reflection; serious thought; contemplation; meditation. Syn. *nilay-nilay, pagninilay-nilay; bulay-bulay, pagbubulay-bulay; pag-iisip na mabuti.*

limit (li-mit), n. 1. frequent occurrence; frequency. Syn. *dalás, kadalasán; kalimitan, pagkamalimit.* 2. closeness; compactness; density. Syn. *sinsín, kasinsinán.*

limitado (li-mi-ta-do), adj. (Sp.) limited; restricted; kept within limits. Syn. *may-takdâ, natátakdaán.*

limitasyón (li-mi-tas-yón), n. (Sp. *limitacion*) 1. limitation. Syn. *takdâ, pagtatakdâ, katakdaán.* 2. restriction. Syn. *pagbabawal, kabawalán.*

limlím (lim-lím), n. sitting on eggs by the hen to hatch them; hatching of eggs by the hen. Syn. *halimhím, paghalimhím, yupyóp o pagyupyóp sa itlóg ng inahín.*

limón (li-món), n. (Sp.) 1. lemon tree. 2. the fruit of this tree. Cf. *dayap, bilulo, kahél.* 3. lemon drop (candy).

limós (li-mós), I. n. 1. act of giving alms. Syn. *paglilimós, pagbibigáy ng limós.* 2. anything given to beggars as help; alms. Syn. *palimós.* Cf. *abuloy.*
—II. adj. referring to anything given as alms. Syn. *palimós.*

limot (li-mot), n. 1. a forgetting or having forgotten; oblivion. Syn. *pagkawalâ sa isip (alaala).* 2. forgetfulness. Syn. *pagkamalimutín.* 3. (by extension) overlooking of offenses; pardon. Syn. *pagpapatawad.*

limót (li-mót), I. n. 1. act of picking up (something) from the floor or ground.

Syn. *pulot, pagpulot.* 2. picking up or learning (something) from another or others. 3. any article of value found accidentally while walking in the street and taken for oneself. Syn. *bagay na nápulot.*
—II. adj. 1. found accidentally by someone. Syn. *nápulot.* 2. referring to fallen fruits that were picked up from the ground; distinguished from those picked from the branches.

limpák (lim-pák), n. 1. a big piece, esp. of meat. Syn. *malakíng piraso o tipák.* 2. a big amount or quantity, as of money. Syn. *malakíng halagá.*

limpiyá (lim-pi-yá), n. (Sp. *limpia*) 1. act of cleaning or shining something, as shoes, boots, etc. Syn. *linis, paglilinis.* 2. the manner shoes, boots, etc. were cleaned or polished. Syn. *pagkakálinis.*

linabán (li-na-bán), v. to scoop out the greasy or fatty scum from. Cf. *halagapan, sagapan ng iskoma.*

linamnám (li-nam-nám), n. 1. deliciousness; tastiness; pleasing taste; appetizing flavor. Syn. *saráp.* 2. taste; flavor. Syn. *lasa.* See **namnám.**

lináng (li-náng), I. n. 1. cultivation of land for planting. Syn. *saka, pagsasaka.* 2. field under cultivation; farm. Syn. *saka, sakahán; tániman; bukid, bukirín.* 3. development or enrichment, as of a language, culture, etc. Syn. *pagpapaunlád, pagpapayaman.*
—II. adj. 1. tilled or cultivated, referring to a field or piece of land. 2. well-developed, as a language. Syn. *maunlád, mayaman.*

linasa (li-na-sa), n. (Sp. *linaza*) linseed; flaxseed.

linaw (li-naw), n. 1. clarity or clearness, as of a mirror, liquid, vision, eyes, speech, etc. Cf. *liwanag, kaklaruhan.* 2. a clarifying or being clarified; clarification. Syn. *pagliwanag,   pagpapaliwanag, pagkakápaliwanag.*

lindól (lin-dól), n. earthquake. Syn. *yaníg ng lupà.*

linimento (li-ni-men-to), n. (Sp.) liniment. Syn. *panghaplás.*

lining (li-ning), n. careful weighing of a matter in one's mind; serious thought about something; contemplation; reflection. Syn. *nilay, pagninilay, pagninilay-nilay; muni-muni, pagmumunimuni.*

linis (li-nis), n. 1. act of cleaning (something). Syn. *paglilinis.* 2. state or condition of being clean; cleanness; cleanliness. Syn. *kalinisan.*

linláng (lin-láng), n. 1. act of playing a trick on somebody. Syn. *paglinláng, panlilinláng, panloloko, pandarayà.* 2. a trick or trickery done on someone; fraud; deceit. Syn. *dayà, pandarayà, laláng.*

linolyo (li-nol-yo), n. (Sp. *linóleo*) linoleum. Syn. *linolyum.*

linotipya (li-no-tip-ya), n. (Sp. *linotipia*) 1. linotype (machine). 2. act or art of linotyping. Syn. *paglilinotipya.*

linsad (lin-sad; lin-sád), I. n. 1. dislocation, as of the joints of bones. Syn. *lisók.* 2. derailment, as of a train. Syn. *diskaril, pagkadiskaríl.*

—II. adj. 1. dislocated, as of bones. Syn. *luminsád, nálinsád; lumisók, nálisók.* 2. derailed, referring to a train. Syn. *diskarilado, nadiskaríl.*

lintâ (lin-tâ), n. (Zool.) 1. water leech. Cf. *limatik.* 2. a person who preys on others; bloodsucker. Syn. *manghuhuthót, buwaya (fig.).*

linták (lin-ták), interj. an exclamation expressive of disgust or surprise. Syn. *Putris!*

lintík (lin-tík), n. 1. lightning; flash of lightning. Syn. *kidlát.* 2. a curse or insulting word. Cf. *mura, tungayaw.*

lintikán (lin-ti-kán), v. (Colloq.) to come to a disastrous end; suffer a setback. Syn. *madisgrasya, mabigô.*

lintóg (lin-tóg), n. 1. blister. Syn. *pautós, libtós, lintós.* 2. any swelling on the skin like a blister. Syn. *paklóy, pamamaklóy.*

lintós (lin-tós), n. an open blister. Syn. *lapnós.*

linya (lin-ya), n. (Sp. *linea*) 1. a long, thin mark made with pencil, ink, etc.; line. Syn. *guhit, raya.* 2. file; row. Syn. *pila, hanay, hilera.* 3. regular route of vehicles and other transports. Syn. *ruta, daán.* 4. a line of printed words, esp. in poetry. Syn. *taludtód.* 5. a printed line in prose. Syn. *talatà.* 6. profession, occupation, or business. Syn. *opisyo, propesyón, gáwain, tungkulin, trabaho.* 7. boundary line; limit. Syn. *hangganan, hanggahan.*

lingá (li-ngá), n. (Bot.) sesame (the plant and its seed).

lingà (li-ngà), var. **lingâ**, n. act or manner of looking for someone. Syn. *pagpapalingún-lingón.*

lingap (li-ngap), n. 1. protective care; a caring for. Syn. *kandili, arugâ, kalingà, andukâ, tangkilik.* 2. compassionate care; pity. Syn. *awà, pagkaawà.* 3. affectionate care; love. Syn. *pagmamahál.*

lingát (li-ngát), n. 1. forgetfulness; absent-mindedness. Syn. *limot, pagkalimot.* 2. negligence; inattentiveness; lack of attention or care. Syn. *pagpapabayà, kapabayaán, pagkaligtâ.*

lingkaw (ling-kaw; ling-káw), n. scythe. Cf. *karit, lilik.*

lingkís (ling-kís), I. n. 1. act of crushing or squeezing a prey by coiling around its body, as by a python or a boa constrictor. Syn. *mahigpít na pagpulupot o pagsalabíd sa katawán ng bíktimá.* 2. (by extension) a very tight hug or embrace. Syn. *nápakahigpít na yakap o yapós.*

—II. adj. 1. crushed or squeezed in the coils of a python or a boa constrictor, referring to a victim. 2. embraced or hugged tightly in one's arms. Syn. *yakáp o yapós nang mahigpít.*

lingkód (ling-kód), n. 1. servant or attendant; servitor. Syn. *utusán, tagapaglingkód, serbidór, tagasilbí.* 2. act of serving someone. Syn. *paglilingkód, pagsisilbí.* 3. helper; assistant. Syn. *katulong, kátulungín.* 4. adherent; follower; disciple. Syn. *tagasunód, tauhan, disipuló, alagád.*

linggatong (ling-ga-tong), n. mental perturbation or trouble. Syn. *baklá, pagkabaklá; ligalig, pagkaligalig; guló o pagkaguló ng isip; bagabag, pagkabagabag.*

linggít (ling-gít), n. littleness; smallness; tininess. Syn. *liít, kaliitán.*

linggo (ling-go; ling-gó), n. 1. week; a period of seven days, from Sunday to Saturday. 2. (L-) Sunday; the first day of the week. Syn. *Domingo*.

Linggo de Ramos, var. Domingo de Ramos, Palm Sunday. Syn. *Linggo ng Palaspás*.

língguhan (líng-gu-han), I. adj. & adv. 1. weekly; once a week; every week. Syn. *linggú-linggó, tuwíng linggo, bawa't linggo*. 2. every Sunday. Syn. *tuwíng (araw ng) Linggo, bawa't Linggo*.
—II. n. a weekly publication, as a magazine.

linggú-linggó (ling-gú + ling-gó), adj. & adv. 1. weekly; every week; once a week. Syn. *língguhan, tuwíng linggo, bawa't linggo*. 2. every Sunday. Syn. *tuwíng araw ng Linggo, bawa't araw ng Linggo*.

lingguwahe (ling-gu-wa-he), var. lengguwahe, n. (Sp. *lenguaje*) language; idiom; speech. Syn. *wikà, salitâ, idyoma*.

lingguwístiká (ling-gu-wís-ti-ká), n. (Sp. *linguística*) linguistics. Syn. *aghámwikà, agwikà, linggistiká*.

lingíd (li-ngíd), adj. secret; hidden; unknown; not known; concealed. Syn. *lihim, tagô, kublí, sekreto*.

lingón (li-ngón), n. act of looking back to see something behind or as a response to someone calling from the back. 2. (Fig.) show of gratitude. Syn. *pagkilala ng utang na loób*.

lipá (li-pá), n. 1. (*Bot.*) a shrub or small tree (*Laportea Meyeniana Warb.*), the leaves of which when touched cause intense irritation. Also called *lipáng-kalabáw, lipáng-lalaki*. 2. (L-) name of a city in the province of Batangas.

lipád (li-pád), n. 1. act or manner of flying; flight. Syn. *paglipád, pagpailanláng sa papawirín*. 2. a trip by air, as in an airplane. Syn. *paglalakbáy sa himpapawíd, pagsakáy sa eroplano*. 3. time or schedule of flight, as of an airplane. Syn. *oras o takdáng oras ng paglipád*.

lipanà (li-pa-nà), I. n. act of roving; extensive wandering, as of a group of government agents looking for someone, or a group of pickpockets looking for their would-be victims. Syn. *lisaw, paglisaw,* *masaklaw na paglilibót o paggagalâ, pagpapalibut-libot*.
—II. adj. roving or wandering over a wide area for a certain purpose or activity. Syn. *nagkalat, nagpalibut-libót*.

lipas (li-pas), n. 1. passing away, as of time. Syn. *daán, pagdaán, pagdaraan*. 2. loss of potency, as of a drug or medicine. Syn. *pagkawalâ ng bisà*. 3. loss of the original taste or savor. Syn. *tabáng, pagtabáng*. 4. a becoming out of fashion. Syn. *pagkawalâ sa moda o uso*. 5. a ceasing or calming down, as of typhoon, anger, etc. Syn. *kalma, pagkalma; hinahon, paghinahon*. 6. a coming to an end. Syn. *tapos, pagkatapos; wakás, pagwawakás*. 7. loss of validity; lapsing. Syn. *pasó, pagkapasó*. 8. loss of popularity. Syn. *hinà, paghinà, pagkawalâ ng popularidád*.

lipás (li-pás), adj. 1. obsolete. Syn. *dî na ginágamit*. 2. no longer in vogue; old-fashioned. Syn. *walâ na sa moda o uso*. 3. out of season, as fruits. Syn. *dî na panahón*. 4. no longer valid; lapsed. Syn *pasó na*. 5. no longer effective; having lost potency. Syn. *walâ nang bisà*. 6. overripe, as fruits. Syn. *labis na ang pagkahinóg*. 7. having lost popularity. Syn. *mahinà na, hindî na populár*. 8. no longer strong or intense. Syn. *kalma na, kalmado na, hintô na*. 9. having come to an end; ended. Syn. *tapós na*.

lipat (li-pat), n. 1. transfer; act of moving from one place to another; change of the place of residence. Syn *paglipat o pagbago ng tirahan, pagtirá sa ibáng lugár*. 2. removing or putting something in another place. Syn. *paglalagáy sa ibáng lugár*. 3. act of transferring something from one container to another. Syn. *salin, pagsasalin*. 4. endorsement. Syn. *endoso, pag-iindoso, paglilipat*.

lipì (li-pì), n. 1. ancestry; lineage. Syn. *angkán*. 2. tribe. Syn. *tribu*. 3. race. Syn. *lahì*.

lipol (li-pol), n. 1. a losing or being lost; disappearance. Syn. *pagkawalâ, waglít, pagkáwaglít*. 2. extinction; annihilation; extermination. Syn. *puksâ, pagpuksâ, pagkapuksâ*.

lipon (li-pon), *n.* a small group or crowd.
Syn. *kalipumpón, lipumpón, kulumpón.* 2.
a small gathering. Syn. *muntíng pagtitipon.*

lipós (li-pós), *adj.* full; fully covered with.
Syn. *punô, batbát.*

lipós-dálitâ (li-pós + dá-li-tâ), *adj.* 1. very
poor; suffering from indigency. Syn. *hiráp
na hiráp sa buhay, nagdáralitâ nang labis.*
2. broken-hearted; full of sorrows. Syn.
sawíng-palad.

lipumpón (li-pum-pón), *n.* a small group,
crowd, or gathering. Syn. *lipon, kulumpón,
umpukan.*

lípunan (lí-pu-nan), *n.* 1. society in general;
association. Syn. *samahán, kapisanan.* 2.
meeting or gathering. Syn. *pagtitipon.* 3.
fashionable society. Syn. *sosyedád.*

lipyâ (lip-yâ), *n.* the part of a plow attached
to the share for turning over the soil;
moldboard.

lira¹ (li-ra), *n.* (Sp.) lyre. Syn. *kudyapî.*

lira² (li-ra), *n.* (Eng.) lira; a monetary unit
in Italy, made up of a silver coin,
originally equal to 19.3 cents.

lirik (li-rik), *n.* (Eng.) 1. lyric; lyric poem.
Syn. *tuláng-awit.* 2. lyrics; words of a song.
Syn. *titik o letra (ng awit).*

lírikó (lí-ri-kó), I. *adj.* (Sp *lírico*) lyric;
lyrical. Syn. *paawít.*
—II. *n.* lyricist; writer of lyrics or lyric
poetry.

lirip (li-rip), *n.* deep thought; careful
analysis or study before acting; effort to
comprehend or realize the truth or
importance of. Syn. *lining, paglilining; pag-
iisip na mabuti; nilay, pagnilay-nilay.*

liryo (lir-yo), *n.* (Sp *lirio*) lily (the plant,
its bulb, or flower).

lisâ (li-sâ), *n.* (*Entom.*) egg of a louse; nit.
Syn. *itlóg ng kuto.*

lisan (li-san), *n.* 1. departure; act of leaving
or going away; start of a journey or trip.
Syn. *alís, pag-alís; yao, pagyao.* 2.
abandonment; act of leaving (someone)
behind. Syn. *iwan, pag-iiwan,
pagpapabayà.*

lisénsiyá (li-sén-si-yá), *n.* (Sp. *licencia*)
license. Cf. *permiso, pahintulot,
kapahintulután.*

lisik (li-sik), *n.* 1. fierce look or glaring of

the eyes in anger. Syn. *pandirilat ng mga
matá (sa galit).* 2. glitter or sparkle of the
eyes. Syn. *kisláp ng mga matá.*

lislís (lis-lís), I. *n.* 1. act of pulling or rolling
up a woman's dress or skirt maliciously.
Syn. *bulislís, pagbulislís.* 2. state or
condition of being raised or rolled up,
referring to a woman's dress or skirt. Syn.
bulislís, pagkabulislís.
—II. *adj.* 1. rolled up or blown up,
referring to someone's dress or skirt. Syn.
nakabulislís, nakalislís. 2. with or having
one's dress or skirt rolled up or blown up.
Syn. *nakalislís o nakabulislís ang barò o saya.*

liso (li-so), *adj.* (Sp.) plain; simple;
unadorned. Syn. *payák, yano, simple.*

lisók (li-sók), I. *n.* state or condition of being
dislocated or sprained, referring to bones.
Syn. *linsád o paglinsád ng kasúkasuán.* Cf.
pilay, pagkapilay.
—II. *adj.* dislocated or sprained, referring
to bones.

lisól (li-sól), *n.* (Sp.) lysol; a liquid mixture
of soap and cresol, used as an antiseptic
or disinfectant.

lista¹ (lis-ta; lis-tá), *n.* (Sp.) 1. a listing or
being listed. Syn. *paglilistá, pagkakálistá;
pagtatalâ, pagkakátalâ.* 2. a list or roll. Syn.
tálaan, lístahan. 3. notes. Syn. *talâ, nota.*

lista² (lis-ta; lis-tá), *adj.* (Sp.) clever or alert;
prompt or quick to act, referring to a
woman. Syn. *alistó, maliksí, maagap.*

listo (lis-to), *adj.* (Sp.) clever or alert;
prompt or quick to act, referring to a man.
Syn. *alistó, maliksí, alertó, maagap.*

listón (lis-tón), *n.* (Sp.) 1. hatband. 2. lath
or slat, used as decorative moldings on
window frames, walls, etc. Cf. *moldura.*
3. ribbon. Syn. *laso.*

lisyâ (lis-yâ), *adj.* 1. wrong; mistaken;
erroneous; misleading. Syn. *malî, di-tamà,
di-wastô.* 2. out of alignment. Syn. *lihís,
walâ sa hanay o linya.*

litanya (li-tan-ya), *n.* (Sp. *letanía*) litany.

litas (li-tas), *n.* 1. a short cut or opening on
each lower side of a shirt, *barong-tagalog,*
or the like. Syn. *bitas.* 2. placket; placket
hole. Syn. *aleta.*

litáw (li-táw), I. *n.* 1. a coming out into view;
appearance. Syn. *labás, paglabás,*

pagpapakita. 2. act of presenting or showing oneself publicly. Syn. *sipót*, *pagsipót; haráp, pagharáp; pagpapakita*. 3. a jutting out; protruding. Syn. *uslî, pag-uslî*. 4. emergence or coming up, as from the surface of water. Syn. *ultaw, pag-ultáw, sulpót, pagsulpót*. 5. state or condition of being visible, jutting out, or embossed. 6. the part of something that is visible, jutting out, or raised. Syn. *ultáw, labás, uslî*.

—II. *adj*. 1. visible; obvious; evident; apparent. Syn. *kita, nákikita; lantád, nakalantád*. 2. jutting out; protruding. Syn. *uslî, nakauslî; ultáw, nakaultáw*. 3. raised on the surface; embossed. Syn. *umbók, nakaumbók; alsado, naka-alsá*. 4. prominent; notable; popular; well-known. Syn. *kilalá, bantóg, populár, tanyág*.

literál (li-te-rál), *adj*. (Sp.) literal; word for word. Syn. *letra por letra*.

literato (li-te-ra-to), I. *n*. (Sp.) a literary man; writer. Syn. *mánunulát*.

—II. *adj*. 1. literate; able to read and write. Syn. *marunong bumasa at sumulat; nakabábasa at nakasúsulat*. 2. educated. Syn. *edukado, nag-aral, may-pinag-aralan*.

literatura (li-te-ra-tu-ra), *n*. (Sp.) literature. Syn. *pánitikán*.

litid (li-tid), *n*. ligament; tendon.

litigasyón (li-ti-gas-yón), *n*. (Sp. *litigacion*) 1. litigation; act or process of carrying on a lawsuit. Syn. *pagdedemanda, pagsasakdál*. 2. a lawsuit. Syn. *usapín*.

litis (li-tis), *n*. 1. trial or investigation in court. Syn. *pagsisiyasat o pagdiníg ng usapín sa húkuman*. 2. careful examination or inquiry about something. Syn. *pagsusuring mabuti*.

litó (li-tó), I. *n*. confusion or distraction of the mind, as in counting. Syn. *limang, pagkalimang*. 2. perplexed or confused state of the mind; bewilderment. Syn. *tarantá, pagkatarantá, guló o pagkaguló ng isip*.

—II. *adj*. 1. confused or distracted, as in counting. Syn. *limáng, nalimang*. 2. perplexed, dazed, or bewildered. Syn. *tarantá, natátarantá, guló ng isip, tuliró*.

litograpiya (li-to-gra-pi-ya), var. **litograpya**,

n. (Sp. *litografía*) lithography.

litógrapó (li-tó-gra-pó), *n*. (Sp. *litógrafo*) lithographer.

litratista (li-tra-tis-ta), var. **ritratista**, *n*. (Sp. *retratista*) used colloquially: photographer. Syn. *tagakuha ng larawan, potógrapó*.

litrato (li-tra-to), var. **ritrato**, *n*. (Sp. *retrato*) used colloquially: picture; portrait; photograph. Sy. *larawan; potograpya*.

litro (li-tro), (Sp.) 1. liter (litre). 2. an instrument or container for measuring a capacity equal to one liter.

litsiyas (lit-si-yas), *n*. (Bot., Ch.) lychees.

litsón (lit-són), *n*. (Sp. *lechón*) 1. a roast pig, usually a suckling (either oven-roasted or in a skewer cooked over live coals). 2. act or manner of roasting a pig. Syn. *paglitsón, paglilitsón*. 3. a dish of roast pig. Syn. *ulam na litsón*.

litsugas (lit-su-gas), *n*. (Sp. *lechugas*) lettuce.

litúrhiyá (li-túr-hi-yá), *n*. (Sp. *liturgia*) liturgy.

liwag (li-wag), *n*. 1. slowness; sluggishness. Syn. *bagal, kabagalan; kuyad, kakuyaran; kupad, kakuparan*. 2. delay. Syn. *abala, pagka-abala; atraso, pagkaatraso*.

liwalíw (li-wa-líw), *n*. pleasure trip; excursion; vacationing or outing. Syn. *pamamasyál, paglilibáng, pagbabakasyón*.

liwanag (li-wa-nag), *n*. 1. that which makes possible to see; light; brightness. Syn. *kaliwanagan*. Cf. *sinag, ilaw*. 2. clearness; clarity; lucidity. Syn. *linaw, kalinawan*. 3. easiness to understand. Syn. *kadaliáng máunawaan*. 4. (Fig.) clear result, as in: *Walâ pang liwanag ang kaniláng úsapan*. There is no clear result yet in their discussion.

líwasan (lí-wa-san), *n*. 1. plaza. Syn. *plasa*. 2. park. Syn. *parke*. 3. a roundabout way or route; bypass; detour. Syn. *líkuan*.

liwaywáy (li-way-wáy), *n*. 1. dawn; daybreak. Syn. *pamimiták ng araw, madalíng-araw, bukáng-liwaywáy*. 2. the beginning, as of an age or era. Syn. *simulâ*. 3. a slight trace; ray (*fig*.) as of hope. Syn. *silahis, banaag*. 4. (L-) a feminine name. 5. (L-) name of a weekly Tagalog magazine.

liyáb   **looban[1]**

liyáb (li-yáb), var. **liáb,** n. 1. big flame; blaze.
Syn. *alab, lagabláb.* 2. (by extension)
outburst, as of anger. Syn. *sikláb (fig.),*
silakbó.

liyabe (li-ya-be), n. (Sp. *llave*) 1. general
term for wrench. 2. knuckles; knuckle-
duster; brass knuckles. 3. key. Syn. *susì,*
yawe.

liyabero (li-ya-be-ro), .n. (Sp. *llavero*). 1.
keymaker; locksmith. Syn. *pandáy-kabán.*
2. key ring. Syn. *anilyo ng susì, liyabera.*

liyád (li-yád), var. **liád,** I. n. 1. act of
protruding the stomach by bending the
body backward. Syn. *hiyád, paghiyád.* 2.
the position of the body with the stomach
jutting out and the back bent backward.
—II. *adj.* bent backward with the stomach
jutting out. Syn. *hiyád, nakahiyád.*

liyag (li-yag), n. 1. darling; beloved; dear.
Syn. *giliw, mahal, sinta, irog, paraluman,*
mutya. 3. sweetheart. Syn. *kasintahan,*
kasuyo, katipan. 3. love or affection for a
person of the opposite sex; a holding dear
in one's heart. Syn. *mahal,´ pagmamahal.*

liyamado (li-ya-ma-do), I. *adj.* (Sp. *llamado*)
at an advantage. Syn. *nakahihigit,*
nakalalamang. 2. in racing or cockfighting,
referring to a horse or a cock which is
preferred to win, hence, having greater
amount of bets. Ant. *dehado.*
—II. *n.* (in racing or cockfighting) a horse
or a cock having the biggest amount of
bets.

liyanera (li-ya-ne-ra), n. (Sp. *llanera*)
molding pan for custard or the like.

liyebo (li-ye-bo), n. (Sp. *llevo*) in Math., a
number carried over to the next left
column, as in addition.

liyempo (li-yem-po), n. a cut of meat from
the flank.

liyo (li-yo), I. n. dizziness; vertigo. Syn. *hilo,*
pagkahilo; lula, pagkalula.
—II. *adj.* dizzy; giddy. Syn. *hilo, nahihilo;*
lula, nalulula.

liyon (li-yon), var. **leon,** n. (Zool.) lion.

loa (lo-a), var. **luwa,** n. (Sp.) 1. poetic verse
in praise of the Holy Virgin and the saints.
2. the act of delivering or reciting this
praise.

lobo[1] (lo-bo), n. (Sp.) wolf.

lobo[2] (lo-bo), n. (Sp. *globo*) balloon. Syn.
balún, globo.

lokalidád (lo-ka-li-dád), n. (Sp. *localidad*)
locality; place; region. Syn. *poók, purók,*
dako.

loko[1] (lo-ko), I. *adj.* (Sp. *loco*) insane;
demented; mad; foolish. Syn. *ulól, sirâ ang*
ulo.
—II. *n.* madman. Syn. *taóng baliw.*

loko[2] (lo-ko), n. act of fooling someone.
Syn. *goyò, panggogoyò; linláng; dayà,*
pandarayà.

lokomotibo (lo-ko-mo-ti-bo), n. (*Hispanized*
Eng.) locomotive; locomotor. Syn. *makiná*
ng tren.

logro (lo-gro), n. in cockfighting, a bet offer
that gives a higher percentage of winning.

lóhiká (ló-hi-ká), n. (Sp. *lóhica*) logic; sound
sense; reason. Syn. *katwiran.*

lóhuwá (ló-hu-wá), n. (Ch.) a confection
of puffed dough with sugar and usually
covered with sesame or puffed rice.

lola (lo-la), n. 1. grandmother. Syn. *abwela,*
lelang, impó. 2. (*Colloq.*) a term usually
used in addressing any old woman. Cf.
indâ.

lolo (lo-lo), n. 1. grandfather. Syn. *abwelo,*
lelong, ingkóng. 2. (*Colloq.*) a term usually
used in addressing any old man.

lomo (lo-mo), n. (Sp.) loin.

lona (lo-na), I. n. (Sp.) canvas; a strong,
coarse cloth. Syn. *kambás.*
—II. *adj.* made of canvas. Syn. *yarì sa lona.*

longganisa (long-ga-ni-sa), n. (Sp. *longaniza*)
a kind of pork sausage. Cf. *suriso (tsuriso),*
hatdóg.

longhitúd (long-hi-túd), n. (Sp. *lungitud*)
longitude.

loób (lo-ób), n. 1. inside; interior; inner part.
Syn. *interyór.* 2. will; state of mind;
volition; disposition. Syn. *kalooban,*
kagustuhan, kaibigán. 3. courage; valor.
Syn. *tapang, giting, lakás ng loób.* 4.
manners; behavior. Syn. *asal, ugalì.*

looban[1] (lo-o-ban), n. 1. inner part of a
residential district. Syn. *interyór.* 2.
premises. Syn. *bakuran.* 3. a fenced lot or
yard planted with various kinds of trees
and plants. Syn. *hardín, halamanan,*
tániman.

looban² (lo-o-ban). v. to plunder; rob by force. Syn. *pagnakawan*.

loók (lo-ók), n. 1. bay or gulf. Syn. *golpo, baiya, baé*. 2. middle part of a bay or gulf. Cf. *laot*.

loro (lo-ro), n. (Sp.) 1. (*Ornith.*), parrot. Cf. *kalangay, katala*. 2. (*Içhth.*) parrotfish (*Family scaridae*). Also, *isdáng loro*.

loryat (lor-yat), n. (Ch.) sumptuous Chinese banquet or dinner.

losa¹ (lo-sa), n. (Sp. *loza*) porcelain. Syn. *porselana*.

losa² (lo-sa) n. (Sp. *losa*) tiled slab. Syn. *baldosa*.

lote (lo-te), n. (Sp.) 1. lot; parcel of land (in real estate). Syn. *lagáy ng lupà* (*colloq.*), *sulár*. Cf. *bakuran, looban*. 2. a number of things regarded as group; lot. Cf. *bahagi*.

loteriya (lo-te-ri-ya), var. **loteryá**, n. (Sp. *lotería*) 1. lottery. Syn. *sápalarán*. 2. raffle. Syn. *ripa, paripa*.

lotus (lo-tus), n. (Eng.) lotus (the plant or its flower).

luád (lu-ád), var. **luwád**, 1. n. sticky soil, used in pot making; clay. Syn. *lupanglagkít*. 2. Cf. *pila*.
—II. *adj*. made of clay. Syn. *yarì sa luwád*.

lubák (lu-bák), n. depression or pothole on the surface, esp. of roads. Syn. *bakô, ukà; mababaw na butas o hukay*.

lubag (lu-bag), n. 1. a calming down, as of emotion or anger. Syn. *hinahon, paghinahon*. 2. lull; cessation; mitigation; calmness. Syn. *hupâ, paghupâ; hignáw, paghignáw; hulaw, paghulaw; lipas, paglipas; humpáy, paghumpáy; hinà, paghinà*.

lubalob (lu-ba-lob), n. 1. act of wallowing in or as in mud. Syn. *lunoy, paglulunoy*. See **lublób**. 2. abandonment or addiction to vice. Syn. *pagpapakabuyó sa bisyo*.

lubáy (lu-báy), n. cessation; relaxation; calming down. Syn. *hintô, paghintô; tigil, pagtigil; lubág, paglubág; hulaw, paghulaw*. 2. leniency; laxity. Syn. *luwág, kaluwagán, pagkamuwág*. 3. looseness; state of not being stretched. Ant. *bagtíng, kabagtingán*.

lubhâ¹ (lub-ha), n. seriousness or gravity, as of sickness, etc. Syn. *lalâ, kalalaán; grabe, kagrabihan; bigát, kabigatán; selan,* *kaselanan*.

lubhâ² (lub-hâ), adv. extremely; too; very, as in *lubháng malakí*, extremely big. Syn. *labis, masyado, totoó, nápaka*.

lubid (lu-bid), n. 1. rope. Syn. *talì, panalì* (*colloq.*). Cf. *pisì*. 2. act or manner of making a rope or ropes. Syn. *paglubid, paglulubid*. 3. the manner a rope was made. Syn. *pagkakálubid*. 4. (*Fig.*) act of inventing or fabricating, as of lies, excuses, etc. Syn. *paglikhâ o pag-imbento, paggagawâ-gawaan*.

lublób (lub-lób), I. n. 1. act of drowning a person in water, as by pushing him down into it. Syn. *paglulubóg sa tubig upang malunod*. 2. act of dipping something in water or liquid. Syn. *sawsaw, pagsasawsáw*. 3. act of wallowing in mud or in water. Syn. *lubalob, paglubalób*. 4. abandonment of self to vice. Syn. *pagpapakalulóng sa bisyo*.
—II. *adj*. 1. dipped or immersed in water or liquid. Syn. *nakalubóg, nakababad*. 2. abandoned or addicted to vice. Syn. *baón* (*sa bisyo*).

lubóg (lu-bog). I. n. 1. setting, as of the sun. Syn. *paglubóg*. 2. sinking, as of a ship in the sea. Syn. *paglubóg*. 3. state or condition of being submerged or sunk. 4. a place submerged in water. 5. a depression or hollow in the ground. Syn. *lubák, hukay*. 6. (by extension) loss of popularity or influence. Syn. *pagkawalâ ng katanyagan o popularidád*. 7. bankruptcy. Syn. *pagbagsák o paghapay ng puhunan, lubós na pangangalugi*.
—II. *adj*. 1. flooded; covered with water, as a low place. Syn. *sanaw, may-sanaw, may-tubig*. 2. sunken or submerged, as a ship. Syn. *lumubóg, nakalubóg*. 3. already sunken, as the sun. Syn. *lumubóg na, nakalubóg na*. 4. low or deep, as a place. Syn. *mababà, malalim*. 5. sunken or hollow, as a person's cheek. Syn. *malalim, humpák*. 6. having lost one's popularity or influence Syn. *bagsák na o patáy na* (*colloq.*). 7. bankrupt; financially broke. Syn. *bagsák na o hapáy na ang puhunan*.

lubós (lu-bós), I. *adj*. complete; full; absolute. Syn. *buô, ganáp*.

lubrikante

lugás

—II. *adv.* completely; totally; absolutely. Syn. *lahát, láhatan, puspusan, ganáp.*

lubrikante (lu-bri-kan-te), *n. & adj.* (Sp. *lubricante*) lubricant. Syn. *pampadulás.*

lubugán ng araw, to lose hope. Syn. *mawalán ng pag-asa.*

lúbusan (lú-bu-san), I. *adj.* complete; full; absolute.
—II. *adv.* completely; totally; fully; absolutely.

lukbán (luk-bán), *n.* (*Bot.*) grapefruit; pomelo (the plant or its fruit). Syn. *suhâ.*

lukbutan (luk-bu-tan), *n.* 1. pocket. Syn. *bulsa.* 2. pocketbook; billfold; wallet. Syn. *pitaka, kartera, portamoneda.*

luklók (luk-lók), *n.* 1. act or manner of sitting. Syn. *upô, pag-upô.* 2. the assumption or taking over of the responsibility of an office or position of a newly elected or appointed official. Syn. *simulâ o pagsisimulâ ng panunungkulan.*

luklukan (luk-lu-kan), *n.* 1. a place or thing to sit on. Syn. *úpuan, likmuan.* 2. the seat of a chair, bench, etc. Syn. *uupán.* 3. seat of honor. Cf. *trono.*

lukmô (luk-mô), *n.* act or manner of sitting oneself comfortably, as on a sofa. Syn. *upô, pag-upô.*

lukob (lu-kob), *n.* 1. act of covering or sheltering (something) with or as with the wings. Syn. *yupyóp, pagyupyóp; yungyóng, pagyungyóng.* 2. act of giving protection to someone. Syn. *tangkilik, pagtangkilik.* 3. placing someone under one's power or authority. Syn. *sakop, pagsakop.*

lukóng (lu-kóng), *n.* 1. concavity, as of plates, platter, etc. Ant. *landáy, kalandayán.* 2. the hollow of the palm of the hand.

lukot (lu-kot), *n.* 1. a crushing or rumping into creases or wrinkles. Syn. *kuyumos, pagkuyumos; yukos, pagyukos.* 2. a cease or wrinkle, as in clothes, etc. Syn. *yukos, kulubót.*

luksâ (luk-sâ), I. *n.* 1 period of mourning. Syn. *pagluluksâ, panahón ng pagluluksâ.* 2. expression or feeling of grief for the death of a dear one; mourning. Syn. *pagdadalamhatì o pamimighatî sa pagyao ng isáng minámahál.* 3. mourning clothes,

usually black ones, worn during the period of mourning. Syn. *itím na damít-panluksâ.*
—II. *adj.* 1. in mourning clothes; wearing black clothes as a sign of mourning. Syn. *nakaluksâ, nakaluto, nakaitím na damít.* 2. grieving over the death of a dear one. Syn. *namímighatî o nagdádalamhatì sa pagyao ng isáng mahál sa buhay.*

luksáng-parangál (luk-sáng + pa-ra-ngál), *n.* necrological services for the dead.

lukso (luk-so; luk-só), *n.* 1. act or manner of jumping; jump; leap. Syn. *lundág, paglundág; talón, pagtalón.* 2. the height or distance of a jump. Syn. *layô o taás ng lundág.* 3. a sudden leap or spring due to fright. Syn. *tiplág, igtád.*

luksóng-tiník (luk-sóng + ti-ník), *n.* a children's game, locally known as "jump-the-spines."

lukú-lukó (lu-kú + lu-kó), *adj.* slightly demented. Syn. *medyú-medyó, may-sirà ang ulo, sintú-sintô.*

lugà (lu-gà), *n.* smelly pus secretion in the ear.

lugamì (lu-ga-mì), *n.* 1. a falling into misfortune; set back in one's life. Syn. *pagkapahamak, pagkapalungì, pagkasadlák sa dusa.* 2. state or condition of being in a vicious or degraded mode of life. Syn. *pagkagumon sa bisyo o hamak na kabuhayan.* 3. complete failure in life. Syn. *lubós na pagkabigô sa buhay.*

lugamók (lu-ga-mók), *adj.* fallen flat on the ground due to being excessively drunk or to over exhaustion. Syn. *nakabulagtâ (sa pagkalasíng o kapaguran).*

lugár (lu-gár), var. **lugál**, *n.* (Sp.) 1. place; position. Syn. *puwesto, kinálalagyán, kinároroonan.* 2. site; place; location. Syn. *poók, dako.* 3. territory. Syn. *teritoryo, sakop, nasasakupan.* 4. vacancy or vacant position, as in office. Syn. *bakante, bakanteng puwesto.* 5. time; chance; opportunity. Syn. *panahón, pagkakataón.* 6. district; area. Syn. *distrito, purók, poók.*

lugás (lu-gás), I. *n.* 1. act of breaking (something) into bits. Syn. *durog, pagdurog.* 2. act of pounding, grinding, or milling (grains) into grits. Syn. *pagbabayó, paggiling, pagkikiskís.* 3. act of flailing or

beating out grains from the stalks;
threshing. Syn. *giík, paggiík*. 4. a falling
off, as of hair, feathers, etc. Syn. *lugon,
panlulugon*. 5. state or condition of being
broken into small bits. Syn. *pagkadurog,
kadurugán*. 6. condition of being fallen off,
as hair or feathers. Syn. *lugon, panlulugon,
pagkalugon*.
—II. *adj*. 1. broken into small bits. Syn.
duróg. 2. threshed or beaten out from the
stalks, referring to grains. Syn. *giík o nagiík
na*. 3. fallen off, as hair, feathers, etc. Syn.
lugón.

lugaw (lu-gaw), *n*. 1. act of cooking rice
porridge or gruel. Syn. *paglulugaw*. 2. rice
porridge or gruel. Syn. *nilugaw (linugaw)*.
Cf. *aruskaldo, sampurado, puspás*.

lugay (lu-gay), *n*. act of disengaging or
loosening a woman's bun and allowing it
to hang loosely. Syn. *pagkalág sa pusód o
tirintas ng buhók ng babae*.

lugi (lu-gi), I. *n*. 1. loss or amount of loss in
a business transaction. Syn. *halagá ng
nalugi o nawalâ sa puhunan*. 2. failure in
business. Syn. *pagkalugi, pangangalugi*.
—II. *adj*. at a loss; resulting in a loss;
losing, as in *luging pagbibilí*, selling at loss.
—III. *adv*. at a cost below the cost price.
Syn. *palugí, nang walâ sa puhunan*.

lugit (lu-git), *n*. 1. extension of time or
deadline given to a person in the payment
of Kis debt, taxes, etc. Syn. *palugit, pataán,
plaso*. 2. an additional length added as
allowance for shrinkage. Syn. *patagana*.
3. a handicap given a player in games, as
in racing. Syn. *palamáng, partida*.

luglóg[1] (lug-lóg), I. *n*. 1. act of washing or
rinsing the inside of a container, esp. a
bottle, by shaking water in it. 2. act of
shaking something to make it fall, as fruits
from the branches of a tree. Syn. *yugyóg,
pagyugyóg*.
—II. *adj*. 1. washed or rinsed, referring to
a container, esp. a bottle, shaken with
water inside it. 2. fallen, as fruits. Syn.
laglág. 3. shaken or rocked, as passengers
in a vehicle. Syn. *tigtíg, liglíg*.

luglóg[2] (lug-lóg), I. *n*. a kind of *pansit*, better
known as *palabok*, the noodles of which
are dipped in boiling stock. Also called

pansit-palabok, pansít-luglóg.
—II. *adj*. said of a certain kind of *pansit*,
the noodles of which are dipped in boiling
stock then added with condiments.

lugmók (lug-mók), I. *n*. 1. act of lying lazily
or helplessly. Syn. *handusáy, paghandusáy;
lupasay, paglupasay*. 2. state or condition
of being bedridden due to illness or
infirmity. Syn. *ratay, pagkaratay*.
—II. *adj*. 1. helplessly prostrate. Syn.
*lupasáy, nakalupasay; handusáy,
nakahandusáy*. 2. bedridden. Syn.
nakaratay.

lugó (lu-gó), *n*. extreme weakness due to
sickness or frustration. Syn. *labis na
panghihinà*.

lugód (lu-gód), *n*. delight; pleasure;
satisfaction. Syn. *tuwâ, galák, kasiyahan,
ligaya*.

lugon (lu-gon), *n*. falling off of hair or
feathers. Syn. *lagas, pagkalagas, o
panlalagas (ng buhók o balahibo)*.

lugpô (lug-pô), I. *n*. state or condition of
being helplessly prostrate or bedridden.
Syn. *gupò, pagkàgupò; lugmók,
pagkalugmók*.
—II. *adj*. helplessly prostrate or
bedridden. Syn. *lupasáy, nakalupasáy;
lugmók, nakalugmók; handusáy,
nakahandusáy*.

lugsô (lug-sô), I. *n*. 1. a sudden caving in or
collapse. Syn. *guhò, pagguhò; lagpák,
paglagpák; bagsák, pagbagsák; gibâ,
pagkágibâ*. 2. a structure or part of a
structure that has caved in or collapsed. 3.
(*Fig*.) a deflowering or taking away the
virginity of a woman. Syn. *pagsasamantalá
sa puri ng isáng babae, gahís o paggahís sa
babae*.
—II. *adj*. 1. caved in; fallen down;
collapsed. Syn. *gumuhò, lumagpák,
bumagsák, nágibâ*. 2. deflowered; raped or
violated, referring to a woman. Syn.
pinagsamantalahán, ginahís, ginahasà.

luhà (lu-hà), *n*. tear or tears.

luho (lu-ho), *n*. (Sp. *lujo*) 1. luxury. Syn.
rangyâ, karangyaán. 2. extravagance;
careless or wasteful spending. Syn.
kabulagsakán, pagkabulagsák.

luhód (lu-hód), *n*. 1. act or manner of

kneeling. Syn. *pagtitiklóp ng tuhod;* *pagluhód.* 2. kneeling position of a person, as in prayer. Syn. *pagkakáluhód.* 3. manner of respecting elders by kneeling and kissing the hand. Syn. *paggalang sa pamamagitan ng pagluhód at pagmamano.* 4. a falling down on one's knees as a sign of submission or surrender. Syn. *pagsukò.*

luhog (lu-hog), n. a humble, earnest request; supplication. Syn. *pamanhík, pamamanhík; hinaíng, daíng, karaingan; samò, pagsamò; pagmamakaamò; pagmamakaawà.*

lulà (lu-là), n. vertigo; seasickness; dizziness. Syn. *hilo, pagkahilo; liyó, pagkaliyó.* 2. fear of height. Syn. *sawan, pagkasawan.*

lulan (lu-lan), I. n. 1. act of loading a vehicle with cargo. Syn. *pagkakarga, paglululan.* 2. load; cargo; freight. Syn. *karga, kargada, kargamento.* 3. act of riding a passenger vehicle. Syn. *sakáy, pagsakáy.* 4. act of taking in passengers. Syn. *pagsasakáy, pagpapasakáy.* 5. passengers.Syn. *pasahero, mga sakáy.* 6. capacity or accommodation, as of a vehicle. Syn. *kapasidád, dami ng malálamán.* 7. content, as of tank, crate, big box, etc. Syn. *lamán.*

—II. *adv. & prep.* aboard; on board. Syn. *nakalulan, sakáy, nakasakáy.*

—III. *adj.* can be accommodated. Syn. *malálaman, kasya, magkakasya.*

lulay (lu-lay), n. lullaby. Syn. *kanta o awit na pampatulog.*

lulód (lu-lód), n. (Anat.) 1. shin; the front part of the leg between the ankle and the knee. 2. shin-bone; tibia. Syn. *butó sa lulód.*

lulon (lu-lon), n. 1. act of swallowing food. Syn. *lunók, paglunók.* 2. an enveloping or engulfing, as by a big wave or waves.Syn. *sakmál, pagsakmál; lamon, paglamon* (colloq.)

lulón (lu-lón), I. n. 1. act of rolling a mat, carpet, paper, or the like into a tube-like form. Syn. *rolyo, pagrorolyo; balumbón, pagbabalumbón; bilo, pagbibilo.* 2. a roll, as of mat, carpet, etc. Syn. *rolyo, balumbón, bilo.*

—II. *adj.* rolled. Syn. *nakalulón; balumbón, nakabalumbón; rolyo, nakarolyo.*

lulóng (lu-lóng), I. n. 1. act of going too

near a place of danger. Syn. *paglapit sa panganib.* 2. involvement of oneself into a certain activity one has to bear up with despite its undesirability. Syn. *subò, pagsubò, pagkapasubò.*

—II. *adj.* deeply involved in. Syn. *napasubò.*

lumà (lu-mà), *adj.* 1. old; not new. Syn. *dati.* 2. used; second-hand. Syn. *gamít na, sigunda-mano.* 3. referring to the remaining crops of the previous year. Syn. *laón.* 4. of or belonging to a time long past. Syn. *matandâ.* 5. out-of-date; old-fashioned; antiquated. Syn. *lipás na; walâ na sa moda.*

lumakí ang ulo, v. to become conceited or vain. Syn. *magíng hambóg o palalò.*

lumagay sa estado, v. to get married. Syn. *mag-asawa.*

lumanay (lu-ma-nay), n. 1. moderation in movement or action. Syn. *hinay, kahinayan; hinhín, kahinhinán; banayad, kabanayaran.* 2. mildness or gentleness in voice or speech. Syn. *hinahon, kahinahunan.*

lumat (lu-mat), n. 1. dilatoriness; delay; lateness; tardiness. Syn. *atraso, abala, luwát, bagal, antala.* 2. slowness; sluggishness. Syn. *bagal, kupad.*

lumay (lu-may), n. 1. moderation or gentleness in speech or action. Syn. *lumanay, hinay.* 2. (Gram.) penultimate level in syllabic stress. Syn. *kalumayan, pagkamalumanay; kabanayaran.*

lumbák (lum-bák), n. shallow pond or pool.Syn. *lubák, sanaw.*

lumbago (lum-ba-go), n. (Sp., Med.) lumbago; rheumatic pain or backache in the lower part of the back. Syn. *rayuma sa likód sa dakong baywáng.*

lumbá-lumbá (lum-bá + lum-bá), var. **lumbalumbá,** n. dolphin, an aquatic carnivorous animal (*Delphinus malayanus* Less.).

lumbáy (lum-báy), n. sadness; loneliness; melancholy; sorrow. Syn. *lungkót, kalungkutan, dalamhatì, pighatî, hapis, dusa.*

lumbó (lum-bó), n. a dipper made of coconut shell. Cf. *tabò.*

lumbóy (lum-bóy), n. (Bot.) 1. a species of

native blackberries known as black plum, Java plum (*Syzygium cumini* Skeels). 2. the berries of this plant. Syn. *duhat*.

lumì (lu-mì), n. penultimate syllabic stress with a glottal vowel ending.

lumikhâ (lu-mik-hâ), I. *v.* 1. to create; bring into being. Syn. *lumaláng*. 2. to invent. Syn. *umimbento*. 3. to coin, as a new word. Syn. *bumuô, magbuô*.
—II. *n.* (L-) the Creator; God; the Supreme Being. Syn. *ang Lumaláng, ang Maylikhâ*.

luminaryo (lu-mi-nar-yo), n. (Sp. *luminario*) luminary; famous intellectual. Syn. *bantôg na taong matalino*.

lumó (lu-mó), n. 1. deep sympathy or pity for the pathetic plight of someone; tragic feeling of grief or sorrow. Syn. *matindíng pagkaawà o pagkahabág*. 2. extreme feeling of weakness. Syn. *matindíng panghihinà o panlalambót ng katawán*.

lumot (lu-mot), n. (*Bot.*) 1. a kind of algae commonly found in brackish water at the mouth of streams and in fishponds (*Enteromorpha intestinalis*). 2. a kind of lichen that grows esp. on trunks of coconut trees (*Usnea Philippina Wainio*). Also called *lumot-kahoy*.

lumpiyâ (lum-pi-yâ), n. (Ch.) a kind of dish or viand made from shrimps, meat, and vegetables wrapped or rolled up in thin wrappers made from flour, and eaten fresh or fried.

lumpo (lum-po; lum-pó), I. *adj.* invalid; crippled or maimed. Syn. *baldado, salantâ ang katawán*.
—II. *n.* an invalid; cripple. Syn. *taong baldado*.

lúnademiyél (lú-na-de-mi-yél), n. (Sp. *luna de miel*) honeymoon. Syn. *pulutgatâ*.

lunán (lu-nán), n. (*Gram.*) place. Syn. *dako, lugár*.

lunas (lu-nas), n. 1. remedy; cure. Syn. *gamót, panggamót; remedyo, panremedyo*. 2. antidote. Syn. *pag-asa*. 3. a means that corrects a wrong, etc. Syn. *paraán, remedyo*.

lunátiko (lu-ná-ti-ko), I. *adj.* (Sp. *lunático*) lunatic; insane. Syn. *loko, balíw, sirâ ang ulo (isip)*.

—II. *n.* a lunatic or insane person. Syn. *balíw, loko, taong balíw o loko*.

lunaw (lu-naw), n. 1. the change or changing from solid or semisolid state to liquid state. Syn. *lusaw, pagkalusaw; tunaw, pagkatunaw*. 2. liquid state or quality. 3. liquid; any liquid substance. 4. soft or liquefied mud. Syn. *lusáw na putik*.

lundág (lun-dág), n. 1. jump; leap. Syn. *luksó, talón*. 2. omission, as of a word in a line. Syn. *palyo*.

lunday (lun-day), n. a boat or banca without outriggers or covering. Syn. *bangkáng waláng-katig*.

lundô (lun-dô), I. n. 1. state or condition of being slack in a rope. 2. sag; place of sagging; sunken or depressed place. 3. the degree or amount of sagging. 4. (*Gram.*) stress in pronunciation. Syn. *diín*.
—II. *adj.* slack or loose, esp. at the middle; relaxed; not tight. Syn. *malubáy, di-banát*.

lúnduyan (lún-du-yan), n. 1. center, as of activities. Syn. *sentro*. 2. focus; center point of attraction, attention, etc. Syn. *támpulan*.

Lunes (Lu-nes), n. (Sp.) Monday.

luningníng (lu-ning-níng), n. 1. brightness; brilliance; scintillation. Syn. *liwanag, ningníng, kisláp*. 2. splendor; pomp. Syn. *dilág, karilagán; dingal, karingalan*. 3. (L-) a feminine name.

lunó (lu-nó), I. n. 1. molting; shedding or casting of skin, scales, etc. of crabs, shrimps, snakes, and the like. Syn. *hunós, paghuhunós*. 2. state or condition in which these animals have just molted. 3. softness or physical weakness of the body. Syn. *kalambután at panghihina ng katawán*.
—II. *adj.* 1. in a state or condition of having just molted, referring to crabs, shrimps, snakes, etc. 2. soft and weak physically, referring to a person. Syn. *mahinà at malambót ang katawán*.

lunók (lu-nók), n. act of swallowing something. Syn. *lulón, paglulón*.

lunod (lu-nod), n. 1. a drowning or being drowned; death by drowning. Also, *pagkalunod*. 2. a soaking or being soaked; saturation. Syn. *pagkatigmák, pagkababad (sa tubig)*.

lunos lupák

lunos (lu-nos), n. 1. compassion; pity. Syn. *awà, pagkaawà; habág, pagkahabág.* 2. sorrow; grief; affliction. Syn. *lungkót, pagkalungkót; pighatî, pamimighatî, kapighatián.*

lunot (lu-not), n. overripeness of fruits. Syn. *labis na pagkahinóg.*

lunoy (lu-noy), n. 1. prolonged stay in water, as of bathers. Syn. *matagál na pagbababad sa tubig.* 2. complete abandonment of oneself, as in vices. Syn. *lubalob, paglulubalob.*

lunsád (lun-sád), n. 1. act of alighting from a vehicle. Syn. *babâ, pagbabâ; panaog, pagpanaog.* 2. unloading of cargo. Syn. *diskarga, pagdidiskarga.* 3. a launching, as of one's candidacy. Syn *bunsód, pagbubunsód.*

lunsód (lun-sód), var. lungsód, n. city. Syn. *siyudád.*

luntian (lun-ti-an), var. lungtian, I. n. & adj. green. Syn. *berde.*

—II. adj. greenish. Syn. *medyo berde, maberde-berde.*

lungab (lu-ngab), n. deep hollow or cavity, as in stone wall or the like. Syn. *malalim na ukà.*

lungad (lu-ngad), n. belching of milk or other liquid food from the mouth of a baby. Cf. *suka, pagsuka.* 2. milk or any liquid food belched out from the mouth of babies.

lungál (lu-ngál), adj. (Tag.) already dead when born; still-born. Syn. *patáy na nang ianák.*

lungangì (lu-nga-ngì), n. position of the head that is drooped or bent down upon the chest, as when one is very sleepy or unconscious.

lungáw (lu-ngáw), n. a large hole or excavation in the ground; dugout. Syn. *malakíng hukay o lunggâ.*

lungayngáy (lu-ngay-ngáy), I. adj. drooping or bent down upon the chest, referring to an unconscious person's head. Cf. *lungangî, nakalungangî.*

—II. n. state or condition of being drooped or bent down, referring to the head of an unconscious person. Cf. *lungangî.*

lungkót (lung-kót), n. 1. sadness; sorrow; unhappiness; grief. Syn. *pighatî, lumbáy, dalamhatî, hapis.* 2. loneliness, as of a remote place. Syn. *pangláw, kapanglawán.*

lunggâ (lung-gâ), n. 1. burrow; hole dug in the ground by snakes, rats, etc. 2. cave. Syn. *lungáw.* 4. hideout; hiding place. Syn. *taguán.*

lunggatî (lung-ga-tî), n. earnest desire; fervent wish or ambition. Syn. *bagay na pinakamimithî, mataós na hángarin o pangarap.*

lungì (lu-ngì), n. 1. a falling into disrepute, dishonor, or disgrace. Syn. *pagkasirà ng pangalan, pagkápalagáy sa kahihiyán.* 2. a falling into misfortune or disaster. Syn. *pagkápahamak, pagkasawî, pagkápanganyayà.*

lungos (lu-ngos), n. 1. (Geog.) headland; promontory; cape; peninsula. Syn. *tangos, tangwáy, imus.* 2. projection; the part that projects or sticks out. Syn. *ungós, uslî.*

lungoy (lu-ngoy), n. supplication; entreaty. Syn. *samò, luhog, daíng, hinaíng, pamanhík, pakiusap.*

luom (lu-om), n. 1. lack of air in a closed room. Syn. *kawalán ng hangin sa loób.* 2. state or condition of being oppressively hot and sultry, as in an unventilated room. Syn. *kaalinsangan (sa loób).* 3. suffocation due to lack of air in an unventilated room.

luóy (lu-óy), adj. 1. withered or faded, referring to a flower or bud of a plant. Syn. *lanta, nalanta.* 2. unsuccessful. Syn. *bigô, nabigô; unsiyamî, naunsiyamî.*

lupà (lu-pà), n. 1. soil; earth, as in *tabunan ng lupà,* to cover with earth. 2. earth; world. Syn. *mundo, daigdíg.* 3. land; landed property, as in: *May lupà siyá sa Mindanáw.* He has land in Mindanao. 4. land; country; nation, as in *umuwî sa sariling lupà,* to return to one's native land. Syn. *bayan, bansá (bansâ).* 5. downstairs; ground floor; basement, as in: *Nanaog siyá sa lupà.* He went downstairs. Syn. *silong, ibabâ (ng bahay).*

lupák (lu-pák), I. n. 1. act of pounding rice in a wooden mortar until fully husked. Syn. *luba, pagluba.* 2. act of pounding boiled green bananas (sabá species) into a mash called *nilupák.*

lupagì

—II. *adj.* 1. fully husked or crushed by pounding in a wooden mortar, referring to rice. Syn. *lubá*. 2. pounded into a mash, said of boiled green bananas.

lupagì (lu-pa-gì), *n.* 1. act or manner of sitting with the buttocks flat on the floor or ground. Syn. *pag-upô nang pasalampák*. 2. sitting position with the buttocks flat on the floor or ground. Syn. *upóng pasalampák*.

lupaín (lu-pa-ín), *n.* 1. land; country, as in *nasa ibáng lupaìn*, in a foreign land. 2. landed estate or property; hacienda. Syn. *pag-aaring lupà*. 3. territory; land under the rule of a distant government. Syn. *teritoryo, sakóp na lupà*.

lupalop (lu-pa-lop), *n.* 1. land; country; nation. Syn. *bansá, nasyón, lupaín*, as in *banyagang lupalop*, foreign land. 2. region; territory. Syn. *rehiyón, teritoryo*. 3. landed estate or property; hacienda. Syn. *lupaín, pag-aaring mga lupà*. 4. continent. Syn. *kontinente*.

lupang-tinubuan (lu-pang + ti-nu-bu-an), *n.* motherland; fatherland; native land; mother country. Syn. *ináng-lupà, lupang sarili, sariling-bayan*.

lupasay (lu-pa-say), *n.* 1. act or manner of sitting with one's haunches flat on the floor or ground. Syn. *lupagì, paglupagì*. 2. such a sitting position. 3. act or manner of lying lazily with the arms and legs stretched flat on the floor or ground. Syn. *bulagtâ, pagbulagtâ*.

lupaypáy (lu-pay-páy), I. *n.* 1. state or condition of being utterly frustrated or dejected. Syn. *panghihinà ng loób, pagkasirà ng loób, pagkawalâ ng pag-asa*. 2. extreme weakness due to loss of hope. Syn. *labis na panghihinà*.

—II. *adj.* extremely weak due to exhaustion or dejection. Syn. *labis na nanghihinà ang katawán*.

lupî (lu-pî), I. *n.* 1. act or manner of folding something. Syn. *tupî, pagtutupî; tiklóp, pagtitiklóp*. 2. a fold; plait or pleat; hem. Syn. *tupî, tiklóp*. 3. the way or manner a thing is folded. Syn. *pagkakálupî, pagkakátupî, pagkakátiklóp*.

—II. *adj.* folded. Syn. *nakalupî, nakatupî*.

lupíg (lu-píg), I. *adj.* 1. subjugated; overpowered; vanquished; conquered. Syn. *gahís, supíl*. 2. suppressed. Syn. *sugpô, sawatâ*. 3. oppressed. Syn. *siíl, sinísiíl; apí, ináapí*.

—II. *n.* state or condition of being subjugated or overpowered.

lupít (lu-pít), *n.* 1. cruelty; brutality. Syn. *bangís, kabangisán; bagsík, kabagsikán*. 2. mercilessness. Syn. *kawaláng-habág*.

lupon (lu-pon; -pón), *n.* 1. committee. Syn. *komité*. 2. board; council. Syn. *konseho*. 3. commission. Syn. *komisyón*.

lurâ (lu-râ), var. **durâ**, *n.* 1. spit; saliva; sputum; spittle. Syn. *laway*. 2. act of spitting. Syn. *paglurâ, pagdurâ*.

luráy (lu-ráy), *adj.* mangled; mutilated. Syn. *gutáy*.

lurok (lu-rok), *n.* full or thorough understanding, as of something that puzzles one's mind. Syn. *unawà, pagunawà; tarók, pagtarók*.

lusak (lu-sak), *n.* 1. deep, sticky mud; wet soggy earth; slush. 2. (by extension) wretched or miserable life. Syn. *hamak na buhay (pamumuhay)*.

lusaw (lu-saw), *n.* 1. a melting or being melted; liquefying or being liquefied; change from solid to liquid state. Syn. *tunaw, pagkatunaw*. 2. liquid state or quality. 3. a watery place. Syn. *sanaw*. 4. beating, as of eggs. Syn. *batí, pagbatí, pagbabatí*.

luses (lu-ses), var. **lusis**, *n.* (Sp. *luces*) Roman candle, a kind of sparkler.

Lusipér (Lu-si-pér), *n.* (Eng., Sp.) Lucifer; Satan. Syn. *Satanás*.

luslós[1] (lus-lós), *n.* (Med.) hernia; rupture. Syn. *erniyá*.

luslós[2] (lus-lós), I. *n.* a falling down, as of pants due to the loose waistline. Syn. *usós, pag-usós; lawít, paglawít*.

—II. *adj.* referring esp. to pants that has fallen down due to the loose waistline.

lusob (lu-sob), *n.* attack; assault; invasion. Syn. *salakay, atake*.

lusog (lu-sog; -sóg), *n.* 1. good health; healthiness. Syn. *buti o husay ng katawán*. 2. obesity; fatness. Syn. *tabâ, katabaán*. 3. luxuriance or vigor, as of plants. Syn. *tabâ,* *katabaan.* 4. progressiveness. Syn. *unlád, kaunlarán; progreso, kaprogresuhan.*

lusong (lu-song), n. 1. a descending or going down from a height to a lower place. Syn. *babâ, pagbabâ; panaog, pagpanaog.* 2. a stepping into water, as in bathing in a river. Syn. *lusok, paglusok.*

lusóng (lu-sóng), n. a big wooden mortar for pounding rice and other grains. Syn. *báyuhan.*

lusót (lu-sót), I. n. 1. a passing through a hole or through a narrow or crowded place. Syn. *pagdaán, pagdaraán; lampás, paglampás.* 2. act of passing ahead of another or others, as in a race. Syn. *lampás, paglampás.* 3. a piercing through (a wall, board, etc.), as by an arrow, bullet, etc. Syn. *tagós, pagtagós; lagós, paglagós; lampás, paglampás.* 4. a slipping through without attracting notice. Syn. *puslít, pagpuslít.* 5. an unexpected success, as in competitive examination. Syn. *diináasahang tagumpáy.* 6. narrow escape, as of a prisoner passing several check points or guards. Syn. *ligtás, pagkaligtás.*

—II. *adj.* 1. pierced through, as by an arrow, bullet, etc. Syn. *tágusan, tinagusán; lágusan, nilagusán.* 2. able to pass through the hole or tight situation. Syn. *lampás, nakalampás, lumampás.* 3. with or having a hole due to being torn or broken, as the wicker seat of a chair. Syn. *butás, maybutás.* 4. able to penetrate through. Syn. *lagós, lumagós; tagós, tumagós.*

lustáy (lus-táy), I. n. 1. embezzlement. Syn. *dispalko, pagdispalko.* 2. misappropriation of fund; incorrect or dishonest use of money.

—II. *adj.* 1. embezzled. Syn. *dispalkado, dinispalko.* 2. misappropriated. Syn. *ginugol sa masamâ o malíng paraán.*

lusután (lu-su-tán), v. 1. to pass through, referring to a hole or narrow opening. 2. to pierce through. Syn. *tagusán, lagusán, lampasán.* 3. to overtake; pass ahead of another or others, as in a race. Syn. *lampasán.* 4. to cause something to pass through by inserting. Syn. *sulután.* 5. to pass or slip through without being noticed.

lutang (lu-tang), I. n. 1. act of floating, as in swimming. 2. state or condition of being afloat or adrift. Syn. *pangíngibabaw sa tubig.* 3. a being prominent or manifest. Syn. *litáw, pagkalitáw, kalitawán.*

—II. *adj.* afloat; floating. Syn. *nakalutang.*

lutás (lu-tás), *adj.* 1. finished; completed; terminated. Syn. *tapós na, yarî na.* 2. solved, referring to a problem. Syn. *sagót na, nasagót na.* 3. solved, as a crime. Syn. *kilalá na ang may-kasalánan.* 4. remedied. Syn. *nalunasan na, naremédyuhán na.*

lutò (lu-tò), I. n. 1. act or manner of cooking food; preparation of food by cooking. Syn. *paglulutò.* 2. a particular kind of cooked food or dish. Syn. *putahe.*

—II. *adj.* cooked; prepared by cooking, referring to food.

lutóng (lu-tóng), n. brittleness or crispiness, as of crackers, cracklings, etc.

lútong-makáw (lú-tong + ma-káw), *adj.* (Fig.) rigged.

lutuán (lu-tu-án), n. 1. cooking utensil like pot, frying pan, casserole, etc. 2. stove. Syn. *kalán.* 3. kitchen. Syn. *kusinà.*

luwa (lu-wa), var. *loa,* n. (Sp. *loa*) a poetic verse in praise of the Holy Virgin and the saints.

luwâ (lu-wâ), I. n. 1. ejection of something from the mouth. Syn. *pagpapalabás ng lamán ng bibig.* Cf. *bugá, pagbubugá.* 2. a sticking or bulging out, as of the eyes. Syn. *ulwâ, pag-ulwâ; uslî, pag-uslî.* 3. something belched or ejected from the mouth. 4. the part of something that's sticking or bulging out. Syn. *ulwâ, bahaging nakaulwâ.*

—II. *adj.* sticking or bulging out. Syn. *nakaluwâ, nakaulwâ, nakauslî.*

luwád (lu-wád), var. *luád,* I. n. clay; sticky soil, used in pot making. Syn. *lúpang-lagkít.* Cf. *pila.*

—II. *adj.* made of clay. Syn. *yarì sa luwád.*

luwág (lu-wág), n. 1. spaciousness, as of a room. Syn. *luwáng, kaluwangán.* 2. looseness or bigness of size, as of clothes and other wearing apparel. Syn. *lakí, kalakihan.* 3. laxity, as in the enforcement of laws. Ant. *higpít, kahigpitán.* 4. a being loose, as of a tie, binding, or knot. 5. ease; comfort;

convenience. Syn. *ginhawà, kaginhawahan*.
6. freedom from restriction. Syn. *layà, kalayaan; layaw, kalayawan*. 7. easiness to do or perform. Syn. *alwán, kaalwanán; dalî, kadalián*.

luwál¹ (lu-wál), n. 1. outside or exterior, as of a town. Syn. *labás; dakong labás*. 2. sudden appearance or coming out, as from darkness. Syn. *biglâng paglitáw o paglabás*. 3. a being born; a coming into being. Syn. *silang, pagsilang*. 4. a giving birth. Syn. *pag-anák, panganganák*.

luwál² (lu-wál), n. (*Econ.*) payment made by someone for another with the understanding that it would be reimbursed sooner or later. Syn. *abono*.

luwalhatì (lu-wal-ha-tì), n. glory; great pleasure or satisfaction. Syn. *glorya, labis na ligaya o kasiyahan*.

luwáng (lu-wáng), n. 1. width. Syn. *lapad*. 2. spaciousness. Syn. *luwág, kaluwagán*. 3. extensiveness; vastness. Syn. *lawak, kalawakan; lapad, kalaparan; lakí, kalakihán*. 4. bigness, as of a crack, hole, well, excavation, etc. Syn. *lakí, kalakihán*. 5. size or measurement, as of shoes, coats, pants, etc. Syn. *sukat, lakí*.

luwás (lu-wás), n. a trip from a town or province to the city. Syn. *paglalakbáy o pagtungo sa lunsód (siyudád)*. 2. exportation of goods from one country to another. Syn. *eksportasyón, paghuhulog ng kalakal sa ibáng bansá*. 3. exports; goods exported.

luwát (lu-wát), n. 1. long time; long duration of time. Syn. *tagál, katagalán; laon, kalaunan*. 2. delay; lateness. Syn. *atraso, kaatrasuhan*.

luya (lu-ya), n. (*Bot.*) 1. ginger plant. 2. the rootstalk of this plant, used for flavoring food and in medicine.

luylóy (luy-lóy), I. n. 1. state or condition of being flabby and hanging loosely. Syn. *pagkaluylóy*. 2. the part of a thing or the thing itself that hangs loosely due to being flabby.
—II. *adj.* hanging loosely due to being flabby. Cf. *lawít, nakalawít*.

M

M, m (ma), n. 1. the tenth letter of the *abakada* (Pilipino alphabet). 2. the type of impression representing this letter. 3. a symbol for the tenth in a group or series.

ma- (ma), *pref.* used to form: 1. adjectives denoting: a) abundance, as in *mayaman*, rich, wealthy; *mabunga*, laden with fruits; *marami*, many, plenty; *mabulaklak*, with or having many flowers; b) quality, as in *maganda*, beautiful; *masama*, bad; *matalino*, talented; c) plural forms of adjectives with the first syllable of the root reduplicated, as in *magaganda, masasama, matatalino*, etc. 2. verbs denoting: a) ability or capacity to do or perform, as in *magawa*, to be able to do; *masabi*, to be able to say or tell; to be able to get; b) functions, as in *maligo*, to take a bath; *mahiga*, to lie down; *matulog*, to sleep; c) idea of becoming into a certain state, as in *masira*, to become destroyed; *mawala*, to be or become lost; *mamatay*, to die; d) involuntary or unintentional acts, as in *makita*, (to be seen accidentally; *makuha*, to get or obtain unintentionally), etc.

máaarì (má-a-a-rì), I. *adj.* 1. that can be; possible; probable. 2. can be used. Syn. *magágamit*.
—II. *adv.* may possibly be.

maabala (ma-a-ba-la), I. *v.* 1. to become delayed or late. Syn. *maatraso, mahuli*. 2. to become unnecessarily troubled or inconvenienced. Syn. *magambala*.
—II. *adj.* causing much inconvenience, bother, or delay. Syn. *nagdulot ng maraming abala*.

maabót (ma-a-bót), *v.* 1. to be able to reach, as a distant place. Syn. *maratíng, masapit*. 2. to be able to reach or take (something) by extending one's hand. Syn. *madukwáng, makuha sa pamamagitan ng pagdukwáng*. 3. to be able to attain or gain through effort. Syn. *matamó, makamít*.

maakit (ma-a-kit), *v.* 1. to be able to persuade or induce. Syn. *mahikayat*. 2. to be persuaded or induced. Syn. *sumang-*

ayon, mapasang-ayon. 3. to be able to attract or allure. Syn. *mapahangá.* 4. to be or become attracted or allured. Syn. *humangá.*

maaksayá (ma-ak-sa-yá), I. *v.* 1. to become wasted. Syn. *masayang.* 2. to be misused or misappropriated. Syn. *malustáy.*
—II. *adj.* 1. wasteful in using materials. Syn. *mapag-aksayá, mapagtapón.* 2. wasteful in spending. Syn. *mapaglustáy, masyadong mapággasta, gastadór.*

maakyát (ma-ak-yát), *v.* 1. to be able to ascend, as an incline or slope. Syn. *maahon.* 2. to be able to climb, as a tree. Syn. *maadyó.* 3. to be able to go up a stair. Syn. *mapanhík.*

maadhikâ (ma-ad-hi-kâ), I. *adj.* 1. ambitious. Syn. *mapághangád, mapágmithí.* 2. thrifty; economical. Syn. *matipíd, mapág-impok.*
—II. *v.* to be able to attain (an ambition) by one's effort. Syn. *mapágtiyagaán.*

maaga (ma-a-ga), *adj. & adv.* early.

maagap (ma-a-gap), *adj.* 1. never late; punctual; prompt; always on time. Syn. *husto sa oras, nasa oras.* 2. alert; watchful. Syn. *listo, alisto.*

maagaw (ma-a-gaw), *v.* to be able to grab, snatch, or take away forcibly. Syn. *makuha sa pamamagitan ng pagsunggáp o pagdaklót.*

maagiw (ma-a-giw), *adj.* full of sooty cobwebs. Syn. *punó ng agiw, maraming agiw.*

maalaala (ma-a-la-a-la), *adj.* thoughtful; considerate. Syn. *maálalahanin, mapag-alaala, mapagmahál.*

máalab (ma-a-lab), *adj.* 1. easily set on fire; flammable. Syn. *madaling magningas.* 2. ardent; passionate. Syn. *maapóy, mainapóy, mainit.*

maalalahanín (ma-a-la-la-ha-nín), *adj.* thoughtful; considerate. Syn. *mapagmahál, maalaala.*

maalam (ma-a-lam), *adj.* 1. bright or talented, as a student. Syn. *matalino, marunong, talentó.* 2. wise; clever; tricky. Syn. *tuso.*

maalamát (ma-a-la-mát), *adj.* rich in legends.

maalapaap (ma-a-la-pa-ap), *adj.* full of clouds; cloudy. Syn. *maulap.*

maalat (ma-a-lat), *adj.* 1. salty; containing salt. Syn. *may-asín, lasang-asín.* 2. too salty. Syn. *sobra sa alat (asin).*

maalikabók (ma-a-li-ka-bók), *adj.* full of dust; dusty.

maalindóg (ma-a-lin-dóg), *adj.* beautiful; charming; pretty; attractive. Syn. *magandá, kaakit-akit.*

maalinsangan (ma-a-lin-sa-ngan), *adj.* sultry; warm, said of weather. Syn. *mainit, mabanás.*

maalintana (ma-a-lin-ta-na), *adj.* thoughtful; considerate. Syn. *maalalahanín, mapag-alaala.*

maalingasaw (ma-a-li-ga-saw), *adj.* smelly; having or giving out unpleasant smell. Syn. *mabahò, namamahò, nangangamóy.*

maalingasngás (ma-a-li-ngas-ngás), *adj.* scandalous; shameful. Syn. *nakahíhiyâ.*

maalisán (ma-a-li-sán), *v.* 1. to be able to remove or take away something from. 2. to be deprived, as of one's power.

maalíw (ma-a-líw), *v.* 1. to be able to comfort or console. Syn. *málibang, maalò.* 2. to be comforted or consoled. 3. to be or become amused or happy. Syn. *matuwâ, masiyahán.*

maaliwalas (ma-a-li-wa-las), *adj.* 1. clear or bright, as the sky. Syn. *maliwanag.* 2. clear; without obstructions; open. Syn. *tahaw.* 3. happy; without any trace of worry (said esp. of face). Syn. *masayá.* 4. spacious and well-ventilated. Syn. *presko, mahangin.*

maalwán (ma-al-wán), I. *adj.* 1. easy, as in *maalwang trabaho,* easy work. Syn. *madalî, magaán.* 2. comfortable, as in *maalwáng buhay,* comfortable life. Syn. *maginhawa.*
—II. *adj.* easy; easily, as in *maalwang gawin,* easy to do. Syn. *madali, magaan, maginhawa.*

maamò (ma-a-mò), I. *adj.* 1. tame; domesticated. Syn. *mabaít, di-mailap.* 2. docile; easily managed; obedient. Syn. *masunurin.*
—II. *v.* to be able to appease; be able to calm down. Syn. *mapaamò, mapahinahon.*

ma- . . . **-an,** a prefix-suffix combination used in forming verbs and nouns.

maanakán (ma-a-na-kán), *v.* to be able to beget a woman with a child.

maani | **maayos**

maani (ma-a-ni), I. *adj*. with or having abundant harvest. Syn. *maraming ani*.
—II. *v*. to be able to harvest.

maanták (ma-an-ták), *adj*. smarting or sharp, referring to pain. Syn. *masakít, makirót, mahapdí*.

maantala (ma-an-ta-la), *v*. to be or become delayed; be late. Syn. *maatraso, mahulí, mabimbín, maabala*.

maantót (ma-an-tót), *adj*. with or having repulsive odor of spoiled meat or stagnant water in a pool. Cf. *mabahò*.

maáng (ma-áng), *n*. feigned or pretended ignorance. Syn. *pagkukunwarí ng kawaláng malay*.

maangal (ma-a-ngal), *adj*. 1. vociferous; clamorous. Syn. *masalitâ, madaldál, maablá*. 2. disposed or inclined to complaining. Syn. *mareklamo, mapagreklamo*.

maanggó (ma-ang-gó), *adj*. with or having the odor of fermented milk.

maangháng (ma-ang-háng), var. **mahangháng**, *adj*. 1. hot to taste. 2. with or having peppery taste. 3. pungently objectionable or unacceptable, referring esp. to expressions. Syn. *masakít o nakasasakít*.

maanghít (ma-ang-hít), *adj*. with or having sweaty odor of the armpit.

maangót (ma-a-ngót), *adj*. with or having the stench of stagnant water in a pool.

maapulá (ma-a-pu-lá), *v*. 1. to be able to check, stop, or prevent. 2. to be checked; stopped, or prevented. Syn. *mapigil, masugpô*.

maaraw (ma-a-raw), *adj*. bright with sunlight; sunny. Syn. *mainit ang araw*.

maarì (ma-a-rì), I. *v*. to be able to own or possess. Syn. *maangkín, puweding ariin*.
—II. *adj*. with or having much possessions or properties. Syn. *maraming ari-arian (pag-aari)*.

máari (má-a-ri), *adj*. 1. allowable; permissible. Syn. *puwede, mapa-híhintulutan, mapápayagan*. 2. possible; that can happen. Syn. *posible, maaaring mangyari*.

maárimuhanán (ma-á-ri-mu-ha-nán), I. *adj*. 1. thrifty; economical; provident. Syn. *matipíd, mapagtipid*. 2. saving. Syn.

maimpók, mapag-impok. Also, *mapag-arimuhanán*.
—II. *v*. to be able to use sparingly. Syn. *matipíd, magamit nang matipíd*.

maarók (ma-a-rók), *v*. 1. to be able to sound the depth of (water) by diving. Syn. *masisid ang lalim*. 2. to be able to understand (the meaning of). Syn. *máunawaan, máintindihán*.

maarte (ma-ar-te), *adj*. 1. having or showing appreciation of beauty; artistic. Syn. *artistikó*. 2. expressive of artistic beauty. Syn. *masining, nasa arte*. 3. referring to a person who is too demonstrative or artificial in one's action.

maarugâ (ma-a-ru-gâ), I. *adj*. referring to a person who is very kind and helpful towards the helpless and the needy. Also, *mapag-aruga*. Syn. *makandilì, mapagkandilì, maalaga*.
—II. *v*. to be able to help someone, as by adopting or taking care of. Syn. *maampón, makandili*.

maasap (ma-a-sap), *adj*. full of smoke; smoky. Syn. *mausok, maasó*.

maasikaso (ma-a-si-ka-so), *adj*. 1. attentive to one's duty or obligation. Syn. *di-pabayâ sa trabaho, masipag*. 2. with or having much work. Syn. *matrabaho, magawain, maraming trabaho*.

maasim (ma-a-sim), *adj*. 1. sour. Syn. *lasang-suka*. 2. rancid; spoiled by fermentation Syn. *panís, kulasim*.

maatim (ma-a-tim), *v*. to be able to tolerate, suffer, or endure. Syn. *matiís, mapagtiisán; maagwanta*.

maatraso (ma-a-tra-so), I. *v*. 1. to become late or delayed. Syn. *mabalam, mabimbín, máhuli*. 2. to be able to cause the delay of.
—II. *adj*. with or having much arrears as in the payment of one's debt or loan. Syn. *maraming atraso*.

maawà (ma-a-wà), *v*. to pity; have pity on; be compassionate or merciful to. Syn. *magdaláng-awà, kaawaan*.

maawaín (ma-a-wa-ín), *adj*. full of mercy; merciful; compassionate. Syn. *máhabagin*.

maaya (ma-a-ya), *adj*. pleasant. Syn. *aliwalas, magandá, kaigá-igaya, masayá*.

maayos (ma-a-yos), I. *adj*. 1. in order;

orderly; in good condition; well-arranged. Syn. *nasaayos*. 2. peaceful; quiet. Syn. *tahimik, waláng-guló*.
—II. *v*. 1. to be able to keep in order; be able to arrange well. Syn. *mailagay sa ayos*. 2. to be able to settle amicably, as a quarrel or trouble.

mabábatá (ma-bá-ba-tá), *adj*. that can be suffered or endured. Syn. *matitiís, mapagtitiisán*.

mababaw (ma-ba-baw), *adj*. 1. shallow; not deep. Syn. *di-malalim, mababà*. 2. superficial; not thorough. Syn. *mahinà*.

mabakás (ma-ba-kás), *v*. 1. to be able to notice. Syn. *mapansin, máhalatâ, mapuná*. 2. to be able to trace the path of. Syn. *matuntón, mataluntón*.

mabaklá (ma-bak-lá), *v*. to be or become worried about something. Syn. *mabahalá, mag-alaalá, matigatig*.

mabagal (ma-ba-gal), *adj*. slow in action or movement; sluggish. Syn. *makupad*.

mabagsík (ma-bag-sík), *adj*. 1. fierce; cruel. Syn. *malupít*. 2. strict. Syn. *mahigpit*. 3. potent or effective, as a drug. Syn. *mabisà*. 4. strong, as a drink. Syn. *matapang*.

mabahò (ma-ba-hò), *adj*. with or having offensive odor; fetid; stinking. Syn. *mabantót, maantót; masamâ ang amóy*.

mabaít (ma-ba-ít), I. *adj*. 1. kind; sympathetic; generous; helpful. Syn. *mabuti, matulungín, maawain*. 2. tame; not wild; domesticated. Syn. *maamò, di-mailáp*.
—II. *n*. (*Colloq.*) mouse. Syn. *dagâ*.

mabalasik (ma-ba-la-sik), *adj*. fierce; savage. Syn. *mabangís, mabagsík*.

mabalat (ma-ba-lat), *adj*. full or covered with birthmarks; with or having many birthmarks.

mabanás (ma-ba-nás), *adj*. sultry; suffocatingly warm. Syn. *maalinsangan, mainit, maalisís* (Bats.).

mabantót (ma-ban-tót), *adj*. with or having the repulsive odor of putrid water or spoiled meat. Syn. *maantót, mabaho*.

mabangis (ma-ba-ngis), *adj*. ferocious; fierce. Syn. *mabalasik, malupit*.

mabangó (ma-ba-ngó), *adj*. fragrant; aromatic; sweet-smelling. Cf. *masamyó,*

mahalimuyák.

mabarkada (ma-bar-ka-da), *adj*. with or having many members in one's gang. Syn. *maraming kabarkada*.

mabasag-ulo (ma-ba-sag + u-lo), *adj*. full of troubles; troublesome. Syn. *maligalig, maraming basag-ulo o ligalig*.

mabató (ma-ba-tó), I. *adj*. full or covered with stones; stony. Syn. *maraming bató*.
—II. *v*. to be able to hit or strike with something, esp. with a piece of stone. Syn *mahagis, mapukól ng bató*.

mabenta (ma-ben-ta), *adj*. with or having plenty of sales. Syn. *mabilí*.

maberde (ma-ber-de), *adj*. 1. green or greenish. Syn. *luntî, luntian*. 2. (*Fig.*) lewd or indecent, referring to expressions. Syn. *malaswâ, mahalay*.

mabibíg (ma-bi-bíg), *adj*. talkative; vociferous. Syn. *madaldal, masalita*.

mabikas (ma-bi-kas), *adj*. 1. stylish; well-dressed; smartly dressed. Syn. *magara (ang kasuután), makisig*. 2. graceful esp. of body movement; dignified in manners.

mabida (ma-bi-da), *adj*. with or having many stories or anecdotes to tell. Syn. *makuwento*. 2. talkative. Syn. *madaldál, masalitâ*.

mabigát (ma-bi-gát), *adj*. 1. heavy; weighty. 2. serious; critical or grave. Syn. *malubhâ, malalâ*. 3. hard to tackle with. Syn. *mahirap*.

mabilí (ma-bi-lí), I. *adj*. 1. fast-selling, referring to goods. Syn. *mabilís ipagbilí*. 2. with or having plenty of sales. Syn. *malakás ang tindá, marami ang namimilí*.
—II. *v*. to be able to buy or purchase. Syn. *maaaring bilhin*.

mabilís (ma-bi-lís), I. *adj*. 1. fast; swift; speedy. Syn. *matulin*. 2. fast or ahead of time, as a watch. Syn. *adelantado sa oras*.
—II. *adv*. in a fast manner; swiftly; speedily; quickly; rapidly. Syn. *matulin, nang matulin*.

mabilog (ma-bi-log), I. *adj*. 1. round; spherical. Syn. *bilog na parang bola*. 2. circular; shaped like a circle.
—II. *v*. to be able to make into a round object, like a ball, or into a circular figure, like a circle.

mabinì (ma-bi-nì), *adj*. modest or coy in movement or speech, referring esp. to a woman. Syn. *mahinhín*.

mabintóg (ma-bin-tóg), var. mapintóg, *adj*. 1. inflated, as a balloon. 2. fat; fleshy; plump; chubby. Syn. *maumbók, matambók, matabâ*.

mabirò (ma-bi-rò), *adj*. full of jokes; fund of joking. Syn. *palabiró, mapagbiró*.

mabisà (ma-bi-sà), *adj*. effective; efficacious; potent.

mabisyo (ma-bis-yo), *adj*. vicious; having bad habits. Syn. *bisyoso*.

mabituin (ma-bi-tu-in), *adj*. full of stars; starry. Syn. *maraming bituin*.

mabiyayà (ma-bi-ya-yà), *adj*. 1. gainful; beneficial. Syn. *mapakinabang, kapakípakinabang; matubò; pinagtútubuan nang malaki*. 2. bountiful. Syn. *masaganá*. 3. full of grace. Syn. *mapagpalà*.

mábukáng-bibíg (mábu-káng + bi-bíg), var. mábukámbibíg, *v*. to happen to mention; be mentioned in passing. Syn. *másambít, masabi nang hindî sinasadyâ*.

mábukód-tangì (má-bu-kód + ta-ngì), *v*. to be taken as an exception from others; be an exception from. Syn. *máibá sa marami*.

mabuhay (ma-bu-hay), I. *v*. 1. to live or be able to live or exist. 2. to become alive. 3. to be able to support the existence, as of one's family.
  —II. *interj*. (M-) Long live! Syn. *Biba!*

mabulas (ma-bu-las), *adj*. robust; luxuriant; healthy. Syn. *malusóg*.

mabulo (ma-bu-lo), var. mabolo, I. *n*. (Bot.) 1. a species of tree (*Diospyros discolor Willd*.), with hard dark-colored wood and edible fruits. 2. the fruit of this plant. Syn. *talang*.
  —II. *adj*. downy, wooly, or hairy, referring to certain fruits or leaves of plants.

mabunyî (ma-bun-yî), *adj*. illustrious; distinguished. Syn. *dakilà, tanyág, marangál, mahál*.

mabunga (ma-bu-nga), *adj*. 1. laden with fruits; with or having many fruits. Syn. *maraming bunga*. 2. fruitful; profitable. Syn. *mapakinabang, maraming pakinabang*.

maburirì (ma-bu-ri-rì), *adj*. too meticulous in doing something. Syn. *makutiltîl*.

maburok (ma-bu-rok), *adj*. chubby; round and plump. Syn. *matambók, mabintóg, maumbók*.

mabusisi (ma-bu-si-si), *adj*. too meticulous in doing something. Syn. *makuriri, maburiri, makutiltil*.

mabuti (ma-bu-ti), *adj*. 1. good; better than average. Syn. *mahusay, magalíng*. 2. healthy; sound; vigorous, as one's body. Syn. *malusog, malakás*. 3. kind; generous; benevolent; helpful. Syn. *mabaít, matulungín*. 4. proper; fit; becoming. Syn. *bagay, nababagay, tumpák; ayos*. 5. respectful. Syn. *magalang*. 2. dutiful; obedient. Syn. *masunurin*.

mabuwáy (ma-bu-wáy), *adj*. in an unstable or shaky state.

maka- (ma-ka-), *pref*. used to form: 1. verbs, meaning "to be able to do, make, or perform," as in *makakuha*, to be able to get; *makagawâ*, to be able to work; *makatalón*, to be able to jump. 2. adjectives, expressing: a) in favor of; pro- (usually hyphenated before proper nouns), as in *maka-Pilipino*, pro-Pilipino; *maka-Inggles*, pro-English; and before nouns or adjectives (without hyphen), as in *makabago*, modernistic; *makalumá*, old-fashioned; b) as much or as many times as, as in *makalimá*, as many times as five; *makaanim*, six times; *makapitó*, seven times.

makaalít (ma-ka-a-lít), *v*. 1. to be in conflict or discord with someone. Syn. *mákagalít, mákalaban*. 2. to be an opponent of someone in a court suit. Syn. *mákausapín, makalaban sa usapín, mákaasuntó*.

makabago (ma-ka-ba-go), I. *adj*. modern; modernistic; up-to-date.
  —II. *v*. to be able to change one's place (of residence). Syn. *makalipat, makaibá ng lugár*.

makabansá (ma-ka-ban-sá), var. makabansá, *adj*. nationalistic; patriotic. Syn. *makabayan*.

makabayan (ma-ka-ba-yan), *adj*. nationalistic; patriotic. Syn. *makabansá*.

makabigát (ma-ka-bi-gát), *v*. 1. to cause an added weight to. Syn. *makáragdág ng bigát*. 2. to cause or to be the cause of gravity or seriousness, as of one's illness. Syn.

makalubhâ, makalalâ. 3. to become an added burden or responsibility to (someone). Syn. *maging karagdagang hirap, makapagpahirap.*

makabihag (ma-ka-bi-hag), *v.* 1. to be able to hold (someone) as a captive. 2. to be able to charm or fascinate. Syn. *makaakit, makabighanì.*

makabuhay (ma-ka-bu-hay), I. *n.* a species of vine (climbing plant), the stem of which has a very bitter substance that is much used for medicinal purposes (*Tinospora rumphi Boerl.*).
—II. *v.* 1. to be able to sustain life. 2. to be able to enliven. Syn. *makasiglá, makapagbigáy-siglá.*

makabuluhán (ma-ka-bu-lu-hán), *adj.* meaningful; important. Syn. *mahalagá, importante.*

makadaóp-palad (ma-ka-da-óp + pa-lad), *v.* to be able to shake hands with (someone), hence, to have a chance or opportunity to be introduced to or be acquainted with (someone).

makademonyo (ma-ka-de-mon-yo), *adj.* devilish; wicked.

makadiwà (ma-ka-di-wà), *adj.* 1. meaningful. Syn. *malamán, makahulugán.* 2. (*Gram.*) of or having the nature of a verb; verbal.

maka-Diyós (ma-ka + Di-yós), *adj.* godly; religious; pious. Syn. *banál, madásalin.*

makáekstra (ma-ká-eks-tra), *v.* to be able to work as extra laborer or an extra performer in a show or the like.

makaharì (ma-ka-ha-rì), *adj.* 1. kingly; royal; regal; majestic. 2. dictatorial; domineering; autocratic.

makahayop (ma-ka-ha-yop), *adj.* bestial; brutal; savage. Syn. *malupít.*

makainá (ma-ka-i-ná), *adj.* very fond of one's mother.

maka-Inggles (ma-ka + Ing-gles), *var.* maka-Ingles, I. *adj.* pro-English.
—II. *v.* to be able to speak English or talk in English. Syn. *makapágsalita ng Ingglés.*

makaisá (ma-ka-i-sá), *v.* 1. to be able to do, make, manufacture, or finish one. Syn. *makagawâ o makatapos ng isá.* 2. (*Colloq.*) to be able to crack a joke.

makaisáng-dibdib (ma-ka-i-sáng + dib-dib), *v.* to be married to; be or become one's spouse.

makálalaki (ma-ká-la-la-ki), *v.* to be able to domineer another man.

makalamáng (ma-ka-la-máng), *v.* to be able to surpass or have an advantage over another. Syn. *makahigít, makabentaha.*

makalangit (ma-ka-la-ngit), *adj.* heavenly; holy; divine. Syn. *banal.*

makalawá (ma-ka-la-wá), *adv.* the day after tomorrow.

makálawá (ma-ka-la-wa), *adj. & adv.* twice; two times.

makalipas (ma-ka-li-pas), *v.* 1. to be able to pass or end, as one's anger, etc. Syn. *makaraán, matapós.*
—II. *adv.* after (a certain period of time). Syn. *makaraán, pagkatapos.*

makáloko (ma-ká-lo-ko), *v.* to be able to deceive or fool someone. Syn. *makálinláng, makádayà.*

makalolo (ma-ka-lo-lo), *adj.* very fond of one's grandfather.

makalumà (ma-ka-lu-mà), *adj.* old-fashioned; out-of-date; antiquated. Syn. *sáunahín, sinauna.*

makalupà (ma-ka-lu-pà), *adj.* earthly; worldly.

maká-makalwá (ma-ká + ma-kal-wá), *adv.* every two days. Syn. *tuwíng makalwá.*

makamulatan (ma-ka-mu-la-tan), *v.* to happen to see or experience since one's childhood. Syn. *kagisnán*

makamundó (ma-ka-mun-dó), *adj.* worldly; earthly. Syn. *makalupà.*

makán (ma-kán), *n.* (*Bot.*) a variety of highland rice.

makandili (ma-kan-di-li), I. *v.* to be able to adopt or take under one's protective care. Syn. *maampon, makupkóp, matangkilik.*
—II. *adj.* with or having many persons under one's care. Syn. *maraming kinákandili.*

makapag- (ma-ka-pag-), *pref.* used to form verbs meaning "to be able to," as in *makapág-asawa,* to be able to marry or get a wife or husband; *makapágsalitâ,* to be able to talk.

makapag- (ma-ka-pag-), *pref.* used to form

verbs meaning "to have a chance or opportunity to," as in *makápag-aral*, to have a chance or opportunity to study or go to school; *makápag-asawa*, to have a chance to marry or get a wife or husband.

makapág-atikhâ (ma-ka-pág + a-tik-ḥâ), *v.* to be able to save for the future by means of consistent frugality.

makapág-isá (ma-ka-pág + i-sá), *v.* to be able to live or stay alone in a place. Syn. *makatiráng mag-isá.*

makapangyarihan (ma-ka-pang-ya-ri-han), *adj.* with or having much power; powerful. Syn. *malakás.*

makapunô (ma-ka-pu-nô), I. *n.* 1. the fruit of a certain species of coconut tree, having thick, soft, edible, white meat, which is usually made into sweets. 2. the coconut palm that bears this fruit.
—II. *v.* to be able to fill up a container, as a bag, box, sack, etc.

makaraán (ma-ka-ra-án), I. *v.* to be able to pass. Syn. *makalampás.*
—II. *adv.* after. Syn. *matapos, pagkatapos.*

makarinyo (ma-ka-rin-yó), *adj.* very affectionate.

makasalanan (ma-ka-sa-la-nan), I. *adj.* full of sin; sinful; wicked; immoral.
—II. *n.* sinner.

makasarili (ma-ka-sa-ri-li), I. *adj.* selfish; egoistic; conceited. Syn. *sakím, makamkám.*
—II. *v.* to be able to obtain or get all for one's own. Syn. *matamóng lahát.*

makasaysayan (ma-ka-say-sa-yan), *adj.* historical.

makasím (ma-ka-sím), *adj.* sourish.

makatà (ma-ka-tâ), *n.* poet. Syn. *poeta.*

makatao (ma-ka-ta-o), *adj.* humane; kind. Syn. *mabaít, maawaín.*

makatarungan (ma-ka-ta-ru-ngan), *adj.* just; lawful; legal; justified. Syn. *legál, náaalinsunod sa batás.*

makatás (ma-ka-tás), I. *adj.* juicy; succulent; sappy.
—II. *v.* to be able to extract the juice of.

makatí (ma-ka-tí), *adj.* itchy.

makatló (ma-kat-ló), *adv.* three days from now.

makatlô (ma-kat-lô), *v.* to be able to divide

into three equal parts. Syn. *mapagtatló.*

makatuwiran (ma-ka-tu-wi-ran), *adj.* 1. full of argument; too argumentative. Syn. *maargumento, mahilig sa pakikipagtalo.* 2. reasonable; just.

makaurì (ma-ka-u-rì), *adj.* (Gram.) adjectival; having the nature or function of an adjective.

makawikà (ma-ka-wi-kà), *adj.* 1. language-minded, referring to a person. 2. tending to serve a certain language.

makiling (ma-ki-ling), *adj.* 1. partial; biased; prejudiced. 2. fond of; given to. Syn. *mahilig.*

mákiná (má-ki-ná), *n.* (Sp. *maquina*) 1. machine (in general). 2. sewing machine. 3. engine; motor. Syn. *motór.*

makináng (ma-ki-náng), *adj.* brilliant; lustrous; shiny. Syn. *makintab.*

makinarya (ma-ki-nar-ya), *n.* (Sp. *maquinaria*) machinery.

mákiní-kinitá (má-ki-ní + ki-ni-tá), *v.* to have an imaginary vision of; have a mental image of. Cf. *máguniguní.*

makinilyá (ma-ki-nil-yá), *n.* (Sp. *maquinilla*) 1. typewriting machine; typewriter. 2. the manner by which something was typewritten. Syn. *pagkakámakinilyá.* 3. a machine hair cutter. Syn. *makinilyá sa buhók.* 4. the manner by which the hair was cut or clipped with this machine.

makinis (ma-ki-nis), *adj.* 1. smooth; fine; well-polished. Syn. *pino.* 2. shiny, as a surface. Syn. *makintáb.*

makintáb (ma-kin-táb), *adj.* shiny; glossy; well-polished. Syn. *makináng.*

makipág- (ma-ki-pág-), *prefix* meaning: 1. to engage or challenge, as in *makipág-away.* 2. to join, as in *makipag-agawan.*

makipágbálitaktakan (ma-ki-pág-bá-li-tak-ta-kan), *v.* to engage another in a heated debate or discussion. Syn. *makipágtalo nang máinitán.*

makipágbasag-ulo (ma-ki-pág-ba-sag + u-lo), *v.* to start trouble or fight with someone. Syn. *makipág-away.*

makipágkápuwâ (ma-ki-pág-ká-pu-wâ), *var.* **makipágkápwâ**, *v.* to be friendly with. Syn. *makipágkaibigan.*

makipágsápalarán (ma-ki-pág-sá-pa-la-rán),

v. to take a chance; try one's luck.

makipagsará (ma-ki-pag-sa-rá), *v.* to close a deal or contract with. Syn. *makipagkásundô.*

makipágsiyám (ma-ki-pág-si-yám), *v.* 1. to attend or participate in the observation of the ninth day or ninth anniversary of someone's death. 2. to attend a nine-day novena.

makipot (ma-ki-pot), *adj.* 1. narrow, referring to things like holes, streets, doors, windows, etc. 2. tight or undersized, referring to pants, shoes, hats, dresses, etc. Syn. *masikíp.*

makisama (ma-ki-sa-ma), *v.* 1. to join in company with another or with a group. Syn. *makisabáy.* 2. to share with someone in the same room, house, vehicle, or the like. Syn. *makisunò.* 3. to live with another as a common-law wife or husband. 4. to try to be friendly or compatible with another or others. Syn. *makibagay.*

makisamá (ma-ki-sa-má), *v.* 1. to work as a tenant farmer in an hacienda. 2. to join in a business partnership with someone. Syn. *makisosyo, makibakas.*

makisig (ma-ki-sig), *v.* elegant; smartly dressed; stylish. Syn. *postoryoso, mabikás, magarà.*

makisláp (ma-kis-láp), *adj.* brilliant; shining with luster. Syn. *makináng.*

makitid (ma-ki-tid), *adj.* narrow; not wide; small in width as compared to length. Cf. *makipot.*

makiutang-na-loób (ma-ki-u-tang + na + lo-ób), *v.* to ask or request a favor. Syn. *makisuyò, makiusap.*

makopa (ma-ko-pa), *n.* (*Bot.*) 1. Malay tersana rose apple tree (*Syzygium malaccense Linn.*), cultivated for its fleshy, edible fruits. 2. the fruit of this tree.

maktól (mak-tól), *n.* peevish behavior. Cf. *sumpóng.*

makulay (ma-ku-lay), *adj.* colorful.

makulít (ma-ku-lít), *adj.* stubbornly repetitious or insistent.

makunat (ma-ku-nat), *adj.* 1. ductile; pliant. 2. hard, as meat. Syn. *matigás.* 3. (*Slang*) stingy; closefisted. Syn. *kuripot.*

makupad (ma-ku-pad), *adj.* sluggish; slow or

slow-moving, referring to a person. Syn. *mabagal, makuyad, mahinang kumilos.*

makursunadahan (ma-kur-su-na-da-han), *v.* to happen to be the choice of someone's caprice or vagary. Syn. *mágustuhán.*

makuskós-balungos (ma-kus-kós + ba-lungos), *adj.* too particular to unnecessary details or trifles. Syn. *marekubeko, makuntil-butil, mabusisi.*

makuwarta (ma-ku-war-ta), I. *adj.* moneyed; having much money; rich; wealthy. Syn. *masalapî, mayaman, mapilak.*

—II. *v.* to be able to turn into cash, as by selling; be able to sell. Syn. *maipagbilí.*

makuwento (ma-ku-wen-to), *adj.* 1. fond of telling or talking about one's experience or about oneself. 2. with, having, or containing many stories.

makuyad (ma-ku-yad), *adj.* slow; slow-moving, referring to a person. Syn. *mabagal, makupad.*

madagtâ (ma-dag-tâ), *adj.* full of sap; sappy. Cf. *makatás.*

madahilán (ma-da-hi-lán), I. *adj.* with or having or giving many reasons or excuses. Syn. *makatwiran, maraming katwiran o dahilan.*

—II. *v.* to be able to use as a reason or excuse. Syn. *maidahilán, maikatwiran.*

madalâ (ma-da-lâ), *v.* to be scared away due to a previous unfortunate experience.

madalang (ma-da-lang), I. *adj.* 1. few; not many. Syn. *iilán, kakauntî, hindî marami.* 2. set far apart; not close together; scattered. Syn. *awáng-awáng, layú-layô, agwát-agwát, hiwá-hiwaláy.* 3. thin, referring to hair. Syn. *manipís.* 4. not often; rare. Syn. *bihirà.*

—II. *adv.* rarely; unfrequently; not often. Syn. *bihirà, ama, amang-ama.*

madalás (ma-da-lás), I. *adj.* 1. often; frequent. Syn. *malimit.* 2. fast; rapid. Syn. *mabilís.*

—II. *adv.* often; frequently; repeatedly.

madalaw (ma-da-law), I. *adj.* with or having many visitors. Syn. *maraming dalaw (dumadalaw), mapanauhin, mabisita.*

—II. *v.* to be able to visit. Syn. *mabisita.*

madaldál (ma-dal-dál), *adj.* talkative; loquacious. Syn. *masalitâ, maablá, masatsát.*

madalî   **mag-**

madalî (ma-da-lî), I. *adj.* 1. easy to do or make; not difficult. Syn. *maalwang gawin*. 2. quick; prompt; immediate. Syn. *mabilís, ágaran*.
—II. *adv.* 1. easily; without much difficulty. Syn. *maalwán*. 2. promptly; quickly; immediately; soon. Syn. *agád, kapagdaka*.

madaling-araw (ma-da-ling + a-raw), *n.* the early hours before dawn. Syn. *dapit-umaga*.

madalî't-sabi (ma-da-lí't + sa-bi), *adv.* 1. therefore; consequently. Syn. *anupá't, kaya ngâ, samakatwíd*. 2. in short. Syn. *sa maikling salitâ, sa madaling salitâ*.

madamdamin (ma-dam-da-min), *adj.* 1. emotional; sensitive; easily offended. Syn. *magagalitin*. 2. full of feelings. See **maramdamin**.

madamó (ma-da-mó), var. **maramó**, *adj.* covered with grass; grassy.

madamot (ma-da-mot), var. **maramot**, *adj.* 1. selfish. Syn. *sakím, masakím, makamkám*. 2. stingy; miserly. Syn. *kuripot, hidhíd*.

madásalin (ma-dá-sa-lin), *adj.* prayerful. Syn. *mapagdasál, paládasál*.

madayà (ma-da-yà), var. **marayá**, I. *adj.* 1. full of tricks; tricky; fraudulent. 2. given to cheating or defrauding others. Syn. *mapanlinláng*.
—II. *v.* to be able to cheat or defraud. Syn. *malinláng*.

madehado (ma-de-ha-do), I. *adj.* in cockfighting and horse racing, with the majority of winning animals coming from the entries having the lesser bets. Ant. *maliyamado*.
—II. *v.* to be able to surpass. Syn. *madaíg*.

madiín (ma-di-ín), var. **mariín**, *adj.* 1. heavily pressed, as in printing. Syn. *matindí*. 2. emphatic; with emphasis.

madilat (ma-di-lat), *adj.* wide-open (s.o. eyes).

madiláw (ma-di-láw), *adj.* yellow or yellowish.

madilihénsiya (ma-di-li-hén-si-ya), *adj.* with or having the ability to find ways and means of obtaining something badly needed. Syn. *mahusay magdilihénsiyá*.

madilim (ma-di-lim), *v.* 1. dark; gloomy. 2. *(Fig.)* uncertain. Syn. *waláng-katíyakan; malabò*. 3. melancholic; sad. Syn. *malungkót*.

madingal (ma-di-ngal), var. **maringal**, *adj.* pompous; magnificent.

madiwà (ma-di-wà), *adj.* full of meaning; meaningful. Syn. *makahulugán, puno ng kahulugán*.

madlâ (mad-lâ), I. *indef. pron.* all; everyone; everybody; the public; the people. Syn. *ang tanán, mga tao, ang publikó*.
—II. *adj.* all of; everyone of. Syn. *lahát*.

madrastra (ma-dras-tra), *n.* (Sp.) stepmother. Syn. *ale, ináng pangumán, tiyahin*. Cf. *padrasto*.

madre (ma-dre), *n.* (Sp.) nun. Cf. *mongha*. 2. *(Carp.)* the principal piece or log.

madrekakáw (ma-dre-ka-káw), var. **marikakáw**, *n.* (Bot.) a timber tree better known as *kakawate*.

madrina (ma-dri-na), *n.* (Sp.) female sponsor; godmother. Syn. *ninang, iniiná*.

madugô (ma-du-gô), var. **marugô**, *adj.* 1. involving bloodshed; bloody. 2. bleeding; full or covered with blood.

madulà (ma-du-là), *adj.* full of drama; dramatic; exciting.

madulás (ma-du-lás), *adj.* 1. slippery. 2. *(Fig.)* elusive. Syn. *mailáp*.

madumí (ma-du-mí), var. **marumí**, *adj.* dirty; untidy. Syn. *punô ng dumí, salaulá* (s.o. persons).

madunong (ma-du-nong), var. **marunong**, *adj.* 1. talented; intelligent; erudite. Syn. *matalino*. 2. wise; shrewd; crafty; cunning. Syn. *tuso*.

madungis (ma-du-ngis), var. **marungis**, *adj.* with or having dirty face or skin. Syn. *marusing*.

madusing (ma-du-ngis), var. **marusing**, *adj.* with or having dirt on the face. Syn. *marungis, amusin*.

madyik (mad-yik), *n.* (Eng.) magic. Syn. *mahiyá, mahiká, salamangka*.

maestra (ma-es-tra), *n.* (Sp.) female teacher. Syn. *gurong babae*.

mag- (mag-); *pref.* used to form: 1. nouns, expressing a) relationship between two persons, as in *mag-amá, mag-iná, mag-*

asawa, magkasama, etc.; b) relation of
three or more persons, with the first
syllable of the root or wordbase
reduplicated, as in *mag-aamá, mag-iiná,
magkakapatíd, magkakasama,* etc.; c)
occupation or trade, with the first syllable
of the root or wordbase reduplicated, as
in *mag-aararó, magsasaká, magbubukid,
magtitindá,* etc. 2. verbs, expressing: a) act
of doing or performing something, as in
*magsaka, magtrabaho, magtinda, maglinis,
magsulát,* etc.; b) continuous or repeated
acts, with the first syllable of the root or
wordbase reduplicated, as in *magtatalón,
maghihiyáw, magsasalitâ, magsusulát,
magtatawa,* etc.; c) simultaneous or
mutual acts, with *–an, -han,* and *–nan*
suffixed to the root, as in *magtawanan,
magbiruán, magtakbuhan, magsalitaan,
magpaligsahan, magmurahán,* etc.

magâ (ma-ga), var. **pagâ,** I. *adj.* swollen;
inflamed. Syn. *namamágâ.*
—II. *n.* 1. state or condition of being
swollen or inflamed. Syn. *pamamaga.* 2.
the swollen or inflamed part.

magaán (ma-ga-án), *adj.* 1. light; not heavy;
having little weight.

mag-aani (mag + a-a-ni), *n.* harvester; reaper
(esp. of grains).

mag-aaráw (mag + a-a-ráw), *n.* daily wage
earner; temporary daily worker.

mag-aasín (mag + a-a-sín), *n.* 1. salt maker
or manufacturer. 2. salt dealer or vendor.

mag-abot (mag + a-bot), *v.* 1. to be touching
each other end to end or side to side,
referring to two things. Cf. *magkahugpóng,
magkadikít.* 2. to be in contact or come
face to face with each other, as in a certain
place. Syn. *magkatagpô, magkita,
magpangita.* 2. to be in a hand-to-hand
struggle or fight. Syn. *magkatuluyan ng
labanán, magkasagupà.*

mag-akalà (mag + a-ka-là), *v.* 1. to plan or have
a plan about something. Syn. *magbalak,
magpanukalà.* 2. to suspect; have a suspicion
about something. Syn. *maghinala.* 3. to have
an idea or presumption about something.
Syn. *magpalagáy.*

mag-adyá (mag + ad-yá), *v.* to redeem, as
from sin or evil. Syn. *magligtás.*

magagalíng (ma-ga-ga-líng), *adj.* referring to
persons or things that are good or
excellent. Syn. *mahuhusay.*

magagalitín (ma-ga-ga-li-tín), *adj.* easily
angered or irritated; irritable. Syn.
madalíng magalit, mainitin ang ulo.

mag-agam-agam (mag + a-gam + a-gam), *v.*
to have a doubt or misgiving about
something. Syn. *mag-alinlangan.*

mag-agaw-buhay (mag + a-gaw + bu-hay),
v. 1. to be hovering between life and
death; be dying. Syn. *maghingalô.* 2. *(Fig.)*
to be almost exhausted or used up. Syn.
magmatirá.

magahís (ma-ga-hís), *v.* 1. to be able to
overpower or subdue. Syn. *malupig.* 2. to
be or become overpowered or subdued.
Syn. *masupit, madaíg.*

magahól (ma-ga-hól), *v.* to lack time; be or
become late or delayed. Syn. *magipít sa
panahón, kapusín sa oras, mahulí.*

mag-alaala (mag + a-la-a-la), *v.* to give
(something) as a gift or present. Syn.
maghandóg, magregalo.

mag-alaalá (mag + a-la-a-lá), *v.* to be worried
about. Syn. *mabahalà.*

magalák (ma-ga-lák), *v.* to rejoice; be happy
or glad. Syn. *matuwâ.*

magalang (ma-ga-lang), *adj.* respectful;
polite; courteous. Syn. *mapitagan.*

mag-álanganin (mag + á-la-nga-nin), *v.* 1.
to be in doubt or uncertain. Syn. *magduda,
mag-alinlangan.* 2. to be hesitant or
undecided. Syn. *mag-atubili, mag-urung-
sulong.* 3. to be insufficient or lacking.
Syn. *kapusín, magkulang.*

magaláw (ma-ga-láw), *adj.* shaky; moving
too much. Syn. *maalóg, maugà.*

mag-ale (mag + a-le), *n.* 1. the aunt and her
niece or nephew. Syn. *magtiyá.* 2. the
relation between an aunt and her niece
or nephew. 3. the stepmother and her
stepchild. 4. the relation between the
stepmother and her stepchild.

mag-alimpuyó (mag + a-lim-pu-yó), *v.* 1. to
whirl violently. Syn. *mag-umikot.* 2. to be
excited or stirred violently, as with anger.
Syn. *magpuyós, magsikláb.*

magalíng (ma-ga-líng), *adj.* 1. very good;
excellent. Syn. *mahusay, mabuti.* 2.

efficient. Syn. *episyente*. 3. effective. Syn. *mabisà*. 4. strong; vigorous; healthy. Syn. *malakás, malusog*. 5. able; expert; skilled. Syn. *dalubhasà, esperto*. 6. (with *na*) already well, referring to a sick person.

nagalíng-galíng (ma-ga-líng + ga-líng), *adj.* slightly better. Syn. *mahusáy-husáy, mabutí-butí*.

nagalingín (ma-ga-li-ngín), *v.* to consider or approve as appropriate or good. Syn. *mabutihin, kilalanin o ipalagáy na mahusay*. 2. to appreciate. Syn. *mahalagahín*.

nag-álisan (mag + á-li-san), *v.* to leave or go away at the same time or in group or groups. Syn. *magyauhan, maglisanan*.

nagalit (ma-ga-lit), *v.* to be or become angry. Syn. *mayamót, mag-init ang ulo*.

nagalitín (ma-ga-li-tín), *adj.* easily made angry; irritable. Syn. *mainitín ang ulo*. See **magagalitín**.

nag-alsa-balutan (mag + al-sa + ba-lu-tan), *v.* to leave in anger and without any warning. Syn. *lumayas nang galít at waláng abug-abóg*.

nag-amá (mag + a-má), *n.* 1. the father and his child. 2. the relation between the father and his child. Syn. *magtatay*.

nag-amaín (mag + a-ma-ín), *n.* 1. the uncle and his niece or nephew. Syn. *magtiyó*. 2. the relation between an uncle and his niece or nephew. 3. a stepfather and his stepchild. 4. the relation between a stepfather and his stepchild. Syn. *magamáng pangumán, magtiyuhin*.

nag-amáng-binyág (mag + a-máng + bin-yág), *n.* 1. the godfather at baptism and his godchild. Syn. *magninong sa binyág, mag-amá sa binyág*. 2. the relation between a godftaher and his godchild.

nagamit (ma-ga-mit), *v.* to happen to use; be used unintentionally.

nag-amot (mag + a-mot), *v.* to give, contribute, or sell a small portion of one's goods to another. Syn. *magbahagi o magbigáy ng kauntí*.

nagamót (ma-ga-mót), I. *v.* to be able to cure or remedy. Syn. *mapagaling, malunasan*. 2. (*Fig.*) to remedy or solve, as a problem. Syn. *malutas, malunasan*.
—II. *adj.* well-supplied with medicines;

with or having plenty of medicines. Syn. *marami o saganà sa gamót*.

mag-amóy- (mag + a-móy-), a combining form, meaning "to have the smell of," as in *mag-amóy-pawis, mag-amóy-kandila*, etc.

mag-ampón (mag + am-pón), *v.* to adopt (a child); take into one's own family by adoption. Cf. *mag-arugâ*.

magana (ma-ga-na), *adj.* 1. with or having a good appetite. 2. that gives or yields much profit or gain. Syn. *matubò, mapakinabang*.

mag-anak (mag + a-nak), *n.* family. Syn. *pamilya*.

mag-anák (mag + a-nák), *v.* to give birth; produce offspring. Syn. *magkaanák*. 2. to act as a sponsor at a wedding, baptism, confirmation, etc. 3. to produce; multiply. Syn. *dumami*.

maganánsiyá (ma-ga-nán-si-yá), *adj.* very profitable or gainful. Syn. *matubò, mapakinabang*.

magandá (ma-gan-dá), *adj.* beautiful; lovely; pretty; comely; good-looking; attractive. Syn. *kaakit-akit, kaigá-igaya, marikit*.

magandahán (ma-gan-da-hán), *v.* to be fascinated or attracted by the beauty of. Syn. *mahalina o mabighanì ng kagandahan*.

magandahin (ma-gan-da-hin), *v.* to appreciate; consider or accept as something good. Syn. *mabutihin, ipalagáy na mabuti o magalíng*.

magandáng-kaloobán (ma-gan-dáng + ka-lo-o-bán), I. *adj.* kindhearted; generous; benevolent.
—II. *n.* kindheartedness; benevolence; generosity.

mag-antabáy (mag + an-ta-báy), *v.* to slow down in order to wait for someone following behind. Syn. *magdahan-dahan*.

magantihán (ma-gan-ti-hán), *v.* 1. to be able to repay or reciprocate (a good act). Syn. *mabayaran, matumbasán*. 2. to be able to retaliate or revenge against. Syn. *mapághigantihán*.

mag-antisipo (mag + an-ti-si-po), *v.* to give an advance partial down payment for something one is intending to buy.

mag-angkin (mag + ang-kin), *v.* to possess, as a certain quality or characteristic. Syn. *magtagláy*.

magapì (ma-ga-pì), *v.* 1. to be able to break with the hand, referring to a small branch. Syn. *mabalì.* 2. to be able to subdue or overpower. Syn. *malupig, masupil.* 3. to be subdued or overpowered.

mag-apuháp (mag + a-pu-háp), *v.* to seek or find by groping or as by groping. Syn. *maghagiláp.*

magarà (ma-ga-rà), *adj.* 1. dressy; elegant. Syn. *bihís na bihís, makisig, pustura.* 2. pompous; stately. Syn. *maringal.*

mag-aral (mag + a-ral), *v.* 1. to study in school; go to school. Syn. *pumasok sa páaralán.* 2. to learn to do (something).

mag-aráw (mag + a-ráw), *v.* to work on a daily basis. Syn. *magtrabaho nang arawán.*

mag-arì (mag + a-rì), *v.* 1. to possess or own (something). Syn. *mag-angkín, magmayarì.* 2. (*Colloq.*) to pretend like (something), as in *mag-aring loko,* to pretend like a fool.

magaríl (ma-ga-ríl), *v.* to stammer; speak indistinctly like someone learning a foreign language. Syn. *mautál.*

mag-asawa (mag + a-sa-wa), I. *v.* to marry; get married; have a husband or wife. Syn. *magmahabang-dulang (fig.), humaráp sa dambaná (fig.).*
—II. *n.* a married couple; husband and wife. Syn. *magkabiyak.*
—III. *adj.* married, referring to a man and a woman. Syn. *kasál.*

magasgás (ma-gas-gás), *v.* to become worn-out by constant use or by friction. Cf. *mapudpód.*

magasín (ma-ga-sín), *n.* (Eng.) 1. magazine. Syn. *rebista.* 2. magazine (in a rifle or pistol).

magasláw (ma-gas-láw), *adj.* coarse or rough in manners. Syn. *maharót, magasó.*

magasó (ma-ga-só), *adj.* mischievous; naughty; prankish. Syn. *malikót, maharót, makarós.*

magaspáng (ma-gas-páng), *adj.* 1. rough or coarse to the touch. Syn. *maaligasgás.* 2. coarse; consisting of rather large particles; not fine in texture, as in *magaspáng na buhangin,* coarse sand. 3. having relatively large diameter in relation to length; thick, as in *magaspáng na sinulid,* thick thread.

4. lacking in refinement; vulgar. Syn. *bastós.*

magastós (ma-gas-tós), I. *v.* to be able to spend. Syn. *magugol.*
—II. *adj.* 1. involving much expense; expensive. Syn. *magugol.* 2. spending much. Syn. *mapággugol, gastadór.*

mag-atang (mag + a-tang), *v.* to help someone put a load on the head.

mag-atas (mag + a-tas), *v.* to issue an order or command. Syn. *mag-utos.*

mag-ate (mag + a-te), *n.* the relation between a girl or a woman and her younger or older sister, or her younger brother. Syn. *magmanang.*

mag-atubilì (mag + a-tu-bi-lì), *v.* to be hesitant; vacillate; be irresolute. Syn. *mag-urung-sulong, magbantulót.*

magawâ (ma-ga-wâ), I. *v.* to be able to do, make, or perform. Syn. *matupád, maisagawâ, matrabaho.*
—II. *adj.* with or having much work; busy. Syn. *matrabaho, abalá sa trabaho.*

mag-ayos (mag + a-yos), *v.* 1. to arrange or put things in good order. 2. to do oneself up; dress up. Syn. *magbihis.* 3. to do or arrange, as one's hair. Syn. *magsukláy.* 4. to settle (a dispute) amicably. Syn. *mag-aregló.*

magayót (ma-ga-yót), *adj.* tough or leathery to the bite, referring esp. to tubers.

mag-ayuno (mag + a-yu-no), *v.* to fast; abstain from food, partially or totally. Syn. *magkulasyón.*

magbakasakalî (mag-ba-ka-sa-ka-lî), *v.* to do or go at some risk; take a chance; venture. Syn. *makipagsápalarán, magpasumalá.*

magbadhâ (mag-bad-hâ), *v.* to indicate; be a sign or indication of.

magbadyá (mag-bad-yá), *v.* to show or express. Syn. *magpakilala.*

magbago (mag-ba-go), *v.* 1. to reform oneself; change one's ways or manners. 2. to become different; be changed or altered. Syn. *mag-ibá.*

magbagong-buhay (mag-ba-gong + bu-hay), *v.* to change one's ways of life. Also, *magpanibagong-buhay.*

magbahág-buntót (mag-ba-hág + bun-tót), *v.* 1. to have one's tail folded between the legs, said of dogs. 2. (*Fig.*) to be or become afraid. Syn. *matakot, mangupiti.*

nagbahagi (mag-ba-ha-gi), *v.* 1. to give someone a portion of what one has. Syn. *magparte.* 2. to divide and distribute proportionally or according to a plan or agreement, apportion. Syn. *maghati.*

nagbaít (mag-ba-ít), *v.* to be good; act properly (s.o. children).

nagbalae (mag-ba-lae), *n.* the relation between the parents of a married couple.

nagbalak (mag-ba-lak), *v.* 1. to plan. Syn. *magpanukalà.* 2. to make a try. Syn. *magtangkâ.*

nagbalagtasan (mag-ba-lag-ta-san), *v.* to engage each other in a poetical joust.

nagbalangkás (mag-ba-lang-kás), *v.* 1. to make or form the framework of. 2. to plan; decide on how something is to be done. Syn. *magbalak, magpanukalà.* 3. to form an outline or rough draft of. Syn. *magbangháy.*

nagbalátkayô (mag-ba-lát-ka-yô), *v.* to disguise oneself; hide one's identity by means of disguise. 2. to pretend to be. Syn. *magkunwarî, magpanggáp.*

nagbalát-sibuyas (mag-ba-lát + si-bu-yas), *v.* to be very sensitive to criticism. Syn. *maging lubháng maramdamin.*

nagbalík-loób (mag-ba-lík + lo-ób), *v.* to return or revert to one's former belief, practice, conviction, etc. Syn. *bumalík sa dating paniwalà, gawain, atb.*

nagbalikwás (mag-ba-lik-wás), *v.* to rise suddenly or in a hurry, as in fright. Syn. *bumalikwás, biglâ o madaliang bumangon.*

nagbálitaán (mag-bá-li-ta-án), *v.* to exchange news or information with each other or with one another. Cf. *magkuwentuhan.*

nagbanál-banalan (mag-ba-nál + ba-na-lan), *v.* to pretend to be pious or religious. Syn. *magsantú-santuhan.*

nagbantáy (mag-ban-táy), *v.* 1. to act as a guard, watcher, or patrol. Syn. *magtanod, gumuwardiyá.* 2. to watch and wait for a person or thing to come, pass by, or appear. Syn. *mag-abáng.*

nagbantulót (mag-ban-tu-lót), *v.* to vacillate; be hesitant. Syn. *mag-atubilî, mag-urung-sulong.*

nagbangáy (mag-ba-ngáy), *v.* to quarrel with each other. Syn. *mag-away, magbabág.*

magbangháy (mag-bang-háy), *v.* 1. to make a draft or outline of. 2. to conjugate or inflect (a verb).

magbangon (mag-ba-ngon), *v.* 1. to rise or get up, as from bed. Syn. *bumangon.* 2. to organize or found. Syn. *magtatag.* 3. to build or erect. Syn. *magtayô.* 4. to rise in revolt. Syn. *mag-alsá, maghimagsík.*

magbasá (mag-ba-sá), *v.* to read extensively; do much reading.

magbasâ (mag-ba-sâ), *v.* 1. to wet oneself. 2. to moisten clothes for ironing by sprinkling water. Syn. *magwaliglig o magwilig ng damit.* 3. to expose oneself in the rain. Syn. *magpaulán.*

magbatî (mag-ba-tî), *v.* to start talking again with each other, as two persons who have been enemies for sometime. Syn. *magusap na mulî.*

magbawa (mag-ba-wa), *v.* 1. to diminish or mitigate, as pain. Syn. *huminà, bumutíbutí.* 2. to refrain or hold back oneself, as from gambling, drinking, smoking, and the like. Syn. *magpigil.*

magbayáw (mag-ba-yáw), *n.* 1. a man and his brother-in-law or his sister-in-law. 2. the relation between a man and his brother-in-law or sister-in-law.

magbibigas (mag-bi-bi-gas, *n.* rice dealer or vendor. Syn. *nagtitindá ng bigás.*

magbigáy (mag-bi-gáy), *v.* 1. to give something to another or others. Syn. *magkaloób.* 2. to contribute; give donation. Syn. *mag-abuloy.* 3. (Fig.) to be tolerant of the act, desires, or opinions of another or others. Syn. *magparayâ.*

magbigáy-alám (mag-bi-gáy + a-lám), *v.* 1. to let (someone) know; notify what one intends to do. Syn. *magsabi, magpaalam.* 2. to report; notify the authorities. Syn. *magsumbóng.*

magbigáy-buhay (mag-bi-gáy + bu-hay), *v.* to make interesting; give life to. Syn. *magpasiglá.*

magbigáy-daán (mag-bi-gáy + da-án), var. **mabigáydaán,** *v.* 1. to give (someone) a chance or opportunity. Syn. *magbigáy ng pagkakataón.* 2. to cause or be a cause for something to happen. Syn. *maging sanhî.*

magbigáy-gaán (mag-bi-gáy + ga-án), *v.* to lighten; make lighter. Syn. *magpagaán, makagaán.*

magbigáy-loób (mag-bi-gáy + lo-oób), var. **magbigáyloób,** *v.* to give in to someone's request in order to please or give satisfaction. Syn. *magbigáy-kasiyahan.* Cf. *magparayâ.*

magbigáy-lugód (mag-bi-gáy + lu-gód), var. **magbigáylugód,** *v.* to please or give satisfaction to. Syn. *makasiyá, magbigáy-kasiyahan.*

magbihis (mag-bi-his), *v.* to dress oneself; change one's clothes; put on new or clean clothes.

magbinatâ (mag-bi-na-tâ), *v.* 1. to grow up into a young man. Syn. *maging binatâ.* 2. to act like a young man. Syn. *kumilos nang parang binatà.*

magbiruán (mag-bi-ru-án), *v.* to joke with each other or with one another. Syn. *magtuksuhan, magtudyuhan.*

magbitíw (mag-bi-tíw), *v.* 1. to give up a position of employment; resign. Syn. *magdimité.* 2. to utter or say (a word or expression). Syn. *magsabi, magsalitâ.*

magbiyahe (mag-bi-ya-he), *v.* to make a trip; go on a trip; travel. Syn. *maglakbáy.*

magbiyanán (mag-bi-ya-nán), var. **magbiyenán,** *n.* 1. a married man or his wife and his or her parent-in-law. 2. the relation between a married man or his wife and his or her parent-in-law.

magbubukíd (mag-bu-bu-kíd), *n.* 1. farmer. Syn. *mag-aararó.* 2. farm worker. Syn. *trabahadór sa bukid.*

magbukáng-liwaywáy (mag-bu-káng + li-way-wáy), *v.* to begin to be day; dawn.

magbukás (mag-bu-kás), *v.* 1. to open, as a door, window, etc. 2. to begin or start, as a program. Syn. *magsimulâ, mag-umpisá.*

magbuklód (mag-buk-lód), *v.* 1. to make or provide (a broom, barrel, bolo handle, or the like) with a ring reinforcement. Syn. *magsaklâ.* 2. to unite or join together. Syn. *magsama, magkaísâ, magsanib.* 3. to cause to be united or joined together. Syn. *pagkáisahín.*

magbuko (mag-bu-ko), *v.* 1. to bud; put forth buds. Syn. *magsuplíng.* 2. to begin to have young fruits; bear fruits. Syn. *mamunga magkabuko, mamuko.*

magbukód (mag-bu-kód), *v.* 1. to separate or put aside something for someone or for the future. Syn. *magtabí, maghiwaláy.* 2. to live separately, as a newly wed couple from their parents. Syn. *magsarilí.*

magbuhat[1] (mag-bu-hat), *v.* to lift or raise (something). Syn. *mag-angát.*

magbuhat[2] (mag-bu-hat), I. *v.* to come from Syn. *manggaling.*
—II. *adv.* since; from the time of. Syn *magmulâ.*

magbuhay- (mag-bu-hay-), a combining form, meaning "to live the life of."

magbuhay-mayaman (mag-bu-hay + ma-ya man), *v.* to live the life of a rich person live in luxury. Ant. *magbuhay-pulubi.*

magbulaán (mag-bu-la-án), *v.* to lie or tell lie. Syn. *magsinungalíng, magkailâ.*

magbulág-bulagan (mag-bu-lág + bu-la gan), *v.* to pretend to be blind.

magbuláng-gugò (mag-bu-láng + gu-gò), var **mabulánggugò,** *v.* to be very generou with one's money.

magbulay-bulay (mag-bu-lay + bu-lay), *v* to contemplate; muse; meditate. Syn *magnilay-nilay, mag-isíp-isíp.*

magbuntís (mag-bun-tís), *v.* to be or becom pregnant. Syn. *magdalang-tao (fig.).*

magbuntóng-hiningá (mag-bun-tóng + hi ni-ngá), *v.* to sigh; give a sigh. Cf *maghinagpís.*

magbunyág (mag-bun-yág), *v.* to denounc or reveal (a secret). Cf. *magsumbóng.* Syn *magsiwalat.*

magbunga (mag-bu-nga), *v.* 1. to bear fruits Syn. *mamunga.* 2. to produce result. 3. to bear a child. Syn. *mag-anák, magkaanák*

magbuód (mag-bu-ód), *v.* to summarize make a summary of. Cf. *lumagom.*

magbuwís (mag-bu-wís), *v.* 1. to pay one's ta: or taxes. Syn. *magbayad ng buwís.* 2. t sacrifice, as one's life. Syn. *magpará maghandóg.*

magbuyó (mag-bu-yó), *v.* to induce someon to indulge in something undesirable. Syn *magsulsól.*

magka-, a combining form used to forr verbs, meaning: 1. to have or be able t have, as in *magkaroón*, to be able to have; *magkaasawa*, to have a husband or wife; *magkabahay*, to be able to have a house. 2. to come into a certain state; result in, as in *magkatotoó*, to become true; *magkamalî*, to commit an error or mistake; *magkahidwâ*, to have misunderstanding. 3. to come to a certain mutual or simultaneous action (with *–an*, *-han*, and *–nan*), as in *magkahidwaan*, to come to have a misunderstanding, *magkatawanan*, to laugh together or at each other. 4. to get or become, as in *magkasakit*, to get sick, *magkasugat*, to become wounded.

magkaagam-agam (mag-ka-a-gaw + a-gaw), *v.* to have some doubt, misgiving, or foreboding. Syn. *magkaroón ng agam-agam*.

magkaagáw (mag-ka-a-gáw), I. *adj.* competing with each other. Syn. *magkaribál, magkapangagáw*.
　—II. *n.* rivals; two persons or things competing with each other.

magkaalám (mag-ka-a-lám), *adj.* acting together in conspiracy; conspiring with each other. Syn. *magkasabwát*.

magkaalinlangan (mag-ka-a-lin-la-ngan), *v.* to have a doubt; entertain some doubt. Syn. *magduda, magkaduda*.

magkaalít (mag-ka-a-lít), I. *adj.* quarreling with each other. Syn. *magkaaway, magkagalít*.
　—II. *n.* enemies, referring to two persons.

magkaanib (mag-ka-a-nib), *adj.* allied, referring to two persons, nations, etc. Syn. *magkasapî, magkakampí*.

magkaanu-ano (mag-ka-a-ni + a-no), *interrog. pron.* used in asking the relation between two persons, as in: *Magkaanu-ano kayo?* What is your relation to each other? Also used idiomatically, as in *Hindi kami magkaanu-ano.* We are not related to each other.

magkaasawa (mag-ka-a-sa-wa), *v.* to have or be able to have a wife or a husband. Syn. *magkaroón ng asawa*.

magkaaway (mag-ka-a-way), I. *adj.* engaged in a quarrel or fight with each other. Syn. *magkagalít*.
　—II. *n.* enemies, referring to two persons, nations, etc.

magkabagáng (mag-ka-ba-gáng), *adj.* suited, adapted to, or compatible with each other. Syn. *magkasundô, magkabagay*.

magkabagay (mag-ka-ba-gay), *adj.* fit or suited to each other. Syn. *magkaayos, magkatugmâ*

magkabaít (mag-ka-ba-ít), *v.* to have or be endowed with a good sense of behavior. Syn. *magkaisip*.

magkabalát (mag-ka-ba-lát), I. *adj.* 1. of or having the same complexion. Syn. *magkakulay ng balat*. 2. of the same or belonging to the same race. Syn. *magkalahì*.
　—II. *v.* to grow or develop skin, as a wound. Syn. *tubuan o magkaroón ng balát*.

magkabanggâ (mag-ka-bang-gâ), *adj.* 1. involved in a collision, as two persons or vehicles. 2. quarreling with each other. Syn. *magkalaban, magkatunggalî*.

magkabarkada (mag-ka-bar-ka-da), *adj.* of the same gang; belonging to the same gang.

magkabarò (mag-ka-ba-rò), I. *adj.* of the same sex; belonging to the same sex (s.o. two women).
　—II. *v.* to have or be able to have or own a dress.

magkabatî (mag-ka-ba-tî), *adj.* on speaking terms with each other, hence, in good terms with each other.

magkabibíg (mag-ka-bi-bíg), *v.* to have a say; have the right to censure or express disapproval.

magkabi-kabilâ (mag-ka-bi + ka-bi-lâ), *adj. & adv.* at all sides; on every side; all around. Syn. *sa kabí-kabilâ, sa lahat ng panig*.

magkabilâ (mag-ka-bi-lâ), *adj.* both sides.

magkábisalà (mag-ká-bi-sa-là), *v.* 1. to fail. Syn. *mabigô*. 2. to err; make an error; be mistaken. Syn. *magkamalî*. 3. to miss. Syn. *magkamintís*.

magkabudhî (mag-ka-bud-hî), I. *v.* have conscience.
　—II. *adj.* of or having the same conscience.

magkabyáw (mag-kab-yáw), *v.* to mill sugar cane. Syn. *mag-iló*.

magkakandilâ (mag-ka-kan-di-lâ), *n.* candle manufacturer or dealer.

magkakapangyarihan (mag-ka-ka-pang-ya-ri-han), *v.* to have or be endowed with power or authority. Syn. *magkaroón o magtamó ng kapangyarihan*.

magkakapatíd (mag-ka-ka-pa-tíd), I. *n.* 1. brothers and sisters. 2. the relation among brothers and sister.
—II. *v.* to have a brother or sister. Syn. *magkaroón ng kapatíd*.
—III. *adj.* of or having the same parents, referring to more than two children.

magkakapit-bahay (mag-ka-ka-pit + ba-hay), I. *n.* neighbors.
—II. *v.* to have a neighbor. Syn. *magkaroón ng kapit-bahay*.
—III. *adj.* belonging to the same neighborhood.

magkadahilán (mag-ka-da-hi-lán), *v.* to have a cause or reason for (an action). Syn. *magkaroón ng dahilán*.

magkadaís (mag-ka-da-ís), *adj.* near or close to each other. Syn. *magkalapít, magkatabí*.

magkadamay (mag-ka-da-may), var. **magkaramay**, *adj.* sharing each other's happiness, sorrow, or hardship.

magkadiwà (mag-ka-di-wà), I. *adj.* having or expressing the same meaning, spirit, or idea. Syn. *magkapareho ng diwà*.
—II. *v.* to have sense or meaning.

magkadugô (mag-ka-du-gô), var. **magkarugo**, I. *adj.* 1. of or having the same type of blood. Syn. *makapareho ng dugô*. 2. (*Colloq.*) of or belonging to the same race. Syn. *magkalahì, magkalipì*.
—II. *v.* 1. to be able to have or obtain blood. Syn. *makakuha ng dugô*. 2. to be stained or filled with blood. Syn. *maduguán, malagyan o mámantsahán ng dugô*.

magkagalít (mag-ka-ga-lít), I. *v.* to quarrel with each other. Syn. *mag-away*.
—II. *adj.* not in good terms with each other; quarreling with each other. Syn. *magkaaway*.

magkagayón (mag-ka-ga-yón), *v.* to be or become like that; come to that state or condition. Syn. *maging gayón*.

magkaguló (mag-ka-gu-ló), *v.* to be thrown into confusion; be in commotion or turmoil. Syn. *maging maguló*.

magkagutom (mag-ka-gu-tom), *v.* to suffer or die from starvation or hunger, referring to many persons. Syn. *magtiís o magkamatay sa gutom*.

magkahalagá (mag-ka-ha-la-gá), I. *v.* 1. to cost; have a price of. Syn. *magkapresyo*. 2. to be of value; become important. Syn. *maging mahalagá*.
—II. *adj.* of or having the same price or value. Syn. *magkapresyo, magkapareho ng presyo*.

magkahambíng (mag-ka-ham-bíng), *adj.* similar or analogous to each other. Syn. *magkatulad, magkawangis*.

magkahanay (mag-ka-ha-nay), *adj.* 1. of or belonging to the same row, line, or file, referring to two persons or things. Syn. *magkahilera, magkalinyá*. 2. of or belonging to the same rank. Syn. *magkaranggo*.

magkahanggán (mag-ka-hang-gán), I. *adj.* adjacent to each other. Syn. *magkanugnóg, magkatabí*.
—II. *n.* neighbors, referring to two persons or families. Syn. *magkapit-bahay*.

magkahawig (mag-ka-ha-wig), *adj.* similar to each other; having semblance or similarity to each other. Syn. *magkawangis, magkatulad*.

magkahidwâ (mag-ka-hid-wâ), *adj.* in contrast with each other. Syn. *magkakontra, magkasalungát*.

magkahinagap (mag-ka-hi-na-gap), I. *v.* to have an idea or notion about something. Syn. *magkahinuhà*.
—II. *adj.* with or having the same idea or notion with each other.

magkahinalà (mag-ka-hi-na-là), I. *v.* to have a suspicion; be suspicious. Syn. *magkasapantahà, magkasospetsa*.
—II. *adj.* with or having the same suspicion with each other.

magkahinanakít (mag-ka-hi-na-na-kít), *v.* to have a personal feeling of resentment against someone, esp. against a friend or relative. Syn. *maghinampó, sumamâ ang loób*.

magkahiwaláy (mag-ka-hi-wa-láy), I. *adj.* 1. separated or placed separately from each other. Syn. *magkaibá ng lugar o kinálalagyán*. 2. living separately from each other, as a husband and his wife. Syn. *hiwaláy*.
—II. *adv.* separately.

magkáhusto (mag-ká-hus-to), *v*. 1. to suffice; be sufficient. Syn. *magkasya, magsapát*. 2. to fit; be the proper size, shape, etc. Syn. *magkasya o tumamà ang sukat o lakí*.

magkaibig (mag-ka-i-big), *v*. to have a wish or desire for (something). Syn. *magkagusto*.

magkaibigan (mag-ka-i-bi-gan), I. *adj*. having friendly relations with each other. —II. *n*. friends, referring to two persons. Syn. *magkatoto*.

magkáibigán (mag-ká-i-bi-gán), *v*. to fall in love with each other. Syn. *magkaroón ng pagmamahál sa isá't isá*.

magkáigi (mag-ká-i-gi), *v*. to be compatible with each other. Syn. *magkásundô, magkatugmâ*.

magkailâ (mag-ka-i-lâ), *v*. to tell a lie; refuse to tell the truth. Syn. *magsinungalíng, maglihim*.

magkáinitán (mag-ká-i-ni-tán), var. **magakáinitán**, *v*. to come to a heated debate or discussion.

magkaintindihan (mag-ka-in-tin-di-han), *v*. to come to an understanding; be able to understand each other. Syn. *magkáunawaán*.

magkáinggitan (mag-ká-ing-gi-tan), *v*. to envy each other; be envious of each other. Syn. *magkápanaghilián*.

magkaisá (mag-ka-i-sá), *adj*. united; in agreement with each other or with one another; having the same belief or stand. Syn. *magkadamdamin, magkapaniwalà*.

magkaisip (mag-ka-i-sip), *v*. to have or develop common sense; be sensible. Syn. *magkabaít*.

magkalaban (mag-ka-la-ban), I. *adj*. 1. opposing or fighting each other; in conflict with each other. Syn. *magkatunggalî*. 2. opposed or contrary to each other. Syn. *magkakontra, magkasalungát*. —II. *n*. the protagonists in a conflict or quarrel.

magkalaguyò (mag-ka-la-gu-yò), I. *n*. a man and his paramour. —II. *adj*. living together, referring to a man and his mistress.

magkalagyô (mag-ka-lag-yô), I. *adj*. of or having the same name. Syn. *magkapangalan, magkapareho ng pangalan*. —II. *n*. two persons of the same name; namesakes. Syn. *magtukayo, magkatukayo*.

magkalahì (mag-ka-la-hì), *adj*. of or belonging to the same nationality or race. Syn. *magkakabayan, magkalipi*.

magkalamat (mag-ka-la-mat), *v*. to have or develop a slight crack. Syn. *magkabiták*.

magkalarawan (mag-ka-la-ra-wan), I. *v*. to have or get possession of a picture. Syn. *magkaroón ng larawan o retrato*. —II. *adj*. having similar facial features; looking alike. Syn. *magkatulad, magkamukhá*.

magkalarô (mag-ka-la-rô), I. *adj*. playing together, referring to two persons. —II. *n*. playmates, referring esp. to two children.

magkalás (mag-ka-lás), *v*. 1. to undo, e.g. a binding, knot, or the like. Syn. *magkalág, magtastás*. 2. to break off, as an engaged couple, by agreement.

magkalayô (mag-ka-la-yô), *adj*. far from each other. Syn. *magkahiwaláy, magkaagwát*.

magkalipumpón (mag-ka-li-pum-pón), *v*. to gather together in small groups. Syn. *magkuyug-kuyog*.

magkálituhan (mag-ká-li-tu-han), *v*. to become confused all together. Syn. *magkáhirahan*.

magkáliwaan (mag-ká-li-wa-an), *v*. 1. to turn to the left at the same time. Syn. *maglíkuan sa kaliwâ*. 2. to conclude a sale by paying cash. Syn. *magbayarán ng kas*. 3. (*Fig.*) to be unfaithful to each other, referring to a husband and wife. Syn. *magtaksil sa isá't isá*.

magkáliwanag (mag-ká-li-wa-nag), var. **magkáliwanagán**, *v*. to come to an understanding; be able to settle matters once and for all. Syn. *magkáunawaán, magkáintindihan*.

magkaloób (mag-ka-lo-ób), *v*. 1. to grant; give what is asked. Syn. *magbigáy*. Syn. *maggawad*. 3. to have a special consideration for. Syn. *magkaroón ng pagtatangí*.

magkamá (mag-ka-má), *v*. to fit or fix something into another. Syn. *magkabít, maglapat*.

magkamág-arál (mag-ka-mág + a-rál), *n.* classmates. Syn. *kapwà istudyante o mag-aarál*. Cf. *magkaeskuwela,magkaklase*.

magkamág-anak (mag-ka-mág + a-nak), *adj.* related to each other; belonging to the same family.

magkamalasakit (mag-ka-ma-la-sa-kit), *v.* to have concern for. Syn. *magkaroón ng malasakit*.

magkamalay (mag-ka-ma-lay), *v.* to become conscious; come to one's senses; regain consciousness. Syn. *matauhan, manumbalik ang malay o ang pagkatao*.

magkamalî (mag-ka-ma-lî), *v.* to commit an error; make a mistake; mistaken.

magkamatay (mag-ka-ma-tay), *v.* to die in great numbers, as during an epidemic. Cf. *mapeste*.

magkámayan (mag-ká-ma-yan), *v.* to shake hands with one another.

magkamayroón (mag-ka-may-ro-ón), *v.* 1. to be able to have, acquire, or possess (something). Syn. *magkaroón, magtamó*. 2. (*Colloq.*) to become rich or wealthy; have much money. Syn. *yumaman, maging mayaman*.

magkáminsán (mag-ká-min-sán), *adv.* sometimes; once in a while. Syn. *kung minsán, paminsán-minsán*.

magkamít (mag-ka-mít), *v.* to receive; be awarded or given. Syn. *magtamó, tumanggáp*.

magkamukhâ (mag-ka-muk-hâ), *adj.* similar to each other; having the same appearance; looking alike. Syn. *magkatulad, magkapareho*.

magkanayon (mag-ka-na-yon), *adj.* from, of, or living in the same barrio. Syn. *magkabaryo*.

magkandarapà (mag-kan-da-ra-pà), *v.* to stumble repeatedly as one hurries to get or reach for something. Syn. *magkangsusungabà*.

magkanduhapang (mag-kan-du-ha-pang), *v.* to be in such a hurry to get or reach something.

magkaní-kanyá (mag-ka-ní + kan-yá), var. **magkanyá-kanyá**, *v.* to have a separate job or work to do for each one of a group; have each one of a group do different or separate work.

magkano (mag-ka-no), *interrog. pron.* How much?

magkanugnóg (mag-ka-nug-nóg), *adj.* adjacent or contiguous to each other, as two towns, provinces, etc. Syn. *magkaratig, magkatabi*.

magkanulô (mag-ka-nu-lô), *v.* to betray; be a traitor to. Syn. *magtaksíl*.

magkáng- (mag-káng-), *pref.* used to form verbs from roots with the first syllable reduplicated, meaning to happen or come to a certain state or condition due to haste or some unavoidable circumstances, as in *magkáng-aantók, magkanggagalit, magkambabalí*, etc. Note: *magkáng-* becomes *magkám-* before roots beginning with b and p, and becomes *magkán-* before roots beginning with d, l, r, s, and t.

magkáng-aantók (mag-káng + a-an-tók), *v.* to become sleepy, as from a long wait.

magkánggagalit (mag-káng-ga-ga-lit), *v.* to be or become very angry; be provoked to extreme anger. Cf. *magkángyayamót*.

magkapakundangan (mag-ka-pa-kun-da-ngan), *v.* to have respect, regard, or reverence for. Syn. *magkagalang, magkapitagan*.

magkapág-asa (mag-ka-pág + a-sa), I. *v.* to have hope.

—II. *adj.* with or having the same hope.

magkapalad (mag-ka-pa-lad), I. *v.* to have luck; be lucky. Syn. *magkasuwerte*.

—II. *adj.* 1. destined to be or become husband and wife. 2. of or having the same fate or destiny. Syn. *magkasuwerte*.

magkapalagáy-loób (mag-ka-pa-la-gáy + lo-ób), var. **magkapalagáyang-loób**, *adj.* having trust with each other; trusting each other.

magkápalít (mag-ká-pa-lít), *v.* to happen to use one instead of another.

magkapanabáy (mag-ka-pa-na-báy), I. *adj.* happening or occurring at the same time. Also, *magkasabáy*.

—II. *adv.* at the same time. Syn. *nang sabáy*.

magkapanahón (mag-ka-pa-na-hón), I. *v.* to have or be able to have time. Syn. *magkaoras, magkaroón ng panahón*.

—II. *adj.* contemporary; of the same or

about the same age. Syn. *magkaedád*, *magkasinggulang*.

nagkapantáy (mag-ka-pan-táy), *adj.* of or having the same height, length, or rank, referring to two persons or things. Syn. *magkasinghabà* (for length), *magkasingtaás* (for height), *magkasingranggo* (for rank).

nagkapangagáw (mag-ka-pa-nga-gáw), *adj.* competing or contending with each other; fighting each other for recognition or supremacy. Syn. *magkalaban*, *magkatunggalî*.

magkapangalan (mag-ka-pa-nga-lan), I. *adj.* of, with, having, or bearing the same name. Syn. *magkapareho ng pangalan*, *magkatukayo* (for persons only).
—II. *v.* 1. to have or be given a name. Syn. *magkangalan*. 2. (*Fig.*) to become famous. Syn. *matanyág*, *mabantóg*.

magkapangkát (mag-ka-pang-kát), *adj.* of or belonging to the same group or committee. Syn. *magkalupón*, *magkagrupo*.

magkapara (mag-ka-pa-ra), *adj.* similar to each other; alike. Syn. *magkatulad*, *magkapareho*.

magkapareha (mag-ka-pa-re-ha), *adj.* 1. acting together as partners, as in a dance. Syn. *magkatuwang*, *magkatambàl*. 2. those which are used as a pair, as shoes, slippers, socks, and the like. Syn. *magkapares*.

magkapareho (mag-ka-pa-re-ho), *adj.* similar to each other; alike. Syn. *magkatulad*, *magkapares*.

magkaparte (mag-ka-par-te), I. *adj.* referring to two persons who share in the partition or division of something. Syn. *magkahatì*, *magkabahagi*.
—II. *v.* to have or be able to have a part or role, as in a drama or play. Syn. *magkaroón ng gagampanán sa drama o dulà*. 2. to have or be able to have a share in the partition or division of something. Syn. *magkaroón ng bahagi o parte*.

magkapatíd (mag-ka-pa-tíd), I *adj.* related to each other by having the same parents. Syn. *magkaputol* (*colloq.*).
—II. *n.* 1. two brothers or two sisters; also, a brother and his sister. 2. the relation between two brothers, or two sisters, or of a brother and his sister.

magkapisan (mag-ka-pi-san), *adj.* 1. living together as husband and wife. Syn. *magkasama*, *nagsasama*. 2. living together in the same room, house, or place. Syn. *magkasama o magkasunò sa tirahan*. 3. deposited in the same place or container. Syn. *magkasama sa lugár o sisidlán*.

magkapit-bahay (mag-ka-pit + ba-hay), var. **magkapitbahay**, *adj. & n.* referring to two persons who are neighbors to each other.

magkáputúl-putól (mag-ká-pu-túl + pu-tól), *v.* to be cut or severed into several pieces. Syn. *magkápatíd-patíd*.

magkapuwáng (mag-ka-pu-wáng), *v.* 1. to have a space between. Syn. *magkapatláng*. 2. to have a vacancy, as in an office. Syn. *magkabakante*. 3. to have a chance. Syn. *magkaroón ng pagkakataón*.

magkaramay (mag-ka-ra-may), *adj.* 1. sharing each other's sorrow or misfortune. 2. involved together, as in committing a crime. Syn. *magkasangkót*.

magkarambola (mag-ka-ram-bo-la), *v.* (in billiards) to play caroms. Syn. *maglarô ng karambola*. 2. to be involved in a collision, as of three cars, one of which hitting the two others one after the other.

magkaribál (mag-ka-ri-bál), I. *adj.* referring to two persons competing with each other for recognition, supremacy or favor. Syn. *magkaagáw*.
—II. *v.* to have a rival. Syn. *magkaroón ng karibál*.

magkasabáy (mag-ka-sa-báy), I. *adj.* 1. at the same time; simultaneous. 2. said of two persons leaving together on a trip. Syn. *magkasama*.
—II. *adv.* 1. simultaneously; at the same time. 2. together. Syn. *magkasama*.

magkasabuwát (mag-ka-sa-bu-wát), var. **magkasabwát**, *adj.* conniving or in connivance with each other. Syn. *magkasapakát*, *magkainalám*.

magkasakít (mag-ka-sa-kít), *v.* to get sick; be or become sick; have an ailment. Syn. *magkaroon ng sakit o karamdaman*, *maratay sa baníg*.

magkasagutan (mag-ka-sa-gu-tan), *adj.* referring to two persons engaged in a debate or heated discussion with each other. Syn. *magkatalo*, *magkadebate*.

magkasál (mag-ka-sál), *v*. to join a couple in wedlock; perform a marriage ceremony. Syn. *magkasá*.

magkasala (mag-ka-sa-la), *v*. to commit a crime or sin. Syn. *makágawâ ng kasalanan o krimen*.

magkasalabíd (mag-ka-sa-la-bíd), *adj*. entangled or twisted together, as two ropes, wires, or the like. Syn. *magkapulupot*, *magkapilipit*.

magkasalapî (mag-ka-sa-la-pî), *v*. to have plenty of money; be or become rich or wealthy. Syn. *magkakuwarta*, *yumaman*.

magkasalisí (mag-ka-sa-li-sí), *adj*. 1. placed or set alternately, referring to two things. Syn. *magkasalit*. 2. with one having just arrived after the other has gone.

magkasalít (mag-ka-sa-lít), *adj*. placed or done alternately. Syn. *magkasalisí*.

magkasalíw (mag-ka-sa-líw), *adj*. 1. singing together, referring to two singers, usually having different voices. Syn. *magkaduweto*. 2. referring to a singer and the accompanist performing together at the same time.

magkasaliwâ (mag-ka-sa-li-wâ), *adj*. 1. going in opposite direction. Syn. *magkasalungát*. 2. referring to a pair in which one happened to be used interchangeably with the other. Syn. *magkapalít*.

magkasalo (mag-ka-sa-lo), *adj*. partaking food together; eating together, specially on the same plate.

magkasalubong (mag-ka-sa-lu-bong), *adj*. going in the direction towards each other.

magkasama (mag-ka-sa-ma), I. *adj*. 1. together; in company with each other. Syn. *magkasabay*. 2. combined or put together. Syn. *magkahalò*, *magkalahók*.
—II. *adv*. together at the same time. Syn. *magkasabay*.
—III. *n*. two persons in company with each other.

magkasamá (mag-ka-sa-má), I. *adj*. referring to the relation between a landlord and a tenant. 2. referring to two persons who are partners in a business enterprise. Syn. *magkasosyo*, *magkabakas*.
—II. *n*. 1. the landlord and the tenant. 2.

the relation between the landlord and the tenant. 3. partners, as in business (s.o. two persons). Syn. *magkasosyo*.

magkasangá (mag-ka-sa-ngá), I. *v*. to have or develop a branch. Syn. *magsangá magkaroón o tubuan ng sanga*.
—II. *adj*. meeting or intersecting each other, as two rivers, streets, and the like. Syn. *magkasalikop*.

magkasangkót (mag-ka-sang-kót), *adj*. both involved or implicated in an affair. Syn. *magkadawit*, *kapwà kasangkót o kadawit*.

magkasanggá (mag-ka-sang-gá), I. *adj*. playing together as partners in a game, gambling, or contest. Syn. *magkakampí*, *magkapanig*, *magkasapì*.
—II. *n*. the two players playing together as partners or teammates in a game.

magkasanggól (mag-ka-sang-gol), *v*. to have a baby; give birth to a baby. Syn. *magkaanák*.

magkasapakát (mag-ka-pa-kát), *adj*. conniving or in connivance with each other. Syn *magkasabuwát*, *magkainalám*.

magkasapantahà (mag-ka-sa-pan-ta-hà), *v*. to have reason or cause to suspect. Syn. *magkahinalà*, *magkaroón ng hinalà o sapantahà*.

magkasapì (mag-ka-sa-pì), I. *adj*. 1. referring to two persons who are both members of the same organization or society. Syn. *magkaanib*. 2. referring to two pieces of flat objects, as boards or the like, which are nailed, glued, or pasted together face to face to make strong or thick.
—II. *n*. any two members of the same organization or society; co-members.

magkasarili (mag-ka-sa-ri-li), *v*. to have something of one's own. Syn. *magkaroón ng sariling pag-aarì*.

magkasayáw (mag-ka-sa-yáw), I. *adj*. dancing together; dancing with each other.
—II. *n*. any two persons or a pair dancing together.

magkasi (mag-ka-si), I. *adj*. in love with each other, referring to a man and a woman. Syn. *magkasuyò*, *magkasintahan*.
—II. *n*. a man and a woman who are in love with each other; lovers; sweethearts.

nagkasintahan (mag-ka-sin-ta-han), *adj. &*
n. referring to a man a woman who love
each other. See magkasi.

nagkasinggulang (mag-ka-sing-gu-lang),
adj. of the same age. Syn. *magkasintandâ.*

nagkasiping (mag-ka-si-ping), *adj.* close to
each other; very near to each other. Syn.
magkatabí, magkasigbáy, magkaabáy.

nagkasirâ (mag-ka-si-râ), *v.* to break
relations with each other. Syn. *magkagalit.*

nagkasiyá (mag-ka-si-yá), *v.* 1. to suffice;
be sufficient. Syn. *magsapát, sumapát;*
maghusto, magkáhusto. 2. to be the proper
size or shape for; be fit for, as a pair of
shoes. Syn. *magkáhusto, maghusto.* 3. to be
enough to fill or contain, as in container.
Syn. *malamán, makayang malamán.* 4.
(*Colloq.*) to be satisfied with. Syn.
masiyahán.

magkasubukán (mag-ka-su-bu-kán), *v.* to be
able to determine or find out who of the
two is better, as by direct confrontation.
Syn. *magkásukatán, magkakilanlanan.*

magkasubuán (mag-ka-su-bu-án), *v.* to be
forced together in an affair which is both
of them should think twice before doing
so. Syn. *magkatuluyan.*

magkásukatán (mag-ká-su-ka-tán), *v.* to be
able to determine or find out who is the
better of the two. Syn. *magkásubukán.*

magkasundô (mag-ka-sun-dô), *adj.*
compatible; in agreement with each
other; capable of existing with each other.
Syn. *magkasuwatò; magkabagáng.*

magkasunò (mag-ka-su-nò), *adj.* 1. riding
together in the same vehicle. Syn.
magkaangkás, magkasama (sa sasakyán). 2.
living together in the same room, house,
etc. Syn. *magkasama sa tirahan.*

magkasunód (mag-ka-su-nód), *adj. & adv.*
following each other; one after another.

magkasuwerte (mag-ka-su-wer-te), I. *v.* to
have good luck; be or become lucky. Syn.
magkapalad, galingín.
—II. *adj.* 1. of or having the same fate or
destiny. Syn. *magkadistino.* 2. destined to
become husband and wife.

magkasuyò (mag-ka-su-yò), *adj. & n.*
referring to a man and a woman who love
each other. Syn. *magkasintahan, magkasi.*

magkatabí (mag-ka-ta-bí), *adj.* very near or
close to each other. Syn. *magkasigbáy,*
magkasiping, magkaratig.

magkataklób (mag-ka-tak-lób), *adj.* referring
to two things with one serving as the
cover of the other. Syn. *magkasuklób.*

magkatagís (mag-ka-ta-gís), *adj.* engaged
with each other in a fight. Syn.
magkalaban, magkatunggalî.

magkatagpô (mag-ka-tag-pô), *adj.* 1.
referring to two persons who had a
previous agreement to meet each other
at a certain place and time. Syn.
magkatiyáp. 2. converging or meeting at
a certain point, as two streets or rivers.
Syn. *magkasalikop.*

magkatalamitam (mag-ka-ta-la-mi-tam), *adj.*
referring to two persons who are
intimately in contact with each other.
Syn. *magkasalamuhà.*

magkatalik (mag-ka-ta-lik), *adj.* referring to
two persons who are engaged in an
intimate or private conversation with
each other.

magkatalo (mag-ka-ta-lo), *adj.* engaged in a
debate or heated discussion with each
other. Syn. *magkadebate, magkasagutan,*
magkadiskusyón.

magkatambál (mag-ka-tam-bál), 1. *adj.*
paired with each other, as in dance. Syn.
magkapareha, magkatuwáng. 2. referring to
two things which are used in pairs, as
slippers. Syn. *magkapares, magkatuwáng.*

magkatáwanan (mag-ká-ta-wa-nan), *adj.*
referring to two persons looking at each
other from a distance. Syn. *magkatinginan*
sa malayò.

magkátaón (mag-ká-ta-ón), *v.* to happen or
occur by chance. Syn. *mangyari o*
maganáp nang hindî ináasahan o sa isang
pagkakataón.

magkatapát (mag-ka-ta-pát), *adj.* 1. fronting
each other; opposite each other. Syn.
magkaharap. 2. (*Colloq.*) destined for each
other. Syn. *magkadestino, magkasuwerte.*

magkatawáng-tao (mag-ka-ta-wáng + ta-o),
v. 1. to take the form of a human being.
Syn. *magmukháng-tao.* 2. to come into
being; be created, as a human being. Syn.
maging tao.

magkatinig (mag-ka-ti-nig), I. *v*. 1. to have voice. Syn. *magkaboses*. 2. to be able to speak; have the right to voice one's opinion. Syn. *makapágsalitâ.*
—II. *adj*. 1. of or having the same or similar voice. Syn. *magkaboses, magkapareho ng boses o tinig.* 2. of or having the same tune. Syn. *magkahimig.*

magkatinginan (mag-ka-ti-ngi-nan), *adj*. referring to two persons looking at each other.

magkatipán (mag-ka-ti-pán), I. *adj*. 1. referring to two persons who have agreed to meet each other at a certain place and time. Syn. *magkatiyâp.* 2. referring to an engaged couple. Syn. *magkasunduan nang pakasál.*
—II. *n*. 1. any two persons who have agreement to meet each other at a certain place and time. 2. a couple engaged to be married.

magkatipo (mag-ka-ti-po), I. *adj*. 1. of or belonging to the same kind or group. Syn. *magkaurì.* 2. having the same characteristics of a group or class. Syn. *magkahalimbawà.* 3. in printing, of or having the same kind or type.
—II. *v*. in printing, to be able to have types.

magkátipun-tipon (mág-ka-ti-pun + ti-pon), *v*. to happen to meet together, at a certain place. Syn. *magkásama-sama.*

magkátitigán (mag-ká-ti-ti-gán), *v*. to happen to be staring at each other. Syn. *magkátinginan nang matagál at waláng kuráp.*

magkátiwalà (mag-ká-ti-wa-là), *v*. 1. to give or leave something in trust to someone. 2. to have trust or confidence in someone. Also, *magtiwalà.*

magkatiyáp (mag-ka-ti-yáp), *adj. & n.* referring to any two persons having an agreement to meet each other at a certain place and time. Syn. *magkatipán.*

magkatokayo (mag-ka-to-ka-yo), *var*. **magkatukayo**, I. *adj*. referring to two persons having the same name. Syn. *magkapangalan.*
—II. *n*. any two persons having the same name, namesakes.

magkatoto (mag-ka-to-to), *adj. & n.* referring to any two persons having close family relations with each other. Syn. *matapát na magkaibigan.*

magkátotoó (mag-ká-to-to-ó), *v*. 1. to become true; come out true. Syn. *magíng totoó o katotohanan.* 2. to happen. Syn. *maganáp, mangyari.*

magkatugón (mag-ka-tu-gón), *adj*. referring to two things that correspond to each other.

magkatulad (mag-ka-tu-lad), *adj*. similar to each other. Syn. *magkapareho, magkaparis.*

magkátulung-tulong (mag-ká-tu-lung + tu-long), *v*. to be able to work all together.

magkatunggalî (mag-ka-tung-ga-lî), *adj. & n.* referring to any two persons contending or fighting with each other. Syn. *magkalaban, magkagalít, magkaalít.*

magkátuwaan (mag-ká-tu-wa-an), *v*. to have fun, referring to a group of persons. Syn. *magkásayahan.*

magkatuwáng (mag-ka-tu-wáng), *adj. & n.* 1. referring to two persons who are co-sponsors at a wedding, baptism, or confirmation. 2. referring to any two persons helping each other in carrying a load. Syn. *magkasuong.* 3. referring to a pair dancing together. Syn. *magkapareha.*

magkauban (mag-ka-u-ban), *v*. to have gray hair. Syn. *magkaroón o tubuan ng uban o puting buhók.*

magkaukol (mag-ka-u-kol), *adj*. destined for each other, as a couple. Syn. *magkasuwerte, magkakapalaran.*

magkaugalì (mag-ka-u-ga-lì), I. *adj*. of or having the same conduct or behavior. Syn. *magkapareho ng ugalì.*
—II. *v*. to have or develop a certain kind of conduct.

magkaugmâ (mag-ka-ug-mâ), *adj*. 1. fit or well-adjusted to each other, as a tenon and mortise. Syn. *magkasukát.* 2. compatible; capable of existing with each other. Syn. *magkasundô, magkabagáng.*

magkaulayaw (mag-ka-u-la-yaw), *adj*. having a pleasant and intimate conversation with each other, referring to two persons.

magkaulirat (mag-ka-u-li-rat), *v*. to come to one's senses after having lost consciousness. Syn. *magkamalay, magkamalay-tao.*

magkáunawaán (mag-ká-u-na-wa-án), *v.* to be able to understand each other. Syn. *magkaintindihan.*

magkaurì (mag-ka-u-rì), I. *adj.* of or belonging to the same kind or class. Syn. *magkaklase.*
—II. *v.* to develop class; be of high class.

magkausap (mag-ka-u-sap), *adj.* talking together or with each other. Syn. *naguusap.*

magkawalà (mag-ka-wa-là), *v.* to get lost; be or become lost, referring to many things.

magkáwalay (mag-ká-wa-lay), *v.* to be or become separated from each other. Syn. *magkálayô, magkáhiwaláy.*

magkawangkî (mag-ka-wang-kî), *adj.* of or having similar appearance or features. Syn. *magkawangis, magkatulad.*

magkawangis (mag-ka-wa-ngis), *adj.* resembling each other. Syn. *magkawangkî.*

magkáwaták-waták (mag-ká-wa-ták + wa-ták), *v.* 1. to be or become widely scattered or separated. Syn. *magkáhiwá-hiwaláy.* 2. to become disunited. Syn. *magkálayú-layô.*

magkáwindang-windáng (mag-ká-win-dang + win-dáng), *v.* to be or become torn into small pieces. Syn. *magkásirâ-sirâ.*

magkayarî (magkayarî), *adj.* referring to two persons who have an agreement or misunderstanding with each other.

magkita-kita (mag-ki-ta + ki-ta), *v.* to see or meet one another as in a certain place. Syn. *magkatagpú-tagpô, magharáp-haráp.*

magkomadre (mag-ko-ma-dre), var. **magkumadre**, *adj. & n.* referring to a female sponsor and the mother or father of her godchild.

magkompadre (mag-kom-pa-dre), var. **magkumpadre**, *adj. & n.* referring to a male sponsor and the father or mother of his godchild.

magkomunyón (mag-ko-mun-yón), *v.* to have or take Holy Communion; go to Communion. Syn. *makinabang.*

magkonsiderasyón (mag-kon-si-de-ras-yón), *v.* to give consideration; be considerate. Syn. *magkaroón o magbigáy ng konsiderasyón.*

magkukulambô (mag-ku-ku-lam-bô), *n.* a mosquito net dealer or vendor. Syn. *magtitindá ng kulambó o moskitero.*

magkukultí (mag-ku-kul-tí), I. *adj.* referring to a person who tans (leather).
—II. *n.* tanner. Also, *mangungultí.*

magkukuweró (mag-ku-ku-we-ró), *adj. & n.* referring to someone who deals in leather. Syn. *magbabalát.*

magkulang (mag-ku-lang), *v.* 1. to lack or be insufficient. Syn. *magkapós, kapusín, kulangin.* 2. to be lacking; have a part or portion of something missing. Syn. *mawalan, mabawasan.* 3. to make an error. Syn. *magkámalî.* 4. to fail to satisfy or please.

magkulay (mag-ku-lay), *v.* 1. to color; put color, as in drawing or painting. Syn. *magkulór.* 2. to dye (clothes). Syn. *magtinà.*

magkulóng (mag-ku-lóng), *v.* 1. to confine, keep, or hold in captivity; put in prison. Syn. *magbilanggô.* 2. to hide or shut oneself, as in a room. Syn. *magtagó o magsará sa kuwarto.* 3. to surround something, as within a circle.

magkulubóng (mag-ku-lu-bóng), *v.* 1. to use or wear a veil. Syn. *magpindóng.* 2. to cover oneself, including the head, with or as with a blanket.

magkumpíl (mag-kum-píl), *v.* to officiate in the confirmation of someone.

magkumpisál (mag-kum-pi-sál), *v.* 1. to admit a fault, crime, etc.; confess. Syn. *magtapát ng kasalanan.* 2. to make one's confession to a priest; confess. Syn. *mangumpisál.*

magkumpleanyo (mag-ku-ple-an-yo), *v.* to celebrate one's birthday. Syn. *magdaos ng kaarawán.*

magkunwâ (mag-kun-wâ) var. **magkunwarî**, *v.* to make a false show of; pretend to be (something); feign; simulate. Syn. *magkunyarî.*

magkunyarî (mag-kun-ya-rî), *v.* to pretend to be something. See **magkunwâ**.

magkurù-kuró (mag-ku-rù + ku-ró), *v.* to think seriously about; contemplate or ponder upon; reflect; meditate. Syn. *magisip-isip.*

magkusà (mag-ku-sà), v. to act voluntarily; have initiative; do something without being told.

magkuya (mag-ku-ya), adj. & n. referring to an older brother and his younger brother or sister. Cf. mag-ate.

magdaán (mag-da-án), v. 1. to pass through or by a place. Syn. dumaán. 2. slip by or elapse, as time. Syn. lumipas.

magdahan-dahan (mag-da-han + da-han), v: 1. to act or move slowly. Syn. mag-atay-atay. 2. to work slowly and carefully.

magdahilán (mag-da-hi-lán), v. to offer, make, or give excuses.

magdahóp (mag-da-hóp), v. to be wanting in money or other necessities in life. Syn. maghirap (sa buhay), magdálitâ.

magdalá (mag-da-lá), v. 1. to bring or carry (something) with oneself. Syn. magtagláy. 2. to deliver or take (something) to someone or to a place. Syn. maghatíd.

magdalagá (mag-da-la-gá), v. to grow up into a young teen-age girl.

magdalamhatì (mag-da-lam-ha-tì), v. to feel deep sorrow or distress; be very sad; grieve or lament. Syn. magdamdám nang labis.

magdaláng-awà (mag-da-láng + a-wà), v. to have compassion or pity. Syn. magdaláng-habág, maawà, mahabág.

magdaláng-tao (mag-dá-lang + ta-o), v. to be or become pregnant. Syn. magbuntís.

magdalás-dalás (mag-da-las + da-las), v. to hurry up; rush. Syn. magdalí-dalì, mag-apurá.

magdalí-dalì (mag-da-lí + da-lì), v. to hurry up; move or act fast. Syn. mag-apurá, magmadalî.

magdálitâ (mag-dá-li-tâ), v. to become poor or indigent; suffer misery or poverty. Syn. maghirap, mamulubi.

magdamág (mag-da-mág), I. n. the whole night. Syn. buóng gabí.
—II. adj. & adv. whole night; all night.

magdamagan (mag-da-ma-gan), adj. & adv. during the whole night.

magdamay (mag-da-may), v. 1. to implicate someone falsely. Syn. magsangkót, magdawit. 2. to cause someone or something to be also affected or involved.

magdamayán (mag-da-ma-yán), v. to help

each other or one another. Syn. magtulungán, mag-ábuluyán.

magdamdám (mag-dam-dám), v. to feel slighted or offended. Syn. maghinanakít, masaktán ang kaloobán.

magdanas (mag-da-nas), v. to experience; have an experience of; undergo. Syn. makáranas, makáramá.

magdaóp-kamáy (mag-da-óp + ka-máy), var. **magdaupkamáy**, v. 1. to clasp or hold together one's hands. 2. to clasp each other's hand; shake each other's hand. Syn. magkamáy.

magdaragát (mag-da-ra-gat), n. seaman; navigator; mariner.

magdarayà (mag-da-ra-yà), n. a deceiver; cheat; swindler; defrauder; impostor. Syn. manlilinláng, manunubà.

magdasál (mag-da-sál), v. to pray; say a prayer or prayers. Syn. manalangin.

magdawit (mag-da-wit), v. to implicate (someone), as in a crime. Syn. magsangkót.

magdiborsiyó (mag-di-bor-si-yó), v. to get a divorce; separate legally, said of a husband and wife. Syn. maghiwaláy nang legál o sa pamamagitan ng diborsiyó.

magdibuho (mag-di-bu-ho), v. to draw a picture or pictures; make a design or drawing of. Syn. magdrowing.

magdikta (mag-dik-ta), v. 1. to speak or read something aloud for someone to write; give someone a dictation. 2. to give orders or instructions with or as with authority. Syn. mag-utos, magmando.

magdiín (mag-di-ín), v. 1. to press down something with or as with one's hand. 2. to give emphasis on; emphasize. Also, magbigáy-diín.

magdilidili (mag-di-li-di-li), v. to meditate; reflect; examine one's conscience. Syn. magbulay-bulay, magwarì-warì.

magdiwáng (mag-di-wáng), v. 1. to celebrate; have a convivial good time. Syn. magsayá. 2. to commemorate (an anniversary, holiday, or the like) with ceremony or festivity.

magdoktór (mag-dok-tór), v. 1. to study medicine for a doctor's degree; be a doctor. Syn. mag-aral ng pagdodoktór o panggagamót, mag-aral ng medisina. 2. to practise medicine. Syn. manggamót. 3. to get or hire a doctor (for someone who is sick). Syn. *kumuha o tumawag ng doktor, magpagamót sa doktór.*

magduda (mag-du-da), *v.* to doubt; have a doubt. Syn. *mag-alinlangan, magkaroón ng duda o alinlangan.*

magdulot (mag-du-lot), *v.* 1. to give or offer (food), esp. to a sick person. 2. to serve food, as in a restaurant. 3. to cause or be the cause of. Syn. *maging dahilán o sanhî, magbigáy.*

magdumalî (mag-du-ma-lî), *v.* to hurry up; rush or be in a hurry. Syn. *magmadalî, magdalí-dalì, mag-apurá.*

magdunúng-dunungan (mag-du-núng + du-nu-ngan), *v.* 1. to pretend to know much; have pretension of having wisdom. Syn. *magkunwaríng marunong, magkunwáng maraming nalalaman.* 2. to pretend to know about something. Syn. *magkunwáng may-nalalaman.*

magdurado (mag-du-ra-do), *v.* 1. to overlay (a metal) with a thin layer of gold; gild. Syn. *magtubóg sa gintô.* 2. to coat or color (something) with gold.

magdusa (mag-du-sa), *v.* 1. to suffer. Syn. *magtiís, maghirap, magbatá.* 2. to be punished for a crime or wrong done. Syn. *magtamo ng parusa, mapárusahan.*

maggalít-galitan (mag-ga-lít + ga-li-tan), *v.* to pretend to be angry. Syn. *magkunwáng galit.*

maggayák (mag-ga-yák), *v.* 1. to dress up. Syn. *magbihis.* 2. to prepare (for a trip). Syn. *maghandâ.* 3. to beautify by putting decoration; embellish; adorn. Syn. *magpalamuti, magdekorasyón.*

maggurò (mag-gu-rò), *v.* to be a teacher; teach children in school. Syn. *magtitser.*

maghabilin (mag-ha-bi-lin), *v.* to leave something to someone for temporary safekeeping.

maghabol (mag-ha-bol), *v.* 1. to lay a claim on something. 2. to make an appeal to a higher court. Syn. *umapelá.* 3. to add a note or supplementary information to a letter, article, or book. Syn. *magpahabol.*

maghakà (mag-ha-ka), *v.* 1. to make a supposition. Syn. *magpalagáy.* 2. to have

a suspicion. Syn. *magsapantahà, maghinalà, magsospetsa.*

maghagiláp (mag-ha-gi-láp), *v.* to grope or search blindly and uncertainly for something. Syn. *mag-apuháp.*

maghahalamán (mag-ha-ha-la-mán), *n.* horticulturist; gardener. Syn. *hardinero.*

maghain (mag-ha-in), *v.* 1. to prepare or set the table. Syn. *maghandâ ng pagkain sa mesa.* 2. to offer or propose. Syn. *maghandóg.*

maghalagá (mag-ha-la-gá), *v.* 1. to set or give price of. Syn. *turingan ang halagá o presyo, magpresyo.* 2. to set an estimated value of (property, etc.) for the purpose of taxation. Syn. *magtasa.*

maghalál (mag-ha-lál), *v.* to select (a person) for an office by voting in an election; elect someone from among the candidates for the position to be filled.

maghalimbawà (mag-ha-lim-ba-wà), *v.* to give or cite an example. Syn. *magbigáy o bumanggít ng halimbawá.*

maghambóg (mag-ham-bóg), *v.* to be boastful, proud, or vain. Syn. *magmayabáng.*

maghamok (mag-ha-mok), *v.* to engage each other in a hand-to-hand fight. Cf. *maglaban, magtunggalî.*

maghamón (mag-ha-món), *v.* to make or issue a challenge.

maghanáp (mag-ha-náp), *v.* 1. to look or search for something missing or lost. 2. to look or find, e.g. work. 3. to expect something, as from another or others. Syn. *umasa.*

maghanapbuhay (mag-ha-nap-bu-hay), *v.* to work for a living; earn something for a living. Syn. *magtrabaho.*

maghanay (mag-ha-nay), *v.* 1. to put or arrange (things) in a row. 2. to form in line. Syn. *maghilera, humilera.* 3. to present one by one in an orderly manner. Cf. *maglahad.*

magha-maghapon (mag-ha + mag-ha-pon), *adv.* all day every day.

maghapon (mag-ha-pon), *adv. & adj.* all day; whole day.

maghapunan (mag-ha-pu-nan), *v.* to take or eat one's supper. Syn. *kumain ng hapunan.*

maghápunan¹ (mag-há-pu-nan), *adv. & adj.* whole day every day.

maghápunan² (mag-há-pu-nan), *v.* to perch or roost simultaneously, referring to birds and fowls.

magharáp (mag-ha-ráp), *v.* 1. to present or submit (something) to someone as evidence or proof. Syn. *magbigáy, magpresenta.* 2. to face or confront each other; meet each other. Syn. *magkita, magtagpô.* 3. to file, as a case in court. 4. to render or submit, as a report.

magharì (mag-ha-rì), *v.* 1. to reign or rule as a king; be a king. 2. to predominate; prevail; preponderate. Syn. *manatili, umiral, manaig.*

magharí-harian (mag-ha-rí + ha-ri-an), *v.* 1. to be a puppet king. 2. to pretend to be a king. Syn. *magkunwáng harì.* 3. to be domineering.

maghasík (mag-ha-sík), *v.* 1. to sow seeds for growing. Syn. *magsabog ng binhî.* 2. to cause to scatter or spread. Syn. *magkalat.*

maghatíd-dumapit (mag-ha-tíd + du-ma-pit), *v.* to indulge in idle talk or rumors about others; be a gossip. Syn. *magtsismís, magmahabang-dilá* (fig.).

maghátinggabí (mag-há-ting-ga-bí), *v.* to be midnight.

maghikahós (mag-hi-ka-hós), *v.* 1. to become poor or needy. Syn. *mamulubi, maghirap, magdalitâ.* 2. to lack the needed supply; be insufficient in. Syn. *magipít sa pangangailangan, magkulang.*

maghikáp (mag-hi-káp), *v.* 1. to go around a place aimlessly. Syn. *maglibót, magpagalá-galà.* 2. to travel or make trips to distant places. Syn. *maglakbáy o maglagalág sa ibá't ibáng dako.*

maghigantí (mag-hi-gan-tí), *v.* to revenge; take vengeance.

maghilom (mag-hi-lom), *v.* to heal or dry up, referring to a wound; become cicatrized. Syn. *gumalíng, mabahaw, matuyo, magpeklat.*

maghimagsik (mag-hi-mag-sik), *v.* to revolt; rise in rebellion against. Syn. *mag-alsá, magbangon.*

maghimalâ (mag-hi-ma-lâ), *v.* 1. to perform a miracle; work miracles. Syn. *magmilagro.* 2. to turn or become miraculous.

maghimatón (mag-hi-ma-tón), var. **maghimatóng**, *v.* 1. to give or point to someone the direction or way to a certain place. 2. to give or send over information or news about something. Syn. *magbalitá.*

maghimutók (mag-hi-mu-tók), *v.* to sigh. Syn. *magbuntóng-hiningá, maghinagpís.*

maghinakdál (mag-hi-nak-dál), *v.* to feel being ignored or unjustly treated by someone less expected to do so. Syn. *maghinanakít.*

maghinagap (mag-hi-na-gap), *v.* to have preconceived idea or opinion about something. Syn. *mag-akalá, magpalagáy.*

maghinagpis (mag-hi-nag-pis), *v.* to sigh. Syn. *maghimutók, magbuntong-hiningá.*

maghinalà (mag-hi-na-là), *v.* 1. to be suspicious about; have suspicion. Syn. *magsapantahà.* 2. to accuse (someone) falsely. Syn. *magparatang.*

maghinanakít (mag-hi-na-na-kít), *v.* to feel resentment against a friend or someone who is close to oneself. Syn. *magdamdám, maghinampó.*

maghinay-hinay (mag-hi-nay + hi-nay), *v.* to act, move, speak, etc. with moderation. Syn. *magdahan-dahan.*

maghintáy (mag-hin-tay), var. **mag-antáy**, *v.* 1. to wait. 2. to look forward to; anticipate. Syn. *umasa.*

maghinuhà (mag-hi-nu-hà), *v.* to infer; make deduction. Syn. *mag-akalà, magsapantahà.*

maghingá (mag-hi-ngá), *v.* (Colloq.) to express (reluctantly) a feeling of resentment one has suppressed or kept to oneself for sometime. Cf. *magtapát.*

maghingaló (mag-hi-nga-ló), *v.* to be in a moribund state; be in the pangs of death; hover between life and death.

maghipag (mag-hi-pag), *adj. & n.* referring to the relation between a man and his sister-in-law. Cf. *magbayáw.*

maghirap (mag-hi-rap), *v.* 1. to become poor; be in poverty. Syn. *magdálitâ.* 2. to suffer hardship or difficulty. Syn. *magdusa, magtiis ng hirap, dumanas ng hirap.*

maghiwaláy (mag-hi-wa-láy), *v.* 1. to separate a part or portion of something.

Syn. *magbukód*. 2. separate from each other, as a husband and his wife. 3. to branch out, as a river, street, etc. Syn. *magsangá, sumangá*. 4. to get away from each other. Syn. *maglayô*.

naghubú't-hubád (mag-hu-bú't + hu-bád), *v*. to undress completely, leaving the body entirely naked.

naghudas (mag-hu-das), *v*. to be a traitor. Syn. *magtaksíl*.

naghulapí (mag-hu-la-pí), *v*. to add a suffix; provide with a suffix. Syn. *maglagáy o gumamit ng hulapí*.

naghulip (mag-hu-lip), *v*. to make replacement for something that has been destroyed or lost.

naghulog (mag-hu-log), *v*. to drop or let drop or fall to the ground. Syn. *maglagpák, magbagsák*. 2. to pay the installment of one's loan or debt. Syn. *maghurnál*. 3. (*in Carp.*) to use a plumb line, as in testing whether a wall, post, etc. is vertically set or not. Syn. *gumamit ng panghulog*.

naghumpáy (mag-hum-páy), *v*. to cease or stop. Syn. *maghintô, humintô*.

naghunusdilì (mag-hu-nus-di-lì), *v*. to think deeply before acting.

naghusay (mag-hu-say), *v*. 1. to put things in order; arrange. Syn. *mag-ayos, mag-imis*. 2. to settle or end a dispute amicably. Syn. *mag-areglo*.

nag-ibá (mag + i-bá), I. *v*. 1. to change, as one's belief or stand. Syn. *magbago*. 2. to become changed. Syn. *maibá, mabago*.
—II. *adj*. not related to each other. Syn. *di-magkamag-anak, di-magka-anu-ano*.

nagibâ (ma-gi-bâ), *v*. to be able to demolish, destroy, or wreck completely. Syn. *mawasák*.

nag-ibayo (mag + i-ba-yo), *v*. to become double; be increased twofold. Syn. *madoble ang lakí o dami*.

nag-íbigan (mag + í-bi-gan), *v*. to love each other. Syn. *magmáhalan*.

magigì (ma-gi-gì), *adj*. meticulous; scrupulous; finical.

magiít (ma-gi-ít), *adj*. insistent; persistent in demand or assertion. Syn. *mapilit*.

magilalás (ma-gi-la-lás), *v*. to be suddenly astonished or surprised. Syn. *mamanghâ*.

magilas (ma-gi-las), *adj*. 1. gallant. Syn. *galante*. 2. smart; stylish. Syn. *makisig, magarà*.

magiliw (ma-gi-liw), *adj*. tender and loving; affectionate. Syn. *mapagmahál, mapanuyò*.

magim- (ma-gim-), var. **magin-**, *pref*. meaning "to be or become," as in *magimbatà*, to become young or be born.

magimbál (ma-gim-bál), *v*. to be greatly disturbed, as by loud and confused noise. Syn. *mabulahaw*.

magimbatá (ma-gim-ba-tá), *v*. 1. to be born, referring to a child. Syn. *ipanganák, isilang*. 2. to be or become young, at least in the physical sense.

mag-imbót (mag + im-bót), *v*. to covet things not one's own.

mag-imikan (mag + i-mi-kan), *v*. 1. to be in talking terms again after a long silence. Syn. *magbatián*. 2. to talk or say something at the same time.

mag-impó (mag + im-pó), *adj. & n*. referring to a grandmother and her grandchild. Syn. *maglola*.

magin- (ma-gin-), var. **magim-**, *pref*. meaning "to be or become," and used with roots beginning with t or d, as in *magintao, magindapat*, etc.

mag-iná (mag + i-ná), *adj. & n*. referring to a mother and her child. Cf. *mag-amá*.

magináw (ma-gi-náw), I. *adj*. cold, referring to the weather. Syn. *malamíg*.
—II. *v*. to feel cold.

magindapat (ma-gin-da-pat), *v*. to be worthy or meritorious. Also, *magíng dapat*.

maginhawa (ma-gin-ha-wa), *adj*. 1. providing comfort; comfortable. 2. convenient; easy to do, use, get, etc. Syn. *maalwán, madalî*. 3. well-off; fairly rich. Syn. *mariwasá*.

maginoó (ma-gi-no-ó), I. *n*. gentleman.
—II. *adj*. well-bred, courteous, gracious, and considerate, referring to a man; honorable. Syn. *marangál*.

magintao (ma-gin-ta-o), *v*. to be born or created, referring to a person. Also, *magíng tao*.

maging (ma-ging), *v*. 1. to be or become. 2. (*Idiom.*) *Maging sino ka man*. Whoever you are.

mag-ingat (mag + i-ngat), v. 1. to be careful. Syn. *maging maingat.* 2. to have, keep, or possess, as firearm. Syn. *maghawak, magmay-arì.*

magipít (ma-gi-pít), v. to find oneself in a tight situation. Syn. *málagáy sa álanganin.* 2. to lack time. Syn. *kapusín sa oras o panahón.* 3. to lack space or room. Syn. *magsikíp, masikipán.* 4. to lack money for expenses. Syn. *kapusín sa gugulín.* 5. to be cornered. Syn. *mapikot.*

mag-irapán (mag + i-ra-pán), v. to look at each other angrily; exchange angry looks at each other. Syn. *magtínginan nang pairáp.*

mag-isá (mag + i-sá), I. v. 1. to be alone. 2. to unite together; be united into one. Syn. *magsama-sama.*
—II. adj. & adv. alone; without any companion. Syn. *solo, waláng kasama.*

mag-isáng-dibdíb (mag + i-sáng + dib-díb), v. to be married. Syn. *magpakasál, humaráp sa dambaná (fig.).*

mágisíng (má-gi-síng), v. to be or become awakened.

mag-isíp (mag + i-síp), v. to think deeply and seriously; study well in one's mind. Syn. *magmuni-muning mabuti.*

mag-isíp-isíp (mag + i-síp + i-síp), v. to study seriously and long enough before acting.

mágisnán (má-gis-nán), v. to happen to see or find upon waking.

magiting (ma-gi-ting), adj. brave; patriotic; heroic.

mágitlá (má-git-lá), var. **mágiklá**, v. to be suddenly surprised, startled, or scared. Syn. *mágulat, mabiglâ.*

mágitnâ (má-git-nâ), v. to be or happen to be in the middle or at the center. Syn. *masentro, mápagitnâ.*

mag-iwan (mag + i-wan), v. 1. to leave something behind or before leaving. 2. to leave something undone. Syn. *magtirá.*

magiwang (ma-gi-wang), adj. too wobbly or shaky, as an old, dilapidated cart.

mag-iwi (mag + i-wi), v. 1. to take care of someone's animal or animals (horses, carabaos, pigs, or the like), on condition that the caretaker would have a share from said animals or from their offsprings. 2. (Colloq.) to harbor or entertain, e.g.

hard feelings. Syn. *magtagláy, magkimkim.*

maglaán (mag-la-án), v. to reserve somethin for the future or for someone; mak reservation for. Syn. *magreserba.*

maglabás (mag-la-bás), v. 1. to bring ou something. Syn. *magdalá sa labás.* 2. to pu out something, as from one's pocket. Syn *dumukot.* 3. to put out or publish, as magazine or newspaper. Syn. *maglathalá* 4. to present, as a show or drama. Syn *magtanghál, magpalabás.*

maglabulabo (mag-la-bu-la-bo), v. to figh one another; engage in a free-for-all fight

maglakad (mag-la-kad), v. to undertake th job of selling something. Syn. *magbili maglako.* 2. to work for the approval of attend to personally.

maglakád-lakád (mag-la-kád + la-kád), v. t take a short walk; walk leisurely. Syn *mamasyál-masyál.*

maglakás-lakasan (mag-la-kás + la-ka-san) v. to pretend to be strong. Syn *magkunwáng malakás.*

maglakás-loób (mag-la-kás + lo-ób), v. to tr to be brave; be brave enough to.

maglakbáy (mag-lak-báy), v. to travel; g on a trip; make a journey. Syn. *magbiyahe*

maglagá (mag-la-gá), v. 1. to extract th essence, flavor, etc., of by boiling; decoct 2. to cook by boiling in plain water, a corn, sweet potatoes, or the like. 3. t stew, as meat.

maglagabláb (mag-la-gab-láb), v. to burs into flame. Syn. *magliyáb.*

maglagak (mag-la-gak), v. 1. to deposi (money), as in a bank. Syn. *magdeposito* 2. to leave something in the care o someone temporarily. Syn. *maghabilin.* 3 to make a deposit for something as guarantee. Syn. *magdeposito.* 4. to put u a bail for. Syn. *magpiyansa.*

maglagalág (mag-la-ga-lág), v. to trave extensively; make trips from place t place. Syn. *maglibót, magpalibut-libot.*

maglagî (mag-la-gî), v. to be always in certain place. Syn. *maglumagák.*

maglahò (mag-la-hò), v. to disappear o vanish mysteriously. Syn. *mawalâ.* 2. t be erased, as from one's mind. Syn *mapawì, makatkát.*

naglamán (mag-la-mán), v. 1. to grow or develop flesh, as a wound. 2. to develop tuber or rootstock, as potatoes, radish, etc. 3. to be able to hold or contain a certain amount or quantity of. Syn. maglulan.

naglámangan (mag-lá-ma-ngan), v. to try to take advantage of each other; try to undo each other.

naglamat (mag-la-mat), v. to have a light crack, referring esp. to chinaware or glassware. Syn. magkalamat, magkabiták.

naglamay (mag-la-may), v. 1. to keep a night vigil; stay awake the whole night. Syn. magpuyát. 2. to work overtime at night. Syn. magtrabaho sa buóng gabí.

naglambingan (mag-lam-bi-ngan), v. to fondle each other affectionately.

naglandás (mag-lan-dás), v. 1. to pass through a certain unbeaten path. 2. to open a path or trail through. Syn. gumawâ ng landás.

naglandî (mag-lan-dî), v. to flirt; play at love, referring to a woman. Syn. magkiri, maglantód.

naglantád (mag-lan-tád), v. to cause something to be exposed or revealed. Syn. maghayág, magbunyág.

naglangó (mag-la-ngó), v. to drink alcoholic liquor habitually or excessively; drink to excess. Syn. maglasíng.

naglapà (mag-la-pà), v. to kill (animals) for meat; butcher. Syn. magkatay.

naglapì (mag-la-pì), v. to use an affix; provide with an affix.

naglápitan (mag-lá-pi-tan), v. to get close or approach (someone or something) at the same time. Syn. magdáisan.

naglarawan (mag-la-ra-wan), v. 1. to describe; give the description of. 2. to make or draw a picture of. Syn. magdrowing.

naglawá (mag-la-wá), v. 1. to be or become flooded. Syn. magbahâ, bumahâ. 2. to be or become sticky with dirt. Syn. manggitatà.

naglayág (mag-la-yág), v. 1. to travel by water or sea; have voyage or trip in a boat or ship. 2. to miss one's regular monthly menstruation; have late menstruation.

naglayás (mag-la-yás), v. 1. to run away from home. 2. to travel from place to place in vagabondage. Syn. maggalâ, maglibót.

maglibíng (mag-li-bíng), v. 1. to bury (a dead body); entomb. 2. to attend or join a funeral. Syn. makipaglibíng.

maglibót (mag-li-bót), v. to go from place to place; travel around. Syn. maggalâ, magpagalá-galà.

maglikás (mag-li-kás), v. 1. to help people to evacuate to a safe place. 2. to evacuate to a safe place.

maglikát (mag-li-kát), v. to stop or cease. Syn. maghumpáy, humumpáy; magtigil, tumigil.

magligalig (mag-li-ga-lig), v. 1. to trouble oneself. Syn. mag-abala. 2. to have a fit of bad temper or ill humor, usually said of children. Syn. mag-alboroto.

magligtás (mag-lig-tás), v. 1. to save (someone) from danger or harm. Syn. magsalbá. 2. to deliver or redeem, as from sin, punishment, etc. Syn. tumubós, maghangò, humangò.

maglihí (mag-li-hí), v. to conceive, referring to a woman. Cf. magdaláng-tao, magbuntís.

maglihim (mag-li-him), v. to keep something to oneself; not tell others what one knows; keep (something) secret. Syn. magkailâ, di-magtapát.

maglihís (mag-li-hís), v. 1. to mislead; misguide. Syn. magligáw. 2. to make erroneous. Syn. magmalî, maglisyâ.

maglilo (mag-li-lo), v. to be unfaithful or disloyal. Syn. magtaksíl, magtraidór.

maglimá-limá (mag-li-má + li-má), v. to be in groups of five.

maglimayón (mag-li-ma-yón), v. to roam around without purpose. Syn. maglakuwatsa.

maglináng (mag-lí-náng), v. 1. to cultivate a farm, be a farmer. Syn. magbukid, magararo. 2. to improve or develop by study or training. Syn. magsanay.

maglinaw (mag-li-naw), v. 1. to clear up; become clear. Syn. magliwanag. 2. to talk things over. Syn. mag-intindihan, magunawaán.

maglining (mag-li-ning), v. to think deeply or seriously about; reflect. Syn. magnilay, maglimì.

maglingíd (mag-li-ngíd), v. to hide something from oneself; not to tell the truth; be secretive. Syn. *maglihim, magkailâ.*

maglipana (mag-li-pa-na), *v.* to roam about in great number; be found everywhere.

maglitáw (mag-li-táw), *v.* to show or bring out (something), as proof or evidence. Syn. *magpakita, maglabás.*

maglítawan (mag-lí-ta-wan), *v.* to appear or show up at the same time. Syn. *maglábasan, magsiputan.*

magliwalíw (mag-li-wa-líw), *v.* to go outing; take a pleasure trip. Syn. *mag-iskursiyón.*

magliyág (mag-li-yág), *adj. & n.* referring to lovers or sweethearts. Syn. *magkasintahan, magnobya o magnobyo, magkasuyò.*

maglola (mag-lo-la), *adj. & n.* referring to the relation between a grandmother and her grandchild.

maglolo (mag-lo-lo), *adj. & n.* referring to the relation between a grandfather and his grandchild.

maglubag (mag-lu-bag), *v.* to mitigate or calm down; ease up or relax. Syn. *huminà, humuláw.*

magmakisig (mag-ma-ki-sig), *v.* 1. to dress up oneself smartly; be stylish. Syn. *magmagarâ.* 2. to act in a spirited or gallant manner. Syn. *magmagilas.*

magdunúng-dunungan (mag-du-núng + du-nu-ngan), *v.* to pretend to know much. See **magmarunóng.**

magmaestra (mag-ma-es-tra), *v.* to teach (children) in school; be a teacher, referring to a female. Syn. *maggurò (manggurò).*

magmagaling (mag-ma-ga-ling), *v.* 1. to pretend to be good. Syn. *magkunwáng mahusay o magalíng.* 2. to be boastful; assume an air of importance. Syn. *maghambóg, magmayabáng.* 3. to ingratiate or bring oneself into someone's favor. Syn. *magmapurí.*

magmagandáng-loob (mag-ma-gan-dáng + lo-ob), *v.* 1. to do someone a favor. 2. to be kindhearted or generous.

magmahál (mag-ma-hál), *v.* 1. to love; hold someone dear to one's heart. 2. to raise the price of goods. Syn. *magtaás ng presyo o halagá.* 3. to become dear or high in price. Syn. *tumaás ang presyo o halagá.*

magmalabís (mag-ma-la-bís), *v.* 1. to be abusive, as in vice. Syn. *mag-abuso.* 2. to be abusive or cruel. Syn. *magmalupít.* 3. to be scurrilous or abusive in an indecent manner. Syn. *magbastós, magmasagwâ.*

magmalakí (mag-ma-la-kí), *v.* to be contemptuously proud; put on airs; act in a superior manner. Syn. *magmagalíng, magmataás.*

magmalasakit (mag-ma-la-sa-kit), *v.* to have concern or interest for the good or welfare of. Syn. *magkaroón ng malasakit.*

magmalay-tao (mag-ma-lay + ta-o), *v.* to become conscious; regain consciousness. Also, *magkamalay-tao.* Syn. *panumbalika ng malay.*

magmaliw (mag-ma-liw), *v.* to disappear; fade. Syn. *maglahô, mawalâ, mapawi, maparam.*

magmana (mag-ma-na), *v.* 1. to inherit; receive an inheritance. 2. to have, get, or possess some characteristic. Syn. *kumuha (colloq.), tumulad.*

magmanang (mag-ma-nang), *adj. & n.* referring to an older sister and her younger sister or brother. Cf. *magmanong.*

magmando (mag-man-do), *v.* 1. to command; give an order or orders. Syn. *mag-utos.* 2. to exercise authority or power over; be in charge. Syn. *mamahalà.*

magmano (mag-ma-no), *v.* to kiss the hand of an elder. Syn. *humalik sa kamáy ng matandâ.*

magmanugáng (mag-ma-nu-gáng), *v.* to be or become a father-in-law or mother-in-law.

magmapurí (mag-ma-pu-rí), *v.* 1. to tell others in order to ingratiate or bring oneself into someone's favor. Syn. *magsipsíp (slang).* 2. to be boastful of one's accomplishment or work. Syn. *magmagalíng.*

magmarunóng (mag-ma-ru-nóng), *v.* to act as if one has much knowledge or understanding of something; pretend to know much. See **magdunúng-dunungan.**

magmásarapan (mag-má-sa-ra-pan), *v.* to enjoy mutual happiness or satisfaction.

magmasibâ (mag-ma-si-bâ), *v.* to be avaricious or greedy. Syn. *maging masibà o maramot, magmatakáw.*

magmasíd (mag-ma-síd), v. 1. to observe; make an observation about something. Syn. *magmatyág*. 2. to look around in search for something.

magmataás (mag-ma-ta-ás), v. to act in a haughty or proud manner; be contemptuously proud. Syn. *magmalakí, magíng palaló o mapágmataás*.

magmatigás (mag-ma-ti-gás), v. 1. to stand pat or be firm, as in one's stand, belief, or decision. Syn. *manindigan*. 2. to be obstinate or hard-headed; be stubborn. Syn. *magsutil, magsuwaíl*.

magmatuwíd (mag-ma-tu-wíd), var. **magmatwíd**, v. to give one's reason; explain one's side; justify one's act. Syn. *mangatuwiran, magpaliwanag*.

magmatyág (mag-mat-yág), v. to observe or watch secretly or closely. Syn. *magmasíd nang lihim (o palihim)*.

magmisa (mag-mi-sa), v. to officiate in a Mass; say or celebrate a Mass.

magmongha (mag-mong-ha), v. to enter a nunnery; be a nun. Syn. *magmadre*.

magmonghe (mag-mong-he), v. to retire from the world and live in solitary self-denial for religious reasons; be a monk.

magmukmók (mag-muk-mók), v. to sulk; be sulky. Syn. *magmaktól*.

magmulâ (mag-mu-lâ), I. v. to come from; start or originate from. Syn. *manggaling, magbuhat*.

—II. *adv.* since. Syn. *mulâ noón, magbuhat noón*.

—III. *prep.* from; since.

magmulat (mag-mu-lat), v. 1. (followed by ng *matá*) to open the (one's) eyes. 2. to make one aware of the facts, real reason or cause of. Syn. *magbukás ng isip*.

magmulto (mag-mul-to), v. to haunt or appear frequently to a person, said of a dead person or his spirit.

magmunakalà (mag-mu-na-ka-là), var. of **magmunukalà**, v. to submit or present a plan or suggestion; suggest or propose (something). Syn. *magmungkahì*.

magmuni-muni (mag-mu-ni + mu-ni), var. **magmunimuni**, v. to think rationally; meditate or reflect. Syn. *mag-isíp-isíp*.

magnanakaw (mag-na-na-kaw), n. thief; burglar; stealer.

magnanay (mag-na-nay), adj. & n. referring to a mother and her child. Syn. *mag-iná*. Cf. *mag-amá, magtatay*.

magnet (mag-net), n. (Eng.) magnet. Syn. *batubalanì*.

magneto (mag-ne-to), n. a small machine for producing electricity; magnet.

magnilay-nilay (mag-ni-lay + ni-lay), v. to give full thought before acting.

magninang (mag-ni-nang), adj. & n. referring to a godmother and her godchild. Syn. *mag-iníná*.

magninong (mag-ni-nong), adj. & n. referring to a godfather and his godchild. Syn. *mag-ináamá*.

magnobena (mag-no-be-na), v. to cite prayers of devotion during a nine-day period of a novena; pray the novena; hold or attend a novena.

magngalit (mag-nga-lit), v. 1. to grind (the teeth) in anger. Syn. *magngitngít*. 2. to make a grating or grinding sound, as with one's teeth.

magpa- (mag-pa-), pref. used to form verbs, meaning: 1. to ask or request someone to do something, as in *magpakuha, magpagawâ*, etc. 2. to allow that something be done on oneself, as in *magpaóperá, magpahuli, magpaabot*, etc.

magpaalaala (mag-pa-a-la-a-la), v. 1. to remind someone about something. Syn. *magpagunitâ*. 2. to give someone an advice. Syn. *magpayo*.

magpaalam (mag-pa-a-lam), v. 1. to bid (someone) good-bye. 2. to let someone know what one intends to do. Syn. *magsabi*.

magpaamò (mag-pa-a-mò), v. 1. to tame or cause to be tamed, referring to an animal. 2. to make less strict or severe. Syn. *magpabaít*.

magpaanák (mag-pa-a-nák), v. 1. to assist at a delivery, as a midwife. 2. to get or have someone as sponsor, esp. at one's own wedding.

magpaaninaw (mag-pa-a-ni-naw), v. to explain something to someone; make someone understand; make something clear to someone. Syn. *magpaunawà, magpaliwanag*.

magpaaral (mag-pa-a-ral), *v.* to send someone to school at his own expense; finance the education of someone.

magpaaraw (mag-pa-a-raw), *v.* 1. to expose oneself under the heat of the sun. Syn. *magbilád sa araw.* 2. to wait for the sun to shine, as when one intends to dry something in the open air. Syn. *maghintáy ng pagsikat ng araw.* 3. to wait till morning comes, as when someone is benighted. Syn. *magpaumaga, maghintáy ng umaga.*

magpaayuda (mag-pa-a-yu-da), *v.* to ask or request for help or succor. Syn. *magpasaklolo, humingî ng tulong o saklolo.*

magpabasa (mag-pa-ba-sa), *v.* 1. to hold a passion reading, as during Holy Week. 2. to allow someone to read something, as from one's own book.

magpabatà (mag-pa-ba-tà), *v.* 1. to reduce one's age. 2. to make oneself look young or younger.

magpabayà (mag-pa-ba-yà), *v.* 1. to be neglectful of one's duty or responsibility. 2. to let others do what they want.

magpabinyág (mag-pa-bin-yág), *v.* 1. to have oneself baptized. 2. to have one's child baptized. Syn. *pabinyagán.*

magpaka- (mag-pa-ka-), *pref.* used to form verbs to express voluntary action performed to the best of one's ability, as in *magpakabuti,* to do one's best.

magpakabaít (mag-pa-ka-ba-ít), *v.* to behave properly; be very good in one's behavior. Syn. *magpakabuti.*

magpakatao (mag-pa-ka-ta-o), *v.* to act like a good man; behave with the dignity of a good man.

magpakatatag (mag-pa-ka-ta-tag), *v.* to be very firm or stable. Syn. *magpakatibay.*

magpakatayog (mag-pa-ka-ta-yog), *v.* 1. to be very or extremely high or aloft. Syn. *magpakataás.* 2. to be very haughty or arrogant. Syn. *magpakapalalò.*

magpakatinô (mag-pa-ka-ti-nô), *v.* 1. to behave properly; conduct oneself with seriousness or integrity.

magpakaulól (mag-pa-ka-u-lól), *v.* to be crazy about. Syn. *magpakahibáng, magpakaloko.*

magpakilala (mag-pa-ki-la-la), *v.* 1. to introduce oneself or someone to another or others. 2. to reveal or show, as one's intention or desire. Syn. *magpahiwatíg.*

magpakipot (mag-pa-ki-pot), *v.* 1. to make narrow or narrower. Syn. *magpakitid.* 2. to make small or smaller, as a hole. Syn. *magpalift.* 3. (Colloq.) to pretend to have no interest or liking for something offered.

magpakitang-gilas (mag-pa-ki-tang + gi-las), *v.* to display or show one's gallantry or excellence in order to impress. Syn. *magparangyâ, magpasikat* (fig.).

magpakitang-tao (mag-pa-ki-tang + ta-o), *v.* to show off, as one's ability. Syn. *magpasikat* (fig.).

magpakumbabâ (mag-pa-kum-ba-bâ), *v.* to be humble; humble oneself. Syn. *magpakababà, magpakaabâ.*

magpakundangan (mag-pa-kun-da-ngan), *v.* to give consideration or due respect for others.

magpadanas (mag-pa-da-nas), var. **magparanas,** *v.* to make or cause someone to experience something. Syn. *magpadamá (magparamá).*

magpagaán (mag-pa-ga-án), *v.* 1. to cause oneself (or someone) to reduce or lose weight, as by exercising or dieting. Syn. *magpapayat.* 2. to make lighter in weight. Syn. *magpababà ng timbáng.* 3. to make severe or harsh. Syn. *magpabawa, magpaluwág.* 4. to make less hard or less difficult. Syn. *magpaalwán, magpadalî, magpaginhawa.*

magpagabí (mag-pa-ga-bí), *v.* to wait until night comes. Syn. *maghintáy ng gabí.*

magpagál (mag-pa-gál), *v.* to spend time and effort uselessly. Syn. *mag-aksayá ng panahón at pagod.*

magpagalá-galà (mag-pa-ga-lá + ga-là), *v.* to wander around; go from one place to another without any purpose. Syn. *magpalibut-libot.*

magpagalíng (mag-pa-ga-líng), *v.* 1. to make oneself well again or get well; have oneself recovered from sickness. Syn. *magpalakás.* 2. to cause one to recover from sickness; make one recover. Syn. *makagamót, makalunas.* 3. to make someone develop excellence or expertness in a certain kind of work or play. Syn. *magpahusay*, *magpabuti*.

magpágalingan (mag-pá-ga-li-ngan), *v.* to try to outshine each other. Syn. *magpásikatán* (fig.).

magpágandahan (mag-pá-gan-da-han), *v.* to compete with each other or with one another in beauty. Syn. *magpáligsahan sa gandá*.

magpagawâ (mag-pa-ga-wâ), *v.* 1. to have something constructed or erected, as a house, etc. Syn. *magpatayô, magpatirik*. 2. to have something be made or done by someone. Syn. *magpayarì*. 3. to have something be made to order. Syn. *magpasadyâ*. 4. to hire workmen to undertake some kind of work. Syn. *magpatrabaho*.

magpaginhawa (mag-apa-gin-ha-wa), *v.* 1. to make someone enjoy the ease or comfort of life. Syn. *magpaalwán, magpasaráp*. 2. to give or cause relief from pain or suffering. Syn. *magpabawa ng sakit o kirot*. 3. to make one comfortable or at ease. 4. to make something enjoyable to do or make. Syn. *magpagaán, magpaalwán, magpadalî*.

magpagunitâ (mag-pa-gu-ni-tâ), *v.* 1. to give an advice or reminder. Syn. *magpayo*. 2. to remind someone about something. Syn. *magpaalaala*.

magpagusót (mag-pa-gu-sót), *v.* to cause or be the cause of trouble or disorder. Syn. *magpagulo, makaguló; magpaligalig, makaligalig*.

magpahabol (mag-pa-ha-bol), *v.* 1. to have someone or something be pursued. Syn. *magpatugis*. 2. to add something to what has been done or made. Syn. *magdagdág*. 3. to add a postscript to (a letter).

magpahalagá (mag-pa-ha-la-gá), *v.* to value; give importance to.

magpahalatâ (mag-pa-ha-la-tâ), *v.* to signify one's intention indirectly. Syn. *magpahiwatig*.

magpahanggán (mag-pa-hang-gán), *prep.* until; up to a certain time. Syn. *hanggáng sa*.

magpahapon (mag-pa-ha-pon), *v.* 1. to wait until afternoon comes. Syn. *maghintáy ng hapon*. 2. to serve supper or evening meal.

magpaharáp (mag-pa-ha-ráp), *v.* 1. to order (someone) to appear before (a court or a person in authority). 2. to order the presentation, as of an evidence.

magpahátinggabí (mag-pa-há-ting-ga-bí), *v.* to wait until midnight comes, or until very late in the night. Syn. *magpaabot ng hátinggabí*.

magpahilagà (mag-pa-hi-la-gà), *v.* to go or move northward. Also, *pahilagà*.

magpahinay-hinay (mag-pa-hi-nay + hi-nay), *v.* to act, move, or speak in a slow, lazy manner. Syn. *magpabagal-bagal, magpaatay-antay*.

magpahintú-hintô (mag-pa-hin-tú + hin-tô), *v.* to stop intermittently. Syn. *magpatigil-tigil*.

magpahingaláy (mag-pa-hi-nga-láy), *v.* to rest or relax for a while. Syn. *mamahingáng sandalî*.

magpahiwatig (mag-pa-hi-wa-tig), *v.* to hint; give a hint. Syn. *magpahalatâ*.

magpahulaw (mag-pa-hu-law), *v.* 1. to make calm or less intense. Syn. *magpahiná, magpahignáw*. 2. to wait until the typhoon or storm calms down.

magpáhulí (mag-pá-hu-lí), *v.* 1. to stay behind (intentionally), as in leaving on a trip. Syn. *magpaiwan*. 2. to go to school or to one's place of work late. Syn. *pumasok nang hulí sa oras*.

magpaibáng-araw (mag-pa-i-báng + a-raw), *v.* to postpone; put off till a later date or time. Syn. *magpaliban, ipagpaliban*.

magpailandáng (mag-pa-i-lan-dáng), *v.* to cause a thing to fly or be thrown asunder. Syn. *magpatilapon*.

magpailangláng (mag-pa-i-lang-láng), *v.* to soar up in the air.

magpaimbabáw (mag-pa-im-ba-báw), *v.* to pretend not to have a liking for. Syn. *magkunwáng áayáw*.

magpaimbulóg (mag-pa-im-bu-lóg), *v.* to fly high in the air; soar. Syn. *magpailangláng*.

magpainút-inót (mag-pa-i-nút + i-nót), *v.* to work little by little. Syn. *magpautáy-utáy*.

magpairal (mag-pa-i-ral), *v.* to enforce; cause to be put into practice. Syn. *magpatupád*.

magpaiya (mag-pa-i-ya), *v.* to give all that a person wants.

magpalaan (mag-pa-la-an), *v.* to ask or request someone to reserve or set apart something for a certain occasion or purpose. Syn. *magpareserba*.

magpalabuy-labuy (mag-pa-la-buy + la-boy), *v.* to go around in vagrancy. Syn. *magpagalá-galà, magbagamundo*.

magpalakad-lakad (mag-pa-la-kad + la-kad), *v.* to walk to and from in a leisurely manner. Syn. *magpahakbáng-hakbáng*.

magpalaki (mag-pa-la-ki), *v.* 1. to bring up or rear from infancy, said of a child. 2. to make grow up or be fully developed. 3. to large or larger; enlarge. 4. to overemphasize; exaggerate. Syn. *magpalabis, magpasobra*. 5. to wait until oneself is big enough. Syn. *maghintáy na lumakí*.

magpálagayan (mag-pá-la-ga-yan), *v.* to consider each other as. Syn. *magturingán*.

magpalahì (mag-pa-la-hì), *v.* to breed; raise or cause to reproduce a certain breed (s.o. animals).

magpalamay (mag-pa-la-may), *v.* to allow or permit workers to work overtime at night.

magpalasáp (mag-pa-la-sáp), *v.* to cause (someone) to experience something. Syn. *magparanas, magpatikím*.

magpalathalà (mag-pa-lat-ha-là), *v.* to cause (something) to be published (in a newspaper or magazine).

magpalawig (mag-pa-la-wig), *v.* to delay or lengthen the time or period. Syn. *magpatagál*.

magpalayà (mag-pa-la-yà), *v.* to make or set free; liberate, as a nation. 2. to let go; set free. Syn. *magpakawalâ*.

magpaliban (mag-pa-li-ban), *v.* to put off until later; postpone; defer. Syn. *magpaibáng-araw*.

magpalibut-libot (mag-pa-li-but + li-bot), *v.* to go from one place to another repeatedly or continuously. Syn. *magpagalá-galà*.

magpalikú-likô (mag-pa-li-kú + li-kô), *v.* to move, walk, or run in a zigzag.

magpaliguy-ligoy (mag-pa-li-guy + li-goy), *v.* to go around the bush; beat the bush.

magpalimbág (mag-pa-lim-bág), *v.* to cause a written matter to be printed or published; have one's work published or printed. See **magpalathalà**.

magpálinawán (mag-pá-li-na-wán), *v.* to clarify things with each other. Syn. *magpáliwanagán*.

magpalingá-lingâ (mag-pa-li-ngá + li-ngâ), *v.* to look at all sides, as in searching for someone. Syn. *magpatingín-tingín sa kabí-kabilâ*.

magpalingún-lingón (mag-pa-li-ngún + li-ngón), *v.* to look back very often or repeatedly.

magpalipas (mag-pa-li-pas), *v.* 1. to let pass or lapse. Syn. *magparaán*. 2. to wait until a storm, or the like, has subsided. Syn. *maghintáy na lumipas o mawalâ*.

magpalugód (mag-pa-lu-gód), *v.* to make happy; cause one to become happy. Syn. *magpatuwâ, makatuwâ*.

magpaluhà (mag-pa-lu-hà), *v.* to make (someone) shed tears; make one cry. Syn. *makaluhà*.

magpalumagak (mag-pa-lu-ma-gak), *v.* to stay or remain temporarily, as in someone's place or house.

magpaluwál (mag-pa-lu-wál), *v.* to pay for someone's debt or obligation with the understanding that said amount would be repaid later. Syn. *mag-abono*.

magpamalay (mag-pa-ma-lay), *v.* 1. to make someone conscious about something; let (someone) know about something indirectly. 2. to cause someone to become conscious or regain consciousness. See **magpamalay-tao**.

magpamalay-tao (mag-pa-ma-lay + ta-o), *v.* to make one regain consciousness.

magpamata (mag-pa-ma-ta), *v.* to make someone be aware of the facts, real reasons, etc.; open someone's eyes. Syn. *magpaunawà, magpaintindí, magpamulat*.

magpamayá-mayâ (mag-pa-ma-yá + ma-yâ), *v.* to wait for a while.

magpamukhâ (mag-pa-muk-hâ), *v.* 1. to face or cover with a new surface. 2. to tell (something) frankly or face to face to someone

magpamulat (mag-pa-mu-lat), *v.* 1. to open someone's eyes; make one aware of the facts, real reasons, etc. of. Syn.

magpamatá, magpaliwanag, magpaunawà. 2. to make or cause a person to open his eyes.

magpanaón (mag-pa-na-ón), *v.* to agree to meet at a certain place and time. Syn. *magtiyáp.*

magpanapúl (mag-pa-na-púl), *v.* to be both present at the beginning or start of.

magpanata (mag-pa-na-ta), *v.* to have or make a vow.

magpanhík-manaog (mag-pan-hík + ma-na-og), *v.* to go up and down the stairs repeatedly. Syn. *mag-akyát-manaog.*

magpantig (mag-pan-tig), *v.* to divide words into syllables; syllabify; syllabicate; syllabize.

magpanting (mag-pan-ting), *v.* (with *ang tainga*) to get hurt and as a result become red from anger.

magpanutô (mag-pa-nu-tô), *v.* to lead or guide. Syn. *mag-akay.*

magpangita (mag-pa-ngi-ta), *v.* 1. to happen to meet each other. Syn. *magpanagpô, magkátagpô.* 2. to agree to meet or see each other at a certain place. Syn. *magtagpô.*

magpapél (mag-pa-pél), *v.* 1. to use paper. Syn. *gumamit ng papél.* 2. to play the role of a certain character in a play or drama. Syn. *gumanáp.*

magparamdám (mag-pa-ram-dám), *v.* to make a hint. Syn. *magpahiwatig.*

magparanas (mag-pa-ra-nas), var. **magpadanas**, v. to make one feel or experience something. Syn. *magparamá.*

magparang- (mag-pa-rang-), a combining form meaning "to look like" or "act like," as in *magparang-bata*, to look like a child. Cf. *magmukháng-.*

magparayâ (mag-pa-ra-yâ), *v.* to be tolerant of the act, desires, or opinions of another or others; forego something graciously in favor of another or others. Syn. *magbigáy.*

magpárituhán (mag-pá-ri-tu-hán), *v.* to come here all together at the same time. Syn. *magdátingan dito.*

magpariwarà (mag-pa-ri-wa-rà), *v.* to cause misfortune, damage, or injury to. Syn. *magpahamak.*

magpasabi (mag-pa-sa-bi), *v.* to send word to. Syn. *magpabalità.*

magpásakalyé (mag-pá-sa-kal-yé), *v.* to play the introductory music before the actual rendition of the song.

magpasakit (mag-pa-sa-kit), *v.* to do something that would hurt the feeling, esp. of a loved one.

magpasinayà (mag-pa-si-na-yà), *v.* 1. to open or start for the first time. Syn. *magsimulâ, mag-umpisá.* 2. to celebrate the first public use of; inaugurate. Syn. *maginagurá.* 3. to install in office with ceremony. Syn. *magtalagá.*

magpasintabì (mag-pa-sin-ta-bì), *v.* to beg apology for taking exception to someone's opinion or stand. Syn. *humingî ng paumanhín sa pagpapasubalì.*

magpasiyám (mag-pa-si-yám), *v.* to hold a nine-day devotional prayers (novena) in memory of a dead relative or for some religious purpose. Syn. *magpanobena.*

magpasubalì (mag-pa-su-ba-lì), *v.* to take exception; express opinion to. Syn. *tumutol*

magpátagalan (mag-pá-ta-ga-lan), *v.* to hold a contest of endurance; compete with each other in endurance.

magpaulík-ulík (mag-pa-u-lík + u-lík), *v.* to be hesitant. Syn. *magpaurung-sulong; magbantulót, mag-atubilì.*

magpaumaga (mag-pa-u-ma-ga), *v.* to wait until morning comes. Syn. *maghintáy ng umaga.*

magpaumanhín (mag-pa-u-man-hín), *v.* to forgive or excuse someone's fault. Syn. *magpatawad.*

magpawaláng-sala (mag-pa-wa-láng + sa-la), *v.* to declare (a person) not guilty; acquit or exonerate after finding that a person is not guilty. Also, *pawaláng-sala.*

magpawaláng-saysáy (mag-pa-wa-láng + say-sáy), *v.* 1. to annul; make null and void. Syn. *magpawaláng-bisà.* 2. to give no importance to. Syn. *magpawalánghalagá.*

magpawili (mag-pa-wi-li), *v.* to cause someone to have continued interest in.

magpilit (mag-pi-lit), *v.* 1. to try or strive hard to attain something. Syn. *magsikap na mabuti.* 2. to insist; be insistent. Syn. *maggiit.*

magpinsán (mag-pin-sán), *adj. & n.* referring to the relation between two cousins.

magpisan-pisan (mag-pi-san + pi-san), *v.* to live or stay together in the same place. Syn. *magsama-sama.*

magpítagan (mag-pí-ta-gan), var. **magpítaganan**, *v.* to be courteous or respectful; show respect or courtesy. Syn. *maging mapítagan o magalang, gumalang, magbigáy-galang.*

magpugad (mag-pu-gad), *v.* to build a nest. 2. (*Fig.*) to live or hide in or as in a den. Also, *mamugad.*

magpugal (mag-pu-gal), *v.* 1. to tie (an animal) to a post, tree, or the like. Syn. *maggapos.* 2. to cause (someone) to be confined (in the house, hospital, etc.) unnecessarily. Syn. *magtali* (*fig.*).

magpumiglás (mag-pu-mig-lás), *v.* to extricate oneself from the tight hold of someone by force; struggle to free oneself from someone's tight hold.

magpumilit (mag-pu-mi-lit), *v.* to try or strive hard in order to attain one's desire or wish. Syn. *magsikap na mabuti.* 2. to be insistent; insist on or upon. Syn. *maging magiit.*

magpuri (mag-pu-ri), *v.* to worship (God) in words or songs.

magpurihán (mag-pu-ri-hán), *v.* to praise each other or one another.

magsa- (mag-sa-), *pref.* used in the formation of verbs, meaning: 1. to act out the role of, as in *magsadoktor*, to act the role of a doctor: 2. to imitate the act of or be like, as in *magsapusà*, to be like a cat: 3. to act in a certain way or manner, as in *magsawaláng-kibô*, to keep silent or pretend not to know anything: 4. to translate into another language, as in *magsa-Kastilà*, to translate into Spanish.

magsaahas (mag-sa-a-has), *v.* to behave like a snake; be a traitor.

magsaalang-alang (mag-sa-a-lang + a-lang), *v.* to take into account or consideration.

magsabalikat (mag-sa-ba-li-kat), *v.* to undertake; assume the responsibility of doing or performing. Syn. *magsagawâ.*

magsabibig (mag-sa-bi-big), *v.* 1. to say or utter. 2. to put into one's mouth.

magsabulâ (mag-sa-bu-lâ), *v.* (*Fig.*) to come

to naught. Syn. *waláng-mangyari, mabigô, máuwî sa wala.*

magsákit (mag-sá-kit), *v.* to persevere; be steadfast in purpose. Syn. *magtiyagâ.*

magsalin (mag-sa-lin), *v.* 1. to transfer something from one container to another. Syn. *maglipat ng lamán sa ibáng lalagyán.* 2. to transcribe, as shorthand notes. 3. to make a copy of (something) in writing or type-writing. Syn. *kumopya.* 4. to translate, as one language into another. Syn. *maghulog* (*sa ibáng wikà*).

magsalitâ (mag-sa-li-tâ), *v.* 1. to talk or speak; say something. Syn. *umimík.* 2. to say what one knows. Syn. *magsabi ng nálalaman, magtapát, magpahayag.* 3. to deliver a speech; give a talk. Syn. *magtalumpatì.* 4. to give a lecture. Syn. *magpanayám.*

magsaloób (mag-sa-lo-ób), *v.* to entertain (something) in one's mind. Syn. *magsaisip, mag-akalá.*

magsama (mag-sa-ma), *v.* 1. to live together, as husband and wife. Syn. *magpisan.* 2. to bring with or take in company, as an adviser or consultant. Syn. *magdalá.* 3. to include or enclose. Syn. *maglakip, magpaloób.* 4. to go together (to a certain place). Syn. *magsabáy.*

magsamantalá (mag-sa-man-ta-lá), *v.* 1. to take advantage of. 2. to take a chance or chances. Syn. *magsápalarán, makipagsápalarán.*

magsanaw (mag-sa-naw), *v.* to be or become flooded; turn into a pool of water. Syn. *magbahâ.*

magsandugô (mag-san-du-gô), *v.* (*Fig.*) to unite or merge for a common cause, as two political parties. Syn. *magsanib, magkáisá.*

magsangá (mag-sa-ngá), *v.* 1. to have or grow a branch or branches. Syn. *magkasangá, tubuan ng sangá.* 2. to branch out, as a river.

magsangkót (mag-sang-kót), *v.* to implicate or involve. Syn. *magdamay, magdawit.*

magsanggaláng (mag-sang-ga-lang), *v.* 1. to defend or protect oneself. Syn. *magtanggól sa sarili.* 2. to plead for someone's cause.

magsápalarán (mag-sá-pa-la-rán), *v.* to take chances or risk; venture. Also, *makipagsápalarán.* Syn. *mag-alasuwerte.*

magsapanganib (mag-sa-pa-nga-nib), *v.* to put in danger; cause danger to; endanger. Syn. *maglagáy sa panganib.*

magsapól (mag-sa-pól), var. magsapúl, *v.* to start at the very beginning.

magsará (mag-sa-rá), *v.* 1. to close or shut (a window, door, or the like). Syn. *magpiníd.* 2. to close down; stop entirely, as a business establishment. 3. to become closed. Syn. *sumará, puminíd.*

magsarilí (mag-sa-ri-lí), *v.* 1. to live independently, as from one's parents; be free from parental care and support. 2. to have independence, as a nation. Syn. *lumayá, magkasarinlán.*

magsasaká (mag-sa-sa-ká), *n.* farmer; agriculturist. Syn. *magbubukíd, mag-aararó.*

magsaulián (mag-sa-u-li-án), *v.* to return what each other gave.

magsaulo (mag-sa-u-lo), *v.* to commit (something) to memory; memorize. Syn. *magmemorya.*

magsawà (mag-sa-wà), *v.* 1. to be supplied to excess; to satiate; surfeit or be overindulged. 2. to lose interest, as in one's work. Syn. *mawalán ng gana.*

magsayá (mag-sa-yá), *v.* to celebrate; be merry or cheerful; rejoice. Syn. *magdiwáng, matuwâ, magalák.*

magsayáng (mag-sa-yáng), *v.* to be wasteful. Syn. *mag-aksayá.*

magsaysáy (mag-say-sáy), *v.* 1. to declare or explain; relate or tell (what happened). Syn. *magsabi, magsalitâ.* 2. to give a statement. Syn. *magpahayag.*

magselos (mag-se-los), *v.* to be jealous. Syn. *manibughô.*

magsermón (mag-ser-món), *v.* 1. to deliver a sermon; preach. 2. to give someone a long lecture. Syn. *mangaral.*

magsikap (mag-si-kap), *v.* 1. to be diligent or persevering. Syn. *magtiyagâ.* 2. to work hard. Syn. *magsipag.*

magsikíp (mag-si-kíp), *v.* 1. to be or become tight-fitting. Syn. *sumikíp, kumipot.* 2. to become too crowded; be filled to overcapacity. Syn. *mapunó, magsiksikan.*

magsikláb (mag-sik-láb), *v.* 1. to burst into flame; flare up. Syn. *maglagabláb.* 2. to burst into sudden action or feeling. Syn. *sumilakbô.*

magsiksík (mag-sik-sík), *v.* 1. to put into force; press hard into a hole, container, etc. Syn. *magsaksák.* 2. to press oneself into a crowd. Also, *sumiksík, gumitgít.*

magsilang (mag-si-lang), *v.* to give birth, referring to a woman. Syn. *manganák, mag-anák.*

magsilbi (mag-sil-bi), *v.* 1. to serve. Syn. *maglingkód.* 2. to be of use as. Syn. *magamit.*

magsilong (mag-si-long), *v.* 1. to take (something) to the shelter so as to protect from the heat of the sun or from rain or storm. 2. to take shelter, as during a rain. Syn. *sumilong.*

magsimbá (mag-sim-bá), *v.* to attend or hear Mass. Also, *sumimbá.*

magsimót (mag-si-mót), *v.* to get all that were left; leave nothing of what were left. Syn. *magsaíd.*

magsimpán (mag-sim-pán), *v.* 1. to save (money) for the future. Syn. *mag-impók.* 2. to economize; practise thrift. Syn. *magtipíd.* 3. to harbor or hold in mind, as a grudge. Syn. *magtaním sa isip (fig.).*

magsimulâ (mag-si-mu-lá), *v.* to start; begin; commence. Syn. *mag-umpisá.*

magsinop (mag-si-nop), *v.* 1. to save for the future. Syn. *mag-impók, magsimpán.* 2. to practise thrift. Syn. *magtipíd.*

magsinungalín (mag-si-nu-nga-lín), var. magsinungalíng, *v.* 1. to tell a lie or falsehood. Syn. *magbulaán.* 2. to deny what one knows. Syn. *magkailâ, maglihim.*

magsingkahulugán (mag-ka-sing-ka-hu-lu-gán), *adj.* of or having the same meaning. Syn. *magkakahulugán.*

magsipag (mag-si-pag), *v.* to work hard or diligently; be industrious. Cf. *magsikap, magtrabahong mabuti.*

magsiping (mag-si-ping), *v.* 1. to sit, lie, or sleep together side by side. Syn. *magtabí, magsibáy.* 2. to have or get someone to lie, sit, or sleep beside oneself.

magsipsíp (mag-sip-síp), *v.* (Slang) to bring oneself into someone's favor; ingratiate. Syn. *magmapurí, magmagalíng.*

magsiraán (mag-si-ra-án), v. to defame or attack each other's reputation. Also, *magsiraáng-puri.*

magsisi (mag-si-si), v. to repent; feel or express regret over some past deeds.

magsisihán (mag-si-si-hán), v. to blame each other or one another.

magsiwalat (mag-si-wa-lat), v. to reveal or disclose, as a secret. Syn. *magbunyág, maglantád.*

magsiyasat (mag-si-ya-sat), v. to conduct an investigation or an inquiry; investigate. Syn. *mag-imbestigá.*

magsukáb (mag-su-ks), v. to be a traitor. Syn. *magtaksíl, maglilo.*

magsukal (mag-su-kal), v. to scatter weeds, rubbish, etc. around. Syn. *magkalat ng damó o basura.*

magsukatán (mag-su-ka-tán), v. 1. to use a pattern of measurement. Syn. *gumamit ng padróng sukatán.* 2. to try to outdo each other in strength. Syn. *magsubukán (ng lakás).*

magsuklób (mag-suk-lób), v. 1. to put on something as a cover, e.g. a hat on one's head. 2. (in gambling) to share with each other in a capital investment, as two bankers. Syn. *magsosyo, magbakas.*

magsukob (mag-su-kob), n. 1. to share together in a blanket, umbrella, etc. 2. to have or allow someone to share with oneself in a cover or shelter.

magsudlóng (mag-sud-lóng), v. to add something to increase length. Syn. *magdugtóng, maghugpóng.*

magsuga (mag-su-ga), v. to graze or feed livestock on growing grass by fastening with a rope or tether.

magsugapà (mag-su-ga-pà), v. to be or become an addict.

magsuhay (mag-su-hay), v. to support or hold up in place with or as with a prop, e.g. a house, to prevent it from failing or leaning to a side. Cf. *magtukod.*

magsulát (mag-su-lát), v. 1. to be busy writing many things. 2. to take writing as a profession; be a writer.

magsulit (mag-su-lit), v. 1. to make a report about something. Syn. *mag-ulat.* 2. to submit something to someone. Syn. *magharáp.* 3. to give a test or examination.

Syn. *mag-iksamin, magbigáy ng iksamin o pagsusulit.*

magtaká (mag-ta-ká), v. to be astonished or surprised; wonder. Syn. *mágulat, manggilalas, mámanghâ.*

magtákapan (mag-tá-ka-pan), v. to bawl at each other angrily. Syn. *mágsígawan, maghíyawan, magmurahán nang malakás.*

magtakdâ (mag-tak-dâ), v. 1. to limit; set a limit. Syn. *magtasa, maglimití.* 2. to put as a provision (in a law or ordinance). Syn. *magtadhanâ, maglagdâ.*

magtákipan (mag-tá-ki-pan), v. to help each other by covering up each other's secret, mistake, or misdeed.

magtaksíl (mag-tak-síl), v. 1. to be a traitor to someone. Syn. *maglilo, magsukáb, magtraidór.* 2. to be unfaithful to one's wife or husband. Syn. *maglilo.*

magtakwíl (mag-tak-wíl), v. to disown; repudiate; cast off. Syn. *magtatwâ.*

magtadhanâ (mag-tad-ha-nâ), v. 1. to destine, as by fate. Syn. *magtalagá.* 2. to put or include as a provision (in an agreement or contract). Syn. *magtakdâ, maglagdâ.*

magtagál (mag-ta-gál), v. 1. to take a long time. 2. to last a long time. 3. to be delayed a long time. Syn. *maatraso nang matagál.*

magtagís (mag-ta-gís), v. 1. to hone; sharpen on a hone. Syn. *maglagis.* 2. to fight each other. Syn. *maglaban, magtunggalî, magsukatán ng lakás.*

magtagláy (mag-tag-láy), v. 1. to bring or carry along with oneself. Syn. *magdalá.* 2. to possess or own. Syn. *mag-arì, magmay-arì, mag-angkín.* 2. to contain. Syn. *maglamán.*

magtagò (mag-ta-gò), v. 1. to hide (oneself). Syn. *magkublí.* 2. to hide or keep something secret. Syn. *maglihim, maglingíd.* 3. to save or put aside for the future. Syn. *magtirá para sa kinabukasan.* 4. to put away and return to the proper place. Syn. *magligpit.*

magtagós (mag-ta-gós), v. to penetrate through and through. Syn. *maglagós.*

magtagpó (mag-tag-pó), v. 1. to meet each other or together, at a certain time and place. Syn. *magkita.* 2. to have or keep a tryst. Syn. *magtipán*. 3. to meet at a certain point, as two lines. Syn. *magsalikop*. 4. to meet or confront each other. Syn. *magharáp*.

magtagubilin (mag-ta-gu-bi-lin), *v*. 1. to make a recommendation; recommend. Syn. *magrekomenda*. 2. to give advice or counsel. Syn. *magpayo*. 3. to give instruction on what to do about something. Syn. *mag-utos*.

magtagumpáy (mag-ta-gum-páy), *v*. 1. to win; be victorious. Syn. *manalo, magwagí*. 2. to be successful. Syn. *magkapalad*.

magtaguyod (mag-ta-gu-yod), *v*. 1. to support or patronize. Syn. *tumangkilik*. 2. to promote or develop. Syn. *magpaunlad*. 3. to propagate or spread. Syn. *magpalaganap*.

magtálakan (mag-tá-la-kan), *v*. to shout loudly and continuously at each other. Syn. *magsígawan, maghíyawan*.

magtálakayán (mag-tá-la-ka-yán), *v*. to have objective discussion on a certain subject, referring to a number of persons; exchange views with one another. Syn. *magpálitang-kuró*.

magtalagá (mag-ta-la-gá), *v*. 1. to assign something for a certain purpose. Syn. *maglaán*. 2. to induct or install, as an elected or appointed official, or officers of an organization. Syn. *magpasumpâ sa tungkulin*. 3. to assign a person to a certain place or position. Syn. *maglagáy sa tungkulin*.

magtálastasan (mag-tá-las-ta-san), *v*. 1. to have an understanding with each other. Syn. *mag-únawaan, mag-intindihan*. 2. to communicate with each other. Syn. *magbálitaán*.

magtalik (mag-ta-lik), *v*. to have an intimate talk with each other.

magtalo (mag-ta-lo), *v*. 1. to argue or debate with each other. Syn. *magdiskusyón, magdebate, magpáliwanagán*. 2. (*Colloq.*, usually with *ang kalooban*) to be undecided; be hesitant. Syn. *mag-alinlangan, mag-urung-sulong, mag-atubili*.

magtalusirà (mag-ta-lu-si-rà), *v*. to break one's promise. Syn. *sumirà sa pangako*.

magtamà (mag-ta-mà), *v*. 1. to set or make

right; correct. Syn. *magwastô, magtumpák*. 2. to cause something to fit another. Syn. *maglapat*. 3. to insert or fit, as into a hole. Syn. *magpasok*. 4. to happen to be compatible to each other. Syn. *magkáwastô, magkasundô*.

magtamasa (mag-ta-ma-sa), *v*. to enjoy the abundance, health, happiness, etc. of. Cf. *matamó, magtamán*.

magtamó (mag-ta-mó), *v*. to obtain or acquire; receive, as a reward or prize. Syn. *magkamít, tumanggáp*.

magtanan (mag-ta-nan), *v*. 1. to run away; escape. Syn. *tumakas, lumayas*. 2. to elope, referring to lovers.

magtánawan (mag-tá-wa-nan), *v*. 1. to look at each other from a distance. 2. to look together at a distance, referring to a number of persons. Syn. *magtínginan sa malayò*.

magtandâ (mag-tan-dâ), *v*. 1. to mark; put a mark or sign on. Syn. *maglagáy ng tandâ o marka*. 2. to bear in mind; remember. Syn. *magsaisip*. 3. to learn a lesson. Syn. *matuto*.

magtaním (mag-ta-ním), *v*. 1. to plant; raise crops. 2. (*Fig.*) to harbor or entertain in one's mind. Syn. *magkimkím, magtagláy*.

magtaning (mag-ta-ning), *v*. 1. to fix the date or time, as to when an occasion is to happen or take place. 2. to make a provision or provisions, as in a contract. Syn. *magtakdâ, magtadhanâ*.

magtantán (mag-tan-tán), *v*. to stop; put an end to. Syn. *magtahán, magtigil, maghintô*.

magtánungan (mag-tá-nu-ngan), *v*. 1. to ask questions at the same time, referring to a number of persons. 2. to exchange questions with each other; ask questions to one another.

magtangá-tangahan (mag-ta-ngá + ta-nga-han), *v*. 1. to pretend stupidity. Syn. *maghangál-hangalan*. 2. to pretend ignorance about something. Syn. *magmaáng-maangan*.

magtanggól (mag-tang-gól), *v*. 1. to defend oneself. Syn. *magsanggaláng*. 2. to protect someone, as from harm. Syn. *mangalagà*. 3. to appear in behalf of an accused in court; be the lawyer of. Syn. *maging* *mánananggól o abogado ng o ni.*

magtanghál (mag-tang-hál), *v.* 1. to exhibit; have an exhibition of. 2. to exalt; extoll. Syn. *magpapuri.*

magtangì (mag-ta-ngì), *v.* to consider or regard (someone) with special favor or consideration.

magtaób (mag-ta-ób), *v.* 1. to cause (something) to be inverted or turned upside down, as a plate, cup, drinking glass, etc. 2. (*Fig.*) to defeat or subdue, referring esp. to a champion. Syn. *matalo.* 3. (in gambling) to make bankrupt, referring to a banker. Syn. *magtumbá, magbagsák.*

magtaón (mag-ta-ón), *v.* 1. to make something coincide with another. Syn. *magsabay.* 2. to make an appointment with each other.

magtapáng-tapangan (mag-ta-páng + ta-pa-ngan), *v.* to try to be brave; pretend to be brave. Syn. *magkunwáng matapang.*

magtapát (mag-ta-pát), *v.* 1. to tell the truth; be frank. Syn. *magsabi ng totoó (katotohanan).* 2. confess one's guilt. Syn. *umamin (ng kasalanan).* 3. to pass through the direct way in going to a certain place; take the direct route. Syn. *dumaán o magdaán sa túwirang landás.* 4. to express openly with sincerity, as one's love. Syn. *magpahayag.* 5. to give the equivalent, as of a word. 6. to put or place something directly opposite, above or under another. Syn. *maglagáy sa tapát.*

magtapós (mag-ta-pós), *v.* 1. to complete; bring to an end; conclude. Syn. *magwakás.* 2. to graduate or be graduated from school or college.

magtatag (mag-ta-tag), *v.* to organize; establish; found. Syn. *magtayô, magbuô, magpundár, mag-órganisá.*

magtatalák (mag-ta-ta-lák), *v.* to shout angrily and continuously. Syn. *maghihiyáw, magsisigáw.*

magtatwâ (mag-tat-wâ), *v.* 1. to disown; disclaim. Syn. *magtakwíl.* 2. to deny; refuse to tell. Syn. *magkailâ, maglihim.*

magtawá (mag-ta-wá), *v.* to laugh continuously or repeatedly.

magtawagán (mag-ta-wa-gán), *v.* 1. to call

each other, as by telephone. 2. to call each other by such term or name which they are both familiar with.

magtawíd-dagat (mag-ta-wíd + da-gat), *v.* to go abroad; make a trip across the sea. Cf. *mangibáng-bayan.*

magtawíd-gutom (mag-ta-wíd + gu-tom), *v.* to save from hunger; keep supplied with bare necessities for existence. Syn. *mag-agdóng-buhay.*

magtayô (mag-ta-yô), *v.* to build; construct; erect; set up. Syn. *magtirik, gumawâ.* 2. to establish; organize; found. Syn. *magtatag, magpundár, magbuó.*

magtika (mag-ti-ka), *v.* to resolve to do or not to do; make a firm determination.

magtíkisan (mag-tí-ki-san), *v.* to stand pat against each other. Syn. *magmátigasan.*

magtigil (mag-ti-gil), *v.* to stop; cease. Syn. *maghintô, maghumpáy, maglikát.*

magtiím (mag-ti-ím), *v.* to press tightly, esp. one's lips or teeth. Syn. *mag-iting.*

magtiís (mag-ti-ís), *v.* to bear, endure, or suffer. Syn. *mag-agwanta, magbatá.* 2. to persevere; be steadfast in one's purpose. Syn. *magtiyagâ.*

magtimpî (mag-tim-pî), *v.* 1. to hold or control one's temper. Syn. *magpigil.* 2. to refrain from doing.

magtimplá (mag-tim-plá), *v.* 1 to fill a doctor's prescription by mixing together the required or needed ingredients. 2. to add a certain flavor to food to make it more appetizing. 3. to prepare or make, as coffee, by adding sugar and milk in the right proportion. 4. to mix colors, paints, etc. to a proper proportion.

magtindíg (mag-tin-díg), *v.* 1 to erect; build; construct. Syn. *magtayô, maggawâ, magtirik.* 2 to establish; found. Syn. *magtatag.* 3. to stand up. Also, *tumindíg.*

magtinggál (mag-ting-gál) *v.* to store up (goods). Syn. *mag-imbák.*

magtínginan (mag-tí-ngi-nan), *v.* 1. to look at each other. 2. look at something at the same time. Syn. *magtánawan.* 3. (*Fig.*) to look after each other's welfare. Syn. *magmálasakitán.*

magtipán (mag-ti-pán), *v.* to have a date or an appointment with each other. 2. to agree to meet each other at a certain time and place. Syn. *magtiyáp*.

magtirá (mag-ti-rá), *v*. to set aside for later use. Syn. *magbukód, magtagò, magtabí*. 2 to leave something undone or unfinished. Syn. *mag-iwan*. 3 to live or reside in. Syn. *tumirá, tumahán*.

magtirik (mag-ti-rik), *v*. 1. to construct; build; erect, Syn. *magtayô, gumawâ, magtindíg*. 2. to set upright, as a post, candle, or the like. 3. (*Colloq.*) to light, as a candle. Syn. *magsindi*.

magtitigán (mag-ti-ti-gán), *v*. to stare at each other. Syn. *magdilatán*.

magtiwalâ (mag-ti-wa-lâ), *v*. 1. to have trust or confidence in someone. Syn. *magkumpiyansa*. 2. to leave something in trust or in the care of someone temporarily. Syn. *maghabilin*. 3. to be confident about. Syn. *manalig, umasa*.

magtiwalág (mag-ti-wa-lág), *v*. to dismiss or cause one to be dismissed (from work). Syn. *magsisante*.

magtiyá (mag-ti-yá), *adj. & n*. referring to an aunt and her niece or nephew. Cf. *magtiyó*.

magtiyakan (mag-ti-ya-kan), *v*. to have assurance from each other; assure each other. Syn. *magsiguruhán*.

magtiyagâ (mag-ti-ya-gâ), *v*. to be diligent or persevering and careful in one's work, etc.; be painstaking. Syn. *magsikap, magtiís, magsipag*.

magtiyáp (mag-ti-yáp), *v*. to agree to meet or do something at a certain time and place. Syn. *magtipán*.

magtiyó (mag-ti-yó), *adj. & n*. referring to an uncle and his niece or nephew. Cf. *magtiyá*.

magtotohanan (mag-to-to-ha-nan), *v*. 1. to be serious or frank to each other. 2. to play against each other seriously. Syn. *maglaban nang totohanan*.

magtotoó (mag-to-to-ó), *v*. to be true to one's word; make true one's promise; be sincere. Syn. *magmatapát*.

magtubal (mag-tu-bal), *v*. to be or become dirty, referring to someone's clothes. Syn. *maging marumí*.

magtukakî (mag-tu-ka-kî), *v*. to feel very

sleepy. Syn. *mag-antok*.

magtugmâ (mag-tug-mâ), *v*. 1. to make (a word) rhyme with. 2. to become compatible with another. Syn. *magkásundô*. 3. to be or become correct. Syn. *máwastô, tumamá*.

magtúlaan (mag-tú-la-an), *v*. to have poetry declamation. Syn. *magbígkasan ng tulâ*.

magtúligsaan (mag-tú-lig-sa-an), *v*. to criticize or attack each other publicly. Syn. *mag-átakihán, magmurahán*.

magtulóy (mag-tu-lóy), *v*. to go on; continue; proceed.

magtulungán (mag-tu-lu-ngán), *v*. to help each other or one another.

magtumbalík (mag-tum-ba-lík), *v*. to overturn; fall upside down. Syn. *magtuwaník*.

magtumpák (mag-tum-pák), *v*. to correct; put in order; set right. Syn. *magtugmâ, magwastô*.

magtumulin (mag-tu-mu-lin), *v*. to walk or run very fast. Syn. *lumakad o tumakbó nang matulin*.

magtungo (mag-tu-ngo), *v*. to go to someone or to a certain place. Syn. *magpuntá, pumuntá*.

magtuós (mag-tu-ós), *v*. 1. to make an accounting of. 2. to settle matters or disputes with each other.

magturing (mag-tu-ring), *v*. 1. to give as a price for. Syn. *maghalagá, magpresyo*. 2. to consider (someone or something) as. Syn. *magpalagáy*. 3. to give one's answer, esp. to a riddle. Syn. *sumagót*.

magturò (mag-tu-rò), *v*. 1. to teach; be a teacher; work as a teacher. Syn. *maggurò, magtitser*. 2. to point something to someone; show the direction of by pointing with the hand. 3. to teach how something is to be done.

magtuwáng (mag-tu-wáng), *v*. 1 to be partners, as in a dance. Syn. *magpareha*. 2. to help each other in carrying a load with the hands or with a pole. Syn. *mag-usong*. 3. to act as co-sponsors in a wedding, baptism, or confirmation.

magtuwíd (mag-tu-wíd), *v*. 1. to make straight; straighten. 2. to correct; make or set right; put in order. Syn. *magtumpák, magtugmâ, magwastô*.

mag-ukol (mag + u-kol), *v.* 1. to set aside something for; intend something for. Syn. *magtalagá.* 2. to devote; give one's time, energy, etc. to some purpose, activity, or person.

mag-ugát (mag- + u-gát), *v.* 1. to take roots; begin to grow roots. Syn. *tubuan ng ugát, magkaugát.* 2. (Fig.) to start or begin from. Syn. *magsimulâ, mag-umpisá.*

magugol (ma-gu-gol), *adj.* costly or expensive to maintain or make. Syn. *magastós.*

magulang (ma-gu-lang), I. *n.* parent; one's father or mother.
—II. *adj.* 1. mature (s.o. fruits). Syn. *mahihinóg na.* 2. old or mature, as a person. Syn. *may-edád na.* 3. (Fig.) showing a crafty or wily nature, referring to a person. Syn. *mapágsamantalá sa kapwà.*

mágulat (má-gu-lat), *v.* 1. to be surprised. Syn. *magtaká, mamanghâ.* 2. to be scared or frightened. Syn. *matakot, masindák.*

magulay (ma-gu-lay), *adj.* with or having plenty of vegetables; well-supplied with vegetables.

mag-ulî (mag + u-lî), *v.* 1. to return or give back something taken or borrowed. Syn. *magsaulî.* 2. to be back to the former state or condition. Syn. *manag-ulî, mabalík sa dati.*

mag-ulián (mag + u-li-án), *v.* 1 to return or give back what was given by each other. Syn. *magsáulián.* 2. to dote; be forgetful or weakminded because of old age.

maguló (ma-gu-ló), I. *adj.* 1. in a disorderly state or condition; in a mess. Syn. *walâ sa ayos, waláng kaayusan, halú-halò.* 2. causing trouble; troublesome, referring to persons. Syn. *maligalig, mapanligalig.*
—II. *v.* 1. to be in a disorderly state or condition; be in disorder. 2. to become distressed or worried, as one's mind. Syn. *mataranta, maligalig.*

magulumihanan (ma-gu-lu-mi-ha-nan), *v.* to be baffled or bewildered by something seen. Syn. *masindakanan.*

mágulungan (má-gu-lu-ngan), *v.* to be run over, as by a vehicle, Cf. *másagasaan.*

mag-umaga (mag + u-ma-ga), *v.* to be morning. Syn. *maging umaga, sumapit ang umaga.*

mágumon (má-gu-mon), *v.* to be or become addicted to (vice, etc.). Syn. *mábuyó.*

mag-unahán (mag + u-na-hán), *v.* to try to get ahead of each other.

mágunámgunam (má-gu-nám-gu-nam), *v.* to seem to realize something that pleases one's mind. Cf. *máguniguní.*

magunaw (ma-gu-naw), *v.* to come to an end, referring to the world.

mag-únawaán (mag + ú-na-wa-án), *v.* to try to come to an understanding, as by conferring with each other. Syn. *mag-intindihan.*

máguniguní (ma-gu-ni-gu-ní), *adj.* imaginative; full of imagination. Cf. *mapángarapin.*

mágunitâ (má-gu-ni-tâ), *v.* to happen to remember or recall to one's mind. Syn. *máalaala.*

mágupiling (má-gu-pi-ling), *v.* to fall asleep lightly. Syn. *maidlíp, máhipíg.*

mag-úsapan (mag + ú-sa-pan), *v.* to talk together lengthily.

magusót (ma-gu-sót), I. *v.* 1. to be crumpled or wrinkled, as newly ironed clothes. Syn. *malukot.* 2. to become entangled, as thread. Syn. *magkásalá-salabíd.* 3. to be able to crumple with one's hand or hands. Syn. *malukot, mayukos.*
—II. *adj.* intricate; disorderly; entangled. Syn. *masalimuót, maguló.*

mágustuhán (má-gus-tu-hán), *v.* to happen to like; have or develop a liking for. Syn. *maibigan.*

mag-utáy-utáy (ma-u-táy + u-táy), *v.* to move, act, or do something little by little. Syn. *mag-atay-atay, mag-untí-untî.*

mag-uwián (mag + u-wi-án), *v.* to go home together at the same time, as workers after their dismissal.

magwakás (mag-wa-kás), *v.* 1. to end or finish what is being done. 2. to come to an end. Syn. *magtapós, matapós.*

magwagí (mag-wa-gí), *v.* 1. to win; triumph; be victorious. Syn. *manalo.* 2. to be successful. Syn. *magtagumpáy.*

magwaláng-anumán (mag-wa-láng + a-nu-mán), *v.* to be unconcerned or unmindful of. Syn. *magwaláng-bahalà.*

magwaláng-bahalà (mag-wa-láng + ba-ha-là), v. 1. to be irresponsible or indifferent. 2. to pay no heed or attention to. Syn. *magwaláng-asikaso*.

magwaláng-kibô (mag-wa-láng + kibô), v. to remain silent; pretend to know nothing about by keeping silent. Syn. *manahimik*.

magwalat (mag-wa-lat), v. 1. to cause destruction, esp. to houses, crops, properties, etc. Syn. *magwasák*. 2. to misappropriate, as one's family resources. Syn. *magwaldás, maglustáy*.

magwari-warì (mag-wa-ri + wa-rì), v. to think about deeply or seriously before acting or deciding. Syn. *mag-isip-isip, magnilay-nilay, magmuni-muni*.

magwastô (mag-was-tô), v. to correct; put in order; make right. Syn. *magtumpák, magsaayos, magtamà*.

magwikà (mag-wi-kà), v. 1. to say or tell something to someone. Syn. *magsabi*. 2. to rebuke; express disapproval of; reprove. Syn. *magalit, magsalitâ*.

magyabáng (mag-ya-báng), v. 1 to be boastful or arrogant. Syn. *maghambóg*. 2. to tell lies or falsehood. Syn. *magsinungaling, magkailâ*.

magyakág (mag-ya-kág), v. to invite (others) vocally to go to a certain place. Syn. *magyayâ*.

magyayâ (mag-ya-yâ), v. to invite (persons) to go somewhere or to do something. Syn *magyakág*.

mahabà (ma-ha-bà), adj. 1. long in measurement; measuring much from end to end. 2. long in distance. Syn. *malayô*. 3. long time. Syn. *matagál, maluwát, malaon*.

máhabaán (má-ha-ba-án), adj. 1. of long distance. Syn. *málayuán*. 2. of great duration. Syn. *mátagalan, málaunán, máluwatán*.

mahábagin (ma-há-ba-gin), adj. compassionate; easily aroused to pity; merciful. Syn. *maawaín*.

mahabá-habâ (ma-ha-bá + ha-bâ), adj. a little longer. Syn. *medyo mahabà; mahaba nang bahagyà*.

mahablangka (ma-ha-blang-ka), var. mahablangko, n. a kind of rice or corn pudding.

mahabol (ma-ha-bol), v. 1 to be able to pursue or run after, 2. to be able to appeal (a case) to a higher court. Syn. *maiapelá*.

mahakà (ma-ha-kà), v. to be able to comprehend or get the idea of. Syn. *maisip, mawarì*.

mahadlangán (ma-had-la-ngán), v. to be able to prevent, avoid, or intercept. Syn. *mapigil, maharang, masansalà*.

mahagap (ma-ha-gap), v. to be able to understand or get an idea or notion about. Syn. *máunawaan*.

máhagilap (má-ha-gi-lap), v. to happen to get hold of at the moment of need. Syn. *máapuhap*.

mahagíp (ma-ha-gíp), v. 1. to be able to get hold or catch quickly while moving fast. 2. to be sideswept, as by a fast running vehicle. Cf. *mádagil, másagì*.

mahagwáy (ma-hag-wáy), adj. somewhat tall in stature. Syn. *medyo mataás o matangkád*.

mahahabà (ma-ha-ha-bà), adj. long, referring to a number of things. Ant. *maiiklî*.

mahál (ma-hál), I. adj. 1. dear; costly; expensive. Syn. *mataás ang presyo o halagá*. 2. much loved; beloved; dear. Syn. *minámahál, inúibig, ginígiliw*. 3. much valued; well-esteemed; very important to someone. Syn. *mahalagá, importante*. 4. noble; important, referring to a person. Syn. *dakilà, marangál*.
—II. n. (used as a term of affection) Dear. Syn. *sinta, irog, giliw, mutyâ*.

mahalagá (ma-ha-la-gá), adj. 1. valuable; important. Syn. *importante*. 2. costly; expensive. Syn. *mahál, mamáhalin*.

mahalagahín (ma-ha-la-ga-hín), v. 1. to think highly of; prize or esteem. 2. to consider important or valuable.

mahalaman (ma-ha-la-man), adj. with or having many plants.

mahalán (ma-ha-lán), v. to set a high price for; sell at a high price. Syn. *taasán ang halagá, ipagbili nang mahál*.

máhalan (má-ha-lan), n. mutual love; love for each other; act of loving each other. Also, *pagmamáhalan*.

máhalatâ (má-ha-la-tâ), v. to be or happen to be noticed or found out, as from one's words of action. Syn. *mápuná, mápansín*.

mahalay (ma-ha-lay), I. adj. indecent; obscene; lewd. Syn. bastós, masagwâ.
—II. v. to be able to violate the purity of; be able to rape. Syn. magahasà.

máhalili (má-ha-li-li), v. to happen to assume or take the position formerly held by someone. Syn. mápalít, mákapalít.

mahalimbawà (ma-ha-lim-ba-wà). adj. full of examples; with or having many examples.

mahalimuyak (ma-ha-li-mu-yak), adj. fragrant; giving off fragrance. Syn. mabangó.

mahalín (ma-ha-lín), v. to love or hold dear to one's heart.

mahalina (ma-ha-li-na), v. to be fascinated or attracted, as by someone's beauty. Syn. mabighanì, mabalanì, maakit. 2. to be convinced. Syn. mahikayat, maganyák.

máhalintulad (má-ha-lin-tu-lad), v. to happen to have or meet the same fate as someone. Also, matulad, mákatulad.

mahaling (ma-ha-ling), v. to be passionately fond of something; be mad about something; be obsessed with. Syn. mahibáng, mahumaling.

mahalumigmig (ma-ha-lu-mig-mig), adj. 1. humid, as air. Syn. úmidó, maúmidó. 2. damp; moist. Syn. basá-basâ, malagihay.

mahambál (ma-ham-bál), v. to feel deep sorrow or pity for; be very sad about. Syn. mahabág, maawà, magdaláng habag o awà.

mahamóg (ma-ha-móg), adj. wet or damp with dew; dewey. Syn. masereno.

mahanap (ma-ha-nap), v. to be able to find.

mahandugán (ma-han-du-gán), v. 1. to be able to give or offer (someone) a gift or present. Syn. maregaluhan. 2. to be able to dedicate (a poem, song, etc.) to. Syn. maalayan, mapatungkulán.

máhandusáy (má-han-du-sáy), v. to be fallen flat or prostrate on the floor or ground. Syn. mátimbuwáng, mábulagtâ.

máhantád (má-han-tád), v. to be known to many, as a secret. Syn. mábunyág, máhayág. 2. to be exposed to view. Syn. málantád.

mahangháng (ma-hang-háng), var. maangháng, adj. pungent to the taste; peppery.

mahangin (ma-ha-ngin), adj. 1. windy. 2. (Fig.) boastful; given to bragging. Syn. hambóg.

mahanginan (ma-ha-ngi-nan), v. to be exposed to the wind. Syn. málantád sa hangin.

mahangò (ma-ha-ngò), v. 1 to be able to remove from the stove or fire, referring to something being cooked. Syn. maahon, maalis sa apóy. 2. to be able to redeem, as from sufferings, hardships, or difficulties. Syn. matubós.

mahapdî (ma-hap-dî), adj. sharp and piercing, referring to pain in the eyes, wounds, etc. Syn. makirót, maanták.

mahapis (ma-ha-pis), v. to feel despondent or dejected. Syn. malumbáy, mamighatî, malungkót.

mahapò (ma-ha-pò), v. 1. to get very tired or exhausted. Syn. mapagod na mabuti. 2. to be short-winded; to be breathing with quick, labored breaths; pant with difficulty. Syn. humingal, maghaból ng hiningá.

maharang (ma-ha-rang), v. to be able to block or prevent the passage of. Syn. mahadlangán.

máharáp (má-ha-ráp), v. to be able to attend to, as a work. Syn. máasikaso.

maharlikà (ma-har-li-kà; -ka), I. adj. of noble birth; aristocratic; noble. Syn. mahál, dakilà, marangál, mabunyî.
—II. n. nobleman; peer. Syn. mahál na tao.

maharós (ma-ha-rós), adj. overactive, said esp. of a child. Syn. makarós, maharót, malikót.

maharót (ma-ha-rót), adj. overactive; recklessly impetuous. Syn. makarós, maharós, malikót.

mahasà (ma-ha-sà), v. to be well-trained; gain much experience. Syn. masanay, mabihasa.

máhatulan (má-ha-tu-lan), v. to be given a sentence by a judge. Syn. másentensiyahán.

mahawa (ma-ha-wa), adj. full of stain. Syn. mamantsa, malalin.

mahawakan (ma-ha-wa-kan), v. 1. to be able to hold with one's hand. Syn. matanganán, matabanan. 2. to be able to hold or occupy, as an office or position.

mahawás (ma-ha-wás), *adj*. 1. slender or slim (s.o. a person's body). Syn. *mahagwáy, balingkinitan, patpatin*. 2. somewhat oval or elongated (s.o. face). Syn. *taluhabâ, medyo-habâ*.

mahayap (ma-ha-yap). *adj*. 1. keen; sharp. Syn. *matalas, matalím*. 2. harsh; severe; biting, as a language, criticism; etc. Syn. *masakít, nakasásakit*.

mahibáng (ma-hi-báng), *v*. 1. to be delirious or out of one's senses due to high fever. Syn. *magmangmáng*. 2. to be mad about; be crazy about. Syn. *mahaling*.

mahibuan (ma-hi-bu-an), *v*. to be able to seduce or tempt someone to do something undesirable. Syn. *masulsulán, maudyukán*.

mahiká (ma-hi-ká). *n*. (Hispanized) magic. Syn. *madyik*.

mahikayat (ma-hi-ka-yat), *v*. 1. to be able to persuade or convince. Syn. *mahimok maamuki*. 2. to be or become persuaded or convinced.

mahigingan (ma-hi-gi-ngan), *v*. to hear or to be heard vaguely. Syn. *máulinigan*.

mahigít (ma-hi-gít), I. *adv*. over; more than; in excess of. Syn. *sobra sa, labis sa*.
—II. *v*. 1. to be able to pull or draw tight. Syn. *mahila, mabatak, mabanat*. 2. to become pulled or drawn tight.

mahigpít (ma-hig-pít), *adj*. 1. strict; punctilious. Syn. *istrikto*. 2. tight, as a knot, tie, fitting, etc. Syn. *hapít, higkót, maigtíng*. 3. tight-fitting. Syn. *makipot, masikíp*. 4. stiff, as a contest or game.

máhigpitan (má-hig-pi-tan), *adj*. 1. urgent or pressing, as need. 2. close or very close, as a competition or contest.

mahilig (ma-hi-lig), *adj*. with or having an inclination or propensity to something; fond of. Syn. *maapisyón, magústuhin*.

mahiligín (ma-hi-li-gín), *adj*. fond of; inclined towards. Syn. *magustuhin, maibigín, matuwaín*.

mahimalâ (ma-hi-ma-lâ), *adj*. miraculous; mysterious. Syn. *mahiwagà*.

mahimasmasán (ma-hi-mas-ma-sán), *v*. to regain consciousness from a fainting spell. Syn. *matauhan, magkamalay-tao*.

mahimbíng (ma-him-bíng), *adj*. 1. deep or sound (as a sleep). Syn. *malalim (colloq.)*. 2. sleeping soundly, referring to a person. Syn. *tulóg na tulóg*.

máhimbíng (má-him-bíng) *v*. to fall asleep soundly. Syn. *makatulóg nang mahimbíng*.

máhimigan (má-hi-mi-gan), *v*. to happen to get a vague idea of something from what is heard from someone. Syn. *máhigingan, mahìwatigan*.

máhimláy (má-him-láy), *v*. to fall asleep lightly for a short time. Syn. *máidlíp, máhipíg*.

mahimok (ma-hi-mok), *v*. 1. to be able to induce or persuade. Syn. *mahikayat, maamukî*. 2. to be induced or persuaded.

mahinà (ma-hi-nà), *adj*. 1. weak; sickly; feeble. Syn. *malambót ang katawán, lúlugú-lugó*. 2. incapable of hard work. Syn. *waláng-kaya*. 3. slow; not fast, as a run. Syn. *marahan, mabagal*. 4. of little amount; small; meager, as one's income. Syn. *maliít, kákaunti*. 5. soft; weak; not loud, as one's voice. Cf. *mababà*. 6. poor; inferior, as certain kinds of goods. Syn. *mababang-urì, mababang-klase*. 7. dull or slow, as sales. Syn. *matumal, di-mabilí*. 8. not heavy; light, as rain. Syn. *di-malakás*. 9. not very effective. Syn. *di-mabisà*. 10. weak; not strong, as coffee. Syn. *matabáng*. 11. not fertile, as soil. Syn. *payát*. 12. not vigorous; not healthy, as plants. Syn. *payát, bansót*. 13. poor or dull, as a student. Syn. *mapuról (ang ulo)*.

mahinahon (ma-hi-na-hon), I. *adj*. calm, as in one's speech, action, or conduct.
—II. *adv*. in a calm manner; calmly.

mahinalà (ma-hi-na-là), *adj*. full of suspicions; suspicious. Also, *mapaghinalà*.

mahinay (ma-hi-nay), I. *adj*. slow and calm, as in the manner of speaking. Syn. *marahan, mahinahon, banayad*.
—II. *adv*. in a slow or calm manner.

mahinhín (ma-hin-hín), *adj*. modest; decent in one's act or behavior, referring esp. to a woman. Syn. *mabini, mayumì*.

mahintáy (ma-hin-táy), *v*. 1. to be able to wait for. Syn. *maantáy*. 2. to be able to rely or depend from. Syn. *maasahan*.

máhingî (má-hi-ngî), *v*. to get or obtain (something) as a favor from someone.

máhirám (má-hi-rám), v. 1. to be borrowed; happen to be borrowed. 2. to have a chance to borrow (a thing). Also, makáhirám.

mahirang (ma-hi-rang), v. to be able to select, choose, or appoint (a person or thing). Syn. mapilì.

mahirap (ma-hi-rap), adj. 1. poor; needy; indigent. Syn. dukhâ, marálitá, pobre. 2. hard to do, make, solve, etc.; difficult. Syn. mabigát (colloq.).

mahirapan (ma-hi-ra-pan), v. 1. to encounter hardship or difficulty. Syn. dumanas ng hirap. 2. to experience pain, injury, etc. Syn. magtiís, masaktán.

mahirati (ma-hi-ra-ti), v. to be or become accustomed; get used to. Syn. masanay, mamihasa.

mahistrado (ma-his-tra-do), n. (Sp. magistrado) magistrate. Cf. hukóm, huwés.

máhitâ (má-hi-tâ), v. to get as an unsatisfactory result or consequence from one's good deed. Syn. mápalâ, mátamó.

mahiwagà (ma-hi-wa-gà), adj. mysterious; miraculous; puzzling. Syn. kataká-taká, mahimalâ, kahimá-himalá.

máhiwaláy (má-hi-wa-láy), v. to be or become separated from. Also, mápahiwaláy. Syn. mápalayô, málayô.

máhiwatigan (má-hi-wa-ti-gan), v. to have an inkling or a vague idea of. Syn. máhigingan, máulinigan.

mahiyâ (ma-hi-yâ), v. 1. to be ashamed. 2. to be embarrassed. Also, mápahiyâ.

máhiyá (má-hi-yá), n. (Sp. magia) magic. Cf. salamangka.

mahíyain (ma-hí-ya-in), adj. shy; timid; bashful. Also, mahihíyain, mahinhín.

máhiyáng (má-hi-yáng), v. to be suited or agreeable to one's health, as weather, medicine, etc. Also, mákahiyáng.

mahiyás (ma-hi-yás), adj. with, having, or possessing many jewelry. Syn. maalahas.

mahubarán (ma-hu-ba-rán), v. 1. to be stripped of one's upper clothing; be undressed from the waist up. 2. to be able to undress someone of his upper clothing.

mahubog (ma-hu-bog), v. 1. to be bent down by force of weight, as a tree branch laden with fruits. Syn. mahutok. 2. to be able to shape into an arc or arch. Syn.

mabalantók.

mahugong (ma-hu-gong), adj. making o creating too much humming sound, as a motor or machine. Syn. maugong maingay.

mahulaan (ma-hu-la-an), v. 1. to be able to guess correctly, as the answer to a riddle or puzzle. Syn. maturingan. 2. to be able to predict or tell, as the fortune o someone.

mahuli (ma-hu-li), I. v. 1. to be able to catch, as an animal. Syn. madakíp. 2. to be able to arrest or apprehend, as a fugitive. Syn. maaresto, madakíp.

—II. adj. with or having a big catch. Syn maraming huli.

máhulí (má-hu-lí), v. 1. to be left behind Syn. maiwan. 2. to be or become late o delayed. Syn. maatraso.

máhulihan (má-hu-li-han), v. 1. to be caught with something being pilfered. 2 to be able to find out or discover something that a person is secretive of Syn. másubukan.

mahulò (ma-hu-lò), v. to be able to think rationally. Syn. maisip.

mahulog (ma-hu-log), v. 1. to fall (from a height). Syn. bumagsák, lumagpák. 2. to fail to pass, as in an examination. Syn di-pumasá, bumagsák, mábagsák, lumagpák málagpák. 3. (Fig.) to be tricked or dupe into.

mahumál (ma-hu-mál), v. to be unable to speak clearly, usually with a nasal twang due to cold, fright, or sense of guilt. Syn magaríl.

mahumalíng (ma-hu-ma-líng), v. to be obsessed with or passionately fond of. Syn mahibáng.

mahampák (ma-ham-pák), v. to becom hollow or sunken, as cheeks, stomach, etc Also, humumpák.

mahunâ (ma-hu-nâ), adj. 1. weak; easil broken, damaged, or destroyed; fragile Syn. masiraín, mabasagín; marupók. 2 susceptible to sickness; weak. Syn masasakitín

mahusay (ma-hu-say), I. adj. 1. efficient competent; able; proficient. Syn. episyente may-kaya, may-kakayahán, sanáy. 2. i good order; well-arranged. Syn. *maayos, nasa ayos*. 3. good; having the right qualities. Syn. *mabuti, maayos, magalíng*. 4. effective; reliable. Syn. *mabisà, magalíng, mapagtitiwalaan*. 5. well; not sick. Syn. *magaling na; walâ nang sakit*. 6. kind; friendly. Syn. *mabaít*. 7. real; genuine; true. Syn. *tunay; di-palsipikado*. 8. satisfying. Syn. *kasiyá-siyá*. 9. well-behaved. Syn. *mabaít, mabuti*. 10. talented. Syn. *marunong, magalíng, matalino*.

—II. *v*. 1. to be able to put in order; be able to arrange. Syn. *maayos, mailagáy sa ayos*. 2. to be able to settle amicably, as a trouble between two persons. Syn. *maayos, mapagkásundô*.

náhusayán (má-hu-sa-yán), *adv*. in a friendly manner; amicably. Syn. *sa maayos na paraán*.

nahustó (ma-hus-to), *v*. 1. to be able to complete. Syn. *makumpleto*. 2. to become complete.

nahutok (ma-hu-tok), *v*. 1. to be able to bend down, as a slender branch, by pulling. Syn. *mahubog, mabayók*. 2. to be or become bent by force of weight. 3. (*Fig.*) to be able to control, as a misguided child. Syn. *masugpô, maakay sa mabuti*.

mai- (ma-i-), *pref*. added to roots to form verbs, meaning "to be able to." See **ma-**.

maiabót (ma-i-a-bót), *v*. to be able to give or hand over (a thing) to someone personally. Syn. *maibigáy*.

maiakyát (ma-i-ak-yát), *v*. 1. to be able to bring (something) upstairs. Syn. *maipanhík*. 2. to be able to carry to a high place. Syn. *madalá sa itaás*. 3. to be able to carry along in climbing a high place. Syn. *maiahon*. 4. to be able to drive (a vehicle) up an inclined road. Syn. *maiahon, mapaahon*.

maiadyá (ma-i-ad-yá), *v*. to be able to save or protect from danger, etc. Syn. *mailigtás*.

maiagap (ma-i-a-gap), *v*. to be able to put or place something in the front or ahead of others. Syn. *maiuna*.

maiahon (ma-i-a-hon), *v*. 1. to be able to remove from the fire or stove, referring to something being cooked. Syn. *mahangò*. 2. to be able to bring up to a

high place, as by climbing. Syn. *maiakyát*.

maiangkóp (mai-ang-kóp), *v*. to be able to fit or adapt something properly to another. Syn. *maiakmâ, maiagpang*.

maiayuda (ma-i-a-yu-da), *v*. to be able to give, as aid or succor. Syn. *maisukoro, maisaklolo, maitulong*.

maibá (ma-i-bá), *v*. 1. to be able to change or make different. Syn. *mabago*. 2. to become changed. Syn. *mag-ibá*.

maibabâ (ma-i-ba-bâ), *v*. 1. to be able to bring downstairs. Syn. *maipanaog*. 2. to be able to bring down from a height, as with rope. Syn. *maihugos*. 3. to be able to lower or make lower, as prices. 4. to be able to land or make a landing, as an airplane. Syn. *mapababâ, mapalapág*. 5. to be able to put down something, as on the floor or land. Syn. *mailapág, maipatong*. 6. to be able to harvest or pick, as fruits. Syn. *mapitás, maputi, maani*. 7. to be able to unload a passenger or passengers. Syn. *mailunsád, maiibís*. 8. to be able to unload a cargo. Syn. *maidiskarga, mailunsád*.

maibagay (ma-i-ba-gay), *v*. to be able to fit or make compatible with. Syn. *maiangkóp, maikmâ*.

maibagsák (ma-i-bag-sák), *v*. 1. to be able to overthrow, as a regime or government. Syn. *maigupô*. 2. to be able to knock down, as in boxing. Syn. *mapatumbá*. 3. to be able to cause someone to fail in an examination. Syn. *maihulog, mailagpák*.

maibalík (ma-i-ba-lík), *v*. 1. to be able to return something borrowed or stolen from someone. Syn. *maisaulî*. 2. to be able to restore (a thing) to its former position or place. Syn. *maisaulî sa dati*. 3. to be able to bring back something that one brought with him on a trip. 4. to be able to drive back, as a car, to where it came from.

maibaling (ma-i-ba-ling), *v*. to be able to turn or make a turn to a side or direction . Syn. *maipaling, maikiling, maipihit*.

máibalità (má-i-ba-li-tà), *v*. to happen to tell someone about an incident or happening. Syn. *másabi*.

maibangon (ma-i-ba-ngon), *v*. 1. to be able to help someone to rise or stand up from a lying position. Syn. *maitayô, maitindíg*.

2. to be able to construct or erect, as a building. Syn. *magawâ, maitayó, maitirik.*

maibaón (ma-i-ba-ón), *v.* to be able to bury (a dead person). Syn. *mailibíng.* 2. to be able to sink, as a dagger. Syn. *maisaksák, maitarak.*

maibukód (ma-i-bu-kód), *v.* to be able to separate (something) from another or others. Syn. *maihiwaláy.*

maikailâ (ma-i-ka-i-lâ), *v.* to be able to deny or not tell the truth. Syn. *mailihim, mailingíd.*

maikaít (ma-i-ka-ít), *v.* to be able to deny or refuse to give. Syn. *maitanggí.*

maikatuwiran (ma-i-ka-tu-wi-ran), var. **maikatwiran,** *v.* to be able to use as a reason or argument for. Syn. *maimatwíd, maidahilán.*

maikiling (ma-i-ki-ling), *v.* to be able to incline or recline to a side, as one's head or body. Syn. *maihilig.*

maikilos (ma-i-ki-los), *v.* to be able to move, as one's body. Syn. *maigaláw.*

maiklî (ma-ik-lî), *adj.* 1. short; not long; lacking the regular or sufficient length. Syn. *maigsî, mautdó.* 2. short or brief, as of time. Syn. *madalî.*

maidlíp (ma-id-líp), *v.* to take a nap. Syn. *mahipíg, humipíg.*

maigâ (ma-i-gâ), *v.* to become dry or drained of water due to evaporation. Syn. *matuyuán ng tubig.*

maigaya (ma-i-ga-ya), *v.* 1. to be delighted with what is being seen or experienced. Syn. *másiyahán, mawili.* 2. to be or become attracted or induced. Syn. *maakit, mabighaní.*

maigi (ma-i-gi), *adj.* 1. well; in good health. Syn. *malusog.* 2. in good or satisfactory condition; favorable; comfortable. Syn. *kasiyá-siyá, maginhawa.* 3. fine; good; all right (in general). Syn. *mabuti, mahusay, magaling.*

maigiit (ma-i-gi-it), *v.* to be able to insist on. Syn. *maipilit.*

maigitáw (ma-i-gi-táw), *v.* to be able to cause something to appear partly or fully. Syn. *mailitáw, mailabás, maiultáw.*

maigsî (ma-ig-sî), *adj.* short; not long; lacking the usual or required length. Syn.

maiklî, kulang sa habà, kapós.

maigsí-igsî (ma-ig-sí + ig-sî), *adj.* a little bi shorter. Syn. *maiklí-iklî.*

maigtíng (ma-ig-tíng), *adj.* 1. tight, as a bite tie, or knot. Syn. *mahìgpít.* 2. very clos or keen, as a contest or competition. Syn *mahigpít; mainit (fig.).*

maigtingan (ma-ig-ti-ngan), *adj.* very clos or tight, as a contest or competition. Se **maigtíng.** Syn. *máhigpitan, máinitan.*

maiguhit (ma-i-gu-hit), *v.* 1. to be able t use in drawing a line or lines. Syn *maipangguhit.* 2. to be able to draw th picture or portrait of. Syn. *mailarawan maidrowing.*

maihablá (ma-i-ha-blá), *v.* to be able t accuse in court. Syn. *maidemanda maisakdál.*

maihabol (ma-i-ha-bol), *v.* 1. to be able t add as a postscript to. Cf. *maidagdág.* 2. t be able to appeal, as to higher court o justice. Syn. *maiapelá.*

maihadláng (ma-i-had-láng), *v.* to be abl to use or put as an obstacle across the way Syn. *maihalang, maiharang.*

maihalál (ma-i-ha-lál), *v.* to be able to elec or vote for. Syn. *maiboto.*

maihalang (ma-i-ha-lang), *v.* to be able t use or put as an obstacle across the way Syn. *maiharang, maihadláng.*

maihalili (ma-i-ha-li-li), *v.* to be able to use as a replacement or substitute for. Syn *maipalít, maitorno.*

maihalimbawà (ma-i-ha-lim-ba-wà), *v.* 1. to be able to use or cite as an example. Syn *magamit o mabanggít na halimbawà.* 2. to be able to compare with. Syn *maihalintulad.*

maihambíng (ma-i-ham-bíng), *v.* to be able to compare with another. Syn *maihalintulad, maitulad, maiwangis.*

maihanap (ma-i-ha-nap), *v.* to be able to find something for someone. Also *maipaghanáp.*

maihandâ (ma-i-han-dâ), *v.* 1. to be able to prepare (something) for use. Syn. *maiprepará, maigayák.* 2. to be able to give as food to one's guest in a party.

maihandóg (ma-i-han-dóg), *v.* 1. to be able to offer as gift or present. Syn. *mairegalo.*

2. to be able to sacrifice as one's life. Syn. *maipará*. 3. to be able to dedicate, as a song or poem. Syn. *maialay, maipatungkól*.

maiharáp (ma-i-ha-ráp), *v*. 1. to be able to submit or present. Syn. *maipresenta*. 2. to be able to cause a thing to face the front. 3. to be able to bring someone in the presence of. Syn. *maisama o madalá sa haráp*. 4. to be able to show or present. Syn. *maipakita*.

maihawig (ma-i-ha-wig), *v*. to be able to compare with. Syn. *maihambíng, matulad, maihalintulad*.

maihayág (ma-i-ha-yág), *v*. 1. to be able to express or declare openly. Syn. *masabi nang háyagan o lántaran*. 2. to be able to announce or disclose the decision or result of.

maihimatón (ma-i-hi-ma-tón), *v*. to be able to give someone an idea of the place where a person or thing could be found.

maihinaíng (ma-i-hi-na-íng), *v*. to be able to supplicate or beg humbly. Syn. *maisamò, maipakiusap, maipamanhík*.

maihingá (ma-i-hi-ngá), *v*. 1. to be able to breathe the air out of one's lungs. 2. (*Fig.*) to be able to express or unbosom one's ill feeling against a friend or to one close to oneself. Syn. *maipagtapát ang samá ng loób*.

maihingî (ma-i-hi-ngî), *v*. to be able to ask or request for something (from another) to be given to someone.

maihirám (ma-i-hi-rám), *v*. 1. to be able to borrow (something) for someone. Cf. *maiutang*. 2. to be able to use for borrowing something, as a library card for borrowing books. Syn. *magamit sa paghirám*.

maihulapì (ma-i-hu-la-pì), *v*. to be able to add as a suffix. Cf. *mailapì, maipanlapì, maiunlapì*.

maíibá (ma-í-i-bá), *adj*. that which can be changed or made different. Syn. *mabábago*.

maíibabâ (ma-í-i-ba-bâ), *adj*. that which can be lowered or made lower.

maíibayo (ma-í-i-ba-yo), *adj*. that which can be doubled. Syn. *madódoblé*.

maíiklián (ma-í-ik-li-án), *adj*. that which can be made shorter. Syn. *maíigsián*,

maúutduhán.

maíilagan (ma-í-i-la-gan), *adj*. avoidable; that which can be avoided. Syn. *maíiwasan*.

maíilít (ma-í-i-lít), *adj*. subject to consfiscation; that which can be consfiscated. Syn. *másasamsám, maíembargo*.

mailaán (ma-i-la-án), *v*. to be able to keep in reserve for. Syn. *maireserba, maipatagana*.

mailakad (ma-i-la-kad), *v*. 1. to be able to use for walking, as one's weak feet or legs. 2. to be able to work personally for the approval of.

mailagan (ma-i-la-gan), *v*. 1. to be able to parry off, as a blow. Syn. *masanggá, masalág*. 2. to be able to avoid. Syn. *maiwasan*.

mailáp (ma-i-láp), *adj*. wild; untamed; undomesticated.

mailarawan (ma-i-la-ra-wan), *v*. 1. to be able to describe. Syn. *madeskribí*. 2. to be able to make a picture of. Syn. *maidibuho, maidrowing, maipinta*.

mailathalà (ma-i-lat-ha-là), *v*. to be able to publish. Syn. *maipalimbag*.

mailawan (ma-i-la-wan), *v*. to be able to provide or set up with a light or lights. Syn. *malagyán ng ilaw*. 2. to be lighted; be bright with a light.

mailiban (ma-i-li-ban), *v*. 1. to be able to postpone. Also, *maipagpaliban*. 2. to be the cause of one's absence. Syn. *maipalyá*.

mailigpít (ma-i-lig-pít), *v*. 1. to be able to gather and keep together. Syn. *malikom*. 2. to be able to keep for future use. Syn. *maitagò*. 3. (*Fig.*) to be able to kill or murder. Syn. *mapatáy*. 4. (*Colloq.*) to be able to arrest. Syn. *mahulí, maaresto*.

mailunsád (ma-i-lun-sád), *v*. 1. to be able to unload, as a passenger or cargo. Syn. *maibabâ, maidiskarga*. 2. to be able to launch. Syn. *maibunsód*.

mailusót (ma-i-lu-sót), *v*. to be able to insert a thing through a small hole or opening. Syn. *maisuót, maipasok*. 2. (*Fig.*) to be able to carry successfully through a tight situation.

mailuwál (ma-i-lu-wál), *v*. to be born. Syn.

maianák, maisilang.

maimbót (ma-im-bót), I. **v.** to be able to covet.
—II. **adj.** selfish; covetous; greedy. Syn. *makamkám, sakím.*

maimis (ma-i-mis), I. **adj.** neat and orderly, referring to a person. Syn. *malinis at areglado.*
—II. **v.** to be able to clear away things and put them in their proper places. Syn. *mailigpit.*

maimot (ma-i-mot), **adj.** 1. frugal. Syn. *matipíd, mapagtipíd.* 2. niggardly; stingy. Syn. *kuripot, maramot.*

maimpluwénsiyá (ma-im-plu-wén-si-yá), **adj.** very influential; having great influence; powerful. Syn. *malakás (fig.), makapangyarihan.*

mainam (ma-i-nam), **adj.** nice; good; fine. Syn. *mabuti, mahusay.*

mainaman (ma-i-na-man), **v.** 1. to be satisfied with the good or fine qualities of. Syn. *magandahán.* 2. (Fig.) to suffer the full consequences of. Syn. *masasaan.*

maíndahin (ma-ín-da-hin), **adj.** 1. too sensitive to criticism. Syn. *marámdamin.* 2. easily affected by the feeling of hardship, etc. Syn. *mapagurín.*

maindayog (ma-in-da-yog), **adj.** 1. rhythmic; full of rhythm. 2. bombastic; flowery, said of speech. Syn. *mabulaklák.*

maindultuhán (ma-in-dul-tu-hán), **v.** to be given pardon or amnesty.

mainín (ma-i-nín), **v.** to be fully cooked, said of rice after having been kept for sometime over live coal or charcoals. Syn. *malutong mabuti ng bagá sa kanin.*

mainíp (ma-i-níp), **v.** to be bored or impatient; be tired of waiting. Syn. *mayamót o mapagod sa paghihintáy.*

maínipin (ma-í-ni-pin), **adj.** easily bored or tired of waiting. Syn. *mayámutin o mapagurin sa paghihintáy.*

maínisin (ma-í-ni-sin), **adj.** easily annoyed or exasperated; irritable. Syn. *mayámutin, masuyaín, magagalitín, pikón (slang).*

mainit (ma-i-nit), **adj.** shining brightly, referring to the sun. Syn. *maaraw.* 2. hot; having much heat, as fire. Syn. *nakapápasò.* 3. hot and humid; warm as

climate. Syn. *alinsangan, maalinsangan, mabanas, maalisis.* 4. violent; raging, as battle. Syn. *masidhî, mainapóy.* 5. (usuall with *ang ulo*) easily aroused or excited esp. to anger. Syn. *bugnutin, magalitín.*

máinitán (má-i-ni-tán), I. **adj.** heated o fiery, as a debate.
—II. **adv.** heatedly; with anger vehemence, etc.

mainít-inít (ma-i-nít + i-nít), **adj.** lukewarm tepid. Syn. *malahiningá, maligamgám.*

mainitín (ma-i-ni-tín), **adj.** 1. referring t something that easily becomes hot. Syr *madalíng uminit.* 2. (usually with *ang ulo* hot-headed; hot-tempered. Syn *magagalitín.*

mainó (ma-i-nó), **v.** to be able to point o call the attention of someone abou something that is not well-done. Syr *mapuná, mapansin.*

mainsulto (ma-in-sul-to), **v.** 1. to be able t insult. Syn. *malait, maalipustâ.* 2. to b insulted; feel insulted.

máintindihán (má-in-tin-di-hán), **v.** 1. to b able to understand or comprehend. Syr *máunawaan.* 2. to be understood.

mainút-inót (ma-i-nút + i-nót) **v.** to be abl to do, make, finish, etc. little by little Syn. *mauntí-untî.*

maingat (ma-i-ngat), **adj.** careful; cautious circumspect.

maingatan (ma-i-nga-tan), **v.** 1. to be abl to take care of. Syn. *maalagaan mapangalagaan.* 2. to be able to keep, a one's possession. Syn. *matagláy, maangkín*

maingay (ma-i-ngay), **adj.** 1. noisy; full o noise. 2. creating or making much noise Syn. *maguló, nagkákaguló, malinggál.*

maingganyo (ma-ing-gan-yo), **v.** to b tempted or enticed; be lured. Syn *matuksó, mabighanì, maakit.*

mainggitin (ma-ing-gi-tin), **adj.** envious o other's success. Syn. *mapanághilim.*

maipá (ma-i-pá), **adj.** chaffy; full of chaff.

maipaalaala (ma-i-pa-a-la-a-la), **v.** to be abl to remind something to another. Syn *maipagunitâ.*

maipaaninaw (ma-i-pa-a-ni-naw), **v.** t cause something to be understood by on as by explaining. Syn. *maipaunawà.*

maipabago (ma-i-pa-ba-go), v. 1. to be able to have a thing made again or in a different way. Syn. *maipagawáng mulî.* 2. to be able to have a thing transferred to another place.

maipabalík (ma-i-pa-ba-lík), v. 1. to be able to cause a thing to be returned to whom it was borrowed. Syn. *maipasaulî.* 2. to be able to have a thing returned to its former place.

maipabasa (ma-i-pa-ba-sa), v. to be able to have a story, book, etc. read by someone.

maipabatíd (ma-i-pa-ba-tíd), v. 1. to be able to make known to somebody. Syn. *maipaalam.* 2. to be able to explain something to someone. Syn. *maipaliwanag, maipaunawà.*

maipabigáy (ma-i-pa-bi-gáy), v. to be able to ask or request someone to give (a thing) to another.

maipabukas (ma-i-pa-bu-kas), v. to be able to postpone for tomorrow. Also, *maipagpabukas.*

maipakahulugán (ma-i-pa-ka-hu-lu-gán), v. to be able to interpret as or give as a meaning of.

maipakaón (ma-i-pa-ka-ón), v. to be able to have someone fetched by another. Syn. *maipasundô.*

maipakasál (ma-i-pa-ka-sál), v. to be able to cause the marriage of someone to another.

maipakatawán (ma-i-pa-ka-ta-wán), v. to be able to authorize the performance of a certain duty by a representative or deputy.

maipakilala (ma-i-pa-ki-la-la), v. 1. to be able to introduce someone to another. 2. to be able to succeed in explaining something to somebody. Syn. *maipaliwanag.* 2. to be able to show or prove one's ability, sincerity, etc. Syn. *maipakita, mapatunayan.*

maipadamá (ma-i-pa-da-má), v. to be able to cause something to be felt or experienced by someone. Syn. *maiparanas.*

maipagawâ (ma-i-pa-ga-wâ), v. 1. to be able to have a thing made or manufactured. 2. to be able to have something constructed or built, as a house or building. Syn.

maipatayô. 2. to be able to have a thing repaired or mended. Syn. *maipakumpuní, maipaayos.*

maipagbigáy-alám (ma-i-pag-bi-gáy + a-lám), v. 1. to be able to report something to someone in authority. Syn. *maipagsumbóng.* 2. to be able to have something relayed to someone.

maipagbilin (ma-i-pag-bi-lin), v. to be able to send an oral message to someone through somebody. Syn. *maipasabi.*

maipagkaít (ma-i-pag-ka-ít), v. to be able to refuse or deny to give. Syn. *maipagdamót.*

maipaglaban (ma-i-pag-la-ban), v. to be able to fight for. Syn. *maipagtanggól.*

maipagpaliban (ma-i-pag-pa-li-ban), v. to be able to postpone or put off for an indefinite period. Syn. *maipagpaibáng-araw.*

maipagpalít (ma-i-pag-pa-lít), v. to be able to exchange (something) with another. Also, *maipalít.*

maipagpasalamat (ma-i-pag-pa-sa-la-mat), v. to be a cause for someone to extend or express thanks to.

maipahayag (ma-i-pa-ha-yag), v. 1. to be able to declare or announce. Syn. *maiproklamá.* 2. to be able to express, as one's intentions. Syn. *masabi.*

maipailalim (ma-pa-i-la-lim), v. 1. to able to put below or under something. 2. to be able to put under the authority or supervision of someone.

maipalamuti (ma-i-pa-la-mu-ti), v. to be able to put or use as a decoration. Syn. *maidekorasyón, maiadorno, maigayák.*

maipaling (ma-i-pa-ling), v. to be able to turn or cause to turn to a side. Syn. *maibaling.*

maipaliwanag (ma-i-pa-li-wa-nag), v. to be able to explain or made clear. Syn. *maipalinaw.*

maipamana (ma-i-pa-ma-na), v. to be able to bequeath or leave something to someone as an inheritance.

maipanalo (ma-i-pa-na-lo), v. to be able to carry on to victory. Syn. *maipágtagumpáy, maipágwagî.*

maipandiwà (ma-i-pan-di-wà), v. to be able

to use as a verb.

maipanlapì (ma-i-pan-la-pì), v. to be able to add or use as an affix (to a word). Syn. *mailapì*.

maipantáy (ma-i-pan-táy), v. to be able to make something equal to the length, height, standard, or rank of another.

maipantíg (ma-i-pan-tíg), v. to be able to use or add as a syllable to a word.

maipanukalà (ma-i-pa-nu-ka-là), v. to be able to submit or present as proposal. Syn. *maimungkahi*.

maipangakò (ma-i-pa-nga-kò), v. to be able to promise.

maipangalan (ma-i-pa-nga-lan), v. to be able to give as a name for. Syn. *maingalan*.

maipareho (ma-i-pa-re-ho), v. 1. to be able to compare a thing with another. Syn. *maiparis, maitulad*. 2. to be able to make in the same manner or shape of another.

maiparte (ma-i-par-te), v. 1. to be able to give someone his or her share. Syn. *maibahagi*. 2. (Colloq.) to be able to report (a thing) to. Syn. *maisuplóng, maisumbóng*.

maipasiyá (ma-i-pa-si-yá), v. to be able to give as a decision.

maipasok (ma-i-pa-sok), v. 1. to be able to bring (something) inside. Syn. *madalá sa loob*. 2. to be able to put, insert, or thrust (a thing) inside. Syn. *maisuót, maipaloób, mailusót, maisulót*. 3. to be able to get an employment for someone. Syn. *maihanap ng trabaho*. 4. to be able to have or help someone enter school. 5. to be able to present successfully, as a resolution or amendment.

maipasyál (ma-i-pas-yál), v. to be able to take someone with oneself for a walk.

maipayo (ma-i-pa-yo), v. to be able to give as an advice.

maipilì (ma-i-pi-lì), v. to be able to select (something) for someone. Syn. *maihirang*.

maipilit (ma-i-pi-lit), v. to be able to force something on someone. Syn. *maigiit*.

maipis (ma-i-pis), adj. full or infested with cockroaches.

maipon (ma-i-pon), v. 1. to be able to collect or gather together. Syn. *matipon, makolekta*. 2. to be or become accumulated, as work. Syn. *mátambák*.

maipuná (ma-i-pu-ná), v. to be able to give as a critism to.

maipuslít (ma-i-pus-lít), v. to be able to smuggle something.

maipuwesto (ma-i-pu-wes-to), v. 1. to be able to put in place. 2. to be able to secure an employment for.

mairamay (ma-i-ra-may), v. to be able to implicate. Syn. *maisangkót*.

mairaos (ma-i-ra-os), v. 1. to be able to hold or celebrate. 2. to be able to finish.

maireklamo (ma-i-rek-la-mo), v. 1. to be able to denounce. 2. to be able to make a complaint about something.

maireto (ma-i-re-to), v. to be able to pit one with another. Syn. *mailaban*.

mairugin (ma-i-ru-gin), adj. affectionate; loving; amorous. Syn. *mapagmahál*.

maís (ma-ís), n. (Sp. *maiz*) corn; maize.

maisaád (ma-i-sa-ád), v. to be able to tell or state. Syn. *masabi*.

maisaalang-alang (ma-i-sa-a-lang + a-lang), v. to be able to consider.

maisaayos (ma-i-sa-a-yos), v. to be able to arrange or put in order.

maisabog (ma-i-sa-bog), v. 1. to be able to sow, as seeds. Syn. *maihasík*. 2. (by extension) to be able to distribute. Syn. *maipamahagi, maipamudmod*. 3. to be able to scatter, as garbage, etc. Syn. *maikalat*.

maisagád (ma-i-sa-gád), v. 1. to be able to sink (a thing) to the bottom or limit. Syn. *maisukdól*. 2. to be able to continue or carry on up to the end. Syn. *maihayón*.

maisaglít (ma-i-sag-lít), v. to be able to bring or take something to a place or to someone and be back right away. Syn. *madalá o maihatíd na madalî*.

maisahán (ma-i-sa-hán), v. (Fig.) to be able to win a point against. Syn. *mapuntusán*.

maisá-isá (ma-i-sá + i-sá), v. 1. to be able to count one by one. Syn. *mabilang na isá-isá*. 2. to be able to do, undertake, or finish one after another.

maisalaysáy (ma-i-sa-lay-sáy), v. to be able to narrate or tell, as a story. Syn. *maikuwento*.

maisalig (ma-i-sa-lig), v. to be able to base something from. Syn. *maibatay*.

maisalin (ma-i-sa-lin), v. 1. to be able to

maisaliwâ   **maitakdâ**

pour or transfer the contents of one container to another. Syn. *mailiwat, mailipat ng lalagyán*. 2. to be able to copy or rewrite. Syn. *makopya*. 3. to be able to translate (a word, sentence, story, or the like) into another language.

maisaliwâ (ma-i-sa-li-wâ), *v*. to be able to reverse the position.

maisama (ma-i-sa-ma), *v*. to be able to take along someone. Syn. *maisabáy*. 2. to be able to add something to a mixture. Syn. *maihalò, maidagdág*. 3. to be able to enclose or include, as in a letter. Syn. *mailakip*. 4. to be able to include, as with a group. Syn. *maibilang*.

maisamò (ma-i-sa-mò), *v*. to be able to request earnestly. Syn. *maipamanhík, mailuhog*.

maisangkót (ma-i-sang-kót), *v*. to be able to implicate, as in an affair or trouble. Syn. *maidamay, maidawit*.

maisangguní (ma-i-sang-gu-nì), *v*. to be able to consult (a problem) to someone for advice. Syn. *maihingî ng payo*.

maisaulî (ma-i-sa-u-lî), *v*. to be able to return something borrowed or taken. 2. to be able to restore (a thing) to its former place. Syn. *maibalík*.

maisaysáy (ma-i-say-sáy), *v*. to be able to narrate or tell, as a story. Syn. *maisalaysáy, maikuwento*.

maisdâ (ma-is-dâ), var. **maistâ**, *adj*. with or having plenty of fish; well-supplied with fish.

maisigáw (ma-i-si-gáw), *v*. to be able to communicate something to someone by shouting. Syn. *maihiyáw*.

maisilang (ma-i-si-lang), *v*. to be born.

maisip (ma-i-sip), *v*. to be able to think about or recall into one's mind. Syn. *maalaala*.

máisipan (má-i-si-pan), *v*. to happen to think of. See **máisip**. Syn. *máalaala*.

maisiwalat (ma-i-si-wa-lat), *v*. to be able to expose or reveal. Syn. *maibunyág*.

maisulat (ma-i-su-lat), *v*. 1. to be able to use for writing, as a pencil or pen. Syn. *magamit sa pagsulat*. 2. to be able to write or put in writing. 3. to be able to write about something to someone. Syn.

mailiham.

maisulit (ma-i-su-lit), *v*. 1. to be able to give or submit. Syn. *maiharáp, maibigáy*. 2. to be able to pass, as an examination or test. Syn. *maipasá*.

maisumpâ (ma-i-sum-pâ), *v*. 1. to be able to curse or wish evil upon someone. 2. to be able to make a vow. Syn. *maiparata, maipangakò*.

maisunód (ma-i-su-nód), *v*. 1. to be able to do something in compliance with certain requirements or orders. Syn. *maialinsunod*. 2. to be able to do (a thing) after a thing is done or finished. 3. to be able to do or make in the same pattern or way another was done. Syn. *magawáng katulad ng*. 4. to be able to cause or make (a vehicle, etc.) follow another or others. Syn. *mapasunód*. 5. to be able to take along something left by someone who has gone ahead. Cf. *maihabol*.

maisusog (ma-i-su-sog), *v*. to be able to introduce as an amendment to. Syn. *maienmyenda*.

maitaán (ma-i-ta-án), *v*. 1. to be able to save or reserve (something) for someone or for future use. Syn. *mailaán*. 2. to be able to set, as a trap or snare.

maitaás (ma-i-ta-ás), *v*. 1. to be able to raise or lift, as a heavy object. Syn. *maangát, maiangát*. 2. to be able to put or place (a thing) on a higher place. Syn. *mailagáy sa mataás o itaás*. 3. to be able to raise, as a flag. 4. to be able to show by raising, as one's hands. 5. to be able to promote in rank, as an employee. Syn. *maiasenso*.

maitabí (ma-i-ta-bí), *v*. 1. to be able to put a thing near or beside another. Syn. *mailapit*. 2. to be able to have someone sit, lie, or sleep beside or close to oneself. Syn. *maisiping, maisigbáy, maiabáy*. 3. to be able to put away and keep in its proper place. Syn. *mailigpít, maitagó*.

maitakas (ma-i-ta-kas), *v*. to be able to take away (a person or thing) without the knowledge of other persons. Syn. *maitanan*.

maitakdâ (ma-i-tak-dâ), *v*. 1. to be able to set as a limit. 2. to be able to set the time or schedule of.

maitagò (ma-i-ta-gò), *v*. 1. to be able to hide (something) in a secret place. Syn. *maikublí*. 2. to be able to keep (something) in secrecy. Syn. *mailihim*. 3. to be able to put away and keep in the proper place. Syn. *mailigpít*.

maitagubilin (ma-i-ta-gu-bi-lin), *v*. 1. to be able to recommend. Syn. *mairekomenda*. 2. to be able to give as an advice. Syn. *maipayo*.

maitaguyod (ma-i-ta-gu-yod), *v*. to be able to support, as a project. Syn. *matangkilik*.

maitalagá (ma-i-ta-la-gá), *v*. 1. to be able to induct or install, as officers of an association. Syn. *mapanumpâ*. 2. to be able to assign something to someone. Syn. *maiukol*.

maitamà (ma-i-ta-má), *v*. 1. to be able to correct or make right. Syn. *maitumpák*, *maiwastô*. 2. to be able to put or place (something) correctly or properly. Syn. *mailagáy sa ayos*. 3. to be able to insert or put into, as in a hole. Syn. *maipasok*, *maisuót*, *mailusót*.

maitambál (ma-i-tam-bál), *v*. to be able to pair (a person or thing) with another. Syn. *maipareha*, *maituwáng*.

maitampók (ma-i-tam-pók), *v*. to be able to exalt or hold in high esteem. Syn. *maitanghál*.

maitanóng (ma-i-ta-nóng), *v*. 1. to be able to ask or inquire about. Syn. *mausisà*. 2. to be able to include as a question in an examination.

maitanggí (ma-i-tang-gí), *v*. 1. to be able to deny the truth of. Syn. *maikailâ*, *mailihim*. 2. to be able to refuse to give. Syn. *maikaít*.

maitangì (ma-i-ta-ngì), *v*. to be able to regard with special consideration or favor.

maitaón (ma-i-ta-ón), *v*. to be able to set or schedule something to coincide with. Syn. *maisabáy*.

maitapát (ma-i-ta-pát), *v*. 1. to be able to put (something) directly in front of or opposite another. Syn. *mailagáy sa tapát*. 2. to be able to give as an equivalent to. Syn. *maitumbás*.

maitapon (ma-i-ta-pon), *v*. 1. to be able to throw or cast away. 2. to be able to deport (someone). Syn. *maidestiyero*.

maitatwâ (ma-i-tat-wâ), *v*. to be able to repudiate, disclaim, or deny. Syn. *maitanggî*, *maikailâ*.

maitikom (ma-i-ti-kom), *v*. to be able to close or shut off, as one's mouth, an umbrella, etc. Syn. *maisará*, *maipiníd*.

maitim (ma-i-tim), I. *adj*. black; dark. —II. *v*. to be able to blacken or make black. Also, *mapaitím*.

maitindíg (ma-i-tin-díg), *v*. 1. to be able to help (someone) to stand up. Syn. *maitayô*. 2. to be able to build, construct, or set up. Syn. *magawá*, *maitayô*, *maitirik*. 3. to be able to organize or found. Syn. *maitatag*, *maipundár*.

maitingalâ (ma-i-ti-nga-lâ), *v*. to be able to raise or tilt upward, as one's face. Syn. *maitungháy*.

maitirik (ma-i-ti-rik), *v*. 1. to be able to build, construct, or erect, as a house. Syn. *magawâ*, *maitayô*. 2. to be able to set upright, as a candle. Syn. *maitayô*.

maititik (ma-i-tik-tik), *v*. 1. to be able to write or put in writing. Syn. *maisulat*. 2. to be able to jot down. Syn. *maitalâ*, *mailistâ*.

maitodo (ma-i-to-do), *v*. to be able to bet all of one's money in a single game. Syn. *maitayáng lahát*. 2. to be able to give or exert all of one's strength, knowhow, etc. Syn. *maibuhos na lahát*.

maitugón (ma-i-tu-gón), *v*. to be able to give as an answer or reply. Syn. *maisagót*.

maitulad (ma-i-tu-lad), *v*. 1. to be able to compare one thing with another. 2. to be able to make something by copying from another. Syn. *maigaya*, *maihawig*, *maipareho*.

maitumbás (ma-i-tum-bás), *v*. to be able to give as an equivalent of.

maitumpák (ma-i-tum-pák), *v*. to be able to correct or make right. Syn. *maitamà*, *maiwastô*.

maitustós (ma-i-tus-tós), *v*. 1. to be able to give as support. Syn. *maitangkilik*. 2. to be able to supply or furnish, as the needed materials. 3. to be able to prolong, as the string of a kite by loosening it.

maitutok (ma-i-tu-tok), *v*. to be able to point (a gun) closely at someone.

maituwíd (ma-i-tu-wíd), *v*. 1. to be able to

straighten. Syn. *maideretso*. 2. to be able to correct. Syn. *maitumpák, maiwastô*.

maiukol (ma-i-u-kol), *v.* to be able to devote or set apart for a certain purpose. Syn. *mailaan, maitalagá, maitungod*.

maiugnáy (ma-i-ug-náy), *v.* to be able to connect or associate a thing with another. 2. to be able to connect or join one thing with another. Syn. *maihugpóng, maidugtóng*.

maiurong (ma-i-u-rong), *v.* 1. to be able to drive or manipulate backward, as a vehicle. Syn. *maiatrás*. 2. to be able to revoke or withdraw. Syn. *mabawì*. 3. to be able to reset a schedule to an earlier period or time.

maiuyan (ma-i-u-yan), *v.* to be able to give as a replacement for something lost. Syn. *maiabono, maipaluwál*.

máiwaglít (má-i-wag-lít), *v.* to happen to lose or mislay.

maiwalay (ma-i-wa-lay), *v.* 1. to be able to separate one from another. Syn. *maihiwaláy, mailayô*. 2. to be able to wean, as a child. Syn. *maawat sa pagsuso (sa iná)*.

maiwan (ma-i-wan), *v.* to be left behind, as in a race.

maiwanan (ma-i-wa-nan), *v.* to forget to bring along in one's departure or trip. Syn. *mákalimutang dalhín*.

maiwasan (ma-i-wa-san), *v.* to be able to avoid. Syn. *mailagan, malayuán*.

máiyák (má-i-yák), *v.* to be forced to cry due to pity or hurt feeling. Also, *mápaiyák*. Syn. *máluhá*.

mala- (ma-la-), *pref.* used to form adjectives meaning: 1. "half-, semi-, or partially as in *malasado*. 2. like, similar to, or somewhat resembling, as in *mala*-Hitler, similar to Hitler.

malaab (ma-la-ab), *adj.* 1. flaming; bursting with flames. Syn. *maliyáb, maningas*. 2. ardent; fervent. Syn. *marubdób*.

malaanan (ma-la-a-nan), *v.* to be able to keep something in reserve for someone or for a certain purpose. Syn. *mataanan, mahandaán*.

malaawoy (ma-la-a-woy), *adj.* not yet fully dried, referring esp. to firewood.

malabág (ma-la-bág), *v.* to be able to violate,

referring to order or a law. Syn. *masuway, di-masunód*.

malabanan (ma-la-ba-nan), *v.* to be able to oppose or fight against. Syn. *masalungát, makontra*.

malabasán (ma-la-ba-sán), *v.* to be able to disentangle oneself from.

malabay (ma-la-bay), *adj.* with or having abundant foliage, referring to a tree or its branches. Syn. *madahon*.

málabí (má-la-bí), *v.* 1. to be left unused or unconsumed, as food, materials, etc. Syn. *di-maubos, mátirá*. 2. to survive; be left alive. Syn. *makaligtás*.

malabigà (ma-la-bi-gà), I. *adj.* gossipy; given to gossips. Syn. *masatsat, matsismís*.
—II. *n.* a gossiper. Syn. *dalahirà, tsismoso (sa), daldalero (ra)*.

malabis (ma-la-bis), I. *adj.* excessive; exorbitant.
—II. *adv.* very much; too much.

malabnáw (ma-lab-náw), *adj.* like water; thin, referring esp. to soup and other like food, as opposed to *malapot*.

malabò (ma-la-bò), *adj.* 1. turbid or muddy, as water. Syn. *maputik*. 2. not clear; indistinct; not heard clearly. Syn. *di-malinaw, waláng-linaw*. 3. faint, dim, or obscure, as a light. Syn. *malamlám, di-maliwanag*. 4. not certain; doubtful. Syn. *waláng-katiyakan, di-tiyák*. 5. confused; disordered. Syn. *maguló*.

malabó (ma-la-bó), *adj.* 1. spongy in consistency, as fruits or tubers. 2. loamy, as soil.

malabór (ma-la-bór), *v.* with or having many intricate decorations.

malabsâ (ma-lab-sâ), *adj.* too soft to eat, as vegetables due to overcooking, and fruits due to being overripe. Syn. *malabsák*.

malabuhók (ma-la-bu-hók), *adj.* somewhat like hair; hairlike. Syn. *parang buhók*.

malák (ma-lák), *n.* 1. idea or notion (about something); knowledge. Syn. *alam, kaalaman; batíd, kabatiran*. 2. intelligence; understanding. 3. awareness; consciousness. Syn. *malay, kamalayan*.

malakad (ma-la-kad), *v.* 1. to be able to reach (a certain distance or destination) by walking. Syn. *maratíng o maabot sa* *lakad.* 2. *(Colloq.)* to be able to work for the approval of.

malakanin (ma-la-ka-nin), *adj.* with or having the consistency of cooked rice. Syn. *maligat.*

Malakanyán (Ma-la-kan-yán), var. **Malakanyáng,** *n.* the name given to the official residence of the President of the Philippines, which, during the American Regime, was originally called Malacañan Palace.

malakás (ma-la-kás), *adj.* 1. strong; able or capable of lifting heavy weight. 2. robust; vigorous; healthy. Syn. *malusog.* 3. durable; strong; tough. Syn. *matibay.* 4. loud, as noise, sound, or voice. Syn. *matunóg, matagintíng.* 5. strong or heavy, as rain. 6. fast-selling, as merchandise or goods. Syn. *mabilí.* 7. hard, strong, or heavy, as a fist blow. Syn. *matindí.* 8. fast; swift. Syn. *mabilís, matulin.* 9. *(Colloq.)* influential. Syn. *maimpluwensiyá.* 10. hard to capture; well-armed, as a fort. Syn. *matibay.* 11. powerful. Syn. *makapangyarihan.* 12. forceful; effective. Syn. *mabisà.*

malakasán (ma-la-ka-sán), *v.* 1. to be able to make loud or louder, as one's voice. 2. to be able to make fast or faster, as a vehicle. Syn. *mabilisán, matulinan.*

malakí (ma-la-kí), *adj.* 1. big; large. 2. vast; expansive; extensive. Syn. *malawak, malapad, masakláw, maluwáng.* 3. full-grown. Syn. *sapát na sa gulang.* 4. wide, as a hole. Syn. *maluwáng.* 5. important. Syn. *mahalagá.* 6. high, as water during a flood. Syn. *mataás.* 7. great; of high status, as a man. Syn. *dakilà, mataás.*

malakí-lakí (ma-la-kí + la-kí), *adj.* a little bit bigger or larger in size or amount; big enough. Cf. *maramí-ramí.*

malakukó (ma-la-ku-kó), *adj.* tepid; lukewarm. Syn. *maligamgám, malahingá, mainít-init.*

malaganap (ma-la-ga-nap), *adj.* widespread; found or occurring in many places. Syn. *laganap, kalat, palasak.*

malagas (ma-la-gas), *v.* 1. to fall off, as hair, leaves, fruits, etc. Syn. *mahulog.* 2. *(Fig.)* to be killed, as soldiers during war.

malagatâ (ma-la-ga-tâ), *adj.* like coconut milk.

malagatas (ma-la-ga-tas), *adj.* milk-like in consistency or color.

málagáy (má-la-gáy), *v.* 1. to be put or placed in a certain condition or situation. 2. to be put as bet on. Syn. *mápusta, mátayâ.*

malagkit (ma-lag-kit), I. *adj.* 1. sticky. Syn. *madikít.* 2. *(Fig.)* sharp, as a look. Syn. *matalim (fig.).*
—II. *n.* a species of rice having glutinous consistency.

malagihay (ma-la-gi-hay), *adj.* halfdry; semidry, as clothes on a line. Syn. *malá-malá.*

malagím (ma-la-gím), I. *v.* to feel deep sorrow or distress; be very sad.
—II. *adj.* grievous; deplorable; atrocious.

malaginlín (ma-la-gin-lín), *v.* to be pushed to one side, as clothes in a line. Syn. *masaginsín.*

malaglág (ma-lag-lág), *v.* 1. to fall or drop, as a fruit from a tree. Syn. *mahulog, lumagpák.* 2. to fail, as in an examination. Syn. *mábagsák.*

malaglagán (ma-lag-la-gán), *v.* 1. *(Med.)* to have an abortion. Syn. *makunan.* 2. *(Colloq.)* to happen to lose (a certain amount). Syn. *mawalán.*

malagô (ma-la-gô), *adj.* 1. tall, as grasses. Syn. *mataás.* 2. luxuriant in growth. Syn. *mayabong.* 2. long, as hair. Syn. *malambâ, mahabà.* 3. *(Fig.)* prosperous; flourishing; progressive. Syn. *maunlád.*

malagom (ma-la-gom), *v.* 1. to be able to get all. Syn. *makuhang lahát.* 2. to be able to monopolize.

malagót (ma-la-gót), *v.* 1. to be able to break or cut a rope, wire, etc. with a snap. Syn. *mapatíd.* 2. to break or part suddenly, as a string, wire, rope, or the like. 3. *(Fig.)* to be suddenly ended. Syn. *biglâng matapos.* 4. (with *ang hiningá*) to die. Syn. *mamatáy.*

málagpák (má-lag-pák), *v.* 1. to happen to fall or drop. Syn. *mahulog, mábagsák.* 2. to fail to pass, as in an examination. Syn. *di-pumasá, mábagsák.*

malagpasán (ma-lag-pa-sán), var. **malampasán,** *v.* 1. to be able to surpass or exceed. Syn. *mahigtán, malaluan.* 2. to be able to pass through or go beyond. Syn.

madaanan, malagusán, malusután. 3. to be able to overtake, as in racing. Syn. maunahan.

málahian (má-la-hi-an), v. to be inbred with a certain stock.

malahiningá (ma-la-hi-ni-ngá), adj. tepid or lukewarm, referring to water or liquid. Syn. malakukò, mainít-init.

málahiran (má-la-hi-ran), v. to happen to be soiled or stained slightly by or as by a moving dirty object. Syn. mábahiran, mámantsahán.

malait (ma-la-it), v. to be able to vilify. Syn. maalimurà, maalipustâ.

malalâ (ma-la-lâ), adj. aggravated; grown more serious or dangerous; grave. Syn. malubhâ, grabe.

malaláng (ma-la-láng), v. to be able to create. Syn. malikhâ.

malalim (ma-la-lim), adj. 1. deep, as a river, sea, or the like. 2. profound; hard to understand. Syn. mahirap unawain.

malalin (ma-la-lin), adj. full of stain. Syn. mahawa, mamantsá.

malalós (ma-la-lós), v. to be taken or affected all together without exception. Syn. matodas.

malaluan (ma-la-lu-an), v. 1. to be able to surpass or exceed. Syn. mahigtán, malampasán. 2. to be surpassed or exceeded.

malamad (ma-la-mad), adj. membranous, said esp. of meat.

malá-malá (ma-lá + ma-lá), var. malamalá, adj. almost dry, referring esp. to clothes. Syn. malagihay.

malaman (ma-la-man), v. to come to know; have the knowledge of. Syn. mabatíd.

malamán (ma-la-mán), I. adj. 1. fleshy; full of flesh or meat, as opposed to mabutó. 2. containing much; having much contents, as can, box, etc. 3. (Fig.) full of meaning; meaningful. Syn. makahulugán.
—II. v. to be able to contain. Syn. magkasya, maghusto.

malamáng (ma-la-máng), I. adv. more or most probably.
—II. adj. 1. with or having more than others do. Syn. lamáng, nakalálamáng. 2. better than; having advantages. Syn. higít,

nakahíhigít.

malamat (ma-la-mat), adj. full of cracks; having cracks.

malamay (ma-la-may), v. to be able to do by working overtime at night.

malambíng (ma-lam-bíng), adj. 1. melodious; sweet-sounding. 2. affectionate; loving. Syn. mapagmahál, magiliw. 3. with or having the characteristic of a child wanting to be caressed or fondled. Syn. malamyós, malantóng.

malambót (ma-lam-bót), adj. 1. soft; tender; not hard. 2. pliant; bending easily. Syn. sunúd-súnuran, madalíng mahutok o mabaluktót. 3. easily swayed or turned. Syn. maluwág.

malamíg (ma-la-míg), adj. 1. cold; having low temperature as opposed to mainit. 2. cold or chilly. Syn. magináw. 3. indifferent; lacking interest or enthusiam. Syn. waláng-siglá, matabáng ang loób. 4. cool; somewhat cold. Syn. presko, aliwalas. 4. calm; not excited. Syn. mahinahon.

malamlám (ma-lam-lám), adj. 1. dim; somewhat dark; not bright, hazy. Syn. malabò, kulabô. 2. gloomy; sad; melancholy or melancholic. Syn. malungkót, mapangláw. 3. languid; lifeless. Syn. matamláy, waláng-siglá.

malamók (ma-la-mók), adj. full of mosquitoes; infested with mosquitoes.

malamóg (ma-la-móg), v. 1. to be or become softened by or as by overhandling, as fruits. Syn. mabugbóg. 2. to be debilitated by or as by beating. Syn. manghinà sa bugbog. 3. to be able to beat mercilessly.

malampasán (ma-lam-pa-sán), v. 1. to be able to surpass or exceed. Syn. mahigtán, malaluan. 2. to be able to overtake and get ahead of. Syn. maunahan, malusután. 3. to be pierced or penetrated through and through. Syn. malagusán, matagusán.

malamukot (ma-la-mu-kot), I. adj. fleshy, as fruits, like mangoes. Cf. malamán.
—II. v. to become crumpled or wrinkled, as one's clothes. Syn. malukot.

malamuray (ma-la-mu-ray), v. 1. to able to mangle to pieces. Syn. maluráy, magutáy.

2. to be mangled to pieces. Syn. *magkaluráy-luráy, magkagutáy-gutáy.*

malamuyot (ma-la-mu-yot), *v.* (Fig.) to be able to persuade or induce. Syn. *mahikayat.*

malamyâ (ma-lam-yâ), *adj.* referring to the manner of talking like a baby who wants to be caressed or fondled. Cf. *malambíng.*

malandás (ma-lan-dás), I. *adj.* slippery. Syn. *madulás.*
—II. *v.* to be able to trace or follow as a trail.

malandáy (ma-lan-dáy), *adj.* shallow or with slight concavity, referring esp. to plates or similar objects, as opposed to *malukóng.*

malandî (ma-lan-dî), *adj.* sensuous, voluptous (s.o. women). Syn. *makirí, hitád.*

malansá (ma-lan-sá), *adj.* 1. fishy; having a fishy taste or smell. Syn. *amóy-isdâ.* 2. obscene or offensive to decency, referring esp. to language. Syn. *malaswâ.*

malantá (ma-lan-tá), *v.* to become faded or withered. Syn. *maluóy, matuyót, malaing.*

malantík (ma-lan-tík), *adj.* gracefully bent or curved, said of eyelashes, fingers, hips, etc.

malantód (ma-lan-tód), *adj.* coquettish. Syn. *malandî, haliparót, makirí.*

malangaw (ma-la-ngaw), *adj.* full of house flies. Cf. *mabangaw.*

malanggám (ma-lang-gám), *adj.* full of ants; infested with ants.

malangís (ma-la-ngís), I. *v.* to be able to make into oil. Syn. *magawáng langís.*
—II. *adj.* 1. with or having plenty of oil; well-supplied with oil. Syn. *saganá sa langís.* 2. oily. Syn. *makintáb o nangingintáb sa langis.*

malaon (ma-la-on), I. *adj.* for a long time, as in *malaong walâ,* absent for a long time.
—II. *adj.* long, referring to time, as in *malaong pagkawala,* long absence. Syn. *matagál, maluwát.*

malaón (ma-la-ón), *v.* to be left unused or unconsumed long after a new harvest, referring to rice and other grains. Syn. *malumà, pag-abutan ng bagong ani.*

malaós (ma-la-ós), *v.* 1. to be or become overripe, said of fruits. Syn. *malayót.* 2.

to lose potency or productivity due to old age or overuse.

malao't-mádalî (ma-la-o't + má-da-lî), *adv.* in the long run; finally; in the end.

malapad (ma-la-pad), *adj.* of considerable width; wide; broad. Cf. *maluwáng, malawak, malakí.*

malapandiwà (ma-la-pan-di-wà), *adj.* (Gram.) verbal, as in *malapandiwang ugát,* verbal root.

malapit (ma-la-pit), I. *adj.* 1. near; close (in time and space); not far. Syn. *katabí.* 2. close in feeling. Syn. *matalik.*
—II. *adv.* almost; nearly. Syn. *halos.*

malapít (ma-la-pít), *adj.* 1. friendly. Syn. *mabaít.* 2. intimate; close to. Syn. *matalik.*

málapitán (má-la-pi-tán), *adj. & adv.* at a close range or distance, as opposed to *málayuán.*

malapít-lapít (ma-la-pít + la-pít), *adj. & adv.* a bit nearer.

malapók (ma-la-pók), *v.* to become decayed or rotten, referring esp. to wood. Syn. *magatô, magapók.*

malapot (ma-la-pot), *adj.* thick; viscous, like syrup, glue, paint, etc., as opposed to *malabnáw.*

malas (ma-las), I. *n.* 1. act of observing or looking intently at someone or something. Syn. *masíd, pagmamasíd.* 2. bad luck; stroke of bad luck. Syn. *samâ, kabuwisitan, kawaláng suwerte.*
—II. *adj.* unlucky; unfortunate. Syn. *sinásamâ, minámalas.*

malasa (ma-la-sa), *adj.* tasty; savory; palatable. Syn. *masaráp.*

malasakit (ma-la-sa-kit), *n.* care or concern for someone or something; solicitude. Also, *pagmamalasakit.*

malasado (ma-la-sa-do), *adj.* rare; underdone; half-cooked; soft-boiled (s.o. eggs).

malasebo (ma-la-se-bo), *adj. & n.* referring to a tamarind fruit that is about to become ripe. Syn. *malaapog.*

malasin (ma-la-sin), *v.* 1. to observe intently; watch attentively. Syn. *masdáng mabuti.* 2. to be unlucky or unfortunate; suffer bad luck. Syn. *samaín; samaíng-palad.*

malaswâ (ma-las-wâ), *adj*. indecent or obscene, referring to language. Syn. *bastós*.

malát (ma-lát), I. *n*. hoarseness (of voice). Also, *pamamalát*. Syn. *paos, pamamaos; pagaw, pamamagaw*.

—II. *adj*. hoarse; having a rough, husky voice, like that of a person who has cold. Also, *namámalát*. Syn. *paós, namámaos; pagáw, namámagaw*.

malatâ (ma-la-tâ), *adj*. 1. soft, as of food. Syn. *malambót*. 2. flabby, as muscles. Syn. *luylóy*. 3. weak, as of sickly person. Syn. *mahinà*.

malatak (ma-la-tak), *adj*. full of residue of dregs, said of liquid. Syn. *matining*.

malatè (ma-la-tè), I. *adj*. swampy.

—II. *n*. (M-) name of a political district in the city of Manila.

malatubá (ma-la-tu-bá), I. *adj*. with or having red feathers; red-feathers; referring to a rooster.

—II. *n*. a red-feathered rooster. Cf. *alimbuyugin, lasak, mayahin*.

malatubà (ma-la-tu-bà), *adj*. indifferent; unconcerned; inattentive. Syn. *waláng-bahalà; waláng-malasakit*.

malaunan (ma-la-u-nan), *v*. 1. to take a long time. Syn. *matagalán*. 2. to be or become delayed or late. Syn. *maluwatán, maatraso*.

malawak (ma-la-wak), *adj*. vast; extensive; covering a large area. Syn. *malapad, maluwáng*.

málawakân (má-la-wa-kân), *adv*. extensively; in an extensive manner.

malaway (ma-la-way), I. *adj*. full of saliva.

—II. *n*. (*Ichth*.) the common slipmouth (*Leiognathus equulus*).

malawig (ma-la-wig), *adj*. of long duration. Syn. *matagál, maluwát*.

malawít (ma-la-wít), *adj*. low or too low, referring to something that is hanging or suspended. Cf. *malawláw*.

malawláw (ma-law-láw), *adj*. too long, referring to sleeves or legs of pants. Cf. *mahabà, malawít*.

malay (ma-lay), *n*. 1. consciousness, as in *mawalan ng malay*, to lose consciousness. 2. knowledge; understanding; know-how. Syn. *alam, kaalaman, kabatiran*.

Maláy (Ma-láy), *n*. (Eng.) 1. Malay citizen. 2. Malay language. Also, *Malayo*.

malayà (ma-la-yà), *adj*. 1. independent; having political liberty; not under the control of a foreign government. Syn. *maykasarinlán, nagsásarilí*. 2. free; loose; not confined; not tied; not shut in or up. Syn. *kawalà, alpás*. 3. free to decide for oneself. Syn. *waláng nakasásakop, nagsasarilí*. 4. not confined in prison. Syn. *hindî nakabilanggô, kawalà*. 5. (*Colloq*.) not married; unmarried. Syn. *waláng-asawa*. 6. still single. Syn. *dalaga o binatà pa*.

malayaw (ma-la-yaw), *adj*. pampered; too free to do whatever one likes. Cf. *malayà*.

malayò (ma-la-yò), *adj*. far; far away; distant; remote; far off, as opposed to *malapit*.

malayô (ma-la-yô), *adj*. aloof, esp. from friends, relatives, and other persons who are supposed to be friendly; unfriendly; reserved and cool to others.

malayog (ma-la-yog), *adj*. high up in the air. Syn. *matayog*.

malay-tao (ma-lay + ta-o), *n*. consciousness. See **malay**.

málayuán (má-la-yu-án), *adj. & adv*. in a manner far from each other, as opposed to *málapitán*.

maleta (ma-le-ta), *n*. (Sp.) valise; suitcase; portmanteau.

maletín (ma-le-tín), *v*. (Sp.) a small valise, suitcase, or portmanteau. See **maleta**.

malî (ma-lî), I. *adj*. wrong; incorrect; mistaken; erroneous. Syn. *di-wastô, di-tamà, lisyâ, sala*.

—II. *n*. mistake; error; blunder; oversight. Syn. *kamálian, pagkakámalî*.

malibág (ma-li-bág), *adj*. thick with dirt, referring to a person's skin.

maliban (ma-li-ban), *adj*. with or having many absences. Syn. *maraming liban o palyo, mapalyo*.

máliban[1] (má-li-ban), I. *conj*. unless; except; if not. Syn. *kung hindî, habang hindî*.

—II. *prep*. except; but; with the exception of.

máliban[2] (má-li-ban), *v*. to be postponed.

malibáng (ma-li-báng), *v*. 1. to be attracted by something interesting. Syn. *maákit*. 2.

to be entertained or amused. Syn. *maalíw.*

malibog (ma-li-bog), *adj.* lustful; sensual.

malibot (ma-li-bot), *v.* 1. to be able to go around a certain place. Syn. *magalà, magalugad, magaygáy.* 2. to be able to visit one by one. Syn. *madalaw na isá-isá.*

malikhâ (ma-lik-hâ), *v.* 1. to be able to make or create. Syn. *magawá.* 2. to be created. Syn. *malaláng.*

malikmatà (ma-lik-ma-tà), *n.* 1. power of invisibility. Syn. *tagibulag.* 2. vision; apparition; phantasm. Syn. *guniguní, pangitain.* 3. transfiguration. Syn. *pagbabagong-anyô, transpigurasyón.*

malikót (ma-li-kót), *adj.* 1. naughty; mischievous. Syn. *pilyo, may-katô sa katawán, galawgáw.* 2. restless; always moving; mobile. Syn. *waláng-tigil, di-mapakalí.* 3. (with *ang kamáy*) inclined to stealing petty objects. Syn. *mapáng-umít, paláumít.*

malig (ma-lig), *n.* 1. culture; development by study, training, etc.; civilization. Syn. *kalinangan, kabihasnán, kultura.*

maligalig (ma-li-ga-lig), I. *adj.* 1. troublesome; causing trouble or disturbance. Syn. *maguló, mapangguló.* 2. tumultuous; very noisy and disorderly; unruly; boisterous. Syn. *nagkákaguló.* —II. *v.* to become troubled or disturbed. Syn. *maguló.*

maligamgám (ma-li-gam-gám), *adj.* 1. tepid or lukewarm (s.o. water or liquid). Syn. *mainít-inít, malahiningá.* 2. restless; uneasy. Syn. *di-mapakalí, balisá.*

maligasgás (ma-li-gas-gás), *adj.* rough or coarse to the touch, referring to a surface. Cf. *magaspáng.*

maligat (ma-li-gat), *adj.* of or having viscous or sticky quality when cooked, referring esp. to rice or tubers.

maligáw (ma-li-gáw), *v.* 1. to lose one's way; be lost on the way. 2. to be misguided. Syn. *málisyâ.*

maligawan (ma-li-ga-wan), *v.* to be able to court or woo, referring to a woman.

malígawin (ma-lí-ga-win), *adj.* prone to being lost on one's way.

maligaya (ma-li-ga-ya), *adj.* having a feeling of joy, contentment, pleasure, etc.; happy.

Syn. *masayá, nagágalák, natútuwâ.*

maligno (ma-lig-no), I. *n.* (Sp.) 1. evil spirit. Syn. *demonyo.* 2. mystery; something mysterious. Syn. *himalâ, kababalaghán.* —II. *adj.* malign; malignant; evil. Syn. *masamâ, nápakasamâ.*

maligoy (ma-li-goy), *adj.* 1. roundabout; circuitous; not direct. Syn. *palikú-likô, hindí túwiran, pasikut-sikot.* 2. verbose; wordy; longwinded. Syn. *masalitâ.*

maligsí (ma-lig-sí), *var.* **maliksí**, *adj.* agile; quick and easy in movement; quick-moving; fast and active. Syn. *mabilís kumilos.*

máligtaán (má-lig-ta-án), *v.* 1. to happen to omit; be omitted unintentionally. 2. to miss; be overlooked; fail to see or include. Also, *mákaligtaán.*

malihim (ma-li-him), *adj.* secretive; not frank or open. Syn. *masekreto, mapáglihim.*

málihís (má-li-hís), *v.* 1. to be deviated or deflected from. Syn. *másinsáy.* 2. to be or become erroneous or incorrect. Syn. *mámalî, málisyâ.* 3. to be misguided. Syn. *máligáw.*

maliín (ma-li-ín), *v.* to make wrong; consider (a thing) wrong. Also, *imalî.*

maliít (ma-li-ít), *adj.* 1. small; relatively small in size. Syn. *muntî.* 2. small in number. Syn. *kákauntî.*

malilang (ma-li-lang), *n.* 1. sulphur. Syn. *asupré.* 2. gunpowder. Syn. *pulburá.*

malilim (ma-li-lim), *adj.* 1. shady; referring to a place. Also, *nalíliliman.* 2. that which gives shade, as a big tree. 3. cloudy; referring to the sky, hence, cool.

malilimutin (ma-li-li-mu-tin), *adj.* 1. forgetful; having poor memory. Cf. *úlianin.* 2. negligent; neglectful. Syn. *pabayâ, mapágpabayâ.*

málimalî (má-li-ma-lì), *adj.* senile; absent-minded due to old age. Syn. *úlianin.*

malî-malî (ma-lî + ma-lî), *adj.* with or having many errors or mistakes; full of mistakes. Syn. *maraming malî.*

malimang (ma-li-mang), *v.* to be confused in counting; make a mistake in counting. Syn. *malitó o magkámalî sa pagbilang.*

malimit (ma-li-mit), I. *adj.* 1. set or placed too close to each other or to one another.

Syn. *masinsín*. 2. frequent; often. Syn. *madalás*.

—II. *adv*. 1. closely; in a manner close to each other or to one another. 2. often; frequently.

malimot (ma-li-mot), *v*. to be able to forget.

malimutan (ma-li-mu-tan), *v*. 1. to happen to forget; be forgotten. Syn. *mákaligtaán*. 2. to happen to neglect; be neglected. Syn. *mapábayaán*.

malina (ma-li-na), *n*. (*Old Tag.*) nymph. Syn. *nimpa*.

malináb (ma-li-náb), *adj*. full of fatty scum on the surface, referring to liquids, esp. broth.

malinamnám (ma-li-nam-nám), *adj*. delicious; very tasty or savory. Cf. *masaráp*.

malináng (ma-li-náng), *v*. 1. to be able to cultivate (a farm). Syn. *mabukid*, *matamnán*. 2. to be able to develop, as a language. Syn. *mapaunlád*. 3. to be able to develop, as by training. Syn. *masanay*.

malinaw (ma-li-naw), I. *adj*. 1. clear; transparent. Syn. *aninaw, naaáninaw*. 2. bright, as a light. Syn. *maliwanag*. 3. obvious; evident; distinct; manifest; unmistakable. Syn. *di-mapágáalinlanganan, waláng-duda, tiyák, maliwanag*.

malining (ma-li-ning), *v*. to be able to consider or study cautiously or carefully. Syn. *mapág-isipang mabuti*.

malinis (ma-li-nis), I. *adj*. 1. clean; neat; not dirty. Syn. *waláng-dumí*. 2. clean; pure. Syn. *dalisay, puro*. 3. morally clean. —II. *v*. to be able to clean.

malinláng (ma-lin-láng), *v*. to be able to cheat, deceive, or defraud. Syn. *mapáglalangán, madayà*.

malintâ (ma-lin-tâ), *adj*. infested with leeches, as a river.

malintikán (ma-lin-ti-kán), *v*. (*Colloq.*) to meet an unforeseen failure or disappointment. Syn. *mápahamak*.

malintóg (ma-lin-tóg), *adj*. 1. swollen. Syn. *namámagâ*. 2. blistered. Syn. *may-paltós*.

málingát (má-li-ngát), *v*. to happen to forget or neglect for a moment what one is doing; be distracted momentarily. Syn.

makalimot na sandalî.

malinggít (ma-ling-gít), *adj*. small; quite small. Syn. *maliít*.

málingunán (má-li-ngu-nán), *v*. to happen to see as one looks at the back. Syn. *mákita sa paglingón*.

malipák (ma-li-pák), *adj*. having callouses; full of callouses. Syn. *makalyo*.

malipol (ma-li-pol), *v*. 1. to be able to exterminate or wipe out. 2. to become lost, extinct, or wiped out. Syn. *mapuksâ, maubos, mawaláng lahát*.

malipós (ma-li-pós), *v*. to be fully covered with; be full of.

maliputô (ma-li-pu-tô), *adj*. short-bodied, referring to a person. Syn. *pandák*.

malirip (ma-li-rip), *v*. to be able to realize or understand the truth or facts about something. Syn. *máunawaan, máintindihán*.

maliróy (ma-li-róy), *adj*. viscous; gelatinous. Syn. *malambót na parang gulaman*.

malisâ (ma-li-sâ), I: *adj*. with or having many nits (louse eggs); full of nits. Syn. *maraming lisâ, punó ng lisâ*.

—II. *v*. to be able to rummage or search thoroughly; be able to comb, as a place. Syn. *magalugad*.

malisya (ma-lis-ya), *n*. (*Sp. malicia*) malice. Syn. *masamáng hángarin*.

málisyâ (má-lis-yâ), *v*. 1. to be wrong or mistaken. Syn. *mámalí*. 2. to be misguided. Syn. *máligáw*.

maliw (ma-liw), *n*. 1. end; conclusion; usually used in the negative, as in *waláng maliw*, without end. Syn. *katapusan, wakás*. 2. loss or disappearance, as of intensity. Syn. *lipas, paglipas, pagkawalâ, pagkapawî*.

maliwag (ma-li-wag), *adj*. 1. requiring a long time to do or finish. Syn. *maluwát gawín*. 2. quite slow. Syn. *mabagal*. 3. difficult; hard; not easy. Syn. *mahirap*.

maliwalas (ma-li-wa-las), shortened form of **maaliwalas**, *adj*. 1. spacious and well-ventilated, usually said of rooms. Syn. *maluwáng at presko*. 2. clear or bright, usually said of the sky or faces of persons. Syn. *maliwanag, masayá*.

maliwanag (ma-li-wa-nag), *adj*. 1. clear as

the sky. Syn. *aliwalas*. 2. bright or luminous, as a light, moon, etc. 3. clear; easy to understand; easily understood. Syn. *malinaw, madalíng intindihín o unawain*.

maliyáb (ma-li-yáb), *adj*. 1. giving off a strong, vivid light; incandescent. Syn. *maliwanag*. 2. easily set on fire; that which burns readily or quickly; inflammable. Syn. *madalíng magliyáb*.

maliyamado (ma-li-ya-ma-do), *adj*. in horse racing and cock-fighting, with the majority of the winning horses and cocks coming from those highly preferred or favored in the betting, as opposed to *madehado*.

malmâ (mal-mâ), *adj*. in an advanced or serious stage; serious or aggravated; grave. Also, *malmák*. Syn. *lalâ, malalâ, malubhâ, grabe, seryoso, talamák*.

malubák (ma-lu-bák), *adj*. full of hollows or holes, referring to roads; bumpy; full of bumps. Syn. *bakú-bakô, mabakó*.

málubalob (má-lu-ba-lob), *v*. 1. to be immersed completely in water, liquid, or mud. Syn. *málublób, málubóg*. 2. to be addicted to a certain vice.

malubáy (ma-lu-báy), *adj*. 1. not tight; loose; relaxed; slack; not well-stretched, as a rope, clothesline, etc. as opposed to *mabagting*. 2. lax; not strict nor closely enforced; not rigorous. Syn. *hindî istrikto, hindî mahigpít, maluwág*.

malubhâ (ma-lub-hâ), *adj*. 1. serious; in a critical condition (s.o. a sick person). Syn. *pátawirin, mabigát ang karamdaman*. 2. in an advanced state; grave or aggravated. Syn. *lalâ, malalâ, grabe*.

malukóng (ma-lu-kóng), *adj*. concave; deeply hollowed, as plates or dishes, as opposed to *malandáy*.

malukuban (ma-lu-ku-ban), *v*. to be able to dominate or put under one's power or authority. Syn. *masakop, mapailaliman*.

malugà (ma-lu-gà), *adj*. having much pus in the ear.

málugamì (má-lu-ga- mì), *v*. to fall into a degraded condition or misfortune. Syn. *mápahamak, mápasamâ*.

málugmók (má-lug-mók), *v*. 1. to collapse;

fall down helplessly. Cf. *máhandusáy, mápahandusáy; máhigâ, mápahigâ*. 2. (with *sa banig*) to be bedridden. Syn. *máratay (sa banig)*.

malugód (ma-lug-gód), I. *v*. to be delighted, pleased, or satisfied. Syn. *matuwâ, magalák, másiyahán*.
—II. *adj*. happy; pleased; delighted; satisfied. Syn. *masayá, nasísiyahán, natútuwâ*.
—III. *adv*. with pleasure, delight, or satisfaction.

maluho (ma-lu-ho), *adj*. luxurious; fond of luxury. Syn. *marangyâ, mahilig sa karangyaán*.

malumà (ma-lu-mà), *v*. 1. to become old or be worn out, as by use. 2. to become outmoded; be out of fashion. Syn. *mawalâ sa moda*.

malumanay (ma-lu-ma-nay), I. *adj*. 1. slow and soft, referring to the manner of speaking. Syn. *marahan at mahinà*. 2. calm or restrained. Syn. *mahinahon*.
—II. *adv*. 1. slowly and softly. 2. with calm and restrain. Syn. *nang mahinahon*.

malumat (ma-lu-mat), *adj*. slow in movement or action. Syn. *mabagal, makupad*.

malumay (ma-lu-may), *adj*. (Gram.) 1. penultimate, referring to a syllabic stress. 2. level or unstressed, referring to pronunciation.

malumbáy (ma-lum-báy), I. *v*. to be sad or lonely. Syn. *mamighatî, magdalamhatî, malungkót*.
—II. *adj*. sad; lonely. Syn. *malungkót, nalúlungkót*.

malumì (ma-lu-mì), *adj*. (Gram.) grave, referring to an accent; with or having a grave accent, referring to a final vowel.

malumot (ma-lu-mot), *adj*. full or covered with moss; mossy.

malundô (ma-lun-dô), *adj*. hanging down closely, esp. in the middle, due to weight or pressure; sagging.

maluningning (ma-lu-ning-ning), *adj*. shining brightly; brilliant. Syn. *maningning, makisláp, makináng*.

malungkót (ma-lung-kót), I. *v*. to be sad or lonely. Syn. *malumbáy, mamighatî*.

—II. *adj.* sad; lonely; sorrowful. Also, *nalúlungkôt.*

malunggáy (ma-lung-gáy), n. (*Bot.*) a small tree, the young leaves, flowers and pods of which are commonly used as vegetable (*Moringa oleifera Lam.*); also, the leaves, flowers and pods of this tree.

malupà (ma-lu-pà), *adj.* 1. full of soil or earth; dirty with soil or earth. Syn. *punô ng lupà.* 2. with or having much land; in possession of much land. Syn. *maraming pag-aaring lupà.*

malupít (ma-lu-pít), *adj.* cruel; brutal; fierce; inhuman. Syn. *mabagsík, mabangís.*

malurit (ma-lu-rit), *adj.* stubbornly repetitious; insistent. Syn. *makulit, mapilit.*

malusak (ma-lu-sak), I. *v.* to become muddy, referring to a watery place. Syn. *magputik, manggitatà sa putik.*

—II. *adj.* muddy; filthy with mud. Syn. *nanggigitatà sa putik.*

malusóg (ma-lu-sóg), *adj.* 1. healthy; having good health; sound-bodied. Syn. *malakás ang katawán.* 2. progressive; prosperous. Syn. *maunlád.*

malutang (ma-lu-tang), *adj.* 1. full of or covered with floating matters or objects. 2. referring to something that floats easily.

malutóng (ma-lu-tóng), *adj.* brittle; crisp; crispy.

maluwág (ma-lu-wág), *adj.* 1. wide or spacious as a room. Syn. *maluwáng.* 2. loose, as a binding, tie, or knot, as opposed to *mahigpit, maigting.* 3. too big or large for, as shoes, slippers, pants, hats, etc. Syn. *maluwáng, malaki.* 4. not full; with only few attending, as opposed to *siksikan, punúng-punô.* 5. not strict; lax, as in the enforcement of an order, law, etc. Syn. *di-mahigpit, di-istrikto.* 6. easy; not hard to tackle with. Syn. *madali, magaan.*

maluwalhati (ma-lu-wal-ha-ti), I. *adj.* glorious.

—II. *adv.* happily; successfully. Syn. *matagumpáy.*

maluwáng (ma-lu-wáng), *adj.* 1. wide; broad. Syn. *malapad.* 2. spacious; roomy. Syn. *maluwág.* 3. too big or large for the size

of, as shoes, slippers, etc.

máluwás (má-lu-wás), *v.* to be able to go to the city. Also, *mapáluwás.*

maluwát (ma-lu-wát), I. *adj.* 1. long in time; requiring a long time. Syn. *matagál, malawig.* 2. late; delayed. Syn. *hulí, atrasado.*

—II. *adv.* 1. for a long time. Syn. *matagál, malaon.* 2. lengthily. Syn. *mahabà, matagál.*

maluylóy (ma-luy-lóy), *adj.* too flabby; hanging or dangling loosely.

mam[1] (mam), n. a child's word used when asking for water to drink. See **mamam.**

mam[2] (mam), n. (*Eng.*) 1. Madam. 2. (*Colloq.*) mom; mother.

mam- (mam) : pref. used as a variant of *mang-,* before roots beginning with *b* and *p,* which may be omitted sometimes. See **man-** and **mang-.**

mamà (ma-mà), n. 1. (*Colloq.*) man; any man. *Ang mamang iyón ay kilalá ko.* I know that man. 2. Mister. Syn. *ginoó.* 3. (*Colloq.*) stepfather. Syn. *tiyuhin, amáng pangumán.*

mamád (ma-mád), *adj.* 1. soft and somewhat swollen due to over-exposure to water or liquid (s.o. hands, feet, and other parts of the body). See **babád.** 2. (*Fig.*) without feeling. Syn. *manhíd, hindî na nakakáramdám.* 3. not well pressed or ironed, referring to clothes. Syn. *manhíd.*

mamadór (ma-ma-dór), n. (*Sp.*) nursing bottle. Syn. *boteng pásusuhán.*

mamahò (ma-ma-hò), *adj.* to stink; give out repulsive or foul odor. Syn. *mangamóy, magkaamóy.*

mamalagì (ma-ma-la-gì), *v.* 1. to stay or remain permanently in a certain place. Syn. *manatili.* 2. to remain unchanged; be always the same. Syn. *di-magbago.*

mamalasakit (ma-ma-la-sa-kit), *adj.* solicitous; showing care, attention, or concern. Also, *mapágmalasakit.*

mamalî (ma-ma-lî), *adj.* having or committing many errors or mistakes. Syn. *maraming malî.*

mámalî (má-ma-lî), *v.* to be mistaken; commit an error or mistake. Also, *magkamalî.*

mamalità (ma-ma-li-tà), *v.* to spread gossip about somebody.

mamalò (ma-ma-lò), *v.* to punish (someone) by whipping.

mamam (ma-mam), *n.* a baby's word when asking for water to drink. See **mam**.

mámamahayág (má-ma-ma-ha-yág), *n.* newspaperman. Syn. *peryodìsta.*

mámamalakaya (má-ma-ma-la-ka-ya), *n.* fisherman, esp. one who uses a *palakaya.*

mámamangkâ (ma-ma-mang-kâ), *n.* boatman. Syn. *bangkero.*

mámamatay-sunog (má-ma-ma-tay + su-nog), *n.* fireman; fire fighter. Syn. *bumbero.*

mámamatay-tao (má-ma-ma-tay + ta-o), *n.* murderer; assassin.

mámamayán (má-ma-ma-yán), *v.* citizen; loosely, a native or inhabitant of a place. Cf. *taong-bayan.*

mamana (ma-ma-na), *adj.* having received much inheritance.

mamanaag (ma-ma-na-ag), *v.* 1. to glimmer; appear or be seen dimly or faintly. 2. to have or give a faint manifestation of. Syn. *mábakas, málarawan.*

mamanata (ma-ma-na-ta), *v.* to take a religious vow.

mamanatag (ma-ma-na-tag), *v.* 1. to stay or remain calm. Syn. *huminahon.* 2. to have confidence in oneself. Syn. *magtiwalà sa sarili.* 3. (Fig.) to die; pass away. Syn. *mamatáy, sumakabiláng-buhay, mamayapà (fig.).*

mamanhík (ma-man-hík), *v.* to ask earnestly; implore or entreat. Syn. *sumamò, makiusap.* 2. to make a formal proposal to the parents of an engaged woman for the marriage of one's son. Also, *mamánhikan.*

mamangkâ (ma-mang-kâ), *v.* 1. to go boating. 2. to take a boat; sail by boat.

mamanginoón (ma-ma-ngi-no-ón), *v.* 1. to work as a servant or slave; serve a master. Syn. *magpaalilà, magpaalipin.* 2. to work under someone. Syn. *manlingkuran, manilbihan.*

mamangláw (ma-mang-láw), *v.* to feel lonely or sad; be lonesome or melancholy. Syn. *maging malungkót.*

mamaos (ma-ma-os), *v.* to become hoarse, referring to one's voice. Syn. *mamalát, mamagaw.*

mamarali (ma-ma-ra-li), *v.* to be bragging about oneself or about something one has done. Syn. *mamarangyâ.*

mamarati (ma-ma-ra-ti), *v.* 1. to stay or remain in a place. Syn. *manatili, mamalagì, mamirme.* 2. to remain unchanged; be always the same. Syn. *di-magbago.*

mamasko (ma-mas-ko), *v.* to ask for a gift or gifts during Christmas season, as from one's godparents.

mamasukan (ma-ma-su-kan), *v.* to be employed; work as an employee. Syn. *manilbihan.*

mamasyál (ma-mas-yál), *v.* 1. to take a walk; walk for pleasure; promenade. Also, *magpasyál.* 2. to take a pleasure trip from one place to another. Syn. *magliwaliw.*

mamatáy (ma-ma-táy), *v.* 1. to die; be dead; stop living; pass away. Syn. *pumanaw, yumao, sumakabiláng-buhay.* 2. to stop functioning, as a machine or motor. Syn. *humintô.* 3. to fade away; become instinct. Syn. *mawalâ, malipol.* 4. to become extinguished, as a light. 5. to be out of business, as a store. Syn. *bumagsák (fig.).*

mamatayán (ma-ma-ta-yán), *v.* 1. to have someone die, as in one's family. 2. (Colloq.) to lose, as one's hope. Syn. *mawalán.*

mamay (ma-may), *n.* a term for grandfather in Southern Tagalog provinces. Syn. *lolo.*

mamáy (ma-máy), *n.* wet nurse. Syn. *sisiwa.*

mámayâ (má-ma-yâ), *adv.* at a later time during the day. See **mayá-mayâ.**

mamayagpag (ma-ma-yag-pag), *v.* to be bragging or boasting about something.

mamayan (ma-ma-yan), *v.* to live or reside in the town proper. Syn. *tumira sa bayan.*

mamayani (ma-ma-ya-ni), *v.* 1. to prevail over or against; be victorious; win; triumph. Syn. *magtagumpay.* 2. to be prevalent; predominate. Syn. *manaig, mangibabaw.*

mamayang gabi. tonight; this coming night.

mamayapa (ma-ma-ya-pa), *v.* to die; be dead; pass away; breathe one's last. Syn. *mamatay, sumakabilang-buhay.*

mamaybay (ma-may-bay), v. to pass along the side of a road, river, etc., follow the shoreline or a sea. Syn. *manggilid*.

mamaywang (ma-may-wang), var. **mamayawang**, v. to stand with one's arms akimbo.

mambabae (mam-ba-ba-e), v. to take on a mistress. Syn. *mangalunya*.

mambabasa (mam-ba-ba-sa), n. a newspaper or magazine reader or readers.

mambabatas (mam-ba-ba-tas), n. lawmaker; legislator. Syn. *mambabatas, lehislador*.

mambagabag (mam-ba-ga-bag), v. to break up the quiet or serenity of; cause uneasiness or anxiety to.

mambatikos (mam-ba-ti-kos), v. to criticize (others) severely. Syn. *manuligsa*.

mambola (mam-bo-la), v. (Slang) 1. to make jokes. Syn. *mambiro*. 2. (Colloq.) to flatter; praise beyond the truth.

mambubutang (mam-bu-bu-tang), n. a gangster; tough guy. Syn. *butangero*.

mambuko (ma-bu-ko), v. to contradict another just for the fun of it. Syn. *mangontra*.

mambugabog (mam-bu-ga-bog), v. to disturb or break up the peace of. Syn. *mambulabog, manggulo*.

mambulahaw (mam-bu-la-haw), v. to cause disturbance; break up the silence or peace of. Syn. *mambulabog, mambugabog*.

mamera (ma-me-ra), I. adj. 1. costing one centavo each (a piece). 2. consisting of one-centavo pieces.

—II. adv. at one centavo each.

mami (ma-mi), n. a kind of Chinese dish consisting principally of noodles with condiments and broth.

mamihasa (ma-mi-ha-sa), v. to be in the habit of; be accustomed or trained to. Syn. *masanay, mahirati*.

mamilaylay (ma-mi-lay-lay), v. (used poetically) to come out from one's mouth; be uttered. Syn. *mamutawi*.

mamili[1] (ma-mi-li), v. to go shopping or marketing; buy things needed. Syn. *mamalengke, mamaraka*.

mamili[2] (ma-mi-li), v. to pick one's choice; choose or select the best. Also, *pumili*.

mamiligro (ma-mi-li-gro), v. to be in danger of. Syn. *manganib*.

mamilit (ma-mi-lit), v. to force on someone something against his will. Syn. *mamuwersa*.

mamimili (ma-mi-mi-li), n. 1. buyer or purchaser. Syn. *tagabili, tagapamili*. 2. customer or regular customer. Syn. *suki, parokyano*.

mamimintas (ma-mi-min-tas), n. faultfinder; one given to finding faults of others. Syn. *pintasero, mamumula, palapuna*.

maminsala (ma-min-sa-la), v. to cause damage or injury to. Syn. *manira*.

mamintas (ma-min-tas), v. to be critical of other's faults or mistakes. Syn. *mamula*.

mamintuho (ma-min-tu-ho), v. 1. to make a love proposal to (a woman). Syn. *manligaw, lumigaw*. 2. to ingratiate oneself to by doing some kind of favor. Syn. *manuyo*.

mamiso (ma-mi-so), I. adj. costing one peso each.

— II. adv. at one peso each.

mamitas (ma-mi-tas), v. to pick or gather fruits, flowers, etc. Syn. *mamupol*.

mamitig (ma-mi-tig), v. 1. to become tired from standing, sitting, lying, etc. Syn. *mangawit, mangalay*. 2. to become numbed due to fatigue. Syn. *mangimay, mamanhid*.

mamon (ma-mon), n. a kind of sponge-like cake or muffin.

mamukadkad (ma-mu-kad-kad), v. to open or unfold fully, referring to flowers. Also, *bumukadkad*.

mamukhaan (ma-muk-ha-an), v. to recognize or be able to recognize someone, esp. by the feature of the face. Syn. *makilala (sa mukha)*.

mamukod (ma-mu-kod), v. to be distinctively different from others.

mamudmod (ma-mud-mod), v. to distribute or dole out things for free. Syn. *mamigay*.

mamuhay (ma-mu-hay), v. to live or reside in a certain place or locality. Syn. *manirahan, manahanan*.

mamuhi (ma-mu-hi), v. to have a strong dislike or distaste for; be repugnantly against. Syn. *masuklam, mapoot*.

mamula (ma-mu-la), v. 1. to become red; redden. 2. to blush or flush, as from anger, shame, etc.

mamula (ma-mu-la), v. to be critical of a person or a thing. Syn. *mamintas.*

mamulaklak (ma-mu-lak-lak), v. 1. to flower; bloom; blossom. 2. (*Fig.*) to be or become productive. Syn. *umunlad.*

mamulagat (ma-mu-la-gat), v. to stare, as in fear, admiration, wonder, or anger. Syn. *mapadilat.*

mamulat (ma-mu-lat), v. 1. to have one's eyes opened. Syn. *mabuksan ang mga mata.* 2. (*Fig.*) to be born in a certain condition or environment. 3. to begin to learn what is right or wrong. Syn. *matuto, mabuksan ang isip.*

mamulubi (ma-mu-lu-bi), v. 1. to lead the life of a beggar. Syn. *magbuhay-pulubi.* 2. to become very poor. Syn. *maghirap sa buhay, magdalita.* 3. to be financially broke; suffer complete financial loss. Syn. *mabangkarote.*

mamumuhunan (ma-mu-mu-hu-nan), n. capitalist; investor. Syn. *kapitalista.*

mamumuna (ma-mu-mu-na), n. critic: *mamumunang pampanitikan,* literary critic.

mamumuslit (ma-mu-mus-lit), n. smuggler. Syn. *kontrabandista.*

mamumuwis (ma-mu-mu-wis), n. taxpayer.

mamuna (ma-mu-na), v. to criticize a person or his work. Syn. *mamintas, mamula.* 2. to be a critic.

mamuno (ma-mu-no), v. 1. to lead; be at the head of. Syn. *manguna.* 2. to be the head or chief, as of an office. Syn. *maghepe.* 3. to be the president or presiding officer, as of an association. Syn. *mangulo.*

mamuntikanan (ma-mun-ti-ka-nan), v. to be on the brink or verge of. Syn. *mamingit.*

mamunga (ma-mu-nga), v. 1. to bear fruits. 2. (*Fig.*) to bear result. Syn. *panggalingan, pagbuhatan.*

mamungay (ma-mu-ngay), v. to be or become lambent, referring to the eyes. Also, *pumungay.*

mamuo (ma-mu-o), v. 1. to coagulate; thicken into a mass. Syn. *makulta.* 2. to become solidified or to harden. Syn. *tumigas.*

mamura (ma-mu-ra), v. to be scolded or

reproached. Syn. *makagalitan.*

mamurok (ma-mu-rok), v. to become chubby, as cheeks. Syn. *umumbok, tumambok, manambok.*

mamusarga (ma-mu-sar-ga), v. 1. to burst open, as popped grains of corn. 2. to become swollen, as the lips bitten by a bee.

mamutawi (ma-mu-ta-wi), v. to be uttered or said; happen to say or utter. Syn. *masabi, mabanggit.*

mamuti[1] (ma-mu-ti), v. to gather or pick (fruits). Syn. *mamitas, manguha.*

mamuti[2] (ma-mu-ti), v. to become white or whitish. Syn. *pumuti, maging maputi.*

mamutiktik (ma-mu-tik-tik), v. 1. to be fully laden, as with flowers or fruits. Syn. *mahitik.* 2. to be teeming, as with ants; swarm with. Syn. *kumuyaw, kumuto.* 3. to be thickly crowded, as with people. Syn. *magsikip sa dami.*

mamutla (ma-mut-la), v. to become pale; turn pale. Syn. *maging maputla.*

man (man), I. adv. 1. also; too; likewise. Syn. *rin, din.* 2. even if. Syn. *kahit, maski.* —II. conj. though; although. Syn. *bagaman.*

man- (man-), pref. (var. of **mang-**) used before words beginning with d, l, s, and t, but with the last two usually omitted, to form: (a) verbs, as in *mandukot, manlaban, manabik* (fr. *sabik*), *manalo* (fr. *talo*), etc.; (b) nouns, with the first syllable of the root reduplicated, as in *mandudula, manloloko, manunugal, mananalo,* etc.

mana[1] (ma-na), I. n. inheritance; legacy; heritage; bequest; patrimony. Also, *pamana.* —II. adj. inherited; acquired or received as an inheritance. Syn. *namana, minana.*

mana[2] (ma-na), adv. 1. consequently; as a result; therefore, as in: *Hindi siya nakapag-aral; mana'y wala siyang nalalaman.* He was not able to study; consequently he knows nothing. 2. (with *pa*) preferably; the better. Syn. *mabuti pa, lalong mabuti.*

manabi (ma-na-bi), v. 1. to go or pass along the side, as of a road, shoreline, etc. Syn. *manggilid; mamaybay sa gilid.* 2. (Colloq.) to move one's bowel; defecate. Syn.

dumumi, tumae.

anabik (ma-na-bik), v. to be eager or anxious; be enthusiastic about. Also, masabik.

anaka-naka (ma-na-ka + na-ka), adv. 1. now and then; occasionally; once in a while; from time to time. Syn. paminsanminsan. 2. seldom; infrequently. Syn. bihira, madalang.

anakawan (ma-na-ka-wan), v. 1. to be able to steal (something) from. 2. to have something stolen from. Syn. mapágnakawan.

anakít (ma-na-kít), v. 1. to inflict or cause injury to someone. 2. to be aching all over, as one's body.

anakop (ma-na-kop), v. to conquer and occupy, as a foreign territory; put under one's control or authority.

anakot (ma-na-kot), v. to intimidate; threaten with harm or violence; cow.

anada (ma-na-da), n. (Sp.) flock; herd. Syn. kawan. 2. a large group, as of people. Syn. barkada.

anadyâ (ma-nad-yâ), v. to do something to another or others intentionally. Syn. manikís.

anagalog (ma-na-ga-log), v. to speak or talk in Tagalog.

anaganà (ma-na-ga-nà), v. 1. to be in abundance; be plentiful l. Syn. sumaksâ. 2. to be well-off financially; become prosperous. Syn. umunlád ang buhay.

anaghilì (ma-nag-hi-lì), v. to be envious; have envy on someone. Syn. mainggít.

anaghóy (ma-nag-hóy), v. to lament; wail; cry in grief or pain. Syn. dumaíng.

anagimpán (ma-na-gim-pán), v. (poetic) to have a pleasant, dreamy thought about something; daydream.

anagót (ma-na-gót), v. 1. to be responsible for. 2. to be a guarantor. Syn. gumarantiya. 3. to answer back; talk back; reply pertinently. Also, magsasagót.

anahanan (ma-na-ha-nan), v. to live or reside in a certain place or locality. Syn. manirahan.

anahî (ma-na-hî), v. to work with a needle and thread; sew.

anahimik (ma-na-hi-mik), v. 1. to be

quiet; be silent. Syn. tumahimik, huwág mag-ingáy. 2. to calm down; be peaceful. Syn. huminahon, pumayapà. 3. to withdraw from active service; retire. Syn. mamahingá, magretiro. 4. (Fig.) to die; pass away. Syn. mamatáy.

manaíg (ma-na-íg), v. to prevail; triumph. Syn. managano.

manalantâ (ma-na-lan-tâ), v. 1. to cause physical disability. 2. to cause destruction or great damage to (crops, etc.). Syn. maminsalà.

manalangin (ma-na-la-ngin), v. to pray; say a prayer or prayers. Syn. magdasál.

manalapî (ma-na-la-pî), I. adj. 1. costing fifty centavos each. 2. with each one receiving fifty centavos. Syn. tigmamánalapî. 3. consisting of fifty-centavo pieces.

    —II. adv. at fifty centavos each.

manalát (ma-nal-lát), v. to become scarcely supplied; opposed to managanà. Also, magsalát.

manalaytáy (ma-na-lay-táy), v. 1. to pass through or flow in capillaries or tiny vessels, as blood in the body. Cf. umagos. 2. to flow or pass through a long, thin object, as clothesline, telephone wire, or the like. Syn. manuláy.

manaliksík (ma-na-lik-sík), v. to do research work; make researches. Also, magsaliksík.

manalig (ma-na-lig), v. 1. to believe. Syn. maniwalà. 2. to have faith or trust in. Syn. magtiwalà.

manalo (ma-na-lo), v. to win; be victorious; triumph. Syn. magwagí, magtagumpáy.

manambitan (ma-nam-bi-tan), v. to make an earnest plea. Syn. manawagan.

manambulat (ma-nam-bu-lat), v. to be scattered or thrown about accidentally, as seeds from a container. Syn. sumabog.

mánamnám (má-nam-nám), var. mánamnamán, v. to have a taste or savor of something. Syn. málasahan, mátikmán.

manampalasan (ma-nam-pa-la-san), v. 1. to cause damage or destruction. Syn. manirà, maminsalà. 2. to be wasteful or extravagant. Syn. mag-aksayá.

manampalataya (ma-nam-pa-la-ta-ya), v. to believe, as in God; have an abiding faith in. Syn. maniwalà, manalig.

mánanakop (má-na-na-kop), n. 1. conqueror. 2. *Dakilang Mananakop:* the Great Redeemer.

mánanalaysáy (má-na-na-lay-sáy), n. historian. Syn. *istoryadór*.

mánanaliksík (má-na-na-lik-sík), n. researcher.

mánanalin (má-na-na-lin), n. translator. Also, *tagasalin*.

mánanalinghagà (má-na-na-ling-ha-gà), n. allegorist.

mánanambáng (má-na-nam-báng), n. waylayer. Syn. *mánghaharang*.

mánanansô (má-na-nan-sô), n. a cheat; swindler. Syn. *mánggagantsó, mánunubà, mánunuwitik*.

mánananggál (má-na-nang-gál), n. in Philippine folklore, an evil spirit, said to be in the form of man with only the upper part of the body roaming around for victims during night. Cf. *aswang, mangkukulam*.

mánananggól (má-na-nang-gól), n. 1. defender. Syn. *tagapágtanggól*. 2. lawyer; attorney. Syn. *abogado*.

mánanayáw (má-na-na-yáw), n. professional dancer; taxi dancer. Syn. *baylerina*.

manang (ma-nang), n. 1. an appellation given to an older sister. 2. elder sister. Syn. *ate*. 3. a female religious devotee.

manangan (ma-na-ngan), v. (Colloq.) to rely or depend on. Syn. *magtiwalà, umasa*.

mananghalì (ma-nang-ha-lì), v. to take or eat one's lunch. Syn. *kumain ng tanghalian*.

manangis (ma-na-ngis), v. to weep. Cf. *umiyák*.

manaog (ma-na-og), v. 1. to go down the stairs, opposed to *pumanhík, umakyát*. 2. to alight or step down, as from a vehicle, opposed to *sumakay, lumulan*. Syn. *bumabâ, umibís, lumunsád*.

manapá (ma-na-pá), adv. preferably; much the better. See **maná**.

manariwà (ma-na-ri-wà), v. to freshen; become fresh.

manás (ma-nás), I. n. dropsy, beriberi. Also, *pamamanás*.

—II. adj. with or having dropsy or beriberi. Syn. *may-manás, namámanás*.

manatili (ma-na-ti-li), v. 1. to stay or remain in the same place, state, or status. Sy mamalagì. 2. to remain unchanged. Sy di magbabago.

manaw (ma-naw), v. (poetic form *pumanaw*) 1. to die; pass away. Sy *mamatáy, sumakabiláng-buhay, bawian buhay*. 2. to disappear. Syn. *mawal lumipas, malipol*.

manawà (ma-na-wà), v. 1. to supply satiety or excess; overindulge. Als *magsawà*. 2. to lose interest, as in on work. Syn. *mawalán ng interés o gana*.

manawagan (ma-na-wa-gan), v. to issue call or make an appeal for hel cooperation, etc.

mándadangkál (mán-da-dang-kál), va **mândarangkál**, n. praying mantis. Sy *sambá-sambá*.

mandagit (man-da-git), v. to snatch or sei swiftly by or as by swooping, as a bird prey. Cf. *manilà*.

mandalà (man-da-lâ), n. a stack or large pi of rice in stalks kept temporarily in th open field for threshing. Syn. *sipo talapok* (in some Southern Tagalc provinces).

mandambóng (man-dam-bóng), v. commit robbery. Syn. *manloób, magnakau*

mandamus (man-da-mus), n. (Eng. mandamus; a writ or written order issue by a higher court to a lower court. Syr *utos ng mataás na húkuman sa mababan húkuman*.

mandamyento (man-dam-yen-to), n. (Sp *mandamiento*) warrant; order. Syn. *utos kautusán*.

mándaragit (mán-da-ra-git), va **mándadagit**, n. bird of prey. Syn. *ibon máninilà*.

mandarin (man-da-rin), n. (Ch.) 1. (M Mandarin, the Chinese dialect spoken b officials and the educated class. 2 mandarin orange (the tree or its fruits) Cf. *dalandán, dalanghita (naranghita) sintunis*.

mandayuhan (man-da-yu-han), v. t migrate; leave one's own country and settle in another. Cf. *mangibáng-bayan*.

mandigmâ (man-dig-mâ), v. to attack th enemy in war.

andilat (man-di-lat), v. to stare; look steadily with wide-open eyes.

andín (man-dín), adv. 1. unexpectedly; suddenly; at once, as in: *Nang magkita kamí, mandín ay tumayô siyá't kinamayán akó.* When we met each other, he suddenly stood up and shook hands with me. Syn. *agád, kaagád.* 2. it seems; perhaps. Syn. *warì, tila, marahil.* 3. even then; nevertheless; yet; still. Syn. *gayón pa man.*

andiri (man-di-ri), v. to feel intense dislike for something foul or filthy. Syn. *manrimarim.*

ando (man-do), n. (Sp.) command; order. Syn. *utos.*

ándudulà (mán-du-du-là), n. playwright; dramatist. Syn. *dramaturgo.*

andumog (man-du-mog), v. to attack (physically) at the same time, referring to a group or number of persons. Cf. *mandaluhong.*

andurò (man-du-rò), v. 1. to prick someone with something pointed. 2. (Colloq.) to try to cow or frighten someone. Syn. *manakot.*

ándurukot (mán-du-ru-kot), n. 1. pickpocket. 2. kidnapper.

anhík-manaog (man-hík + ma-na-og), adj. said of person who goes up and down the stairs repeatedly. Syn. *akyát-manaog.*

anhíd (man-híd), I. n. 1. numbness. Also, pamamanhíd. Syn. *ngimay, pangingimay; mitig, pamimitig.* 2. fatigue. Syn. *ngawit, pangangawit; ngalay, pangangalay.*

—II. adj. numb; deprived of the power of feeling. Also, namámanhíd. Syn. *ngimáy, nangíngimay; mitíg, namímitig.*

anî (ma-nî), n. (Bot.) 1. the peanut plant. 2. the pod or seed of this plant.

anibago (ma-ni-ba-go), v. to feel new about something; be unfamiliar or unaccustomed to. Syn. *mábaguhan.*

anibaláng (ma-ni-ba-láng), I. adj. mature or nearly ripe, referring to a fruit, esp. mango, santól, or the like.

—II. n. 1. a mature or nearly ripe fruit. 2. state or condition of being mature or nearly ripe.

anibasib (ma-ni-ba-sib), v. to rush forward in violent attack, as a mother pig when someone tries to get her sucklings.

manibela (ma-ni-be-la), n. (Sp. *manivela*) steering wheel.

manibughô (ma-ni-bug-hô), v. to be jealous. Syn. *magselos.*

manibulos (ma-ni-bu-los), v. to have full confidence or trust. Syn. *lubós na magtiwalà.*

manikíp (ma-ni-kíp), v. to be or become tight; feel tightness, as in one's breast while breathing. Also, *magsikíp.*

manikís (ma-ni-kís), v. to annoy someone by doing something that he hates. Syn. *manadyâ.*

manikluhód (ma-nik-lu-hód), v. to beg for forgiveness. Syn. *magmakaawà.*

manikmát (ma-nik-mát), v. to snatch or grab suddenly with the mouth. Cf. *manakmál.*

maniksík (ma-nik-sík), v. to press or force oneself, as in a crowd.

maniktík (ma-nik-tík), v. to watch or observe closely or secretly; spy on someone. Syn. *magmanmán.*

manigás (ma-ni-gás), v. to become hard or stiff. Also, *tumigás.*

manigíd (ma-ni-gíd), v. to be piercing or penetrating, as pain, cold, or the like. Also, *sumigid.*

manigò (ma-ni-gò), adj. 1. lucky; fortunate. Syn. *masuwerte, mapalad.* 2. prosperous. Syn. *masaganà.*

manifl (ma-ni-íl), v. 1. oppress; treat with cruelty. Syn. *mang-apí, magmalupít.* 2. to kill someone by strangling. Syn. *manakál.*

manilà (ma-ni-là), v. to attack, kill, and then eat, as lions, bears, and the like do with other small animals.

maniláw (ma-ni-láw), v. to turn or become yellow.

manilbihan (ma-nil-bi-han), v. to do menial work for others. Syn. *magpaalilà.*

Manilenya (Ma-ni-len-ya), I. adj. of or from Manila, referring to a woman. Syn. *tagá-Maynilà.*

—II. n. a woman native or resident of Manila.

Manilenyo (Ma-ni-len-yo), I. adj. of or from Manila, referring to a man. Syn. *taga-Maynilà.* Cf. *Manilenya.*

—II. n. a male native or resident of Manila.

manimbáng (ma-nim-báng), v. 1. to poise or balance oneself, as on the stilts. 2. to try to be compatible, as with one's companion, chief, etc. Syn. *makisama, makibagay.*

manindíg (ma-nin-díg), v. to stand on end, as one's hair when afraid. Syn. *mangalisag.*

maníndigan (ma-nín-di-gan), v. 1. to guarantee or be responsible for someone. Syn. *managót.* 2. to stand pat; refuse to be intimidated or cowed. Syn. *magmatigás.* 3. to defend one's right, stand, or belief.

máninilà (má-ni-ni-là), n. animal that attacks and eats other animals; animal that preys on other animals.

maningaláng-pugad (ma-ni-nga-láng + pu-gad), v. (*Fig.*) to begin to have interest in the opposite sex, referring to boys in their puberty.

maningas (ma-ni-ngas), adj. 1. easily set on fire; flammable; that which burns readily or quickly. Syn. *madalíng mag-alab o magningas.* 2. giving out bright flames. Syn. *maalab.*

maningkád (ma-ning-kád), v. 1. to become brightly colored. Also, *tumingkád.* 2. (*Fig.*) to be or become colorful. Syn. *maging makulay.*

maninghál (ma-ning-hál), v. to shout angrily at someone. Syn. *mambulyáw.*

maningíl (ma-ni-ngíl), v. to collect debts or bills. Syn. *mangobrá.*

maningníng (ma-ning-níng), adj. bright; brilliant. Syn *makisláp.*

manipís (ma-ni-pís), adj. 1. thin; not thick. Syn. *di-makapál.* 2. having little flesh. Syn. *payát.*

manirà (ma-ni-rà), v. 1. to cause destruction or ruin. Syn. *magwasák.* 2. to talk falsely about someone; slander. Syn. *manirang-puri, magpasamâ ng kapwà.*

manirahan (ma-ni-ra-han), v. 1. to live or reside in a certain place or locality. Syn. *manahanan.* 2. to stay temporarily at the place of someone. Syn. *manuluyan.*

maniwalà (ma-ni-wa-là), v. 1. to believe, as in what someone says. 2. to believe in God and His teachings. Syn.

manampalataya, sumampalataya. 3. t trust; have faith or confidence in. Syn *magtiwalà.*

maniyák (ma-ni-yák), v. to be so sure about consider as a certainty or without doubt Syn. *maniguro.*

manlabán (man-la-bán), v. to fight bac furiously.

manlagas (man-la-gas), v. to fall off, as hai leaves, fruits, etc. Syn. *manlugon* (fo hair), *manghulog, mangalaglág.*

manlait (man-la-it), v. to speak evil o someone; insult; vilify. Syn. *mandustâ mang-alipustâ.*

manlalaki (man-la-la-ki), v. to commi adultery; be guilty of adultery, referrin to a married woman. Cf. *mambabae.*

manlamáng (man-la-máng), v. to take advantage of another or others. Syn *magsamantalá sa kapwà.*

manlibák (man-li-bák), v. to laugh or scof at; mock. Syn. *manuyâ, mangutyâ, mang uyám.*

manligaw (man-li-gaw), v. to make love to court; woo. Syn. *manuyò (sa dalaga) upang máibig.*

manliít (man-li-ít), v. 1. to become small Also, *lumiít.* 2. to shrink, as in shame.

manlililok (man-li-li-lok), n. sculptor. Syn *eskultór.*

manlilimbág (man-li-lim-bág), n. printer.

manlimahid (man-li-ma-hid), v. to be untidily dressed.

manlinláng (man-lin-láng), v. to deceive, cheat, or swindle others. Syn. *mandayà, manuwitik.*

manlitó (man-li-tó), v. to distract or mislead someone's attention. Syn. *manlinláng.*

manloko (man-lo-ko), v. to fool or cheat someone. Syn. *mandayà.*

manloób (man-lo-ób), v. to commit robbery or banditry. Syn. *manulisán.*

manlupig (man-lu-pig), v. to conquer; subjugate; vanquish.

manmán (man-mán), n. 1. a spying on someone; careful or secret watching on the activities of someone. Syn. *subaybáy, pagsubaybáy.* 2. a person assigned to spy on someone. Syn. *ispiyá.*

mano (ma-no), n. (*Sp.*) 1. act of kissing the

hands of elders as a sign of respect. Also, *pagmamano*. 2. right or right turn (in traffic), opposed to *silya o kaliwâ*. 3. the right of a player or players to be first in playing the game, as in batting in baseball. 4. coating or layer, as of paint: *unang mano*, first coating. Syn. *pahid*. 5. quire or a set of 24 or 25 sheets, as of paper of the same size and stock.

manók (ma-nók), n. 1. chicken (live). 2. chicken meat or a dish of this. 3. (*Fig.*) a protégé or person for whom one's support is given, as in an election. Syn. *kandidato*, *pambatò*, *batà* (*colloq.*).

mánonoód (má-no-no-ód), n. 1. audience. 2. spectator; onlooker. Syn. *mirón*, *usyoso*.

manong (ma-nong), n. 1. an appellation given to an elder brother or male cousin. Syn. *kuya*. 2. a male religious devotee.

manoód (ma-no-ód), v. 1. to attend or see a show, concert, game, etc. 2. to be a spectator or onlooker in. Syn. *magmirón*, *mag-usyoso*.

mansana (man-sa-na), var. **mansanas**, n. (Sp. *manzana*) apple tree or its fruit.

mansanilya (man-sa-nil-ya), n. (Sp. *manzanilla*) the common chamomile (*Matricaria chamomilla Blanco*); a medicinal plant.

mansanitas (man-sa-ni-tas), n. (*Bot.*) 1. a small tree, widely scattered in the Philippines (*Rhamnus jujuba Linn.*), the shape of its fruit is like an apple but very much smaller. 2. the fruit of this tree.

manta (man-ta), n. (*Sp.*) 1. blanket; coverlet. Syn. *makapál na kumot*. 2. cloak; mantle. Syn. *kapa*.

manták (man-ták), interj. think of that; would you believe. *Manták mo! Sinabi niyá sa akin iyón!* Think of that! He told me about it! Syn. *birò mo; akalain mo; mantakin mo* (all used colloquially).

mantekado (man-te-ka-do), var. **mantikado**, I. adj. (Sp. *mantecado*) with lard or butter, as in ice cream, biscuit, etc.
—II. n. ice cream. Syn. *sorbetes*.

mantél (man-tél), n. (*Sp.*) tablecloth. Syn. *tapete*.

mantikà (man-ti-kà), n. (Sp. *manteca*) lard.

mantikilya (man-ti-kil-ya), n. (Sp.

mantequilla) butter.

mantilya (man-til-ya), n. (Sp. *mantilla*) 1. veil over head; scarf for the head. Syn. *talukbóng*, *pindóng*. 2. saddlecloth.

mantsá (man-tsá), var. **mansá**, n. (Sp. *mancha*) stain. Syn. *lalin*, *bahid*.

manubà (ma-nu-bà), v. to engage in swindling people. Syn. *manansô*, *manggantso*.

manubíg (ma-nu-bíg), v. to urinate; micturate. Syn. *umihî*.

manubok (ma-nu-bok), v. 1. to spy on someone. 2. to catch (someone) by surprise.

manukalà (ma-nu-ka-là), var. **munukalà**, **panukalà**, n. 1. proposal; proposition. Syn. *mungkahî*. 2. plan; project. Syn. *balak*, *proyekto*.

manukan (ma-nu-kan; má-nu-kan), n. poultry farm; chicken farm.

manukín (ma-nu-kín), v. (*Colloq.*) to sponsor or support, as a candidate in an election. Syn. *tangkilikin*, *ikandidato*, *batain* (*colloq.*)

manuksó (ma-nuk-só), v. to make jokes at someone; say something that is meant to amuse. Syn. *magbirô*.

manudyô (ma-nud-yô), v. to tease or make fun of in a playful, good natured way; banter. Syn. *mangantiyáw*.

manugang (ma-nu-gang), n. son-in-law or daughter-in-law.

manulad (ma-nu-lad), v. to be imitating or copying others. Syn. *manggaya*, *manggagád*.

manuligsâ (ma-nu-lig-sâ), v. to speak or write against; attack verbally. Syn. *mangatake*.

manulót (ma-nu-lót), v. 1. to poke or thrust someone with or as with a stick through a hole or small opening. Syn. *manundót*. 2. to ingratiate or bring oneself into someone's favor by telling on others.

manulsól (ma-nul-sól), v. to incite or instigate someone to do something undesirable. Syn. *mang-upat*, *mang-udyók*.

manuluyan (ma-nu-lu-yan), v. to board or stay temporarily in someone's place.

manumbalik (ma-num-ba-lik), v. to be restored or returned to the former state or status. Syn. *manag-ulî*.

mánumbrahán (má-num-bra-hán), *v.* to be appointed to a certain position or office. Syn. *máhirang*.

manumpâ (ma-num-pâ), *v.* 1. to take an oath; swear solemnly. 2. to utter a curse or curses on; blaspheme; curse.

mánunubà (má-nu-nu-bà), *n.* 1. swindler; racketeer. Syn. *mánanansô, manggagantsó, mánunuwitik, mánlilinláng.* 2. one who does not pay his debts purposely. Cf. *balasubas.*

mánunubok (má-nu-nu-bok), *n.* 1. a spy. Syn. *ispiyá.* 2. a person who has the habit of prying into others' privacy. Syn. *máninilip.*

mánunubos (má-nu-nu-bos), *n.* 1. savior; redeemer. Syn. *tagapagligtás.* 2. (Ang M-) the Redeemer; Our Lord Jesus Christ.

mánunukat-lupà (má-nu-nu-kat + lu-pà), *n.* surveyor; land surveryor. Syn. *agrimensór.*

manunuklás (ma-nu-nuk-lás), *n.* explorer. Syn. *esplorador, manggagalugad.* 2. inventór. Syn. *imbentor, manlilikhâ.* 3. discoverer. Syn. *ang tumuklás o nakátuklás.*

mánunuksó (má-nu-nuk-só), *n.* 1. a person fond of joking others; habitual joker. Syn. *mambibirò, palábirò, taong mapágbirò.* 2. tempter. Also, *mápanuksó.*

mánunudyó (má-nu-nud-yó), *n.* a person who makes fun of others in a playful, good-natured way. Syn. *mángangantiyáw.*

mánunugal (má-nu-nu-gal), *n.* gambler. Syn. *sugaról, hugadór.*

mánunugmâ (má-nu-nug-mâ), *n.* versifier.

mánunulà (má-nu-nu-là), *n.* 1. versifier; poetaster. Syn. *mánunugmâ.* 2. declaimer. Syn. *mambibigkás.*

mánunulát (má-nu-nu-lát), *n.* writer; author; journalist. Syn. *peryodista.*

mánunuligsâ (má-nu-nu-lig-sâ), *n.* a person who speaks or writes against others. Syn. *mámbabatikos.*

mánunulsól (má-nu-nul-sól), *n.* agitator; instigator; incendiary. Syn. *mang-uupat, mang-uudyók.*

mánunúnog (má-nu-nu-nog), *n.* firebug; arsonist; pyromaniac. Syn. *máninilab.*

mánunuyà (má-nu-nu-yà), *n.* a person who mocks or ridicules others. Syn. *mángungutyâ, mang-uuyam.*

manungaw (ma-nu-ngaw), *v.* to look out of the window. Also, *dumungaw, sumungaw, mamintanà.*

manungayaw (ma-nu-nga-yaw), *v.* to scold loudly. Syn. *magmurá nang malakás.*

manúngkulan (ma-núng-ku-lan), *v.* to hold or perform a job; hold an office or position. Syn. *manúparan, tumupád ng tungkulin.*

manuót (ma-nu-ót), *v.* to penetrate or pierce into.

manurì (ma-nu-rì), *v.* to be a critic, esp. a literary critic.

manurot (ma-nu-rot), *v.* to point or poke an accusing finger at someone.

manutok (ma-nu-tok), *v.* to hold up (someone) at the point of a gun. Syn. *mangholdap.*

mánuwál (má-nu-wál), var. *manwál,* I. *n.* (Sp. *manual*) handbook; manual.
—II. *adj.* manual; done by the hand. Syn. *gawâ ng kamáy, pangkamáy.*

manuyâ (ma-nu-yâ), *v.* to make a sarcastic remark or remarks against someone; mock or ridicule. Syn. *mangutyâ, mang-uyám.*

manuyò (ma-nu-yò), *v.* 1. to ingratiate oneself to someone by doing him favors. 2. to show love to a woman by being very solicitous or accommodating to her.

manyapa (man-ya-pa), *conj.* & *adv.* (often **manyapa't** or **manyapa ba't**) just because. Syn. *dahil lamang; dahil lamang ba.*

manyari (man-ya-ri), *conj.* because; due to. Distinguished from *mangyari.*

manyempo (man-yem-po), *v.* to take advantage of a favorable time or opportunity to accomplish what one wants to do.

Mang (Mang), *adj.* (shortened form of Mamà) used as a respectful term of address antiponed to the given name of a man, as in Mang Juan, Mang Tacio, etc.

mang- (mang-), var. **man-, mam-,** *pref.* used before words that begin with the vowels and the consonants k, g, h, m, n, ng, w and y, with k often omitted to form verbs and nouns, which in the latter case, the first syllable is reduplicated.

manga- (manga-), a combining form of particle antiponed to roots to form verbs in the plural form, as in *mangatuwà*, *mangawalâ*. Distinguished from **mga**, a pluralizing particle for nouns. (Note: In his study about this particle (*manga-*), the author made reference to this as misleading. In the *ma-* and *mag-* verbs, as *matuwâ*, *magtawá*, etc., he contends that in making these verbs plural, (e.g. *mangatuwâ*, *mangagtawá*), *manga-* is not really the pluralizing particle but *–ang-*, which is infixed or inserted between the two initial letters of the prefixes *ma-* and *mag-*; hence, *matuwâ* becomes **mangatuwâ** and *magtawá* becomes **mangagtawá**).

mangá (ma-nga), *art.* the plural of *ang*, usually written *mga*, and often preceded with *ang*: *ang mga*.

mang-aagaw (mang- + a-a-gaw), *n.* 1. snatcher. Cf. *mandurukot*. 2. usurper. Syn. *mangangamkám*.

mang-aawit (mang + a-a-wit), *n.* singer; professional singer. Syn. *manganganta*.

mang-abâ (mang + a-bâ), *v.* to look down on or upon; despise. Syn. *manghamak*, *mangmatá* (*fig.*).

mang-abala (mang + a-ba-la), *v.* to bother; trouble; disturb. Syn. *mang-istorbo*, *mangguló*. 2. to cause someone or something to be delayed. Syn. *mang-atraso*.

mangabayo (ma-nga-ba-yo), *v.* to ride on horseback. Syn. *magsakay o sumakáy sa kabayo*.

mang-abuso (mang + a-bu-so), *v.* 1. to take advantage of someone's weakness or ignorance. Syn. *magsamantala sa kapwa*. 2. to rape (a woman). Syn. *manggahasá*.

mang-akit (mang + a-kit), *v.* 1. to charm; fascinate; attract. Syn. *manghalina*, *manggayuma*, *mambighani*. 2. to cause someone to be induced or persuaded. Syn. *manghikayat*.

mangakò (ma-nga-ko), *v.* to promise; make a solemn pledge or promise; give one's word. Cf. *sumumpa*, *manumpa*.

mangag- (ma-ngag-), plural of prefix **mag-**. See also note under **manga-**.

mangangaw (ma-nga-ngaw), *v.* 1. to appropriate something not his own Syn.

mangamkam. 2. to snatch or grab something from someone. Also, *mang-aagaw*.

mangagím- (ma-nga-gím), var. of pref. **mangaging**, used before roots beginning with b and p.

mangagimbala (ma-nga-gim-ba-la), *v.* 1. to be born, referring to a number of babies. Syn. *ipanganak*, *isilang*. 2. to be or become young, referring to a number of persons. Syn. *magsibatà*.

mangagin- (ma-nga-gin), var. of pref. **mangaging-**, (used before roots beginning with d, l, r, s, and t). See **mangagim-** and **mangaging-**.

mangagindapat (ma-nga-gin-da-pat), *v.* to be or become worth, proper, or meritorious, referring to a number of persons or things. Syn. *maging karapat-dapat*.

mangagintao (ma-nga-gin-ta-o), *v.* to be created or born, referring to a number of persons. Syn. *magkatawáng-tao*.

mangaging- (ma-nga-ging-), plural form of pref. **maging**. See also **mangagim-** and **mangagin** .

mangahás (ma-nga-hás), *v.* 1. to be bold enough to do something prohibited or dangerous; expose oneself to danger or risk. Syn. *maglakás-loob*. 2. to do something not his duty. Syn. *manghimasok*.

mangahiyâ (ma-nga-hi-yâ), *v.* to be ashamed or feel ashamed, referring to a number of persons.

mangain (ma-nga-in), *v.* to graze; be eating on growing grass. Also, *manginain*.

mangalagà (ma-nga-la-gà), *v.* to take care of oneself. Syn. *mag-ingat (sa sarili)*.

mangalap (ma-nga-lap), *v.* 1. to enlist new members, as for a society or organization. 2. to recruit or enlist men, as for the army or navy. 3. to cut trees into logs. Syn. *magtroso*.

mangalat (ma-nga-lat), *v.* to ravel or unravel; become ravelled or unravelled. Also, *makalás*.

mangalat (ma-nga-lat), *v.* 1. to become scattered all around. Also, *kumalat*. Syn. *sumabog*. 2. distribute; cause something to be distributed to many persons or

mangalay   **mangasím-ngasím**

places. Syn. *mamigáy, mamahagì.*

mangalay (ma-nga-lay), *v.* to become tired or fatigued. Syn. *mangawit.*

mangaligkíg (ma-nga-lig-kíg), *v.* to shiver or shake, as with cold. Syn. *manginig sa ginaw.*

mangalingasaw (ma-nga-li-nga-saw), *v.* to emit or give out a strong, offensive odor; stink. Syn. *kumalat ang bahò, mamahò.*

mangalirang (ma-nga-li-rang), *v.* 1. to be extremely dried; shrink or curl due to extreme dryness. Syn. *mangluntóy.* 2. to become extremely thin and weak. Syn. *mangayayat at manghinang mabuti.*

mangalisag (ma-nga-li-sag), *v.* to stand on end, referring to hair, as in fright. Cf. *mangilabot.*

mangalóg (ma-nga-lóg), *v.* to shake, as one's knees when extremely tired or frightened. Syn. *mangatóg.*

mangalumatá (ma-nga-lu-ma-tá), *v.* to feel weak, esp. due to lack of sleep.

mangalumbabà (ma-nga-lum-ba-ba), *v.* to support one's chin with the palm of the hand.

mangalunyâ (ma-nga-lun-ya), *v.* to commit adultery, referring to a married man; have a concubine or paramour. Syn. *mambabae.*

mangálungî (ma-ngá-lu-ngi), *v.* to fall into misfortune or despair, referring to a number of persons. Syn. *mangapahamak, mangasawî.*

mangaluóy (ma-nga-lu-óy), *v.* to become withered, as flowers. Syn. *mangalantá.*

mangamatáy (ma-nga-ma-táy), *v.* to die, referring to a number of persons, animals, or plants. Syn. *magkamatay.*

mangambá (ma-ngam-bá), *v.* 1. to have fear of imaginery danger; imagine something evil would come; have a premonition of something wrong. Syn. *mag-alaalá, mabahalà.* 2. to be in danger of. Syn. *manganib.*

mangamkám (ma-ngam-kam), *v.* to appropriate something not his own. Syn. *mang-akin, mangagaw.*

manganák (ma-nga-nák), *v.* to give birth; bring forth a child. Syn. *magsilang ng sanggól, umanák.*

manganib (ma-nga-nib), *v.* to be in danger.

Syn. *mamiligro, málagáy sa panganib.*

manganinag (ma-nga-ni-nag), *v.* 1. to be translucent or partially transparent. Also, *máaninag.* 2. to be reflected or partially visible through a translucent medium. Syn. *másinág.*

manganino (ma-nga-ni-no), *v.* to have inferiority complex. Syn. *masilóng.*

manganlóng (ma-ngan-lóng), *v.* to take shelter or cover; hide oneself behind or under something. Syn. *mangublí.*

mangangalakál (ma-nga-nga-la-kál), *n.* 1. merchant; trader. Syn. *komersiyante.* 2. businessman. Syn. *negosyante.*

mangangathâ (ma-nga-ngat-hâ), *n.* 1. writer; author. Syn. *manunulat.* 2. composer; music composer. Syn. *kompositór.*

mangaón (ma-nga-ón), *v.* to go and fetch persons for a certain purpose. Syn. *manundô.*

mangapâ (ma-nga-pâ), *v.* to be groping or searching about, as in the dark. Syn. *magapuháp.* 2. to catch fish with one's hands by or as by groping under, esp. in mud or between rocks.

mangapál (ma-nga-pál), *v.* to be or become thick, opposed to *numipís.* 2. to thicken or become callous, as the skin. Syn. *mangalyo, magkakalyo.* 3. to increase in number; be numerous. Syn. *dumami, maging marami.*

mang-apí (mang + a-pí), *v.* to oppress others who are less fortunate. Syn. *manghamak, mandustâ.*

mangapós (ma-nga-pós), *v.* 1. to be or become short of; be lacking or insufficient. Syn. *magkulang, kulangin.* 2. (with *ang hiningá*) to be hard of breathing. Syn. *humingal.*

mangaral (ma-nga-ral), *v.* 1. to give moral or religious advice; preach. Syn. *magsermón.* 2. to give counsel or advice to others. Syn. *magpayo.*

mangarap (ma-nga-rap), *v.* to dream; have a dream or dreams. Syn. *managinip.*

mangasera (ma-nga-se-ra), *v.* to live in a boarding house; be a boarder in.

mangasím (ma-nga-sím), *v.* to become sourish. Also, *magkulasím.*

mangasím-ngasím (ma-nga-sím + nga-sím),

adj. somewhat sour or sourish.

nangasiwà (ma-nga-si-wà), *n.* to take charge of; manage or direct. Syn. *mamahalà*.

nangatóg (ma-nga-tóg), *v.* to shake or tremble, as knees due to cold, fear, or tiredness.

nangawit (ma-nga-wit), *v.* to feel tired or fatigued due to long waiting, standing, or sitting. Syn. *mangalay*.

nangayayat (ma-nga-ya-yat), *v.* to grow or become thin, said of persons or animals. Also, *pumayat*.

nangayupapà (ma-nga-yu-pa-pà), *v.* to be humble to accept one's mistake, defeat, etc. Cf. *magpakumbabâ*.

nangkók (mang-kók), *n.* (*Ch.*) big bowl. Syn. *tasón*.

nangkukulam (mang-ku-ku-lam), *n.* witch; bewitcher. Syn. *manggagaway*.

nanggá (mang-gá), *n.* (*Bot.*) 1. mango tree. 2. the heart-shaped fruit of this tree.

nanggagá (mang-ga-gá), *v.* 1. to practise or commit usurpation. Syn. *mangamkám*. 2. to commit rape on a woman or girl. Syn. *manggahasà (sa babae)*.

nanggagád (mang-ga-gád), *v.* 1. to copy or imitate someone's work. Syn. *mangopya, manggaya*. 2. to falsify or counterfeit. Syn. *manghuwád, pumalsipiká*. 3. to ape, mimic, or imitate what another is doing. Syn. *manggaya, mamadyá*.

nanggagamot (mang-ga-ga-mot), *n.* doctor; physician. Syn. *doktór*.

nanggagantso (mang-ga-gan-tso), *n.* swindler; cheat. Syn. *mánunubà, mánanansô, mánunuwitik*.

nanggagawà (mang-ga-ga-wà), *n.* worker; workman; laborer. Syn. *trabahadór, obrero*.

nanggahasà (mang-ga-ha-sà), *v.* 1. to use force. Syn. *mandahás, mamuwersa*. 2. to commit rape on woman or girl. Syn. *manggagá, manggahís*.

nanggaling (mang-ga-ling), *v.* to come or originate from. Syn. *magbuhat, magmulâ*.

nanggas (mang-gas), *n.* (*Sp. manga*) sleeve. Syn. *kamáy (ng kasuutáng pang-itaas)*.

nanggilalas (mang-gi-la-las), *v.* to wonder; be seized with admiration, wonder, or surprise; marvel. Syn. *mámangkâ, humangà, magtaká*.

nanggipupos (mang-gi-pu-pos), var.

manggipuspós, *v.* to be overcome by disconsolation or low spirit. Syn. *magdalamhatì*.

manggo (mang-go), *n.* (*Sp. mango*) handle, as a knife, bolo, revolver, etc. Syn. *hawakán, tatangnán, puluhan*.

manggulang (mang-gu-lang), *v.* to take advantage of someone's ignorance or lack of experience. Syn. *manlamáng, magsamantalá sa kapwà*.

manggulat (mang-gu-lat), *v.* 1. to take someone by surprise. Syn. *manggitlá*. 2. to show off. Syn. *magpasikat (fig.)*.

mangguló (mang-gu-ló), *v.* to cause or create trouble. Syn. *manligalig, mambasag-ulo*.

manghâ (mang-hâ), I. *n.* state or condition of being amazed or surprised; feeling caused by something amazing. Syn. *taká, pagtataká*.
—II. *adj.* amazed; surprised. Syn. *gulát, nagtátaká*.

manghahabi (mang-ha-ha-bi), *n.* a person who weaves (cloth); weaver. Syn. *tagahabi*.

manghahalal (mang-ha-ha-lal), *n.* elector; a qualified voter. Syn. *botante, elektór*.

manghalay (mang-ha-lay), *v.* 1. to put someone to shame; dishonor. Syn. *manghiyâ*. 2. to dishonor or rape a woman. Syn. *manggahasà (ng babae)*.

manghalina (mang-ha-li-na), *v.* 1. to win over to one's side by inducement; attract or entice. Syn. *mang-akit, manghikayat*. 2. to charm, as with one's beauty. Syn. *manggayuma, mambighanì*.

manghihilot (mang-hi-hi-lot), *n.* 1. midwife. Also, *hilot*. Syn. *komadrona*. 2. massager; massagist. Syn. *masahista*.

maghihimagsik (mang-hi-hi-mag-sik), *n.* rebel.

manghilakbót (mang-hi-lak-bót), *v.* to be attacked with sudden fright or horror. Syn. *mabiglâ sa takot, masindák*.

manghimalay (mang-hi-ma-lay), *v.* to pick or gather spikes of rice grains left on the field by harvesters or reapers; glean. Syn. *mamulot ng uhay na naiwan sa pag-aani*.

manghimasok (mang-hi-ma-sok), *v.* to interfere in someone's business or affair; meddle in something one is not concerned about. Syn. *makialam*.

manghimok (mang-hi-mok), *v.* to win over others by enticement or persuasion. Syn. *manghikayat*.

manghinà (mang-hi-nà), *v.* to become or grow weak; lose strength. Syn. *manlambót*. 2. to lose speed. Syn. *bumagal*. 3. to lose intensity; wane. Syn. *magbawa, umuntós*.

manghinawà (mang-hi-na-wà), *v.* 1. to lose one's appetite for a certain kind of food that a person eats too often. Syn. *magsawà na sa kinákain, mawalan ng gana sa kinain*. 2. to lose one's interest in. Syn. *manghinabáng, mawalán ng interés o malasakit*.

manghinayang (mang-hi-na-yang), *v.* to regret the failure to obtain something that is very much desired; feel regret for not having taken advantage of a certain situation or chance.

manghiningá (mang-hi-ni-ngá), *v.* to pick small particles of food left between the teeth with or as with a toothpick. Syn. *mag-alís ng tingá*.

manghinulí (mang-hi-nu-lí), *v.* to pick one's ears of dried earwax or cerumen.

manghingâ (mang-hi-ngî), *v.* 1. to ask or request for something without paying for it. 2. to beg (for alms). Syn. *magpalimós*.

manghiyâ (mang-hi-yâ), *v.* 1. to put someone to shame. 2. (Colloq.) to refuse or deny someone's request.

manghuhulà (mang-hu-hu-là), *n.* soothsayer; fortuneteller; prophet.

manghuhuthót (mang-hu-hut-hót), *n.* 1. profiteer. Syn. *mapágsamantalá sa negosyo*. 2. swindler. Syn. *manggagantsó, mananansó*. 3. exploiter. Syn. *mánanamantalá*.

manghuhuwad (mang-hu-hu-wad), *n.* counterfeiter; falsifier. Syn. *palsipikadór*.

manghulà (mang-hu-là), *v.* 1. to guess; make guesses. 2. to predict; make predictions; prophesy or foretell. 3. to practise fortune telling; be a fortuneteller.

mangibá (ma-ngi-bá), *n.* to feel strange or unfamiliar, as among strangers or in a new place. Syn. *manibago*. 2. to cry or feel shy in the presence of a stranger or other people, said of children. Syn. *mangilala*.

mangibáng-bayan (ma-ngi-báng + ba-yan *v.* 1. to live or reside in another tow Syn. *tumirá o manirahan sa ibáng bayan*. to travel abroad. Syn. *maglakbáy-baya mangibáng-bansâ*.

mangibig (mangibig), *v.* to propose love make love to; court. Syn. *manligav lumigaw*.

mangilala (ma-ngi-la-la), *v.* to cry or feel sh in the presence of a visitor or strange referring to a child. Syn. *mangibá*.

mangilin (ma-ngi-lin), *v.* 1. to fast; g without or with very little food. Syn. *mo ayuno, magkulasyón*. 2. to observe as holiday.

mangimbuló (ma-ngim-bu-ló), *v.* 1. to fe jealous or envious of someone. Sy *mainggít*. 2. to feel inferior to; look upo someone with inferiority complex. Sy *manganino, mamalahibo*.

mangimì (ma-ngi-mì), *v.* to feel shy to sa or express one's opinion against someon esp. in respect for him. Syn. *maumí makimî*.

mang-imot (mang + i-mot), *v.* to try to as or request someone to give oneself a ve small amount of something. Sy *manghingî ng kauntî*.

manginain (ma-ngi-na-in), *v.* to feed or gra on growing grass, referring to livestoc Also, *mangain*.

manginoón (mangi-no-ón), *v.* to be under boss or master; serve a master or boss. Sy *manlingkuran, mamasukan*.

mangingibig (má-ngi-ngi-big; má-ngi-ng bíg), *n.* suitor; wooer. Syn. *manliligaw*.

mangingikil (má-ngi-ngi-kil), *n.* extortionis chiseler. Syn. *mangunguwart(manghuhuthôt, mangagantso, manananső*.

mangingisdâ (ma-ngi-ngis-dâ), colloq. va **mangingistâ**, *n.* fisherman. C *mámumukót, mámimingwít, mámamalakay*

mangipot (ma-ngi-pot), *v.* 1. to becom narrow or narrower, as a hole, opposed t *manluwáng, lumuwáng*. 2. to become sma or smaller in size, as of clothes, shoes, et Syn. *lumiít, sumikíp*.

mangirót (ma-ngi-rót), *v.* to be smarting or penetratingly painful, as a wound c cut. Syn. *umanták, manganták*.

mangisá-ngisá (ma-ngi-sá + ngi-sá), *adj.* few; quite few; not many. Syn. *kakauntî, ûlán*.

nangisáy (ma-ngi-sáy), *v.* to shake or wriggle violently, as in convulsion or in death. Syn. *mangisíg, magpapalág-palág ang katawán*.

nángitî (má-ngi-tî), *v.* to happen to smile. Also, *mápangitî*.

nangitím (ma-ngi-tím), *v.* to become black or dark; darken. Also, *umitím*.

nangitlóg (ma-ngit-lóg), *v.* 1. to lay an egg or eggs, as birds and chickens. 2. to spawn, as fish.

nangiyakis (ma-ngi-ya-kis), *v.* to rub one's body against something to relieve itching.

nángiyák-ngiyák (má-ngi-yák + ngi-yák), *v.* to be almost crying. Syn. *máluhá-luhá*.

nangmang (mang-mang), *adj.* ignorant; illiterate; uneducated. Syn. *waláng pinag-aralan, di-nag-aral, ignorante, hindi marunong bumasa't sumulat*.

nangmatá (mang-ma-tá), *v.* (Fig.) to look down on or upon; belittle or regard as inferior. Syn. *manghamak*.

nanguha (ma-ngu-ha), *v.* to pick or gather (fruits, flowers, etc.) Syn. *mamitás, mamupól*.

nangulila (ma-ngu-li-la), *v.* to be or become lonely.

nangulo (ma-ngu-lo), *v.* 1. to preside, as in a meeting. Syn. *maging tagapangulo*. 2. to act as a leader; lead or head, as in a campaign, etc. Syn. *manguna, maglider*. 3. to manage or administer. Syn. *mamahalà, mangasiwà*.

nangulubót (ma-ngu-lu-bót), *v.* to become wrinkled.

nangumpisál (ma-ngum-pi-sál), *v.* to confess.

nangumusta (ma-ngu-mus-ta), *v.* to inquire about the health of someone.

nanguna (ma-ngu-na), *v.* 1. to lead; take the lead; be at the head of. Also, *umuna, magpáuná*. 2. to be the first; win. Syn. *manalo, magtagumpáy*.

nangunót (ma-ngu-not), *v.* to be or become wrinkled; form wrinkles. Syn. *mangulubót*.

nangupas (ma-ngu-pas), *v.* to lose color or brilliance; fade. Also, *kumupas*.

nangupit (ma-ngu-pit), *v.* to steal in small

quantities; filch. Syn. *mang-umit*.

mangurakot (ma-ngu-ra-kot), *v.* 1. (Slang). to lose, fail, or be defeated dismally. 2. to steal; loot.

mangurit (ma-ngu-rit), *v.* to pinch someone with the nails of the thumb and the forefinger. Syn. *mangurót*.

mangurót (ma-ngu-rót), *v.* to pinch someone with the nails of the thumb and the forefinger. Syn. *mangurit*.

mangusap (ma-ngu-sap), *v.* to talk or speak. Syn. *magsalitâ*.

mang-utô (mang + u-tô), *v.* to make a fool of someone. Syn. *mang-ulól, manloko*.

mangutyâ (ma-ngut-yâ), *v.* to ridicule or mock (someone). Syn. *manuyâ, manlibák*.

mang-uyám (mang + u-yám), *v.* to scoff or ridicule someone. Syn. *mang-utô, manuyâ, manlibák*.

Mangyán (Mang-yán), *n.* (*Anthrop.*) a member of a non-Christian tribe living principally in the island of Mindoro.

mangyari (mang-ya-ri), I. *v.* to happen or occur; take place. Syn. *maganáp*.
—II. *conj.* (with 'y) because; due to the fact that. Syn. *sapagka't*.

maóng (ma-óng), I. *n.* 1. denim cloth; a coarse, twilled cotton cloth. 2. an overall, uniform, etc. made of denim.
—II. *adj.* made of denim. Syn. *yarì sa maóng*.

maós (ma-ós), colloq. var. of **paos**, *n.* hoarseness of voice. Syn. *malat, pamamalat*.

mapa (ma-pa), *n.* (*Sp.*) 1. map. 2. (*Colloq.*) map-like stain or dirt on clothes, paper, etc. caused by liquid spilt over it.

mapa- (ma-pa), *pref.* used to form verbs, meaning (a) to be able to cause someone to do or perform something, as in: *mapaalís*, to be able to send away; (b) to be able to make (something) into a certain state or condition, as in: *mapabuti*, to be able to improve or make better.

mápa- (mápa-), *pref.* used to form verbs, meaning to become, result into, or happen to be in a certain condition or state, as in: *mápasama*, to happen to be included or become a part of; *mápasamâ*, to result or end up into some kind of disappointment or failure.

mapaabót (ma-pa-a-bót), *v.* to be able to extend or lengthen in order to reach a certain distance or point.

mapaakyát (ma-pa-ak-yát), *v.* 1. to be able to ask or order someone to climb a tree, etc., or to go upstairs. 2. to be able to drive upward a slope, as a car. Syn. *mapaahon*.

mapaaga (ma-pa-a-ga), *v.* to be able to set or schedule (an event, etc.) earlier.

mapaamin (ma-pa-a-min), *v.* to be able to make (someone) confess or admit one's guilt or crime. Syn. *mapágtapát ng kasalanan*.

mapaamò (ma-pa-a-mò), *v.* to be able to tame or domesticate. Syn. *maansó, mapabaít*.

mapabaít (ma-pa-ba-ít), *v.* to be able to tame or domesticate, said of animals. Syn. *mapaamò*.

mapabalità (ma-pa-ba-li-tà), *v.* to become widely known; be known wide over. Syn. *mápabantóg, mápatanyág*.

mápabantóg (má-pa-ban-tóg), *v.* to become well-known. Syn. *mápatanyág*.

mapabulaanan (ma-pa-bu-la-a-nan), *v.* to be able to prove as untrue, said of a statement, accusation, etc. Syn. *mapasinungalingan*.

mapabunga (ma-pa-bu-nga), *v.* to be able to cause (a tree) to bear fruits. Also, *mapamunga*.

mapabuti (ma-pa-bu-ti), *v.* to be able to improve or make better. Syn. *mapahusay; magawang lalong mahusay o mabuti*.

mapakialám (ma-pa-ki-a-lám), *adj.* given to the habit of meddling. Syn. *mapanghimasok*.

mapakiusapan (ma-pa-ki-u-sa-pan), *v.* to be able to request or persuade (a person to do a certain thing. Syn. *mapakisuyuan*.

mapaklá (ma-pak-la), *adj.* acrid in taste, as of young guava fruits.

mapaknit (ma-pak-nit), *v.* to be able to detach, or be detached, referring to things glued or attached surface to surface. Syn. *matukláp, mapuknát*.

mapadako (ma-pa-da-ko), *v.* to happen to be in or near a certain place. Syn.

mápaginda, mápalapit, mápapunta.

mapadamay (ma-pa-da-may), var. **maparamay**, *v.* 1. to be involved o implicated, as in trouble, crime, etc. Syn *másangkót, mápasangkót; mádawit mápadawit*. 2. to happen to be included Syn. *mápasama, mápahalò*.

mápadpád (má-pad-pád), *v.* 1. to be carried or blown away by or as by the wind. Syn *matangáy*. 2. to happen to be in a certain place. Cf. *máligáw, mápaligáw*.

mapág- (ma-pág-), *pref.* used to form (a) verbs, meaning to be able to make (something) into a certain state, as i mapágkasya, mapágbuti, etc. (b) adjectives, meaning having the habit o nature of, as in mapagmahal, mápághimal mápaghinalà, mapagmagalíng, etc.

mapág-akalà (ma-pág + a-ka-là), *adj.* given to the habit of imputing or attributin, something to someone. Syn mapágparatang, mapagbintáng, mapág hinalà.

mapagál (ma-pa-gál), *v.* to be easily tired Syn. *mapagod na madalî*.

mapagaling (ma-pa-ga-ling), *v.* 1. to be able to make (a person) recover from sickness 2. to be able to cure or heal (a cut o wound). Syn. *mapaghilom*. 3. to be able to improve or make better. Syn mapagbuti, mapahusay.

mapagáng (ma-pa-gáng), *v.* 1. to becom extremely dry due to overheating o overcooking, referring to food. Cf matustang mabuti. 2. (Fig.) to be bored o impatient, as from waiting too long. Syn mainíp o mayamót sa kahihintay.

mapág-árimuhanán (ma-pág + á-ri-mu-ha nán), var. **mapág-árimuhunán**, *adj* penny-wise; careful or thrifty in regard t small matters. Syn. *mapágtipíd sa malili na bagay*.

mapág-arugâ (ma-pág + a-ru-gâ), *adj* referring to a person who is very helpfu in taking under his loving care those who are helpless and needy. Syn. *mapág ampón, mapágkupkóp, mapágkandili matulungín*.

mapág-asa (ma-pág + a-sa), *adj.* full of hope very hopeful.

napág-asá (ma-pag + a-sá), *adj.* too dependent on the help of others. Syn. *paláasá*.

napagbakasakalì (ma-pag-ba-ka-sa-ka-lì), *adj.* inclined to taking chances. Syn. *mapág-alasuwerte*.

napágbago (ma-pág-ba-go), *v.* to be able to cause (someone) to change (his ways).

napagbalát-kayô (ma-pag-ba-lát + ka-yô), var. **mapágbalátkayô**, *adj.* given to the habit of feigning to be what one is not. Syn. *mapágkunwâ, mapágkunwarî*.

napágbatá (mápagbatá), *adj.* able or having the capacity to bear hardship; used to suffering. Syn. *mapágtiís*.

napágbigáy (ma-pág-bi-gáy), *adj.* 1. generous; liberal; unselfish. Syn. *mapagkaloób, bukás-palad*. 2. complaisant; willing to please; obliging; tolerant. Syn. *matulungín, mapágpaubayà*.

napágbintáng (ma-pág-bin-táng), *adj.* inclined to accuse others falsely. Syn. *mapághinalà, mapágparatang*.

napágbirô (ma-pág-bi-rô), *adj.* fond of jokes; given to joking. Syn. *palábirô*.

napágbuti (ma-pág-bu-ti), *v.* to be able to do or make in the best way one can. Syn. *mapághusay*.

napágkaibigan (ma-pág-ka-i-bi-gan), *adj.* friendly, said of one who can easily make friends with others. Syn. *palákaibigan*.

napágkailâ (ma-pág-ka-i-lâ), *adj.* very secretive; given to refusing or denying the truth. Syn. *mapáglihim, mapáglingíd*.

napágkaít (ma-pág-ka-ít), *adj.* given to the habit of denying or refusing to give something to others. Syn. *mapágmaramót*.

mapágkalingà (ma-pág-ka-li-ngà), *adj.* very helpful or generous to others. Syn. *matulungín*.

mápagkalokohan (má-pag-ka-lo-ko-han), *v.* to be very fond of. Syn. *mápagka-humalingan*.

mapágkaloob (ma-pág-ka-lo-ób), *adj.* very generous. Syn. *mapágbigáy*.

mápagkamalán (má-pag-ka-ma-lán), *v.* to be mistaken for.

mapagkánulô (ma-pag-ká-nu-lô), *adj.* treacherous; disloyal; perfidious. Syn. *taksíl, traidór*.

mapágkapwà (ma-pág-kap-wà), *adj.* friendly. Syn. *mapágkaibigan*.

mapágkasya (ma-pág-kas-ya), *v.* to be able to make something suffice for a certain use or purpose. Syn. *mapághusto, mapágsapát*.

mapagkáwanggawâ (ma-pag-ká-wang-ga-wâ), *adj.* generous in giving to the poor; charitable. Syn. *matulungin sa mahihirap*.

mápagkitá (má-pag-ki-tá), *v.* to be seen very often. Syn. *makita nang malimit*.

mapágkunwarî (ma-pág-kun-wa-rî), *adj.* prone to the habit of pretending to be what he is not. Syn. *mapágpanggáp, mapágkunwâ, mapágbalatkayô*.

mapágkusà (ma-pág-ku-sà), *adj.* with or having initiative. Also, *maykusà*.

mapághanáp (ma-pág-ha-náp), *v.* too faultfinding or critical of others. Syn. *maintasin, mapamintás*.

mapághandaán (ma-pág-han-da-án), *v.* to be able to prepare for.

mapághanguan (ma-pág-ha-ngu-an), *v.* to be able to use as a basis of. Syn. *mapágbantayan*.

mapágharáp-haráp (ma-pág-ha-ráp + ha-ráp), *v.* to be able to have or cause (a number of persons) to meet one another. Syn. *mapágtagpú-tagpô*.

mapághari-harian (ma-pág-ha-rí + ha-ri-an), *adj.* domineering; inclined to rule or control by strength or power. Syn. *mapánduminá*.

mapághimagsík (ma-pág-hi-mag-sík), *adj.* 1. rebellious; defying authority. Syn. *mapánlabán, mapándigmâ*. 2. insolent. Syn. *suwaíl, matutól*.

mapághimalâ (ma-pág-hi-ma-lâ), *adj.* miraculous. Syn. *mapágmilagró, milagroso*.

mápaghinalaan (má-pag-hi-na-la-an), *v.* to be suspected of; be the subject of someone's suspicion. Syn. *mápag-suspetsahán*.

mápaghinanakitán (má-pag-hi-na-na-ki-tán), *v.* to be the object of someone's resentment or reproachful feeling.

mapághunos-dilì (ma-pág-hu-nos + di-lì), var. **mapághunusdilì**, *adj.* cautious or calm in one's act or disposition; given to the habit of thinking cautiously before making a decision. Syn. *mahinahon, hindî pabiglá-biglâ.*

mapág-imbót (ma-pág + im-bót), *adj.* covetous; selfish; greedy; avaricious. Syn. *sakím, masakím; kamkám, makamkám.*

mapág-impók (ma-pág + im-pók), *adj.* frugal; saving; economical. Syn. *matipíd, mapágtipíd.*

mapagin- (ma-pa-gin-), *pref.* var. of **mapaging,** used before words beginning with d and t.

mapagíndapat (ma-pa-gín-da-pat), *v.* to be able to make someone or something suitable or appropriate for. Syn. *mapagíng karapat-dapat.*

mapagínhawa (ma-pa-gín-ha-wa), *v.* to be able to give comfort or ease to. Syn. *mabigyán ng ginhawa.* 2. to be able to make easy or easier to do or make. Syn. *mapaalwán, mapagaán, mapadalî.*

mapagíng (ma-pa-gíng), *v.* to be able to make someone or something into a certain state or status. Syn. *magawâ.*

mapág-isá (ma-pág + i-sá), *v.* to be able to unite into a single unit. Syn. *magawang isá na lamang.*

mápag-isá (má-pag + i-sá), *v.* to be left alone. Syn. *maiwang nag-iisá.*

mapág-isá-isá (ma-pág + i-sá + i-sá), *v.* to be able to separate individually.

mapág-isíp (ma-pág + i-síp), *adj.* 1. often in a pensive mood; inclined to thinking deeply or seriously. 2. with or having a certain mind. Syn. *paláisíp.*

mápag-itingan (má-pag + i-ti-ngan), *v.* to be the focus, as of one's ire or anger. Syn. *mápagbuntunán.*

mapág-iwan (ma-pág + i-wan), *v.* to be left behind by others.

mapáglaanan (ma-pág-la-a-nan), *v.* to be able to keep something in reserve for. Syn. *mapágtaanan, mapághandaan.*

mapáglangís (ma-pág-la-ngís), *adj.* referring to a person who has the habit of ingratiating oneself by flattery or insincere praise. Syn. *mapágmapurí.*

mapágmagalíng (ma-pág-ma-ga-líng), *v.* 1. given to bragging, esp. about one's work or oneself. Syn. *mapághambóg.* 2. given to the habit of ingratiating oneself by flattery

or insincere praise. Syn. *mapágmapurí.*

mapágmalasakit (ma-pág-ma-la-sa-kit), *adj.* referring to a person who is sincerel▮ concerned for the good or welfare c▮ another. Syn. *mapágkandili.*

mapágmapurí (ma-pág-ma-pu-rí), *adj.* give▮ to the habit of ingratiating oneself b▮ flattery or insincere praise. Syn. *mapág▮ magalíng.*

mapágmarunóng (ma-pag-ma-ru-nong), *ad▮* referring to a person who has the habit ▮ trying to impress others with what h▮ knows. Also, *mapágdunung-dunungan.*

mapágmasdán (ma-pág-mas-dán), *v.* to b▮ able to observe (a person or thing▮ intently. Syn. *matingnáng mabuti.*

mapágmasíd (ma-pág-ma-síd), *adj▮* observant; keenly; quick to notice. Sy▮ *mapúnahin, mapágmalas, mapánsinin.*

mapágmatá (ma-pág-ma-tá), *adj.* inclined t▮ belittling others. Syn. *mapánghamak.*

mapágmataás (ma-pág-ma-ta-ás), *adj▮* haughty; too proud of oneself; arrogan▮ Syn. *palalò, mapágmalakí.*

mapágmatigás (ma-pág-ma-ti-gás), *adj▮* stubborn; obstinate. Syn. *sutíl, matigás an▮ uló, suwaíl.*

mapágmatuwíd (ma-pág-ma-tu-wíd), va▮ **mapágmatwíd,** *adj.* apt to argue▮ argumentative; contentious. Syn. *palá▮ tutól, palákontra.*

mapágmatyág (ma-pág-mat-yág), *adj.* give▮ to observing others closely or secretl▮ secretly watchful or alert.

mapagod (ma-pa-god), *v.* to be or becom▮ tired or weary.

mapágpabayâ (ma-pág-pa-ba-yâ), *adj.* ▮ negligent; neglectful. Also, *pabayâ.* 2▮ careless; inattentive. Syn. *waláng-ingat.*

mapágpakasakit (ma-pág-pa-ka-sa-kit), *adj▮* referring to a person who makes sacrific▮ or who perseveres by doing difficult wor▮ to help another. Syn. *mápagpakahirap.*

mapágpakitang-tao (ma-pág-pa-ki-tang + ta▮ o), *adj.* given to ostentation; ostentatiou▮ showy; pretentious. Syn. *pasikat▮ mapágpasikat; mapágparangyâ.*

mapágpakumbabâ (ma-pág-pa-kum-ba-bâ▮ *adj.* humble; modest; not proud. Syr▮ *mababang-loób, hindî mapágmataás.*

mapágpakundangan (ma-pág-pa-kun-da-ngan), *adj*. 1. considerate of others' rights. Syn. *mapágbigáy*. 2. showing regard, esp. for elders; respectful. Syn. *magalang, mapitagan*.

mapágpakunwarî (ma-pág-kun-wa-rî), var. **mapágpakunyarî**, *adj*. prone to the habit of pretending to be what one is not.

mapágpahamak (ma-pág-pa-ha-mak), *adj*. referring to a person who causes others to fail, be injured, etc. Cf. *mapágpasamâ*.

mapágpalà (ma-pág-pa-là), I. *adj*. helpful. Syn. *matulungín*.
—II. *v*. to be able to help (someone in need). Syn. *matulungan*.

mapágpanggáp (ma-pág-pang-gáp), *adj*. pretentious; given to the habit of claiming to be what one is not.

mapágpasiyahán (ma-pág-pa-si-ya-hán), *v*. to be able to render a decision on. Syn. *madisisyunán, mahatulan*.

mapágsino (ma-pág-si-no), *v*. to be able to recognize who the person is. Syn. *mákilala, mámukhaán*.

mapágsisihan (ma-pág-si-si-han), *v*. to be able to repent or feel sorry for (the wrong or sin done).

mapágsiyá (ma-pág-si-yá), *v*. to be able to recognize who one is. Syn. *mapágsino, mákilala*.

mapágtamà (ma-pág-ta-mà), *v*. 1. to be able to fit or adjust correctly or exactly. 2. to be able to correct or make right. Syn. *maiwastô*.

mapágtibay (ma-pág-ti-bay), *v*. to be able to approve, as a resolution, appointment, bill, etc.

mapágtimpî (ma-pág-tim-pî), *adj*. having self-control. Syn. *mahinahon, hindî mapusok, hindî pabiglá-biglâ*.

mapagtítiwalaan (ma-pag-tí-ti-wa-la-an), *adj*. trustworthy; reliable; that can be trusted. Syn. *maáasahan*.

mapágtiwalà (ma-pág-ti-wa-là), *adj*. referring to a person who is trustful of others.

mapágtiyagaán (ma-pág-ti-ya-ga-án), *v*. to be able to persevere or continue steadily in doing a hard work. Syn. *mapág-tiisáng gawín*.

mapágtulungan (ma-pág-tu-lu-ngan), *v*. 1. to be able to do or make by helping each other. 2. to be able to fight together against someone.

mapágwaláng-bahalà (ma-pág-wa-láng + ba-ha-là), *adj*. habitually unconcerned, indifferent, or disinterested.

mapágyaman (ma-pág-ya-man), *v*. to be able to preserve or take good care of, as a treasure. Syn. *maalagaang mabuti*.

mápahamak (má-pa-ha-mak), *v*. 1. to suffer an injury or damage. Syn. *mapinsalà*. 2. to meet failure or disappointment. Syn. *mabigô*.

mapahusay (ma-pa-hu-say), *v*. to be able to improve or make better. Syn. *mapabuti, mapaigi*.

mapaibig (ma-pa-i-big), *v*. to be able to win the love of.

mapaít (ma-pa-ít), *adj*. bitter.

mapaiyák (ma-pa-i-yák), *v*. to be able to make (someone) cry. Syn. *mapaluhà*.

mápaiyák (má-pa-i-yák), *v*. to be unable to control one's tears. Syn. *mápaluhâ*.

mápalâ (má-pa-lâ), *v*. to get or receive (something) unwittingly as a result of what one has done. Syn. *mápamá*.

mapalakí (ma-pa-la-kí), *v*. 1. to be able to enlarge or make bigger. 2. to be able to support until fully grown, as one's child.

mapalad (ma-pa-lad), *adj*. lucky; fortunate. Syn. *masuwerte*.

mápalaran (má-pa-la-ran), *v*. to be lucky enough to have, see, meet, etc. Syn. *másuwertihan, mátaunán*.

mapaligaya (ma-pa-li-ga-ya), *v*. to be able to make (someone) happy. Syn. *mabigyáng-kasiyahan*.

mápalingát (má-pa-li-ngát), *v*. to be distracted or have one's mind drawn away from for a moment.

mapalot (ma-pa-lot), *adj*. having the odor of urine; urinous. Syn. *mapanghí*.

mápalulóng (má-pa-lu-lóng), *v*. to be deeply involved, as in a certain activity. Cf. *mápasubò*.

mapalungî (ma-pa-lu-ngî), *v*. to fall into a misfortune. Syn. *mápahamak, madisgrasya*.

mapam- (ma-pam-), pref. var. of **mapang-**, used before words beginning with b and p. See **mapang-**.

mápamá (má-pa-má), v. to get or receive as a result of one's effort, as in doing favor for someone. Syn. mátamó, mápalâ.

mápamahál (má-pa-ma-hál), v. 1. to be loved; be held dear in one's heart. Also, mámahál. 2. to be paying or buying something at a much higher price.

mapámahiín (ma-pá-ma-hi-ín), adj. superstitious; full of superstitions.

mapamatahán (ma-pa-ma-ta-han), v. to be able to make someone understand, referring esp. to one who is ignorant.

mapamigyán (ma-pa-mig-yán), v. to be able to give something to everyone. Syn. mabigyáng lahát.

mapamihag (ma-pa-mi-hag), adj. captivating; charming; fascinating. Syn. mapáng-akit, kaakit-akit, kabighá-bighanì.

mapamímilian (ma-pa-mí-mi-li-an), adj. referring to a number of things from which one can select from. Syn. mapagpipilian.

mápaminsalà (má-pa-min-sa-là), adj. destructive; causing damage or injury. Syn. mápanirà.

mapamukhaán (ma-pa-muk-ha-án), v. to be able to accuse or blame (someone) face to face. Syn. maparatangan nang hárapan.

mapan- (ma-pan-) : pref. var. of mapang-, used before words beginning, with d, l, r, s, and t. See mapáng-.

mápanaginip (má-pa-na-gi-nip), v. to dream about. Syn. mápangarap.

mápanahón (má-pa-na-hón), v. to be timely.

mapanatili (ma-pa-na-ti-li), v. to be able to maintain or keep in the same place or condition. Syn. mapamalagí.

mapanibago (ma-pa-ni-ba-go), v. to be able to change; be made again. Syn. maibá, magawáng mulî.

mapanibughuin (ma-pa-ni-bug-hu-in), adj. prone to be jealous. Also, pánibughuin. Syn. mapagselos, seloso.

mápanibulos (má-pa-ni-bu-los), v. to be concentrated or focused on a person or thing, as one's love, attention, trust, etc. Syn. mápabuhos (colloq.).

mápanikís (má-pa-ni-kís), adj. referring to a person who has the habit of purposely doing things that others don't like. Syn.

mápanadyâ.

mapaniíl (ma-pa-ni-íl), adj. cruel and unjust tyrannical. Syn. malupít at waláng katarungan.

mapanilà (ma-pa-ni-là), adj. referring t animals that prey on other smaller o weaker animals.

mapanirà (ma-pa-ni-rà), adj. 1. destructive causing damage or injury to plants property, etc. Syn. mapaminsalà. 2 referring to a person who has the habit c discrediting others. Syn. mapágpasamâ s kapwà.

mapanisi (ma-pa-ni-si), adj. expressin reproach, blame, or censure; reproachful

mapániwalaín (ma-pá-ni-wa-la-ín), adj easily made to believe; easily deceive credulous. Syn. madalíng maniwalà.

mápaniyák (má-pa-ni-yák), adj. referring t a person who has the habit of accusing c blaming others without any reservation Syn. mápamiho, mápaniguro.

mapanlikhâ (ma-pan-lik-hâ), adj. creative inventive. Syn. mapag-imbento.

mapanot (ma-pa-not), v. to be or becom entirely bare of hair, referring to a person head. Syn. makalbó. 2. to become entirel without trees, referring to a mountain.

mapantayán (ma-pan-ta-yán), v. to be ab to equal.

mápanuksó (mà-pa-nuk-só), adj. 1. fond c joking others. Syn. mabirô, palábirô mápanudyó. 2. fond of tempting others.

mápanudyó (má-pa-nud-yó), adj. incline to make jokes or banter. Syn. mápanuksó palábirô.

mápanulsól (má-pa-nul-sól), adj. referrin to a person given to the habit of incitin others to do wrong. Syn. mapáng-upat mapáng-udyók.

mápanumbát (má-pa-num-bát), adj referring to a person who always make mention of past favors he has done fo others as a means of telling that they ar ungrateful. Syn. mápanuntón.

mápanurì (má-pa-nu-rì), adj. too particula about details; critically inclined.

mápanuto (má-pa-nu-to), v. to be guide properly; be on the right direction. Sy mátumpák ng landás.

mápanuyâ (má-pa-nu-yâ), adj. sarcastic;
sneering; expressing scorn or contempt.
Syn. mapáng-uyám.

mápanuyò (má-pa-nu-yò), adj. referring to
a person who has the habit of ingratiating
oneself to someone by doing favors.

mapang- (ma-pang-), pref. used to form
adjectives, meaning tending to cause a
certain act or state, as in: mapáng-apí,
abusive. (Note: mapáng- is used before
words beginning with vowels and with the
consonants k, g, h, m, n, ng, w, and y;
mapáng- becomes mapám- before words
beginning with b or p, and becomes
mapán- before words that begin with d, l,
r, s, and t).

mapáng-akit (ma-páng + a-kit), adj.
attractive; charming; captivating. Syn.
mapánghalina.

mapangahás (ma-pa-nga-hás), adj. daring;
recklessly bold. Also, pangahás. Syn.
waláng-takot, malakás ang loób, mapusok.

mapangalanan (ma-pa-nga-la-nan), v. to be
able to give or provide with a name. Syn.
mabigyán ng pangalan.

mapanganib (ma-pa-nga-nib), adj.
dangerous; risky; perilous. Syn. peligroso,
delikado.

mápanganyayà (má-pa-ngan-ya-yà), v. to
fall into a misfortune.

mapáng-apí (ma-páng + a-pí), adj. abusive;
tending to abuse or maltreat. Syn.
mapáng-abuso, mapáng-alipin.

mapangaralan (ma-pa-nga-ra-lan), v. to be
able to advise or counsel; be able to give
advice. Syn. mapág-payuhan.

mapangarap (ma-pa-nga-rap), adj. full of
dreams; dreamy. Syn. mapanaginip.

mapangkó (ma-pang-kó), v. to be able to
hold close to one's breast. Cf. makalong,
makandóng.

mapángganyák (ma-páng-gan-yák), adj.
seductive; alluring; captivating. Syn.
mapáng-akit, mapáng-halina, mapánghikayat.

mapanghál (ma-pang-hál), v. to become
cool, referring esp. to cooked rice after
having been kept too long on a plate or
in the pot. Cf. matigáng.

mapánghalina (ma-páng-ha-li-na), adj.
attractive; charming; captivating. Syn.
mapáng-akit.

mapanghí (ma-pang-hi), adj. having the
smell of urine. Syn. mapalot, amóy-ihì.

mapangítan (ma-pa-ngí-tan), v. to consider
(a person or thing) ugly. Syn. di magandahán.

mapangláw (ma-pang-láw), adj. 1. solitary;
lonely; unhappy; sad; melancholy;
gloomy. Syn. malungkót. 2. unfrequented;
uninhabited; deserted. Syn. liblíb.

mapáng-uyám (ma-páng + u-yám), adj.
sarcastic, referring to a person.

mapaos (ma-pa-os), var. mamaos, v. 1. to
have a hoarse voice. 2. to become hoarse,
referring to one's voice. Syn. mamalát,
mamagaw.

mapapag- (ma-pa-pag-), pref. used to form
verbs, meaning to be able to make or
require (a person) to do a certain kind of
work, as in: napapág-araro, to be able to
require (someone) to plow.

mapapág-aral (ma-pa-pág + a-ral), v. to be
able to support one in his studies; be able
to make someone study or go to school.
Syn. mapapasok sa páaralán.

mápara (má-pa-ra), v. to be likened to. Syn.
mátulad, mákatulad; máparis, mákaparis.

maparaán (ma-pa-ra-án), I. adj. 1.
resourceful; good at thinking of ways to
do things; methodical. Syn. maraming
paraán. 2. with or having many methods.
Syn. masistema.
—II. v. to be able to make or let (a person
or thing) pass. Syn. mapadaán,
mapayagang dumaán. 2. be able to push
through, as certain papers for approval.

maparam (ma-pa-ram), v. 1. to disappear,
as pain. Syn. mawalâ, mapawî. 2. to cause
to disappear.

máparamay (má-pa-ra-may), var.
mápadamay, v. to happen to be involved
or implicated. Syn. mápasangkót,
mápadawit. 2. to happen to be included.
Syn. mápasama.

maparangalán (ma-pa-ra-nga-lán), v. to be
able to honor.

maparatíng (ma-pa-ra-tíng), v. to be able to
have something reach a certain
destination. Syn. mapaabót.

maparatingán (ma-pa-ra-ti-ngán), v. (Fig.)

mapariwarà   **mapatáy**

to be able to bribe. Syn. *masuhulan*, *mapabagsakán* (fig.).

mapariwarà (ma-pa-ri-wa-rà), *v.* to meet a misfortune. Syn. *mápahamak, máparoól.*

máparoól (má-pa-ro-ól), *v.* to meet a misfortune; be unfortunate. Syn. *mápahamak.*

mapartihán (ma-par-ti-hán), *v.* to be able to give a share to. Syn. *mabahaginan, mahatian.*

mápasa- (má-pa-sa-), pref. used to form verbs, meaning, (a) to happen to be given to, as in: *mapasáakin,* to happen to be given to me. (b) to happen to go to, as in *mápasá-Amériká,* to happen to go to America.

mápasadlák (má-pa-sad-lák), *v.* to happen to fall into a misfortune. Syn. *mápahamak, mápanganyayà.*

mapasagót (ma-pa-sa-gót), *v.* 1. to be successful in having someone give his answer. 2. to be forced to answer. Syn. *mapilitang sumagót.*

mápasaisip (má-pa-sa-i-sip), *v.* to be in one's mind; be reminded of. Syn. *máalaala, mágunitâ.*

mápasaiyó (má-pa-sa-i-yó), *v.* to happen to be given to you. Syn. *mábigáy o mapunta sa iyó.*

mápasalin (má-pa-sa-lin), *v.* 1. to be transferred into another container, referring to the contents of certain receptacle. Syn. *mápalipat sa ibáng sisidlán.* 2. to be translated into another language, as a story, novel, etc.

mápasanib (má-pa-sa-nib), *v.* 1. to be joined, coalesced, or united with; as an occasion. 2. to be or become a member. Syn. *mápasapî, mákaanib.* 3. to overlap accidentally with another.

mapasapit (ma-pa-sa-pit), *v.* to be able to have a thing reach its destination. Syn. *maparatíng, mapaabót.*

mapasiglá (ma-pa-sig-lá), *v.* to be able to make lively or animated. Syn. *mabigyáng-buhay.*

mapasinayaan (ma-pa-si-na-ya-an), *v.* to be able to inaugurate. Syn. *mainagurahán.*

mapasláng (ma-pas-láng), *v.* 1. to be able to insult. Syn. *mainsulto.* 2. to be able to

murder or kill. Syn. *mapatáy.*

mapasó (ma-pa-só), *v.* to lapse; lose force; end. Syn. *mawalán ng bisà, malipasan.*

mapasò (ma-pa-sò), *v.* to be scalded or burned, referring to skin.

mapasukan (ma-pa-su-kan), *v.* 1. to be able to have something inserted into. Syn. *masuutan.* 2. to be able to get into. Also, *mapasok.* 3. to be able to introduce something into, as an amendment to a law. Syn. *masusugan.*

mapasunód (ma-pa-su-nód), *v.* 1. to be able to cause someone to obey one's order. 2. to be able to send someone to follow another who has already gone ahead.

mapasyalán (ma-pas-ya-lán), *v.* to be able to make a short visit to someone who lives not too far from one's place.

mapatalsík (ma-pa-tal-sík), *v.* to be able to dismiss or be successful in having someone dismissed from his place of work.

mapatanyág (ma-pa-tan-yág), *v.* to be able to cause someone to becóme famous or prominent. Syn. *mapabantóg.*

mápatangì (má-pa-ta-ngì), *v.* to be an exception from. Syn. *mápaibá.*

mápataón (má-pa-ta-ón), *v.* to happen to coincide with a certain event or happening. Syn. *mápasabáy.*

mapatatag (ma-pa-ta-tag), *v.* 1. to be able to stabilize, as prices of commodities. 2. to be able to make firm or stable. Syn. *mapatibay.*

mápatatág (má-pa-ta-tág), *v.* to be founded or established. Syn. *mápatayô, máorganisá, mabuô.*

mapatawad[1] (ma-pa-ta-wad), *v.* 1. to be able to pardon or forgive someone. Syn. *mapágpaumanhinán.*

mapatawad[2] (ma-pa-ta-wad), *v.* to be able to give (someone) a discount in the purchase of. Syn. *mabigyán ng bawas o diskuwento.*

mapatáy (ma-pa-táy), *v.* 1. to be able to kill or murder, referring to a person. 2. to be able to slaughter, as an animal. Syn. *makatay.* 3. to be able to put out or extinguish, as light, fire, etc. Cf. *masugpô.* 4. to be able to get rid of or wipe out. Syn. *malipol, mapuksâ.*

mápatayong

mapisâ¹

mápatayong (má-pa-ta-yong), v. to be unnecessarily postponed or temporarily suspended or delayed, as the approval of certain papers. Syn. *mabimbín*.

mapatdán (ma-pat-dán), v. 1. to have something cut off or stopped suddenly. Cf. *mawalán*. 2. (with ng *hiningá*) to stop breathing, hence to die. Syn. *mamatáy*.

mapatibayan (ma-pa-ti-ba-yan), v. to be able to prove that something is true or false. Syn. *mapatunayan*.

mapatid (ma-pa-tid), v. to be able to trip or make someone stumble by tripping the feet intentionally.

mapatíd (ma-pa-tíd), v. 1. to snap or break suddenly, as a tight clothesline or rope; be cut off unexpectedly. Syn. *malagót*. 2. to be able to cut off or break apart, as a rope, wire, etc. Syn. *malagót*. 3. (with *ang hiningá*) to stop breathing, hence to die. Syn. *mamatáy*, *malagután ng hiningá*.

mapatnubayan (ma-pat-nu-ba-yan), v. to be able to lead or guide.

mapatubigan (ma-pa-tu-bi-gan), v. to be able to irrigate, referring to a certain land area.

mapatunayan (ma-pa-tu-na-yan), v. to be able to prove that something is true or false. Syn. *mapatibayan*, *mapatotohanan*.

mápawakawak (má-pa-wa-ka-wak), v. 1. to meet a misfortune; be unfortunate. Syn. *mápahamak*. 2. to be abandoned to the mercy of the elements. Also, *máwakawak*.

mápawaglít (má-pa-wag-lít), v. to be lost, mislaid, or misplaced. Syn. *mawalâ*, *málagáy sa ibáng lugár*.

mápawalay (má-pa-wa-lay), v. to be or become separated from. Syn. *mápahiwaláy*, *mápalayô*.

mapayapà (ma-pa-ya-pà), I. adj. peaceful; free from disturbance or disorder. Syn. *tahimik*, *matahimik*, *waláng guló o ligalig*.
—II. v. to be able to pacify or calm down. Syn. *mapatahimik*, *mapahinahon*.

mapeligro (ma-pe-li-gro), adj. full of dangers. Syn. *mapanganib*.

mapera (ma-pe-ra), adj. having much money; moneyed; rich; wealthy. Syn. *makuwarta*, *mayaman*, *masalapî*, *makapál ang bulsá* (fig.).

mápikít (má-pi-kít), v. 1. to close one's eyes unconsciously; hence, to fall asleep. Syn. *mákatulóg*, *mápaidlíp*. 2. (Fig.) to die. Syn. *mamatáy*, *sumakabiláng-buhay* (fig.).

mapikón (ma-pi-kón), v. (Slang) to be provoked to anger. Syn. *mapiká*, *magalit*.

mapikot (ma-pi-kot), v. to be able to corner or force into a corner. Syn. *makubkób*, *mapágsalikupan*.

mapiho (ma-pi-ho), v. to be certain or sure about. Syn. *matiyák*, *masiguro*.

mapiít (ma-pi-ít), v. 1. to be able to corner, surround, or encircle. Syn. *makubkób*, *mapikot*, *mapaligiran*. 2. to be cornered, surrounded, or encircled. Syn. *makulóng*, *mapikot*, *makubkób*.

mápiít (má-pi-ít), v. to be imprisoned. Syn. *mabilanggò*, *makulóng sa bilangguan*.

mapilak (ma-pi-lak), adj. having much money; rich; wealthy. Syn. *mapera*, *masalapî*, *mayaman*, *makuwartá*.

mapilit (ma-pi-lit), I. adj. insistent; persistent in demands or assertions. Also, *mapágpumilit*. Syn. *magiít*.
—II. v. 1. to be able to force someone to do something against his will. Syn. *maubligá*, *mapuwersa*. 2. to be forced to do something against one's will.

mapinsalà (ma-pin-sa-là), v. 1. to suffer as a result of; be prejudiced by. Syn. *mápahamak*. 2. to be or become damaged or injured. Syn. *masirà*, *masaktán*.

mapintás (ma-pin-tás), adj. too faultfinding; too critical of others or of others' work. Also, *mápamintás*, *mapintasin*.

mapipi (ma-pi-pi), v. 1. to become dumb or speechless. 2. to become dumbfounded. Syn. *matilihan*, *mápatigagal*.

mapipî (ma-pi-pî), v. 1. to be able to flatten, as by pressing or pounding. 2. to become flat or flattened; be pressed flat.

mapirat (ma-pi-rat), v. to be pressed flat, referring esp. to things like tomatoes, eggs, and soft fruits. Syn. *mapisâ*.

mápirmí (má-pir-mí), v. 1. to be or become permanent, as in one's position or office. Syn. *maging permanente o pirmihan*. 2. to be fixed or settled in one's situation or position. Syn. *mamalagì*, *mátigil*.

mapisâ¹ (ma-pi-sâ), v. to become pressed or

crushed flat, as tomatoes, eggs, etc. Syn. *mapirat.*

mapisâ² (ma-pi-sâ), *v.* to be or become hatched, referring to eggs. Syn. *magsisiw, magkasisiw.*

mapítagan (ma-pí-ta-gan), I. *adj.* respectful; courteous. Syn. *magalang.*

—II. *adv.* respectfully; courteously; in a respectful or courteous manner.

mapoót (ma-po-ót), *v.* to feel hate; regard someone with extreme dislike or hatred. Syn. *mamuhî, masuklám.*

mapukaw (ma-pu-kaw), *v.* to be able to arouse (from sleep). Syn. *magising.* 2. to be aroused (from sleep). Syn. *magisíng.* 3. to be able to arouse from inaction. Syn. *mapakilos.*

mapuknát (ma-puk-nát), *v.* 1. to be able to detach or remove, referring esp. to things glued or pasted. Syn. *matukláp, mabakbák.* 2. to be or become unglued or detached.

mapuksâ (ma-puk-sâ), *v.* 1. to be able to exterminate or destroy totally. Syn. *malipol, matodas.* 2. to be or become exterminated or totally destroyed.

mapulaan (ma-pu-la-an), *v.* to be able to criticize adversely. Syn. *mapintasán, mapistaán.*

mapuláng-mapulá (ma-pu-láng + ma-pu-lá), *adj.* very, very red. Syn. *nápakapulá.*

mapulá-pulá (ma-pu-la + pu-la), *adj.* somewhat red; reddish.

mapulós (ma-pu-lós), *v.* 1. to be able to include all, without any exception. 2. to be all included, without any exception. Syn. *malahát, mapanáy.*

mapúnahin (ma-pú-na-hin), *adj.* 1. observant; quick to notice. Syn. *mapánsinin, mapagmasíd.* 2. too critical or faultfinding. Syn. *mapintasin, mápamulà.*

mapunlâ (ma-pun-lâ), *adj.* having plenty of seedlings.

mapunò (ma-pu-nò), *adj.* covered with trees; planted with many trees.

mapunyagî (ma-pun-ya-gî), *adj.* hardworking; industrious; diligent; painstaking. Syn. *matiyagâ, masipag.*

mapungay (ma-pu-ngay), *adj.* having an air of sentimental tenderness; wistful; melancholy, referring to eyes; languishing, as a look.

mapunggál (ma-pung-gál), *v.* to be broken off at the base, referring esp. to horns of animals.

mapuról (ma-pu-ról), *adj.* 1. dull; blunt; not sharp or keen. Syn. *di-matalas, waláng talím.* 2. (with *ang ulo*) dullheaded; mentally slow. Syn. *mahinà ang ulo.*

mápuruhan (má-pu-ru-han), *v.* to be hit or affected directly or critically.

mapusok (ma-pu-sok), *adj.* passionate; ardent; vehement. Syn. *maalab, masidhî, maapóy, mainit.*

mapuspós (ma-pus-pós), *v.* to be replete or completely filled with. Syn. *mapunô, malipós.*

mápusuan (má-pu-su-an), *v.* to fall in love with; have a strong feeling or passionate affection for. Syn. *máibigan.*

mapusyáw (ma-pus-yáw), *adj.* 1. pale or light in color. Syn. *maputlâ ang kulay.* 2. (*Fig.*) shameful; disgraceful. Syn. *nakahihiyâ, kahiya-hiyâ.*

maputi (ma-pu-ti), *v.* to be able to pick or harvest, referring to fruits. Syn. *mapitás, maani.*

maputî (ma-pu-tî), *adj.* white; of white color.

maputí-putî (ma-pu-tí + pu-tî), *adj.* somewhat white; whitish.

maputlâ (ma-put-lâ), *adj.* pale; wan.

maputós (ma-pu-tós), *v.* to be fully filled up; be crowded or fully covered with. Syn. *masiksík, mapunóng mabuti.*

marák (ma-rák), *adj.* thin and pale, referring esp. to face.

maragsâ (ma-rag-sâ), *adj.* (*Gram.*) marked with a circumflex accent, referring to a final vowel of a word.

maragundóng (ma-ra-gun-dóng), *adj.* with, having, or giving out loud, rolling sounds, as that of thunder. Cf. *mahugong.*

marahan (ma-ra-han), I. *adj.* 1. slow in action or movement. Syn. *mabagal, makupad.* 2. soft; low; not loud or harsh, as in the way one speaks. Syn. *mahinà, mahinay.*

—II. *adv.* 1. slowly. 2. softly.

marahás (ma-ra-hás), *adj.* 1. drastic; acting with force or violence. Syn. *mahigpít.* 2. ruthless; cruel; without pity. Syn. *malupít,*

marahil   **máriwarà**

waláng-awà, waláng-habág.

marahil (ma-ra-hil), *adv.* perhaps; probably; possibly; maybe. Syn. *siguro, bakâ, bakâ sakali.*

marahuyò (ma-ra-hu-yò), *v.* to be attracted, charmed, or enticed. Syn. *maakit, mabighanì, mahalina.*

maraingán (ma-ra-i-ngán), *v.* to be able to supplicate or beg humbly and earnestly from. Syn. *mapamanhikan, masamuan, mapagmakaawaan, mahingán ng tulong.*

maralitâ (ma-ra-li-tâ), *adj.* poor; needy; indigent; destitute; impoverished. Syn. *dukhâ, hikahós o dahóp sa buhay.*

máramá (má-ra-má), var. **mádamá,** *v.* to feel or be felt or experienced. Syn. *máram-damán, máranasan.*

máramay (má-ra-may), *v.* 1. to be implicated or involved, as in crime. Syn. *másangkót, mádawit.* 2. to be unwittingly included. Syn. *másama, mápasama.*

maramdamin (ma-ram-da-min), *adj.* sensitive; easily offended. Syn. *madalíng magdamdám, matampuhin, balát-sibuyas (fig.).*

marami (ma-ra-mi), var. **madami,** I. *adj.* many; plenty; numerous.

—II. *n.* a large number (of persons or things); many.

máramihán (má-ra-mi-hán), var. **mádamihán,** *adj. & adv.* in large numbers.

maramot (ma-ra-mot), *adj.* 1. selfish. Syn. *sakím, makamkám.* 2. stingy; miserly. Syn. *kuripot.*

marangál (ma-ra-ngál), *adj.* 1. honorable; respectable. Syn. *kagalang-galang.* 2. noble; illustrious. Syn. *dakilà, mabunyî.*

marangyâ (ma-rang-yâ), *adj.* pompous; ostentatious. Syn. *magarbo, pasikat (colloq.).*

marapat (ma-ra-pat), I. *adj.* 1. deserving; worthy. Syn. *karapat-dapat.* 2. fit; proper. Syn. *bagay, nábabagay.* 3. necessary; essential. Syn. *kailangan, mahalagà.*

—II. *v.* must; ought to; should. Syn. *dapat, kailangan.*

máratay (má-ra-tay), *v.* to be confined in bed; be or become bedridden. Syn. *magkasakit nang matagál.*

marawal (ma-ra-wal), *adj.* 1. abject; pitiful;

miserable. Syn. *kahabág-habág, kaawá-awá.* 2. despicable; contemptible. Syn. *kasuklám-suklám.*

marikit[1] (ma-ri-kit), *adj.* very pretty; of extreme beauty. Syn. *nápakagandá, marilág, nápakarilág.*

marikit[2] (ma-ri-kit), *adj.* burns readily or easily; easily set on fire; flammable. Syn. *maliyáb, madalíng magliyáb o magdikit.*

marihuwana (ma-ri-hu-wa-na), *n.* (Sp. *mariguana*), the marijuana plant; the narcotic obtained from this plant.

mariín (ma-ri-ín), I. *adj.* 1. emphatic; said with force or firmness. Syn. *matigás (colloq.), mahigpít, matindí.* 2. (Gram.) with or having an acute accent on the last syllable; oxytone. Syn. *may-diín.*

—II. *adv.* an emphatic manner; emphatically.

marilág (ma-ri-lág), *adj.* very beautiful; exquisite. Syn. *napakagandá, marikít.*

mariláw (ma-ri-láw), var. **madilaw,** I. *adj.* yellow; with or having a yellow color.

—II. *n.* (M-) name of a town in the province of Bulacan, usually spelled Marilao.

marimarim (ma-ri-ma-rim), *v.* to have an intense dislike for something nasty. Syn. *madiri, mandiri.*

marimba (ma-rim-ba), *n.* (Eng.) marimba, a musical instrument somewhat like a xylophone.

marimlán (ma-rim-lán), *v.* to be beclouded or darkened. 2. to be confused or muddled up, as one's mind.

marina (ma-ri-na), I. *n.* (Sp.) fleet; navy. Syn. *hukbóng-dagat.*

—II. *adj.* naval. Syn. *pandagat.*

márindí (má-rin-dí), *v.* to be deafened by or as by a loud noise. Syn. *matulíg.*

máriníg (ma-ri-nig), var. **máringíg,** *v.* to hear or be able to hear. Also, *mápakinggán.*

maringal (ma-ri-ngal), *adj.* grand; splendid; magnificent; resplendent. Syn. *dakilà, marilág.*

mariposa (ma-ri-po-sa), *n.* (Sp.) 1. butterfly. Syn. *paruparó.* 2. a species of big moth; often mistaken for a big butterfly. 3. bowtie.

máriwarà (má-ri-wa-rà), *v.* to meet a misfortune; be unfortunate. Syn.

mápahamak.

mariwasâ (ma-ri-wa-sâ), *adj.* prosperous; rich, wealthy; well-to-do. Syn. *may-kaya (sa buhay), mayaman, masalapî, makuwarta.*

marmol (mar-mol; mar-mól), I. *n.* (*Sp.*) marble.
—II. *adj.* made of marble. Syn. *yarí sa marmól.*

marón (ma-rón), var. **marún,** *adj. & n.* (*Eng. & Sp.*) maroon; dark brownish red.

marpil (mar-pil; mar-píl), I. *n.* (Sp. *marfil*) ivory. Syn. *garing.*
—II. *adj.* made of ivory. Syn. *yarì sa garing.*

Marso (Mar-so), *n.* (Sp. *Marzo*) March, the third month of the year.

Marte (Mar-te), *n.* (*Sp.*) the planet Mars.

Martes (Mar-tes), *n.* (*Sp.*) Tuesday.

martir (mar-tir; mar-tír), *n.* (*Sp.*) martyr.

marubdób (ma-rub-dób), *adj.* 1. burning brightly; flaming. Syn. *maningas, maalab, maliyáb.* 2. ardent; fervent; enthusiastic. Syn. *masigasig, masiglá, maapóy, maalab.*

marugô (ma-ru-gô), *adj.* bloody; full of blood.

marumí (ma-ru-mí), var. **madumí,** *adj.* 1. dirty; untidy; unclean. Syn. *salaulà.* 2. obscene; nasty; indecent. Syn. *bastós, malaswâ, mahalay.*

marunong (ma-ru-nong), var. **madunong,** *adj.* 1. intelligent; wise; erudite; endowed with intellect; talented. Syn. *matalino, matalas ang isip.* 2. crafty; cunning; shrewd. Syn. *tuso.*

marungis (ma-ru-ngis), var. **madungis,** *adj.* dirty or unclean, referring esp. to a person's face.

marupok (ma-ru-pok), *adj.* 1. fragile; easily broken or destroyed. Syn. *mabasagin, mahuna.* 2. weak in structure. Syn. *mahinà, siraín, mahunâ.* 3. weak of body; easily sick; sickly. Syn. *mahinà ang katawán, masasaktín.* 4. morally weak. Syn. *mahiná ang loób, madaling matuksó.*

marurok (ma-ru-rok), *adj.* high; lofty. Syn. *matayog, mataás.*

maruyà (ma-ru-ya), var. **marhuyà,** *n.* (Sp. *marjuya*) banana or sweet potato fritter.

mas (mas), *adv.* (*Sp.*) 1. much, as in *mas mabuti,* much better. 2. more, as in: *mas*

magandá, more beautiful. Syn. *higít, lalò.*

masa (ma-sa), *n.* (*Sp.*) 1. dough. 2. act or manner of kneading (flour) into dough. Also, *pagmasa, pagmamasa, pagkakamasa.* 3. populace; common people. Syn. *karaniwang mga tao.*

másaád (má-sa-ád), *v.* to be stated, as in a document. Syn. *mábanggít.*

másabak (má-sa-bak), *v.* to be unexpectedly involved, as in a fight, contest, work, etc. Syn. *másubò, mápalaban.*

másabáy (má-sa-báy), *v.* to happen or occur at the same time with another (event or happening). Also, *mápasabáy.*

masabi (ma-sa-bi), *v.* to be able to tell, say, or utter. Syn. *mabigkás, mawikà, masalitâ.*

masabík (ma-sa-bík), *v.* to be very eager; have an eager craving or desire for.

masabihan (ma-sa-bi-han), *v.* 1. to be able to inform. Syn. *mabalitaan.* 2. to be able to reprimand. Syn. *mapangaralan, makagalitan, mapagsabihan.*

masabog (ma-sa-bog), *adj.* with or having many things scattered all around. Syn. *makalat, maraming kalat.*

masabón (ma-sa-bón), I. *v.* 1. to be able to soap or wash with soap. 2. to be soaped or washed with soap. 3. (*Fig.*) to be scolded or reprimanded. Syn. *mákagalitan.*
—II. *adj.* 1. with or having plenty of soap; well-supplied with soap. 2. soapy; full of soap.

masakím (ma-sa-kím), *adj.* selfish; avaricious. Syn. *maramot; makamkám, mapangamkám; maimbót, mapág-imbót.*

masakit (ma-sa-kit), *adj.* diligent; persevering. Syn. *matiyagá, masikap.*

masakít (ma-sa-kít), *adj.* 1. painful; causing pain; aching. Syn. *makirót, maanták.* 2. hurting. Syn. *nakasásakit.*

masákitin (ma-sá-ki-tin), var. **masasaktin,** *adj.* referring to a person who easily gets sick; sickly. Syn. *mahinà ang katawán, madalíng magkasakit.*

masakláp (ma-sak-láp), *adj.* 1. bitter. Syn. *mapaít.* 2. painful; hurting. Syn. *masakit, nakasásakít.*

masakláw (ma-sak-láw), I. *adj.* 1. comprehensive; including much; inclusive. Syn. *maraming sakláw.* 2.

extensive; having great extent; vast. Syn.
malawak.

—II. *v.* 1. to be able to include or take
into one's jurisdiction. Syn. *masakop.* 2.
to be included or be a part of. Syn.
mápasama, magíng bahagi.

masakop (ma-sa-kop), *v.* 1. to be able to
occupy as a territory. 2. to be occupied as
by an enemy, referring to a territory. 3. to
be or become a part of; be included as a
part of. Syn. *magíng bahagi.*

másaksihán (má-sak-si-hán), *v.* to be able
to witness or see. Syn. *mákita.*

masakyán (ma-sak-yán), *v.* 1. to be able to
ride (an animal or vehicle). 2. (*Fig.*) to
be able to comprehend or understand.
Syn. *máunawaan, máintindihán.*

masadlák (ma-sad-lák), *v.* to fall into a
certain misfortune. Syn. *mápahamak.*

masadyâ (ma-sad-yâ), *v.* 1. to be able to do
(something) intentionally. Syn. *matikís,
makusà.* 2. to be able to go to a certain
person or place with a certain specific
mission or purpose.

masagabal (ma-sa-ga-bal), *adj.* full of
impediments or obstacles. Syn. *mabalakid.*

masaganà (ma-sa-ga-nà), *adj.* 1. abundant;
plentiful. Syn. *pasasa.* 2. prosperous;
wealthy. Syn. *maunlad ang buhay,
mayaman.*

másagap (má-sa-gap), *v.* (*Fig.*) to be able to
pick up, as rumor or any information
circulating around.

masagót (ma-sa-gót), *v.* 1. to be able to
answer. Syn. *matugón.* 2. to be able to
guarantee or answer for someone. Syn.
magarántiyahan.

maságutin (ma-sá-gu-tin), *adj.* referring to
a person who has the habit of answering
back. Syn. *palásagót, mapágsagót.*

masagwâ (ma-sag-wâ), *adj.* 1. vulgar; not
defined; coarse. Syn. *magaspáng, pangit.*
2. indecent; indecorous; obscene;
immodest; morally offensive. Syn. *bastós,
mahalay, malaswâ.*

masagwil (ma-sag-wil), *adj.* full of
impediment or obstacles. Syn. *masagabal.*

masahe (ma-sa-he), *n.* (Sp. *masaje*) massage;
act or manner of massaging. Also,
pagmasahe, pagmamasahe.

masahin (ma-sa-hin), *v.* to knead into
dough.

masahod (ma-sa-hod), *v.* 1. to be able to
catch with an open hand or hands, as a
falling or dropping object. Syn. *masalo.*
2. to happen to fall or drop into a
receptacle or container. 3. to be able to
receive, as one's salary. Syn. *matanggáp.*

masahóg (ma-sa-hóg), *adj.* with or having
many ingredients, referring esp. to a dish
(of food). Syn. *marikado.*

masahól (ma-sa-hól), I. *v.* to be able to
defeat or subdue. Syn. *malupig, masupil.*
2. to be defeated or subdued.

—II. *adj. & adv.* worse than. Syn. *higít na
masamâ.*

masaíd (ma-sa-íd), *v.* 1. to be able to use,
consume, or eat all. Syn. *magamit o maubos
na lahát.* 2. to be all used, consumed, or
eaten; have nothing left.

masalakay (ma-sa-la-kay), *v.* to be able to
invade or attack. Syn. *malusob, maatake.*

másalamín (má-sa-la-mín), *v.* (*Fig.*) to be
noticed or observed, as from someone's
face. Syn. *mákita, mahalatâ.*

masalantâ (ma-sa-lan-tâ), *v.* 1. to be or
become physically injured or disabled,
referring esp. to a person. Syn. *mabalda,
malumpó.* 2. to be or become greatly
damaged or destroyed. Syn. *lubháng
mapinsalà o mápahamak.*

masalapî (ma-sa-la-pî), I. *adj.* 1. having
much money; rich; wealthy. Syn.
mayaman, makuwarta, mapilak, mapera.

—II. *v.* to be able to turn into cash.

masaliksík (ma-sa-lik-sík), I. *v.* 1. to be able
to investigate or find out the cause, etc.
about something by searching for clues.
2. to be able to make an extensive
research about (something).

—II. *adj.* fond of research. Syn.
mapágsaliksík.

masalimuót (ma-sa-li-mu-ót), *adj.*
complicated; intricate. Syn. *magusót,
maguló.*

másalin (má-sa-lin), *v.* 1. to be transferred
or poured into another container,
referring to water, liquid, grains, etc. Syn.
málipat ng lalagyán o sisidlán. 2. to be
translated into another language. 3. to be

transferred to another, as a duty or responsibility. Syn. *malipat sa iba*.

masalitâ (ma-sa-li-tâ), I. *adj*. talkative; loquacious; too vocal. Syn. *madaldál, matabíl*.
—II. *v*. to be able to say or utter, as a word. Syn. *masabi, mabigkás*.

másaloób (má-sa-lo-6b), *v*. to be thinking about; be reminded of. Syn. *máalaala, mágunita*.

masalto (ma-sal-to), *adj*. full of omission; with or having many parts ommitted. Syn. *mapalyo*.

masalunga (ma-sa-lu-nga), *v*. to be able to go against (a current, wind, or the like). Syn. *masalubong*.

másama (má-sa-ma), *v*. 1. to be or become included. Also, *mákasama*. 2. to be or become a part of a mixture. Syn. *máhalò, mápahalò; másahóg, mápasahóg*. 3. to be included in a group or gang. Syn. *mabarkada, mákabarkada*.

masamâ (ma-sa-mâ), *adj*. 1. bad; wicked; evil; sinful. Syn. *makasalanan*. 2. immoral; morally wrong or wicked. Syn. *imorál, bastós*. 3. harmful; injurious; destructive. Syn. *nakapípinsala, mápaminsalà*.

masamantalá (ma-sa-man-ta-lá), *v*. to be able to take advantage of the time or opportunity of.

masambá (ma-sam-bá), *v*. to be able to worship or adore.

másambít (má-sam-bít), *v*. to happen to mention or say in passing. Syn. *mábanggit, másabi*.

masamyô (ma-sam-yô), I. *adj*. sweet smelling; sweet-scented; aromatic; fragrant. Syn. *mahalimuyak, mabangó*.
—II. *v*. to be able to smell or inhale the sweet odor or fragrance of. Syn. *máamóy ang bangó*.

masanay (ma-sa-nay), *v*. 1. to be able to train. 2. to be trained or accustomed; be used to. Syn. *mahirati*.

másangkót (má-sang-kót), *v*. to be involved or implicated. Syn. *máparamay; mádawit*.

masanghíd (ma-sang-híd), *adj*. having a strong, disagreeable odor. Syn. *masangsáng*.

masangsáng (ma-sang-sáng), *adj*. with or

having a strong, disagreeable odor. Syn. *masanghíd*.

másapantahà (má-sa-pan-ta-hà), *v*. to happen to presume; have a suspicion. Syn. *máipalagáy, máakalà, máhagap*.

masapit (ma-sa-pit), *v*. 1. to be able to reach a certain place or destination. Syn. *maratíng, maabót*. 2. to be the result or outcome of. Also, *kásapitan, káhi-natnán*.

masaráp (ma-sa-ráp), *adj*. 1. tasty; palatable; delicious. Syn. *malasa, malinamnám*. 2. enjoyable; pleasing; comfortable. Syn. *kasiyá-siyá, maginhawa*.

masarili (ma-sa-ri-li), *v*. to be able to have or get something for oneself exclusively. Syn. *maaring lubós*.

masariwà (ma-sa-ri-wà), I. *adj*. referring to a certain time or period during market day when there are plenty of fresh vegetables, fish, etc. that can be bought.
—II. *v*. (*Fig.*) to be able to remind someone about something one had experienced before. Syn. *maungkát sa alaala*.

masasaan (ma-sa-sa-an), *v*. to bear the brunt of; suffer the most of. Syn. *mabigatán*.

masasaktin (ma-sa-sak-tin), *adj*. often sick; sickly; not healthy. Syn. *mahinà ang katawán, malimit magkasakít, sákitin*.

masasál (ma-sa-sál), *adj*. intense; fast and strong, as the beating of the heart. Syn. *masidhi, mabilis at malakas*.

masatsát (ma-sat-sát), *adj*. 1. fond of idle talk or gossip. Syn. *matsismís*. 2. talkative; loquacious. Syn. *madaldál*.

másaulì (má-sa-u-lì), *v*. 1. to be restored to the former place or position. Syn. *mábalík sa dating kinálalagyán*. 2. to be returned to the (former) owner, as a stolen, lost, or borrowed article. Syn. *mábalík sa may-arì*.

masaulo (ma-sa-u-lo), *v*. to be able to memorize; be able to commit to memory. Syn. *matandaán*.

masawatâ (ma-sa-wa-tâ), *v*. 1. to be able to stop or check. Syn. *masawáy, mapahintô, mapatigil*. 2. to be stopped or checked. Syn. *mahintô, matigil, mapigil*.

masawî (ma-sa-wî), *v*. 1. to be unfortunate or unlucky. Syn. *mabigô*. 2. to die. Syn. *mamatáy*.

masayá (ma-sa-yá), *adj.* happy; joyous; cheerful; gay; merry. Syn. *maligaya, malugód.*

masayahin (ma-sa-ya-hin), *adj.* with or having a cheerful or happy disposition.

masayang (ma-sa-yang), *v.* to be or become wasted. Syn. *maaksayá.*

maskí (mas-kí), var. **miskí**, *conj. & adv.* (Sp. *masque*) although; even then; even if. Syn. *kahit na; kulubmán, kahiman.*

masdán (mas-dán), *v.* to look at attentively; observe very well. Also, *pagmasdán.* Syn. *tingnáng mabubuti.*

masebo (ma-se-bo), *adj.* fatty; full of fat. Syn. *matabâ, mamantikà.*

masekreto (ma-se-kre-to), I. *adj.* secretive; not frank or open. Syn. *malihim, mapáglihim.*
—II. *v.* to be able to talk secretly with. Syn. *makausap nang sekreto o lihim.*

maselang (ma-se-lang), var. **maselan**, *adj.* 1. fastidious; not easy to please. Syn. *dilikado, pihikan.* 2. oversensitive; easily disgusted. Syn. *maramdamin, lubháng maramdamin.* 3. serious; in grave condition. Syn. *malubhâ, nasa malubháng kalagayan.*

masereno (ma-se-re-no), *adj.* wet or damp with night dew. Syn. *mahamóg (sa gabí).*

maseta (ma-se-ta), *n.* (Sp. *maceta*), 1. small mace or mallet. Syn. *malyete.* 2. small flowerpot. Syn. *maliit na pasô.*

masibà (ma-si-ba), *adj.* 1. voracious; gluttonous; greedy. Syn. *matakaw.* 2. avaricious; covetous. Syn. *masakim, makamkám, maimbót.*

masibol (ma-si-bol), *adj.* healthy (in growth). Syn. *malusog.*

masikap (ma-si-kap), *adj.* diligent; painstaking; attentive to one's work; assiduous; persevering. Syn. *masigasig, matiyagá, masipag, masikháy.*

masikháy (ma-sik-háy), *adj.* painstaking; assiduous; diligent; persevering. Syn. *matiyagá, masikap, masigasig.*

masikat (ma-si-kat), *adj.* shiny; brilliant, referring esp. to the sun. Syn. *mainit (gaya ng araw), maluningning.*

masikip (ma-si-kip), *adj.* 1. crowded; overcrowded. Syn. *gipit, siksikan.* 2. tight-fitting; too small for one's size. Syn.

makipot, maliit.

masikmurà (ma-sik-mu-rà), *v.* (Fig.) to be able to stomach or bear. Syn. *mabatá, matiís, makain (fig.).*

masíd (ma-síd), *n.* close look; careful observation. Cf. *tingin, malas.*

masidhî (ma-sid-hî), *adj.* intense; profound. Syn. *matindí.*

masigabo (ma-si-ga-bo), *adj.* loud and prolonged, said of applause or clapping of hands.

masigalót (ma-si-ga-lót), *adj.* 1. full of problems; problematic. Syn. *masuliranin.* 2. with or having many disputes or disagreements. Syn. *mahidwaan.*

masigasig (ma-si-ga-sig), *adj.* diligent; assiduous; painstaking. Syn. *matiyagâ, masikap, masipag.*

masigid (ma-si-gid), *adj.* 1. intense. Syn. *matindí.* 2 pungent; sharp and piercing; painful; poignant. Syn. *makirót, masakít, maanták.*

masigíng (ma-si-gíng), *adj.* arrogant; haughty. Syn. *palalò.*

masiglá (ma-sig-lá), *adj.* animated; lively; full of enthusiasm. Syn. *magaán ang katawán.*

masigwá (ma-sig-wá), *adj.* stormy. Syn. *mabagyó.*

masiíl (ma-si-íl), *v.* 1. to be able to oppress or be oppressed. Syn. *maapí, mapágmalupitán.* 2. to be able to choke or suffocate by strangling with the hands. Syn. *masakál.*

masilakbó (ma-si-lak-bó), *adj.* passionate; fiery. Syn. *maapoy, mainapóy, marubdób, maalab.*

másilág (má-si-lág), *v.* to be seen through a translucent object. Syn. *máaninag, masinág.*

masilaw (ma-si-law), *v.* 1. to be able to dazzle (someone) as with the glare of a strong light. 2. to be dazzled with or as with a strong light. Syn. *masuló.* 3. to feel inferior to what one considers better than oneself. Syn. *manganino, mamalahibo.*

másilayan (má-si-la-yan), *v.* to be seen briefly. Syn. *makitang sandalì, mámataan.*

masilya (ma-sil-ya), *n.* (Sp. *masilla*) 1. putty used to fill cracks or holes esp. in wood or lumber in furniture making. Syn. *pamatse.* 2. the act or manner of filling or covering cracks or holes with putty. Also, *pagmamasilya o pagkakámasilya.*

masimbahin (ma-sim-ba-hin), *adj.* given to the habit of regularly attending or hearing mass. Also, *palásimbá.*

masimót (ma-si-mót), *v.* 1. to be able to use or consume every bit of. Syn. *maubos na lahát.* 2. to be used or consumed entirely.

masimpán (ma-sim-pán), *adj.* thrifty; given to the habit of saving for the future. Syn. *matipid, mapag-impók, masinop.*

masimsím (ma-sim-sím), *v.* to be able to enjoy the pleasant taste of something by sipping little by little.

masinág (ma-si-nág), *v.* 1. to be able to see through a translucent or transparent object. 2. to be able to trace or copy by using tracing paper.

masindák (ma-sin-dák), *v.* to be suddenly filled with terror or fright. Syn. *biglág matakot, mabiglâ.*

masindakin (ma-sin-da-kin), *adj.* easily frightened or made afraid. Syn. *mabíglain, matatakutin.*

masining (ma-si-ning), *adj.* showing artistic skill and ability; artistic. Syn. *maarte, may-arte, nasa arte.*

masinop (ma-si-nop), *adj.* 1. clean and orderly, referring to a person. Syn. *malinis at maayos.* 2. thrifty; frugal; economical. Syn. *matipíd, maimpók, mapág-impók.*

másinsáy (ma-sin-say), *v.* 1. to be mistaken or erroneous. Syn. *mamalî, málisyâ.* 2. to be violative of. Syn. *málabág.*

masinsín (ma-sin-sín), *adj.* close together; thickly set, opposed to *madalang.* Syn. *malimit, tabí-tabí, lapít-lapít.*

masintahin (ma-sin-ta-hin), *adj.* affectionate; loving. Syn. *mapágmahál, mairugín.*

masipag (ma-si-pag), *adj.* industrious; hard-working. Syn. *masikháy, masikap.*

masiphayò (ma-sip-ha-yò), *v.* to be disappointed; fail; meet failure; be unsuccessful. Syn. *mabigô, masawî.*

masirà (ma-si-rà), *v.* 1. to be able to break, destroy, or damage. Syn. *magibâ, mawasák.* 2. to become spoiled, as cooked food. Syn.

mabulók, mapanis. 3. to become ripped or torn apart, as clothes. Syn. *mapunit, mawakwák.* 4. to be out of order, as a clock, electric fan, sewing machine, etc. 5. to be broken or unfulfilled, as a promise. Syn. *di matupád.* 6. to be destroyed or damaged, as by a typhoon. Syn. *mawasák, mapinsalà.* 7. (with *ang ulo o isip*) to become insane or deranged. Syn. *maloko.*

masisté (ma-sis-té), var. **masistí,** *adj.* full of jokes; fond of joking. Syn. *mabirô, palabirô.*

masistema (ma-sis-te-ma), *adj.* systematic; orderly in one's ways of doing things. Syn. *maparaán.*

maso (ma-so), *n.* (Sp. *maʒo*) 1. a big wooden hammer; mallet. 2. sledge hammer. 3. a strike or hard blow with a mallet or sledge hammer.

masolo (ma-so-lo), *v.* to be able to get or obtain all for oneself. Syn. *masarili.*

masorahín (ma-so-ra-hín), *adj.* easily bored or annoyed. Syn. *maínisin, mayámutin, bugnutin, magalitín.*

masubhán (ma-sub-hán), *v.* 1. to be doused or extinguished with water, referring to live coals or charcoals or a small fire. 2. (with *ang galit*) to be quickly pacified.

másubò (má-su-bò), *v.* to be or become involved in an act one is not too willing to do. Also, *mápasubò.* Syn. *málulóng, mápalulóng.*

masukal (ma-su-kal), *adj.* 1. full of or scattered with weeds, garbage, rubbish, and other useless things. Syn. *makalat, mabasura.* 2. over-grown with weeds, grasses, and other growths. Syn. *magubat, naggúgubat.*

masuklám (ma-suk-lám), *v.* 1. to feel hate against. Syn. *mapoót, mamuhî.* 2. to feel a strong dislike for; be disgusted. Syn. *masuyà, maínis.*

masukól (ma-su-kól), *v.* 1. to be able to catch in the act of doing something wrong. Syn. *máhuli sa akto.* 2. to be cornered; be driven into a corner; be surrounded. Syn. *mapikot, makulóng.*

masugid (ma-su-gid), *adj.* 1. faithful; true. Syn. *matapát.* 2. persistent. Syn. *matiyagâ.*

masugpô

matabáng

3. earnest; eager; ardent; zealous; active. Syn. *masigasig, maalab, masiglá*.

masugpô (ma-sug-pô), *v.* 1. to be able to stop, suppress, or check. Syn. *mapatigil, mapigil, mapahintô*. 2. to be stopped, suppressed, or checked. Syn. *matigil, mahinto*.

masulat (ma-su-lat), I. *v.* to be able to write down or put into writing. Syn. *maisulat*. —II. *adj.* 1. with or having many letters. 2. full or filled up of writings.

masuliranín (ma-su-li-ra-nín), *adj.* with or having many problems. Syn. *maproblema, maraming súliranin o problema*.

másulit (má-su-lit), *v.* 1. to be submitted, as a report. Syn. *maiharáp, máharap*. 2. to be recovered or regained, as capital in business. Syn. *mábalik, mabawî*.

masulong (ma-su-long), *adj.* progressive. Syn. *maunlad*.

másulyapán (má-sul-ya-pán), *v.* to happen to see suddenly and briefly; have a quick glimpse of. Syn. *másilayan*.

masumikap (ma-su-mi-kap), *adj.* attentive to one's work or duty; diligent; persevering. Syn. *matiyagâ, mapagtiyaga*.

másumpungán (má-sum-pu-ngán), *v.* 1. to find accidentally or by chance. Syn. *mátagpuán, mákita nang hindî sinásadyâ*. 2. to have a sudden fancy of doing something. Syn. *biglâng mágustuháng gawín*.

masunók (ma-su-nók), *v.* to be fed up with. Syn. *masuyà, magsawà*.

masunód (ma-su-nód), *v.* 1. to be followed, as an order or instruction. Syn. *matupád*. 2. to have one's way. Syn. *makapangyari*.

masunurin (ma-su-nu-rin), *adj.* obedient; docile. Syn. *di-matigas ang ulo*.

masungit (ma-su-ngit), *adj.* 1. easily bored; irritable; cross; ill-tempered. Syn. *mainitin ang ulo, magagalitin*. 2. stern; cruel. Syn. *malupit, marahas*. 2. unfavorable; harsh; inclement; rough, as the weather. Syn. *masama*.

masuong (ma-su-ong), *v.* to be forced to do something against odds, opposition, danger, or difficulties. Syn. *masubo, mapasubo; malulong, mapalulong*.

masupil (ma-su-pil), *v.* 1. to be able to

subjugate or dominate. Syn. *malupig*. 2. to be able to discipline or control. Syn. *masugpo, masuheto*. 3. to be dominated, disciplined, or controlled.

masuwerte (ma-su-wer-te), *adj.* lucky; fortunate. Syn. *mapalad, ginágalíng*.

masuyà (ma-su-yà), *v.* 1. to be supplied to excess. Syn. *magsawà, masunók (sa pagkain)*. 2. to be disgusted; feel annoyed. Syn. *mainís, mayamót*.

masuyò (ma-su-yò), I. *adj.* full of affection; affectionate. Syn. *mapagmahál*. —II. *v.* to be able to win the affection or love of, as by being helpful.

masyado (mas-ya-do), I. *adj.* (Sp. *demasiado*) excessive; too much. Syn. *sobra, labis*. —II. *adv.* very; extremely; too; excessively.

matá (ma-tá), *n.* 1. eye; organ of sight in man and animals. Syn. *paningin*. 2. the node or knot, as in bamboos. Syn. *buko*. 3. bud of a potato. 4. the hard center of a boil. 5. mesh, as of a net. Syn. *butas*.

mataan (ma-ta-an), *v.* to watch; keep an eye on. Syn. *bantayan, matyagán*.

mataás (ma-ta-ás), *adj.* 1. high; tall (said of persons). Syn. *matangkád, tangkaro*. 2. up in the air; high above. Syn. *matayog*. 3. high or elevated, as land. 4. high in rank or position. 5. with or having greater intensity, as fever. Syn. *malakás (colloq.)*. 6. eminent; noble; important (said of persons). Syn. *mahalagà, eminente, importante, dakilà*. 7. acute, as in pitch; sharp, as in voice. Syn. *matinís*. 8. high in cost; dear. Syn. *mahál*. 9. arrogant; haughty; too proud. Syn. *palalò*.

mataás-taás (ma-ta-ás + ta-ás), *adj.* 1. with or having a height a little higher than another or others. Syn. *mataas nang kauntî*. 2. with or having a pitch a little higher than ordinary.

matabâ (ma-ta-bâ), *adj.* 1. having much flesh; fat. 2. plump; attractively fat. Syn. *maburok, mapintóg, mabilog, maumbók*. 3. having much fat; fatty. Syn. *mamantika*. 4. productive; fertile, said of soil.

matabáng (ma-ta-báng), *adj.* 1. tasteless; insipid. Syn. *waláng-lasa*. 2. lacking a certain specific flavor; not sufficiently flavored (said of food). Syn. *kulang sa timpla*. 3. lacking enthusiasm; cold; not cordial. Syn. *malamig (fig.)*, *waláng-siglá*.

matabihán (ma-ta-bi-hán), *v.* 1. to be able to sit, or sleep close or beside someone. Syn. *masipingan, masigbayán*. 2. to be able to provide with an edge or border. Syn. *magiliran, malagyán ng tabí o gilid*.

matabíl (ma-ta-bíl), *adj.* too talkative; fond of talking too much. Syn. *madaldál, masalitâ*.

matabsing (ma-tab-sing), *adj.* 1. saltish; brackish, said of sea-water. Syn. *maalát-alát*. 2. sourish. Syn. *mangasím-ngasím*.

matakaw (ma-ta-kaw), *adj.* greedy; gluttonous; avaricious; voracious. Syn. *masibà*. 2. covetous. Syn. *makamkám, sakím*.

matakbuhán (ma-tak-bu-hán), *v.* 1. to be able to run or participate, as in a certain race. 2. (*Fig.*) to be able to seek aid or help from in time of necessity or need. Syn. *mahingán ng tulong, malapitan, madulugán*.

matakot (ma-ta-kot), *v.* 1. to be able to frighten or make afraid. 2. to be or become afraid.

matadero (ma-ta-de-ro), *n.* (*Sp.*) slaughterhouse; abattoir. Syn. *patayan o katayán ng hayop*.

matadór (ma-ta-dór), *n.* (*Sp.*) bull-fighter. Syn. *torero, toreador*.

matagál (ma-ta-gál), I. *adj.* over-extended in time; requiring a long time; of long duration. Syn. *malaon, maluwát*.
—II. *adv.* for a long time.

matagalán (ma-ta-ga-lán), *v.* 1. to take or require a long time. Syn. *máluwatan, malaunán*. 2. to be able to bear or endure. Syn. *matiís, maagwanta*.

mataginting (ma-ta-gin-ting), *adj.* sonorous; giving or causing a hard, metallic sound. Cf. *makalansíng*.

matagnî (ma-tag-nî), *adj.* full or covered with patches, referring to clothes and the like. Syn. *matagpî*.

mátagpuán (má-tag-pu-án), *v.* 1. to be able to find (a person or thing) in a certain place. Syn. *masumpungán, mákita*. 2. to

happen to find or discover. Syn. *mátuklasan*.

matagtág (ma-tag-tág), I. *v.* to be able to unfasten or detach. Syn. *mabakbák, mapuknát, matukláp*. 2. to be able to dismantle. Syn. *matanggál, makalás*. 3. to be dismissed or separated, as from one's work. Syn. *mátiwalág, másesante, matanggál, maalís*. 4. to be shaken, as a vehicle passing through a rugged road. Syn. *maalóg, matigtíg*. 4. to be unfastened, detached, or dismantled.
—II. *adj.* shaky, as an old, delapidated vehicle. Syn. *maalóg, makalóg, matigtíg*.

matagumpáy (ma-ta-gum-páy), *adj.* 1. successful; having attained success. 2. fortunate. Syn. *mapalad, masuwerte*. 3. prosperous. Syn. *maunlád*.
—II. *adv.* successfully; with success.

matagurián (ma-ta-gu-ri-án), *v.* to be able to give an appellation or nickname to. Syn. *mapalayawan, mabansagán*.

matahimik (ma-ta-hi-mik), I. *adj.* 1. peaceful; quiet. Syn. *payapà, mapayapà*. 2. calm; composed. Syn. *mahinahon*.
—II. *adv.* peacefully; calmy; quietly. Syn. *mahinahon, mapayapà*.

matahín (ma-ta-hin), *v.* (*Fig.*) to belittle; look down or upon; despise. Syn. *hamakin*.

matahô (ma-ta-hô), *v.* 1. to know or learn about; be able to find out. Syn. *málaman, mabaít*. 2. to be able to understand or comprehend. Syn. *máunawaan, maintindihán*.

mataimtim (ma-ta-im-tim), I. *adj.* sincere; fervent; heartfelt. Syn. *matapát, tapátpusò, taós-pusò, mataós*.
—II. *adv.* sincerely; fervently. Syn. *nang matapát, nang taós-pusò*.

matalampák (ma-ta-lam-pák), *v.* to be able to say or tell something openly or frankly to someone.

matalas (ma-ta-las), *adj.* 1. sharp or keen, referring to blades. Syn. *matalím*. 2. clear, as one's eyes. Syn. *malinaw*. 3. (with *ang tainga*) clear of hearing. Syn. *mauliníg, mahusay ang pandiníg*. 4. (with *ang ulo o isip*) talented. Syn. *marunong, matalino*.

matalastás (ma-ta-las-tás), *v.* 1. to be able

to learn or to know about. Syn. *mabatíd*, *málaman*. 2. to be understood. Syn. *máunawaan*, *máintindihán*.

matalaw (ma-ta-law), *adj.* 1. high; of more than normal height, referring esp. to gamecocks or of the height of their flight in combat. 2. at an advantage over another. Syn. *nakahíhigit*, *nakalálamáng*.

matalbóg (ma-tal-bóg), *adj.* referring to something that rebounds or bounces well.

matalik (ma-ta-lik), I. *adj.* 1. intimate; close; very familiar. Syn. *malapit*. 2. true; faithful. Syn. *tapát*, *matapát*.
—II. *adv.* intimately; in an intimate manner.

matalím (ma-ta-lím), *adj.* sharp; keen. Syn. *matalas*, *mahayap*.

matalima (ma-ta-li-ma), *v.* to be able to comply with. Syn. *masunód*, *matupád*.

matalino (ma-ta-li-no), *adj.* 1. intelligent; talented. Syn. *marunong*, *magaling ang ulo*. 2. shrewd; crafty; cunning; wise. Syn. *tuso*.

matalinghagà (ma-ta-ling-ha-gà), *adj.* 1. figurative; metaphorical. Syn. *makahulugán*, *metaporiko*. 2. allegorical; symbolical. Syn. *mapanagisag*. 3. mysterious. Syn. *mahiwagà*.

matalisik (ma-ta-li-sik), *adj.* erudite; scholarly; learned. Syn. *marunong*, *matalino*.

matalós (ma-ta-los), *v.* 1. to know or come to know; have the knowledge about. Syn. *málaman*, *mabatíd*. 2. to be able to know or understand. Syn. *máunawaan*, *máintindihán*, *matantô*.

mataluntón (ma-ta-lun-tón), *v.* to be able to trace or follow up a line, path, etc. Syn. *matuntón*.

matamán (ma-ta-mán), I. *adj.* assiduous; diligent; persevering; painstaking. Syn. *matiyagâ*, *masikap*.
—II. *adv.* assiduously; diligently.

matamasa (ma-ta-ma-sa), *v.* to enjoy the abundance of.

matambád (ma-tam-bád), *v.* to be or become exposed to view; be seen in the open. Syn. *mailantad*, *mahayag*.

matambók (ma-tam-bók), *adj.* bulging; having a convex. Syn. *maumbok*.

matamís (ma-ta-mís), I. *adj.* 1. sweet; having

the taste of sugar. 2. pleasant; gratifying; sweet, as one's voice. Syn. *malambíng*.
—II. *n.* 1. sugar. Syn. *asukal*. 2. a course of sweets; dessert; sweetmeat; candy.

matamisín (ma-ta-mi-sín), *v.* 1. to make into sweets or sweetmeat. Syn. *gawíng matamís*. 2. to take or eat as a dessert. Syn. *himagasin*. 3. (*Fig.*) to prefer; like better; choose rather. Syn. *masarapín*, *mabutihin*.

matamláy (ma-tam-láy), *adj.* 1. disposed; slightly ill. Syn. *mabigát o masamá ang katawán*, *masamá ang pakiramdám*. 2. languid; lifeless. Syn. *waláng-siglá; lúlugú-lugó*. 3. dull or sluggish, as sales of goods. Syn. *mahinà*, *hindî mabilí*, *matumal*.

matamó (ma-ta-mó), *adj.* receiving much from; gainful. Syn. *mapakinabang*.

matampalasan (ma-tam-pa-la-san), *v.* to be destroyed, damaged, or spoiled. Syn. *masirà*, *mawasák*. 2. to be or become wasted. Syn. *masayang*, *maaksayá*. 3. to be able to destroy.

matampok (ma-tam-pok), *v.* to be exalted; be raised in status, dignity, power, or honor. Syn. *mátanghál*, *mátanyág*.

matampuhin (ma-tam-pu-hin), *adj.* sulky; easily made sullen or sulky. Syn. *maramdamin*.

matandâ (ma-tan-dâ), I. *adj.* 1. old; aged; old age. Syn. *may-edad na*, *magulang na*. 2. made or produced sometime ago; not new. Syn. *lumà*. 3. former. Syn. *dati*.
—II. *n.* an aged person; an old man or woman.

matandaán (ma-tan-da-án), *v.* 1. to be able to remember or recollect. Syn. *máalaala*, *mágunitâ*. 2. to be able to mark with a sign; be able to put a marker. Syn. *malagyán ng tandá o panandâ*.

matándain (ma-tán-da-in), *adj.* 1. with, having, or possessing a good or retentive memory; not forgetful, opposed to *malimutin*. 2. referring to a person who has the tendency to look prematurely old. Syn. *madalíng magmukháng matandâ*.

matánimin (ma-tá-ni-min), *adj.* (*Fig.*) easily offended. Syn. *maramdamin*, *mahinákitin*.

mátanóng (má-ta-nóng), I. *v.* to be able to ask questions about something.

—II. adj. asking too many questions; full of questions; inquisitive. Syn. mausisà, maraming itinátanóng.

mátantán (má-tan-tán), v. to be stopped, as from talking, moving, etc. Syn. mátigil, máhintô.

matantô (ma-tan-tô), v. to realize or be able to realize; come to know or understand. Syn. málaman, máunawaan, máintindihán, mabatíd, matalastás.

mátanyág (má-tan-yág), v. to be or become popular; be prominent or well-known. Syn. mábantóg, mábalità, magíng kilalá.

mátangá (má-ta-ngá), v. to look or happen to look at someone or something amazingly. Syn. mátungangà.

matangkád (ma-tang-kád), adj. tall, referring to a person. Syn. mataás, mahagwáy ang katawán.

matangkilik (ma-tang-ki-lik), I. v. to be able to patronize, protect, or support. Syn. maitaguyod, makalingà, matulungan.

—II. adj. with or having many persons under one's patronage. Syn. maampón, maraming ampón.

matanghalian (ma-tang-ha-li-an), v. 1. to be late or delayed in the morning: Also, matanghalianan. 2. to be able to eat or take as one's dinner (midday meal). Syn. makain sa pananghalian.

matangì (ma-ta-ngì), I. prep. (with sa or kay) except; excepting; with the exception of. Syn. máliban sa, máliban kung, liban sa o kung.

—II. conj. unless. Syn. kung hindî, máliban kung.

matáng-lawin (ma-táng + la-win), adj. hawk-eyed; keen-sighted. Syn. matalas ang matá (paningín).

matáng-manók (ma-táng + ma-nók) with or having eyes that can't see in the dark. Syn. malabò sa dilím ang matá.

matangos (ma-ta-ngos), adj. prominent, referring esp. to a nose.

matáng-pusà (ma-táng + pu-sà), I. n. (Ichth.) fish called sea bass (Lates calcarifer).

—II. adj. 1. keen-sighted, esp. at night. Syn. malinaw ang matá sa gabí. 2. almond-eyed; slant-eyed. Syn. singkít.

matao (ma-ta-o), adj. 1. crowded with people; with or having many people; well-attended, as a meeting. 2. populous; well-populated.

mátaón (má-ta-ón), v. to happen or occur at the same time with another; happen to coincide with. Also, mápataón. Syn. másabáy.

mataós (ma-ta-ós), I. adj. sincere; true; heartfelt genuine. Syn. tapát, matapát, tunay.

—II. adv. sincerely; truly; genuinely.

matapang (ma-ta-pang), adj. 1. brave courageous; valiant; game. Syn. malakás ang loób, waláng-takot, buô ang loób. 2 strong; pure; not diluted, as wine, vinegar. etc. Syn. puro, waláng-halò.

matapát (ma-ta-pát), I. adj. 1. sincere; true; genuine. Syn. tunay. 2. faithful; loyal. Syn. tapát na loób.

—II. adv. sincerely; truly; genuinely. 2. faithfully.

—III. v. 1. to be able to tell someone the whole truth about. Syn. masabi nang tápatan. 2. to be able to go to a certain place by taking the direct or shortest way.

matápatin (ma-tá-pa-tin), adj. truthful; honest; frank or open. Also, tapát, matapát.

matapobre (ma-ta-pob-re), adj. (Sp.) said of rich persons, usually ones who have snobbish attitude towards the poor. Syn. mapánghamak sa mga dukhâ.

matarantá (ma-ta-ran-tá), v. to be or become confused or be unable to decide on what to do. Syn. matuliró, malitó o maguló ang isip, matarka.

mataras (ma-ta-ras), adj. sharp-tongued; referring esp. to a woman. Cf. mataray.

mataray (ma-ta-ray), adj. termagant; shrewish or evil-tempered, referring to a woman.

matarík (ma-ta-rík), adj. steep; having a sharp slope.

matarók (ma-ta-rók), v. 1. to be able to sound the depth, as of a river or sea. Syn. maarók, masukat ang lalim. 2. to be able to comprehend or understand the meaning or mystery of. Syn. máunawaan.

matatakutín (ma-ta-ta-ku-tín), adj. easily frightened or made afraid. Also, matakutín.

matatag (ma-ta-tag), var. matatag, adj. 1.
stable; firm. Syn. matibay. 2. unchanging;
constant; steady. Syn. waláng pagbabago,
di-nabábago, pirmihan.

matatap (ma-ta-tap), v. 1. to be able to know
or learn about. Syn. málaman, mabatíd,
matantô, matalós. 2. to come to understand.
Syn. máunawaan, máintindihán.

matatás (ma-ta-tás), adj. able to speak
fluently; fluent in speech. Syn. mahusay
o maliwanag magsalitâ.

matauhan (ma-ta-u-han), v. to regain
consciousness. Syn. magkamalay-tao. 2. to
be able to provide with personnel,
referring to an office.

matáy (ma-táy), adv. (Colloq.) repeatedly;
always; every time; from time to time.
Syn. lagì, palagì; paulit-ulit; mulî't mulî;
tuwî na, tuwí-tuwî na.

mátayô (má-ta-yô), v. 1 to be erected, built,
or constructed. Syn. mátirik, magawâ, 2.
to be founded or established. Syn.
mátatag, mápatatag.

matayog (ma-ta-yog), adj. high; loftly; more
than normal height. Syn. mataás, malayog.

matemátiká (ma-te-má-ti-ká), n. (Sp.
matemática) mathematics. Syn.
aghambilang (agbilang).

materya (ma-ter-ya), n. (Sp. materia) 1.
matter. Syn. bagay. 2. material. Syn. gamit,
kagamitán; sangkáp, panangkáp.

materyál (ma-ter-yál), I. n. (Sp. material)
material. Syn. sangkáp, panangkáp; gamit,
kagamitán.
—II. adj. material; physical or of the body.
Syn. panlupà, pangkatawán, makalupà.

matibay (ma-ti-bay), adj. 1. not easily
broken or destroyed; strong; durable;
opposed to mahunâ, marupók. 2. firmly set
or built. Syn. matatag. 3. physically strong,
as one's body. Syn. malakás, malusog. 4.
morally strong. Syn. matapát.

matikas (ma-ti-kas), adj. with or having
good bearing. Syn. magandá ang
pangangatawán.

matigáng (ma-ti-gáng), v. to become arid or
extremely dry, referring esp. to land or
soil.

matigás (ma-ti-gás), adj. 1. solid and
compact; resistant to pressure; hard. 2.

(with ang katawán) lazy. Syn. tamád. 2.
(with ang ulo) hard-headed; stubborn.
Syn. sutil. 3. (with ang pusò) heartless;
without pity. Syn. waláng-awà, waláng-
habág, malupít.

matigatig (ma-ti-ga-tig), v. to be worried,
anxious, or uneasy. Syn. mabalisa, mag-
alaalá, maligalig, mabahalà.

matigíb (ma-ti-gíb), v. to be or become
overloaded, overcrowded or filled to full
capacity. Cf. masiksík.

matigilan (ma-ti-gi-lan), v. to become
suddenly confused and undecided; be
temporarily immobile due to surprise or
amazement.

matigmák (ma-tig-mák), v. to become
soaked or thoroughly drenched, as with
blood. Syn. mapuyog, mapigtâ.

matigtíg (ma-tig-tíg), I. adj. too shaky or
jerky, as an old, dilapidated vehicle. Syn.
maalóg.
—II. v. to be able to shake or jerk, as by
pulling repeatedly. 2. to be or become
shaken, as passengers in an old,
dilapidated vehicle.

matíisin (ma-tí-i-sin), adj. patiently tolerant
of hardship; forebearing; used to suffer
hardships. Syn. mapágbatá, mapágtiís.

matilamsík (ma-ti-lam-sík), adj. 1.
spattering; splattering; making splashes or
splatters. 2. covered or marked with
splashes or spatters.

matilihan (ma-ti-li-han), v. to waver or
hesitate in amazement or doubt. Syn.
matigilan.

matimbáng (ma-tim-báng), I. v. 1. to be able
to weigh. 2. to be weighed 3. to be able
to balance. Syn. mapagpareho ang timbáng.
—II. adj. weighty; heavy. Syn. mabigát. 2.
of great significance or importance. Syn.
mahalagá, importante.

matimpî (ma-tim-pî), adj. having self-
control or restraint. Syn. mahinahon;
mapágpigil.

matimtiman (ma-tim-ti-man), adj. shy and
reserved; modest in one's act or action,
said of ladies. Syn. mahinhín.

matimyás (ma-tim-yás), adj. pure or
genuine, usually said of love or affection.
Syn. malinis at tapát.

matindí   **matsakáw**

matindí (ma-tin-dí), *adj.* 1. intense; severe;
serious; grave. Syn. *mabigát, malalâ,
malubhâ.* 2. strong; with force. Syn.
malakás.

matiník (ma-ti-ník), *adj.* 1. thorny; full or
covered with thorns; prickly, as some
plants like cactus. 2. spiny, as some fish.
3. full of obstacles, difficulties, problems,
etc.; thorny. Syn. *masúliranín, mabalakíd,
maproblema.*

matinig (ma-ti-nig), *adj.* 1. with of voice;
having loud voice.

matining (ma-ti-ning), *adj.* 1. with or having
much sediment or dregs. Syn. *malatak.* 2.
calm and quiet; serene; tranquil.

matinís (ma-ti-nís), *adj.* shrill; high-pitched,
referring esp. to voice. Cf. *matagintíng.*

matinô (ma-ti-nô), *adj.* 1. mentally healthy;
of sound mind; sane; sensible. Syn. *may-
isip, maliwanag ang isip* 2. showing good
sense; sound; reasonable, as a policy. Syn.
makatwiran, may-katwiran.

mátinuan (ma-ti-nu-an), *adj.* sensible;
intelligent, as in: *mátinuang pag-uusap,*
sensible-conversation.
—II. *adv.* in a sensible manner;
intelligently; wise.

matingkád (ma-ting-kád), *adj.* 1. vivid;
bright or brilliant, referring esp. to colors.
2. intense, as the heat of the sun. Syn.
matindí, masidhí. 3. very colorful. Syn.
nápakakulay.

matipíd (ma-ti-píd), I. *adj.* thrifty;
economical; saving; frugal. Syn. *maimpók,
mapág-impók.*
—II. *v.* to be able to save something for
the future by economizing.

mátipok (má-ti-pok), *v. (Slang)* 1. to be
caught, as by a policeman. Syn. *máhuli.*
2. to be killed, as in a gun battle. Syn.
mápatáy.

matipunò (ma-ti-pu-nò), *adj.* stocky;
thickset; stout. Syn. *balisaksakin (ang
katawan), siksík (ang katawán).*

mátirá (má-ti-rá), I. *v.* to be left unfinished,
undone, or unused. Syn. *máiwang di-tapós
o di-nagamit.* 2. to be left as surplus or
excess. Syn. *lumabis, sumobra.* 3. to be
lucky to remain alive, unhurt, etc. Syn.
makaligtás. 4. to stay or remain (in the

house, office, etc.) while others leave.
Syn. *maiwan, magpaiwan.* 5. to be almost
consumed or used up. Syn. *maubos halos*
—II. *adj.* almost used up or consumed
Syn. *halos ubós.*

matirahán (ma-ti-ra-hán), *v.* to be able to
live in; be livable or fit to live in.

mátirik (má-ti-rik), *v.* 1. to be erected o
constructed. Syn. *mátayô, mátindíg.* 2. t
be forced to stop, as on a flooded roa
due to mechanical trouble, referring to
motorized vehicle. Syn. *mábahura.*

matiwalà (ma-ti-wa-là), *adj.* with or havin
much trust or confidence in. Syn
makumpiyansa.

mátiwangwáng (má-ti-wang-wáng), *v.* 1. t
be left totally exposed in the open. Syn
mábuyangyáng. 2. to be left undone o
unattended, as a work abandoned by
worker. Syn. *mápabayaan.*

matiwasáy (ma-ti-wa-sáy), I. *adj.* in peace
peaceful; calm; serene; tranquil. Syn
payapà, mapayapà; tahimik, matahimik.

matiyagâ (ma-ti-ya-gâ), *adj.* painstaking
diligent; attentive to one's work. Syn
masikap, matamán.

mátiyempuhán (má-ti-yem-pu-hán), *v.* t
chance on or upon; find, meet, or com
upon by chance. Syn. *mátaunán.* 2. to b
caught in the act of. Syn. *máhuli sa akto*

matodas (ma-to-das), *v.* 1. to be al
consumed, used up, or lost. Syn. *maubo
na lahát.* 2. *(Colloq.)* to be all killed. Syn
mamatáy na lahát.

matón (ma-tón), *n. (Sp.)* bully; goon; thug
cutthroat. Syn. *butangero.*

matríkulá (ma-trí-ku-lá), *n. (Sp. matricula*
matriculation; tuition fee.

mátrimonyo (má-tri-mon-yo), *n. (Sp*
matrimonio) matrimony; marriage. Syn
kasál, pag-aasawa.

matrís (ma-trís), *n. (Sp. matriz)* the uterus
womb. Syn. *bahay-batà.*

matrisidyo (ma-tri-sid-yo), *n. (Sp*
matricidio) matricide; act of killing one'
mother. Sn. *pagpatáy sa sariling iná.*

matsakáw (mat-sa-káw), *n. (Ch.)* smal
pieces of bread, usually *pan-de-agwa,* cu
into small pieces and oven-baked to mak
crispy.

matsíng (mat-síng), n. the common species of small monkey. Syn. *tsunggo, unggóy*.

mátsoke (má-tso-ke), v. to be bumped, as by a vehicle. Syn. *mábanggâ, mábunggô*. 2. to be pitted against a strong opponent. Syn. *mápalaban*.

matsora (mat-so-ra), I. adj. (Sp. *machorra*) barren or infertile, referring to female animals, like cows, carabaos, horses, etc. Syn. *di-nag-áanák*.
—II. n. a barren female animal.

matubig (ma-tu-big), adj. 1. full of water; plenty of water; well-supplied with water. 2. containing too much water; watery.

matubigán (ma-tu-bi-gán), v. (Fig.) to be suddenly hesitant, as at the sight of something frightening. Syn. *matigilan*.

matubò (ma-tu-bò), adj. lucrative; gainful; profitable; remunerative. Syn. *mapakinabang, kapakí-pakinabang, magana, maganansiyá*.

mátuka (má-tu-ka), v. 1. to be given to someone, as an assignment. Cf. *máukol, máibigáy*. 2. to be assigned as to a certain duty. Syn. *mátalagá*.

mátuklasán (má-tuk-la-sán), v. to be able to discover. Syn. *mádiskubré*.

matukoy (ma-tu-koy), v. to be able to mention or refer to specifically. Syn. *mabanggít nang tíyakan*.

matuksó (ma-tuk-só), v. 1. to be able to tempt to commit something wrong. Syn. *masulsulán*. 2. to be or become tempted. Syn. *mahikayat*. 3. to be able to crack jokes at. Syn. *mabirò, masisté*.

matugnás (ma-tug-nás), v. to become melted or liquefied. Syn. *matunaw, malusaw*.

matugnáw (ma-tug-náw), v. to be completely burned. Syn. *mapugnáw*.

matugunán (ma-tu-gu-nán), v. 1. to be able to answer or be accountable or responsible for. Syn. *masagután, mapanagután*. 2. to be able to supply the need of.

matulain (ma-tu-la-in), adj. poetic; full of poetry.

matularan (ma-tu-la-ran), v. to be able to imitate or copy. Syn. *magaya, makopya, maparisan*.

matulíg (ma-tu-líg), v. to be temporarily deafened or confused due to much noise. Syn. *matuliró o matarantá sa ingay*.

matulin (ma-tu-lin), I. adj. fast; swift; speedy. Syn. *mabilís*.
—II. adv. swiftly; speedily; fast.

matulis (ma-tu-lis), adj. 1. sharp-pointed. Syn. *mahayap ang dulo*. 2. pointed as a nose. Syn. *matangos*. 3. (Fig.) severe; biting; sharp, as in one's language. Syn. *masakít, nakasásakít, mahayap*.

matulog (ma-tu-log), v. to sleep; go to sleep. Also, *tumulog*.

matulugín (ma-tu-lu-gín), adj. inclined or disposed to sleep long and often.

matulungín (ma-tu-lu-ngín), adj. helpful to others. Cf. *maawaín*. Syn. *madamayín*.

matuluyan (ma-tu-lu-yan), v. to become inevitable. Syn. *di-maiwasan*. 2. to be forced to; be unheeded. Syn. *mapilitan*.

matumal (ma-tu-mal), adj. 1. dull (said of business). Syn. *di-mabilí*. 2. slack (said of sales). Syn. *mahinà*. 3. slow. Syn. *mabagal*.

matumbók (ma-tum-bók), v. to be able to hit with or as with a cue.

matunóg (ma-tu-nóg), adj. 1. clear and strong in sound; resonant; sonorous. Syn. *malakás ang tunóg*. 2. (Fig.) famous; well-known; renowned. Syn. *bantóg, tanyág*.

mátunugán (má-tu-nu-gán), v. (Fig.) to get wind of; find out; to know about in time. Syn. *mátuklasán; máamuyán (fig.)*.

mátungkól (má-tung-kól), v. to be about (something). Syn. *máhinggíl*.

matupád (ma-tu-pád), v. 1. to become true. Syn. *magkátotoó*. 2. to be able to fulfill (a promise, duty, or task). Syn. *magawâ, maganáp, maisagawâ*. 3. to be able to comply with. Syn. *masunód*.

mátuto (má-tu-to), v. to learn; be able to learn; acquire knowledge about something. Syn. *magkaroón ng kaalaman o kabatiran*.

matutol (ma-tu-tol), adj. with or having many objections. Syn. *maraming tutol o kontra*.

matuwâ (ma-tu-wâ), v. to be glad; feel happy. Syn. *magalák, malugód*.

matuwaín (ma-tu-wa-ín), adj. having a liking or affection for; fond of. Syn. *mahilig, magustuhin, maibigín*.

matuwíd (ma-tu-wíd), I. adj. 1. straight; not

curved or crooked. Syn. *tuwíd, deretso*. 2.
direct. Syn. *tápatan, deretso*. 3. right;
correct; reasonable. Syn. *tamà, tumpák,
makatwiran*.

matuyô (ma-tu-yô), *v*. 1. to dry up; be or
become dry, referring to a watery place or
any wet object. 2. to wither or become
withered. Syn. *matuyót*. 3. to become a
tubercular. Syn. *maging tísikó*.

matuyót (ma-tu-yót), *v*. to be extremely dry
or withered. Syn *mangalirang*.

matwíd (mat-wíd), *n*. reason; common
sense; right thinking. Syn. *katwiran,
sentido común*.

matyág (mat-yág), *n*. 1. close or secret watch
or observation. Syn. *manmán,
pagmamanmán*. 2. the person assigned to
undertake such a job. Syn. *lihim na bantáy
o tanod*.

mauban (ma-u-ban), *adj*. full of or having
gray hair; gray-headed. Also, *ubanin*.

maukilkíl (ma-u-kil-kíl), *adj*. insistent. Syn.
mapilit.

máudlót (má-ud-lót), *v*. to be suddenly
stopped or withdrawn. Syn. *biglâng
máhintô*.

maugát (ma-u-gát), I. *adj*. 1. rooty; having
many roots, referring to plants. 2. veiny;
having or showing many veins, as in some
arms or legs.
—II. *v*. (Fig.) to be able to trace the origin,
as of one's family.

máugmâ (má-ug-mâ), *v*. to be in harmony
with. Syn. *mábagay, mátugmâ, máangkóp*.

maugnayin (ma-ug-na-yin), *adj*. coherent;
consistent.

maugong (ma-u-gong), *adj*. having or
producing roaring sound. Syn. *mahugong*.

mauhaw (ma-u-haw), *v*. 1. to be or become
thirsty. 2. (Fig.) to be very eager or
desirous of. Syn. *manabík*.

maulán (ma-u-lán), *adj*. having much rain;
rainy.

máulanán (má-u-la-nán), *v*. to be or become
wet by the rain; be exposed to the rain.
Syn. *mabasâ ng ulán, málagay sa ulanán*.

maulap (ma-u-lap), *adj*. cloudy; full of
clouds. Syn. *maalapaáp*.

maulî (ma-u-lî), *v*. to be returned or reverted
to the former position or state. Syn.

mábalík sa datì.

maulila (ma-u-li-la), *v*. 1. to lose one's
parents by death; be left an orphan; be
left without a mother or father. 2. to be
left alone, as by friends. Syn. *mápag-isá*.

maulo (ma-u-lo), *adj*. 1. talented; gifted;
having talent. Syn. *matalino, marunong,
mautak*. 2. wise; crafty; shrewd; cunning.
Syn. *tuso*.

maulól (ma-u-lól), *v*. to become insane or
demented. Syn. *maloko o maloka, masirà
ang ulo o isip*.

maulop (ma-u-lop), *adj*. foggy; misty. Cf.
maulap.

maulukan (ma-u-lu-kan), *v*. to be able to
cajole or persuade by pleasant words or
by flattery. Sy. *mahikayat, mahimok*.

maumagahan (ma-u-ma-ga-han), *v*. to be
found in the morning still with a task
unfinished. Syn. *umagahin, abutin ng
umaga*.

maumbók (ma-um-bók), *adj*. bulgy; having
a bulge. Syn. *matambók*.

maumíd (ma-u-míd), *v*. to be unable to
speak due to shame or shyness.

máuná (má-u-ná), *v*. 1. to be the first to go,
do, or start. Also, *magpáuná*. 2. to be
ahead of another or others. Also, *umuna*.

máunawaan (má-u-na-wa-an), *v*. 1. to
understand what a thing is all about. Syn.
malaman. 2. to be understood. Syn.
máintindihán.

maunawaín (ma-u-na-wa-ín), *adj*. said of a
person who easily understands;
understanding.

maunlád (ma-un-lád), *adj*. progressive;
prosperous; well-developed. Syn.
progresibo, masulong.

maunlapian (ma-un-la-pi-an), *v*. to be able
to add a prefix to.

maunós (ma-u-nós), *adj*. stormy.

maunsiyamî (ma-un-si-ya-mî), *v*. 1. to
become stunted or arrested in growth.
Syn. *mabansót, mapuril*. 2. to fail; meet
failure. Syn. *mabigô*.

máupasalà (má-u-pa-sa-là), *v*. to be forced
to vituperate or scold (someone) severely.
Syn. *máalimurà*.

mausál (ma-u-sál), *v*. to be able to say
silently and repeatedly, as prayers.

mausìsà (ma-u-si-sà), I. *adj.* too inquisitive;
inclined to ask so many questions. Syn.
matanóng, mapagtanóng, palátanóng.
—II. *v.* to be able to inquire or ask
(someone) about something by way of
reminding.

mausok (ma-u-sok), *adj.* 1. smoky; giving
off much smoke. Syn. *maasap, maasó.* 2.
full or filled of smoke.

mautak (ma-u-tak), *adj.* 1. brainy;
intelligent; talented. Syn. *matalino,
marunong.* 2. wise; cunning; clever;
shrewd; crafty. Syn. *tuso.*

mautás (ma-u-tás), *v.* 1. to be completed or
finished. Syn. *matapos.* 2. to be able to
kill. Syn. *mapatáy.*

mautáy-utáy (ma-u-táy + u-táy), *v.* to be
able to do or finish little by little. Syn.
mauntí-untî, mainút-inót.

máutô (má-u-tô), *v.* to be fooled. Syn.
máloko, máulól.

máuwì (má-u-wì; -wî), *v.* 1. to end up in
something not expected. Syn. *mápunta,
máipapunta.* 2. to be home or come home
unexpectedly.

mauwido (ma-u-wi-do), *adj.* with or having
ear or talent for music.

máuyám (má-u-yám), *v.* to be ridiculed or
mocked. Syn. *mátuyâ, málibák, máaglahì.*

máwaksí (má-wak-sí), *v.* 1. tó be rid of from
one's hand by shaking or jerking. 2. to be
renounced or forgotten. Syn. *mátakwíl,
mátatwâ, malimot.* 3. to be lost; be
misplaced. Syn. *máwaglít, mawalâ.*

mawalâ (ma-wa-lâ), *v.* 1. to be misplaced or
mislaid; be lost. Syn. *máwaglít, malipol.* 2.
to be lost, as in one's way. Syn. *máligáw.*
3. to disappear; vanish. Syn. *maparam,
mapawì, maalís, maglahò* (*fig.*). 4. (with *sa
sarili*) to be unable to control oneself. Syn.
makalimot, di-makapágpigil.

mawaláng- (ma-wa-láng-), a combining
form, meaning to lose, as in: *mawaláng-
bisà*, to lose potency. Also written
separately: *mawalán ng.*

mawaláng-galang (ma-wa-láng + ga-lang),
v. to lose respect for.

máwangis (má-wa-ngis), *v.* to be similar to.
Syn. *mátulad, mákatulad; mákaparehó;
mákawangis.*

mawarì (ma-wa-rì), *v.* to be able to meditate
or reflect on.

máwatasan (má-wa-ta-san), *v.* to be able to
hear or understand clearly. Syn. *máriníg
na mabuti, máintindiháng mabuti.*

máwili (má-wi-li), *v.* to be happily engrossed
in doing, hearing, seeing, reading, etc.
something; be interested or attracted to.

may (may), *v.* 1. to have; own; possess, as
in: *May bahay silá sa Baguio.* They have
(own) a house in Baguio. 2. to have or be
affected with, as in: *May lagnát siyá.* He
has fever. 3. there is; there are, as in: *May
pag-asa pa.* There is still hope.

may- (may-), *pref.* used to form (a)
adjectives, meaning having, possessing,
suffering, etc., as in: *may-asawa*, married;
may-sugat, wounded; *may-sakít*, sick, etc.
(b) nouns (prefixed to roots without
hyphen), as in: *maybahay*, wife; *maysakít*,
patient.

maya (ma-ya), *n.* (*Ornith.*) sparrow (general
name for all species).

mayabang (ma-ya-bang), *adj.* boastful;
braggart. Syn. *hambóg, palalò, mahangin*
(*colloq.*).

mayabong (ma-ya-bong), *adj.* thick with
leaves, as a branch or a tree; luxuriant in
growth. Cf. *malabay.*

may-akdâ (may + ak-dâ), *n.* 1. author; writer
of a literary work. Syn. *maykathâ.* 2.
(*Mus.*) composer.

mayakyák (ma-yak-yák), *adj.* talkative;
loquacious. Syn. *masalità.*

mayahin (ma-ya-hin), I. *adj.* with or having
red feathers; red-feathered, referring to a
rooster.
—II. *n.* a red-feathered rooster. Cf.
talisayin, malatubâ, alimbuyugin, bulik.

mayaman (ma-ya-man), *adj.* rich; wealthy;
well-to-do. Syn. *masalapî, makuwarta,
mapilak, mariwasâ.*

maya-maya (ma-ya + ma-ya), var.
mayamaya, *n.* 1. (*Ichtc.*) red snapper
(*Lutianus sp.*) 2. a kind of rice cake often
eaten with grated coconut. Syn. *puto-
maya.*

mayámayâ (ma-yá-ma-yâ), *adv.* by and by;
after a while; in a little while. Syn.
pagkailáng sandalî.

mayamò   **may-lapì**

mayamò (ma-ya-mò), *adj*. 1. covetous; selfish; greedy. Syn. *sakím, masakím; maramot; maimbót*. 2. ostentatious. Syn. *marangyâ, mapágmarangyâ*.

mayámutin (ma-yá-mu-tin), *adj*. easily annoyed or displeased. Syn. *maínisin, masuyaín, magalitín, masúklamin*.

mayana (ma-ya-na), *v*. (*Bot*.) a branched annual herb propagated both as ornamental and medicinal plant; its variously blotched or colored leaves are used as poultice for bruises, swellings, etc.

may-angkóp (may + ang-kóp), var. **may-pang-angkóp**, *adj*. (*Gram*.) with or having a ligature.

mayapá (ma-ya-pá), *adj*. 1. tasteless; insipid; flavorless. Syn. *waláng-lasa*. 2. juiceless. Syn. *wálang-katás, di-makatás*.

mayapós (ma-ya-pós), *v*. to be able to embrace tightly; be able to hug. Syn. *mayakap nang mahigpít*.

mayapyáp (ma-yap-yáp), *adj*. given to useless or idle talk. Syn. *madaldál, masalitâ.-*

may-aral (may + a-ral), *adj*. with, having, or teaching a moral lesson or lessons.

may-arì (may + a-rì), *n*. owner; proprietor.

mayasáng (ma-ya-sáng), *adj*. brittle due to being too dry, referring esp. to materials like rattan, bamboo, or the like. Cf. *malutóng*.

mayá't-mayâ (ma-yá't + ma-yâ), *adv*. now and then; every now and then; every so often.

mayaw (ma-yaw), *n*. 1. harmony; accord. Syn. *pagkakasundô*. 2. absence of noise; silence. Syn. *katahimikan*.

may-bahay (may + ba-hay), I. *adj*. having a house.

maybahay (may-ba-hay), *n*. wife.

may-baít (may + ba-ít), *adj*. prudent; sensible; circumspect; using one's common sense. Syn. *may-isip*.

may-bisà (may + bi-sà), *adj*. 1. having an effect; producing effect or result; efficacious. Syn. *mabisà, may-epekto*. 2. operative; in effect; active. Syn. *umiiral*.

may-bukadura (may + bu-ka-du-ra), *v*. (*Colloq*.) with or having the ability to speak well. Syn. *mahusay magsalitâ*.

may-budhî (may + bud-hî), *adj*. kind; understanding; conscientious. Syn. *mabaít, maawaín, matulungín, maúnawaín*.

may-buhay (may + bu-hay), *adj*. 1. alive; living. Syn. *buháy*. 2. active; lively; full of life. Syn. *masiglá*.

may-kabá (may ka-bá), *adj*. 1. apprehensive; fearful; showing fear. Syn. *natátakot, nagáalaalá*. 2. with or having premonition about something. Syn. *may-agam-agam, may-kutób*.

Maykapál (May-ka-pál), *n*. Creator; God; the Supreme Being. Syn. *Ang Lumikhâ*.

maykapangyarihan (may-ka-pang-ya-ri-han), *n*. 1. a person exercising power or command. 2. an agent of the law. Syn. *alagád ng batás*.

may-karamdaman (may + ka-ram-da-man), *adj*. sick; ailing; indisposed. Syn. *may-sakít*.

maykathâ (may-kat-hâ), *n*. 1. author or writer of a literary work. Syn. *may-akdâ, ang sumulat*. 2. (*Mus*.) composer. 3. creator or inventor. Syn. *maylikhâ*.

may-katwiran (may + kat-wi-ran), *adj*. reasonable; according to reason; with or having reason. Syn. *nasa-katwiran, makatwiran*.

may-kaya (may + ka-ya), *adj*. 1. capable; able; competent; with or having ability. Also, *may-kakayahán*. 2. wealthy; rich; well-to-do. Syn. *mayaman, makuwarta, masalapî*.

may-kusà (may + ku-sà), *adj*. with or having initiative. Syn. *marunong magkusà*.

may-diín (may + di-ín), *adj*. with a stress; stressed, as a syllable.

may-diwà (may + di-wà), *adj*. with or having sense or meaning. Syn. *may-kahulugán*.

maygawâ (may-ga-wâ), *n*. 1. maker; manufacturer. Syn. *tagagawâ, manggagawà*. 2. owner. Syn. *may-arì, maykanyá*. 3. a person responsible for an act. Syn. *maykagagawán*.

may-isip (may + i-sip), *adj*. 1. thoughtful; attentive. Syn. *maasikaso*. 2. understanding; considerate. Syn. *maúnawain, maálalahanín*. 3. sensible; kind. Syn. *maybaít, mabaít*.

may-lapì (may + la-pì), *adj*. with or having

an affix. Also, *may-panlapî*.

maylikhâ (may-lik-hâ), n. 1. (M-) God, the Creator. 2. inventor; creator. Syn. *imbentór*.

maylupà (may-lu-pà), n. land owner.

may-malay (may + ma-lay), *adj.* 1. aware of; having knowledge about. Syn. *alám, nalalaman*. 2. conscious; able to feel and think. Syn. *may-malaytao*. 3. (*Colloq.*) old enough to know what is right and wrong. Syn. *may-isip, dî na musmós*.

may-ngalan (may + nga-lan), var. **may-pangalan**, *adj.* 1. with or having a name. 2. noted; well-known; famous. Syn. *kilalá, tanyág, bantóg, populár, sikát*.

Mayo (Ma-yo), n. (*Sp.*) May, the fifth month of the year.

Mayón (Ma-yón), n. the name of the famous volcano in Albay.

mayór (ma-yór), *adj.* (*Sp.*) main; principal. Syn. *pángunahín*.

mayór-de-edád (ma-yór + de + e-dád), *adj.* of age; of legal age. Syn. *nasa-edád, nasa-gulang, nasa-hustong gulang*.

mayoriya (ma-yo-ri-ya), n. (*Sp. mayoriá*) majority. Syn. *nakarárami*.

mayroón (may-ro-ón), I. *v.* 1. have; own; possess, as in: *Mayroón siláng lupà sa lalawigan*. They have land in the province. 2. to have or be affected with, as in: *Mayroón siyáng lagnát*. He has fever. 3. there is still a chance.
—II. *adj.* 1. with or having (something), as in: *mayroóng talino*, having talent. 2. having money; rich; wealthy. Syn. *mayaman, makuwarta*.
—III. *n.* have; person who is relatively rich or wealthy, as in: *ang mga mayroón at ang mga walâ*, the haves and the have-nots.

maysakít (may-sa-kít), n. patient, as in a hospital. Syn. *pasyente*.

may-sákit (may + sá-kit), *adj.* diligent; painstaking; persevering. Syn. *may-tiyagâ, matiyagâ*.

maysala (may-sa-la), n. 1. offender; culprit; sinner; criminal. Syn. *ang nagkasala o may-kasalanan, kriminal, salarín*.

may-salapî (may + sa-la-pî), *adj.* rich; wealthy; well-to-do. Syn. *makuwarta,*

mayaman.

may-suwerte (may + su-wer-te), *adj.* lucky; fortunate. Syn. *masuwerte, mapalad, may-portuna*.

may-taning (may + ta-ning), *adj.* limited; given a certain limit. Syn. *may-takdâ*.

may-ulo (may + u-lo), *adj.* 1. with, having, or provided with a head. 2. (*Fig.*) with talent; having talent; talented. Syn. *matalino, may-talino; marunong, may-dunong*. 3. with, having, or provided with a heading or title. Syn. *may-títuló, may-pamagát*.

mayumì (ma-yu-mì), *adj.* 1. tender or soft to the touch. 2. modest in manner, referring esp. to a woman; sedate; demure. Syn. *mahinhín o mabining kumilos*.

may-urì (may + u-rì), *adj.* 1. of good class or quantity. Syn. *mahusay na klase*. 2. of high social rank. Syn. *may mataás na urì*.

may-utak (may + u-tak), *adj.* brainy; with or having brains; intelligent; talented. Syn. *matalino, marunong, intelihente*.

may-uwido (may + u-wi-do), *adj.* having talent for music.

mekanismo (me-ka-nis-mo), n. (*Sp. mecanismo*) 1. machinery. Syn. *makinarya*. 2. mechanism; means or way by which something is done. Syn. *paraán, kaparaanán, pamamaraán*. 3. system of parts working together, as parts of a machine. Syn. *kayarian*.

médikó (mé-di-kó), n. (*Sp. médico*) 1. physician; doctor. Syn. *manggagamot, doktór*. 2. (*Colloq.*) herb doctor. Syn. *erbularyo*.

medida (medi-da), n. (*Sp.*), 1. measure; measurement. Syn. *sukat*. 2. tape measure.

medisina (me-di-si-na), n. (*Sp. medicina*) 1. any drug used to cure disease; medicine. Syn. *gamót, panggamót*. 2. the science and art of curing diseases. Syn. *panggagamót*.

meditasyón (me-di-tas-yón), n. (*Sp. meditacion*) meditation. Sy. *bulay-bulay, pagbubulay-bulay; nilay-nilay, pagninilay-nilay*.

medya (med-ya), n. & *adj.* (*Sp. media*) half; one half. Syn. *kalahatî*.

medya-agwa (med-ya + ag-wa), var. **medyaagwa**, n. (*Sp. media agua*) awning;

also, the lower extension of the roof.

medya-luna (med-ya + lu-na), var. **medyaluna**, n. (Sp. *media luna*) half-moon.

medya-notse (med-ya + not-se), var. **medyanotse**. n. (Sp. *medianoche*) 1. midnight. Syn. *hatinggabí*. 2. midnight repast.

medyas (med-yas), n. (Sp. *medias*) stockings; socks.

medyo (med-yo), (Sp. *medio*) , I. *adj.* half; semi-. Cf. *mala*—
—II. *adv.* somewhat; to some extent; in some degree; rather.

medyú-medyó (med-yú + med-yó), *adj.* somewhat demented or crazy. Syn. *may-pagkalokó-lokó.*

mehora (me-ho-ra), n. (Sp. *mejora*) improvement made esp. on a property.

meme (me-me), n. a child's term for sleep. Syn. *tulog.*

memorable (me-mo-ra-ble), *adj.* (Sp.) 1. memorable; not to be forgotten. Syn. *di-malílimot.* 2. notable. Syn. *dakilà.*

memorandum (me-mo-ran-dum), n. (Sp. & Eng.) 1. a short list. Syn. *maiklíng tálaan o listahan.* 2. a short note or report. Syn. *maiklíng ulat.* 3. a circular letter. Syn. *palibot-liham, palibot-sulat.*

memorya (me-mor-ya), n. (Sp. *memoria*) 1. memory; remembrance. Syn. *alaala, gunità.* 2. act or process of remembering; memorizing. Syn. *pagsasaulo.*

memoryal (me-mor-yal), I. *adj.* (Sp. *memorial*) memorial; commemorative. Syn. *pang-alaala, panggunita, taga-pagpagunita.*
—II. n. a monument. Syn. *bantayog, monumento.*

menór (me-nór) I. *adj.* (Sp.) 1. of minor importance. Syn. *di-lubháng mahalagá.* 2. young; not yet of age. Syn. *walâ pa sa edád o gulang.* 3. (Mus.) of minor key.
—II. n. 1. a child of minor age. Syn. *batang walâ pa sa edád o hustong-gulang.* 2. (Mus.) minor key. 3. (in automobile driving) medium rate acceleration.

menos (me-nos), *adj.* (Sp.) less; of less value, effect, degree, etc. Syn. *di-masyadô, di-gaanó.*

mensahe (men-sa-he), n. (Sp. *mensaje*) message sent to someone. Syn. *pahatíd, balità.*

mensuwál (men-su-wál), *adj.* (Sp. *mensual*) mensal; monthly. Syn. *búwanan, buwán-buwán.*

mentál (men-tál), *adj.* (Sp.) mental; of the mind; for the mind. Syn. *pandiwà, pang-isip, pangkaisipán.*

mentalidád (men-ta-li-dád), n. (Sp.) 1. mentality; mental capacity. Syn. *isip, pag-iisip, kaisipán.* 2. mental attitude; opinion. Syn. *kuru-kurò, palagáy, opinyón.*

mentór (men-tór), n. (Sp.) 1. teacher. Syn. *maestro, gurò.* 2. a wise, loyal adviser. Syn. *matalino't matapát na tagapayo.*

menú (me-nú), n. (Sp.) 1. menu; list of food served at a meal. Syn. *tálaan ng mga putahe.* 2. the food served.

menudénsiyá (me-nu-dén-si-yá), n. (Sp. *menudencıa*) animal entrails, usually cooked as a special dish.

menudo (me-nu-do), var. minudo, n. (Sp.) a dish of pork meat with liver cut into small cubes, cooked with cubes of potatoes, tomatoes, pepper, etc. in a little sauce.

merkado (mer-ka-do), n. (Sp. *mercado*) market. Syn. *palengke, pámilihan.*

merkuryo (mer-kur-yo), n. (Sp. *mercurio*) 1. (Min.) mercury. Syn. *asoge.* 2. (M-) Mercury, the messenger of the gods in the Roman mythology. 3. Mercury, the smallest planet in the solar system.

merengge (me-reng-ge), var. **meringge**, n. (Sp. *merengue*) meringue, a small cake made of egg white beaten stiff and mixed with sugar and often filled with fruit, etc.

méritó (mé-ri-tó), n. (Sp.) 1. merit; goodness. Syn. *buti, kabutihan.* 2. special quality. Syn. *katangian.* 3. worth; value. Syn. *halagá, kahalagahan.*

mersenaryo (mer-se-nar-yo), I. *adj.* (Sp. *mercenario*) 1. working for payment only. Syn. *mukháng kuwarta, sa kuwarta lamang.* 2. hired. Syn. *upahán, inúupahan.*
—II. n. 1. a professional soldier serving another country for pay. Syn. *sundalong ı pahán.*

meryenda   **minoridád**

meryenda (mer-yen-da), var. minandál, mirindál, n. (Sp. *merienda*) snack.

mesa (me-sa), n. (*Sp.*) table. Syn. *lamesa, hapág.*

meseta (me-se-ta), var. mesita, n. (*Sp.*) a small table. Syn. *muntíng mesa.*

Mesiyás (Me-si-yás), var. Mesyás, (Sp. *Mesías*) Messiah. Syn. *Tagapagligtas.*

mestisa (mes-ti-sa), var. mistisa, n. (Sp. *mestiza*) a woman or girl mestizo; mestiza.

metáporá (me-tá-po-rá), n. (Sp. *metáfora*) metaphor. Syn. *paghahambíng, hambingan.*

metastasis (me-tas-ta-sis), n. (*Sp.*) 1. change of form. Syn. *pagbabagong-anyô.* 2. (*Biol.*) metabolism. Syn. *metabolismo.* 3. (*Rhetoric*) metastasis; an abrupt transition from one subject to another. Syn. *bigl

ng pagbabago ng paksâ.*

metro (me-tro), n. (*Sp.*) 1. meter; unit of measure equal to 100 centimeters. 2. a meter stick. 3. an instrument or apparatus for measuring rate of flow of water, gas, etc. Syn. *kontadór.*

metsado (met-sa-do), var. mitsado, n. (Sp. *mechado*) a dish of stuffed, rolled meat.

meyor (me-yor), n. (*Eng.*) mayor (of a town or city). Syn. *alkalde.*

mga (ma-ngá), I. *art.* used as a pluralizing article for nouns.

—II. *adv.* about; nearly; approximately, as in: *mga sampû,* about ten.

mi (mi), n. (Sp. *Mus.*) mi, the third note in the musical scale.

mike (mi-ke), var. miki, n. (*Ch.*) a kind of noodle made from wheat flour and usually used in making *pansít.*

mikrobyo (mi-krob-yo), n. (Sp. *microbio*) microbe; germ.

miga (mi-ga), n. (*Sp.*) 1. crumbs, as of bread. 2. the soft, inner part of bread. Cf. *masa.*

milagro (mi-la-gro), n. (*Sp.*) miracle. Syn. *himalâ, hiwagà.*

milisya (mi-lis-ya), n. (Sp. *milicia*) militia; army composed of citizens instead of professional soldiers.

militante (mi-li-tan-te), adj. (*Sp.*) militant; warlike. Syn. *mapanlabán, mapandigmâ, matapang.*

militár (mi-li-tár), I. n. (*Sp.*) military man; soldier. Syn. *kawal, sundalo, taong-hukbó.*

—II. *adj.* 1. military; pertaining to the army. Syn. *panghukbó, pang-militár.* 2. for war; suitable for war. Syn. *pandigmâ.*

milyahe (mil-ya-he), n. (Sp. *millaje*) 1. mileage; total number of miles traveled or covered. 2. milestone; milepost. Cf. *kilometrahe.*

milyón (mil-yón), n. & *adj.* (Sp. *millión*) million. Syn. *angaw, sanlibong-libo.*

milyonarya (mil-yo-nar-ya), var. milyunarya, n. (Sp. *millonaria*) a woman millionaire; very wealthy woman.

míminsán (mí-min-sán), *adv.* just once; only once. Syn. *minsán lamang.*

mina (mi-na), n. (*Sp.*) 1. mine; mineral deposit. 2. a buried explosive used to destroy the enemy or its fortifications. 3. any great source of supply.

minámahál (mi-ná-ma-hál), *adj.* dear; beloved; held dear to one's heart. Syn. *inúirog, sinísinta, ginígiliw.*

minana (mi-na-na), *adj.* inherited; passed over to someone by inheritance. Syn. *námana.*

minandál (mi-nan-dál), var. minindál, mirindál, n. (Sp. *merienda*) 1. snack; light meal or repast, usually taken between regular meals. 2. act of taking a snack.

minerba (mi-ner-ba), n. (Sp. *minerva*) 1. (M) Minerva, an ancient Roman goddess of wisdom, technical skill, and invention. 2. a kind of small printing machine or press.

minero (mi-ne-ro), n. (*Sp.*) miner; mine digger. Syn. *magmiminá.*

mínimó (mí-ni-mó), I. *adj.* (*Sp.*) minimum; least; lowest; smallest. Syn. *pinakamaliít, pinakamababà.*

—II. *n.* the lowest or smallest quantity, number, degree, etc.

ministeryo (mi-nis-ter-yo), n. (Sp. *ministerio*) ministry; department, as of education. Syn. *departamento, kágawarán.*

ministro (mi-nis-tro), n. (*Sp.*) 1. department head or secretary; minister. Syn. *kalihim pangkagawarán.* 2. a diplomatic officer to a nation, lower than an ambassador; minister. Cf. *sugò.* 2. a church minister; clergyman; pastor. Syn. *pastór.*

minoridád (mi-no-ri-dád), n. (*Sp.*) minority

minsán   **misteryoso**

of age. Syn. *kakulangán sa edád.*

minsán (min-sán), *adv.* once; one time. Syn. *isáng beses.*

mínsanan (mín-sa-nan), *adv.* all at the same time; all at once; at a single time. Syn. *láhatan.*

mintís (min-tís), I. *adj.* (*Sp.*) 1. wrong or mistaken, as an answer or guess. Syn. *malî, lisyâ, hindî tamà.* 2. having failed to hit at something aimed at. Syn. *lihís, sala, hindî tumamà.* 3. failed to explode, as a firecracker, shell, or bomb. Syn. *palyado, paltós, hindî pumutók.*
—II. *n.* 1. a wrong answer or guess; mistake. 2. a miss or failure to hit a target. 3. failure to explode.

minú-minuto (mi-nú + mi-nu-to), *adv.* minute after minute; every minute. Syn. *bawa't minuto.*

minúskulá (mi-nus-ku-la), *n.* (*Sp. menuscula*) small letter; lower case (in printing), Syn. *munting titik, maliít na titik o letra.*

minús-minós (mi-nús + mi-nós), I. *adj.* 1. somewhat demented or crazy. Syn. *medyú-medyó, loko-loko, kuláng-kuláng.* 2. silly; stupid; easily deceived. Syn. *lokohín, tangá.*
—II. *n.* a silly person; simpleton; fool. Syn. *taong hangál o lokó-lokó.*

minutero (mi-nu-te-ro), *n.* (*Sp.*) the minute hand of a watch or clock. Cf. *segundaryo, oraryo.*

minuto (mi-nu-to), *n.* (*Sp.*) one sixtieth of an hour; minute. Syn. *sandalî.*

minyatura (min-ya-to-ra), I. *n.* miniature; something represented in a small scale. Syn. *maliít na modelo o larawan.*
—II. *adj.* miniature; done on a very small scale. Syn. *muntî, maliít.*

mira (mi-ra), *n.* (*Sp. mirra*) myrrh.

mirákuló (mi-rá-ku-ló), *n.* (*Hispanized Eng.*) miracle; wonder; something marvelous. Syn. *milagró, himalâ, kababalaghán.*

mirasól (mi-ra-sól), *n.* (*Bot., Sp.*) sunflower.

mirón (mi-rón), *n.* (*Sp.*) spectator; onlooker; bystander. Syn. *mánonood, taong osyoso.*

miryenda (mir-yen-da), *n.* (*Sp. merienda*) light repast between meals. Syn. *minandál, mirindál.*

Misa (Mi-sa), *n.* (*Sp.*) Mass; Holy Mass.

Misa-de-galyo, *n.* Midnight Mass.

Misál (Mi-sál), *n.* (*Sp.*) book of prayers or devotions; Missal.

Misa Mayór, *n.* High Mass.

misantropiyá (mi-san-tro-pi-yá), var. **misantropya**, *n.* (*Sp. misantropía*) misanthropy; hatred or mistrust of all people.

Misa Rekyém, *n.* Requiem Mass.

Misa Resada, *n.* Low Mass.

miserable (mi-se-ra-ble), *adj.* (*Sp.*) 1. miserable; unhappy. Syn. *malungkót.* 2. pitiful. Syn. *kaawá-awá.* 3. poor. Syn. *dukhâ, marálitâ.*

misis (Mi-sis), *n.* 1. mistress; married woman. Syn. *Ginang.* 2. wife, as in: *Siyá ang misis ko.* She is my wife.

mismo (mis-mo), I. *adj.* very; the same, as in: *sa mismóng araw na iyón*, in that same (very) day.
—II. *pron.* himself or herself; themselves; as in: *siyá mismo*, he himself.

misó (mi-só), *n.* (*Ch.*) boiled, mashed beans, used as ingredient in saute or in making a certain kind of sauce for *pesà.*

misogamya (mi-so-gam-ya), *n.* (*Sp. misogamia*) misogamy; hatred of marriage.

misógamó (mi-só-ga-mó), I. *n.* (*Sp.*) misogamist; a person who hates marriage. Syn. *taong ayaw ng pag-aasawa.*
—II. *adj.* misogamous (s.o. persons who hate marriage). Syn. *ayaw mag-asawa.*

misóhinó (mi-só-hi-nó), I. *adj.* (*Sp. misógino*) misogynous (s.o. men who hate women). Syn. *ayaw sa babae.*
—II. *n.* misogynist; woman hater.

misohinya (mi-so-hin-ya), *n.* (*Sp. misoginia*) misogyny; hatred of women.

mister (mis-ter), *n.* (M-) Mister. Syn. *Ginoó.* 2. husband, as in: *Siyá ang mister ko.* He is my husband.

misteryo (mis-ter-yo), *n.* (*Sp. misterio*) 1. mystery; secret. Syn. *hiwagà, lihim.* 2. something that cannot be understood; wonder. Syn. *himalâ, kababalaghân, milagro.*

misteryoso (mis-ter-yo-so), *adj.* (*Sp. misterioso*) mysterious. Syn. *mahiwagà, mahimalâ.*

místikó (mís-ti-kó), I. n. (Sp. *místico*) a
believer in mysticism; mystic.
—II. *adj.* mystic; mystical.

mistulá (mis-tu-lá), I. *adj.* 1. real; true. Syn.
tunay, talagá. 2. very similar; closely
similar or identical; very much the same.
Syn. *katulad na katulad, kaparehung-
kapareho.*
—II. *adv.* truly; in fact; really; indeed. Syn.
tunay, talagá.

miswá (mis-wá), n. (*Ch.*) 1. very fine and
tender noodles made from flour and
resembling vermicelli. 2. a dish, the chief
ingredient of which is this kind of
noodles.

misyón (mis-yón), n. (Sp. *mision*) 1.
diplomatic delegation; mission Syn. *mga
sugò.* 2. errand; mission. Syn. *layon, sadyâ,
pakay.* 3. a person's calling or purpose in
life. Syn. *layon, láyunin; hangád, hángarin.*
4. duty or assignment given to someone.
Syn. *tungkulin.*

misyonero (mis-yo-ne-ro), n. var.
misyunero, n. (Sp. *misionero*) missioner;
missionary.

mitád (mi-tád), I. n. (Sp.) half-and-half. Syn.
hatián.
—II. *adj.* equal, referring to two; half
each.

mithî (mit-hî), n. ambition; ardent desire
or wish. Syn. *lunggatî, pita, pithayà,
pangarap* (*fig.*).

mitig (mi-tig), n. numbness due to fatigue.
Syn. *manhíd, pamamanhíd.*

miting (mi-ting), n. (*Eng.*) a gathering of
people to decide or discuss certain
matters; meeting; conference. Syn.
pulong, pagpupulong, kumperénsiyá.

mito (mi-to), n. (*Sp.*) myth; legend. Syn.
alamát.

mitolóhiyá (mi-to-ló-hi-yá), n. (Sp.
mitología) mythology; myths. Syn. *mga
alamát.* 2. mythology: study of myths. Syn.
paláalamatan.

mitsá (mit-sá), n. (Sp. *mecha*) 1. wick, as of
a candle, oil or gas lamp, firecracker, etc.
2. (*Carp.*) tenon. 3. (*Fig.*) immediate
cause, as of war. Syn. *titis* (*fig.*).

miyembro (mi-yem-bro), var. **membro**, n.
(Sp. *miembro*) 1. member, as of society or

organization. Syn. *kasapî, kaanib.* 2.
member, as of a board. Syn. *kagawád.*

miyentrás (mi-yen-trás), *adv.* (Sp. *mientras*)
while; in the meantime. Syn. *habang,
samantala.*

Miyérkulés (Mi-yér-ku-lés), n. (Sp.
Miercoles) Wednesday.

miyopya (mi-yop-ya), n. (Sp. *miopía*)
myopia; nearsightedness. Syn. *pagkakorta-
bista.*

mo (mo), *pron.* 1. (used prepositively) your,
as in: *Aklát mo ba ito?* Is this your book?
2. you, as in: *Sinabi mo.* You said it. 3. by
you, as in: *Ginawâ mo*, done by you.

moka (mo-ka), n. (*Sp.*) 1. mocha: coffee
(any variety). Syn. *kapé.* 2. ice cream
flavored with coffee or with coffee and
chocolate.

moda (mo-da), I. n. (*Sp.*) 1. fashion; mode;
style. Syn. *uso.* 2. prevailing custom or
habit. Syn. *ugalì, kaugalián.*
—II. *adj.* fashionable; in vogue. Syn. *uso,
nasa uso o moda.*

modelo (mo-de-lo), n. (*Sp.*) 1. model;
example. Syn. *húwaran, halimbawà.* 2. a
woman who models clothes; mannequin.
Syn. *manikín.* 3. a style or design, as of
cars.

moderno (mo-der-no), I. *adj.* modern. Syn.
makabago.
—II. n. 1. a person who has modern idea
and tastes. 2. anything made in
accordance to modern design.

modista (mo-dis-ta), n. (*Sp.*) dressmaker;
modiste; milliner; seamstress. Syn.
kosturera, mánanahì.

modo (mo-do), n. (*Sp.*) 1. good manners and
right conduct; civility; respect. Syn.
galang, respeto. 2. (*Gram.*) mode. Syn.
panagano.

mohón (mo-hón), var. **muhón**, n. (Sp.
mojon) landmark; boundary mark of a
piece of land. Syn. *musón.*

molde (mol-de), n. (*Sp.*) 1. mold; casting
mold. Syn. *hulmá, hulmahan, bubuán.* 2.
act or manner of shaping something in a
mold. Syn. *pagmolde, pagmomolde,
paghuhulma.*

molékulá (mo-lé-ku-lá), var. **molékuló**, n.
(Sp. *molecula*) molecule.

molestiyá

mukhâ

molestiyá (mo-les-ti-yá), n. (Sp. *molestia*). 1. bother; inconvenience. Syn. *abala, kaabalahan; gambalà, kagambalaan*. 2. act of asking favor from someone. Syn. *pakikiutang na loób, paghingî ng tulong*. 3. molest; harass. 4. assault; abuse sexually.

monarka (mo-nar-ka), n. (Sp. *monarca*) monarch; king or emperor. Syn. *harî, emperadór*.

monasilyo (mo-na-sil-yo), var. **munisilyo**, n. (Sp. *monacillo*) acolyte. Syn. *sakristan*.

monasteryo (mo-nas-ter-yo), n. (Sp. *monasterio*) monastery. Cf. *abadiyá*.

monógamó (mo-nó-ga-mó), I. n. (Sp.) monogamist, a person who practises or advocates monogamy.
—II. *adj.* monogamous.

monólogó (mo-nó-lo-gó), n. (Sp.) monologue; soliloquy. Syn. *pagsásalitáng mag-isá (waláng kausap)*.

monopolyo (mo-no-pol-yo), n. (Sp. *monopolio*) monopoly. Syn. *pagsasarili, pagkakamkám*.

monosílabá (mo-no-sí-la-bá), var. **monosílabó**, n. (Sp.) monosyllable. Syn. *salitáng iisahing pantíg*.

Monsenyór (Mon-sen-yór), n. (Sp. *Monseñor*) Monsignor.

monte (mon-te), n. (Sp.) 1. a kind of card game. 2. mountain. Syn. *bundók*.

monumento (mo-nu-men-to), n. (Sp.) monument. Syn. *bantayog*.

mongha (mong-ha), n. (Sp. *monja*) nun. Cf. *madre*.

monghe (mong-he), n. (Sp. *monje*) monk. Cf. *paré, ermitanyo*.

Mora (Mo-ra), n. a Muslim woman or girl.

morado (mo-ra-do), var. **murado**, I. *adj.* of purple color.
—II. n. 1. purple; violet. Syn. *lila, biyuleta*. 2. a kind of plant with purple leaves and flowers.

morál (mo-rál), n. (Sp.) 1. morals; behavior; conduct. Syn. *asal, ugalì*. 2. morale. Syn. *sigla, lakás ng loób*. 3. something good that can be learned from. Syn. *buti, kabutihan; aral; liksiyón*.

moralidád (mo-ra-li-dád), n. (Sp.) morality. Syn. *kagandahang-asal, kabutihang-asal*.

moralista (mo-ra-lis-ta), n. (Sp.) 1. moralist;

teacher or writer on morals. Syn. *gurò o mánunulát tungkól sa moralídad*. 2. a person who leads a moral life. Syn. *taong malinis ang buhay*.

morkón (mor-kón), n. (Sp. *morcon*) a large, homemade sausage. Cf. *relyeno*.

morena (mo-re-na), I. *adj.* (Sp.) brunette; having black or dark-brown hair and eyes, and a dark complexion, referring to a woman or girl. Cf. *kayumanggí*.
—II. n. a woman or girl having such hair, eyes, and complexion; brunette.

morge (mor-ge), var. **murge**, n. (Sp. *morgue*) morgue.

Moro (Mo-ro), n. (Sp.) Moro, member of a group of Moslem Malay tribes living in the southern Philippines. Syn. *Muslim*. 2. their Malay language; Maguindanao. 3. a male horse having dark-brown hair. Cf. *bayo, astanyo*.

moro-moro (mo-ro + mo-ro), var. **moromoro**, n. a comedy or stage play depicting Christians and Mohammedans fighting each other, resulting always in the defeat of the latter; play acting. Syn. *komedya*.

morpina (mor-pi-na), n. (Sp. *morfina*) a kind of drug made from opium; morphine.

mortalidád (mor-ta-li-dád), n. (Sp.) 1. mortality; loss of life in a large scale. Syn. *pagkakamatay*. 2. rate of death. Syn. *dami ng namámatáy*.

mortuwaryo (mor-tu-war-yo), n. (Sp. *mortuario*) 1. funeral parlor. Syn. *punerarya*. 2. morgue. Syn. *morge*.

moskitero (mos-ki-te-ro), var. **muskitero**, n. (Sp. *mosquitero*) mosquito net. Syn. *kulambô*.

mosyón (mos-yón), n. (Sp. *mocion*) 1. motion; proposal. Syn. *mungkahî, panukalà*. 2. motion; movement. Syn. *kilos, galáw*.

motibasyón (mo-ti-bas-yón), n. (Sp. *motivacion*) act of inducing; motivation. Syn. *pagganyák, pangganyák*.

motibo (mo-ti-bo), n. (Sp. *motivo*) motive, cause or reason for doing something. Syn. *layon, láyunin; hangád, hángarin; dahilán; katwìran*.

mukhâ (muk-hâ). I. n. 1. (*Anat.*) the front

part of the head; face. 2. look or expression
of the face; countenance. Syn.
pagmumukhâ, ayos ng mukhâ. 3. the main
surface or side of a thing. Syn. *pamukhâ,
haráp.* 4. the marked or finished side or
surface, as of cloth. Syn. *karayagán.* 5. the
front side; frontage. Syn. *haráp, harapán;
patsada; delantera.* 6. (Fig.) dignity; self-
respect; prestige. Syn. *dangál, karangalan,
dignidád.*
—II. *adj.* (with –ng) like; similar to. Syn.
katulad, kawangis, kagaya.
—III. *adv.* (with –ng) seemingly;
apparently. Syn. *tila, animo, parang.*

mukháng- (muk-háng-): a combining form,
meaning like or similar to, as in: *mukháng-
aso,* like a dog.

mukmók (muk-mók), n. sullen or
withdrawn behavior due to resentment;
sulkiness. Syn. *maktól, pagmamaktól;
tampó, pagtatampó.*

muktâ (muk-tâ), n. (Colloq.) idea;
knowledge or understanding, as in: *Walâ
akóng muktâ tungkól sa bagay na iyán.* I
have no idea about that matter. Syn. *alam,
kaalaman; batíd, kabatiran; malay,
kamalayan.*

muktô (muk-tô), var. **mugtô,** I. *adj.* swollen,
referring to eyes due to long crying or
oversleeping. See also **puktô, pugtô.**
—II. n. swelling of the eyes due to long
crying or oversleeping. Also, *pamumuktô,
pamumugtô.*

mudmód (mud-mód), n. distribution of
things to each and everyone around. Syn.
pamamahagi, pamimigáy. See **budbód.**

mugmóg (mug-móg), *adj.* 1. swollen and
painful due to mauling or beating. Syn.
bugbóg, lamóg at masakít. 2. too soft due
to overhandling, as fruits. Syn. *lamóg.*

muhì (mu-hì), n. intense feeling of
annoyance, dislike, or disgust, bordering
on hatred. Syn. *matindíng yamót.*

mula (mu-la), n. (Zool., Sp.) mule. Cf.
kabayo, buriko, asno.

mulâ (mu-lâ), I. n. 1. source; origin. Syn.
pinagbuhatan, pinanggagalingan. 2. start or
beginning. Syn. *simulâ, umpisâ.* 3. cause
or reason. Syn. *sanhí, dahilán.*
—II. *adj.* obtained, based, or derived from.

Syn. *galing, kuha, batay.*

mulabe (mu-la-be), var. **molabe,** n. (Bot.) a
species of Philippine hard wood
belonging to the first class or group. Syn.
mulawin.

mulagà (mu-la-gà), n. an empty, fixed look
with the eyes wide open; stare. Syn.
mulagat, pandirilat, titig.

mulagat (mu-la-gat), n. a steady, intent look
or gaze. See **mulagà.**

mulalà (mu-la-la), n. 1. stupidity; lack of
intelligence. Syn. *katangahán, kahangalán.*
2. innocence; lack of cunning. Syn.
kawaláng-malay, kainosentihán.

mulán (mu-lán), *v.* (Colloq.) to start; begin.
Syn. *simulán, umpisahán.*

mulapì (mu-la-pì), n. (Gram.) prefix. Syn.
unlapì.

mulat (mu-lat), n. 1. act of opening the eyes.
Also, *pagmulat.* Cf. *dilat, pagdilat.* 2. the
extent to which the eyes are opened. Syn.
pagkámulat.

mulát (mu-lát), I. *adj.* 1. open; not closed,
referring to the eyes; opposed to *pikít.* 2.
awake; not sleeping. Syn. *gisíng, hindî
tulóg.* 3. educated; civilized; well-
informed. Syn. *nag-aaral, may-pinag-
aralan, edukado.*
—II. n. state or condition of being open,
referring to eyes.

mulatan (mu-la-tan), *v.* to teach or train
while still young, referring to a child. Syn.
turuan habang batà pa.

mulá't-mulâ (mu-lá't + mu-lâ), *adv.* from the
very beginning. Syn. *mulá't-sapúl.*

mulato (mu-la-to), n. & *adj.* (Sp.) mulatto.
Syn. *mestisong Negro.*

mulá't-sapúl (mu-lá't + sa-púl), *adv.* from the
very start or beginning. Syn. *mula't-mulâ.*

mulawin (mu-la-win), n. (Bot.) 1. a
Philippine hardwood, commercially
known as molave. 2. the tree from which
this hardwood is obtained.

muleta (mu-le-ta), n. (Sp.) crutch or
crutches. Syn. *sakláy.*

mulî (mu-lî), *adv.* again; once more; at a
second time. Syn. *ulî, minsan pá.*

mulî't-mulî (mu-lî't + mu-lî), *adv.* again and
again.

mulmól (mul-mól), n. 1. loose ends of

threads worn-out by long use or by friction. Also, *himulmól.* 2. short, fine hair. Syn. *balahibo.*

multa (mul-ta), n. (*Sp.*) 1. fine; penalty. Syn. *rekargo.* 2. the payment of fine or penalty.

multo (mul-to), n. (Sp. *muwerto*) 1. ghost; specter. Syn. *impakto.* 2. (*Colloq.*) the spirit soul (of a dead person). Syn. *káluluwá.*

mumo (mu-mo), n. some particles of cooked rice (*kanin*) left on the table or plate after eating.

mumò (mu-mò), var. **momò,** n. 1. child's term for ghost or specter. Syn. *mamaw.*

mumog (mu-mog), n. 1. act of washing or rinsing the mouth with water. 2. act of gargling (the throat) with water or liquid.

mumuntî (mu-mun-tî), *adj.* plural form of *muntî,* as in: *mumuntíng bagay,* small things or matters.

mumurahin (mu-mu-ra-hin), *adj.* 1. cheap; not expensive; opposed to *mamahalin.* 2. of little value or worth. Syn. *di-mahalagá.*

muna (mu-na), *adv.* 1. first, as in: *Gawín muna natin itó.* Let's do this first. 2. yet; at the present time; presently, as in: *hindî muna,* not at the present time. 3. before; beforehand, as in: *Sabihin muna natin sa kanyá.* Let's tell him beforehand.

munakala (mu-na-ka-la), var. **munukala,** n. 1. plan. Syn. *balak.* 2. proposal. Syn. *mungkahì.* 3. project; project proposal. Syn. *proyekto, panukalang-gawain.*

mundiyál (mun-di-yál), *adj.* (Sp. *mundial*) extending throughout the world; worldwide. Syn. *pandaigdíg, ng buóng daigdíg.*

mundo (mun-do; mun-dó), n. (*Sp.*) 1. the earth; world. Syn. *daigdíg.* 2. the universe. Syn. *sansinukob.*

muni (mu-ni), n. 1. reflection; careful thinking before acting; rationalized thinking. Syn. *bulay, pagbubulay-bulay; nilay, pagnininlay-nilay.* 2. thought; idea. Syn. *isip, kaisipán; kurò, kuru-kurò.*

muniknîk (mu-nik-nîk), n. a swarming or teeming, as of bees, locusts, ants, or the like. Syn. *muninì, mutiktîk.*

muni-muni (mu-ni + mu-ni), var. **munimuni,** n. 1. long rationalized

thinking; deep thought. Syn. *malalim na pagbubulay-bulay, matagál na pagnininlay-nilay.* 2. solemn reflection about something serious. Syn. *dili-dili, pàgdidili-dili.*

munisipyo (mu-ni-sip-yo), n. (Sp. *municipio*) 1. municipality; town. Syn. *bayan.* 2. municipal building; town hall.

munisyón (mu-nis-yón), n. (Sp. *municion*) materials used in war; munition. Syn. *mga kagamitáng pandigmâ, mga gamit sa digmâ, mga sandata.*

muntalà (mun-ta-là), n. 1. asteroid; planetoid. Cf. *planeta.* 2. a man-made satellite.

muntî (mun-tî), I. *adj.* 1. small; tiny; little. Syn. *maliit.* 2. negligible; that can be disregarded. Syn. *di-gaanó, waláng-gaanó.* —II. *adv.* (usually with *na*) almost; nearly. Syn. *halos.*

muntîk (mun-tîk), var. **kamuntîk na,** *adv.* (with *na*), almost; nearly. Syn. *halos, muntî na.*

munyekà (mun-ye-kà), var. **munyika,** n. (Sp. *muñeca*) 1. doll. Syn. *manikà, munikà.* 2. puppet.

mungkahì (mung-ka-hì), n. 1. a motion or proposition for discussion in a meeting or assembly. Syn. *panukalà, mosyón, resolusyón.* 2. suggestion or proposal. Syn. *suhestiyón.*

munggo (mung-go) n. 1. the chicken pea. 2. the bean of this plant; green gram.

mungot (mu-ngot), n. frown; frowning. Syn. *simangot, pagsimangot.*

muók (mu-ók), n. 1. fierce fighting; hand-to-hand fight or battle. Also, *pamuók, pagpapamuók.* Syn. *mahigpít na labanán.*

muóg (mu-óg), var. **moóg,** n. 1. fort; fortification; bastion. Syn. *kutà, matibay na tanggulan.* 2. den; lair; hide-out. Syn. *taguán, kublihan, pugad (fig.).*

mura[1] (mu-ra), *adj.* cheap; having low price; inexpensive; opposed to *mahál.* Syn. *mababà ang halagá o presyo.*

mura[2] (mu-ra), n. 1. slanderous attack. Syn. *tuligsâ, atake.* 2. scolding or blaming with angry words. Syn. *alipustâ, pag-alipustâ.*

murà (mu-rà), I. *adj.* 1. still young, tender, and fresh, as green vegetables. Syn.

sariwa't malambót. 2. young; unripe, as fruits. Syn. hiláw, bubót. 3. immature; not fully developed; still young. Syn. batà pa. 4. (of color) light, as in: berdeng murà, light green. Syn. mapusyáw.

–II. v. very young coconut fruit. Syn. buko.

muralya (mu-ral-ya), n. (Sp. muralla) rampart; thick walls, as of a fortress.

musa (mu-sa), n. (Sp.) muse. Syn. diwatà, lakambini, paraluman.

musang (mu-sang), n. a kind of wild or mountain cat with repulsive odor.

musangsáng (mu-sang-sáng), var. busangsáng, adj. 1. swollen or distended, as the thick lips of a person. Syn. namámalikaró. 2. split open at the end, as the badly beaten head of a chisel handle. Syn. salsál, busalsál.

muskada (mus-ka-da), n. (Bot., Sp.) nutmeg.

muskitero (mus-ki-te-ro), var. **moskitero**, n. (Sp. mosquitero) mosquito net. Syn. kulambô.

muskulado (mus-ku-la-do), var. **masculado**, adj. (Spanish-influenced) muscular; having well-developed muscles. Syn. malamán, matipunô.

músiká (mú-si-ká), n. (Sp. música) music; the art or science of making musical sounds by vocal or instrumental rendition. Syn. sining o aghám ng pag-awit o pagtugtóg. 2. a musical composition. Syn. tugtugin.

Muslím (Mus-lím), n. & adj. Moslem. Syn. Moro.

musmós (mus-mós), adj. 1. very young; of immature mind. Syn. nápakabatà pa. 2. innocent, as a child. Syn. inosente, walâ pang muwáng o malay.

musón (mu-són), n. (Sp. mojon) landmark; boundary mark of a piece of land. Syn. muhón.

mustasa (mus-ta-sa), var. **mostasa**, n. (Sp. mostaza) mustard.

mustra (mus-tra), n. (Sp. mostrar) 1. sign or signal with the hand or hands. Syn. senyás, hudyát. 2. sample; example. Syn. halimbawà.

mutà (mu-tà), n. (Sp. mota) gummy secretion in the eyes; mote.

mutawì (mu-ta-wì), n. coming out of words from the mouth or lips of a person.

mutiktík (mu-tik-tík), n. 1. a being fully laden, as with flowers or fruits. Syn. hitik, pagkahitik. 2. a teeming or swarming, as of bees, ants, etc. Syn. muninì, pamumuninì. 3. a being thickly crowded, as with people. Syn. pagkapunúng-punô.

mutsatsa (mut-sat-sa); n. (Sp. muchacha) a girl or woman servant; maid; maidservant; housemaid. Syn. alilang babae, utusáng babae.

mutso (mut-so), adj. (Sp. mucho) with or having much money; rich; wealthy. Syn. mayaman, mapera, makuwalta, masalapî.

mutyâ (mut-yâ), I. n. 1. darling; sweetheart. Syn. giliw, sintá, irog, mahál. 2. amulet; charm; talisman. Syn. galíng, antíng-antíng. –II. adj. 1. dear; beloved. Syn. mahál, minámahál. 2. alone; only one; single. Syn. solo, nag-íisá.

muwák (mu-wák), n. (Colloq.) knowledge; understanding; idea about something. Syn. alam, nalalaman; batíd, kabatiran.

muwál (mu-wál), adj. full or filled up, esp. with food (s.o. mouths). Syn. punô o punúng-punô ang bibíg. Also, namúmuwalán.

muwáng (mu-wáng), n. knowledge or understanding about something. Syn. malay, kamalayan; alam, kaalaman; batíd, kabatiran.

muwebles (mu-we-bles), n. (Sp. muebles) furniture. Syn. (mga) kasangkapan (pambahay o pantanggapan).

muwelye (mu-wel-ye), n. (Sp. muelle) 1. (Mech.) spring. Syn. ispiríng. 2. pier; dock; wharf. Syn. piyér, daungán, pantalán.

muwestra (mu-wes-tra), n. (Sp. muestra) 1. sample; example. Syn. halimbawà. 2. mode; pattern. Syn. húwaran, modelo, ulirán, parisán. 3. sign or signal, as with the hand or hands. Syn. senyás, hudyát. See mustra.

muyangit (mu-ya-ngit), n. molasses, syrup honey, or any thick liquid ashering along the sides of a container. Syn. kayat.

N

N, n (na), *n.* 1. the eleventh letter of the *abakada* (Pilipino alphabet). 2. the type or impression representing this letter. 3. a symbol for the eleventh in a group or sequence.

na (na), I. *adv.* 1. already, as in: *Umalis na sila.* They have left already. 2. now, as in: *Lumakad na tayo.* Let's go now. 3. more, any more: as in: *Wala na siyang kuwarta.* He has no more money or he has no money any more.

—II. as lig., used to connect (a) a modifier having a final consonant with the word it modifies (usually not expressed in English), as in: *masarap na pagkain,* tasty food; *matapang na lalaki,* brave man. (b) an adverb with a verb, but may also be omitted, as a child who runs fast, *batang malakas (na) tumakbo.* See **nang** and **–ng.**

na- (na-), *pref.* used in forming (a) the past tense of *ma-* verbs, as in: *natalo* (fr. *matalo*), *nawala* (fr. *mawala, nasawi*), etc. (b) verbal adverbs, as in: *narito, naririto* (fr. *dito*), *nariyan, naririyan* (fr. *diyan*), *naroon, naroroon* (fr. *doon*), etc.

naáabala (na-á-a-ba-la), *adj.* being delayed, referring to a person or to the work he is doing. Syn. *naátraso.*

náaakmâ (ná-a-ak-mâ), *adj.* 1. put or placed in position; attached, fitted, or adjusted in place. Syn. *nakaakmâ, nakakabít.* 2. right; proper, as in: *náaakmang pasiyá,* right decision.

naáalaala (na-á-a-la-a-la), *adj.* that can be recalled in one's mind; possible of recalling to one's mind.

náaalaala (ná-a-a-la-a-la), *adj.* still in one's mind. Syn. *nasa isip pa, hindî pa nákakalimutan.*

naáapí (na-á-a-pí), *adj.* being maltreated or taken advantage of. Syn. *pinagsásamantalahán, tinátrato nang masamâ.*

naáarì (na-á-a-rì), *adj.* that can be possessed or owned. Syn. *máaaring maarì.*

naáasahan (na-á-a-sa-han), *adj.* 1. dependable; reliable. Syn. *mapaníniwalaan, mapananaligan.* 2. trustworthy.

Syn. *mapagtítiwalaan.* 3. that can be depended or relied on.

nabâ (na-bâ), *v.* (poetic form of *bumabâ*) to go down; come down. Syn. *manaog, pumanaog.*

nábabakás (ná-ba-ba-kás), *adj.* 1. that can be traced, as footsteps and fingerprints. 2. detectable or noticeable, as one's poverty from the way he is dressed. Syn. *nápupuná, nápapansín.*

nábabagay (ná-ba-ba-gay), *adj.* fit; fitting; proper; suitable. Syn. *angkóp, náaangkóp.*

nábabago (ná-ba-ba-go), *adj.* referring to something that a person is not yet familiar with. Syn. *náiibá.*

nábabaguhan (ná-ba-ba-gu-han), *adj.* referring to a person who still feels unfamiliar or new to a place or to the use of something being handled by him. Syn. *naníníbago.*

nabál (na-bál), *adj.* (Sp.) of or pertaining to warships or to the navy. Syn. *pandagat, ng hukbóng-dagat.*

nabalam (na-ba-lam), *adj.* delayed; having been delayed. Syn. *atrasado, naatraso.*

nabalo (na-ba-lo), past tense of **mabalo,** to become a widow or widower.

nábanggít (ná-bang-gít), *adj.* mentioned; having been mentioned.

nábiktimá (ná-bik-ti-má), *adj.* victimized; having been victimized.

nabigasyón (na-bi-gas-yón), *n.* (Sp. *navegación*) navigation; sailing. Syn. *paglalayág.*

nabighanì (na-big-ha-nì), *adj.* charmed or seduced; having been charmed or seduced. Syn. *naakit, nahikayat.*

nabimbín (na-bim-bín), *adj.* delayed; having been delayed. Syn. *naabala, naatraso.*

nabinat (na-bi-nat), var. **nabaynat,** *adj.* referring to a person who suffered a relapse.

nabingí (na-bi-ngí), *adj.* referring to a person who has gone deaf.

nabúbuhay (na-bú-bu-hay), *adj.* 1. referring esp. to plants that can be propagated or made to grow, as under a certain condition or climate. Syn. *napatútubo.* 2. able to support the living, as of one's family. Syn. *nasúsustentuhán.*

nabuhay (na-bu-hay), *adj.* restored to life; has come back to life.

nabuwág (na-bu-wág), *adj.* 1. demolished; torn down. 2. has become disbanded or dissolved, as an association, office, etc.

naka (na-ka), *pref.* used to form (a) past tense of *maka*-verbs, as in: *nakatapos*, was able to finish. (b) verbal adjectives, as in: *nakabitin*, hanging; *nakatayo*, standing.

nakakaábala (na-ka-ka-á-ba-la), *adj.* referring to someone or something that causes delay or disturbance. Syn. *nakaáatraso, nakabábalam.*

nakaáaburido (na-ka-á-a-bu-ri-do), *adj.* causing desperation or despair.

nakaáakit (na-ka-á-a-kit), *adj.* 1. attractive; charming. Syn. *kaakit-akit, nakabíbighani.* 2. convincing. Syn. *kapaní-paniwalà.*

nakaáalíw (na-ka-á-a-líw), *adj.* 1. interesting. 2. comforting; consolatory.

nakaáawà (na-ka-á-a-wà), *adj.* pitiful; deserving pity or compassion. Also, *nakákaawà.*

nákaaway (ná-ka-a-way), *adj.* referring to a person with whom one has had a quarrel or fight. Syn. *nákabasag-ulo, nákagalít.*

nakabábalám (na-ka-bá-ba-lám), *adj.* referring to something that causes delay. Syn. *nakaáatraso.*

nakábahagi (na-ká-ba-ha-gi), *adj.* was able to get one's share from. Syn. *nakáparte, nakáamot.*

nakabantáy (na-ka-ban-táy), *adj.* watching; guarding; in duty, referring to a guard or watchman. Syn. *nakatanod.*

nakabíbigát (na-ka-bí-bi-gát), *adj.* causing a burden to someone; burdensome. Syn. *pampabigát.*

nakabíbighanì (na-ka-bí-big-ha-nì), *adj.* 1. charming; attractive. Syn. *kaakit-akit, nakaáakit.* 2. enticing; convincing.

nakabingit (na-ka-bi-ngit), *adj.* on the edge or verge of.

nakabúbuhay (na-ka-bú-bu-hay), *adj.* able to sustain life.

nakabúbuti (na-ka-bú-bu-ti), *adj.* that which serves to improve, remedy, or make better. Syn. *nakagágalíng, naka-pagpápabuti.*

nakabuká (na-ka-bu-ká), *adj.* open, referring esp. to a mouth, wound, etc.

nakabukadkád (na-ka-bu-kad-kád), *adj.* fully open or spread out, referring esp. to mats, flowers, wings, etc. Syn. *nakaladlád.*

nakabukás (na-ka-bu-kás), *adj.* open; not closed, as doors, windows, books, drawers, etc. Ant. *nakasará, nakapiníd.*

nakabukód (na-ka-bu-kód), *adj.* 1. separated or set aside, as for a certain purpose. Syn. *nakahiwaláy.* 2. living separately, as a newly married couple, from their parents.

nakabungad (na-ka-bu-ngad), *adj.* at the entrance or threshold of. Syn. *nasa-bungad.*

nakaburol (na-ka-bu-rol), *adj.* lying in state, said of a dead person. -

nakabuti (na-ka-bu-ti), I. *v.* past tense of *makabuti.*
—II. *adj.* referring to something that served to improve, remedy, or make better. Syn. *nakagalíng, nakapágpabuti.*

nakábuwaya (na-ká-bu-wa-ya), *adj.* said of one who was able to swindle or defraud someone. Syn. *nakásubà, nakátansô.*

nakabuyangyáng (na-ka-bu-yang-yáng), *adj.* exposed in the open. Syn. *nakahantád.*

nakákaalam (na-ká-ka-a-lam), *adj.* referring to someone who has the knowledge of something. Syn. *nakákabatid, nakáka-intindí.*

nakákaawa (na-ká-ka-a-wa), *adj.* pitiful; deserving pity or compassion.

nakákabasa (na-ká-ka-ba-sa), *adj.* able to read; with or having the ability to read. Also, *nakábábasa.*

nakákabatà (na-ká-ka-ba-tà), *adj.* 1. said of something that causes a person to look younger. Syn. *nakapagpápabatà.* 2. younger, referring to one's sister or brother.

nakákabuti (na-ká-ka-bu-ti), *adj.* referring to something that serves to improve or give something good to someone.

nakákakabá (na-ká-ka-ka-bá), *adj.* that which serves to give someone a premonition of something unpleasant.

nakákakilos (na-ká-ka-ki-los), *adj.* able to move; free to move. Syn. *nakákagaláw.*

nakákakita (na-ká-ka-ki-ta), *adj.* 1. able to see, referring to a person or to his eyes.

2. able to earn something for one's living. Also, *kumíkita*.

nakákagalák (na-ká-ka-ga-lák), *adj.* that which serves to make someone happy. Syn. *nakákatuwâ, nakákaligaya*.

nakákagalíng (na-ká-ka-ga-líng) , *adj.* 1. with or having the potency to cure a disease or sickness, as a medicine. 2. that which serves to give a person or thing something good or beneficial. Syn. *nakákábuti*.

nakákagalit (na-ká-ka-ga-lit), *adj.* that which causes someone to become angry. Syn. *nakapagbápagalit*.

nakákagulat (na-ká-ka-gu-lat), *adj.* causing surprise or shock. Syn. *nakákataká, nakákabiglâ*.

nakákahalina (na-ká-ka-ha-li-na), *adj.* attractive; charming. Syn. *nakákaakit, kaakit-akit, kahalí-halina*.

nakákahambál (na-ká-ka-ham-bál), *adj.* pitiful; lamentable. Syn. *nakákaawà, nakákahabág*.

nakákahigít (na-ká-ka-hi-gít), *adj.* with or having an advantage over another or others; in a better position or standing than another or others. Syn. *nakálalamáng*.

nakákahilì (na-ká-ka-hi-lì), *adj.* referring to a person or thing that invites envy to another or others.

nakákahirá (na-ká-ka-hi-rá), *adj.* confusing; distracting. Syn. *nakákalitó*.

nakákahiyâ (na-ká-ka-hi-yâ), *adj.* shameful; disgraceful.

nakákain (na-ká-ka-in), *adj.* fit to eat; eatable; can be eaten.

nakákainip (na-ká-ka-i-nip), *adj.* causing boredom or impatience.

nakákainís (na-ká-ka-i-nís), *adj.* 1. annoying; vexing; irritating. Syn. *nakákayamót, nakayáyamót*. 2. tending to suffocate; suffocating.

nakákainggít (na-ká-ka-ing-gít), *adj.* that which causes envy.

nakákalamáng (na-ká-ka-la-máng), *adj.* with or having an advantage; in a better position than another or others. Syn. *nakákahigít*.

nakákalibáng (na-ká-ka-li-báng), *adj.*

interesting; entertaining; amusing. Syn. *nakákawili, kawili-wili*.

nakákalimot (na-ká-ka-li-mot), *adj.* forgetting; forgetful.

nakákalitó (na-ká-ka-li-tó), *adj.* confusing. Syn. *nakákahirá*.

nakákalugód (na-ká-ka-lu-gód), *adj.* enjoyable; interesting. Syn. *nakakatuwâ nakákawili*.

nakákaluhâ (na-ká-ka-lu-hâ), *adj.* referring to something that causes one to cry or shed tears.

nakákalungkót (na-ká-ka-lung-kót), *adj.* said of an incident that causes someone to become lonely.

nakákamatáy (na-ká-ka-ma-táy), *adj.* deadly; fatal; mortal.

nákakapanahón (ná-ka-ka-pa-na-hón), *adj.* 1. referring to someone who is of the same age with another. 2. living or happening at the same time or period with another.

nakákatawá (na-ká-ka-ta-wá), *adj.* referring to something funny; laughable. Syn. *katawá-tawá*.

nakákatiyák (na-ká-ka-ti-yák), *adj.* referring to someone who is sure about something. Syn. *nakákasiguro*.

nákakatulad (ná-ka-ka-tu-lad), *adj.* somewhat similar to another. Syn. *nákakahawig*.

nakákatulad (na-ká-ka-tu-lad), *adj.* able to copy or imitate something. Syn. *nakákakopya*.

nákakatumbás (ná-ka-ka-tum-bás), *adj.* representing the equivalent of. Syn. *nákakatimbáng, nákakapareho*.

nakákatuwâ (na-ká-ka-tu-wâ), *adj.* pleasing; enjoyable. Syn. *nakákagalák, nakákaligaya*.

nakakatuyâ (na-ka-ka-tu-yâ), *adj.* using sarcasm; sarcastic. Syn. *nakakauyám*.

nakákawalâ (na-ká-ka-wa-lâ), *adj.* said of anything that serves to remove, erase, remedy, or relieve stain, pain, etc. Syn. *nakákaalís*.

nakakawili (na-ka-ka-wi-li), *adj.* interesting; entertaining.

nakakíkilabot (na-ka-kí - ki-la-bot), *adj.* horrible; causing or tending to cause horror.

nakakúkutyâ (na-ka-kú-kut-yâ), *adj.*

degrading; humiliating; disgraceful; shameful. Syn. *nakákahiyâ*.

ákadaúp-palad (ná-ka-da-úp + pa-lad), *adj.* referring to someone whom another has shaken hands with. Syn. *nákakamáy*.

akadipá (na-ka-di-pá), *adj.* said of a person whose arms are stretched out horizontally at the sides.

akagágambalà (na-ka-gá-gam-ba-là), *adj.* disturbing; causing annoyance or distraction.

akagáganyák (na-ka-gá-gan-yák), *adj.* enticing; convincing. Syn. *nákákaakit, nakahíhikayat*.

akagiginhawa (na-ka-gi-gin-ha-wa), 1. said of anything that gives relief, as from pain; soothing. Also, *nakapagpápaginhawa.* 2. providing or giving comfort; comfortable.

akagitáw (na-ka-gi-táw), *adj.* seen on the surface; with or having a part or portion protruding outside. Syn. *nakalitáw, nakauslî.*

akagúgulantáng (na-ka-gú-gu-lan-táng), *adj.* shocking.

akaguhit (na-ka-gu-hit), *adj.* drawn or illustrated, as a picture. Syn. *nakalarawan.*

akagumon (na-ka-gu-mon), *adj.* 1. helplessly confined, as in bed. Syn. *nakaratay.* 2. wallowing or addicted to, as in a vice.

akaháhabág (na-ka-há-ha-bág), *adj.* pitiful; deserving pity or compassion. Syn. *nakaáawà.*

akaháhalina (na-ka-há-ha-li-na), *adj.* 1. attractive; charming. Syn. *nákákaakit, kaakit-akit.* 2. convincing; enticing.

akaháhambál (na-ka-há-ham-bál), *adj.* deplorable; pitiful. Syn. *nakalúlungkót, nakaáawà.*

nakahain (na-ka-ha-in), *var.* **nakahayin**, *adj.* said of food set or prepared on the table.

nakahambalang (na-ka-ham-ba-lang), *adj.* lying flat or idly across a way or on the center of a place. Syn. *nakabulagtâ sa gitnâ.*

nakahandâ (na-ka-han-dâ), *adj.* prepared or made ready for use. Syn. *nakalaán, preparado.*

nakahapon (na-ka-ha-pon), *adj.* referring to a bird, chicken, etc. roosting on branch, pole, or perch. Syn. *nakadapò.*

nakaharáp (na-ka-ha-ráp), *adj.* 1. facing at someone or at something; opposed to *nakatalikod.* 2. present; in attendance.

nakahíhikayat (na-ka-hí-hi-ka-yat), *adj.* convincing; enticing; persuasive. Syn. *nákákaakit, nakaáakit.*

nakahíhigít (na-ka-hí-hi-gít), *adj.* at an advantage over another or others; in a better position than another or others. Syn. *nakalálamáng.*

nakahíhinayang (na-ka-hí-hi-na-yang), *adj.* referring to something that is regretted if lost, not taken advantage of, or the like.

nakahilig (na-ka-hi-lig), *adj.* inclined; sloping. Syn. *nakahapay, nakatagilid.*

nakahilís (na-ka-hi-lís), *adj.* slanting; oblique. Syn. *nakahirís, nakahiwid.*

nakaíiníp (na-ka-í-i-níp), *adj.* boring; tedious; long and wearisome. Also, *nakákainíp.*

nakalálayà (na-ka-lá-la-yà), *adj.* free; not confined, as a criminal; at large.

nakalamáng (na-ka-la-máng), *adj.* referring to a player who has gained an advantage over his opponent. Syn. *nakahigít.*

nakalantád (na-ka-lan-tád), *adj.* exposed in the open. Syn. *nakahayág.*

nakalata (na-ka-la-ta), *adj.* preserved in cans; canned.

nakalayà (na-ka-la-yà), *adj.* said of a person who has been freed or released, as from imprisonment.

nakalibíng (na-ka-li-bíng), *adj.* burried. Cf. *nakabaón.*

nakalílitó (na-ka-lí-li-tó), *adj.* confusing; distracting. Syn. *nakahíhirá.*

nakalimot (na-ka-li-mot), I. *adj.* referring to a person who has forgotten someone or something.
—II. *v.* past tense of *makalimot.*

nakaluklók (na-ka-luk-lók), *adj.* seated. Syn. *nakaupô.*

nakalugay (na-ka-lu-gay), *adj.* hanging loosely, referring to woman's hair. Cf. *nakalayláy.*

nakalulan (na-ka-lu-lan), *adj.* 1. riding, as in a vehicle. Syn. *nakasakáy.* 2. placed in a container. Syn. *nakalamán.* 3. loaded, as cargo. Syn. *nakakarga.*

nakalúlumbáy (na-ka-lú-lum-báy), *adj.*

saddening; distressing. Syn. *nakalúlungkót.*

nakalúlunos (na-ka-lú-lu-nos), *adj.* deplorable; pitiful. Syn. *nakaáawà.*

nakalusót (na-ka-lu-sót), *adj.* able to pass through without being noticed. Syn. *nakalampás.*

nakámalay (na-ká-ma-lay), *adj.* referring to a person who was able to have an idea or inkling about something secret,. Syn. *nakáhiwatig.*

nakamámanghâ (na-ka-má-mang-hâ), *adj.* astonishing; surprising.

nakamatá (na-ka-ma-tá), *adj.* gazing or looking intently at someone or something. Syn. *nakatitig.*

nakamatáy (na-ka-ma-táy), I. *adj.* said of a person who has committed murder. Also, *nakápatáy.*

—II. *n.* (with *ang*) murderer; assassin.

nákamatayán (ná-ka-ma-ta-yán), *adj.* said of something left unfinished or undone by the untimely death of someone.

nákamít (ná-ka-mít), *adj.* said of something that one was able to get or obtain. Syn. *nátamó.*

nakapág- (na-ka-pág-): past form of the prefix *makapag-.*

nakapag-áalaalá (na-ka-pag + á-a-la-a-lá), *adj.* that which causes someone to worry about.

nakapag-áalinlangan (na-ka-pag + á-a-lin-la-ngan), *adj.* said of something that gives someone reason to have a doubt. Syn. *nakapagdúduda.*

nakapag-aral (na-ka-pag + a-ral), I. *adj.* referring to someone who was able to study or get educated.

—II. *v.* past tense of *makapag-aral*, to be able to study or get educated.

nakapagdáramdam (na-ka-pag-dá-ram-dam), *adj.* said of something that causes one to feel hurt or slighted. Syn. *nakapaghíhinanakít.*

nakapaghíhinalà (na-ka-pag-hí-hi-na-là), *adj.* that tends to cause suspicion. Syn. *nakapagdúduda.*

nakapaglílingkód (na-ka-pag-lí-ling-kód), *adj.* said of someone who is able to serve or do favors for others.

nakapagngíngitngít (na-ka-pag-ngí-ngit-ngít), *adj.* said of something that causes feeling of suppressed rage or anger.

nakapagpápabaít (na-ka-pag-pá-pa-ba-ít), *adj.* said of something that causes a perso to become kind or well-behaved.

nakapagpápadalisay (na-ka-pag-pá-pa-da-li say), *adj.* said of something that purifies

nakapagpápahinà (na-ka-pag-pá-pa-hi-nà *adj.* said of something that serves to mak (a person or thing) weaker; opposed t *nakapagpápalakás.*

nakapagpápaibá (na-ka-pag-pá-pa-i-bá), *ad,* that which causes something to becom changed or different.

nakapagpápalayà (na-ka-pag-pá-pa-la-yà *adj.* said of someone who has the authorit to set a person free, as from confinemer or prison.

nakapagpápalinaw (na-ka-pag-pá-pa-li naw), *adj.* that which serves to make clea Syn. *nakapagpápaliwanag.*

nakapagpápalusóg (na-ka-pag-pá-pa-lu sóg), *adj.* healthful; good for the health nutritive.

nakapagpápamatá (na-ka-pag-pá-pa-ma-tá) *adj.* that which serves as an eye opene educational or instructive.

nakapagpáparangál (na-ka-pag-pá-pa-ra ngál), *adj.* dignifying. Also, *nakákarangá*

nakapagpápasayá (na-ka-pag-pá-pa-sa-yá) *adj.* that which gives joy or happiness.

nakapagpápasiglá (na-ka-pag-pá-pa-sig-lá) *adj.* inspiring; stimulating.

nakapagpápasiyá (na-ka-pag-pá-pa-si-yá) *adj.* said of someone who has the authorit or is able to decide. Syn. *may-karapatán* *may-kakayaháng magpasiyá.*

nakapagpápatapang (na-ka-pag-pá-pa-ta pang), *adj.* referring to something tha makes one courageous.

nakapagpápatibay (na-ka-pag-pá-pa-ti-bay) *adj.* 1. said of something that serves t give strength or enduring quality. Syn *nakapagpápalakás.* 2. with or having th authority to make approval, as o appointments, laws, etc.

nakapagpápatingkád (na-ka-pag-pá-pa-ting kád), *adj.* that which gives color o brightness; that which makes somethin colorful.

nakapagpápatunay (na-ka-pag-pá-pa-tu-nay), *adj.* that serves to prove the truth about something. Syn. *nakapagpápatotoó*.

nakapagtátaká (na-ka-pag-tá-ta-ká), *adj.* causing surprise or wonder; surprising.

nakapagtúturò (na-ka-pag-tú-tu-rò), *adj.* 1. instructive; educational. 2. that which teaches moral lesson. 3. able to teach (s.o a teacher, instructor, and the like).

nakapaling (na-ka-pa-ling), *adj.* veered to one side or direction. Syn. *nakabaling*.

nakapanánabík (na-ka-pa-ná-na-bík), *adj.* referring to something that tends to cause keen eagerness or desire.

nakapandídiri (na-ka-pan-dí-di-ri), *adj.* loathsome. Also *nakadídiri*.

nakapangíngilabot (na-ka-pa-ngí-ngi-la-bot), *adj.* horrible; terrific; frightening.

nákar (ná-kar), I. *n.* (Sp. *nácar*) mother-of-pearl.
—II. *adj.* of or made of mother-of-pearl.

nakaraán (na-ka-ra-án), I. *adj.* past; bygone. Syn. *nakalipas, lumipas*.
—II. *n.* 1. past; anything that is gone or past. 2. (*Gram.*) the past tense.

nakarárami (na-ka-rá-ra-mi), I. *adj.* of or belonging to the majority. Syn. *nakahíhigít sa bilang*. –II. *n.* (the) majority. Syn. *mayoriya (mayorya)*.

nakarírimarim (na-ka-rí-ri-ma-rim), *adj.* said of something a person loathes for being foul or filthy. Syn. *nakadídiri*.

nákariringgán (ná-ka-ri-ring-gán), *adj.* misheard.

nakasalíg (na-ka-sa-líg), *adj.* based on. Syn. *nakabatay*.

nákasama (ná-ka-sa-ma), *adj.* said of a person who was with someone on. Syn. *nákasabáy*.

nakasamâ (na-ka-sa-mâ), *adj.* said of a thing that caused bad effect on someone or something, opposed to *nakabuti*.

nakasásabík (na-ka-sá-sa-bík), *adj.* that which causes someone to long for with eagerness.

nakasásakít (na-ka-sá-sa-kít), *adj.* causing physical or moral pain; hurtful. Syn. *nakasúsugat* (*fig.*).

nakasásawà (na-ka-sá-sa-wà), *adj.* tiring or boring. Also, *nakapagsásawà*.

nakasimangot (na-ka-si-ma-ngot), *adj.* frowning.

nakasísilaw (na-ka-sí-si-law), *adj.* dazzling, as an extremely bright light.

nakasísindák (na-ka-sí-sin-dák), *adj.* horrible; terrifying; dreadful.

nakasísirang-puri (na-ka-sí-si-rang + pu-ri), *adj.* referring to something that destroys or harms the good name or reputation of.

nakasísiyá (na-ka-sí-si-yá), *adj.* said of anything that gives satisfaction or contentment to someone; satisfying. Syn. *nakapagbibigáy-kasiyahan, nakalúlugód*.

nakasulit (na-ka-su-lit), *adj.* 1. said of an examinee who has successfully passed. Syn. *nakapasá*. 2. referring to a bill collector who was able to remit his collection.

nakasúsunók (na-ka-sú-su-nók), *adj.* detestable to one's smell.

nakasúsura (na-ka-sú-su-ra), *adj.* annoying; causing annoyance. Syn. *nakayáyamót, nakabúbuwisit*.

nakatadhanâ (na-ka-tad-ha-nâ), *adj.* 1. destined for a certain purpose. Syn. *nakatakdâ*. 2. given as a provision, as in a contract, law, etc.

nakatagò (na-ka-ta-gò), *adj.* hidden; kept in a hidden place.

nakatanod (na-ka-ta-nod), *adj.* keeping watch; standing on guard. Syn. *nakabantáy, nakaguwardiyá*.

nakatangá (na-ka-ta-ngá), *adj.* watching or looking at something in a stupid manner. Syn. *nakatungangà*.

nakatapos (na-ka-ta-pos), *adj.* 1. referring to someone who was able to finish or complete his studies. Also, *nakapagtapós*. 2. said of one who was able to finish doing something. Syn. *nakayarì*.

nakatátaás (na-ka-tá-ta-ás), *adj.* of higher rank or standing, as a chief in an office.

nakatátandâ (na-ka-tá-tan-dâ), *adj.* 1. older than. Syn. *nakahíhigít sa edad (gulang)*. 2. able to remember. Syn. *nakakáalaala, nakakágunitâ*.

nakatátantô (na-ka-tá-tan-tô), *adj.* able to understand; understanding. Syn. *nakaúunawà*.

nakatawa (na-ka-ta-wa), *adj.* that laughs; laughing.

nakátikím (na-ká-ti-kím), *adj.* said of someone who was able to taste or experience something. Syn. *nakáranas*.

nakatitik (na-ka-ti-tik), *adj.* written; put in writing. Syn. *nakasulat*.

nakatitig (na-ka-ti-tig), *adj.* staring; looking staringly at someone or something.

nakatítiís (na-ka-tí-ti-ís), *adj.* 1. able to endure or suffer a certain kind of hardship. Syn. *nakatátagál*. 2. tolerant; with or having tolerance.

nakatiwangwáng (na-ka-ti-wang-wáng), *adj.* lying idly in the open; idle or not in use.

nakatugón (na-ka-tu-gón), *adj.* 1. said of someone who was able to write an answer to someone's letter. Syn. *nakasagót*. 2. (*Fig.*) was able to comply, as to a certain requirement.

nakatungangà (na-ka-tu-nga-ngà), *adj.* staring at someone with one's mouth open; doing nothing.

nakatútulíg (na-ka-tú-tu-líg), *adj.* 1. defeaning. Syn. *nakabíbingí*. 2. of much noise as to cause defeaning; very loud or noisy.

nakatútuwâ (na-ka-tú-tu-wâ), *adj.* of such nature as to cause joy or happiness. Syn. *nakasísiyá, nakagágalák*.

nákatuwaán (ná-ka-tu-wa-án), *adj.* said of something that had become the caprice of someone. Syn. *nákahumalingan*.

nakaw (na-kaw), I. *adj.* referring to something stolen or pilfered. Syn. *umít, náumít, inumít*.

—II. *n.* anything stolen or pilfered.

nakawán (na-ka-wán), *n.* robbery, esp. in band. Cf. *loobán*.

nakawín (na-ka-wín), *adj.* said of something that can easily be stolen.

nakawíwili (na-ka-wí-wi-li), *adj.* arousing interest; interesting. Also, *kawilí-wili, nakákawili*.

nakayag (na-ka-yag), *adj.* said of someone who has been induced to do something usually undesireable. Syn. *nayakag, nahikayat*.

nakayáyamót (na-ka-yá-ya-mót), *adj.* tiresome; annoying; boring. Syn. *nakaíinís*.

nakayukayok (na-ka-yu-ka-yok), *adj.* crestfallen; with drooping crest or bowed head. Syn. *nakalungayngáy*.

nakayukô (na-ka-yu-kô), var. **nakaukô,** *adj.* with bowed head, as in shame. Syn. *nakatungó*.

naki-, past form of the pref. *maki-*.

nakiayon (na-ki-a-yon), I. *v.* past tense of *makiayon*, which means to join another or others in expressing similar to sentiments or views or to agree with another or others.

—II. *adj.* said of someone who expressed agreement with another or others.

nákikilala (ná-ki-ki-la-la), *adj.* familiar or known to. Also, *kilalá*.

nakikipamayan (na-ki-ki-pa-ma-yan), *adj.* living with others in a certain community or locality, referring esp. to a non-resident of the place.

nakíkiramay (na-kí-ki-ra-may), *adj.* said of someone who expresses condolence for the misfortune of another. Syn. *nakíkidalamhatì*.

nakíkisama (na-kí-ki-sa-ma), *adj.* 1. living temporarily with someone in the same room or house. Syn. *nakíkisunò*. 2. living as a common-law wife of a man. 3. trying to be compatible with another by being good to. Syn. *nakíkipag-kapwà, nakíkibagay*.

nákikita (ná-ki-ki-ta), *adj.* 1. seen; visible. 2. (*Colloq.*) said of an amount one is able to earn, as by working or from business.

nákilala (ná-ki-la-la), *adj.* recognized; known. Also, *kilalá*.

nakipág-, past form of the prefix *makipág-*.

nakipágbasag-ulo (na-ki-pág-ba-sag + u-lo), *adj.* said of one who had a quarrel or fight with another. Syn. *nakipág-away*.

nakipisan (na-ki-pi-san), *adj.* referring to someone who decided to live with another in the same house. Syn. *nakisunò, nakisama*. 2. said of a woman who lived with a man as a common-law wife.

nakiramay (na-ki-ra-may), *adj.* said of one who condoled someone or expressed sympathy with another in grief.

nakisuyò (na-ki-su-yò), *adj.* referring to someone who requested a favor from another. Syn. *nakiusap*.

nakít (na-kít), *v.* poetic form of *sumakít*, to become painful.

nákita (ná-ki-ta), I. *adj.* said of someone or something that was seen or found. Syn. *nátagpuán*.

—II. *v.* past form of *mákita*, to be seen or be able to see. Syn. *mátagpuán*

nákitaan (ná-ki-ta-an), I. *v.* past form of *mákitaan*, to happen to observe or be able to observe something from.

—II. *adj.* said of someone whose private part was seen by another or others. Syn. *nábosohan*.

naknák (nak-nák), I. *adj.* abscessed or filled with pus, usually said of cuts or wounds. Syn. *may-nanà*, *nagnánana*.

—II. *n.* 1. state or condition of being abscessed in body tissues; abscess.

Nakú (Na-kú), *interj.* (fr. *Iná ko!*) an exclamation expressing surprise, wonder, fear, pain, etc. (usually used with *pô*, *nakú pô!*)

nakunan (na-ku-nan), *adj.* referring to a woman who had an abortion. Syn. *naagasan*, *nalaglagán*.

nadaíg (na-da-íg), *adj.* surpassed or excelled by another.

nádagdág (ná-dag-dág), I. *adj.* referring to something which was added to another unintentionally. Syn. *náhalò*, *násama*.

—II. *n.* the amount unintentionally added to something.

nádamá (ná-da-má), *v.* past form of *mádamá*, to be able to feel. Syn. *náramdamán*.

nádaramá (ná-da-ra-má), *adj.* tangible; that can be felt or touched. Syn. *náhihipò*.

nag-, past form of the prefix *mag-*.

nag-, *pref.* used before verb roots with the first syllable reduplicated, expressing the present progressive form of *mag-* verbs.

nag-áalaalá (nag + á-a-la-a-lá), *adj.* worried about something. Syn. *nabábahalà*.

nag-áalab (nag + á-a-lab), *adj.* afire; aflame; ablaze; burning. Syn. *naglíliyáb*, *nagníningas*, *nasúsunog*.

nag-áalinlangan (nag + á-a-lin-la-ngan), *adj.* 1. doubting; in doubt. Syn. *nagdúduda*. 2. hesitant. Syn. *nag-áatubilí*.

nag-áanák (nag + á-a-nák), *adj.* 1. said of a woman who or a female animal that bears young. 2. said of a person acting as sponsor, as in baptism or confirmation.

nag-áaral (nag + á-a-ral), *adj.* studying, as a student.

nag-áawitan (nag + á-a-wi-tan), *adj.* singing together at the same time, referring to a group of persons. Syn. *nagkákantahan*.

nag-ábot (nag + á-bot), *adj.* 1. referring to two persons who happened to meet each other in a certain place. Syn. *nagkita*, *nagkátagpô*. 2. said of two enemies who happened to come into physical contact. Syn. *nagkásagupà*, *nagkábanggâ*.

nagágamit (na-gá-ga-mit), *adj.* that can be used; usable.

nagbábakâ-sakalì (nag-bá-ba-kâ + sa-ka-lì), *adj.* taking a chance or chances. Syn. *nakikipagsápalarán*.

nagbábago (nag-bá-ba-go), *adj.* that changes; changing. Syn. *nag-íibá*, *naíibá*.

nagka-, past form of the prefix *magka-*.

nagkáibigán (nag-ká-i-bi-gán), *adj.* said of two persons who happened to like or love each other. Syn. *nagkágustuhan*.

nagkailâ (nag-ka-i-lâ), *adj.* said of someone who did not tell the truth. Syn. *nagsinungalíng*.

nagkáisá (nag-ká-i-sá), *adj.* referring to two persons or groups who have agreed to unite for a certain purpose. Syn. *nagkásundô*.

nagkaít (nag-ka-ít), *adj.* said of someone who refused to give in to another's request.

nagkamalay (nag-ka-ma-lay), *adj.* said of a person who was able to regain consciousness.

nagkásala (nag-ká-sa-la), *adj.* said of a person who committed a sin or crime.

nagkusà (nag-ku-sà), *adj.* said of a person who did something without being told.

nagdahilán (nag-da-hi-lán), *adj.* said of a person who fabricated an excuse or excuses for not being able to do something.

naghíhirap (nag-hí-hi-rap), *adj.* suffering, as from poverty, injury, pain, etc. Syn. *nagtítiís*.

naghóy (nag-hóy), poetic form of the verb *tumaghóy* o *managhóy*.

nagì (na-gì), *v.* poetic form of *sumagì*, to graze or touch lightly against something in passing.

nag-ibá (nag + i-bá), I. *adj.* referring to a person who, or a thing that, has changed. Syn. *nagbago*.
—II. *v.* past form of *mag-ibá*.

nag-ibayo (mag + i-ba-yo), *v.* past tense of *mag-ibayo*, to become doubled in number or amount.

nagim- (na-gim-), past form of the prefix *magim-*.

nagin-: past form of the prefix *magin-*, a var. of *maging*.

nagipít (na-gi-pít), I. *v.* past tense of *magipít*.
—II. *adj.* 1. referring to someone who became very poor or financially broke. Syn. *naghirap*. 2. said of someone who got into a tight situation.

naging (na-gíng), *v.* past tense of *maging*.

nágising (ná-gi-síng), *adj.* said of a person who was awakened, as by a loud noise.

nagmana (nag-ma-na), I. *v.* past tense of *magmana*.
—II. *adj.* referring to a person who inherited something from someone.

nagpa- (nag-pa-), past form of the prefix *magpa-*.

nagpababà (nag-pa-ba-bà), I. *adj.* that which caused (someone or something) to become lower in height, rank, grade, etc.
–II. *v.* past tense of *magpababà*.

nagpaka-: past form of the prefix *magpaka-*.

nagpakabuti (nag-pa-ka-bu-ti), I. *v.* past tense of *magpakabuti*, to do one's best.
—II. *adj.* said of one who did his best. Syn. *nagpakahusay*.

nagsalitâ (nag-sa-li-tâ), I. *v.* past tense of *magsalitâ*.
—II. *adj.* referring to a person who spoke or was a speaker, as in a program. Syn. *nagtalumpatì*.

nagsásalitâ (nag-sá-sa-li-tâ), I. *n.* (*Gram.*) first person; the person speaking.
—II. *adj.* talking or speaking.

nagsásama (nag-sá-sa-ma), *adj.* 1. referring to a woman and a man who live together as wife and husband. 2. said of someone who takes another in going regularly to a certain place. 3. referring to someone who mixes or adds something to a mixture. Syn. *nagháhalò*, *nagsásahóg*.

nagsísisi (nag-sí-si-si), *adj.* repenting; repentant; feeling sorry for one's wrongdoing.

nagsísisihán (nag-sí-si-si-hán), *adj.* blaming each other.

nagsúsulatán (nag-sú-su-la-tán), *adj.* writing or corresponding with each other or with one another. Syn. *naglílihamán*.

nagtayô (nag-ta-yô), *adj.* 1. referring to someone who built or constructed something, esp. a house or building. Syn. *gumawâ*, *nagtindíg*, *yumarì*. 2. said of someone who founded or organized something, as a society or association. Syn. *nagtatág*.

nagúgutom (na-gú-gu-tom), *adj.* 1. hungry. 2. starving; suffering severely from hunger.

nágumon (ná-gu-mon), *adj.* said of a person who has become addicted to a vice, etc. Syn. *nálulóng*, *nábaón* (*fig.*).

nágupò (ná-gu-pò), *adj.* said of a person who became bed-ridden.

nag-úunahán (nag + ú-u-na-hán), *adj.* trying to get ahead of each other or of one another.

nagwakás (nag-wa-kás), *adj.* that which came to an end. Syn. *natapos*, *nagtapós*.

nagwas (nag-was), *n.* (Sp. *enaguas*) petticoat; underskirt; half slip. Cf. *kamisón*.

náhaán (ná-ha-án), var. **náhan**, *adv.* used colloquially for *násaán*, where is, are or were. Also, *ahan*.

nahadlangán (na-had-la-ngán), *adj.* having been stopped or prevented, as from entering or proceeding to a certain place.

naháhalatâ (na-há-ha-la-tâ), *adj.* that can be noticed or detected; noticeable.

náhalili (ná-ha-li-li), *adj.* 1. said of a person who, or a thing that, was put in place of another. Syn. *nápalít*. 2. said of someone who alternates with another. Syn. *pumápalít*, *humáhalili*, *tumútorno*.

náhan (ná-han), *adv.* colloquial form of *násaan* where is (are or were). Also, *ahan*.

nahíhibáng (na-hí-hi-báng), *adj.* 1. mentally unbalanced or deranged; crazy; insane. 2. in a state of delirium; delirious.

nahíhirapan (na-hí-hi-ra-pan), *adj.* having

a hard time or difficulty; suffering, as from pain, etc. Syn. *nagtítiís*.

nahíhiyâ (na-hí-hi-yâ), *adj.* ashamed; feeling shame.

náhulí (ná-hu-lí), I. *v.* past tense of *máhulí*, to be or become late.
—II. *adj.* said of a person who, or thing that, came late. Syn. *naatraso*.

náhulihan (ná-hu-li-han), *adj.* said of a person from whom a stolen thing or things were found.

naibá (na-i-bá), I. *v.* past tense of *maibá*, to be able to change or make different. Syn. *mabago*.
—II. *adj.* said of a person or thing that was changed or made different.

naik (na-ik), *n.* 1. an outlying district of a city or town; suburb. Syn. *arabál*. 2. (N-) a town in Cavite.

naigâ (na-i-gâ), *adj.* said of water or liquid that has dried up by evaporation. Syn. *natuyô*.

náiibigan (ná-i-i-bi-gan), *adj.* said of a person or thing that someone has a liking for. Syn. *nágugustuhán*.

náiintindihán (ná-i-in-tin-di-hán), *adj.* that can be understood or comprehended; comprehensible; understandable. Syn. *náuunawaan*.

naíingatan (na-í-i-nga-tan), *adj.* 1. that can be prevented from happening by being careful. Syn. *naiiwasan*. 2. that can be owned or possessed. Syn. *naáari*.

naíinggít (na-í-ing-gít), *adj.* feeling envy; envious. Syn. *nahihilî, nananaghilî*.

nais (na-is), I. *n.* desire; wish; purpose; preference. Syn. *gusto, ibig, layon, láyunin*.
—II. *v.* (Colloq.) to have a liking for.

naisahán (na-i-sa-hán), *v.* past tense of *maisahán*, to be able to gain or win a point against. Syn. *mapuntusán*.

naisin (na-i-sin), *v.* to prefer or like better. Syn. *ibigin, gustuhin*.

náisip (ná-i-sip), *v.* past tense of *máisip*, to happen to think of or about.

náisipan (ná-i-si-pan), *v.* past tense of *máisipan*, to happen to think of doing.

naitútumpák (na-i-tú-tum-pák), *adj.* that can be corrected or made right.

naiwan (na-i-wan), *v.* past tense of *maiwan*, to happen to be left behind.

naiwanan (na-i-wa-nan), *v.* past tense *maiwanan*, to forget to bring. Syn. *nákalimutang dalhín*.

nálalabí (ná-la-la-bí), *adj.* that which remains unused or unfinished. Syn. *nátitirá*.

nalalaman (na-la-la-man), I. *adj.* having knowledge about; known to; known by. Syn. *alám, batíd*.
—II. *n.* something one knows; knowhow; knowledge; understanding. Syn. *kabátiran*.

nalinláng (na-lin-láng), *adj.* said of someone who was cheated or deceived. Syn. *nádayà, nágantsô*.

naloka (na-lo-ka), I. *v.* past tense of *maloka*, to become crazy or insane, referring to a woman. Syn. *nasirâ ang ulo*.
—II. *adj.* said of a woman who became crazy or insane.

náloko (ná-lo-ko), *v.* past tense of *máloko*, to be fooled or deceived. Syn. *nálinláng*.

nalúlumbáy (na-lú-lum-báy), *adj.* feeling sad; lonely; sorrowful. Syn. *nalúlungkót*.

nalúlungkót (na-lú-lung-kót), *adj.* sad; lonely; sorrowful. Syn. *nalúlumbáy*.

námamalayan (ná-ma-ma-la-yan), *adj.* aware of; conscious of.

namámangláw (na-má-mang-láw), *adj.* feeling lonely or sad. Syn. *nalúlungkót*.

namámasukan (na-má-ma-su-kan), *adj.* employed; working for wages or salary.

namámasyál (na-má-mas-yál), *adj.* taking a walk; promenading. Also, *nagpápasyál*.

namámatáy (na-má-ma-táy), *adj.* that dies; liable to perish or die; mortal. Syn. *may-kamatayan*.

namámayapà (na-má-ma-ya-pà), *adj.* dead; already dead. Syn. *patay na*.

naman¹ (na-man), *adv.* 1. (with *na*) again; anew, as in: *nang magkita na naman kami*, when we met again. Syn. *ulî, mulî, minsán pa*. 2. (preceded with *man*) in the same or like manner; also; similarly; too, as in: *Siyá man namán ay malî*, He too is wrong. Syn. *din o rin*. 3. (with *man*) ever; at all; in any case; by any means or chance, as in: *Kung akó man namán ay nagkamalî*, if at all I made a mistake. Syn. *sakalî*. 4. instead, as in: *Kung walâ niyán, itó namán* *ang gamitin mo.* If there is none of that, use this instead. 5. else, as in: *Kung hindî ka paróroón, saán namán ang tungo mo?* If you are not going there, where else are you going? 6. next; after, as in: *Itó namán ang gawín.* Do this next. Syn. *kasunód, pagkatapos.* 7. really; truly, as in: *Magandá namán siyá.* She is really beautiful. Syn. *talagá, tunay.*

Namán² (Na-mán), *interj.* 1. Again! Once again! *Na namán!* 2. Really! Syn. *Siyá nga ba!*

namanatag (na-ma-na-tag), *adj.* referring to a person who had come to rest (had died). Syn. *namatay, yumao, sumakabiláng-buhay.*

námanghâ (ná-mang-hâ), *v.* past tense of *mámanghâ,* to be or become surprised or shocked. Syn. *nagtaká, nátungangá.*

námataan (ná-ma-ta-an), *v.* past tense of *mámataan,* to happen to see briefly. Syn. *násilayan.*

namatáy (na-ma-táy), I. *v.* past tense of *mamatáy,* to die; be dead. Syn. *namayapà, sumakabiláng-buhay.*

—II. *adj.* said of a person who died.

—III. *n.* (with *ang*) the deceased.

namatayán (na-ma-ta-yán), I. *v.* past tense of *mamatayán.*

—II. *adj.* referring to a person who has a relative who has just died.

namihasa (na-mi-ha-sa), I. *v.* past tense of *mamihasa,* to become accustomed or used to.

—II. *adj.* accustomed or used to, said of a person. Syn. *nasanay, nahirati.*

namímilipit (na-mí-mi-li-pit), *adj.* writhing, as in pain.

namímilí (na-mí-mi-lí), *adj.* referring to a person who is out marketing. Syn. *namámalengké.*

namímilì (na-mí-mi-lì), *adj.* inclined to be particular in choosing; choosy.

namin (na-min), *pron.* 1. (postpositive, exclusive of the person addressed) our; ours. 2. we, as in: *Kukunin namin iyán.* We shall get that.

naminsalà (na-min-sa-là), *v.* past tense of *maminsalà,* to do harm or destruction; be destructive or harmful; cause damage or damages.

namnám (nam-nám), *n.* 1. savor; taste. Syn. *lasa, panlasa.* 2. sense of feeling. Syn. *damá, pandamá.*

námukhaán (ná-muk-ha-án), *v.* past tense of *mámukhaán,* to happen to know someone by face. Syn. *mákilala sa mukhâ.*

namukód (na-mu-kód), *adj.* said of a person or thing that stood out among others.

namuhay (na-mu-hay), *v.* past tense of *mamuhay,* to live a certain way of life.

namulubi (na-mu-lu-bi), *v.* past tense of *mamulubi,* to become poor like a beggar. Syn. *maghirap ang buhay.*

namúmukód (na-mú-mu-kód), *adj.* that stands out; outstanding; distinctive.

namúmurok (na-mú-mu-rok), *adj.* round and plump; chubby, as in: *mga pisngíng namúmurok,* chubby cheeks.

namúmusangsáng (na-mú-mu-sang-sáng), *adj.* 1. badly swollen, as the lips of a person which was bitten by a bee. Syn. *namúmusargá.* 2. forcibly opened or spread out as the badly beaten head of a chisel handle. Syn. *busalsál.*

namúmutiktík (na-mú-mu-tik-tík), *adj.* teeming or swarming with. Syn. *kumúkutô, kumúkuyaw.*

nana (na-na), *n.* aunt, as in: *Nana Juana,* Aunt Juana.

nanà (na-nà), *n.* pus, a thick, yellowish-white secretion found in wounds or boils.

nanabáng (na-na-báng), *adj.* having lost one's interest in or appetite for. Also, *tinabangán, nawalán ng gana.*

nanánabík (na-ná-na-bík), *adj.* eagerly desirous.

nanánadyâ (na-ná-nad-yâ), *adj.* said of someone who intentionally does something that another does not like in order to annoy him. Syn. *nanínikís.*

nanánaghóy (na-ná-nag-hóy), *adj.* wailing or crying long and loud due to grief or pain. Syn. *nanánangis.*

nanánagót (na-ná-na-gót), I. *adj.* 1. responsible or obliged to account for. 2. referring to a person who acts as a guarantor for another or others.

—II. *n.* the person who acts as a guarantor.

nanánaíg (na-ná-na-íg), *adj.* predominant;

prevailing. Syn. *nangíngibabaw*, *nakapangíngibabaw*, *nakapangyáyari*.

nanánalig (na-ná-na-lig), *adj.* believing; having faith in. Syn. *naníniwalà*, *nagtitiwalà*.

nanánampalataya (na-ná-nam-pa-la-ta-ya), *adj.* believing in God and His teaching. Also, *sumásampalataya*. Syn. *naníniwalà*.

nanánangan (na-ná-na-ngan), *adj.* with or having a firm belief in. Syn. *may-matibay na paniniwalà, nanínindigan*.

nanánapatan (na-ná-na-pa-tan), *adj.* 1. serenading. Syn. *nagháharana*. 2. said of a person who goes and sings from house to house asking for contributions or alms.

Nanang (Na-nang), *n.* appellation used in addressing one's mother.

nanaw (na-naw), *v.* poetic form of *pumanaw*, (1) to disappear. Syn. *naparam, nawalâ*. (2) to die; pass away. Syn. *namatáy*.

nanay (na-nay), *n.* 1. mother. Syn. *ina*. 2. also used as an appellation in addressing one's mother. 3. (in Bats. and other Southern Tagalog provinces) the term for grandmother. Syn. *lola*.

nanáy-nanayan (na-náy + na-na-yan), *n.* & *adj.* referring to a foster mother.

nandiné (nan-di-né), var. **nandiní**, *adj.* referring to a person who, or a thing that, is present here or in the place where the speaker is. Also, *nárine (nárini), nandíriné (nandíriní), naririné (naririní)*.

nandíritó (nan-dí-ri-tó), var. **náriritó**, *adj.* said of a person who, or a thing that, is present here or in the place where the speaker is.

nandíriyán (nan-dí-ri-yán), var. **náririyán**, *adj.* said of a person who, or a thing that, is present there or in the place where the second person is. Also, *nandiyán, náriyán*.

nandoón (nan-do-ón), var. **nandóroón**, *adj.* referring to a person who, or a thing that, is there or in a place far off from both the speaker and the person spoken to.

nanínindigan (na-ní-nin-di-gan), *adj.* firm in one's conviction.

nanínirahan (na-ní-ni-ra-han), I. *adj.* living or residing in a certain place or locality. Syn. *nanánahanan*.
—II. *n.* resident. Syn. *mámamayán*.

naninirang-puri (na-ní-ni-rang + pu-ri), *adj.* said of a person who slanders or speaks slander against another or others. Syn. *nanínirà, nagpápasamâ*.

naníniwalà (na-ní-ni-wa-là), *adj.* 1. said of someone who believes something is true or real. 2. with or having faith or trust in. Syn. *may-tiwalà, nagtítiwalà*.

nanónoót (na-nó-no-ót), var. **nanúnoót**, *adj.* penetrating or intense, as cold. Syn. *nanínigíd*.

nang (nang), I. *conj.* 1. in order that; so that; is in: *Magtrabaho ka nang may makain*. Work in order that you may have something to eat. 2. when; at the time of, as in: *Walâ siyá nang kamí'y dumatíng*. He was away when we arrived. 3. and, as in: *Kumain siyá nang kumain*. He ate and ate.
—II. *adv.* 1. more (*colloq.*), as in: *walâ nang pag-asa*, no more hope. 2. already, as in: *Nakaalís nang lahát silá*. All of them have already gone. 3. in a certain manner (expressed by specific adverbs), as in: *umiyák nang malakás*, to cry loudly, *dumatíng silá nang hulí*, they came late.

nang- (nang-), past form of the prefix *mang-*.

nanga- (na-nga-), past form of the prefix *manga-*.

nangakò (na-nga-kò), I. *v.* past tense of *mangako*, to promise; make a promise.
—II. *adj.* said of a person who promised to do something.

nangág- (na-ngág-), past form of the prefix *mangag-*.

nangág-abalá (na-ngág + a-ba-lá), I. *v.* past tense of *mangág-abalá*, to waste time; go out of one's ways, as to help others, referring to a group of persons.
—II. *adj.* said of persons who waste time or who went out of their way to help another or others.

nangagím- (na-nga-gím-), past form of the prefix *mangagím*.

nangagín- (na-nga-gín-), past form of the prefix *mangagin*.

nangagíng- (na-nga-gíng-), past form of the prefix *mangagíng*.

nanganák (na-nga-nák), I. *v.* past tense of *manganak*, to give birth; bring forth a child.

—II. *adj*. said of a woman has just given birth to a child.

nanganay (na-nga-nay), I. *v*. past tense of *manganay*, to give birth to one's first child (s.o. a woman).

—II. *adj*. said of a woman who gave birth to her first child.

nangángailangan (na-ngá-nga-i-la-ngan), *adj*. in need of; needing.

nangángalagà (na-ngá-nga-la-gà), *adj*. said of someone who takes care of oneself. Syn. *nag-úingat*.

nangángalay (na-ngá-nga-lay), *adj*. feeling tired or fatigued. Syn. *nangángawit*, *namímitig*.

nangángalingasaw (na-ngá-nga-li-nga-saw), *adj*. stinking; emitting a disagreeable odor. Syn. *namámahò*.

nangánganinag (na-ngá-nga-ni-nag), *adj*. transparent. Syn. *napaglálagusán ng paningín*.

nangángaral (na-ngá-nga-ral), *adj*. 1. giving moral or religious advice. 2. didactic; didactical.

nangángarap (na-ngá-nga-rap), *adj*. dreaming. Syn. *nanánaginip*.

nangayayat (na-nga-ya-yat), *v*. past tense *mangayayat*, to grow thin or thinner. Also, *pumayát*, *namayat*.

nangkâ (nang-kâ), var. **langkâ**, *n*. (Bot.) jack fruit (*Artocarpus, hetenophyllus Lam.*).

nanggahasà (nang-ga-ha-sà), I. *v*. past tense of *manggahasà*. (1) to use force. Syn. *mamuwersa, daanín sa lakás*. (2) to violate or rape (a woman).

—II. *adj*. said of a man who has committed rape.

—III. *n*. (usually with *ang*) rapist.

nanggaling (nang-ga-ling), I. *v*. past tense of *manggaling*, to come or originate from. Syn. *nagbuhat, nagmula*.

—II. *prep*. (with *sa* or *kay*) from. Syn. *mulâ o buhat sa* (*kay*).

nanghíhinà (nang-hí-hi-nà), *adj*. getting weak or weaker. Also, *humíhinà*.

nanghíhinayang (nang-hí-hi-na-yang), *adj*. feeling sorry for not having taken advantage of an opportunity, etc.

nanghíhiyâ (nang-hí-hi-yâ), *adj*. said of a person who disgraces others or put others to shame.

nangíngibá (na-ngí-ngi-bâ), *adj*. said of a person who feels new or unfamiliar about something. Syn. *nanínibago*.

nangíngibabaw (na-ngí-ngi-ba-baw), *adj*. predominant; prevailing; preponderant. Syn. *nanánaíg; naghához* (fig.).

nangíngibáng-bayan (na-ngí-ngi-báng + ba-yan), *adj*. said of persons who immigrate or live in a town or country not his own.

nangíngilala (na-ngí-ngi-la-la), *adj*. said of a child who cries when taken or held by other persons unfamiliar to him.

nangíngimbuló (na-ngí-ngim-bu-ló), *adj*. with or having inferiority complex. Syn *nangánganino*.

nangúnguna (na-ngú-ngu-na), *adj*. 1. ahead; leading. Syn. *nanánalo, nakákalamáng*. 2. acting as the leader of a group. Syn. *namúmunò*.

nangúngupahan (na-ngú-ngu-pa-han), I. *adj*. paying rent; renting.

—II. *n*. tenant. Syn. *ingkilino*.

nangúngusap (na-ngú-ngu-sap), 1. that speaks; speaking or talking. Syn. *nagsásalitâ*. 2. (Fig.) that seems to speak; expressive, as in: *nangúngusap na tingín*, expressive look.

—II. *n*. (Gram.) the speaker; first person. Syn. *ang nagsásalitâ*.

napa- (na-pa-), past form of the prefix *mapa-*.

nápaagá (ná-pa-a-gá), *adj*. that happened or occurred earlier than expected or usual.

nápaanó (ná-pa-a-nó), *v*. (Colloq.) What happened? *Nápaanó ka?* What happened to you? Syn. *Anó ang nangyari?*

nápabutí (ná-pa-bu-tí), *adj*. referring to someone or something that turned out better than expected; opposed to *nápasamâ*.

nápaka- (ná-pa-ka-), pref. for adjectives expressing superlative degree.

nápakabago (ná-pa-ka-ba-go), *adj*. very new; opposed to *nápakalumà*.

nápakabulaan (ná-pa-ka-bu-la-an), *adj*. very untruthful or dishonest. Syn. *nápakasinungaling*.

nápakabuti (ná-pa-ka-bu-ti), *adj*. very kind, very good. Syn. *nápakabaít*.

nápakasamâ (ná-pa-ka-sa-mâ), adj. very bad.

nápakagalíng (ná-pa-ka-ga-líng), adj. very good; excellent. Syn. nápakahusay.

nápakagiting (ná-pa-ka-gi-ting). adj. very brave. Syn. nápakatapang.

nápakahamak (ná-pa-ka-ha-mak), adj. very lowly. Syn. nápakaabâ.

nápakahusay (ná-pa-ka-hu-say), adj. very good; excellent. Syn. nápakagalíng, nápakabuti, nápakainam.

nápakamakasarili (ná-pa-ka-ma-ka-sa-ri-li), adj. egoistic or self-centered. Syn. lubháng makasarili.

nápakamahál (ná-pa-ka-ma-hál), adj. 1. very dear or important to someone. Syn. mahál na mahál. 2. very dear or high in price; very costly. Syn. nápakataás ang presyo o halagá.

nápakamalas (ná-pa-ka-ma-las), adj. very unlucky. Syn. nápakawaláng suwerte, nápakasinásamâ.

nápakatagál (ná-pa-ka-ta-gál), adj. too long, referring to time. Syn. nápakalaon, nápakaluwát.

nápakatalino (ná-pa-ka-ta-li-no), adj. very talented; with or having exceptional talent. Syn. nápakarunong, nápakagalíng ang ulo (utak).

nápakatibay (ná-pa-ka-ti-bay), adj. very strongly built; that can not be easily broken or destroyed.

nápakatuso (ná-pa-ka-tu-so), adj. very cunning; too clever in deceit. Syn. lubháng matalino.

nápakawaláng-hiyâ (ná-pa-ka-wa-láng + hi-yâ), adj. without any shame at all. Syn. nápakakapál ang mukhâ.

nápakayabang (ná-pa-ka-ya-bang), adj. very arrogant or boastful. Syn. nápakahambóg.

napakita (na-pa-ki-ta), adj. said of someone who showed up or appeared in the open in order to be seen. Syn. lumantád.

nápadamay (ná-pa-da-may), v. past tense of mápadamay, to happen to be included or involved, as in a crime, or as a victim in a fire, accident, etc.

napag- (na-pag-), past form of the prefix mapag-.

napag-ábot (na-pag + á-bot), v. past tense of mapag-ábot, to be able to make two

things touch each other end to end or side to side. Cf. mapaghugpóng, mapagdikít.

napagim- (na-pa-gim-), past form of the prefix mapagim-.

napagimbatà (na-pa-gim-ba-tà), v. past tense of mapagimbatà, to be able to make (a person) look young or younger.

napagin- (na-pa-gin-), past form of the prefix mapagin-.

napaging- (na-pa-ging-), past tense of the prefix mapaging-.

napágyaman (na-pág-ya-man), v. past tense of mapágyaman, to be able to utilize something not so usable by careful management or expertise.

nápapanahón (ná-pa-pa-na-hón), adj. timely; fit for the present time or occasion.

napáparam (na-pá-pa-ram), adj. evanescent; vanishing. Syn. nawáwalâ, napápawî.

napápawì (na-pá-pa-wì), adj. 1. that can be erased or obliterated. Syn. nabúburá, nakákatkát. 2. that vanishes or disappears. Syn. nawáwalâ, napáparam.

napatunayan (na-pa-tu-na-yan), v. past tense of mapatunayan, to be able to prove that an allegation is true, as by a witness or an evidence. Syn. napatotohanan.

napawì (na-pa-wì), I. v. past tense of mapawì, to become erased or eradicated.
—II. adj. erased or eradicated. Syn. naburá.

napugnáw (na-pug-náw), adj. burned or razed to ashes. Syn. natupok.

nara (na-ra), I. n. (Bot.) the narra tree (Ptecarpus indicus); also, its hard lumber or wood.
—II. adj. made of narra.

naranghá (na-rang-há), n. & adj. (Sp. naranja) orange (color).

naranghada (na-rang-ha-da), adj. (Sp. marangjada) orange-colored; tangerine.

naranghita (na-rang-hi-ta), n. (Bot.) a species of orange tree (Citrus nobilis Lour.); also, its fruit.

nárarapat (ná-ra-ra-pat), adj. proper; fitting; appropriate. Syn. bagay, nábabagay.

narkótikó (nar-kó-ti-kó), I. adj. (Sp. narcotico) narcotic; capable of producing narcosis.

—II. *n.* 1. any drug that causes profound sleep, lethargy, or relief from pain; narcotic. 2. a person addicted to narcotics.

nárine (ná-ri-né), var. **nárini**, *adj.* said of a person who or thing that, is present here or in the place where the speaker is. Also, *nandírine, (nandírini), náririne (náririni)*.

náriritó (ná-ri-ri-tó), var. **náritó**, *adj.* said of someone who, or something that, is present here or in the place where the speaker is. See **nárine**.

náririyán (ná-ri-ri-yán), var. **náriyán**, *adj.* said of someone who, or something that, is present there or in the place where the person addressed is.

nároón (ná-ro-ón), var. **nároroón**, *adj.* said of someone who, or something that, is present there or in the place far both from the speaker and the person addressed.

nars (nars), *n.* (*Eng.*) nurse.

nasa (na-sa), *prep.* 1. in; inside; within, as in: *nasa kuwarto*, in (inside) the room. 2. in; included or contained in, as in: *nasa sulat*, in (contained in) the letter. 3. on; according to, as in: *nasa oras*, on time. 4. in someone's possession, as in: *nasa kanyá*, in his possession.

nasà (na-sà), *n.* wish; desire; purpose; intention. Syn. *nais, hangád, layon*.

násaán (ná-sá-án), *adv.* 1. (used interrogatively) where; in or at what place, as in: *Násaán siyá ngayón?* Where is he now? 2. (with *man*) whenever, as in: *násaán man siyá*, wherever he is.

nasain (na-sa-in), *v.* to desire or wish for. Syn. *hangarín, mithiín*.

nasanay (na-sa-nay), *adj.* said of a person who has been trained or used to a certain act or situation. Syn. *nahirati*.

Nasareno (Na-sa-re-no), *n.* (Sp. *Nazareno*) 1. Nazarene; a native or inhabitant of Nazareth. 2. the Nazarene; Jesus.

nasarili (na-sa-ri-li), *v.* past tense of *masarili*, to be able to own something alone by oneself.

násasaád (ná-sa-sa-ád; *adj.* stated or mentioned, as in a document.

nasásabík (na-sá-sa-bík), *adj.* eagerly desirous. Also, *nanánabík*.

nasásayang (na-sá-sa-yang), *adj.* said of something that is being wasted. Cf. *nátatapon*.

nasawatâ (na-sa-wa-tâ), *v.* past tense of *masawatâ*. 1. to be able to stop or check. Syn. *napigil, naampát*. 2. to be able to prohibit or restrain from doing. Syn. *nasawáy*.

nasawáy (na-sa-wáy), *v.* past tense of *masawáy*, to be able to prohibit or restrain from doing something.

nasawî (na-sa-wî), *v.* past tense of *masawî*, 1. to be unfortunate; meet with a misfortune. 2. to die, as in an accident. Syn. *namatáy*.

nasimót (na-si-mót), *adj.* said of something that has been totally consumed or used up. Syn. *nasaíd*.

nasirà (na-si-rà), *adj.* 1. referring to something that has been spoiled, damaged, or destroyed. 2. that which failed to materialize; broken, as a promise, plan, etc. Syn. *di-natupád, nabigô*. 3. (with *ang ulo*) said of a person who became insane or demented. Syn. *naloko, naulól*.

nasnás (nas-nás), I. *adj.* frayed; threadbare, said esp. of clothes due to overuse. Cf. *nisnís, gasgás*.

—II. the part or portion that is frayed or threadbare.

nasúsulat (na-sú-su-lat), *adj.* that can be written or put in writing. Also, *naisúsulat*.

nasúsupok (na-sú-su-pok), *adj.* that can be carbonized, as by burning partially.

nasúsuyà (na-sú-su-yà), *adj.* said of someone who is already fed up or disgusted about something. Syn. *sawâ na*.

nasyón (nas-yón), *n.* (Sp. *nacion*) nation. Syn. *bansá (bansâ)*.

nata (na-ta), *pron.* 1. (postpositive of *ata*) our; ours (dual: the speaker and the person addressed), as in: *Aklát nata itó*. This is our book. 2. us, as in: *Dalhin nata ito*. Let us bring this.

natagalán (na-ta-ga-lán), I. *v.* past tense of *matagalán*, to be or become delayed unnecessarily. Syn. *naluwatán*.

—II. *adj.* said of something that was delayed unnecessarily.

nátagpuán (ná-tag-pu-án), *adj.* said of

something that was found unintentionally or by accident.

ámataan (ná-ma-ta-an), I. *adj.* 1. referring to a person or animal that was wounded or hit with a stone, bullet, etc. 2. referring to a target that someone succeeded in hitting.

—II. *v.* past tense of *matamaan*. 1. to be able to hit successfully with or as with a bullet. 2. to be able to guess the right answer to a question, or the winning number or numbers in a lottery or the like.

átamó (ná-ta-mó), I. *adj.* referring to something that a person was able to get, obtain, or receive as a result of. Syn. *nátanggáp, nákamit.*

—II. *v.* past tense of *mátamó*.

átampók (ná-tam-pók), *adj.* referring to someone who or something that, was declared or hailed outstanding.

átanáw (ná-ta-náw), I. *adj.* 1. said of someone who, is looking out from or as from a window. Also, *tumátanáw.* Syn. *nádungaw, dumúdungaw.* 2. that refers to someone or something that was seen from afar. Syn. *nátanawán.*

—II. *v.* past tense of *mátanáw*, to be able to see from afar, or be seen from a far distance.

atantiyá (na-tan-ti-yá), *v.* past tense of *matantiyá*, to be able to make an approximate calculation or estimate of.

atantô (na-tan-tô), *v.* past tense of *matanto*, to understand, know, or realize. Syn. *nálaman, náunawaan, náintindihán.*

átaón (ná-ta-ón), *v.* past tense of *mátaón*, to happen or occur at the same time with another or by coincidence. Also, *nápataón, násabáy, nápasabáy.*

atapos (na-ta-pos), I. *v.* past tense of *matapos*. 1. to be able to finish. Syn. *nayarì.* 2. to come to an end; be ended. Syn. *nagwakás.* 3. to finish or complete, as a course in college.

—II. *adj.* said of something that someone had finished or completed.

atarók (na-ta-rók), *v.* past tense of *matarók*, to be able to understand, as one's intention or purpose. Syn. *máunawaan.*

atauhan (na-ta-u-han), *v.* past tense of

matauhan, to regain consciousness. Syn. *magkamalay-tao.*

nátaunán (ná-ta-u-nán), *v.* past tense of *mátaunán*, to happen to see or find someone in a certain mode, state, or condition.

natigatig (na-ti-ga-tig), *v.* past tense of *matigatig*, to be worried about something. Syn. *nabalino, nabalisa.*

natin (na-tin), *pron.* 1. (postpositive of *atin*) our; ours (inclusive of the person addressed), as in: *Bahay natin itó.* This is our house (this house is ours). 2. us (dual; inclusive of the person addressed), as in: *Gawín natin itó.* Let us make this.

nátirá (ná-ti-rá), I. *adj.* 1. living or residing in a certain place. Also, *tumítirá .* Syn. *nátahán, tumátahán.* 2. said of things left unused, undone, uneaten, etc. Syn. *naiwáng hindî tapós, hindî nagamit, hindî nakain.*

—II. *n.* 1. something left over; left-over. Syn. *labis, sobra.* 2. a person or persons living or residing in a certain place. Syn. *ang nakatirá o tumítirá.*

natiyák (na-ti-yák), *v.* past tense of *matiyák*, to be able to ascertain or be sure about. Syn. *nasiguro.*

nátukahan (ná-tu-ka-han), I. *v.* past tense of *mátukahan*, to be assigned or given a certain responsibility.

—II. *adj.* assigned or given a certain responsibility, referring to a person.

natukoy (na-tu-koy), *v.* past tense of *matukoy*, to be able to mention or refer to openly. Syn. *mabanggít.*

natukóy (na-tu-kóy), *v.* past tense of *matukóy*. 1. to be able to find, locate, or pinpoint the exact location of something. Syn. *natiyák ang kinálalagyán.* 2. to be able to guess accurately. Syn. *nasagót nang tíyakan.*

natuksó (na-tuk-só), I. *v.* past tense of *matuksó*, to be or become tempted or induced; be allured, esp. to something immoral or sensually pleasurable. Syn. *nabighanì (sa masamâ).*

—II. *adj.* said of a person who has been tempted or allured to something immoral.

nátulog (ná-tu-log), I. *adj.* 1. sleeping. Also, *nátutulog.* 2. (*Colloq.*) said of capital that was not utilized; did not earn. Syn. *hindi kumíta*.

—II. *v.* past tense of *matulog*, to go to sleep.

nátunugán (ná-tu-nu-gán), *v.* past tense of *mátunugán*, to happen to find out or discover (something) just on time.

natupád (na-tu-pád), I. *v.* past tense of *matupád*. 1. to be able to fulfill or carry out. 2. to be fulfilled or carried out. Syn. *naganáp*.

—II. *adj.* fulfilled; carried out. Syn. *nagawâ, naisagawâ*.

naturalesa (na-tu-ra-le-sa), *n.* (Sp. *naturaleza*) 1. nature; inborn character of a person. Syn. *likás na (katutubong) ugalì*. 2. essential quality or character of a thing. Syn. *sariling katangian*.

naturingan (na-tu-ri-ngan), *v.* past tense of *maturingan*. 1. to be able to give or guess the answer (to a riddle). 2. to be able to give or quote the price of. Syn. *nahalagahán*.

nátutóp (ná-tu-tóp), *adj.* caught red-handed. Syn. *náhuli sa akto*.

náubos (ná-u-bos), *adj.* said of things, e.g. supplies, that had been totally used, consumed, or eaten. Syn. *nasaíd*.

naulila (na-u-li-la), I. *adj.* said of a person who was orphaned by the death of his parents.

—II. *v.* past tense of *maulila*, to be or become orphaned.

—III. *n.* a person or persons left orphaned.

náuná (ná-u-ná), I. *v.* past tense of *máuná*, to go or leave ahead of another or others. Syn. *nagpáuná, umuna*.

—II. *adj.* said of a person who went ahead of another or others.

—III. *n.* predecessor; forerunner.

náunawaan (ná-u-na-wa-an), *v.* past tense of *máunawaan*, to be able to understand. Syn. *náintindihán*.

náuukol (ná-u-u-kol), I. *adj.* (with *sa* or *kay*) said of something intended for a certain person or for a certain purpose. Syn. *pará sa o kay*.

—II. *prep.* about; concerning; regarding. Syn. *tungkól, hinggíl*.

nawâ (na-wâ), I. *aux. v.* (used idiomatically in expressing a wish, hope, or prayer) may:

as in: *Nawá'y pagpalain ka ng Diyós!* Ma God bless you!

—II. *interj.* (usually with *Siya*) *Siyá naw* So be it! Amen!

náwaglít (ná-wag-lít), *adj.* referring something that cannot be found located when needed; misplaced. C *nawalâ*.

nawalâ (na-wa-lâ), I. *v.* past tense of *mawal* 1. to be or become lost; be missing. Syn *nalipol*. 2. to disappear or vanish, as pai etc. Syn. *napawì, lumipas*. 3. (with *sa isi alaala, loób*) to be forgotten. Syn. *nalimo nalimutan*.

—II. *adj.* 1. that cannot be located found; lost; missing. Syn. *nalipol*. having disappeared or vanished.

nawalán (na-wa-lán), I. *v.* past tense *mawalán*, 1. to lose (something). 2. to b completely without or devoid of, as ligh water, or the like.

—II. *adj.* 1. said of someone who los something. 2. completely without; devoi of.

—III. *n.* a person who lost something.

náwalay (ná-wa-lay), I. *v.* past tense *máwalay*, to be separated from. Syn *náhiwaláy, nápahiwaláy*.

—II. *adj.* said of someone who got lost o separated, as from his companions.

náwikà (ná-wi-kà), *v.* past tense of *máwik* to happen to say or utter. Syn. *násab nábigkás, násalitâ*.

náwikaan (ná-wi-ka-an), *v.* past tense o *máwikaan*, to be reproved or blamed. Syn *másisi*.

nay (nay), *n.* (short for *inay* or *nanay*), use as an endearing appellation for mother.

nayaníg (na-ya-níg), *adj.* shaken, as by a earthquake. Syn. *naalóg, naugà*.

nayarì (na-ya-rì), I. *v.* past tense of *mayar* to be able to finish doing or makin something. Syn. *natapos*.

—II *adj.* referring to something that person finished making or manufacturing

—III. *n.* things that a person or a factor was able to finish, as within a certai period.

nayon (na-yon), *n.* barrio; small village Syn. *baryo*.

ebera (ne-be-ra), *n.* (Sp. *nevera*) icebox; refrigerator. Syn. *repreheradór, aisbaks.*

egosyante (ne-gos-yan-te), *n.* (Sp. *negociante*) businessman; merchant; dealer. Syn. *komersiyante, mángangalakál.*

egosyo (ne-gos-yo), *n.* (Sp. *negocio*) 1. business; commercial enterprise. 2. commerce; trade. Syn. *kálakalán, pangangalakal, komersiyó.*

Jegra (Neg-ra), *n.* (*Sp.*) a Negro woman or girl; Negress.

Jegrito (Ne-gri-to), *n.* (*Sp.*) a member of a wandering mountain tribe in the Philippines, with dark complexion and curly hair. Syn. *Ita, Ayta.*

Iegro (Ne-gro), I. *n.* (*Sp. & Eng.*) a member of the dominant black race of Africa and the United States; Negro.
—II. *adj.* negro; black (s.o. persons).

Jené (Ne-né), *n.* an affectionate appellation for a young girl.

Jeneng (Ne-neng), *n.* an affectionate term for a teenage girl.

epotismo (ne-po-tis-mo), *n.* (Sp.) nepotism; favoritism given to relatives, esp. in matters of appointment. Syn. *paboritismo sa paghirang sa tungkulin sa mga kamág-anak.*

Jeptuno (Nep-tu-no), *n.* (*Sp.*) 1. Neptune, the god of the sea in Roman mythology. 2. Neptune, the third largest planet in the solar system.

érbiyós (nér-bi-yós), *n.* (Sp. *nervios*) 1. feeling of nervousness or fear. Syn. *takot, pagkatakot.* 2. nervous breakdown, as in: *Namatáy siya nerbiyós.* He died of nervous breakdown.

Jeto (ne-to), I. *adj.* net; left over after certain deductions have been made, as in: *netong tubò,* net profit. Syn. *linis o malinis* (*colloq.*).
—II. *n.* net amount, profit, income, price, etc.

Jeutrál (ne-u-trál), var. **niyutrál**, *adj.* (Sp.) neutral; not taking side in war or in a quarrel. Syn. *waláng kiníkilingan.*

Ji¹ (ni), *prep.* (used before a person's name) 1. of; also expressed by 's, suffixed to the name of a person, as in *iná ni Nena,* mother of Nena or Nena's mother. 2. by,

as in: *ginawâ ni Juán,* made by Juan. 3. even (used as an emphatic or an intensive article), as in: *Si Juan ay hindî dumatíng.* Even Juan did not come. Syn. *kahit, kahit na, maging.*

ni² (ni), *conj.* usually used in the form *ni ... ni,* neither . . . nor, as in *ni ikáw ni akó,* neither you nor I.

nibél (ni-bél), *n.* (Sp. *nivel*) level, an instrument for determining whether a surface is on an even horizontal plane or for just adjusting a surface to such a plane.

nikník (nik-ník), *n.* (*Entom.*) a species of a tiny blood-sucking insect that usually infests animals, esp. horses.

nido (ni-do), *n.* (*Sp.*) 1. (food) edible bird's nest. 2. (N-) a brand name of a kind of powdered milk.

nigò (ni-gò), *n.* 1. good luck or fortune. 2. prosperity. See **manigò**.

niíg (ni-íg), *n.* private or intimate conversation; tete-a-tete. Also, *pagniniíg.*

niím (ni-ím), *v.* poetic form of *tumiím,* to close or be closed tightly (s.o. lips or teeth). See **tiím.**

nilà (ni-là), *pron.* (postpositive of *kanilá*), 1. (used as a possessive after noun): their; theirs, as in: *Ito'y awto nilá.* This is their auto. 2. (used after a verb) by them; they, as in: *Ito'y ginawâ nila.* This is made by them or they made this.

nilagà (ni-la-gà), var. **linagà**, I. *adj.* 1. cooked by boiling; boiled (s.o. corn, sweet potatoes, and the like). 2. cooked in water with condiments (s.o. meat); stewed.
—II. *n.* 1. boiled corn or sweet potatoes. 2. stewed meat.

nilagyán (ni-lag-yán), var. **linagyán**, *v.* past tense of *lagyán, v.* 1. to fill, as a container. Syn. *sidlán, lamanán (lamnán).* 2. to put or provide, as with decorations.

nilait (ni-la-it), var. **linait**, *v.* past tense of *laitin,* to revile; abuse with words; vilify. Syn. *minura, dinustâ.*

nilaláng (ni-la-láng), I. *adj.* 1. created as by God. Syn. *nilikhâ.* 2. made-up; fabricated; invented; false. Syn. *gawá-gawâ, gawâ-gawaan; likhâ, nilikhâ.*
—II. *n.* anything created, animate or inanimate; any creation by God. Syn.

nilikhâ. 2. anything made-up or fabricated.

nilamon (ni-la-mon), I. *v*. past tense of *lamunin*. 1. to devour or eat (something) voraciously. 2. *(Fig.)* to engulf totally as by fire, big waves, or the like.
—II. *adj*. 1. said of something devoured or eaten voraciously, as by a hungry dog. 2. engulfed, as by big waves.

nilang (ni-lang), *v*. poetic form of *sumilang*, 1. to be born; come into being, as a child. Syn. *ipanganák*. 2. to rise or appear, as the sun, moon, etc. Syn. *sumikat*.

nilapastangan (ni-la-pas-ta-ngan), *v*. past tense of *lapastanganin*. 1. to blaspheme. 2. to revile. Syn. *minura, nilait*.

nilapitan (ni-la-pi-tan), I. *v*. past tense of *lapitan*.
—II. *adj*. said of a person or thing approached by someone.

nilay (ni-lay), *n*. thinking seriously about; meditation; reflection; contemplation.

nilikhâ (ni-lik-hâ), I. *v*. past tense of *likhaín*, to create.
—II. *adj*. 1. created by God. Syn. *nilaláng*. 2. made-up; fabricated; invented. Syn. *gawá-gawâ, gawá-gawaan*.
—III. *n*. all things created by God; any creation by God. Syn. *nilaláng*.

nilináng (ni-li-náng), I. *v*. past tense of *linangín*.
—II. *adj*. 1. cultivated; planted to crops. Syn. *sinaka*. 2. well-developed, as by proper training. Syn. *pinaunlád*.

nilinaw (ni-li-naw), I. *v*. past tense of *linawin*, to clarify; make clear. Syn. *niliwanag*.
—II. *adj*. made clear by someone.

nilinláng (ni-lin-láng), I. *v*. past tense of *linlangín*.
—II. *adj*. swindled; defrauded. Syn. *dinayà, nádayà*.

nilisan (ni-li-san), var. **linisan**, 1. to leave a person or place temporarily. Syn. *iniwang pansamantalá*. 2. to abandon. Syn. *iniwan, pinabayaan, nilayasan*.
—II. *adj*. said of a person, place, or anything that someone has abandoned.

nilitis (ni-li-tis), var. **linitis**, I. *v*. past tense of *litisin*, to try in court.
—II. *adj*. referring to a case in court that has been tried or investigated.

niloób (ni-lo-oób), var. **linoób**, *v*. past tense of *loobín*, to be so by the will (of God).

nilooban (ni-lo-o-ban), var. **linooban**, I. *v*. past tense of *looban*, to rob or plunder.
—II. *adj*. victimized by robbers. Syr. *ninakawan, pinagnakawan*.

nimbo (nim-bo) *n*. *(Sp.)* halo; nimbus. Syr. *sinag*.

nimpa (nim-pa), *n*. (Sp. *ninfa*) nymph. Syr. *diwatà*.

niná (ni-ná), *prep*. plural of *ni*.

ninang (ni-nang), *n*. a female sponsor (at wedding, baptism, or confirmation); godmother. Syn. *iníná, madrina*.

ninikat (ni-ni-kat), *adj*. (poetic form c *sumisikat*) rising and shining, referring t the sun, moon, etc.; getting or becomin popular, as an artist.

nino (ni-no), *pron*. postpositive of *kanino* whose: as in: *Lapis nino ito?* whose penc is this?

ninombrahán (ni-nom-bra-hán), I. *v*. pas tense of *nombrahán*, to appoint to certain position or office. Syn. *hinirang*.
—II. *adj*. said of a person who has bee appointed to a certain position or office as by the President.

ninong (ni-nong), *n*. a male sponsor (at wedding, baptism, or confirmation); godfather. Syn. *ináamá, padrino*.

ninunò (ni-nu-nò), *n*. ancestor; forefathe Also, *nunò*.

ninya (nin-ya), *n*. (Sp. *niña*) a derogator term of a much pampered young girl o daughter, esp. of a Spanish mestizo famil

Ninyo (Nin-yo), *n*. (Sp. *Niño*) Young Jesus Jesus as a child in the manger.

ninyó (nin-yó), *pron*. (postpositive of *inyó* plural of *iyó* and *mo*) 1. your; yours, as in *Tungkulin ninyó iyán*. That is your duty 2. you; by you, as in *ginawá ninyó*, mad by you.

ningas (ni-ngas), var. **dingas, lingas**, flame; small blaze. Cf. *liyáb, alab*.

ningas-bao (ni-ngas + ba-o), *adj*. fleeting passing swiftly; not lasting, said esp. o someone's interest in some kind of work See **ningas-kugon**.

ningas-kugon (ni-ngas + ku-gon), *adj*. o

short duration; not lasting or enduring. Syn. *pánandalian*.

ningníng (ning-níng), n. brilliance; radiance; sparkle; splendor. Syn. *luningníng, kisláp*.

nipa (ni-pa), n. *(Bot.)* 1. nipa; palm *(Nypa fruticans)*. 2. the leaves of this palm, usually used as thatching materials. Syn. *pawid*.

nipís (ni-pís), n. 1. thinness, as of cloth, paper, board, etc.; opposite of *kapál*. 2. thinness (of persons and animals). Syn. *kapayatán*. 3. thinness or sparseness, as of hair. Syn. *dalang, kadalangan*.

Niponggo (Ni-pong-go), n. 1. a Japanese citizen. Syn. *Hapones*. 2. the Japanese language.

nirí (ni-rí), I. *pron*. this, referring to a person or thing near the speaker. Syn. *nitó, niyarí*. —II. *adj*. of this.

nisnís (nis-nís), I. *adj*. frayed or worn out along the edge, usually said of cloth or any woven material.
—II. n. the frayed part or portion of cloth, etc., esp. along the edge.

nita (ni-ta), v. poetic form of *kumita*. 1. to earn (a certain amount). 2. (with *ng liwanag*) to be born, as a child.

nitó (ni-tó), I. *pron*. this, referring to a person or thing near the speaker. Syn. *nirí, niyarí*.
—II. *adj*. of this; by this. Syn. *nirí*.

nitò (ni-tò), n. *(Bot.)* a long, slender forest vine, used esp. in making baskets, etc.

nitso (nit-so), n. (Sp. *nicho*) 1. niche; a hollow in the wall for a statue, vase, etc. 2. tomb; vault for burial; sepulcher.

niyá (ni-yá), pron. (postpositive of *kaniyá*): 1. his or her, as in: *Ito'y kuwarta niya*. This is his (her) money. 2. by him; by her, as in *ginawâ niyá*, made by him (her).

niyán (ni-yán), I. *pron*. that, referring to a person or thing far from the addressed, as in: *Walâ akó niyán*. I don't have that.
—II. *adj*. of that; by that, as in: *sinulat niyáng batang iyán*, written by that child.

niyaón (ni-ya-ón), *adv*. when; at the (that) time; during the time when, as in: *niyaóng walâ ka pa*, when you were still away. Syn. *noón, nang*.

niyarí (ni-ya-rí), I. *pron*. this, referring to oneself or to a person or thing near the speaker. See **nirí**.
—II. *adj*. this; of this.

niyebe (ni-ye-be), n. (Sp. *nieve*) snow.

niyóg (ni-yóg), n. *(Bot.)* 1. coconut palm tree. 2. coconut fruit.

niyón (ni-yón), I. *pron*. that, referring to a person not present or away, as in: *Gusto ko niyón*. I like that.
—II. *adj*. of that, as in: *bahay niyóng lalaking iyón*, in the house of that man.
—III. *adv*. at that time, during that time: as in: *niyóng walâ pa siyá*, at the time when he was still away. Syn. *nang, noon*.

niyugan (ni-yu-gan), n. coconut grove or plantation.

Noa (No-a), n. (in the Bible) Noah. Syn. *Noé, Nowé*.

Nob. (Nob.), n. abbrev. of **Nobyembre**, November (Nov.).

nobato (no-ba-tò), var. **nobatos**, I. n. (Sp. *novato*) greenhorn; novice; beginner. Syn. *baguhan*. –II. *adj*. inexperienced.

nobedád (no-be-dád), n. *(Sp. novedad)* novelty; new or unusual thing or experience. Syn. *bagay o karanasang bago o di-pangkaraniwán*.

nobela (no-be-la), n. (Sp. *novela*) novel. Syn. *kathambuhay*.

nobelista (no-be-lis-ta), n. (Sp. *novelista*) novelist. Syn. *mángangathambuhay*.

nobena (no-be-na), n. (Sp. *novena*) in the Rom. Catholic Church, the recitation of prayer during a nine-day period for a certain religious purpose; novena.

nobenta (no-ben-ta), n. & *adj*. (Sp. *noventa*) ninety. Syn. *siyamnapu*.

nobisyo (no-bis-yo), n. (Sp. *novicio*) 1. novice; beginner. Syn. *baguhan, nobatos*. 2. a person on probation in a religious group or order; also, a recent convert. Syn. *nobisyado*.

noblesa (no-ble-sa), n. (Sp. *nobleza*) nobility; nobleness. Syn. *pagkamarangál, karangalán; pagkaonorable, kaonorablehan*.

nobya (nob-ya), n. (Sp. *novia*) 1. bride. Syn. *babaing kakasalin, babaing bagong-kasál*. 2. fiancee; sweetheart. Syn. *kasintahan; katipán, kasuyò*.

Nobyembre (Nob-yem-bre), n. (Sp. *Noviembre*) November, the eleventh month of the year.

nobyo (nob-yo), n. (Sp. *novio*) 1. groom; bridegroom. Syn. *lalaking kakasalin o bagong kasál*. 2. fiancé. Syn. *katipán, kasintahan*.

noli-me-tángeré (no-li + me + tán-ge-ré), n. (*Lat.-Sp.*) 1. malignant ulcer; cancerous skin disease. 2. (*Noli Me Tangere*) the title of one of Rizal's famous novels.

nombra (nomm-bra), I. n. (Sp. *nombrar*) act of appointing a person to an office or position. Syn. *paghirang*.

—II. adj. (*Colloq.*) designated or appointed by.

nomenklatura (no-men-kla-tu-ra), n. (Sp. *nomenclatura*) names used in a branch of learning or activity; nomenclature. Syn. *mga pangalan o katawagán*.

nominasyón (no-mi-nas-yón), n. (Sp. *nominacion*) a nominating or appointing; nomination. Syn. *paghirang, pagkakáhirang*.

noó (no-ó), n. (*Anat.*) forehead.

noón (no-ón), adv. 1. at that time; during that time; at or during the time of. 2. when. Syn. *nang*.

normál (nor-mál), adj. normal; natural; common; regular. Syn. *karaniwán, pangkaraniwán, natural, regulár*.

norte (nor-te), n. & adj. (*Sp.*) north. Syn. *hilagà*.

nota (no-ta), n. (*Sp.*) 1. note (in music). 2. short letter or memorandum; note. 3. mark or grade in class or in a subject. Syn. *marka, grado*. 4. unfavorable record or reputation. Syn. *masamáng pangalan o reputasyón*. 5. notes or list about something. Syn. *talâ, listahan*. 6. explanatory note or notes; annotation (on a book, notebook, etc.).

notable (no-ta-ble), I. adj. (*Sp.*) 1. notable; remarkable. Syn. *mahalagá, importante*. 2. distinguished. Syn. *tanyág, bantóg, kilalá, litáw*.

—II. n. a notable person. Syn. *taong tanyág (kilalá, bantóg, litáw)*.

Notsebuwena (Not-se-bu-we-na), n. (Sp. *Nochebuena*) Christmas Eve. Syn. *Bisperás*

ng *Paskó*.

nukleo (nu-kle-o), n. (Sp. *nucleo*) nucleus; central part. Syn. *ubod, pinakaubod*.

nugnóg (nug-nóg), n. 1. border or boundary. Syn. *hangganan*. 2. end or extremity. Syn. *dulo, duluhan, hangganan*.

nulo (nu-lo), adj. (*Sp.*) null; void; without legal force; not binding. Syn. *waláng-bisà*.

númeró (nú-me-ró), n. (*Sp.*) number. Syn. *bilang*.

nunál (nu-nál), n. (*Sp. lunar*) mole; congenital spot on the human skin. Syn. *taling*.

nunò (nu-nò), n. 1. forefather; ancestor. Syn. *ninunò*. 2. grandfather or grandmother. Syn. *lolo o lola; lelong o lelang*. 3. (in folklore) an evil or mischievous spirit, said to be found in anthills. Also called *nunò sa punsó*.

nunò sa talampakan, great-great grandparent.

nunò sa tuhod, great-grandparent.

nunsiyó (nun-si-yó), n. (Sp. *nuncio*) papal; ambassador; papal nuncio; nuncio. Syn. *sugò o kinatawan ng papa*.

nungka (nung-ka), adv. (Sp. *nunca*) never; not at all. Syn. *di-kailanmán, hindíng-hindî, talagáng hindî*.

nutnót (nut-nót), I. adj. frayed; worn out by friction or rubbing. Syn. *nunót, nisnís, mulmulín*.

—II. n. 1. fibers worn away or frayed. Syn. *mulmól, himulmól*. 2. the worn out or frayed part or portion.

nutrisyón (nu-tris-yón), n. (Sp. *nutricion*) anything that nourishes; nourishment; food. Syn. *pagkain*.

nuwebe (nu-we-be), n. & adj. (Sp. *nueve*) nine. Syn. *siyám*.

nuynóy (nuy-nóy), n. 1. serious thought or thinking; reflection; meditation. Syn. *bulay-bulay, pagbubulay-bulay; nilay-nilay, pagninilay-nilay*. 2. act of mentioning or repeating one by one things that a person wants to blame on another. Syn. *pagbanggít sa isá-isá*.

NG

NG, ng (nga), *n*. 1. the twelfth letter of the *abakada* (Pilipino alphabet). 2. the type or impression representing this letter. 3. a symbol for the twelfth in a group or series.

ng (nang), *prep*. 1. of; from, as in: *mámamayán ng Maynilà*, citizen of (from) Manila; also expressed by 's, as in: *ang anák ng Pangulo*, the President's son. 2. by; of, as in: *kuwento ng kaibigan ko*, story by my friend. 3. sometimes *ng* is not expressed in English, as in: *Umínóm siyá ng alak*, he drinks wine.

-ng, lig. variant of **na**, used as a suffix.

ngâ (ng²), *adv*. 1. really; certainly; truly; in fact, as in: *Tunay ngâ iyón*. That's really true. 2. (*Colloq.*) kindly; please, as in: *Bigyán mo ngâ siyá ng pagkain*. Please (kindly) give him food.

ngabáy (nga-báy), *n*. a holding on a handrail, as in passing a narrow hanging bridge or in going downstairs. Also, *pangangabáy*.

ngabngáb (ngab-ngáb), *n*. a scraping off (something) with teeth, as when a dog bites off thin meat from a big bone. Cf. *kabkáb*.

ngangák (nga-ngák), *n*. 1. loud crying as a child. Syn. *palakat, palahaw, atungal*. 2. an empty foolish talk; babble. Syn. *ablá, daldál, satsát*. 3. boast or boasting, brag or bragging. Syn. *kahambugán, paghahambóg*.

ngalan (nga-lan), *n*. 1. name of a person, animal, or thing. Also, *alan, pangalan*. 2. word or term by which anything is called. Syn. *tawag, katawagán*. 3. name or title. Syn. *pamagát, títuló*. 4. (*Fig.*) good name; honor; fame; reputation. Syn. *dangál, karangalan; kabantugan, katanyagan*.

ngalandakan (nga-lan-da-kan), *n*. boasting or proud spreading, esp. of one's achievements or good things done. Syn. *parali, pamamarali, pagmamapurí*.

ngalangalá (nga-la-nga-lá), *n*. (*Anat.*) roof of mouth; palate.

ngalay (nga-lay), *n*. muscular tiredness or weariness due to long waiting, standing, sitting, etc. Syn. *ngawit, pangangawit;*

mitig, pamimitig.

ngalingali (nga-li-nga-li), *n*. state or condition of being almost at the point or verge of extreme eagerness to do something. Syn. *pagkaibig na ibig*.

ngalirang (nga-li-rang), var. **kalirang**, *n*. 1. extreme dryness, as of leaves. Syn. *labis na pagkatuyô*. 2. state or condition of being very thin, referring esp. to a person. Syn. *labis na kapayatán (pangangayayat)*.

ngalisag (nga-li-sag), var. **kalisag**, *n*. standing of hair on end due to fear. Cf. *kilabot, pangingilabot*.

ngalit (nga-lit), *n*. gritting or gnashing of teeth in anger. 2. subdued anger or fury, usually manifested by the gritting of one's teeth. Syn. *ngitngít, pagngingitngít*.

ngalitngít (nga-lit-ngít), *n*. 1. sound produced in gritting or gnashing the teeth. 2. creaking sound as that produced by rusty hinges. Syn. *langitngít*.

ngalngál (ngal-ngál), *n*. 1. loud crying, as of a child. Syn. *angal, atungal, palakat, palahaw*. 2. a babbling; meaningless talk. Syn. *daldál, satsát, ablá*. 3. a complaining; complaint. Syn. *reklamo, pagrereklamo*.

ngalos (nga-los), *n*. extreme weakness due to being too tired.

ngalót (nga-lót), *n*. grinding or crushing noisily with the teeth; chewing or masticating, esp. of hard food. Cf. *nguyâ, pagnguyâ*.

ngalumatá (nga-lu-ma-tá), *n*. languishing look or expression of the eye due to lack of sleep. Also, *pangangalumatá*.

ngalumbabà (nga-lum-ba-bà), *n*. pensive position of a person, with the chin or cheeks supported by the palms of the hands. Also, *pangangalumbabà*.

ngalutngót (nga-lut-ngót), *n*. noise produced when munching something. Syn. *langutngót*.

ngambá (ngam-bá), *n*. misgiving; doubt; fear. Syn. *alinlangan, kabá, pangambá*.

nganák (nga-nák), *n*. a giving birth (to a child). Syn. *silang, pagsisilang*.

nganay (nga-nay), *n*. a giving birth to one's first child. See *pangangay*.

nganí (nga-ní), *n*. 1. a faltering or hesitation. Syn. *atubili, pag-aatubili*. 2. loathing or loathsome. Syn. *diri, pandidiri*.

nganib (nga-nib), *n.* an obsolescent root, meaning danger, from which *panganib, manganib, panganiban,* etc. are derived.

nganino (nga-ni-no), *n.* feeling of inferiority or inadequacy; inferiority complex.

nganinganí (nga-ni-nga-ní), *n.* 1. respect; courtesy. Syn. *galang, paggalang; pitagan, pamimitagan.* 2. apprehensive feeling or reluctance, as in touching something dirty. Syn. *diri, pandidiri.*

ngangá (nga-ngá), I. *n.* 1. act or manner of opening one's mouth. Also, *pagngangá, pagkakángangá.* 2. the open position of the mouth. 3. state or condition by which the mouth is opened.
—II. *adj.* 1. open, referring to one's mouth. Also, *nakangangá.* 2. gaping; wide-open, as a big cut or wound.

ngangà (nga-ngà), *n.* 1. a preparation of ikmo leaves, areca nut, and lime for chewing, known locally as *buyò* or *hitsó.* 2. the chewing or mastication of this preparation. Also, *pangangà.*

ngángayón (ngá-nga-yón), *adv.* just now; only now or this time. Syn. *ngayón lamang.*

ngapa (nga-pa), *n.* clumsy or awkward manner of doing something due to the confused state of the mind or to the lack of experience about it.

ngapós (nga-pós), *adj.* lacking; short of (something).

ngasáb (nga-sáb), *n.* 1. act or manner of opening and closing one's mouth noisily, as animals do while eating. 2. the sound thus produced. 3. (*Fig.*) long, senseless babbling. Syn. *daldál, ngasngás, satsát.*

ngasím (nga-sím), *n.* sourish taste of food. Also, *pangangasím.*

ngasngás (ngas-ngás), *n.* 1. idle talk; rumors; gossip. Syn. *tsimís, sitsiryá.* 2. babble; useless talk. Syn. *daldál, satsát.* 3. a boasting or bragging. Syn. *kahambugán, paghahambóg.*

ngatâ (nga-tâ), I. *n.* grinding or crushing into pulp with the teeth; mastication; chewing.
—II. *adj.* chewed; masticated. Also, *nginatâ.*

ngatál (nga-tál), var. **katál**, I. *n.* a trembling as of the hands, body, voice, etc.

ngatngát (ngat-ngát), I. *n.* 1. act of gnawing; biting or tearing away bit by bit with the teeth. Cf. *kabkáb.* 2. part or portion that has been gnawed.

ngatóg (nga-tóg), I. *n.* a shaking or trembling from cold or exhaustion, esp. of the knees.
—II. *adj.* shaking or trembling, esp. from cold or exhaustion. Also, *nangangatóg.*

ngawâ (nga-wâ), *n.* 1. loud, continuous crying, as of a child. Syn. *angal, atungal, palakat.* 2. empty, foolish talk; babble. Syn. *daldál, satsát; ablá.*

ngawit (nga-wit), *n.* tiredness or weariness due to long waiting, sitting, standing, etc. Syn. *ngalay, pangangalay.*

ngayón (nga-yón), I. *adv.* now; at present; at this moment or time. Syn. *sa kasalukuyan.*
—II. *n.* present; present time; today; this day.

ngayon din, right away; at once; right now. Cf. *agád, kapagdaka.*

ngayún-ngayón (nga-yún + nga-yón), *adv.* (usually with *lamang*) just now; only a moment ago. Syn. *ngángayón.*

ngayupapâ (nga-yu-pa-pâ), *n.* humble submission of oneself, esp. to one in authority. Syn. *pakumbabâ, pagpapa-kumbabâ.*

ngibá (ngi-bá), I. *n.* tendency of a child to cry when held by someone not known to him.
—II. *v.* poetic form of *mangibá* or *umibá,* to change or transfer, as one's place of residence.

ngibì (ngi-bì), *n.* pursing of lips, as when a child is about to cry. Syn. *hibî.*

ngibit (ngi-bit), *n.* facial expression of contempt indicated by twisting the lips and showing the teeth.

ngiki (ngi-ki), *n.* chill; fit of shivering; ague; algor. Syn. *matindíng gináw, kaliglíg sa gináw.*

ngilin (ngi-lin), *n.* 1. abstinence. Also, *pangilin, pangingilin.* 2. observation of holidays.

ngilngíl (ngil-ngíl), I. n. act or manner of talking with another in an angry, growling tone. Cf. *angil*.

ngiló (ngi-ló), I. n. sensation of tingling discomfort on the teeth.

—II. *adj*. said of a person who feels a tingling discomfort on the edges of his teeth. Syn. *nangingiló*.

ngima (ngi-ma), n. thin coating of putrefied food subtances on the surface of teeth; plaque.

ngimay (ngi-may), n. numbness due to fatigue; insensitiveness caused by anesthesia. Syn. *manhíd, pamamanhíd*.

ngimbuló (ngim-bu-ló), n. a feeling of inferiority complex or inadequancy, esp. to a rival. Syn. *panganganino*.

ngimì (ngi-mì), var. **kimì**, n. 1. shy attitude or character; timidity; shyness; bashfulness. 2. reserved attitude in respect for someone, consideration or respect. Syn. *alang-alang, pag-aalang-alang*.

nginain (ngi-na-in), n. feeding or grazing on growing grass, as of animals in a pasture. Also, *panginginain*.

nginíg (ngi-níg), I. n. a trembling or shivering, as from fear, cold, etc. Syn. *ngatál, pangangatál*. –II. *adj*. trembling or shivering, referring to voice, hands, or body of a person. Also, *nangínginíg*.

ngingì (ngi-ngì), n. the space or angle between two fingers or toes.

ngipin (ngi-pin), n. 1. (*Anat*.) tooth. 2. a toothlike part of saw, comb, etc.

ngisbî (ngis-bî), n. sour expression of the lips, as in sobbing. Cf. *hibî*.

ngisi (ngi-si), n. silly laugh; giggle; grin. Syn. *ngisngís, tawang-aso*.

ngisngís (ngis-ngís), I. n. 1. a person given to giggling. Syn. *taong palátawá*. 2. silly laugh; giggle; grin. Syn. *ngisi, tawang-aso*.

—II. *adj*. fond of giggling. Syn. *ngisí, bungisngís*.

ngitî (ngi-tî), n. smile. Syn. *umis* (*Bats*.).

ngitlóg (ngit-lóg), v. poetic variant of *mangitlóg* or *umitlóg*, to lay an egg or eggs.

ngitngít (ngit-ngít), n. 1. intensity of emotion; rage; fury. Syn. *matindíng galit*. 2. intensity or inclemency, as of weather.

ngiwî (ngi-wî), I. n. 1. state or condition of being twisted or wry, referring esp. to a person's mouth or face. 2. a person with a twisted or wry face or mouth.

—II. *adj*. 1. twisted or wry, referring to someone's mouth or face. 2. distorted or turned to one side, as an object. Syn. *tabingî, hiwíd*.

ngiyáw (ngi-yáw), n. the characteristic vocal sound made by cats; mew; meow. Syn. *ingáw*.

ngongò (ngo-ngò), var. *ngungò*, I. n. a person who cannot speak distinctly due to a nasal defect.

—II. *adj*. with or having a voice that seems to come from a clogged nose. Cf. *humál*.

ngudngód (ngud-ngód), n. 1. act of pushing or shoving the head of someone that the nose or face would strike against something. 2. an accidental striking of the nose or snout against something, as when falling face down. Cf. *sungabà*.

ngulila (ngu-li-la), n. feeling of loneliness due to being alone. Also, *pangungulila*.

ngulimbát (ngu-lim-bát), var. **kulimbát**, n. act of stealing something. Syn. *nakaw, pagnanakaw*.

ngulimlím (ngu-lim⸲lím), I. n. cloudiness; state or condition of being cloudy. Also, *pangungulimlím, kakulimlimán*.

—II. *adj*. cloudy; darkened with clouds, referring to the sky.

nguni't (ngu-ni't), *conj*. (fr. *ngunì* and *at*, which by common practice now takes the form *ngunit*), but. Syn. *subali't* (also *subalit*), *dátapwa't* (also *dátapwát*).

ngunót (ngu-nót), var. **kunót**, I. n. a wrinkle or wrinkles, as on someone's forehead.

—II. *adj*. wrinkled; with or having wrinkles.

ngusngós (ngus-ngós), n. tip of the nose. Syn. *tungkî ng ilóng*. 2. snout of an animal. Syn. *ngusò*. 2. green immature string beans locally known as *paayap*.

—II. *adj*. (by extension) still young and innocent. Syn. *musmós*.

ngusò (ngu-sò), n. 1. snout (of an animal). 2. the upper lip of a person. 3. the human mouth esp. one that is large and prominent. 4. (by extension) the act of

ngutngót

pointing a person or thing by protruding the lips towards the person or object. Also, *pangungusò*.

ngutngót (ngut-ngót), n. 1. insistent request or pleading in a whimpering tone. 2. whimpering cry. Syn. *ungót, nguyngóy*.

nguyâ (ngu-yâ), n. 1. act of chewing or grinding (food) with the teeth. Cf. *ngatá, ngalót*. 2. the manner (something) has been chewed or masticated. Also, *pagkakánguyâ*.

nguyapit (ngu-ya-pit), var. **ngunyapit**, n. 1. act or manner of climbing a tree by holding on with the hands from branch to branch. Syn. *ukyabit*. 2. act of holding on something to prevent oneself from falling or from drowning.

nguyngóy (nguy-ngóy), n. 1. sulky, continuous weeping. 2. the sound of continuous weeping.

O

O, o (pronounced like 'O' in *omelet, object*, etc.), n. 1. the thirteenth letter of the *abakada* (Pilipino alphabet). 2. the type or impression representing this letter 3. the symbol for the thirteenth in a group or series.

O! *interj.* 1. O! Oh! 2. (used in referring to something being given or offered to someone) here, as in: *O, kunin mo itó!* Here, take this! Syn. *heto.*

o, *conj.* or. Syn. *o kayâ, dili kayâ*.

o, *adv.* then; now, as in: *O, anó ang nangyari sa iyó?* Now, what happened to you?

oasis (o-a-sis), n. (*Sp., Eng.*) oasis, fertile place in a desert.

obalo (o-ba-lo). n. & adj. (Sp. *óvalo*) oval.

obaryo (o-bar-yo), n. (*Anat.*, Sp. *ovario*) ovary. Syn. *bahay-itlóg*.

obispo (o-bis-po), n. (*Sp.*) bishop.

obituwaryo (o-bi-tu-war-yo), var. **obitwaryo**, n. (Sp. *obituario*) obituary; notice of death. Syn. *patalastás ng pagkamatáy*.

oblasyón (ob-las-yón; o-blas-yón), n. (Sp. *oblacion*) oblation; an offering to God.

Syn. *handóg o alay sa Diyós*.

obligá (o-bli-gá), n. (Sp. *obligár*) act of bringing about something by compulsion.

obligasyón (o-bli-gas-yón), n. (Sp. *obligacion*) 1. obligation or duty under the law; responsibility. Syn. *tungkulin, katungkulan; sagutin, pananágutan*.

obra (o-bra), n. (*Sp.*) 1. work; employment. Syn. *trabaho, empleyo, gawá, tungkulin*. 2. work; something made or done. Syn. *gawâ, likhâ, yarì, trabaho*. 3. literary work. Syn. *kathâ, akdâ*.

obrá (o-brá), I. adj. possible; acceptable; allowable; permissible. Syn. *puwede, maaarì; matátanggáp*.

obra-maestra (o-bra + ma-es-tra), n. (*Sp.*) masterpiece. Also written, *obra maestra*. Syn. *akdáng-gurò, likháng-gurò*.

obrero (o-bre-ro), n. (*Sp.*) worker; laborer. Syn. *trabahadór, manggagawà*.

obserba (ob-ser-ba), n. (Sp. *observar*) 1. observation; fact of being seen or noticed. 2. observance, as of laws, rules, etc. Syn. *pagtalima, pagsunód, pagtupád, paggalang* 3. celebration; observation. Syn. *pagdiriwang, pagdaraos*.

okasyón (o-kas-yón), n. (Sp. *occasion*) 1. occasion; chance; opportunity Syn. *pagkakátaón*. 2. an event; celebration. Syn. *pangyayari, pagdiriwang*. 3. need or exigency. Syn. *pangangailangan*.

okasyonál (o-kas-yo-nál), adj. (Sp. *ocasional*) 1. occasional; once in a while. Syn. *minsán-minsán, paminsán-minsán, manakánaká, bihirà*. 2. for some special time or purpose. Syn. *pantangì, pang-espesyál, pambihirà*.

óke (ó-ke), var. **okey**, I. adj. (*Eng.*, *colloq.*) okay; all right. Syn. *tamà, areglado* (*colloq.*).

—II. n. approval; endorsement. Syn. *patibay, pagpapatibay*.

okoy (o-koy), var. **ukoy**, (*Ch.*) a kind of food consisting of grated potatoes, squash, green papaya, mongo bean sprouts, etc. with pork, shrimps, mixed with batter and deep fried in lard or oil; it is usually eaten with vinegar and garlic sauce.

okra (o-kra), n. (*Eng.*) okra: the plant or its pods, used as vegetable in soups, stew, etc.

okre

okre (o-kre), n. (Sp. *ocre*) ocher; yellow or brown earth used as pigment.

oksidentál (ok-si-den-tál), I. *adj.* (Sp. *occidental*) occidental; western; of the west. Syn. *kanluranin, sa o ng kanluran.*
—II. n. native of the west; Occidental; Westerner. Syn. *taga-Kanluran, Kanluranin.*

oksiheno (ok-si-he-no), n. (Sp. *oxigeno*) oxygen.

oktaba (ok-ta-ba), n. 1. (*Mus.*, Sp. *octava*) octave. 2. (*Poetry*) octave; a group of eight lines of verse. 3. postponement. Syn. *pagpapaliban.*

oktabo (ok-ta-bo), *adj. & n.* (Sp. *octavo*) eighth.

Oktubre (Ok-tu-bre), n. (Sp. *Octubre*) October, the tenth month of the year.

okupá (o-ku-pá), n. (Sp. *ocupar*) an occupying or being occupied; taking possession of a place. Syn. *pagtirá, pagtahán.* 2. occupation by seizure or conquest. Syn. *pagsakop.*

okupasyón (o-ku-pas-yón), n. (Sp. *ocupacion*) 1. means of livelihood; occupation. Syn. *hanapbuhay, trabaho, gawain, empleyo.* 2. act of occupying a territory, as by an enemy. Syn. *pagsakop, pananakop.* 3. occupying a place, as a house. Syn. *pagtirá, pagtahán, pag-okupá.* 4. being busy. Syn. *kaabalahan, karamihan ng trabaho o gawain.*

oda (o-da), n. (*Sp.*) ode. Cf. *tulâ.*

odit (o-dit), var. **awdit**, n. (*Eng.*) audit; examination and checking of accounts or financial records. Also, *pag-oodit.*

ohales (o-ha-les). var. **ohalis, uhalis**, n. (Sp. *ojales*) 1. buttonhole. 2. act or manner of making a buttonhole or buttonholes. Also, *pag-oohales, pagkákaohales.*

ohetes (o-he-tes), var. **uhetes**, n. (Sp. *ojetes*) eyelet or eyelets.

ohò (o-hò), *adv., interj. & n.* (used as an affirmative answer showing respect for elders or superiors, but less formal than *opò*) Yes, Sir, Yes, Madam. Syn. *Opò.* Cf. *Oo.*

óleó (ó-le-ó), n. (*Sp.*) 1. oil. Syn. *langis* 2. (*Colloq.*) oil painting.

oliba (o-li-ba), n. (Sp. *oliva*) 1. the olive tree. 2. the fruit of this tree.

olímpikó (o-lím-pi-kó), *adj. & n.* (Sp. *olimpico*) olympic; olympics.

olpaktoryo (ol-pak-tor-yo), I. n. (Sp. *olfactorio*) 1. olfactory; organ of smell. Syn. *pangamóy.* 2. sense of smell.
—II. *adj.* olfactory; of the sense of smell.

omega (o-me-ga), n. (*Sp., Eng.*) 1. omega; the twenty-fourth and final letter of the Greek alphabet. 2. end. Syn. *wakás, katapusán.*

omnipotente (om-ni-po-ten-te), I. *adj.* (Sp. *omnipotente*) omnipotent; having all power. Syn. *lubós na makapangyarihan.*
—II. n. (O-) Omnipotent. Syn. *Ang Dakilang Maykapangyarihan; Ang Diyós.*

onda (on-da), n. (*Sp.*) wave; ripple.

onse (on-se), n. & *adj.* (Sp. *once*) 1. eleven. Syn. *labing-isá.* 2. (*Slang*) a swindling or being swindled.

oo (o-o), *adv. & n.* (used as an affirmative answer in familiar conversation with a younger person or with an equal) yes.

opensibo (o-pen-si-ba), n. (Sp. *ofensivo*) 1. that which attacks; attacking; offensive. 2. causing resentment or anger; insulting. Syn. *pampagalit, nakagágalit.* 3. hurting feelings. Syn. *nakasúsugat ng damdamin.*

operasyón (o-pe-ras-yon), n. (Sp. *operacion*) 1. surgical operation. Also, *pag-operá, pag-ooperá.* Syn. *tistís, pagtistís.* 2. the part of the body that has been operated on 3. management or administration, as of business. Syn. *pamamahalà, pangangasiwà, pagpapalakad.* 4. state of being operative. Syn. *iral, pag-iral.* 5. act or manner of operating or running a machine. Syn. *pagpapatakbó, pagpapaandár, pagpapalakad.* 6. way or manner or functioning, as a machine. Syn. *andár, pag-andár; takbó, pagtakbó.* 7. (*Mil.*) a maneuvering; strategy.

opereta (o-pe-re-ta), n. (*Sp., Eng.*) a short, amusing musical play; operetta.

opinyón (o-pin-yón), n. (Sp. *opinion*) 1. opinion; what one thinks about something. Syn. *palagáy, kuru-kurò.* 2. formal judgement as by an expert; professional advice. Syn. *pasiyá, hatol, payo.* 3. belief about something. Syn. *paniwalà, paniniwalà.*

opisyál (o-pis-yál), I. n. (Sp. *oficial*) officer; official; a person who holds an administrative position. Syn. *punò*, *pinunò*. —II. *adj.* official; authorized; legal.

opisyo (o-pis-yo), n. (Sp. *oficio*) occupation; work; means of livelihood. Syn. *hanapbuhay*, *trabaho*, *gawain*.

opò (o-pò), *adv.*, *interj.* & n. (short of "*oo pô*") Yes, Sir; Yes, Madam. Syn. *ohò*. Cf. *oo*.

oportunidád (o-por-tu-ni-dád), n. (Sp.) opportunity; chance. Syn. *pagkakátaón*.

oposisyón (o-po-sis-yón), n. (Sp. *oposicion*) 1. act of opposing; resistance. Syn. *pagtutol, pagsalungát, pagkontra, paglaban*. 2. the political party opposed to the party in power. Syn. *tagasalungát, partidong tagasalungát*.

opresyón (o-pres-yón), var. **opresiyón**, I. n. act of oppressing; cruel or unjust treatment. Syn. *pag-apí, pang-aapí; pagsiíl, paniniíl; kalupitán, pagmamalupít*. 2. a being oppressed or maltreated. Syn. *pagkaapí, kaapihán*.

opsiyonál (op-si-yo-nál), var. **opisyunál**, *adj.* (Sp. *opcional*) optional; left to one's choice. Syn. *di-sápilitán*.

óptikó (óp-ti-kó), n. (Sp. *óptico*) optician, person who makes and sells eyeglasses and other optical instruments. Syn. *manggagawà ng salamín sa matá*.

ora (o-ra), n. (Sp. *hora*) hour. Note: *Ora* is rarely used except in the borrowings *kada ora, por ora, ora mismo*, etc; *oras* is used instead.

oras (o-ras), n. (Sp. *hora*) 1. hour, as in: *limáng oras na atraso*, five hours late. 2. time, as in: *Anóng oras ang datíng nilá?* At what time will they arrive? 3. (*Fig.*) destined hour, as of one's death. Also, *takdáng oras*.

orasán (o-ra-sán), n. 1. a time piece; watch or clock. Syn. *relo o relos*. 2. chronometer.

orasyón (o-ras-yón), n. (Sp. *oracion*) 1. prayer; orison. Syn. *dasál, pagdarasál; dalangin, panalangin*. 2. evening prayer; vesper; angelus. 3. invocation; calling upon God in prayer. Syn. *pananalangin, pagtawag sa Diyós*. 4. incantation used in conjuring. Syn. *bulóng*.

oratorya (o-ra-tor-ya), n. (Sp. *oratoria*) oratory; eloquence; skill in public speaking. Syn. *husay o kahusayan sa pagtatalumpatì*.

oratoryo (o-ra-tor-yo); n. (Sp. *oratorio*) 1. small chapel; oratory. Syn. *silíd-dásalan, silíd-pánalanginán*. 2. (*Mus.*) oratorio.

orbe (or-be), n. (Sp.) orb; globe. Syn. *globo*.

orden (or-den), n. (Sp.) 1. order; command. Syn. *utos, kautusán, mando*. 2. law. Syn. *batas*. 3. rule; regulation, Syn. *pátakarán, kautusán, pamamalakád*. 4. arrangement; order. Syn. *ayos, kaayusan*. 5. clerical office; religious order.

ordenansa (or-de-nan-sa), var. **ordinansa**, n. (Sp. *ordenanza*) ordinance; rule or law by authority. Syn. *kautusán*.

ordíl (or-díl), n. (*Eng.*) 1. ordeal; something hard to do. Syn. *pahirap, bagay na mahirap gawín*. 2. a very hard punishment or experience. Syn. *pahirap, napakahirap na parusa o karanasán*.

ordinaryo (or-di-nar-yo), *adj.* (Sp. *ordinario*) ordinary; customary; common; usual; regular. Syn. *karaniwan, pangkaraniwan*.

oréganó (o-ré-ga-nó), var. **oríganó**, n. (*Sp.*, *Eng.*) organo; the plant and also the leaves which are used for seasoning.

organ (or-gan), n. (*Eng.*) 1. organ (musical instrument). Syn. *organo*. 2. organ (functional part of the body of a person, animal, or plant). Syn. *bahagi, parte, o sangkáp*. 3. a means of spreading news or information. Syn. *tagapamanság, tagapagsalitâ*. 4. newspaper or magazine. Syn. *páhayagán, diyaryo, mágasín*.

orgánikó (or-gá-ni-kó), *adj.* 1. organic; of the body organ. Syn. *ng o sa bahagi ng katawán*. 2. vital; organic. Syn. *mahalagá, importante*. 3. fundamental. Syn. *saligán, batayán*.

organisasyón (or-ga-ni-sas-yón), n. (Sp. *organización*) 1. an organizing or being organized; organization. Syn. *pagtatag, pagtatayô, pagbuô, pagpupundár*. 2. state or manner by which something was organized. Syn. *pagkakátatág, pagkakátayô, pagkakábuô, pagkakápundár*. 3. association; society; club. Syn. *samahán, kapisanan*.

organismo (or-ga-nis-mo), *n.* (*Sp.*)
organism; any living thing. Syn. *lahat ng
bagay na may-buhay, bagaháy* (newly
coined).

orihinál (o-ri-hi-nál), I. *adj.* 1. first; earliest;
original: as in: *ang orihinál na presyo,* the
original price. 2. former; at the first time,
as in: *orihinal na sukat,* former
measurement. Syn. *dati.* 3. native, as in:
orihinal na mga mamamayán, native
citizens. Syn. *katutubò, taál.* 4. not copied;
not translated; original, as in: *orihinál na
mga akdâ,* original work (writings). Syn.
sarili, sariling-gawâ, sariling-sinulat.
—II. *n.* the first or original copy or work
of someone; original.

oriyá (o-ri-yá), var. **uriyá,** *n.* (*Sp. orillo*)
selvage; selvedge.

oro (o-ro), *n.* (*Sp.*) gold. Syn. *gintô.*

ortograpiya (or-to-gra-pi-ya), var.
ortorapya, *n.* (Sp. *ortografia*) 1. orthography; correct spelling. Syn. *wastóng
pagbabaybáy.* 2. orthography, art or
science of spelling. Syn. *palábaybayan,
palátitikán.*

oryentál (or-yen-tál), I. *adj.* (Sp. *oriental*)
orienta; eastern. Syn. *silanganín, sa o sa
dakong silangan.*
—II. *n.* (O-) Oriental; Easterner. Syn.
taga-Silangan.

oryentasyón (or-yen-tas-yón), *n.* (Sp.
orientación) orientation; familiarization
with and adaptation to a situation or
environment. Syn. *pagsasanay.*

oryente (or-yen-te), I. *adj.* (Sp. *oriente*)
orient; east.
—II. *n.* (O-) the Orient; the East. Syn.
Silangan.

osilasyón (o-si-las-yón), *n.* Sp. *oscilación*)
oscillation; swinging to and fro. Syn. *ugóy,
pag-úgoy, pag-ugúy-ugóy.*

osmosis (os-mo-sis), *n.* (*Eng., Sp.*) osmosis;
diffusion of fluids through a membrane
or porous partition. Cf. *siníp, pagsiníp.*

oso (o-so), *n.* (*Sp.*) bear.

ostentasyón (os-ten-tas-yón), *n.* (Sp.
ostentacion) ostentation; a showing off.
Syn. *karangyaán, pagmamarangyâ.*

óstiyá (ós-ti-yá), *n.* (Sp. *hostia*) host, the
bread or water used in the Mass of the

Roman Catholic Church.

ostrasismo (os-tra-sis-mo), *n.* (Sp.
ostracismo) 1. ostracism; temporary
banishment. Syn. *pagpapatapon,
pagdidestiyero.* 2. exclusion from one's
favor. Syn. *pagtatakwíl.*

osyoso (os-yo-so), I. *adj.* (Sp. *ocioso*) looking
on; watching but not participating. Syn.
nanónoód, tumítingín-tingín, nagmimirón.
—II. *n.* 1. act of onlooking. Also, *pag-
oosyoso.* Syn. *panonoód, pagmimirón.* 2. an
onlooker; spectator; bystander. Syn. *mirón.*

otokalesa (o-to-ka-le-sa), *n.* (fr. auto +
calesa) a Pilipino innovation of a
motorized vehicle during the Japanese
regime in the Philippines which became
the precursor of the now popular jeepney.

otograpiya (o-to-gra-pi-ya), var. **otograpya,
awtograpiya,** *n.* autography; a person's
own handwriting. Syn. *sariling sulat-
kamáy.*

otomátikó (o-to-má-ti-kó), var. **awtomátikó,**
adj. (Sp. *automático*) 1. moving or acting
by itself; automatic. 2. done without
thought or attention; automatic. Syn.
kusà, pakusà.

otonomíya (o-to-no-mí-ya), var. **otonomya,
awtonomíya,** *n.* (Sp. *autonomia*) autonomy;
self-government; independence. Syn.
pagsarilí, kasarinlán, kalayaan.

otoridád (o-to-ri-dád), var. **awtoridad,** *n.*
(Sp. *autoridad*) 1. authority; power;
control. Syn. *kapangyarihan.* 2. a
recognized expert on a certain line. Syn.
esperto o dalubhasang sanggunian. 3. a
person or persons who exercise power or
command. Syn. *(ang) maykapangyarihan.*
4. permission. Syn. *kapahintulután.*

otorisasyón (o-to-ri-sas-yón), var.
awtorisasyón, *n.* (Sp. *autorización*) 1.
authorization; giving right, power, or
authority. Syn. *pagbibigáy-kapangyarihan,
pagbibigáy-karapatán.* 2. permission;
authorization. Syn. *permiso, pahintulot.* 3.
act of giving permission. Syn.
pagpapahintulot.

otsenta (ot-sen-ta), *n. & adj.* (Sp. *ochenta*)
eighty. Syn. *walumpû.*

otso (ot-so), *n. & adj.* (Sp. *ocho*) eight. Syn.
waló.

ow! (ow), *interj.* an exclamation expressing
(a) sudden pain, as in: Ouch! *Aray!* (b)
doubt or disbelief: Oh!

oy! (oy), *interj.* an exclamation used to
attract or call the attention of someone:
Hey! Syn. *Hoy!* 2. a sudden utterance or
ejaculation made by someone who
unexpectedly made a mistake. Syn. *Ay!*

oyaye (o-ya-ye), var. **oyayi, uyayi,** *n.* 1.
cradlesong; lullabye. 2. (in some Southern
tagalog Provinces, particularly in
Batangas) cradle or hammock. Syn.
duyan.

oyò (o-yò), var. **uyò,** *n.* (not common) low
tide. Syn. *kati.*

P

P, p (pa), *n.* 1. the fourteenth letter of the
abakada (Pilipino alphabet). 2. the type
or impression representing this letter. 3.
a symbol for the fourteenth in a group or
series.

pa (pa), *adv.* 1. still, as in: *Kumakain pa siyá.*
He is still eating. 2. more; much more, as
in: *higít pa sa riyán,* more than that. 3. yet,
as in: *hindî pa tapós,* not yet finished.

pa- (pa-) pref. used to form 1. adverbs and
adjectives, expressing manner, position,
or direction, as in: *patayô,* in an erect or
standing manner; *pababâ,* downward;
pasilangán, eastward, toward the east. 2.
verbs, meaning: (a) to request or ask
someone to do a thing, as in: *Pabilí ka ng
gatas.* Ask someone to buy milk for you.
(b) to let or have someone do something
for oneself, as in: *Pakuha ka ng larawan.*
Have someone take your picture.

paá (pa-á), *n.* 1. (*Anat.*) foot or leg. 2. the
part of a garment that covers the leg. 3.
one of the supports of a piece of furniture,
as a table, chair, etc. Cf. *tukod.* 4. foot or
base, as of a mountain. Syn. *punò, paanán.*
5. leg of animal, esp. hog or cow, used for
food. Syn. *pata.*

paabangán (pa-a-ba-ngán), *v.* to ask or
request someone to wait for a certain
person or thing in a certain place. Cf.

pabantayán.

paabutin (pa-a-bu-tin), *v.* 1. to cause or
make a rope, wire, or the like reach a
certain point, distance, or limit. 2. to ask
or request someone to get or reach for
something by extending the hand. Cf.
padukwangín.

paakay (pa-a-kay), *v.* to allow oneself to be
led or guided by someone, esp. by the
hand.

paakbáy (pa-ak-báy), *adj. & adv.* with or
having an arm over the shoulders of
another.

paakit (pa-a-kit), *v.* to allow oneself to be
charmed or attracted, as by someone's
beauty, eloquence, etc. Syn. *pabighanì.*

paakyát (pa-ak-yát), *adv.* 1. upstairs; up the
stairs. Syn. *papanhík.* 2. upward; upwards.
Syn. *pataás, paitaás.*

paagahán (pa-a-ga-han), *n.* an agreement
among a number of persons in which
everyone tries to be earlier than the rest.

paagusán (pa-a-gu-san), *n.* a gutter, channel,
canal, or ditch used to carry off water from
one place to another; drainage.

paahón (pa-a-hón), *adv.* upward a slope or
an inclined plane; toward a higher place
or position. Syn. *paakyát.*

paalaala (pa-a-la-a-la), *n.* 1. a reminding.
Also, *pagpapaalaala.* 2. a reminder. Syn.
tagapágpaalaala, tagapágpagunitâ. 3.
admonition; advice. Syn. *payo, pagunita.*

paalabin (pa-a-la-bin), *v.* to set on fire, as
with certain substances. 2. to stir up anger,
strife, riot, etc.

paalakbáy (pa-a-lak-báy), *adj. & adv.* with
or having an arm placed over the
shoulders of another.

paalagá (pa-a-la-gá), I. *adj.* said of a person
or thing put under the care of someone.
Syn. *pinaáalagaan.*
    —II. *v.* to have oneself taken care of, as
by a nurse.

paalalahanan (pa-a-la-la-ha-nan), *v.* 1. to
remind (someone). 2. to warn or caution
(someone) against specific faults;
admonish. Syn. *pagsabihan.*

paalam (pa-a-lam), I. *n.* 1. farewell; good-
bye, as in: *hulíng paalam,* last farewell. 2.
notice. Syn. *patalastás.* 3. act of informing

paalatin   **pabalagbág**

or letting someone know about something. Syn. *pagpapatalastás.*

—II. *interj.* Good-bye! Syn. *Gudbay!*

paalatin (pa-a-la-tin), *v.* to make salty or saltier.

paalilà (pa-a-lilà), *v.* 1. to work as a servant of someone. Syn. *magtrabaho bilang utusán (alila).* 2. to allow oneself to be treated like a servant; serve (someone) like a servant. Cf. *paalipin.*

paalís (pa-a-lís), I. *adj.* going away; leaving for a certain place; set to go or leave. Also, *áalis.*

—II, *v.* to cause something to be removed away from oneself, as one's shoes, clothes, gray hair, etc.

paaminin (pa-a-mi-nin), *v.* to make one confess or admit a fault, crime, etc. Syn. *papagtapatín ng kamalian, kasalanan, atb.*

paampunan (pa-am-pu-nan), *n.* 1. orphanage. 2. asylum. Syn. *asilo.*

paamuin (pa-a-mu-in), *v.* to tame or domesticate, as a wild animal. Syn. *mansuhín, pabaitín.*

paanán (pa-a-nán), *n.* 1. foot or base, as of a mountain, bridge, or the like. Cf. *punò.* 2. the end of a bed, grave, etc. toward which the feet are directed; opposed to *ulunán.*

paanás (pa-a-nás), *adj. & adv.* in whispers.

paandáp-andáp (pa-an-dáp + andáp), *adj.* flickering. Syn. *pakisláp-kisláp, pakuráp-kuráp.*

paandaran (pa-an-da-ran), *v.* to túrn on (an electric fan, etc.) towards someone. 2. (*Fig.*) to make a vain display in order to impress (someone). Cf. *pasikatan (fig.).*

paano (pa-a-no), var. **papaano**, I. *adv.* how; in what manner, as in: *Paano nangyari iyón?* How did it happen?

—II. *conj.* because of; on account of; by reason of; due to. Syn. *pagkát, sapagkát.* **Paano man,** however.

paanyaya (pa-an-ya-ya), *n.* invitation (usually written or formal). Syn. *imbitasyón.*

paangkín (pa-ang-kín), *v.* to allow oneself to be claimed as someone's own, referring esp. to a child.

paapí (pa-a-pí), *v.* to allow oneself to be mistreated.

paaralán (pa-a-ra-lán), *n.* school: *páaraláng elementarya,* elementary school; *mataás na páaralán,* high school.

paatay-atay (pa-a-tay + a-tay̆), *adv.* slowly, in a slow way or manner. Syn. *dahan-dahan, padahan-dahan.*

paatubili (pa-a-tu-bi-li; -li), I. *adj.* hesitant. Syn. *pabantulót.*

—II. *adv.* hesitantly; in a hesitant manner.

paawít (pa-a-wít), *adv.* in a melodious manner.

paayap (pa-a-yap), *n.* (*Bot.*) a variety of string beans having meaty pods that are eaten as a vegetable when still immature; also called *kibal* in some Southern Tagalog provinces.

paayón (pa-a-yón), *adj. & adv.* 1. in a parallel position or line with another; along or following the same line or direction. 2. in conformity with; not against.

pabaák (pa-ba-ák) *adv.* into halves, as in: *nabasag nang pabaák,* broken into halves.

pababâ (pa-ba-bâ), I. *adj.* 1. going down; descending, as a balloon, airplane, etc. 2. getting lower or cheaper; on the downward trend; decreasing, as prices. Syn. *pamurá, minumura.* 3. about to go downstairs. Syn. *papanaóg.* 4. about to get down or alight, as from a bus. Syn. *palunsád.*

—II. *adv.* downward.

pabakasakalí (pa-ba-ka-sa-ka-lí), *adv.* by taking a chance; at some risk.

pabagsák (pa-bag-sák), *n.* (*Fig.*) bribe; payola. Syn. *suhol, parating (fig.)*

pabagtás (pa-bag-tás), *adv.* across, crosswise: *Tumakbó siyáng pabagtás sa kalye.* He ran across the road. Syn. *patawíd.*

pabagu-bago- (pa-ba-gu + ba-go), *adj.* 1. always or ever changing; not constant. Syn. *paibá-ibá, papalít-palít.* 2. with or having the habit of always transferring from one place to another. Syn. *palipat-lipat.*

pabalagbág (pa-ba-lag-bág), I. *adj.* 1. transversal or transverse; lying crosswise. 2. contradictory. Syn. *laban, salungát.*

—II. *adv.* 1. crosswise; across; athwart.

Syn. *pahalang*. 2. in a contrary manner. Syn. *pasalungát*.

—III. *n.* the cross pieces in a trellis work.

pabalandra (pa-ba-lan-dra), *adv.* in the manner like bouncing or hitting against a wall.

pabalantok (pa-ba-lan-tok), *adj. & adv.* in the form of an arch. Syn. *paarko*.

pabaláng (pa-ba-láng), *adv.* (*Colloq.*) 1. in a careless manner. Syn. *padaskul.* 2. in an unmannerly way. Syn. *pabastós.*

pabalát (pa-ba-lát), I. *n.* 1. covering material, esp. for books. 2. cover, as of a book. 3. wrappers for *lumpiyâ.* 4. anything used as superficial covering. Syn. *pambalot.*

—II. *adj.* referring to something used for covering books, *lumpiya*, etc.

pabalát-bunga (pa-ba-lát + bu-nga), I. *n.* something said or done in pretext or without sincerity; pretended offer or invitation. Cf. *pagpapakunyarî, pagpapakunwarî.*

—II. *adj.* said or done in pretext or without sincerity. Cf. *pakunyarî, pakunwarî.*

pabalát-kayô (pa-ba-lát + ka-yô), *adj.&adv.* in a surreptitious manner; in disguise; incognito.

pabalbál (pa-bal-bál), I. *adj.* slangy; having the nature of slang.

—II. *adv.* slangily; in a slangy manner.

pabale (pa-ba-le), I. *n.* 1. something sold or bought on credit. Syn. *pautang.* 2. partial salary given or paid in advance to someone.

—II. *adj.* 1. sold or bought on credit. Syn. *pautang, inutang.* 2. referring to partial salary paid in advance.

pabalikukô (pa-ba-li-ku-kô), I. *adj.* distorted. Syn. *pabaluktót, papilipít.*

—II. *adv.* in a distorted manner. Syn. *nang baluktot o pabaluktot, nang pilipit o papilipit.*

pabalighô (pa-ba-lig-hô), *adj. & adv.* in an absurd or contrary manner. Syn. *pabalintuná.*

pabaligtád (pa-ba-lig-tád), *adj.* 1. reverse; inverted. 2. turned inside-out, as a coat, dress, and the like.

—II. *adv.* in reverse. Syn. *pasaliwa.* 2. in

an upside-down position. Syn. *patiwarik.*

pabalintunà (pa-ba-lin-tu-nà), *adj. & adv.* in a manner contrary to fact or expectation. Syn. *pabalighô.*

pabalíng (pa-ba-líng), *adj. & adv.* sidewise; sideways; obliquely.

pabalità (pa-ba-li-tà), *n.* news or message from someone. Cf. *pabilin, pasabi.*

pabango (pa-ba-ngo), *n.* perfume.

pabaon (pa-ba-on), *n.* provisions (money, food, or supplies) given to someone going on a trip.

pabasa (pa-ba-sa), *n.* an invitational Passion reading.

pabatíd (pa-ba-tíd), *n.* 1. message; information sent or given to someone. Syn. *pabalità, pasabi.* 2. announcement; notice. Syn. *babalâ, paunawà, patalastás.*

pabawás (pa-ba-was), *adj.* decreasing; diminishing. Syn. *pauntî, pakauntî, paliít, papaliít.*

pabayà (pa-ba-yà; -ya), *adj.* 1. negligent; neglectful; not attentive to one's duty or work. Syn. *walang-asikaso.* 2. careless, esp. of one's body or habit. Syn. *waláng-ingat, bulagsák.*

pabaybáy (pa-bay-báy), *adv.* by spelling or mentioning letter by letter. 2. by going one by one or from one to another. 3. by mentioning one by one. 4. by tracing or following the route.

pabigáy (pa-bi-gáy), *n. & adj.* referring to something sent or given to someone through another. Syn. *pahatíd.*

pabiglá-biglá (pa-big-lá + big-lâ), *adv. & adj.* with or having the habit of acting or doing things in a hurry or without much thought.

pabilin (pa-bi-lin), I. *n.* 1. message delivered or to be delivered to someone. Syn. *pasabi.* 2. an order or requisition for goods. Syn. *pidido, pabilí.*

—II. *adj.* that which refers to goods being ordered or requisitioned. Syn. *pabili.*

pabilíng-bilíng (pa-bi-líng + bi-líng), *adj.* continuously turning from side to side; restless. Syn. *balisá, hindî mápalagáy.*

pabilíg (pa-bí-log), I. *adj.* 1. round or rounded, as a ball. 2. circular, as a flat figure.

—II. *adv.* 1. in the form of a circle. 2. in the form of a ball.

abinyág (pa-bin-yág), n. 1. baptismal party or celebration. Also, *binyagan.* 2. baptism. Also, *binyag, pagbibinyag.* 3. baptismal fee. Syn. *bayad sa binyág o pagpapabinyág.*

abirô (pa-bi-rô), *adv.* jokingly; in a joking manner. Syn. *patuksó.*

abitin (pa-bi-tin), n. 1. a kind of game, usually held during Maytime festivals, in which the participants compete with each other by trying to grab as many hanging objects, as their prizes, from a square lattice of bamboo strips made to move up and down with a rope held by someone. 2. the hanging objects, usually different kinds of fruits, toys, and many others, that serve as prizes for the participants in this game; they are also called *bitin.*

abo (pa-bo), n. (Sp. *pavo*) turkey.

abor (pa-bor), n. (Sp. *favor*) 1. favor; kindness. Syn. *kagandahang-loób, kabutihan o kabutihang-lóob.* 2. favor; help. Syn. *tulong.* 3. favoritism; bias. Syn. *panig, pagpanig; kampí, pagkampi; kiling, pagkiling; pagtatangí.* 4. a conforming. Syn. *pagsang-ayon.*

—II. *adj.* in conformity with; agreeable to; in favor. Syn. *sang-ayon, kasang-ayon.*

aborable (pa-bo-ra-ble), *adj.* (Sp. *favorable*) 1. good for; advantageous; favorable. Syn. *mabuti, makabubuti, mainam.* 2. agreeable or conforming to. Syn. *sang-ayon, kasang-ayon, sumásang-ayon.*

aborito (pa-bo-ri-to), I. n. a person or thing regarded with special liking; favorite.

—II. *adj.* held in special regard; preferred; favorite.

pábriká (pá-bri-ká), n. (Sp. *fabrica*) factory; manufacturing plant or establishment. Syn. *págawaan.*

pabugsu-bugsô (pa-bug-su + bug-sô,) *adj. & adv.* with sudden, intermittent force. Cf. *pabiglá-biglâ at malakás, paulit-ulit at malakás.*

pábula (pá-bu-la), n. (Sp. *fabula*) 1. fable; made-up story that teaches a lesson or lessons. Syn. *kuwento o káthang may-aral.* 2. a legend. Syn. *alamát.* 3. a lie; fabricated statement. Syn. *kasinungalingan.*

pabulaan (pa-bu-la-an) n. a statement said to refute or disapprove something. See **pabulà.**

pabulalás (pa-bu-la-lás), *adj. & adv.* 1. in an angry, loud manner. 2. in the form of an interjection.

pabulóng (pa-bu-lóng), *adj. & adv.* in whispers. Syn. *paanás.*

pabulyáw (pa-bul-yáw), *adj. & adv.* in an angry and loud voice, as in giving order or command. Syn. *pagalít at malakás.*

pabuntóng-hiningá (pa-bun-tóng + hi-ni-ngá), *adj. & adv.* in sighs; with sighs.

pabuód (pa-bu-ód), *adj. & adv.* in a brief or summarized form; briefly.

pabusabos (pa-bu-sa-bos), *v.* to allow oneself to be treated like a slave. Syn. *paalipin.*

pabusisî (pa-bu-si-sî), *adj. & adv.* in a too meticulous manner. Syn. *pakutiltíl.*

pabuti (pa-bu-ti), *adj. & n.* referring to someone or something that tends to improve or make better.

pabuyà (pa-bu-yà), n. 1. tip given to a waiter, porter, etc. Syn. *tip.* 2. reward. Syn. *gantimpalà.* 3. gratification; recompense. Syn. *bigáy-palà, ganting-pagál.*

paká-, pref. used in forming verbs that express the idea of being too much or more than necessary, as in: *pakálayô,* to go too far; *pakátulinan,* to make too fast.

pakabíg (pa-ka-bíg), *adj. & adv.* towards oneself, as in: *hilahin nang pakabíg,* to pull towards oneself.

pakabutihin (pa-ka-bu-ti-hin), *v.* to do one's best; do or make (a thing) in the best way one can. Syn. *pakahusayin, pakagalingin.*

pakakak (pa-ka-kak), n. a kind of sound or noise producer, used by blowing with the mouth like a horn or trumpet. Cf. *tambulì.*

pakagát (pa-ka-gát), I. *v.* to allow oneself to be bitten, as by a dog.

—II. *adj. & adv.* by biting. Syn. *sa kagát, sa pamamagitan ng kagát o pagkagát.*

—III. n. (Fig.) something used as a lure; enticement.

pakain (pa-ka-in), I. *adj.* given or provided with free food. Syn. *may-pagkain, libré pagkain.*

—II. n. 1. fodder (for animals like carabaos, cows, etc.). 2. feed (for fowls).

Syn. *patukà, pamatukâ.* 3. act of giving fodder or feed to animals. Syn. pagpapakain. 4. time of feeding (animals). Syn. *oras ng pagpapakain.*

pákainín (pá-ka-i-nín), I. *adj.* referring to a person who relies on someone for support. —II. *n.* a dependent.

pakaingatan (pa-ka-i-nga-tan), *v.* to be very careful about.

pakaisipin (pa-ka-i-si-pin), *v.* to think deeply or seriously before finally deciding.

pakaliwâ (pa-ka-li-wâ), I. *v.* to turn or move to the left; opposed to *pakanan.* —II. *adj. & adv.* toward the left; going to the left.

pakanâ (pa-ka-nâ), *n.* 1. plot; evil scheme; conspiracy. Syn. *sápakatan, sábwatan, masamáng balak.* 2. trick; stratagem; scheme. Syn. *taktikâ.* 3. creation or intention to deceive. Syn. *laláng.*

pakanan (pa-ka-nan), *v.* to go, move, or turn to the right.

pakantá (pa-kan-tá), I. *adj.* referring to a song requested by someone. Syn. *paawit.* —II. *adj. & adv.* by singing or in a manner like singing. Syn. *paawit.*

pakapâ (pa-ka-pâ), I. *adj. & adv.* by groping; by feeling about blindly. —II. *v.* to allow oneself to be searched by someone. Syn. *pakapkáp.*

pakasál (pa-ka-sál), I. *v.* to marry or be married to someone; get married. Also, *magpakasál.* —II. *n.* 1. wedding celebration. Also, *kasalan.* 2. marriage fee. Syn. *bayad sa kasál.*

pakaskás (pa-kas-kás), *n.* a kind of sugar cake made from *tuba* (buri palm juice) and coconut milk with little salt, usually poured into a small, shallow *buri* leaf container where it is molded before marketing.

pakaw (pa-kaw), *n.* 1. hook or clasp, as of an earring. Syn. *kawit, kalawit.* 2. a hoop or ring attached to the nose of an animal. Syn. *tagikaw.* 3. bolt or bar for locking a door, window, etc. Syn. *barál, tarangká.*

pakay (pa-kay), *n.* purpose or aim. Syn. *layon, layunin.* 2. errand; mission. Syn. *sadyâ.*

pakbet (pak-bet), *n.* (Ilok.) a kind o vegetable dish popular among th Ilocanos. Cf. *bulangláng.*

pakete (pa-ke-te), *n.* (Sp. *paquete*) packag Syn. *kaha, kartón.*

pakí (pa-kí), *n.* (Slang) 1. short for *pakialam* interference or meddling in other's affair or business, as in: *walâ kang pakí* you hav no business or right to interfere or medd with. 2. short for *pakiusap* or *pakisuy* please or kindly do this for me.

paki- (pa-ki-), *pref.* used in forming (a nouns denoting a request for favor asked as in: *pakisuyo,* a request or favor asked (b) adjectives referring to somethin requested, as in: *pakibilí,* bought o someone's request. (c) verbs, suffixed wit *an, han, in,* or *hin,* meaning please or b obliging enough to, as in: *pakikuha,* pleas get; *pakitawagan,* please call someone *pakisamahan sa,* please accompany to *pakidalhín,* please bring.

pakialám (pa-ki-a-lám), *n.* an interfering o meddling. Also, *pakikialám.*

pakiki- (pa-ki-ki), *pref.* used in formin nouns denoting (a) cooperation, as in *pakikisama* (comradeship). (b sympathetic feeling, as in: *pakikiramay pakikidalamhatí.* (c) request or specia favor, as in *pakikisuyò, pakikiusap.*

pakikiapíd (pa-ki-ki-a-píd), *n.* adultery concubinage. Syn. *pakikilaguyò.*

pakikibaka (pa-ki-ki-ba-ka), *n.* 1. a campaign against something evil. Syn *pakikilaban o pakikipaglaban sa masama.* 2 participation in a war or battle. Syn *pakikidigmâ.*

pakikibagay (pa-ki-ki-ba-gay), *n.* act o acting in harmony or in compatibility with another or others. Syn. *pakikisama pakikiisá.*

pakikidalamhatì (pa-ki-ki-da-lam-ha-tì), *n.* expression of one's sympathy or condolence to someone who has lost a loved one. Syn. *pakikiramay.*

pakikilaguyò (pa-ki-ki-la-gu-yò), *n.* adultery; concubinage. Syn. *pakikiapíd.*

pakikinabang (pa-ki-ki-na-bang), *n.* 1. prospect of gaining something, as from one's work or investment. Syn. *pagtutubò.*

2. act of sharing in the Lord's supper, as by taking Communion. Syn. *pagkokomunyón*.

akikipágbakasakalì (pa-ki-ki-pág-ba-ka-sa-ka-lì), n. act of taking a chance or risk. Also, *pagbabakásakalì*. Syn. *pakikipágsápalarán*.

akikipágbálitaktakan (pa-ki-ki-pág-bá-li-tak-ta-kan), n. act of engaging another or others in an angry or heated debate.

akikipágkapwà (pa-ki-ki-pág-kap-wà), n. act of maintaining friendly relations with another or others.

akikipág-íbigan (pa-ki-ki-pág + í-bi-gan), n. a person's love affair with another. Syn. *pakikipágmáhalan*.

akikipáglibíng (pa-ki-ki-pág-li-bíng), n. act of joining or going with the funeral of someone.

akikipágsiyám (pa-ki-ki-pág-si-yám), n. act of attending or participating in a nine-day novena.

akikiramay (pa-ki-ki-ra-may), var. pakikidamay, n. 1. sharing of sympathy with someone; expression of condolence. 2. act of helping another or others. Syn. *pagtulong, pagdamay*.

akikisama (pa-ki-ki-sa-ma), n. 1. act of living with another or others in the same room or house. Syn. *pakikipisan, pakikisunò*. 2. act of living with someone, as a man with his common-law wife. 3. manner or attitude of getting along with people. Syn. *pakikipágkapwà, pakikipagkapwà-tao*.

akikiusap (pa-ki-ki-u-sap), n. act of requesting a favor from someone. Syn. *pakikisuyò*.

akimkím (pa-kim-kím), I. n. money or gift given to a godchild by his/her godparent(s) after the baptism or confirmation.
—II. *adj.* referring to something given as a gift to one's godchild after baptism or confirmation.
—III. *adv. & adj.* with one's close hand.

akinabang (pa-ki-na-bang), n. 1. interest, as of money deposited in a bank. Syn. *tubò*. 2. gain or profit, as from business or capital investment. Syn. *tubò*. 3. benefit; advantage. Syn. *palà, kabutihan, pama*. 4.

(P-) Holy Communion. Syn. *komunyòn, pangongomunyón*.

pakipkíp (pa-kip-kíp), I. n. present or gift given by a godparent to his/her newly baptized or confirmed godchild. Syn. *pakimkím*.
—II. *adj. & adv.* by holding closely under one's arms.

pakipot (pa-ki-pot), n. (*Slang*) pretended dislike for something.

pakiramdám (pa-ki-ram-dám), n. 1. feeling; sense of feeling. Syn. *damá, pandamá*. 2. sensation (physical or sensual). Syn. *damdám*. 3. perception. Syn. *hiwatig, pagkahiwatig*.

pakiskis (pa-kis-kis), I. n. & *adj.* referring to unhusked rice (*palay*) ordered or requested to be milled Syn. *pagiling*.
—II. *adj. & adv.* by rubbing or grazing against something.

pakisláp (pa-kis-láp), n. & *adj.* that which is used to make a thing glitter. Also, *pampakisláp*.

pakita (pa-ki-ta), I. *v.* to appear or show up in the presence of someone.
—II. n. 1. display; sample in an exhibit. Syn. *muwestra*. 2. a sample showing of a coming picture or film. 3. a showing off. Syn. *pasikat, pagpapasikat* (*fig.*).

pakitang-gilas (pa-ki-tang + gi-las), n. a showing off; vain display. Syn. *pasikat, pagpapasikat; parangyâ, pagpaparangyâ*.

pakitang-loób (pa-ki-tang + lo-ób), n. 1. show of kindness, good will, or concern. Syn. *kagandahang-loób, kabutihan, malasakit*. 2. pretended goodwill or concern. Syn. *pakunwaríng pagmamalasakit o kabutihan*.

pakitang-tao (pa-ki-tang + ta-o), n. 1. hypocrisy; pretense. Syn. *pagkukunyarî*. 2. ostentation; showiness; boastful exhibition. Syn. *pagmamarangyâ, pagpapasikat, paghahambóg*.

pakiusap (pa-ki-u-sap), n. 1. request for favor. Syn. *pakisuyò*. 2. appeal; entreaty. Syn. *samo, pamanhík*.

pakiwari (pa-ki-wa-ri), n. vague thought or idea; notion. Syn. *palá-palagáy, hinagap*.

pakla (pak-la), n. 1. acridity in taste, esp. of immature fruits like guava. 2. painfulness or bitterness to someone's feeling. Syn. *sakláp, kasaklapán.*

paklí (pak-lí), n. 1. answer; reply. Syn. *sagot, tugon.* 2. retort; repartée. Syn. *ganting-sagót.* 3. rebuttal; refutation; objection. Syn. *tutol, pasubalì.*

paknit (pak-nit), I. *adj.* 1. forcibly detached, referring to something pasted, glued, etc. Also, *napaknit.* 2. peeled off, as the bark of a tree. Syn. *tukláp, natukláp.*
—II. n. 1. act of detaching or peeling off something forcibly. Syn. *pagpaknit, pagtukláp.* 2. state or condition of being detached or peeled off forcibly. Syn. *pagpaknit, pagkatukláp.* 3. the part or portion from which something has been forcibly detached or peeled off.

paknót (pak-nót), I. *adj.* totally devoid of growth, as a head, top of a mountain, etc.; denuded. Syn. *panót.*
—II. n. 1. state or condition of being denuded or devoid of growth. Syn. *pagkapaknót, pagpanot.* 2. the part or portion that has been denuded or devoid of growth. Syn. *panot.*

pakò (pa-kò), n. 1. nail. 2. act or manner of fastening something with a nail or nails. Syn. *pagpako, pagkakapako.*

pakô (pa-kô), n. (Bot.) fern.

pakpák (pak-pák), n. 1. wing (in general). 2. any of the big feathers that cover the wings of birds and domestic fowls. Syn. *bagwis.*

pakrús (pa-krús), I. *adv.* crosswise; in the form of a cross.
—II. n. (Carp.) crosspiece.

paksâ (pak-sâ), n. 1. topic; subject; theme, as of one's speech. Syn. *tema.* 2. object; aim; purpose. Syn. *layon, láyunin.*

paksíw (pak-síw), I. n. a dish of fish or meat cooked in vinegar with salt and ginger or garlic. Also called *pinaksíw.*
—II. *adj.* cooked in vinegar with salt and ginger or garlic.

paktura (pak-tu-ra), n. (Sp. *factura*) 1. invoice; bill of lading. 2. price list. Syn. *tálaan ng mga presyo o halagá.* 3. market price. Syn. *halaga o presyo sa pamilihan.*

pakulô (pa-ku-lô), n. (Slang) a bragging or boasting. Syn. *pasikat, pagpapasikat.*

pakumahog (pa-ku-ma-hog), *adj.* & *adv.* in a hurry. Syn. *nagmámadalî, nag-áapurá.*

pakumbabâ (pa-kum-ba-bâ), I. n. humbleness; humility. Syn. *kababaang loób.*
—II. *adv.* in a humble manner; humbly; with humility.

pakundangan (pa-kun-da-ngan), n. respect; courteous regard for. Syn. *paggalang, pitagan, pamimitagan, respeto.*

pakunsuwelo (pa-kun-su-we-lo), n. & *adj.* referring to something given in order to give comfort or consolation to someone.

pakunwâ (pa-kun-wâ), var. **pakunwarî**, I. *adj.* simulated; pretended; disguised; feigned.
—II. *adv.* simulatedly; in a pretended or disguised manner.

pakupás (pa-ku-pás), *adj.* 1. fading, referring to colors. 2. waning or fading out, as strength, popularity, etc. Syn. *palipás.*

pakupyâ (pa-kup-yâ), *adj.* (Gram.) circumflex; marked with a circumflex accent.

pakusâ (pa-ku-sa), I. *adj.* voluntary; intentional. Syn. *sinadyâ, tinikis.*
—II. *adv.* voluntarily; intentionally.

pakutyâ (pa-kut-ya), *adj.* & *adv.* by making sarcastic remarks. Syn. *patuyâ, pauyám.*

pakwán (pak-wán), n. (Bot.) water-melon plant (*Citrullus vulgaris Schrad.*), the fruit of this plant.

pakyáw (pak-yáw), I. n. 1. wholesale buying or purchase. 2. contract labor, as in building a house.
—II. *adj.* 1. bought or purchased by wholesale. 2. undertaken or being undertaken by contract.

padabóg (pa-da-bóg), *adj.* & *adv.* in a sulky manner accompanied by stamping the feet.

padakilain (pa-da-ki-la-in), v. to make great.

padako (pa-da-ko), I. v. to go towards a certain place.
—II. *prep.* toward; towards; in the direction of.

padahan-dahan (pa-da-han + da-han), *adj.* & *adv.* in a slow manner.

padaíg (pa-da-íg), v. to allow oneself to be surpassed, beaten, etc. Syn. *pahigit,* *palampas, patalo, pasupil, pagapì.*

padaíng (pa-da-íng), *adv.* 1. in a groaning voice. Syn. *pahaluyhóy.* 2. in a pleading voice. Syn. *pasamô.*

padalá (pa-da-lá), I. *n.* 1. act of sending a letter, etc., as by mail. Syn. *pahatid, pagpapahatid.* 2. anything sent by someone to another. Syn. *pahatid.*
—II. *adj.* sent (by someone). Syn. *pahatid.*
—III. *v.* 1. to allow oneself to be brought to a certain person or place. Syn. *pahatid.* 2. (*Fig.*) to allow oneself to be carried away, as by one's emotion.

padaláng (pa-da-láng), *adj.* decreasing in number; getting fewer.

padalíin (pa-da-li-ín), *v.* to make easier or faster to do. Syn. *paalwanin, paginhawahin.*

padalus-dalos (pa-da-lus + da-los), I. *adj.* done hurriedly and carelessly. Syn. *pawardi-wardi.*
—II. *adv.* hastily; rashly; in haste, in a hurried, careless manner.

padaluyán (pa-da-lu-yán), *n.* 1. drain or a system of drains; conduit. Syn. *páagusán.* 2. canal; ditch. Syn. *bambáng, kanál.* 3. gutter. Syn. *alulód.*

padamá (pa-da-má), *n. & adj.* (fr. *dama*) referring to an act or gesture tending to convey something indirectly to someone.

padamdám (pa-dam-dám), *var.* **paramdám**, *n. & adj.* referring to something said or done to give a hint or insinuation to someone. Cf. *pahiwatig, padamá.*

padapuan (pa-da-pu-an), *v.* to let something be alighted on, as by a fly, bird, etc. Syn. *pahapunan.*

padarág (pa-da-rág), *adj. & adv.* in or with an angry voice, usually accompanied by the stamping of feet. Cf. *padabóg.*

padasál (pa-da-sál), *var.* **parasál**, I. *n.* prayers or a novena offered for the soul of the dead or for a certain occasion.
—II. *adv.* by praying; in a prayerful manner.

padaskól (pa-das-kól), I. *adj.* done hastily and carelessly.
—II. *adv.* carelessly and hastily; in a careless, hasty manner.

padatingán (pa-da-ti-ngán), *var.* **paratingán**, *v.* 1. to bribe; give someone a bribe. 2. to

leave something in a certain place or condition in order to be seen by someone arriving. Also, *padatnan (paratnan).*

padaúp-palad (pa-da-úp + pa-lad), *adj. & adv.* with one's hands or palms clasped together.

padér (pa-dér), *n.* (Sp. *pared*) stone wall or fence.

padilát (pa-di-lát), *adj. & adv.* with wide-open eyes.

padipá (pa-di-pá), *var.* **paripá**, *adj. & adv.* with the arms stretched out sidewise.

padpád (pad-pád), I. *n.* 1. a shipwreck. Syn. *labí ng bapór na nawasak sa dagat.* 2. a person or thing saved from a wrecked ship. 3. a being blown away by the wind. 4. (by extension) a non-native resident in a place. Syn. *dayo, dayuhan.*
—II. *adj.* 1. cast ashore from a wreck, referring to persons or things. 2. non-native of a place. Syn. *dayuhan.*

padastro (pa-das-tro), *n.* (*Sp.*) stepfather. Syn. *amang-pangumán, tiyuhin.*

padre (pa-dre), *n.* (*Sp.*) 1. priest. Syn. *pare.* 2. (as a title in addressing a priest) Father. 3. used colloquially for *kumpadre.*

padrino (pa-dri-no) *n.* (*Sp.*) 1. male sponsor in baptism, confirmation, or wedding; godfather. Syn. *ninong; inaamá sa binyág, sa kumpil, o sa kasál.* 2. an influential person to whom one approaches for help in obtaining choice position, etc.

padrón (pa-dron), *n.* (*Sp.*) pattern; cut design used by tailors and dressmakers.

padugô (pa-du-gô), I. *n.* 1. bloodletting. 2. something used by or given to someone to increase the volume of his blood. Also, *pampadugô.* 3. something taken to induce menses. Syn. *pamparegla.*
—II. *adj.* 1. that tends to increase the volume of blood. Syn. *pamaparagdág-dugô.* 2. that causes bleeding. 2. that induces menstruation. Syn. *pamparegla.*

padyák (pad-yák), *n.* 1. thump or thumping of feet, as in marching. 2. the sound of this thumping of foot or feet. 2. stamping of the foot or feet, as in anger. Cf. *tarang, pagtaráng.* 3. rhythmic stamping of the foot or feet, as in dancing.

paekes-ekes (pa-e-kes + e-kes), *var.* **paekis-**

.ekis, *adv.* in a zigsag way or manner; waveringly; unsteadily, as in: *lumakad nang paekes-ekes*, to walk unsteadily. Cf. *pahapay-hapay*, *paese-ese*.

paeksamin (pa-ek-sa-min), var. **paiksamin**, I. *v.* to submit oneself to a medical or physical examination. Also, *magpaeksamen* (*magpaiksamin*).

—II. *n.* 1. act of submitting oneself to a medical or physical examination. Also, *pagpapaeksamin*, *pagpapaiksamin*. 2. the ordinary fee charged by a doctor in conducting such an examination. 3. test or examination being given by a teacher to his/her students. 4. a competitive or qualifying examination, as that given by the Civil Service Commission.

paekstra-ekstra (pa-eks-tra + eks-tra), *adj.* without permanent work; often hired as a casual or temporary worker.

pag (pag), *conj.* if; in case that. Syn. *kung*, *kapag*. 2. when; at any time that. Syn. *pagka*, *kapág*.

pag- (pag-), *pref.* used to form (a) verbal nouns from roots, as in: *pagdating*, arrival; *pag-alis*, departure; *pagtulog*, act of sleeping. etc. (b) verbal nouns that express act or manner of doing a thing, with the first syllable of the root duplicated, as in: *pagsasalita*, act or manner of talking; *pagbabasá*, act or manner of reading, etc. (c) verbs suffixed with *–an* or *–han* and *–in* or *–hin*, as in: *pag-aralan*, to study; *pagpasiyahán*, to decide; or render a decision on.

pagâ (pa-gâ), I. *adj.* swollen. Also, *namamagâ*.

—II. *n.* 1. state or condition of being swollen. Also, *pamamagâ*. 2. a swollen part or portion of the body; swelling. Cf. *bukol*, *umbók*.

pag-aagaw-buhay (pag + a-a-gaw + bu – hay), *n.* a hovering between life and death; state or condition of being in death throes. Syn. *paghihingaló*.

pag-aagaw-dilim (pag + a-a-gaw + di-lim), *n.* the time just before dark; dusk. Syn. *takipsilim*.

pag-aagaw-liwanag (pag + a-agaw + li-wa-nag), *n.* dawn; twilight. Syn. *bukáng-liwaywáy*.

pag-aagaw-tulog (pag + a-a-gaw + tu-log), *n.* state or condition of being half-awake or half-asleep.

pag-aaláala (pag + a-a-lá-a-lá), *n.* worry; anxiety; uneasy feeling about something. Syn. *pagkabahalà*, *pagkabalisa*, *di-pagkapalagáy*.

pag-aalab (pag + a-a-lab), *n.* a being aflame or in fire. Syn. *pagningingas*, *pagliliyáb*. 2. a being greatly aroused, as with anger. Syn. *pagngingitngít*.

pag-aalagà (pag + a-a-la-gà), *n.* 1. act of taking care, as of patient, a child, etc. 2. act of being careful, as of one's health. Syn. *pag-iingat*. 3. raising or breeding, as of animals.

pag-aalang-alang (pag + a-a-lang + a-lang), *n.* consideration or respect, as for elders. Syn. *pagbipítagan*.

pag-aalangán (pag + a-a-la-ngán), *n.* vacillation; irresolution; indecision. Also, *pag-aalanganin*. Syn. *pag-aatubilí*, *pag-uurong-sulong*.

pag-aalay (pag + a-a-lay), *n.* act of offering or dedicating something to someone. Syn. *paghahandóg*.

pag-aalinlangan (pag + a-a-lin-la-ngan), *n.* doubt; entertainment of doubt. Syn. *duda*, *pagdududa*.

pag-aalíw (pag + a-a-líw), *n.* taking one's time to have recreation or amusement. Syn. *paglilibáng*.

pag-aalmusál (pag + a-al-mu-sál), var. **pag-aamusal**, *n.* act or time of eating one's breakfast. Syn. *pag-aagahan*, *pagkain ng agahan o almusál*.

pag-aalsá (pag + a-al-sá), *n.* 1. a rising in revolt; rebellion. Syn. *pagbabangon*. 2. declaration of a labor strike; refusal of workers to return to work for the failure of the management to give their demands. Syn. *pagwewelga*. 3. the act of lifting or raising a heavy weight, as with a lever or a system of pulleys. Syn. *pagtataás*, *pang-aangát*.

pagaán (pa-ga-án), I. *adj.* getting lighter; decreasing in weight.

—II. something that tends to reduce weight. Also, *pampagaán*.

pag-aanák (pag + a-a-nák), n. 1. giving birth to a child or children. Also, *panganganák, pagkakaanák*. 2. the act of standing as a sponsor in a wedding, baptism, or confirmation. Syn. *pagnininong, pagnininang*.

pag-aapóy (pag + a-a-póy), n. 1. act of building a fire. 2. a bursting into flame. Syn. *pagdidingas, pagliliyáb*. 3. a becoming very hot, as with fever. Syn. *pag-iinit na lubha*. 4. a becoming very intense, as with anger. Syn. *pagngingitngit*.

pag-aapurá (pag + a-a-pu-rá), n. 1. act of urging someone to hurry up. 2. act of moving fast, as in going to a certain place or destination. Syn. *pagmamadalì*. 3. act of doing something in a hurry. Syn. *pagdadali-dalì*.

pag-aaral (pag + a-a-ral), n. 1. act of going to school, as a student. Syn. *pagpasok sa paaralán*. 2. act of studying one's lesson in a class. 3. act of learning how something is to be done or made. 4. critical investigation or examination of. Syn. *pagsusuring mabuti*.

pag-aarì (pag + a-a-rì), n. 1. property or possession. Also, *arì, ari-ariaǹ*. 2. act of acquiring or possessing something as one's own; owning. Also, *pagmamay-arì*.

pag-aárimuhanán (pag + a-á-ri-mu-ha-nán), var. **pag-aarimuhunan**, n. avoidance of waste by careful planning and use; economy. Syn. *pagtitipid*.

pag-aasal-hayop (pag + a-a-sal + ha-yop), n. the act of behaving like a beast. Syn. *pag-uugaling-hayop*.

pag-aasawa (pag + a-a-sa-wa), n. act of getting married. Syn. *pagpapakasál*.

pag-aatang (pag + a-a-tang), n. act of helping another in putting a load on the head or shoulder.

pag-aatas (pag + a-a-tas), n. act of giving instructions or orders to someone. Syn. *pag-uutos*.

pag-aáwitan (pag + a-á-wi-tan), n. act of singing together or at the same time. Syn. *pagkakántahan*.

pag-abante (pag + a-ban-te), n. 1. act of moving forward. Syn. *pagsulong, paglakad*. 2. act of gaining advantage in score against one's opponent, as in basketball,

etc. Syn. *paglamáng*. 3. the possibility, as of supplies, to last up to a certain time. Syn. *pagsapát, paghuhusto*.

pag-abutan (pag + a-bu-tan), v. to be left unused until new ones are supplied.

pag-abutin (pag + a-bu-tin), v. 1. (with *ang kinikita*) to make both ends meet. 2. to make both ends touch each other. 3. to cause two persons to meet each other unexpectedly.

pagák (pa-gák), I. *adj.* rough and husky, referring to voice.
—II. n. the sound of a rough and husky voice; any similar sound.

pag-akay (pag + a-kay), n. 1. act of guiding or leading someone by holding the hand. 2. moral guidance. Syn. *pagpapatnubay*.

pag-akdâ (pag + ak-dâ), n. act of writing a story, novel, poem, or the like.

pag-akit (pag + a-kit), n. 1. act of charming or attracting someone, as by one's beauty. Syn. *paghalina, pagbighanì*. 2. act of inducing or persuading someone to join in something. Syn. *paghikayat*.

pag-akó (pag + a-kó), n. 1. act of assuming the responsibility of someone's duty. Syn. *pag-akín*. 2. confession or admission, as of one's guilt. Syn. *pag-amin*.

pag-akyát (pag + ak-yát), n. 1. act or time of going upstairs. Syn. *pagpanhik*. 2. act or manner of climbing a tree. Syn. *pagadyó*. 3. act or manner of climbing or ascending (a slope). Syn. *pag-ahon*. 3. rise or increase in height. Syn. *pagtaas*. 5. rise or promotion, as in rank or position. Syn. *pag-asenso, pagtaás*.

pagahís (pa-ga-hís), v. 1. to allow oneself to be subdued or conquered. Syn. *palupig*. 2. to allow oneself to be raped. Syn. *pagahasà*.

pagál (pa-gál), I. *adj.* tired; fatigued. Syn. *pagod, napápagod*.
—II. n. 1. trouble or delay incurred in doing something. Syn. *abala*. 2. fatigue or tiredness in doing something. Syn. *pagod, pagkapagod*.

pagalà (pa-ga-là), I. *adj.* 1. stray or wandering, referring esp. to domestic animals. Syn. *ligaw, kawala, alpas*. 2. given to wandering or roving around. Syn. *libot,*

pagalakin

pag-apulà

palibut-libot, lagalág.

—II. n. 1. a rover; wanderer; vagrant. Syn. lagalág, layás, palayas. 2. (Ornith.) pelican (bird).

pagalakin (pa-ga-la-kin), v. to make someone happy.

pagalá-galà (pa-ga-lá + ga-là), adj. moving from place to place; wandering; roving. Syn. pagalà, palibot, palibut-libot. 2. nomadic, said of some tribes. Syn. lagalág.

pag-alinlanganan (pag + a-lin-la-nga-nan), v. to doubt; have a doubt about. Syn. pagdudahan.

pag-alintana (pag + a-lin-ta-na), n. 1. a minding, as of one's health. Syn. pagasikaso. 2. act of taking notice about something. Syn. pagpansín. 3. feeling of being hurt or slighted, as by someone's remark. Syn. pagdamdám, pagdaramdám.

págalingan (pá-ga-li-ngan), n. 1. a contest or competition of ability to do something. Syn. pahusayán. 2. recovery room or ward.

pagalít (pa-ga-lít), adv. in an angry manner; angrily.

pag-aliw (pag + a-liw), n. act of entertaining or amusing someone. Syn. paglibáng.

pagalugad (pa-ga-lu-gad), adj. & adv. by searching all over a certain place.

pag-amin (pag + a-min), n. confession or admission of one's guilt. Syn. pagtatapát (ng kasalanan).

pagamit (pa-ga-mit), I. adj. provided or supplied with tools, instruments, supplies, furniture, etc. Syn. pakasangkapan.

—II, v. to allow oneself to be used as a tool by someone. Syn. pakasangkapan.

pag-amot (pag + a-mot), n. act of requesting someone to share a small part or portion of something he bought.

pagamutan (pa-ga-mu-tan), n. 1. medical clinic; dispensary. Syn. klíniká, dispensaryo. 2. infirmary; hospital. Syn. impirmarya, hospitál (ospitál).

pagana (pa-ga-na), I. n. 1. the regular or standard wage given to workers. Syn. pasahod. 2. appetizer. Also, pampagana.

—II. adj. that stimulates appetite. Also, pampagana.

paganapin (pa-ga-na-pin), v. 1. to let or allow someone to perform a certain

function. Syn. patuparin, papanungkulin. 2. to assign a person to perform a certain role, as in a drama. Syn. papágpapelin.

pag-aninaw (pag + a-ni-naw), n. act of trying to see something through haze.

paganitó (pa-ga-ni-tó), adj. & adv. 1. in this way or manner. 2. like this.

paganiyán (pa-ga-ni-yán), var. paganyan, adj. & adv. in that way or manner (referring to procedure being done by someone who is being pointed by the speaker). 2. like that (referring to something near the person addressed).

pagano (pa-ga-no), I. adj. (Sp.) pagan; heathen; not Christian. Syn. hindi Kristiyano, di-binyagan.

—II. n. pagan; one who worships false goods. Syn. taong di-binyagan.

paganoon (pa-ga-no-on), adj. & adv. 1. in that way or manner (referring to something far from both the person addressed and the speaker). 2. like that (referring to something far from the speaker and the person addressed).

pagáng (pa-gáng), I. adj. 1. too dry, referring esp. to rice cooked too long over live coals. Cf. tigang. 2. tired and bored, as from long waiting.

—II. n. state or condition of being too dry, referring esp. to rice cooked too long over live coals.

pag-angkóp (pag + ang-kóp), n. act of adapting or fitting oneself to a certain condition or requirement. Syn. pagbagay, pakikibagay.

pagapáng (pa-ga-páng), adj. & adv. by creeping or crawling; in a creeping or crawling manner.

pag-apaw (pag + a-paw), n. 1. overflow of water, as from a river. Syn. pagbahâ. 2. a flowing over the rim of a container. Syn. pagsobra, paglabis. 3. a becoming overcrowded, as with people. Syn. pagkapunó o pagkasiksik na mabuti.

pagapì (pa-ga-pì), v. to allow oneself to be defeated or subdued. Syn. palupig, patalo, padaig.

pag-apulà (pag + a-pu-là), n. act of stopping or checking the progress or spread, as of something harmful. Syn. pagsugpo, pagpigil.

págaraán (pá-ga-ra-án), n. 1. competition in the manner of dressing. Syn. *pákisigán*. 2. contest in stateliness or pomposity. Syn. *paringalan*.

pag-arók (pag + a-rók), n. act of sounding the depth of. Syn. *pagtarók*.

pagás (pa-gás), adj. hoarse or husky, referring to voice. Syn. *paós, namámaos; pagáw, namámagaw*.

pag-asa (pag + a-sa), n. 1. hope; feeling that what one is dreaming about would be realized, as in: *Hindi pa siya nawáwalán ng pag-asa*. He has not yet lost hope. 2. expectation; anticipation. Syn. *inaasahan*. 3. source of hope, or someone from whom something may be hoped for. 4. reliance on someone or something.

pag-asám (pag + a-sám), n. expectation or anticipation of something wholesome or enjoyable. Syn. *pananabik*.

pagaspás (pa-gas-pás), n. 1. flapping or shaking, as of wings. 2. a fluttering movement or shaking, as of a flag atop a pole. Syn. *pagaypáy, wagaywáy, wasiwas*. 3. the flapping sound as that made by wings.

pag-atrás (pag + a-trás), n. 1. act of moving backward, as of a vehicle. Syn. *pag-urong*. 2. retreat; act of withdrawing or going back, as of an army in defeat. Syn. *pagbalík, pag-urong*. 3. a backing out, as from one's promise.

pag-atupag (pag + a-tu-pag), n. act of attending to one's work diligently; serious attention given to something being done. Syn. *pag-asikaso*.

pagáw (pa-gáw), adj. 1. hoarse or husky, referring to voice. 2. with or having hoarse or husky voice, referring to a person. Syn. *paós, namámaos; malát, namamalát*.

pagawaan (pa-ga-wa-an), n. factory; manufacturing plant. Syn. *pábrika*.

pagawaran (pa-ga-wa-ran), v. to order the awarding of honor or reward to. Syn. *pabigyán*.

pag-awas (pag + a-was), n. overflow or overflowing, as of liquid from a container. Syn. *pagsobra, paglabis, pag-apaw*.

pag-awat (pag + a-wat), n. 1. act of separating or pacifying two or more persons engaged in a quarrel or fight. 2. act of weaning a child. Syn. *pagwawalay sa (pagsuso sa) ina*.

pag-away (pag + a-way), n. act of starting or provoking a fight or quarrel with another.

pag-awit (pag + a-wit), n. 1. act or manner of singing. Syn. *pagkanta*. 2. one's turn in singing.

pag-ayáw (pag + a-yáw), n. 1. refusal to fight; a running away from a fight. Syn. *dipaglaban; pag-urong sa laban*. 2. refusal to accept (a bribe, gift, offer, etc.). Syn. *pagtanggí sa ibinibigáy*. 3. a backing out, as from an agreement. Syn. *pagtatalusirà, pakikipagtalusirà*.

pag-ayáw-ayawin (pag + a-yáw + a-ya-win), v. to divide or distribute proportionally among a number of persons or things.

pag-ayon (pag + a-yon), n. 1. willingness or readiness to agree. Syn. *pag-sang-ayon, pagpayag*. 2. compliance in accordance with the rules, laws, agreement, etc. Syn. *pag-alinsunod*. 3. fact of placing oneself in a parallel position with another. Syn. *pag-agapay*.

pagayón (pa-ga-yón), adj. & adv. 1. in that way or manner. 2. like that.

pagaypáy (pa-gay-páy), n. flapping of wings; shaking of leaves being blown by the wind. Syn. *pagaspás*.

pagayún-gayón (pa-ga-yun + ga-yon), adj. doing nothing; idle; lazy; indolent. Syn. *waláng-ginágawa, tamád, batugan*.

pagbabâ (pag-ba-bâ), n. 1. act of going down the stairs. Syn. *pagpanaog*. 2. act of alighting or getting down, as from a vehicle. Syn. *paglunsád, pag-ibís, pagpanaog*. 3. act or manner of landing, as of an airplane. Syn. *paglapág*. 4. act of going down a slope. Syn. *paglusong*. 5. decrease, as of prices. Syn. *pagmura*. 6. decrease or becoming lower, as temperature or fever. Syn. *paghulaw, pagbabawa*.

pagbabakásakalì (pag-ba-ba-ka-sa-ka-lì), n. act of taking a chance or chances. Syn. *pakikipagsápalaran*.

pagbabaga (pag-ba-ba-ga), n. a becoming aglow or red-hot, as a result of great heat or fire. Syn. *pamumulá sa init.*

pagbabago (pag-ba-ba-go), n. 1. change. Syn. *pagpapalít.* 2. renewal. 3. an amending or being amended; amendment. Syn. *pagsususog.* 4. reform; reformation; improvement. Syn. *pagpapabuti, reporma.*

pagbabagong-buhay (pag-ba-ba-gong + bu-hay), n. 1. act of changing one's ways of life. Syn. *pagpapanibagong-buhay.* 2. reincarnation.

pagbabagong-loób (pag-ba-ba-gong + lo-ób), n. change of heart, mind, affection, etc.

pagbabagu-bago (pag-ba-ba-gu + ba-go), n. 1. frequent changing or revision. Syn. *pagpapalít-palít.* 2. frequent transfer or changing of place. Syn. *pagpapalipat-lipat.*

pagbabálagtasan (pag-ba-bá-lag-tasan), n. the encounter of two or more poets in a poetical debate or joust. Cf. *pagtatalo, pagkakátiwaranan.*

pagbabalangkás (pag-ba-ba-lang-kás), n. 1. formulation of a plan. Syn. *pagpaplano, pagbabalak.* 2. construction of the frame work of. Syn. *pagtatayô ng balangkás.* 3. conjugation, as of a verb or verbs. Syn. *pagbabangháy.*

pagbabalát (pag-ba-ba-lát), n. 1. act of peeling or trimming away the rind, skin, or covering of. Syn. *pagtatalop.* 2. act of providing with a cover, as a book. Syn. *pagpapabalat.* 3. growth or development of new skin. Syn. *pagkakaroón o pagtubo ng bagong balát.* 4. the shedding of skin or scales of snakes, crabs, and the like. Syn. *paghuhunos.* 5. act of dealing in leather or hides.

pagbabalát-kalabáw (pag-ba-ba-lát + ka-la-báw), n. insensitiveness to criticism, jokes, insult, etc.

pagbabalát-kayô (pag-ba-ba-lát + ka-yô), n. act or manner of disguising. 2. hypocrisy. Syn. *pagkukunwarî.*

pagbabalát-sibuyas (pag-ba-ba-lát + si-bu-yas), n. sensitiveness to criticism, jokes, insult, etc.

pagbabalík (pag-ba-ba-lík), n. 1. act of returning something a person borrowed from another. Syn. *pagsasaulí.* 2. a return to one's home. Syn. *pag-uwí.* 3. return to

the former state or condition. Syn. *pananag-ulì.* 4. act of returning something to its former place. Syn. *pagsasauli o paglalagáy sa dating lugár.*

pagbabálitaán (pag-ba-ba-li-ta-an), n. exchanging of news or information with each other or with one another.

pagbabálitaktakan (pag-ba-ba-li-tak-ta-kan), n. act or manner of exchanging heated arguments. Syn. *pagtatalo nang mainitán.*

pagbabatá (pag-ba-ba-tá), n. patient endurance of something hard or painful; bearing of pain, distress or injury; suffering Syn. *pagtitiis.*

pagbaka (pag-ba-ka-), n. act or manner of campaigning against something evil.

pagbakás (pag-ba-kás), n. 1. act of tracing or following the footsteps, trails, tracks, etc. of. Syn. *pagtalunton.* 2. the leaving of an imprint or mark on a surface. Syn. *pagmarka, pagmamarka.*

pagbagay (pag-ba-gay), n. act or manner of adapting oneself to certain condition, happening, etc.

pagbait (pag-ba-it), n. 1. a becoming tame or domesticated, referring to a wild animal. Syn. *pag-amò.* 2. change from being cruel to being good or kind. Syn. *pagbuti.*

pagbalangkás (pag-ba-lang-kás), n. 1. act of planning. 2. Syn. *pagplano, pagbabalak.* 2. (Const.) act or manner of constructing the framework of. Syn. *pagbabanghay.* 3. act of preparing the outline of. 4. (Gram.) act of conjugating; conjugation.

pagbalík (pag-ba-lík), n. 1. return to one's house, town, or country. Syn. *pag-uwi.* 2. act of retreating. Syn. *pag-urong.*

pagbalikat (pag-ba-li-kat), n. 1. act of taking or carrying something on one's shoulder. Syn. *pagpasán, pagpapadalá sa balikat.* 2. act of assuming the burden of. Also, *pagsasabalikat.*

pagbaligtád (pag-ba-lig-tád), n. 1. act of turning oneself upside-down. Syn. *pagtuwarik, pagsirko, pagtumbalík.* 2. act of reversing a decision, position, etc. Syn. *pagsaliwa.* 3. act of turning something inside-out, referring to a coat, jacket, etc.

pagbalong (pag-ba-long), n. the flow or coming out of water from the earth, as in a well or spring. Syn. *pagbukál*.

pagbangay (pag-ba-ngay), n. act of starting a quarrel or fight with another. Syn. *pag-away*.

pagbangháy (pag-bang-háy), n. 1. act of making an outline of. Syn. *pagguhit ng balangkas*. 2. act of making a rough draft of. Syn. *pagbuburador, paggawa ng burador*. 3. act of constructing the framework of. Syn. *pagbanglakas, pagbabanglangkas*. 4. (*Gram*.) act of conjugating; conjugation. Syn. *pagbalangkas*. 5. construction, as of a sentence. Syn. *pagbuo, paggawa*.

pagbasa (pag-ba-sa), n. act or manner of reading something.

pagbatá (pag-ba-tá), n. patient endurance; ability to suffer or endure something hard, painful, etc. Syn. *pagtiis, pag-agwanta*.

pagbatà (pag-ba-tà), n. 1. a becoming young or younger (in appearance). Syn. *pagmumukháng batà*. 2. act of sponsoring someone as a candidate. Syn. *pagmamanók* (*fig*.).

pagbatì (pag-ba-tì), n. act of beating or mixing something with or as with a beater.

pagbatikos (pag-ba-ti-kos), n. act or manner of attacking another verbally. Syn. *pagtuligsâ*.

pagbawì (pag-ba-wì), n. 1. retraction, as of one's statement, promise, etc. Syn. *pag-uurong*. 2. getting back or recall of what one has given to another. Syn. *pagkuhang mulî*. 3. retaliation of one's defeat or loss, as in boxing, basketball, and the like. 4. regain, as of one's loss in gambling.

pagbayaran (pag-ba-ya-ran), v. 1. to pay for (something one bought). 2. to recompense, as for one's sin or crime.

pagbaybáy (pag-bay-báy), n. 1. act of spelling a word or words. 2. act of passing along the border or side of a road, seashore, river, etc. Syn. *pamamaybáy*. 3. act of mentioning one by one; enumeration. Syn. *pag-isa-isá*.

pagbibigáy (pag-bi-bi-gáy), n. 1. act of giving or handing over something to someone. Syn. *pag-aabót*. 2. act of bestowing or awarding something to someone. Syn.

pagkakaloób, paggagawad. 3. act of giving in to someone's request or desire as a friendly gesture or as a matter of pity.

pagbibigáy-dangál (pag-bi-bi-gáy + da-ngál), n. act of giving honor, as to one's country, by doing something great.

pagbibigáy-galang (pag-bi-bi-gáy + ga-lang), n. act or manner of paying respect to someone.

pagbibigáy-loób (pag-bi-bi-gáy + lo-ób), n. act of giving into someone's request, desire, etc. in order to please or as a gesture of friendship.

pagbibimbín (pag-bi-bim-bín), n. act of delaying action on something.

pagbibintáng (pag-bi-bin-táng), n. act of accusing someone. Syn. *pagpaparatang*.

pagbibinyág (pag-bi-bin-yág), n. 1. act of baptizing a person. 2. act of giving someone a nickname.

pagbibitíw (pag-bi-bi-tíw), n. 1. resignation from one's office or position. Syn. *pagdidimití*. 2. act or manner of releasing one's hold on something.

pagbidahan (pag-bi-da-han), v. to narrate a story or stories to. Syn. *pagkuwentuhán*.

pagbigkás (pag-big-kas), n. 1. act or manner of pronouncing a word or words. 2. delivery, as of a poem, speech, etc.

pagbigyán (pag-big-yán), v. 1. to give someone a chance. Syn. *bigyán o pagkaloobaːn ng pagkakátaón*. 2. to give in to someone's request as a gesture of friendship or out of pity.

pagbilís (pag-bi-lís), n. increase in speed or velocity. Syn. *pagtulin*.

pagbimbín (pag-bim-bín), n. act of delaying something unnecessarily. Syn. *pag-atraso*.

pagbitay (pag-bi-tay), n. execution; putting someone to death by hanging or by electrocution.

pagbubukáng-liwaywáy (pag-bu-bu-kang + li-way-way), n. the beginning of dawn or daybreak.

pagbubuklód (pag-bu-buk-lód), n. 1. act of providing the handle of a bolo, knife, and the like with a metal ring reinforcement. Syn. *pagsasalita, pagbabalangkat*. 2. act of unifying two or more groups. Syn. *pag-iisa*. 3. act of joining a man and a woman in marriage. Syn. *pagkakasál*.

pagbubuhay- (pag-bu-bu-hay +), a combining form, meaning act of living a certain way of life.

pagbubuhay-alamáng (pag-bu-bu-hay + a-la-máng), n. act or manner of living a miserable life.

pagbubulaán (pag-bu-bu-la-án), n. act of telling a lie or lies. Syn. *pagsisinungaling, di-pagsasabi ng katotohanan*.

pagbubulsa (pag-bu-bul-sa), n. 1. act of putting something in one's pocket. 2. act of appropriating something for one's own. 3. act of providing (a coat, pants, etc.) with pockets.

pagbubuntis (pag-bu-bun-tis), n. a becoming pregnant; pregnancy. Syn. *pagdadaláng-tao*.

pagbubuntóng-hiningá (pag-bu-bun-tóng + hi-ni-ngá), n. act of sighing. Syn. *paghihinagpis*.

pagbubunyág (pag-bu-bun-yág), n. act of exposing an anomaly, secret, etc. Syn. *paghahayág, pagsisiwalat*.

pagbubunyî (pag-bu-bun-yi), n. jubilation; happy celebration, as in victory; rejoicing. Syn. *pagsasayá, pagkakatuwâ*. 2. glorification; giving high honor to; exaltation. Syn. *pagtatanghál, pagpaparángal*.

pagbubunga (pag-bu-bu-nga), n. 1. bearing of fruits, as of plants and trees. Also *pamumunga*. 2. a producing of result.

pagbubuwág (pag-bu-bu-wág), n. 1. demolition or destruction, as of a wall. Syn. *pagwawasák*. 2. disbandment or abolition, as of an office or organization. Syn *paglalanság*.

pagbubuwís (pag-bu-bu-wís), n. payment of taxes. Syn. *pagbabayad ng buwís*.

pagbubuyó (pag-bu-bu-yó), n. act of seducing or persuading someone to do something wrong. Syn. *pagsusulsól*.

pagbuká (pag-bu-ká), n. 1. a becoming open, as flowers. Syn. *pagbukad*. 2. a becoming open or bursting apart, as the ground during a strong earthquake. Syn. *pagnganga*. 3. the spreading out, as of wings. Syn. *pag-unat*.

pagbukakà (pag-bu-ka-kà), n. act or manner of opening or spreading the legs wide

apart. Syn. *pagkaka, pagkaang na mabuti*.

pagbukadkád (pag-bu-kad-kád), n. becoming fully open (s.o. flowers).

pagbukál (pag-bu-kál), n. 1. flowing of water, as from a spring. 2. (Med.) eruption or breaking out in rash, as of some kind of skin diseases. Syn. *pagsingáw*.

pagbukó (pag-bu-kó), n. act of blocking or contradicting the plan, proposal, etc. of another or others.

pagbuhatan (pag-bu-ha-tan), v. 1. to be the source or origin of. Syn. *panggalingan, pagmulán*. 2. to be the cause of. Syn. *maging dahilán ng*. 3. (with ng kamáy) to hurt or punish someone by or as by whipping. Syn. *saktán*.

pagbulay-bulay (pag-bu-lay + bu-lay), var. **pagbubulay-bulay**, n. act of meditating or thinking deeply about something. Syn. *pagnilay-nilay, pagninilay-nilay*.

pagbuô (pag-bu-ô), n. 1. act of adding together to find the total. Syn. *pagsuma*. 2. act of organizing or creating a committee, etc. Syn. *pagtatatag, paglikhâ*. 3. act of repairing or restoring something into good condition. Syn. *pagkumpuni*.

pagbusabos (pag-bu-sa-bos), n. act or manner of treating someone like a slave. Syn. *pag-alipin*.

pagbuti (pag-bu-ti), n. 1. recovery from sickness. Syn. *paggaling*. 2. change from bad to good; change for the better. Syn. *paghusay*. 3. progress or growth, as of one's business. Syn. *pag-unlad*.

pagka (pag-ka), *conj.* 1. when, as in: *Pumáparito siya pagka mayroón siyang kailangan*. He comes here when he needs something. Syn. *kapág, sakalì*. 2. if, as in: *Pupunta ako roón pagka sumama siyá*. I will go there if he would go. Syn. *kung*.

pagka- (pag-ka-), pref. used in forming: 1. nouns, expressing (a) a certain fact, state, or condition, as in: *pagkamasamâ*, fact or state of being bad. (b) reason or cause, as in: *pagkamatáy*, reason or cause of the death. (c) manner by which something was done, with the ka- syllable duplicated, as in: *pagkakáburá*, manner by which something was erased. 2. adverbs, expressing time after the action of the pagkaabâ

pagkabayani

root, as in: *pagkaalis*, after departing (leaving); *pagkatapos*, afterwards.

pagkaabâ (pag-ka-a-bâ), n. state or condition of being poor, humble, unfortunate, etc. Syn. *pagkakaawá-awà*.

pagkaaburido (pag-ka-a-bu-ri-do), n. confused state of the mind. Syn. *pagkaguló o kaguluhán ng isip*.

pagkaakit (pag-ka-akit), n. 1. a being charmed or attracted, as by a woman's beauty. Syn. *pagkabighani*. 2. a being persuaded or induced. Syn. *pagkakahikayat, pagkaganyák*.

pagkáalaala (pag-ka-a-la-a-la), n. remembering; recollection; coming back of something to one's mind. Syn. *pagkágunitâ, pagkápanumpabalik sa gunitâ*.

pagkaalangán (pag-ka-a-la-ngán), var. **pagkaalanganin**, n. 1. fact or state of being medium-sized. Syn. *pagkakaraniwán ang lakí*. 2. fact or state of being insufficient. Syn. *pagkakulang, kakulangán*. 3. fact or state or being inappropriate for someone or something. Syn. *pagka-di-bagay*.

pagkaani (pag-ka-a-ni), adv. after harvest; after the harvest season. Syn. *pagkaraán o pagkatapos ng anihán*.

pagkaantala (pag-ka-an-ta-la), n. delay; fact or state of being delayed. Syn. *pagkabalam, pagkaatraso, pagkaatrasado*.

pagkaawà (pag-ka-a-wà), n. pity; feeling of sorrow or compassion for the suffering or misfortune of another or others. Syn. *habág, pagkahabág*.

pagkabá (pag-ka-bá), n. palpitation or rapid beating, as of the heart, esp. when one has a premonition of something frightening.

pagkababae (pag-ka-ba-ba-e), n. womanly qualities; womanliness; fact or state of being a woman. Syn. *pagiging babae*.

pagkabagabag (pag-ka-ba-ga-bag), n. fact, state, or condition of being worried or distressed. Syn. *pagkabahalà*.

pagkabagót (pag-ka-ba-gót), n. 1. exasperation; extreme annoyance or irritation. Syn. *matinding yamot o galit*. 2. impatience; boredom. Syn. *pagkainip*.

pagkabalino (pag-ka-ba-li-no), n. worry; anxiety; state or condition of being worried or restless. Syn. *pagkabahalà*.

pagkabalintunà (pag-ka-ba-lin-tu-nà), n. state or condition of being contrary to fact; absurdity. Syn.*pagkabalighô*.

pagkabalisa (pag-ka-ba-li-sa), n. restlessness; uneasiness. Syn. *pagka-dí-mapalagáy*.

pagkabalo (pag-ka-ba-lo), n. 1. loss or death of one's wife or husband. Syn. *pagkamatáy ng asawa*. 2. fact, state, or condition of being a widow or, widower. Syn. *pagkabiyudo (da)*.

pagkabanál (pag-ka-ba-nál), n. saintliness; piety; holiness. Also, *kabánalan*.

pagkabantulót (pag-ka-ban-tu-lót), n. fact or state of being hesitant; hesitancy. Syn. *pag-uurung-sulong, pag-aatubilí, pag-uulík-ulík*.

pagkábanggit (pag-ká-bang-git), n. act or manner by which a thing was mentioned or referred to in passing. Syn. *pagkáuntág, pagkátukoy, pagkásabi*.

pagkabao (pag-ka-ba-o), n. 1. death or loss of one's wife or husband. Syn. *pagkamatáy ng asawa*. 2. fact or state of being a widow or widower. Syn. *pagkabalo*.

pagkabaog (pag-ka-ba-og), n. 1. a becoming barren or sterile, referring to a woman or female animal. Syn. *pagkamatsora*. 2. a being barren or sterile; barrenness; sterility. Also, *kabaugan*.

pagkabatà (pag-ka-ba-tà), I. n. 1. fact or state of being a child. Syn. *pagiging batà*. 2. childhood; state or time of being a child. Syn. *kabataan*.
—II. adv. from (one's) childhood. Syn. *mulâ sa pagkabatà*.

pagka-Bathalà (pag-ka + Bat-ha-là), n. fact or state of being God; Divinity. Syn. *pagka-Diyós*.

pagkabatíd (pag-ka-ba-tíd), I. n. knowledge or understanding about something that happened. Syn. *pagkaalam, pagkaunawà*.
—II. adv. after having learned about; after knowing or learning about.

pagkabatugan (pag-ka-ba-tu-gan), n. fact, quality, or state of being lazy or slothful; laziness; slothfulness. Syn. *pagkatamád, katámaran*.

pagkabayani (pag-ka-ba-ya-ni), n. 1.

heroism. Also, *kabayanihan*. 2. bravery; great courage. Syn *pagkamagiting*, *kagitingan*; *pagkamatapang*, *katapangan*.

pagkabiglâ (pag-ka-big-lâ), n. 1. fact or state of being caught unaware; unawareness. 2. fact or quality of being too sudden. 3. loss of one's temper.

pagkabigô (pag-ka-bi-gô), n. disappointment; frustration; failure. Syn. *pagkásiphayò*.

pagkabihasá (pag-ka-bi-ha-sá), n. fact or state of being well-trained or accustomed to a certain situation or condition.

pagkabinatà (pag-ka-bi-na-tà), n. fact, state, or period of being a bachelor; bachelorhood. Syn. *pagiging binatà*, *pagkabagongtao*.

pagkabinibini (pag-ka-bi-ni-bi-ni), n. fact, state, or period of being a bachelor girl; maidenhood. Syn. *pagkadalaga*.

pagbukáng-liwayway (pag-ka-bu-káng + li-way-way), adv. after the break of day; after dawn.

pagkabuhay-mulî (pag-ka-bu-hay + mu-lî), var. **pagkabuhay-na-mulî**, n. a coming back to life; regaining of one's life; resurrection.

pagkabulag (pag-ka-bu-lag), I. adv. after becoming blind; after losing one's sight. —II. n. 1. state or condition of being blind. 2. cause of one's blindness.

pagkabulang-gugò (pag-ka-bu-lang + gu-gò), n. (Fig.) gallantry in spending money for friends and for social activities.

pagkabundát (pag-ka-bun-dát), I. n. state or condition of being very full or fully glutted. Syn. *pagkabusog na mabuti*. —II. adv. after eating or having eaten too much. Syn. *matapos mabundat o kumain nang nápakarami*.

pagkabuyó (pag-ka-bu-yó), n. fact or state of being or having been induced to indulge in something undesirable. Syn. *pagkásubò*, *pagkápasubò*.

pagkakáayaw (pag-ka-ká-ayaw), n. act or manner by which someone refused an offer. Syn. *pagkakátanggí*. 2. act or cause of one's refusing to fight or withdrawal from a fight.

pagkakahalagá (pag-ka-ka-ha-la-gá), n.

increase of price or value. Syn. *pagkataas ng presyo o halaga*.

pagkakáhawig (pag-ka-ká-ha-wig), n. similarity; likeness to each other; semblance. Syn. *pagkakáwangis*, *pagkakátulad*.

pagkakaibá (pag-ka-ka-i-bá), n. peculiarity; oddness. Syn. *kakaibhan*, *pagkakatuwa*, *kakatuwaan*.

pagkakaibigan (pag-ka-ka-i-bi-gan), n. friendship. Syn. *pagiging magbakaibigan*.

pagkakáigi (pag-ka-ká-i-gi), n. compatibility; fact or state of being compatible. Syn. *pagkakásundô*, *pagka-kásuwatò*.

pagkakailâ (pag-ka-ka-i-lâ), n. act of denying knowledge about something which one really knows about. Syn. *di pagtatapát*.

pagkakáinisan (pag-ka-ká-i-ni-san), n. feeling of dislike or hatred for each other or for one another. Syn. *pagkakáyamutan*.

pagkakáisá (pag-ka-ká-i-sá), n. 1. fact or state of being united; unity. Syn. *kaisahán*. 2. agreement; harmony. Syn. *pagka-kasundô*, *kasunduan*. 3. union; association. Syn. *samahán*.

pagkakálayô (pag-ka-ká-la-yô), n. fact or state of being separated from each other, as a husband and his wife. Syn. *pagkakáhiwaláy*. 2. state or condition of being far or away from each other.

pagkakalikhâ (pag-ka-ká-lik-hâ), n. the way or manner a thing was created. Syn. *pagkakálalâng*.

pagkakáligtás (pag-ka-ká-lig-tás), n. act or manner by which a person or thing has been saved from danger, damage, etc.

pagkakálutás (pag-ka-ká-lu-tás), n. act or manner by which a problem was or has been solved.

pagkakamál (pag-ka-ka-mál), n. accumulation or amassment, as of wealth.

pagkakamalay (pag-ka-ka-ma-lay), n. 1. becoming conscious; regaining of one's consciousness. Syn. *panunumbalik ng malay*. 2. the time or period during which a child has come to understand what is right and wrong.

pagkakámalî (pag-ka-ká-ma-lî), n. 1. commission of an error or errors; making a mistake or mistakes. 2. error or mistake committed.

pagkakánulô (pag-ka-ká-nu-lô), n. a betraying; betrayal. Syn. *pagtataksíl.*

pagkakápareho (pag-ka-ká-pa-re-ho), n. 1. fact, state, or quality of being the same; similarity. Syn. *pagkakátulad, pagkakáparis.* 2. the act or manner a thing was copied or made in the same manner as another.

pagkakáratay (pag-ka-ká-ra-tay), n. confinement in bed; time of illness. Syn. *pagkakasakit.*

pagkakasala (pag-ka-ka-sa-la), n. 1. sin. Syn. *kasalanan.* 2. crime. Syn. *paglabág sa batas.*

pagkakasirâ (pag-ka-ka-si-râ), n. 1. state or condition of being in controversy. Syn. *pagkakagalit.* 2. controversy; quarrel; dispute. Syn. *sigalót, sígalutan; away, pag-aaway.*

pagkakásundô (pag-ka-ká-sun-dô), n. 1. understanding or agreement with each other. Syn. *pagkakaunawaan.* 2. reconciliation. Syn. *pagkakabatiang-muli.* 3. act or manner by which someone was fetched by another from a certain place. Syn. *pagkakákaón.*

pagkakátaón (pag-ka-ká-ta-ón), n. 1. chance; opportunity. Syn. *oportunidad.* 2. hope; possibility. Syn. *pag-asa, posibilidad.* 3. coincidence; chance occurrence. Syn. *di-sinasadyang pangyayari.* 4. occasion. Syn. *pangyayari.*

pagkakátatag (pag-ka-ká-ta-tag), n. act or manner by which something was organized or founded. Syn. *pagkakábuô, pagkakátayô.*

pagkakáwanggawâ (pag-ka-ká-wang-ga-wâ), n. act of charity. Syn. *pagtulong sa mga nangangailangan.*

pagkakáwangis (pag-ka-ká-wa-ngis), n. resemblance; similarity. Syn. *pagkakátulad, pagkakáwangkí.*

pagkadalaga (pag-ka-da-la-ga), n. state or period of being a maiden; maidenhood. Syn. *pagiging dalaga.*

Pagkadiyós (Pag-ka-di-yós), var. **pagka-Diyos**, n. divine quality or nature; divinity. Syn. *pagkabathalà.*

pagkadungô (pag-ka-du-ngò), n. 1. fact, condition, or quality of being shy or timid;

timidity; shyness. 2. stupidity; lack of intelligence. Syn. *pagkatangá, katangahán.*

pagkagawî (pag-ka-ga-wî), n. 1. an unexpected visit or coming to a certain place. Also, *pagkápagawî.* 2. a becoming used or accustomed to a certain habit. Syn. *pagkasanay, pagkahirati.*

pagkagising (pag-ka-gi-sing), adv. after waking up or having been awakened from sleep. Syn. *matapos magisíng.*

pagkágitlá (pag-ka-git-la), n. a feeling of sudden fright or shock. Syn. *pagkágulat.*

pagkagiyagis (pag-ka-gi-ya-gis), n. fact or state of being restless or worried. Syn. *pagkadí-mapalagáy.*

pagkágumon (pag-ká-gu-mon), n. state or condition of being deeply addicted, as to a certain vice.

pagkágupiling (pag-ká-gu-pi-ling), n. a falling into a light, restful sleep. Syn. *pagkáidlíp, pagkápahipíg.*

pagkahapò (pag-ka-ha-pò), n. 1. panting due to extreme tiredness. Syn. *paghingal, pangangapós ng hiningá.* 2. extreme tiredness. Syn. *matinding pagod.*

pagkahátinggabí (pag-ka-há-ting-ga-bí), adv. after midnight.

pagkahayág (pag-ka-ha-yag), I. adv. after announcing or having announced something. Syn. *pagkasabi.*
—II. n. fact or state of being known to many or exposed to the public.

pagkahenyo (pag-ka-hen-yo), n. fact or state of being a genius.

pagkahibáng (pag-ka-hi-báng), n. 1. state of delirium; temporary disorder of the mind. Also, *kahibangan.* 2. craziness about someone or something. Syn. *pagkahaling, kahalingán.*

pagkáhilig (pag-ká-hi-lig), n. inclination or propensity for something. Syn. *pagkakagusto.*

pagkahinayang (pag-ka-hi-na-yang), n. feeling of regret for the loss of something important or valuable, or for failure to take advantage of something desirable. Also, *panghihinayang.*

pagkain (pag-ka-in), n. 1. food (in general). 2. feed; fodder. Syn. *pagkain, pamakain.* 3. food for fowls. Syn. *patukâ, pamatukâ.*

4. act of manner of eating.

pagkainá (pag-ka-i-ná), n. 1. fact or state of being a mother; motherhood. Syn. *pagiging iná*. 2. the quality or character of a mother.

pagkainip (pag-ka-i-nip), n. impatience or displeasure due to long waiting; boredom. Syn. *pagkayamót, pagkabagót*.

pagkainis (pag-ka-i-nis), n. 1. suffocation; asphyxiation; death due to lack of air. 2. feeling of annoyance or intense dislike for something. Syn. *pagkayamót*.

pagkainitan (pag-ka-i-ni-tan), v. to be or become the object of someone's ire or anger. Syn. *pagbuntunán ng galit*.

pagkainggit (pag-ka-ing-git), n. envy; resentful dislike of another who has something desirable. Syn. *panaghilì, pananaghilì*.

pagkaísahán (pag-ka-í-sa-hán), v. 1. to join or unite together against someone or something. Also, *pagkáisa-isahán*. 2. to approve unanimously.

pagkaitán (pag-ka-i-tán), v. to refuse to give; deny what is being asked or requested by someone.

pagkalagak (pag-ka-la-gak), adv. 1. after placing or putting something in a safe place. Syn. *pagkalagay*. 2. after depositing or having been deposited in a bank, as one's money. Syn. *pagkadepósitó, matapos maideposito*. 3. after paying or having paid the bail or bond for the temporary release of an accused. Syn. *pagkapiyansa, pagkapágpiyansa*.

pagkalahì (pag-ka-la-hì), n. 1. one's family lineage or descent. 2. citizenship; status of one's citizenship. Syn. *pagkamámamayán*.

pagkalalaki (pag-ka-la-la-ki), n. 1. manhood; state of being a man. 2. manliness; manly character or quality.

pagkalaláng (pag-ka-la-láng), adv. after creating or having been created. Syn. *pagkalikhâ, matapos malikhâ o malaláng*.

pagkalantá (pag-ka-lan-tá), n. fact or state of being withered, referring to flowers, leaves, etc.

pagkalaós (pag-ka-la-ós), n. 1. fact or state of being already overriped (s.o. fruits).

Also, *kalausán*. 2. state or condition of having lost potency or productiveness.

pagkalapastangan (pag-ka-la-pas-ta-ngan), n. fact, quality, or character of being discourteous, disrespectful, or irreverent; disrespectfulness; discourtesy; irreverence. Syn. *pagkawaláng-galang, kawalang-galang*.

pagkalikhâ (pag-ka-lik-hâ), n. act or manner by which a person created something. Also, *pagkakalikhâ*.

pagkaligalig (pag-ka-li-ga-lig), n. 1. a being preoccupied or bothered. Syn. *pagkaabala*. 2. state or condition of being disturbed. Syn. *pagkagulo*. 3. state or condition of being worried or in distress. Syn. *pagkabahalà, pagkabagabag, pagkabalisa*.

pagkaligáw (pag-ka-li-gáw), n. a being lost in one's way; loss of one's direction; inability to find one's way. Syn. *pagkawalâ sa daán*. 2. state or condition of being mistaken in one's belief or discretion, etc. Syn. *pagkálisyâ, pagkáhidwâ*.

pagkalimang (pag-ka-li-mang), n. mistake or loss of order in the manner of counting. Syn. *pagkahirá, pagkalito*.

pagkalimot (pag-ka-li-mot), n. 1. temporary loss of memory. Syn. *pansamantaláng pagkawalâ ng alaala*. 2. failure to recall something to one's mind; inability to remember.

pagkalingà (pag-ka-li-ngà), n. act or manner of helping someone by supporting or taking under one's care. Syn. *pagkandilì, pag-arugâ, pagkupkóp*.

pagkalingâ (pag-ka-li-ngâ), n. act or manner by which a person turned his head to one side or at the back in order to see someone or something. Cf. *pagkalingón*.

pagkalingát (pag-ka-li-ngát), n. intentional neglect of one's duties or responsibilities. Syn. *pagpapabayà*.

pagkalipas (pag-ka-li-pas), adv. after the lapse or passing away, as of time. Syn. *pagkaraán*.

pagkalisyâ (pag-ka-lis-yâ), n. 1. fact, state, or quality of being improper; impropriety. 2. fact, state, or condition of being incorrect; incorrectness. Syn. *pagkamalî, kamalián*. 3. fact or state of being violative of. Syn. *pagkalabág*.

pagkalitó (pag-ka-li-tó), n. 1. distraction, as in counting. Syn. *pagkalimang, pagkahirá*. 2. fact or state of being confused; confused state of the mind. Syn. *pagkataranta*.

pagkaliwâ (pag-ka-li-wâ), n. 1. act or manner of turning to the left. Syn. *pagpihit o, paglikô sa kaliwâ*. 2. (Colloq.) concubinage. Syn. *pakikiagulò, pangangalunyà, pagtataksil sa asawa*.

pagkalooban (pag-ka-lo-o-ban), v. 1. to give, as a gift or present. Syn. *bigyan*. 2. to confer, as an honor or award. Syn. *gawaran, bigyán*.

pagkálubalob (pag-ká-lu-ba-lob), n. state or condition of being deeply involved, as in a certain vice. Also, *pagkápalubalob*.

pagkalubós (pag-ka-lu-bós), n. fact or state of being complete or absolute. Also, *kalubusán*.

pagkálugamì (pag-ká-lu-ga-mì), n. a falling into a misfortune or complete failure in life. Syn. *pagkapahamak*.

pagkálulóng (pag-ka-lu-long), n. deep involvement into something undesirable. Syn. *pagkásubò, pagkápasubò*.

pagkalunsád (pag-ka-lun-sád), adv. 1. after alighting or having alighted, as from a vehicle. Syn. *pagkababâ, pagkaibís*. 2. after unloading or having been unloaded. Syn. *pagkadiskarga*.

pagkaluráy (pag-ka-lu-ráy), I. adv. after mutilating or having been mutilated; after mangling or having been mangled. Syn. *pagkagutáy, pagkadurog*.

pagkamaáarì (pag-ka-ma-á-a-rì), n. a being possible; possibility. Syn. *posibilidad*.

pagkamaáarì (pag-ka-ma-á-a-rì), n. possibility to be owned or possessed. Syn. *posibilidad na maarì*.

pagkamaaga (pag-ka-ma-a-ga), n. a being early; earliness.

pagkamaagap (pag-ka-ma-a-gap), n. a being on time; punctuality; promptness. Also, *kaagapan*.

pagkamaaya (pag-ka-ma-a-ya), n. fact or state of being pleasant. Syn. *pagkakalugúdlugód*.

pagkamabagsík (pag-ka-ma-bag-sík), n. 1. ferocity; fierceness. Also, *kabagsikán*. Syn. *pagkamabangís, kabangisán*. 2. potency or strongness, as of poison.

pagkamabaít (pag-ka-ma-ba-ít), n. fact or state of being kind; kindness. Also, *kábaìtán*.

pagkamabigát (pag-ka-ma-bi-gát), n. 1. fact, state, or quality of being heavy; heaviness. Also, *kabigatán*. 2. gravity or seriousness, as of one's sickness. Syn. *pagkagrabe, pagkamalubhá, pagkalalâ*.

pagkamabuwenas (pag-ka-ma-bu-we-nas), n. state or quality of being lucky; good luck; streak of good luck. Syn. *pagkamasuwerte, pagkaginágalíng*.

pagkamakabayan (pag-ka-ma-ka-ba-yan), n. nationalistic feeling or effort; nationalism. Syn. *pagkamakabansâ, diwang makabansâ o makabayan*.

pagkamakulay (pag-ka-ma-ku-lay), n. fact, state, or quality of being colorful; colorfulness.

pagkamadámdamin (pag-ka-ma-dám-da-min), n. 1. the quality of being full of feelings, usually said of expressions. 2. (var. **pagkamaramdamin**) sensitiveness, esp. to criticism. Syn. *pagkabalát-sibuyas* (fig.).

pagkamadiwà (pag-ka-ma-di-wà), n. fact, state, or quality of being full of meaning; meaningful.

pagkamagiliw (pag-ka-magi-liw), n. quality of being affectionate; tender and loving attribute of a person. Syn. *pagkamapágmahál*.

pagkamagiliwín (pag-ka-ma-gi-li-wín), n. inclination or fondness for something. Syn. *pagkamatuwaín, pagkamagustuhin*.

pagkamagulang (pag-ka-ma-gu-lang), n. 1. state or quality of being mature, referring esp. to fruits. 2. fact or state of being a parent; parenthood. Syn. *pagigíng magulang*. 3. authority or responsibility of a parent. 4. (Colloq.) the character of a person who takes advantage of others. Syn. *pagkasuwitik*.

pagkamahangin (pag-ka-ma-ha-ngin), n. 1 fact or condition of being windy; windiness. Also, *kahangínan*. 2 (Fig.) boastfulness. Syn. *pagkahambóg, kahambugán*.

pagkamahiwagà (pag-ka-ma-hi-wa-gà), n. fact or state of being mysterious; mysteriousness. Syn. *pagkamahimalâ*.

pagkamaíndahin (pag-ka-ma-ín-da-hin), n. sensitiveness to little hardship or tiredness or to insult or criticism. Syn. *pagkamarámdamin*.

pagkamaínipin (pag-ka-ma-í-ni-pin), n. tendency to become easily bored or impatient, due esp. to long waiting.

pagkamalabò (pag-ka-ma-la-bò), n. 1. fact, state, or quality of being turbid or muddy, referring to water. Cf. *pagkamaputik*. 2. obscurity, as of meaning. Syn. *pagkadímáunawaan, pagkadí-máintindihán*. 3. state or quality of being dim; dimness, as of light. Syn. *pagkamalamlám*. 4. dimness of vision due to nearsightedness or farsightedness. Syn. *kahinaan ng matá o paningín*. 5. uncertain state or condition, as of an agreement; uncertainty. Syn. *kawaláng-katiyakan, pagkawaláng-katiyakan*.

pagkamalamán (pag-ka-ma-la-mán), n. 1. state or quality of being fleshy; fleshiness. 2. state or quality of being meaty; meatiness. 3. fact or state of being meaningful; meaningfulness. Syn. *pagkamadiwà, pagkamakahulugán*.

pagkámalán (pag-ká-ma-lán), v. 1. to be mistaken for someone or something else. Also, *ipagkámalí*. 2. to identify or recognize incorrectly.

pagkamalas (pag-ka-ma-las), n. state or condition of being unlucky or unfortunate. Also, *kamalasan*.

pagkámalas (pag-ká-ma-las), n. the way or manner a person observed something. Syn. *pagkákita, pagkámasíd*.

pagkamalíkhain (pag-ka-ma-lík-ha-in), n. 1. fact or state of being constantly moving. Syn. *pagkawaláng-tigil, pagkamagasláw*. 2. mischievousness. Syn. *kapilyuhán*.

pagkamaligoy (pag-ka-ma-li-goy), n. long-windedness, as of speech, writing, etc. Also, *kaliguyan*.

pagkamalimí (pag-ka-ma-li-mí), n. reflective or thoughtful habit before acting or making a decision. Also, *pagkamapáglimì*.

pagkámalín (pag-ká-ma-lín), v. to cause someone to make an error or mistake. Also, *papagkámalín*.

pagkamalín (pag-ka-ma-lín), v. (fr. *kamál*) to cause someone to accumulate or amass a fortune or wealth.

pagkamaluwát (pag-ka-ma-lu-wát), n. 1. state or condition of being long in time or duration. Syn. *pagkamatagál, pagkamalaon*. 2. state or condition of being long delayed. Syn. *pagkabalam, pagkaatraso*.

pagkamámamahayág (pag-ka-má-ma-ma-ha-yág), n. the work or status as a newspaperman.

pagkamámamayán (pag-ka-má-ma-ma-yán), n. status or condition of being a citizen; citizenship.

pagkamánunulát (pag-ka-má-nu-nu-lát), n. ability, status, or quality as a writer.

pagkámanghâ (pag-ká-mang-hâ), n. feeling of wonder or great surprise; amazement. Syn. *panggigilalas, pagtataká,pagkágulat*.

pagkamaparaán (pag-ka-ma-pa-ra-án), n. quality or nature of being methodical or systematic. Syn. *pagkamasistema*.

pagkamapilit (pag-ka-ma-pi-lit), n. fact, character, or nature of being insistent; insistency. Syn. *pagkamagiít*.

pagkamarahás (pag-ka-ma-ra-hás), n. fact or state of being ruthless or harsh; ruthlessness; cruelty; harshness. Syn. *pagkamalupít,pagkamabangís*.

pagkamarálitâ (pag-ka-ma-rá-li-tâ), n. state or condition of being poor or impoverished. Also, *karalitaán*. Syn. *pagkamahirap, kahirapan; pagkadukhâ, karukhaán*.

pagkamaramdamin (pag-ka-ma-ram-da-min), n. state or quality of being sensitive; sensitiveness. Syn. *pagkabalát-sibuyas* (*fig.*).

pagkamatahimik (pag-ka-ma-ta-hi-mik), n. 1. quietness; stillness; silence. Syn. *pagkawaláng-ingay,kawaláng-ingay*. 2. calmness; peacefulness. Syn. *pagkamapayapà, pagkamahinahon, pagkapanatag*.

pagkamatamán (pag-ka-ma-ta-mán), n. assiduous quality or ability. Syn. *pagkamatiyagâ; pagkamasigasig*.

pagkamataós (pag-ka-ma-ta-ós), n. fact or state of being heartfelt or sincere. Syn. *pagkamatapát*.

pagkamataras (pag-ka-ma-ta-ras), n.

pagkamatáy   **pagkápintóng**

sharped-tongued manner or contemptuousness in speech, esp. of women. Syn. *pagkamataray*.

pagkamatáy (pag-ka-ma-táy), I. *adv.* after dying or passing away; after the death of. Syn. *matapos mamatáy, pagkapanaw*. —II. n. 1. death; end of life in any form. Syn. *pagsakabiláng-buhay, pagpanaw, pagyao*. 2. cause of death. Syn. *sanhî ng kamatayan*. 3. (*Fig.*) loss, as in: *pagkamatáy ng pag-asa*, loss of hope. 4. state or condition of being extinguished or put out, as light.

pagkamatunóg (pag-ka-ma-tu-nóg), n. 1. fact, state, or quality of being loud-sounding or sonorous. Also, *katunugán*. 2. (*Fig.*) state or quality of being famous, well-known, or popular; popularity. Syn. *pagkabantóg, kabantugán, pagkatanyág, katanyagán*.

pagkamuhî (pag-ka-mu-hî), n. feeling of intense dislike, hatred, anger, etc. Syn. *pagkapoót, matindíng pagkagalit*.

pagkamulat (pag-ka-mu-lat), *adv.* after opening one's eyes.

pagkamulát (pag-ka-mu-lát), n. 1. fact or state of being educated. Syn. *pagkamáy-pinag-aralan, pagkaedukado*. 2. fact of being awake or aware about the truth or reality of things.

pagkamusmós (pag-ka-mus-mós), n. 1. immaturity of mind. Syn. *pagkamurang-isip, pagkabatang-isip*. 2. innocence for being still a child. Syn. *pagkainosente, pagkawaláng-malay, pagkawaláng-baít*.

pagkandilî (pag-kan-di-lì), n. act of taking someone under one's protective care. Syn. *pagtangkilik, pag-arugâ, pagkupkóp, pag-ampón*.

pagkaón (pag-ka-ón), n. act of fetching or summoning someone from a certain place. Syn. *pagsundô, pagtawag*.

pagkapaláasá (pag-ka-pa-lá-a-sá), n. the habit of being too dependent on someone for support or aid.

pagkapalagáy-loób (pag-ka-pa-la-gáy + lo-ób), n. fact or quality of having confidence in oneself.

pagkapalalò (pag-ka-pa-la-lò), n. arrogance; haughtiness.

pagkapalamara (pag-ka-pa-la-ma-ra), n. fact or state of being traitor. Syn. *pagkataksíl; pagkatraidór, pagkasukáb*.

pagkapalasák (pag-ka-pa-la-sák), n. fact or state of being widespread or common. Syn. *pagigíng palasák*.

pagkapalibhasà (pag-ka-pa-lib-ha-sà), n. state or quality of being lowly in rank, position or station in life. Syn. *pagkahamak, pagkamarálitâ, pagkamahirap*.

pagkápasangkót (pag-ká-pa-sang-kót), n. state or condition of being involved or implicated; involvement. Syn. *pagkáparamay, pagkápadawit*.

pagkápatáy (pag-ká-pa-táy), n. the act or manner by which someone was killed or murdered. Also, *pagkakápatáy*.

pagkápatibay (pag-ká-pa-ti-bay), n. 1. the act or manner by which something was or has been made strong or stronger. 2. the act or manner by which something was or has been approved. Also, *pagkakápatibay*.

pagkapawì (pag-ka-pa-wì), I. *adv.* 1. after erasing or having been erased. Syn. *pagkaburâ; matapos maburâ*. 2. after disappearing or having disappeared, as pain. Syn. *pagkawalâ, pagkalipol, pagkaalís*. —II. n. state or condition of being erased or obliterated. Syn. *pagkaburá*. 2. disappearance, as of pain. Syn. *pagkawalâ, pagkalipol*.

pagkapayák (pag-ka-pa-yák), n. 1. state or quality of being simple or plain; simplicity. Also, *kapayakán*. Syn. *pagkasimple, kasimplihán*. 2. state or quality of being without mixture; purity. Syn. *pagkapuro, pagkawaláng-halò*.

pagkapkáp (pag-kap-káp), n. act or manner of running the hands over the body of someone, as in looking for something hidden in the body. Cf. *paghalughóg*.

pagkapihikan (pag-ka-pi-hi-kan), n. choosiness, esp. in food; fastidiousness. Syn. *pagkamaselang o pagkamapilì (sa pagkain o sa ibá pang bagay)*.

pagkápintóng (pag-ká-pin-tóng), n. 1. temporary delay, as of papers to be signed by someone. Syn. *pagkábimbín*. 2. state or condition of being stored or deposited, as in a warehouse.

pagkapipi (pag-ka-pi-pi), *n.* state or condition of being dumb; dumbness.

pagkapipî (pag-ka-pi-pî), *n.* state or condition of being forcibly flattened.

pagkaraan (pag-ka-ra-an; -ra-án), *adv.* 1. after the lapse or passing, as of time, etc. Syn. *pagkalipas.* 2. after a person or thing has passed (a certain place). Syn. *matapos dumaán o makaraán, pagkadaán.*

pagkaraka (pag-ka-ra-ka), *adv.* at once; immediately; without delay. Syn. *kaagád, kapagdaka.*

pagkasalungát (pag-ka-sa-lu-ngát), I. *adv.* after opposing or having expressed one's opposition to. Syn. *pagkatutol, pagkakontrá.*
—II. *n.* fact, state, or condition of being opposed or contradictory to. Syn. *pagkalaban, pagkakontrá, pagkatutol.*

pagkasanay (pag-ka-sa-nay), I. *adv.* after training or having been trained. Syn. *pagkahirati, matapos masanay o mahirati.*
—II. *n.* a becoming trained or being trained or used to a certain kind of work, condition or situation.

pagkasawî (pag-ka-sa-wî), *n.* 1. misfortune; bad luck. Also, *kasawián, kasawiáng-palad.* 2. despair; loss of hope. Syn. *kawaláng-pag-asa.* 3. loss of life; death. Syn. *pagkamatáy, kamatayan.*

pagkasílang (pag-ka-sí-lang), *adv.* 1. after rising or having risen, referring to the sun, moon, and the like. Syn. *pagkasikat, matapos sumikat.* 2. after being born or having been born, referring to a child. Syn. *pagkalitáw sa maliwanag, matapos isilang o ipanganák.* 3. after giving birth, referring to a woman. Syn. *pagkaanák, pagkapanganák.*

pagkásilay (pag-ká-si-lay), *n.* a brief sight of something. Cf. *pagkákita, pagkámasíd, pagkátanáw.*

pagkasiphayò (pag-ka-sip-ha-yò), *n.* state or condition of being a failure; lack of success. Syn. *pagkabigô.*

pagkásiyahín (pag-ká-si-ya-hín), *v.* to make sufficient. Syn. *pagsapatín, paghustuhín.*

pagkasugapà (pag-ka-su-ga-pà), *n.* fact, state, or habit of being addicted to a certain vice, esp. to narcotics. Also, *kasugapaan.*

pagkasugpô (pag-ka-sug-pô), I. *adv.* after suppressing or having been suppressed. Syn. *pagkapigil, pagkaapulà, pagkasawatâ.*
—II. *n.* state or condition of being suppressed or checked.

pagkásumpóng (pag-ká-sum-póng), *n.* 1. unexpected attack, as of a heart disease, etc. Syn. *pagkáatake.* 2. an unexpected find or discovery, as of a remedy or cure for a certain mysterious disease. Syn. *pagkátagpô, pagkátuklás.*

pagkasunód (pag-ka-su-nód), I. *adv.* after following or having followed one who has gone ahead.
—II. *n.* 1. state or condition of being in accordance, as with certain requirements, rules, etc. Syn. *pagigíng sunód.* 2. realization, as of a plan. Syn. *pagkatupád, pagigíng totoó.*

pagkásungabà (pag-ká-su-nga-bà), *n.* a stumbling or fall in walking or running, with the face striking on something. Also, *pagkápasungabà.* Cf. *pagkásubasob, pagkápasubasob.*

pagkasupók (pag-ka-su-pók), *n.* state or condition of being carbonized or totally burned. Cf. *pagkasunóg.*

pagkasura (pag-ka-su-ra), *n.* feeling of annoyance. Syn. *pagkayamót, pagkabuwisit.*

pagkatahô (pag-ka-ta-hô), *n.* knowledge or understanding about something. Syn. *pagkabatíd, pagkáunawà, pagkáintindi.*

pagkatanyág (pag-ka-tan-yág), *n.* state or condition of being prominent, well-known, or popular. Syn. *pagkapopulár, pagkabantóg, pagkabalità, pagkakilalá.*

pagkatao (pag-ka-ta-o), *n.* 1. human nature; personality. Syn. *personalidád.* 2. family background.

pagkatapos (pag-ka-ta-pos), I. *adv.* 1. after. Syn. *pagkaraán, pagkalipas.* 2. afterwards; later. Syn. *pagkaraan, sa dakong hulí.* 3. at the end or conclusion of. Syn. *sa katapusán.* 4. after the completion or finishing of. Syn. *pagkayarì, pagkagawâ.*
—II. *n.* 1. end; a coming to an end; conclusion. Syn. *pagwawakás, katapusán.*

2. condition of being completed or finished. Syn. *pagkayarì.*

pagkatawán (pag-ka-ta-wán), n. act or manner of representing someone, as in a conference, etc.

pagkátayô (pag-ká-ta-yô), n. 1. fact or reason behind the founding or establishment of. Syn. *pagkátatag, pagkábuô.* 2. the position or manner a person stands. Also, *pagkakátayô.* Syn. *pagkátindíg, pagkakátindíg.* 3. the purpose or reason for the erection or construction of. Syn. *pagkátirik, pagkakátirik.*

pagkati (pag-ka-ti), n. the receding of tide; ebb. Syn. *pagliít ng tubíg sa dagat.*

pagkatigáng (pag-ka-ti-gáng), n. extreme dryness; aridity, esp. of soil. Syn. *labis na pagkatuyô.*

pagkatigatig (pag-ka-ti-ga-tig), n. state or condition of being worried or uneasy; worried feeling; unsettled state of mind. Syn. *pagkabalisa, di-pagkápalagáy.*

pagkatiwalî (pag-ka-ti-wa-lî), n. 1. fact or state of being erroneous or contrary to the truth or fact. Syn. *pagkamalî, pagkalisyâ, pagkalabág sa katotohanan.* 2. fact or state of being anomalous or irregular; irregularity. Syn. *pagkairegulár.*

pagkatiyak (pag-ka-ti-yak), I. adv. after having been sure about. Syn. *matapos matiyák; pagkasiguro.*

—II. n. fact or state of being sure; freedom from doubt. Syn. *pagkasiguro, kasiguruhan.*

pagkátuto (pag-ká-tu-to), I. adv. after learning or knowing the manner or method of doing something.

—II. n. ability to learn. Syn. *kakayaháng matuto.*

pagkatuyô (pag-ka-tu-yô), I. adv. after drying or having been made dry. Syn. *matapos matuyô.*

—II. n. 1. a becoming dry. 2. state or condition of being dry. 3. (Colloq.) consumption; tuberculosis. Syn. *tisis; tíbi (colloq.), tuberkulosis.*

pagkauhaw (pag-ka-u-haw), n. 1. a desire for something to drink; thirst. Also, *uhaw, kauhawan.* 2. (Fig.) thirst or strong desire for something (other than water). Syn. *pananabík, masidhíng pagnanasà.*

pagkaulila (pag-ka-u-li-la), n. 1. a being orphaned; loss of one's mother or father or both. 2. loneliness for being alone or left alone. Also, *pangungulila.*

pagkaulirán (pag-ka-u-li-rán), n. the character or quality of a person that is worthy of emulation.

pagkaumíd (pag-ka-u-míd), n. state of being unable to speak or talk due to fear, shyness, or shame.

pagkáunlád (pag-ká-un-lád), n. the state, condition, or extent of progress or advancement made. Syn. *pagkáprogreso, pagkásulong.*

pagkaúnsiyamì (pag-ka-ún-si-ya-mì), n. failure to materialize. Syn. *pagkabigó.*

pagkaupós (pag-ka-u-pós), n. 1. state or condition of being sunk to the hilt. Syn. *pagkakábaón nang sagád o sapák.* 2. state or condition of being reduced to a butt or stub, as a candle, cigar, cigarette, etc. 3. complete loss of strength due to exhaustion. Syn. *lubós na panghihinà dahil sa pagod.*

pagkautangan (pag-ka-u-ta-ngan), v. to be indebted from; have a loan from. Syn. *magkautang sa.*

pagkautás (pag-ka-u-tás), I. n. 1. a coming to an end; completion. Syn. *pagkatapos, pagkayarì.* 2. end of one's life; death. Syn. *pagkamatáy.*

—II. adv. after completing or finishing. Syn. *pagkatapos, pagkayarì.* 2. after killing or having been killed.

pagkawagás (pag-ka-wa-gás), n. 1. state or condition of being pure; purity. Syn. *pagkadalisay, kadalisayan.* 2. state or condition of being sincere; sincerity. Syn. *pagkatapát, pagkamatapát.*

pagkawalâ (pag-ka-wa-lâ), n. 1. a becoming lost or extinct; disappearance. Syn. *pagkalipol.* 2. a losing or being lost, as of one's right, property, etc. 3. a misplacing or being misplaced. Syn. *pagkáwaglít, pagkápawaglít.* 4. lack or absence, as of trust, love, etc. Syn. *kawalán.* 5. unexpected absence or nonattendance. Syn. *di-inaasahang pagliban o di-pagharáp.* 6. effort to free oneself from being tied or confined. Syn. *pag-aalpás.*

pagkawaták-waták (pag-ka-wa-ták + wa-ták), n. state or condition of being widely separated or scattered, as members of a group. Syn. *pagkakálayú-layô, pagkakáhiwá-hiwaláy.*

pagkilala (pag-ki-la-la), n. 1. act of identifying a person or thing. 2. recognition or acknowledgement, as of fact or truth. Syn. *pagtanggáp.*

pagkilatis (pag-ki-la-tis), n. act of appraising the value, importance, or ability of. Syn. *pag-urì.*

pagkít (pag-kít), n. wax; beeswax.

pagkita (pag-ki-ta), n. 1. act or manner of earning (money) for one's living, as by working. Syn. *paggawa.* 2. earning of interest, as money deposited in a bank. Syn. *pagtubò.*

pagkubabaw (pag-ku-ba-baw), n. act or manner of climbing on top of another, as in coitus or copulation among animals. Syn. *pagbabá.*

pagkukulang (pag-ku-ku-lang), n. 1. lack; shortage; insufficiency. Also, *kakulangán.* Syn. *pagkakapós, kakapusán.* 2. neglect, as of one's duty; negligence. Syn. *pagpapabayà, kapabayaán.* 3. fault or mistake. Syn. *pagkakámalî, kamalian.*

pagkukumamot (pag-ku-ku-ma-mot), n. haste or hurry in order to be on time. Syn. *pagmamadalî, pagkukumahog.*

pagkukunwâ (pag-ku-kun-wâ), var. **pagkukunwarî**, n. act of pretending to be what one is not; pretense; false claim. Syn. *pagkukunyarî.*

pagkupas (pag-ku-pas), n. 1. a fading; loss of color or brilliance; discoloration. Syn. *pagkawalâ ng kulay.* 2. loss of vigor, popularity, etc. Syn. *paglipas, paghinà.*

pagkuwán (pag-ku-wán), adv. then; soon after. Syn. *pagkatapos, matapos.*

pagdaanan (pag-da-a-nan), v. 1. to pass over or through. Syn. *daanan.* 2. (Colloq.) to experience; have a taste or experience of. Syn. *pagdanasan, danasin.*

pagdaka (pag-da-ka), adv. at once; immediately; instantly. Syn. *agád, kaagád, agád-agád, biglâ, kagyát.*

pagdakilà (pag-da-ki-là), n. 1. a becoming great or high in rank. 2. recognition of someone's greatness or eminence.

pagdadahilán (pag-da-da-hi-lán), var. **pagdarahilán**, n. act of making excuses or false reason to justify one's shortcoming.

pagdadahóp (pag-da-da-hóp) var. **pagdarahóp**, n. 1. state or condition of being poor or needy. Syn. *paghihirap, paghihikahós.* 2. lack or insufficiency, as of commodities, and other necessities. Syn. *pagkukulang, pagsasalát.*

pagdadalamhatì (pag-da-da-lam-ha-tì), n. feeling of extreme sorrow; state or condition of being unhappy. Syn. *matindíng lungkót, pagtitiís ng lungkót o dusa, paghihinagpís.*

pagdadaláng-tao (pag-da-da-láng + ta-o), n. state or condition of being pregnant; pregnancy. Syn. *pagbubuntís.*

pagdadamay (pag-da-da-may), var. **pagdaramay**, n. act of including or implicating someone in a misdeed or crime. Syn. *pagsasangkót, pagdadawit.*

pagdadamayán (pag-da-da-ma-yán), var. **pagdaramayán**, n. 1. act of expressing a common sympathetic feeling or condolence for each other. 2. act of helping each other in time of need or danger. Syn. *pagtutulungán.*

pagdadamdám (pag-da-dam-dám), var. **pagdaramdám**, n. feeling of being slighted or insulted. Syn. *paghihinanakít, pagsamâ ng loób.*

pagdagás (pag-da-gás), n. act of fetching someone when a close relative falls very ill or dies. Syn. *mádaliang pagsundô sa malapit na kaanak ng maysakít o ng namatáy.*

pagdagís (pag-da-gís; pag-dag-is), n. act of exerting efforts in moving one's bowels or in giving birth. Syn. *pag-irí.*

pagdagison (pag-da-gi-son), n. act of moving closer to each other or to one another.

pagdagsâ (pag-dag-sâ), n. 1. the coming or arrival of goods in great abundance in the market. Syn. *pagdatíng o pagkakaroón ng maraming kalakal sa pámilihan.* 2. the coming or arrival of a great number of people, as in attending a big rally or meeting. Syn. *pagdarátingan ng nápakaraming tao.*

pagdaíng (pag-da-íng), n. 1. a moaning;
expression of sorrow or pain. Syn.
pagtaghóy. 2. expression of one's complaint
to win pity or sympathy, as from an
authority. Syn. *pagreklamo, pagrereklamo*.

pagdalang (pag-da-lang), n. 1. a becoming
sparse. Syn. *pagkauntî*. 2. a becoming
widely separated, as the growth of plants;
opposed to *pagsinsín*. 3. a becoming
infrequent, as of one's visit to a friend;
opposed to *paglimit*.

pagdalangin (pag-da-la-ngin), n. 1. act of
praying. Syn. *pagdarasál*. 2. act of asking
for something through prayer or
supplication. Also, *pananalangin*.

pagdalumat (pag-da-lu-mat), n. act of
thinking deeply about something. Syn.
paglirip.

pagdamután (pag-da-mu-tán), v. 1. to be
selfish to. Also, *pagmaramután*. 2. (*Fig.*)
to accept even if too small or insignificant
in value or amount, referring to
something being given to someone.

pagdapit (pag-da-pit), n. the religious
ceremony in which a priest and an acolyte
fetch a dead person from the house to the
church for blessing before being finally
taken to the cemetery for burial.

pagdaraán (pag-da-ra-án), n. 1. act of passing
through a certain place. 2. a passing by,
as of time. Syn. *paglipas*.

pagdarahóp (pag-da-ra-hóp), var.
pagdadahóp, n. 1. state or condition of
being poor or needy. Syn. *paghihirap,
paghihikahós*. 2. lack or insufficiency, as
of commodities or other necessities. Syn.
pagkukulang, pagsasalát.

pagdarálitâ (pag-da-rá-li-tâ), var.
pagdadálitâ, n. state or condition of being
in dire need; extreme poverty. Syn. *labís
na paghihirap sa buhay*.

pagdaramdám (pag-da-ram-dám), var.
pagdadamdám, n. feeling of being slighted
or insulted. Syn. *paghihinanakít, pagsamâ
ng loób*.

pagdibdíb (pag-dib-díb), n. act of taking
something to heart or seriously. Syn.
pagsasa-pusò.

pagdidili-dili (pag-di-di-li + di-li), n.
meditation; reflection. Syn. *pagbubulay-*

bulay, pagwawari-wari.

pagdidilím (pag-di-di-lím), n. advent or
coming of darkness; becoming dark.

pagdilág (pag-di-lág), n. a becoming
gorgeous or beautiful. Syn. *pagdikít,
paggandá*.

pagdilimán (pag-di-li-mán), var. **pagdimlán**,
v. (usually with *ng paningín*). 1. to have
one's sight suddenly obscured or dimmed.
Syn. *panlabuan ng paningín*. 2. to have a
blackout or momentary lapse of
consciousness.

pagdiníg (pag-di-níg), var. **pagdingíg**, n. 1.
act of hearing or listening to what is being
said or asked. Also, *pakikiníg*. 2. act of
listening or obeying what one is being
told to do. Syn. *pagsunód*. 3. hearing or
investigation of a case by a judge. Syn.
pagsisiyasat.

pagdiriwang (pag-di-ri-wang), n. celebrating
or feasting; celebration; festivity. Syn.
pagsasayá, selebrasyón.

pagdiyós (pag-di-yós), n. 1. a deifying or
looking upon as god; deification. 2.
idealization; adoration.

pagdududa (pag-du-du-da), n. a doubting;
doubt. Syn. *alinlangan, pag-aalinlangan*.

pagdudunúng-dunungan (pag-du-du-núng +
du-nu-ngan), n. act of pretending to know
very well.

pagdudusa (pag-du-du-sa), var. **pagdurusa**,
n. 1. suffering; patient endurance of
hardship. Syn. *pagtitiís*. 2. deserved
punishment for one's crime.

pagduláng (pag-du-láng), n. 1. search, as for
knowledge. Syn. *paghahanáp, pagtuklás*. 2.
mine-prospecting.

pagdulóg (pag-du-lóg), n. 1. act of attending
or appearing in the presence of someone
in authority. Syn. *pagharáp*. 2. act of
appearing before a civil authority in order
to be married, usually without parental
consent. 3. act of taking one's place at
the dining table, as during a banquet.

pagdurugô (pag-du-ru-gô), n. flow of blood,
as from a cut or wound; bleeding;
hemorrhage. Also, *pagdugô*.

pagdusahan (pag-du-sa-han), v. to make one
suffer for his or her guilt or crime.

pagdustâ (pag-dus-tâ), n. act of oppressing

someone. Syn. *paghamak, pag-apí.*

page (pa-ge), var. **pagi,** n. ray (fish).

paggabáy (pag-ga-báy), n. act of guiding someone morally or physically. Syn. *pagpatnubay, pag-akay.*

paggabí (pag-ga-bí), n. the approach of night.

paggalang (pag-ga-lang), n. respect; show of respect; courteous regard for elders. Syn. *pamimítagan, pítagan.*

paggana (pag-ga-na), n. 1. act of earning money, as by working. Syn. *pagkita sa trabaho.* 2. bearing or earning of interest, as money in a bank. Syn. *pagtubò.*

pagganáp (pag-ga-náp), n. 1. act of performing one's duty or responsibility. Syn. *pagtupád, paggampán.* 2. act of performing a role, as in a play. Syn. *pagpapapél.* 3. act of performing on stage. Syn. *paglabás.*

paggawâ (pag-ga-wâ), n. 1. act of making something; manufacture. Syn. *pagyarì.* 2. act or manner of working. Syn. *pagtrabaho, pagtatrabaho.* 3. construction or erection, as of a house, building, etc. Syn. *pagtatayô.* 4. labor, as partner of "capital." 5. commission, as of a crime.

paggaygáy (pag-gay-gáy), n. act of visiting or going over one by one. Syn. *pag-isá-isá.*

paggiliw (pag-gi-liw), n. affection; love. Syn. *pag-ibig, pagmamahál.*

pagginhawa (pag-gin-ha-wa), n. 1. relief from pain, sickness, etc. Syn. *pagbuti, paggalíng.* 2. improvement or ease attained in life. Syn. *paggaán ng buhay.* 3. a becoming prosperous or wealthy. Syn. *pagunlád ng buhay, pagyaman.*

paggitáw (pag-gi-táw), n. a coming out or appearance, as from hiding, long absence, etc. Syn. *pagsipót, paglitáw, paglabás.*

paggitnâ (pag-git-nâ), n. 1. act of moving or placing oneself in the middle or center of. Syn. *pagsentro.* 2. *(Colloq.)* entry or participation, as in politics. Syn. *pagpasok, pagsali.*

paggunaw (pag-gu-naw), n. the power, attributed to God, to cause deluge or great flood.

paggunitâ (pag-gu-ni-tâ), n. 1. act of

recollecting or recalling of something to one's memory. Syn. *pag-alaala.* 2. a celebration in memory of someone or something; commemoration.

paggupò (pag-gu-pó), n. 1. a falling down or collapse, as of a weak structure. Syn. *pagbagsák, paglugsô.* 2. a becoming bedridden. Syn. *pagkáratay sa baníg, pagkakasakít nang malubhâ.*

paghahakà (pag-ha-ha-kà), n. 1. idea, supposition. Syn. *pag-aakalà, pagwawarì.* 2. suspicion. Syn. *hinalà, paghihinalà; suspetsa, pagsususpetsa; sapantahà, pagsasapantahà.*

paghahapunan (pag-ha-ha-pu-nan), n. 1. act of eating one's supper or evening meals. Syn. *pagkain ng hapunan.* 2. time for supper or for eating one's evening meals.

paghaharáp (pag-ha-ha-ráp), n. 1. a coming face to face with each other. Syn. *pagkikita.* 2. hostile encounter; confrontation. Syn. *pagsasagupà, pagpapanagupà.* 3. submission, as of one's report, suggestion, or the like; presentation. Syn. *pagpipresenta, pagsusubmití.* 4. filing, as of a complaint against someone.

paghaharí-harian (pag-ha-ha-rí + ha-ri-an), n. 1. act of pretending as a king. 2. act of ruling like a king. 3. act of bullying others. Syn. *pandodominá.*

paghaláw (pag-ha-láw), n. 1. selection or picking out things considered preferable or more desirable than the others. Syn. *pagpilì, pamimilì.* 2. adaptation or condensation, as of a literary work of an author.

paghalimuyak (pag-ha-li-mu-yak), n. emission of sweet smell or fragrance. Syn. *pamamangó, pagsamyô.*

paghalina (pag-ha-li-na), n. act of fascinating or attracting someone, as by one's charm. Syn. *pagbalanì, pagbighanì, pag-akit.*

paghamak (pag-ha-mak), n. act of belittling the ability or low condition in life of someone. Syn. *pagmaliít, pagdustâ, pagalipustâ.*

paghambingin (pag-ham-bi-ngin), v. to use as a model; copy from. Syn. *pagtularan.*

paghanapán (pag-ha-na-pán), v. 1. to

demand something from. Also, *hanapan*. 2. to expect something from. Syn. *asahan*.

paghanapin (pag-ha-na-pin), *v.* to look or search for assiduously.

paghandugán (pag-han-du-gán), *v.* to make an offering to; have something dedicated to. Syn. *pag-alayan*.

paghantóng (pag-han-tóng), *n.* a coming to an end. Syn. *pagwawakás, pagkatapos*.

paghangà (pag-ha-ngà), *n.* 1. admiration; high esteem. Syn. *mataás na pagpapalagáy*. 2. amazement; astonishment. Syn. *pagtataká, panggigilalas, pagkámanghâ*.

paghangò (pag-ha-ngò), *n.* 1. removal from the fire or stove of the food being cooked. Syn. *pag-ahon*. 2. the act of adapting or reproducing from the original of a literary work. Syn. *paghalaw, pagbabatay*. 3. act of redeeming someone from poverty, hardship, etc. Syn. *pagtubós*.

paghapon (pag-ha-pon), *n.* 1. act of alighting or perching, as of a bird, on a tree. Syn. *pagdapò*. 2. act of roosting or settling down on a roost, as of fowls, during night. 3. (Rare) act of eating supper (evening meals). See **paghahapunan**.

pagharà (pag-ha-rà), *n.* act of placing oneself in the middle of a place, thus blocking the way of others behind.

pagharian (pag-ha-ri-an), *v.* to rule or reign over. 2. to be overwhelmed or overpowered, as by fear, etc. Syn. *pangibabawan, panaigán*.

paghatirín (pag-ha-ti-rín), *v.* to ask or allow someone to deliver something to. Also, *papághatirín*. Syn. *pagdalahín, papágdalhín*.

paghawakin (pag-ha-wa-kin), *v.* 1. to make someone hold something. Syn. *pagtanganin, papágtanganin*. 2. to give or authorize someone to hold or occupy, as a certain important position. Syn. *bigyán ng tungkulin*.

paghehele-hele (pag-he-he-le + he-le), *n.* pretension of dislike. Syn. *pagkukunwaríng ayaw*.

paghibík (pag-hi-bík), *n.* 1. act of begging humbly and earnestly; pleading; supplication. Syn. *pagsamò, pagmamakaawà*. 2. sobbing; lamentation. Syn.

pagtaghóy, pagdaíng.

paghibò (pag-hi-bò), *n.* act of persuading someone to do wrong; seduction. Syn. *pagsulsól, pag-upat, pag-akit sa masamâ*.

paghikap (pag-hi-kap), *n.* act of going or travelling around or from place to place. Syn. *paglibot, paglibót; paggalà, paggagalâ*.

paghihikahós (pag-hi-hi-ka-hós), *n.* fact or state of being in dire need; indigence; poverty. Syn. *paghihirap, pagdarálitâ, pamumulubi*.

paghihigantí (pag-hi-hi-gan-tí), *n.* act of taking revenge against someone; vengeance; vendetta. Syn. *benggansa, pagbenggansa*.

paghihilík (pag-hi-hi-lík), *n.* act of snoring in sound sleep.

paghihimagsik (pag-hi-hi-mag-sik), *n.* act of rising in revolt; rebellion; revolution. Syn. *pagbabangon, pag-aalsá*.

paghihimatón (pag-hi-hi-ma-tón), *n.* 1. act of giving someone an information or idea about something. Syn. *pagbabalità, pagpapabatíd*. 2. act of helping someone by giving or pointing the place or direction to a certain place. Syn. *pagtuturò ng daán*.

paghihimutók (pag-hi-hi-mu-tók), *n.* forceful expression of resentment, disappointment, distress, or deep sorrow. Syn. *paghihinagpís*.

paghihinagap (pag-hi-hi-na-gap), *n.* act of entertaining an idea or notion about something. Syn. *pag-aakalà, paghihinuhà*.

paghihinanakít (pag-hi-hi-na-na-kít), *n.* reproachful feeling of someone towards a friend or a relative who acted unfavorably against oneself. Syn. *pagdaramdám, pagtatampó*.

paghihintáy (pag-hi-hi-táy), *n.* 1. act of waiting for someone or something to come. Syn. *pag-aantabáy, pag-aabáng*. 2. length or duration of waiting.

paghihingalô (pag-hi-hi-nga-lô), *n.* death agony; moribund state. Syn. *pag-aagaw-buhay*.

paghihirap (pag-hi-hi-rap), *n.* 1. suffering from pain, hardship, or difficulty. Syn. *pagtitiís*. 2. state or condition of poverty or indigence. Syn. *pamumulubi*,

pagdarálitâ. 3. labor in childbirth. Syn.
paghilab ng tiyán sa panganganák. 4. patient
endurance of hardship to attain a certain
wish or dream. Syn. *pagpapakasakit*.

paghilî (pag-hi-lì), *n*. act of making or
causing someone to become envious. Syn.
pag-inggít.

paghimagsikán (pag-hi-mag-si-kán), *v*. to
rebel against. Syn. *pag-alsahán*,
pagbangunan.

paghimalaán (pag-hi-ma-la-án), *v*. to show
or perform miracle to someone. Syn.
pagmilagruhán.

paghimláy (pag-him-láy), *n*. act of lying
down to take a nap or short sleep. Syn.
pag-idlíp, paghipíg.

paghinakdalán (pag-hi-nak-da-lán), *n*. to
unbosom one's hurt feeling to (someone).
Syn. *pagdaingán o paghingahán ng samâ ng
loób*.

paghingá (pag-hi-ngá), *n*. act or manner of
breathing; respiration. See **hingá**.

paghingî (pag-hi-ngî), *n*. 1. act of requesting
or asking, as for help or favor. Syn.
paghilíng, pakikiusap. 2. act of asking or
requesting someone to give oneself a gift
or something free of charge.

paghirang (pag-hi-rang), *n*. 1. act of picking
or selecting the best from. Syn. *pagpilì,
pamimilî*. 2. act of selecting or appointing
someone to a certain position or office.
Syn. *pagnonombra, paglalagáy sa tungkulin*.

paghubog (pag-hu-bog), *n*. 1. act of bending
down something, as a branch laden with
fruits. Syn. *paghutok*. 2. act of shaping
something into an arch by bending or
curving. Syn. *pag-arko, pag-aarko*. 3. act
of training someone to develop a certain
habit or conduct. Syn. *pagsanay*.

paghuhukóm (pag-hu-hu-kóm), *n*. 1. trial
in court. Syn. *paglilitis*. 2. pronouncement
of sentence, as by a judge. Syn. *paghatol,
paglalagdâ ng hatol, pagsesentensiyá*. 3. last
judgment of God.

paghulas (pag-hu-las), *n*. 1. melting or
liquefaction, as of ice. Syn. *pagtutubíg,
untí-untíng pagkalusaw o pagkatunaw*. 2.
oozing. Syn. *pagtulas, pagtagas*.

paghulaw (pag-hu-law), *n*. 1. diminution or
decrease of intensity. Syn. *pag-untós*,

paglubág. 2. cessation, as of rain, storm,
etc. Syn. *paghintô, pagtigil, pagtilà* (of rain),
paglipas.

paghulò (pag-hu-lò), *n*. act of understanding
something seriously before acting or
deciding.

paghumpáy (pag-hum-páy), *n*. cessation or
stopping in doing something continuously
or repeatedly. Syn. *pagtigil, paghintô*.

paghusayin (pag-hu-sa-yin), *n*. to do one's
best. Syn. *pagbutihin*.

paghutok (pag-hu-tok), *n*. 1. act of bending
something by force. Syn. *pagbaluktót,
paghubog*. 2. act of disciplining or
controlling the action or conduct of
someone by force or by proper guidance.
Syn. *pagsugpô*.

pagi (pa-gi), var. **page**, *n*. ray; ray fish.

pag-ibá (pag + i-bá), *n*. 1. act of changing
the shape, system, appearance, etc.;
alteration. Syn. *pagbago, pagbabago*. 2. act
of substituting something with another.
Syn. *pagpapalit*. 3. transfer or changing,
as of one's residence. Syn. *paglipat*.

pag-ibig (pag + i-big), *n*. love; strong
affection for; devotion to a person or
persons. Syn. *pagmamahál, pagsinta,
paggiliw, pag-irog*.

pag-iíbigan (pag + i-í-bi-gan), *n*. 1. love
affair. Syn. *pagmamáhalan, pagsusúyuan*.
2. love for each other. Syn. *pagmamahál
sa isá't isá*.

pag-ilandáng (pag + i-lan-dáng), *n*. 1.
sudden flight, as of something
accidentally thrown. Syn. *pagtilampon,
pagtalsík*. 2. upward propulsion, as of water
from a fountain. Syn. *pagtilandóy*.

pag-iláp (pag + i-láp), *n*. a becoming wild,
esp. of a previously domesticated or tamed
animal.

pag-imbák (pag + im-bák), var. **pag-iimbák**,
n. act of storing goods, as in a bodega.
Syn. *pagtitinggál*. 2. act of conserving or
preserving food for commercial purposes,
as by canning or packing. Syn. *pagsasalata*.

pag-imbáy (pag + im-báy), *n*. 1. gentle
trotting or gait of a horse. Syn. *pagtrote*.
2. the characteristic swaying of the arms
in walking. Cf. *kampáy, pagkampáy*.

pag-imík (pag + i-mík), *n*. breaking of

silence by talking after having been silent for sometime. Syn. *pagsisimuláng umimík o magsalitâ.*

pag-inam (pag + i-nam), n. improvement; change from bad to good. Syn. *pagbuti, paghusay.*

pagindapatin (pa-gin-da-pa-tin), *v.* to consider favorably; make acceptable to.

pag-initan (pag + i-ni-tan), *v.* 1. to use for heating water, food, etc. over a fire, as a pot, casserole, or the like. 2. (*Colloq.*) to be the object of one's ire or anger; get mad at.

pag-inó (pag + i-nó), n. act of calling attention of someone or about something. Syn. *pagpuná, pagpansín.*

pag-ingatan (pag + i-nga-tan), *v.* 1. to be careful about; take good care of. Syn. *pangalagaan.* 2. to do or make carefully. Syn. *gawín nang maingat.*

pag-iral (pag + i-ral), n. 1. a being in operation or in force; taking effect; effectivity. Syn. *pagkakabisà.* 2. existence; a being in use or in vogue. Syn. *pananatili, pamamalagì.* 3. predominance; prevalence. Syn. *pananaíg, pangingibabaw.*

pag-irap (pag + i-rap), n. a sullen look or glance at someone. Syn. *paingós na tingín o pagtingín.*

pag-iríng (pag + i-ríng), n. act of treating someone with disdain or scorn. Syn. *paghamak, pag-alipustâ, pagdustâ.*

pag-irog (pag + i-rog), n. love or affection for someone. Syn. *pagmamahál, pagsintá, pagsuyò, pagliyág, paggiliw.*

pag-isahín (pag + i-sa-hín), *v.* to combine into one; unite. Syn. *buuín, pagsamá-samahin.*

pag-isip (pag + i-sip), n. act of thinking, as of a plan, ways and means, etc.

pagispis (pa-gis-pis), n. 1. a soft flapping, as of leaves. 2. the soft sound thus produced. Syn. *lawiswís.*

pagitan (pa-gi-tan), n. 1. space or distance between two objects or places; gap. Syn. *puwáng.* 2. interval of time; period of time between two events, etc; intervening period. 3. extent of differences between two qualities or conditions. Syn. *pagkakáibá.* 4. something placed between

two things, as a wall or partition.

pagitnâ (pa-git-nâ), *v.* 1. to go to the center; place oneself in the middle. Also, *pumagitnâ.* Syn. *sumentro.*

pagiwang-giwang (pa-gi-wang + gi-wang), *adj.* wobbling; moving unsteadily from side to side, as a dilapidated cart.

pag-iwas (pag + i-was), n. 1. act of avoiding contact or meeting someone. Syn. *pagilag.* 2. avoidance from being involved, as in trouble, etc. Syn. *pag-ilag, pangingilag, paglayô.* 3. evasion, as from paying taxes.

paglabág (pag-la-bág), n. 1. act of violating a law, agreement, rule, etc. Syn. *pagsuwáy, di-pagsunód.* 2. an instance of breaking a law, etc.; violation; infraction; infringement.

paglabás (pag-la-bás), n. 1. act of going out, as from a room, house, etc.; opposed to *pagpasok.* 2. appearance or coming out, as from hiding. Syn. *paglitáw, pagsipót.* 3. a jutting out, as from a hole. Syn. *pagultaw, pag-litáw, pag-uslî.* 4. release, as from prison. Syn. *paglayà.* 5. issue or coming out, as a publication. Syn. *pagkápalathalâ.* 6. act of performing or acting, as on the stage. Syn. *pagganáp (sa tanghalan).*

paglaboy (pag-la-boy), n. act of wandering aimlessly from one place to another, vagrancy; vagabondage. Syn. *pagpapagalá-galà, paglilibót nang waláng kasaysayan, pagbabagamundo.*

paglakad (pag-la-kad), n. 1. act or manner of walking. Syn. *paghakbang.* 2. act or time of leaving for a mission; departure; start, as of a trip. Syn. *pag-alís.* 3. progress or development, as of work, business, etc. Syn. *takbó, pagtakbó.* 4. the working or running condition, as of a machine. Syn. *andár, pag-andár.* 5. passing, as of time. Syn. *lipas, paglipas; daán, pagdaán.*

paglakí (pag-la-kí), n. 1. growth; increase in size, as of a child. 2. growth, as of plant. Syn. *paglagô.* 3. growth, development, or progress, as of business. Syn. *pag-unlád.* 4. increase in area. Syn. *pagluwáng, paglapad.* 5. a bulging or swelling. Syn. *pamamagá, pag-umbók, pagtambók.* 6. increase, as of income, expenses, etc. Syn.

paglagabláb

paglakás, pagdami.

paglagabláb (pag-la-gab-láb), n. a bursting in flame. Syn. *pagsikláb, bigláng paglalaáb o pagdiringas.*

paglagáy (pag-la-gáy), n. 1. act of placing oneself in a certain place or position. Syn. *pagpuwesto.* 2. (with *sa estado o sa magalíng*) act of marrying or getting married. Syn. *pag-aasawa, pagharáp sa dambanà* (fig.), *pagmamahabang dulang* (fig.).

paglagì (pag-la-gì), n. act of staying permanently in a certain place or position. Syn. *pagpirmí, pananatili.*

paglagô (pag-la-gô), n. 1. growth or luxuriant growth, as of plants. Syn. *paglambâ, paglakí, pagtubò, pagtaás, pagyabong.* 2. progress or growth, as of a business enterprise. Syn. *pag-unlád.* 3. increase, as of capital. Syn. *paglakí (ng puhunan).*

paglait (pag-la-it), n. a vilifying or being vilified; vilification; calumniation. Syn. *pag-alimurà, pag-alipustâ.*

paglalâ (pag-la-lâ), n. a becoming grave or serious, as of an illness; aggravation. Syn. *paglubhâ, pagbigát.*

paglalabás (pag-la-la-bás), n. 1. act of putting or drawing out something, as from one's pocket. Syn. *pagdukot.* 2. act of showing something, as proof. Syn. *pagpapakita, paghaharáp.* 3. presentation or showing, as of a play or drama; staging. Syn. *pagtatanghál.* 4. a publishing or publication, as of a magazine. Syn. *paglalathalà.* 5. exportation, as of goods to other countries. Syn. *pagluluwás (ng kalakal).* 6. withdrawal, as of money from a bank. Syn. *pagkuha.*

paglalakad (pag-la-la-kad), n. 1. act of undertaking the promotion or sale of. Cf. *pag-aahente.* 2. act of negotiating for the approval of something by one in authority through influence or connection.

paglalakás-loób (pag-la-la-kás + lo-ób), n. show of courage or fearlessness. Syn. *pagmamatapáng, pagpapakita ng tapang o kawaláng-takot.*

paglalakbáy (pag-la-lak-báy), n. 1. act of going on a trip or journey. Syn. *paglilibót sa ibá't ibáng dako.* 2. a trip, journey, or

paglalamyâ

travel taken or made by someone. Cf. *pagliliwalíw.*

paglalagáy (pag-la-la-gáy), n. 1. act of putting or placing a thing on something. Syn. *pagpapatong, paglalagak.* 2. act of depositing money, as in a bank. Syn. *pagdedepósitó, paglalagak.* 3. act of attaching or providing a thing with something, as a chair with a new leg or legs. Syn. *pagkakabít.* 4. installation, as of a telephone line, etc. Syn. *pagkakabít.* 5. installation, as of officers of an association. Syn. *pagtatalagá o pagluluklôk (sa tungkulin).* 6. act of putting something in a container. Syn. *pagsisilíd.* 7. act of putting something inside a hole, room, etc. Syn. *pagpapasok.* 8. (Fig.) act of giving a bribe. Syn. *pagsusuhol, pagpaparatíng.*

paglalahad (pag-la-la-had), n. 1. detailed explanation or presentation of facts. Syn. *pagpapaliwanag.* 2. act of showing or presenting something openly, as one's hands. Syn. *paglaladlád.* 3. (Rhet.) exposition; expository writing.

paglalahò (pag-la-la-hò), n. 1. eclipse (of the moon or sun). Syn. *eklipse.* 2. sudden disappearance. Syn. *bigyáng pagkawalâ o pagkalipol.*

paglalalin (pag-la-la-lin), n. 1. act of contaminating someone, as with a disease. Syn. *paghahawa.* 2. act of staining something, as with some kind of color.

paglalamán (pag-la-la-mán), n. 1. growth of flesh, as in a cut or wound; hence, a becoming healed. Syn. *paghihilom, paggalíng, pagkatuyô.* 2. act of filling a container. Syn. *pagsisilíd.* 3. act of stuffing or filling the inside of, as a cushion, sandwich, etc. Syn. *pagpapalamán.* 4. growth or development of tubers or rootstocks, like potatoes. Also, *pagkakalamán.* 5. accommodation, as of a certain number of persons in a room. Syn. *pagkakasya.*

paglalambing (pag-la-lam-bing), n. act of showing one's affectionate desire to be caressed.

paglalamyâ (pag-la-lam-yâ), n. act or manner of talking like a baby who wants to be caressed.

paglalandî (pag-la-lan-dî), n. coquetry; flirting.

paglalantád (pag-la-lan-tád), n. 1. act of making known; revelation. 2. a public disclosure; exposé. 3. act of showing something in the open.

paglaláng (pag-la-láng), n. a creating; creation.

paglalangán (pag-la-la-ngán), v. to be deceived by trickery; swindle; defraud.

paglalapit (pag-la-la-pit), n. 1. act of placing something near or close another. 2. submission or presentation, as of an offer or proposal to someone in authority for comment or approval.

paglalarawan (pag-la-la-ra-wan), n. 1. act of portraying something in picture; drawing or sketching. 2. act of giving an account of something in words; a describing or description.

paglalatang (pag-la-la-tang), n. increase in intensity. Syn. *pagsidhî, pagtindî.*

paglalathalà (pag-la-lat-ha-là), n. act or job of publishing; publication. Syn. *pagpupublikâ.*

paglalayág (pag-la-la-yág), n. 1. act of sailing in the sea; voyage; trip by boat or ship. Syn. *paglalakbáy-dagat.* 2. delayed or irregular discharge of the menses. Syn. *pagka-atraso ng regla.*

paglalayás (pag-la-la-yás), n. act of traveling to many places without real purpose; vagabondage. Syn. *paglilimayón.*

paglamáng (pag-la-máng), n. 1. act of surpassing another. Syn. *paghigít, paglalò, paglampás.* 2. act of taking advantage of another. Syn. *pagsasamantalá.*

paglamayan (pag-la-ma-yan), v. 1. to keep vigil for; keep awake during the usual hour of sleep, as in keeping vigil for. Syn. *pagpuyatán.* 2. to have a work done overtime during night.

paglambingán (pag-lam-bi-ngán), v. to act affectionately or tenderly towards someone.

paglamíg (pag-la-míg), n. 1. loss or decrease of heat, as of hot iron, food, etc. 2. a becoming cold or colder, as of temperature during night. Syn. *paggináw.* 3. waning or loss, as of interest,

enthusiasm, etc. Syn. *pagkawalâ ng siglá.*

paglamlám (pag-lam-lám), n. 1. dimming or becoming dim, as of light. Syn. *paglabò, panlalabò; pagkulimlím, pangungulimlím.* 2. loss of animation, enthusiasm, etc. Syn. *pagtamláy, pananamláy.*

paglanság (pag-lan-ság), n. 1. act of dismantling or breaking something into parts, referring esp. to machinery. 2. disorganization or abolition, as of an office. Syn. *pagbuwág.*

paglantád (pag-lan-tád), n. 1. a coming out in the open; making oneself known. Syn. *paghayág, pagpapakilala.* 2. act of showing oneself in the open. Syn. *pagpapakita.*

paglaon (pag-la-on), n. a being delayed or unnecessarily prolonged. Syn. *pagluwát, pagluluwát; pagtagál, pagtatagál.*

paglapastangan (pag-la-pas-ta-ngan), n. act or statement of disrespect or irreverence. Syn. *pagwawaláng-galang, pagwawaláng-pítagan, pagwawaláng-pakundangan.*

paglapit (pag-la-pit), n. 1. act of approaching or getting close or nearer a person, place, or thing. Syn. *pagdaís.* 2. a becoming near or nearer. 3. act of approaching or seeing someone to ask for help or favor. Syn. *paghingî ng tulong o pabór.*

paglasóg (pag-la-sóg), n. act of breaking (bones, etc.) into pieces. Syn. *pagdurog.*

paglatag (pag-la-tag), n. 1. a rolling out, as a sheet of metal. 2. a falling flat or prostrate, as the body of an exhausted person.

paglawak (pag-la-wak), n. an expanding; spread or expansion.

paglayà (pag-la-yà), n. 1. release or freedom from confinement or prison. 2. attainment of liberty or independence from a ruling nation; emancipation.

paglayô (pag-la-yô), n. 1. act of going away to a far place. 2. act of getting away or separating from someone. 3. a keeping away from; avoidance.

paglibák (pag-li-bák), n. mockery; derision.

paglibáng (pag-li-báng), n. 1. act of distracting the attention of someone in order to confuse. 2. act of consoling or cheering up a person in distress or in sorrow. 3. act of entertaining someone.

paglibingán (pag-li-bi-ngán), *v.* to use (a place) for burying a dead person.

paglikás[1] (pag-li-kás), *n.* act of withdrawing from a place of danger to a safer place of safety; evacuation. Syn. *ebakuwesyón*.

paglikás[2] (pag-li-kás), *n.* 1. widespread occurrence, as of a certain communicable disease. Syn. *pagkalat.* 2. eruption or breaking out in a rash, as of a certain kind of skin disease. Syn. *pagsingáw, pagbukál.*

paglikat (pag-li-kat; -kát), *n.* a waning or cessation of intensity. Syn. *paghupâ, paghipâ, paglubag, paghintô.*

paglikhâ (pag-lik-hâ), *n.* 1. act of creating or inventing; invention, creation. Syn. *pag-imbento.* 2. creation, as by God. Syn. *paglaláng.*

paglikom (pag-li-kom), *n.* 1. act of collecting or gathering things together. Syn. *pag-ipon, pag-iipon; pagtipon, pagtitipon.* 2. act of putting and keeping things together after using. Syn. *pagliligpít.*

pagligaw (pag-li-gaw), *n.* act, manner, or period of courtship; wooing. Also, *panliligaw.* Syn. *pangingibig.*

pagligaya (pag-li-ga-ya), *n.* a becoming happy; change from loneliness to happiness.

pagliham (pag-li-ham), *n.* act or time of writing or sending a letter to someone. Syn. *pagsulat, pagpapadalá ng sulat o liham.*

paglihihán (pag-li-hi-hán), *v.* to be the object of one's craving when a woman is conceiving.

paglihiman (pag-li-hi-man), *v.* to be secretive to; keep a secret from. Syn. *pagkailaán.*

paglihís (pag-li-hís), *n.* 1. act of deviating from the straight or direct way. Syn. *pagsinsáy.* 2. act of violating a law, ordinance, or the like. Syn. *paglabág.*

paglilim (pag-li-lim), *n.* the time when the light of the sun becomes subdued, hence, cooler, because of being shaded or covered with thick clouds. Syn. *paglilom, paglamíg ng sikat ng araw.*

paglililo (pag-li-li-lo), *n.* act or instance of disloyalty or treachery. Syn. *pagtataksíl.*

paglililom (pag-li-li-lom), *n.* the time when the sun gets shaded or covered with clouds.

paglilimayón (pag-li-li-ma-yón), *n.* act of gallivanting around. Syn. *pagbubulakból, pagpapalabuy-laboy, paglalakuwatsa.*

paglilimì (pag-li-li-mì), *n.* deep thinking, serious thought; contemplation. Syn. *pagninilay-nilay, pagbubulay-bulay.*

paglilimután (pag-li-li-mu-tán), *n.* act of forgetting each other or one another, said of lovers.

paglilináng (pag-li-li-náng), *n.* act of maintaining a farm; cultivation of land for planting. Syn. *pagbubukid, pagtataním, pag-aararo.* 2. development, as of a language. Syn. *pagpapaunlád.*

paglilinaw (pag-li-li-naw), *n.* act of clearing a misunderstanding. Also, *paglilinawán.* Syn. *pag-uúnawaán.*

paglilining (pag-li-li-ning), *n.* careful or serious consideration or thinking about something before acting. Syn. *paglilimì, masusíng pagsasaalang-alang.*

paglilingkód (pag-li-ling-kód), *n.* 1. act of serving or working for someone. 2. manner or kind of service done or being done for someone. 3. time or period of service, as in an office.

paglilirip (pag-li-li-rip), *n.* serious or deep thinking about, something; careful study or analysis. Syn. *masusing pag-aaral o pagsasaalang-alang; paglilimì.*

paglilitis (pag-li-li-tis), *n.* investigation or trial of a case in court; court hearing. Syn. *imbestigasyón, pagsisiyasat.*

pagliliwalíw (pag-li-li-wa-líw), *n.* pleasure trip; vacationing; excursion.

pagliliwanag (pag-li-li-wa-nag), *n.* 1. a becoming clear or bright, as of a dark room, after providing it with a light. 2. a becoming clear to someone's understanding.

paglilok (pag-li-lok), *n.* act of carving a figure or statue from wood, stone, or metal; the work of a sculptor. Syn. *pag-ukit.*

pagliluhan (pag-li-lu-han), *v.* to betray; be disloyal to. Syn. *pagtaksilán.*

paglimahím (pag-li-ma-hín), *v.* 1. to divide into five (equal) parts. 2. to increase something five times. Also, *limahín.*

aglimì (pag-li-mì), n. serious study, thought, or consideration about something a person wants to do. Syn. *masusing pag-iisip, pag-aaral, o pagsasaalang-alang.*

aglimit (pag-li-mit), n. 1. a becoming frequent or often, as one's visit. Syn. *pagdalás.* 2. a becoming dense or closer to one another; opposed to *pagdalang.* Syn. *pagsinsín.*

aglimot (pag-li-mot), n. act or attempt to forget or put something out of one's mind. Syn. *pagwawaglít sa isip o sa alaala.*

aglináng (pag-li-náng), n. 1. act of cultivating a field for planting. Syn. *pagsaka.* 2. act of developing or enriching, e.g., a language. Syn. *pagpapayaman, pagpapaunlád.*

aglinaw (pag-li-naw), n. 1. a clearing or becoming clear, as of muddy water after the dregs have settled down. Cf. *pagtining.* 2. recovery, as of one's sight. Syn. *pagliliwanag.* 3. a clarifying or being clarified; clarification. Syn. *pagliwanag, pagpapaliwanag.*

aglingap (pag-li-ngap), n. 1. protective care given to someone. Syn. *pagkalingà.* 2. compassion; pity. Syn. *awà, habág.*

aglipanà (pag-li-pa-nà), n. act of spreading all over a certain place, referring esp. to plainclothes men, pickpockets, and the like. Syn. *pagkalat, paglisaw.*

aglipas (pag-li-pas), n. 1. passing or lapsing, as of time. Syn. *pagdaán, paglampás.* 2. a becoming out of fashion or style. Syn. *pagkawalâ sa moda.* 3. loss of potency or effectivity. Syn. *pagkawalâ ng bisà.* 4. a subsiding or decrease of intensity. Syn. *paghupâ, pag-untós, pagtigháw, paghintô, pagtigil.* 5. a calming down, as of anger. Syn. *paghinahon, pagkalma.*

aglipós (pag-li-pós), n. act of overwhelming someone, as with joy or happiness. Syn. *pagpuspós.*

aglirip (pag-li-rip), n. effort to understand or realize the truth or significance of. Syn. *paglining, paghulò.*

aglitáw (pag-li-táw), n. 1. a jutting or sticking out, as from a hole, small opening, etc. Syn. *pag-ultáw, pag-uslî,*

pagsulpót. 2. a coming out into sight; appearance. Syn. *paglabás, pagpapakita, paglantád.* 3. a coming back or return, as from a long hiding or absence. Syn. *pagsipót.*

pagliwanag (pag-li-wa-nag), n. 1. a becoming clear or bright, as of a room after opening the windows or providing it with a light. 2. act of explaining something to make it clear; clarifying. Syn. *pagpapaliwanag.*

pagliyág (pag-li-yág), n. expression of love or affection for the opposite sex. Syn. *pag-ibig, pagmamahál, pagsinta, pag-irog.*

paglubág (pag-lu-bág), n. a calming down; decrease of intensity. Syn. *pagkalmá, paghupâ, pag-untós, pagtigháw.*

paglubáy (pag-lu-báy), n. 1. a loosening, as of a tight rope, bite, grip, etc. Syn. *pagluwág.* 2. a ceasing or stopping, as of a long crying, laughing, joking, etc. Syn. *paghintô, pagtigil, pagtahán, paghumpáy, pagtugot.*

paglubhâ (pag-lub-hâ), n. a becoming grave or serious; change from bad to worse. Syn. *paglalâ, paggrabe.*

paglubóg (pag-lu-bóg), n. 1. a sinking or going down the surface of water, soft ground, mud, etc. Cf. *pagbaón.* 2. setting or sinking, as of the sun, moon, etc.; opposed to *pagsikat.* 3. a waning or loss, as of popularity.

paglubós (pag-lu-bós), n. act of carrying on something to completion. Syn. *pagtapos, pagkumpleto.*

paglukob (pag-lu-kob), n. 1. act of protecting someone by or as by covering with the body. 2. act of controlling or putting under one's power or authority; domination. Syn. *pagsakop.*

paglugár (pag-lu-gár), var. **paglugál**, n. act of taking one's proper or right place. Syn. *paglagáy sa lugár.*

paglugon (pag-lu-gon), n. a falling off, as of hair. Syn. *paglagas, panlalagas.*

pagluhà (pag-lu-hà), n. 1. act of crying; shedding of tears. Syn. *pag-iyák.* 2. suffering, esp. from misfortune. Syn. *paghihirap, pagtitiís.*

pagluhód (pag-lu-hód), n. 1. act, time, or

duration of kneeling, as in praying. 2. (*Fig.*) act of begging for mercy. Syn. *paghingî ng tawad, pagmamakaawà.*

pagluhog (pag-lu-hog), n. act of begging humbly and earnestly; supplication. Syn. *pagsamò, pagmamakaawà.*

paglulukó (pag-lu-lu-kó), n. 1. act of doing foolishness. 2. neglect of one's duty. Syn. *pagpapabayâ sa tungkulin.*

pagluluksâ (pag-lu-luk-sâ), n. 1. act or period of wearing mourning clothes. 2. mourning period for a deceased person.

paglulunsád (pag-lu-lun-sád), n. 1. act of unloading cargoes, passengers, etc. Syn. *pagdidiskarga, pag-iibís.* 2. act of launching, as of one's candidacy in an election. Syn. *pagbubunsód.*

paglulunggatî (pag-lu-lung-ga-tî), n. fervent wish or the effort to attain, e.g., success. Syn. *taimtím na láyunin o pagsisikap.*

paglulupasáy (pag-lu-lu-pa-sáy), n. act or manner of lying flat on the floor or ground, as in complete exhaustion, unconsciousness, laziness, etc. Cf. *paglulupagî.*

paglulupít (pag-lu-lu-pít), n. act of cruelty or brutality. Also, *pagmamalupít.*

paglulustáy (pag-lu-lus-táy), n. misuse or embezzlement of fund. Syn. *pagdidespalko.*

pagluluwál (pag-lu-lu-wál), n. act or time of giving birth (said of pregnant women). Syn. *pag-aanák, panganganák, pagsisilang (ng sanggól).*

pagluluwát (pag-lu-lu-wát), n. delay; a becoming or being delayed. Syn. *pagtatagál, pagkaatraso.*

paglungayngáy (pag-lu-ngay-ngáy), n. drooping of head due to loss of consciousness, complete exhaustion, etc.

paglungkót (pag-lung-kót), n. a becoming sad or lonely.

paglunggatián (pag-lung-ga-ti-án), v. to make effort to attain a fervent wish or ambition. Syn. *pagsumikapan.*

paglupig (pag-lu-pig), n. act of conquering or subjugating an enemy or opponent. Syn. *pagsupil, pagtalo, pagdaíg.*

pagluráy (pag-lu-ráy), n. act of mangling, mutilating, or tearing into small pieces. Syn. *pagmungláy, pagdurog, paggutáy.*

paglusóg (pag-lu-sóg), n. 1. healthy growth as of a person's body. Syn. *pagtabâ paglakás ng katawán.* 2. progress o development, as of a business enterprise Syn. *pag-unlád, paglagô.*

paglusong (pag-lu-song), n. 1. act of goin down an incline; descent. Syn. *pagbabá* 2. act of stepping or getting down i water, as in taking a bath in a river. Syn *paglusok.*

paglustáy (pag-lus-táy), n. misuse of fund embezzlement. Syn. *pagdespalko.*

paglutang (pag-lu-tang), n. 1. act o remaining afloat (on water). 2. risin above the surface of water or liquid. Syn *pangingibabaw sa tubig.*

paglutas (pag-lu-tas), var. **paglutás**, n. 1. ac of finishing or completing something Syn. *pagtapos.* 2. act of solving or findin the solution to a problem, crime, etc. Syn *pagremedyo, paglunas.*

paglutók (pag-lu-tók), n. a becoming brittle referring esp. to materials, due to bein very dry. Cf. *paglutóng.*

pagluwág (pag-lu-wág), n. 1. a becomin more spacious or roomy; increase of roor or space. Syn. *paglakî ng lugár, pagluwáng paglawak.* 2. a loosening, as of joint knots, bindings, attachments, etc. An *pagsikip, paghigpít.* 3. a becoming loose du to the increase of size, as of shoes, hat etc. Syn. *pagluwáng.* 4. a becoming le strict; relaxation, as of rules, regulation or the like. Syn. *pagginhawa, pag-alwán.*

pagluwál (pag-lu-wál), n. 1. a coming int being, as of a child. Syn. *pagsilang.* 2. coming out or appearance, as fron darkness. Syn. *paglitáw, paglabás.*

pagluwát (pag-lu-wát), n. a long o unnecessary delay. Syn. *pagtagál, paglaor*

pagmaáng-maángan (pag-ma-áng + ma-a ngan), v. to feign ignorance to; preten to know nothing about to someone. Syn *pagkunwariáng waláng-nálalaman.*

pagmagalingán (pag-ma-ga-li-ngán), v. to b boastful to; speak too highly about onese to. Syn. *paghambugán, pagmahanginán.*

pagmalakihán (pag-ma-la-ki-hán), v. to b overly proud to. Syn. *pagmataasán pagpalaluan.*

pagmamabutí (pag-ma-ma-bu-tí), n. act of bringing oneself into someone's favor; ingratiation. Syn. *pagmamagalíng.*

pagmamakaawà (pag-ma-ma-ka-a-wà), n. humble pleading for pity or mercy; act of begging for mercy.

pagmamakasarili (pag-ma-ma-ka-sa-ri-li), n. selfishness; egoism; egotism; self-conceit. Syn. *labis na pagpapahalagá sa sarili, pagkapalalò, kapalaluán.*

pagmamagalíng (pag-ma-ma-ga-líng), n. 1. act of bragging or boasting. Syn. *paghahambóg.* 2. act of bringing oneself into someone's favor or good graces; ingratiation. Syn. *pagsisipsíp (fig.).*

pagmamagandáng-loób (pag-ma-ma-gandáng + lo-ób), n. act of helping another graciously, as by giving a gift, doing someone a favor, or the like.

pagmamahál (pag-ma-ma-hál), n. 1. act of loving someone; love or affection for someone. Syn. *pag-ibig.* 2. act of increasing the price of a commodity. Syn. *pagtataás ng halagá.*

pagmamalabís (pag-ma-ma-la-bís), n. 1. abuse, as of authority. Syn. *pag-aabuso.* 2. unjust or corrupt practice.

pagmamalakí (pag-ma-ma-la-kí), n. vain pride; show of arrogant pride. Syn. *pagmamataás.*

pagmamalasakit (pag-ma-ma-la-sa-kit), n. concern for the good or protection of someone or something. See *malasakit.*

pagmamalinís (pag-ma-ma-li-nís), n. practice or habit of cleanliness; also, pretension of being clean.

pagmamaliw (pag-ma-ma-liw), n. *(poetic)* loss or disappearance. Syn. *paglalahò, pagkawalâ.*

pagmamaramót (pag-ma-ma-ra-mót), n. act or instance of being selfish or stingy. Also, *karamutan.*

pagmamarunóng (pag-ma-ma-ru-nóng), n. pretension of being wise or intelligent. Also, *pagdudunúng-dunungan.*

pagmamasíd (pag-ma-ma-síd), n. 1. act of observing what is happening or going around; observation. Syn. *pagmamalas, pag-oobserba.* 2. the work of an observer or supervisor.

pagmamataás (pag-ma-ma-ta-ás), n. 1. vain pride; exaggerated self-esteem. Syn. *nagmamalakí.* 2. haughtiness; arrogance. Syn. *paghahambóg, kahambugán.*

pagmamatigás (pag-ma-ma-ti-gás), n. act of being firm in one's words, belief, or stand; firm stand or belief.

pagmamatuwíd (pag-ma-ma-tu-wíd), var. pagmamatwíd, n. act or manner of expressing one's reasons or arguments in favor or against something; argumentation. Syn. *pangangatuwiran.*

pagmamatyág (pag-ma-mat-yág), n. silent or secret observation; act of spying on someone. Syn. *lihim o tahimik na pagmamasíd o pagsubaybáy.*

pagmano (pag-ma-no), n. act of kissing the hand of an elder as a sign of respect.

pagmaramután (pag-ma-ra-mu-tán), v. to be selfish to.

pagmasakitan (pag-ma-sa-ki-tan), v. to have protective concern for. Syn. *pagmalasakitan.*

pagmasdán (pag-mas-dán), v. to look at or observe intently. Syn. *tingnán o obserbaháng mabuti.*

pagmatá (pag-ma-tá), n. *(Fig.)* act of belittling someone. Syn. *paghamak.*

pagmimirón (pag-mi-mi-rón), n. the act of watching an event or a gambling game without taking any active part.

pagmimithî (pag-mi-mit-hî), n. a fervent or vehement desire or wish for the attainment of something. Syn. *paghahangád.*

pagmithián (pag-mit-hi-án), v. to be the object of one's fervent desire or wish.

pagmukhaín (pag-muk-ha-ín), v. 1. to make alike or similar to each other. Syn. *pagparehuhin.* 2. to make one look like something.

pagmulat (pag-mu-lat), n. act of opening one's eyes. Cf. *pagdilat.*

pagmumukhâ (pag-mu-muk-hâ), n. countenance; expression of the face (used disparagingly).

pagmumulat (pag-mu-mu-lat), n. 1. (usually with *ng matá*) act of opening the eyes. See **pagmulat.** 2. *(Fig.)* act of opening a person's eyes or making him see or understand what is really happening. Syn.

pagpapamatá, pagpapamulat.

pagmumuni-muni (pag-mu-mu-ni + mu-ni),
n. long, continuous thinking; long,
careful study of something in one's mind.
Syn. *pagninilay-nilay.*

pagmumúntikanan (pag-mu-mún-ti-ka-
nan), n. fact or state of being almost a
failure or success, depending on what the
result is. Cf. *pamimiligró.*

pagmumurang-sibuyas (pag-mu-mu-rang +
si-bu-yas), n. *(Fig.)* the act of a woman
who has passed middle age to dress up
elegantly in order to look younger and
more attractive to suitors.

pagnamnám (pag-nam-nám), n. act of
tasting the savor of. Syn. *paglasáp,
pagtikím.*

pagnanais (pag-na-na-is), n. fervent desire
or wish. Syn. *paghahangád.*

pagnanasà (pag-na-na-sà), n. desire or wish.
Syn. *paghahangád.*

pagniniíg (pag-ni-ni-íg), n. long intimate
conversation; tete-a-tete. Cf.
pagpapanayam; pagtatalamitam.

pagninilay (pag-ni-ni-lay), n. contemplation
or reflection; deep thought. Syn.
pagdidilidili, pagbubulay-bulay.

pagngakngák (pag-ngak-ngák), n. 1. act of
crying aloud sulkingly, esp. by a child. 2.
act of speaking out of turn. 3. act of
chattering or talking too much and in a
foolish way.

pagngalingalí (pag-nga-li-nga-lí), n. too
much eagerness in trying to attain, do,
finish, something.

pagngalitin (pag-nga-li-tin), v. 1. to cause
someone to become furious (with anger).
2. to cause someone to grit his teeth, as
in anger.

pagngapa (pag-nga-pa), n. act of groping in
the dark. 2. the condition a person
experiences when he is at a loss on what
to do.

pagngawâ (pag-nga-wâ), n. 1. act of talking
too much. 2. act of crying long and loud.

pagngingitngít (pag-ngi-ngit-ngít), n.
suppressed feeling of rage or fury.

pagod (pa-god), n. tiredness; weariness;
fatigue. Also, *kapaguran, pagkapagod.* Syn.
pagál, pagkapagál; hapò, pagkahapò.

pagóng (pa-góng), var. **pag-ong**, n. (Zool
turtle. Cf. *pawikan.*

pagpakitaan (pag-pa-ki-ta-an), v. to sho
(something) to someone; prov
something to someone by showing c
demonstrating.

pagpakitaang-gilas (pag-pa-ki-ta-ang + g
las), v. to impress someone with one's vai
display of ability. Syn. *pagpasakitan.*

pagpakuan (pag-pa-ku-an), v. 1. to use (
thing) for nailing on something. Syr
gamiting pakuán o pámakuán. 2. *(Fig.)* t
be the main object or target of.

pagpakundanganan (pag-pa-kun-da-nga
nan), v. to regard with respect c
consideration; consider or treat wit
deference or courtesy. Syn. *igalang.*

pagpág (pag-pág), I. n. act of shakin
something to get rid of dust, water, etc
Also, *pagpapagpág.*
—II. adj. rid of dust, etc. by shaking.

pagpaguran (pag-pa-gu-ran), v. 1. to get c
obtain by exerting efforts; work for i
order to attain or obtain. Syn. *paghirapa
pagpakahirapan.*

pagpahayagan (pag-pa-ha-ya-gan), v. t
express to; make a declaration of one
intention to. Cf. *pagtapatán.*

pagpahimakasán (pag-pa-hi-ma-ka-sán), i
to bid goodbye or farewell to. Syn
pagpaalaman.

pagpalain (pag-pa-la-in), v. 1. to protect an
help; take care of. Syn. *tangkilikin
ampunín, alagaan.* 2. to bless or be blessed

pagpalibhasà (pag-pa-lib-ha-sà), n. act c
underestimating or belittling someone
Syn. *paghamak.*

pagpaling (pag-pa-ling), n. 1. act of turnin
to one side. Syn. *pagbaling, pagpihit.* 2. ac
inclining or leaning slightly to a side. Syn
pagkiling, pagtagilid, paghilig.

pagpalya (pag-pal-ya), n. 1. omission o
skipping in typing or printing. Syn
pagsalto, pagpalyo. 2. failure to explode
as a firecracker. Syn. *di-pagputók, di
pagsabog, pagmimintís.* 3. act of absentin
oneself from school, work, etc.; non
attendance. Syn. *pagliban, di-pagpasok.*

pagpanaw (pag-pa-naw), n. 1. mysteriou
disappearance or loss. Syn. *mahiwagan,*

pagkawalâ o pagkalipol. 2. departure. Syn. *paglisan, pagyao, pag-alís.* 3. death. Syn. *pagkamatáy, kamatayan.*

pagpandáy (pag-pan-dáy), n. 1. act of shaping red-hot metal, esp. iron, into a certain form by beating on the anvil. 2. *(Fig.)* act of training (someone) very well. Syn. *pagsanay na mabuti.*

pagpanibulos (pag-pa-ni-bu-los), n. act of having complete trust and confidence in someone. Syn. *lubós na o lúbhang pagtitiwalà.*

pagpansín (pag-pan-sín), n. 1. act of calling the attention of someone about something. Syn. *pagpuná.* 2. act of finding fault of others; censuring; criticism. Syn. *pagpintás, pamimintás.*

pagpanghál (pag-pang-hál), n. 1. act of allowing food to become cool unnecessarily due to being left uneaten while still hot. 2. act of making someone wait too long.

pagpangit (pag-pa-ngit), n. a becoming ugly; change from being beautiful or handsome to being ugly; opposed to *paggandá.*

pagpapa- (pag-pa-pa-), pref. used in the formation of nouns denoting: (a) act of having something done, as in: *pagpapagupít,* act of having one's hair cut; (b) act of causing something to be in a certain state or condition, as in: *pagpapasamâ,* act of causing something to deteriorate or turn from good to bad.

pagpapaalam (pag-pa-pa-a-lam), n. 1. act of notifying or informing someone. Syn. *pagpapabatíd, pagpapasabi, pagpapabalità.* 2. act or effort of trying to acquire more knowledge. Syn. *pagpaparunong, pagpapatalino.* 3. act of bidding someone goodbye. Also, *pamamaalam.*

pagpapaamin (pag-pa-pa-a-min), n. act of making a person confess of his crime. Syn. *pagpapatugâ ng kasalanan.*

pagpapaanák (pag-pa-pa-a-nák), n. 1. act of helping or assisting (a woman) in childbirth or delivery. 2. act of having or getting someone as sponsor or godparent in one's baptism, confirmation, or wedding.

pagpapaaninaw (pag-pa-pa-a-ni-naw), n. act

of explaining or clarifying something to someone. Syn. *pagpapaliwanag.*

pagpapaapí (pag-pa-pa-a-pí), n. act of allowing oneself to be mistreated by another or others.

pagpapaayos (pag-pa-pa-a-yos), n. 1. act of having a place put in good order. 2. act of having oneself fixed up, as in a beauty shop or parlor. 3. act of asking or hiring someone to make repairs on one's house, etc. Syn. *pagpapakumpuní.* 4. an order for the amicable settlement of (a case, etc.). Syn. *pagpapaareglo.* 5. act of requesting for the amicable settlement, as of a case in court.

pagpapabagu-bago (pag-pa-pa-ba-gu + ba-go), n. act of changing one's place of residence, office, etc. very often. Syn. *pagpapalipat-lipat.*

pagpapabaít (pag-pa-pa-ba-ít), n. 1. act of taming or domesticating (a wild animal). Syn. *pagpapaamò.* 2. act of befriending someone, thus making him good and kind.

pagpapabalam (pag-pa-pa-ba-lam), n. act of causing the delay of the early completion of something being done or undertaken. Syn. *pagpapaabala, pagpapaantala, pagpapaatraso, pagpapatagál, pagpapalaon.*

pagpapabalík (pag-pa-pa-ba-lík), n. 1. act of telling or urging someone to return or go back home. Syn. *pagpapauwî.* 2. act of telling someone to return a thing borrowed, taken, or stolen from another. Syn. *pagpapasaulì.* 3. act of causing a vehicle to run or turn backward. Syn. *pagpapaurong.*

pagpapabalikat (pag-pa-pa-ba-li-kat), n. act of giving someone the full responsibility of performing a certain big task. Syn. *pagpapakatawán.*

pagpapabatá (pag-pa-pa-ba-tá), n. act of causing someone to suffer or endure something hard. Syn. *pagpapaagwanta, pagpapatiís.*

pagpapabatà (pag-pa-pa-ba-tà), n. 1. a deceptive act of trying to make one's age younger, as by changing the date of one's birth. 2. act of trying to make oneself look younger, as by using make-up, etc. 3. act of trying to get the patronage or support of an influential person in order to be assured of victory, as of a candidate in an election. Syn. *pagpapapanók* (fig.), *pagpapatangkilik*.

pagpapabayà (pag-pa-pa-ba-yà), n. 1. act of neglecting one's duty, etc.; neglect; negligence. 2. abandonment, as of one's family. Syn. *pagtatakwíl*. 3. tolerance or consent for the continuance of something undersirable. Syn. *pagkukunsinti*, *pagtutulirá*.

pagpapabayani (pag-pa-pa-ba-ya-ni), n. 1. act of undertaking or managing a cooperative project whereby labor is rendered for free. Syn. *pagpapalusong*, *pagpapasaknóng*. 2. act of working or offering one's services for free.

pagpapabigáy-alam (pag-pa-pa-bi-gáy + a-lam), n. a request to notify someone about something. Syn. *pagpapabatíd*, *pagpapasabi*, *pagpapabalità*.

pagpapabilin (pag-pa-pa-bi-lin), n. 1. act of sending an order for the purchase of something through another. Syn. *pagpapabilí*, *pagpapapidido*. 2. a request for relaying an information to someone. Syn. *pagpapasabi*, *pagpapabalità*.

pagpapabinyág (pag-pa-pa-bin-yág), n. 1. act of having oneself baptized or christened. Syn. *pagpapabautismo*. 2. act of having one's child baptized. 3. (*Colloq.*) act of having oneself circumcised. Syn. *pagpapatulì*.

pagpapabukadkád (pag-pa-pa-bu-kad-kád), n. act of allowing or waiting for a flower, for example, to open its petals fully.

pagpapabukas (pag-pa-pa-bu-kas), n. postponement of something to be done for the next day. Syn. *pagpapaliban sa kinabukasan* (*sa súsunód na araw*).

pagpapabukas-bukas (pag-pa-pa-bu-kas + bu-kas), n. act or habit of postponing or putting off things till later; procrastination. Syn. *pagpapaliban-liban ng araw*.

pagpapabulà (pag-pa-pa-bu-là), n. a refuting or proving to be false or wrong; disproof of a claim or argument; refutation. Syn. *pagpapasinungaling*.

pagpapabulos (pag-pa-pa-bu-los), n. a

request for a second or more helping o food.

pagpapabuntót (pag-pa-pa-bun-tót), n. 1 act of asking or requesting someone t follow closely a person wherever he goes act of making someone trail another. Syn *pagpapatugaygáy saán man tumungo*. 2. ac of providing or furnishing with a tail referring esp. to a kite. 3. act of addin something to what someone has alread said. Syn. *pagpapahabol sa sinabi*.

pagpapabusabos (pag-pa-pa-bu-sa-bos), n act of allowing oneself to be treated lik a slave. Syn. *pagpapaalipin*.

pagpapábutihán (pag-pa-pá-bu-ti-hán), n act of competing with each other or on another in doing something. Syn *pagpapáhusayán*, *pagpapágalingan*.

pagpapaka- (pag-pa-pa-ka-), pref. used t form nouns denoting an act or effort t attain fully a certain desire, good or bad as in *pagpapakabuti*, *pagpapakasamâ*.

pagpapakababà (pag-pa-pa-ka-ba-bà), n. 1 act or manner of being too humble o lowly in one's habit or character. 2. act o placing oneself down too low.

pagpapakabaít (pag-pa-pa-ka-ba-ít), n. th act or effort of a person in trying to behav in the best manner he could. Syn *pagpapabuti ng ugalì*.

pagpapakahaling (pag-pa-pa-ka-ha-ling), n act of allowing oneself to be madly o passionately fond of. Syn. *pagpa pakahibáng*.

pagpapakahibáng (pag-pa-pa-ka-hi-báng) n. fact or state or being madly o passionately obsessed with or fond o someone or something. Syn. *pagpa pakahaling*.

pagpapakahirap (pag-pa-pa-ka-hi-rap), n act or effort of working very hard to attai a purpose or goal. Syn. *pagpapakasakit*.

pagpapakahulugán (pag-pa-pa-ka-hu-lu gán), n. act of interpreting or giving meaning to; interpretation. Syn *pagbibigáy-kahulugán*.

pagpapakaimbí (pag-pa-pa-ka-im-bí), n. ac of being too mean or ignoble.

pagpapakainam (pag-pa-pa-ka-i-nam), n act of doing the best one can. Syn *pagpapakahusay, pagpapakabuti.*

pagpapakamatáy (pag-pa-pa-ka-ma-táy), n. act of killing oneself intentionally; suicide. Syn. *pagkitíl sa sariling buhay.*

pagpapakarunong (pag-pa-pa-ka-ru-nong), n. the act or effort to study hard in order to know much. Syn. *pagpapakatalino.*

pagpapakasakit (pag-pa-pa-ka-sa-kit), n. act of persevering; perseverance. Syn. *pagpapakahirap.*

pagpapakasanay (pag-pa-pa-ka-sa-nay), n. act or effort to train oneself very well. Syn. *pagpapakadalubhasà.*

pagpapakasangkapan (pag-pa-pa-ka-sang-ka-pan), n. act of allowing oneself to be the tool of. Syn. *pagpapasangkalan.*

pagpapakasawî (pag-pa-pa-ka-sa-wî), n. act of killing oneself or committing suicide. Syn. *pagpapatiwakál, pagpapakamatáy.*

pagpapakataás (pag-pa-pa-ka-ta-ás), n. 1. act of climbing or flying too high. Syn. *pagpapakatayog.* 2. excessive arrogance. Syn. *labis na paghahambóg o pagmamataás.*

pagpapakatinô (pag-pa-pa-ka-ti-nô), n. act or manner of behaving sensibly or righteously. Syn. *pagpapakabaít, pagpapakabuti.*

pagpapakayaman (pag-pa-pa-ka-ya-man), n. act or effort to accummulate excessive wealth. Syn. *labis na pagpapayaman.*

pagpapakilala (pag-pa-pa-ki-la-la), n. 1. a manifesting; a signifying or showing, as of one's intention; manifestation. Syn. *pagpapahayag, pagpapakita.* 2. introduction, as of a friend, speaker, etc.

pagpapakilos (pag-pa-pa-ki-los), n. 1. act of making something move. Syn. *pagpapagaláw, pagpapatinag.* 2. act of putting something into motion, circulation, or use; mobilization.

pagpapakisig (pag-pa-pa-ki-sig), n. act or manner of dressing oneself elegantly. Syn. *pagpapagarà; pagpapabihis nang magarà o makisig.*

pagpapakita (pag-pa-pa-ki-ta), n. 1. act of appearing or showing oneself in the presence of someone. Syn. *pagharáp, paglantád.* 2. act of showing or presenting something to someone. Syn. *paghaharáp.* 3. act of showing or signifying, as one's

intention or purpose. Syn. *pagpapakilala.* 4. act of showing or presenting to the public. Syn. *pagpapalabás, pagtatanghál.*

pagpapakiyáw-kiyáw (pag-pa-pa-ki-yáw + ki-yáw), n. act or manner of being uselessly fussy about something.

pagpapakuha (pag-pa-pa-ku-ha), n. 1. act of requesting or requiring someone to get, obtain, or procure something. Syn. *pagpapahanap.* 2. (with ng *larawan*) act of having one's picture taken by someone.

pagpapakumbabâ (pag-pa-pa-kum-ba-bâ), n. act or manner of showing humbleness in one's words or behavior, esp. in the presence of a superior.

pagpapakundangan (pag-pa-pa-kun-da-ngan), n. 1. act of showing respect, consideration, reverence, etc., esp. to an elder, royalty, or authority. Syn. *pagpipitagan, paggalang.* 2. act of recognizing the importance or significance of. Syn. *pagpapahalagá, pagbibigáy-halagá.*

pagpapakunwarî (pag-pa-pa-kun-wa-rî), n. a pretending; false; claim; pretense. Syn. *pagkukunyarî, pagbabalát-kayô.*

pagpapadalus-dalos (pag-pa-pa-da-lus + da-los), n. reckless haste in doing something. Syn. *pagpapabiglá-biglâ.*

pagpapadamá (pag-pa-pa-da-má), var. **pagpaparamá**, n. act of causing someone to feel or experience something. Syn. *pagpapadanas.*

pagpapadamdám (pag-pa-pa-dam-dám), var. **pagpaparamdám**, n. act or manner of hinting something to someone.

pagpapadanak (pag-pa-pa-da-nak), var. **pagpaparanak**, n. act of causing blood to flow or shed copiously. Syn. *pagpapabahâ* (ng *dugô*).

pagpapadanas (pag-pa-pa-da-nas), var. **pagpaparanas**, n. act of causing someone to experience something. Syn. *pagpaparamá, pagpapatikím* (colloq.).

pagpapadasál (pag-pa-pa-da-sál), var. **pagpaparasál**, n. act of holding an invitational prayers or novena in honor or commemoration of a dear one. Syn. *pagpapanobena.*

pagpapagabí (pag-pa-pa-ga-bí), n. 1. act of waiting for the night to come. Syn.

paghihintáy ng gabí. 2. act of passing the night in a certain place. Syn. *pagpapalipas o pagpaparaán ng gabí.*

pagpapagamit (pag-pa-pa-ga-mit), n. 1. act of allowing someone to use something. Syn. *pagpapahintulot na gumamit.* 2. act of supplying or providing (a person or persons) with tools, apparatus, equipment, etc. Syn. *pagpapakasangkapan, pagbibigáy ng kagamitán o kasangkapan.* 3. act of allowing oneself to be used as a tool by someone. Syn. *pagpapakasangkapan.*

pagpapagibík (pag-pa-pa-gi-bík), n. act of calling or shouting for help or succor. Syn. *pagpapadaló.*

pagpapagitáw (pag-pa-pa-gi-táw), n. a request or order for someone to appear or come out in the open in order to be seen. Syn. *pagpapalabás.*

pagpapagulang (pag-pa-pa-gu-lang), n. 1. act of allowing fruits to become matured. Cf. *pagpapahinóg.* 2. (*Colloq.*) act of allowing oneself to be taken advantage by another. Syn. *pagpapalamáng.* 3. act of waiting or allowing oneself to be of age or to grow old. Syn. *pagpapatandâ.* 4. act of making oneself look old.

pagpapagunitâ (pag-pa-pa-gu-ni-tâ), n. act of reminding someone about something. Syn. *pagpapaalaala.*

pagpapagurán (pag-pa-pa-gu-rán), n. act of tiring each other or one another.

pagpapagusót (pag-pa-pa-gu-sót), n. act of causing confusion, disorder, or trouble. Syn. *pagpapaguló, pagpapaligalig.*

pagpapahabág (pag-pa-pa-ha-bág), n. act of begging for pity or mercy. Syn. *pagmamakaawà.*

pagpapahalagá (pag-pa-pa-ha-la-gá), n. 1. recognition of the merit, worth, or importance of. Syn. *pagbibigáy-halagá (-merito o –importansiyá).* 2. a requirement or order for the fixing of the prices, as of certain commodities. Syn. *pagpapapresyo, pagpapalagáy ng presyo o halagá.*

pagpapahalatâ (pag-pa-pa-ha-la-tâ), n. act of showing or signifying one's intention indirectly. Syn. *pagpapahiwatig.*

pagpapahamak (pag-pa-pa-ha-mak), n. act of causing someone to suffer injury, loss, damage, etc. Syn. *pagpapasamâ, pagpinsalà.*

pagpapahanap (pag-pa-pa-ha-nap), n. 1. act of asking or requesting someone to look for something. 2. an order for the search or finding of someone wanted or lost.

pagpapahangín (pag-pa-pa-ha-ngín), n. (*Fig.*) act of boasting or bragging about oneself. Syn. *paghahambóg, pagpapasikat.*

pagpapahapon (pag-pa-pa-ha-pon), n. 1. act of offering or serving supper (for guests). Also, *pagpapahapunan.* Syn. *pagpapakain ng hapunan.* 2. act of waiting for the afternoon to come. Syn. *paghihintáy ng hapon.*

pagpapaharáp (pag-pa-pa-ha-ráp), n. 1. act of asking or telling someone to face towards a certain direction. 2. act of asking or urging someone to attend or be present, as in a meeting. Syn. *pagpapadaló.* 3. an order for someone to appear or be present, as in a court hearing.

pagpapahatíd (pag-pa-pa-ha-tíd), n. 1. act of sending (a letter, etc.) to someone. Syn. *pagpapadalá.* 2. act of asking or requesting someone to accompany oneself to a certain person or place. Syn. *pagpapasama.* 3. act of subscribing to a periodical, etc. for a specified period of time. Syn. *pagpaparasyón.* 4. act of sending a news or information to someone through another. Syn. *pagpapabalità, pagpapasabi.*

pagpapahátinggabí (pag-pa-pa-há-ting-ga-bí), n. 1. act of waiting for midnight to come. Syn. *paghihintáy ng hátinggabí.* 2. act of passing the midnight in a certain place. Syn. *pagpaparaán ng hátinggabí.*

pagpapahayag (pag-pa-pa-ha-yag), n. 1. act of declaring or expressing one's stand or views. Syn. *pagsasabi.* 2. act of announcing or declaring something to the public; proclamation. Syn. *pagpoproklamá.*

pagpapahele-hele (pag-pa-pa-he-le + he-le), n. act of pretending not to like. Syn. *pagpapakunwaríng ayaw.*

pagpapahibás (pag-pa-pa-hi-bás), n. act of waiting or allowing the intensity of typhoon, fever, or the like to subside. Syn. *pagpapabawa, pagpapahulaw.*

pagpapahignáw (pag-pa-pa-hig-náw), n. act of waiting or allowing the intensity to

pagpapahimakás

pagpapalakí

subside or calm down. Syn. *pagpapatigháw, pagpapahulaw.*

pagpapahimakás (pag-pa-pa-hi-ma-kás), n. act of bidding one's last farewell, referring to a dying person. Syn. *pagsasabi o pagbigkás ng huling paalam.*

pagpapahindî (pag-pa-pa-hin-dî), n. act of denying a request. Syn. *di-pagpayag sa kahilingan.*

pagpapahirap (pag-pa-pa-hi-rap), n. 1. act of making something difficult to do or make: opposed to *pagpapagaán, pagpapaalwán, pagpapadalî.* Syn. *pagpapabigát ng gawín.* 2. act of causing difficulty or suffering to someone; maltreatment; oppression. Syn. *pagpaparusa.*

pagpapahirati (pag-pa-pa-hi-ra-ti), n. act of causing or making someone to become accustomed or habituated to a certain act or situation. Syn. *pagpapamihasa, pagpapasanay.*

pagpapahiwatig (pag-pa-pa-hi-wa-tig), n. act of giving someone a hint; an insinuating. Syn. *pagpaparamdám.*

pagpapahiyáng (pag-pa-pa-hi-yáng), n. act of doing something different from what one ordinarily does to offset the bad luck he has suffered for long. Cf. *paghahanáp ng suwerte.*

pagpapahusay (pag-pa-pa-hu-say), n. 1. act of making improvements or causing something to be improved. Syn. *pagpapabuti, pagpapaayos.* 2. an order for the amicable settlement, as of a case. Syn. *pagpapaareglo.* 3. act of allowing or requesting for the amicable settlement of one's case. Syn. *pagpayag o pag-sang-ayon na paareglo.*

pagpapaibá (pag-pa-pa-i-bá), n. a request or order for the change or transfer of. Syn. *pagpapabago, pagpapalipat.*

pagpapaibig (pag-pa-pa-i-big), n. act of trying to attract the affection of someone.

pagpapaigi (pag-pa-pa-i-gi), n. 1. act of doing something to improve the quality or condition of; improvement of. 2. act of having or causing something to be repaired. Syn. *pagpapakumpuní.* 3. act of waiting for sufficient time to recover or recuperate from an ailment. Syn.

pagpapagalíng, pagpapalakás.

pagpapaimbabáw (pag-pa-pa-im-ba-báw), n. a pretended or feigned gesture of goodness. Syn. *pagpapakunyaring buti o kabutihan.*

pagpapaintindi (pag-pa-pa-in-tin-di), n. act of explaining something to someone; act of making someone understand the meaning of. Syn. *pagpapaunawà, pagpapalinaw, pagpapaliwanag.*

pagpapaisip (pag-pa-pa-i-sip), n. act of causing someone to think of something.

pagpapaiya (pag-pa-pa-i-ya), n. act of allowing someone to do what he likes. Syn. *pagpapabayà, pagpapaubayà.*

pagpapalà (pag-pa-pa-là), n. act of favoring someone with a good fortune.

pagpapalabò (pag-pa-pa-la-bò), n. 1. act of making water turbid. Cf. *pagpapaputik.* 2. act of making a light dim. Syn. *pagpapalamlám, pagpapadilím.* 3. act of causing a statement, etc. hard to understand. Syn. *pagpapahirap unawain.*

pagpapalabuy-laboy (pag-pa-pa-la-buy + la-boy), n. act of wandering aimlessly from place to place; vagrant way of life; vagabondage. Syn. *paglalakuwatsa, pagpapalibut-libot.*

pagpapalakad (pag-pa-pa-la-kad), n. 1. act of urging someone to go or leave. Syn. *pagpapaalís.* 2. act of driving a vehicle. Syn. *pagmamaneho, pagpapatakbó.* 3. act of managing or running (a business). Syn. *pamamahalà, pangangasiwà.* 4. act of securing the help of someone in getting the approval of.

pagpapalakás (pag-pa-pa-la-kás), n. 1. act of practising or exercising to develop physical strength. Syn. *pagsasanay, pageersisyo.* 2. act of winning to one's side more and more followers to gain political strength or influence, as a candidate. 3. act or resting well and eating good food to regain one's health after an illness. Syn. *pagpapagalíng.* 4. act of causing a vehicle to run fast or faster. Syn. *pagpapatulin, pagpapabilís.* 5. increasing the volume of sound, music, etc.

pagpapalakí (pag-pa-pa-la-kí), n. 1. act of making a plant or the like to grow up.

Syn. *pagpapatubò*. 2. act of enlarging or increasing the size of. 3. exaggeration. Syn. *pagpapalabis, pagpapasobrá*. 4. act of nurturing and educating a child. Syn. *pagbuhay at pagpapaáral sa isáng batà*.

pagpapalagáy (pag-pa-pa-la-gáy), n. 1. act of having or causing something to be placed or set up in a certain place. 2. the way or manner a person regards another.

pagpapalait (pag-pa-pa-la-it), n. act of allowing one self to be vilified by another. Syn. *pagpapamura, pagpapaalimurà*.

pagpapalalò (pag-pa-pa-la-lò), n. 1. act of showing arrogance or haughtiness. Syn. *paghahambóg*. 2. act of exaggerating something. Syn. *pagpapalabis, pagpapasobra*. 3. act of allowing oneself to be surpassed by another or others. Syn. *pagpapahigít, pagpapalampás, pagpapadaíg*.

pagpapalamáng (pag-pa-pa-la-máng), n. 1. act of sacrificing one's right in favor of another or others. 2. act of allowing oneself to be surpassed by another or others. Syn. *pagpapadaíg, pagpapahigít, pagpapalalò*. 3. act of allowing oneself to be taken advantage by someone.

pagpapalaon (pag-pa-pa-la-on), n. act of delaying action for an indefinite time. Syn. *pagpapatagál*.

pagpapalaot (pag-pa-pa-la-ot), n. 1. act of going or sailing into the middle of the sea. Syn. *pagtungo o pagpunta sa laot (gitnâ ng dagat)*. 2. (Fig.) act of involving oneself too deeply into something. Syn. *pagpapakasubò, pagpapakabuyó*.

pagpapalarawan (pag-pa-pa-la-ra-wan), n. 1. act of having one's picture drawn or taken with a camera. Syn. *pagpaparetrato*. 2. act of asking someone to describe something.

pagpapalasáp (pag-pa-pa-la-sáp), n. 1. act of making someone enjoy the taste or flavor of something. Syn. *pagpapatikím*. 2. act of causing someone to have an experience of something. Syn. *pagpapadanas*.

pagpapalawak (pag-pa-pa-la-wak), n. 1. act of increasing the area or expanse, as of a field. Syn. *pagpapaluwáng, pagpapalapad*. 2. act of expanding the area or scope of; enlargement on or upon a topic, idea, etc.

Syn. *pagpapasakláw*.

pagpapalawig (pag-pa-pa-la-wig), n. act of causing the unnecessary delay of. Syn. *pagpapaatraso, pagpapatagál, pagpapalaon*.

pagpapalayà (pag-pa-pa-la-yà), n. 1. act of letting loose or setting free, for example, a tied or caged animal. Syn. *pagpapakawalâ, pagpapaaalpás*. 2. act of releasing or giving freedom to a prisoner. Syn. *pagpapalabás*. 3. act of giving independence to a country under the rule of another. Syn. *pagbibigáy ng kalayaan o independénsiyá*.

pagpapalayaw (pag-pa-pa-la-yaw), n. 1. act of pampering or coddling, esp. a child. Syn. *labis na pagpapasunód*. 2. act of giving someone a nickname.

pagpapalibák (pag-pa-pa-li-bák), n. act of allowing oneself to be the victim of mockery or derision by someone. Syn. *pagpapatuyâ, pagpapakutyâ, pagpapauyám*.

pagpapaliban (pag-pa-pa-li-ban), n. a postponing; postponement. Syn. *pagpapaibáng-araw*.

pagpapaligpít (pag-pa-pa-lig-pít), n. 1. act of asking someone to put or keep away things in their proper places. Syn. *pagpapaimis, pagpapatagò sa mga kalat*. 2. (Colloq.) an order to liquidate or murder someone. Syn. *pagpapapatáy*.

pagpapaliguy-ligoy (pag-pa-pa-li-guy + li-goy), n. act of beating around the bush.

pagpapalihís (pag-pa-pa-li-hís), n. 1. act of causing something to deviate from. Syn. *pagpapasinsáy, pagpapalikó, pagpapaiwas*. 2. act of making something erroneous or incorrect. Syn. *pagpapamalî*.

pagpapaliít (pag-pa-pa-li-ít), n. 1. act of making a thing small or smaller; act of reducing the size. Syn. *pagpapalinggít*. 2. a minimizing; making something appear not too important. Syn. *di-lubháng pagpapahalagá*.

pagpapalimì (pag-pa-pa-li-mì), n. act of telling someone to consider a thing reflectively before deciding or acting. Syn. *pagpapaisip na mabuti, pagpapamuni-muni, pagpapanilay-nilay*.

pagpapalimlím (pag-pa-pa-lim-lím), n. act of having or causing a hen to hatch her eggs; act of allowing a hen to sit on her eggs. Syn. *pagpapahalimhím, pagpapapisâ ng mga itlóg sa inahín.*

pagpapalináng (pag-pa-pa-li-náng), n. 1. act of having one's land or field cultivated and planted with crops. Syn. *pagpapasaka.* 2. act of causing the development of ability or talent by training or practice. Syn. *pagpapasanay, pagpapaunlád.*

pagpapalinaw (pag-pa-pa-li-naw), n. 1. act of allowing or waiting for the water or liquid to clear up. Syn. *paghihintáy na luminaw.* 2. act of explaining or clarifying something in order to be understood. Syn. *pagpapaliwanag.* 3. act of causing the eyes, light, etc. to become clear.

pagpapalingá-lingâ (pag-pa-pa-li-ngá + li-ngâ), n. act of looking sideways or right and left repeatedly, as if searching for someone or something. Syn. *pagtingín-tingín o pagpapatingín-tingín sa kabí-kabilâ.*

pagpapalipas (pag-pa-pa-li-pas), n. 1. act of allowing or causing the effectivity to lapse. Syn. *pagpapasó.* 2. act of allowing or waiting for the time, anger, etc. to pass. Syn. *pagpapalampás, pagpaparaán.*

pagpapálitan (pag-pa-pá-li-tan), n. 1. act of exchanging things with each other or with one another. 2. the act or practice of bartering.

pagpapalitán (pag-pa-pa-li-tán), v. to change all or everything. Syn. *palitáng lahát.*

pagpapaliwanag (pag-pa-pa-li-wa-nag), n. 1. act of clarifying or explaining something to make easy to understand; clarification; explanation. Syn. *pagpapalinaw, pagpapa-unawà.* 2. act of making a place bright or brighter, as by putting more lights. 3. act of causing a light to become bright or brighter.

pagpapaluklók (pag-pa-pa-luk-lók), n. 1. act of offering or giving someone a seat; act of making someone sit. Syn. *pagpapaupô.* 2. *(Legal)* act of ordering or allowing someone to assume office or position, thus lifting a previous restraining order.

pagpapalugit (pag-pa-pa-lu-git), n. act of extending the date of maturity.

pagpapalugód (pag-pa-pa-lu-gód), n. act of giving someone pleasure or delight. Syn.

pagbibigáy-kasiyahan.

pagpapalunes (pag-pa-pa-lu-nes), n. act of postponing something till Monday. Syn. *pagpapaliban hanggáng Lunes.*

pagpapalusog (pag-pa-pa-lu-sog), n. 1. act or manner of improving one's health, as by eating good food and observing other health practices. Syn. *pagpapalakás ng katawán.* 2. act or means of improving life, business, etc. Syn. *pagpapaunlád.*

pagpapaluwág (pag-pa-pa-lu-wág), n. 1. act of making a place more spacious. Syn. *pagpapaluwáng.* 2. act of causing a tie, binding, knot, screw, etc. to loosen; opposed to *pagpapahigpít, pagpapahapit, pagpapaigtíng.* 3. a request or order for the relaxation of rules and regulations. 4. act of giving comfort, convenience, and ease to someone. Syn. *pagpapaginhawa, pagpapaalwán.*

pagpapaluwalhatì (pag-pa-pa-lu-wal-ha-tì), n. a glorifying; giving glory to.

pagpapaluwát (pag-pa-pa-lu-wát), n. act of causing something to be delayed unnecessarily. Syn. *pagpapatagál, pagpapalaon, pag-abala.*

pagpapamakalawá (pag-pa-pa-ma-ka-la-wá), var. **pagpapamakalwá**, n. act of postponing something till the day after tomorrow.

pagpapamalas (pag-pa-pa-ma-las), n. act of showing one's love, concern, ability, etc. Syn. *pagpapakita.*

pagpapamalay (pag-pa-pa-ma-lay), n. 1. act of making someone conscious or aware of something. Cf. *pagpapagunitâ, pagpa-paalaala.* 2. act of causing someone to have a hint or idea about something. Syn. *pagpapahiwatig.*

pagpapamalí-malî (pag-pa-pa-ma-lí + ma-lî), n. act of committing errors or incon-sistencies in one's statements or answers.

pagpapámanhikan (pag-pa-pá-man-hi-kan), n. an old Filipino custom whereby the parents of a suitor ask formally for the hand of a prospective bride of their son from her parents. Syn. *pagmamátandaan.*

pagpapamanihalá (pag-pa-pa-ma-ni-ha-lá), n. act of giving or leaving one's affairs or business to the care or management of someone.

pagpapamasíd-masíd (pag-pa-pa-ma-síd + ma-síd), n. act of observing things around a place enjoyably. Also, *pagmamasíd-masíd.*

pagpapamatá (pag-pa-pa-ma-tá), n. act of opening someone's eyes; making one aware of the facts, real reasons, etc. Syn. *pagpapamulat sa katotohanan at ibá pa.*

pagpapamukhâ (pag-pa-pa-muk-hâ), n. act of accusing a person face to face. Syn. *pagpaparatang nang hárapan.*

pagpapamulat (pag-pa-pa-mu-lat), n. 1. act of making someone open his eyes. Syn. *pagpapabukás ng matá.* 2. act of making one aware of the facts, real reasons, etc. Syn. *pagpapamatá.*

pagpapanata (pag-pa-pa-na-ta), n. act of making a vow. Syn. *pagdedebosyón.*

pagpapanatili (pag-pa-pa-na-ti-li), n. act of maintaining something in the same position, state, or condition. Syn. *pagpapamalagì.*

pagpapanibago (pag-pa-pa-ni-ba-go), n. act of changing; change; renewal. Syn. *pagbabago, pag-uulit.*

pagpapanibagong-buhay (pag-pa-pa-ni-ba-gong + bu-hay), n. act of changing one's way of life; fresh start in life. Also, *pagbabagong-buhay.*

pagpapanig-panig (pag-pa-pa-nig + pa-nig), n. act of grouping together cooperatively in opposition to another group or groups. Syn. *pagpapangkát-pangkát.*

pagpapantáy-paá (pag-pa-pan-táy + pa-á), n. (Fig.) death; the act or fact of dying; permanent ending of a personss's life. Syn. *pagkamatáy.*

pagpapantíng-taingá (pag-pa-pan-tíng + ta-i-ngá), n. fact of having one's ears flushed and heated with anger. Syn. *pagsisikláb o pag-iinit sa galit.*

pagpapanumbalik (pag-pa-pa-num-ba-lik), n. act of causing the regain of one's consciousness, old habit, former ailment, etc. Syn. *pagpapanág-ulì.*

pagpapangalan (pag-pa-pa-nga-lan), n. act of giving a person or thing a name. Syn. *pagngangalan, pagbibigáy ng pangalan.*

pagpapanganyayà (pag-pa-pa-ngan-ya-yà),

n. act of causing someone to suffer damage or injury. Syn. *pagpapahamak.*

pagpapanggáp (pag-pa-pang-gáp), n. act of pretending to be what one is not; pretense; pretension. Syn. *pagkukunwâ, pagkukunwarî, pagkukunyarî.*

pagpaparamay (pag-pa-pa-ra-may), var. **pagpapadamay,** n. act of asking for soliciting help. Syn. *pagpapatulong.*

pagpaparamdám (pag-pa-pa-ram-dám), n. 1. act of hinting or insinuating; insinuation. Syn. *pagpapariníg, pagpapasaríng.* 2. act of making someone feel or experience something. Syn. *pagpaparamá, pagpapadanas.*

pagpaparanas (pag-pa-pa-ra-nas), var. **pagpapadanas,** n. act of making or causing someone to experience something. Syn. *pagpapadamá.*

pagpaparangál (pag-pa-pa-ra-ngál), n. act of honoring or giving honor to someone. Syn. *pagbibigáy-dangál.*

pagpaparayâ (pag-pa-pa-ra-yâ), n. 1. act of giving in to someone's request, as a matter of friendliness, kindness, etc. Syn. *pagbibigáy (fig.).* 2. act of allowing oneself to be taken advantage of by another as a gesture of sportsmanship. Syn. *pagpapalamáng.*

pagpaparuól (pag-pa-pa-ru-ól), n. act of causing someone to meet a misfortune. Syn. *pagpapahamak.*

pagpapasabi (pag-pa-pa-sa-bi), n. act of sending or causing a person to bring or relay a message or news to someone; act of informing someone through another. Syn. *pagpapabalità.*

pagpapasabík (pag-pa-pa-sa-bík), n. act of causing someone to be very eager about something.

pagpapasalamat (pag-pa-pa-sa-la-mat), n. act of thanking someone; expression of appreciation or gratitude for a favor received. Syn. *pagkilala ng utang na loób.*

pagpapasalin (pag-pa-pa-sa-lin), n. 1. act of causing the transfer of water, liquid, grains, etc. from one container to another. Cf. *pagpapalipat.* 2. act of causing a poem, story, etc. translated into another language.

pagpapasalunò (pag-pa-pa-sa-lu-nò), n. a request for someone to meet another on the way. Syn. *pagpasalubong.*

pagpapasamâ (pag-pa-pa-sa-mâ), n. 1. act of making someone bad in the eyes of others. Syn. *paninirà, paninirang-puri.* 2. act of causing someone to become bad or ignoble.

pagpapasamakalawá (pag-pa-pa-sa-ma-ka-la-wá), n. act of postponing a scheduled work or occasion until the day after tomorrow.

pagpapasaríng (pag-pa-pa-sa-ríng), n. act of making an innuendo or indirect remark implying something derogatory. Syn. *pagpaparunggít, pagpapariníg, pagpapatutsada.*

pagpapasariwà (pag-pa-pa-sa-ri-wà), n. 1. act of making or causing flowers, leaves, or plants to look fresh again. Also, *pagpapanariwà.* 2. (Fig.) act of recalling or renewing to one's memory something long forgotten. Syn. *pagpapaalaala, pagpapagunitâ.*

pagpapasasà (pag-pa-pa-sa-sà), n. act of enjoying the great abundance of; indulgence. Syn. *pagpapakasawà.*

pagpapasaulo (pag-pa-pa-sa-u-lo), n. act of having or causing a list of words, a sentence, poem, etc. to be memorized. Syn. *pagpapamemorya.*

pagpapasayá (pag-pa-pa-sa-yá), n. act of causing someone or an occasion to become happy, gay, or cheerful. Syn. *pagpapaligaya, pagpapagalák, pagpapalugód.*

pagpapasikat (pag-pa-pa-si-kat), n. 1. act of waiting for the sun or moon to rise. Syn. *pagpapasilang, paghihintáy na sumikat o sumilang.* 2. boasting or showing off. Syn. *paghahambóg, pagpapakitang-gilas.*

pagpapasikut-sikot (pag-pa-pa-si-kut + si-kot), n. act of beating around the bush; speaking or talking about a certain subject without getting to the point. Syn. *pagpapaliguy-ligoy.*

pagpapasimunò (pag-pa-pa-si-mu-nò), n. act of leading or starting an undesirable affair. Syn. *pagpupromotór.*

pagpapasiyá (pag-pa-pa-si-yá), var. **pagpapasyá,** n. 1. act of making up one's mind or making a decision. 2. act of deciding or rendering a decision, as by a judge. Syn. *paghatol, paggagawad ng hatol.*

pagpapasiyám (pag-pa-pa-si-yám), n. act of holding a nine-day novena in memory of a loved one. Syn. *pagpapadasál ng siyám na araw sa alaala ng isáng mahál na sumakabiláng-buhay.*

pagpapasubalì (pag-pa-pa-su-ba-lì), n. act of taking exception; act of giving or expressing a dissenting opinion. Syn. *pagsalungat, pagtutol, pagsalangsáng.*

pagpapasunod (pag-pa-pa-su-nod), n. 1. act of having or causing another to follow or go after someone. Syn. *pagpapabuntót (fig.), pagpapasubaybáy.* 2. act of enforcing obedience or requiring fulfillment, as of an order. Syn. *pagpapatalima.* 3. treatment accorded to subordinates. Syn. *pagtrato.*

pagpapatadhanà (pag-pa-pa-tad-ha-nà), n. a requirement for the inclusion of a provision in an ordinance or law. Syn. *pagpapatakdâ bilang tadhanâ o probisyón.*

pagpapatagál (pag-pa-pa-ta-gál), n. act of causing the prolongation of time in doing something. Syn. *pagpalaon, pagpapaluwát.*

pagpapatahimik (pag-pa-pa-ta-hi-mik), n. act of causing a person or persons to be quiet, calm, or peaceful. Syn. *pagpapapayapà, pagpapatiwasáy.*

pagpapatandâ (pag-pa-pa-tan-dâ), n. act of allowing oneself to become old, as before getting married. Syn. *paghihintáy na tumandâ.* 2. act of causing someone to put a mark or marker on something. Syn. *pagpapalagáy ng tandâ o panandâ.* 3. act of making someone remember something. Syn. *pagpapagunitâ.*

pagpapatangáy (pag-pa-pa-ta-ngáy), n. 1. act of allowing oneself to be carried by or as by the current. Syn. *pagpapatianód.* 2. act of causing something to be carried by the current, wind, or the like. 3. act of allowing oneself to be carried or influenced as by one's emotion. Syn. *pagpapaimpluwensiyá.*

pagpapatanghalì (pag-pa-pa-tang-ha-lì), n. 1. act of offering or serving dinner or midday meals. Also, *pagpapatanghalian.* Syn. *pagkain ng tanghalian.* 2. act of waiting till late in the morning, as in going to office, waking up, etc.

pagpapatao (pag-pa-pa-ta-o), n. 1. act of having someone stay in the house temporarily as a guard or caretaker during the absence of the owner. 2. act of causing a place to be occupied with inhabitants; populating, as a newly developed place. 3. act of supplying an office with personnel. 4. act of demanding a better treatment, as from an employer.

pagpapataupû (pag-pa-pa-ta-u-pû), var. **pagpapatawpû** (fr. *tao* + *pô*), n. a native custom of saying "*tao pô*," usually accompanied by knocking at the door, when one visits or drops at someone's house, in order to call the attention of whoever is inside.

pagpapatawad (pag-pa-pa-ta-wad), n. 1. act of pardoning a person for a crime or offense done. Syn. *pagpapaumanhín.* 2. in the Roman Catholic Church, the remission of temporal or purgatorial punishment after a person's guilt has been forgiven. 3. act of giving a discount in the purchase of. Syn. *pagbibigáy ng diskuwento o bawas sa halagá.*

pagpapatawag (pag-pa-pa-ta-wag), n. 1. act of requesting someone to call for (a doctor, taxi, etc.). Syn. *pagpapasundô.* 2. act of allowing a person to use one's telephone (apparatus) in calling someone. Syn. *pagpapagamit sa teléponó.* 3. act of allowing oneself to be called by a certain name. 4. an order for the recall or return, as of an envoy to his home office. Syn. *pagbabalík, pagpapauwî.* 5. a request or call, as for a meeting. Syn. *pagpapapulong, pagpapamiting.*

pagpapátayan (pag-pa-pá-ta-yan), n. act of killing each other or one another, as in war or battle. Syn. *pag-uútasan.*

pagpapatayín (pag-pa-pa-ta-yín), v. to kill all. Syn. *pag-uutasín.*

pagpapatay-patay (pag-pa-pa-tay + pa-tay), n. lack of animation, spirit, or interest in action, movement, or in doing something.

pagpapatayung-tayong (pag-pa-pa-ta-yung + ta-yong), n. act or habit of postponing or putting off something being done now

and then. Syn. *pagpapaliban-liban ng ginágawá sa tuwí-tuwí na.*

pagpapatibay (pag-pa-pa-ti-bay), n. 1. act of strengthening or making a thing stronger (materially). 2. act of making a person stronger morally and physically. Syn. *pagpapalakás.* 3. passage or approval, as of a law, amendment, etc. Syn. *pag-aaprobá.* 4. act of giving approval, sanction, or consent. Syn. *pagsang-ayon, pagpayag, pagpapahintulot.* 5. act of proving that a thing is true or right. Syn. *pagpapatunay, pagpapatotoó.*

pagpapatingín (pag-pa-pa-ti-ngín), n. 1. act of telling or allowing someone to look at something. 2. act of consulting or seeking the advice, as of a doctor. Syn. *pagkunsulta (sa manggagamot).*

pagpapatirapâ (pag-pa-pa-ti-ra-pâ), n. a falling down forward intentionally in supplication. Cf. *paglulumuhód.*

pagpapatiwakál (pag-pa-pa-ti-wa-kál), n. act of committing suicide. Syn. *pagbatáy sa sarili, pagpapakamatáy.*

pagpapatukoy (pag-pa-pa-tu-koy), n. a request or demand for someone to mention something for clarification. Syn. *pagpapabanggít.*

pagpapatuksó (pag-pa-pa-tuk-só), n. 1. act of allowing oneself to be tempted into doing something undesirable. Cf. *pagpapahibò, pagpapasulsól.* 2. act of allowing oneself to be teased or joked by others. Syn. *pagpapabirò.*

pagpapatugmâ (pag-pa-pa-tug-mâ), n. 1. act of making a word rhyme with another. Syn. *pagpaparima.* 2. act of having a wrong or error corrected by someone. Syn. *pagpapatumpák.*

pagpapatumpík-tumpík (pag-pa-pa-tum-pík + tum-pík), n. act or manner of being artfully hesitant, esp. in accepting an offer. Syn. *pagpapakunwá-kunwaríng áayáw o waláng-gusto.*

pagpapatunay (pag-pa-pa-tu-nay), n. 1. clear manifestation or proof. Syn. *maliwanag na katibayan.* 2. act of proving that something is true; proving the validity of. Syn. *pagpapatotoó.*

pagpapatungkól (pag-pa-pa-tung-kól), n. 1

act of giving someone something to do. Syn. *pagpapatrabaho, pagpapagawâ.* 2. act of dedicating something to someone. Syn. *paghahandóg, pag-aalay.*

pagpapatupád (pag-pa-pa-tu-pád), n. 1. act of enforcing obedience or causing the carrying out of an order, provision, or a contract, etc. Syn. *pagpapasunód.* 2. an order for the accomplishment or fulfillment of a task, etc. Syn. *pagpapaganáp.*

pagpapatuwáng (pag-pa-pa-tu-wáng), n. 1. act of asking or requesting another to help oneself in carrying a heavy load together. Syn. *pagpapatulong sa pagbuhat o pagdadalá ng isáng bagay na mabigát.* 2. act of requesting someone to be one's co-sponsor at a wedding, baptism, or confirmation.

pagpapaubayà (pag-pa-pa-u-ba-yà), n. 1. act of relinquishing one's own right or responsibility to another. 2. act of leaving or letting someone do, decide, act, etc. alone by himself.

pagpapauliuli (pag-pa-pa-u-li-u-li), n. act of going around a place aimlessly. Syn. *pagpapagalá-galâ, pagpapalibut-libot.*

pagpapaumaga (pag-pa-pa-u-ma-ga), n. act of waiting for the morning to come.

pagpapauna (pag-pa-pa-u-na), n. 1. act of telling or urging someone to go ahead of another or others. Syn. *pagpapaalís na máuná.* 2. act of allowing another or others to be ahead of oneself or allowing oneself to be left behind.

pagpapaunlád (pag-pa-pa-un-lád), n. act of developing or improving, e.g. one's knowledge, language, etc. Syn. *pagpapaprogreso.*

pagpapauntós (pag-pa-pa-un-tós), n. act of allowing or waiting for the intensity, as of a typhoon, to subside or mitigate. Syn. *pagpapahupâ, pagpapahulaw, pagpapalubag.*

pagpapaurong (pag-pa-pa-u-rong), n. 1. act of driving a vehicle backward. Syn. *pagpapaatrás.* 2. act of allowing a fabric to shrink. 3. act of telling or urging someone to retreat or go back. Syn. *pagpapabalík.* 4. an order for the revocation, as of an order or permit. Syn. *pagpapabawì.* 5. act of resetting a scheduled activity earlier than previously

announced. Also, *pag-uurong.*

pagpapaurong-sulong (pag-pa-pa-u-rong + su-long), n. 1. act of moving forward and backward repeatedly. 2. irresolution; hesitation. Syn. *pagsasalawahan, pagbabantulót.*

pagpapautáy-utáy (pag-pa-pa-u-táy + u-táy), n. act of working, moving, or doing something little by little. Syn. *pagpapainút-inót, pag-iinút-inót.*

pagpapawaláng-sala (pag-pa-pa-wa-láng + sa-la), n. acquittal; freeing a person from guilt or fault. Also, *pagpapawaláng-kasalanan.*

pagpapawaláng-saysáy (pag-pa-pa-wa-láng + say-sáy), n. act of giving no importance or value to; act of disregarding something for lack of merit. Syn. *pagpapawaláng-halagá.*

pagparangalan (pag-pa-ra-nga-lan), v. to take pride in showing off something to someone. Syn. *pagparangyaán, paghambugán.*

pagparatangan (pag-pa-ra-ta-ngan), v. to make imputations against; make false accusation against. Syn. *pagbintangán, pagsapantahaan.*

pagparisan (pag-pa-ri-san), n. to use as a model; copy from. Syn. *pagtularan, pagparehuhan, paggayahan.*

pagparisin (pag-pa-ri-sin), v. to compare each other. Syn. *pagtularin, pagparehuhin.*

pagparito (pag-pa-ri-to), n. act of coming here (to this place).

pagpariyan (pag-pa-ri-yan), n. act of going there (to the place of the person spoken to).

pagparoón (pag-pa-ro-ón), n. act of going there (to the place far from both the speaker and the person spoken to). Syn. *pagpunta o pagtungo roón.*

pagpaparoó't-parito (pag-pa-pa-ro-ó't + pa-ri-to), n. act of going back and forth repeatedly. Syn. *pagpapabalík-balik.*

pagparunggitán (pag-pa-rung-gi-tán), v. to make a sly hint or insinuation against someone. Syn. *pagpasaringán, pagparinggán.*

pagpasá- (pag-pa-sá-), pref. used to form nouns, meaning act of going to a certain place, as in *pagpasábayan, pagpasáilog*.

pagpasabihan (pag-pa-sa-bi-han), *v.* to send word or notice to, esp. through a messenger. Syn. *pagpatalastasán*.

pagpasalamatan (pag-pa-sa-la-ma-tan), *v.* to thank; express one's gratitude for a favor or kindness done by someone. Also, *pasalamatan*.

pagpasaringán (pag-pa-sa-ri-ngán), *v.* to make a sly hint or insinuation against someone. Syn. *pagparunggitán, pagparinggán*.

pagpasasaan (pag-pa-sa-sa-an), *v.* to take full advantage of enjoying the abundance of.

pagpasiyahán (pag-pa-si-ya-hán), *v.* to decide; make or render a decision. Syn. *hatulan, disisyunán*.

pagpasláng (pag-pas-láng), *n.* 1. act of insulting someone. Syn. *pag-alipustá, paglait, pagdustâ*. 2. act of committing murder. Syn. *pagpatáy (ng tao)*.

pagpaták (pag-pa-ták), *n.* falling or dropping, as of rain, fruit from a tree, etc. Syn. *paglagpák*.

pagpatáy (pag-pa-táy), *n.* 1. killing of a person by another; homicide; murder; assassination. Syn. *homisidyo, asasinasyón*. 2. killing of an animal for food; butchering; slaughtering. Syn. *pagkatay*. 3. act of destroying or putting an end to. Syn. *pagsugpô*. 4. act of causing an engine, etc. to stop. Syn. *pagpapahintô, pagpapatigil*. 5. act of putting out, as fire or light. Syn. *pagsusubá* (for fire); *pagsasará* (for electric light); *paghihip* (for candle light or the like).

pagpatol (pag-pa-tol), *n.* 1. act of taking advantage of someone inferior to oneself. 2. act of paying attention to someone of inferior rank or someone not worth it.

pagpatúng-patungin (pag-pa-túng + pa-tu-ngin), *v.* to place all things on top of one another. Syn. *salansanín*.

pagpayag (pag-pa-yag), *n.* 1. act of giving permission. Syn. *pagpapahintulot*. 2. act of giving in to a request. Syn. *pagsang-ayon, pagbibigáy, pagpapaunlák*.

pagpayapà (pag-pa-ya-pà), *n.* 1. act of pacifying; pacification. Syn. *pagpapatahimik, pagpapatiwasáy*. 2. return to peacefulness or tranquility. Syn. *pagtahimik, pagtiwasáy*.

pagpikit (pag-pi-kit; -kít), *n.* act of closing the eyes; opposed to *pagmulat*.

pagpikot (pag-pi-kot), *n.* act of surrounding or cornering to prevent escape. Syn. *pagsalikop*. 2. act of cornering or putting into a tight situation. Syn. *paggipit*.

pagpigapit (pag-pi-ga-pit), *n.* act of putting someone under stress or in tight situation. Syn. *paggipít*.

pagpiho (pag-pi-ho), *n.* act of making sure or certain; assurance. Syn. *pagtiyák, pagsiguro*.

pagpiít (pag-pi-ít), *n.* 1. act of cornering or putting someone in a tight situation. Syn. *paggipít*. 2. act of putting someone in prison. Syn. *pagbibilanggô*.

pagpilitan (pag-pi-li-tan), *v.* to do one's best or strive hard to do, make, get, or obtain. Syn. *pagsumikapan*.

pagpintíg (pag-pin-tíg), *n.* 1. light throbbing or beating, as of the pulse or heart. Syn. *pagtibók*. 2. act of hitting or striking (a ball, etc.) lightly. Syn. *pagpalò nang mahinà*.

pagpintuhò (pag-pin-tu-hò), *n.* adoration; worship. Syn. *mataós na paghangà, pagsambá*.

pagpipigil (pag-pi-pi-gil), *n.* 1. act or manner of holding something in one's hands. Syn. *paghahawak, pagtatangan*. 2. act of controlling one's anger, etc. Syn. *pagkokontrolá*.

pagpipirá-pirasuhin (pag-pi-pi-rá + pi-ra-su-hin), *v.* to cut or break (a big piece) into many smaller pieces. Syn. *paghatí-hatiin*.

pagpipitagan (pag-pi-pi-ta-gan), *n.* courteous regard for someone; respect. Syn. *paggalang*.

pagpirmé (pag-pir-mé), *n.* 1. act of keeping oneself motionless in one's position. Syn. *di-paggaláw, di-pagkibô*. 2. act of staying permanently in one place. Syn. *pagtigil nang pálagián*.

pagpisan (pag-pi-san), *n.* 1. act of staying or living in the same room, house, etc. with another. Syn. *pagsunò, pakikisunò*. 2. act of living with another, as a woman with a man, or the other way around. Syn. *pagsama, pakikisama*.

pagpitada (pag-pi-ta-da), n. act of blowing or sounding a siren, as during air raids.

pagpitaganan (pag-pi-ta-ga-nan), v. to respect; show respect to. Syn. *igalang, irespeto.*

pagpukaw (pag-pu-kaw), n. act of rousing a person from sleep. Syn. *paggising.*

pagpuksâ (pag-puk-sâ), n. act of wiping out; annihilation; extermination. Syn. *paglipol, pagtodas, pag-ubos.*

pagpuga (pag-pu-ga), n. a getting away from; breaking loose, as from prison; escape. Syn. *pagtakas, pagtanan, paglayas.*

pagpugos (pag-pu-gos), n. act of washing the dirty portion of clothes or a piece of cloth with clean water.

pagpugot (pag-pu-got), n. act of cutting the head of a person; beheading or decapitating. Syn. *pagputol sa ulo.*

pagpulà (pag-pu-là), n. act of criticizing a person or thing; finding fault with another or others. Syn. *pagpintás, pamimintás; pagpistâ, pamimistâ.*

pagpulás (pag-pu-lás), n. 1. sudden flight or start. Syn. *bigláng pag-alís o pagtakas.* 2. leaving or departure without notice. Syn. *waláng paalam na pag-alís o paglisan.*

pagpumilitan (pag-pu-mi-li-tan), v. strive hard to do, get, obtain, etc. Also, *pagpilitan.*

pagpuná (pag-pu-ná), n. 1. act of making a comment or observation. Syn. *pagpansín.* 2. act of criticizing adversely; finding fault with; censuring. Syn. *pagpintás, pagpulà.*

pagpunta (pag-pun-ta), n. 1. act of going to a certain place. Syn. *pagtungo, pagparoón.* 2. act of attending a meeting, etc. Syn. *pagdaló.*

pagpunyagián (pag-pun-ya-gi-án), v. to strive hard to do, get, or attain. Syn. *pagpumilitan.*

pagpupugay (pag-pu-pu-gay), n. 1. act of taking off one's hat. 2. act of greeting or saluting someone by taking off one's hat.

pagpupulaán (pag-pu-pu-la-án), n. act of critcizing each other adversely. Syn. *pagpipintasan, pagpipistaan.*

pagpupúlasan (pag-pu-pú-la-san), n. 1. simultaneous flight or start, as of frightened people. Syn. *bigláng pag-aálisan*

o pagtatákasan. 2. simultaneous leaving or departure, as of a number of persons. Syn. *pag-aálisan, paglilísanan.*

pagpupumilit (pag-pu-pu-mi-lit), n. 1. act of striving hard to do, get, or obtain something. Syn. *pagpipilit.* 2. insistence. Syn. *paggigiít.*

pagpupúnahan (pag-pu-pú-na-han), n. act of criticizing each other adversely. Syn. *pagpipíntasan, pagpupulaán.*

pagpupunyagî (pag-pu-pun-ya-gî), n. persistent effort to do or attain something; act of striving hard. Syn. *pagsisikap, pagpapakasakit, pagpapakahirap.*

pagpupusakál (pag-pu-pu-sa-kál), n. complete abadonment of oneself to vice. Syn. *pagpapakasugapà, pagpapakagumon.*

pagpuputa (pag-pu-pu-ta), n. the immoral act of a prostitute or harlot. Syn. *pagbuburikák.*

pagpuputong (pag-pu-pu-tong), n. 1. act of putting something on the head. 2. act or ceremony of crowning a queen or a king; coronation. Syn. *pagkokorona.*

pagpupuwera (pag-pu-pu-we-ra), n. act of excluding a person or thing. Syn. *di-pagsasama, paghihiwaláy.*

pagpupuyát (pag-pu-pu-yát), n. act of staying awake during night; act of keeping a night vigil. Syn. *paglalamay, di-pagtulog sa gabí.*

pagpupuyós (pag-pu-pu-yós), n. 1. act of starting a fire by friction, that is by rubbing two hard objects together. 2. (Fig.) intense feeling, esp. of anger. Syn. *pagngingitngít.*

pagrahuyò (pag-ra-hu-yò), n. act of influencing or persuading someone to do something undesirable. Syn. *paghikayat, pagganyák.*

pagsabát (pag-sa-bát), n. 1. a butting in or into others' conversation. Syn. *pagsabád.* 2. act of intercepting someone on the way. Syn. *pagharang.* 3. act of contradicting the statement, etc. of another. Syn. *pagsalungát.*

pagsabihan (pag-sa-bi-han), n. 1. to advise someone to be wary or cautious. Syn. *paalalahanan, pagunitaán.* 2. to reprimand; reprove formally. Syn. *kagalitan,* *pangaralan*. 3. to inform. Syn. *balitaan*.

pagsakitan (pag-sa-ki-tan), *v.* to strive hard or exert efforts in order to attain. Syn *pagsikapan, pagtiyagaán, paghirapan*.

pagsakop (pag-sa-kop), *n.* 1. occupation of a conquered territory. 2. inclusion of someone or something within one's jurisdiction. Syn. *pagsakláw*.

pagsaksí (pag-sak-sí), *n.* 1. act of seeing or witnessing an occurrence personally or with one's own eyes. 2. act of testifying as a witness. Syn. *pagtestigo*.

pagsadyâ (pag-sad-yâ), *n.* 1. doing something intentionally or on purpose. Syn. *pagtikís*. 2. act of visiting or going to a certain person or place for a specific purpose. 3. act of making something in accordance to a certain detailed specification, as of made-to-order shoes, clothes, etc.

pagsagád (pag-sa-gád), *n.* 1. act of reaching the highest peak, as of one's fame, greatness, success, etc. Syn. *pag-abot sa tugatog*. 2. act of penetrating or reaching up to the other side, as of a wall. Syn. *pagtagós, paglagós*. 3. act or ability to reach one's destination. Syn. *pag-abot, pagsapit*. 4. act of reaching or touching down the bottom of. Syn. *pagsayad o pag-abot sa ilalim*. 5. complete exhaustion or tiredness. Syn. *lubós na pagod o pagkapagod*. 6. state or condition of being in dire need. Syn. *matindíng paghihirap o pagdarálità*.

pagsaganà (pag-sa-ga-nà), *n.* 1. increase, esp. of crops or of goods in the market, to a proportion more than sufficient. Syn. *pagsaksâ, pagdagsâ*. 2. a becoming rich; change from being poor to being rich. Syn. *pagyaman*.

pagsagap (pag-sa-gap), *n.* 1. act of scooping off fat, spume, etc. from the surface of liquid. Syn. *pagsalap, paghalagap*. 2. act of inhaling, e.g. fresh air. Syn. *paglangháp, pagsangháp*. 3. (*Fig.*) act of picking up rumors or information circulating around. Syn. *pamumulot ng mga tsismis o mga balità*.

pagsagkâ (pag-sag-kâ), *n.* act of preventing or stopping, e.g. a person's intention to do something. Syn. *pagpigil, paghadláng*.

pagsagì (pag-sa-gì), *n.* 1. a grazing; light touch or rub against something in passing, intentional or otherwise. 2. (with *sa alaala*) a coming to one's mind; sudden occurrence in one's mind. Syn. *pagkágunitâ, pagkáalaala*.

pagsagila (pag-sa-gi-la), *n.* 1. act of rushing to a certain place. Syn. *mádaliang pagtungo sa*. 2. sudden occurrence in one's mind. Syn. *bigláng pagsagì sa isip; bigláng pagkáalaala*. 3. sudden occurrence or taking place. Syn. *bigláng pangyayari*.

pagsagót (pag-sa-gót), *n.* 1. act or manner of answering a letter, question, argument, telephone call, or the like. Syn. *pagtugón*. 2. act of returning a blow, attack, etc. Syn. *pagganti*. 3. act of assuming the responsibility of another. Syn. *pananagót, paggarantiyá*.

pagsalakay (pag-sa-la-kay), *n.* act of attacking or invading the enemy. Syn. *paglusob, pag-atake*.

pagsalamangka (pag-sa-la-mang-ka), *n.* 1. cunning or craft used in deceiving. 2. a clever act of deception; sleight. 3. magic performance. Also, *pagsasalamangka*.

pagsalamín (pag-sa-la-mín), *n.* 1. (*Fig.*) act of looking up to someone as a model. 2. act of using or wearing, as one's eyeglasses.

pagsalawahanan (pag-sa-la-wa-ha-nan), *v.* to have doubt about someone or something; mistrust. Syn. *pag-alinlangan, pagdudahan*.

pagsalbahe (pag-sal-ba-he), *n.* 1. act of abusing or raping a woman. Syn. *paggahasà*. 2. (*Colloq.*) act of making a fool of someone. Syn. *pagloko*.

pagsalimuót (pag-sa-li-mu-ót), *n.* a complicating or becoming complicated. Syn. *paggusót*.

pagsalitaán (pag-sa-li-ta-án), *v.* 1. to reprimand. Syn. *pagwikaan, kagalitan*. 2. to talk to. Syn. *kausapin*.

pagsalíw (pag-sa-líw), *n.* 1. act of singing with another, as a duet. Syn. *pagduweto*. 2. act of accompanying a singer on the piano, guitar, etc.; act of playing or singing an accompaniment for or to. Syn. *pagkompanya, pag-akompanya*.

pagsaliwâ (pag-sa-li-wâ), *n.* 1. reversion or

reversal, as of an action, decision, position, etc. Syn. *pagbaligtád*. 2. act of interchanging one for another in a pair.

pagsaloób (pag-sa-lo-ób), var. **pagsasaloób**, n. act of entertaining something in one's mind or heart. Syn. *pagsasaisip*.

pagsalooban (pag-sa-lo-o-ban), v. 1. to suspect someone. Syn. *paghinalaan*, *pagsuspetsahán*. 2. to have an intention to do something to. Syn. *pagbalakan*.

pagsalubong (pag-sa-lu-bong), n. 1. act of meeting someone on the way. 2. act of receiving or welcoming someone who has just arrived. 3. act of meeting someone's demand halfway. 4. act of going against the current, wind, etc. Syn. *pagsalunga*.

pagsalunò (pag-sa-lu-nò), n. act of meeting someone on the way, esp. for fear that he may get lost. Syn. *pagsalubong*. Cf. *pagsundô*, *pagkaón*.

pagsalunga (pag-sa-lu-nga), n. 1. act of going against the current, wind, etc. Syn. *pagsubà*. 2. (*Fig.*) fight against poverty, difficulties, etc. Syn. *pakikipaglaban*.

pagsama (pag-sa-ma), n. 1. act of accompanying someone in going to a certain place. Syn. *paghahatíd*. 2. act of going with another or others in going to a certain place. Syn. *pagsabáy*. 3. act of living with another or others in the same room or house. Syn. *pagsunò*, *pakikisunò*. 4. act of riding or sharing a ride in someone's vehicle. Syn. *pag-angkás*, *pakikiangkás*. 5. act of living with another as a wife or husband. Syn. *pagpisan*, *pakikipisan*. 6. act of mixing or mingling with others. Syn. *paghalò*, *pakikihalò*. 7. act of joining as a member of a society. Syn. *pagsapì*, *pakikisapì*. 8. act of joining with others, as in waging a campaign against something evil. Syn. *pakikiisá*. 9. act of going with the current. Syn. *pagpapatianód*.

pagsamâ (pag-sa-mâ), n. 1. change from good to bad or worse. Cf. *paglalâ*, *paglubhâ*. 2. reason for one's becoming bad.

pagsamantalá (pag-sa-man-ta-lá), n. 1. act of taking advantage, as of someone's ignorance. Cf. *paglamáng*. 2. act of making use of the opportunity at hand.

pagsambá (pag-sam-bá), n. 1. worship; adoration. Syn. *pananampalataya*, *adorasyón*. 2. true devotion. Syn. *katapatan*. 3. belief. Syn. *paniniwalà*, *pananalig*, *pagsampalataya*.

pagsambít (pag-sam-bít), n. mention or reference about something in one's speech. Syn. *pagbanggít*.

pagsambót (pag-sam-bót), n. 1. act of catching something with the hand. Syn. *pagsaló*. 2. act of taking over the duty or position left by another. Syn. *paghalili*. 3. recovery of one's loss in gambling or business. Syn. *pagbawì*.

pagsamò (pag-sa-mò), n. act of begging humbly and earnestly; supplication. Syn. *pagluhog*, *pamamanhík*, *pagmamakaawà*, *pananambitan*.

pagsampalataya (pag-sam-pa-la-ta-ya), n. 1. religious belief; worship. Also, *pananampalataya*. Syn. *pagsambá*. 2. faith. Syn. *tiwalà*, *pagtitiwalà*. 3. belief; conviction that certain things are true. Syn. *paniniwalà*, *pananalig*.

pagsamyó (pag-sam-yó), var. **pagsamyô**, n. 1. emission of sweet odor or fragrance. Syn. *pagbangó*, *paghalimuyak*. 2. act of smelling or inhaling the fragrance of. Syn. *pag-amóy*, *paglangháp*.

pagsandál (pag-san-dál), n. 1. act of leaning one's back against something. 2. an inclining or tendency to incline against something, as a post against a wall. Syn. *pagsandíg*. 3. (*Fig.*) dependence upon someone. Syn. *pag-asa sa ibá*.

pagsang-ayon (pag-sang + a-yon), n. acquiescence; assent; consent; concurrence. Syn. *pagpayag*, *pagpapahintulot*.

pagsangkutsa (pag-sang-kut-sa), n. act of frying (leafy vegetebles, etc.) lightly with spices in a little fat.

pagsanggunì (pag-sang-gu-nì), n. act of consulting or seeking the advice of someone. Syn. *pagkunsulta*; *paghingî ng payo*.

pagsangháp (pag-sang-háp), n. act of inhaling, esp. through the mouth. Syn. *paglangháp*, *pagsagap* (*ng hangin*).

pagsanghíd (pag-sang-híd), n. emission of strong, disagreeable odor. Syn. *pagbahò*, *pagsangsáng*, *pagkakaamóy*.

pagsangsáng (pag-sang-sáng), n. emission of strong, pleasant odor. Syn. *paghalimuyak, pagsingáw ng bangó.*

pagsansalà (pag-san-sa-là), n. act of forbidding; prohibition; interdiction; injunction. Syn. *pagbabawal, pagpigil.*

pagsanto (pag-san-tò), n. (*Colloq.*) too much respect for (someone). Syn. *labis na paggalang.*

pagsapantahà (pag-sa-pan-ta-hà), n. 1. a conjecturing or guessing. Syn. *paghakà, pagpapalagáy.* 2. act of suspecting. Syn. *pagsusospetsa, paghihinalà.*

pagsapit (pag-sa-pit), n. 1. act of reaching or arriving at a certain place or destination. Syn. *pagdatíng.* 2. time of arrival at a certain place. Syn. *oras ng datíng.* 3. a coming to a certain limit or state. Syn. *pag-abot, paghantóng.*

pagsariwà (pag-sa-ri-wà), n. 1. regain of new health and vigor, esp. of plants. Syn. *pananariwang mulî.* 2. (*Fig.*) with *sa alaala*: act of reminding someone about something. Syn. *pagpapaalaala, pagpapagunitâ.*

pagsasa- (pag-sa-sa-), pref. used to express: **(a)** act of translating into another language, as in: *pagsasa-Kastilà,* translation into Spanish; **(b)** act or manner of imitating the act or habit of, as in: *pagsasa-pagóng,* act of moving like a turtle; **(c)** act of implementing, as in: *pagsasagawâ,* implementation or putting into practice; **(d)** adaptation or writing into, as in: *pagsasanobela,* adaptation into a novel.

pagsasaalang-alang (pag-sa-sa-a-lang + a-lang), n. act of taking something into consideration.

pagsasabalikat (pag-sa-sa-ba-li-kat), n. act of assuming the full responsibility of undertaking or performing a certain kind of important work. Cf. *pagsasakatuparan.*

pagsasabi (pag-sa-sa-bi), n. 1. act of saying or telling something. Syn. *pagsasalitâ, pagpapahayag.* 2. act of telling something to someone. Cf. *pagbabalità.*

pagsasaka (pag-sa-sa-ka), n. cultivation of land for raising crops; farming; agriculture. Syn. *pagbubukid, paglilináng, agrikultura.*

pagsasakit (pag-sa-sa-kit), n. constant, careful effort in order to attain an ambition; diligence; perseverance. Syn. *pagtitiyagâ, pagtitiís.*

pagsasákripisyo (pag-sa-sá-kri-pis-yo), n. 1. act of offering something as a sacrifice. Syn. *paghahandóg ng sákripisyo.* 2. sacrifice; doing something difficult. Syn. *pagpapakasakit.*

pagsasagawâ (pag-sa-sa-ga-wâ), n. act of putting into action or realization; implementation. Syn. *pagsasakatuparan.*

pagsaságutan (pag-sa-sá-gu-tan), n. 1. act of answering each other, as in writing, by telephone, etc. Syn. *pagtutúgunan.* 2. (in debate) act of arguing with each other. 3. verbal controversy or noisy altercation. Syn. *pagtatáltalan, pagmumurahán, pagbabálitaktakan.*

pagsasalát (pag-sa-sa-lát), n. 1. period or time of scarcity. Syn. *pagdarahóp, paghihikahós.* 2. personal experience of being in want or in need. Syn. *pagdarálitâ, paghihirap.*

pagsasalawahan (pag-sa-sa-la-wa-han), n. 1. fact or state of being inconstant or fickle. 2. act of being confused. Syn. *pagaalinlangan.* 3. act of hesitating or vascillating. Syn. *pagbabantulót, paguurung-sulong, pag-uulík-ulík.*

pagsasalaysáy (pag-sa-sa-lay-sáy), n. the act or manner of narrating; telling a story or giving an account of a happening; narration. Syn. *pagkukuwento.*

pagsasalin (pag-sa-sa-lin), n. 1. act of pouring or transferring water, liquid, grains, etc. from one container to another. 2. translation of one language to another. Also, *pagsasalin-wikà.* 3. transcription, as of stenographic notes. 3. endorsement, as of a recommendation, circular, etc. Syn. *paglilipat.* 4. act of making a copy or copies from. Syn. *pagkopya, paggawâ ng kopya o sipî.* 5. act of turning over an office, function, or the like to a successor. Syn. *paglilipat.*

pagsasalitâ (pag-sa-sa-li-tâ), n. 1. act or manner of talking. 2. act or manner of delivering a speech. Syn. *pagtatalumpatî, pagdidiskursó.*

pagsasaloób (pag-sa-sa-lo-ób), n. 1. act of putting something inside. Syn. *pagpapasok, pagpapaloób*. 2. act of putting something into one's mind. Syn. *paglalagáy sa isip, pagsasaisip*.

pagsasama (pag-sa-sa-ma), n. 1. act of going or leaving together. Syn. *pag-alís na magkasama, pagsasabáy*. 2. act of living together, as a husband and his wife. Syn. *pagpipisan*. 3. act of putting or combining a thing with another. Syn. *paghahalò, paglalahók*. 4. act of including something in a letter, etc. Syn. *paglalakip*. 5. act of accompanying someone to a certain place. Syn. *paghahatíd*.

pagsasamantalá (pag-sa-sa-man-ta-lá), n. 1. act of taking advantage, as of someone's ignorance, etc. 2. act of taking the chance or opportunity of.

pagsasangkót (pag-sa-sang-kót), n. act of implicating someone in an affair. Syn. *pagdaramay, pagdadawit*.

pagsasápalarán (pag-sa-sá-pa-la-rán), n. act of taking a risk or chance. Also, *pakikipagsápalarán*. Syn. *pagbabakásakalì, pag-aalasuwerte*.

pagsasapantahà (pag-sa-sa-pan-ta-hà), n. 1. act or instance of suspecting; suspicion. Syn. *paghihinalà, pagdududa, pasusospetsa*. 2. act of making a conjecture or guess; presumption. Syn. *pag-aakalà, paghihinuhà*.

pagsasarilí (pag-sa-sa-ri-lí), n. 1. act of living on one's own or independently from one's parents. Syn. *pamumuhay na mag-isá*. 2. independence or autonomy, as of a nation. Syn. *paglayà, kalayaan, independénsiyá, kasarinlán*.

pagsasayá (pag-sa-sa-yá), n. merry-making; feasting; rejoicing; merriment; gaiety and fun; celebration. Syn. *pagdiriwang, pagkakátuwaan*.

pagsasayáng (pag-sa-sa-yáng), n. act of wasting time, money, materials, etc. Syn. *pag-aaksayá*.

pagsaulian (pag-sa-u-li-an), v. 1. to recover or regain, as one's health, consciousness, etc. 2. to have a thing returned to.

pagsaulo (pag-sa-u-lo), n. act of memorizing or putting into one's mind or memory. Syn. *pagmemorya*.

pagsawaan (pag-sa-wa-an), v. 1. to have surfeit (from a certain kind of food) due to overindulgence. 2. to lose interest in or have no more liking for (something) due to constant or long use.

pagsayad (pag-sa-yad), n. 1. a running aground, as of a boat or ship. Syn. *pagsadsád*. 2. act or manner by which a hanging object touches the ground or bottom of. 3. (*Fig.*) state or condition of being financially broke. Syn. *pagkagipít (sa buhay), paghihirap*.

pagseséntimyento (pag-se-sén-tim-yen-to), n. feeling of being slighted or insulted. Syn. *pagdaramdám*.

pagsibol (pag-si-bol), n. robust growth, as of a young man. Syn. *pagbulas (ng katawán)*.

pagsiból (pag-si-ból), n. a sprouting or germination of seeds. Syn. *pagtubò ng butó o binhî*.

pagsikat (pag-si-kat), n. 1. act or time of rising, as of the sun, moon, stars, etc. Syn. *pagsilang*. 2. a becoming popular or well-known; rise to popularity. Syn. *pagtanyág*.

pagsikíl (pag-si-kíl), n. harassment; persecution. Syn. *pagpapahirap, pagmamalupít*.

pagsidhî (pag-sid-hî), n. a becoming more intense; intensification. Syn. *pagtindí, paglalâ*.

pagsigáw (pag-si-gáw), n. 1. act of shouting or crying out aloud. Syn. *paghiyáw, pagpalahaw, pagpalakat*. 2. (*Fig.*) act of confessing; disclosure of one's participation in a crime, secret dealing, etc. Syn. *pagtatapát*.

pagsige (pag-si-ge), var. **pagsigi**, n. act of continuing or going ahead, as with one's trip, plan, etc. Syn. *pagtulóy, pagpapatuloy*.

pagsiglá (pag-sig-lá), n. a becoming more animated or lively. Syn. *pagkakaroón ng buhay (fig.)*.

pagsiíl (pag-si-íl), n. 1. act of oppressing; oppression. Syn. *pag-apí, pang-aapí, pagpapahirap*. 2. act of strangling a person with the hand. Syn. *pagsakál*.

pagsilakbó (pag-si-lak-bó), n. sudden outburst, as of anger, passion, or the like.

Syn. *pagsikláb*. 2. sudden flight, as of thick dust or smoke. Syn. *pagsigabo*.

pagsilang (pag-si-lang), n. 1. act or time of rising, as of the sun, moon, and the like. Syn. *pagsikat*. 2. a being born; birth; nativity. Syn. *pagiging tao*, *paglitáw sa maliwanag*.

pagsimsím (pag-sim-sím), n. 1. act of tasting the sweetness of something by sipping it little by little. Syn. *pagnamnám nang untî-untî*. 2. enjoyment with gusto, as of something pleasant.

pagsinag (pag-si-nag), n. the appearance of the rays, as of the sun, moon, etc. Syn. *pagbanaag*, *pamamanaag*.

pagsino (pag-si-no), n. act of asking who a person is.

pagsintá (pag-sin-tá), n. 1. love; tender feeling for. Syn. *pag-ibig*, *pagmamahál*, *pag-irog*. 2. act of standing on hind feet, as what a dog does in front of his master.

pagsingkád (pag-sing-kád), n. the act of reaching the full extent. Syn. *pagsukdól*, *pag-abót sa sukdulan*.

pagsipót (pag-si-pót), n. 1. appearance or coming out, as from hiding or long absence. Syn. *paglitáw*, *paggitáw*. 2. an unexpected arrival of someone, as in a meeting. Syn. *di-ináasahang pagdatíng*.

pagsisi (pag-si-si), n. act of cutting, chopping, or splitting firewood.

pagsisikap (pag-si-si-kap), n. act of working hard; constant and careful effort; diligence or perseverance. Syn. *pagsisipag*, *pagtitiyagâ*.

pagsisilang (pag-si-si-lang), n. act of giving birth or bringing forth a child. Syn. *pag-aanák*, *panganganák*.

pagsisimpán (pag-si-sim-pán), n. 1. act or habit of saving for the future; thrift. Syn. *pagtitipíd*, *pagtitipon para sa hinaharáp*.

pagsisimulâ (pag-si-si-mu-lâ), n. act or time of beginning or starting; start or beginning of; commencement. Syn. *pag-uumpisá*.

pagsisinóp (pag-si-si-nóp), n. 1. act or habit of maintaining oneself neat and clean. 2. act or habit of being thrifty. Syn. *pagtitipíd*, *pagsisimpán*.

pagsisintahan (pag-si-sin-ta-han), n. love affair; mutual love or affection for each other. Syn. *pagmamahalan*, *pag-iibigan*.

pagsisinungalín (pag-si-si-nu-nga-lín), var. **pagsisinungalíng**, n. act or habit of telling a lie or lies. Syn. *pagbubulaán*.

pagsisiraán (pag-si-si-ra-án), n. act of slandering each other. Also, *pagsisiraáng-puri*.

pagsisisi (pag-si-si-si), n. repentance; feeling of sorrow for one's fault or wrongdoing; contrition; remorse; compunction.

pagsisisihán (pag-si-si-si-hán), n. act of blaming each other.

pagsisiwalat (pag-si-si-wa-lat), n. act of revealing or disclosing a secret, an anomaly, etc. Syn. *pagbubunyág*.

pagsisiyám (pag-si-si-yám), n. 1. act of holding devotional prayers or a novena during a nine-day period, usually for some special religious purpose or in memory of a deceased person. Syn. *pagnonobena*. 2. the period during which rains fall continuously for nine days.

pagsubaybáy (pag-su-bay-báy), n. 1. act of secretly observing the act or movement of someone. Syn. *pagmanmán*, *pagmamanmán*. 2. act of carefully following up the progress of. 3. act of going with someone in order to protect.

pagsubok (pag-su-bok), n. 1. act of watching someone secretly; a spying on someone. Syn. *lihim na pagmamanmán*. 2. act of making a try. Syn. *pag-ato*. 3. act of savoring the taste of. Syn. *pagtikím*. 4. an experimenting. Syn. *pag-iiksperimento*.

pagsukdól (pag-suk-dól), n. act of reaching the highest point or farthest distance possible. Syn. *pagsagád*.

pagsugat (pag-su-gat), n. 1. act of injuring someone by cutting, stabbing, shooting, etc. 2. act of wounding or injuring the feeling, reputation, etc. of.

pagsugid (pag-su-gid), n. act of becoming diligently faithful or persistent, as a lover or follower. Syn. *pagsigasig*.

pagsuling (pag-su-ling), n. act of wandering around a place aimlessly, as in a dazed state of mind or in bewilderment.

pagsulong (pag-su-long), n. 1. a moving forward; advance. Syn. *pag-abante*, *paglakad*, *pagtulak*. 2. progress; advance;

improvement. Syn. *pag-unlád, progreso.*

pagsulpót (pag-sul-pót), n. 1. sudden jutting
or sticking out from a hole, or small
opening. Syn. *pag-uslî, pag-ulpót, pag-
ultáw, paglitáw.* 2. sudden appearance or
coming out, as of a person long absent.
Syn. *biglâng paglitáw-pagsipót.*

pagsumpâ (pag-sum-pâ), n. 1. act of taking
an oath. Also, *panunumpâ.* 2. act of
cursing someone.

pagsunód (pag-su-nód), n. 1. act of
following another (or others) who has
(have) departed ahead. 2. act of obeying
someone, a rule, command, or order. Syn.
pagtalima. 3. act of deciding something in
accordance with. Syn. *pag-alinsunod.*

pagsungaw (pag-su-ngaw), n. 1. act of
looking or peeping out from the window,
door, or hole. Syn. *pagdungaw.* 2. act of
appearing or showing oneself from an
opening, as window, door, or hole. Syn.
paglitáw, pag-ultáw, pagpapakita.

pagsupil (pag-su-pil), n. 1. act of disciplining
or bringing under control. Syn.
pagdisiplina. 2. act of dominating or
subjugating. Syn. *paglupig, pagdominá,
pagpapasukò.*

pagsuplíng (pag-sup-líng), n. 1.
development of a new branch. Syn.
pagsangá. 2. act of having offspring;
reproduction. Syn. *pagkakaanák.*

pagsurot (pag-su-rot), n. 1. a menacing
attempt to thrust one's finger at the eyes
of someone. 2. angry reference about
someone's ingratitude. Syn. *pagsumbát.*

pagsusubukán (pag-su-su-bu-kán), n. 1. act
of spying or watching each other secretly.
Syn. *lihim na pagmamánmanan.* 2.
simultaneous act of making a try. Syn. *pag-
aatuhán.* 3. act of competing with each
other, esp. in strength or talent. Syn.
pagsusukatán.

pagsusulát (pag-su-su-lát), n. writing; act of
writing as a profession.

pagsusulit (pag-su-su-lit), n. 1. a set of
questions asked in an examination or test.
Syn. *mga tanóng o katánungan sa iksamin.*
2. act of giving an examination or test.
Syn. *pag-iiksamin, pagpapaiksamin.* 3. act
of making a report, accounting, or

explanation about something. Syn. *pag-
uulat, pagpapaliwanag.* 4. act of submitting
something. Syn. *pagbibigay, paghaharáp.* 5.
act of returning something previously
entrusted to oneself. Syn. *pagsasaulì.*

pagsusulong (pag-su-su-long), n. 1. act of
pushing something forward. Syn.
pagtutulak. 2. act of pushing or going
ahead, as with one's plan or project. Syn.
pagtutulóy, pagpapatuloy.

pagsusumakit (pag-su-su-ma-kit), n. diligent
effort to attain or accomplish a wish or
dream. Syn. *pagsusumikap.*

pagsusumikap (pag-su-su-mi-kap), n.
diligent effort in order to attain or
accomplish a wish or dream. Syn.
pagsusumakit.

pagsusuplíng (pag-su-sup-líng), n. 1. growth
of new shoots or branches. Syn.
pagsasangá. 2. act of having offspring;
reproduction. Syn. *pag-aanák,
pagkakaanák.*

pagsusúyuan (pag-su-sú-yu-an), n. love
affair. Syn. *pag-iibigan, pagmamáhalan.*

pagsuyò (pag-su-yò), n. 1. act of bringing
oneself into someone's favor or good
graces, any ingratiatory act. Also,
panunuyò. 2. affection. Syn. *pag-ibig,
pagmamahál.*

pagsuysóy (pag-suy-sóy), n. act of prodding
or reminding someone to act or do
something.

pagtakipsilim (pag-ta-kip-si-lim), n.
beginning of dusk or nightfall. Also,
pagtatakipsilim. Syn. *pag-aágaw-dilím,
pagdadapithapon.*

pagtaksilán (pag-tak-si-lán), v. 1. to be a
traitor to; act treacherously against
someone. Syn. *pagtraidurán.* 2. to betray,
as one's friend. Syn. *ipagkánulô.* 3. to be
unfaithful, esp. to one's wife or husband.
Syn. *pagliluhan.*

pagtagál (pag-ta-gál), n. 1. prolongation or
being prolonged, as of time. Syn. *paglaon,
pagluwát.* 2. ability or power to resist or
endure pain, strain, or stress. Syn. *pagtiís,
pagbatá, pag-agwantá.*

pagtaghóy (pag-tag-hóy), n. loud grief;
lamentation. Also, *pananaghóy.* Syn.
pagdaíng.

pagtahimik (pag-ta-hi-mik), n. 1. act of keeping silent. Syn. *pagwawaláng imik o kibô*. 2. a becoming calm or peaceful; calming down. Syn. *pagpayapà, pagtiwasáy*. 3. (*Fig.*) act of getting married. Syn. *pag-aasawa*.

pagtahô (pag-ta-hô), n. act of understanding; knowing all about something. Syn. *pag-unawà, pag-intindí, pagbatíd*.

pagtalagá (pag-ta-la-gá), n. 1. act of getting ready or prepared for any eventuality. Syn. *paghandâ*. 2. dedication of oneself to some kind of work or service. Syn. *paglaán*.

pagtalampák (pag-ta-lam-pák), n. act of telling something openly to someone. Syn. *pagsasabi nang táhasan o lantarán*.

pagtalikód (pag-ta-li-kód), n. 1. act of turning about, as to face the other way; a turning of one's back. 2. a shift or reversal of allegiance, religion, opinion, or belief; a turning-about-face.

pagtaliin (pag-ta-li-in), v. 1. to tie together. Cf. *papágtaliin*. 2. to ask, request, or allow someone to tie something. Also, *papágtaliin*. 3. (*Fig.*) to join or unite a man and a woman in wedlock. Syn. *ikasál*.

pagtalima (pag-ta-li-ma), n. 1. doing what one is told to do; obedience. Syn. *pagsunód*. 2. fulfilling, as of one's promise; fulfillment. Syn. *pagtupád*.

pagtalimuwáng (pag-ta-li-mu-wáng), n. act of feigning ignorance about a fact or something one knows about. Syn. *pagkailâ, pagkakailâ*.

pagtalós (pag-ta-lós), n. act of understanding or knowing about something. Syn. *pag-unawà, pag-intindí*.

pagtalunan (pag-ta-lu-nan), n. to debate on; argue about; decide a problem by discussion or debate. Syn. *pagdiskusyunán, pagtalakayan, pagdebatihan*.

pagtamán (pag-ta-mán), n. act of experiencing, esp. hardship. Syn. *pagdanas*. See pagtatamán.

pagtamasa (pag-ta-ma-sa), var. pagtatamasa, n. enjoyment of wealth or abundance. Syn. *pagpapasasà*.

pagtamaulî (pag-ta-ma-u-lî), var. pagtatamaulî, n. 1. retraction; taking

back. Syn. *pagbawì*. 2. change of mind o decision. Syn. *pagbabagong-loób pagbabagong-isip*.

pagtambád (pag-tam-bád), n. 1. act o exposing oneself to view. Syn. *paglantád paghantád, paglitáw, pagpapakita, paglabás* 2. sudden exposure of something to view

pagtamláy (pag-tam-láy), n. 1. loss or losing of interest in something. Syn *paghihinawà, panghihinabáng*. 2. lassitude weariness; languor. Syn. *panlalambót ng katawán; panghihinà*.

pagtampalasan (pag-tam-pa-la-san), n. ac of destroying something. Syn. *pagsirà, pagwasák*.

pagtanáw (pag-ta-náw), n. act of looking a someone or something from a distance. Syn. *pagtingín sa malayò*.

pagtantán (pag-tan-tán), n. a stopping o desisting, esp. from talking. Syn. *pagtigil, paghintô, pagtahán, paglikát*.

pagtantô (pag-tan-tô), n. act of knowing or understanding. Syn. *pag-unawà, pag-intindí, pagbatid*.

pagtangá (pag-ta-ngá), n. act of being present but doing nothing, as a spectator or bystander. Syn. *pagtungangà*.

pagtangkilik (pag-tang-ki-lik), n. patronage; support given by a patron or sponsor. Syn. *pagtataguyod*.

pagtanggáp (pag-tang-gáp), n. 1. act of receiving something being given or offered. 2. act of admitting or confessing, as one's crime. Syn. *pag-amin*. 3. acceptance or approval. Syn. *pagsang-ayon, pagpapatibay*. 4. a welcoming; kind reception for a new arrival or arrivals. Syn. *pagsalubong*.

pagtangis (pag-ta-ngis), n. act of weeping. Cf. *pag-iyák, pagluhà*.

pagtao (pag-ta-o), n. 1. act of considering or treating someone as a human being. Syn. *pagtrato bilang tao*. 2. act of staying in the house as a watcher during the absence of the other members of the family. Syn. *pagpapaiwan sa bahay bilang bantáy*.

pagtapatán (pag-ta-pa-tán), v. 1. to be frank to; tell the truth to. 2. to confess to; make a confession to.

pagtapusín (pag-ta-pu-sín), *v.* 1. to urge or allow someone to finish or complete what he is doing. 2. to support (a student) until he graduates. 3. to allow or permit a student to graduate. Also, *papágtapusín.*

pagtarók (pag-ta-rók), *n.* 1. act of sounding the depth, as of a sea. Syn. *pag-arók, pagsukat ng lalim.* 2. act of understanding well after studying carefully. Syn. *pag-unawang mabuti.*

pagtatabí (pag-ta-ta-bí), *n.* 1. act of sitting, lying, or sleeping together or near each other. Syn. *pagsisiping.* 2. act of putting or keeping something, as a vehicle, at or near the side of the road. 3. act of keeping or saving something for someone or for future use. Cf. *pagtatagò, pagliligpít.*

pagtataká (pag-ta-ta-ká), *n.* amazement; great surprise; astonishment; wonderment. Syn. *panggigilalas, pagkámanghâ.*

pagtatakdâ (pag-ta-tak-dâ), *n.* 1. act of putting a limit to. Syn. *pagtatasa, paglilimití.* 2. a scheduling or fixing of time. Syn. *pagtataning.*

pagtatakíp-butas (pag-ta-ta-kíp + bu-tas), 1. (*Fig.*) act of providing a substitute for someone who is unable to attend a function as a performer. 2. literally, act of covering or plugging a hole. Syn. *pagpapasak.*

pagtatakípsilim (pag-ta-ta-kíp-si-lim), *n.* beginning of twilight or nightfall. Syn. *pagdadapithapon, pag-aagaw-dilím.*

pagtataksíl (pag-ta-tak-síl), *n.* 1. act of perfidy or treason; treachery; disloyalty. Syn. *pagtatraidor, paglililo, pagsusukáb, pagpapalamara.* 2. disloyalty to one's spouse. Syn. *paglililo.*

pagtatadhanà (pag-ta-tad-ha-nà), *n.* 1. act of providing or including a certain provision or provisions in an act, ordinance, agreement, etc. Syn. *paglalagdâ, pagtatakdâ.* 2. predetermination of someone's fate.

pagtatagál (pag-ta-ta-gál), *n.* 1. long duration of time before something is finished or completed. Syn. *pagluluwát.* 2. long delay. Syn. *matagál na atraso.* 3. prolongation of time.

pagtatág-aráw (pag-ta-tág + a-ráw), *n.* the beginning or coming of summer or hot season. Syn. *pagtatág-inít.*

pagtatággutom (pag-ta-tág-gu-tom), *n.* occurrence of famine or starvation.

pagtatáglamíg (pag-ta-tág-la-míg), *n.* coming of the cold season or winter.

pagtatagláy (pag-ta-tag-láy), *n.* 1. state or condition of having something in one's possession. Syn. *pagdadalá.* 2. act of owning or having, as certain personal chracteristics. Syn. *pag-aangkín.*

pagtatagò (pag-ta-ta-gò), *n.* 1. act of hiding or keeping oneself out of sight. Syn. *pagkukublí.* 2. act of keeping a secret, etc. Syn. *paglilihim, paglilingíd.* 3. act of keeping something out of sight. Syn. *pagliligpít.* 4. act of saving (money, food, etc.) for the future. Syn. *pagsisimpán, pag-iimpók.*

pagtatág-ulán (pag-ta-tág + u-lán), *n.* coming of rainy season. Syn. *pag-uúlanan.*

pagtatagumpáy (pag-ta-ta-gum-páy), *n.* act or instance of success or victory. Syn. *pagwawagí.*

pagtataingang-kawalì (pag-ta-ta-i-ngang + ka-wa-lì), *n.* (*Fig.*) act of pretending deafness to an appeal or request of another or others. Syn. *pagbibingí-bingihan.*

pagtatalagá (pag-ta-ta-la-gá), *n.* 1. act of assigning a person (to work) in a certain place. 2. induction or installation, as of officers of an association. Syn. *pagpapanumpâ sa tungkulin.* 3. act of setting apart something for a certain purpose. Syn. *paglalaán.*

pagtatalamitam (pag-ta-ta-la-mi-tam), *n.* act of intermingling together intimately.

pagtatálampakan (pag-ta-tá-lam-pa-kan), *n.* act of accusing each other or one another face to face.

pagtatálastasan (pag-ta-tá-las-ta-san), *n.* 1. act of understanding each other or one another. Syn. *pag-uúnawaán, pag-iintindihan.* 2. act of communicating with each other or with one another, as by telephone, etc. Cf. *pagbabálitaán.*

pagtatalik (pag-ta-ta-lik), *n.* a private intimate conversation between two persons; tete-a-tete. Syn. *pagniniíg, pag-uulayaw.*

pagtatalo (pag-ta-ta-lo), n. verbal dispute or controversy; debate; heated discussions. Syn. *debate*, *pagdedebate;diskusyón*, *pagdidiskusyón*.

pagtatalusirà (pag-ta-ta-lu-si-rà), n. act of breaking one's promise or backing out from one's promise. Syn. *pagtalikód o pagsirà sa pangakò*.

pagtatamán (pag-ta-ta-mán), n. 1. diligence; perseverance. Syn. *tiyagâ*, *pagtitiyagâ*. 2. act of obtaining or acquiring something through constant efforts. Syn. *pagtatamô*, *pagkakamít*.

pagtatandâ (pag-ta-tan-dâ), n. 1. act of remembering; putting something into one's mind or memory. Syn. *pagsasaalaala*, *paglalagáy sa isip*. 2. ability to remember or memorize. Syn. *pagmemorya*. 3. act of providing (a place, etc.) with a marker. Syn. *paglalagáy ng panandâ*. 4. (Colloq.) act of learning a lesson from one's past experience.

pagtatangí-tangì (pag-ta-tangí + ta-ngì), n. unequal treatment or regard for others.

pagtatapáng-tapangan (pag-ta-ta-páng + ta-pa-ngan), n. pretended bravery or valor. Syn. *paglalakás-lakasan ng loób*.

pagtatapát (pag-ta-ta-pát), n. 1. act of telling the truth; confession. Syn. *pagsasabi ng katotohanan*. 2. faithfulness; fidelity; opposed to *pagtataksíl*, *paglililo*. 3. act of taking the direct or straight route from a place to another. 4. frankness; sincerity.

pagtatapós (pag-ta-ta-pós), n. 1. act of completing or finishing something being made. Syn. *pagyarì*. 2. conclusion. Syn. *pagwawakás*. 3. graduation from school or college. Syn. *graduwasyón*. 4. the last day of a nine-day novena or celebration. Syn. *hulíng araw ng pagsisiyám*. 5. final stage of anything. Syn. *hulíng yugtô*.

pagtatayu-tayo (pag-ta-ta-yu + ta-yo), n. act, manner, or habit of doing things exclusively among ourselves, that is, among relatives or close friends.

pagtawad (pag-ta-wad), n. 1. in buying, the act of asking or requesting for a reduction or discount in price. Syn. *paghingî ng bawas o diskuwento*. 2. (Fig.) a belittling, as of the importance of something. Syn. *paghamak*.

pagtawanán (pag-ta-wa-nán), v. tо laugh mockingly at someone.

pagtayog (pag-ta-yog), n. 1. rise of the flight, as of a kite. Syn. *pagtaás*. 2. rise to prominence. Syn. *pagtanyág*, *pagbantóg*.

pagtibók (pag-ti-bók), n. beating or throbbing, as of the heart; pulsation. Syn. *pagpintíg*.

pagtigíb (pag-ti-gíb), n. 1. act of overloading (a vehicle) with or as with passengers. Syn. *pagpunóng mabuti*. 2. act of overburdening someone as with pain or suffering. Syn. *paglipós*, *pagbatbát*, *pagpuspós*.

pagtiís (pag-ti-ís), n. 1. act of bearing or suffering (pain, hardship, etc.) with fortitude. Syn. *pagbatá*, *pag-agwanta*. 2. act of refraining from giving help to someone suffering pain, hardship, etc. Cf. *pagtikís*.

pagtingín (pag-ti-ngín), n. 1. act of looking. Cf. *pagtanáw*, *pagmalas*, *pagmasíd*. 2. personal point of view about something; viewpoint or mental attitude. Syn. *palagáy*, *opinyón*, *pananáw*. 3. regard; respect and affection; esteem. Syn. *pagpapahalagá*, *paghangà*. 4. observation. Syn. *pagmamasíd*.

pagtitimpî (pag-ti-tim-pî), n. self-control; moderation or control of one's emotion, desires, actions, etc. Syn. *pagpipigil*, *pagpapakahinahon*.

pagtitínginan (pag-ti-tí-ngi-nan), n. 1. act of looking at each other. Syn. *pagmamásiran*, *pagtatánawan*. 2. act of looking simultaneously or at the same time. 3. regard or concern for each other or for one another. Syn. *pagpapálagayan*.

pagtitiwalà (pag-ti-ti-wa-là), n. 1. trust or confidence in someone. Also, *tiwalà*. Syn. *kumpiyansa*, *pagkukumpiyansa*, *pananalig*. 2. act of entrusting something to someone. Also, *pagkakátiwalà*.

pagtiwalaan (pag-ti-wa-la-an), v. 1. to have confidence or trust in; rely on. Syn. *panaligan*, *paniwalaan*. 2. to entrust something to. Syn. *paghabilinan*, *pagkumpiyansahán*.

pagtiwasáy (pag-ti-wa-sáy), n. a becoming peaceful, calm, or tranquil. Syn. *pagtahimik*, *pagpayapà*.

pagtiyáp (pag-ti-yáp), n. act of making an appointment or agreement with another to meet together in a certain place and time. Syn. *pagtipán*.

pagtotoó (pag-to-to-ó), n. fulfillment or making true one's words or promise. Syn. *pagtupád*. 2. act of performing something seriously (without intention to deceive).

pagtugón (pag-tu-gón), n. act or manner of replying or answering. Syn. *pagsagót*.

pagtugot (pag-tu-got), n. a stopping or cessation. Syn. *pagtigil, paghintô, pagtahán, paglikát*.

pagtulâ (pag-tu-lâ), n. act or manner of reciting or delivering a poem; recitation of poetry. Syn. *pagbigkás ng tulâ*.

pagtulad (pag-tu-lad), n. act, means, or instance of imitating or copying someone or something. Syn. *paggaya, pagparis, pagkopya, paggagád, paghuwád*.

pagtuntón (pag-tun-tón), n. 1. act of tracing or retracing a line, path, route, etc. Syn. *pagtaluntón*. 2. act of following the trail or footprints of. Syn. *pagbakás*. 3. rigorous following of a rule, regulation, order, etc. Syn. *pagsunód, pag-alinsunod, pagtalima*. 4. act of finding or determining the origin, source, date, etc. of someone or something by tracing.

pagturing (pag-tu-ring), n. 1. act of answering a riddle. Syn. *pagtuód; pagsagót*. 2. act of making mention or remark about something. Syn. *pagbanggít*. 3. act of making a price offer for, as in an auction sale. Syn. *pagtawad*.

pagturól (pag-tu-ról), n. act of mentioning or pointing out. Syn. *pagbanggít, pagsasabi*.

pagtutuwíd (pag-tu-tu-wíd), n. 1. act or manner of making a thing straight; straightening. Syn. *pagpapatuwíd, pagdideretso*. 2. act of correcting an error or mistake. Syn. *pagwawastô, pagtutumpák*.

pag-ukulan (pag + u-ku-lan), v. 1. to set aside something for. Syn. *paglaanan, pagtaanan*. 2. to spend or devote, as one's time, effort, consideration, in doing something.

pag-uhâ (pag + u-hâ), n. crying of a newly born baby. Cf. *pag-iyák*.

pag-ulán (pag + u-lán), n. 1. the coming or falling of rain. Also, *pagkakaulán*. 2. a falling or pouring like rain, as of bullets.

pag-ulapan (pag + u-la-pan), v. (Fig.) to lose, as one's hope. Syn. *mawalán*.

pag-ulila (pag + u-li-la), n. (Fig.) act of leaving someone alone in despair.

pag-uná-unahin (pag + u-ná + u-na-hin), v. to do things one by one or one after another.

pag-unawà (pag + u-na-wà), n. act of understanding or knowing the meaning of. Syn. *pag-intindí*.

pag-unlád (pag + un-lád), n. 1. advancement; development; improvement. Syn. *pagbuti*. 2. progress; prosperity. Syn. *pagsulong, progreso*.

pag-unsiyamì (pag + un-si-ya-mì), colloq. var. **pag-usyami**, n. act of disappointing someone, as by not giving in to his request. Syn. *pagbigô, pagsiphayô*.

pag-untág (pag + un-tág), n. 1. act of reminding someone about something forgotten or neglected. Syn. *pagpapaalaala, pagpapagunitâ, pag-ungkát*. 2. act of mentioning something in passing. Syn. *pagbanggít*.

pag-untól (pag + un-tól), n. sudden, temporary stop or cessation. Syn. *bigláng pagtigil o paghintô*.

pag-ungkát (pag + ung-kát), n. 1. act of reminding someone about something forgotten or neglected. Syn. *pag-untág, pagpapaalaala, pagpapagunitâ*. 2. act of recalling or mentioning again something relevant to a previous happening.

pag-upasalà (pag + u-pa-sa-là), n. act of speaking to or about a person in a bitter, abusive language; vituperation. Syn. *pagmura, paglait, pag-alipustâ, pag-insulto, pagdustâ*.

pag-upat (pag + u-pat), n. act or instance of instigating or inciting a person to do something undesirable; instigation. Syn. *pag-apuyo, pagsulsól, pag-udyók*.

págupitan (pá-gu-pi-tan), n. a barber's place of business; barbershop.

pagupuin (pa-gu-pu-in), v. 1. to destroy or demolish, as a structure. Syn. *gibain, wasakin, paguhuin*. 2. (Fig.) to make bedridden, as with sickness. Syn. *paratayin*.

pag-urì

pag-urì (pag + u-rì), n. 1. act of classifying things, as to kind, quality, origin or nature. Syn. *pagklasipiká*. 2. a test or analysis to determine the quality or purity, as of jewelry.

pagurin (pa-gu-rin), v. to make (someone) tired; cause (a person) to become tired. Syn. *pagalín, hapuin*.

pag-urí-uriin (pag + u-rí + u-ri-in), v. to classify or arrange according to kind, quality, or purity.

pag-urong (pag + u-rong), n. 1. backward movement. Syn. *atrás, pag-atrás*. 2. retreat; going back. Syn. *pagbalík*. 3. shrinking, as in fabrics. Syn. *pag-iklí, pag-utdó*. 4. admission of defeat; refusal to fight anymore. Syn. *pagsukò, pagpapatalo*. 5. revocation or withdrawal, as of one's promise or commitment. Syn. *pagbawì, pagtalikód (fig.)*.

pag-usapan (pag + u-sa-pan), v. to discuss or talk about, as in a meeting or conference; make as a subject of discussion. Syn. *talakayin, pagtalakayan (sa pulong o miting)*.

pag-usig (pag + u-sig), n. 1. act of conducting an inquiry or investigation about something. Syn. *pagsiyasat, pagsisiyasat*. 2. persecution. Syn. *pagpapahirap*.

pag-usisà (pag + u-si-sà), n. 1. act of inquiring about the status of something. Syn. *pagtatanóng, pag-alám*. 2. act of making an inquiry or investigation about something. Syn. *pagsiyasat*.

pag-utusan (pag + u-tu-san), v. to be at one's service or command.

pag-uukol (pag + u-u-kol), n. 1. act of putting something aside for a certain purpose. Syn. *paglalaán, pagtataán*. 2. act of giving or devoting one's time, effort, thought, etc. for a certain enterprise or purpose.

pag-uugalì (pag + u-u-ga-lì), n. 1. act of making something as a habit. 2. personal conduct, habit, or behavior. Syn. *kustumbre, kaugalián*.

pag-uugnáy (pag + u-ug-náy), n. 1. act of joining or connecting two things together or one thing with another. Syn.

pag-uyám

pagkakabit, paghuhugpóng. 2. act of associating one thing with another.

pag-uulap (pag + u-u-lap), n. formation of clouds; a becoming cloudy, referring to the sky. Also, *pagkakaulap*.

pag-uulayaw (pag + u-u-la-yaw), n. a private or intimate conversation between two persons; tete-a-tete. Syn. *pagniniíg*.

pag-uúlianin (pag + u-ú-li-a-nin), var. pag-uulyanin, n. the foolish or childish condition caused by old age; dotage; senility.

pag-uulík-ulík (pag + u-u-lík + u-lík), n. hesitancy or hesitation; indecision; tendency to hesitate. Syn. *pag-aatubilí (pag-aatubili), pag-uurung-sulong, pagbabantulót*.

pag-uumpísá (pag + u-um-pi-sá), n. 1. a commencing; start; beginning. 2. time of commencing or starting. Syn. *pagsisimulá*.

pag-uunahán (pag + u-u-na-hán), n. a contest of speed in doing something or in getting first to a certain destination.

pag-uúnawaán (pag + u-ú-na-wa-án), n. 1. a conferring or discussing with each other; bargaining to reach an agreement; negotiation. 2. act of understanding each other. Syn. *pag-iíntindihan*.

pag-uunlapì (pag + u-un-la-pì), n. act of using prefix or providing with a prefix. Syn. *pagpipripeho*.

pag-uupat (pag + u-u-pat), n. act of inducing or instigating someone to do something undesirable. Syn. *pagsusulsól, pag-aapuyo*.

pag-uurì (pag + u-u-rì), n. 1. a classifying, as to kind, variety, origin, or nature. Syn. *pagkaklásipiká*. 2. a test or analysis to determine the quality or purity, as of jewelry.

pag-uurung-sulong (pag + u-u-rung + su-long), n. hesitancy; hesitation; indecision; vacillation. Syn. *pag-aatubilí*.

pag-uusap (pag + u-u-sap), n. 1. act of talking or conversing with each other. 2. act of holding a meeting or conference. Syn. *pagmimiting, pagpupulong*.

pag-uwî (pag + u-wî), n. act or time of going home or returning to one's home. Syn. *pagbabalík sa sariling tahanan o bayan*.

pag-uyám (pag + u-yám), n. 1. act of mocking or ridiculing someone. Syn. *pag-*

aglahì, *paglibák*. 2. something said to ridicule or mock someone.

pagwagaywáy (pag-wa-gay-wáy), n. a waving or fluttering in the air, as of a flag being blown by the wind. Syn. *pagwasiwas*.

pagwaláng-bahalà (pag-wa-láng + ba-ha-là), n. lack of concern for; nonchalant attitude towards a person or thing. Also, *pagwawaláng-bahalà*.

pagwarì (pag-wa-rì), n. act of thinking deeply about something.

pagwawakás (pag-wa-wa-kás), n. a coming to an end. Syn. *pagtatapós*.

pagwawagí (pag-wa-wa-gí), var. **pagwawagî**, n. act of winning; triumph; victory. Syn. *pagtatagumpáy*.

pagwawalâ (pag-wa-wa-lâ), n. 1. act of struggling to free oneself from being tied or confined in a cell or prison. Syn. *pagaalpás*, *pagpipilit makawalâ*. 2. act of losing something. Syn. *paglilipol*.

pagkawaláng-kibô (pag-ka-wa-láng + ki-bô), n. 1. silence. Syn. *pagwawaláng-imík*, *di-pag-imík*. 2. unconcerned attitude; indifference. Syn. *pagwawaláng-bahalà*, *di-pakikialám*.

pagwawangkî (pag-wa-wang-kî), n. act of comparing one thing with another. Syn. *pagtutulad*, *pagwawangis*.

pagwawari-warì (pag-wa-wa-ri + wa-rì), n. long, deep thought; long-careful thinking. Syn. *pagninilay-nilay*, *pagbubulay-bulay*.

pagwawastô (pag-wa-was-tô), n. act of correcting an error or mistake. Syn. *pagtutumpák*, *pagtatamà*.

pagwikaan (pag-wi-ka-an), v. to reprove severely; reprimand. Syn. *pagsabihan*, *kagalitan*.

pagyabong (pag-ya-bong), n. luxuriant growth, as of plants. Syn. *paglabay ng mga dahon*.

pagyamanin (pag-ya-ma-nin), v. 1. to treasure; value highly, as a treasure. 2. to preserve well, as a tradition.

pagyao (pag-ya-o), n. 1. act of leaving for a certain place; departure. Syn. *pagyaon*, *pag-alís*, *paglisan*. 2. death. Syn. *pagkamatáy*, *pagpanaw*, *pagsakabiláng-buhay*.

pagyurak (pag-yu-rak), n. 1. act of crushing, destroying, or hurting by or as by treading on heavily. Syn. *pagyapáw*, *pagyasák*. 2. violation, as of someone's right. Syn. *paglabág*.

paha (pa-ha), n. (Sp. *faja*) 1. girdle; waistband. Syn. *bigkís*. 2. band wrapper for rolled matter, like newspapers and magazines sent by mail.

pahabâ (pa-ha-bâ), I. adj. 1. long and narrow; elongate. Also, *habâ*. 2. longitudinal. Syn. *paayón*. 3. becoming or getting longer. Also, *humáhabà*.
—II. adv. & adj. lengthwise; lengthways; longitudinally.

pahabág (pa-ha-bág), v. to ask for pity or compassion. Syn. *paawà*, *magmakaawà*.

pahabilin (pa-ha-bi-lin), I. n. something left to someone for temporary safekeeping. Cf. *patiwalà*, *pabahalà*.
—II. adj. referring to something entrusted to someone for temporary safekeeping.

pahabol (pa-ha-bol), I. n. 1. postscript (to a letter). 2. something added or to be added to complement an anticipated lack or shortage. Syn. *pandagdág*, *pampunô*.
—II. adj. referring to something prepared to complement an anticipated lack or shortage of.

pahaból (pa-ha-ból), adj. in a manner like pursuing or running after someone. Syn. *pahagád*, *patugís*.

pahakbáng (pa-hak-báng), adj. by stepping forward.

pahadláng (pa-had-láng), I. adj. running across; crosswise. Syn. *pahaláng*.
—II. adj. in a contrary manner. Syn. *pasalungát*, *pakontra*.
—III. v. to allow oneself to be stopped or prevented from doing something. Syn. *papigil*.

pahagibís (pa-ha-gi-bís), adj. & adv. with lightning speed. Syn. *paharurót*, *pahaginít*.

pahalakhakín (pa-ha-lak-ha-kín), v. to make one laugh loudly; make one burst into laughter. Syn. *patawanin nang malakás*.

pahalagahán (pa-ha-la-ga-hán), var. **pahalaghán**, v. 1. to order or require the setting of the price for. 2. to value;

appreciate the value of; give importance to. 3. to cause the assessment or valuation, as of a property. Syn. *patasahan*.

pahaláng (pa-ha-láng), I. *adj*. 1. horizontal; parallel to the horizon. Syn. *pahigâ*. 2. crosswise; lying across. Syn. *pahadláng*.

—II. *adv*. 1. horizontally. 2. in a crosswise manner.

pahaláw (pa-ha-láw), *adj. & adv*. done, made, adapted, etc. superficially or in a superficial manner. Syn. *pahapáw*.

pahalina (pa-ha-li-na), *v*. to allow oneself to be fascinated, attracted, or charmed, as by the beauty of someone. Syn. *pabighanì, paakit, pagayuma, pabalanì*.

pahalubiluhin (pa-ha-lu-bi-lu-hin), *v*. to let or allow someone to mingle or intermingle with a group or crowd. Syn. *pahaluin*.

pahám (pa-hám), I. *adj*. erudite; learned; scholarly, referring to a person. Syn. *dalubhasà, pantás, esperto*.

—II. *n*. a highly learned person; sage. Syn. *pantás, dalubhasà*.

pahamak (pa-ha-mak), *n. & adj*. 1. referring to a person who, or a thing that, causes failure, injury, destruction, etc. to another. 2. a saboteur or a traitor.

pahambaláng (pa-ham-ba-láng), *adv*. athwart; obliquely; crosswise; across. Syn. *pahaláng, pahadláng*.

pahambíng (pa-ham-bíng), I. *adj*. (Gram.) comparative. Syn. *patulád, pahalintulad*.

—II. *adv*. comparatively; in a comparative manner; by comparison.

pahantarín (pa-han-ta-rín), *v*. to tell (someone) to come out in the open. Syn. *palantarín, palitawín*.

pahangain (pa-ha-nga-in), *v*. to attract or impress someone, as by one's beauty, charm, wisdom, etc.; win the admiration of.

páhanginán (pá-ha-ngi-nán), *n*. 1. a place or an open space where things are exposed to the wind in order to dry. Syn. *pátuyuan sa hangin, yángyangan*. 2. act or manner of trying to outwit each other in bragging or boasting.

pahapáw (pa-ha-páw), I. *adj*. superficial, as in: *pahapáw na pag-aaral*, superficial study.

—II. *adv*. in a superficial manner; superficially.

pahapáy (pa-ha-páy), *adv*. in an inclining or leaning position, as in: *Pahapáy siyáng umupô sa sopá*. He sat in an inclining position on the sofa. Syn. *pasandál, pahilig*.

pahapon (pa-ha-pon), I. *n. & adj*. referring to a supper or a party hosted by someone. Also, *pahapunan*.

—II. *v*. 1. to allow oneself to be alighted on by a bird or fowl. Syn. *padapô*. 2. to wait for the afternoon to come. Also, *maghapon*. Syn. *maghintáy ng hapon*.

paharáp (pa-ha-ráp), I. *adj*. facing forward; facing the front. Also, *nakaharáp*.

—II. *adv*. 1. with the face forward or facing the front. 2. toward the front.

paharapín (pa-ha-ra-pín), *v*. 1. to make someone face forward or to the front; opposed to *patalikurín*. 2. to order or require someone to be present in; make one appear before someone. Cf. *padaluhín, papuntahín*.

pahás (pa-hás), *n*. (Zool.) a species of turtle smaller than *pawikan* but larger than the ordinary *pagóng*.

pahát (pa-hát), *adj*. 1. insufficient; not enough; lacking; inadequate. Syn. *disapát, kapós, kulang*. 2. still young. Syn. *batà pa, musmós, paslít*. 3. inexperienced. Syn. *walâ pang karanasán, baguhan*.

pahatdán (pa-hat-dán), *v*. to send someone a letter, telegram, news, etc. Syn. *padalhán, pahatirán*.

pahatíd (pa-ha-tíd), I. *n*. 1. news or message sent through a messenger, mail, telegraph, etc. Syn. *balità, pabalità*. 2. anything sent by someone to another, as gifts, letters, telegrams, etc. Syn. *padalá*.

—II. *adj*. sent (by). Syn. *padalá, ipinadalá*.

—III. *v*. allow oneself to be accompanied by someone to a certain place. Syn. *pasama*.

pahátinggabí (pa-há-ting-ga-bí), *v*. to stay or remain till midnight. Syn. *magpaabot o paabot ng hátinggabí*.

pahayag (pa-ha-yag), *n*. 1. statement; declaration. Syn. *sabi, salitâ, wikà*. 2. answer. Syn. *sagót, kasagutan; tugón, katugunan*. 2. proclamation;

announcement; manifesto. Syn. *patalastás*.

áhayagán (pá-ha-ya-gán), n. 1. newspaper, magazine, or periodical. Syn. *diyaryo*, *peryódikó*, *mágasín*, *rebista*. 2. act of expressing each other's opinion, belief, etc. Syn. *pagtatápatan ng paniwalà o nilóloób*.

ahayop (pa-ha-yop), adj. 1. beastly; bestial; cruel, as in: *pahayop na pakikitungo*, cruel (bestial) treatment. Syn. *makahayop*. 2. (*Colloq.*) of poor quality, as in: *pahayop na trabaho*, work of poor quality.

ahesusán (pa-he-su-sán), var. **pahiruhan**, v. to say the prayer "Jesus, Mary, Joseph" as an aid to a dying person.

ahibík (pa-hi-bík), adv. in a pleading manner. Syn. *pasamô*.

ahikap (pa-hi-kap), adj. fond of wandering or gallivanting around. Syn. *pagalà*, *palalibót*.

ahikayat (pa-hi-ka-yat), v. to allow oneself to be persuaded. Syn. *pahimok*, *paamukì*, *pahibò*, *pakayag*.

ahid (pa-hid), n. 1. act of wiping off something with or as with a rag. Syn. *punas*, *pagpunas*. 2. act or method of cleaning a surface by wiping with a rag. Syn. *punas*, *pagpunas*. 3. application of thin coating (of paint, oil, etc.) with or as with a brush. 4. a layer or coating of paint, oil, etc. applied on a surface. Syn. *mano*.

ahigâ (pa-hi-gâ), I. adj. 1. with the body flat on the surface; lying down. Also, *nakahigâ*. 2. parallel to the plane of the horizon; horizontal.
—II. adv. 1. horizontally. 2. in a lying position; lying down.

ahigantí (pa-hi-gan-tí), I. adv. in a revengeful or vengeful manner. Syn. *pabenggansa*.
—II. v. to allow someone to take revenge against oneself.

ahigít (pa-hi-gít), I. n. 1. extra amount added. Syn. *palabis*, *pasobra*. 2. allowance, as for shortage. Syn. *patagana*.
—II. v. 1. to allow self to be pulled with or as with a rope. Syn. *pahatak*, *pahila*, *pabatak*. 2. to allow self to be surpassed or

left behind. Syn. *padaíg*, *palamáng*.
—III. adv. by pulling with or as with a rope. Syn. *pabaták*, *pahaták*, *pahilá*.

pahila (pa-hi-la), I. n. load or cargo being pulled, hauled, towed or tugged.
—II. adj. said of things being towed, hauled, or tugged for someone. Syn. *paremolke*, *paarastre*.
—III. v. 1. to allow self to be pulled by someone. Syn. *pahatak*, *pabatak*. 2. (*Colloq.*) to accept an invitation to go to a certain place or to do something. Syn. *payakayag*, *payayà*, *pakayag*.

pahilagâ (pa-hi-la-gâ), I. adj. bound north; going north or northward; northbound. Syn. *panorte*.
—II. adv. northward; toward the north.

pahilatâ (pa-hi-la-tâ), adj. & adv. by lying down lazily or in abandon.

pahilíg (pa-hi-líg), I. adj. inclined or leaning. Also, *hilig*, *nakahilig*. Syn. *tagilíd*, *nakatagilid*.
—II. adv. in an inclining position.

pahilíng (pa-hi-líng), I. adj. in the manner of a request. Syn. *papakiusap*.
—II. n & adj. referring to the small quantity of goods or merchandise added for free to what a buyer bought, usually on his own request. Cf. *patawad*.

pahilís (pa-hi-lís), I. adj. 1. slanting; inclining; oblique (said esp. of lines). Syn. *pahilíg*, *pahapáy*. 2. in a manner like playing a violin. 3. (*Gram.*) acute, referring to accents.
—II. adv. slantingly; slantwise; obliquely.
—III. n. a slanting line or lines among other intersecting lines. Cf. *pakrús*, *pahaláng*.

pahilom (pa-hi-lom), n. & adj. referring to something that hastens cicatrization or healing up of cuts or wounds. Also, *pampahilom*.

pahimakás (pa-hi-ma-kás), n. 1. last farewell. Syn. *hulíng paalam o pamamaalam*. 2. parting word. Syn. *hulíng pangungusap*. 3. last will. Syn. *hulíng habilin*.

pahimalâ (pa-hi-ma-lâ), adv. miraculously.

pahimutók (pa-hi-mu-tók), adv. with a sigh; in a sighing manner. Syn. *pabuntóng-*

hiningá, pahinagpís.

páhiná (pá-hi-ná), *n.* (Sp. *página*) page, as of book, magazine, notebook, etc. Syn. *mukhâ* (*colloq.*).

pahinakdál (pa-hi-nak-dál), *adv.* in a manner that expresses pain, dissatisfaction, etc.; complainingly. Syn. *pasumbóng, pahinanakít.*

pahinagpís (pa-hi-nag-pís), *adv.* in a sighing manner; with a doleful sigh. Syn. *pahimutók, pabuntóng-hiningá.*

pahinahunin (pa-hi-na-hu-nin), *v.* to make calm or sober, referring to an angry person. Syn. *payapain, papayapain.*

pahinain (pa-hi-na-in), *v.* 1. to make weak or weaker, physically. 2. to make slow or slower; reduce the speed. Syn. *pabagalin, padahanin.* Ant. *patulinin, pabilisín.* 3. to make lower; tone down or soften, as music. Also, *hinaan.* 4. to make weak, referring to materials. Syn. *parupukín.*

pahinanakít (pa-hi-na-na-kít), *adv.* with a feeling of resentment; in a manner expressing complaint, dissatisfaction, etc. Syn. *pahinakdál.*

pahinasyón (pa-hi-nas-yón), *n.* (Sp. *paginacion*) 1. pagination; paging; numbering the pages of. Syn. *pagpapáhiná.* 2. act or process of forming a page or pages for printing. Syn. *pagpapáhiná, pagbubuô ng mga páhiná.* 3. way the pages of a book, etc. were numbered. Syn. *pagkakánumero sa mga páhiná.*

pahináy-hinay (pa-hi-náy + hi-nay), I. *adj. & adv.* in an easy and slow manner. Syn. *padahán-dahan.*

pahindî (pa-hin-dî), I. *adj. & adv.* by denying or refusing to say "yes." Syn. *patanggî.*
—II. *n.* refusal; denial. Syn. *pagtanggî.*

pahintú-hintô (pa-hin-tú + hin-tô), I. *adj.* stopping and resuming again repeatedly or at intervals; intermittent. Syn. *patigil-tigil.*
—II. *adv.* intermittently.

pahintulot (pa-hin-tu-lot), *n.* 1. consent; permission. Also, *kapahintulután.* Syn. *pagsang-ayon, pagpayag.* 2. permit; license. Syn. *permiso, lisénsiyá.*

pahinuhod (pa-hi-nu-hod), I. *v.* to acquiesce; agree or accept quietly. Syn.

sumang-ayon nang waláng-kibó.
—II. *n.* acquiescence. Also, *pagpahinuho∎* Syn. *pakumbabáng pagsang-ayon.*

pahingá (pa-hi-ngá), I. *n.* rest; relaxatio∎ time for rest or relaxation. Als∎ *pagpapahingá, pamamahingá.* 2. (Colloq∎ retirement from work or employmen∎ Syn. *retiro, pagriretiro, pagkakáretiro.*
—II. *adj.* 1. on leave; on vacation. Sy∎ *namámahingá, nagbábakasyón.* 2. restin∎ Syn. *nagpápahingá.*

pahingî (pa-hi-ngî), I. *adj. & n.* referring ∎ something given or obtained for free. Sy∎ *bigáy.*
—II. *v.* (Colloq.) (P-) Please give me. M∎ I have some please?

pahirap (pa-hi-rap), *n.* 1. act of inflictin∎ severe pain on someone; torture. ∎ anything done or given to someone ∎ order to suffer. Syn. *parusa.* 3. that whic∎ causes difficulties, hardships, or sufferin∎ Syn. *pampahirap.*

pahirís (pa-hi-rís), I. *adj.* slanting; in ∎ slanting position; oblique. Syn. *pahilí∎ patagilid, pahiwíd.*
—II. *adv.* in a slanting position; oblique∎

pahiwatig (pa-hi-wa-tig), *n.* hin∎ insinuation; indication; warning. Sy∎ *paramdám, babalâ.*

pahiyás (pa-hi-yás), I. *adj. & n.* referring ∎ gems or jewelry given or furnished ∎ someone by another. Syn. *paalahas.*
—II. *n.* beautiful and expensive dec∎ rations. Syn. *mamáhali't magagandá∎ palamuti.*

pahò (pa-hò), *n.* (Bot.) a species ∎ Philippine mango (Mangifera longipe∎ Griff) that bears small fruits with b∎ seeds. 2. the fruit of this tree. Cf. *pik∎ kalabáw (kinalabáw).*

pahulaan (pa-hu-la-an), *v.* 1. to ask a pers∎ to guess what an unseen or hidden thir∎ is. 2. to make someone guess or tell th∎ answer by guessing. 3. to consult ∎ fortuneteller or a soothsayer about th∎ fate or fortune of someone.

pahuthót (pa-hut-hót), I. *adv. & adj.* b∎ sucking. Syn. *pahithít, pasipsíp.*
—II. *v.* (Slang) to allow oneself to b∎ swindled or taken advantage of by or ∎

by a swindler or profiteer.

aibabâ (pa-i-ba-bâ), I. v. 1. to go down. Syn. *pumanaog, manaog.* 2. to go down a slope. Syn. *lumusong.*

—II. *adj.* going or coming down.

aibabaw (pa-i-ba-baw), v. 1. to climb on or over the top. Also, *pumaibabaw.* 2. to rise on the top or surface; opposed to *pailalim.*

aibabawan (pa-i-ba-ba-wan), v. 1. to cover the surface or top with. Syn. *latagan o patungan sa ibabaw.* 2. to climb over the top, as in coitus. Syn. *patungan, babahán (babhán).*

aibá-ibá (pa-i-bá + i-bá), adj. with or having one's habit, method place, etc. changed very often. Syn. *pabagu-bago, papalít-palít.*

aibáng-, a combining form, used in the formation of verbs, as in: *paibáng-bayan,* to go to a foreign country.

aibayo (pa-i-ba-yo), v. to go to the other or opposite side of a river, mountain, etc. Syn. *tumawid sa kabilâ ng.*

aibigin (pa-i-bi-gin), v. 1. to attract or win over someone's love or affection. 2. to let or allow someone to select what he wants.

aikit (pa-i-kit), n. 1. the distance around; circumference. Syn. *paikot, paligid, palibot, kabilugan.* 2. act or manner of causing a wheel, top, or the like to rotate or turn fast. Syn. *paikot, pagpapaikot.* 3. a complete round, as in a circular field. Syn. *ligid, paligid.*

aiklî (pa-ik-lî), I. adj. getting or becoming short or shorter. Syn. *paigsî, pautdó.*

—II. *adj. & n.* referring to something used to shorten or make a thing shorter. Also, *pampaiklî.*

aikóm (pa-i-kóm), adv. & adj. by folding (s.o. wings, umbrella, etc.). Syn. *patikóm, patiklóp.*

aikot (pa-i-kot), I. n. 1. the distance around; circumference. Syn. *paikit, paligid, palibot, kabilugan.* 2. the things, conditions, circumstance, etc. that surround a given place or person. Syn. *paligid, kapaligirán.* 3. act or manner of causing a wheel, top, etc. to rotate or turn very fast.

—II. *adv.* by going or running around (a place). Syn. *paligid, palibot.*

paikúd-ikód (pa-i-kúd + i-kód), adj. & adv. walking with a limp; limping. Syn. *paikáikâ, papiláy-piláy, pahingkúd-hingkód.*

paikutin (pa-i-ku-tin), v. to cause (something) to rotate or turn round and round, as a top, by spinning. Syn. *paikitin, painugin.*

paidlíp (pa-id-líp), adj. & adv. by taking a nap or a short, light sleep. Syn. *pahipíg, pahimláy.*

paig (pa-ig), n. 1. boredom due to a long wait. Syn. *pagkainíp dahil sa matagál na paghihintáy.* 2. overdryness, esp. of food due to overexposure to heat or fire. Syn. *tigang, pagkatigang.*

paigtád (pa-ig-tád), adj. & adv. by leaping or jumping suddenly. Syn. *palundagin, patalunín.*

pailalím (pa-i-la-lím), I. adv. in a treacherous or perfidious manner; traitorously. Syn. *pataksíl, patraidór.* 2. secretly. Syn. *palihím, nang lihim.* 3. towards the bottom or underneath.

—II. *adj.* characterized by treachery; perfidious.

pailanláng (pa-i-lan-láng), var. **pailangláng,** I. v. to fly high or soar up in the air. Also, *magpailanláng, magpailangláng.*

—II. *adj. & adv.* by soaring up in the air.

pailapín (pa-i-la-pín), v. to make wild; cause (an animal) to become wild.

pailayá (pa-i-la-yá), adj. & adv. going towards the direction of the upper part of the town.

paimbabáw (pa-im-ba-báw), I. adj. superficial; not sincere; hypocritical. Syn. *pakunwarî, pabalát-kayô.*

paimbî (pa-im-bî), adv. in an ignoble manner. Syn. *sa hamak o imbíng paraán.*

paimbót (pa-im-bót), adj. & adv. with selfish motives; characterized by covetousness or greediness.

paimpít (pa-im-pít), adj. (Phon.) guttural, said of sound.

pain (pa-in), n. 1. bait (for catching fish, rats, etc.). 2. decoy. Syn. *pangatî.* 3. nest egg.

painamin (pa-i-na-min), v. to make good or

painan

better; improve. Syn. *pabutihin.*

painan (pa-i-nan), *v.* 1. to provide a hook, trap, etc. with a bait. 2. to lure (a person or an animal) into a trap by using a decoy. Syn. *katiín.* 4. to place an egg in a nest to induce a hen to lay eggs.

painít (pa-i-nít), I. *adj.* getting or becoming hotter or warmer (s.o. weather).

—II. *n.* unnecessary exposure of self to the heat of the sun. Also, *pagpapainít.*

painugin (pa-i-nu-gin), *v.* to cause a thing to rotate very fast; spin, as a top. Syn. *paikutin nang mabilís.*

painút-inót (pa-i-nút + i-nót), *adv.* 1. slowly. Syn. *dahan-dahan.* 2. little by little. Syn. *untí-untí.*

paingat (pa-i-ngat), *n. & adj.* referring to something given to another to be taken care of or for safekeeping. Syn. *paalagà.*

pairalin (pa-i-ra-lin), *v.* 1. to make predominant or prevalent. Syn. *panatilihin, panaigín.* 2. to enforce. Syn. *ipatupád.*

pairáp (pa-i-ráp), *adv. & adj.* with a sullen, scoffing look.

pairog (pa-i-rog), *n.* 1. something given or granted as a favor. Syn. *bigáy-loób.* 2. act of granting the favor asked or requested by someone. Syn. *pagbibigáy, pagbibigáy-loób.*

pais (pa-is), *n.* 1. act or method of cooking food, esp. small fish, wrapped in banana leaf, either by roasting or by boiling. 2. such food cooked in this manner; also called *pinais.*

paisahe (pa-i-sa-he), *n.* (Sp. *paisaje*) 1. landscape painting. Syn. *nakapintáng tánawin.* 2. quoted passage or excerpt from a literary work of an author. Syn. *halaw, hangò.*

paisano (pa-i-sa-no), var. **paysano,** I. *n.* (Sp.) 1. fellow countryman; compatriot. Syn. *kababayan.* 2. civilian. Syn. *sibilyán.*

—II. *adj.* 1. of or from the same country or locality. Syn. *kababayan, magkababayan.* 2. civilian; non-military.

paisip (pa-i-sip), *v.* to get someone to think of a means, plan, etc. Also, *magpaisip.*

paít (pa-ít), *n.* 1. bitter quality or taste, as of gall; bitterness. 2. disagreeableness;

pal‹

harshness; severity. Syn. *lupít, kalupitán*

paitaás (pa-i-ta-ás), I. *v.* 1. to go upstairs. 2 to rise upward in the air. Syr *pumailanláng.* 3. to rise or appear on th‹ surface (of water). Syn. *lumutang paibabaw.*

—II. *adv. & adj.* 1. upward; going upwar or rising; towards the top. 2. goin‹ upstairs. Syn. *paakyát, papanhík.*

paiwâ (pa-i-wâ), I. *adj.* 1. (Gram.) grav‹ referring to an accent. Cf. *pahilís, pakupy‹* 2. traitorous or treacherous (s.o. acts Syn. *patraidór, pataksíl, pasaksák sa likód*

—II. *adv.* in a traitorous or treacherou manner; in a manner like stabbin‹ someone on the back.

paiwan (pa-i-wan), *v.* 1. to stay or remai at home or in the office while others leav or depart for a certain place. 2. to allo‹ self to be left behind, as in a race. Als‹ *magpaiwan* (for both senses).

paiwás (pa-i-wás), I. *adj.* tending or tryin to avoid or evade. Cf. *pailág, palayô.*

—II. *adv.* in an evasive manner; evasivel‹

paiwi (pa-i-wi), *n. & adj.* referring to a animal or animals given to another t take care of, on an agreement that th owner and the caretaker would sha‹ equally in the offspring.

paiya (pa-i-ya), *n.* toleration; willingness t allow other people to do what they lik to satisfy themselves.

páiyakan (pá-i-ya-kan), *n. & adj.* (Colloq referring to a practice of selling or buyin things in an installment plan. Sy‹ *hulugán.*

paiyák-iyák (pa-i-yák + i-yák), *adj. & ad‹* by crying pretentiously.

pala (pa-la), *n.* (Sp.) 1. spade; shovel. 2 (Fig.) hired or paid applauders. 3 (i gambling) a planted bettor, who ‹ conspiracy with the banker, puts sha‹ wager in order to attract more bettors.

palá (pa-lá), I. *interj.* 1. used to expres surprise, unawareness, etc., more or le equivalent to English "so," as in: *Iká‹ palá!* So, it's you! 2. oh!, as in: *Siyá ng palá, hindî ko nasabi iyón sa iyó.* Oh, yes! was not able to tell you about it.

—II. *adv.* so; so then.

palà (pa-là), *n.* 1. grace; blessing. Syn. *grasya, biyayà.* 2. favor granted. Syn. *kaloób.* 3. gain or benefit. Syn. *tubò, pakinabáng.*

palâ (pa-lâ), *n.* 1. reward. Syn. *gantimpalà.* 2. retribution. Syn. *hitâ, náhitâ; pamá, nápamá.*

palá- (pa-lá-), *pref.* used to express: (a) addiction to or having the habit of, as in: *paláinóm ng alak,* having the habit of drinking wine; (b) arrangement, system or style of, as in *paláugnayan,* syntax; *palábaybayan,* spelling system.

palaán (pa-la-án), I. *n. & adj.* referring to something ordered or requested to be reserved for someone or for the future.
—II. *v.* to request for oneself the reservation of. Also, *magpalaán.*

paláasá (pa-lá-a-sá), *adj.* too dependent on others; with or having the habit of depending too much on others.

palabà (pa-la-bà), *n.* the halo of the moon.

palabagín (pa-la-ba-gín), *v.* 1. to make someone violate, disobey, or go against (a law, rule, order, etc.). Syn. *pasuwayín.* 2. to make violative of.

palaban (pa-la-ban), I. *n.* a game, contest, or fight sponsored by someone. Cf. *patorneo, paboksíng, pasabong, pasugál, patimpalák.*
—II. *adv.* in opposition or contrast with; contradictory.

palábangáy (pa-lá-ba-ngáy), *adj.* quarrelsome; fond of quarrel. Syn. *paláawáy, basag-ulero.*

palabás (pa-la-bás), I. *n.* 1. show; public entertainment or performance. 2. exit; a way out; doorway or passage leading to the outside.
—II. *adj.* on the way out; getting or coming out.
—III. *adv.* outward; towards the outside. Syn. *papuntá sa labás.*

palábatî (pa-lá-ba-tî), *adj.* with or having the habit of greeting or talking with people, even to strangers, as a friendly gesture, sociable or friendly. Syn. *mapágkapwà, mapágkaibigan, palákaibigan.*

palábigasan (pa-lá-bi-ga-san), *n.* 1. milled rice container or bin. Syn. *sisidlán ng bigás.*

2. *(Fig.)* a person from whom another or others always ask for help or support. 3. rice granary.

palábigkasan (pa-lá-big-ka-san), *n.* 1. phonics. 2. phonetics. Syn. *palátinigan, ponétiká.* 3. prosody.

palabok (pa-la-bok), *n.* 1. kind of *pansít* or noodle dish, also known as *pansít-luglóg.* 2. a kind of thick sauce, used to flavor *pansít-luglóg.* 3. flowery elaboration in one's expression or language.

palaboy (pa-la-boy), I. *n.* vagrant; tramp; idle wanderer. Syn. *taong lagalág (layás); bagamundo, hampaslupà.*
—II. *adj.* wandering; vagrant; at large. Syn. *layás, libót, galà, lagalág.*

palabúy-laboy (pa-la-búy + la-boy), *adj.* free to wander around in vagrancy; straying. Syn. *pagalágalà, palibút-libot.*

palakâ (pa-la-kâ), *n.* (Zool.) 1. frog. 2. toad, also called *palakáng-kati, palakáng-lupà.*

palakad (pa-la-kad), *n.* 1. policy; way of management; regulation. Syn. *pátakarán, pamamalakad, pasunód, reglamento.* 2. administration; management. Syn. *pangangasiwà.* 3. mission or errand for which one was sent.

palakad-lakad (pa-la-kad + la-kad), *adj.* walking to and fro.

palakat (pa-la-kat), *n.* loud, shrill shout or cry; bowl; wail. Syn. *hiyawán, sigawán, palahawan.*

palakaya (pa-la-ka-ya), *n.* 1. a kind of wide-spreading net outfit, provided with floaters and pulled by boats, usually used for deep-sea fishing. 2. the act or method of fishing with this kind of outfit.

palakí (pa-la-kí), I. *adj.* getting bigger, becoming larger.
—II. *adj. & n.* referring to a person or animal reared or raised to maturity by someone.

palakip (pa-la-kip), *n. & adj.* referring to something included or enclosed in or as in a letter on request by someone.

palaklák (pa-la-klák), *adj. & adv.* by drinking in big gulps.

palakól (pa-la-kól), *n.* 1. ax. Cf. *palatáw, putháw.* 2. the act or manner of using an ax. Also, *pagpalakól.*

palakpák (pa-lak-pák), n. 1. clap or clapping of hands. 2. the sound produced by clapping the hands. 3. applause; approval or praise shown by clapping the hands.

palad (pa-lad), n. 1. palm (of the hand). 2. fate; fortune; luck. Also, *kapalaran.* Syn. *suwerte, portuna, tadhanà.*

paladpád (pa-lad-pád), n. a blowing or being blown by a strong wind, referring esp. to things like a galvanized iron sheet. Cf. *salipadpád.*

palág (pa-lág), n. 1. convulsive movement of the body, as in instant death. Cf. *kisáy, kawág.* 2. wriggling or wiggling, as of fish. Syn. *paság.* 3. shaking of the head, hands, or even the body, as in getting rid of dust, drops of water, etc.

palaganapin (pa-la-ga-na-pin), v. to make widespread; propagate; make popular; popularize. Syn. *pakalatin.*

palagáy (pa-la-gáy), n. opinion; personal view; viewpoint; idea. Syn. *kurò, kuru-kurò.* 2. supposition; surmise. Syn. *akalà, sapantahà, hinuhà.*

palágayá (pa-lá-ga-yá), adj. fond or having the habit of imitating others. Syn. *palágagád, mapággagád.*

palagayang-loób (pá-la-ga-yang + lo-ób), n. trust or confidence in each other. Syn. *pagtitiwalà sa isá't isá.*

palagáy-loób (pa-la-gáy + lo-ób), adj. confident; sure of oneself. Syn. *may-tiwalà, nagtítiwalà.*

palagì (pa-la-gì), adv. always; all the time; at all times; continuously. Syn. *parati, pirmí.*

palágitlingan (pa-lá-git-li-ngan), n. the rules or system of hyphenation.

palaguín (pa-la-gu-ín), v. 1. to make or allow to grow, referring to plants, hair, etc. Syn. *patubuin, palambaín, pahabain.* 2. (in gambling or business) to make one's small capital grow by putting it as a bet or as an investment with the hope of winning or gaining.

palagyô (pa-lag-yô), I. adj. (Gram.) nominative, as in: *kaukuláng palagyô,* nominative case.
—II. n. nickname. Syn. *palayaw, tagurî.*

palahad (pa-la-had; -hád), adj. & adv. by extending openly, as one's hand. Syn. *palantád.* 2. by explaining or narrating. Syn. *pasalaysáy.*

palahaw (pa-la-haw), n. loud cry or shout. Syn. *sigáw, hiyáw, palakat.*

palahì (pa-la-hì), adj. & n. referring to an animal or animals raised or bred from a different stock or species.

paláisdaan (pa-lá-is-da-an), n. 1. fishpond. 2. fishery; fishing ground. Syn. *pángisdaan.*

paláisíp (pa-lá-i-síp), adj. 1. said of a thinker or one who is always in deep thought. Also, *mapág-isíp.* 2. inventive. Syn. *mapanlikhâ.*

paláisipan (pa-lá-i-si-pan; -pán), n. 1. riddle. Syn. *bugtóng.* 2. a question or problem that puzzles; puzzle.

palalò (pa-la-lò), adj. arrogant; too proud; haughty. Syn. *mapágmataás, mapágmalakí, hambóg, mayabang.*

palamán (pa-la-mán), n. something used to fill or stuff; stuffing. Also, *panlamán.*

palamara (pa-la-ma-ra), I. n. one guilty of treason; traitor. Syn. *traidór, lilo, taksíl.*
—II. adj. traitorous; treacherous; ingrate; ungrateful. Syn. *lilo, sukáb, mapagkánulô.*

palámasíd (pa-lá-ma-síd), adj. observant. Also, *mapágmasíd.*

palámatá (pa-lá-ma-tá), adj. referring to a person who looks on others with disdain. Also, *mapágmatá.*

palamíg (pa-la-míg), I. adj. 1. getting cold or chilly. Syn. *pagináw.* 2. referring to something that refreshes.
—II. n. something that refreshes; refreshments. Syn. *pampalamíg, pampapresko.*

palamlamín (pa-lam-la-mín), v. to make dim, as a light. Syn. *palabuin.*

palamon (pa-la-mon), I. n. & adj. (derogative) referring to a person wholly dependent on someone for support. Syn. *pakain, pákainín.*
—II. n. 1. animal feed. 2. act or time of feeding animals. Also, *pagpapalamon.* Syn. *pagpapakain.*

palamuti (pa-la-mu-ti), n. ornament; decoration. Syn. *gayák, adorno, dekorasyón.*

palanas (pa-la-nas), n. 1. a vast tract of level

palansák   **palátulaan**

land; wide plain. Cf. *kapatagan*. 2. a level,
stony river bank. Syn. *batuhán, nguni't
pantay na baybayin ng ilog*.

palansák (pa-lan-sák), I. *adj.* 1. *(Gram.)*
collective, as in: *pangngalang palansák*,
collective noun. 2. as a whole; including
all; without exception. Syn. *láhatan,
waláng pilì-pilì, kasamang lahát (malakí't
maliít)*.
—II. *adv.* collectively; as a whole or
group.

palantarín (pa-lan-ta-rín), *v.* to tell, ask, or
urge a person to come out in the open.
Syn. *palabasín, pahayagín*.

palangkâ (pa-lang-kâ), n. 1. a lever; bar for
raising a weight at one end or side. Syn.
panikwás, panikwát. 2. pole for carrying
weight on both ends. Syn. *pingga, pásanan*.
3. packsaddle.

palanggana (pa-lang-ga-na), n. (Sp.
palangana) basin; washbasin. Cf. *batyâ*.

palaot (pa-la-ot), *v.* 1. to go or sail far into
the middle of the sea; go towards the high
seas. Also, *pumalaot*. 2. to get involved,
as in politics. Syn. *lumahók, pumagitnâ*.

palapà (pa-la-pà), n. *(Bot.)* the frond or
compound leaf of a palm or banana plant.
See **balabà**.

palápantigan (pa-lá-pan-ti-gan), n. *(Gram.)*
the rules or system of providing words (of
a language) into syllables.

palapít (pa-la-pít), I. *adj. & adv.* getting
nearer; approaching.
—II. *adv.* on the way towards a person,
thing, or place. Also, *papalapit*.

palápuná (pa-lá-pu-ná), *adj.* observant;
critical of others' mistakes or
shortcoming. Also, *mapágpuná,
mapúnahin*.

palarâ (pa-la-râ), n. tinsel; tin foil.

palarawán (pa-la-ra-wán), I. *adj.* descriptive.
—II. *adv.* descriptively; in a descriptive
manner.

palarin (pa-la-rin), *v.* 1. to be lucky; meet
with good fortune. Syn. *suwertihín, galingín*.
2. to be successful. Syn. *magtagumpáy*.

palarô (pa-la-rô), I. n. 1. a series of games
sponsored by someone. 2. an invitational
gambling session. Syn. *pasugál*.
—II. *adj. & n.* referring to a game or

gambling sponsored by someone.
—III. *adv.* playfully; in a playful manner.

palasak (pa-la-sak), *adj.* 1. ordinary;
common; usual. Syn. *karaniwan,
pangkaraniwan*. 2. in vague or fashion.
Syn. *uso, moda*. 3. prevalent; widespread.
Syn. *kalát, laganap*.

palasáp (pa-la-sáp), n. *& adj.* referring to
something that a person was made to
undergo or experience. Syn. *paranas*.

palásingsingan (pa-lá-sing-si-ngan), n. ring
finger. Cf. *hinlalakí, hintuturo, hinlalatò,
kalingkingan*.

palasô (pa-la-sô), n. arrow. Syn. *tunod*.

palaspás (pa-las-pás), n. palm leaves, usually
woven into various shapes and figures and
taken to the church during Palm Sunday
for blessing.

palásurián (pa-lá-su-ri-án), n. 1. *(Gram.)*
analogy. 2. *(Ling.)* semasiology; semantics.
Syn. *semántiká*.

palásuwáy (pa-lá-su-wáy), *adj.* 1.
disobedient. Syn. *sutíl, matigás ang ulo
(fig.), masuwayín*. 2. rebellious. Syn.
mapánghimagsík.

palasyo (pa-las-yo), n. (Sp. *palácio*) palace.
Syn. *bahay-harì (colloq.)*.

palaták (pa-la-ták), n. 1. clap of the tongue.
2. the clacking sound produced by the
clap of the tongue.

palátandaan (pa-lá-tan-da-an), n. 1. sign;
token; indication; symbol or mark. Syn.
sagisag. 2. marker; landmark. Syn. *muhón*.

palátawá (pa-lá-ta-wá), *adj.* fond of
laughing; with or having the habit of
laughing. Also, *mapágtawá*.

palathalà (pa-lat-ha-là), n. 1. press release.
2. advertisement.
—II. *adj.* published for someone.

palátinigan (pa-lá-ti-ni-gan), n. *(Gram.)*
phonetics. Syn. *ponétiká*.

palátitikan (pa-lá-ti-ti-kan), n. orthography;
system of spelling. Syn. *palábaybayan,
ortograpiya (ortograpya)*.

palátugmaan (pa-lá-tug-ma-an), n. the
science or system of rhythm or
rhythmical forms; rhythmics.

palátulaan (pa-lá-tu-la-an), n. 1. the art or
system of writing poems. 2. theory of
poetry; poetics.

palátuldikan (pa-lá-tul-di-kan), n. 1. the rules or system of accentuation.

palátuntunan (pa-lá-tun-tu-nan), n. 1. program (of activities). Syn. *programa*. 2. (Rare) guiding principle. Syn. *pánuntunan*.

palátunugan (pa-lá-tu-nu-gan), n. 1. (*Ling.*) phonemics. Syn. *ponémiká*. 2. phonetics. 3. science of sound.

palátuusan (pa-lá-tu-u-san; pa-lá-tu-u-sán), n. system of accounting.

paláugatan (pa-lá-u-ga-tan), n. (*Ling.*) etymology. Syn. *pámuhatán*.

paláugnayan (pa-lá-ug-na-yan), n. (*Gram.*) syntax.

paláwikaán (pa-lá-wi-ka-án), n. the system or study of the structure and development of a particular language.

palawig (pa-la-wig), *adj.* referring to something that causes unnecessary delay. Also, *pampalawig*.

palawít (pa-la-wít), I. n. decorative hangings, as tassels and fringes.
—II. *adv. & adj.* in a hanging position. Syn. *pabitín, palayláy, palawingwíng*.

palay (pa-lay), n. (*Bot.*) 1. the rice plant (*Oriza sativa*). 2. the unhusked grain of this plant, distinguished from *bigás*.

palayan (pa-la-yan), n. rice field.

palayaw (pa-la-yaw), n. 1. nickname. Syn. *tagurî, tawag*. 2. pampering treatment. Also, *pagpapalayaw*. Syn. *labís na pagpapasunód*.

palayô (pa-la-yô), *adv. & adj.* going away; getting farther away. Also, *papalayô*.

palayók (pa-la-yók), var. **palyók**, n. 1. earthen cooking pot. 2. potful, as in: *isáng palayók na kanín*, a potful of rice.

palayón (pa-la-yón), *adj.* (*Gram.*) objective, as in: *kaukuláng palayón*, objective case.

palaypaláy (pa-lay-pa-láy), *adj.* gentle or soft, as of breeze or blow of wind.

paldo (pal-do), var. **pardo**, I. n. (*Sp. fardo*) bale; large package or bundle of things for shipment. Syn. *bulto*.
—II. *adj.* (*Colloq.*) with or having much money; rich; wealthy. Syn. *makuwalta* (*makuwarta*), *mapera, mayaman, masalapî, makapál ang bulsá (fig.)*.

palengke (pa-leng-ke), n. (*Sp. palenque*) market; market place. Syn. *pámilihan, merkado, baraka*.

palî (pa-lî), n. (*Anat.*) spleen.

paliban-liban (pa-li-ban + li-ban), *adv.* 1. very irregular in attendance; often absent. Syn. *papalya-palya; malimit na hindî pumápasok*. 2. often postponed; having been postponed several times.

palibhasà (pa-lib-ha-sà), I. *conj.* because; because of the fact that; due to the fact that; on account of the fact that.
—II. n. (Rare) a belittling or speaking slightly of someone. Also, *pagpalibhasà*. Syn. *paghamak, pagdustâ*.

palibís (pa-li-bís), *adv.* 1. sloping downward. Syn. *patalibís, pababâ, palusóng*. 2. towards the hillside.

palibot (pa-li-bot), I. n. environ; surrounding. Syn. *paligid, kapaligiran*. 2. circumference. Syn. *paikot*. 3. a single round, as in a racing track. Syn. *ligid, libid*.
—II. *adj.* 1. wandering; going from one place to another. Syn. *galâ, pagalà*. 2. fond of travel; well-traveled (s.o. a person).

palibut-libot (pa-li-but + li-bot), *adj.* circulating around, as news. 2. wandering around, as a person looking for someone. Syn. *pagalá-galà*.

palikás (pa-li-kás), I. n. an order for the evacuation of. Also, *pagpapalikás*.
—II. *adj.* getting ready or preparing to evacuate.

palikero (pa-li-ke-ro), n. philanderer; rake; libertine; Don Juan.

palikì (pa-li-kì), n. 1. act of courting or making love without serious intention. Cf. *panliligaw*. 2. a woman's suitor. Syn. *manliligaw*.

palikô (pa-li-kô), *adj.* 1. that turns or curves towards a certain direction, as a street. 2. about to make a turn on a bend or curve, as a running vehicle.

palikpík (pa-lik-pík), n. (*Ichth.*) fin.

palikú-likô (pa-li-kú + li-kô), *adj.* winding or tortuous, as a road. Syn. *pakurbá-kurbá, balú-baluktót*.

pálikuran (pá-li-ku-ran), n. public toilet. Syn. *kubeta, kumón, kasilyás*.

paliga (pa-li-ga), n. an invitational

tournament, as of basketball games.

paligayahin (pa-li-ga-ya-hin), *v.* to make (someone) happy; cause someone to become happy. Syn. *pasayahín, dulutan ng ligaya, lugód, o tuwâ.*

paligid (pa-li-gid), *n.* 1. circumference. 2. a single round around a place. Syn. *ikot, paikot.* 3. environ; surrounding. Syn. *kapaligirán.*

paligò (pa-li-gò), *n.* 1. act of taking a bath; bathing. 2. water or any liquid preparation to be used for bathing. Also, *pampaligò.*

páligsahan (pá-lig-sa-han), *n.* 1. contest or competition under certain rules. Syn. *timpalák, patimpalák.* 2. any ordinary contest. Syn. *páhusayán, págalingan, pábutihán.*

palihán (pa-li-hán), *n.* anvil. Cf. *pukpukan, sangkalan.*

palihím (pa-li-hím), *adv.* in secret; secretly. Syn. *pasekreto, nang sekreto; patagô, nang patagô.* 2. treacherously. Syn. *patraidór, nang pasaksák sa likód (fig.).*

palihís (pa-li-hís), *adj.* deviating or turning aside from the right course, direction, etc. Syn. *paliwás, pasinsáy.*

pálimbagan (pá-lim-ba-gan), *n.* printing shop; printery.

palimít (pa-li-mít), *adj.* 1. getting or becoming closer to each other. Syn. *pasinsín.* 2. becoming more frequent. Syn. *padalás.*

palimós (pa-li-mós), *n. & adj.* referring to something given to someone as alms.

paling (pa-ling), *n.* 1. turn or turning of the head to one side. Syn. *baling.* 2. act of turning slightly from the direct or straight course. 3. the amount or degree of inclination or divergence from.

palingá-lingâ (pa-li-ngá + li-ngâ), *adj.* turning one's head repeatedly at all sides. Cf. *palingún-lingón.*

palipád-hangin (pa-li-pád + ha-ngin), *n.* 1. (*Fig.*) an utterance, usually insincere, expressing one's love or appreciation within the hearing distance of a woman. 2. bluff; statement to impress or deceive someone. Syn. *bola (colloq.), kahambugán, pagpapasikat.*

páliparan (pá-li-pa-ran), *n.* airfield; airport.

2. a wide, open field for flying kites.

palipás (pa-li-pás), *adj.* 1. passing away; calming down, as rain, storm, anger, etc. Syn. *palubag, pagkalmá.* 2. becoming obsolete; passing out of general use; obsolescent. 3. losing potency, as medicine. 4. becoming out of date or of style.

palipas-gutom (pa-li-pas + gu-tom), *n. & adj.* referring to something eaten to stave off hunger. Also, *pampalipas-gutom.*

palís (pa-lís), I. *n.* act of wiping or sweeping away (dust or the like) with or as with a duster.
—II. *adj.* wiped or swept away. Cf. *palispís.*

palít (pa-lít), *n.* 1. exchange; barter. Also, *pálitan.* 2. substitute or replacement. Syn. *halili, kahalili.* 3. change; changing. Syn. *pagbabago, pagbago.* 4. an amount of money in lower denominations given in exchange of one having higher denomination. Syn. *suklî.*

palitada (pa-li-ta-da), *n.* (*Sp.*) 1. cement mortar used in masonry. Syn. *templadang semento.* 2. cement pavement. 3. the act or manner of paving (a surface) with cement. Syn. *pagsisemento, pagkakásemento.*

palitán (pa-li-tán), *v.* 1. to change or replace something with another. Syn. *halinhán.* 2. to change (someone's money) with coins or money of lower denominations. Cf. *suklián.*

palitáw (pa-li-táw), I. *n.* a kind of cake made from the starch of glutinous rice with sugar and eaten with grated coconut meat.
—II. *adj. & adv.* with a portion jutting or sticking out.

palito (pa-li-to), *n.* (*Sp.*) toothpick. Syn. *panghiningá, pantingá.* 2. match stick.

paliwanag (pa-li-wa-nag), *n.* 1. explanation; clarification. Also, *pagpapaliwanag.*

palò¹ (pa-lò), *n.* (*Sp.*) 1. act of whipping or beating, esp. a child, with a stick, belt, or the like, usually in castigation. 2. a strike or hit given with a bat, as in baseball and indoor baseball. 3. the turn of a player to bat in baseball or indoor baseball. Syn. *pagpalò.* 4. act of manner of hitting or beating something with or as with a hammer. Syn. *pukpók, pagpukpók.* 5. act of hitting or striking someone with or as with a stick. Syn. *hampás, bugbóg, buntál, gulpí.* 6. an accidental hitting or collision as of one's head against something. Syn. *bunggô, umpóg, salpók.*

palò² (pa-lò), *n. & adj.* referring to a person who is attracted by the beauty or handsomeness of the opposite sex.

paloma (pa-lo-ma), *n.* (rarely used) dove; pigeon. Syn. *kalapati.*

palong (pa-long), *n.* cockscomb.

palós (pa-lós), *n.* (*Ichth.*) a variety of large, edible, salt-water eel; conger; congĕr eel. Cf. *igat, duhól, kalabukab.*

palosebo (pa-lo-se-bo), var. **palusebo**, *n.* 1. a kind of game involving competition of skill in climbing a high, slippery bamboo pole, at the top of which is placed a prize the contestant is supposed to get upon reaching it. 2. the high, slippery bamboo pole used in this game.

palot (pa-lot), *n.* the oppressive odor (smell) of urine. Syn. *panghí.*

palpál (pal-pál), *n.* 1. a big handful of food forced into the mouth. 2. any thing that obstruct free passage of water or the like in a tube, pipe or a hole. Syn. *bará, pasak.*

palso (pal-so), *adj.* (Sp. *falso*) 1. forged; counterfeit; falsified; spurious. Syn. *huwád, hinuwád.* 2. not well-done; badly done; poorly made. 3. bad; not good. Syn. *masamâ.*

paltík (pal-tík), *n.* 1. a kind of homemade gun, usually common in the province of Cavite. 2. (*Bats.*) a slingshot. Syn. *tiradór.* 3. act of hitting or shooting with a slingshot. Syn. *pagtiradór.* 4. a quick stroke or blow with the end of a whip or lash. Syn. *labtík, pilantík.*

paltók (pal-tók), *n.* a high level land, esp. on a plain; highland. Syn. *kataasan; gulód.*

paltós¹ (pal-tós), I. *n.* blister, as that caused by burns or scalding. Syn. *libtós, lintóg, lintós.*

—II. *adj.* blistered; with or having a blister or blisters.

paltós² (pal-tós), I. *n.* 1. a mistake; wrong answer or guess. 2. a miss or failure to hit (a target). Syn. *mintís, sala.* 3. failure to explode, as a firecracker. Syn. *pagmintís, pagmimintís.* 4. inability or failure to succeed. Syn. *pagkabigô.*

—II. *adj.* 1. wrong or mistaken, as an answer or guess. Syn. *malî, lisyâ.* 2. didn't hit the mark; missed. Syn. *sala, lihís, ditumamà, mintís.* 3. didn't explode, as a firecracker. Syn. *di-pumutók, palyado.*

palubág (pa-lu-bág), I. *adj.* calming down; getting lower in intensity. Syn. *pahinâ, pakalmá, pauntós, pahupâ.*

—II. *n & adj.* referring to something that reduces intensity. Also, *pampalubag.* Syn. *pampakalmá, pampahinà, pampahupâ.*

palubág-loób (pa-lu-bág + lo-ób), *n.* 1. something given or offered to pacify, appease, or calm down someone. Syn. *pampahinahon.* 2. consolation prize, as in a lottery. Also, *pampalubág-loób.*

palubáy (pa-lu-báy), *adj.* getting lower or reduced in intensity. Syn. *palubág, pahinâ, pahupâ.*

palubhâ (pa-lub-hâ), *adj.* getting serious; becoming worse; worsening. Syn. *palalâ, pagrabe.*

palubóg (pa-lu-bóg), *adj.* 1. sinking; getting lower and lower to the bottom of. 2. declining; on the decline; becoming less and less popular. 3. becoming or getting bankrupt. 4. sinking, as the sun in the late afternoon.

—II. *n.* a lead weight or weights used in fishing; sinker. Syn. *pabigát.*

palukob (pa-lu-kob), *v.* 1. to allow oneself to be under the shelter or protection of. 2. to allow oneself to be under the authority or power of. Syn. *pasakop, pailalim.*

palugit (pa-lu-git), *n.* time extension given to someone in the payment of (debt, loan, taxes, etc.). Syn. *pataan, plaso.*

palugsô (pa-lug-sô), *n.* 1. a trick to deceive. Syn. *patibóng.* 2. a trap or snare. Syn. *bitag, umang, silò.* 3. sabotage. Syn. *sabotahe, pagsabotahe, pagpapahamak.*

palugurín (pa-lu-gu-rín), *v.* to give someone pleasure or delight; make someone delighted or pleased. Syn. *paligayahin, pagalakín, pasayahín.*

paluhód (pa-lu-hód), *adj. & adv.* by kneeling; on bended knees. Syn. *patiklóptuhod.*

paluhóg (pa-lu-hóg), *adj. & adv.* in an earnest, humble manner. Syn. *nang buóng pagpapakumbabâ, nang pasamô.*

pálulóng (pá-lu-lóng), *v.* to get involved (in an affair) too seriously. Syn. *pásubò, pábuyó.*

palumat-lumat (pa-lu-mat + lu-mat), *adj.* hesitant; slow in acting, choosing, or deciding. Syn. *pabantú-bantulót.*

palumbayin (pa-lum-ba-yin), *v.* to make lonely; cause someone to become sad. Syn. *palungkutín, dulutan ng kalungkutan.*

palumpón (pa-lum-pón), *n.* cluster, as of flowers, leaves, or the like. Syn. *pumpón.*

palumpóng (pa-lum-póng), *n.* 1. shrub; bush. 2. thick growth of bushes; thicket.

paluningningín (pa-lu-ning-ni-ngín), *v.* to cause something to sparkle or scintillate. Syn. *pakinangín, pakislapín.*

palungkutín (pa-lung-ku-tín), *v.* to make sad or gloomy; cause someone to become sad or lonely. Syn. *dulutan ng lungkót.*

palupalò (pa-lu-pa-lò), *var.* **paló-palò,** *n.* wooden club used for beating laundry. Syn. *pamugbóg.*

palupasáy (pa-lu-pa-sáy), *adv.* 1. with the haunches flat on the floor. Syn. *palupagî.* 2. with the body flat on the floor. Syn. *pahandusáy.*

palupo (pa-lu-po), *n.* 1. ridge of a roof. Also **pálupuhán.** 2. the plain galvanized iron sheet or the like used to cover the ridge of a roof.

palusóng (pa-lu-sóng), I. *adj.* 1. referring to a person (or persons) who is (are) descending or going down from a higher to a lower place. Syn. *pababâ, palapág.* 2. said of the part of a main road or highway that descends or slopes down evenly.

—II. *n.* 1. a downward slope or descent in a thoroughfare. Syn. *salida.* 2. a way down or downward.

palusót (pa-lu-sót), I. *adj. & n.* referring to something that someone was able to smuggle or carry through a tight restriction or situation.

—II. *adj. & adv.* by passing through a narrow opening or hole. Syn. *palagós.*

páluwagan (pá-lu-wa-gan), *n.* 1. act or practice of helping each other or one another, esp. by lending money. Syn. *páutangán.* 2. the purpose of savings and loan associations; also, such an association.

paluwál[1] (pa-lu-wál), I. *n.* 1. act of advancing a sum of money for the payment of something in favor of someone. Also, *pagpapaluwál.* Syn. *pagaabono.* 2. the amount of money advanced by someone for the payment of something bought by another.

—II. *adj.* advanced by someone for another, referring esp. to payment of money.

paluwál[2] (pa-lu-wál), *adj.* delivered by or as by a doctor, referring to a baby. Syn. *paanák.*

paluwás (pa-lu-wás), I. *adj.* referring to a person (or persons) who is (are) going to the city.

—II. *adv.* towards the (direction of) city. Syn. *palunsód, pasiyudád.*

paluwatín (pa-lu-wa-tín), *v.* to delay action unnecessarily. Syn. *patagalín, bimbinín.*

palya (pal-ya), I. *n.* (Sp. *falla*) 1. omission; skip. Syn. *laktáw, lakdáw.* 2. a blank space, esp. one left unfilled. Syn. *puwáng, patláng, blangko.* 3. absence; failure to attend or be present. Syn. *liban.* 4. failure to explode, as a firecracker.

—II. *adj.* 1. absent; unabled to attend or be present. Syn. *liban, di-pumasok, di-nakapasok.* 2. failed to explode, as a firecracker. Syn. *palyado, di-pumutók.*

pam- (pam-), *pref.* used as a variant of *pang-,* in words beginning with "b" and "p," as in: *pambatà* (for children), *pambansà* (national), *pampánguluhán* (presidential), *pamburá* (eraser).

pama (pa-ma), *n.* (Sp. *fama*) 1. fame. Syn. *kabantugan.* 2. benefit; profit. Syn. *pakinabang, kapakinabangan.*

pamakalawá (pa-ma-ka-la-wá), *v.* to wait for the day following tomorrow. Also, *magpamakalawá.*

pámakuán (pá-ma-ku-án), *n.* (Carp.) structural pieces of timber, usually horizontal, to which wall boards, roofings, etc. are nailed.

pamagát (pa-ma-gát), *n.* 1. title or heading, as of story, novel, poem, book, etc. Syn.

título. 2. nickname; alias. Syn. *palayaw*.

pamagitanan (pa-ma-gi-ta-nan), *v.* to mediate; act as a go-between or mediator between two persons in dispute.

pamago (pa-ma-go), *n.* first fruits or harvest of the season.

pamahál (pa-ma-hál), *adj.* getting dear or dearer; becoming costly; increasing in price or cost. Syn. *pataás ang halagá*.

pámahalaán (pá-ma-ha-la-án), *n.* (*Pol.*) government. Syn. *gobyerno*.

pamahaw (pa-ma-haw), *n.* (Rare) 1. breakfast. Syn. *almusál, amusál, agahan*. 2. a light meal between regular meals; repast. Syn. *minandál, mirindál, meryenda*.

pamahay (pa-ma-hay), *adj.* 1. for house or household use. Also, *pambahay*. 2. for housing allowance.

pamahayag (pa-ma-ha-yag), *n.* 1. proclamation. Syn. *proklamasyón*. 2. announcement. Syn. *patalastás*. 3. demands asked by demonstrators.

pamahayan (pa-ma-ha-yan), *v.* 1. to live or reside in; make as one's residence. 2. to be or become the site of a housing project. Syn. *maging pámahayán*. 3. to become filled or covered with or as with water, referring to a low place. Syn. *panirahán, tigilan*.

pamahid (pa-ma-hid), *n. & adj.* 1. referring to a piece of rag, a napkin, handkerchief, towel, or the like used for cleaning or wiping. Syn. *pamunas*. 2. referring to something used for rubbing, as ointment, alcohol, etc. Syn. *panghaplás*.

pamahiín (pa-ma-hi-ín; pá-ma-hi-ín), *n.* superstition. Syn. *superstisyón, abusyón*.

pamain (pa-ma-in), *n. & adj.* 1. referring to something used as a bait. Cf. *pangatí*. 2. said of a nest egg.

pamalakâ (pa-ma-la-kâ), *n. & adj.* referring to a net, hook, etc. used for catching frogs. Syn. *pampalakâ, panghuli ng palakâ*.

pamalakaya (pa-ma-la-ka-ya), *n. & adj.* referring to a net, boat, or any kind of fishing gear used for deep-sea fishing.

pamalas (pa-ma-las), *n.* 1. act of showing or putting out something for someone or for anybody to see. Also, *pagpapamalas*. Syn. *pakita, pagpapakita*.

pamalay (pa-ma-lay), *I. n. & adj.* referring to something that causes someone to become conscious or regain consciousness. Also, *pampamalay*.
—II. *n.* 1. act of causing someone to have knowledge about something by giving him a hint. 2. the hint thus given.
—III. *v.* to make one's presence be noticed. Cf. *pahalatâ*.

pamalí-malî (pa-ma-lí + ma-lî), *adj. & adv.* committing repeated errors; repeatedly committing mistakes.

pamalít (pa-ma-lít), *n. & adj.* 1. referring to a person or thing used as substitute. Syn. *panghalili*. 2. referring to coins made ready for changing money of higher denominations. Syn. *panuklî*.

pamalò (pa-ma-lò), *I. n.* 1. something used for beating or whipping; whip. 2. a bat (in baseball). Syn. *bat*. 3. a wooden club used for beating laundry. Syn. *palupalò, pamugbóg*.
—II. *adj.* used for whipping or for hitting a ball.

pamaltík (pa-mal-tík), *n.* a slingshot. Syn. *tiradór*. See **paltík**.

pamalukagan (pa-ma-lu-ka-gan), *v.* 1. to have one's hair stand on end. Syn. *pangalisagan, panindigán ng balahibo*. 2. to have goose flesh. Syn. *pangilabutan*.

pamamaalam (pa-ma-ma-a-lam), *n.* act of bidding goodbye. Also, *pagpapaalam*.

pamamagitan (pa-ma-ma-gi-tan), *I. n.* mediation; intercession.
—II. *prep.* (with *sa ... ng*) through the means of; by means of.

pamamahagi (pa-ma-ma-ha-gi), *n.* 1. act, manner, or time of distributing things, esp. for free; distribution, as of information, etc. Syn. *pagkakalat, pagpapakalat*.

pamamahalà (pa-ma-ma-ha-là), *n.* 1. management; administration. Syn. *pangangasiwà, pamamatnugot*. 2. term of office, as of an official. Syn. *panahón o taning ng panunungkulan*.

pamamahay (pa-ma-ma-hay), *n.* 1. home; household. Syn. *tahanan*. 2. housekeeping; homemaking; house or home management.

pamamahayag (pa-ma-ma-ha-yag), n. 1. public show of feelings or opinions, as by people in a meeting or parade; public demonstration to bring about change. Syn. *demonstrasyón*. 2. the work of a newspaperman.

pamamahingá (pa-ma-ma-hi-ngá), n. 1. act of resting. Also, *pagpapahingá*. Syn. *pagpapahingaláy*. 2. time or period of rest or relaxation. 3. retirement, as from work. Syn. *pagreretiro*.

pamamahò (pa-ma-ma-hò), n. emission of foul odor, as of rotting meat, carcass, etc. Syn. *pangangamóy, pangangalingasaw ng bahò o masamáng amóy*.

pamamalakad (pa-ma-ma-la-kad), n. 1. management; administration. Syn. *pangangasiwà, pamamatnugot*. 2. regulation or policy being enforced, as in a certain office. Syn. *pasunód, tuntunin, pánuntunan, regulasyón*.

pamamalagì (pa-ma-ma-la-gì), n. 1. continuous stay, as in a certain place. Syn. *pananatili*. 2. permanence or permanency. Syn. *pagkapálagián*. 3. perpetuity. Syn. *kawaláng-pagbabago*.

pamamalahibo (pa-ma-ma-la-hi-bo), n. (Fig.) inferiority complex. Syn. *panganganino, pagkasilóng*.

pamamalát (pa-ma-ma-lát), n. state or condition of having a hoarse voice; hoarseness of voice. Syn. *pamamaos, pamamagaw*.

pamamanaag (pa-ma-ma-na-ag), n. 1. faint appearance of light, as from the moon. Syn. *bahagyáng pagliliwanag*. 2. the break of day; sunrise. Syn. *pagbubukáng-liwaywáy; pamimiták ng araw*. 3. (Fig.) faint manifestation, as of hope.

pamamanata (pa-ma-ma-na-ta), n. devotional promise; religious vow. Syn. *matapát na pangakò o pangangakò; debosyóng banál*.

pamamanatag (pa-ma-ma-na-tag), n. 1. complete rest or retirement, as from political involvement. Syn. *lubós na pamamahingá*. 2. end of life; death. Syn. *pagkamatáy, kamatayan*.

pamamanhík (pa-ma-man-hík), n. 1. entreaty; earnest request; supplication.

Syn. *samò, pagsamò*. 2. persuasion by imploring. Syn. *pakikiusap, pakikisuyò*. 3. same as *pamamánhikan*.

pamamánhikan (pa-ma-mán-hi-kan), n. the practice or custom of asking formally for the hand of a prospective bride by the parents of the bridegroom by going to the house of the girl's parents.

pamamanihalà (pa-ma-ma-ni-ha-là), n. act of managing or supervising an office, business concern, etc. Also, *pamamahalà*. Syn. *pangangasiwà, pamamatnugot*.

pamamanság (pa-ma-man-ság), n. act of bragging or boasting. Syn. *paghahambóg, pagpapasikat*.

pamamangláw (pa-ma-mang-láw), var. pamamanláw, n. feeling of melancholy or solitude; loneliness.

pamamaraan (pa-ma-ma-ra-an; -ra-án), n. system; way or manner of doing something; method; means; process. See paraán.

pamamaralì (pa-ma-ma-ra-lì), n. 1. act of boasting or bragging about one's successes or accomplishments. Syn. *paghahambóg, pagpaparangyâ, pagpapasikat*. 2. act of spreading rumors or gossips about others; act of telling on others. Syn. *paninirà, paninirang-puri*.

pamamarati (pa-ma-ma-ra-ti), n. unchanged state or condition. Syn. *pananatili, kawaláng pagbabago*.

pamamasláng (pa-ma-mas-láng), n. act of insolence or irreverence. Syn. *kapusungán, kawaláng-galang*. 2. an abusive act; assault.

pamamatnubay (pa-ma-mat-nu-bay), n. 1. guiding; guidance. Syn. *pag-akay, pag-aakay, pagpapanuto*. 2. leadership. Syn. *pamumunò, pangungulo, pangunguna, pamamatnugot*.

pamamayagpág (pa-ma-ma-yag-pág), n. 1. flapping of wings of fowls or birds. Cf. pagaspás. 2. boastfulness of one who has attained success. Syn. *paghahambóg*.

pamamayani (pa-ma-ma-ya-ni), n. predominance; prevalence; preponderance. Syn. *pananatili, pananaíg, pangingibabaw, paghaharì*.

pamamayapà (pa-ma-ma-ya-pà), n. end of

life; death. Syn. *pagkamatáy pagsakabiláng-buhay, pagyao, pagpanaw.*

pamana (pa-ma-na), *n.* inheritance; legacy; heritage; bequest.

pamanhikán (pa-man-hi-kán), *v.* 1. to entreat; ask or request (someone) earnestly. Syn. *pakiusapan, pakisuyuan.* 2. to persuade by imploring.

pamanság (pa-man-ság), *n.* 1. something a person is boasting or bragging about. Syn. *pamalità, panabi, pamarali.* 2. public declaration or statement. Syn. *pahayag.* 3. name or term for. Syn. *panawag, katawagán, tagurí.*

pamansíng (pa-man-síng), *n.* a fishing rod attached with a line and hook. Syn. *pamingwít.*

pámantayan (pá-man-ta-yan), I. *n.* standard; basis of comparison. Syn. *sukatán, batayán, saligán.*

—II. *adj.* standard; used as a standard, as in: *pámantayang oras,* standard time.

pamangkín (pa-mang-kín), *n.* 1. niece or nephew; child of one's brother, sister, or cousin. 2. stepson or stepdaughter; stepchild. Syn. *anák na pangumán.*

pamanggít (pa-mang-gít), *adj.* (*Gram.*) relative, as in: *panghalíp pamanggít,* relative pronoun.

pamanghâ (pa-mang-hâ), *adv.* in an amazed manner; amazingly. Cf. *pataká, pagulát.*

pamanguhín (pa-ma-ngu-hín), *v.* 1. to use, referring to a certain kind of perfume. 2. to fill with sweet odor; make fragrant. Also, *pabanguhín.*

pamaraan (pa-ma-ra-an; -án), *n.* 1. trick; stratagem. 2. way; method; system. Also, *paraán, pamamaraán.* 3. (*Gram.*) manner, as in: *pang-abay na pamaraan,* adverb of manner.

pamarali (pa-ma-ra-li), *n. & adj.* referring to a derogatory remark made by someone against another. Syn. *panirà, panirang-puri.* 2. referring to something that someone is boasting about. Syn. *ang ipinagháhambóg o ipinagmámagalíng.*

pamaram (pa-ma-ram), *n. & adj.* referring to something used to quench or stop thirst, hunger, pain, etc. Syn. *pamawî.*

pamarisan (pa-ma-ri-san), *v.* to imitate;

make as one's model. Syn. *tularan, gawíng modelo o húwaran.*

pamasahe (pa-ma-sa-he), *n.* transportation money or allowance. Also, *pampasahe.*

pamasko (pa-mas-ko), *n. & adj.* 1. referring to something special, as clothes, shoes, etc., for someone's use on Christmas Day. 2. referring to something given to or received by as Christmas gift. Also, *papaskó.*

pamatíd-gutom (pa-ma-tíd + gu-tom), *n. & adj.* anything eaten or that can be eaten to stave off hunger.

pamatláng (pa-mat-láng), *n.* (*Print.*) a device used for making spaces; spacer.

pamatlíg (pa-mat-líg), I. *adj.* (*Gram.*) demonstrative, as in: *panghalíp pamatlíg,* demonstrative pronoun.

—II. *n.* (*Gram.*) a demonstrative pronoun or adjective.

pamatnubay (pa-mat-nu-bay), *n. & adj.* referring to a thing used as a guide.

pamawì (pa-ma-wì), I. *n.* 1. eraser; eradicator. Syn. *pamburá.* 2. anything used to quench or satisfy. Syn. *panlunas, pamatíd, pang-alís.*

—II. *adj.* used for erasing.

pámayanán (pá-ma-ya-nán), *n.* community. Syn. *komunidád.*

pamaypáy (pa-may-páy), *n.* 1. folding fan. Syn. *abaniko.* 2. anything used as a folding fan.

pambababae (pam-ba-ba-ba-e), *n.* the act of maintaining a mistress or mistresses. Syn. *pangangálunyâ.*

pambababoy (pam-ba-ba-boy), *n.* act of making a fool of another by talking of nasty or indecent things. Syn. *panlalaswâ.*

pambabae (pam-ba-ba-e), *adj.* 1. of or for women or girls; female. 2. (*Gram.*) feminine, as in: *kasariáng pambabae,* feminine gender.

pambalaki (pam-ba-la-ki), *adj.* (*Gram.*) neuter, as in: *kasariáng pambalaki,* neuter gender.

pambálaná (pam-bá-la-ná), *adj.* (*Gram.*) common: as in *pangngalang pambálaná,* common noun.

pambalanì (pam-ba-la-nì), *n. & adj.* referring to a person's charm or magnetism

pambalarilà   **pamista**

that easily attracts others. Syn. *panghalina, pang-akit.*

pambalarilà (pam-ba-la-ri-là), *adj.* 1. grammatical. Syn. *panggramátiká.* 2. referring to grammar. Syn. *ukol sa balarilà o gramátiká.*

pambansá (pam-ban-sá; -sà), *adj.* national; of or for the nation.

pambigáy-kaya (pam-bi-gáy + ka-ya), *n. & adj.* referring to something that someone intends to give to a bride as a dowry. Syn. *pandote, pambilang o pamilang* (Bats.).

pambihirà (pam-bi-hi-rà), I. *adj.* 1. uncommon, extraordinary. Syn. *di-karaniwán, di-pangkaraniwan.* 2. rare; rarely found. Syn. *madalang, úlán.*
—II. *adv.* rarely; seldom; not often; infrequently.

pambunsód (pam-bun-sód), I. *n.* 1. a tool or machine used for launching something. 2. something done or prepared to launch or introduce a project, etc.
—II. *adj.* introductory; serving to introduce; preliminary. Syn. *pansimulá, panimulá.*

pambungad (pam-bu-ngad), I. *n.* 1. introduction; introductory remarks. Syn. *páunáng salitá.* 2. frontispiece. Syn. *pamukhá, pangmukhá.* 3. anything placed in front for better effect or attraction.
—II. *adj.* 1. introductory; opening, as of a speech. Syn. *panimulá, pansimulá.* 2. that which is placed in front for better effect or attraction.

pamburol (pam-bu-rol), I. *n.* 1. a dress or clothes for the dead lying in state. 2. *(Fig.)* the best dress or clothes a person has.
—II. *adj.* referring to a dress or clothes intended for a person when he dies. Also, *pamurol.*

pamigáy (pa-mi-gáy), *adj.* given or distributed free of charge.

pamilí (pa-mi-lí), I. *n.* 1. money for marketing. 2. things bought, esp. from the market. Also, *pinamilí.*
—II. *adj.* 1. referring to a certain amount of money for buying things in the market. Syn. *pamalengke.* 2. referring to things bought by someone in the market.

pámilihan (pá-mi-li-han), *n.* 1. market;

market place. Syn. *palengke, merkado; baraka, bárakahán.* 2. shopping center. Syn. *sentro ng kalakal.*

pamilya (pa-mil-ya), *n.* (Sp. *familia*) family. Syn. *mag-anak, angkán.*

pamilyár (pa-mil-yár), *adj.* (Sp. *familiar*) 1. familiar; known to all. Syn. *kilala ng lahát.* 2. intimate; close, as in: *Pamilyar kong kaibigan ang dalawá.* The two are my familiar friends. Syn. *matalik.*

pamimihasa (pa-mi-mi-ha-sa), *n.* state or condition of being used or accustomed to. Syn. *pagkasanay, pagkahirati.*

pamimilì (pa-mi-mi-lì), *n.* act or manner of selecting (the best) from a group of persons or things; selection; choosing.

pamimilit (pa-mi-mi-lit), *n.* act or manner of forcing someone to do or accept something against his or her will. Syn. *pamumuwersa.*

pamimintás (pa-mi-min-tás), *n.* act of finding faults with others. Syn. *pamumulà, pamimistà.*

pamimintuhò (pa-mi-min-tu-hò), *n.* act of admiring, loving, veneration, or worship. Syn. *panunuyò.*

pamimiták (pa-mi-mi-ták), *n.* (with *ng araw*) break of day; dawn; daybreak.

pamimítagan (pa-mi-mí-ta-gan), *n.* respect; show of respect. Syn. *paggalang.*

páminsanan (pá-min-sa-nan), *adv.* all at the same time. Syn. *láhatan.*

paminsán-minsán (pa-min-sán + min-sán), *adj. & adv.* once in a while.

paminta (pa-min-ta), *n.* (Sp. *pimienta*) 1. black pepper. 2. the black berries from which this powdered pepper is obtained. 3. the plant that bears these berries.

pamintón (pa-min-tón), *n.* (Sp. *pimenton*) pimiento; ground red pepper.

páminggalan (pá-ming-ga-lan), *n.* 1. cupboard. Syn. *pamingganan.* 2. pantry; larder. Syn. *banggerahán.*

pamisa (pa-mi-sa), *n. & adj.* referring to a requiem or mass offered by someone for the repose of the soul or souls of the dead.

pamista (pa-mis-ta), *n. & adj.* referring to a person's best clothes, shoes, and other wearing apparel used or worn in attending fiestas. Also, *pamiyesta, pampiyesta.*

pamitaganan

pamitaganan (pa-mi-ta-ga-nan), v. to respect; show one's respect to (or for). Syn. *igalang.*

pampa- (pam-pa-), pref. meaning: (a) causing or intended to cause a certain condition or state, as in *pampatulog.* (b) a device, tool, or instrument used for a certain purpose, as in *pampatigil.*

pampaalaala (pam-pa-a-la-a-la), n. & adj. referring to something that causes someone to be reminded of. Syn. *pampagunitâ.*

pampaalab (pam-pa-a-lab), n. & adj. 1. referring to a something that causes fire to burn ablaze. Syn. *pampaliyáb, pampaningas, pampalagabláb.* 2. that which causes fervor or enthusiasm. Syn. *pampasigasig, pampasiglá.*

pampabangó (pam-pa-ba-ngó), n. & adj. referring to an aromatic substance used to give aroma or fragrance, as a perfume.

pampadamá (pam-pa-da-má), var. **pamparamá,** n. & adj. that which makes someone feel or experience something.

pampadubdób (pam-pa-dub-dób), var. **pamparubdób,** n. & adj. 1. referring to something used for feeling a fire in order to increase the blaze. Syn. *pampaliyáb, pampaalab.* 2. (Fig.) that which makes ardent, fervent, or eager. Syn. *pampasigasig, pampaalab, pampasiglá.*

pampagalíng (pam-pa-ga-líng), n. & adj. 1. referring to something that treats or cures a person of his (her) sickness. 2. that which makes a person or thing better. Syn. *pampabuti, pampahusay.*

pampahignáw (pam-pa-hig-náw), n. & adj. referring to something that reduces the intensity of. Syn. *pampahupâ, pampabawa, pampahulaw.*

pampahirap (pam-pa-hi-rap), n. & adj. referring to anything that causes poverty, difficulties, hardships, or sufferings.

pampalabò (pam-pa-la-bò), n. & adj. 1. that which causes (water) to become turbid or muddy. 2. said of a device or means used to make light dim or dark. Syn. *pampalamlám, pampadilím.* 3. referring to something said or done that obscures the meaning of. Syn. *pampahirap unawain*

pampánitikán

(intindihín).

pampálagián (pam-pá-la-gi-án), I. adj. permanent; lasting. Also, *pálagián, pámalagián.*

—II. adv. permanently. Syn. *pirmihan.*

pampalipas (pam-pa-li-pas), n. & adj. referring to something that a person does to pass away the time. Syn. *pamparaán, pamparaos.*

pampaliwanag (pam-pa-li-wa-nag), n. & adj. referring to something that makes a place clear or bright, as lamps. 2. that which is given or said to clarify or explain the meaning of. Syn. *pampalinaw, pampaunawa.* 3. referring to something that makes the eyes or vision clear. Syn. *pampalinaw.*

pampalubág-loób (pam-pa-lu-bág + lo-ób), n. & adj. that which serves as a consolation.

pampalugód (pam-pa-lu-gód), n. & adj. that which gives delight, pleasure, or satisfaction. Syn. *pampagalák, pampatuwâ, pampaligaya.*

pampalumanay (pam-pa-lu-ma-nay), n. & adj. referring to something that makes a person act, move, or speak in a gentle, suave manner. Syn. *pampahinay.*

pampalumat (pam-pa-lu-mat), n. & adj. that which causes unnecessary delay in doing. Syn. *pampaluwát, pampatagál, pampaabala.*

pampalumbáy (pam-pa-lum-báy), n. & adj. that which makes a person sad or lonely. Syn. *pampalungkót, pampahapis, pampadalamhatì.*

pampám (pam-pám), I. adj. (Orig. unknown) engaging in promiscuous sexual intercourse for pay, referring to a woman. —II. n. prostitute; whore; harlot. Syn. *puta, kalapating mababà ang lipád* (fig.); *burikák.*

pampanág-aráw (pam-pa-nág + a-ráw), adj. for or suitable for summer. Also, *pantag-aráw.*

pampanág-ulán (pam-pa-nág + u-lán), adj. for or suitable for rainy season. Also, *pantag-ulán.*

pampánitikán (pam-pá-ni-ti-kán), adj. having to do with literature; literary. Syn. *panliteratura.*

pampanuto (pam-pa-nu-to), n. & adj. that which serves as a guide.

pampáng (pam-páng), n. bank; border or side of a river.

pamparaán (pam-pa-ra-án), var. **pampadaán**, n. & adj. referring to something done or being done to pass away time, tiredness, etc. Syn. pampalipas, pamparaos.

pampasabog (pam-pa-sa-bog), n. & adj. referring to something that causes explosion, or that which causes something to burst or explode. Syn. pampasambulat.

pampasakit (pam-pa-sa-kit), n. & adj. referring to something said or done that hurts the feeling of others. Syn. pampasamâ ng loób, pampasugat ng damdamin.

pampataká (pam-pa-ta-ká), n. & adj. that which is said, done, or shown to make others wonder. Syn. pampamanghâ.

pampatalisik (pam-pa-ta-li-sik), n. & adj. said of something that makes someone erudite. Syn. pampatalino.

pampatigháw (pam-pa-tig-háw), n. & adj. referring to something that reduces the intensity of. Syn. pampahulaw, pampahipâ.

pampatulog (pam-pa-tu-log), n. & adj. hypnotic; soporific.

pampawili (pam-pa-wi-li), n. & adj. that which keeps a person or persons to have continued interest in something.

pampayì (pam-pa-yì), var. **pamayì**, n. & adj. said of something used to erase or eradicate writings or dirt on surfaces, etc. Syn. pamawì, pampawì.

pamplete (pam-ple-te), n. & adj. referring to a certain amount of money for fare or transportation allowance. Syn. pampasahe, pamasahe.

pampuná (pam-pu-ná), var. **pamuná**, n. & adj. that which a person often uses to criticize others. Syn. pamintas, pamulà.

pamukhâ (pa-muk-hâ), n. 1. a design or illustration on or for the title page or frontispiece of a book. Syn. portada, pamortada. 2. the main façade, as of a building. 3. a strong statement of accusation hurled against someone face to face.

pamukhaán (pa-muk-ha-án), v. 1. to accuse (a person) face to face. Syn. paratangan nang hárapan. 2. to provide or decorate the front, as with a certain design or decoration. Syn. patsadahan.

pamukól (pa-mu-kól), n. & adj. referring to a piece of stone or the like used for hitting someone or something by throwing. Syn. pamató, pambató, panghagis.

pamukot (pa-mu-kot), n. & adj. referring to a kind of dragnet used in deep-sea fishing.

pamuksâ (pa-muk-sâ), I. n. that which destroys totally or eradicates; exterminator; killer.
—II. adj. that which is used to eradicate or destroy totally. Syn. pamatáy, pampalipol.

pamukulan (pa-mu-ku-lan), I. v. to have one's breasts grow bigger during puberty, referring to girls.
—II. adj. said of a young girl whose breasts have started to grow bigger.

pamudmód (pa-mud-mód), adj. & adv. by distributing or doling out sparingly to individuals.

pamugaran (pa-mu-ga-ran), var. **pagpugaran**, v. 1. to use as one's nest, as by a hen or bird. 2. to frequent (a place); make or use a place as one's haunt.

pamugot (pa-mu-got), n. & adj. said of a device or tool used for decapitating or cutting off heads. Also, pampugot.

pámuhatán (pá-mu-ha-tán), n. 1. etymology; origin and development of a word. 2. source; origin. Syn. pinanggalingan, pinagmulán.

pámuhayán (pá-mu-há-yán), n. livelihood; living condition.

pamuhunanan (pa-mu-hu-na-nan), v. to make investment in; invest capital in. Syn. pangapitalán.

pámulaan (pá-mu-la-an), n. 1. etymology. Syn. pámuhatán. 2. starting place. Syn. úmpisahan. 3. source; origin. Syn. pinanggalingan, pinagbuhatan.

pamulaklakín (pa-mu-lak-la-kín), v. 1. to wait for or allow a plant or plants to bear flowers. Syn. hintayín o hayaang mamulaklák. 2. to make or allow someone to pick or gather flowers. Syn. papangunin o papamitasín ng (mga) bulaklák.

pamulahán (pa-mu-la-hán), v. (usually with ng mukha) to blush; have one's face turned red, as from shame, excitement, etc.

pamulatan (pa-mu-la-tan), v. (Fig.) to make one open his eyes; make one understand what is right and wrong. Syn. paunawaan.

pamulî (pa-mu·lî), adv. & adj. again; once again; once more. Also, mulî.

pamumukadkád (pa-mu-mu-kad-kád), n. the time during which flowers are in full bloom.

pamumukaw (pa-mu-mu-kaw), n. the act or habit of waking up persons while asleep. Syn. panggigising.

pamumuko (pa-mu-mu-ko), n. 1. time or season during which plants begin to bud. 2. the act of picking or gathering young coconut fruits. Syn. pangunguha ng buko o muráng niyóg.

pamumukó (pa-mu-mu-kó), n. the act or habit of contradicting or disappointing others. Syn. pangunguntra, panghihiyà.

pamumukód (pa-mu-mu-kód), n. 1. state or quality of being particularly apart or different from all others; singularity; individuality. Also, pamumukód-tangì. 2. distinction; difference. Syn. kaibhán o pagkakáibá sa lahát.

pamumuksâ (pa-mu-muk-sâ), n. massacre; wholesale and pitiless slaughter or killing of people or animals. Syn. waláng awang pagpatáy sa mga tao o hayop.

pamumugad (pa-mu-mu-gad), n. 1. act of building and living in a nest. Also, pagpupugad. 2. nesting season.

pamumuhay (pa-mu-mu-hay), n. 1. livelihood; means of living. Syn. kabuhayan. 2. way of life; living condition.

pamumuhunan (pa-mu-mu-hu-nan), n. investment of capital; capitalization. Syn. pangangapitál.

pamumulá (pa-mu-mu-lá), n. 1. a becoming red or reddish, referring to things. Also, pagpulá. 2. a blushing or reddening, as of one's face due to shame, etc.

pamumulà (pa-mu-mu-là), n. act or habit of criticizing others or their work. Syn. pamimintás, pamimistâ.

pamumulaklák (pa-mu-mu-lak-lák), n. the time or season during which plants and

trees bloom or bear flowers.

pamumulubi (pa-mu-mu-lu-bi), n. state or condition of being impoverish or of living the life of a beggar. Syn. labis na paghihirap o pagdarálitâ.

pamumuná (pa-mu-mu-ná), n. the art, habit, or work of a critic; criticism.

pamumunò (pa-mu-mu-nò), n. 1. act of managing or acting as chief, as of an office. Syn. paghehepe, pangangasiwà, pamamahalà. 2. leadership. Syn. paglilider. 3. act of heading or presiding a group. Syn. pangungulo.

pamumunga (pa-mu-mu-nga), n. 1. bearing of fruit, as of a tree; fruition. 2. season of bearing fruit. 3. (Fig.) bearing of children. Syn. pangangának.

pamumuri (pa-mu-mu-ri), n. 1. act of praising others. 2. something said in praise of someone.

pamumusyáw (pa-mu-mus-yáw), n. partial loss of color or brilliance; fading away of color. Syn. pangungupas.

pamumutawì (pa-mu-mu-ta-wì), n. a coming out from the mouth, said of words.

pamumuti (pa-mu-mu-ti), n. act or manner of picking or gathering fruit from a tree. Syn. pamimitás o pangunguha ng bunga.

pamumutiktík (pa-mu-mu-tik-tík), n. a swarming or crowding in great numbers. Syn. pagkutô sa dami.

pamumutlâ (pa-mu-mut-lâ), n. 1. a becoming pale or wan. 2. condition of being pale; paleness. Also, kaputlaán.

pamumutók (pa-mu-mu-tók), n. 1. a bursting or popping, as of corn being roasted. Syn. pamumusá. 2. repeated or continuous explosions. 3. a cracking or breaking, as the surface of land due to extreme dryness. Syn. pagkakabiták, pamimiták.

pamunô (pa-mu-nô), var. pampunô, n. & adj. referring to something intended to complete or fill up the need, lack, or insufficiency of. Syn. panghustó.

pamunuan (pa-mu-nu-an), v. 1. to head or lead. Syn. pangunahan. 2. to direct or manage. Syn. pamahalaan, pangasiwaan.

pamutat (pa-mu-tat), n. & adj. referring to something used as a side dish or eaten as *hors d'oeuvres.* See putat. Cf. *pamulutan, pampulutan.*

pamutawiin (pa-mu-ta-wi-in), *v.* to say or utter. Syn. *sabihin, bigkasin.*

pamutiktikán (pa-mu-tik-ti-kán), *v.* to be filled thickly with or as with ants. Syn. *pamuninian.*

pamutol (pa-mu-tol), var. **pamputol,** *n. & adj.* referring to a tool or instrument used as a cutter or for cutting.

pamuuín (pa-mu-u-ín), *v.* 1. to cause liquid to coagulate or milk to curdle. 2. to cause something to become hard or solidified.

pan-, prefix used as a variant of pang- before words beginning with "d" and "t," as in *pandiwà* (verb), *pantukoy* (article), and the like.

panà (pa-nà), *n.* 1. bow and arrow. 2. act or manner of shooting with the bow and arrow. Also, *pagpanà, pagkakápanà.*

panabangán (pa-na-ba-ngán), *v.* to lose one's taste, interest, desire, or liking for. Syn. *mawalán ng gana o gusto.*

panabáy (pa-na-báy), *adv.* at the same time; simultaneously.

panabi (pa-na-bi), *n.* (*Colloq.*) statement or utterance one uses to tell on others. Syn. *pamarali.*

panabikán (pa-na-bi-kán), *v.* to have extreme eagerness for.

panabikín (pa-na-bi-kín), *v.* to make someone very eager to see, get, or experience something.

panabing (pa-na-bing), var. **pantabing,** *n. & adj.* said of a blanket, bed sheet, or the like, used in the same manner a curtain is used.

panaká-nakâ (pa-na-ká + na-kâ), *adj. & adv.* once in a while; occasionally. Syn. *paminsán-minsán.*

panakáw (pa-na-káw), *adv.* 1. by stealing. 2. secretly. Syn. *palihím, patagô.*

panakíp (pa-na-kíp), var. **pantakíp,** *n. & adj.* referring to anything used to cover a jar, pot, or the like. Syn. *panaklób, pantaklób.*

panakíp-butas (pa-na-kíp + bu-tas), *n. & adj.* referring to anything used to fill or cover a hole. Syn. *pamasak.* 2. (*Fig.*) referring to a person who takes the place of another or is assigned in place of

another who fails to come or be present in an occasion.

panakláw (pa-nak-láw), *n. & adj.* said of the signs [ ] and ( ), called brackets and parentheses, respectively. Syn. *panaklóng.*

panaklolo (pa-nak-lo-lo), var. **pansaklolo,** *n. & adj.* said of men, material, and other things made ready or available for aid or relief to victims of accidents or disasters. Syn. *pansokoro, pantulong.*

panaklóng (pa-nak-lóng), *n.* (Gram.) parentheses.

panakot (pa-na-kot), var. **pantakot,** *n. & adj.* 1. referring to something that someone uses for threatening or scaring another or others. 2. said of anything set up in a field to scare crow. Syn. *pátakót.*

panaderiya (pa-na-de-ri-ya; -yá), var. **panaderyá,** *n.* (Sp. *panadería*) bakery. Syn. *tínapayán.*

panadero (pa-na-de-ro), *n.* (Sp.) baker. Syn. *magtitinapáy.*

panág- (pa-nág-), pref. meaning "for" or "suitable for," as in: *panág-aráw, panág-ulán.* Syn. *pantág-.*

panagano (pa-na-ga-no), *n.* 1. (Gram.) mood; mode. 2. prevalence; widespread occurrence. Also *pananagano.* Syn. *pananaíg, paglaganap; paghaharì* (fig.), *pangingibabaw.*

panaganong pasakalî, subjunctive mood.

panaganong paturól, indicative mood.

panaganong pautós, imperative mood.

panaganong pawatás, infinitive mood.

panagkâ (pa-nag-kâ), var. **pansagkâ,** *n. & adj.* that which is used to prevent or stop something from slipping, spreading, continuing, or from being realized.

panaghilì (pa-nag-hi-lì), *n.* envy. Syn. *inggít, pagkainggít, kainggitán.*

panaghóy (pa-nag-hóy), *n.* pitiful cry of grief and pain; wailing. Syn. *daíng, pagdaíng.*

panagimpán (pa-na-gim-pán), *n.* (poetic form of **panaginip**) 1. dream. Syn. *pangarap.* 2. ambition. Syn. *lunggatí, mithî, hángarin.*

panaginip (pa-na-gi-nip), *n.* 1. dream. Syn. *pangarap.* 2. ambition; aspiration. Syn. *mithî, mithiin; lungatî, lungatiin.*

panagisag (pa-na-gi-sag), *n. & adj.* referring

to something used as a symbol for.

panagót (pa-na-gót), n. & adj. 1. that which refers to something used as a guarantee, security or bond. Syn. pampiyansa. 2. referring to a prepared answer or answers to some expected questions to be asked.

panág-ulian (pa-nág + u-li-an), v. to regain, as one's consciousness, good health, etc. Syn. panúmbalikan.

panagurî (pa-na-gu-rî), n. (Gram.) predicate.

panágutan (pa-ná-gu-tan), var. **pananágutan**, n. 1. responsibility. Also, ságutin. 2. obligation; duty. Syn. tungkulin.

panagutín (pa-na-gu-tín), v. to hold someone responsible for, make someone accountable for.

panahóg (pa-na-hóg), var. **pansahóg**, n. & adj. 1. in cooking, referring to something added to a dish as an ingredient. Syn. panghalò. 2. said of a seasoning ingredient added to food. Syn. rikado, panrikado.

panahón (pa-na-hón), n. 1. time; period of time; era; epoch. 2. season. Also, kapanáhunan. 3. climate; weather. Syn. klima. 4. (Gram.) tense. Also, pánahunan.

panahóng kasalukuyan, present; present time.

panahóng dárating, future; time to come. Syn. hináharáp; panahóng hináharáp.

panahóng háharapín, future; future time. Syn. panahóng dáratíng.

panahóng lumipas, past; past time. Syn. panahóng nagdaán.

panahóng pandáratíng, 1. future. 2. (Gram.) future tense.

panahóng pangkasalukuyan, 1. present; present time. 2. (Gram.) present tense.

panahóng panghináharáp, 1. future; time to come. 2. (Gram.) future tense.

panahóng pangnagdaán, 1. past; past time. 2. (Gram.) past tense.

pánahunan (pá-na-hu-nan), I. n. 1. (Gram.) tense. See **panahón.** 2. climatology; science dealing with climate.

—II. adj. seasonal; coming regularly at a certain season. Syn. maysadyáng panahón.

panalakay (pa-na-la-kay), var. **pansalakay**, n. & adj. said of weapons or arms used in attacking enemies or enemy positions.

Syn. pang-atake, panlusob.

panalág (pa-na-lág), var. **pansalág**, n. & adj. said of something held by the hand to parry off blows. Syn. pananggá, pansanggá.

panalangin (pa-na-la-ngin), n. 1. prayer. Syn. dasál. 2. something prayed for or requested in one's prayer.

panalig (pa-na-lig), var. **pananalig**, n. 1. trust; confidence; faith. Syn. tiwalà, pagtitiwalà, kumpiyansa. 2. belief. Syn. paniwalà, paniniwalà.

panalinghagà (pa-na-ling-ha-gà), n. 1. figure of speech; metaphor. Syn. metáporá. 2. idiomatic expression. 3. allegory; symbolical narration or description. See **pananalinghagà.**

panalitâ (pa-na-li-tâ), n. 1. word, as a unit of speech. 2. (Gram.) speech, as in: mga bahagi ng pananalitâ, parts of speech.

panalo (pa-na-lo), I. n. 1. win or victory, as in games or contest. Syn. tagumpáy. 2. winnings, as in gambling. 3. a victor or winner, as in battle.

—II. adj. victorious; successful. Syn. nanalo, nagtagumpáy.

panamà (pa-na-mà), I. n. 1. (Colloq.) chance or hope, as in: Walâ kang panamà sa kanyá. You have no chance against him. 2. compatibility, as of two persons. Syn. pagkakásundô, pagkakátumpák.

—II. adj. compatible or in agreement with each other. Syn. magkasundô, magkasuwatò.

panambitan (pa-nam-bi-tan), n. 1. supplication; doleful entreaty; petition or prayer. Syn. daíng, hinaíng. 2. lamentation; loud grief. Syn. pananaghóy, pananangís.

panamlayán (pa-nam-la-yán), v. (usually with ng katawán) 1. to feel cool to; lose interest in. Syn. panabangán, mawalán ng gana o interés. 2. to lose vigor or vitality; feel weak. Syn. manghinà, makáramdám ng panghihinà (ng katawán).

panamnamín (pa-nam-na-mín), v. to cause a person to experience or have a taste of something. Syn. palasapín, padanasin, patikimín.

pananabáng (pa-na-na-báng), n. 1. loss of interest in; becoming indifferent. Syn. panlalamíg (fig.), paghihinawà, pagkawalâ *ng gana o interes.* 2. a becoming tasteless. Syn. *pagkawalâ ng lasa.*

pananabát (pa-na-na-bát), n. act or habit of entering in others' conversation. Syn. *paghalò o pakikihalò sa úsapan ng ibá.*

pananabík (pa-na-na-bík), n. keen desire or interest in; eagerness or longing for.

pananakít (pa-na-na-kít), n. 1. act or habit of hurting others. Cf. *pagpapahirap (sa kapwà).* 2. feeling of pain, as of someone's back, etc. Cf. *pangingirót.*

pananakot (pa-na-na-kot), n. intimidation; act of making someone afraid by threatening.

pananadyâ (pa-na-nad-yâ), n. act of doing something against someone intentionally. Syn. *paninikís.*

pananaganà (pa-na-na-ga-nà), n. 1. abundance or plentifulness, as of crops or harvests. 2. enjoyment of wealth and abundance. Syn. *pagtatamasa ng kayamanan at kasaganaan.*

pananaghóy (pa-na-nag-hóy), n. act of wailing or moaning, as in pain or suffering. Also, *pagtaghóy.* Syn. *pagdaíng.*

pananagimpán (pa-na-na-gim-pán), n. (poetic form of **pananaginip**) act of dreaming.

pananaginip (pa-na-na-gi-nip), n. act or instance of dreaming. Syn. *pangangarap.*

pananagót (pa-na-na-gót), n. act or habit of replying rudely or impertinently; answering or talking back. Syn. *pagsagút-sagót.* 2. act of assuming responsibility for something. 3. act of serving or acting as a guarantor for someone.

pananahimik (pa-na-na-hi-mik), n. 1. act of keeping still or quiet. Syn. *pagwawaláng-kibô o pagwawaláng-imík.* 2. act of resting, as from active participation in; retirement. Syn. *pamamahingá, pagreretiro.*

pananaíg (pa-na-na-íg), n. predominance; preponderance; prevalence. Syn. *pangingibabaw, pananatili, paghaharì.*

pananalangin (pa-na-na-la-ngin), n. act of praying. Syn. *pagdarasál.*

pananalapî (pa-na-na-la-pî), n. 1. finance, as in: Kagawarán ng Pananalapî, Department of Finance. 2. funds; financial status, as of a city or municipality. Syn. *pondo.* 3. currency; the money in circulation in a country. Syn. *kuwarta o salaping umiiral.*

pananalát (pa-na-na-lát), n. 1. lack of supply; scarcity. Syn. *pagkukulang o kakulangán (sa mga pángunahíng kailangan).* 2. financial crisis; depression. Syn. *paghihirap sa salapî, depresyón.*

pananalaytáy (pa-na-na-lay-táy), n. 1. smooth capillary flow, as of blood in the veins and arteries. Cf. *panunulay.* 2. act of passing along the side or edge of. Syn. *pananaluntón, pamamaybáy.*

pananaliksík (pa-na-na-lik-sík), n. 1. act or manner of searching very well for something. Syn. *masusing paghahanáp.* 2. research; act or manner of doing research. Also, *pagsasaliksík.*

pananalig (pa-na-na-lig), n. 1. trust; confidence; faith. Syn. *tiwalà, pagtitiwalà, kompiyansa.* 2. belief. Syn. *paniwalà, paniniwalà.*

pananalinghagà (pa-na-na-ling-ha-gà), n. 1. use of figures of speech or allegory. 2. metaphor. Syn. *metápora.*

pananalitâ (pa-na-na-li-tâ), n. 1. act, manner or style of speaking; diction; discourse. Also, *pagsasalitâ.* 2. speech, as in: bahagi ng pananalitâ, part of speech. See **panalitâ.**

pananámbitan (pa-na-nám-bi-tan), n. act of making a humble request or supplication, esp. in prayers. Syn. *pagmamakaawà, pagsamò, pagsusumamò.*

pananamláy (pa-na-nam-láy), n. 1. a becoming cool or waning of interest. Syn. *panlalamíg ng loób, pagkawalâ ng gana.* 2. feeling of debility; lassitude or langour. Syn. *panlalambót o panghihinà ng katawán.* 3. a becoming dull, as of sales in the market. Syn. *pagtumal ng kalakal, paghinà ng benta o pagbibilí.*

pananámpalasan (pa-na-nám-pa-la-san), n. act, manner, or habit of destroying things; destruction. Syn. *paninirà, pagwawasák.* 2. act of wasting money and other things. Syn. *paglustáy, paglulustáy; pag-aksayá, pag-aaksayá.*

pananámpalataya (pa-na-nám-pa-la-ta-ya), n. belief and faith in God; worship. Syn.

paniniwalà, pagsambá.

pananangan (pa-na-na-ngan), n. 1. act of holding tightly on something to prevent self from falling, sliding, etc. Syn. *pangangapit.* 2. (*Fig.*) act of depending on something for aid or authority or for basis of one's action. Syn. *panghahawakan.* 3. firm stand or strong argument. Syn. *paninindigan.*

pananangis (pa-na-na-ngis), n. act of weeping continuously.

pananaog (pa-na-na-og), n. 1. act or time of getting down the stairs or from the house. Also, *pagpanaog.* 2. act of getting down or alighting, as from a vehicle. Syn. *paglunsád, pag-ibís.* 3. act of getting down from a tree. Syn. *pagbabâ.* 4. release, as of a court decision or order.

pananariwà (pa-na-na-ri-wà), n. 1. a refreshing or being refreshed, as of plants after being watered or after a rain. 2. improvement, as of one's health. Syn. *paglusóg o pagbuti ng katawán.*

pananata (pa-na-na-ta), n. 1. act of making a vow or religious devotion. 2. solemn promise not to do something. Syn. *matapát o taimtím na pangakò; pagsumpâ, panunumpâ.*

pananatili (pa-na-na-ti-li), n. 1. continuous existence. Syn. *pagpapatuloy na pag-iral.* 2. prevalence. Syn. *pananaíg.* 3. stay; time spent in place. Syn. *pagtirá, paninirahan, pagtigil.*

pananáw (pa-na-náw), n. 1. sight; eyesight; vision. Syn. *paningín.* 2. mental attitude; standpoint; viewpoint; point of view. Syn. *paninindigan.*

panandâ (pa-nan-dâ), n. & adj. referring to something used as a marker or sign to indicate a place. 2. said of a person's memory, as in: *Mahinà ang kanyáng panandâ.* He has a poor memory. 3. (specifically) that which refers to bookmarks, tablets, or gravestone, etc.

panandalî (pa-nan-da-lî), adj. brief; short or of short duration.

pananím (pa-na-ním), I. n. & adj. referring to seeds or seedlings used for propagation or for planting. Also, *pantaním.*
—II. n. crop; food plants. Syn. *halaman.*

pananóng (pa-na-nóng), I. n. 1. an interrogation mark or sign (?). 2. an interrogative; word, construction, or element that asks a question. 3. formal questions or set of questions used in tests or examinations. Syn. *mga katanungan.*
—II. adj. that which refers to things used in asking questions, esp. those commonly asked in tests or examinations.

panantô (pa-nan-tô), var. **pantantô,** n. & adj. referring to something that a person uses in order to understand the problem of others. Syn. *pang-unawà.*

pananggí (pa-nang-gí), n. & adj. referring to a word, term, or phrase used in denying or rejecting something.

pananghalian (pa-nang-ha-li-an), n. 1. act or time of eating one's lunch. Also, *pananánghalian.* 2. food for lunch.

panangì (pa-na-ngì) var. **pantangì,** adj. 1. (*Gram.*) proper, as in: *pangngalang panangì,* proper noun. 2. for special use or occasion.

panangis (pa-na-ngis), var. **pananangis,** n. act of weeping or crying continuously.

panao (pa-na-o), var. **pantao,** adj. (*Gram.*) personal, as in: *panghalíp panao,* personal pronoun.

panaog (pa-na-og), n. 1. act or time of going downstairs or down a ladder. Syn. *pagbabâ, paglapág.* 2. act of alighting from a vehicle. Syn. *paglunsád, pag-ibis.* 2. discharge of the menses, or the period when this occurs.

panaón (pa-na-ón), I. n. coincidence; chance happening or occurrence. Syn. *di-inaasahang pagkakásabáy o pangyayari.*
—II. adj. simultaneous; at the same time; happening or occurring at the same time. Syn. *sabáy, magkasabáy.*

panapos (pa-na-pos), var. **pantapos,** n. & adj. said of something said or done to end or bring to end a program, etc. Syn. *pangwakás.*

panará (pa-na-rá), var. **pansará,** n. & adj. 1. referring to a device used for locking doors, windows, drawers, etc., as a key, latch, or the like. Syn. *pansusì, panusì, pantrangka, pang-aldaba.* 2. referring to shutters, movable doors, and the like used to close windows, doorways, etc.

panarili (pa-na-ri-li), var. **pansarili**, *adj*. for one's own use; personal.

panata (pa-na-ta), *n*. vow; solemn promise or devotion. Syn. *matapát o taimtím na pangakò, sumpâ.*

panatag (pa-na-tag), I. *adj*. 1. tranquil; calm; serene; quiet; peaceful. Syn. *payapà, mapayapà; tiwasáy, matiwasáy; tahimik, matahimik.* 2. secure; free from fear, doubt, or anxiety. Syn. *ligtás, walâ nang takot o pag-aalinlangan.*

panatang-makabayan (pa-na-tang + ma-ka-ba-yan), *n*. loyalty pledge to one's country; patriotic pledge of loyalty to one's nation. Also, *panatang makabayan.*

panátikó (pa-ná-ti-kó), I. *adj*. (Sp. *fanatico*) fanatic; fanatical; zealous beyond reason. Syn. *labis na mapániwalaín.*
—II. *n*. a fanatical person; fanatic.

panatili (pa-na-ti-li), var. **pananatili**, *n*. continuous stay; permanence in a certain state or condition; prevalence. Syn. *pamamalagì, patulóy na kalagayan o pag-iral.*

panatismo (pa-na-tis-mo), *n*. (Sp. *fanatismo*) fanaticism; unrealistic enthusiasm or zeal.

panauhan (pa-na-u-han), *n*. 1. (*Gram.*) person; as in: *unang panauhan*, first person. 2. (*Theat.*) character; dramatis personae, as in *pángunahíng panauhan sa drama*, principal character in the play (drama).

panauhin (pa-na-u-hin), I. *n*. visitor; guest; caller. Syn. *bisita, dalaw.* 2. an invited guest, as a speaker.
—II. *adj*. guest; invited; performing by invitation, as in: *panauhing artista*, guest artist.

panaw (pa-naw), var. **pagpanaw**, *n*. 1. sudden disappearance. Syn. *bigláng pagkawalâ, pagkaparam, paglalahò.* 2. departure. Syn. *alís, pag-alís; yao, pagyao.* 3. lost of one's life; death. Syn. *pagkamatáy, pagyao, pagsakabiláng-buhay.*

panawain (pa-na-wa-in), *v*. to gratify with more than enough so as to weary or disgust; satiate; surfeit. Syn. *papágsawain.*

panawan (pa-na-wan), *v*. 1. to lose or be deprived of (one's life). Syn. *mawalán (ng buhay).* 2. to be left alone in solitude, as by the death of a loved one. Syn. *maulila, ulilahin.*

panawíd-buhay (pa-na-wíd + bu-hay), var. **pantawíd-buhay**, *n. & adj.* said of anything eaten by a person to survive in time of crisis or depression. Syn. *pangagdóng-buhay.*

panáy (pa-náy), *adj*. 1. all; only, as in: *panáy na salitâ, waláng gawâ*, all (only) words, without action or deed. 2. all; without exception, as in: *Panáy na Pilipino and dumaló.* Those who attended are all Filipinos. 2. unmixed; undiluted; pure; of only one kind, as in: *panáy na asukal*, pure sugar. Syn. *puro, waláng-halò.* 4. continuous; without stop or letup; without ceasing, as in: *Panáy ang ulán kagabí.* The rain last night was continuous. Syn. *waláng-tigil, waláng-hintô, tulúy-tulóy.* 5. full; fully covered with; filled up, as in *Panáy langgám ang asukal.* The sugar is full of ants.

panayám (pa-na-yám), *n*. 1. a prepared talk on a certain subject; lecture, as in: *bumasa ng panayám*, to read a lecture. 2. a meeting of two people to talk about something important; interview. Also, *pagpapanayám.* 3. a meeting to discuss a particular subject; conference. Syn. *komperénsiyá, pulong, pagpupulong.*

pánayam (pá-na-yam), *adj*. continuous; going on without interruption or break. Syn. *waláng-likát, waláng-hintô, tulúy-tulóy.*

pandák (pan-dák), *adj*. 1. short of stature; lacking in height; opposed to *matangkád.* 2. (*Slang*) insufficient; of little amount. Syn. *kulang, kákauntî.* 3. (*Slang*) matchless; incomparable to. Syn. *waláng-laban, sapal (colloq.)*

pandakót (pan-da-kót), *n. & adj.* referring to a shovel-like receptacle or pan used for collecting dust, rubbish, etc., as a dustpan.

pandadagit (pan-da-da-git), var. **pandaragit**, *n*. act of swooping and seizing a victim or victims, as by a bird of prey; snatching while in flight.

pandadahás (pan-da-da-hás), var. **pandarahás**, *n*. 1. use of force or violence against another. Syn. *paggamit ng lakás o puwersa sa kapwà.* 2. act of committing a crime of force against a woman or girl;

rape. Syn. *panggagahasà (sa babae)*.

pandadalâ (pan-da-da-lâ), *n.* act of
discouraging, scaring off someone from
doing something again by punishing him.

pandadayuhan (pan-da-da-yu-han), var.
pandarayuhan, *n.* immigration;
emigration. Syn. *pangingibáng-bansâ*,
pangingibáng-bayan.

pandaigdíg (pan-da-ig-díg), *adj.* 1.
international; between or among nations.
Syn. *pangmundo*. 2. worldwide. Syn.
laganap sa buóng mundo.

pandalawá (pan-da-la-wá), *adj.* 1. in second
place or position. Also, *pangalawá*,
ikalawá. 2. for two; for the use of two. Syn.
pará sa dalawá.

pandamá (pan-da-má), *n.* sense of touch or
feeling. See **pandamdám**.

pandamdám (pan-dam-dám), *n.* 1. (*Gram.*)
interjection. exclamation. Syn. *bulalás*. 2.
sense of touch or feeling. Syn. *pakiramdám*, *pandamá*.

pandán (pan-dán), *n.* (*Bot.*) a species of
screwpine (*Pandanus odoratissimus Linn.*),
the leaves of which are much used in the
manufacture of mats, baskets, bags, etc.

pandangál (pan-da-ngál), *adj.* honorary, as
in: *pangulong pandangál*, honorary
president.

pandarambóng (pan-da-ram-bóng), *n.* act of
plundering; pillage; robbery; piracy. Syn.
pagnanakaw, panloloób.

pandaskól (pan-das-kól), var. **pandaskúl**, *n.*
& adj. referring to something intended for
everyday use, as working clothes. Cf.
pantrabaho.

pandáw (pan-dáw), *n.* 1. act or time of
visiting a trap, snare, fish coral, or the like
to see if there is a catch. 2. a short,
unexpected visit by a man to his
paramour. Syn. *sandalíng pagdalaw*.

pandáy (pan-dáy), *n.* 1. smith; metalworker;
blacksmith. 2. act of making or shaping
metal objects, like tools and the like, by
hammering while the metal is still red-hot
and soft. 3. (by extension) act of training
someone very well. Syn. *pagsanay na mabuti*.

pandesál (pan-de-sál), var. **pandisál**, *n.* (*Sp.*
pan de sal) the common salt bread; French
bread.

pandewang (pan-de-wang), var.
pamandewang, *n. &.* *adj.* referring to
something used for wiping the anus after
moving the bowels, as toilet paper. Syn.
pang-iwang.

pandidiri (pan-di-di-ri), *n.* extreme dislike
or abhorrence, esp. for things dirty.

pandilatan (pan-di-la-tan), *v.* to look at
someone with wide-open, angry eyes. Syn.
tingnán nang matalím (padilát).

pandiníg (pan-di-níg), var. **pandingíg**, *n.*
hearing; sense of hearing.

pandiwà (pan-di-wà), I. *n.* (*Gram.*) verb.
Syn. *berbo*.
—II. *adj.* for the brain or mind. Syn. *pang-
isip, pangkaisipán, pang-utak*.

pandiwang kátawanín, intransitive verb.
Syn. *berbo intransitibo*.

pandiwang palipát, transitive verb. Syn.
berbo transitibo.

pandiwang pangatníg, linking verb;
copulative verb. Syn. *berbo kopulatibo*.

pandiwarì (pan-di-wa-rì), *n.* (*Gram.*)
participle; verbal adjective. Syn. *pang-
uring makadiwà*.

pandiwaring pangngalan, verbal noun.

pandiwaring pang-urì, verbal adjective.

pandóng (pan-dóng), *n.* head covering,
usually a piece of cloth, paper, or the like
for protection against the heat of the sun,
from rain, etc. Syn. *kulubóng, talukbóng,
kubóng*.

panduduhagi (pan-du-du-ha-gi), var.
panduruhagi, *n.* act of oppressing people;
oppression. Syn. *pang-aapí, panghahamak*.

pandudurò (pan-du-du-rò), *n.* 1. act or habit
of pricking others with or as with a pin.
Syn. *panunusok, panunundós, panunundót*.
2. (*Colloq.*) act of boasting in order to
impress.

pandudustâ (pan-du-dus-tâ), var.
pandurustâ, *n.* act of treating others
ignominiously. Syn. *panghahamak, pang-
aalipustâ*.

pandurukot (pan-du-ru-kot), var.
pandudukót, *n.* 1. the act or work of a
pickpocket. 2. kidnapping.

panhík (pan-hík), *n.* 1. act of going upstairs.
Syn. *pag-akyát sa bahay*. 2. time to go
upstairs. Syn. *oras ng akyát*. 3. a coming

in, as of income from business. Syn.
pagkita (ng kuwarta), akyát (ng kuwarta).
3. rise or ascent, as of supply of water in
the house. Syn. *akyát, sampá*.

panhík-panaog (pan-hík + pa-na-og), *adj.*
said of a person who goes up and down
the stairs repeatedly or continuously. Syn.
akyát-manaog, akyát-panaog.

panibago (pa-ni-ba-go), I. *n.* a remaking or
renewing; making anew. Syn. *pag-ulit, pag-
uulit*.
—II. *adj.* 1. new; not the same as before;
renewed, as in: *panibagong pagsisikap*,
renewed effort. Syn. *bago, mulî*. 2.
another; different, as in: *panibagong
simulâ*, another start.
—III. *adv.* again; anew, as in: *gawíng
panibago*, to make anew.

panibukas (pa-ni-bu-kas), *n.* 1.
postponement of something for the next
day. Syn. *pagpapabukas*. 2. the next day;
tomorrow, as in: *Maghintáy tayo ng
panibukas*. Let's wait for the next day.

panibulos (pa-ni-bu-los), *n.* 1. complete
trust and confidence. Syn. *lubós na
pagtitiwalà o kumpiyansa*. 2. unrestrained
freedom of activity; complete
abandonment to. Syn. *pagkápasubò,
pagkápalulóng*. 3. a new serving of food
during meals.

panikalâ (pa-ni-ka-lâ), *n.* an ironical
expression or talk; irony.

panikbí (pa-nik-bí), *n.* upper canine tooth;
eyetooth. Syn. *pangito*.

panikì (pa-ni-kì; pá-ni-kì), *n.* (Zool.) a kind
of large fruit bat. Cf. *báyakan, kabág,
kabág-kabág*.

panikluhód (pa-nik-lu-hód), *n.* 1.
supplication; entreaty; humble request,
petition, or prayer. Syn. *pakiusap,
pamanhík*. 2. a falling on one's bended
knees, as in begging for pardon. Syn.
pagmamakaawà.

panig (pa-nig), *n.* 1. a specific place in an
area; side; part. Syn. *dako, lugár, bandá,
bahagi, parte*. 2. either of the two surfaces
of a thing. Syn. *mukhâ*. 3. either one of
the two sides or parties in a contest,
conflict, etc. 4. the position, stand, or
attitude of one opposing another. Syn.

paninindigan. 5. a taking side with
someone in a quarrel, debate, etc. Syn.
kampí, pagkampí.

panigan (pa-ni-gan), *v.* to take sides with.
Syn. *kampihán*.

panihalà (pa-ni-ha-là), *n.* 1. management or
disposition. Syn. *pamamahalà*. 2.
responsibility. Syn. *pananagutan*. 3.
proposal; suggestion. Syn. *panukalà,
mungkahì*.

paniíl (pa-ni-íl), var. **pansiíl**, *n. & adj.*
referring to something that is used or
made to cause fire. Syn. *panunog*.

panilaw (pa-ni-law), var. **pansilaw**, *n. & adj.*
1. said of a very bright light used to dazzle
or dim the vision of someone. 2. referring
to something that a person uses to
fascinate or attract someone, as costly
jewelry, etc.

panimbangán (pa-nim-ba-ngán), *v.* 1. to try
to get along with or be compatible with.
Syn. *pakibagayan*. 2. to balance oneself on.

panimdím (pa-nim-dím), *n.* 1. repressed ill-
feeling or resentment. Syn. *samâ ng loób,
hinanakít, pagdaramdám*. 2. sorrow;
sadness; grief. Syn. *lungkót, dalamhatì*. 3.
misgivings that bother someone's mind.
Syn. *agam-agam, balisa, bagabag, balino,
pangambá*.

panimulâ (pa-ni-mu-lâ), I. *adj.* preliminary;
leading to something more important.
Syn. *páuná, pamáuná*. 2. introductory;
opening, as in: *panimuláng pagbibilí*,
opening sale.
—II. *n.* start; beginning, as in: *Itó'y
panimulâ lamang*. This is only the start
(beginning). Syn. *umpisá*.

paninda (pa-nin-da; pa-nin-dá), I. *n.* things
for sale, esp. those displayed in stores and
markets; goods or merchandise for sale.
Syn. *kalakal (sa tindahan o palengke)*.
—II. *adj.* for sale; intended for selling.

paninibago (pa-ni-ni-ba-go), *n.* an affected
change of feeling brought about by one's
new experience in another place, work,
etc.; feeling of unfamiliarity or strangeness
about something new. Syn. *pangingibá*.

paninibughô (pa-ni-ni-bug-hô), *n.* jealousy
or an instance of this. Syn. *selos,
pagseselos*.

paninikíl (pa-ni-ni-kíl), n. 1. act or instance of oppressing others; any oppressive act, esp. of someone in authority. Syn. *pangaapí*. 2. act of putting others in a tight position. Syn. *panggigipít*.

paninikíp (pa-ni-ni-kíp), n. 1. feeling of tightness, as in one's breast. 2. a becoming tight or smaller in reference to a certain size, as of shoes, etc. Syn. *pagliít, pagkipot*.

paninikís (pa-ni-ni-kís), n. act or instance of provoking another or others intentionally, or of doing something against another or others without provocation. Syn. *pananadyâ*.

paninikluhód (pa-ni-nik-lu-hód), n. 1. a humble, earnest request; supplication. Syn. *pagmamakaawà, pagmamakaamò*. 2. a falling on one's knees, as in begging for pardon. Syn. *paglulumuhód*.

paniniktík (pa-ni-nik-tík), n. spying; the work of a detective, spy, or secret agent. Syn. *lihim na pagmamanmán o panunubok*.

paninigíd (pa-ni-ni-gíd), n. penetrating effect of the extreme coldness of weather or of smarting pain.

paninindák (pa-ni-nin-dák), n. terrorizing; causing another or others to be affected with sudden fear. Syn. *pananakot*.

paniningaláng-pugad (pa-ni-ni-nga-láng + pu-gad), n. the act or period during which a teenage boy starts courting girls.

paniningkád (pa-ni-ning-kád), n. state of brightness in color.

paniningíl (pa-ni-ni-ngíl), n. act of collecting payments for debt or loan. Syn. *pangongobra*.

paniniphayò (pa-ni-nip-ha-yò), n. act of disappointing another or others, as by not giving what is requested. Syn. *pambibigô, panghihiyâ* (*colloq.*).

paninirà (pa-ni-ni-rà), n. 1. act or process of destroying things; destruction; vandalism. Syn. *bandalismo*. 2. act of making slanderous statement against another or others; defamation; malefaction. Also, *paninirang-puri*.

paniniwalà (pa-ni-ni-wa-là), n. 1. belief. Also, *paniwalà*. 2. faith; trust; confidence. Syn. *tiwalà, pagtitiwalà*.

paningkáw (pa-ning-káw), n. & adj. 1.

referring to implements used for harnessing beasts of burden. 2. referring to an animal used as a beast of burden. Cf. *pantrabaho*.

paningín (pa-ni-ngín), n. 1. eyes. Syn. *(mga) matá*. 2. vision; sight, as in: *mawalán ng paningín*, to lose one's sight. 3. (*Colloq.*) opinion; personal view; viewpoint. Syn. *palagáy, kurò, kuru-kurò*.

panipì (pa-ni-pì), I. n. (*Gram.*) quotation marks.
—II. n. & adj. referring to a device or machine used for copying or making duplicate copies of. Syn. *pangopya*.

panís (pa-nís), adj. 1. stale; sourish; spoiled, referring to cooked food. Syn. *sirâ, bulók*. 2. (*Colloq.*) slightly demented or crazy. Syn. *medyú-medyó*.

panit (pa-nit), n. 1. act of shaving the crown of the head. Syn. *panot, pagpanot*. 2. part of the head left bare by shaving; tonsure. Syn. *anit, panot, satsát*. 3. an excoriating or being excoriated. Syn. *paglapnós, pagkalapnós, pagkapaknít*. 4. an excoriated spot on the surface of the body; abrasion. Syn. *paknít, lapnós*.

panitik (pa-ni-tik), I. n. 1. (*Lit.*) pen. Syn. *panulat*. 2. ability to write; literary ability. Syn. *kakayahán sa pagsusulát, panulat*.
—II. adj. used for literary writing, said of a pen. Syn. *panulat, pansulat*.

pánitikán (pá-ni-ti-kán), n. literature. Syn. *literatura*.

paniwalà (pa-ni-wa-là), n. 1. belief. Also, *paniniwalà*. 2. spiritual belief. Syn. *sampalataya, pananampalataya*. 3. trust; confidence; faith. Syn. *tiwalà, pagtitiwalà*. 4. personal opinion. Syn. *sariling palagáy o kuru-kurò*.

panlabás (pan-la-bás), adj. 1. external; outer; outside; exterior, as in: *gandáng panlabás*, external beauty. 2. for external or outer use, as clothes. 3. having to do with foreign countries or international affairs; foreign; external, as in: *pálitang panlabás*, foreign exchange. 4. (*Theat.*) for or suitable for showing. Also, *pampalabás*. Syn. *pananghál, pantanghál*.

panlahát (pan-la-hát), adj. of or for all; for everybody; general, as in: *sa kabutihang* *panlahát*, for the good of all.

panlahì (pan-la-hì), *adj.* of or characteristic of a race or ethnic group; racial. Syn. *panlipì*.

panlalait (pan-la-la-it), *n.* act of vilifying; vilification. Syn. *pang-aalimurà, pang-aalipustâ*.

panlalamáng (pan-la-la-máng), *n.* act or instance of taking advantage of another or others. Syn. *pagsasamantalá sa kapwà*.

panlalamíg (pan-la-la-míg), *n.* 1. feeling of cold in one's body. 2. loss of interest or enthusiasm. Syn. *pagkawalâ ng gana o siglâ*.

panlalangís (pan-la-la-ngís), *n. (Fig.)* act of ingratiating oneself (to someone) by flattery or by being servile. Also, *paglalangís*. Syn. *pagmamapurí*.

panlalapastangan (pan-la-la-pas-ta-ngan), *n.* act of committing irreverence or blasphemy. Syn. *pagwawaláng-galang, pagwawaláng-pítagan*.

panlapì (pan-la-pì), I. *n.* affix. Syn. *apiho*.
—II. *adj.* said of a syllable or word used as an affix.

panlibáng (pan-li-báng), *n. & adj.* referring to something used to amuse or entertain. Syn. *pang-alíw*. 2. said of a trick or anything used to distract the attention of another or others. Syn. *panlimang, panghirá*.

panlilíít (pan-li-li-íit), *n.* a becoming small; decrease in size, volume, or amount. Syn. *paglinggít*. 2. feeling of embarrassment due to certain situation, like committing errors or of having inferiority complex.

panlililo (pan-li-li-lo), *n.* any act of disloyalty or unfaithfulness. Syn. *pagtataksíl, pagtatraidór, pagsusukáb*.

panlilisik (pan-li-li-sik), *n.* (with *ng matá*) a fierce or angry stare. Syn. *pandidilat ng (mga) matá sa galit*.

panlipunan (pan-li-pu-nan; -nán), *adj.* social; of, about, or pertaining to society. Syn. *sa, ng, o ukol sa lipunán*.

panlulumó (pan-lu-lu-mó), *n.* fact or state of being weak and depressed due to disappointment or frustration. Syn. *panlalambót ng katawán*.

panlunán (pan-lu-nán), *adj.* (Gram.) designating or of a case expressing location or place; locative.

panlunsád (pan-lun-sád), *n. & adj.* referring to a device used for unloading cargoes. Syn. *pandiskarga*. 2. referring to things used or fit for use in inaugurating or launching something. Syn. *pampasinayà, pambukás, pansimulâ*.

panlupaypayán (pan-lu-pay-pa-yán), *v.* to feel weak and depressed; lose spirit or enthusiasm due to disappointment or frustration. Cf. *panlumúhán*.

panonoód (pa-no-no-ód), *n.* act of watching or seeing a show, program, etc. for enjoyment or entertainment.

panót (pa-nót), *adj.* bald; baldheaded. Syn. *kalbo*.

pansamantalá (pan-sa-man-ta-lá), I. *adj.* temporary.
—II. *adv.* temporarily.

pansangkapuluan (pan-sang-ka-pu-lu-an), *adj.* for the entire archipelago.

pansangkatauhan (pan-sang-ka-ta-u-han), *adj.* for the whole humanity.

pansimunò (pan-si-mu-nò), *adj* .(Gram.) nominative; subjective.

pansín (pan-sín), *n.* 1. attention; notice. 2. observation. Syn. *pagkákita, pagkápuná*. 3. criticism; critical view; comment; appraisal. Syn. *puná*.

pansining (pan-si-ning), *adj.* done for artistic effect; for the sake of arts.

pansít (pan-sít), *n.* (Ch.) a general term for several kinds of Chinese dish of noodles, some of which are the following: *pansít-bihon, pansít-kantón, pansít-kiyamlo, pansít-gisado, pansít-langláng, pansít-luglóg, pansít-malabón, pansít-miki, pansít-molo, pansít-palabok, pansít-sútanghón*.

pansól (pan-sól), *n.* 1. source of a stream; spring. Syn. *bukál*. 2. (P-) name of a well-known hot spring in Barrio Pansol near Los Baños, Laguna.

pantál (pan-tál), *n.* 1. a slightly swollen part of the skin as that caused by insect bite. 2. a wale, welt, or wheal caused by whipping or lashing. Syn. *latay, banil*.

pantalán (pan-ta-lán), *n.* wharf; dock; pier. Syn. *daungán, muwelye, piyér*.

pantalón (pan-ta-lón), *n.* (Sp.) trousers. Syn. *salawál*.

pantánghalan

panumbát

pantánghalan (pan-táng-ha-lan), n. & adj. referring to a drama or play written for the stage. Syn. pandúlaan.

pantás (pan-tás), I. n. wise man; sage; savant. Syn. pahám, taong pahám.
—II. adj. erudite; learned; scholarly. Syn. pahám, dalubhasà.

pantás-aghám (pan-tás + ag-hám), n. scientist. Syn. dalúb-aghám, siyentípikó.

pantástikó (pan-tás-ti-kó), adj. fantastic; odd; unreal. Syn. kakatwâ, di-kapaní-paniwalà.

pantás-wikà (pan-tás + wikà), n. linguist; philologist. Syn. dalubwikà, lingguwista.

pantáy (pan-táy), adj. 1. of or having the same length; of equal length. Syn. magkasinghabà. 2. of or having the same height; of equal height. Syn. magkasintaás. 3. of the same rank; with or having the same or equal rank. Syn. magkaranggo; pareho ng ranggo o antás. 4. level; flat. Syn. patag.

pantáy-balikat (pan-táy + ba-li-kat), I. adj. as high or as tall as the height of one's shoulder. Syn. sintaás o kasintaás ng balikat.
—II. n. a height as high as one's shoulder.

pantáy-kawayan (pan-táy + ka-wa-yan), adj. as high as a standing bamboo. Syn. sintaás o kasintaás ng kawayan.

pantáy-paá (pan-táy + pa-á), adj. (Fig.) dead, referring to a person. Syn. patáy (na); walâ nang hiningá.

pantáy-pantáy (pan-táy + pan-táy), adj. 1. all of the same length. Syn. magkakapareho ng habà, pare-pareho ng habà. 2. all of the same height. Syn. magkakapareho ng taás; magkakasintaás. 3. equa:, referring to a number of persons or things. Syn. pare-pareho, magkakapareho.

pantíg (pan-tíg), n. (Gram.) syllable. Syn. sílabá.

pantíng (pan-tíng), n. a blushing or flushing with or as with anger or rage. Syn. sikláb ng galit. 2. a hard flip or snap on the ear. Syn. malakás na pitík sa taingá.

pantitík (pan-ti-tík), n. & adj. 1. said of a pen, brush, etc. used for lettering. Syn. panletra. 2. said of a literary pen. Syn. panulat.

pantiyón (pan-ti-yón), n. (Sp. panteon)

cemetery. Syn. sementeryo, kamposanto, líbingan.

pantóg (pan-tóg), n. (Anat.) bladder; urinary bladder.

pantukoy (pan-tu-koy), n. (Gram.) article.

panubalì (pa-nu-ba-lì), n. & adj. referring to a word or words that express adversative correlations, as ngunì, dátapwâ, subalì, etc.

panubíg (pa-nu-bíg), var. panunubíg, n. urination; time to urinate. Syn. pag-ihì, oras ng pag-ihì.

panukà (pa-nu-kà), var. pansukà, n. & adj. referring to vinegar used as condiment or preservative, as green mangoes, tamarind, etc., used as condiment in cooking sinigáng. Syn. paasim, pampaasim.

panukalà (pa-nu-ka-là), n. 1. plan. Syn. balak, plano. 2. proposal; proposition; suggestion. Syn. mungkahì, suhestiyón. 3. motion, as one presented in a meeting. Syn. mungkahì.

panukalang-batás (pa-nu-ka-lang + ba-tás), n. (Legis.) draft of a proposed law to be presented for approval by a legislative body; bill.

panudyó (pa-nud-yó), var. pantudyó, n. & adj. referring to a remark or remarks that a person often uses in joking or teasing another or others. Syn. panuksó, pantuksó, pambirò.

pánulaan (pá-nu-la-an), n. the art of writing poems; poetry.

panulat (pa-nu-lat), n. & adj. 1. referring to several devices for writing, as a pen, pencil, fountain pen, etc. Syn. pansulat. 2. referring to a literary writer's style or his ability to write.

pánuldikan (pá-nul-di-kan), n. the system of accentuation used in a certain language. Also, called palátuldikan.

panulukan (pa-nu-lu-kan), n. corner or intersection, as of two streets. Syn. kanto.

panumbalik (pa-num-ba-lik), var. panunumbalik, n. 1. return or restoration to a former place, condition, status, etc. Syn. pananaulì. 2. regain or recovery, as of one's good health.

panumbát (pa-num-bát), n. & adj. referring to something that a person can use to accuse another of being ungrateful. Syn. *pansuwát, panuwát.*

panumpâ (pa-num-pâ), n. & adj. referring to words or statement that a person uses in swearing or taking an oath.

panuntán (pa-nun-tán), v. to follow as an example; be guided by. Also, *panuntunán.*

panunubà (pa-nu-nu-bà), n. the act or instance of swindling. Syn. *pandarayà.*

panunubok (pa-nu-nu-bok), n. act or manner of spying on someone; secret observation of what another or others are doing. Syn. *lihim na pagmamanmán.*

panunuklás (pa-nu-nuk-lás), n. devotion of one's time and efforts to discover new things or ideas.

panunuksó (pa-nu-nuk-só), n. 1. the act or habit of making fun with others by joking or teasing. Syn. *pambibirò, panunudyó.* 2. act of causing someone to fall into temptation. Cf. *panunulsól, panghihibò, pang-uupat.*

panunuligsâ (pa-nu-nu-lig-sâ), n. act of criticizing or attacking another or others publicly; verbal attack or criticism. Syn. *pang-aatake, pagmumurá.*

panunulót (pa-nu-nu-lót), n. act of making a joke with someone by poking him with something through a hole or space between the slats of the floor. 2. act of ingratiating or bringing oneself into someone's favor or good graces by means of intrigue. Syn. *pagpapasamà sa kapwà upang mapabutí ang sarili.*

panunuluyan (pa-nu-nu-lu-yan), n. temporary sojourn or stay in someone's place.

panunumbalik (pa-nu-nu-num-ba-lik), n. return or restoration to the former place, condition, status, etc. Syn. *pananag-ulì, pananaulì.*

panunumbát (pa-nu-num-bát), n. act of accusing another of being ungrateful. Syn. *panunuwát.*

panunuót (pa-nu-nu-ót), n. a piercing or penetrating effect, as of cold. Syn. *paninigíd, pàgsigíd.*

panunupil (pa-nu-nu-pil), n. act of domineering; domination. Syn. *panduduminá, paghaharí-harian.*

panunurì (pa-nu-nu-rì), n. 1. the act, art, or responsibility of a critic. 2. critical analysis made by a critic; criticism, as in: *panunuring pampánitikán,* literary criticism.

panunuyâ (pa-nu-nu-yâ), n. act of making sarcastic remarks against others; mockery. 2. any sarcastic remark directed against someone. Syn. *pangungutyâ, pang-uuyám.*

panunuyò (pa-nu-nu-yò), n. 1. act of bringing oneself into someone's good graces by doing him favors; ingratiation. Syn. *pagmamapurí, pagmamabutí.* 2. act of trying to win the love or affection of a girl by giving gifts and doing favors.

panuring (pa-nu-ring), 1. n. (Gram.) modifier.
—II. var, **panturing,** n. & adj. referring to a prepared or specific answer to a question or a riddle. Syn. *panagót, pansagót.*

panustós (pa-nus-tós), var. **pantustós,** n. & adj. 1. referring to supply or provisions for future need or continuous use. Cf. *panlaan.* 2. said of fund to finance or support someone's studies or livelihood. Syn. *panustento.*

panuto (pa-nu-to), n. & adj. 1.referring to a moral or spiritual guide. Syn. *patnubay, pamatnubay.* 2. said of an indicator or pointer, as an arrow sign. Syn. *panurò, panturò.*

panutsá (pa-nut-sá), n. (Sp. Mex. *panocha*) 1. a cake of brown sugar moulded in or as in a half coconut shell. 2. a small flat cake of molasses with peanuts.

panyô (pan-yô), n. (Sp. *paño*) 1. handkerchief. 2. scarf or kerchief for the head. Syn. *bupanda, bandana.*

pang-, pref. used in variation with **pam-** and **pan-,** before words beginning with the vowels *a, e, i, o, and u,* and some consonants like *k, g, h, m, n, ng, w, and y,* to form: (1) nouns denoting instruments, tools, utensils, etc., as in: *pang-ahit, pang-ipit, panghisò, pangkahig, panggamót,* etc. (2) nouns expressing a habit or habitual act, profession, or the like, before words with the initial syllable reduplicated, as in: *pang-aagaw,* *panggagamót, pangwawasák,* etc. (3) adjectives meaning "used or utilized for a certain purpose," as in: *pang-ani, pang-umaga, panggawâ, pang-araw, pangnayon, pangmádalian,* etc.

pang (fr. *pa + ng*) *adv.* (used usually with *walâ*) yet, as in: *walâ pang asawa,* without a spouse yet.

pangá (pa-ngá), *n.* 1. jaw. 2. jawbone.

pang-aabâ (pang-a-a-bâ), *n.* a despising or looking down on someone; humble treatment of another. Syn. *panghahamak, pangmamatá (fig.)*

pang-aapí (pang + a-a-pí), *n.* maltreatment of others; oppression. Cf. *pang-aalipin.*

pang-aapíd (pang + a-a-píd), var. **pakikiapíd,** *n.* unfaithfulness of a husband to his wife or of a wife to her husband; adultery. Syn. *pangangálunyâ, pagtataksíl sa asawa.*

pang-abay (pang + a-bay), *n.* (Gram.) adverb. Syn. *adberbiyó.*

pang-abay pamanahón, adverb of time.

pang-abay pamaraán, adverb of manner.

pang-abay pamítagan, adverb of respect.

pang-abay panáng-ayon, adverb of affirmation.

pang-abay pananggí, adverb of negation.

pang-abay panlunán, adverb of place.

pang-abay panulad, adverb of comparison.

pang-abay pánunuran, adverb of order.

pang-abay pang-agam, adverb of doubt.

pang-abay panggaanó, adverb of quantity.

pang-abot (pang + a-bot), *n.* 1. a coming in contact with each other, said of two things. Syn. *paglapat, paglalapat.* 2. a being abreast with each other, as two runners. 3. an accidental meeting, as of two persons in a certain place. Syn. *pagkikita.*

pang-akít (pang + a-kít), *n. & adj.* 1. said of a person's personality, beauty, etc. that attracts or charms another or others. Syn. *panghalina, pambalanì, panggayuma, pambighanì.* 2. referring to something used to attract or win over another to one's side. Syn. *panghikayat.*

pangagáw (pa-nga-gáw), *adj.* competing with each other; in competition with each other.

pang-agdón (pang + ag-dón), *n. & adj.* 1. referring to anything used by a person to

complete or finish something under stress. Syn. *pantapos, pangkumpleto.* 2. that which is used to tide over one's need until a better time comes.

pangahás (pa-nga-hás), var. **mapangahás,** *adj.* daring; bold. Syn. *waláng-takot, waláng-gulat, malakás ang loób.*

pangál (pa-ngál), *adj.* tired or fatigued, esp. due to long waiting or continuous talking. Syn. *pagód na sa pagkainip o kásasalitâ.*

pangalan (pa-nga-lan), *n.* name. Syn. *ngalan, tawag.*

pangalandakan (pa-nga-lan-da-kan), *n.* something that a person is bragging about.

pangalawá (pa-nga-la-wá), var. **pangalwá,** *n. & adj.* 1. second. Syn. *ikalawá.* 2. referring to someone's assistant or deputy. Syn. *katulong.*

pangalisag (pa-nga-li-sag), var. **pangangalisag,** *n.* 1. standing of hair on end, esp. due to fear. Syn. *pamamalukag.* 2. goose flesh. Syn. *pangilabot, pangingilabot.*

pangambá (pa-ngam-bá), *n.* 1. fear; feeling of fear. Syn. *takot, pagkatakot.* 2. doubt; feeling of doubt. Syn. *alinlangan, pag-aalinlangan; duda, pagdududa.* 3. apprehension; misgiving; premonition. Syn. *agam-agam, kabá.*

panganák (pa-nga-nák), var. **panganganák,** *n.* act, time, or manner of giving birth. Syn. *pagsisilang ng sanggól.*

panganay (pa-nga-nay), I. *n.* 1. the first-born child of a couple. Syn. *unang anák.* 2. (Fig.) first fruit or product, as of one's pen. —II. *adj.* born first in a family; first-born, referring to a child; oldest among a couple's children.

panganib (pa-nga-nib), *n.* 1. danger; peril. Syn. *peligró.* 2. terror; cause of great fear. Syn. *kilabot, taong kinatatákutan.*

panganino (pa-nga-ni-no), var. **panganganino,** *n.* feeling of inferiority; inferiority complex. Syn. *pangungupete, pamamalahibo (fig.).*

panganorin (pa-nga-no-rin), *n.* 1. thin, high clouds. Syn. *mataas at manipis na ulap.* 2. the atmospheric space beyond the clouds; sky. Syn. *alangaang, himpapawíd, papawirín, langit.*

pangangailangan

pang-araw-araw

pangangailangan (pa-nga-nga-i-la-ngan), n.
1. need; want; demand. 2. necessity; lack.
Syn. *kawalán*. 3. time or condition of
need. Syn. *pagkagipít, kagipitan*. 4. lack of
money; a being poor. Syn. *pagdarálitâ,
karálitaán*.

pangangalagà (pa-nga-nga-la-gà), n. 1. act
of taking care, as of one's health. Cf. *pag-
iingat*. 2. act of keeping something from
destruction; conservation. Cf.
pagpapanatili sa mabuting kalagayan.

pangangalap (pa-nga-nga-lap), n. 1. a
campaigning, as for votes. Syn.
pangangampanya. 2. act of soliciting or
collecting, as of contribution. Syn.
pangingilak. 3. recruitment or enlistment,
as of young men for military service. 4.
cutting of trees into logs; logging. Syn.
pagtotroso.

pangangaliwâ (pa-nga-nga-li-wâ), n. 1. act
of passing along the left side of (a road,
etc.). 2. (*Colloq.*) act of double-crossing
another. Syn. *panloloko, panlilinláng,
pandarayà*. 3. (*Fig.*) unfaithfulness to one's
spouse. Syn. *pagtataksíl sa asawa,
pangangálunyâ*.

pangangalumatá (pa-nga-nga-lu-ma-tá), n.
1. state or condition of having dark rings
around the eyes due to lack of sleep. 2.
feeling of tiredness or exhaustion due to
loss of sleep. Syn. *panlalambót ng katawán
dahil sa puyat*.

pangangalumbabà (pa-nga-nga-lum-ba-bà),
n. act of resting the chin on one's palm
or palms or on the back of the hands, as
when one is in a pensive mood.

pangangálunyâ (pa-nga-nga-ngá-lun-yâ), n.
concubinage. Syn. *pakikiagulò, pakikiapíd*.

pangangaluykóy (pa-nga-nga-luy-kóy), n. a
shivering from cold; feeling extreme cold.
Syn. *pangangaligkíg*.

pangangambá (pa-nga-ngam-bá), n. 1. fear;
feeling of uneasiness or disquiet due to
doubt or misgiving. 2. (*Colloq.*) state of
being in danger. Syn. *pamimiligro,
panganganib*.

pangangamote (pa-nga-nga-mo-te), n. 1. act
of digging or gathering sweet potatoes. 2.
(*Fig.*) unsuccessful attempt; failure. Syn.
pagkabigô.

panganganák (pa-nga-nga-nák), n. act of
giving birth to a child; childbirth;
delivery.

panganganay (pa-nga-nga-nay), n.
childbirth or delivery of one's first child.
Syn. *una o primerong panganganák*.

panganganínganí (pa-nga-nga-ní-nga-ní), n.
repulsive feeling towards something dirty
or loathsome. Syn. *pandidiri*.

pangangantiyáw (pa-nga-ngan-ti-yáw), n.
act of bantering; a good-natured teasing,
ridicule, or joking. Syn. *panunudyó,
panunuksó*.

pangangapâ (pa-nga-nga-pâ), n. 1. act of
groping for something, as in the dark. Syn.
pag-aapuháp. 2. the act or manner of
catching fish with the hands in a shallow,
rocky place, usually near the side of a
river. Syn. *pangangapkáp*.

pangangapit-bahay (pa-nga-nga-pit + ba-
hay), n. the act or habit of visiting
neighbors. Syn. *pangangahanggán*.

pangangaral (pa-nga-nga-ral), n. 1. act of
preaching, as by a priest. Syn. *pagsesermón*.
2. act or duty of giving moral advice. Cf.
pagpapayo.

pangangarap (pa-nga-nga-rap), n. 1. act of
dreaming. Syn. *pananaginip*. 2. fond hope
or aspiration for something big;
daydreaming.

pangangatwiran (pa-nga-ngat-wi-ran), n. 1.
act of arguing or giving one's reason or
reasons to justify his point. Syn.
pagpapaliwanag. 2. reason or argument
given or presented to support one's stand
or side. Syn. *paliwanag*.

pangangayupapá (pa-nga-nga-yu-pa-pá), n.
humble submission to another's wish or
wishes. Cf. *pagpapakumbabâ*.

pangaral (pa-nga-ral), n. 1. parental advice.
Syn. *payong-magulang*. 2. teachings; moral
lessons contained in a sermon.

pangarap (pa-nga-rap), n. 1. dream. Syn.
panaginip. 2. (*Fig.*) fervent wish or desire;
ambition. Syn. *láyunin, ambisyón*.

pang-araw-araw (pang + a-raw + a-raw), adj.
1. daily; everyday; done everyday, as in:
pang-araw-araw na trabaho, daily work. 2.
for everyday use, as clothes. Syn. *gamit o
ginágamit sa araw-araw*.

pangát (pa-ngát), *n. & adj.* referring esp. to small fish cooked in little water and vinegar with salt to taste. See, **pinangát**.

pang-atin (pang + a-tin), *adj.* referring to something exclusively for ourselves.

pangatníg (pa-ngat-níg), *n. (Gram.)* conjunction. Cf. *pang-ugnáy*.

pangatníg pamukód, disjunctive or alternative conjunction.

pangatníg panapós, final conjunction.

pangatníg paninsáy, adversative conjunction.

pangatníg panlinaw, illative conjunction.

pangatníg pantulong, subordinate conjunction.

pangatníg pantuwáng, coordinate conjunction.

pangatníg panubalì, conditional conjunction.

pangatníg panulad, comparative conjunction.

pangatníg pang-angkóp, copulative conjunction.

pangaw (pa-ngaw), *n.* 1. anything that holds in check, as handcuffs, fetters, manacles, shackles, and the like. Syn. *kalso, kalang*.

pangawíng (pa-nga-wíng), I. *n.* 1. a hook used to hold, catch, or link something to another. Syn. *kalawit, pangalawit*. 2. a verb that links.
—II. *adj.* linking, as in: *pandiwang pangawíng*, linking verb.

pangkapwâ-tao (pang-kap-wâ + ta-o), *adj.* serving to foster friendly relations among men; for fostering friendship with others.

pangkaraniwan (pang-ka-ra-ni-wan), *adj.* common; ordinary.

pangkasalukuyan (pang-ka-sa-lu-ku-yan), *adj.* 1. *(Gram.)* present. 2. of the present; of the present time. Syn. *ngayón*.

pangkát (pang-kát), *n.* 1. group. Syn. *grupo*. 2. band or gang. Syn. *barkada, barkadahán, gang*. 3. section, as of an office. Cf. *sangáy*.

pangkátaón (pang-ká-ta-ón), *adj.* 1. of, for, or pertaining to a special occasion. Syn. *pantangì, pang-espesyál*. 2. occurring on a particular occasion; occasional. Syn. *pambihirà*.

pangkáwanggawâ (pang-ká-wang-ga-wâ), *adj.* for charity.

pangkinábukasan (pang-ki-ná-bu-ka-san), *adj.* for the future; pertaining to the future. Syn. *pará sa hináharáp, panghináharáp*.

pangko (pang-ko), I. *n.* 1. act of carrying or holding a child on one's arm or arms close to the breast. 2. a child carried or held in this manner.
—II. *adj.* carried or held in one's arm or arms. Cf. *kargá*.

panggabí (pang-ga-bí), *adj.* 1. said of a worker whose duty is during nights. 2. nocturnal.

panggáp (pang-gáp), var. **pagpapanggáp**, *n.* act of pretending to be what one is not; pretension. Syn. *pagkukunwarî, pagkukunwâ, pagkukunyarî*.

panggigilalás (pang-gi-gi-la-lás), *n.* feeling of extreme astonishment or surprise. Syn. *lubós na pagtataká*.

panggigipuspós (pang-gi-gi-pus-pós), *n.* feeling of intense disconsolation.

pangginggera (pang-ging-ge-ra), *n.* a woman whose vice is playing *panggingge*.

panggugulang (pang-gu-gu-lang), *n. (Fig.)* act of taking advantage of another or others. Syn. *panlalamáng*.

panghabang-buhay (pang-ha-bang + bu-hay), *adj.* for the duration of one's life; for life.

panghál (pang-hál), *adj.* 1. referring to food that has become cool due to being left uneaten. 2. tired of long waiting.

panghalíp (pang-ha-líp), *n.* 1. *(Gram.)* pronoun. 2. a substitute or alternate. Syn. *panghalili, pamalít*.

panghalíp paarî, possessive pronoun.

panghalíp pamanggít, relative pronoun.

panghalíp pamatlíg, demonstrative pronoun.

panghalíp panakláw, indefinite pronoun.

panghalíp pananóng, interrogative pronoun.

panghalíp panao, personal pronoun.

panghangà (pang-ha-ngà), *n. (Gram.)* exclamation mark.

panghapon (pang-ha-pon), *adj.* 1. afternoon; of, in, or for the afternoon, as in: *mga klaseng panghapon*, afternoon classes. 2. assigned to work in the afternoon, said of employees. Cf. *panggabí*.

panghawakan (pang-ha-wa-kan), *v.* to rely (upon) as basis of one's statement or action. Syn. *pagbatayan*, *pagsaligan*.

panghí (pang-hí), n. the smell or odor of urine. Syn. *palot*.

panghibò (pang-hi-bò), n. *& adj*. referring to a statement or praise used to gratify the vanity of someone.

panghihimasok (pang-hi-hi-ma-sok), n. interference in others' affairs; meddling. Syn. *pakikialám*.

panghihinawà (pang-hi-hi-na-wà), n. loss of interest in something. Syn. *pagkawalâ ng gana*.

panghihinayang (pang-hi-hi-na-yang), n. regret for something lost.

panghihiningá (pang-hi-hi-ni-ngá), n. act of picking small particles of food left between the teeth, esp. after eating. Syn. *pagpapalito, pagtitinga*.

panghilakbutan (pang-hi-lak-bu-tan), v. to be affected with a sudden feeling of fear or horror.

panghimasukan (pang-hi-ma-su-kan), v. to meddle or interfere with. Syn. *pakialamán*. See **manghimasok**.

panghinaan (pang-hi-na-an), v. 1. (with ng *katawán*) to feel weak. Syn. *manlambót o panlambután (ng katawan)*. 2 (with ng *loób*) to lose courage; be discouraged.

panghinabangán (pang-hi-na-ba-ngán), v. to lose interest in. Syn. *mawalán ng gana o interés*.

panghináharáp (pang-hi-ná-ha-ráp), adj. 1. (Gram.) future. 2. for the future.

panghinawaan (pang-hi-na-wa-an), v. to lose interest or enthusiasm in. Cf. *pagsawaan*. Syn. *panghinabangán*.

panghinayangan (pang-hi-na-ya-ngan), v. to regret the loss of or one's failure in.

panghulapì (pang-hu-la-pì), n. *& adj*. referring to a word, syllable or syllables used as a suffix. Cf. *pang-unlapì, panggitlapì*.

pangibabawan (pa-ngi-ba-ba-wan), v. 1. to be above or on top of. 2. to dominate or overwhelm. Syn. *pagharian*.

pangiki (pa-ngi-ki), n. chill; malarial chill. See **ngiki**.

pangikig (pa-ngi-kig), var. **pangkikig**, n. *& adj*. referring to a feather or a small stick attached with a small piece of cotton on one end for use in cleaning the inside of ears, or for relieving itchiness inside by rotating it over and over.

pang-igaya (pang + i-ga-ya), I. adj. that tends to motivate or induce. Syn. *pang-akit, panghalina*.

—II. n. motivation; inducement.

pangil (pa-ngil), n. 1. eyetooth; upper canine tooth. Syn. *pangito*. 2. tusk, as of an elephant. 2. fang, as of snakes.

pangilabutan (pa-ngi-la-bu-tan), v. to have goose flesh due to chill, fear, shock, etc. Cf. *pangalisagan*.

pangilak (pa-ngi-lak), I. n. 1. act of soliciting contribution or raising funds thru contributions. Also, *pangingilak*. 2. the amount of funds thus raised or solicited.

—II. adj. raised or solicited by someone, referring to funds.

pangilagan (pa-ngi-la-gan), v. to avoid by or as by being careful. Syn. *iwasan, pagingatan*.

pang-ilán (pang + i-lán), interrog. pron. what is the place or number of a person or thing in a row or series?

pangilin (pa-ngi-lin), n. 1. period of fasting; abstinence. Syn. *ayuno, pag-aayuno; kulasyón, pagkukulasyón*. 2. day of freedom from work; holiday; official holiday. Syn. *piyesta opisyál*.

pangimay (pa-ngi-may), var. **pampangimay**, I. adj. that produces or causes anesthesia; anesthetic (anaesthetic).

—II. n. anything, as drug, etc., that produces or causes anesthetic. Syn. *pamanhíd, pampamanhíd*.

pangimbuló (pa-ngim-bu-ló), var. **pangingimbuló**, n. feeling of shyness or inferiority towards another whom one considers with high esteem or respect. Cf. *pangimì*.

panginigán (pa-ngi-ni-gán), v. (with ng *katawán*) to shake or tremble in fear or with cold. Syn. *pangatalán*.

panginoón (pa-ngi-no-ón), n. 1. the master or owner, as of an animal. Syn. *amo, mayarì*. 2. (P-) Master or Lord, referring to Jesus Christ. 3. (Colloq.) boss; chief. Syn. *hepe, punò*.

pangingibá (pa-ngi-ngi-bá), n. 1. feeling of

unfamiliarity in a new place or environment. Syn. *paninibago*. 2. fit of bad temper or annoyance, esp. of a child, in the presence of unfamiliar faces or strangers. Syn. *pangingilala*.

pangingibabaw (pa-ngi-ngi-ba-baw), n. 1. a floating or rising of something on the surface of water or liquid. Syn. *paglutang*. 2. predominance; prevalence. Syn. *pananaíg, pamamayaní, paghaharì*.

pangingibáng-bayan (pa-ngi-ngi-báng + ba-yan), n. 1. act of travelling abroad. 2. act of living or residing in another town or country. Syn. *paninirahan sa ibáng bayan o bansâ*.

pangingibig (pa-ngi-ngi-big), n. courtship. Syn. *panliligaw*.

pangingilabot (pa-ngi-ngi-la-bot), n. appearance of goose flesh due to fear or cold.

pangingilag (pa-ngi-ngi-lag), n. avoidance by being careful; exercise of care to prevent something undesirable to happen. Syn. *pag-iingat*.

pangingilala (pa-ngi-ngi-la-la), n. the unfavorable reaction of a child upon seeing a stranger or an unknown person. Syn. *pangingibá*.

pangingimì (pa-ngi-ngi-mì), n. a feeling of shame or shyness to talk to someone because of respect. Syn. *pag-aálang-alang*.

pang-isá (pang + i-sá), adj. 1. (*Gram.*) singular. 2. for use by one person or for one thing; single, as a bed, room, etc.

pángisdaan (pá-ngis-da-an), n. place where persons can catch fish from; fishing ground.

pangit (pa-ngit), adj. 1. ugly; unsightly; unpleasant to the sight. 2. bad; unpleasant; disagreeable. Syn. *masamâ*.

pangita (pa-ngi-ta), n. a face-to-face meeting. Syn. *pagkikita, pagpapangita*.

pangitain (pa-ngi-ta-in), n. omen; sign of something to happen. Syn. *tandâ, palátandaan, babalâ*.

pangitî (pa-ngi-tî), adj. & adv. with a smile; in a smiling manner.

pang-iwang (pang + i-wang), var. **pandewang**, n. & adj. said of anything used for wiping the anus after moving the bowels, as toilet paper.

pangláw (pang-láw), var. **panláw**, n. 1 feeling of melancholy or solitude loneliness. 2. solitude or loneliness, as c a place. Syn. *lungkót* (for both senses).

pangmarami (pang-ma-ra-mi), I. adj. 1 (*Gram.*) plural; containing or designatin more than one; opposed to *pang-isá*. 2. fo or intended for many persons or things. —II. n. the form of a word in the plura number; plural.

pangngalan (pang-nga-lan), I. n. (*Gram.* noun. —II. n. & adj. referring to a word or word intended to be given as a name or name for. Syn. *pampangalan*.

pangngalang pambálana, common noun.

pangngalang pandiwarì, verbal noun.

pangngalang pantangi, proper noun.

pangngalang pariralà, noun phrase.

pangngalang sugnáy, noun clause.

pangô (pa-ngô), adj. 1. snub; flat and turne up; snubby, said of the nose. 2. having snub nose; snubnosed, said of a person Syn. *sarát* (for both senses).

pangód (pa-ngód), adj. 1. blunt; dull; no sharp, said of cutting or bladed tools. Syn *pulpól, mapuról*. 2. dull-headed; mentall slow. Syn. *mahinà ang ulo*.

pangós (pa-ngós), n. act of chewing suga cane.

pang-ukol (pang + u-kol), I. n. (*Gram.* preposition. Syn. *preposisyón*. —II. n. & adj. referring to something reserved or intended for someone. Syn *panreserba, panlaán*.

pang-ugnáy (pang + ug-náy), n. (*Gram.*) 1. connective. 2. conjunction. Syn *pangatníg*.

pangulay (pa-ngu-lay), var. **pangkulay**, n. & adj. referring to a certain matter or substance used for dyeing or coloring. Syn. *pangkolór, pangolór; pantinà, paninà*.

pangulo (pa-ngu-lo), n. 1. president. Syn. *presidente*. 2. presiding officer; chairman. Syn. *tagapangulo*.

pangulubutín (pa-ngu-lu-bu-tín), v. to make wrinkled; cause to become wrinkled.

panguluhan (pa-ngu-lu-han), v. 1. to head or lead. Syn. *pangunahan, paglideran*. 2. to preside. Syn. *pamatnugutan*.

pangumán (pa-ngu-mán), var. **pangamán**, adj. referring to a person related to someone by a previous marriage, usually used as a combining form, as in: *amáng-pangumán* (stepfather), *ináng-pangumán* (stepmother), etc.

pangunahan (pa-ngu-na-han), v. 1. to lead or head; be the leader or head of. Syn. *pamunuan*. 2. to do or act before someone does. Syn. *máuná, magpáuná*.

pángunahín (pá-ngu-na-hín), adj. 1. first-class; of the best quality. Syn. *primera klase*. 2. principal; most important; chief; main, as in: *pángunahíng kailangan*, principal need.

pang-unawà (pang + u-na-wà), n. 1. understanding; ability to understand; sense of understanding. Syn. *pang-intinde*.

pangunguna (pa-ngu-ngu-na), n. 1. state or condition of being ahead or first. 2. act of starting ahead of others. Syn. *pagpapáuná*. 3. act of leading; leadership. Syn. *pamumunò*.

pangungusap (pa-ngu-ngu-sap), n. 1. (*Gram.*) sentence. 2. statement; declaration. Syn. *pahayag*. 3. way or manner of talking (speaking). Syn. *pagsasalitâ*. 4. promise; word, as in: *sirain ang pangungusap*, to break one's word. Syn. *pangako, salitáng binitawan*.

pangungusap na hugnayan, complex sentence.

pangungusap (na) pasalaysáy, same as *pangungusap (na) pasaysáy*.

pangungusap (na) pasaysáy, declarative sentence.

pangungusap (na) patanóng, interrogative sentence.

pangungusap (na) pautos, imperative sentence.

pangungusap (na) payák, simple sentence.

pangungusap (na) tambalan: compound sentence.

pang-urì (pang + u-rì), I. n. 1. (*Gram.*) adjective. Syn. *adhetibo*.
—II. n. & adj. referring to a device or instrument used for assaying metals, esp. gold or silver.

pangusap (pa-ngu-sap), n. reprimand; formal reproof. Syn. *pangaral*.

pangusapin (pa-ngu-sa-pin), v. to cause or allow to say something; make one talk or speak. Syn. *pagsalitaín, pápagsalitaín*.

pang-uupat (pang + u-u-pat), n. instigation; incitement. Syn. *pang-uudyók, panunulsól*.

pang-uuyám (pang + u-u-yám), n. act of mocking another or others; sarcastic remark; mockery; ridicule. Syn. *panunuyâ, panlilibák*.

pangwakás (pang-wa-kás), I. adj. final; last; concluding, as in: *pangwakás na bilang*, final number. Syn. *pangkatapusan*.
—II. n. the concluding part or portion; end; conclusion. Syn. *wakás, katapusán*.

pangwarì (pang-wa-rì), n. 1. way of thinking. 2. opinion.

pangyarihan (pang-ya-ri-han), v. to be or become the scene of an event or happening.

pangyayari (pang-ya-ya-ri), n. 1. happening; occurrence; event; incident. 2. case; circumstance.

paos (pa-os), var. **pamamaos**, n. hoarseness of voice. Syn. *pagaw, pamamagaw; malát, pamamalát*.

Papa¹ (Pa-pa), n. (*Sp., eccl.*) Pope.

papa² (pa-pa), n. standard width of textile or cloth. Syn. *antso, lapad o luwáng (ng tela)*.

papa³ (pa-pa), n. (*Eng.*) papa; father. Syn. *tata, tatay, itáy, tatang, dadi*.

papà (pa-pà), n. (in baby talk) food. Syn. *pagkain*.

papák (pa-pák), n. act of eating viands only, that is, without rice or bread, esp. not during regular meal time.

papag (pa-pag), n. bamboo bed or bench.

papág- (pa-pág-), pref. used in combination with the suffixes –in and –hin, meaning to allow or cause one to do, make or perform something, as in: *papág-aralin*, to send to school to study; *papáglinisin*, to cause someone to do some cleaning.

papág-alabin (pa-pág + a-la-bin), v. 1. to cause fire to burn brightly. Syn. *papágliyabín, papágningasin*. 2. to cause a person to become aflame with anger. Syn. *papág-apuyín sa galit*.

papág-anakín (pa-pág + a-na-kín), v. 1. to cause or let a woman bear a child, or a female animal to have offspring. 2. to get someone to act as sponsor or godparent.

papág-apuyín (pa-pág + a-pu-yín), *v.* 1. to tell someone to build a fire. Syn. *Papágparikitín ng apóy*. 2. to make the fire burst into flame. Syn. *papágdingasin, papág-alabin, papágliyabín*. 3. (Fig.) to make more intense or ardent. Syn. *pasidhíin, paalabin (fig.)*.

papagayán (pa-pa-ga-yán), var. **papaganyán, papaganiyán**, *adv.* 1. in that way or manner. Syn. *sa ganyáng paraán*. 2. in that or toward that direction.

papagayón (pa-pa-ga-yón), *adv.* 1. in that way or manner. Syn. *sa gayóng paraán*. 2. towards that direction.

papagkásunduín (pa-pag-ká-sun-du-ín), *v.* to reconcile or settle the quarrel or dispute of (two persons).

papág-ingatin (pa-pág + i-nga-tin), *v.* 1. to cause or tell someone to be careful about something. 2. to let or allow someone to carry, hold, or own, as a gun, etc.

papág-isahín (pa-pág + i-sa-hín), *v.* 1. to let one alone in a place or in going to a certain place. Syn. *bayaang mag-isá o nagiisá*. 2. to order the unification of. Syn. *iutos ang pag-iisá o pagsasamasama*.

papág-isíp-isipín (pa-pág + i-síp + i-si-pín), *v.* to give someone sufficient time to think or study seriously about something. Syn. *papágbuláy-bulayin*.

papáglamayin (pa-pág-la-ma-yin), *v.* 1. to cause someone to attend a night vigil. 2. to cause or allow someone to work overtime during nights; assign a worker on a night duty.

papáglapitín (pa-pág-la-pi-tín), *v.* to cause two persons to be near or close to each other.

papáglayuín (pa-pág-la-yu-ín), *v.* to tell or cause two persons engaged in a quarrel to separate from each other. Syn. *papághiwalayín, awatin*.

papáglubagín (pa-pág-lu-ba-gín), *v.* 1. to make calm, as one's emotion. Syn. *pahinahunin, payapain*. 2. to cause the intensity of (something) to lower or diminish. Syn. *pahupaín, pahulawin*.

papáglubayín (pa-pág-lu-ba-yín), *v.* to cause someone to stop doing or continuing.

Syn. *pahintuín, patigilin*.

papágmagalingín (pa-pág-ma-ga-li-ngín), *v.* 1. to cause someone to become boastful. Syn. *papághambugín, papágpasikatin*. 2. to allow one to ingratiate oneself to someone by doing favors. Syn. *papágmapurihín*.

papágmasirín (pa-pág-ma-si-rín), *v.* to cause or allow someone to make an ocular observation of something. Syn. *papág obserbahín*.

papágmukhaín (pa-pág-muk-ha-ín), *v.* to cause someone to look like something. Syn. *papághitsurahin*.

papágningningín (pa-pág-ning-ni-ngín), *v.* to make brilliantly beautiful.

papágngitngitín (pa-pág-ngit-ngi-tín), *v.* to cause someone to seethe with controlled anger. Cf. *papágngalitin*.

papágpanggapín (pa-pág-pang-ga-pín), *v.* to make or allow someone to pretend to be what he is not. Syn. *papágkunwariín, papágkunyariín*.

papágpasasain (pa-pág-pa-sa-sa-in), *v.* to let or make someone enjoy fully the abundance of. Cf. *papágsawain*.

papágpisanin (pa-pág-pi-sa-nin), *v.* to make or allow a man and a woman to live together as husband and wife. Syn. *papágsamahin*.

papágsarilihín (pa-pág-sa-ri-li-hín), *v.* 1. to make a nation or country independent; allow a nation or country to become independent. Syn. *palayain, bigyán ng kalayaan o independensiyá*. 2. to make free from parental care and support; make a son or daughter live independently from his or her parents. Syn. *pabukurín*.

papágsikapin (pa-pág-si-ka-pin), *v.* to make or advise someone to be diligent in order to attain his aim or dream. Syn. *papágtiyagaín, papágsipagin*.

papágsimpanín (pa-pág-sim-pa-nín), *v.* to advise or urge someone to save for the future. Syn. *papág-impukín*.

papágsimulaín (pa-pág-si-mu-la-ín), *collo.* var. **papágsimulín**, *v.* to make someone start or begin. Syn. *papág-umpisahín*.

papágsiwalatin (pa-pág-si-wa-la-tin), *v.* to cause or allow someone to expose or reveal an anomaly, secret, etc. Syn.

papágbunyagín.

papágtagalín (pa-pág-ta-ga-lín), *v.* to delay unnecessarily. Syn. *papágluwatín, paluwatín, palaunin.*

papágtagpuín (pa-pág-tag-pu-ín), *v.* to cause two persons to meet or encounter each other in a certain place. Syn. *papágkitain.*

papágtibayin (pa-pág-ti-ba-yin), *v.* to cause or let a council, legislative body, etc. to approve a proposal or a bill into an ordinance or law. Syn. *papág-aprobahín.*

papágtiisín (pa-pág-ti-i-sín), *v.* to make or cause someone to suffer or bear something hard or difficult. Syn. *papágbatahín, papág-agwantahín, papágdanasin ng hirap.*

papágtimpiín (pa-pág-tim-pi-ín), *v.* to cause or advise someone to exercise self-control, temperance, or moderation in one's acts or practices. Syn. *papágmahinahunin, papágpigilin.*

papágtotohanín (pa-pág-to-to-ha-nín), *v.* to make someone do something seriously, that is, without joking or intention to deceive.

papág-usigin (papág + u-si-gin), *v.* to require or order a prosecutor to conduct a hearing of a case. Syn. *papágsiyasatin.*

papágwagiín (pa-pág-wa-gi-ín), *v.* to declare someone a winner. Syn. *papanalunin, papágtagumpayín.*

papágwangisin (pa-pág-wa-ngi-sin), *v.* to make each other look alike. Syn. *papágtularin, papágwangkiín.*

papágwariin (pa-pág-wa-ri-in), *v.* to make or cause someone to reflect or think seriously about something. Syn. *papág-isiping mabuti.*

papait (pa-pa-it), *n. (Ilok.)* a kind of viand having a slightly bitter taste, popular among the Ilocanos.

papalabás (pa-pa-la-bás), *adj.* 1. getting out; on the way to the outside. Syn. *patungo o papunta sa labás.* 2. leading to the outside (s.o. a door, passage, etc.) Also, *palabás.*

papalapít (pa-pa-la-pít), *adj.* coming or getting nearer; approaching. Also, *lumálapit.*

papalayô (pa-pa-la-yô), *adj.* going away.

papalít-palít (pa-pa-lít + pa-lít), *adj.* said of someone who has the habit of changing

his opinion, position, clothing, etc. very often. Syn. *pabagu-bago, paibá-ibá.*

papaloób (pa-pa-lo-ób), *adj.* 1. going inside, said of a person. Syn. *papasók, papunta sa loób.* 2. said of a way or passage going inside (a room, house, building, etc.).

papanabikín (pa-pa-na-bi-kín), *v.* to cause someone to be eagerly desirous of something.

papanagutín (pa-pa-na-gu-tín), *v.* to make someone responsible for.

papanaigín (pa-pa-na-i-gín), *v.* to consider (something) to be above all others. Syn. *papangibabawin.*

papanámpalatayahin (pa-pa-nám-pa-la-ta-ya-hin), *v.* to make one believe in God or His teachings. Syn. *pasambahín.*

papanaóg (pa-pa-na-óg), *adj.* 1. said of a person who is about to go down the stairs or is already on the way down the stairs. 2. said of a way or passage used in going down the stairs or from any high place. Syn. *papababâ.*

papanatagin (pa-pa-na-ta-gin), *v.* to make calm or peaceful. Syn. *papanahimikin.*

papanatilihin (pa-pa-na-ti-li-hin), *v.* to perpetuate; let or allow to stay unchanged. Syn. *papamalagiin.*

papanawin (pa-pa-na-win), *v. (Poetic)* to make disappear.

papanhík (pa-pan-hík), *adj.* 1. said of a person going upstairs or about to go upstairs. Syn. *paakyát (sa bahay).* 2. said of a way or passage used in going upstairs.

papanimdimín (pa-pa-nim-di-mín), *v.* to cause someone to be in anguish. Syn. *papamighatiín, papágdamdamín, pagpágdalamhatiín.*

papanúmbalikin (pa-pa-núm-ba-li-kin), *v.* to cause something to be returned to its place, position, condition, or status. Syn. *papanság-uliin.*

papangahasín (pa-pa-nga-ha-sín), *v.* to cause someone to do something dangerous or not familiar to him.

papangilabutin (pa-pa-ngi-la-bu-tin), *v.* to cause someone to have goose flesh due to cold, fear, etc.

papangunahan (pa-pa-ngu-na-han), *v.* to cause a group to be led or headed by someone.

papangyarihin (pa-pang-ya-ri-hin), *v.* to cause to happen; allow to occur. Syn. *bayaang mangyari o maganáp.*

paparamí (pa-pa-ra-mí), *adj.* increasing in number; becoming or getting numerous. Syn. *dumárami.*

papariní (pa-pa-ri-ní), I. *adj.* 1. said of `a person or thing who or that is coming to this place, that is, where the speaker is. Syn. *paparitó.* 2. said of a street or thoroughfare going to the place where the speaker is.
—II. *adv.* toward this place, as in: *tumakbó siyáng papariní.* He ran toward this place.

papariyán (pa-pa-ri-yán), I. *adj.* 1. said of a person who or a thing that is going to that place. 2. said of a road, street, etc. leading to that place. Syn. *patungo o papunta riyán.*
—II. *adv.* toward that place.

paparoón (pa-pa-ro-ón), I. *adj.* going there; leading to that place.
—II. *adv.* toward that place.

papás (pa-pás), *adj.* 1. low or almost flat, said of roof structure. Syn. *papâ, mapapâ.* 2. flattened to the ground as by a strong wind or typhoon, referring to a ricefield, sugar cane plantation, etc.

pápatay-patay (pá-pa-tay + pa-tay), *adj.* slow moving, referring to a person. Syn. *mabagal kumilos o magpasiyá.*

papawirín (pa-pa-wi-rín), *n.* the high space above; firmament; the sky. Syn. *panganorin, alangaang, himpapawíd.*

papayaó (pa-pa-ya-ó), *adj.* leaving; about to go or leave. Syn. *papaalís, paalís.*

papél¹ (pa-pél), var. **papíl**, *n.* (*Sp.*) 1. paper. 2. (*Colloq.*) reputation; record, as in: *Basâ ang kanyáng papél.* He has a bad record.

papél² (pa-pél), *n.* (in a play or drama) the role given to an actor or actress. Syn. *parte o bahaging ginágampanán.*

papél-de-bangko (pa-pél + de + bang-ko), *n.* (*Sp.*) bank note.

papél-de-hapón (pa-pél + de + ha-pón), *n.* a kind of thin but strong paper usually used for covering or clothing kites.

papeles (pa-pe-les), *n.* (*Sp.*) papers or documents pertinent to a certain record or case. Syn. *mga dokumento o kasulatan.*

papikít-pikit (pa-pi-kít + pi-kit), *adj. & adv.* with the eyes winking continuously or repeatedly. Syn. *pakuráp-kuráp.*

papiláy-piláy (pa-pi-láy + pi-láy), I. *adv.* with a limp; in a limping manner. Syn. *pahingkúd-hingkód.*
—II. *adj.* walking with a limp, referring to a person or animal.

papiliin (pa-pi-li-in), *v.* to let choose; make (someone) choose. Syn. *bayaang pumilì o mamili.*

papulà (pa-pu-là), *v.* to allow oneself to be adversely criticized. Syn. *papintás.*

papuná (pa-pu-ná), I. *adj. & adv.* in the manner of criticism. Syn. *papintás, papulâ.*
—II. *v.* to allow oneself to be criticized or judged disapprovingly. Syn. *papulà, papintás.*

papuntá (pa-pun-tá), I. *adj.* 1. said of a person who is going or about to go to a certain place. Syn. *patungó.* 2. said of a road or the like going toward a certain direction or place. Syn. *patungó.*
—II. *adv.* towards a certain place or direction.

papunuán (pa-pu-nu-án), var. **papunán**, *v.* 1. to cause a container to be fully filled up. Syn. *palamnán nang punô, pahustuhán ng lamán.* 2. to cause the completion of something by adding the amount still needed. Syn. *pahustuhán, pakumpletuhan.*

papurihan (pa-pu-ri-han), *v.* 1. to praise; laud; extol. 2. to honor. Syn. *parangalán.*

paputók (pa-pu-tók), *n.* 1 a firecracker or firecrackers. Syn. *rebentadór (labintadór).* 2. explosive; dynamite. Syn. *dinamita, pampasabog.* 3. firework rocket. Syn. *kuwitis.*

paputungan (pa-pu-tu-ngan), *v.* to cause (someone) to be crowned, as a queen or king. Syn. *pakoronahan.*

para¹ (pa-ra), *prep.* (*Sp.*) 1. (with *sa, kay,* or *kiná*) 1. for; meant for or belonging to (someone), as in: *para sa iyó,* for you; *para kay* Juan, for Juan. 2. like; similar to; same as. Syn. *tulad o kagaya ng (ni).*

para² (pa-ra), I. *interj.* (Sp. *parar*) Stop! Syn. *Tigil! Hintô!*
—II. *n.* 1. a stopping or coming to a stop, as a vehicle. Syn. *hintô, paghintô; tigil, pagtigil.* 2. the act of stopping a vehicle.

Syn. *pagpapahintô, pagpapatigil*. 3. the signal or act of signaling a vehicle to stop.

para³ (pa-ra), var. **pará**, I. *adj.* only; just, as in: *para isá lamang*, just one only.

—II. *n.* act of sacrificing (something) for a cause. Also, *pagpapará*.

paraán (pa-ra-án), I. *n.* 1. method; manner of doing; process; procedure; means. Also, *pamamaraán*. 2. act or manner of sewing something. Syn. *tahî, pagtahî*. 3. a going over superficially, as by reading something. 4. permission given to someone to pass through a place. Syn. *pahintulot sa pagdaraán*.

—II. *adj.* about to pass; shall or will be passing. Syn. *dáraán, magdáraán*.

—III. *v.* 1. to allow or ask someone to fetch oneself from a certain place by passing over said place. Syn. *pasundô o pakaón sa pagdaraán*. 2. (imperatively) Let me pass.

parábolá (pa-rá-bo-lá), var. **parábulá**, *n.* (*Sp.*) 1. parable; brief story that teaches moral or spiritual lessons. Syn. *katháng may-aral*. 2. (*Sp.-Eng.*) in Geometry, parabola.

parák (pa-rák), *adj.* 1. meaningless; useless. Syn. *waláng-kahulugán, waláng-kabuluhán, waláng-kasaysayan*. 2. coquettish; flirtatious; frivolous. Syn. *landî, hitâd*.

parada (pa-ra-da), *n.* (*Sp.*) 1. parade. Cf. *prusisyón*. 2. act of parking a vehicle at a certain place. Syn. *himpíl, paghimpíl*. 3. the way or manner a vehicle is parked. Syn. *himpil, pagkakáhimpil; parke, pagkakáparke*. 4. the unloading of merchandise in a certain place where they are sold in bulk; also, the merchadise thus unloaded. 5. (in cockfighting) the total amount of bets put on a gamecock. Syn. *buóng pusta ng kalabang manók*.

paragala (pa-ra-ga-la), *n.* (*Sp.*) tip given for service; gratuity. Syn. *pabuyà, tip, porpina (propina), bigáy-palà*.

paragás (pa-ra-gás), I. *v.* to allow oneself to be hurriedly called or summoned, esp. when a close relative dies. Syn. *pasundóng mádalian*.

—II. *adj. & adv.* by calling or summoning someone hurriedly, esp. a close relative.

Syn. *sa pamamagitan ng mádaliang pagsundô*.

—III. *adj. & n.* referring to a person sent hurriedly to call or summon a close relative of dead person.

paragos (pa-ra-gos), *n.* 1. a kind of sled (sledge), usually pulled by a carabao. Syn. *kareta*. 2. a crudely made harrow, used in breaking big lumps of earth after plowing a field. Syn. *kalmót*. Cf. *suyod*.

paraiso (pa-ra-i-so), *n.* (*Sp.*) 1. (P-) Paradise; garden of Eden. 2. paradise; heaven. Syn. *langit*. 3. state or condition of great happiness. Syn. *labis na kaligayahan*. 4. (*Bot.*) an ornamental shrub or small tree known as Chinese umbrella tree or China tree (*Melia azedarach* Linn.).

parait (pa-ra-it), *n.* 1. ally. Syn. *kakampí, kapanalig, kaanib*. 2. alliance. Syn. *pagkakáisá, kaisahán, kásunduan, alyansa*.

parali (pa-ra-li), *n.* 1. injurious remark against another; defamation. Syn. *paninirà o pagpapasamâ sa kapwà*. 2. a boasting or bragging about one's accomplishments or successes. Syn. *paghahambóg, pagmamagalíng*.

paralis (pa-ra-lis), *n.* 1. a short cylinder of metal or wood, used as a roller on which a heavy object can be moved easier from one place to another along a surface. 2. go-between; intermediary. Syn. *tagapamagitan*. 3. a go-between in an illicit love affair. Syn. *bugaw*.

paralisado (pa-ra-li-sa-do), *adj.* (Sp. *paralizado*) 1. paralyzed, referring to a person. Syn. *lumpó*. 2. rendered inactive; brought into a condition of helpless activity.

parálisís (pa-rá-li-sís), *n.* (*Sp.*) partial or complete loss of the power of motion or sensation; paralysis. Syn. *pagkalumpó, pagkaparalisá*.

parálitaín (pa-rá-li-ta-ín), var. **papagdálitaín**, *v.* to make poor; make someone suffer from poverty. Syn. *papághirapin*.

paraluman (pa-ra-lu-man), *n.* 1. muse. Syn. *musa, diwatà, lakambini*. 2. a beautiful lady. Syn. *magandáng dalaga*. 3. (*Old Tag.*) magnetic needle; mariner's compass.

param (pa-ram), *n.* disappearance, as of pain,

paramá   parilya

etc. Also, *pagkaparam*. Syn. *pagkawalâ*,
pagkapawî, *pagnamaliw*, *paglalahò*.

paramá (pa-ra-má), *n. & adj.* referring to
something done to make another feel or
experience something. Also, *pamparamá*.

paramdám (pa-ram-dám), I. *n.* insinuation;
something said or done to give a hint to
someone. Syn. *pahiwatig*.
—II. *v.* to cause someone to feel one's
presence.

paramtán (pa-ram-tán), *v.* 1. to clothe; put
clothes on; dress. Syn. *baruan, bihisan.* 2.
to give or provide with clothing
allowance. 3. to cover with cloth or paper,
as a kite. Syn. *pabalatán.*

parang[1] (pa-rang), *n.* a wide, open field;
meadow; prairie.

parang[2] (pa-rang), *prep.* (*para* + *-ng*) like;
same as; similar to, as in: *parang batà*, like
a child (behaving like a child.).

parangál (pa-ra-ngál), I. *n.* 1. an honor given
or awarded to someone. Syn *kaloób na
karangalan.* 2. a program, ceremony, or
celebration in honor or memory of
someone. 3. something that gives honor
to someone.
—II. *adj.* held or given in honor or
memory of someone.

parangyâ (pa-rang-yâ), var. **pagpaparangyâ**,
n. boastful exhibition; ostentation;
worthless pomp or show; vainglory. Syn.
pasikat, pagpapasikat (fig.).

paraos (pa-ra-os), *n.* 1. celebration
sponsored by someone. Syn. *pagdiriwang.*
2. act of doing something just to pass away
the time. Also, *pagpaparaos.*

parapara (pa-ra-pa-ra), *adv.* (collective form
of *para*) all, without exception; wholly;
entirely; altogether. Syn. *lahát-lahát, paré-
parehó, waláng itinatangì.*

parapernál (pa-ra-per-nál), *adj.* (Sp.
parafernal) paraphernal; said of right,
properties, etc. given over to the control
of the wife.

parapernalya (pa-ra-per-nal-ya), *n.* 1.
paraphernalia; personal belongings. Syn.
pansariling mga kagamitán. 2. equipment;
outfit; paraphernalia. Syn. *mga kagamitán
o kasangkapan.*

parasol (pa-ra-sol), *n.* (Eng.) a kind of light
umbrella; parasol. Syn. *munting payong.*

paratang (pa-ra-tang), *n.* false accusation or
imputation. Syn. *bintáng.*

parati (pa-ra-ti), *adv.* always; at all times.
Syn. *lagì, palagì; tuwî na, tuwí-tuwî na.*

paratíng (pa-ra-tíng), *n.* 1. message sent to
someone. Syn. *pahatíd-balità, paabot-balità.*
2. (*Colloq.*) bribe. Syn. *suhol, pabagsák
(fig.), lagáy (colloq.).*

paráw (pa-ráw), *n.* a kind of large native
sailboat.

parayà (pa-ra-yà), var. **padayà**, *v.* to allow
oneself to be fooled, cheated, or swindled.
Syn. *paloko, palinláng, pagantso.*

parkas (par-kas), *n.* (Sp. *parca*) goddesses of
fate (as used by Balagtás in his *Florante at
Laura*).

pare (pa-re), *n.* (short for *kumpare*) used as
a form of address for the godfather of one's
child, or for the father of a child one has
sponsored. 2. used also as a form of address
for a male person whose name is not
known to the addresser.

parè (pa-rè), var. **parì**, *n.* (Sp. *padre*) priest.
Syn. *padre.*

pareha (pa-re-ha), *n.* (Sp. *pareja*) 1. a pair,
as of dancers. Syn. *tambál.* 2. running
competition; race. Syn. *karera, páligsahan
sa takbuhan.* 3. a pair, as of shoes. Syn.
pares.

pareho (pa-re-ho), *adj.* (Sp. *parejo*) 1. equal.
Also, *magkapareho.* 2. similar to each
other; identical. Syn. *kaparis, magkaparis;
katulad, magkatulad; kawangis,
magkawangis.*

pares (pa-res), *n.* 1. partners or a pair, as in
dancing. Syn. *pareha.* 2. a pair, as of shoes,
etc. 3. set, as of furniture. Syn. *huwego.*

párián (pá-ri-án), *n.* (OTag.) 1. plaza. Syn.
plasa, líwasan. 2. market place. Syn.
baraka, palengke, pámilihan, merkado.

parikalá (pa-ri-ka-lá), *n.* (OTag.) sarcastic
irony. Syn. *panunuyà.*

parikalâ (pa-ri-ka-lâ), *n.* presumption;
supposition. Syn. *palagáy, palá-palagáy,
kurú-kurò.*

parihabâ (pa-ri-ha-bâ), I. *n.* rectangle. Syn.
rektángguló.
—II. *adj.* rectangular.

parilya (pa-ril-ya), *n.* (Sp. *parrilla*) 1. grill;

gridiron. 2. a frame of metal bars attached
at the back of a vehicle for carrying extra
luggage. 3. (Colloq.) a man's chest, esp.
the width of the body from shoulder to
shoulder.

pariníg (pa-ri-níg), var. **paringíg**, n. an
indirect derogatory reference to someone;
innuendo. Syn. *pasaríng, patutsada.*

paripá (pa-ri-pá), var. **padipá**, I. adj. & adv.
with the arms extended sidewise.
—II. n. the position of the arms extended
sidewise.

parirala (pa-ri-ra-la), n. 1. (Gram.) phrase.
Syn. *prase.* 2. common expression by
someone. Syn. *bukáng bibíg.* 3. a boasting.
Syn. *paghahambóg, pagmamagalíng,
pagpapasikat.*

paris (pa-ris), I. n. 1. a comparing. Syn.
tulad, patutulad. 2. same as *pares*, which
see.
—II. adj. similar to; like; identical to. Syn.
tulad, katulad; gaya, kagaya.

parisidyo (pa-ri-sid-yo), n. (Sp. *paricidio*) 1.
parricide; killing of one's own father or
mother, or both. Syn. *pagpatáy sa
magulang.* 2. a killer of one's own father
or mother, or both. Syn. *mámamatay o ang
nakamatáy ng sariling magulang.*

paris-paris (pa-ris + pa-ris), adj. 1. in pairs;
pair by pair. Syn. *paré-pareha, tambál-
tambál.* 2. with all looking similar or alike
to each other. Syn. *magkakapareho,
magkakatulad.*

parisukát (pa-ri-su-kát), I. n. (Geom.)
square.
—II. adj. said of a plane figure having four
equal sides and four equal angles. Syn.
kuwadrado (for both n. and adj.).

parito (pa-ri-to), I. n. a coming to this place:
as in: *Kailán ang parito mo?* When will be
your coming here? Also, *pagparito.*
—II. v. (imper.) Come here; come to this
place.

pariwarà (pa-ri-wa-rà), n. & adj. referring
to a person who causes another or others
to suffer a misfortune. Syn. *pahamak.*

pariyán (pa-ri-yán), I. v. (imper.) go there;
go to that place. Syn. *pumunta (ka) riyán.*
—II. adj. going to that place, referring to
a person.

—III. adv. toward that place. Syn. *papunta
riyán.*

parokya (pa-rok-ya), n. (Sp. *paroquia*) 1.
parish. 2. parish church.

paról (pa-ról), n. (Sp. *farol*) 1. lantern. 2.
street lamp, esp. one with a glass shade.
3. (Eng.) parole. Syn. *pansamantaláng
pagpapalayà sa isáng bilanggô.*

parola (pa-ro-la), n. (Sp. *farola*) 1.
lighthouse. 2. a large street lamp.

paroól (pa-ro-ól), n. & adj. referring to
something that causes someone to suffer
a misfortune. Syn. *pariwarà.*

paroón (pa-ro-ón), I. v. to go there; go to
that place.
—II. adj. going there; heading for that
place. Syn. *pupunta o patungo roón.*
—III. adv. towards that place.

paroó't-parito (pa-ro-ó't + pa-ri-to), adj. &
adv. back-and-forth; to-and-fro. Syn.
pabalik-balik.

parte (par-te), n. (Sp.) 1. side; particular part
or location in a certain place. Syn. *panig,
dako, bahagi.* 2. share or part, as in a
division. Syn. *kabahagi, kaparte.* 3. role or
part, as of an actor in a play. Syn. *papél*
(colloq.). 4. a part or portion, as of a thing
cut into pieces. Syn. *bahagi, piraso,
kapiraso.* 5. act or manner of dividing a
thing into shares or parts. Syn. *bahagi,
pagbabahagi.* 6. act of reporting an
anomaly, etc. Syn. *sumbóng, pagusumbóng;
suplóng, pagsusuplóng.* 7. sometimes used
as a variant of *parté.*

partikulár (par-ti-ku-lár), I. adj. (Sp.
particular) 1. specific; particular; separate
from others. Syn. *tangì, nátatangì, náiibá.*
2. private; personal. Syn. *pansarili,
personál.*
—II. n. particulars; details; items of
information; specifications. Syn. *mga
detalye.*

partido (par-ti-do), n. (Sp.) 1. political party.
Syn. *lapian.* 2. one's relative or relation;
kinsman or kinswoman. Syn. *kamág-anak;
kaanak.* 3. used as a variant of *partida.*

parubdób (pa-rub-dób), n. & adj. referring
to something used for increasing the blaze
or flame of fire. Also, *pamparubdób.* Syn.
paningas, pampaningas.

parugô (pa-ru-gô), var. **padugô**, I. *n.* bloodletting; phlebotomy.

—II. *n* .& *adj.* 1. referring to something that causes bleeding. Also, *pampadugô*. 2. referring to food, drug, etc. that increases the blood of a persons. Syn. *pamparami ng dugô*.

parunungin (pa-ru-nu-ngin), *v.* to make talented; cause someone to become talented. Syn. *patalinuhin*.

parunggít (pa-rung-gít), *n.* an indirect derogatory reference to someone; innuendo; sly hint against someone; insinuation. Syn. *pasaríng, pariníg, paringíg*.

paruparó (pa-ru-pa-ró), *n.* (*Entom.*) butterfly. Cf. *paparó, aliparó*.

parusa (pa-ru-sa), *n.* 1. punishment; penalty; chastisement. Cf. *pahirap*. 2. fine; penalty. Syn. *multa*.

paryente (par-yen-te), *n.* (Sp. *pariente*) relative; relation. Syn. *ának, kaának, kamág-ának*.

pasa (pa-sa), I. *n.* (Sp. *pasar*) 1. act of passing something to another, as in basketball. Syn. *paglilipat o paghahagis sa ibá*. 2. act of giving or handing over something to another. Syn. *pagbibigáy o pag-aabót sa ibá*.

—II. *adj.* (*Colloq.*) passable; acceptable. Syn. *puwede, matátanggáp*.

pasá (pa-sá), I. *n.* (Sp. *pasar*) 1. a passing, as in an examination. Also, *pagpasá*. 2. the number of successful candidates in an examination. Syn. *ang nagsipasá o mga pumasá*.

—II. *adj.* 1. passed or successful (in an examination). Syn. *pasado, nakapasá, nakasulit*. 2. approved. Syn. *aprobado*.

pasâ (pa-sâ), I. *n.* bruise; contusion.

—II. *adj.* bruised; with or having contusion. Syn. *lamóg, bugbóg*.

pasa- (pa-sa-), *pref.* meaning "to go to," as in: *pasalalawigan*, to go to the province.

pasaán (pa-sa-án), *adv.* where; to what place (one will or would go), as in: *Pasaán ba siyá?* Where will he go? *Kung pasaán siyá, ay hindi ko nalalaman.* To what place he would go, I don't know.

pasabi (pa-sa-bi), *n.* a message sent to or left for someone. Syn. *bilin, pabilin*.

pasabog¹ (pa-sa-bog), *n.* & *adj.* referring to things that are made to explode, as firecracker, dynamite, etc. Also, *pampasabog*.

pasabog² (pa-sa-bog), *n.* sowing of seed in the field done by someone for another. Syn. *pahasík*.

pasak (pa-sak), *n.* 1. an object used to stop up a hole; plug. Syn. *tapón, panapón*. 2. anything that clogs the hole of a tube, pipe, etc. Syn. *bará*.

pasaka (pa-sa-ka), *n.* land being cultivated (by someone) for another.

pasakalì (pa-sa-ka-lì), I. *adj.* & *adv.* by taking a chance.

—II. *adj.* (*Gram.*) subjunctive, said of a verb form expressing supposition, etc.

pasakalye (pa-sa-kal-ye), *n.* (Sp. *pasacalle*) an introductory music to a song rendition.

pasakbát (pa-sak-bát), *adj.* & *adv.* by carrying with a band slung from a shoulder and made to hang around the neck.

pasakit (pa-sa-kit), *n.* suffering or torment, caused esp. by a lover. Cf. *dalamhatì, pagtitiís*.

pasakláw (pa-sak-láw), I. *v.* to allow oneself to be under the authority or jurisdiction of someone. Syn. *pasakop o pailalim sa kapangyarihan ng o ni*.

—II. *adj.* & *adv.* in a comprehensive or inclusive manner.

pasaklolo (pa-sak-lo-lo), I. *v.* to call or ask for help (succor). Syn. *magpasaklolo, humingî ng tulong o saklolo*.

—II. *n* .& *adj.* referring to a person or persons sent to give succor or help to someone in danger.

pasakop (pa-sa-kop), *v.* to allow oneself to be under someone. Syn. *pasaklaw, pailalim*.

pasada (pa-sa-da), *n.* (Sp.) 1. a trip or run of a passenger vehicle on its regular route. Syn. *biyahe*. 2. a going over something superficially, as in reading a manuscript. Syn. *pagpaparaán* (*colloq.*) *pahapyáw na pagbasa*. 3. act or manner of doing something briefly, as in ironing or sewing clothes.

pasado (pa-sa-do), *adj.* 1. passel having obtained passing mark or grade in an examination. Syn. *nakapasá, pumasá*. 2.

pasadór

approved, as an appointment paper. Syn. *aprobado, pinagtibay.* 3. obsolete; discarded; no longer in use. Syn. *lipás na, hindî na uso, hindî na ginágamit.* 4. overdue. Syn. *lampás na sa taning o takdáng panahón.* 5. past, as the time indicated in a clock or watch, as in: *pasado alás singko,* past five o'clock.

pasadór (pa-sa-dór), *n.* *(Sp.)* 1. sanitary napkin used by women having menstruation. Syn. *sapula, panapula.* 2. a wet, clean rag or towel used for moistening clothes while being ironed or pressed.

pasadyâ (pa-sad-yâ), I. *adj.* made-to-order; custom-made, as in: *sapatos na pasadyâ,* made-to-order shoes.
—II. *adv.* intentionally; purposely. Syn. *patikís.*

paság (pa-ság), *n.* 1. a sudden wriggling or shaking motion to free self, as of a live fish held by the hand. Syn. *palág, kawág.* 2. tramping of feet, as in anger or dislike. Syn. *taráng, dabog.* 3. sudden twist or shaking of body in dislike or hate. Syn. *piksí, pigsí.*

pasaglít (pa-sag-lít), *adj. & adv.* 1. in a while; for a while; just for a while. 2. in a hurry; as in: *pasaglít ko siyáng dinalaw.* I visited him in a hurry. Syn. *mádalian.*

pasagság (pa-sag-ság), *adv.* in a hurry; hurriedly, as in: *Pasagság siyáng dumatíng.* He arrived in a hurry. Syn. *nagmámadalî, nag-áapurá.*

pasahe (pa-sa-he), *n.* (Sp. *pasaje*) 1. fare; payment for a ride. Syn. *plete, bayad sa sasakyán.* 2. a portion of something spoken or written; excerpt. Syn. *bahaging hinalaw o sinipî.*

pasahod (pa-sa-hod), *n.* 1. the standard or regular wages for workers in a certain establishment or factory. 2. payment of salaries or wages. Syn. *pagbabayad o bayarán ng suweldo.* 3. payday. Syn. *araw ng suweldo.*

pasal (pa-sal), *n.* 1. extreme hunger. Syn. *matindíng gutom.* 2. weakness caused by extreme hunger. Syn. *panghihinà sa matindíng gutom.*

pasalitâ (pa-sa-li-tâ), I. *adj.* oral; spoken.

pasambá

—II. *adv.* orally; by speech or spoken words.

pasaliwà (pa-sa-li-wà), I. *adj.* 1. opposed or contrary to; running counter to. Syn. *salungát, pasalungát; laban, nálalaban.* 2. interchanged in wearing or using, as a pair of shoes, slippers, etc. Syn. *talipâ, magkatalipâ.*
—II. *adv.* 1. opposing or going against. 2. towards the opposite direction. 3. by using the wrong pairing. Syn. *nang patalipâ.*

pasalubong (pa-sa-lu-bong), *n. & adj.* referring to anything given as a gift to someone by a newly arrived person.

pasalunò (pa-sa-lu-nò), *v.* to request or ask someone to meet oneself on the way home or in going to a certain place. Syn. *pasalubong sa daán.*

pasalungát (pa-sa-lu-ngát), I. *v.* to allow oneself to be opposed or contradicted. Syn. *pumayag na kontrahín o tutulan.*
—II. *adj.* 1. contrary; contradictory; opposed; against. Syn. *kontra, laban, nálalaban.* 2. moving against the direction of (a current, wind, etc.). Syn. *pasalubóng, pakontra.* 3. against the grain, as in planing or sawing.
—III. *adv.* 1. in a contrary manner. Syn. *nang salungát, nang pakontra o nálalaban.* 2. in contrary with; by opposing. 3. in the manner against the grain.

pasamâ (pa-sa-mâ), *adj.* 1. becoming or getting bad or worse. Also, *sumásamâ; nagiging masamâ.* 2. said of something that makes bad or worse. Also, *pampasamâ.*

pasamaín (pa-sa-ma-ín), *v.* 1. to discredit another; harm the reputation of. Syn. *siraan (ng puri o pangalan).* 2. to cause, teach, or help someone to become bad. Syn. *turuang maging masamâ.* 3. to make or do a thing improperly. Syn. *gawín nang pahuwasò.*

pasamano (pa-sa-ma-no), var. **pasimano**, *n.* *(Sp.)* window sill. Syn. *palábabahan.*

pasamantalá (pa-sa-man-ta-lá), *adv.* temporarily; tentatively; provisionally.

pasambá (pa-sam-bá), I. *v.* to cause oneself to be worshipped or highly honored.
—II. *adj. & adv.* by worshipping or paying great respect or homage to.

pasamô

pasamô (pa-sa-mô), *adv.* by begging humbly and earnestly. Syn. *pahibík, paluhóg.*

pasampalatayá (pa-sam-pa-la-ta-yá), *adv.* with a feeling of great adoration or belief; in a manner of worship.

pasán (pa-sán), I. *n.* 1. act of carrying a load on the back or shoulder. Also, *pas-an* (in some Tagalog areas). Cf. *balagwít.* 2. a load carried on one's back or shoulder. 3. *(Fig.)* load or burden of responsibility. Syn. *dálahin, ságutin, pananágutan, tungkulin.* —II. *adj.* 1. carried on the back or shoulder. Syn. *dalá sa likód o sa balikat.* Cf. *balagwít.* 2. under one's responsibility. Syn. *ságutin, nasa-pananágutan.*

pasanhî (pa-san-hî), *adj. (Gram.)* causative.

pásanín (pá-sa-nín), *n. & adj.* 1. referring to a person that someone is under obligation to support or protect. Syn. *ságutin, dálahin.* 2. said of something that a person is supposed to carry on his shoulder.

pasáng-ayon (pa-sáng + a-yon), 1. *adj.* affirmative; saying yes, as in: *sagót na pasáng-ayon,* affirmative answer. —II. *adv.* in the affirmative; affirmatively.

pasang-krús (pa-sang + krús), *n.* a person or thing that someone has to bear up with patience and sacrifice. Syn. *mabigát na dálahin, pahirap.*

pasapyáw (pa-sap-yáw), I. *adj.* superficial (said esp. of cuts or wounds). Syn. *mababaw.* —II. *adv.* superficially. Syn. *mababaw, nang mababaw, pasalapyáw.*

pasarili (pa-sa-ri-li), I. *adj. (Gram.)* reflexive. 2. by appropriating something for one's own. —II. *n.* a reflexive verb or pronoun.

pasaríng (pa-sa-ríng), *n.* an indirect derogatory remark or reference to someone; innuendo; insinuation. Syn. *pariníg, paringíg, patutsada.*

pasas (pa-sas), *n.* (Sp. *pasa*) any of the various kind of sweet, dried grapes, esp. seedless; raisin.

pasasà (pa-sa-sà), I. *adj.* abundantly supplied. Syn. *saganà, nanánaganà.* —II. *n.* state or condition of being abundantly supplied. Syn. *pananaganà.*

pasasa- (pa-sa-sa-), a combining form used to express the future tense of *pasa-*.

pasawatâ (pa-sa-wa-tâ), I. *v.* to allow oneself to be stopped from doing something drastic; heed someone's advice to stop. Syn. *pasawáy.* —II. *adj. & adv.* by advising to stop, or desist from.

Pasko (Pas-ko), *n.* (Sp. *Pascua*) Christmas; Yuletide.

pasko ng pagkabuhay, easter.

pasénsiyá (pa-sén-si-yá), var. **paseyénsiyá, pasyénsiyá,** *n.* (Sp. *paciencia*) 1. patience; calm endurance of pain, trouble, etc. Syn. *tiís, pagtitiís.* 2. steady effort; perseverance. Syn. *tiyagâ, pagtitiyagâ, katiyagaán.* 3. willingness to forgive someone. Syn. *paumanhín, pagpapaumanhín.*

paseo (pa-se-o), *n. (Sp.)* 1. promenading or taking a walk for pleasure. Syn. *pasyál, pamamasyál, pagpapasyál.* 2. a going around, as a band of musicians during a town fiesta. Syn. *libot, paglilibót, pagpapalibut-libot.*

pasikat (pa-si-kat), I. *n.* 1. a showing off. Syn. *parangyâ, pagpaparangyâ.* 2. a bragging or boasting. Syn. *paghahambóg.*

pasikláb (pa-sik-láb), *n.* 1. (Slang) anything done to show off. Syn. *pasikat, pagpapasikat.* 2. anything that causes sudden ignition or bursting into flame. Also, *pampasikláb.*

pasidhî (pa-sid-hî), *adj.* 1. becoming intense. Syn. *patindí.* 2. getting worse. Syn. *palalâ, palubhâ.* 3. that which makes intense or worse. Syn. *pampatindí, pampalalâ, pampalubhâ.*

pasig (pa-sig), *n.* 1. sandy river bank. Also, *pasigan.* 2. (P-) formerly capital town of the Province of Rizal, now a city of the National Capital Region. 3. (P-) the name of a river that passes Manila and empties at the Manila Bay.

pasilay (pa-si-lay), *v.* to appear or show oneself briefly. Syn. *pakitang sandalî.*

pasilyo (pa-sil-yo), *n.* (Sp. *pasillo*) 1. a small passage way, as between rows of benches; aisle. 2. corridor. 3. *(Colloq.)* a small alley or walk between two rows of houses. Syn. *eskinita.*

pasimulán (pa-si-mu-lán), v. 1. to start or begin doing. Also, *simulán*. Syn. *umpisahán*. 2. to cause something to be started. Syn. *paumpisahán*.

pásimundán (pa-si-mun-dán), var. **pásumundán**, n. 1. model; pattern. Syn. *húwaran, tularán, ulirán, hulwaran*. 2. precedent. Cf. *saligán, batayán*.

pasimunò (pa-si-mu-nò), n. one responsible for starting something undesirable; leader, esp. of an undesirable act; perpetrator. Syn. *promutór*.

pasinayà (pa-si-na-yà), n. inauguration; formal celebration of the first public use or appearance of. Syn. *inagurasyón*.

pasintabì (pa-sin-ta-bì), n. 1. due regard or respect for, as in: *isáng pasintabì sa kanyáng katandaán*, a due regard for his old age. 2. an objection to an objection. 3. a begging pardon or excuse. Syn. *paghingî ng paumanhín*.

pasiyá (pa-si-yá), var. **pasyá**, n. decision; judgment. Syn. *disisyón, hatol*.

pasiyám (pa-si-yám), I. n. a novena in memory of a dead person, held on the ninth day of his or her death.
—II. n. & adj. ninth. Syn. *ikasiyám, pansiyám*.

pasláng (pas-láng), I. adj. insolent; impertinent; impudent; irreverent. Syn. *waláng-galang, waláng-pítagan, waláng-pakundangan, pusóng, lapastangan*.
—II. n. 1. act of committing insolence; irreverence. 2. (*Colloq.*) act of killing another; murder. Syn. *pagpatáy sa kapwà*. 3. (*Colloq.*) murderer.

paslít (pas-lít), I. n. a young, innocent child. Syn. *batang musmós o inosente*.
—II. adj. very young; innocent; inexperienced. Syn. *musmós, waláng-muwáng, waláng-malay, inosente*.

pasma (pas-ma), n. (prob. Sp. *pasmo*) an abnormal state of the nerves with manifestation of sweating and slight shaking of the body or any part of it, esp. the hands.

paso (pa-so), n. (*Sp.*) 1. a pass or way; passage; passageway. Syn. *daán, daanán, lagusan, bagtasan*. 2. pace or gait, as of a horse. Cf. *trote, yagyág, imbáy*.

pasò (pa-sò), n. burn or injury on the skin caused by something hot or by scalding; scald. Syn. *banlî* (when caused by hot water or liquid).

pasó (pa-só), I. adj. expired; having elapsed; with no more effect. Syn. *lipás, walâ nang bisà, pasado*.

pasô (pa-sô), n. 1. flowerpot. Syn. *masetera*. 2. an earthen vessel used as food container. Syn. *kamáw*.

pasok (pa-sok), n. 1. a going inside; entry. Syn. *papunta sa loób, pagpasok*. 2. penetration. Syn. *pagbaón, pagtusok*. 3. act or time of going to school or place of work. Syn. *pagpasok, oras ng pagpasok*. 4. (in accounting) entry.

paspasán (pas-pa-sán), v. 1. to clean by sweeping away the dust from, as with a duster. 2. to attack (physically or verbally). Syn. *banatan, tirahin, birahán*. 3. to do something (with haste or hurry). Syn. *gawíng madalî o dalí-dalî*. 4. to attack (a woman) sexually. Syn. *gahisín, gahasain*. 5. to eat something voraciously or in haste. Syn. *lamunin, kaining dalás-dalás*. 6. to drive (a vehicle) with great speed. Syn. *patakbuhín nang matulin*.

pastilyas (pas-til-yas), n. (Sp. *pastillas*) 1. lozenge; pastille; small tablet. Syn. *tabletas, píldurás*. 2. a small candy.

pastól (pas-tól) n. (Sp. *pastor*) 1. shepherd; animal herder. Syn. *pastór, tagapastól*. 2. the act or manner of pasturing animals. Syn. *pagpapastól, pagkakápastól*.

pastór (pas-tór), n. (*Sp.*) 1. pastor; minister; clergyman. Syn. *ministro, kura, klero, parè*. 2. same as *pastól*.

pasubalì (pa-su-ba-lì), n. dissenting opinion; exception expressed against something or against someone. See **pasintabì**.

pasubaybáy (pa-su-bay-báy), I. adj. & adv. by following and observing secretly.
—II. n. & adj. said of a person assigned by someone to follow and observe another secretly.

pasugbá (pa-sug-bá), adj. & adv. by plunging or dashing impetuously into a certain danger. Cf. *pasugód*.

pasugò (pa-su-gò), n. 1. an order for someone to accomplish. Syn. *utos*. 2. message sent through someone. Syn. *pabalità*. 3. errand or mission that someone is to carry out. Syn. *misyón*. 4. messenger sent to deliver something to someone.

pasuling-suling (pa-su-ling + su-ling), *adj. & adv.* going around aimlessly in desperation or bewilderment. Syn. *pagalá-galá*.

pasulóng (pa-su-lóng), I. *adj. & adv.* 1. by advancing forward. Syn. *paabante*. 2. by pushing forward. Syn. *patulák*. —II. *adj.* progressing; making progress. Syn. *umúunlád*.

pasulyáp-sulyáp (pa-sul-yáp + sul-yáp), *adj. & adv.* with the eyes looking fearfully or suspiciously from side to side.

pasumalá (pa-su-ma-lá), I. *adj.* 1. accidental; happening by chance. Syn. *di-sinásadyâ; kátaón*. 2. temporary. Syn. *pansamantalá*. 3. by taking a chance. —II. *adv.* 1. accidentally; in an accidental manner. 2. temporarily.

pasunò (pa-su-nò), I. *v.* to allow someone to share a ride in one's vehicle. Also, *magpasunò*. Syn. *paangkás, magpaangkás*. —II. *n. & adj.* said of a passenger (or passengers) who was made to share a ride in one's own vehicle.

pasuray-suray (pa-su-ray + su-ray), *adj.* reeling or staggering, as in pain or due to being drunk. Syn. *pahapay-hapay*.

pasusog (pa-su-sog), *n.* a proposed amendment.

pasyál (pas-yál), *n.* 1. promenading; taking a walk. Also, *pamamasyál*. 2. a short visit to a certain person or place. Syn. *dalaw, pagdalaw*.

pasyente (pas-yen-te), *n.* (Sp. *paciente*) a sick person under the care of a doctor; patient. Syn. *maysakít*.

pasyón (pas-yón), *n.* (Sp. *pasion*) 1. passion; the story of the agony and suffering of Jesus Christ during the Crucifixion or during the period following the Last Supper. 2. the book or the vernacular verse about the life and death of Jesus.

pata (pa-ta), *n.* (*Sp.*) 1. leg of an animal, usually used for food. 2. a dish of animal leg. 3. a contemptuous term for the human leg. Syn. *biyás* (*colloq.*).

patâ (pa-tâ), I. *n.* fatigue; exhaustion; weariness. Syn. *labis na pagod o pagkapagod*. —II. *adj.* fatigued; exhausted; tired out. Syn. *pagód na pagód, nanghíhiná sa pagod*.

pataás (pa-ta-ás), I. *adj.* rising; going upward. Syn. *tumátaás, umáakyát*. —II. *adv.* upward; toward a high place or position. Syn. *paitaás*.

patabâ (pa-ta-bâ), I. *n.* 1. fertilizer. Syn. *pampatabâ, abono*. 2. anything that makes a person fat or plump; fattener. —II. *adj.* 1. that makes soil rich. Syn. *pampatabâ, nakatátabâ*. 2. that fattens a person or animal.

paták (pa-ták), I. *n.* 1. drop, as of tear, water, or any liquid. 2. a dropping or falling in drops. Syn. *tulò, pagtulò*. —II. *n. & adj.* referring to fruits fallen on the ground. Syn. *laglág, lagpák*.

pataká (pa-ta-ká), I. *n.* any act purposely done to make people wonder or to cause surprise or amazement. Also, *pampataká*. —II. *adj. & adv.* in an amazed or astonished manner.

pataksíl (pa-tak-síl), I. *adj.* by treachery. —II. *adv.* in a treacherous or traitorous manner; treacherously.

patadyóng (pa-tad-yóng), *n.* a kind of wide skirt worn by tucking the upper portion in the waistline.

patag (pa-tag), I. *adj.* level; even; flat, said esp. of the surface of land. Syn. *pantáy, hindî bakú-bakô*. —II. *n.* 1. the state or condition of being level or flat. 2. the part of a ground that is flat or level. 3. the way or manner a land surface was levelled. Also, *pagkakápatag*.

patalampák (pa-ta-lam-pák), I. *v.* 1. to allow oneself to be told harshly or openly about one's fault, etc. 2. to wait to be told openly or frankly about something. —II. *adv.* in an open or frank manner; openly; frankly. Syn. *nang tapát o tápatan, nang lántaran o háyagan*.

patalastás (pa-ta-las-tás), *n.* 1. announcement; notice. Syn. *paunawà, babalà*. 2. communique; report or information sent to someone. Syn. *pahatíd, pabalità*.

patalím   **patáy**

patalím (pa-ta-lím), *n*. 1. any sharp bladed or cutting instrument. 2. *(Colloq.)* steel. Syn. *asero*.

patalinghagà (pa-ta-ling-ha-gà), I. *adj*. figurative.

—II. *adv*. figuratively.

pataliwás (pa-ta-li-wás), *adj*. contrary or against the rule or fact. Syn. *pasalungát, kontra, pakontra*.

pataluntón (pa-ta-lun-tón), *adj*. & *adv*. 1. by following the rule, precept, etc. Syn. *paalinsunod, pasunód*. 2. by tracing or following the way, path, etc. Syn. *pasubaybáy, pataguntón*.

patandaán (pa-tan-da-án), *v*. 1. to cause a thing or a place to be provided with a marker. Syn. *palagyán ng tandâ o panandâ*. 2. to tell or cause someone to remember something.

patangáy (pa-ta-ngáy), I. *v*. to allow oneself to be carried away. Also, *magpatangáy*. Syn. *padalá (sa agos, hangin, atbp.)*.

—II. *adj*. & *adv*. by carrying away.

patangkilik (pa-tang-ki-lik), I. *v*. 1. to allow oneself to be given support or protective help by someone. Syn. *patulong, magpatulong; pakalingà, magpakalingà*. 2. to allow self to be adopted by someone. Syn. *paampón, magpaampón*.

—II. *n*. a request for the patronage or support of. Also, *pagpapapatangkilik*. Syn. *pagpapapataguyod*.

—III. *adj*. & *adv*. in the form or manner of help or patronage.

patanghalì (pa-tang-ha-lì), I. *v*. to wait or stay until noon. Syn. *maghintáy o magpaabot ng tanghalì, magpatanghalì*.

—II. *n*. & *adj*. 1. referring to a lunch or a dinner party offered or given in honor of someone. Also, *patanghalian*. 2. referring to the food given during a lunch or dinner party in honor of someone. Syn. *handâ sa pananghalian*.

patao (pa-ta-o), I. *n*. the act of supplying or providing (an office) with personnel or manpower. Also, *pagpapatao*.

—II. *n*. & *adj*. 1. referring to the personnel provided for by someone to man an office.

pataón (pa-ta-ón), I. *v*. to allow oneself to

be seen by someone in the act of doing something. Syn. *pahuli o magpahuli sa akto*.

—II. *adj*. & *adv*. by coincidence.

patapón (pa-ta-pón), I. *adj*. & *n*. referring to materials that are wasted, hence, no longer needed.

—II. *adv*. in a wasteful manner; wastefully. Syn. *paaksayá, nang paaksayá*.

patapós (pa-ta-pós), I. *adj*. & *adv*. with finality.

—II. *n*. the last day of a novenary celebration in memory of a dead relative, usually at the fortieth day of his or her death.

patas (pa-tas), I. *n*. 1. act or way of piling things in an orderly manner. Syn. *salansán, pagsasalansán, pagkakásalansán*. 2. an orderly pile or heap, as of firewood. Syn. *salansán, talaksán*. 3. a contest or match which ended in a tie or draw. Syn. *laróng nagtablá o nagpatas*.

—II. *adj*. that ended in a draw or tie, said of a game or match. Syn. *tablá, nagtablá*.

—III. *adv*. in a tie or draw; with no one winning.

patatas (pa-ta-tas), *n*. *(Sp.)* potato (the plant and its rootstock). Syn. *papas*.

patatwâ (pa-tat-wâ), var. **patatuwâ**, *v*. 1. to tell or request someone to deny that oneself is in or present. Syn. *pakailâ, magpakailâ*. 2. to allow oneself to be repudiated or disowned by someone. Syn. *patakwíl, magpatakwíl*.

pataw (pa-taw), *n*. 1. fetter; chain or shackle for the feet. 2. weight to keep an object down or under water. Syn. *pabigát*. 3. fine; surcharge; penalty. Syn. *multa, rekargo, patong (colloq.)*.

patawad (pa-ta-wad), *n*. 1. pardon; forgiveness. Also, *kapatawarán*. Cf. *paumanhin, pagpapaumanhin*. 2. absolution or remission of sins. Also, *pagpapatawad ng kasalanan*. 3. a discount given to a buyer. Syn. *diskuwento*.

pátawirin (pá-ta-wi-rin), *adj*. referring to a person who is hovering between life and death; with a slim chance of surviving. Syn. *agaw-buhay, nag-aagaw-buhay*.

patáy (pa-táy), I. *adj*. 1. lifeless; dead, said of a person or animal. Syn. *waláng-buhay;*

hindî na humíhingá. 2. off; not on, as a light, electric fan, faucet, etc. Syn. *sarado, nakasará; hindî bukás.* 3. dried; no longer growing, as plants. Syn. *tuyô, tuyô na.* 4. obsolete; no longer in use, as a word, language, law, etc. Syn. *hindî na ginágamit.*
—II. n. 1. the dead body of a person; cadaver; corpse. Syn. *bangkáy.* 2. the dead body of an animal; carcass. 3. state or condition of being dead. 4. act of killing or murdering a person; butchering of an animal, esp. for meat.

patáy-na-loób (pa-táy + na + lo-ób), *adj.* (Fig.) ungrateful. Syn. *waláng-utang-na-loób.*

patay-patay (pa-tay + pa-tay), *adj.* 1. slow moving; sluggish. Syn. *mabagal kumilos, makuyad, makupad.* 2. lazy; idle. Syn. *tamád, batugan.*

patayúng-tayong (pa-ta-yúng + ta-yong), *adj.* often delayed or postponed unnecessarily.

patente (pa-ten-te), *n.* (Sp.) patent; registered right granted to a person to make or sell a new invention.

paternál (pa-ter-nál), *adj.* (Sp.) 1. paternal; fatherly: as in: *payong paternal,* paternal (fatherly) advice. 2. of a father, as in *paternal na pagmamahál,* paternal love or love of a father. Syn. *ng amá.* 3. related on the father's side of the family, as in: *lolong paternal,* grandfather on the father's side.

paternidad (pa-ter-ni-dad), *n.* (Sp.) 1. state of being a father; fatherhood; paternity. Syn. *pagkaamá, pagigíng amá.* 2. male parentage; paternal origin. Syn. *pinag-amahán.* 3. origin or authorship in general. Syn. *pinagmulán, pinanggalingan, pinagbuhatan.*

paternoster (pa-ter-nos-ter), var. **Pater Noster,** *n.* (Lat.) the Lord's Prayer, esp. in Latin.

pati (pa-ti), *n.* 1. advice; admonition. Syn. *payo.* 2. warning. Syn. *paalaala, pagunitâ.*

patí (pa-tí), I. *adj.* including. Syn. *kasama, kabilang.*
—II. *adv.* also; too; even; likewise. Syn. *din (rin), gayón din.*
—III. *prep.* as well as; in addition to;

besides.

patì (pa-tì), *n.* 1. turn of a debater to answer his opponent. Syn. *pagsagót.* 2. rebuttal; a debater's answer after the turn of his opponent, as in: *hulíng patì,* last rebuttal. Syn. *sagót, paklî.*

patianód (pa-ti-a-nód), *n.* 1. act of allowing self to drift or be carried along by the current. Also, *pagpapaanód.* Syn. *pagpapatangáy sa agos.* 2. a going with the tide (fig.); allowing oneself to be carried along by circumstances.

patibóng (pa-ti-bóng), *n.* 1. snare; trap. Syn. *bitag, silò, umang.* 2. trick; stratagem; a deceptive scheme. Syn. *panlinlang, pandayà, pakanâ.*

patikím (pa-ti-kím), *n.* 1. a small piece or portion of something, esp. food, given to someone as sample for tasting. Also, *pampatikím.* 2. giving someone a chance to experience something. Syn. *padanas, pagpapadanas.*

patid (pa-tid), *n.* 1. act of tripping the foot of someone intentionally. Also, *pagpatid.* 2. a tripping or being tripped. Also, *pagkápatid.*

patíd (pa-tíd), I. *adj.* 1. cut apart; cut off. Syn. *putól, lagót.* 2. disconnected, as telephone line.
—II. *n.* 1. act of cutting apart a rope, wire, etc. Also, *pagpatíd.* Syn. *putol, pagputol; lagót, paglagót.* 2. act of disconnecting the continuity, as of electric current, etc. 3. state or condition of being cut off or disconnected.

patilya (pa-til-ya), *n.* (Sp. *patilla*) sideburns; sidewhiskers.

patimog (pa-ti-mog), I. *v.* to go south (southward). Also, *pumatimog.*
—II. *adj.* going toward the south; southward bound.
—III. *adv.* towards the south. Also, *patimóg.*

patimpalák (pa-tim-pa-lák), *n.* a literary or beauty contest, or the like, sponsored by someone. See *timpalák.*

patindí (pa-tin-dí), I. *adj.* getting serious; becoming intense. Syn. *palubhâ, lumúlubhâ; palalâ, lumálalâ; pabigát, bumíbigát.* 2. that tends to make serious or intense. Also, *pampatindí*. Syn. *pampalubhâ, pampalalâ, pampabigát*.

atinig (pa-ti-nig), n. (*Gram.*) vowel. Syn. *bokál*.

atinô (pa-ti-nô), I. *adj.* said of a person who is becoming sensible, righteous, etc. Syn. *nagkákaisip, nagkákabaít*.
—II. *n. & adj.* referring to something that helps a person become sensible, righteous, etc. Also, *pampatinô*.

atíng (pa-tíng), n. 1. (*Ichth.*) shark. 2. (*Fig.*) a viciously dishonest person; swindler. Syn. *manggagantso, manunubà*. 3. (*Fig.*) usurer. Also, *patíng-kati*. Syn. *usurero*.

atinga (pa-ti-nga), n. 1. partial advance or down payment for an option to buy something. 2. a deposit, usually an amount to guarantee the return of something borrowed, as in buying softdrinks with the bottle to be taken home. Syn. *depósitó*.

atís (pa-tís), n. a kind of native salty fish sauce.

atláng (pat-láng), n. 1. space or distance between; gap. Syn. *agwát, puwáng*. 2.interval, as of time. Syn. *pagitan*. 3. an omission, as in typing or printing. Syn. *palya (palyo)*.

atníg (pat-níg), n. reparteé; witty reply or answer.

atnubay (pat-nu-bay), n. 1. guide; leader; escort. Syn. *giyá, lider, gabáy, tagaakay*. 2. bodyguard. Syn. *tanod, guwardiyá, taliba*. 3. guidance; leadership. Also, *pamamatnubay, pagpatnubay*.

atnugot (pat-nu-got), n. 1. editor. Syn. *editór*. 2. direktor; administrator. Syn. *direktór, tagapangasiwà*.

ato (pa-to), n. (*Sp., Zool.*) 1. wild duck. 2. the common domestic duck. Syn. *itik, bibi*.

atók (pa-tók), I. (*Slang*) n. sure winner in a horse race.
—II. *adj.* sure of winning, referring to a horse.

atol (pa-tol), n. act of dealing with, paying attention to, or even falling in love with someone unworthy or inferior in rank. Also, *pagpatol*. Syn. *pakikitungo sa isáng di-karapat-dapat o mababà ang urì*.

atola (pa-to-la), n. (*Bot.*) 1. a coarse, annual, herbaceous vine (*Luffa Acutangula Roxb.*) commonly cultivated for its edible fruit. 2. the fruit of this vine.

patong[1] (pa-tong), I. n. 1. act of placing one thing on the top of another. Also, *pagpapatong*. 2. the position of two things with one on top of the other. Also, *pagkakápatong*. 3. (*Fig.*) cohabitation, esp. among animals. Syn. *babá, pagbabá*. 4. anything placed on top of another; a super-imposed matter. Syn. *ang nakapatong o nasa ibabaw*.
—II. *adj.* with one on top of another. Also, *magkapatong*.

patong[2] (pa-tong), n. (*Comm.*) 1. interest charged on loans or debts. Syn. *patubò sa utang*. 2. fine or penalty for overdue loan or debt. Syn. *multa, rikargo, pataw*.

patotoó (pa-to-to-ó), I. n. 1. proof; conclusive evidence. Syn. *katibayan, pruweba*. 2. a statement or testimony tending to confirm the truth about something. Syn. *patunay, pagpapatunay*.
—II. *adj. & adv.* in an intentional manner; intentionally. Syn. *nang tótohanan, talagá, sadyâ*.

patotot (pa-to-tot), var. **patutot**, n. prostitute; harlot. Syn. *puta, burikák (colloq.), kalapating mababà ang lipád* (fig.).

patpát (pat-pát), n. a bamboo stick or split; distinguished from *lapát*.

pátpatin (pát-pa-tin), *adj.* tall and thin; slender; slim. Syn. *mahagway, balingkinitan*.

patrón (pa-trón), n. (*Sp.*) 1. a patron or guardian saint. Syn. *santóng pitakasi o tagapag-adyá*. 2. a sponsor, as of a radio or television program. Syn. *tagatangkilik, tagataguyod*.

patsada (pat-sa-da), n. (*Sp. fachada*) 1. (*Arch.*) façade, as of a building. Syn. *haráp, harapán*. 2. frontispiece; title page. Syn. *dahong pambungad (pamukhâ)*.

patse (pat-se), n. (Hispanized Eng., or prob. Sp. *pache*) 1. plaster; poultice. Syn. *tapal, panapa*. 2. patch; piece of material sewn to cover or mend a hole or tear. Syn. *tagpî*. 3. act or manner of plastering or applying with a poultice. Also, *pagpapatse, pagkakápatse*. Syn. *pagtatapal, pagka-kátapal*. 4. act of patching or covering a hole or tear with a patch. Syn. *pagtatagpî*, *pagkakátagpî*.

patubig (pa-tu-big), I. n. 1. (*Agri.*) irrigation system. 2. water supply system.

—II. *adj.* supplied with free water, usually said of house tenants.

patubilíng (pa-tu-bi-líng), n. weathercock; weather vane. Syn. *girimpulá*, *banoglawin*.

pátumanggâ (pá-tu-mang-gâ), n. careful thought or thinking; prudent consideration, as in: *waláng-pátumanggâ*, without careful thought or prudent consideration.

patunay (pa-tu-nay), n. 1. a proving or certifying that something is true. Also, *pagpapatunay*. 2. proof, evidence. Syn. *patotoo*, *katíbayan*, *ebidensiyâ*.

patungkól (pa-tung-kól), n. & *adj.* referring to something dedicated or done in honor or in memory of someone. Syn. *handóg*, *alay*.

patungo (pa-tu-ngo), I. *v.* to go to (a certain place). Syn. *pumunta*, *magpunta*.

—II. *adj.* going or moving towards a certain place. Syn. *papunta*, *púpunta*.

—III. *prep.* towards; in the direction of.

patungó (pa-tu-ngó), *adj.* & *adv.* with the head bowed or lowered. Syn. *paukô o payukô ang ulo*.

patúng-patong (pa-túng + pa-tong), *adj.* 1. placed on top of one another. Also, *magkakapatong*. 2. (*Colloq.*) too many; very many, said of work to do. Syn. *nakatambák nakabuntón*, *nápakarami*.

pátunguhan (pá-tu-ngu-han), n. 1. exodus or simultaneous going of a group or a certain number of people to a certain place. Syn. *púntahan*, *pagpupúntahan*. 2. place where many people usually go, as during summer.

patupat (pa-tu-pat), n. 1. a crudely made cigar or cigarette holder or pipe. 2. a kind of home-made cigar or cigarette.

paturan (pa-tu-ran), *v.* 1. to cause or allow something to be mentioned. Syn. *ipasabi*, *ipabanggít*. 2. to let someone guess the answer, esp. to a riddle. Syn. *ipasagót*; *ipasabi ang sagót*, *paturingan*.

paturing (pa-tu-ring), I. *v.* 1. to allow oneself to be considered as someone's friend, etc.

Also, *magpaturing*. 2. to ask or request tha oneself be called by a certain name.

—II. *n.* a request for an answer to a riddle

patutot (pa-tu-tot), var. patotot , n prostitute; harlot. Syn. *puta*, *buriká* (*colloq.*), *kalapating mababà ang lipád* (*fig.*)

patutsada (pa-tut-sa-da), n. innuendo insinuation; indirect derogatory remark o reference to someone. Syn. *pasaríng pariníg* (*paringíg*).

patyo (pat-yo; pat-yô), n. (Sp. *patio*) 1. court; courtyard. 2. churchyard.

paubayà (pa-u-ba-yà), n. 1. relinquishmen of one's right or responsibility to another 2. act of allowing someone to do, decide act, etc. alone by himself. Also *pagpapaubayà*. (for both senses).

paulit-ulit (pa-u-lit + u-lit), I. *adj.* said done, or made more than once; repeated many times.

—II. *adv.* again and again; more tha once; repeatedly.

paulo (pa-u-lo), *adj.* heaping; overfull. Syn *apaw*, *umáapaw*, *punúng-punô*.

paumaga (pa-u-ma-ga), I. *v.* to let the nigh pass; wait for the night to pass; wait til morning comes. Also, *magpaumaga*.

—II. *n.* act of waiting for the night to pass Also, *pagpapaumaga*. Syn. *pagpaparaán n gabí*.

paumanhín (pa-u-man-hín), n. 1. apology excuse for fault or wrong done, as in *humingî ng paumanhín*, to ask for apology Syn. *patawad*, *pagpapatawad*. 2. ttoleratior of someone's fault with kind understanding. Syn. *paubayà pagpapaubayà*.

paumang (pa-u-mang), I. *n.* & *adj.* refering to a snare or trap set for someone.

—II. *v.* to allow oneself to be pointed closely with a gun. Syn. *patutok*, *magpatutok*.

páuná (pá-u-ná), I. *n.* 1. down payment partial advance payment. Syn. *antisipo*. 2 act of starting something ahead of others. Also, *pagpápáuná*. 3. anything said, made, or done in advance.

—II. *adj.* first, made, done, or said in advance. Syn. *una*, *náuuná*.

—III. *adv.* in advance; beforehand.

páunáng-bayad (pá-u-náng + ba-yad), n.
down payment; partial advance payment.
Syn. *antisipo*. See **páuná**.

páunáng-salitâ (pá-u-náng + sa-li-tâ), n.
introduction. Syn. *introduksiyón*,
pambungad na pangungusap.

paunawà (pa-u-na-wà), n. 1. act of
explaining something to someone in order
to be understood; explanation. Syn.
*paliwanag, pagpapaliwanag; paintindí,
pagpapaintindí*. 2. notice; announcement.
Syn. *patalastás, pabatíd*. 3. warning. Syn.
babalâ. 4. advice. Syn. *payo*.

paunda (pa-un-da), I. n. & adj. referring to
the waves or curls made on someone's
hair. Syn. *alún-alón*.
—II. adv. with curls or waves, referring
to the arranging of hair. Syn. *alún-alón,
paalún-alón*.

pauntî (pa-un-tî), I. adj. getting smaller in
size or in number. Syn. *paliít, pakauntî*.
—II. n. & adj. referring to a thing that
causes something to become smaller in
size or in number. Also, *pampauntî*. Syn.
pampaliít, pampakauntî.

pauntúl-untól (pa-un-túl + un-tól), I. adj.
with several stops; stopping and starting
again at intervals; intermittent. Syn.
pahintú-hintô, patigíl-tigil.
—II. adv. intermittently.

paurá-urada (pa-u-rá + u-ra-da), adv. hastily;
in haste; without preparation. Syn.
pabiglá-biglâ, nang waláng paghahandâ.

páurián (pá-u-ri-án), n. a place or a
laboratory where metal, esp. gold or silver,
can be submitted for assaying.

pausong (pa-u-song), I. v. to ask, request,
or accept the help of another in carrying
a heavy load. Also, *magpausong*.
—II. adj. & adv. 1. by helping another in
carrying a heavy load. 2. by helping each
other in carrying a heavy load.

pautós (pa-u-tós), I. adj. (*Gram.*) imperative,
as in: *pangungusap na pautós*, imperative
sentence.
—II. n. (*Gram.*) 1. the imperative mood.
2. a verb in the imperative.

pawà (pa-wà), I. adj. all; every one; all
together, as in: *Ang buhay ay hindî pawang
kasiyahan*. Life is not all pleasure. Syn.

*lahát, lahát-lahát, taganas, panáy, puro,
para-para*.
—II. adv. all; altogether; entirely, as in:
pawang sirâ, all worn out. Syn. *lubós, lahát,
ganáp*.

pawaláng-bisà (pa-wa-láng + bi-sà), v. to
annul; invalidate; declare null and void.
Syn. *pawaláng-saysáy*.

pawatás (pa-wa-tás), adj. & n. (*Gram.*)
infinitive. Syn. *impinitibo*.

pawî (pa-wî), n. 1. act of erasing something,
as with a rubber, ink eradicator, etc. Also,
pagpawì. Syn. *burá, pagburá, pagbuburá*. 2.
the place where something was erased;
erasure. Syn. *pinagburahán, pinagpawian*.
3. disappearance, as of one's tiredness,
thirst, etc. Syn. *pagkawalâ, pagkaparam*.

pawikan (pa-wi-kan), n. (*Zool.*) a species of
large sea turtle.

pawid (pa-wid), n. (*Bot.*) 1. nipa palm. Syn.
sasá. 2. nipa palm leaves which are usually
used for thatching roofs.

payák (pa-yák), I. adj. 1. (*Gram.*) simple, as
in: *payák na pangungusap*, simple sentence.
Syn. *simple, yano*. 2. pure; without
mixture. Syn. *puro, waláng-halò*. 3. all;
every one; altogether. Syn. *pawà, lahát,
panáy, lúbusan*.

payag (pa-yag), I. n. 1. conformity;
acquiescence. Syn. *sang-ayon, pagsang-
ayon*. 2. consent; approval. Syn.
*pahintulot, pagpapahintulot; patibay,
pagpapatibay*.
—II. adj. in accord with; consenting;
interposing no objection to, said of
persons. Syn. *sang-ayon, sumásang-ayon*.

payagpág (pa-yag-pág), n. 1. flapping of
wings. Cf. *pagaspás*. 2. act of shaking the
body, as of a wet dog trying to shake off
water, dust, etc. Syn. *palagpág*. 3. (*Fig.*) a
bragging or boasting. Also,
pamamayagpág. Syn. *paghahambóg,
pagpapasikat*.

payapà (pa-ya-pà), I. adj. peaceful; calm;
tranquil. Syn. *tahimik, matahimik; tiwasáy,
matiwasáy*.
—II. n. 1. a pacifying or being pacified.
2. state or condition of being calm or
peaceful. Also, *kapayapaán, pagkapayapà*.
Syn. *katiwasayán, pagkatiwasáy*.

payaso (pa-ya-so), n. (Sp.) clown; jester. Syn. bobo, lakayo (lukayo), kómikó, komikero.

payát (pa-yát), adj. 1. thin; skinny; lean. Syn. butó't balát, manipís ang katawán.

payo (pa-yo), n. advice; counsel. Syn. hatol, aral, pangaral.

payola (pa-yo-la), n. (Eng.) 1. payola, bribery. Syn. pagsuhol. 2. bribe given. Syn. suhol, paratíng.

payong (pa-yong), n. umbrella; parasol.

paypáy (pay-páy), n. 1. scapula; shoulder blade. 2. (Colloq.) shoulder, as in: Masakít ang aking paypáy. My shoulder aches. Syn. balikat.

payungyóng (pa-yung-yóng), I. v. 1. to allow oneself to be under the protective shade of the overhanding branches of a tree. 2. to allow oneself to be under the power, control, or jurisdiction of someone. Syn. magpailalim, pasakláw, magpasakláw.
—II. adv. by putting under one's protective care, control, or jurisdiction.

Pebo (Pe-bo), n. (Sp. Febo) 1. Phoebus; Apollo, the god of the sun. 2. (Poetic) the sun personified.

Pebrero (Peb-re-ro), n. (Sp. Febrero) February, second month of the year.

pekas (pe-kas), n. (Sp. pecas) freckles. Cf. anán. 2. (Colloq.) mildew. Cf. amag.

peklát (pek-lát), var. piklát, pilat, n. scar.

pekulyár (pe-kul-yár), adj. (Sp. peculiar) peculiar; strange; odd; unusual. Syn. kaibá, kakaibá; katwâ, kakatwâ; di-karaniwan.

pedágogó (pe-dá-go-gó), n. (Sp.) pedagogue; teacher. Syn. gurò, maestro.

pelíkulá (pe-lí-ku-lá), n. (Sp. pelicula) motion picture film.

peligroso (pe-li-gro-so), var. piligroso, adj. (Sp.) dangerous; risky. Syn. mapanganib.

peluka (pe-lu-ka), n. (Sp. peluca) wig. Syn. pustisong buhók.

pelús (pe-lús), I. n. (Sp. pelusa) velvet. Syn. tersiyopelo.
—II. adj. of or made of velvet. Syn. yarì sa pelús.

peniténsiyá (pe-ni-tén-si-yá), n. (Sp. penitencia) 1. penitence; sorrow for doing wrong. Syn. pagsisisi. 2. penance; sacrifice.

Syn. pagpapakasakit, pagpapahirap sa saril'

penitente (pe-ni-ten-te), I. adj. (Sp. penitent; sorry for doing wrong. Sy» nagsísisi.
—II. n. penitent; a person who is sorr for sins.

penoy (pe-noy), n. hard-boiled duck's egg

penúltimó (pe-núl-ti-mó), adj. (Sp. penultimate; next to the last. Syr pangalawá sa hulí.

pepino (pe-pi-no), var. pipino, n. (Sp.; Bot cucumber.

pera (pe-ra), n. (Sp.-Mex.) 1. centavo. Syr sentimo (sentimós). 2. money (in general Syn. kuwalta (kuwarta). 3. wealth. Syr yaman, kayamanan, pilak, salapî.

perdisyón (per-dis-yón), n. (Sp. perdición 1. perdition; ruin; complete an irreparable loss. Syn. lubós n kapahamakán, lubós na pagkápariwarà. 2 (Theol.) loss of one's soul. Syr pagkápanganyayà ng káluluwá.

peregrinasyón (pe-re-gri-nas-yón), n. (Sp peregrinacion) pilgrimage. Syn. paglalakbá sa isáng banál na lugár.

pergamino (per-ga-mi-no), n. (Sp. parchment paper.

perhuwisyo (per-hu-wis-yo), n. (Sp perjuicio) 1. injury; damage; harm. Syn pinsalà, kapinsalaán, kapahamakán. 2 prejudice.

pero (pe-ro), conj. (Sp.) but; on the othe hand. Syn. subalì, subali't (subalit); nguni nguni't (ngunit); dátapwâ, datapwá' (dátapwát).

perokaríl (pe-ro-ka-ríl), n. (Sp. ferocarri railroad.

perpekto (per-pek-to), adj. (Sp. perfecto perfect; without mistake; having no faul Syn. waláng-malî, tamang lahát.

perpétuwá (per-pé-tu-wá), var. perpetwa adj. (Sp. perpetua) perpetual; forever. Syn waláng-hanggán, waláng-katapusán.

perso.ahe (per-so-na-he), n. (Sp. personaje 1. personage; specifically, character in play, novel, or in history. 2. crew, as of ship. 3. personnel. Syn. tauhan (for all th senses).

personál (per-so-nál), adj. 1. private individual; personal. Syn. sarili, pansaril

2. done in person; directly by oneself. Syn. *hárapan*. 3. about or against someone; personal, as in: *punáng personál*, personal remark. Syn. *tungkól o laban sa kapwà*. 4. (*Gram.*) personal; showing the person, as in: *personál na panghalíp*, personal pronoun. Syn. *panao*.

personalidád (per-so-na-li-dád), n. (*Sp.*) 1. personality; personal quality that makes a person different from another. Syn. *kakanyahán, sariling katangian*. 2. being a person. Syn. *katauhan, pagkatao*.

personipikasyón (per-so-ni-pi-kas-yón), n. (*Sp. personificacion*) 1. personification; a personifying or being personified. Syn. *paglalarawang-tauhan*. 2. embodiment; perfect example. Syn. *tunay na larawan o halimbawà*. 3. a figure of speech in which something is represented as a person. Syn. *pagsasatao, pagbibigáy-katauhan*.

perya (per-ya), n. (*Sp. feria*) fair; exposition; exhibition. Cf. *tanghalan*.

peryódikó (per-yó-di-kó), n. (*Sp. periodico*) periodical; newspaper; journal. Syn. *páhayagán, diyaryo*.

pesà (pe-sà), n. a dish of boiled fish with spices.

peste (pes-te), n. (*Sp.*) 1. plague; pest. Syn. *salot, epidemya*. 2. pest; nuisance. Syn. *pangguló, pambuwisit*.

pesteho (pes-te-ho), n. (*Sp. festejo*) any festive celebration; festivity; festival. Syn. *kasayahan, selebrasyón, pagdiriwang*.

petsa (pet-sa), n. (*Sp. fecha*) date.

petsay (pet-say; -sáy), n. (*Ch.; Bot.*) Chinese cabbage.

piká (pi-ká), n. (*Sp. pica*) a fit of displeasure; pique; irritation; annoyance. Syn. *yamót, pagkayamót; inís, pagkainís*.

pikî (pi-kî), I. *adj.* knock-kneed; opposed to *sakáng*.

—II. *n.* state or condition of being knock-kneed. 2. a knock-kneed person.

pikít (pi-kít), I. *n.* 1. act of closing the eyes. 2. state or condition of being closed (s.o. eyes.)

—II. *adj.* 1. closed, referring to eyes. Also, *nakàpikít*. 2. with or having closed eyes, referring to a person. Syn. *sarado ang mga matá*. 3. asleep; sleeping. Syn. *tulóg,*

natútulog. 4. pretending to be blind. Syn. *nagbubulág-bulagan*.

pikít-matá (pi-kít + ma-tá), I. *adj.* with closed eyes.

—II. *adv.* in a blind manner; blindly.

pikón (pi-kón), adj. (*Sp. picón*) peevish; easily offended or provoked to anger by jokes. Syn. *magagalitín*.

pikot (pi-kot), n. 1. act of surrounding a fugitive, an enemy, etc. for the purpose of capturing. Syn. *kubkób, pagkubkób*. 2. act of forcing someone into an awkward position from which escape is difficult.

pikpík (pik-pík), I. *n.* act or manner of pressing down something to make compact, by or as by striking lightly with the hand. Also, *pagpikpík*.

—II. *adj.* made compact or pressed down by the light strokes of the hand.

piksí (pik-sí), var. **pigsí**, n. flounce; act of flouncing. Also, *pagpiksí*.

pideos (pi-de-os), var. **pidyós**, n. vermicelli.

pigâ (pi-gâ), I. *n.* 1. act of removing water from clothes by wringing or squeezing. 2. act of extracting juice, as from a lemon fruit, by pressing or squeezing. Also, *pagpigâ* (for both senses).

—II. *adj.* 1. wrung of water (s.o. wet clothes, etc.). 2. squeezed of juice (s.o. oranges, etc.).

pighatî (pig-ha-tî), n. profound sorrow; mental anguish or suffering; affliction. Syn. *dalamhatì, matindíng lungkót*.

pigî (pi-gî), n. either half of the rump; buttock.

pigil (pi-gil), n. 1. act of holding tightly in or with one's hand. Also, *pagpigil*. Syn. *tangan o pagtangan nang mahigpít*. 2. detention; confinement or keeping in custody. Syn. *ditiní, pagditiní, pagkulóng*. 3. a stopping or preventing from doing or continuing; suspension. Syn. *pagpapahintô, pagpapatigil, pagsuspende*. 4. control, as of one's temper. Also, *pagpipigil*.

pigíng (pi-gíng), n. 1. act of entertaining or honoring someone by giving a banquet. 2. a banquet given in honor of someone. Syn. *salu-salong handóg sa pinarárangalán*.

pigipit (pi-gi-pit), var. **pigapit**, n. 1. act of causing someone to be in a tight situation.

504

Syn. *paggipít, paglalagáy sa gipít na kalagayan.* 2. act of placing or putting someone under pressure or compulsion. Syn. *pagpilit.*

piglás (pig-lás), *n.* sudden struggle or effort to get free from someone's hold. Syn. *bigláng kilos sa pag-aalpás.*

pigsa (pig-sa; -sá), *n.* boil; abscess.

pigtâ (pig-tâ), I. *n.* a being drenched or wet all over, said of someone's clothes.

—II. *adj.* drenched or wet all over. Syn. *basáng-basâ, puyóg.*

pigtál (pig-tál), I. *n.* a detaching or being detached forcibly, as buttons from one's pants. Also, *pagpigtál, pagkapigtál.* Syn. *pagpigtás, pagkapigtás.*

—II. *adj.* detached or ripped off forcibly. Syn. *pigtás, napigtás.*

pigtás (pig-tás), I. *n.* 1. a detaching or tearing out from, as a page of a book. Syn. *pigtál, pagpigtál; punit, pagpunit.* 2. a ripping or tearing open forcibly, as one's pocket, buttonhole, or the like. Syn. *bigtál, pagbigtál.*

—II. *adj.* 1. detached or torn off, as a page of a book. Syn. *pigtál, napigtál; punít, napunit.* 2. ripped or torn open, as a buttonhole, pocket, etc.

pigura (pi-gu-ra), *n.* (Sp. *figura*) 1. figure; the way a person or thing looks; shape. Syn. *hitsura, hugis, anyô, ayos.* 2. illustration or design, as on a book. Syn. *larawan, dibuho.* 3. (Math.) number. Syn. *número.* 4. (Fig.) a sizing up, esp. in reference to someone's beauty or figure. Syn. *kilatis, pagkilatis (fig.); kaliskís, pagkaliskís (fig.).*

pigurín (pi-gu-rín), *n.* (Sp. *figurín*) 1. mannequin. Syn. *manikín.* 2. decorative statuette. Syn. *maliít na rebulto.* 3. a fashion plate. Syn. *larawan ng mga bagong moda ng damít.* 4. dummy; a tool of another. Syn. *pantalya, taú-tauhan.*

pihado (pi-ha-do), I. *adj.* sure; certain; without doubt. Syn. *tiyák, piho, sigurado, waláng-duda, waláng-alinlangan.*

—II. *adv.* surely; certainly; without doubt. Syn. *tiyák, tíyakan, sigurado.*

pihikan (pi-hi-kan), *adj.* fastidious or choosy, esp. with food. Syn. *tamilmíl sa*

pagkain, maselan o pilian sa pagkain.

pihit (pi-hit), *n.* 1. act of turning one's head or face, or even one's body to one side. Syn. *baling, pagbaling; paling, pagpaling.* 2. change of direction, as of wind. Syn. *pagiibá o pagbabago ng direksiyón.* 3. turning around and around; rotation; gyration. Syn. *ikot, pag-ikot.* 4. act or manner of causing something to turn round and round. Syn. *pagpapaikot.* 5. act of turning a key, handle, knob, or the like, as in opening something. Cf. *pagbubukás.*

piho (pi-ho), I. *adj.* sure; certain. Syn. *pihado, tiyák, sigurado.*

—II. *adv.* surely; certainly; without doubt. Syn. *tiyák, tíyakan, pihado, sigurado.*

piít (pi-ít), I. *n.* 1. confinement in a cell or prison, as of a criminal. Syn. *pagkulóng, pagkukulóng; pagbilanggô, pagbibilanggô; pagpipreso.* 2. being confined in a cell or prison. Syn. *pagkákulóng, pagkábilangô, pagkápreso.*

—II. *adj.* 1. confined in a cell or prison. Syn. *nakakulóng, nakabilanggô.* 2. too crowded or packed too full, as employees in a small room. Syn. *siksikan, gipít na gipít.*

pila¹ (pi-la), *n.* (Sp.) dry cell battery, esp. for flashlights.

pila² (pi-la), *n.* (Sp. *fila*) row; file; line information. Syn. *linya, hilera, hanay.*

pilak (pi-lak), I. *n.* 1. silver (metal). Syn. *plata.* 2. silver coin or money. 3. (Colloq.) money. Syn. *pera, salapî, kuwalta (kuwarta).*

—II. *adj.* made of silver. Syn. *yarì sa pilak.*

pilapil (pi-la-pil), *n.* a small dike or levee made of earth between two paddies of an irrigated field. Syn. *hapila, turundón.*

pilas (pi-las), *n.* 1. act of tearing or detaching a leaf from a book, etc. Syn. *pigtás, pagpigtás; punit, pagpunit.* 2. a small piece or strip of paper, cloth, etc. torn off from a bigger piece. Syn. *piraso.* 3. a sheet, as of typing paper. Syn. *pilyego, pohas.* 4. a tear or laceration in the female sex organ due to childbirth, sexual intercourse, etc. Syn. *punit.*

pilat (pi-lat), *n.* scar. Syn. *peklát (piklát).*

pilay (pi-lay), *n.* 1. sprain; pain at the bone joint due to injury. Syn. *pinsala sa butó.* 2.

pildorás

pina-

bone dislocation. Syn. *linsád o paglinsád ng butó sa kasu-kasuán.* 3. *(Fig.)* disadvantage; lack, as of certain qualifications, etc. Syn. *kakulangán, disbentaha.* 4. walking with a limp. Syn. *pamimiláy, pagpiláy.*

pildorás (pil-do-rás), var. **pildurás**, n. (Sp. *pildora*) pill; tiny ball of medicine.

pileges (pi-le-ges), var. **pleges**, n. (Sp. *pliegue*) plait; pleat. Cf. *tupî, lupî.*

pilete (pi-le-te), n. (Sp. *filete*) hem; piece of cloth usually made by folding the edge and sewn along the border of a garment.

pilì[1] (pi-lì), I. n. 1. act of choosing or selecting the best or those that are needed. Syn. *hirang, paghirang.* 2. that or those selected. 2. cleaning of rice *(bigás)* by picking grass seeds, grains of sand, etc. from it.
—II. adj. chosen or selected from among many; hence, the best.

pilì[2] (pi-lì), n. *(Bot.)* 1. a tropical tree that bears nuts that look like almonds. 2. the nut of this tropical tree.

pilík (pi-lík), n. 1. any of the hairs on the edge of the eyelid; eyelash. 2. all of the hair on the edge of the eyelid or eyelids; eyelashes. Also, *pilikmata.*

pilíg (pi-líg), n. 1. act of shaking the head, as when one tries to dislodge something from inside the ears. 2. the shaking of the body of animals in an effort to shake off water, dust, etc. Syn. *palagpág, payagpág.*

piling (pi-ling), n. 1. side, space, or position close to another. Syn. *tabí, katabí.* 2. act of placing oneself beside or close to another. Syn. *tabí, pagtabí; siping, pagsiping; sigbáy, pagsigbáy.*

piling (pi-líng), n. 1. a banana cluster; distinguished from *buwíg*, the whole bunch. 2. a cluster of fruit, like lanzones, grapes, and the like. Syn. *kumpól.* 3. act of cutting the clusters or hands (of bananas) from the whole bunch.

Pilipina (Pi-li-pi-na), n. & adj. (Sp. *Filipina*) referring to a female native or citizen of the Philippines.

Pilipinas (Pi-li-pi-nas), n. (Sp. *Filipinas*) Philippines; Republic of the Philippines.

Pilipino (Pi-li-pi-no), I. n. (Sp. *Filipino*) a native or citizen of the Philippines, esp. a male. 2. the Filipino national language based on Tagalog. Syn. *wikang pambansá ng Pilipinas.*
—II. adj. of or pertaining to the Philippines or to its citizens.

pilipisan (pi-li-pi-san), n. *(Anat.)* temple (of the head). Syn. *sentido.*

pilipit (pi-li-pit), n. 1. act of twisting something. 2. a single twist in a strand or rope. Syn. *ikid, ayikid.* 3. a twisting, as of the body in pain. Also, *pamimilipit.* 4. a winding or twisting around something, as of vines. Syn. *puluput, pagpuluput, pamumulupot.* 5. act of distorting or perverting the meaning of.

pilit (pi-lit), I. n. 1. act of forcing someone to do, accept, etc. something against his will. Also, *pagpilit.* Syn. *puwersa, pagpuwersa.* 2. insistence, as of one's reasons, etc. Syn. *giít, paggigiít.* 3. exertion of one's full efforts to attain something very hard to do. Also, *pagpupumilit.*
—II. adj. & adv. by force; with full efforts. Syn. *sápilitan, sa puwersahan.*

pilók (pi-lók), I. n. twisting of a foot, often due to a misstep, resulting sometimes in a sprain or dislocation of the ankle joint. Syn. *tapilók, tapiyók.*
—II. adj. twisted (s.o. an arm, ankle, or foot).

pilósopó (pi-ló-so-pó), n. (Sp. *filósofo*) 1. philosopher. 2. *(Colloq.)* a contentious or argumentative person. Syn. *taong mapágdunúng-dunungan.*

piloto (pi-lo-to), n. *(Sp.)* 1. pilot (of a ship); steersman. Syn. *tagaugit.* 2. pilot (of an aeroplane); aviator; flier. Syn. *abyadór, manlilipad.*

pilya (pil-ya), adj. (Sp. *pilla*) naughty or mischievous (s.o. a girl).

pimiyento (pi-mi-yen-to), var. **pimyento**, n. *(Sp.-Eng.)* 1. pimiento. 2. red pepper.

pimpín (pim-pín), n. 1. hedge or hedges (of plants). Syn. *bakod na halaman.* 2. embankment. Syn. *hapila.*

pina- (pi-na-), prefix used in forming the past tense of *pa-...* *-an, pa-...-in, pa-...-han*, and *pa-...-hin* verbs, as in: *pabutihin, pinabuti, pasamahan, pinasamahan;*

pakainin, pinakain, etc. Note: *pina-* is formed from *pa,* infixed with *–in–.*

pinabayaan (pi-na-ba-ya-an), I. *p.t.* of *pabayaan.*
—II. *adj.* left unattended; abandoned.

pinaka- (pi-na-ka-), prefix used in: (a) forming adjectives in the superlative degree from simple adjectives, as in: *pinakamaganda* (fr. *maganda*), most beautiful; *pinakamatulin* (fr. *matulin*), fastest, etc. (b) forming nouns, meaning "one serving as or who acts as," as in: *pinakahepe,* one serving as president, etc.

pinakaabalá (pi-na-ka-a-ba-lá), *adj.* busiest. Syn. *pinakamatrabaho.*

pinakaamá (pi-na-ka-a-má), *n.* one serving as a father.

pinág- (pi-nág-), prefix used as past form of the prefix *pag-* in the formation of *pag-...-in* verbs and its derivatives, as in: *pinágaralan* (pag-aralan), *pinágbuti* (pagbutihin), *pinágsabihan* (pagsabihan), etc.

pinag-áalinlanganan (pi-nag + á-a-lin-la-nga-nan), *adj.* said of a person or thing that someone has a doubt about. Syn. *pinagdúdudahan.*

pinág-aksayahán (pi-nág + ak-sa-ya-hán), I. *adj.* said of something on which someone spent time or money uselessly.
—II. *p.t.* of *pag-aksayahán.*

pinágbilihán (pi-nág-bi-li-hán), var. **pinágbilhán,** I. *n.* & *adj.* 1. referring to the amount of money obtained from the sale of something. Syn. *nápagbilhán.* 2. *(Bus.)* referring to the amount of sales, as in a store, market stall, etc. Syn. *benta, nápagbilhán.* 3. referring to a person to whom something was sold by someone. Syn. *pinágbentahán.*
—II. *p.t.* of *pagbilihán (pagbilhán).*

pinagbúbuhatan (pi-nág-bu-bu-ha-tan), *n.* source; origin. Syn. *simulà, pinagsisimulán; umpisá, pinag-úumpisahán.* 2. cause. Syn. *dahilán, sanhî.*

pinagkásunduan (pi-nag-ká-sun-du-an), *n.* & *adj.* referring to an agreement or understanding made by a group; said of something agreed upon. Syn. *pinagkáisahán, napagkaisahán.*

pinágdaanán (pi-nág-da-a-nán), I. *n.* & *adj.*

referring to a place where one passed. Also, *dinaanán.* 2. *(Colloq.)* referring to something that a person had experienced. Syn. *dinanas, pinágdadanasan.*
—II. *p.t.* of *pagdaanán.*

pinágdusahan (pi-nág-du-sa-han), I. *adj.* & *n.* referring to a crime or any wrong done for which someone had suffered or was punished.
—II. *p.t.* of *pagdusahan.*

pinágmanahan (pi-nág-ma-na-han), I. *n.* & *adj.* referring to certain characteristics that someone has inherited, as from one's parents.
—II. *p.t.* of *pagmanahan.*

pinágmulán (pi-nág-mu-lán), I. *n.* & *adj.* 1. referring to a source or origin. Syn. *pinágbuhatan, pinánggalingan.* 2. referring to a cause that started something. Syn. *naging dahilán o sanhî.*
—II. *p.t.* of *pagmulán.*

pinágpalà (pi-nág-pa-là), I. *n.* & *adj.* referring to a person who is blessed with or as with a good fortune.
—II. *p.t.* of *pagpalain.*

pinágsabihan (pi-nág-sa-bi-han), I. *adj.* 1. said of someone who was told or notified about something. Also, *pinasabihan.* 2. said of someone who was reprimanded. Syn. *kinagalitan.*
—II. *p.t.* of *pagsabihan.*

pinágsalitaán (pi-nág-sa-li-ta-án), I. *adj.* said of someone who was reprimanded or scolded by someone. Syn. *pinágsabihan, kinagalitan.*
—II. *p.t.* of *pagsalitaán.*

pinágsamahan (pi-nág-sa-ma-han), I. *n.* & *adj.* 1. referring to a thing to which another thing was mixed or added. Syn. *pinághaluan,, pináglahukán.* 2. referring to the good relation or friendship that previously existed between two persons.
—II. *p.t.* of *pagsamahan.*

pinágsamantalahán (pi-nág-sa-man-ta-la-hán), I. *adj.* 1. said of someone who was unfairly taken advantage of. 2. referring to a woman who was sexually attacked against her will. Syn. *ginahasà, pinuwersa*
—II. *p.t.* of *pagsamantalahán.*

pinag-úusig (pi-nag + ú-u-sig), I. *n. (Law.*

respondent; defendant. Syn. *ang nakademanda*.

—II. *adj*. 1. being investigated; under investigation. Syn. *sinísiyasat, nasa pagsisiyasat*. 2. being persecuted. Syn. *ináapí, pinahíhirapan*.

pinahirapan (pi-na-hi-ra-pan), I. *adj*. 1. said of a person who was made to suffer difficulties or hardship. 2. said of something that was caused or ordered to be made hard.

—II. *p.t*. of *pahirapan*.

pinál (pi-nál), *n*. (Sp. *final*) finish; end; conclusion; close; finale. Syn. *wakás, katapusán*.

pinalad (pi-na-lad), I. *adj*. lucky. Syn. *mapalad, masuwerte, sinuwerte*.

—II. *p.t*. of *palarin*.

pinalibhasà (pi-na-lib-ha-sà), I. *adj*. belittled. Syn. *hinamak, minatá* (fig.).

—II. *p.t*. of *palibhasain*.

pinamilí (pi-na-mi-lí), *n*. things that someone bought; purchases.

pinamilì (pi-na-mi-lì), I. *adj*. 1. said of someone who was made or allowed to choose or select what he or she wanted. Also, *pinapamilì*.

—II. *p.t*. of *pamiliin*.

pinanigan (pi-na-ni-gan), I. *adj*. said of someone whom another took sides with.

—II. *p.t*. of *panigan*.

pinanuyuan (pi-na-nu-yu-an), I. *adj*. said of someone to whom another tried to ingratiate oneself.

—II. *p.t*. of *panuyuan*.

pinangát (pi-na-ngát), *n*. & *adj*. referring to fish cooked in a little amount of water with vinegar, ginger, and salt, or instead of vinegar, any sour fruit like tomatoes, tamarind, etc. may be used.

pinanggalingan (pi-nang-ga-li-ngan), I. *n*. 1. source; place where a person or thing came from. Syn. *pinagbuhatan*. 2. cause or reason that brought about something. Syn. *dahilán, sanhî*.

—II. *p.t*. of *panggalingan*.

pinangyarihan (pi-nang-ya-ri-han), I. *n*. 1. place where something occurred or took place. 2. setting, as in a play or drama.

—II. *p.t*. of *pangyarihan*.

pinatáy (pi-na-táy), I. *adj*. murdered; put to death.

—II. *p.t*. of *patayín*.

pinawà (pi-na-wà), *n*. unpolished rice.

pinawalán (pi-na-wa-lán), I. *adj*. 1. set free; freed or released from confinement or prison. Syn. *pinalayà*. 2. said of someone whose request was denied by another. Syn. *pinahindián, tinanggihán*.

—II. *p.t*. of *pawalán*.

Pináy (Pi-náy), *n*. & *adj*. (*Colloq.*) referring to a Filipina, esp. one residing abroad, in distinguishing her from other foreign female nationals. Syn. *Pilipina*.

pindanggâ (pin-dang-gâ), *n*. & *adj*. referring to a spinster or old maid (a derogatory term).

pindóng (pin-dóng), var. **pandóng**, *n*. head cover, usually of cloth, paper, and the like for protection against rain, heat of the sun, etc. Syn. *talukbóng, kulubóng, kubóng*.

pindót (pin-dót), *n*. act of pressing something, usually playfully, with a finger or between two fingers. Cf. *pisíl, pagpisíl-pisíl*.

pinilakang-tabing (pi-ni-la-kang + ta-bing), *n*. 1. silver screen; movie screen. 2. movie; motion picture. Syn. *sine, pelíkulá*. Also written, *pinilakang tabing*.

pinipig (pi-ni-pig) var. **pilipig**, *n*. glutinous rice grains slightly toasted and pounded in a mortar into flakes.

pino[1] (pi-no), *adj*. (Sp. *fino*) 1. fine; finely ground or crushed. Syn. *duróg na duróg, pinulbós*. 2. very thin or slender; fine, as thread. 3. fine; smooth, as skin. Syn. *makinis*. 4. polite; courteous; refined in manners. Syn. *magalang, mapitagan*. 5. of delicate composition. Syn. *pulido*. 6. well-polished; glossy. Syn. *makintáb*.

pino[2] (pi-no), *n*. (*Sp*.) pine tree.

Pinóy (Pi-nóy), *n*. & *adj*. referring to a Filipino citizen living abroad, as distinguished from other nationals. Syn. *Pilipino*.

pinsalà (pin-sa-là), *n*. 1. damage; injury; harm. Syn. *kapahamakán*. 2. moral damage. Syn. *sirà, kasiraán*.

pinsan (pin-san), *n*. cousin.

pinsang-buô (pin-sang + bu-ô), *n*. first cousin.

pinsél (pin-sél), n. (Sp. *pincel*) artist's brush; drawing brush.

pinsík (pin-sík), n. (Ch.) a kind of finely chopped meat with shrimps and onions, wrapped in dough.

pinta (pin-ta; -tá), I. n. (Sp.) 1. act or manner of painting something, e.g. a house, table, etc. Also, *pagpipinta*, *pagkakápinta*. 2. paint; paint preparation. Syn. *pintura*. 3. coating of paint on a surface. 4. a painting; oil painting.
—II. *adj.* (with *ni*) painted by.

pintakasi (pin-ta-ka-si), n. 1. patron saint; titular saint of a church. Syn. *patrono*. 2. cockfighting sessions held during a town fiesta. Cf. *pasabong*. 3. object of worship or veneration.

pintas (pin-tas; -tás), n. 1. adverse criticism; fault-finding. Syn. *pistâ*, *pulà*, *krítiká*. 2. fault; defect. Syn. *samâ*, *kasamaán*; *depekto*; *sirà*, *kasiraán*.

pintíg (pin-tíg), n. beat or beating, as of the heart; throb; palpitation. Syn. *tibók*. 2. a light hit or strike, as in baseball. Syn. *kantí*.

pintô (pin-tô), n. 1. door; any movable structure for opening and closing an entrance to a room, etc. 2. a doorway; gate; entrance. Syn. *pintuan*, *pasukán*.

pintog (pin-tog; -tóg), n. inflation; swelling. Syn. *bintóg*.

pintór (pin-tór), n. 1. (Sp.) in Arts, painter; oil painter. 2. house painter. 3. sign painter.

pintuhò (pin-tu-hò), n. 1. adoration; veneration; worship. Syn. *samba*, *pagsamba*. 2. admiration; high regard; esteem. Syn. *hangà*, *paghangà*. 3. object of worship, admiration, or veneration. Syn. *pintakasi*.

pintura (pin-tu-ra), n. (Sp.) 1. paint. Syn. *pampinta*. 2. an oil painting; canvas. 3. the way something was painted. Also, *pagkakápinta*. 4. art of painting. Syn. *siníng ng pagpipintá*.

pinukpók (pi-nuk-pók), I. *p.t.* of *pukpukín*.
—II. n. & *adj.* referring to a kind of abaca cloth made fine by pounding or beating.

pinunò (pi-nu-nò), n. 1. official; officer. Also, *punò*. 2. chief; head; leader. Syn. *hepe*.

pinúpoón (pi-nú-po-ón), *adj.* (*Colloq.*) highly respected; venerated. Syn. *sinásambá*, *iginágalang na mabuti*.

pinya (pin-ya), I. n. (Bot., Sp. *piña*) 1. the pineapple plant. 2. the juicy, edible fruit of this plant.
—II. *adj.* said of fabric made from the fibers obtained from the leaves of pineapple.

pingas (pi-ngas), n. a nick or indentation in the edge of a plate, saucer, drinking glass, etc., usually caused by breakage. Syn. *bungì*.

pingkáw (ping-káw), I. *adj.* 1. crooked or twisted, referring to an arm or arms. 2. with or having crooked or twisted arm (arms), said of a person. Syn. *komang*, *pingkól* (for both senses).
—II. n. state or condition in which a person's arm (or arms) is (are) twisted or crooked.

pingkî (ping-kî), I. n. 1. the condition in which the knees knock each other in walking; knocking together of the knees. 2. a knocking or collision of one thing against another while in motion side by side. Syn. *umpóg*, *umpugan*. 3. striking together, as of two hard stones, to produce fire. Syn. *kiskís*, *pagkikiskís*.
—II. *adj.* 1. knocking together in walking, said of knees. 2. knock-kneed, referring to a person. Syn. *pikî*.

pingga (ping-ga; -gá), n. 1. a bamboo pole or the like used in balancing a load carried on the shoulder. Syn. *pambalagwít*, *bálagwitan*. 2. (in construction) a horizontal beam. Syn. *batangán*. 3. a long lever used for raising or lifting heavy objects. Cf. *panikwás*.

pinggán (ping-gán), n. 1. plate; dish. Syn. *plato*. 2. a plateful, as of food.

pingol (pi-ngol), n. 1. act of pinching and twisting the ear; tweaking. Syn. *piral*, *pagpiral*. 2. the lower lobe or flap of the ear. Syn. *lambî ng taingá*.

pingot[1] (pi-ngot), n. hard tweak or pinch on the ear. Syn. *mariíng piral*.

pingot[2] (pi-ngot), n. a nick at the edge, as of plate or the like. Syn. *pingas*, *bingot*.

pingpóng (ping-póng), var. **pimpóng**, n. (*Eng.*) table tennis; ping-pong.

pipa (pi-pa), n. (Sp.) 1. cigarette pipe. 2. cigar pipe. Syn. *kuwako*.

pipi (pi-pi), I. adj. 1. unable to speak; dumb; mute. Syn. *apáw, hindî makapágsalitâ, dimarunong magsalitâ*. 2. unwilling to speak; silent. Syn. *ayaw magsalitâ*.
—II. n. a person who cannot speak; dumb; deaf-mute.

pipî (pi-pî), I. adj. flattened; pressed flat. Syn. *pisâ, pitpít*.
—II. n. 1. act or manner of causing something to become flattened or pressed flat. 2. state or condition of being flattened or pressed flat.

pipil (pi-pil), n. subjugation; subjection; conquer; defeat. Syn. *lupig, paglupig; talo, pagtalo; pagpapasukò*.

pipino (pi-pi-no), n. (Bot.) cucumber (*Cucumis sativus Linn.*), the plant or its fruit.

pipít (pi-pít), n. (Ornith.) a small, sweet singing bird known as northern willow warbler (*Acanthopneuste borealis*).

pipitsugin (pi-pit-su-gin), n. (Colloq.) 1. novice; greenhorn. Syn. *baguhan, bagitò*. 2. a know-nothing individual. Syn. *sanô, tangá*.

piranha (pi-ran-ha), n. (Ichth.; Eng.) piranha; a small, voracious freshwater fish that attacks other big animals, even man.

piranggót (pi-rang-gót), n. a very small piece or quantity of something. Also, *kapiranggót*. Syn. *piyangót, kapiyangót*.

piraso (pi-ra-so), n. 1. piece; portion cut or broken from a larger piece. Also, *kapiraso*. Syn. *atado, bahagi*. 2. act of cutting or breaking a portion or piece from. Also, *pagpiraso*.

pirat (pi-rat), n. a crushing or being crushed flat by weight or pressure, as of tomatoes and the like.

pirata (pi-ra-ta), n. (Sp.) pirate. Syn. *tulisáng-dagat*.

pirinsá (pi-rin-sá), colloq. var. of **prinsa**, n. (Sp. *prensa*) 1. an old model flat iron made hot with live charcoal. 2. act or manner of pressing clothes with this kind of flat iron. Also, *pagpirinsá, pamimirinsá, pagkakápirinsá*.

piríng (pi-ríng), n. 1. blindfold (for persons).

2. blinder or blinker (for horse). 3. the way or manner a blindfold or blinder was put. Also, *pagkakápiríng*.

pirito (pi-ri-to), var. **prito**, I. n. fried fish or meat.
—II. adj. fried, said of fish or meat. Syn. *ipinipirito*.

pirma (pir-ma), n. (Sp. *firma*) 1. signature; a person's name written by himself. Syn. *lagdâ*. 2. act of signing one's name; the manner one's name was signed. Syn. *paglalagdâ, pagkakálagdâ*.

pirmé (pir-mé), var. **pirmí**, I. adj. (Sp. *firme*) 1. fixed; permanent. Syn. *lagì, palagì, pálagián, permanente*. 2. unchanged. Syn. *di-nagbabago, waláng-pagbabago*.
—II. adv. always; all the time. Syn. *palagì, pálagián*.

pirot (pi-rot), n. a sharp pinch or pressing with a finger or between two fingers in order to crush.

pirurutong (pi-ru-ru-tong), n. (Bot.) a variety of dark-colored glutinous rice.

pisâ¹ (pi-sâ), I. adj. (Sp. *pisar*) hatched (referring to eggs). Syn. *sisiw na, nagsisiw na*.
—II. n. 1. hatching of eggs by the hen; process of hatching eggs. Also, *pagpisâ, pamimisâ*. 2. state or condition of being already hatched, referring to eggs.

pisâ² (pi-sâ), I. adj. 1. crushed or pressed flat by the pressure or weight of something heavy. Syn. *pipî, pirát*. 2. pressed out of supporation or pus, referring to a boil, etc.
—II. n. 1. act of pressing out the pus or supporation (from a boil, etc.). 2. act of breaking or crushing something by pressing with the fingers. 3. state or condition of being broken or crushed, as tomatoes, or of being pressed out of pus or supporation, as a boil.

pisák (pi-sák), I. adj. 1. badly crushed or pressed flat, as tomatoes or the like. 2. badly damaged, referring esp. to an eye or eyes.

pisan (pi-san), I. n. 1. act of living with someone, as a woman with her common-law husband, or vice versa. Also, *pagpisan, pakikipisan*. 2. act of living together, as wife and husband. Syn. *pagpipisan*, *pagsasama.* 3. act of sharing with someone in a house, etc. Syn. *sunò, pagsunò, pakikisunò.* 4. act of putting things together in the same place.

—II. *adj.* living together, as husband and wife. Syn. *magkapisan, magkasama, nagsasama.*

pisara (pi-sa-ra), n. (Sp. *pizarra*) blackboard.

piskál (pis-kál) I. n. (Sp. *fiscal*) in Law, a public or government prosecutor; fiscal.

—II. *adj.* (*Econ.*) fiscal; financial, as in: *taóng piskál*, fiscal year. Syn. *pánuusán.*

piseta (pi-se-ta), var. **peseta**, n. (*Sp.*) 1. a twenty-centavo piece or coin. 2. twenty centavos.

pisì (pi-sì), n. 1. string; cord; twine; packthread. Syn. *leteng, panalì.* 2. (*Fig.*) something to spend; money. Syn. *kuwarta, gastusin, panggastós.* 3. (*Fig.*) patience; calmness to bear, esp. insult. Syn. *pasyensiyá, paumanhín.*

pisik (pi-sik), n. spatter or spattering, as of boiling lard. Cf. *tilamsík.*

pisíl (pi-síl), n. tight hold of the hand; hand pressure, as in holding something. Syn. *higpít ng hawak.*

pisngí (pis-ngí), n. 1. (*Anat.*) cheek. 2. either of the two fleshy side, as of a mango fruit. Syn. *kalamnán (ng manggá).*

piso (pi-so), n. (Mex.–Sp. *peso*) 1. the amount of one peso or 100 centavos; peso. 2. a one-peso bill or coin. Also, *pipisuhin.*

pisón (pi-són), n. (*Sp.*) steamroller; street roller. Syn. *pamatag-daán, pamatag-kalye.*

pispís¹ (pis-pís), n. act of cleaning a surface covered with dust or the like by wiping or sweeping lightly with a duster or a piece of rag. Syn. *palís, pagpalís.*

pispís² (pis-pís), n. small particles or bits of food left on the dining table after eating. Syn. *mismís.*

pista (pis-ta), var. **piyesta**, n. (Sp. *fiesta*) 1. feast day; day of celebration or festivity. 2. holiday. Syn. *pangiling araw.* 3. birthday; birthday anniversary. Syn. *kaarawán, kapanganakan.*

pistón (pis-tón), n. (*Sp.*) 1. piston. 2. the longitudinal fold on each of the legs of pants.

pita (pi-ta), n. 1. something a person wishes to have or attain. Syn. *hangád, hángarin; layon, layunin; pithayà.* 2. the purpose or subject of one's errand or mission. Syn. *pakay.* 3. a request. Syn. *hilíng, kahilingan.*

pitak (pi-tak), n. 1. section or compartment, as in shelf, box, etc. Syn. *butas, kahón.* 2. section or column in a newspaper or magazine. Syn. *tudlíng, kolumná.* 3. a division or section in an irrigated field. Syn. *matá.* 4. (*Fig.*) place; space; room. Syn. *puwáng, lugál (lugár).*

pitakà (pi-ta-kà), n. (Sp. *petaca*) wallet; billfold. Syn. *portamoneda.*

pitada (pi-ta-da), n. (*Sp.*) 1. blast or whistle of a siren. Syn. *ihip (hihip) ng sirena.* 2. toll or tolling of bells. Syn. *ripike.*

pítagan (pí-ta-gan), n. respect; reverence; courtesy. Syn. *galang, paggalang, respeto, pakundangan, alang-alang.*

pitás (pi-tás), I. n. act of picking or removing by pulling as with the fingers; plucking or gathering (flowers, fruits, etc.) Also, *pagpitás, pamimitás.* Syn. *puti, pagputi, pamumuti* (for fruits); *pupól, pagpupól* (for flowers).

—II. *adj.* picked, plucked, or gathered, said of flowers, fruits, etc.

pithayà (pit-ha-yà), n. 1. something a person wants very much; ambition; a long-dreamed wish. Syn. *hangád, hángarin, pangarap, pita, nasà.* 2. request; something asked in a request. Syn. *pakiusap, hilíng, kahilingan.*

pitík¹ (pi-tík), n. 1. snap or strike with a finger; fillip. 2. act of tossing a coin, etc. by snapping the thumb against a finger. 3. a kind of children's game whereby the winner gets the right to hit the hand of the loser with a certain number of fillips as per agreement.

pitík² (pi-tík), n. 1. a carpenter's line marker. Syn. *baktáw.* 2. the act or manner of making a line or lines by using a carpenter's line marker. 3. the marks or line thus made.

pitík³ (pi-tík), n. 1. a strong cord or rope used as a rein or tether for guiding work animals. 2. a sudden jerk of the rein or tether to make the animal move faster. Syn. *labtik.* Cf. *saltík.*

pitís (pi-tís), I. *adj.* very tight; tight-fitting, referring to clothes.

—II. *n.* state or condition of being very tight or tight-fitting, referring to clothes.

pitisyón (pi-tis-yón), *n.* (Sp. *petición*) formal request; petition. Syn. *hilíng, kahilingan*.

pitlág (pit-lág), *n.* sudden dodge or jerk of the body, as when frightened. Syn. *tiplág, igtád*.

pito (pi-to), *n. (Sp.)* 1. act of whistling. Syn. *sipol, pagsipol*. 2. the sound of whistling. 2. whistle. 5. blast of siren. Syn. *pitada, hihip ng sirena*. 6. (*Mus.*) pipe. Syn. *típanó*. 7. a hard rubber or plastic fixture connected to a rubber tube and inserted into the rectume in giving enema to a patient.

pitó (pi-tó), *n.* & *adj.* seven. Syn. *siyete*.

pitóng-bukó (pi-tóng + bu-kó), var. **pitumbukó**, *n.* (*Colloq.*) scorpion. Syn. *alakdán, atang-atang*.

pitpít (pit-pít), I. *n.* act of flattening or crushing something by beating or pounding.

—II. *adj.* flattened or crushed by beating or pounding.

pitserahan (pit-se-ra-han), *v.* 1. to provide with a lapel or lapels. Syn. *solapahan*. 2. to hold or grab by the lapel.

pitso (pit-so; -só), *n.* (Sp. *fecho*) breast of fowl. Cf. *dibdíb*.

pitsón (pit-són), *n.* (Sp. *pichon*) young of a pigeon; squab. Syn. *inakáy ng kalapati*.

piyák (pi-yák), *n.* 1. sudden cry of a fowl when scared or suddenly caught. Cf. *puták*. 2. sudden change of the voice of a person, while speaking, that resembles the sudden cry of a scared fowl.

piyait (pi-ya-it), *n.* 1. state or condition of being crushed or pressed flat between two heavy objects. Syn. *ipit, pagkaipit*. 2. act of crushing or pressing a thing flat between two heavy objects. Syn. *pag-ipit*.

piyansa (pi-yan-sa), *n.* (Sp. *fianza*) security for the release of; bail; bond. Syn. *lagak*.

piyapís (pi-ya-pís), I. *adj.* defeated; vanquished; annihilated; overpowered. Syn. *lupíg, gahís*.

—II. *n.* state or condition of being completely defeated or vanquished.

piyé (pi-yé), *n.* (Sp. *pie*) a measure of length equal to 12 inches; foot. Syn. *talampakan*.

piyeltro (pi-yel-tro), I. *n.* (Sp. *fieltro*) felt.

—II. *adj.* made of felt. Syn. *yari sa piyeltro*.

piyesa (pi-ye-sa), *n.* (Sp. *pieza*) 1. bolt (of cloth). Syn. *rolyo*. 2. (*Mus.*) musical piece. 3. part or spare part, as of a machine, etc.

piyók (pi-yók), *n.* echoic glottal sound of the voice while speaking. Cf. *piyak²*.

piyón (pi-yón), *n.* (Sp. *peon*) 1. laborer; unskilled worker. 2. (in checkers, chess.) pawn. Syn. *pitsa*.

plaka (pla-ka), *n.* (Sp. *placa*) 1. phonograph record; disc. Syn. *disko*. 2. X-ray film. Syn. *negatibo*. 3. battery plate for storage batteries. Syn. *plato*. 4. (*Photog.*) plate. Syn. *negatibo*. 5. ornamental tablet; plaque.

plano (pla-no), *n. (Sp.)* 1. plan; something a person wants to do. Syn. *balak*. 2. plan or a working design, as of building or house to be made. Syn. *disenyo*. 3. an outline; draft. Syn. *krokis*. 4. map or sketch showing direction or location of a place. Syn. *krokis, mapa*. 5. (*Geom.*) plane.

planta (plan-ta), *n. (Sp.)* 1. plant; the equipment, buildings, etc. of a factory or business firm. 2 plant; any tree, shrub, herb, etc. Syn. *halaman*.

plantilya (plan-til-ya), *n.* (Sp. *plantilla*) list of employees to be paid with the amount due each; payroll. Syn. *talaan ng pasahod, peyrol, talaupahan*.

plantsado (plan-tsa-do), var. **plansado**, *adj.* (Sp. *planchado*) 1. ironed or pressed with a flat iron, referring to clothes, etc. 2. plain or flat, referring to galvanized iron sheet. Syn. *liso, dikanalado*. 3. (*Fig.*) neatly dressed, referring to a person.

plasa (pla-sa), *n. (Sp.; Eng.)* plaza; town square; park. Syn. *parke, liwasan*.

plasma (plas-ma), *n. (Sp.; Eng.)* plasma; fluid part of blood.

plastado (plas-ta-do), *n. adj. (Sp.)* 1. tight-fitting. Syn. *hapit, hapit na hapit; lapat, lapat na lapat*. 2. well-pressed; well-ironed, referring to clothes. Syn. *plantsado*. 3. well-dressed; neatly dressed. Syn. *ayós na ayós*. 4. neatly combed, said of hair. 5. fallen flat, as a drunkard. Syn. *tumbado*.

plata

6. *(Fig.)* sick in bed; bedridden. Syn. *ratay o nakaratay sa banig* (*ng karamdaman*).

plata (pla-ta), n. (*Sp.*) 1. silver (metal). Syn. *pilak.* 2. silver coin.

plataporma (pla-ta-por-ma), n. (*Sp. plataforma*) 1. raised flooring or stage for performers, speakers, etc.; platform. Syn. *entablado.* 2. program of action or activity, as of a political party. Syn. *palatuntunan, patakaran, simulain.*

plateria (pla-te-ri-a). var. **plateriyá, plateryá,** n. (*Sp. plateria*) 1. silversmith's shop. 2. (by extension) goldsmith's shop.

platina (pla-ti-na), n. (*Sp.*) 1. in *printing* platen. 2. roller in a typewriter. Syn. *rodilyo.* 3. table of a microscope. 4. lining of a skirt. Syn. *aporo.*

platito (pla-ti-to), n. (*Sp.*) saucer. Syn. *platilyo.*

plato (pla-to), n. (*Sp.*) 1. plate; dish. Syn. *pinggán; palaton* (colloq.). 2. a plateful of food. 3. pan of a balance.

plegarya (ple-gar-ya), n. (*Sp. plegaria*) 1. prayer. Syn. *dasal, panalangin.* 2. tolling of bells, esp. for the dead.

pleges (ple-ges), var. **pileges,** n. (*Sp. pliegue*) 1. fold (in cloth). Syn. *lupî, tupî.* 2. pleat; plait.

plete (ple-te), n. (*Sp. flete*) 1. passenger fare. Syn. *pasahe, bayad sa pagsakáy o sa sasakyán.* 2. freight charge. Syn. *bayad sa paktura.*

plorera (plo-re-ra), n. (*Sp. florera*) 1. flower vase. 2. female florist.

plorete (plo-re-te), n. (*Sp. florete*) 1. fencing foil. Cf. *espada, sablé.* 2. swordsmanship; art of fencing Cf. *eskrima, estukada.*

pluma (plu-ma), n. (*Sp.*) 1. fountain pen. Syn. *pontimpén.* 2. pen point; writing pen. Syn. *asero.*

plumero (plu-me-ro), n. (*Sp.*) 1. feather duster. 2. (*Amer.*) penholder.

pô (pô), n. 1. a respectful answer when one's name is called. 2. a term often used to express respect in talking with an elder or to a superior, esp. when one mishears him or her.

poblasyón (po-blas-yón), n. (*Sp. poblacion*) town proper. Syn. *kabayanan.*

pobre (po-bre), *adj.* poor. Syn. *dukhâ,*

poón

mahirap, maralitâ.

pokus (po-kus), n. (*Eng.*) 1. focus. 2. (*Colloq.*) sleight of hand; magic. Syn. *salamangka.*

podér (po-dér), n. (*Sp.*) power; authority. Syn. *kapangyarihan.*

poesya (po-es-ya), n. (*Sp. poesia*) 1. poetry; poems collectively. Syn. *pánulaan.* 2. poem. Syn. *tulá.*

poge (po-ge), l. *adj.* (*Slang*) handsome. Syn. *makisig, magandá.*

—II. n. (*Slang*) handsome man.

politburo (po-lit-bu-ro), n. (*Eng.*) politburo; executive committee of the Communist Party of the Soviet Union.

politiká (po-li-ti-ka), var. **pulitiká,** n. (*Sp. politica*) 1. politics. 2. policy. Syn. *patakarán, pamalakad, pamamalakad.* 3. tact. Syn. *taktiká, pamamaraán.*

pompiyáng (pom-pi-yáng), var. **pumpiyáng,** n. (*Orig.?*) 1. cymbals. 2. in *huweteng,* daily double (in racing), and other numbers games, the winning pair of numbers represented by the same numeral.

ponda (pon-da), n. (*Sp. fonda*) wayside food store. Cf. *karihan, karinderiya.*

pondilyo (pon-dil-yo), var. **pundilyo, pundiyó,** n. (*Sp. pondillos*) seat of pants.

pondo (pon-dó), var. **pundo,** n. (*Sp. fondo*) 1. fund; sum of money available for use. Syn. *kuwartáng gastusin o gugulin.* 2. bottom. Syn. *ilalim, káilaliman, pusod* (*fig.*). 3. depth; profundity, as of one's arguments. Syn. *lalim.* 4. background. Syn. *karanasán.* 5. end, as of a street. Syn. *dulo.* 6. stay, as in a boarding house. Syn. *tigil, pagtigil.*

ponduhan (pon-du-han), var. **punduhan,** n. 1. station. Syn. *istasyón, himpilan.* 2. parking place. Syn. *páradahán, parkihan.* 3. boarding house; temporary residence. 4. place to anchor; anchorage for sea crafts. Syn. *daungán.*

poók (po-ók), var. **puók,** n. place; district; region; site; location. Syn. *lugár, distrito, dako.*

poón (po-ón), var. **puón,** n. 1. lord; master. Syn. *panginoón, amo.* 2. image of a saint. Syn. *santo.*

poót (po-ót), I. n. 1. wrath; intense anger; rage; indignation. Syn. *matindíng galit, ngitngít, muhi, pagkamuhí.* 2. hate; hatred. Syn. *suklám, pagkasuklám.*

—II. adj. indignant. Syn. *galit na galit, matindi ang galit.*

Pordiyós (Por-di-yós), interj. (Sp. *Por Dios*) By God; My God.

pormasyón (por-mas-yón), n. (Sp. *formación*) 1. formation; creation; organization. Syn. *pagtatatag, pagbubuô, pagtatayô.* 2. erection, as of a building; construction. Syn. *pagtitirik, pagtatayô, pagyari.* 3. formation; shape. Syn. *hugis, anyô.* 4. framework. Syn. *balangkás, kayarian.*

pórmulá (pór-mu-lá), n. (Sp. *fórmula*) 1. formula; set form of rules. Syn. *pátakarán, álituntunin.* 2. medical prescription. Syn. *reseta.*

pornada (por-na-da), var. purnada, n. (Sp. *pornada*) a swindling or being swindled used colloquially. Syn. *pagdayá, pagkadayá; paggantso, pagkagantso; pagsubá, pagkasubá.*

porsado (por-sa-do), adj. (Sp. *forzado*) forced; compelled. Syn. *pilít, napilitan, sapilitán.*

porselana (por-se-la-na), I. n. (Sp. *porcelana*) 1. porcelain; china. 2. porcelain dishes or ornaments, collectively.

—II. adj. made of porcelain.

porsiyento (por-si-yen-to), var. pursiyento, n. (Sp. *por ciento*) 1. per cent; per centum. Syn. *bahagdán.* 2. (Colloq.) rate of interest. Syn. *patubó.* 3. (Colloq.) commission, as of an agent or salesman. Syn. *komisyón.*

portada (por-ta-da), n. (Sp.) 1. the main façade of a building. Syn. *patsada.* 2. front. Syn. *haráp, harapán.* 3. portal; gate. Syn. *pultahan, entrada, pasukán.* 4. cover, as of a book, magazine, or the like. Syn. *balát, pabalát.* 5. title page of a book. Syn. *páhináng pambungad.* 6. frontispiece of a book. Syn. *pambungad na larawan sa aklát.* 7. preface; foreword. Syn. *prepasyo, pambungad na salitâ.*

portal (por-tal), n. (Sp.; Eng.) 1. portal; entrance; gate. Syn. *entrada, pasukán, pultahan.* 2. doorstep. Syn. *bungad ng pintô (pintuan).*

portamoneda (por-ta-mo-ne-da), n. (Sp.) billfold; wallet. Syn. *pitakà, kartera.*

portero (por-te-ro), n. (Sp.) 1. porter; gatekeeper. Syn. *bantáy-pintô, tanod-pintô.* 2. baggage carrier. Syn. *kargadór.*

portuna (por-tu-na), n. (Sp. *fortuna*), 1. fortune; luck. Syn. *suwerte, kapalaran.* 2. success; good luck. Syn. *mabuting kapalaran, tágumpay.* 3. chance; opportunity. Syn. *pagkakátaón.*

posas (po-sas), n. (Sp. *esposas*) 1. handcuff; manacle. Cf. *pangáw.* 2. the way or manner someone is handcuffed or manacled. Syn. *pagkákaposas.*

posesyón (po-ses-yón), n. (Sp. *posesión*) 1. possession; holding. Syn. *paghahawak, pagtataglày.* 2. ownership; possession. Syn. *pagmamay-arì, pag-aarì.* 3. thing possessed; property. Syn. *arì, pag-aarì, arí-arìan.* 4. apartment house for rent. Syn. *aksesorya.* 5. territory held under the rule of a country; possession. Syn. *teritoryo, lupang sakóp o nasásakupan.*

posibilidád (po-si-bi-li-dád), n. (Sp.) 1. a being possible; possibility. Syn. *pagkamáaari.* 2. something that is possible. Syn. *bagay na máaaring mangyari.*

posible (po-sib-le), I. adj. (Sp.) 1. that can be; possible. Syn. *máaari, puwede.* 2. that can happen. Syn. *máaaring mangyari (matupád).* 3. that can be done or made. Syn. *magágawâ.* 4. maybe true; that can be true. Syn. *máaaring tunay, totoo o magkakátotoó.*

—II. adv. possibly; perhaps. Syn. *marahil, máaari.*

posisyón (po-sis-yón), n. (Sp.) 1. position; place where a person or thing is placed. Syn. *lugár; puwesto; lagáy, kinalalagyán; tayô, kinátatayuán.* 2. stand; personal attitude towards a subject. Syn. *paninindigan.* 3. location; site. Syn. *lugár, kinaroroonán, puwesto* 4. the manner a person poses, as for picture taking. Syn. *puwesto, pagkakápuwesto.* 5. a person's relative place, as in society; status or rank. Syn. *lagáy, kalágayan.* 6. post; duty; position; appointment. Syn. *tungkulin, trabaho.*

positibo (po-si-ti-bo), adj. (Sp. *positivo*) 1.

sure; positive. Syn. *tiyák, sigurado*. 2. definite; emphatic. Syn. *tiyák, waláng-alinlangan*.

poso (po-so), n. (Sp. *pozo*) well; deep well. Syn. *balón, kuluóng*.

poso-negro (po-so + ne-gro), n. (Sp. *pozo negro*) cesspool; septic tank.

pospas (pos-pas), var. **puspas**. n. (Ch. ?) chicken porridge. Syn. *aruskaldo, lugaw (nilugaw) na may manók*.

pósporó (pós-po-ró), n. (Sp. *fósforo*) 1. match; match stick. Syn. *palito ng kasapwego o ápuyan*. 2. match box and its contents. Syn. *kasapwego, ápuyan*. 3. (*Chem.*) phosphorus.

postiso (pos-ti-so), var. **pustiso**, I. adj. (Sp. *postizo*) false; artificial, as in: *postisong buhok o ngipin*, false hair or teeth. Syn. *artipisyál, di-tunay*.
—II. n. 1. false hair; wig. Syn. *peluka*. 2. false teeth or denture.

póstumó (pós-tu-mó), adj. (*Sp.*) posthumous; after one's death. Syn. *pagkamatáy*.

postura (pos-tu-ra), var. **pustura**, I. adj. (*Sp.*) well-dressed; elegantly dressed. Syn. *makisig, magarà, bihís na bihís*.
—II. n. posture. Syn. *tindíg, tikas*.

potahe (po-ta-he), var. **putahe**, n. (Sp. *potaje*) special dish or viand. Syn. *ulam, pang-ulam*.

praksiyón (prak-si-yón), n. (Sp. *fración*) 1. fraction; a small part of. Syn. *maliít na bahagi*. 2. (*Math.*) fraction. Syn. *hátimbilang*.

praktikál (prak-ti-kál), adj. (*Sp.; Eng.*) 1. practical; having good sense. Syn. *práktikó, may-isip, matalino*. 2. fit for actual practice; that can be done or made. Syn. *magágawá, maisásagawá*.

praktis (prak-tis), n. (*Eng.*) 1. exercise; physical exercise. Syn. *hersisyo, paghihersisyo; pagpapalakás*. 2. practice; training; rehearsal. Syn. *insayo, pag-iinsayo; sanay, pagsasanay*. 3. the practice or following of one's profession. Syn. *panggagamót o pagdodoktór* (for doctors), *pag-aabogado* (for lawyers). 4. the usual way or custom. Syn. *ugalì, kaugalián*.

pranela (pra-ne-la), I. n. (Sp. *franela*) 1.

frannel; loosely woven cloth. 2. any clothing made of this cloth.
—II. adj. made of flannel.

Pranses (Pran-ses; -sés), n. (Sp. *Frances*) 1. a Frenchman; the French people. 2. the French language.

prangkisya (prang-kis-ya), var. **prankisya**, n. (Sp. *franquicia*) franchise; privilege or right granted by the government or a private company to an individual or group to carry out commercial activities. Syn. *pahintulot o karapatáng ipinágkaloób ng pámahalaán*.

prangko (prang-ko), adj. (Sp. *franco*) frank; open; sincere. Syn. *tapát, matapát, tahás*.

praternál (pra-ter-nál), adj. (*Sp.; Eng.*) fraternal; brotherly. Syn. *pangkapatíd; sa o ukol sa kapatíd*.

praude (pra-u-de), n. (Sp. *fraude*) 1. fraud; dishonest dealing; cheating. Syn. *dayà, pagdarayà, dayaàn*. 2. anomaly. Syn. *katiwalián, anomalya*. 3. something fraudulent or falsified. Syn. *bagay na huwád o palsipikado*.

prayle (pray-le), n. (Sp. *fraile*) friar. Cf. *paré (parì)*.

prehuwisyo (pre-hu-wis-yo), n. (Sp. *prejuicio*) 1. prejudice; bias. Syn. *masamáng palagáy*. 2. harm; injury. Syn. *pinsalà, kapinsalaán*.

premyado (prem-ya-do), adj. (Sp. *premiado*) awarded or given a prize. Syn. *nagka-premyo, nápremyuhán*.

premyo (prem-yo), n. (Sp. *premio*) prize; reward. Syn. *gantimpalà*.

prenda (pren-da), n. (*Sp.*) 1. pledge; security. Syn. *sanglâ, garantiyá*. 2. punishment, as in a certain kind of game. Syn. *parusa*.

preno (pre-no), n. (Sp. *freno*) 1. (*Mech.*) brake. 2. restraint; control. Syn. *pagpipigil*.

prensa (pren-sa), n. (*Sp.*) press; printing press. Syn. *limbagan, palimbagan, imprenta*.

prente (pren-te), n. (Sp. *frente*) 1. front; forepart. Syn. *unahán*. 2. the part that face forward. Syn. *haráp, harapán*.

preparasyón (pre-pa-ras-yón), n. (Sp. *preparación*) 1. act of preparing; preparation. Syn. *paghahandâ*. 2. (*Amer.*) education; learning. Syn. *pinág-aralan, napag-aralan, edukasyón*. 3. a specially prepared medicine. Syn. *gamót na espisípikó*.

presa (pre-sa), var. **presas**, n. (Sp. *fresa*) 1. strawberry (the plant and fruit). 2. the strawberry or dark-red color.

presko (pres-ko), adj. (Sp. *fresco*) fresh; cool (said of weather). Syn. *aliwalas, maaliwalas, malamíg*.

preskripsiyón (pres-krip-si-yón), n. (Sp. *prescripción*) 1. an order for medicine, as by a doctor; prescription. Syn. *reseta*. 2. an order or direction. Syn. *utos, tagubilin*.

presentable (pre-sen-ta-ble), adj. (Sp.) presentable; suitable in appearance, dress, etc. Syn. *magandá, kaakit-akit*.

presentasyón (pre-sen-tas-yón), n. (Sp. *presentación*) 1. presentation; introduction. Syn. *paghaharáp, pagpapakilala*. 2. exhibition; showing; presentation. Syn. *pagpapalabás, pagtatanghál*. 2. something presented or exhibited, as on stage. Syn. *palabás, tanghál*. 4. act of offering or giving. Syn. *pagbibigáy, pagkakaloób, paghahandóg*.

presente (pre-sen-te), I. n. (Sp.) present. Syn. *kasalukuyan*.

—II. adj. present. Syn. *naroón, dumaló, kaharáp*.

presidensiyá (pre-si-den-siyá), n. (Sp. *presidencia*) 1. municipal building. Syn. *munisipyo, bahay-pámahalaán*. 2. presidency. Syn. *pánguluhán, pagkapangulo*.

presidente (pre-si-den-te), n. (Sp.) 1. president, as of a nation. Syn. *pangulo*. 2. chairman; presiding officer. Syn. *tagapangulo*.

presinto (pre-sin-to), n. (Hispanized Eng.) 1. precinct; district. Syn. *distrito, purók*. 2. pooling place; electoral precint. 3. station, as of a police force. Syn. *himpilan, istasyón*.

preso (pre-so), I. n. (Sp.) 1. prisoner. Syn. *bilanggô*. 2. (Colloq.) prison; jail. Syn. *bilangguan, karsel, bilibid*.

—II. adj. imprisoned; in jail. Syn. *nakabilanggô, nakakulóng, nakabilibid; nasa karsél*.

prestihiyó (pres-ti-hi-yó), n. (Sp. *prestigio*) prestige; reputation. Syn. *dangal, karangalan, pagkakilala, reputasyón*.

presupuwesto (pre-su-pu-wes-to), var.

presupwesto, n. (Sp. *presupuesto*) budget; appropriation. Syn. *laang-gugulín, apropriyasyón, badyet*.

presyón (pres-yón), var. **presiyón**, n. (Sp. *presion*) 1. pressure; action of weight or force. Syn. *bigát, tindí, puwersa*. 2. compelling force or influence. Syn. *pamimilit, pamumuwersa, panggigipít*. 3. urgency. Syn. *mahigpít na pangangailangan*. 4. (Colloq.) blood pressure.

presyoso (pres-yo-so), var. **presiyoso**, adj. (Sp. *precioso*) 1. precious; very valuable. Syn. *mahalagá, mamáhalin*. 2. dear; much loved. Syn. *pinakamámahál*.

pretensiyón (pre-ten-si-yón), n. (Sp. *pretensión*) 1. pretension; false claim. Syn. *pagpapanggáp, pagsisinungalíng*. 2. pretense; act of make-believe. Syn. *pagkukunwa, pagkukunwarî, pagkukunyarî*. 3. doing things for show; display. Syn. *pagpaparangyâ, pagmamarangyâ, pagmamagalíng, paghahambóg*.

pribado (pri-ba-do), adj. (Sp. *privado*) 1. private; not public. Syn. *pansarili, panarili, di-pambayan, di-pampublikó*. 2. secret. Syn. *lihim, sekreto*.

pribilehiyó (pri-bi-le-hi-yó), n. (Sp. *privilegio*) privilege; special right, advantage, or favor given to someone. Syn. *tanging karapatán, pabór*.

pribyu (prib-yu), n. (Eng.) preview; first showing. Syn. *unang pagtanghál*.

prima (pri-ma), n. (Sp.) 1. female cousin. Syn. *pinsáng babae*. 2. (Comm.) premium. 3. (Colloq.) female friend. Syn. *kaibigang babae*.

primera (pri-me-ra), I. n. (Sp.) 1. (Mech.) first gear. 2. first place or position, as in racing. 3. (Mus.) highest pitch.

—II. adj., adv. & n. first. Syn. *una*.

primero (pri-me-ro), adj., adv. & n. first. Syn. *una*.

primo (pri-mo), n. (Sp.) 1. cousin; male cousin. Syn. *pinsáng lalaki*. 2. (Colloq.) friend. Syn. *kaibigan*. See **prima.**

prinsa (prin-sa), var. **pirinsá**, n. (Sp. *prensa*) 1. an old model flat iron made hot with live charcoal. 2. act or manner of pressing clothes with this flat iron. Also, *pagprinsa, pagkakáprinsa*.

prinsipál (prin-si-pál), I. n. (Sp., *Eng.*) 1. (*Edu.*) principal; head teacher. Syn. *punong-gurò*. 2. (*Comm.*) capital in an investment. Syn. *puhunan, kapitál.*

prinsipyo (prin-sip-yo), n. (Sp. *principio*) 1. principle; truth as the basis or foundation of other truths. Syn. *batayán, saligán.* 2. principle, as a rule in science. Syn. *tuntunin, pánuntunan, alituntunin.* 3. principle or rule of action or conduct. Syn. *pátakarán, pánuntunan.* 4. principle or fundamental belief or stand. Syn. *simulain, paninindigan.*

prito (pri-to), I. n. (Sp. *frito*) a dish of fried food, as eggs, fish, meat, etc. See. *pritada.* —II, adj. fried.

pro (pro), I. n. (*Eng.*) 1. a person who favors the affirmative side of a question. Syn. *ang pábor o sang-ayon.* 2. an argument or vote in favor of someone or something. 3. (*Colloq.*) a professional, esp. a player distinguished from an amateur. Syn. *propesyonál.* 4. (*Colloq.*) press or public relations officer. Syn. *tagapagbalitá.* —II, adj. favorable; in favor of the affirmative side. Syn. *sang-ayon, kasangayon.*

probabilidád (pro-ba-bi-li-dád), n. (*Sp.*) probability; quality of being likely or probable; a chance. Syn. *pagkakátaón, kalamangáng mangyari.*

probado (pro-ba-do), adj. (Sp. *provado*) proven; tried. Syn. *subók na.*

probetso (pro-bet-so), n. (Sp. *provecho*) benefit; gain; profit. Syn. *pakinabang, pamá.*

probinsiyana (pro-bin-si-ya-na), I. n. (Sp. *provinciana*) a female provincial native. Syn. *babaing tagalalawigan.* —II. adj. with or having the manners, speech, etc. of a provincial woman.

probisyón (pro-bis-yón), n. (Sp., *Eng.*) 1. provision; stock of food and other supplies for use in the future. Syn. *panlaán, panustós.* 2. money, clothes, food, etc. brought by someone on a trip. Syn. *baon.* 3. stipulation or a statement making a condition as in an ordinance, law, or legal agreement or document. Syn. *tadhanâ, kondisyón.*

problema (pro-ble-ma), n. (*Sp.*) 1. problem; a matter of difficulty or doubt. Syn. *súliranín.* 2. matter to cope with; responsibility. Syn. *ságutin, pananágutan.* 3. question to be answered, as in arithmetic. Syn. *tánong, katanungan.*

probokasyón (pro-bo-kas-yón), n. (Sp. *provocacion*) 1. act of provoking; provocation. Syn. *pagpagalit.* 2. something said or done that provokes. Syn. *pampagalit.*

prodigál (pro-di-gál), I. adj. (*Sp.*; *Eng.*) prodigal; wasteful. Syn. *mapágtapón, mapágwaldás, mapáglustáy, bulagsák.*

produksiyón (pro-duk-si-yón), n. (Sp. *produccion*) 1. act or process of producing or manufacturing; production. Syn. *pagyayarí, paggawâ, paglikhâ.* 2. something produced, manufactured, or created. Syn. *gawâ, yari, likhâ, produkto.* 3. raising of crops. Syn. *pagtataním.* 4. crops or products raised from the farm. Syn. *ani.* 5. showing or staging. Syn. *ani.* 5. showing or staging, as of plays or dramas. Syn. *pagtatanghal, pagpapalabas.*

produkto (pro-duk-to), n. (Sp. *producto*) things manufactured, raised, or produced; products. Syn. *yarì, gawâ, bunga, ani.*

progreso (pro-gre-so), n. (*Sp.*) progress; advance; development; improvement. Syn. *pag-unlád, kaunlarán, pagsulong, pagbuti.*

prohibitibo (pro-hi-bi-ti-bo), adj. (Sp. *prohibitivo*) 1. prohibitive; prohibiting or tending to prohibit. Syn. *nagbábawal.* 2. too high, as a price. Syn. *nápakataás.*

proletaryado (pro-le-tar-ya-do), n. (Sp. *proletariado*) proletariat; the working class. Syn. *ang mga manggagawà, ang mga anàk-pawis.*

promedyo (pro-med-yo), n. (Sp. *promedio*) average; common standard. Syn. *pámantayang pangkalahatán.*

prominente (pro-mi-nen-te), adj. (*Sp.*) 1. prominent; well-known. Syn. *tanyág, bantóg, kilaláng-kilalá.* 2. easy to see. Syn. *hayág, lantád, kitang-kita.*

promosyón (pro-mos-yón), n. (Sp. *promoción*) 1. promotion; helping on to success. Syn. *pagpapalaganap, propaganda, pagtataguyod, pagpapaunlád.* 2. promotion or advancement in rank, position, etc. Syn. *pagtaás o pagtataás sa ranggo o tungkulin.*

promotór (pro-mo-tór), n. (*Sp.*) 1. promoter. Syn. *tagapagtaguyod, tagapagpalaganap, propagandista.* 2. leader, esp. of a group engaged in something undesirable.

propaganda (pro-pa-gan-da), n. (*Sp.; Eng.*) propaganda; effort to promote something. Syn. *pagpapalaganap, promosyón.*

propagasyón (pro-pa-gas-yón), n. (*Sp. propagación*) 1. propagation; development. Syn. *pagpapaunlád.* 2. spreading; dissemination. Syn. *pagpapalaganap, pagpapakalat.*

propesyonál (pro-pes-yo-nál), I. n. (*Sp. profesionál*) 1. professional; person engaged in a profession. 2. a professional player, singer, etc.
—II. *adj.* 1. engaged in a certain profession (s.o. lawyers, doctors, engineers, and the like). 2. said of singers, players, etc. who are paid for their performances.

propiyedád (pro-pi-ye-dád), var. **propyedád**, n. (*Sp. propiedad*) property. Syn. *arí-arian, pag-aari.*

prospekto (pros-pek-to), n. (*Sp. prospecto*) 1. prospect; hope; anticipation. Syn. *pag-asa.* 2. chance. Syn. *pagkakátaón.* 2. prospectus. Cf. *katálogó.*

proteksiyón (pro-tek-si-yón), n. (*Sp. protección*) 1. act of protecting; protection. Syn. *pagtatanggól, pagsasanggaláng.* 2. taking care of; caring. Syn. *pangangalagà, pagkupkóp, pagkalingà.* 3. defense; something used to defend. Syn. *pananggól, pananggaláng.*

protesta (pro-tes-ta), n. (*Sp.*) protest; strong objection. Syn. *tutol, pagtutol.*

protestasyón (pro-tes-tas-yón), n. (*Sp. protestación*) 1. protest; protestation. Syn. *tutol, pagtutol.* 2. solemn declaration; strong assertion; protestation. Syn. *sumpâ, pagsumpá.*

prueba (pru-e-ba), var. **pruweba**, n. (*Sp.*) 1. (*Printing*) proof. 2. evidence; proof. Syn. *patunay, katunayan, ebidensyá.* 3. trial; testing. Syn. *subok, pagsubok.* 4. fitting; trying on. Syn. *sukat, pagsusukat.* 5.

sample; sampling. Syn. *muwestra.*

pruta (pru-ta), var. **prutas**, n. (*Sp. fruta*) fruit; fruits. Syn. *bungang-kahoy.*

prutera (pru-te-ra), n. (*Sp. frutera*) 1. fruit bowl or basket. 2. a woman fruit seller. Syn. *tindera ng prutas.*

pû (pû), rare var. of **pô**.

-pû(pû), a suffix meaning tens, times ten, expressed by the suffix –ty, as in: *dalawampû* (twenty), *tatlumpû* (thirty), etc.

publasyón (pu-blas-yón), var. **poblasyón**, n. (*Sp. población*) town proper.

publikasyón (pu-bli-kas-yón), n. (*Sp. publicación*) 1. act of publishing; publication. Syn. *paglalathalà, paglilimbág.* 2. anything that is published; publication. Syn. *ano mang limbág na babasahín.* 3. newspaper. Syn. *diyaryo, páhayagan, peryódikó.* 3. mágazine. Syn. *magasin.*

publikó (pu-bli-kó), I. n. (*Sp. publicó*) 1. the people as a whole; public. Syn. *mga tao, bayan, mga taong bayan, madlâ.* 2. audience; spectators. Syn. *mga nanónoód o nakíkiníg, mga tagapakiníg, mga tagapanoód.*
—II. *adj.* 1. of, for, or belonging to the people as a whole; public. 2. for the use or benefit of all. Syn. *pambayan, pangmadlâ.*

pukaw (pu-kaw), n. act of rousing or causing a person to wake up. Syn. *gising, paggising.*

puki (pu-ki), n. (*Anat.*) the external genital organ of the female; vulva. Syn. *kikì.*

puknát (puk-nát), I. n. 1. act of detaching forcibly something that is glued, pasted, or the like. Syn. *tukláp, pagtukláp; paknít, pagpaknít; bakbák, pagbakbák.* 2. the part of something glued or pasted that is forcibly detached. 3. state of condition of being forcibly detached.
—II. *adj.* forcibly detached, said of something glued, pasted, etc. Syn. *tukláp, bakbák, paknít.*

pukól (pu-kól), n. 1. act of throwing or hitting someone or something, as with a stone, etc. Syn. *bató, pagbató; hagis, paghagis; balibág, pagbalibág.* 2. act or manner of pitching or throwing a ball, as in baseball or indoor baseball. Syn. *hagis,* *paghagis*. 3. (also in baseball) act or manner of hitting the ball. Syn. *palò*, *pagpalò*.

pukos-pukos (pu-kos + pu-kos), var. **pukus-pukos, pukuspukos,** *n.* tricks of a stage magician; legerdemain.

pukpukan (puk-pu-kan), *n.* 1. a block, as of wood where something is beaten or pounded. Cf. *sangkalan*. 2. specifically, an anvil. Syn. *palihán*. 3. (in boxing) exchange of hard blows. Syn. *bakbakan*.

puksâ (puk-sâ), I. *n.* 1. an exterminating; annihilation. Also, *pagpuksa*. Syn. *paglipol*, *pagsaíd*, *pag-ubos* 2. state or condition of being exterminated or annihilated. Also, *pagkapuksa*. Syn. *pagkalipol*, *pagkasaíd*, *pagkaubos*.
—II. *adj.* exterminated; annihilated. Syn.*ubós o said na lahát*.

puktô (puk-tô), I. *n.* state or condition whereby the external portion of the eyes is slightly swollen, due esp. to long crying.
—II. *adj.* slightly swollen, referring to the external portion of the eyes after too much crying. Also, *namúmuktô*.

pukyót (puk-yót), *n.* honeybee; the common hive bee. Syn. *anilan*, *laywán*. See **pukyutan.**

pukyutan (puk-yu-tan), *n.* 1. honeybee. See **pukyot.** Syn. *anilan*, *laywán*. 2. honecomb. Syn. *saray*. See **bahay-pukyutan.**

pudpód (pud-pód), I. *adj.* blunt or worn-out at the business end due to constant use or overuse.
—II. *n.* 1. act of causing the business end of something to become blunt or worn-out by overuse or constant using. Syn. *pudapod*. 2. state or condition of being blunt or worn-out at the business end due to friction or overuse. Also, *pagkapudpód*, *pagkapudapod*.

pueblo (pu-e-blo), var. **puweblo,** *n.* (*Sp.*) a municipality; town or township. Syn. *bayan*, *munisipyo*.

puga (pu-ga), I. *n.* (Sp. *fuga*) 1. escape or escaping; flight; fleeing. Syn. *tanan*, *pagtanan*, *pagtatanan*; *takas*, *pagtakas*, *pagtatakas*. 2. a fugitive. Syn. *pugante*, *takas*.

—II. *adj.* fugitive; having fled or escaped, as from prison. Syn. *takas*, *nakatakas*; *tanan*, *nakatanan*.

pugák (pu-gák), *n.* (*echoic*) sudden burst of sound like that produced by a car's exhaust pipe.

pugad (pu-gad), *n.* 1. nest, as of a bird or fowl. Syn. *saláy*. 2. (*Fig.*) den; lair. Also, *pámugarán*. Syn. *libliban*, *kutâ*. 3. (*Fig.*). home. Syn. *táhanan*.

pugal (pu-gal), I. *n.* 1. act or manner of tying a person or an animal, as on a tree, post, etc. in order not to escape. Cf. *pagtatali*. 2. confinement or a being tied up, as in the house, due to sickness, bad weather, or pressure of much work. Syn. *págkapatali* (*fig.*). 3. the rope or the like tied or bound on a person or animal. Syn. *gapos*.
—II. *adj.* tied up or confined, as in the house, due to sickness. etc. Also, *nakapugal*. Syn. *nakatali*, *nakakulóng*.

pugay (pu-gay), *n.* 1. act of taking off one's hat as a sign of respect or in salute. Also, *pagpupugay*. 2. act or manner of saluting. Syn. *saludo*, *pagsaludo*. 3. (*Fig.*) act of abusing a woman; dishonor done to a woman. Syn. *paggahasà o pagsasamantalá sa babae*.

pugayán (pu-ga-yán), *n.* act of taking off hats simultaneously, as of a group of persons.

pugità (pu-gi-tà), *n.* 1. cuttlefish. 2. octopus.

pugnáw (pug-náw), I. *n.* state or condition of being razed or totally burned. Syn. *tugnáw*, *pagkatugnáw*; *tupok*, *pagkatupok*; *supok*, *pagkasupok*.
—II. *adj.* razed or totally burned; reduced to ashes. Syn. *supók*, *tupók*, *tugnáw*, *naging abó*.

pugo (pu-go), *n.* (*Ornith.*) quail.

pugók (pu-gók), var. **pu-gók,** *adj.* short-necked.

pugón (pu-gón) *n.* (Sp. *fogon*) 1. stove. Syn. *kalán*, *kusinilya*. 2. kiln; furnace. Syn. *humo*.

pugong (pu-gong), *n.* 1. act or manner of tying hair into a knot. Syn. *pusód*, *pagpusód*, *pagpupusód*. 2. the manner hair is tied into a knot. Also, *pagkakapugong*. Syn. *pagkakapusód*. 3. knot of hair worn by a woman; top knot. Syn. *pusód*. 4. a piece of cloth or a handkerchief tied on the hair. 5. act of tying up the mouth of a bag or sack, as after filling it with grains. Also, *pagpugong*. 6. a piece of cord, twine, or the like thus used. Syn. *pamugong*.

pugos (pu-gos), n. act or manner of washing only the soiled portion of a garment or clothing, as under the running water of a faucet. Also, *pagpupugos*.

pugot (pu-got), n. 1. a beheading; decapitation. Also, *pagpugot*. Syn. *pagputol sa ulo*. 2. also, act of cutting off an ear, arm, or thigh, esp. at the base.

pugpóg (pug-póg), I. *adj.* rotten or decayed at the end, as of a piece of wood, pole, or the like. Syn. *gapók*, *gipô*. 2. charred, referring to one end of a firewood, cigar, or cigarette. Syn. *tigpô*.
—II. n. 1. act of trimming or snuffing off the decayed or charred portion of a thing. 2. the portion of a thing that is decayed or charred.

pugtô (pug-tô), I. *n.* state or condition of being severed or cut off violently.
—II. *adj.* severed or cut violently.

puhunan (pu-hu-nan), n. 1. capital in business or gambling; investment. Syn. *kapital*. 2. (Colloq.) assets; resources. Syn. *kayamanan*.

pulá (pu-lá), I. n. 1. red; red color. 2. (of eggs) yolk.
—II. *adj.* red; with or having red color. Syn. *mapulá*.

pulà (pu-là), n. act of finding fault with another; adverse criticism. Syn. *pintás*, *pamimintás; pistâ, pamimistâ*.

pulák (pu-lák), n. act of lopping or cutting off the branches of a tree. Syn. *pusad*, *pagpusad*.

pulad (pu-lad), n. young growth of feathers.

pulag (pu-lag), n. glare of light; dazzling light. Syn. *nakasísilaw na liwanag*, *matindíng liwanag*.

pulahán (pu-la-hán), I. n. 1. (P-) Red; a communist. Syn. *Komunista*. 2. a citizen of the Soviet Union. Syn. *Ruso*.
—II. *adj.* 1. of the Soviet Union; communist. Syn. *komunista*. 2. with or having reddish hue or color.

pulandit (pu-lan-dit), n. spurt or squirt of water or liquid. Syn. *bigláng puslit*, *tilandóg*.

pulanggós (pu-lang-gós), n. a slipping from hold, trap, arrest, etc.

pulapol (pu-la-pol), n. 1. act or manner of smearing something, as with paint, oil, mud, or any sticky liquid. Also, *pagpulapol, pagkakápulapol*. 2. any sticky dirt or liquid smeared on something. Syn. *kapol, kulapol*.

pulás (pu-lás), n. 1. sudden start, as of runners in a race. 2. early start or departure. Syn. *maagang pag-alis o pagyao*.

puláw (pu-láw), n. night vigil over a dead or a seriously sick person. Syn. *lamay*, *paglalamay*.

pulbera (pul-be-ra), n. (Sp. *polvera*) powder box. Syn. *púlbuhan*.

pulbós (pul-bós), I. n. (Sp. *polvos*) 1. powder; face powder. Cf. *blangkete*. 2. act or manner of applying face powder. Also, *pagpupulbós*. 2. any pulverized manner, as dust, ash, etc. Syn. *abó*.
—II. *adj.* pulverized; reduced or ground to powder or dust. Syn. *duróg na duróg*, *pinung-pino*.

pulburá (pul-bu-rá), n. (Sp. *pólvora*) gunpowder.

pulburón (pul-bu-rón), n. (Sp. *polvorón*) a kind of compressed cookies made of starch grit with sugar, milk, butter, etc.

pulgada (pul-ga-da), n. inch (measure). Syn. *dalì*.

pulgás (pul-gás), n. (Sp. *pulga*) flea.

pulikat (pu-li-kat), n. cramp. Syn. *kalambre*, *kisíg* (in some regions).

pulido (pu-li-do), *adj.* (Sp.) 1. polished; refined; neat (s.o. workmanship). Syn. *makinis, pino*. 2. well-behaved; well-mannered. Syn. *mahinhín, pormál*.

pulilan (pu-li-lan), n. 1. lagoon. Syn. *dagat-dagatan, lanaw*. 2. (P-) name of a town in the province of *Bulacán*.

pulò (pu-lò), n. 1. an isolated place, esp. a wooded area in a wide plain. 2. a small place or area separated from other places. Syn. *iláng*. 3. an island. Syn. *isla*.

pulók (pu-lók), n. 1. violent pecking with the beak or bill, esp. of fowls and birds.

2. the neck feathers of birds and fowls.

pulong (pu-long), n. 1. act of talking together; conversation. Syn. *usap, paguusap*. 2. meeting, as of an association. Syn. *miting, pagmimiting*. 3. conference. Syn. *kumperénsiyá*. 4. session, as of a lawmaking body.

pulós (pu-lós), I. adj. 1. all; every one of. Syn. *payák, lahát, taganás, pawà*. 2. full of; covered with. Syn. *puro, punô ng*.
—II. adv. wholly; fully; entirely; completely.
—III. pron. all; everyone. Syn. *lahát, lahát-lahát*.

pulot (pu-lot), I. n. 1. act of picking up something that has fallen or found on the ground, floor, etc. Syn. *dampót, pagdampót*. 2. something found accidentally and taken for one's own. Syn. *bagáy na nápupulot*. 3. act of acquiring or learning something from another, as a matter of experience. 4. an idea, knowledge, etc. learned or acquired from another. Syn. *bagay na nátutuhan sa ibá*.
—II. adj. 1. found accidentally and taken for one's own. 2. not original; learned from another.

pulót (pu-lót), n. thick, dark-colored syrup; molasses.

pulót-gatâ (pu-lót + ga-tâ), n. 1. honeymoon. Syn. *luna-de-miyél*. 2. sweet intimacy. Syn. *pagmamáhalan*.

pulót-pukyutan (pu-lót + puk-yu-tan), n. honey.

pulpól (pul-pól), I. n. state or condition of being already dull or blunt, as the point of a pencil. Cf. *pudpód, salsál*.
—II. adj. already dull or blunt, said esp. of points. Syn. *upód, pudpód*.

pulseras (pul-se-ras), n. (Sp. *pulsera*) bracelet. Syn. *galáng*.

pulso (pul-so; -só), n. (Sp.) 1. regular beating in the arteries caused by the contractions of the heart. Cf. *tibók, pintíg*. 2. the perceptible underlying feelings of the public, group of people, etc. Syn. *damdamin, opinyón*. 3. act of taking the pulse count of a person by holding him on his wrist. Also, *pagpulso*. 4. (Fig.) critical estimate or evaluation of the

feelings or opinions of the public or of a group of peole. Syn. *pagdamá sa damdamin*.

pultahan (pul-ta-han), n. gate; gateway; entrance. Syn. *tárangkahan*.

pultero (pul-te-ro), n. (Sp. *portero*) gatekeeper. Syn. *bantáy-pintó*.

pulube (pu-lu-be), var. pulubi, n. pauper; beggar; mendicant. Syn. *magpapálimos*.

puluhan (pu-lu-han), n. the handle of a bolo, knife, dagger, or the like. Syn. *manggo*. Cf. *hawakán, tatangnán*.

pulumpón (pu-lum-pón), n. 1. a small group. Syn. *kulumpón, lipumpón*. 2. a small pile or heap. Syn. *timbón*.

pulupot (pu-lu-pot), n. 1. a coiling or winding around something. Syn. *pilipit, pagpilipit; ayikid, pag-ayikid; bidbíd, pagbidbíd; salabíd, pagsalabíd*. 2. a rope, wire, twine, etc. coiled around something. Syn. *bagay na nakapulupot o nakasalabíd*. 2. a coil or a number of coils around something. Syn. *pilipit, ikid, ayikid, salabid*.

pulú-pulô (pu-lú + pu-lô), I. adj. 1. divided into small islands. 2. not concentrated in a single place. Syn. *puktú-puktô, putá-putakî*.
—II. adv. from island to island.

pulú-pulutóng (pu-lú + pu-lu-tóng), adj. & adv. in separate groups or bands. Syn. *pangkát-pangkát, hiwá-hiwaláy, grupu-grupo*.

pulutan (pu-lu-tan), n. hors d'oeuvre; appetizer, usually taken with wine. Cf. *pampagana*.

pulutóng (pu-lu-tóng), n. a small, separate group, band, or company. Syn. *kulumpól, kulumpón, lipon*.

pumagitna (pu-ma-git-na), v. (used a present tense and past tense) 1. to place oneself at the center. Also, *gumitnâ, pagitnâ*. Syn. *sumentro, pasentro*. 2. to place oneself between two persons or things. Syn. *pumagitan, lumagáy sa pagitan*. 3. to enter or involve oneself, as in politics.

pumalít (pu-ma-lít), v. (present and past) 1. to act as a substitute for another; replace another; take the place of another. Syn. *humalili*. 2. to have one's money changed into lower denominations. Also, *magpapalít*. Syn. *magpasuklí*.

pumaltós (pu-mal-tós), *v.* (*present* and *past*) 1. to become blistered or scalded. Also, *magpaltós*. 2. to fail; become a failure; fail to realize. Syn. *mabigó*. 3. to miss a target. Syn. *sumalà; magmintís, mumintís*. 4. to fail to explode.

pumalya (pu-mal-ya; -ya), *v.* (*present* and *past*) 1. to be absent; be absent from. Syn. *di pumasok, di dumaló, lumiban*. 2. to skip; have an omission. Syn. *humakdáw, sumalto*. 3. to fail to explode. Syn. *di pumutók, pumaltós*.

pumanatag (pu-ma-na-tag), *v.* (*present* and *past*) to stay calm; calm down. Syn. *tumahimik, manahimik*.

pumanaw (pu-ma-naw), *v.* (*present* and *past*) 1. to disappear. Syn. *mawalá, malipol*. 2. to die; pass away. Syn. *mamatáy, sumakabiláng-buhay*. 3. to depart or leave. Syn. *yumao, yumaon, umalís*.

pumanig (pu-ma-nig), *v.* (*present* and *past*) to side or take sides with. Syn. *kumampí*.

pumangláw (pu-mang-láw), *v.* (*present* and *past*) to become melancholic; turn lonely. Syn. *lumungkót, magíng mapangláw o malungkót*.

pumareho (pu-ma-re-ho), *v.* (*present* and *past*) to imitate another; do what another does. Syn. *tumulad, gumaya, pumaris*.

pumasada (pu-ma-sa-da), *v.* (*present* and *past*) to go out and make trips on one's regular or assigned route getting passengers on the way, referring to a passenger vehicle driver. Also, *magpasada*.

pumasok (pu-ma-sok), *v.* (*present* and *past*) 1. to enter; go inside. 2. to go to school or to one's work. 3. to enter or penetrate. Syn. *sumuót, sumulót, lumusót*.

pumaspás (pu-mas-pás), *v.* (*present* and *past*) 1. to make a sudden burst of speed. Syn. *kumaskás, kumarimot*. 2. (*Colloq.*) to make a furious attack against. Syn. *bumanat, umatake*. 3. to attack a woman sexually. 4. to make fast waving motions, as a flag in the air that is being blown by a strong wind. Syn. *wumasiwas, pumagaspás, wumagaywáy*.

pumatáy (pu-ma-táy), I. *v.* (*present* and *past*)

1. to kill someone; commit murder. Syn. *umutang ng buhay* (*fig.*) 2. to butcher or kill an animal. Syn. *kumatay, magkatay*. —II. *n.* (with *ang*) the murderer or killer.

pumatol (pu-ma-tol), *v.* (*present* and *past*) 1. to accept the challenge of an unworthy opponent. 2. to lower or degrade oneself by paying attention to someone who is inferior or lower in rank.

pumayapà (pu-ma-ya-pà), *v.* (*present* and *past*) 1. to become calm, quiet, peaceful, tranquil, etc. Syn. *tumahimik, kumalma*. 2. to make calm, peaceful. etc. Syn. *patahimikin, pakalmahín*.

pumigil (pu-mi-gil), *v.* (*present* and *past*) 1. to hold something in one's hand. Syn. *humawak, maghawak; tumangan, magtangan*. 2. to hold on something to prevent self from falling, sliding, etc. Syn. *kumapit, tumangan, humawak*. 3. to stop or prevent someone from doing something undesirable. Syn. *sumansalà, sansalain*.

pumilit (pu-mi-lit), *v.* (*present* and *past*) 1. to try hard to do or accomplish something. Also, *magpilit*. 2. to force or compel someone to do something against his will. Syn. *pumuwersa*.

pumintas (pu-min-tas; -tás), *v.* (*present* and *past*) to criticize adversely. Syn. *pumulà, mamulà*.

pumitada (pu-mi-ta-da), *v.* (*present* and *past*) to give forth a long, loud blast or resonant sound, as that of a siren or church bell. Syn. *sumirena, sumilbato, rumipíki* (for church bells).

pumpiyáng (pum-pi-yáng), *n.* (*Ch. ?*) 1. cymbals. 2. (in some kind of numbers game) the winning pair of numbers represented by the same numeral.

pumpón (pum-pón), *n.* 1. bouquet; bunch of flowers. Syn. *bukéy*. 2. cluster of fruits, leaves, etc. Syn. *kumpól, langkáy*.

pumpóng (pum-póng), *n.* 1. file, as of papers. Syn. *buntón, támbak*. 2. cluster, as of leaves. Syn. *kumpól, kulumpól*. 3. (in hide-and-seek) the cry shouted by a player when a member of the opposite team is found or located. 4. a small group. Syn. *lipon, umpók*.

pumukaw (pu-mu-kaw), *v.* (*present* and *past*)
1. to cause someone to wake up (from sleep). 2. to be the one to rouse someone from inaction or lethargy. Syn. *gumising*.

pumulás (pu-mu-lás), *v.* (*present* and *past*)
1. to start suddenly, as runners in a race. Syn. *biglâng kumaskás (ng takbó)*. 2. to depart or leave suddenly for a trip. Syn. *biglâng umalís o lumisan*.

pumuná (pu-mu-na), *v.* (*present* and *past*) 1. to take notice of. Syn. *pumansín*. 2. to criticize adversely; find fault with. Syn. *pumulà, pumintás, pumistá*.

pumunta (pu-mun-ta), *v.* (*present* and *past*) to go to a certain place; leave for a certain place. Syn. *tumungo*.

pumupól (pu-mu-pól), *v.* (*present* and *past*) to get a flower or flowers by picking with the fingers.

pumurba (pu-mur-ba), *v.* (*present* and *past*) to make a try. Syn. *umato, sumubok*.

pumuri (pu-mu-ri), *v.* (*present* and *past*) to compliment; speak well of someone or something; praise.

pumutók (pu-mu-tók), *v.* (*present* and *past*)
1. to burst noisily; explode, as a bomb. Syn. *sumabog, sumambulat*. 2. to burst open, as popcorn. Syn. *bumusá*. 3. to crack or become cracked, as glass, etc. Syn. *mabasag, magkabasag*. 4. to erupt, as a volcano. Syn. *sumabóg*. 5. to split open, as the ground during an earthquake. Syn. *bumuká, ngumangá, bumiták*. 6. to fire or discharge a projectile, as a gun.

puná (pu-ná), *n.* 1. notice or noticing; observation. Syn. *pansín, reparo, obserbasyón*. 2. remark; comment. Syn. *pansin, komentaryo*. 3. adverse criticism; objection. Syn. *kritiká, tutol*.

punado (pu-na-do), *adj.* noticeable; easily seen; conspicuous. Syn. *halatâ, hálatain*.

punas (pu-nas), *n.* 1. act or manner of wiping off dirt with or as with a rag; cleaning something by wiping. Syn. *pahid, pagpahid*. 2. sponge bath. Syn. *banyos*.

punda (pun-da), *n.* (Sp. *funda*) pillowcase. Syn. *damít-unan*.

pundár (pun-dár), *adj.* (Sp. *fundar*) founded or established by. Also, *ipinundár*. Syn. *itinatag, itinayó*.

pundasyón (pun-das-yón), *n.* (Sp. *fundacion*) 1. base; groundwork; foundation, as of a building. 2. the fundamental principle on which something is founded; basis. Syn. *saligán, batayán*. 3. an institution maintained by endowment.

pundi (pun-di), I. *n.* (Sp. *fundir*) 1. a burning or being burnt, as of an electric fuse or bulb. Also, *pagkapundi*. 2. state or condition of being inutile, esp. of a person, due to overwork. etc.
—II. *adj.* burnt; no longer serviceable (s.o. fuse, electric bulb, etc.) Also, *pundido*.

pundilyo (pun-dil-yo), var. **pundiyó**, *n.* (Sp. *fundillos*) seat of pants, drawers, panties, etc. Syn. *puwít ng salawál, kalsunsilyo, atbp*.

punerarya (pu-ne-rar-ya), *n.* (Sp. *funeraria*) funeral parlor.

punit (pu-nit), *n.* 1. act of tearing or ripping (cloth, paper, or the like) with the hands. Also, *pagpunit*. 2. the part or portion that is torn or ripped; tear; rent.

punít-punít (pu-nít + pu-nít), *adj.* badly torn or ripped; lacerated; tattered. Syn. *sirá-sirá*.

punlâ (pun-lâ), *n.* 1. act of planting seeds in a seedbed. 2. young plants in a seedbed; seedlings.

punò (pu-nò), *n.* 1. chief; head; boss. Syn. *hepe*. 2. leader, as of a gang. Syn. *lider, promotór*. 3. base or foot, as of a bridge, mountain, etc. Syn. *paá, paanán*. 4. origin or source, as of a river, spring, etc. Syn. *simulâ, pinagmúmulán*. 5. (a) tree. Syn. *punongkahoy*; (b) trunk (of a tree). 6. cause. Syn. *sanhî, dahilán*.

punô (pu-nô), I. *adj.* 1. full; filled up (s.o. containers). Syn. *hustó na ang lamán*. 2. fully occupied, as a movie house, passenger vehicle, etc. Syn. *walâ nang puwáng o bakante, kargado na*. 3. (Colloq.) soiled, smeared, or covered with (mud, dirt, etc.). Syn. *puro, panay (colloq.)*. 4. (*Fig.*) fed-up; disgusted. Syn. *sawâ na, suya na*.
—II. *n.* state or condition of being already full, filled up, or fully occupied.

punong-abala (pu-nong + a-ba-la), *n.* host or hostess (in a party, celebration, etc.)

punong-bayan   **pungóg**

Syn. *ang may-handâ o may-paanyaya*.

punong-bayan (pu-nong + ba-yan), var. **punungbayan, punumbayan**. *n*. 1. town mayor; president (of a town). Syn. *alkalde, presidente*. 2. provincial capital; capital town. Syn. *kabisera*.

punso (pun-so), *n*. 1. ant hill. 2. hillock; mound.

punta (pun-ta), *n. (Sp.)* 1. act of going to a certain place. Also, *pagpunta*. Syn. *tungo, pagtungo; paroón, pagparoón*. 2. the place or direction to which a person or thing is going. Syn. *patútunguhan, púpuntahán*. 3. headland; promontory; cape. Syn. *tangos, lungos, tangway, imus*. 4. point; pointed end. Syn. *tulis*. 5. end; tip; extremity. Syn. *dulo*. 6. *(Colloq.)* objective; aim; purpose. Syn. *layon, láyunin; tungo, túnguhin; hangád, hangarin*.

puntas (pun-tas), *n. (Sp.)* 1.lace. Syn. *engkahe*. 2. lacework. Syn. *kulado*. 3. bobbinet; bobbin lace.

puntiryá (pun-tir-yá), *n*. 1. aim; act of aiming at a target. Syn. *sipat, pagsipat*. 2. anything aimed at; target. Syn. *bagay na pinatátamaan*. 3. *(Colloq.)* aim; purpose; objective. Syn. *layon, layunin*. 4. marksmanship. Syn. *pagtudlâ*.

punto (pun-to), *n. (Sp.)* 1. *(Gram.)* period. Syn. *tuldók*. 2. tone of voice in speaking; intonation. Syn. *estilo*. 3. a score or point made by a player in a game. Syn. *iskór*. 4. an impressive argument or idea made by someone; point. Syn. *katwiran*. 5. state or condition whereby the point of crystalization or granulation, as of sugar, etc., has been reached.

puntod (pun-tod; -tód), *n*. 1. burial ground; grave. Syn. *libíng, líbingan*. 2. hillock. Syn. *mababang buról*. 3. (by ext., in golf) tee.

puntos (pun-tos), *n. (Sp.)* a point or points (score) made by a player, debater, etc.

punyagî (pun-ya-gî), *n*. persistent effort or efforts; endeavor; perseverance; diligence. Syn. *sikap, pagsisikap; pagsasakit, pagsusumakit; tiyagâ, pagtitiyagâ*.

punyál (pun-yál), *n. (Sp. puñal)* poniard; dagger. Syn. *daga, sundáng, balaráw*.

punyós (pun-yós), *n. (Sp. puño)* wristband; cuff.

pungál (pu-ngál), I. *adj*. broken at the base or foot, as of a tooth, animal horn, and the like. Syn. *pungál*.

–II. *n*. 1. state or condition of being broken at the base or foot. Also, *pagkapungál*. Syn. *punggál, pagkapunggál*. 2. a tooth, horn, etc. that has been broken at the base or foot.

pungás (pu-ngás), *n*. confused or startled state of the mind at waking up, as after a frightening dream. Syn. *alimpungát*.

pungay (pu-ngay), *n*. soft radiance or lambency of the eyes. Syn. *lamlám ng matá*.

pungkol (pung-kol; -kól), I. *adj*. 1. with a maimed arm (or arms); armless. Syn. *putól (ang braso), waláng-braso*. 2. legless, usually said of fowls. Syn. *putól ang paá, waláng-paá*.

punggahan (pung-ga-han), *n*. den; lair; haunt. Syn. *taguán, lunggâ (fig.)*.

punggî (pung-gî), I. *adj*. tailless, referring esp. to a dog. Syn. *waláng-buntót, putól ang buntót*.

—II. *n*. a tailless animal, esp. a dog.

punggók (pung-gók), *adj*. 1. thickset and relatively short; stocky. Syn. *matipunò, báliksaksakin*. 2. short-tailed, referring to an animal. Syn. *putól o maiklî ang buntót*. See **punggî**.

punggós (pung-gós), I. *n*. 1. act of wrapping something in a handkerchief or in piece of cloth by tying its four corners. Syn. *bungkós, pagbungkós*. 2. fact, state, or condition of being wrapped in a handkerchief or the like with the four corners tied together.

—II. *adj*. wrapped in a handkerchief or in a piece of cloth with the four corners tied together. Syn. *bungkós, nakabungós*.

punggot (pung-got; -gót), I. *n*. 1. act of cutting off a small thing, as a twig, small vine, etc., with the fingers. 2. something cut off short with the fingers. 3. state or condition of being cut off very short, with the fingers.

—II. *adj*. cut off short with the fingers.

punglô (pung-lô), var. **punlo**, *n*. bullet. Syn. *bala*.

pungóg (pu-ngóg), *adj*. cut off, too short. Syn. *masyadong maiklî*.

pungól (pu-ngól), var. pung-ol, n. 1. stump of a tree. Syn. tuôd. 2. the root or remaining part of a decayed tooth. Syn. upód o pudpód na ngipin. 3. an almost used up firewood brand. Syn. agipó.

pungós (pu-ngós), n. act of cutting off an ear, cockscomb, etc. with or as with a knife in the manner like using a saw.

pupitre (pu-pi-tre), n. (Sp.) 1. desk; school desk. 2. writing desk or table. Syn. mesang sulatán.

pupò (pu-pò), adj. & adv. much; very much, as in: pupong mabuti, much better. Syn. higít, lalò, mas.

pupog (pu-pog), n. 1. furious and persistent attack, as of a fowl, on an enemy, using beak and feet. 2. (Fig.) a swarming in to see, buy, etc. by a great number of persons (fans, buyers, viewers, etc.). Syn. dagsâ, pagdagsâ. 3. passionate or amorous kisses, as an expression of affection by a lover.

pupól (pu-pól), n. act or manner of picking flowers. Syn. pitás, pamimitás.

puras (pu-raṣ), n. (Bot.) citrus or lemon blossoms. Syn. asahár.

purba (pur-ba), n. (Sp. probar) 1. a try or trying; test; trial. Syn. subok, pagsubok; ato, pag-ato. 2. tasting or savoring. Syn. tikím, pagtikím.

purbado (pur-ba-do), adj. (Sp. probado) tried; tested; proven. Syn. subók (na).

purke (pur-ke), conj. (Sp. porque) because. Syn. dahil, sapagká't.

purgá (pur-gá), n. (Sp.) 1. purgative; laxative; cathartic. Syn. laksante, pampadumí, pampatae. 2. act or manner of taking or giving a purgative. Also, pagpurgá, pagpupurgá.

puri (pu-ri), n. 1. honor; good reputation. Syn. dangál, karangalan, onór. 2. praise; act of praising or lauding. Also, pagpuri. 3. fame. Syn. katanyagan, kabantugan. 4. chastity; purity. Syn. kalinisan, kadalisayan.

puro (pu-ro), I. adj. (Sp.) 1. pure; undiluted; unadulterated. Syn. dalisay, waláng-halò. 2. pure-blooded; of unmixed stock. Syn. lantáy. 3. full of; covered with, as in: puro langgám, full of or covered with ants. 4. with or having the last card or number

(of a pair) being awaited to be drawn in order to win. Syn. namúmuro. 5. causing instant death, as a shot, stab, etc.
—II. n. 1. state or condition of being pure or unadulterated. 2. the last card or number (of a pair) that is being awaited to be drawn in order to win.

purók (pu-rók), n. district. Syn. distrito, poók, sityo.

puról (pu-ról), n. 1. dullness or bluntness, as of bladed tools. Also, kapurulán. Syn. kapangalan, kapaurán. 2. mental slowness; dullness of mind. Syn. hinà ng ulo o isip.

pursigé (pur-si-gé), var. pursigí, n. (Sp. por seguido) 1. diligence. Syn. sigasig, kasigasigan. 2. initiative. Syn. kusà, pagkukusà.

purúk-purók (pu-rúk + pu-rók), I. adj. divided into districts. Syn. distri-distrito.
—II. adv. by districts; in districts.

puruhan (pu-ru-han), v. to hit or be able to hit directly or critically. Syn. tamaan nang tuwiran.

purunggo (pu-rung-go; -gó), n. tiny pieces of broken crystals.

purupót (pu-ru-pót), n. loose bowel movement. Syn. pagtataé.

pusà (pu-sà), n. 1. (Zool.) cat. 2. (Fig.) a betrayer. Syn. taong mapagkánulô.

pusakál (pu-sa-kál), adj. completely addicted or given to a bad practice or habit (s.o. persons). cf. sugapà, gumunggumon.

pusalì (pu-sa-lì), n. the miry place under a batalán, which receives drainage and sewage from the kitchen, etc. Cf. lusak.

pusikit (pu-si-kit), adj. very dark, as in: gabíng pusikit, very dark night.

pusít[1] (pu-sit), n. (Ichth.) squid.

puslít (pus-lít), I. n. 1. act of escaping or running away secretly. Syn. pagtakas nang palihím. 2. a squirting, as of water through a small hole or opening. Syn. tilandóy, pagtilandóy; pulandít, pagpulandít. 3. act of gate-crashing. 4. a gate-crasher; an uninvited guest. 5. act of smuggling goods from or out of a country. 6. contraband; smuggled goods. 7. a person who escaped. Syn. takas.
—II. adj. 1. illegally obtained or taken. Syn. nakaw, ninakaw; kupit, kinupit; ilit,

inilít; umít, inumít. 2. smuggled; taken in
as a contraband. Syn. kontrabando,
palusót. 3. said of an uninvited guest or
gate-crasher.

pusò (pu-sò), n. 1. (Anat.) heart. 2. (Zool.)
the heart of an animal that is eaten or
used for food. 3. (Bot.) the heart or
blossom of a banana plant. 4. (Bot.) ear
of corn. 5. (Fig.) inner most thoughts and
feelings; conscience. Syn. damdamin.

pusok (pu-sok), n. 1. impetuousity;
impulsiveness; acting on sudden
impulsive. Syn. dahás, karáhasán. 2.
harshness; cruelty. Syn. lupit, kalupitán. 3.
bravery; courage; Syn. tapang, katapangan.

pusod (pu-sod), n. 1. (Anat.) navel;
umbilicus. 2. center or heart, as of a city.
Syn. sentro, gitnâ. 2 bottom, as of a river
or sea. Syn. káilaliman, káibuturan.

pusód (pu-sód), n. 1. a kind of hairdo in
which the hair is knotted on the top or
back of the head; bun. Syn. puyód. 2. act
or manner of making this kind of hair do.
Also, pagpusód, pagpupusód. Syn. puyód,
pagpuyód, pagpupuyód.

pusón (pu-són), var. pus-on, n. (Anat.) the
lower, middle part of the abdomen;
hypograstrium. Cf. tiyán.

pusóng (pu-sóng), adj. impudent; brazen;
irreverent. Syn. waláng-galang, waláng-
pitagan, bastós.

puspós (pus-pós), adj. complete; thorough;
replete; full. Syn. tigîb, lipós.

pusta (pus-ta; -tá), n. (Sp. posta, apuesta) 1.
bet or stake in gambling. Syn. tayâ. 2. the
amount of bet or wager. 3. act of betting.
Also, pagpusta. Syn. pagtayâ, pananayâ.

pustà (pus-tà), n. a slice of fish cut crosswise.
Syn. hiwà o gilít (ng isdâ).

pusturyoso (pus-tur-yo-so), adj. (Masc.)
fond of elegant dresses; always well-
dressed. Syn. magarang manamit; mabikas.

pusyáw (pus-yáw), n. 1. discoloration;
softness or paleness of color; slight loss of
color. Syn. kupas, pagkupas. 2. a becoming
less distinct, as of one's popularity, honor,
etc; a fading.

puta (pu-ta), n. (Sp.) whore; harlot;
prostitute. Syn. burikák (slang), patutot,
kalapating mababá and lipád, pampám.

puták (pu-ták), n. cackle of hens or fowls.
Cf. kakak.

putakî (pu-ta-kî), n. state or condition of
being scattered or found separately in
small quantity.

putakti (pu-tak-ti; -tí), n. (Entom.) 1. wasp.
2. hornet.

putahe (pu-ta-he), var. potahe, n. a choice
dish or viand. Syn. ulam, pang-ulam.

putá-putakî (pu-tá + pu-ta-kî), adj. scattered
or found separately in small amount in
different places; not confined to one
place. Syn. puktú-puktó, hiwá-hiwaláy.

putat (pu-tat), n. something taken or eaten
as appetizer or to prevent surfeit. See
pulutan.

puti (pu-ti), n. 1. act of harvesting or picking
fruits. Syn. pangunguha o pamimitás ng
bungangkahoy. 2. the fruits harvested or
picked. 3. act of killing or putting life to
an end. Syn. kitíl o pagkitíl ng buhay.

putî (pu-tî), I. n. 1. white; white color. 2.
whiteness; state or condition of being
white. Also, kaputián. 3. an individual
belonging to the white race. 4. the white
or albumen of eggs. Syn. klaro (if an egg
is uncooked. 5. any white object or
matter. 6. the part or portion of anything
that is white.
—II. adj. 1. white; of white color. Also,
maputî. 2. with or having a light-colored
skin; belonging to the white race.

putik (pu-tik), n. 1. wet, soft, sticky earth;
mud. Syn. lusak. 2. dirt or stain of mud
on anything.

puting-buhók (pu-tíng + bu-hók), n. white
or gray hair. Syn. uban.

puting-tabing (pu-tíng + ta-bing), n. 1.
silver screen. 2. motion pictures
collectively. Syn. pelíkulá.

puting-tainga (pu-tíng + ta-i-nga), var.
puting-taynga, I. n. (Fig.) a stingy or
selfish person. Syn. taong maramot o
kuripot.
—II. adj. 1. stingy; selfish. Syn. maramot,
kuripot.

puting-tiyán (pu-tíng + ti-yán), I. n. (Fig.)
1. a stingy or selfish individual. Syn.
puting-tainga.
—II. adj. stingy; selfish. Syn. maramot,

kuripot, hidhíd.

putlâ (put-lâ), *n.* paleness; lack of color; pallor. Also, *pamumutlâ, kaputlaán.*

puto (pu-to), *n.* a kind of native rice cake cooked by steaming.

puták (pu-tók), *n.* 1. explosion; loud noise caused by bursting. 2. a bursting or blowing up. Syn. *sabog, pagsabog; sambulat, pagsambulat.* 3. discharge or report of a gun or cannon; fire or shot. 4. eruption, as of a volcano. Syn. *sabog, pagsabog.*

puták-sa-buhò (pu-tók + sa + bu-hò), I. *n.* (Fig.) an illegitimate child; bastard. Syn. *anák-sa-labás, anák-sa-ligaw, anák-sa-puwera.*

—II. *adj.* bastard; illegitimate, referring to a child.

putód (pu-tód), *n.* 1. shorts; trunk; knee breeches. Syn. *korto.* 2. drawers. Syn. *kalsunsilyo.*

putól (pu-tól), I. *adj.* 1. cut; cut off; severed. Syn. *patíd, lagót,* 2. disconnected. Syn. *pinutol, nilagót.* 3. with or having a leg or arm or both legs or arms dismembered or cut off.

—II. *n.* an armless person or legless animal.

puto-maya (pu-to + ma-ya), var. putumaya, *n.* a kind of native rice cake made from glutinous rice *(malagkit)* and eaten with grated coconut meat and sugar.

putong (pu-tong), *n.* 1. anything set or placed on the head: specifically, a crown. Syn. *korona.* 2. the act or manner of crowning, e.g. a queen. Syn. *pagkokorona.*

putós (pu-tós), I. *adj.* 1. thickly crowded or crammed, as with people. Syn. *siksikan, punúng-punô.* 2. completely full or filled up, as a bag or sack. Syn. *siksík na siksík, punúng-punô.*

puto-seko (pu-to + se-ko), var. putuseko, *n.* a kind of rice flour biscuit.

putót (pu-tót), I. *adj.* 1. very short; cut off too short. Syn. *maiklíng-maiklî.* 2. heavily burdened, as with work; with or having much work. Syn. *lubháng matrabaho.*

—II. *n.* shorts; short pants; trunks. Syn. *korto, putód.*

putpót (put-pót), *n.* 1. act of winding, coiling, or binding a cord, twine, thread, wire, etc. around something. Syn. *pulupot, pagpulupot; bidbíd, pagbibidbíd.* 2. a cord, twine, thread, etc. coiled or wound around something.

putpután (put-pu-tán), *v.* 1. to call the attention of by blowing or sounding the horn. Syn. *businahan.* 2. to call someone to sounding a whistle. Syn. *silbatuhan.*

putsero (put-se-ro), *n.* (Sp. *puchero*) a dish of boiled meat and vegetables with spices and condiments.

pútubumbóng (pú-tu-bum-bóng), var. puto-bumbóng, *n.* a kind of rice flour cake, made from a certain kind of glutinous rice called *pirurutong,* moulded and steamed in a small bamboo segment. Cf. *puto-sulôt.*

puwáng (pu-wáng), I. *n.* 1. small space between; small opening; gap. Syn. *siwang, awáng, kawang pagitan.* 2. crack; cleavage; split. Syn. *biták, biyák.* 3. vacant space; margin. Syn. *espasyo.* 4. vacancy or opening, as in an office. Syn. *bakante.*

puwede (pu-we-de), I. *adj.* (Sp. *puede*) 1. possible; that can be done, allowed, used, etc. Syn. *máaarì, posible.* 2. permissible; allowable; tolerable.

—II. *adv.* 1. possibly; by any possible means; in any case. 2. perhaps; maybe; by some possibility.

puwente[1] (pu-wen-te), *n.* (Sp. *fuente*) spring of water; fountain. Syn. *bukál, batis, saloy.*

puwente[2] (pu-wen-te), *n.* (Sp. *puente*) bridge. Syn. *tuláy.*

puwera (pu-we-ra), I. *adj.* (Sp. *fuera*) excluded; not included. Syn. *hindî kasama.*

—II. *prep.* except; with the exception of; barring. Syn. *líban o máliban kung.*

—III. *interj.* (P-) Out! Get out! Syn. *Layas! Alis!*

puwersa (pu-wer-sa), *n.* (Sp. *fuerza*) 1. force; strength. Syn. *lakás.* 2. power; compulsion; pressure brought to bear. Syn. *dahás.* 3. military, naval, or air force. Syn. *sandatahán lakás.* 4. (Law) binding power; validity. Syn. *bisà.* 5. (Mil.) fort. Syn. *kutà.*

puwerta (pu-wer-ta), *n.* (Sp. *puerta*) 1. door; doorway. Syn. *pintô, pintuan.* 2. entrance; gate. Syn. *pultahan, tárangkahan.* 3. port; harbor. Syn. *dáungan (daungán).* . See puwerto, sense 1. 4. (Anat.; colloq.) vulva. Syn. pukì.

puwerte (pu-wer-te), I. adj. (Sp. fuerte) 1. strong; with or having powerful effect; vigorous; drastic. Syn. malakás. 2. loud. Syn. malakás.
—II. adv. 1. hard; vigorously. Syn. nang malakás, mapuwersa. 2. loudly; in a loud manner.

puwerto (pu-wer-to), n. (Sp. puerto) 1. harbor: port. Syn. daunga. See puwerta, sense 3. 2. (Colloq.) the entrance to the vagina. Syn. butas ng puki. 3. fort. Syn. kutà.

puwés (pu-wés), conj. (Sp. pues) 1. then; therefore. Syn. kayâ, samakatwíd, anupá't. 2. since; in as much as; because. Syn. yamang, mayamang; pagká't, sapagká't; dahil sa.

puwesto (pu-wes-to), n. (Sp. puesto) 1. stand; stall; booth. Syn. lugár, kinátatayuan. 2. place or space occupied; location; site; position. Syn. kinároroonán; kinálalagyán; lugár. 3. place; rank or position in a sequence, as in: unang puwesto, first place. 4. post; office; station. Syn. upisina, tanggapan. 5. employment; position; appointment. Syn. trabaho, tungkulin. 6. the way or manner a thing is placed or situated. Syn. lagáy, pagkakálagáy.

puwíng (pu-wíng), n. 1. any small foreign body in the eyes. 2. (Fig.) act of disproving or contradicting a statement of another. Syn. pagpapasinungaling.

puwít (pu-wít), n. 1. (Anat.) buttocks; rump. Syn. pigî. 2. the anus. 3. the seat of pants, trousers, etc. 4. the external buttom of pots, vases, drinking glasses, and other containers. Cf. ilalim. 5. (Colloq.) the very last. Syn. káhulí-hulihan.

puwitán (pu-wi-tán), I. n. 1. the rear or posterior end of something. Syn. hulihán, buntót. 2. the last place or position, as in a race. Syn. kulilat. 3. the position or space behind someone. Syn. hulihán. 4. the seat, as of pants, trousers, etc. See puwít.

puyat (pu-yat), n. 1. want or lack of sleep; loss of sleep. Also, pagkapuyat. Syn. kakulangán sa tulog. 2. nightlong

wakefulness, as in keeping night vigil. Also, pagpupuyát. Syn. lamay, paglalamay. 3. act of causing someone to lose sleep. Also, pagpuyat.

puyaw (pu-yaw), n. fresh juice of newly pressed or milled sugar cane. Syn. sariwang katás ng tubó.

puyó (pu-yó), n. 1. cowlick. 2. (with sa pisngí) a small hollow in the cheek; dimple. Syn. biloy, turupyá, butas sa pisngí. 3. a whirl or whirling. Syn. alimpuyó, ipu-ipo.

puyok (pu-yok), n. attack of a fowl (with its beak and feet) against another which is weaker or refuses to fight.

puyód (pu-yód), n. bun; knot of hair on the top of the head. Syn. pusód.

puyog (pu-yog), n. act of drenching or wetting someone thoroughly. Syn. pagpitâ, pagbasáng mabuti.

puyós (pu-yós), n. 1. act of making fire by rubbing two hard objects or by friction. 2. a rapid whirling motion, as of air, water, dust, etc. Syn. alimpuyó. 3. intensity, as of anger. Syn. ngitngít, pagngingitngít.

puyupoy (pu-yu-poy), var. payipoy, n. wagging, as of a dog's tail. Syn. mabilís na kawág o pagkawág ng buntót.

púyusan (pú-yu-san), n. 1. a flint used for starting a fire. Syn. batóng kiskisan. 2. a two-piece set of dry bamboo sticks used for making fire by rubbing one against another.

R

R, r (ra; ere), n. 1. the fifteenth letter of the abakada (Pilipino alphabet). 2. the type or impression representing this letter. 3. a symbol for the fifteenth in a group or series.

raán (ra-án), n. var. daán, used after a vowel in derivative formation, as in: dumáraán (dumádaán).

rábanó (rá-ba-nó), n. (Sp.) radish. Syn. labanós.

rabis (ra-bis), n. (Eng.) rabies; hydrophobia. Syn. haydropobya, idropobya, kamandágaso.

raket¹ (ra-ket), n. (Eng.) 1. racket, as of tennis, badminton, etc. Syn. *raketa.* 2. any fraudulent or illegal scheme; racket. Syn. *dayà, pagdarayà.*

raket² (ra-ket), n. (Eng.) rocket; skyrocket. Syn. *kuwitis.*

raketa (ra-ke-ta), n. (Sp. *raqueta*) racket, as of tennis, badminton, etc. See raket¹, sense 1.

radar (ra-dar; -dár), n. (Eng.) radar.

radikál (ra-di-kál), n. & adj. (Sp. *radical*) radical.

radyasyón (rad-yas-yón), var. **radiyasyón**, n. (Sp. *radiación*) radiation.

radyo (rad-yo), n. 1. wireless telephony or telegraphy; radio. 2. message sent by radio; radiogram. Syn. *radyograma.* 3. the radio receiving set.

radyoaktibo (rad-yo-ak-ti-bo), adj. (Sp. *radioactivo*) radioactive.

radyopono (rad-yo-po-no), n. (Sp. *radiofono*) telephone operated by radio; radiophone; radiotelephone. Syn. *radyoteléponó.*

radyum (rad-yum), n. (Eng.) radium.

raha (ra-ha), n. (Eng.) rajah.

rahuyo (ra-hu-yo; -yò), n. an inducing or being induced; enticement; fascination.

rali (ra-li), n. (Eng.) rally; mass meeting. Syn. *malakíng miting o pamamahayag.*

rambután (ram-bu-tán), n. (Mal.) 1. an evergreen, bushy tree (*Nephelium lappaceum Linn.*) with oblong fruits covered with thick, coarse, wavy hair or soft spines. 2. the fruit of this tree.

ramí (ra-mí), I. n. (Eng.) 1. the ramie plant (*Boehmeria nivea*). 2. the fiber obtained from this plant. 3. cloth made from the fibers of this plant.

—II. adj. made of ramie fibers.

rantso (ran-tso), n. (Sp. *rancho*) 1. a very large farm, used esp. for raising cattle; ranch. 2. large hut or cabin.

ranggo (rang-go), n. (Sp. *rango*) 1. rank; position. Syn. *tungkulin.* 2. class; level; rank. Syn. *urì, klase.*

rangyâ (rang-yâ), n. ostentation; pomposity; magnificence. Also, *karangyaán.*

rápidó (rá-pi-dó), n. (Sp. *rápido*) 1. rapid firing of gun. 2. rapids.

rasa (ra-sa), n. (Sp. *raza*) 1. race; people having the same ancestry. Syn. *lahì.* 2. breed; stock. Syn. *kasta, lipì.*

raso (ra-so), n. (Sp.) a kind of silk-like fabric; satin.

rasón (ra-són), n. (Sp. *razón*) 1. reason; reasoning; argument. Syn. *katwiran, pangangatwiran, paliwanag.* 2. cause; motive. Syn. *dahilán, layon, láyunin.* 3. justification. Syn. *pagbibigáy-katwiran.*

rasonable(ra-so-na-ble), adj. (Sp. *razonable*) 1. reasonable. Syn. *makatwiran.* 2. moderate. Syn. *katamtaman.*

raspahín (ras-pa-hín), v. to rasp; scrape with a rough instrument.

rasyón (ras-yón), n. (Sp. *ración*) ration; fixed allowance of food, etc.

rasyonál (ras-yo-nál), adj. (Sp. *racional*) 1. rational; sensible. Syn. *makatwiran, nasakawiran, may-katwiran.* 2. able to reason clearly. Syn. *nakapangángatwiran.*

rasyonalidád (ras-yo-na-li-dád), n. (Sp. *racionalidád*) rationality; reasonableness. Syn. *pagkamay-katwiran.*

rasyonalismo (ras-yo-na-lis-mo), n. (Sp. *racionalismo*) rationalism. Syn. *pangangatwiran.*

rátilés (rá-ti-lés), var. **arátilés, dátilés**, n. (Bot.) 1. a widely distributed tree in the Philippines (*Mutingia calabura Linn.*) bearing smooth, rounded berry fruits which are very popular among children. 2. the fruit berries of this tree.

ratipiká (ra-ti-pi-ká), n. (Sp. *ratificar*) a ratifying or being ratified; ratification. Syn. *pagpapatibay.*

ratipikasyón (ra-ti-pi-kas-yón), n. (Sp. *ratificacion*) ratification; confirmation; approval. Syn. *pagpapatibay.*

raun (ra-un), n. (Eng.) 1. round, as in boxing. 2. round or tour of duty, as of a doctor in a hospital ward. Syn. *rekurida, libot, paglibot.*

raya (ra-ya), n. (Sp.) 1. line drawn with a pencil, pen, etc. Syn. *guhit, linya.* 2. act or manner of drawing a line or lines. Also, *pagraraya.* Syn. *linya, paglilinya, pagguhit ng raya o linya.*

rayadilyo (ra-ya-dil-yo), n. (Sp. *rayadillo*) stripped cotton duck.

rayama

rayama (ra-ya-ma), n. tete-a-tete; private
conversation. Syn. niíg, pagniniíg; ulayaw,
pag-uulayaw; pagsasárilinan.

rayo (ra-yo), n. (Sp.) 1. ray; beam. Syn.
sinag. 2. spoke, as of a wheel. See rayos.

rayos (ra-yos), n. (Sp.) spokes of a wheel.

rayos-ekes (ra-yos + e-kis), var. rayos-ekis,
n. (Sp.) 1. X-ray. 2. a photograph made
by means of X-rays. Syn. eksréy.

rayot (ra-yot), n. (Eng.) riot; wild, violent
public disturbance. Syn. guló, káguluhan,
pagkakaguló.

rayuma (ra-yu-ma), var. reuma, reyuma, n.
(Sp. reuma) rheumatism. Syn. reyumatismo.

reaksiyón (re-ak-si-yón), n. (Sp. reaccion)
1. reaction; action in response to some
influence. Syn. ganti, tugón, sagót. 2.
chemical reaction. Syn. epekto, pag-ipekto.

reál (re-ál), n. (Sp.) real; Spanish coin.

realidád (re-a-li-dád), n. (Sp.) reality; fact;
truth. Syn. katotohanan, katunayan.

realisá (re-a-li-sá), n. (Sp. realizar) a realizing
or being realized.

realisasyón (re-a-li-sas-yón), n. (Sp.
realizacion) 1. realization; understanding.
Syn. pag-unawà, pagká-unawà; pagtantô,
pagkátantô. 2. act of making real of
something imagined or planned. Syn.
pagtupád, katuparan, pagsasakatúparan.

realistikó (re-a-lis-ti-kó), adj. (Hispanized
Eng.) realistic. Syn. makatotohanan.

rebaha (re-ba-ha), n. (Sp. rebaja) in Comm.,
1. discount; rebate. Syn. tawad, patawad.
2. deduction; reduction. Syn. bawas,
diskuwento.

rebálidá (re-bá-li-dá), n. (Sp. reválida) final,
oral examination for an academic degree.

rebelasyón (re-be-las-yón), n. (Sp.
revelación) 1. act of making known;
revelation. Syn. paghahayág, pagsisiwalat,
pagbubunyag. 2. telling the truth about
something. Syn. pagtatapát. 3. state or
condition of being known or revealed.
Syn. pagkakáhayág, pagkakábunyág,
pagkakásiwalat.

rebelde (re-bel-de), I. n. (Sp.) 1. rebel;
insurgent. Syn. manghihimagsík,
rebulusyunaryo, insurekto. 2. defaulter.
—II. adj. 1. rebellious. Syn.
mapanghimagsík, mapanlabán. 2. stubborn.

rebokasyón

Syn. matigás ang ulo, sutíl.

rebelyón (re-bel-yón), n. (Sp. rebelión)
revolt; rebellion; insurrection. Syn.
panghihimagsík, pagbabangon, pag-aalsá,
insureksiyón, rebulusyón.

rebentadór (re-ben-ta-dór), colloq. var.
labintadór, n. (Sp. reventadór) firecracker.
Cf. paputók.

reberendo (re-be-ren-do), adj. (Sp. reverendo)
reverend; worthy of great respect. Syn.
kagalang-galang, kapita-pítagan.

rebersiyón (re-ber-si-yín), n. (Sp. reversión)
reversion; return to a former condition
or position. Syn. pagbabalík, pagsasauli,
pananag-uli, panunumbalik, pagpapanumbalik.

rebisá (re-bi-sá), n. (Sp. revisar) 1. review;
restudy. Syn. repaso, pagrerepaso,
pagbabalik-aral. 2. inspection; checking;
examination. Syn. pag-iksamin, pagsuri,
pagsusuri, inspeksiyón. 3. revision. Syn.
rebisyón, pagwawastó, pagbabago. 4.audit;
examination and checking of business
accounts. Syn. pagtuós, pagtutuós.

rebisadór (re-bi-sa-dór), n. (Sp. revisador) 1.
reviewer. Syn. tagarepaso. 2. inspector;
examiner; checker. Syn. inspektór,
tagasuri, tagaiksámin. 3. reviser. Syn.
tagaayos, tagapag-ayos. 4. auditor. Syn.
tagatuós, óditór.

rebista (re-bis-ta), n. (Sp. revista) 1. journal;
magazine (publication). Syn. mágasìn.
2. retrial; new trial; rehearing, as of a case
in court. Syn. panibagong bista o paglilitis.

rebisyón (re-bis-yón), n. (Sp. revision) 1.
review; restudy. Syn. repaso, pagrerepaso.
2. act of revising; revision. Syn.
pagbabago, pag-aayos, pagsasaayos,
pagwawastô. 3. inspection; examination;
checking. Syn. pag-iksamin, pagsuri,
pagsusurì. 4. a revised form. Syn. binagong
ayos.

reboká (re-bo-ká), var. rebuká, ribuká, n.
(Sp. revocar) a revoking or being revoked;
revocation. See rebokasyón.

rebokasyón (re-bo-kas-yón), var.
rebukasyón, ribukasyón, n. (Sp.
revocación) 1. revocation; repeal;
cancelling. Syn. pagkansilá, pagpapawaláng-bisà, pagpapawaláng-saysáy. 2.

rebolber

rekord¹

withdrawing. Syn. *pagbawì, pag-uurong.*

rebolber (re-bol-ber), n. *(Sp.; Eng.)* revolver. Cf. *barfl.*

rebolusyón (re-bo-lus-yón), var. **rebulusyón,** n. *(Sp. revolución)* revolution. Syn. *paghihimagsík, hímagsikan, pagbabangon, pag-aalsá; rebelyón.*

rebolusyonaryo (re-bo-lus-yo-nar-yo), var. **rebulusyonaryo, ribulusyonayo,** I. n. *(Sp. revolucionario)* revolutionist; rebel. Syn. *manghihimagsík, rebelde, insurekto.* –II. *adj.* revolutionary; connected with a revolution. Syn. *maghíhimagsík, manghíhimagsik.*

rebosado (re-bo-sa-do), var. **rebusado,** I. *adj.* (Sp. *rebozado)* coated with batter (thin mixture of flour, milk, egg, etc.). —II. n. a dish, esp. for shrimps, coated with batter.

rebyú (reb-yú), n. *(Eng.)* review. Syn. *repaso.*

rekado (re-ka-do), var. **rikado,** n. (Sp. *recado)* seasoning or flavoring material for food. Also, *panrekado (panrikado).*

rekargo (re-kar-go), var. **rikargo,** n. (Sp. *recargo)* fine or additional charge for tax overdue; surcharge. Syn. *multa, patong.*

rekisa (re-ki-sa), var. **rikisa,** n. (Sp. *requisa)* thorough search or inspection of a house or any place for hidden contraband, etc. Syn. *halughóg, paghahalughóg.*

rekisisyón (re-ki-sis-yón), var. **rikisisyón,** n. (Sp. *requisición)* requisition; a formal, written order, esp. for supplies.

rekisito (re-ki-si-to), var. **rikisito,** n. (Sp. *requisito)* requisite; requirement. Syn. *bagay na kailangan o kinákailangan.*

reklamado (re-kla-ma-do), *adj.* reclaimed; filled up, as a wasteland.

reklamadór (re-kla-ma-dór), I. n. (Sp. *reclamadór)* 1. reclaimer. 2. complainant. —II. *adj.* given to complaining; with or having many complaints. Syn. *mareklamo.*

reklamasyón (re-kla-mas-yón), n. (Sp. *reclamacion)* 1. demand; claim, complaint. 2. a reclaiming or being reclaimed; reclamation.

reklamo (rek-la-mo; re-kla-mo), n. 1. claim; demand. Syn. *kahilingan, daìng.* 2. complaint; objection. Syn. *tutol.*

reklusiyón (re-klu-si-yón), var. **reklusyón,**

n. (Sp. *reclusion)* seclusion; confinement.

rekluta (rek-lu-ta; re-klu-ta), var. **rekuluta,** n. (Sp. *recluta)* recruit; a new member. Syn. *bagong kalap na kasapi.*

rekobeko (re-ko-be-ko), var. **rekubeko, rikubeko,** n. (Sp. *recoveco)* a round-about way; unnecessary details, requirements, demand, etc. Syn. *kuskús-balungos, kiyáw-kiyáw.*

rekodo (re-ko-do), var. **rekudo,** n. (Sp. *recodo)* 1. angle. Syn. *angguló.* 2. bend or turn, as of paths, etc. Syn. *likô, paglikô; kurba, kurbada.*

rekoleksiyón (re-ko-lek-si-yón), n. (Sp. *recolección)* 1. recollection; memory; remembrance. Syn. *alaala, gunitâ.* 2. act or power of recalling something to one's mind. Syn. *pag-alaala, paggunitá.*

Rekoleto (Re-ko-le-to) n. (Sp. *Recoleto)* a priest of the Order of the Recollects.

rekomenda (re-ko-men-da; -dá), n. (Sp. *recomendar)* a recommending or being recommended. See **rekomendasyon.**

rekomendado (re-ko-men-da-do), *adj.* (Sp. *recomendado)* recommended. Syn. *itinagubilin, itinatagubilin, inirekomenda.*

rekomendasyón (re-ko-men-das-yón), n. (Sp. *recomendación)* 1. a recommending. Syn. *pagrerekomenda, pagtatagubilin.* 2. something that recommends a person or thing. Syn. *tagubilin.* 3. advice. Syn. *payo.* 4. praise; commendation. Syn. *papuri.*

rekonosido (re-ko-no-si-do), *adj.* (Sp. *reconocido)* recognized; acknowledged; accepted. Syn. *kinikilala, tinátanggáp.*

rekonosimyento (re-ko-no-sim-yen-to), n. (Sp. *reconocimiento)* recognition; acknowledgement; acceptance. Syn. *pagkilala, pagtanggáp.*

rekonsiderasyón (re-kon-si-de-ras-yón), n. (Sp. *reconsideración)* reconsideration. Syn. *muling pagsasaalang-alang.*

rekonsilyado (re-kon-sil-ya-do), *adj.* (Sp. *reconciliado)* reconciled. Syn. *magkasundô na, nagkakásundô na.*

rekonsilyasyón (re-kon-sil-yas-yón), n. (Sp. *reconciliación)* reconciliation. Syn. *muling pagkakásundô, pagbabatiáng mulî ng nagkagalít.*

rekord¹ (re-kord), n. *(Eng.)* 1. record;

register; list of things kept in a file. Syn.
talâ, tálaan. 2. an official record or
account, as of a meeting; minutes. Syn.
katitikan. 3. record of one's
accomplishments or achievements. Syn.
mga nagawâ. 4. the best yet done; highest
success. 5. (*Colloq.*) bad reputation, as of
a person who had served a term in prison.
Syn. *masamáng pangalan.*

rekord² (re-kord), n. (*Eng.*) record;
phonograph disc or record. Syn. *plaka.*

rekorida (re-ko-ri-da), var. **rekurida,
rikurida,** n. (Sp. *recorrida*) a going about
or around one's place of assignment, as a
policeman on his beat. Cf. *libot, paglilibót.*

rekorte (re-kor-te), n. (Sp. *recorte*) clipping;
trimming; cutting. Syn. *pinagtabasan.* 2.
newspaper item or clipping. Syn. *kliping.*

rektánggulo (rek-táng-gu-ló), n. (Sp.
rectángulo) rectangle.

réktipikasyón (rék-ti-pi-kas-yón), n. (Sp.
rectificación) rectification; making right.
Syn. *pagtutuwíd, pagwawastô,
pagtutumpák.*

rekto (rek-to), adj. (Sp. *recto*) 1. straight.
Syn. *tuwíd, matuwid.* 2. upright; honest.
Syn. *tapat, matapát, onesto.*

rektor (rek-tor; -tor), n. (*Sp.; Eng.*) rector.

rekurso (re-kur-so), n. (Sp. *recurso*) 1.
recourse; resort. Syn. *dúlugan, tákbuhan,
lapitán* (all colloq.) 2. means. Syn. *paraán,
kaparaanán.*

rekuwerdo (re-ku-wer-do), var. **rekwerdo,**
n. (Sp. *recuerdo*) memento; remembrance;
keepsake; souvenir. Syn. *alaala.*

rekwa (rek-wa), n. (Sp. *recua*) a great
number; pack or bunch (*fig.*), as in: *isáng
rekwang kasinungalingan,* a pack of lies.

redaksiyón (re-dak-si-yón), n. (Sp.
redacción) editing; reduction. Syn. *éditíng,
pag-eedit.*

redaktor (re-dak-tor; -tór), n. (Sp. *redactor*)
editor. Syn. *éditór, patnugot, direktór.*

redensiyón (re-den-si-yón), n. (Sp.
redención) redemption. Syn. *pagtubós.*

redentor (re-den-tor; tór), n. (*Sp.*)
redeemer. Syn. *tagapágligtás, tagapág-adyá.*

redoblante (re-do-blan-te), n. (*Sp.*) drum
beater; drummer. Syn. *tambulero,
tagatamból.*

redoble (re-do-ble), n. (*Sp.*) 1. redoubling;
double-folding. 2. drum roll.

redoma (re-do-ma), n. (*Sp.*) flask. Syn.
prasko.

reduksiyón (re-duk-si-yón), n. (Sp.
reducción) 1. discount; rebate. Syn. *tawad,
patawad, diskuwento, bawas.* 2. reduction;
deduction; decrease. Syn. *bawas,
pagbabawas.*

redundánsiyá (re-dun-dán-si-yá), n. (Sp.
redundancia) redundance. Syn. *ligoy,
pagkamaligoy, kaliguyan; pagkapaulit-ulit,
pagkamaulit, kaulitán.*

reeleksiyón (re-e-lek-si-yón), n. (Sp.
reelección) reelection. Syn. *mulíng halál,
paghahalál o pagkakáhalál.*

reenkarnasyón (re-en-kar-nas-yón), var.
reinkarnasyón, n. (Sp. *reencarnación*)
reincarnation. Syn. *pagbabago o
pagpapanibagong anyô ng buhay.*

regadera (re-ga-de-ra), var. **rigadera,** n. (*Sp.*)
sprinkler. Cf. *pandilíg.*

regalo (re-ga-lo), colloq. var. **rigalo,** n. (*Sp.*)
gift; present. Syn. *alaala, handóg, bigáy,
kaloób.*

regalya (re-gal-ya), var. **rigalya,** n. (Sp.
regalia) royal pomp. Syn. *dingal,
karingalan, pagkamaringal.*

regata (re-ga-ta), n. (*Sp.*) regatta; boat race.
Syn. *karera ng bangkâ.*

regla¹ (re-gla), n. (*Sp.*) 1. menses;
menstruation. Syn. *sapanahón.* 2. the
blood discharged from the uterus during
menstruation. Syn. *dugô ng sapanahón.*

regla² (re-gla), n. (*Law*) rule; ruling;
regulation; policy. Syn. *tuntunin, alítun-
tunin, patakarán, pasunód, reglamento.*

regla³ (re-gla), n. line; straight line. Syn.
linya, matuwíd na linya o guhit.

reglamento (reg-la-men-to; re-gla-men-to),
n. (*Sp.*) regulation; policy being enforced,
as in a certain establishment. Syn.
pátakarán, tuntunin, palakad, pamalakad.

reguladór (re-gu-la-dór), n. (*Sp.*) 1.
regulator (person); director;
administrator; governor. Cf.
tagapangasiwà. 2. regulator; mechanism
for adjusting movement of machinery,
flow of gases, liquids, electricity, etc.

regulár (re-gu-lár), adj. 1. regular; usual;

ordinary. Syn. *karaniwan, pangkaraniwan.*
2. habitual; steady; permanent. Syn.
pirmihan, pálagián. 3. uniform; not
changing; regular. 4. usual; customary.
Syn. *katamtaman, kainaman.*

regulasyón (re-gu-las-yón), n. (Sp.
regulación) 1. regulation; policy being
enforced. Syn. *palakad, pamamalakad,
reglamento, pátakarán.* 2. rule; law. Syn.
batás, tuntunin.

rehabilitá (re-ha-bi-li-tá), n. (Sp. *rehabilitar*)
a rehabilitating or being rehabilitated.
See **rehabilitasyón.**

rehabilitasyon (re-ha-bi-li-tas-yón), n. (Sp.
rehabilitación) rehabilitation; restoration
to a former standard, rank, etc. Syn.
*pagbabagong-buhay, pagpapanibagong-
buhay.* 2. restoration to a good condition;
rehabilitation. Syn. *pagbabagong-ayos,
pagpapanibagong-ayos; pagbabagong-tatag,
pagbabagong-tatag.*

rehas (re-has), n. (Sp. *reja*) grille; grating,
esp. in a window.

rehente (re-hen-te), n. (Sp. *rejente*) regent.

rehistrado (re-his-tra-do), *adj.* (Sp.
registrado) registered. Syn. *nakatalâ,
itinalâ.*

rehistradór (re-his-tra-dór), n. (Sp.
registrador) 1. registrar; recorder. Syn.
tagatalâ. 2. register; cash register. 3. regis-
tering device; meter. Syn. *kontadór, metro.*

rehistro (re-his-tro), n. (Sp. *registro*) 1.
register; list. Syn. *talaan.* 2. record; entry.
Syn. *talâ.*

rehiyón (re-hi-yón), n. (Sp. *region*) region;
specific area or district. Syn. *dako; lugár;
poók.*

relasyón (re-las-yón), n. (Sp. *relación*)
relation. Syn. *kaugnayan, pagkákaugnay.*

relebo (re-le-bo), colloq. var. **rilyebo,** n. (Sp.
relevo) 1. relief or replacement of a person
in duty. Syn. *pagpapalít o paghahali sa
paglilingkód.* 2. a person who relieves
another in duty. Syn. *kapalit, kahalili,
katumo.*

relikya (re-lik-ya), n. (Sp. *reliquia*) relic; a
thing or piece left from the past. Syn.
matandáng labí (ng lumipas).

relihiyón (re-li-hi-yón), n. (Sp. *religion*) 1.
religion; belief in God or in a divine or

superhuman power. 2. any system of
religious belief or worship. Syn.
pananampalataya.

relihiyosa (re-li-hi-yo-sa), *adj.* (Sp. *religiosa*)
religious, referring to a woman; devoted
to religion. Syn. *banál, madásalin.*

relihiyoso (re-li-hi-yo-so), *adj.* (Sp. *religioso*)
religious, referring to a man; devoted to
religion. Syn. *banál, madásalin, paládasál.*

reló (re-ló), var. **relós, riló, rilós,** n. (Sp.
reloj) watch; clock. Syn. *orasán.*

relohera (re-lo-he-ra), n. (Sp. *relojera*) 1.
watchcase. 2. watch pocket. Syn. *bulsa-
de-relós.*

relohería (re-lo-he-rí-a), var. **reloheriya,** n.
(Sp. *relojeria*) 1. watch or clock store. Syn.
tindahan ng relós. 2. watchmaker's shop;
watch repairer's shop.

relohero (re-lo-he-ro), n. (Sp. *relojero*) 1.
watchmaker;   clockmaker.   Syn.
manggagawà ng relós. 2. watch or clock
dealer.

relyeno (rel-ye-no), var. **rilyeno,** I. n. (Sp.
relleno) stuffed chicken, turkey, fish, etc.
—II. *adj.* stuffed, referring to a chicken,
turkey, fish, etc. Also, *irelyeno.*

rematá (re-ma-tá), n. (Sp. *rematár*)
foreclosure of a mortgaged property for
failure to redeem.

rematse (re-mat-se), var. **rimatse,** n. (Sp.
remache) metal volt or pin with a head
on one end and used to fasten plates or
beams together; rivet. 2. a riveting or
being riveted; act of fastening with a rivet
or rivets. Also, *pagrirem* *atse.*

remedio (re-me-di-o), var. **remedyo,** n. (Sp.
remedio) remedy; relief. Syn. *lunas.* 2.
relief. Syn. *tulong.* 3. (*Law*) means; legal
redress.

remédyuhán   (re-méd-yu-hán),   var.
remédiohán, *v.* 1. to remedy; do
something to correct or put back into
proper condition. Syn. *lunasan.* 2. to
prescribe a remedy or treatment for.

remunerasyón (re-mu-ne-ras-yón), n. (Sp.
remuneración)   remunerating;
compensating; paying. Syn. *pagbabayad.*
2. remuneration; pay; payment;
compensation. Syn. *upa, suweldo, bayad,
sahod.* 3. reward. Syn. *gantimpalà, premyo.*

renasimyento (re-na-sim-yen-to), n. (Sp. *renacimiento*) renascence; renaissance. Syn. *mulíng-pagsilang*.

renda (ren-da), n. (Sp. *rienda*) reins. 2. (*Fig.*) control; power; management. Syn. *ugit, pamamahalà, kapangyarihan*.

rendido (ren-di-do), var. **rindido**, adj. (*Sp.*) 1. confused. Syn. *litó, nalílitó; tarantá, natátarantá*. 2. worn out, fatigued, or exhausted. Syn. *pagód, pagód na pagód, patáng-patá*.

renta (ren-ta), n. (*Sp.*) rent; rental. Syn. *upa, alkilá (arkilá)*.

rentas (ren-tas), n. (*Sp.*) revenue; government income.

renúnsiyasyón (re-nún-si-yas-yón), n. (Sp. *renunciación*) renunciation.

reórganisá (re-ór-ga-ni-sá), n. (Sp. *reorganizar*) a reorganizing or being organized. Syn. *pagtatatag na mulî o pagkakátatag na mulî, mulíng-pagtatatag o mulíng-pagkakátatag*.

reparado (re-pa-ra-do), adj. (*Sp.*) 1. repaired; restored to the former good condition. Syn. *kinumpuní na, inayos na*. 2. already compensated for damage done. Syn. *bayád na, nabayaran na*.

reparasyón (re-pa-ras-yón), n. (Sp. *reparación*) 1. repair or repairing; reparation. Syn. *kumpuní, pagkumpuní, pagkukumpuní*. 2. result of being repaired. Syn. *pagkakákumpuní*. 3. reparations; giving satisfaction of compensation for wrong or damage done. Syn. *pagbabayad-pinsalà*. 2. compensation or payment for wrong or damage done. Syn. *bayad-pinsalà*.

reparo (re-pa-ro), n. (*Sp.*) a noticing or being noticed; observation. Syn. *pansín, pagkápansín; puná, pagkápuná*.

repaso (re-pa-so), n. (*Sp.*) review; restudy. Syn. *balík-aral, pagbabalik-aral*.

reperendum (re-pe-ren-dum), n. (*Eng.; Sp.*) referendum; submission of an issue to the direct vote of the people. Syn. *pagsanggunì sa bayan*.

reperénsiyá (re-pe-rén-si-yá), n. (Sp. *referencia*) 1. reference; something used for information or reference. Syn. *sanggunian*. 2. mention or mentioning. Syn. *banggít,*

pagbanggít; tukoy, pagtukoy.

repertoryo (re-per-tor-yo), n. (Sp. *repertorio*) 1. repertoire. 2. repertory.

repetisyón (re-pe-tis-yón), n. (Sp. *repetición*) repetition. Syn. *pag-ulít, pag-uulit*.

repike (re-pi-ke), n. (Sp. *repique*) peal; continuous ringing of a bell or bells. Syn. *pitada*.

repinado (re-pi-na-do), I. adj. (Sp. *refinado*) refined, said esp. of sugar.
—II. n. refined sugar.

repleksibo (re-plek-si-bo), I. adj. (Sp. *reflexivo*) in Gram., reflexive. Syn. *pansarili*.
—II. n. a. reflexive verb or pronoun.

repleksiyón (re-plek-si-yón), n. (Sp. *reflexion*) reflection.

repolyado (re-pol-ya-do), var. **ripulyado**, adj. (Sp. *repollado*) surrounded, as by a big crowd. Syn. *ligíd na ligíd, nalíligiran*.

repolyo (re-pol-yo), var. **ripulyo**, n. (Sp. *repollo*) 1. cabbage. 2. (*Colloq.*) a crowding or gathering around in great number. Syn. *pagkakalibumbóng, pagkakálibumbungan*. 3. (*Colloq.*) a small group or crowd, as of friends, admirers, etc. Syn. *kalibumbóng*.

reporma (re-por-ma), n. (Sp. *reforma*) reform; improvement. Syn. *pagbabago, pagpapabuti*.

reporsado (re-por-sa-do), adj. (Sp. *reforzado*) reinforced; made stronger by reinforcement. Syn. *pinalakás, sinapian*.

repórt (re-pórt), n. (*Eng.*) 1. report; news. Syn. *balità*. 2. report, esp. in writing, about something done by someone. Syn. *ulat, pag-uulat*. 3. rumor; common talk. Syn. *sabí-sabí, bulúng-bulungan, balità*. 4. act of telling on somebody; informing against. Syn. *sumbóng, pagsusumbóng*.

reporter (re-por-ter), n. (*Eng.*) 1. reporter; newspaper reporter; news correspondent. Syn. *tagapág-balità*. 2. a person who told on someone. Syn. *ang nagsumbóng*.

repositoryo (re-po-si-tor-yo), n. (Sp. *repositorio*) repository; place or container of things stored or kept. Syn. *lágakan, imbakan, lalagyán, taguán, sisidlán*.

representante (re-pre-sen-tan-te), n. (*Sp.*) 1. (*Leg.*) representative; congressman. Syn. *kinatawán, kongresmán*. 2. (*Comm.*)

representasyón   resolusyón

agent; salesman. Syn. *ahente*.

representasyón (re-pre-sen-tas-yón), n. (Sp.
representación) 1. act of representing;
representation. Syn. *pagkatawán*. 2.
representative, as of a certain group, in
some kind of negotiation. Syn. *kinatawán*.
3. presentation or showing, as of a play.
Syn. *pagpapalabás, pagtatanghál*.

represyón (re-pres-yón), n. (Sp. *represión*)
1. repression. Syn. *pagpigil, pagsugpô,
pagsuweto*. 2. being repressed or subdued.
Syn. *pagkasugpô, pagkasuweto, pagkalupig,
pagkasupil*.

repriheradór (re-pri-he-ra-dór), n. (Sp.
refrigeradór) refrigerator. Syn. *repridye-
retor, pridyedér*.

reproduksiyón (re-pro-duk-si-yón), n. (Sp.
reproducción) 1. reproducing or remaking.
Syn. *pag-ulit, pag-uulit, paggawáng mulî*. 2.
copying or reproducing a copy of. Syn.
pagkopya, pagsipì. 3. a copy thus made.
Syn. *kopya, sipì*. 4. reproduction (as of
offspring). Syn. *pagpaparami, pag-aanák*.
4. representation or reshowing, as of a
play. Syn. *mulíng pagpapalabás o
pagtatanghál*

reptíl (rep-tíl), var. **reptilya**, n. *(Sp.)* reptile.

repúbliká (re-pú-bli-ká), n. (Sp. *república*)
republic.

repúhiyó (re-pú-hi-yó), n. (Sp. *refugio*)
refuge; shelter. Syn. *kublihan, taguán,
kanlungan, pánganlungan*.

reputasyón[1] (re-pu-tas-yon), n. (Sp.
refutación) act of refuting; disproof of a
claim, argument or opinion. Syn.
pagpapabulaan, pagpapasinungaling.

reputasyón[2] (re-pu-tas-yón), n. (Sp.
reputación) 1. reputation; what people
think and say about the character of
someone. Syn. *pagkákilala*. 2. the
reputation or name a person has made for
himself. Syn. *pangalan*. 3. fame. Syn.
kabantugán, katanyagán.

repuwerso (re-pu-wer-so), var. **repwerso**, n.
(Sp. *refuerso*) reinforcement. Syn. *patibay,
pampatibay; palakás, pampalakás*.

resepsiyón (re-sep-si-yón), n. (Sp. *recepción*)
1. the act of receiving and entertaining
visitors. Syn. *pagtanggáp, pagharáp*. 2. a
party; reception. Syn. *pagtitipon, salu-salo*.

3. an entertainment; celebration. Syn.
pagdiriwang, kasayahan, katuwaan.

reserba (re-ser-ba), I. n. (Sp. *reserva*) 1.
something reserved for future use; reserve.
Syn. *pondo, laán, panlaán, patagana*. 2. act
of holding or keeping back. Syn.
paglalaán, pagtataán, pagtatagò. 3.
(specifically) spare tire. 4. *(Mil.)* reserves;
troops held back for use in emergencies.
Syn. *panlaáng kawal (sundalo)*.
—II. adj. 1. reserved for future use. Syn.
panlaán. 2. spare; extra.

reseta (re-se-ta), var. **riseta**, n. (Sp. *receta*)
medical prescription; doctor's pres-
cription. Cf. *hatol*.

resibaryo (re-si-bar-yo), n. (Sp. *recibario*) pad
or book of blank receipts.

resibo (re-si-bo), n. (Sp. *recibo*) receipt (for
something received or accepted). Cf.
katibayan.

residénsiyá (re-si-dén-si-yá), n. (Sp.
residencia) 1. residence; abode; home;
house. Syn. *táhanan, tírahan*. 2. a residing,
living, or dwelling. Syn. *pagtahán,
pananahanan; pagtirá, paninirahan*.

residente (re-si-den-te), n. & adj. *(Sp.)*
resident.

resignasyón (re-sig-nas-yón), n. (Sp.
resignación) resignation. Syn. *pagbibitiw
(ng tungkulin)*.

résipé (ré-si-pé), var. **résipí**, n. *(Eng.)* 1.
recipe; direction for preparing dish or
drink. Syn. *panuto sa pagluluto*. 2. medical
prescription. Syn. *reseta*.

resisténsiyá (re-sis-tén-si-yá), n. (Sp.
resistencia) resistance; endurance. Syn.
tibay, lakas, laban, panlaban.

resitasyón (re-si-tas-yón), n. (Sp. *recitación*)
1. recitation; act of reciting. Syn.
pagsasalaysáy, pagkukuwento. 2. reciting of
a prepared lesson by pupils during class.
Syn. *pagsagót sa tanóng*. 3. reciting (a
poem) from memory. Syn. *bigkás,
pagbigkás*.

resolbe (re-sol-be), n. (Sp. *resolver*) a
resolving or being resolved. Syn. *paglutas,
pagkalutas*.

resolusyón (re-so-lus-yón), n. (Sp.
resolución) 1. resolution; thing decided on.
Syn. *pasiyá, kapasiyahan*. 2. resolution or

proposal submitted for approval. Syn. *panukalà, mungkahì.* 3. something a person wants to do; promise. Syn. *pagtitika, pangakò.*

respetable (res-pe-ta-ble), *adj. (Sp.)* respectable; worthy of respect. Syn. *kagalang-galang, kapitá-pítagan, kinaáalang-alangan.*

respeto (res-pe-to), *n. (Sp.)* respect. Syn. *galang, paggalang; pitagan, pamimítagan; alang-alang, pag-aálang-alang.*

respirasyón (res-pi-ras-yón), *n. (Sp. respiración)* respiration; breathing. Syn. *hingá, paghingá.*

responsabilidád (res-pon-sa-bi-li-dád), *n. (Sp.)* 1. responsibility; thing a person is responsible for. Syn. *ságutin, pananágutan.* 2. obligation; duty. Syn. *tungkulin, katungkulan.*

responsable (res-pon-sa-ble), *adj. (Sp.)* 1. responsible; obliged to account for. Syn. *manágót, may-pananágutan.* 2. responsible; reliable; trustworthy. Syn. *mapagtítiwalaan, mapagkákatiwalaan.* 3. deserving credit or blame for. Syn. *may-kagagawán.*

restaurán (res-ta-u-rán), *var.* **restawrán**, *n. (Eng.)* restaurant. Syn. *karehan, karinderiyá.*

restriksiyón (res-trik-si-yón), *n. (Sp. restricción)* 1. restriction; prohibition. Syn. *pagbabawal, paghihigpít.* 2. limitation; restriction. Syn. *pagtatakdâ.*

resulta (re-sul-ta), *n. (Sp.)* result; outcome; consequence. Syn. *bunga, kinálabasán, kinásapitan, kináuwian, wakás.*

resumé (re-su-mé), *n. (Eng.)* 1. résumé; summary. Syn. *buód, lagom.* 2. a summarizing or being summarized. Syn. *pagbubuód, pagkakábuód.*

resureksiyón (re-su-rek-si-yón), *n. (Sp. resurrección)* coming to life again; resurrection. Syn. *pagkabuhay na mulî, mulíng pagkabuhay.*

retaso (re-ta-so), *n. (Sp. retazo)* 1. remnant. Syn. *pinagtabasan, pinaggupitán, pinagputulan.* 2. *(Colloq.)* one's child. Syn. *anák.*

retené (re-te-né), *var.* **retiné**, *n. (Sp. retener)* a detaining or being detained; a confining or being confined. Syn. *pagpigil, pagkakapigil; pagkulóng, pagkakákulóng.* 2. a retaining or delaying. Syn. *pagbimbín, pag-antala.*

retensiyón (re-ten-si-yón), **retinsiyón**, *n. (Sp. retención)* 1. retention; a detaining or being detained. Syn. *pagpigil, pagkápigil.* 2. remain. Syn. *pagpapanatili, pagpapamalagì.* 3. a remaining or staying. Syn. *pamamalagì, pananatili.* 4. ability to remember. Syn. *pagtandâ, pagtatandâ; memorya, pagmemorya, pagmememorya.*

retina (re-ti-na), *n. (Eng., Sp.)* retina.

retirada (re-ti-ra-da), I. *adj. (Sp.)* 1. retired, referring to a woman worker or employee. Syn. *nagretiro na, namámahingá na sa trabaho.* 2. resting; at rest; withdrawn, as soldiers from actual combat. 3. *(Printing)* reprinted. Syn. *mulíng nilimbág.*
—II. *n.* 1. a woman retiree. 2. (in *Printing*) reprint; reprinting.

retirado (re-ti-ra-do), I. *adj.* retired, referring to a worker or employee. Syn. *nagretiro na, namámahingá na.*
—II. *n.* retired employee or officer.

retiro (re-ti-ro), *n. (Sp.)* 1. a retiring, as from one's work or employment. Also, *pagriretiro.* Syn. *pamamahingá sa trabaho.* 2. withdrawal or retreat, as of soldiers, from actual combat. Syn. *pagpapahingá, pamamahingá.*

reto (re-to), *n. (Sp.)* challenge. Syn. *hamon, paghamon, paghahamón.*

retoke (re-to-ke), *var.* **retuke, ritoke**, *n. (Sp. retoque)* a retouching or being retouched (s.o. photographs, painting, etc.).

retóriká (re-tó-ri-ká), *n. (Sp. retórica)* rhetoric. Syn. *sayusay.*

retraksiyón (re-trak-si-yón), *n. (Sp. retracción)* 1. retraction or drawing back. Syn. *pag-urong.* 2. retraction or taking back; withdrawal of one's promise, statement, etc. Syn. *pagtalikód, pagbawì, pag-urong.*

retratista (re-tra-tis-ta) *var.* **ritratista, litratista,** *n. (Sp.)* photographer. Syn. *potógrapó.*

retrato (re-tra-to), *var.* **ritrato, litrato,** *n. (Sp.)* photograph; picture. Syn. *larawan.*

retribusyón (re-tri-bus-yón), *n. (Sp.*

retribución) 1. retribution; return for evil done or sometimes for good done. Syn. *gantì, paggantí.* 2. retribution or act of rewarding. Syn. *paggantí ng utang na loób.* 3. revenge. Syn. *higantí, paghihigantí.* 4. punishment. Syn. *parusa, pagpaparusa.*

retroaktibo (re-tro-ak-ti-bo), *adj.* (Sp. *retroactivo*) retroactive; effective prior to enactment of effectuation of. Syn. *may bisà na bago pa pinagtibay o nápagtibay.*

retuhin (re-tu-hin), *v.* to challenge.

reunyón (re-un-yón), *n.* (Sp. *reunión*) reunion. Syn. *pagtitipun-tipong mulî, pagsasama-samang mulî.*

reyna (rey-na), *n.* (Sp. *reina*) queen.

reyno (rey-no), *n.* (Sp. *reino*) kingdom. Syn. *kaharian.*

ribál (ri-bál), I. *n.* (Sp. *rival*) 1. rival; competitor. Syn. *kalaban, karibál.* 2. state or fact being rivals, esp. in love or courtship. —II. *adj.* rival; competing with each other, esp. in love or courtship. Syn. *kakompeténsiyá, kalaban, karibál, kaagáw.*

ríbalan (rí-ba-lan), *n.* rivalry; competition. Syn. *tunggalian, kompetensiyá, labanán, páligsahan.*

ribete (ri-be-te), *n.* (*Sp.*) in sewing: 1. border; edge, as of a handkerchief. Syn. *gilid.* 2. trimming; embellishment; decoration. Syn. *borlás (burlás).*

ribyú (rib-yú), var. **rebyú**, *n.* (*Eng.*) review; restudy. Syn. *repaso, pagrepaso, pagrerepaso.*

riles (ri-les), *n.* (Sp. *riel*) rails; railway. Syn. *daáng-bakal (daámbakal).*

rima (ri-ma), *n.* (*Sp.*) rhyme. Syn. *tugmâ.*

rimarim (ri-ma-rim), *n.* loathing or disgust, esp. for something dirty. Syn. *diri, pandiri, aní, pagkaani.*

ripa (ri-pa), *n.* (Sp. *rifa*) raffle. Cf. *loterya.*

riple (ri-ple), *n.* (Sp. *rifle*) rifle. Cf. *baríl, eskopeta.*

risés (ri-sés), *n.* (*Eng.*) recess; rest period. Syn. *pamamahingá.*

ritmo (rit-mo), *n.* (*Sp.*) rhythm. Syn. *indayog, aliwíw.*

rito (ri-to), *n.* (*Sp.*) rite; ceremony. Syn. *seremonya.*

ritwal (rit-wal; -wal), var. **rituwál**, *n.* (Sp. *ritual*) form or system of rites; ritual. Syn.

seremonya.

riyesgo (ri-yes-go), *n.* (Sp. *riesgo*) risk; danger. Syn. *peligro, panganib, kapanganibán.*

roka (ro-ka), *n.* (Sp. *roca*) rock. Syn. *malakíng bató.*

rodilyo (ro-dil-yo), *n.* (Sp. *rodillo*) 1. roller. 2. rolling pin.

rolyo (rol-yo), *n.* (Sp. *rollo*) 1. roll or cylindrical bundle, as of paper, cloth, etc. Syn. *balumbón, bilo.* 2. act of rolling something into a cylindrical bundle or into a roll. Syn. *pagbalumbón, pagbabalumbón; pagbilo, pagbibilo.*

rolyú-rolyo (rol-yú + rol-yo), *adj. & adv.* in rolls.

romano (ro-ma-no), *n. & adj.* (*Sp.*) roman.

romansa (ro-man-sa), *n.* (Sp. *romanza*) 1. romance. Syn. *pag-iibigan, pagmamáhalan.* 2. a love story. Syn. *kuwento ng pag-ibig o pag-iibigan.*

romanse (ro-man-se), *n.* (Sp. *romance*) 1. romance; tale. 2. historical ballad; tale of chivalry.

romántiká (ro-mán-ti-ká), I. *adj.* (Sp. *romantica*) romantic. —II. *n.* a romantic woman.

romántikó (ro-mán-ti-kó), I. *adj.* (Sp. *romántico*) romantic. —II. *n.* 1. romanticist. Syn. *romantisista.* 2. a romantic man.

ronda (ron-da), *n.* (*Sp.*) 1. patrolling during night as by a fire brigade. 2. a fire brigade or a member of this who is on night duty. Syn. *bantáy-sunog.*

rondalya (ron-dal-ya), *n.* (Sp. *rondalla*) a string band or orchestra.

roól (ro-ól), *n.* a falling into misfortune; now obsolescent, except in the formation of derivatives, as in *máparoól, ikáparoól, pagkáparoól,* etc.

ropero (ro-pe-ro), var. **rupero**, (*Sp.*) hamper for dirty linen or clothes.

rosa (ro-sa), *n.* (*Sp., Bot.*) 1. rose plant or its flower. 2. (R-) a feminine name.

rosál (ro-sál), *n.* (*Sp., Bot.*) gardenia rose plant or its flower.

rosario (ro-sa-ri-o), var. **rosaryo**, *n.* (*Sp.*) 1. a series of prayers; rosary. 2. act of praying the Rosary. Also, *pagrorosaryo.* 3. a string of beads for keeping count in saying the prayers; rosary. Syn. *dásalang kuwintas*. 4. (R-) a feminine name.

rosas (ro-sas), I. *n. (Sp.)* 1. rose plant; also, its flower. See **rosa**. 2. rose color; pink; purplish red.
—II. *adj.* rose-colored; pink.

rosas-hapón (ro-sas + ha-pón), *n. (Bot.)* chrysanthemum. Syn. *krisántemó*.

roskás (ros-kás), var. **ruskás**, *n.* (Sp. *rosca*) 1. thread on a screw, bolt, nut, etc. 2. the act or manner of threading a screw, nut, bolt, etc. Also, *pagroroskás*.

rosilyo (ro-sil-yo), I. *n.* (Sp. *rosillo*) 1. roan color, esp. of a horse. 2. a roan; roan horse.
—II. *adj.* roan-colored (s.o. horses).

rotasyón (ro-tas-yón), *n.* (Sp. *rotación*) 1. rotation; a turning round and round. Syn. *ikót, pag-ikot; inog, pag-inog*. 2. act of rotating something. Syn. *pagpapaikot, pagpapainog*. 3. rotation, as of workers. Syn. *paghahalí-halilí o túrnuhan ng mga manggagawà*. 4. rotation in planting crops. Syn. *pag-iibá-ibá ng taním o pananim*.

rotonda (ro-ton-da), *n. (Sp.)* a circular plaza, usually at the intersection of two or more thoroughfares. Cf. *krusing, pinagkrusán*.

royalti (ro-yal-ti), *n. (Eng.)* 1. a specified percentage paid to an author, composer, etc.; royalty. 2. a royal person, as a king or queen.

rubí (ru-bí), I. *n. (Sp.)* ruby; a precious stone, red in color.
—II. *adj.* 1. made of ruby. 2. red in color; ruby. Syn. *pulá, mapulá*.

ruler (ru-ler), *n. (Eng.)* 1. ruler; a straight strip of wood or metal used for drawing straight lines. Syn. *regladór, panlinya*. 2. a ruler; person who rules. Syn. *punò, pinunò*. 3. (specifically) a king or queen. Syn. *harì o reyna*.

ruleta (ru-le-ta), *n. (Sp.)* roulette.

rumangyâ (ru-mang-yâ), *v.* (*present* and *past*) to become ostentatious or pompous.

rumba (rum-ba), *n. (Sp.; Eng.)* 1. rumba (a dance). 2. the music for this dance.

rumbo (rum-bo), *n.* (Sp. *rumbo*) used colloquially: gang. Syn. *barkada, barkadahán*.

rumeklamo (ru-mek-la-mo), *v.* (*present* and *past*) to complain; make a complaint. Also, *magreklamo*.

rumhán (rum-hán), var. **dumhán**, *v.* to soil; make dirty.

rumór (ru-mór), *n. (Sp.)* rumor. Syn. *bulúngbulungan, usáp-usapan, balí-balitâ, tsismis*.

rupya (rup-ya), *n.* (Sp. *rupia*) rupee, monetary unit of India, Ceylon, etc.

rurál (ru-rál), *adj. (Sp.; Eng.)* rural; of the open country. Syn. *sa o ukol sa bukid, pambukid*.

rurok (ru-rok), *n.* summit; highest point; top. Syn. *tuktók, taluktók, tugatog*.

Ruso (Ru-so), *n. (Sp.)* 1. Russian (citizen). 2. Russian language.

Rusya (Rus-ya), *n. (Sp.)* Russia.

ruta (ru-ta), *n. (Sp.)* route; itinerary; way or course for traveling. Syn. *daán, daanán, landás*.

ruweda (ru-we-da), *n.* (Sp. *rueda*) 1. wheel. Syn. *gulong*. 2. ring, enclosed space for boxing bout, cockfighting, etc. Syn. *ring*.

ruwina (ru-wi-na), *n.* (Sp. *ruina*) ruins. Syn. *wasak, pagkakawasak, guhò, labí ng mga pagkakawasak*.

S

S, s (Sa; see), *n.* 1. the sixteenth letter of the *abakada* (Pilipino alphabet). 2. the type or impression representing this letter. 3. the symbol for the sixteenth in a group or series.

sa (sa), *prep.* 1. for; intended for; belonging to, as in: *Itó'y sa iyó*. This is for you. 2. to; toward; in the direction of, as in: *Pupunta silá sa bukid*. They will go to the field. 3. in; at, as in: *Walâ siyá sa bahay*. He is not in the house. 4. at; during, as in: *Natutulog siyá sa tanghalì*. He sleeps at noon. 5. in; inside; into, as in: *Ilagáy mo itó sa kahón*. Put this in the box. 6. with; in company with; together with, as in: *Sumama siyá sa akin*. He went with me. 7. from, as in: *Galing silá sa kaniláng páaralán*. They came from their school. 8. to; to a certain condition, degree, etc., as in: *máuwî sa walâ*, to come to naught. 9. on;

upon; at the time of, as in: *sa pagpasok sa kuwarto*, on entering the room. 10. on; upon; on top of, as in: *Ilagáy mo itó sa (ibabaw ng) mesa*. Put this on the table. 11. on; through the use of, as in: *Nabúbuhay silá sa tubig at tinapay*. They live on water and bread. 12. from; of; due to; because of, as in: *Namatáy siyá sa gutom*. He died of (from) hunger. 13. by; at; near; along: as in: *Namahingá siyá sa tabi ng daán*. He took a rest at the side of the road. 14. than, as in: *higít sa limá*, more than five. 15. on; with; on the basis of: as in *Ginawâ niyá iyón sa kapahintulután ng Pangulo*. He did that with the permission of the President. 16. of; from, as in: *Tubò siyá sa Maynilà*. He is a native of Manila.

sá- (sá-), *pref.* used adverbially, meaning "unexpectedly" with something happening at the same time: as in *sá-daratíng silá nang kami'y paalis na*. They came unexpectedly when we were about to leave.

sa- (sa-), *pref.* used before nouns, usually preceded by *may*, meaning "having or possessing the quality or characteristics of" as in: *may sa-tagibulag*, having the qualities of invisibility; *may sa-pagóng*, (possessing the characteristics of a turtle); and the like.

sá-áakyát (sá + á-ak-yát), *v.* to be coincidentally about to go upstairs at the time when something is about to happen. Syn. *sá-pápanhík*.

saab (sa-ab), *n.* a singeing or burning of something superficially over a flame. Syn. *salab, pagsasalab*.

saád (sa-ád), *n.* 1. act of saying, stating, or relating something. Syn. *sabi, pagsasabi*. 2. something that a person said or stated. Syn. *ang sinabi o sinalitâ*.

saán (sa-án), I. *adv.* 1. where; in or to what place, as in: *Saán ka pupunta?* Where are you going? 2. from; from where; from what place or source, as in: *Saán mo iyán kinuha?* Where (from where) did you get that? —II. *conj.* 1. where; in or at what place, as in: *Nalalaman namin kung saán siyá kumain*. We know where he ate. 2. where; in or at the place or situation in which,

as in: *Ilagáy natin siyá kung saán siyá nárarapat*. Let's put him where he should be. 3. to or toward the place to which; where, as in: *Dádalhín ka ng taksi kung saán ka patutungo*. The taxi will take you where you are going. —III. *pron.* what or which place; where, as in: *Saán ka buhat?* Where do you come from (from where are you)?

saanmán (sa-an-mán), I. *adj.* everywhere; anywhere. Syn. *kahit saán, maski saán, kulób saán, sa lahát ng dako*. —II. *conj.* wherever; in, at, or to whatever place or situation.

sabá (sa-bá), *n.* (*Bot.*) 1. a species of banana plant, the fruit of which are usually eaten boiled or made into fritters. 2. the fruit of this plant. Cf. *butuhán, bungulan*.

sabak (sa-bak), *n.* 1. undue haste in attack or assault. Syn. *banat, pagbanat; lanták, paglanták*. 2. blind involvement, as in something one hardly expects to be able to do. Syn. *subò, pagsubò, pagkapasubò*.

sabád (sa-bád), *n.* an interrupting or breaking into the conversation of others; meddling or butting in someone's talk. Also, *pagsabád, pakikisabád*. Syn. *sabát, pagsabát, pakikisabát; paghalò o pakikihalò sa úsapan ng ibá*.

Sábadó (Sá-ba-dó), *n.* (*Sp.*) Saturday.

sabalás (sa-ba-lás), *n.* 1. northeast. Syn. *hilagang-silangan*. 2. northeast wind. Syn. *hanging mulâ sa hilagang-silangan*.

sabana (sa-ba-na), *n.* (*Sp.*) savanna, a treeless plain. Syn. *aliwalas na kapatagan*.

sabáng (sa-báng), *n.* crossing or intersection, as of railroads, rivers, streets, etc. Syn. *krosing, sambát, pinagkrusán*.

sabat (sa-bat), *n.* 1. a meddling or butting into someone's talk or conversation with another. Syn. *sabád, pakikihalò o paghalò sa pag-uusap ng ibá*. 2. a sudden interruption or cutting across someone's way.

sabáw (sa-báw), *n.* broth; clear, thin soup.

sabáy (sa-báy), I. *n.* 1. act of going together or accompanying someone on a trip, etc. Syn. *sama, pagsama*. 2. simultaneous happening or occurrence. Syn. *pangyayari nang magkasabáy*. 3. act of doing

something at the same time or in unison,
as in singing.

—II. *adj.* 1. at the same time;
simultaneous; in unison. See **magkasabáy**.
2. said of two persons leaving or going to
a certain place together at the same time.
Syn. *magkasama, magkasabáy.*

—III. *adv.* simultaneous; at the same time;
in unison.

sabi (sa-bi), I. n.1. statement; something said
by someone. Syn. *pahayag, pangungusap,
deklarasyón.* 2. act of saying something.
Syn. *pagsasalitâ, pagpapahayag.* 3. act of
telling something to someone. Also,
pagsasabi. 4. (Colloq.) words; expression;
statement, as in: *sa karaniwang sabi,* in
simple or common expression.

—II. *adj.* (with *ng* or *si*) according to; as
stated in or reported by. Syn. *alinsunod sa
(o kay).*

sabík (sa-bík), I. *adj.* eager; wanting very
much; keenly desiring; longing very
much. Also, *nanánabík.*

—II. *n.* keen desire for; eagerness. Also,
pananabík, kasabikán. Syn. *matindíng
paghahangád.*

sabíd (sa-bíd), n. 1. an entangling or being
entangling, as one's foot or feet, in a vine,
twine, rope, etc. Syn. *salabíd, pagkásalabíd.*
2. thread, twine, rope, or the like,
entangled on something. Syn. *salabíd.* 3.
an entwining or being entwined. Syn.
pulupot, pamumulupot, pagkakápulupot. 4.
something entwined around something.
Syn. *pulupot.* 5. (Fig.) hindrance;
obstacle. Syn. *balakíd, sagabal, sagwíl.*

sabihan (sa-bi-han), *v.* 1. to notify; give
notice to. Syn. *balitaan.* 2. to admonish;
reprove mildly. Syn. *kagalitan, pangaralan,
pagsabihan.*

sabilá (sa-bi-lá), n. (Bot.) a species of aloe
plant (*Aloe barbadensis Mill.*), having
fleshy, mucilaginous leaves with soft
spines along the edges, and the juice of
which is said to be very effective in
preventing falling of hair.

sabí-sabí (sa-bí + sa-bí), n. rumors; what
someone is telling about another or
others; gossip; hearsay. Syn. *balí-balità,
bulúng-bulungan, tsismis.*

sabit (sa-bit), n. 1. act or manner of hanging
something on a nail, hook, or the like.
Also, *pagsasabit.* 2. something hung in this
manner. Syn. *bagay na nakasabit.* 3. a
being caught on or as on a hook or nail
in a hurry. Syn. *kalawit, pagkákalawit,
pagkápakalawit.* 4. a tear or rip caused in
this manner. Cf. *punit, sirà.*

sabláy (sab-láy; sa-bláy), I. *n.* miss; failure
to hit, guess, answer, etc. Syn. *mintís,
pagmintís, pagmimintís; sala, pagsala; lihís,
paglihís.*

—II. *adj.* wide off the mark; not striking
the target aimed at. Syn. *sala, lihís,
nagmintís, mumintís.*

sablót (sab-lót), n. sudden snatch with the
hand. Syn. *daklót, pagdaklót; saklót,
pagsaklót.*

sabog (sa-bog), n. 1. act of scattering things
all around. Syn. *kalat, pagkakalat.* 2.
planting of seeds by sowing. Syn. *hasík,
paghahasík.* 3. explosion; loud bursting.
Syn. *malakás na putók.* 4. eruption, as of a
volcano. Syn. *putók, pagputók.* 5.
dispersion, as of light. Syn. *kalat, pagkalat.*
6. things scattered all around. Syn. *kalat.*

sabón (sa-bón), n. (Sp. *jabón*) 1. soap. 2. act
or manner of washing something with
soap and water. Also, *pagsabón,
pagsasabón.* 3. (Fig.) a severe or formal
rebuke; reprimand. Syn. *mura, pagmura.*

sabong (sa-bong), n. 1. attack of a cock
against another. Also, *pagsabong.* Syn.
salpók, pagsalpók. 2. cockfighting. Cf.
sultada.

saboy (sa-boy), n. 1. act of splashing or
throwing water, liquid, mud, sand, dust,
etc. at someone or something. Also,
pagsasaboy. 2. splash, as of water or waves
against the side of a boat, etc. Syn. *salpók
ng tubig o alon.* 3. splash or splatter of
water, liquid, mud, etc. on something.

sabsáb (sab-sáb), n. act or manner of eating
voraciously and noisily, as hogs, dogs, and
other animals do. Cf. *lamon, paglamon.*

sabsaban (sab-sa-ban), n. 1. feeding trough
(for hogs, horses, and other animals). Syn.
labangán. 2. manger.

sabukay (sa-bu-kay), n. 1. act of combing
the hair backward with the fingers in a

hurried or careless manner, not for the purpose of arranging it well but just to prevent it from hanging over the face. 2. a sudden, strong sweep or rush, as of waves, against something, sometimes causing it to be overturned or greatly damaged.

sabunot (sa-bu-not), n. act of grabbing and pulling the hair, as in anger. Also, *pagsabunot*. Cf. *gabot*, *paggabot*.

sabungán (sa-bu-ngán), n. cockpit. Syn. *simburyo*.

sábuwatan (sá-bu-wa-tan), var. **sábwatan**, n. conspiracy; secret plot or agreement with another or others for doing something wrong or unlawful. Syn. *sáubatan*, *sápakatan*.

saka (sa-ka), n. 1. cultivation of land; farming; agriculture. Also, *pagsasaka*. Syn. *pagbubukid*, *paglilinang*, *pagbubungkál ng lupà*, *pag-aararo*, *agrikultura*. 2. land being cultivated by a farmer; farmland. Syn. *linang*, *taniman*.

sakâ (sa-kâ), I. adv. 1. then; and then; afterwards, as in: *Ngumití lamang siyá at sakâ umalís*. He just smiled and then left (went away). 2. besides; moreover. Syn. *bukód sa*.
—II. conj. and; also; and also, as in: *Bibigyán kitá ng saging, sakâ manggá*. I'll give you bananas and also mango.

sakáb (sa-káb), n. 1. act or means of getting the facts or truth about something from someone by tricky questioning. Syn. *salakáb*. 2. a kind of basket-like fish trap made of bamboo splits and used in shallow-water fishing. Syn. *salakáb*.

sakada (sa-ka-da), n. (Sp. *sacada*) farm workers or laborers hired from other districts at lower pay than local labor.

sakál (sa-kál), n. 1. a strangling or being strangled; strangulation. Also, *pagsakál*, *pagkakásakál*. Cf. *bigti*, *pagbigti*. 2. fact, state, or condition of being strangled or seized by the neck. Also, *pagkasakál*.
—II. adj. strangled; seized by the neck.

sakalì (sa-ka-lì), adv. 1. if; in case; if by chance it happen. Syn. *kung*, *kung mangyari*, *kung magkátaón*. 2. maybe; perhaps; possibly. Syn. *bakâ*, *marahil*.

sakáng (sa-káng), I. adj. having bowlegs; bow-legged; opposed to *pikî*.
—II. n. 1. state or condition of being low-legged. 2. a bow-legged person.

sakâ-sakalì (sa-kâ + sa-ka-lì), adv. just in case. Syn. *kung sakalì*, *kung magkátaón*.

sakate (sa-ka-te), n. (Sp. *zacate*) a species of grass fodder. Syn. *kumpay*, *damóng pampakain sa hayop*.

sakáy (sa-káy), I. n. 1. act of riding a vehicle or an animal. Also, *pagsakáy*. Syn. *lulan*, *paglulan*. 2. passenger or passengers. Syn. *pasahero*. 3. load or cargo. Syn. *kargada*, *kargamento*, *lulan*. 4. the mounting of type composition on a printing machine for actual running or printing. Syn. *montada*. 5. the number of type forms or compositions needed to be run on the machine to complete the printing of a certain publication.
—II. adj. riding on an animal or vehicle. Syn. *lulan*, *nakalulan*, *nakasakáy*.
—III. adv. & prep. abroad; on board; on board of; in; on. Syn. *nasa*, *nakalulan sa*.

sakbát (sak-bát), I. n. 1. act or means of carrying something on a shoulder and allowing it to hang diagonally at the front and back toward the opposite side of the body, or around the neck and allowing it to hang down on the breast. 2. anything carried in these manners. 3. a band or sash slung from a shoulder downward slanting across the body or around the neck downward over the breast. Syn. *salakbát*, *banda*.
—II. adj. carried in a sling on the shoulder or around the neck downward over the chest.

sakbáy (sak-báy), n. act of placing one's arm around the waist of another in order to support, hold, or guide him. Cf. *akbáy*, *alakbáy*.

sakbót (sak-bót), n. a sudden snatching or grabbing in order to save a person or thing from danger. Cf. *saklót*, *daklót*.

sakdál¹ (sak-dál), n. 1. (*Law*.) formal charge or accusation filed in court; complaint. Syn. *demanda*, *hablâ*. 2. (*Colloq*.) grievance; cause of complaining. Syn. *reklamo*, *hinakdál*. 3. accusation. Syn.

paratang, sumbóng.

sakdál² (sak-dál), I. *adj.* 1. extreme. Syn. *sukdól, sukdulan.* 2. excessive. Syn. *masyado, labis, ubod ng.*

—II. *adv.* extremely; to an extreme degree; very.

—III. *n.* a coming to an end. Syn. *wakás, pagwawakás; tapos, pagkatapós, pagtatapós.*

sakím (sa-kím), I. *adj.* covetous; selfish; avaricious; greedy. Syn. *maimot, maimbót, mapág-imbót, sakré, masibá, matakaw, maramot, makamkám, mapágkamkám.*

—II. *n.* a covetous or selfish person.

sakit (sa-kit), *n.* 1. diligence; consistent effort; perseverance; endeavor. Syn. *sikap, pagsisikap, tiyagâ, pagtitiyagâ; sigasig, pagsisigasig.* 2. interest or concern for. Syn. *malasakit, pagmamalasakit; hasikaso, paghahasikaso.* 3. suffering. Syn. *tiisin, pagtitiís; hirap; dusa, pagdurusa.*

sakít (sa-kít), *n.* 1. sickness; illness; ailment; disease. Syn. *karamdaman.* 2. pain, painfulness; sore, soreness. Syn. *kirót, kakirután; hapdi, kahapdián; anták, kaantakán.*

saklâ (sak-lâ), *n.* a kind of prohibited card game whereby gamblers put bets on pairs of cards pasted on a board placed on a long table. Cf. *monte.*

sakláng (sak-láng), *n.* 1. act, manner, or position of sitting or riding an animal with the legs astraddle. 2. *(Carp.)* trestle; horse. Syn. *kabalyete, kabayo* (colloq.). 3. yoke for work animals. Syn. *pamatok, sakláy, yugo, paód.* 4. any one of the cross pieces or studs on the ridge or top of a roof, esp. of a nipa house. Syn. *sakláy.*

saklâp (sak-láp), *n.* 1. bitterish taste, esp. of unripe or green fruits. Syn. *paklâ, kapaklahán, pagkamapaklâ.* 2. bitterness or painfulness to one's feeling. Syn. *sakít, kirót, paít.*

sakláw (sak-láw), I. *n.* 1. extent, scope, or limit, as of someone's jurisdiction or power. Syn. *lawak, lakí, takdâ.* 2. comprehension or inclusion. Syn. *sakop, pagsakop.*

—II. *adj.* 1. within the extent, scope, or limit of. Syn. *sakóp, nasásakop, nasásakupan.* 2. under the jurisdiction or

power of. Syn. *nasa ilalim ng kapangyarihan.* 3. included; embraced. Syn. *kasama, nápapaloób.*

sakláy (sak-láy), *n.* 1. crutch with a crosspiece on top that fits the armpit. Syn. *muleta.* 2. act of putting or resting an arm or arms on a crutch or crutches. 3. yoke for work animals. Syn. *pamatok, paod, yugo.* 4. any one of the cross pieces or studs used to secure the ridge or top of a roof, esp. of a nipa house. 5. saddle-like device with a pair of studs used for carrying loads on the back of a horse. Syn. *palangkâ.* 6. such loads on the back of a horse. 6. the position of such loads made to hang on both sides of the animal.

saklób (sak-lób), var. **suklób, taklób,** *n.* 1. act or manner of putting on one's hat. Syn. *pagbapatong sa ulo ng sumbrero.* 2. act of covering a receptacle with or as with a lid. 3. any hollow cover, as lids for pots. Syn. *tuntóng, panuntóng; takip, panakip; takób, panakob.* 4. in gambling, partnership or joint venture of two bankers. Syn. *bakasán, sosyohán.* 5. act of putting a picture, a plate, etc. face to face with another.

—II. *adj.* 1. placed together face to face, as two pictures, plates, etc. Syn. *magkasuklób, magkataklób, magkasaklób.* 2. sharing with each other in an investment, esp. as bankers in a gambling venture. Syn. *bakas, magkabakas; sosyo, magkasosyo.*

saklolo (sak-lo-lo), var. **saklulo,** *n.* 1. act of responding to a call for help. Also, *pagsaklolo.* Syn. *pagsukoro.* 2. succor; aid; help; assistance. Syn. *tulong, sukoro.* 3. a person or persons on a mission to give help or assistance to someone or something in distress or in danger.

saklóng (sak-lóng), *n.* 1. stanza or paragraph. Syn. *párapó, tálataán.* 2. var. **saknáng,** brackets, represented by the sign [ ]; also, parentheses, represented by the sign ( ). See **panaklóng.** 3. in harvesting rice, the part or portion of a field which by common practice is supposed to be harvested by someone. See **saknóng.** 4. act of helping another in his work. Syn. *tulong, pagtulong.* 5. one who helps another in his work. Syn. *tulong, katulong.*

saklót (sak-lót), *n.* a sudden snatch or seizing with the hand. Syn. *daklót, pagdaklót; haklít, paghaklít.*

sakmál (sak-mál), I. *n.* 1. act of snatching or seizing suddenly with the big open mouth. Syn. *bigláng sagpáng ng malakíng bungangà.* 2. act of getting possession of something by or as by grabbing. Syn. *sunggáb, pagsunggáb; sagpáng, pagsagpáng.* –II. *adj.* held tightly in the big mouth.

saknóng (sak-nóng), *n.* 1.stanza or paragraph. Syn. *párapó, tálataán, táludturan.* See **saklóng.** 2. in harvesting a ricefield, the portion given to someone for him to harvest. 3. act of helping another in his work. Syn. *tulong, pagtulong; saklóng, pagsaklóng.* 4. one who helps another in his work. Syn. *tulong, katulong.*

sako (sa-ko), *n.* (Sp. *saco*) 1. sack; big bag of coarse material for holding grains. 2. a sackful, as in: *limáng sakong bigás,* five sackfuls of rice.

sakong (sa-kong), *n.* 1. heel (of the human foot). 2. the part of a stocking, socks, etc. worn under the heel of a foot.

sakop (sa-kop), *n.* 1. act of occupying an enemy possession or territory. Also, *pagsakop.* Syn. *okupá, pag-ukopá.* 2. the part of an enemy territory occupied by the conqueror. Syn. *teritoryong okupado ng kaaway.* 3. putting someone under one's jurisdiction or power. Syn. *sakláw, pagsaklaw.* 4. the extent or limit of one's jurisdiction. Syn. *sakláw, nasásakláw.* 5. the part or portion comprising the entire land area of someone's landed property. Syn. *parte, bahagi.*

sakramento (sa-kra-men-to), *n.* (Sp. *sacramento*) sacrament. Cf. *biyayà ng Diyós.*

sakré (sa-kré), *adj.* covetous; avaricious; selfish. Syn. *sakim, masakím, maramot, matakaw, makamkám, makasarili.*

sakriléhiyó (sa-kri-lé-hi-yó), *n.* (Sp. *sacrelegio*) sacrilege. Syn. *kalaspatanganan, kapusungán.*

sakripisyo (sa-kri-pis-yo), *n.* (Sp. *sacrificio*) 1. a sacrificing; doing something difficult

as a means of sacrifice. Syn. *pagpapakasakit, pagsasakripisyo.* 2. thing sacrificed or offered as a sacrifice. Syn. *handóg o hain sa Diyós.*

sakristán (sa-kris-tán), *n.* (Sp. *sacristan*) 1. sacristan; person in charge of the sacristy. 2. altar boy; acolyte. Syn. *munisilyo.*

sakristiya (sa-kris-ti-ya), *n.* (Sp. *sacristía*) sacristy; vestry. Syn. *bestuwaryo.*

sakrosanto (sa-kro-san-to), *adj.* (Sp. *sacrosanto*) sacrosanct; very holy; very sacred. Syn. *nápakabanál, nápakasagrado, sagradung-sagrado, napakasanto, santúngsanto.*

saksák (sak-sák), *n.* 1. act of stabbing; a thrust, as with a knife or any pointed instrument. Also, *pagsaksák.* Syn. *tarak, iwà, ulos.* 2. deep wound made by stabbing. Syn. *malalim na sugat ng patalím.* 3. act of cramming something into a container. Syn. *siksík, pagsisiksík.* 4. (usually with *ng*) the extreme of. Syn. *ubod, sukdulan.* 5. act of piercing or sticking something into, as pins on a pincushion. Syn. *tusok, pagtutusók; durò, pagdudurò.*

saksi (sak-si; -sí), *n.* 1. a seeing or witnessing an incident, appearance, or occurrence of something. 2. a person who was a witness to something that happened. Syn. *ang nakakita o kaharáp sa nangyari.* 3. (*Law*) witness; person who testifies in a court trial. Syn. *testigo.* 4. (*Colloq.*) a member of a certain religious sect.

saktán (sak-tán), *v.* 1. to hurt (someone) or to inflict pain (on someone). 2. to suffer, as from stomachache, toothache, etc.

sakunâ (sa-ku-nâ), *n.* accident; mishap. Syn. *aksidente, disgrasya, kapahamakàn.*

sadista (sa-dis-ta), I. *n.* (Sp.) sadist. —II. *adj.* sadistic.

sadlák (sad-lák), *n.* a falling into misfortune or into shame or dishonor. Syn. *roól, pagkáparoól, pagkasawî, pagkápahamak.*

sadsád (sad-sád), *n.* 1. arrival of a ship, boat, etc. on a shore; docking or landing. Syn. *duóng, pagduóng; pundo, pagpundo.* 2. a running aground, as of a ship. Syn. *sayad, pagsayad, pagsadsád.* 3. a sliding and striking against something. Syn. *balandra, pagbalandra.*

sadyâ (sad-yâ), I. n. 1. act of visiting or going to a certain person or place for a certain special purpose or mission. Also, *pagsasadyâ.* 2. mission; special object or purpose in visiting or going to a certain person or place. Syn. *pakay, layon, láyunin; misyón.* 3. act of doing something intentionally or on purpose. Syn. *tikís, pagtikís; pagsadyâ.* 4. act of making something in accordance to certain specifications or requirements, as made-to-order shoes, etc.
—II. *adj.* 1. intentional; done on purpose. Syn. *sinadyâ; talagáng ginawâ.* 2. made-to-order. Syn. *pasadyâ.*
—III. *adv.* intentionally; deliberately; purposely. Syn. *talagà, kusà.*

sagabal (sa-ga-bal), n. anything that causes obstruction; impediment; obstacle. Syn. *hadláng, sagwíl, balakíd, halang.*

sa-gabi (sa + ga-bi), n. (fr. *gabi*) a special ability attributed to a person who is said to be free from becoming wet. Syn. *katangiang laban sa pagkabasâ.*

sagád (sa-gád), *adj.* sunk to the hilt. Syn. *upós, sampák.* 2. reaching up to the other or opposite side. Syn. *abót sa kabilâ.* 3. penetrating or piercing through and through. Syn. *tagós, tágusan; lágusan; lampás, lámpasan.* 4. reaching up to the bottom. Syn. *abót sa pusod o ilalim, sayad sa ilalim.* 5. having reached the end, as the string kite. Syn. *ubós na o tapos na.* 6. (*Colloq.*) broke; penniless. Syn. *baligtád ang bulsa* (fig.), *walâ nang pera.* 7. having reached the limit, as of one's self-control. Syn. *punô na* (fig.), *hindî na makapagpigil.* 8. all used up or exhausted. Syn. *ubós o saíd na.* 9. fully tired or exhausted. Syn. *pagód na pagód, walâ nang kaya dahil sa lubós na pagkapagod.*
—II. n. 1. state or condition of being sunk to the hilt, having reached up to the end or other side of, or down to the bottom. 2. state or condition of being totally broke or penniless.

sagadsád (sa-gad-sád), I. n. a dragging or being dragged. Syn. *kaladkád, pagkakaladkád.* 2. a sliding or skidding. Syn. *dagusdos, dalusdós.* 3. a sliding and colliding against. Syn. *balandra, pagbalandra.* 4. a running aground, as a ship. Syn. *sadsád, pagsadsád; sayad, pagsayad.* 5. fact, state, or condition of being continuous or uninterrupted up to the end. Syn. *pagkatulúy-tulóy, kawaláng tigíl hanggáng sa matapos.*
—II. *adj.* continuous; uninterrupted up to the end. Syn. *patuloy, tulúy-tulóy, waláng-tigil, waláng-hintô.*
—III. *adv.* in a hurry; hurriedly. Syn. *dalí-dalì, nagmámadalî, nag-áapurá, humáharos.*

sagala (sa-ga-la), n. (Sp. *zagala*) any of the several maiden participants in a *Santakrusan* or Lenten Procession, wearing a certain costume appropriate to her role.

sagalwák (sa-gal-wák), n. 1. strong flow or gush of water, as from a big broken pipe. 2. the sound or noise produced by this. 3. an accidental spilling of water, as from a container. Syn. *salwák.* 4. the water thus spilled.

saganà (sa-ga-nà), *adj.* 1. abundant; plentiful; more than sufficient. Syn. *pasasà.* 2. rich; wealthy. Syn. *mayaman, mariwasâ, nakaririwasâ.*

sagansán (sa-gan-sán), n. 1. act of arranging or placing persons or things close together on one side or end of a row or line. Also, *pagsagansán.* Syn. *saginsín, pagsaginsín.* 2. a row or file of persons or things close together on one side or end.

sagasà (sa-ga-sà), n. 1. a driving or running over someone or something, as with a vehicle. Also, *pagsagasà.* 2. a going through (difficulties, storm, flood, etc.) with determination; running against odds. Syn. *sagupà, pagsagupà; salunga, pagsalunga; salasâ, pagsalasà.*

sagasâ (sa-ga-sâ), *adj.* reckless; rash; heedless of consequences. Syn. *waláng-tarós, mapusok, pabiglá-biglâ, waláng paghuhunus-dilì, padaskúl-daskól.*

sagay (sa-gay), n. coral.

sagkâ (sag-kâ), n. 1. act of preventing or stopping someone from doing something. Syn. *pagpigil, pagsawáy.* 2. anything that prevents or stops someone or something; impediment; obstacle; obstruction. Syn.

sagwíl, balakíd, hadláng, sagabal.

sagì (sa-gì), n. 1. a sideswiping or being sideswiped. Syn. *dagil, pagdagil, pagkadagil.* 2. momentary recollection or remembering, as of something long forgotten. Syn. *pagkáalaala, pagkágunitâ.* 3. (*Colloq.*) a dropping in for a moment at a certain place while passing by. Syn. *sinsáy o pansinsáy na sandalî, saglít, pagsaglít.*

sagilahan (sa-gi-la-han), v. 1. to be momentarily afflicted, as with terror, disease, etc. Syb. *bigláng sumpungín ng takot, karamdaman, atbp.*

sagimsím (sa-gim-sím), n. foreboding; premonition; presentiment. See **salagimsím.** Syn. *pag-aalaalá, pangambá, kabá o kutób ng loób, pagkabalisa.*

saginsín (sa-gin-sín), I. n. 1. act of placing or arranging things close together on one side or end. Syn. *sagansán, pagsagansán.* 2. state or condition of being placed or arranged close together.

—II. adj. arranged or placed together closely; compact. Syn. *dikít-dikít, masinsín.*

saging (sa-ging), n. (*Bot.*) 1. the common name for all the species of banana plants. 2. the fruit of any of these plants.

sagip (sa-gip), n. 1. act of snatching or grasping with the hand a floating object or one being carried away by the current in order to salvage. 2. act of saving or rescuing someone from drowning or from some sort of danger or misfortune. Syn. *pagliligtás.*

sagisag (sa-gi-sag), n. 1. emblem; symbol; insignia. Syn. *palátandaan, símboló.* 2. pen name; pseudonym; *nom de plume.* Also, *sagisag-panulat.*

sagisod (sa-gi-sod), n. act of pushing something forward on the floor or along the ground, with or as with one's foot. Cf. *talisod, pagtalisod.*

sagitsit (sa-git-sit), n. 1. hiss; hissing sound, as of hot oil in a frying pan when spattered with water. Syn. *sirit.* 2. whizzing sound, as of something rushing along the way through the air. Syn. *haginít, hagibis.*

saglít (sag-lít), n. 1. instant moment. Syn. *sandali.* 2. second (part of a minute). Syn.

segundo, sandalî. 3. act of going to a certain person or place in a hurry for a very short time. Also, *pagsaglít.* Syn. *punta o pagpuntang sandalî.*

sagó (sa-gó), n. (*Bot.*) 1. sago palm (*Metroxylon rumphii Mart.*). 2. the starchy granular substance prepared from the pith of this palm, used in making pudding, etc.

sagót (sa-gót), n. 1. act or manner of answering. Also, *pagsagót.* Syn. *tugón, pagtugón.* 2. an answer or reply to a question, letter, etc. Syn. *tugón, katúgunan.* 3. an answer or solution to a problem. Syn. *solusyón.* 4. (*Law*) rebuttal. Syn. *gantíng-matwíd, gantíng-katwiran, pagpapabulaan, pagpapasinungaling.* 5. assumption of another's responsibility. Syn. *pananagót, pag-akò.*

sagpáng (sag-páng) n. 1. sudden snatch with the mouth. Syn. *sakmál, pagsakmál.* 2. (*Fig.*) act of grabbing or accepting at once, as an offer. Syn. *pagtanggáp agád.*

sagrado (sa-gra-do), adj. (*Sp.*) sacred.

sagraryo (sa-grar-yo; sag-rar-yo), n. (*Sp. sagrario*) 1. sanctuary; part of the church about the altar. Syn. *santuwaryo, presbitaryo.* 2. tabernacle. Syn. *tabernákuló.*

sagság (sag-ság), n. 1. sudden departure or rushing to a certain place. Syn. *mádaliang pag-alís o pagtungo sa isáng lugár, pagmamadalî.* 2. height, as of certain activities, in business, etc. Also, *kasagsagán.*

sag-ulì (sag + u-lì), n. restoration or a being restored to the former state or condition. Syn. *pananág-ulì, pagsasaulî sa dating ayos o kalagayan.*

sagunsón (sa-gun-són), n. 1. act of pushing or arranging things close together at one end or side of a place. Syn. *saginsín, pagsaginsín.* 2. act of following or tracing the line or path of. Syn. *taluntón, pagtaluntón.* 3. act of sewing (cloth) with long, loose, temporary stitches. Syn. *tutos, pagtutos.*

sagupà (sa-gu-pà), n. 1. act of facing or meeting one's enemy. Syn. *paglaban o pagharáp sa kaaway.* 2. act of going against the wind, traffic, etc. Syn. *salubong,* *pagsalubong; salunga, pagsalunga.* 3. act of colliding with something frontally. Syn. *banggâ, pagbanggâ.*

sagwâ (sag-wâ), *n.* vulgarity; indecency; immodesty; obscenity. Syn. *halay, kahalayan, kabastusán, kalaswaán.* 2. coarseness; unrefined quality. Syn. *gaspáng, kagaspangán.* 3. ugliness; ugly quality. Syn. *kapangitan.*

sagwák (sag-wák), 1. gushing, as of a big volume of water from a big, broken pipe. Syn. *bulwák, bugalwák.* 2. an accidental spilling of a big volume of water from a big container. Syn. *salwák, ligwák.* 3. water spilled in this manner.

sagwán (sag-wán), *n.* 1. act or manner of propelling a boat with a paddle or paddles. Syn. *gaod, paggaod.* 2. paddle or oar. Also, *panagwán.* Syn. *gaod, paggaod.*

sagwíl (sag-wíl), *n.* 1. obstacle; obstruction. Syn. *sagabal, hadláng, balakíd.* 2. problem; inconvenience; difficulty. Syn. *problema, suliranín.*

sahà (sa-hà), *n.* the sheath of a banana plant. Syn. *upak o talupak ng punong saging.*

sahíg (sa-híg), *n.* 1. floor (of a room, hall, etc.). Syn. *suwelo.* 2. flooring material. Syn. *panahíg, pansahíg.* 3. act of making the floor of. Also, *pagsasahíg.* Syn. *pagsusuwelo.*

sahing (sa-hing), *n.* 1. (*Bot.*) a tree reaching a height of 35 meters, popularly known as *pili* (*Canarium luzonicum Blume*). 2. the soft; sticky, opaque, and slightly yellow substance obtained from this tree, known locally by the Spanish term *brea blanca*, or white pitch in English.

sahod (sa-hod), *n.* 1. the position of an open hand or hands in the act of receiving something from someone; also, the act of receiving something from someone with an open hand or hands. 2. a receptacle used to hold or catch falling objects, flowing water, etc. Also, *panahod, pansahod.* 3. salary; pay; wage. Syn. *suweldo.* 4. act of receiving one's pay or salary. Also, *pagsahod.* Syn. *pagtanggáp ng sahod o suweldo.* 5. payday. Syn. *araw ng suweldo.*

sahóg (sa-hóg), *n.* 1. act of putting or adding

something to mixture. Syn. *halò, paghahalò.* 2. anything added to a mixture, as ingredients in cooking food. Also, *panahóg, pansahóg.*

sahól (sa-hól), *adj.* 1. inadequate in amount, quality, etc.; deficient; Syn. *kulang, kapós, di-sapát.* 2. overpowered; subdued; subjugated. Syn. *talo, lupíg.* 3. wanting or lacking in certain qualities. Syn. *salát.*

saikapat (sa-i-ka-pat), *adj.* one-fourth, distinguished from *sa ika-apat,* on the fourth.

saíd (sa-íd), I. *n.* 1. state or condition of having nothing left. Syn. *kawaláng nátirá.* 2. the use or consumption of everything on hand. Syn. *ubos, pag-ubos, pagkaubos.* —II. *adj.* with everything all used up; exhausted or consumed. Syn. *ubós na lahát; waláng natirá o lumabis.*

sainete (sa-i-ne-te), *var.* **saynete,** *n.* (*Sp.*) one-act farce. Cf. *drama, dulà (dulâ).*

saing (sa-ing), *n.* 1. act or manner of cooking milled rice by boiling or steaming. Also, *pagsasaing.* 2. in some Southern Tagalog areas, the cooking of fish in little water with salt. Syn. *pangát, pagpapangát.*

sala[1] (sa-la) . *n.* 1. fault; guilt; sin. Syn. *kasalanan, pagkakasala.* 2. error; mistake. Syn. *malî, pagkakámalî, kamalian.* 3. a miss or failure to hit a target. Syn. *mintís, pagmintís.* —II. *adj.* 1. wrong; mistaken. Syn. *malî, lisyâ.* 2. off the mark. Syn. *mintís, nagmintís; di-tumamà; lihís, lumihís.* 3. not suitable; bad for; against or contrary to, as some kind of food. Syn. *masamâ sa, bawal.*

sala[2] (sa-la), *var.* **salas,** *n.* (*Sp.*) receiving room; visitors' room.

salà[1] (sa-là), *n.* 1. filtering; straining. Also, *pagsalà, pagsasalà.* 2. irrigation dam.

salaán (sa-la-án), *n.* 1. strainer; filter. Syn. *panalà.* 2. colander.

salab (sa-lab), *n.* act of burning (something) superficially on or over a flame, as animal carcass, to remove the bristles or feathers, or leaves, in order to soften or wither; searing; singeing; scorching. Also, *pagsalab, pagsasalab.* Syn. *daráng, pagdadaráng.*

salabat (sa-la-bat), n. 1. small branches or twigs sticking out confusely in the forest, causing obstruction to those entering it. Syn. *halabat.* 2. things, like branches, twigs, or the like scattered on the way, causing obstruction to passers-by.

salabát (sa-la-bát), n. ginger tea. Syn. *tahó, panggasì.*

salabíd (sa-la-bíd), n. 1. an entangling or being entangled , as of one's foot or feet in a net, vine, twine, etc. 2. something that entangles. 3. a coiling around on something. Syn. *pulupot, pagpulupot.* 4. a coil or coils, as of twine, or the like, on a spool. 5. (by extension) impediment; obstruction; obstacle. Syn. *sagabal, hadláng, balakíd.*

salakáb (sa-la-káb), n. act of obtaining facts or the truth about something from someone by some kind of ruse or tricky questions.

sa-lakasan (sa + la-ka-san), var. **sálakasan,** n. use of superior force or influence.

salakatâ (sa-la-ka-tâ), n. a jolly fellow who always laughs at the slightest provocation. Syn. *taong palatawá.*

salakay (sa-la-kay), n. 1. assault; violent physical attack, as of a person against another. 2. raid, as by police on some gambling houses. 3. (Mil.) raid or air raid, as by bombers. 4. (Mil.) invasion. Syn. *imbasyón.*

salakbát (sa-lak-bát), I. n. a band or sash worn on a shoulder, slanting downward over the chest and back, meeting at the opposite side. 2. anything carried on a shoulder, hanging on the front and back sides. 3. the act or manner of carrying anything in this way.

—II. *adj.* carried on a shoulder and made to hang on the front and back sides.

salakop (sa-la-kop), n. an encircling or a being encircled, as a place, by a cordon of raiders.

salakót (sa-la-kót), var. **salukót,** n. a wide-brimmed, helmet-like covering of the head, usually made of *buri* sheathings or leaves.

salaksák (sa-lak-sák), n. act of prodding or thrusting a pole, etc. repeatedly into a hole or small opening, as in trying to clear a pipe of some obstructions.

salág (sa-lág), n. act or manner of parrying or warding off a blow, etc. with the hand or with something held by the hand. Syn. *sanggá, pagsanggâ.*

salaghatì (sa-lag-ha-tì), var. **salakhatì,** n. 1. feeling of displeasure; resentment. Syn. *hinanakít, samâ ng loób.* 2. affliction; suffering; melancholy. Syn. *dalamhatî, pighatî, dusa.*

salagimsím (sa-la-gim-sím), n. premonition; foreboding. Syn. *agam-agam, kabá, kutób.*

salágintô (sa-lá-gin-tô), n. (Entom.) goldbug; gold beetle. Cf. *salágubang.*

salágubang (sa-lá-gu-bang), n. (Entom.) June bug; June beetle. Cf. *salágintô.*

salalay (sa-la-lay), n. 1. act of placing a thing on something to support or hold it temporarily. Syn. *patong, pagpapatong.* 2. act of placing a container (of food) on another shallow container with water for the purpose of keeping away ants, and other crawling insects. 3. a shallow vessel containing water for the purpose in sense 2. 4. a holder or support on which something rests temporarily. Syn. *patungán, sapín.* 5. the position of a thing held suspended on something to which it has fallen. Syn. *salálak, pagkásalalak.*

salamangka (sa-la-mang-ka), n. sleight of hand; legerdemain; prestidigitation; magic. Syn. *máhiká, madyik.*

salamat (sa-la-mat), I. n. thanks (an expression of gratitude). Also, *pasasalamat.*

—II. *interj.* Thank you! Thanks!

salambáw (sa-lam-báw), I. n. 1. a big lift net supported by a tripod-like contraption made of full length bamboos mounted on a raft, and usually used in rivers. 2. act of tilting upward the front of a two-wheeled vehicle by making the rear heavier. Also, *pagsalambáw.* 3. state or condition of being tilted upward due to being heavier at the rear end, referring esp. to two-wheeled vehicles.

—II. *adj.* tilted upward at the front due to being heavier at the rear. Syn. *mabigát sa likód, tikwás sa haráp.*

salamín (sa-la-mín), I. n. mirror; looking glass. Syn. *espeho*. 2. crystal or glass. Syn. *bubog, kristál*. 3. (for the eyes) eyeglasses; spectacles; goggles. Syn. *antiparas, anteohos*. 4. (of the ear) eardrum; tympanum.

—II. *adj*. of or made of glass.

salamisim (sa-la-mi-sim), n. 1. reminiscence; recollection. Syn. *gunitâ, alaala*. 2. illusion; fantasy; phantasm. Syn. *guniguní*.

salampák (sa-lam-pák), n. 1. act or manner of sitting or lying suddenly and heavily on something, as of one who is very tired. Also, *pagsalampák*. 2. such a position in sitting or lying.

salampáy (sa-lam-páy), n. 1. act or manner of hanging something carelessly, as on a shoulder, clothesline, fence, etc. Syn. *alampáy, pag-aalampáy; sampáy, pagsasampáy*. 2. anything placed or hung in the manner above. 3. neckerchief; shawl or scarf; muffler. Syn. *alampáy*.

salamuhà (sa-la-mu-hà), n. hobnobbing; associating in a familiar way with people; mixing or mingling with. Syn. *halubilo, pakikihalubilo*.

salansán (sa-lan-sán), n. 1. act of piling things one over another in an orderly manner. Syn. *talaksán, pagtalaksán, pagtatalaksán*. 2. a neat pile or heap, as of firewood. Syn. *talaksán*. 3. an orderly arrangement of papers, cards, etc. for reference purposes; file.

salansanán (sa-lan-sa-nán), v. to use a box, cabinet, or the like for filling or keeping files or records.

salansáng (sa-lan-sáng), var. **salangsáng**, n. 1. act of opposing or objecting to someone's opinion or to something being proposed or planned by someone. Syn. *tutol, pagtututol; salungát, pagsalungát*. 2. a contrary position taken by someone against another; opposition; objection.

salantâ (sa-lan-tâ), I. n. 1. an infirm or a physically disabled person. Syn. *taong baldado o inutil*. 2. state or condition of being infirm or physically disabled, referring to a person. Syn. *pagkabaldado, pagkainutil*. 3. state or condition of being badly damaged or ruined, as by typhoon.

—II. *adj*. 1. infirm or physically disabled (s.o. persons). Syn. *baldado, inutil, lumpó*. 2. badly damaged or completely ruined, as by typhoon; devastated. Syn. *wasák na wasák*.

salang (sa-lang), n. 1. act or manner of putting a pot, frying pan, or the like, over a fire or stove, as in cooking. Also, *pagsasalang*. Syn. *sigáng, pagsisigáng*. 2. anything being cooked on a pot, casserole, etc. on a fire or stove.

saláng (sa-láng), n. 1. a very light touch, as with a finger or hand. Syn. *hipò, paghipò*. 2. (*Fig.*) an unintentional mention or reference to something bitter or hurting to someone. Syn. *di-sinásadyáng pagbanggit*.

salanggapáng (sa-lang-ga-páng), I. *adj*. roguish; dishonest; unscrupulous. Syn. *tampalasan, buhóng*.

—II. n. rogue; a dishonest and worthless person.

salapáng (sa-la-páng), n. 1. harpoon. 2. trident (a three-pronged fish spear).

salapaw (sa-la-paw), n. a spreading over, as of vines on a trellis. Syn. *gapang o paggapang sa ibabaw*.

salapî (sa-la-pî), n. (*Mal.*) 1. money (in general). Syn. *pera, kuwarta (kuwalta)*. 2. a fifty-centavo coin.

salapiín (sa-la-pi-ín), v. to sell (a thing) in order to get money or cash from it; turn (something) into cash by selling. Syn. *kuwartahín (kuwaltahín)*.

salapot (sa-la-pot), n. (*Colloq.*) clothes; clothing. Syn. *damít, pananamít*.

salarín (sa-la-rín), n. criminal; culprit; offender. Syn. *kriminál, ang nagkasala o may-kasalanan*.

salas (sa-las), var. **sala**, n. (*Sp.*) receiving room; living room. See **sala²**.

salasà (sa-la-sà), n. a plunging or rushing forward recklessly or without fear, as into a crowd. Syn. *sagasà, pagsagasà*.

sala-salá (sa-la + sa-lá), var. **sala-salá**, I. n. a railing or fence made of interwoven bamboo slats.

—II. *adj*. made of interwoven bamboo slats.

salát¹ (sa-lát), adj. 1. poor; needy. Syn. *mahirap, dukhâ, marálitâ*. 2. in need; in

want. Syn. *hikahós, kapós, dahóp.* 3.
scanty; meager; scarce. Syn. *kákaunti,
kulang na kulang, di-sapát.*

salát² (sa-lát), n. 1. act of running one's hand
or fingers over a surface to identify or look
for something. Cf. *kapâ, pagkapâ.* 2.
nature of a thing perceived through
touch; feel. Syn. *hipò.* 3. *(Fig.)* personal
opinion or judgment about someone's
ability, character, etc. Sy. *taya, tantyá.*

salatan (sa-la-tan), n. 1. southwest. Syn.
timog-kanluran. 2. southwest wind. Syn.
hanging timog-kanluran, habagat.

salaulà (sa-la-u-là), *adj.* 1. with or having
dirty or unsanitary habit. Syn. *ugaling-
baboy, marumi, nakadidiri.* 2. morally
offensive; obscene. Syn. *bastós.*

salawahan (sa-la-wa-han), I. *adj.* 1. fickle;
inconstant. Syn. *pabagu-bago ng isip.* 2.
doubtful; feeling doubt. Syn. *alinlangan,
nag-áalinlangan, may-alinlangan.* 3.
hesitant; vascillating. Syn. *bantulót,
nagbábantulót; urung-sulong, nag-úurongsulong; ulík-ulík, nag-úulik-ulík.*
—II. n. 1. doubt; feeling of doubt. Syn.
*alinlangan, pag-aalinlangan; duda,
pagdududa.* 2. a wavering in opinion or
belief. Syn. *bantulot, pagbabantulót.*

salawál (sa-la-wál), var. **salwál,** n. pants;
trousers; pantaloons. Syn. *pantalón.* 2.
drawers; underpants. Syn. *karsunsilyo
(kalsunsilyo).* 3. panties. Syn. *panti.*

saláwikaín (sa-lá-wi-ka-ín), n. 1. idiomatic
expression. Syn. *kawikaán.* 2. saying;
maxim; adage; proverb. Syn. *kasabihán,
sáwikaín, bukambibíg.*

salawsáw (sa-law-sáw), n. turmoil; melée.
Syn. *guló, pagkakaguló; ligalig, kaligaligan.*

salaysáy (sa-lay-sáy), n. 1. an account of
something that happened; story. Syn.
kuwento, pagkukuwento; bida, pagbibida. 2.
testimony, as of a witness. Syn. *pahayag,
pagpapahayag.* 3. an oral or written report
or account about something. Syn. *ulat,
pag-uulat; repórt, pagrerepórt.*

salba (sal-ba; -bá), n. (Sp. *salvar*) a saving
or rescuing, as from danger, ruin, or death.
Syn. *ligtás, pagliligtás.*

salbabida (sal-ba-bi-da), n. (Sp. *salvavidas*)
life preserver.

salbadór (sal-ba-dór), n. (Sp. *salvador*)
savior; rescuer. Syn. *ang nagligtás o
tagapágligtás.*

salbahe (sal-ba-he), I. *adj.* (Sp. *salvaje*) 1.
savage; wild; undomesticated. Syn.
mailáp, simarón, mabangís. 2. naughty;
mischievous. Syn. *malikót, pilyo.* 3.
notoriously cunning or abusive. Syn.
manloloko, manlilinláng, tuso.
—II. n. a person who is notoriously
cunning or abusive.

salbahihin (sal-ba-hi-hin), *v.* 1. to do
someone a mischief; abuse the confidence
of someone by cheating or cunning
trickery. Syn. *lokohin.* 2. to abuse or
disgrace a woman. Syn. *abusuhin,
gahasain.*

salbasyón (sal-bas-yón), n. (Sp. *salvacion*) a
saving or being saved; salvation;
redemption. Syn. *pagliligtás, kaligtasan,
pagkakáligtás.*

sali (sa-li), n. 1. act of participating in a play,
contest, or competition. Also, *pagsali,
pakikisali.* Syn. *lahók, paglahók, pakikilahók.*
2. an entry or participant. Syn. *kasali,
lahók, kalahók.*

salibád (sa-li-bád), n. 1. a swift, sudden
flight, as of a frightened bird. Syn. *bigláng
lipád.* 2. a swooping flight, as of a bird of
prey in pouncing or snatching a victim.
Syn. *simbád, pagsimbád, bigláng dagit o
pagdagit.*

salibát (sa-li-bát), n. a butting into others'
conversation. Syn. *sabát, pakikisabát.*

salik (sa-lik), n. 1. element; basic part. Syn.
mahalagáng sangkáp o bahagi, elemento. 2.
any one of the four elements of nature:
earth, air, fire, and water. Syn. *elemento.*
3. influence, as in: *mga salik kanluranín,*
western influences. 4. *(Gram.)* syllable.
Syn. *pantíg, silabá.*

salikop (sa-li-kop), n. 1. a converging or
meeting together, forming an angle or
corner, as of two roads or rivers. Syn.
tagpô, pagtatagpô. 2. place or point of
meeting or convergence. Syn. *tagpuan,
pinagtagpuán, pinagsalikupan.* 3. act of
encircling or surrounding a place from
opposite direction, as by a cordon of
raiding policemen. Syn. *kulóng,*

549

pagkulóng; kubkób, pagkubkób; pikot, pagpikot. 4. a closing or folding together, as of the wings of a bird. Syn. *tikom, pagtikom; tiklóp, pagtiklop.* 5. act of folding together, as the hem of a skirt. Syn. *balumbón.*

saliksík (sa-lik-sík), I. *n.* 1. a minute or detailed search or searching. Syn. *halughóg, paghahalughóg.* 2. research; act of doing research. Syn. *pananaliksik.*

—II. *adj.* having been searched all over; gone over minutely for the purpose of finding something. Syn. *halughóg, hinalughóg.*

salida (sa-li-da), *n.* (Sp.) 1. a way out; exit. Syn. *lábasan, daán sa paglabás.* 2. leaving or departure. Syn. *alís, pag-alís; yao, pagyao.* 3. a sallying or rushing forth, as of a vehicle in going down a slope, usually without the aid of the engine. Syn. *takbó o pagtakbó nang patáy ang mákiná.* 4. (a) professional call or visit, esp. of a doctor. Syn. *dalaw, pagdalaw;* (b) the fee for such a call. Syn. *subida.* 5. (*Econ.*) expenditures. Syn. *gugol, gastós.* 6. (*Accounting*) debit. 7. in gambling, money paid out to the winners in excess of the winnings after each game; opposed to *kabig.* 8. downward slope or descent, as of a road. Syn. *lusong, paglusong.*

salig (sa-lig), I. *adj.* (usually with *sa*) based on or from. Syn. *batay o hango (sa).*

—II. *n.* act or manner of basing a thing from another. Also, *pagsalig, pagsasalig.* Syn. *hangò, paghangò; batay, pagbabatay.*

saligáng batás (sa-li-gáng + ba-tás), var. **saligambatás,** *n.* constitution. Syn. *konstitusyón.*

saligawgáw (sa-li-gaw-gáw), *adj.* naughty; mischievous. Syn. *malikót, maharót, pilyo.*

saligutgót (sa-li-gut-gót), I. *n.* intricacy; complexity. Syn. *gusót, kagusután, pagkagusót.* 2. disorder; confusion. Syn. *guló, kaguluhán, pagkaguló; ligalig, kaligaligan, pagkaligalig.*

—II. *adj.* intricate; complicated. Syn. *maguló, maligalig, magusót.*

salilong (sa-li-long), *n.* 1. act of taking shelter, cover, or protection under a shade or under someone's custody. Syn. *pagkublí,*

pangungublí. 2. act of giving shelter, cover, or protection to someone. Syn. *pagkandilí, pagkupkóp, pag-andukâ, pag-arugá, pag-ampón.*

salimbáy (sa-lim-báy), *n.* a swooping flight or glide, as of a flying bird. Syn. *sibád, salibád.*

salimuót (sa-li-mu-ót), I. *adj.* 1. complicated; intricate; entangled. Syn. *maguló, magusót.* 2. knotty; hard to solve. Syn. *mahirap.* 3. problematic. Syn. *masúliranín.*

—II. *n.* 1. intricacy; complexity; complication. Syn. *guló, pagkamaguló, kaguluhán; gusot, pagkamagusót, kagusutan.* 2. disorder; confusion. Syn. *ligalig, kaligaligan; guló, kaguluhán.*

salin (sa-lin), *n.* 1. act of pouring something from one container into another. Syn. *liwat, pagliliwat.* 2. (a) act of making a copy of something by typing or writing. Syn. *kopya, pagkopya; sipì, pagsipì.* (b) such a copy or copies made. Syn. *kopya, sipì.* 3. (a) act of translating a text from one language to another. Also, *pagsasalin.* (b) the translation thus made. Syn. *translesyón, traduksiyón.* 4. a turning over or relinquishment of an office or position to a successor. Syn. *paglilipat ng tungkulin.* 5. transfer of passengers or cargoes from one vehicle to another. Syn. *paglilipat ng mga pasahero o kargada.* 6. endorsement of any communication from one office to another. Syn. *indoso, paglilipat.* 7. transferring of blood from one person to another; transfusion.

salindayaw (sa-lin-da-yaw), *n.* a young male deer whose horns are beginning to branch.

salinlahì (sa-lin-la-hì), var. **salinglahì,** *n.* generation; single stage or degree in the succession of natural descent. Syn. *henerasyón.*

salinwikà (sa-lin-wi-kà), var. **salingwikà,** *n.* language translation.

salíng (sa-líng), *n.* a very light touch, as with a finger. Syn. *alíng, saláng, marahang salát o hipò.* 2. an unintentional mention or reference about something bitter or undesirable to someone. Syn. *ungkát, pag-ungkát.*

salingít (sa-li-ngít), n. act of doing something, e.g. passing, escaping, giving, putting, etc. in a stealthy or sneaking manner, esp. when no one is looking.

saling-pusà (sa-ling + pu-sà), var. salimpusà, adj. & n. referring to a playmate esp. one who is still young and whose participation in the game or play is only to please or placate her or him.

salipadpád (sa-li-pad-pád), n. a swift flight or glide, as of a light, flat object blown by a sudden gust of wind or thrown in the air. Cf. salimbáy, sibád.

salí-sálitaan (sa-lí + sá-li-ta-an), n. (Colloq.) common talk of the people; rumor. Syn. tsismis, usap-úsapan.

salisí (sa-li-sí), I. n. 1. arrival or coming of a person at a certain place after someone being sought has just left. 2. acting, happening, or doing something by turns. Syn. halilí, paghahalilí. 3. the manner by which things are arranged alternately. Syn. sálitan, pagkakásalít-salít.
—II. adj.1. taking each other's turn alternately. Syn. halilí, pálitan. 2. placed or arranged alternatingly. Syn. sálitan. 3. occurring by turns; one after the other; alternate.

salisod (sa-li-sod), n. 1. act or manner of pushing something on the floor or ground with or as with the toes. Cf. tisod, pagtisod; talisod, pagtalisod. 2. act or manner of scraping off or dislodging something on a surface by thrusting with the tongue, snout, etc. Syn. sudasod, pagsudasod; ulaod, pag-ulaod.

salisol (sa-li-sol), n. 1. act or manner of cleaning or scraping off dirt, etc., esp. inside something, with or as with the point of a finger wrapped with cotton or cloth. Cf. salisod, sense 2. 2. the thing used for cleaning or scraping off dirt, etc. in this manner, as a small stick with a small ball of cotton at one point.

salít (sa-lít), n. 1. act of making, doing, or placing things alternately or at intervals with other things. 2. things made, done, or placed alternately or at intervals with other things.

salitâ (sa-li-tâ), n. 1. words; vocable. 2.

language; dialect. Syn. wikà, lengguwahe, diyalekto. 3. statement; remark; brief expression. Syn. pangungusap. 4. narration.

sálitan (sá-li-tan), I. adj. done, made, or placed alternately or at intervals with other things.
—II. adv. alternately; at intervals with other things.

salitáng-ugát (sa-li-táng + u-gát), n. (Gram.) root; root word.

salitre (sa-li-tre), n. (Sp.) saltpeter; potassium nitrate.

salít-salít (sa-lít + sa-lít), adj. done, made, or placed alternately or at intervals with other things. Cf. halí-halilí.

saliw (sa-liw), n. 1. act or manner of placing an accompaniment. Also, pagsaliw (pagsalíw). Syn. akompanya, pag-akompanya. 2. musical accompaniment. Syn. akompanyamiyento.

saliwâ (sa-li-wâ), I. adj. 1. reverse; turned upside down or backward. Syn. baliktád, tumbalik, tiwarík (tuwarik). 2. reverse; contrary in position or direction. Syn. salungát, pasalungát. 3. interchanged, as in pairing or using (shoes, slippers, or the like). Syn. talipâ. 4. misleading; wrong. Syn. malî, lisyâ.
—II. n. 1. fact, state, or condition of being reverse or contrary in position or direction. Syn. salungát, pagkasalungát. 2. state or condition of being wrong or misleading. Syn. malî, pagkamalî, kamalián; lisyâ, pagkalisyâ, kalisyaán.

salmo (sal-mo), n. (Sp.) psalm; hymn. Syn. awit, dalít, himno.

salmón (sal-món), n. (Sp.) 1. (Ichth.) salmon (fish). 2. salmon color; yellowish pink or pale red.

salo (sa-lo), n. act of eating with another or together, esp. on the same plate. Also, pagsalo, pagsasalo, pakikisalo.

saló (sa-ló), n. 1. act of catching something with a hand or hands. Syn. sambót, pagsambót. 2. act or manner of supporting something from under, esp. with one's hands. Syn. sapó, pagsapó; sapupo, pagsapupo. 3. an under support or prop. Syn. tukod, talukod. 4. act of taking over something left by another.

salok (sa-lok), *n.* 1. act of fetching water (for home use) from a well or spring. Syn. *igíb, pag-igíb.* 2. act of bailing out water from a well with a pail or bucket. Syn. *timbâ, pagtimbâ.* 3. act of scooping water with or as with a dipper. Syn. *tabô, pagtabô.* 4. dive or swooping flight, as of a kite in the air. Syn. *sirok, pagsirok.* 5. a small hand net for catching butterflies. Syn. *sakyód, panakyod.* 6. a small scoop net for catching small fish. Syn. *sagap, panagap.*

salón (sa-lón), *n.* *(Sp.)* 1. a big hall. Syn. *bulwagan.* 2. dancing hall; ball room. Syn. *bulwagang sayawan.* 3. cabaret. Syn. *kábarét.*

salong (sa-long), *n.* 1. act of putting a bolo, sword, pistol, etc. into a sheath or scabbard; sheathing. Also, *pagsasalong.* Syn. *pagsasakaluban.* 2. surrender of arms or weapons, as by rebels, as a sign of giving up to the authorities. Syn. *pagsusukô ng sandata.* 3. an agreement to end up hostilities. Syn. *pagkakásundô.*

sáloobín (sá-lo-o-bín), *n.* 1. feeling about something. Syn. *damdamin.* 2. something a person usually entertains in his mind. Syn. *paniwalà, akalà.*

salóp (sa-lóp), *n.* 1. a cubical receptacle for measuring grains equal to three liters. 2. act of measuring grains with a *salóp.* Also, *pagsalóp, pagsasalop, pagtakal sa salóp.* 3. a dry measure equivalent to three liters; ganta.

salot (sa-lot), *n.* epidemic; pestilence; plague. Syn. *peste, epidemya.*

salpák (sal-pák), *n.* 1. act or manner of sitting down precipitately on something. Cf. *salampák, pagsalampák.* 2. act of fitting something into a hole carelessly.

salpók (sal-pók), *n.* 1. a bumping or collision against something. Syn. *banggá, pagbanggá; bunggô, pagbunggô.* 2. attack or assault, as of a cock against another. Cf. *pupog, pagpupog.*

salsal (sal-sa), var. **sarsa**, *n.* *(Sp.)* sauce; gravy.

salsál¹ (sal-sal), I. *adj.* dull or blunt at the business end; not pointed. Syn. *pulpól.*
—II. *n.* 1. act of beating the point in order to make dull or blunt. Also, *pagsalsál.* Syn. *pagpulpól.* 2. state or condition of being blunt or dull, said of a point.

salsál² (sal-sál), *n.* masturbation. Also, *pagsasalsál.*

salta (sal-ta; sal-tá), *n.* *(Sp. saltar)* 1. rise or rising, as of water from a supply pipe below. Syn. *akyát, pag-akyát; sampa, pagsampa.* 2. act of going up a stair or ladder. Syn. *panhík, pagpanhík, akyát.* 3. act of climbing or going up a slope. Syn. *ahon, pag-ahon.* 4. *(Colloq.)* entry or coming in, as of money in the form of income. Syn. *datíng o pagdatíng (ng kuwalta).* 5. in printing, a skip or omission. Syn. *salto, pagsalto; palyo, pagpalyo.* 6. landing, as of invading marines. Syn. *sampa, pagsampa; ahon, pag-ahon.*

salubong (sa-lu-bong), *n.* 1. act of meeting a person or thing in the way. Also, *pagsalubong.* Syn. *salunò, pagsalunò sa daratíng.* 2. act of advancing forward to meet (someone) frontally or in an encounter. Syn. *pagharáp sa (kalaban).* 3. a meeting along the way, as of persons or animals. Syn. *pagkikita o pagtatagpô sa daán.* 4. a welcome reception for a new arrival or arrivals. Also, *pasalubong.* 5. act of meeting half-way, as in deciding a question. 6. a person, party, or group assigned to meet or receive a newly-arrived visitor or visitors. 7. *(Colloq.)* gift or present given by someone who has just returned from a trip. Also, *pasalubong.*

salukbít (sa-luk-bít), *n.* act or manner of tucking something at the waistband of a skirt or pants. Syn. *sukbít, pagsusukbít.* 2. anything tucked at the waistband. Syn. *sukbít, bagay na nakasukbít.*

saluksók (sa-luk-sók), I. *n.* 1. act of inserting or tucking something into a slit or small opening. Syn. *suksók, pagsusuksók.* 2. anything inserted or tucked into a slit or small opening. Syn. *suksók, bagay na nakasuksók.*
—II. *adj.* inserted or tucked into a slit or small opening. Syn. *nakasuksók, nakasukbít.*

saludár (sa-lu-dár), *n.* *(Sp.)* act or manner of receiving or entertaining a visitor or guest. Syn. *pagtanggáp at pakikiharáp sa panauhin, estimá, pag-iistimá*.

saludsód (sa-lud-sód), n. 1. act of dislodging or scraping off a thing by pushing it forward with the flat tip or end of something, as with a trowel. 2. act of pushing a thing forward on a surface with or as with the toes.

salumbabà (sa-lum-ba-bà), n. 1. bib. Syn. *babero (bebero, baberon), sapula*. 2. a strap or bandage used to support the chin. 3. the position of a hand or hands supporting one's chin. See **pangangalumbabà**.

salunò (sa-lu-nò), n. 1. act of meeting someone for fear of being lost or for some other purposes. Also, *pagsalunò*. Syn. *salubong, pagsasalubong*. 2. a person who went to meet someone on the way for a certain purpose. Syn. *taong sásalubong sa isáng dáratíng*.

salunga (sa-lu-nga), n. 1. act of going upstream. Syn. *subà, pagsubà*. 2. a going against the wind, current, water, etc. Syn. *salubong, pagsalubong*. 3. act of suffering or enduring hardship or difficulties. Syn. *pagtitiís*. 4. act of contradicting or opposing. Syn. *salungát, pagsalungát; kontra, pagkontra*.

salungát (sa-lu-ngát), I. n. 1. act of opposing or contradicting someone's opinion, proposal, etc. Syn. *tutol, pagtutol; kontra, pagkontra*. 2. being opposed or against someone or something. Syn. *kontra, pagkontra, pagigíng laban o kalaban*. 3. the negative side in a debate or discussion. Syn. *tutol; laban, kalaban; kontra, kakontra*.

—II. adj. 1. opposed to; against; contrary to. Syn. *kontra, laban, tutol*. 2. against or going against the direction of. Syn. *salungá, pasalungá; salubóng, pasalubóng*.

salungkit (sa-lung-kit), n. 1. act of picking thorn stuck in the flesh with or as with the point of a needle or pin. Syn. *sungkít, pagsungkít*. 2. act of picking off food particles left between the teeth, as with a toothpick. 3. a small hook attached at one end of pole for picking fruits. Syn. *kawit, kalawit*.

salungguhit (sa-lung-gu-hit), n. underscore; underline.

salungsóng (sa-lung-sóng), I. n. 1. act of meeting someone along the way for fear of being lost or for some other reasons. Syn. *salubong, pagsalubong; salunò, pagsalunò*. 2. a person or a party sent to meet someone along the way. Syn. *salunò tagasalunò*. 3. act of following or tracing the path or trail towards a certain place or direction. Syn. *taluntòn, pagtaluntòn* 4. a going against the direction of the wind, stream, or current. Syn. *salunga, pagsalunga; salubong, pagsalubong*.

—II. adj. going against the current, wind, etc. Syn. *salungá, pasalungá; salubóng, pasalubóng*.

salupong (sa-lu-pong), n. a meeting, as of two rivers, streets, etc. at a certain place or point. Syn. *tagpô, pagtatagpô*.

salu-salo (sa-lu + sa-lo), var. **salu-salo**, I. n. a dinner party; banquet. Syn. *bangkete, handaan, piging*.

—II. adj. eating together, referring to a group of friends, visitors, etc. Syn. *magkakasalo*.

salutasyón (sa-lu-tas-yón), n. (Sp. *salutacion*) salutation (as part of a letter); greeting. Syn. *batì, pagbatì, pagbibigáy-galang*.

saluyot (sa-lu-yot), var. **saluyut**, n. (Bot.) 1. an erect, branched, annual herb (*Corchorus capsularis* Linn.), the tops of which are eaten as vegetable, esp. by Ilocanos. Syn. *pasaw*. 2. a dish of this vegetable.

saluysóy (sa-luy-sóy), n. 1. act of following or tracing the path or trail going to a certain place or direction. Syn. *taluntón, pagtaluntón*. 2. (Fig.) act of mentioning past favors done to someone to impress upon him that he deserves a better treatment, etc. Syn. *dalirot, pagdalirot*.

salya (sal-ya; -yá), n. lifting and throwing with force; heaving or pushing away forcefully. Cf. *hagis, paghahagis, malakás na tulak o pagtutulak*.

sama (sa-ma), n. 1. act of going with someone to a certain place. Also, *pagsama*. 2. act of accompanying someone to a certain place. Syn. *hatíd, paghahatíd* 3. inclusion of someone, as in a group

Syn. *sali, pagsasali.* 4. a combining or mixing of one thing to another. Syn. *halo, paghahalo; lahók, paglalahók.* 5. act of living with someone or others in the same house or place. Syn. *sunò, pagsunò, pagsusunò.* 6. act of living together as husband and wife. Syn. *pisan, pagpipisan.*

amâ (sa-mâ), *n.* 1. defect; fault. Syn. *depekto, kapintasan.* 2. misfortune; bad luck. Syn. *kawaláng-suwerte, kamalasan.* 3. shamelessness. Syn. *kawaláng-hiyaán, pagkawaláng-hiyâ.* 4. ugliness. Syn. *kapangitan, pagkapangit.* 5. indecency. Syn. *kabastusan.* 6. (with *ng loób*) resentment. Syn. *hinanakít, paghihinanakít, pagdaramdám.*

amaang-loób (sá-ma-ang + lo-ób), *n.* mutual resentment; bad feeling against each other. Syn. *hínanakitan.* Also written *sámaan ng loób.*

amakalawá (sa-ma-ka-la-wá), *var.* **samakalwá,** *adv.* on the following day after tomorrow; on the day after tomorrow. Syn. *pagkaraán ng dalawáng araw.*

amakatwíd (sa-ma-kat-wíd), *conj. & adv.* therefore; consequently; for this or that reason. Syn. *kayâ, anupá't.*

amahán (sa-ma-hán), *n.* 1. society; association; federation. Syn. *kapisanan, pederasyón, katipunan.* 2. business partnership; corporation. Syn. *korporasyón.* 3. joint partnership in an investment. Syn. *sosyohán, bakasán.*

amaíng-palad (sa-ma-íng + pa-lad), *v.* 1. to be unlucky, meet with bad luck. Syn. *malasin.* 2. to fail; meet with failure; be unsuccessful. Syn. *mabigô.*

amantala (sa-man-ta-la), I. *adv.* meanwhile; meantime; in the meantime that. Syn. *habang, miyentrás.*
—II. *conj.* while; during or throughout that time .

amantalá (sa-man-ta-lá), *n.* act of taking advantage, as of an opportunity. Syn. *paggunáguná.*

amâ-ng-loób (sa-mâ + ng + lo-ób), *var.* **samâ-ng-kaloobán,** *n.* resentment; ill-feeling against another; grievance. Syn. *hinanakít, pagdaramdám.*

ama-sama (sa-ma + sa-ma), I. *adv.* 1.

together; all together; in association; in company with each other. Syn. *magkakasama.* 2. at the same time. Syn. *sabáy-sabáy, magkakasabáy.*
—II. *adj.* all mixed together; combined together. Syn. *halú-halò, magkakahalò; lahúk-lahók, magkakalahók.*

samba (sam-ba; -bá), *n.* 1. adoration; worship. Also, *pagsambá.* 2. spiritual belief. Syn. *sampalataya, pagsampalataya, pananampalataya.*

sambahan (sam-ba-han), *n.* place of worship, as the altar or church. Syn. *poók o lugár na dálanginán.* Cf. *simbahan.*

sambahayán (sam-ba-ha-yán), *n.* 1. household; all the persons living in a house. Syn. *mga taong magkakasama sa isáng bahay.* 2. the whole family. Syn. *buóng pamilya o mag-anak.* 3. a group or cluster of houses.

sambalilo (sam-ba-li-lo), *n.* (Sp. *sombrero*) hat. Syn. *sumbrero.*

sambasambá (sam-ba-sam-bá), *n.* (Entom.) praying mantis. Syn. *mandadangkál (mandarangkál).*

sambayanán (sam-ba-ya-náṇ), *n.* 1. the whole town; the whole population of a town. Syn. *buóng bayan, lahát ng tao sa isáng bayan.* 2. the public in general. Syn. *públikó.*

sambeles (sam-be-les), *n.* a single coin of small denomination in use during the early Spanish regime in the Philippines; the term is now obsolete, except in the common expression *walâ ni sambeles,* completely broke or penniless.

sambeses (sam-be-ses), *adv.* once. Syn. *minsán.*

sambilang (sam-bi-lang), *n.* unit; a group or a number or persons or things considered or counted as one.

sambilat (sam-bi-lat), *n.* a sudden violent seizure or snatching of something, causing it to become torn or ripped to pieces, or to become scattered around. Cf. *saklót, daklót.*

sambít (sam-bít), *n.* act of saying or mentioning something in passing. Syn. *banggít, pagbanggít.* See **sambitlâ.**

sambitlâ (sam-bit-lâ), *n.* 1. sudden,

vehement mention or utterance. Syn. *bigláng sabi*, *bulalas*. 2. ejaculation. Syn. *bulalás*.

sambóng (sam-bóng), n. (*Bot.*) a coarse, tall, erect, halfwoody, strongly aromatic herb (*Blumea balsamefera Linn.*), the juice or the powdered leaves of which are used as a vulnerary.

sambót (sam-bót), I. n.1. act or manner of catching something with a hand or hands. Syn. *salò, pagsalò*. 2. recovery of capital in an investment. Syn. *pag-akyát o pagkabawì ng puhunan*. 3. (*Fig.*) act of taking over something left by another. —II. *adj.* 1. caught by the hand, as a flying ball or the like. Syn. *salo, nasalo*. 2. recovered, referring to one's capital investment. Syn. *bawî, nabawì*.

sambulat[1] (sam-bu-lat), n. 1. sudden grabbing or snatching of things, causing them to become scattered all around. Syn. *sambilat, pagsambilat*. Cf. *daklót, pagdaklót; saklót, pagsaklót*. 2. things scattered all around. Syn. *kalat, mga bagay na nakakálat; sabog, mga bagay na nakasabog*.

sambulat[2] (sam-bu-lat), n. sudden bursting or explosion, as of a volcano. Syn. *sabog, pagsabog*.

samíd (sa-míd), n. 1. sudden effort to dislodge something that blocks the throat, causing choke or suffocation. Also, *pagsamíd, pagkasamíd*. 2. the sound caused by choking.

samláng (sam-láng), I. *adj.* with or having dirty habits. Syn. *salaulà, babúy-babóy*. —II. n. a person who has dirty habits. Syn. *taong salaulà*.

samò (sa-mò), n. supplication; earnest request or petition. Syn. *luhog, pamanhík, pakiusap, pakisuyò, hinaíng, panambitan*.

sampa (sam-pa; -pá), n. 1. act of climbing on top of something. Syn. *salta, akyát, panhík*. 2. act or manner of riding an animal. Syn. *sakáy, pagsakáy*. 3. a coming in, as of money as a means of income. Syn. *panhík o akyát (ng kuwarta)*.

sampaka (sam-pa-ka), var. **tsampaka**, n. (*Bot.*) 1. a small tree cultivated for ornamental purposes and for its highly prized flowers which are made into necklaces (*Mechelia champaca Linn.*). 2. the flowers of this ornamental plant.

sampagita (sam-pa-gi-ta), n. (*Bot.*) 1. a spreading or sprawling, smooth shrub (*Nyctanthes sambac Linn.*), commonly cultivated for ornamental purposes and for its white, fragrant flowers which are strung into necklaces. 2. the flowers of this shrub, now adopted as the national flower of the Philippines.

sampal (sam-pal; -pál), n. a slap or blow on the face of someone with the palm of the hand. Cf. *tampál, pagtampál; sampilóng, pagsampilóng*.

sampalataya (sam-pa-la-ta-ya), n. 1. belief or faith in someone. Syn. *paniwalà, paniniwalà; tiwalà, pagtitiwalà*. 2. act of worship in God; adoration. Syn. *samba, pagsamba*.

sampalok (sam-pa-lok), n. (*Bot.*) 1. the tamarind tree (*Tamarindus indica*). 2. the fruit of this tree.

sampatíg (sam-pa-tíg), I. *adj.* monosyllabic. Syn. *iisahing-pantíg*. —II. n. monosyllable; a monosyllabic word.

sampáy (sam-páy), n. 1. act or manner of hanging clothes to dry on a clothesline, fence, etc. Syn. *pagbibilád sa sampayan, pagsasampáy*. 2. the manner clothes are hung on a clothesline, fence, etc. Syn. *pagkakásampáy*. 3. clothes on a clothesline. Syn. *binilád sa sampayan*.

sampáy-bakod (sam-páy + ba-kod), I. n. 1. clothes hung to dry on a fence. Syn. *mga damít na nakabilád sa bakod*. 2. (*Fig.*) a person or persons being looked upon as belonging to the poor class. —II. *adj.* mediocre or commonplace, referring to someone who pretends to be a poet.

sampíd (sam-píd), n. 1. a clinging, or being caught or held on something as a result of falling on it. Syn. *sabit, pagsabit; sangít, pagsangít*. 2. anything left clinging, caught, or held on something as a result of falling on it. Syn. *bagay na násabit o násangít*. 3. a thick or sticky substance left adhering on the mouth of a container after pouring. Syn. *kayat, sapid*.

sampilóng (sam-pi-lóng), n. a slap with the open hand on the region of the nose and mouth. Cf. *sampál, tampál.*

sampón (sam-pón), var. sampún, adv. including; also; likewise; too. Syn. *gayón din, patí.* See sampû².

sampóy (sam-póy), var. tsampóy, n. (Ch.) a kind of dried, salted fruit.

sampu¹ (sam-pu), n. & adj. ten. Syn. *diyés.*

sampû² (sam-pu), adv. (with ng) also; likewise; too; including. Syn. *sampûn.*

sampurado (sam-pu-ra-do), var. tsamporado, n. (Mex. Sp.) rice porridge with chocolate.

samsám (sam-sám), I. n. 1. confiscation or seizure of property, esp. by someone in authority. Syn. *kompiskasyón, pagkompiska; ilít, pag-ilít; embargo, pagembargo.* 2. anything confiscated or seized by an authority.

—II. adj. confiscated or seized, as by an authority.

samulâ (sa-mu-lâ), n. tradition. Syn. *tradisyón, kaugalián, pinagkáugalián.*

samuól (sa-mu-ól), n.1. act of putting something hurriedly into the mouth, as in trying to avoid being seen by someone. Syn. *bigláng subò o pagsusubò.* 2. anything put into the mouth hurriedly.

samut-samot (sa-mut + sa-mot), I. n. a mixture or collection of varied things, usually in small amount or quantity.

—II. adj. composed of a mixture or collection of varied things in small amount or quantity. Cf. *halu-halò, sari-sari.*

samyó (sam-yó), n. 1. act of inhaling something with gusto. Syn. *langháp, paglangháp.* 2. aroma; fragrance; sweet odor. Syn. *bangó, halimuyák.* 3. spicy odor, as of food being cooked. Syn. *masaráp na amóy.*

San (San), adj. (Sp.) a contraction of *Santo,* used before masculine names of saints.

san- (san-), pref. var. of sang-, meaning isá (one), used before roots beginning with d, l, r, s and t, as in: *sandaán* (one hundred), *santaón* (one year), etc.

sana (sa-na), adv. used to express the wish, desire, hope or expectation of the speaker, as in: *Sana'y umulán:* I wish it would rain.

sanay (sa-nay), n. act or manner of practicing to gain proficiency or expertness; rehearsal; training; exercise. Syn. *praktís, pagpapraktís; insayo, pagiinsayo.*

sanáy (sa-náy), adj. 1. trained; well-trained; experienced; well-experienced. Syn. *maykaranasan na, mahusay na.* 2. accustomed or used to, as to a certain climate, place, etc. Syn. *hiratí na.*

sanaysáy (sa-nay-sáy), n. a short composition on a particular subject; essay.

sandakót (san-da-kót), n. & adj. referring to a handful of things, like salt, rice, and other grains.

sandaigdigan (san-da-ig-di-gan), n. the whole world or universe. Syn. *buóng mundo (daigdíg), sangkalupaán, sansinukób, santinakpán.*

sandál (san-dál), n. 1. act or manner of leaning one's back at something. Also, *pagsandál.* 2. the position of a person with his or her back leaning on something. Also, *pagkakásandál.* 3. the position of a thing placed in a reclining or leaning manner against something. Syn. *sandíg, pagkakásandíg.* 4. anything placed in a reclining or leaning position against something. Syn. *bagay na nakasandál o isinandál.* 5. (Fig.) dependence or reliance on someone for support. Syn. *asa, pag-asa.*

sandalì (san-da-lì), I. n. one inch. Syn. *isáng pulgada.*

—II. adj. of one inch length; with or having an inch length. Syn. *may-habang isáng pulgada.*

sandalî (san-da-lî), I. n.1. moment; an instant, as in: *sandalî lamang,* just a moment. 2. second. Syn. *segundo.* 3. minute. Syn. *minuto.*

—II. adj. & adv. for a moment; in a moment; for a very short time.

sandamák (san-da-mák), I. n. (fr. isáng + damák) a width equal to the width of an open palm of the hand. Cf. *sandapal.*

—II. adj. of or having a width equal to the width of an open palm of the hand. Syn. *sinlapad ng palad.*

sandangkál (san-dang-kál), I. n. (fr. isáng + dangkál) a length equal to the measure from the tip of the thumb to the tip of the middle finger when stretched.

—II. *adj.* with or having a length equal to the measure from the tip of the thumb to the tip of the middle finger when stretched.

sandát (san-dát), I. *adj.* 1. full or replete (after eating); fed fully. Syn. *bundát, busóg na busóg.* 2. satiated. Syn. *sawâ, sawâ na.* —II. *n.* fact or state of being full or replete. Also, *kasandatán, pagkasandát.* Syn. *bundát, kabundatán, pagkabundát.*

sandata (san-da-ta), *n.* 1. arms; weapon. Syn. *armás.* 2. any means of defense. Syn. *panananggól, panananggalang.*

sandíg (san-díg), *n.* 1. a leaning or reclining against something. Also, *pagsandíg.* Syn. *sandál, pagsandál.* Cf. *hilig, paghilig.* 2. (*Colloq.*) a depending or relying on someone. Syn. *asa o pag-asa sa ibá.*

sandiwà (san-di-wà), *n.* (fr. *isáng + di-wà*) 1. one soul or spirit, as in: *sambansâ, sandiwà,* one nation, one soul. 2. unity of purpose. Syn. *sanláyunin.* 3. unification. Syn. *kaisahán, pagkakáisá.*

sando (san-do), *n.* (*Jap.*) sleeveless undershirt. Syn. *kamisetang walang manggás.*

sandók (san-dók), *n.* 1. a ladle, usually made of coconut shell shaped like a big spoon and provided with a handle. Cf. *kawot, kutsarón.* 2. the act or manner of using this spoon-like ladle.

sanduguán (san-du-gu-án), *n.* 1. blood compact. Syn. *kasunduang nilagdaán ng dugô.* 2. alliance; union; coalition. Syn. *pagsasanib, pagsasama-sama, koalisyón, kaisahán, pagkakáisá.*

sanhî (san-hî), *n.* cause; reason; motive. Syn. *dahilán.*

sanib (sa-nib), I. *n.* 1. a joining together, as two forces, factions, parties, etc. for a certain purpose. Syn. *pagsasama, pag-iisá, pagpipisan.* 2. act of placing together two things surface to surface or by overlapping each other. Syn. *patong, pagpapatong.* 3. anything used as a support or under-layer for another. Syn. *sapín.* 4. something joined or added to the side of another to increase the size or width of. Syn. *datig.*

—II. *adj.* 1. joined together as one. Syn. *pinag-isá, pinagsama.* 2. placed together surface to surface or by overlapping each other. Syn. *patong, magkapatong, pinagpatong.* 3. joined together edge to edge. Syn. *datig, magkadatig, pinagdatig.*

sanidád (sa-ni-dád), *n.* (*Sp.*) 1. sanitation; cleanliness. Syn. *kalinisan.* 2. healthiness. Syn. *kalusugan.* 3. (by extension) sanitary inspector; health officer. Syn. *sanitaryo.*

sanlaksâ (san-lak-sâ), *n. & adj.* ten thousand. Syn. *sampunlibo.*

sanlibo (san-li-bo), *n. & adj.* one thousand. Syn. *sampundaán.*

sanlibután (san-li-bu-tán), *n.* the whole world or universe. Syn. *sandaigdigan.*

sanlíng (san-líng), *n.* 1. red ocher (ochere); red earth. Syn. *lupang pulá.* 2. yellow gold. Syn. *gintóng diláw.*

sanlinggó (san-ling-gó), I. *n.* one week; one whole week. Syn. *buóng linggó.* —II. *adv. & adj.* for a week; in or during a week's time.

sanô (sa-nô), *adj.* stupid; dull; not intelligent. Syn. *tangá, hangál, gunggóng, estúpidó, gago, ungás.*

sansalà (san-sa-là), *n.* 1. act of prohibiting or preventing a person from doing or undertaking something. Syn. *pigil, pagpigil; sawáy, pagsawáy.* 2. (*Law*) injunction; interdiction; prohibition. Syn. *bawal, pagbabawal.*

sansán (san-sán), I. *n.* 1. act of piling or placing things one over another in an orderly pile. Syn. *salansán, pagsalansán, pagsasalansán; talaksán, pagtatalaksán.* 2. an orderly or neat file, as of papers. Syn. *salansán, patas, talaksán.* —II. *adj.* placed or arranged in an orderly pile. Syn. *salansán, nakasalansán.*

Sánskrito (Sáns-kri-to), *n.* (*Sp. Sánscrito*) Sanskrit; Sanskrit language.

sansé (san-sé), *n.* (*Ch.*) an appellation for the third eldest sister. Cf. *manang, ate.*

sansinukob (san-si-nu-kob), *var.* **sansinukuban,** *n.* the whole world or universe. Syn. *sandaigdig, sandaigdigan.*

santa (san-ta), I. *n.* 1. a female saint. 2. an image or statue of a female saint. 3. (S-) Saint, usually abbreviated "Sta.", used in

referring to or speaking of a female saint, placed before the name, as in: *Sta. Maria.*
—II. *adj.* holy; sacred, as in: *Santa Krus,* Holy Cross. Syn. *banál.*

santakrús-de-mayo (san-ta-krús + de + ma-yo), *n.* 1. religious festival held during the month of May, highlighted by nightly processions participated in by young ladies of a particular place and some invited beauties.

santán (san-tán), *n.* (*Bot.*) 1. a smooth shrub, planted principally for ornamental purposes (*Ixora stricta Roxb.*). 2. the flower of this shrub having pink or reddish corolla.

santaóng-singkád (san-ta-óng + sing-kád), *n. & adv.* one whole year.

santinakpán (san-ti-nak-pán), *n.* the whole world or universe. Syn. *sandaigdíg, buóng mundo.*

santísimó (san-tí-si-mó), *adj.* (*Sp.; Masc.*) most holy; holiest. Syn. *kábanál-banalan, kásantú-santuhan.*

santo (san-to), *n.* (*Sp.*) 1. a male saint. 2. an image or statue of a male saint. 3. (S-) Saint, usually abbreviated "Sto.", as in: *Sto. Domingo.*
—II. *adj.* holy; saint; sacred.

santuwaryo (san-tu-war-yo), *n.* (*Sp. santuario*) 1. sanctuary; sacred place. Syn. *santong lugár, banál na poók, sagradong poók.* 2. the part of the church near the altar. Syn. *presbiteryo.* 3. place of refuge or protection. Syn. *kanlungan, bublihan.* 4. safety; immunity. Syn. *kaligtasan.*

sang- (sang), *pref.* meaning: (a) one, as in: *sang-angaw,* one million; (b) the whole of, as in: *sangkatauhan,* the whole of mankind.

sangá (sa-ngá), *n.* 1. a twig or branch (of a tree). 2. a branch or tributary, as of a river. 3. (*Colloq.*) a separately located unit or branch of an office, business establishment, etc. Syn. *sangáy, sakursál.*

sangab (sa-ngab), *n.* inhalation or breathing in of smoke, air, vapor, etc., esp. through the mouth. Syn. *langap, sanga, langháp.*

sangág (sa-ngág), I. *n.* 1. act of frying rice. 2. act of roasting popcorn, coffee, etc. Also, *pagsasangág.*

—II. *adj.* roasted or toasted. Also, *sínangág.* Cf. *tostado, tinustá.*

sangandaán (sa-ngan-da-án), *n.* place where two or more roads intersect; road crossing; crossroads. Syn. *krus na daán, pinagkrusán, sabáng.*

sang-angaw (sang + a-ngaw), *n. & adj.* one million. Syn. *sangmilyón.*

sangáy (sa-ngáy), *n.* 1. branch, as of an office, company, business, firm, etc. Syn. *sukursál.* 2. branch, as of a society. Syn. *balangay (balangáy).* 3. a person with the same name as another; namesake. Syn. *taong kapangalan, tukayo.*

sang-ayon (sang + a-yon), I. *n.* 1. the affirmative side in a debate; pro. Syn. *pabór, katig.* 2. a vote or votes in favor or for the affirmative; yes votes. Syn. *botong pabór.* 3. act of agreeing with someone or something. Also, *pagsang-ayon.* Syn. *katig, pagkatig.*
—II. *adj.* 1. affirmative; saying yes. Syn. *kumákatig.* 2. in conformity or agreement with; in favor of. Syn. *kasang-ayon, sumásang-ayon, payag, pumápayag.* 3. based from; inconformity with. Syn. *batay o ibinatay sa.*
—III. *adv.* (followed with *sa,* or with *kay* if followed with the name of a person) according to; as stated by.

Sangkakristiyanuhan (Sang-ka-kris-ti-ya-nu-han), *n.* the entire Christendom.

sangkál (sang-kál), I. *n.* hardening of a woman's breast due to too much accumulation of milk. Also, *pagsangkál, kasangkalán.*
—II. *adj.* hardened due to too much accumulation of milk, referring to the breasts of a nursing mother.

sangkalan (sang-ka-lan), *n.* 1. chopping block; butcher's block. Syn. *tadtaran.* 2. (*Fig.*) a mere excuse or pretext. Syn. *dahilán (lamang).*

sangkalangitan (sang-ka-la-ngi-tan), *n.* 1. heavens; firmament. 2. (*Fig.*) state of great happiness.

sangkáp (sang-káp), *n.* 1. material, as in construction work. Syn. *materyal, materyales, kagamitán.* 2. element; component part; spare part. Syn. *bahagi,* *parte*. 3. condiment; ingredient. Syn. *halò*, *lahók*.

sangkapuluan (sang-ka-pu-lu-an), *n.* the whole archipelago.

sangkatauhan(sang-ka-ta-u-han), *n.* the whole of mankind; all the people of the world; all humanity. Syn. *kalahatán ng tao*, *lahát ng tao sa daigdíg*.

sangkatirba (sang-ka-tir-ba), *adj.* very many; numerous. Syn. *nápakarami, maraming-marami, katakut-takot (na dami)*.

sangkatutak (sang-ka-tu-tak), *adj. (Slang)* too many; numerous, usually said of persons or things considered unnecessary or unimportant.

sangko (sang-ko; -kó), *n. (Ch.)* appellation for the third elder brother. Cf. *kuya, manong, kakâ*.

sangkutsá (sang-kut-sá), *n.* (Sp. *sancochar*) act of sauteing or frying in a little fat until partially cooked. Cf. *gisá, paggigisá*.

sangga (sang-ga; -gá), *n.* 1. a parrying or turning aside an attack, blow, etc. Syn. *salág, pagsalág*. 2. a protective shade or covering, as from the heat of the sun, rain, etc. Syn. *takíp, panakíp; tabing, panabing*. 3. a protective bar that prevents entry into a place. Syn. *halang, hadláng*. 4. a temporary divider or partition, as between two small rooms. Syn. *tabil, tabing, tabikè, dingdíng*.

sanggaláng (sang-ga-láng), *n.* 1. act or manner of defending or protecting oneself or someone. Syn. *tanggól, pagtatanggól*. 2. something that defends; means of defense. Syn. *pananggól, pananggaláng, depensa, pandepensa*. 3. an argument in support of or to justify one's stand. Syn. *katwiran*.

sángganó (sáng-ga-nó), I. *n.* (Sp. *zángano*) 1. loafer; a good-for-nothing fellow; idler. Syn. *lakuwatsero, aligandó, bulakbulero*. 2. an insolent or impertinent fellow.

—II. *adj.* insolent; impudent; impertinent. Syn. *bastós, waláng-galang, pusóng*.

sanggî (sang-kî), *n.* a light touch or contact with something in passing. Cf. *sagì, dagil*. Syn. *alíng, pagkáalíng*. 2. an unintentional mention of something that hurts or that reminds someone of something he or she hates. Syn. *saláng, pagkásaláng*.

sanggól (sang-gól), I. *n.*1. infant; babe; a

very young child. Syn. *musmós, paslít*. 2. a baby; a child. Syn. *batà*.

—II. *adj.* very young, said of a child. Syn. *batang-batà, musmós, paslít*.

sanggumay (sang-gu-may), *n. (Bot.)* a species of orchid (*Dendrobium crumenaltum Sw.*) bearing yellow fragrant flowers that last only for one day.

sanggunì (sang-gu-nì), *n.* seeking of advice or counsel from someone; consultation. Syn. *paghingî ng payo, konsulta, pagkonsulta*.

sanghayà (sang-ha-yà), *n. (poetic)* 1. beauty, esp. of a woman. Syn. *gandá, kagandahan; dikít, kariktán*. 2. dignity; honor. Syn. *dangál, karangalan*.

sanghíd (sang-híd), *n.* strong disagreeable smell. Syn. *bahò, masamáng amóy*.

sanghód (sang-hód), *n.* act of smelling something disagreeable. Cf. *langháp, sangháp*.

sanglâ (sang-lâ), *n.* 1. act of pawning something. 2. mortgage of one's property. Also, *pagsasanglâ*. 3. the property thus pawned or mortgaged; something given as a security. Syn. *prenda*.

sangmaliwanag (sang-ma-li-wa-nag), *n. (Fig.)* the world as a creation of God, as in: *May digmaan noón nang isilang siyá sa sangmaliwanag na itó*. There was war when he was born in this world.

sangsáng (sang-sáng), *n.* strong odor, esp. of perfume, that is often disagreeable to others. Cf. *sanghíd*.

sangyutà (sang-yu-tà), *n. & adj.* one hundred thousand. Syn. *sandaanlibo*.

sapà (sa-pà), *n.* a small brook or rivulet that usually dries up during long dry season. Cf. *saog*.

sapák¹ (sa-pák), *adj.* broken off, esp. at the fork, referring to a branch. Syn. *balî, nabalì*.

sapák² (sa-pak), *adj. (Colloq.)* 1. very beautiful. Syn. *nápakaganda*. 2. very good; excellent. Syn. *magalíng, nápakagalíng*.

sápakatan (sá-pa-ka-tan), *n.* conspiracy; connivance. Syn. *sáubawatan, sábuwatan (sabwatan)*.

sapagká't (sa-pag-ká't), *var.* **sapagkát** (fr. *sapagkâ + at*), *conj.* because; due to; for the reason that.

sapal (sa-pal), I. *n.* 1. that which remains after masticating or chewing the *buyo.* Syn. *sapá.* 2. the pulp or residue, as of coconut meat or the like, after squeezing out the juice from it.
—II. *adj.* referring to a person or thing considered inferior or of no match to another. Syn. *waláng-laban* (*colloq.*), *waláng-panalo* (*colloq.*).

sapalà (sa-pa-là), *var.* **sapalâ,** *adv.* as expected, as in: *Sapalá'y gayón ngâ ang nagyari.* As expected that's the way it happened. 2. to greater degree or extent; muck more, as in: *Malakí itó sapalà kaysa riyán.* This is much bigger than that. 3. possibly; perhaps. Syn. *marahil, malamáng.*

sápalarán (sá-pa-la-rán), I. *n.* 1. game of chance; gambling. Syn. *sugál, huwego.* 2. venture; taking risk. Syn. *pagbabakásakalì, pag-aalásuwerte.* 3. a trying. Syn. *pagsubok, pag-ato.*
—II. *adj.* involving risk or dangerous undertaking. Syn. *alasuwerte.*

sa-panahón (sa + pa-na-hón), *adv.* on time; timely, as in: *wala sa-panahón,* not on time (untimely). Also written *sa panahón.*

sapantahà (sa-pan-ta-hà), *n.* 1. an inkling. Syn. *hiwatig, pagkáhiwatig.* 2. suspicion. Syn. *sospetsa, hinalà, paghihinalà.* 3. presumption; supposition. Syn. *akalà, palagáy.* 4. conjecture; guess. Syn. *hulà.*

sapát (sa-pát), I. *adj.* sufficient; adequate; enough. Syn. *kaysa, husto, katamtaman.*
—II. *adv.* sufficiently; adequately; enough; fairly.
—III. *n.* state or condition of being sufficient.

sapateriya (sa-pa-te-ri-ya), *var.* **sapaterya,** *n.* (Sp. *zapateria*) 1. shoe store. Syn. *tindahan ng sapatos.* 2. shoe repair shop; shoemaker's shop. Syn. *páhulmahan o páayusán ng sapatos.* 3. shoe factory. Syn. *pábriká o págawaan ng sapatos.*

sapatilyá (sa-pa-til-yá), *n.* (Sp. *zapatilia*) 1. a woman's slipper with a higher heel than a *tsinelas.* 2. a leather or rubber washer.

sapatos (sa-pa-tos), *n.* (Sp. *zapatos*) a shoe or shoes.

sapaw¹ (sa-paw), *n.* 1. a spreading over, as of vines on a trellis. Syn. *gapang o* *paggapang sa ibabaw.* 2. the first appearance or surfacing of spikes of grains, esp. of rice plants. Syn. *pangingibabaw ng mga uhay.* 3. spikes of grains that have just appeared or surfaced, as on a ricefield.

sapaw² (sa-paw), *n.* 1. act of cooking eggs by putting on the surface of the rice being cooked in a pot. 2. eggs, or the like, that is being cooked in this manner.

sapí (sa-pí), *n.* 1. act of joining an association, and the like, as a member. Syn. *pagsapì, pagmimiyembro, anib, pag-anib.* 2. stock or share in a corporation or business partnership. Syn. *sosyo, bakas.* 3. something attached or nailed to or against another to reinforce or strengthen it. Syn. *patibay, patigás.* 4. (*Fig.*) amulet. Syn. *antíng-antíng.*

sápilitán (sá-pi-li-tán), I. *adj.* 1. compulsory; obligatory. Syn. *obligado, puwersahan.* 2. required. Syn. *kailangan, kinákailangan.*
—II. *adv.* forcibly; by force.

sapín (sa-pín), *n.* 1. anything placed or laid underneath an object as a support or underlayer. 2. protective covering for the hands, as gloves or mitts. Syn. *guwantís.* 3. a thick holder used to protect the hands when lifting or holding hot objects. Syn. *panghawak sa mainit.* 4. (with *sa paá*) general term for all kinds of footwears.

sapín-sapín (sa-pin + sa-pin), I. *adj.* 1. placed or laid in several layers; with or having several layers; made up of many layers. Syn. *susún-susón, patung-patong.*
—II. *n.* a kind of native blancmange made of several layers, usually of different colors.

sapit (sa-pit), *n.* 1. act or time of reaching a certain place or destination; arrival. Syn. *datíng, pagdatíng; abot, pag-abot.* 2. (*Colloq.*) attainment, as of one's ambition. Syn. *tamó, pagtatamó.* 3. (*Colloq.*) result; outcome. Syn. *bunga* (fig.), *resulta, kinálabasán, kináhinatnán.*

saplót (sap-lót), *n.* clothes or clothing (in general, often in a deprecatory sense).

sapó (sa-pó), I. *n.* 1. act of supporting something from under with the palms of the hands. Syn. *sapupo, pagsapupo.* 2. a temporary support to prevent something heavy from collapsing. Syn. *tukod, talukód, saló.*

—II. *adj.* 1. held or supported from under with the palms of the hand. Syn. *sapupo.* 2. supported under with a prop. Syn. *maytukod, may-saló.*

sapók (sa-pók), *n.* a blow or strike with the closed hand, esp. from the upper direction. Cf. *suntók.*

sapól (sa-pól), var. **sapúl,** I. *adj.* 1. from the beginning or start of. Syn. *buhat o mulâ (sa umpisâ).* 2. straight or direct, as in: *sapól na suntók,* direct blow with the fist. Syn. *túwiran.*

—II. *adv.* 1. since; ever since; from the time of. Syn. *mulâ, magmulâ.* 2. at the beginning or start.

sapot (sa-pot), *n.* 1. cobweb; spider web. Syn. *bahay-gagambá.* 2. a single thread of such web or the substance that it is made of. 3. shroud or black covering for a corpse. 4. mantle or veil (*fig.*), as in: *sapot ng dilím,* mantle of darkness. Syn. *lambóng.*

sapula (sa-pu-la), *n.* 1. bib. Syn. *babero.* 2. anything used like a bib.

sapyáw (sap-yáw), I. *n.* 1. superficial cut or wound caused by a glancing stab or bullet. 2. a kind of lift net, attached on two bamboo crosspieces which are mounted on one side of a banca (native boat). 3. breastplate.

—II. *adj.* superficial or skin-deep, referring to cuts or wounds. Syn. *daplís, dumaplís.*

sará (sa-rá), *n.* (Sp. *cerrar*) 1. act of closing (a door, window, etc.); closure. Also, *pagsasará.* Syn. *piníd, pagpipiníd.* 2. the manner a door, window, etc. was closed. Syn. *pagkakásará, pagkakápiníd.* 3. adjournment or closing, as of a meeting or session. Syn. *hintô, paghintô; piníd, pagpipiníd.* 4. anything used to close a passage or to block entry into a place. Syn. *halang, hadláng.*

sarado (sa-ra-do), *adj.* (Sp. *cerrado*) 1. closed; shut; no longer open. Syn. *nakasará; piníd, nakapiníd.* 2. ended; finished. Syn. *tapós o natapos na.*

saragate (sa-ra-ga-te), var. **sargate,** I. *n.* a rascal; rogue; scoundrel. Syn. *taong salbahe*

o *pilyo.*

—II. *adj.* mischievous. Syn. *pilyo, salbahe.*

saranggola (sa-rang-go-la), var. **saringgola,** *n.* a kind of kite. Syn. *guryón, papagayo, buladór.*

saráp (sa-ráp), *n.* 1. agreeable taste (of food); tastiness; deliciousness (of food). Syn. *linamnám, kalinamnamán.* 2. enjoyment or comfort; satisfaction. Syn. *ginhawa, alwán, kasíyahan.*

sarát (sa-rát), *adj.* with or having a flat nose; snub-nosed, referring to a person. Syn. *pangô ang ilóng,; may ilóng na pangô.* 2. snub; short and turned up; pug, said of the nose. Syn. *pangô.*

saray (sa-ray), *n.* 1. strut or strutting, as of a cock. Syn. *girì, paggirì.* 2. shelves or compartments, as of a bookcase. Syn. *andana, pitak.* 3. storey or floor, as of a building. Syn. *palapág, piso.* 4. beehive. Syn. *bahay-pukyutan, panilan, anilan.*

sardinas (sar-di-nas), *n.* (Sp. *sardina*) 1. sardine. 2. canned sardines. 3. (*Colloq.*) fact, state, or condition of being thickly crowded or filled up to full capacity, often said of passenger vehicles.

sarhento (sar-hen-to), *n.* (Sp. *sargento*) sergeant.

sari (sa-ri), *n.* (*Eng.*) the principal outer garment of a Hindu woman; sari or saree.

sarili (sa-ri-li), *pron.* self; oneself; one's ownself.

—II. *adj.* 1. of one's own; one's own; private. 2. for one's own. Syn. *pansarili.*

sarilihin (sa-ri-li-hin), var. **sarilinin,** *v.* 1. to appropriate something for oneself alone. Syn. *angkinín.* 2. to do (a thing) alone by himself (herself). Syn. *gawíng mag-isá.*

saríng (sa-ríng), *n.* 1. a glancing off; deflected impact. Syn. *daplís, pagdaplís.* 2. an indirect or passing remark or reference. See **pasaríng.**

sarí-sarì (sa-rí + sa-rì), *adj.* of various kinds. Syn. *ibá't-ibá.*

sariwà (sa-ri-wà), I. *adj.* 1. fresh; green or newly harvested, as in: *sariwang gulay,* fresh (or green) vegetables. 2. not spoiled, rotten, or stale; fresh, as in: *sariwang isdâ, karne, atbp.,* fresh fish, meat, etc. 3. new; recent, as in: *sariwang balità,* recent news.

4. cool and refreshing; invigorating, as in: *sariwang hangin*, cool and refreshing air. 5. healthy; vigorous, as in: *sariwang katawán*, healthy body.

—II. n.1. fact or state of being fresh, new, recent, etc.; freshness, as in: *Ang ulá'y nagbigáy sariwà sa mga halaman.* The rain gave freshness to plants. Syn. *kasariwaan.* 2. (*Fig.*) a reminding of something long forgotten. Also, *pagsariwà.* Syn. *pagbuhay sa alaala.*

saro (sa-ro), n. (Sp. *jarro*) 1. jug. Syn. *pitsél.* 2. earthenware mug. Syn. *taro.*

saról (sa-ról), var. **tsaról**, I. n. (Sp. *charol*) patent leather.

—II. *adj.* of or made of patent leather.

sarong (sa-rong; -róng), n. (Eng. fr. Malay *sarung*) sarong, principal garment of Malay men and women, consisting of a long strip of cloth and worn like a skirt.

sarsa (sar-sa), var. **salsa**, n. (Sp. *salsa*) sauce; gravy. Cf. *sawsawan.*

sarsaparilya (sar-sa-pa-ril-ya), n. (Sp. *zarzaparilla*) 1. (*Bot.*) sarsaparilla: a tropical American plant. 2. a bottled, carbonated drink flavored with sarsaparilla.

sarsiyado (sar-si-ya-do), n. (*Sp.*) a dish of fish or meat cooked with tomato sauce and other condiments.

sarsuwela (sar-su-we-la), n. (Sp. *zarzuela*) traditional Spanish musical drama. Syn. *dramang musikál.*

sasá (sa-sá), n. (*Bot.*) 1. a species of nipa palm (*Nypa fruticans Wormb*). 2. the leaves of this palm, usually used for thatching. Syn. *pawid.*

sasâ (sa-sâ), *adj.* 1. enjoying great abundance; having more than enough. Syn. *saganà, masaganà.* 2. satiated; supplied with too much. Syn. *sawà, nagsasawà.*

sasabungin (sa-sa-bu-ngin), I. n. gamecock. Syn. *tandáng na panabong.*

—II. *adj.* trained for fighting, referring to a cock.

sasakyán (sa-sak-yán), I. n. 1. vehicle; means of conveyance or transportation. Syn. *behíkuló.* 2. an animal, as a horse, camel, or the like used for riding.

—II. *adj.* for riding; used for riding, as in: *kabayong sasakyán*, horse for riding.

sasál (sa-sál), n. 1. fit, as of coughing. Syn. *sumpóng, atake.* 2. fury, as of a storm. Syn. *hirit, ngitngít* (*fig.*). 3. intensity or aggravation, as of pain, attack of a disease, etc. Syn. *tindí, katindihàn.*

saserdote (sa-ser-do-te), n. (Sp. *sacerdote*) priest; clergyman. Syn. *parè, pagre, pastór, ministro.*

sastre (sas-tre), n. (*Sp.*) tailor. Syn. *mánanahì.*

Satanás (Sa-ta-nás), n. (*Sp.*) Satan. Syn. *diyablo, dimonyo.*

satín (sa-tín), I. n. (*Sp.*) a fabric of silk, nylon, rayon, or the like having a smooth finish, glossy on the face and dull on the back; satin.

—II. *adj.* of or made of satin.

satsát (sat-sát), n. (Sp. *chacharear*) gossip; idle or gossipy talk; babble. Syn. *tsismís, daldál.*

saulado (sa-u-la-do), *adj.* memorized. Syn. *memoryado.*

saulì (sa-u-lì), n. 1. act of returning a thing borrowed or taken. Also, *pagsasaulì.* Syn. *pagbabalík (ng hinirám o kinuha).* 2. a putting back (of something) into its former or normal state or position. Syn. *pagbabalík sa dating kalágayan o puwesto, pagpapanság-ulì.* 3. (*Colloq.*) act of buying a thing from another at the same price it was bought.

saulo (sa-u-lo), n. act of committing something to memory; memorization. Syn. *memorya, pagmimemorya.*

sauna (sa-u-na), *adj.* of the old generation; of the days long gone, as in: *mga tao sauna*, people of the old generation.

sáunahín (sá-u-na-hín), *adj.* old fashioned; out-of-date; antiquated. Syn. *lipás na, walâ na sa moda.*

sawá (sa-wá), (*Zool.*) boa; constrictor; boa constrictor; python. Syn. *manglilingkís.*

sawâ (sa-wâ), *adj.* 1. satiate; surfeited; cloyed; sated. Syn. *suyâ.* 2. having lost interest in. Syn. *walâ nang gana o interés.*

sawatâ (sa-wa-tâ), I. n. 1. act of telling someone to stop or discontinue what he is doing or what he plans to do. Syn.

sawáy, pagsawáy. 2. prevention; putting something to stop. Syn. *pigil, pagpigil, pagpapahintô.* 3. fact, state, or condition of being checked or stopped.
—II. *adj.* checked; stopped from continuing or further developing.

sawáy (sa-wáy), *n.* act of telling someone to stop from doing something or from intending to do something. See **sawatâ.**

sawî (sa-wî), I. *adj.* 1. unfortunate; unlucky. Syn. *waláng-suwerte, kulang-palad; sinamáng-palad, walang-palad, bigô, sinásamà.* 2. killed, as in war, accident, etc. Syn. *namatáy.*
—II. *n.* 1. a person or persons killed (in war, accident, etc.). 2. fact or state of being unfortunate or unlucky.

sáwikaín (sá-wi-ka-ín), *n.* 1. proverb; maxim; adage. Syn. *kasabihán, saláwikaín.* 2. saying; common expression. Syn. *bukambibig, kawikaán.*

sawiíng-palad (sa-wi-íng + pa-lad), *v.* 1. to prostrate or disappoint, as in one's love for a woman. Syn. *biguín.* 2. to be unfortunate; meet with a misfortune. Syn. *mabigô, samaíng-palad.*

sawsáw (saw-sáw), *n.* act of dipping something, esp. food, in sauce and the like to make it more tasty.

saya (sa-ya), *n.* (*Sp.*) skir:. Cf. *palda.*

sayá (sa-yá), *n.* 1. joy; happiness; gladness. Syn. *tuwâ, katuwaán; galák, kagalakan; ligaya, kaligayahan* 2. merriment; festivity; gaiety. Syn. *pagkakatuwá, pagdiriwang.*

sayad (sa-yad), I. *adj.* with the bottom, side, or top touching a surface. Syn. *lapat, nakalapat; diít, nakadiít; daít, nakadaít.*
—II. *n.* fact or state of having the bottom, side, or top touching the surface of another. Also, *pagsayad, pagkakásayad.* 2. the part of a thing that touches the surface of another. Syn. *bahaging nakasayad (nakadaít).* 3. (*Fig.*) state or condition of being broke or penniless.

sayang (sa-yang), I. *n.* 1. a wasting or being wasted. Also, *pagsayang, pagkasayang.* 2. useless spending or consuming. Syn. *aksayá, pag-aksayá, pag-aaksayá.* 3. failure to take advantage, as of an opportunity. Syn. *pagpaparaán sa pagkakátaón.* 4.

gradual loss, decrease, or destruction by decay, etc.
—II. *adj.* wasted; uselessly spent or consumed, as in: *sayang na mga oras,* wasted hours.
—III. *interj.* (S-) What a pity!

sayáw (sa-yáw), *n.* 1. dance; a particular kind of dance, as the tango, waltz, etc. 2. act, manner, or art of dancing. Also, *pagsayáw.*

saynete (say-ne-te), *n.* (*Sp. sainete*) a kind of humorous play; farce. Cf. *komedya, maiklíng dúlang katatawanán.*

sayód (sa-yód), I. *n.* 1. act of doing or going over something thoroughly. 2. act of consuming or using something entirely.
—II. *adj.* 1. done or gone over thoroughly. 2. consumed entirely. Syn. *ubós na lahát.*

sayote (sa-yo-te), *n.* (*Bot.; Mex. chaiote*) a very leafy vine that bears green, somewhat pear-shaped fruit; the young shoots and fruit of this vine which are used as vegetable.

saysáy[1] (say-sáy), *n.* 1. worth or value. Syn. *halagá, kahalágahan.* 2. significance; importance. Syn. *kabuluhán, importánsiyá.*

saysáy[2] (say-say), *n.* 1. act of telling or relating something to someone in detail. Syn. *sabi, pagsasabi; salaysáy, pagsasalaysáy.* 2. the statement or declaration thus made. Syn. *salaysáy, pahayag.*

sayusay (sa-yu-say), *n.* effective use of words in speaking and writing; orderliness and harmony in expression.

sáyusayan (sá-yu-sa-yan), *n.* rhetoric; art or science of using words effectively in speaking and writing.

sebo (se-bo), *n.* 1. tallow; suet; fat. Syn. *tabâ.* 2. shoe polish.

sekreta (se-kre-ta), *n.* (*Sp. secreta*) detective; secret service man; plainclothesman. Syn. *detektib, tiktík.*

sekreto (se-kre-to), *n. & adj.* (*Sp. secreto*) secret. Syn. *lihim.*

seks (seks), *n.* (*Eng.*) 1. either of two divisions, male or female, with reference to their reproductive functions; sex. Syn. *tauhín.* 2. the urge for sexual gratification or reproduction. Syn. *libog, kalibugan.*

seksi (sek-si), *adj.* *(Eng.)* 1. intending to excite sexual desire; sexy. Syn. *pampalibog.* 2. exciting or having urge for sexual gratification. Syn. *malibog.*

sekta (sek-ta), *n.* (Sp. *secta*) sect. Cf. *pangkát.*

seda (se-da), I. *n.* *(Sp.)* 1. silk fiber produced by silkworms. Syn. *sutlâ.* 2. the thread or fabric made from this fiber.
—II. *adj.* of or made of silk. Syn. *sutlâ, yarì sa sutlâ.*

sedatiba (se-da-ti-ba), var. **sedatibo**, I. *n.* (Sp. *sedativa*) sedative; medicine that lessens pain or excitement. Syn. *kalmante, gamot-pampakalmá.*
—II. *adj.* sedative; soothing; calming. Syn. *pampakalmá, kalmante, pampaginhawa, pampalubag.*

sedentaryo (se-den-tar-yo), *adj.* (Sp. *sedentario*) 1. sedentary; used to sitting most of the time. Syn. *paláupô, laging nakaupô.* 2. keeping one seated much of the time, as a secretarial job. Syn. *kailangang gawín nang paupô.* 3. remaining in one locality; not migratory (said of birds). Syn. *permihan sa isang lugár.*

sedisyón (se-dis-yón), *n.* (Sp. *sedicion*) 1. sedition. Syn. *panunulsól laban sa pámahalaán.* 2. *(Rare)* revolt; rebellion. Syn. *pagbabangon, pag-aalsà laban sa pámahalaán.*

seduksiyón (se-duk-si-yón), *n.* (Sp. *seducción*) act of persuading (someone) to do wrong; seduction. Syn. *panunulsól, pang-uupat, pang-hihibò.*

sédulá (sé-du-lá), *n.* (Sp. *cédula*) 1. residence tax; cedula. 2. residence certificate.

segida (se-gi-da), var. **sigida**, I. *adj.* (Sp. *seguida*) one after another; in succession. Syn. *sunúd-sunód, magkakasunód.*
—II. *adv.* at once; immediately. Syn. *agád, kaagád, agád-agád; pagdaka, kapagdaka.*

según (se-gún), var. **sigún**, I. *prep.* *(Sp.)* according to; in accordance with. Syn. *batay o alinsunod sa.*
—II. *adv.* accordingly; correspondingly.

segunda (se-gun-da), I. *adj.* *(Sp.)* 1. second; coming next after the first. Syn. *pangalawá, ikalawá.* 2. *(Music.)* said of a person singing in the second voice.

—II. *n.* 1. the person or thing that is second. 2. *(Mus.)* a person singing the second voice. 3. (S-) a feminine name.

segurado (se-gu-ra-do), var. **sigurado**, *adj.* 1. insured. Syn. *nakasiguro.* 2. sure; certain. Syn. *tiyák, piho, pihado.* 3. safe; secure. Syn. *ligtás (sa panganib), waláng peligró.* –II. *adv.* surely; assuredly; for certain. Syn. *tiyák, piho, pihado, waláng-alinlangan, waláng-duda.*

seguro (se-gu-ro), var. **siguro**, I. *n.* *(Sp.)* 1. insurance. 2. certainty; assurance. Syn. *katíyakan, kasiguruhán.* 3. security; safety. Syn. *kaligtasan.*
—II. *adv.* perhaps; possibly; probably. Syn. *marahil, may-posibilidád.*

selang (se-lang), *n.* 1. fastidiousness; delicacy; sensitive taste for what is considered improper or offensive. Syn. *dilikadesa, kadilikadesahan.* 2. squeamishness; prudery. 3. seriousness; gravity; critical condition or taste. Syn. *lubhâ, kalubhaán.*

selestiyál (se-les-ti-yál), *adj.* (Sp. *celestial*) celestial; heavenly. Syn. *makalangit.*

selos (se-los), *n.* (Sp. *celos*) 1. jealousy; dislike for rivals. Syn. *panibughô, paninibughô.* 2. envy. Syn. *panaghilî, pananaghilì; inggít, kainggitán, pagkainggít.*

selosa (se-lo-Sa), I. *adj.* (Sp. *celosa*) jealous, referring to a woman. Syn. *pánibughuin.*
—II. *n.* a jealous woman. Syn. *babaing pánibughuin.*

seloso (se-lo-so), I. *adj.* (Masc.; Sp. *celoso*) 1. jealous. Syn. *pánibughuin.* 2.. resentfully envious. Syn. *mainggitin, mapanághiliín.* 3. suspicious. Syn. *mapághinalà.*

selyo (sel-yo), *n.* (Sp. *cello*) 1. postage stamp. 2. seal; stamp. Syn. *panaták, pantaták.*

Semana Santa Holy Week.

sementado (se-men-ta-do), *adj.* (Sp. *cementado*) 1. cemented; paved or covered with cement. 2. concrete; made of concrete. Syn. *kongkreto, yarì sa kongkreto.*

sementeryo (se-men-ter-yo), *n.* (Sp. *cementerio*) cemetery. Syn. *kamposanto, libingan.*

semento (se-men-to), *n.* (Sp. *cemento*) 1. cement (for building construction). 2. a cement-like substance, used in dentistry as to fill cavities. Syn. *pastâ.* 3. (Colloq.) the way or manner a thing was cemented. Syn. *pagkakásemento.*

semilya (se-mil-ya), var. **similya,** n. (Sp. *semillia*) 1. seed. Syn. *binhî, binhíng pamunlâ.* Syn. *butóng pananím.* 2. seedling. Syn. *punlâ.* 3. sperm.

senákuló (se-ná-ku-ló), n. (Sp. *senaculo*) Passion play.

senepa (se-ne-pa), var. **sinepa,** n. (Sp. *cenefa*) 1. (in sewing) decorative border or trimming; edging; lining. Cf. *aporo.* 2. (in building construction) board siding; *facia* board.

sensitibo (sen-si-ti-bo), adj. (Sp. *sensitivo*) 1. receiving impressions readily; sensitive. Syn. *madalíng makádamá.* 2. easily affected. Syn. *madalíng talabán.* 3. easily hurt or offended. Syn. *maramdamin, mapágdamdám.*

sensuwál (sen-su-wál), adj. (Eng.: Sp.) 1. bodily rather than with the mind or spirit. Syn. *pangkatawán.* 2. sensual; sensuous; lustful. Syn. *malibog.*

sentauro (sen-ta-u-ro), n. (Sp.; Gr. Myth.), a monster with a man's head, trunk, and arms, and a horse's body and legs; centaur.

sentenaryo (sen-te-nar-yo), I. adj. (Sp. *centenario*) 1. of a period of 100 years; of a century; centenary. Syn. *ikasandaángtaón.*

—II. n. 1. centenary; a century; period of 100 years. 2. centennial; hundredth anniversary. Syn. *ikasandaáng anibersaryo.*

senténsiyá (sen-tén-si-yá), n. (Sp. *centencia*) 1. sentence; decision of a judge or court on the punishment of a criminal. Syn. *hatol, kahatulán.* 2. the punishment itself. Syn. *parusa.*

sentido (sen-ti-do), var. **sintido,** n. (Sp.) 1. sense or meaning, as of an expression. Syn. *diwà, kahulugán.* 2. (Anat.) the temples. Syn. *pilipisan.*

sentimentál (sen-ti-men-tál), adj. (Sp.; Eng.) 1. sentimental; showing tender, gentle, or delicate feeling. Syn. *madamdamin, punô ng damdamin.* 2. showing such feelings in an excessive or exaggerated way. Syn. *malungkót,*

nápakalungkót. 3. of or resulting from sentiment. Syn. *dahil sa damdamin.*

séntimó (sén-ti-mó), n. (Sp. *céntimo*)) hundredth part of a peso; centavo. Syn. *pera.*

sentimyento (sen-tim-yen-to), var. **sentimiyento,** n. (Sp. *sentimiento*) 1. sentiment; mixture of thought and feeling. Syn. *damdamin.* 2. (by ext.) ill will; grudge; sullen feeling against another, esp. to a friend or relatives. Syn. *hinanakit, samâ-ng-loób, pagdaramdám.*

sentro (sen-tro), n. (Sp. *centro*) 1. center; middle. Syn. *gitnâ, kalágitnaan.* 2. hub or center, as of business. Syn. *lundayan, lunduan, pusod* (fig.). 2. (Colloq.) health center.

senyál (sen-yál), var. **sinyál,** n. (Sp. *señal*) 1. sign; omen; portent. Syn. *pangitain, babalâ, tandâ, palátandaan.* 2. signal; sign giving notice. Syn. *senyás, babalâ, hudyát.* 3. indication; token. Syn. *tandâ, palátandaam.*

senyas (sen-yas; -yás), n. (Sp. *señas*) 1. sign given by gesture, etc. signal. Syn. *babalâ, hudyát.* 2. sign; indication. Syn. *tandâ, palatándaan.*

senyór (sen-yór), var. **sinyór,** n. (Sp. *señor*) 1. mister; sir. Syn. *ginoó.* 2. lord; master. Syn. *panginoón, amo.* 3. gentleman. Syn. *ginoó, maginoó, don.*

senyora (sen-yo-ra), var. **sinyora,** n. (Sp. *señora*) 1. madam; madamme. Syn. *ginang* (if married). 2. mistress. Syn. *ama, panginoóng babae.* 3. a term of endearment for one's wife. Syn. *mahál.* 4. a derogatory term for a woman who hates to work. Syn. *donya, prinsesa.*

senyorita (sen-yo-ri-ta), var. **sinyurita,** n. (Sp. *señorita*) 1. miss; a young lady. Syn. *binibini, dalaga, gining.* 2. a term usually used for a daughter of a rich couple. 3. a derogatory term for a young lady who pretends to be rich and doesn't like to work. Syn. *donyeta.*

senyorito (sen-yo-ri-to), var. **sinyurito,** n. (Sp. *señorito*) 1. a young master. Syn. *batang amo o panginoón.* 2. a young man or gentleman. Syn. *binatà, baguntao.* 3. a derogatory term for a young man who doesn't like to work.

separado (se-pe-ra-do), *adj.* (*Sp.*) 1. separate; apart. Syn. *ibá, hiwaláy.* 2. separated; divorced. Syn. *magkahiwaláy, naghiwaláy; diborsiyado, nagdiborsiyó.*

sepilyo (se-pil-yo), var. **sipilyo,** n. (*Sp. cepillo*) 1. brush; specifically, a hairbrush or toothbrush. Syn. *panghisò* (toothbrush). 2. act or manner of brushing the teeth. Syn. *hisò, panghihisò.* 3. act or manner of brushing hair, felt, etc. Also, *pagsipilyo, pagsisipilyo.* 4. act or manner of planing wood or lumber. Syn. *pagkatám, pagkakatám.*

sepulturero (se-pul-tu-re-ro). n. (*Sp.*) gravedigger.

sepya (sep-ya), I. n. (*Sp.; Eng.*) 1. sepia; dark, reddish-brown color. 2. a photographic print in sepia. —II. *adj.* 1. sepia; dark reddish-brown in color. 2. printed in sepia, referring to a photograph.

seradura (se-ra-du-ra), n. (*Sp. cerradura*) lock. Syn. *kandado.*

serbesa (ser-be-sa), n. (*Sp. cerveza*) beer.

serbidór n. (*Sp. servidor*) 1. server or waiter, as in a restaurant. Syn. *weyter, tagapágsilbí.* 2. servant. Syn. *alilà, utusán.* 3. attendant. Syn. *tagapáglingkód.*

serbidora n. (*Sp. servidora*) 1. waitress, as in a restaurant. Syn. *weytres, babaing tagapágsilbí.* 2. maid; house help. Syn. *alilang babae, mutsatsa, utusáng babae.* 3. a woman attendant. Syn. *babaing tagapáglingkod.*

serbisyo[1] (ser-bis-yo), n. (*Sp. servicio*) 1. service; performance of duties. Syn. *paglilingkód.* 2. help; assistance. Syn. *tulong, pagtulong.* 3. use, benefit, or advantage obtained from something. Syn. *pakinabang, kapakinabangán.* 4. any religious ceremony. Syn. *seremonya, kulto.* 5. the act, manner, or quality of providing services to people, as with water, light, etc. 6. act or manner of serving food to customers, as in a restaurant. Syn. *pagsisilbí.*

serbisyo[2] (ser-bis-yo), n. (*Sp. servicio*) an infant's trainer seat provided with a chamber pot.

serenata (se-re-na-ta), n. (*Sp.*) 1. serenade.

Syn. *harana.* 2. concert. Syn. *konsiyerto.*

sereno (se-re-no), n. (*Sp.*) 1. night watchman. Syn. *tanod panggabí, guwardiyá sa gabí.* 2. night dew. Syn. *hamóg sa gabí.* 3. night cold in the open air. Syn. *lamíg ng gabí sa labás.*

sermon (ser-mon; -món), n. (*Sp., Eng.*) 1. sermon, esp. by a priest. 2. moral lecture. Syn. *pangaral, pangangaral.* 3. (*Colloq.*) long scolding, esp. by a parent. Syn. *mahabang pagmumurá.*

sero (se-ro), n. (*Sp. cero*) 1. zero, the symbol or numeral "0"; clipher. 2. nothing; naught.

serye (ser-ye), n. (*Sp. serie*) series; sequence.

seryoso (ser-yo-so), *adj.* (*Hispanized Eng.*) 1. serious; sincere; not joking or trifling. Syn. *tapát, matapát, hindî nagbíbirô.* 2. showing or having deep concern for or about someone or something.

sesante (se-san-te), I. n. (*Sp. cesante*) 1. a dismissed employee. Syn. *kawaníng inalís o naalis sa trabaho.* 2. an unemployed or jobless person. Syn. *taong waláng trabaho (hanapbuhay).* 3. dismissal of an employee for cause. —II. *adj.* 1. dismissed, referring to an employee. 2. jobless; unemployed. Syn. *waláng trabaho (o hanapbuhay).*

sesenta (se-sen-ta), n. *& adj.* (*Sp.*) sixty. Syn. *animnapú.*

setenta (se-ten-ta), n. *& adj.* (*Sp.*) seventy. Syn. *pitumpú.*

si (si), *art.* used in the nominative case as a marker for the name of a person. Cf. *siná.*

sibà (si-bà), n. gluttony; voracity; voraciousness; greed; greediness; avarice; cupidity. Syn. *takaw, katakawan, kasakimán, kakamkamán.*

sibák (si-bák), I. n. act or manner of hewing, chopping or splitting wood (firewood) into big pieces with or as with an ax. Cf. *tipák, sapák, biyák.* —II. *adj.* 1. chopped, hewed, or split (horizontally) into big pieces (s.o. firewood). 2. hacked or wounded critically, as the head or face of a person.

sibád (si-bád), n. sudden start, as of a car; sudden burst of flight, as of a frightened bird. Syn. *bigláng lipád o takbó.*

sibasib (si-ba-sib), *n.* 1. sudden violent attack, as of a fierce animal. Syn. *bigláng lusob o sagpáng.* 2. a sudden reproach or rebuke, as by an angry person.

sibát (si-bát), *n.* 1. lance; spear. 2. harpoon. Syn. *salapáng.* 3. act or manner of striking or piercing someone or something with a spear, lance, or harpoon. Also, *pagsibát.* Syn. *pagsalapáng.* 4. (*Fig.*) sudden flight or escape, as of a wanted criminal. Syn. *sibád, bigláng pagtakas.*

sibi (si-bi), *n.* 1. awning. Syn. *medya-agwa.* 2. a temporary shed attached to the roof or side of a house. Syn. *ambì, pasibi, hulog.* 3. a small addition to a house by extending the roof and providing it with light walling. Syn. *sulambi.*

sibì (si-bì), *n.* act of pouting or pursing the lips, as of a baby about to cry. Syn. *hibî, paghibî.*

síbiká (sí-bi-ká), var. **síbikó,** *adj.* (*Sp. cívica*) civic; pertaining to the public or the citizens. Syn. *pambayan, pangmámamayán.*

sibíl (si-bíl), *adj.* (*Sp. civil*) civil; of a citizen or citizens; having to do with citizenship. Syn. *pangmamamayán, pambayan.*

sibilisado (si-bi-li-sa-do), *adj.* (*Sp. civilizado*) 1. civilized; with or having a high standard of civilization. Syn. *may-kabihasnán.* 2. cultured; educated. Syn. *may-kalinangán, edukado, nag-aral, may-pinag-aralan.*

sibilisasyón (si-bi-li-sas-yón), *n.* (*Sp. civilizacion*) civilization; civilized condition. Syn. *kabihasnán.* 2. culture or ways of living of a race or nation. Syn. *kalinangán, kultura.* 3. act of civilizing. Syn. *pagsibilisá, pagmumulat sa kabihasnán.*

sibóg (si-bóg), *n.* 1. a being driven into confused flight, as of gamblers raided by the police, or of animals in their den. Syn. *bulabog, pagbulabog.* 2. state or condition of confusion, as of persons and animals being driven out of their dens. Also, *pagkasibóg.* Syn. *pagkabulabog, pagkakaguló.*

sibol[1] (si-bol), *n.* healthy growth, as of a young man, Also, *kasibulan.* Syn. *bulas, kabulasan.*

sibol[2] (si-bol), *n.* spring of fresh water. Syn. *bukál, balong, saluysóy.*

siból (si-ból), I. *n.* 1. a sprouting or germination, as of seeds. Syn. *tubò, pagtubò.* 2. a new growth from a bud, rootstock, germinating seed, etc. Syn. *suloy, supang, tubò.* 3. the appearance or eruption, as of rashes on the skin. Syn. *singáw, pagsingáw.* 4. rashes or any eruption on the skin. Syn. *singáw, bukál.* 5. (*Fig.*) natural growth or development, as of love for another. Syn. *bukál, pagbukál (fig.*), *likás na pagtubò o pagkakaroón.* 6. a being natural or inherent to someone or to something. Syn. *pagkákatutubò.*

—II. *adj.* 1. natural; inherent. Syn. *likás, katutubò.* 2. native; indigenous. Syn. *katutubò, taál, lehítimó.*

sibuyas (si-bu-yas), *n.* (*Sp. cebolla*) onion. Syn. *lansuná.*

sikad (si-kad), *n.* 1. act or manner of kicking. Syn. *tadyák, pagtadyák, sipà, pagsipà.* 2. kick; a blow with a foot or feet. Syn. *tadyák, sipà.* 3. a recoiling or springing back, as of a gun after being fired. Cf. *igkás, pag-igkás.* 4. (*Fig.*) a kicking out or forced dismissal, as of an employee.

sikang (si-kang; -káng), *n.* 1. act of opening the mouth of someone forcibly and putting a wedge between the upper and lower jaws to prevent it from closing. 2. a wedge thus placed in the open mouth. Cf. *kalso, sagká.* 3. a crosspiece or a horizontal prop or support between two posts, walls, etc. so as to prevent them from leaning towards each other. Cf. *tukod, talukod.*

sikap (si-kap), *n.* diligence; zeal; ardent devotion to duty; persistent effort. Syn. *sipag, tiyagâ, sigasig, sikháy.*

sikapat (si-ka-pat), var. **saikapat,** *n.* an old monetary denomination equivalent to twelve and a half centavos.

sikat (si-kat), *n.* 1. rise or appearance, as of the sun, moon, stars, etc. Syn. *silang, pagsilang.* 2. rays, as of the sun, etc. Syn. *banaag.* 3. brightness; brilliance; splendor. Syn. *ningníng, luningníng.* 4. (*Fig.*) rise to popularity; a becoming popular. Syn. *pagtanyág.*

sikdo (sik-do; -dó), *n.* 1. sudden, strong throb or palpitation, as of the heart, pulse,

sikháy

etc. Syn. *biglá't malakás na tibók (ng pusò)*, *pulso, atbp*. 2. sudden feeling of fear. Syn. *kabá, kutób*.

sikháy (sik-háy), n. (*Ch.*) assiduity; diligence; perseverance. Syn. *sikap, tiyagâ, sipag, sigasig*.

sikíl (si-kíl), I. n.1. act of causing someone to suffer hardship or inconvenience. Syn. *gipít, paggipít*. 2. oppression, as by an authority or a ruler. Syn. *pag-apí, pang-aapí*.
—II. *adj.* badly treated; oppressed. Syn. *ginígipít, ináapí*.

sikíp (si-kíp), I. n. 1. lack of space; state or condition of being too crowded. Syn. *kakulangán ng lugár, pagkasiksikan*. 2. tightness; a being tight or tight-fitting, as of a dress, pants, shoes, etc. Syn. *kipot, kakiputan, kaliitán sa sukat*.
–II. *adj.* 1. crowded; over crowded. Syn. *siksikan, punúng-punô*. 2. tight; tight-fitting; small in size for. Syn. *mahigpít, makipot*.

sikitíng (si-ki-tíng), var. tsikitíng, I. n. (*Sp. chiquito ?*) a small kid; a little boy or girl; tot. Syn. *bulilít, batang bulilít*.
—II. *adj.* small or tiny, referring esp. to a boy or girl. Syn. *bulilít*.

sikláb (sik-láb), n. 1. a brief, big flash or spark of fire; sudden burst of flame. Syn. *bigláng ningas*. 2. sudden outburst, as of anger, war, etc. Syn. *silakbó*.

siklát (sik-lát), I. n. 1. act or manner of splitting open a thing forcibly. Syn. *hiklát, paghiklát*. 2. the state or condition of being split open forcibly.
—II. *adj.* split open forcibly.

siklo (sik-lo), n. (*Sp. siclo*) cycle. Syn. *ikot, ligid*.

siklón (sik-lón), n. (*Sp. ciclon*) cyclone; hurricane; tornado. Syn. *buhawì, ipuipo*.

siklót (sik-lót), n. 1. a kind of children's game of tossing, catching or picking up pebbles, shells, etc. played in various ways; jack or jackstones. Syn. *sinták*. 2. act of tossing, catching, or picking up something, as in a game of jacks. 3. a tossing or being tossed about, as by waves. 4. (*Fig.*) a being adversely affected, as by misfortune.

sikmát (sik-mát), n.1. a sudden bite or snatch by or as by a dog. Syn. *sibasib, sagpáng, sakmál*. 2. a sudden angry rebuke or censure. Syn. *bulyáw*.

sikmurà (sik-mu-rà), n. 1. stomach. Syn. *tiyán*. 2. (*Fig.*) sense of delicacy; shame. Syn. *kahihiyán, pagkahiyâ*.

siko[1] (si-ko), n. (*Anat.*) the human elbow.

siko[2] (si-ko), var. tsiko, n. (*Bot.*; Sp.-Mex. *chico ?*) 1. sapodilla tree (*Achras Zapota Linn*.). 2. the fleshy, edible fruit of this tree.

sikolóhiyá (si-ko-ló-hi-yá), n. (*Sp. sicología*) psychology. Syn. *aghám-isip; ag-isip*.

sikot (si-kot), n. 1. a beating around the bush. Syn. *ligoy, kaliguyan, pagpapaliguy-ligoy*. 2. a roundabout way.

siksík (sik-sík), I. n. 1. act of forcing oneself into a crowd, small opening, etc. Syn. *gitgít, paggitgít*. 2. act or manner of stuffing or packing a container, etc. tightly. 3. state or condition of being thickly crowded, crammed, packed, or stuffed tightly. Syn. *pagkapunúng-punô*.
–II. *adj.* thickly crowded, crammed, packed, or stuffed tightly. Syn. *punúng-punô*.

sikulate (si-ku-la-te), var. tsokolate, I. n. 1. chocolate, a bar, paste, powder, or syrup made from cacao seeds that had been roasted and ground. 2. a drink made from chocolate. 3. reddish brown; chocolate (color). Syn. *kulay-tsokolate*.
—II. *adj.* 1. made of flavored chocolate. 2. reddish-brown; of chocolate color.

sikwát[1] (sik-wát), n. lifting or prying up the side or edge of something with or as with a lever. Syn. *tikwás, pagtikwás*. 2. a sudden thrust or stab with or as with a knife. Cf. *saksák, iwà, sakyód*.

sikwát[2] (sik-wat), I. n. (*Slang*) 1. act of stealing or pilfering something. Syn. *umít, pag-umit; nakaw, pagnakaw*. 2. anything pilfered or stolen. Syn. *bagay na nakaw, ninakaw, umít, o inumít*.
—II. *adj.* said of anything stolen or pilfered. Syn. *nakaw, ninakaw, umít, inumít*.

sidhî (sid-hî), n. 1. extreme degree; intensity. Syn. *tindí, katindihán*. 2. gravity;

seriousness. Syn. *lubhâ, kalubhaán; lalâ, kalalaán; grabidád, kagrabihan; bigát, kabigatán.*

sigà (si-gà), I. *adj. (Slang)* 1. gallant; dashing. Syn. *magilas.* 2. brave. Syn. *matapang; kinatátakutan.*

—II. *n.* bully; thug.

sigâ (si-gâ), *n.* 1. fire made by burning garbage, weeds, etc. Syn. *siláb.* 2. bonfire.

sigabo (si-ga-bo), *n.* 1. sudden flight of thick dust, smoke, etc. Syn. *silakbó, pagsilakbó; sigalbó, pagsigalbó.* 2. thick cloud of dust, smoke, etc. Syn. *makapál na ulap, alikabók, usok, atbp.* 2. long outburst, as of applause or clapping of hands.

sigalbó (si-gal-bó), *n.* 1. sudden burst, as of fire, smoke, dust, etc. Syn. *silakbó, pagsilakbó.* 2. sudden flight, as of flame, smoke, etc. belched out from a volcano. Syn. *bugá, pagbugá.*

sigalót (si-ga-lót), **sigalutan,** *n.* 1. dispute; quarrel; controversy; conflict. Syn. *away, pag-aaway; kagalít, pagkakagalit, kagalitan; basag-ulo.* 2. misunderstanding; disagreement. Syn. *di-pagkakáunawaán, di-pagkakásundô, hidwaan.* 3. problem; something hard to solve or to entangle. Syn. *súliranín; problema.*

sigáng (si-gáng), var. **sig-ang,** *n.* 1. act of putting a pot or any cooking utensil on a stove or over a fire in the process of cooking. Syn. *salang, pagsasalang, pagllulutô sa kalán.* 2. anything being cooked in a pot or in any cooking utensil on a stove or over a fire.

sigarilyás (si-ga-ril-yás), *n. (Bot.)* winged beans.

sigasig (si-ga-sig), *n.* 1. diligence; assiduity; perseverance. Syn. *tiyagâ, katiyagaán; sipag, kasipagan; sikap, kasikapan.* 2. persistence. Syn. *pagkamapilit, pagpupumilit.*

sigáw[1] (si-gaw), *n.* 1. shout; loud call or cry; outcry. Syn. *hiyáw, paghiyáw, palakat, palahaw.* 2. a loud call for help or succor. Syn. *malakás na tawag o pagpapadaló.* 3. an angry outburst or shout at someone. Syn. *bulyáw, pagbulyáw.*

sigáw[2] (si-gáw), *n.* 1. forced confession. Syn. *tugâ, pagtugâ.* 2. revelation or disclosure,

esp. of a secret. Syn. *pagtatapát, pagsasabi ng katotohanan.*

sigáw-sigawán (si-gáw + si-ga-wán), *v.* to treat someone like a slave by shouting at him very often. Syn. *hiyáw-hiyawán.*

Sige (Si-ge), I. *interj. (Sp. sigue)* 1. Go ahead! Go on! Syn. *Tuloy!* 2. Try it. Syn. *Subukin mo!*

—II. *n. (Colloq.)* departure; leaving. Syn. *alís, pag-alís; yao, pag-yao; lakad, paglakad (colloq.).*

sigíd (si-gíd), *n.* 1. pungency in taste. Syn. *tapang.* 2. smarting pain. Syn. *anták, kirót, hapdí, sakit.* 3. intensity, as of the coldness of weather. Syn. *tindí, sidhí.*

sigida (si-gi-da), I. *adj. (Sp. seguida)* one after another; in succession; in a row, as in *dalawáng sigida,* two in a row. Syn. *sunód, magkasunód.*

—II. *adv.* at once; immediately; without delay or letup. Syn. *agád, kaagád, agád-agád.*

siglá (sig-lá), *n.* 1. enthusiasm; eager interest; fervor; zeal. Syn. *sigasig, interés.* 2. animation; liveliness. Syn. *buhay, sigsá.*

signál (sig-nál), *n. (Eng.)* signal; sign giving notice about something. Syn. *hudyát, babalâ, senyas, senyál.*

signós (sig-nós), *n. (Sp. signo)* 1. sign; mark. Syn. *tandâ, palátandaan.* 2. fate; destiny. Syn. *suwerte, palad, kapalaran.*

sigunda-mano (si-gun-da + ma-no), *adj. (Sp. segunda mano)* used; second-hand. Syn. *lumà, gamít na.*

sigurista (si-gu-ris-ta), *n. (Sp. segurista)* a person who does things when sure of success. Syn. *taong mapaniguro.*

sigwá (sig-wá), *n.* 1. heavy rain. Syn. *malakás na ulán.* 2. tempest; storm; typhoon. Syn. *bagyó, unós.*

sihà (si-hà), *n.* space between two fingers or toes. Syn. *ngingî.*

sihang (si-hang), var. **siháng,** *n. (Osteol.)* maxilla; jawbone. Syn. *pangá.*

sííl (si-íl), I. *n.* 1. act of killing a person or any small animal by squeezing the neck. Syn. *pagpatáy sa pamamagitan ng sakál (pagsakál).* 2. oppression; cruel or unjust treatment, esp. by a ruler. Syn. *pag-apí, pagpapahirap, pagpaparusa.* 3. suppression, as of a people's right.

—II. *adj*. 1. oppressed; maltreated. Syn. *apí*, *ináapí*. 2. suppressed; crushed. Syn. *sugpô*, *pigíl*.

siím (si-ím), var. sim, *n*. (Eng. *zinc* ?) galvanized iron sheet. Syn. *yero*.

siít (si-ít), *n*. 1. a small dry branch or twig. Syn. *malíít na tuyóng sangá*. 2. a thorny bamboo branchlet.

silá (si-lá), *pron*. 1. they, as in: *Pumarito silá*. They came here. 2. them, as in: *anyayahan mo silá*. Invite them.

silà (si-là), *n*. the act of a fierce animal attacking another animal for the purpose of preying on it.

siláb (si-láb), *n*. 1. act of burning things, as garbage, weeds, grasses, etc.; setting things on fire. Syn. *sunog*, *pagsunog*. 2. conflagration; big fire. Syn. *malakíng sunog o pagkasunog*. 3. bonfire. Syn. *sigâ*.

silabá (si-la-bá), *n*. (*Sp*.) syllable. Syn. *pantíg*.

silakbó (si-lak-bó), *n*. 1. sudden flight, as of thick dust, smoke, etc. Syn. *sigalbó*. 2. sudden outburst, as of anger or passion. Syn. *sikláb*, *pagsikláb*. 3. sudden outburst, as of applause. Syn. *sigabo*.

silag (si-lag), *n*. myopia; shortsightedness; nearsightedness. Syn. *pagkakorta-bista*; *kalabuan ng mata sa malayò*.

silág (si-lág), I. *n*. act of looking at something through a translucent object. Syn. *sinág*, *pagsinág*.

—II. *adj*. seen or can be seen through a translucent object. Syn. *sinág*, *nasisinág*; *aninag*, *náaninag*.

silahis (si-la-his), *n*. (Sp. *celaje*) beams or rays of light coming from the sun. Syn. *sinag*. Cf. *sikat*.

silam (si-lam), *n*. pain or irritation in the eye or eyes, due esp. to soap, shampoo, etc. Syn. *hilam*.

silang (si-lang), *n*. rise or rising, as of the moon, sun, stars, and other planets. Syn. *sikat*, *pagsikat*. 2. birth; a being born; nativity. Syn. *paglitáw sa maliwanag*, *pagigíng-tao*, *pagkakatawáng-tao*, *pagsipót sa sangmaliwanag*.

silangan (si-la-ngan), I. *n*. 1. east. 2. (S-) the East; Orient. Syn. *Oryente*.

—II. *adj*. eastern, as in: *silangang dako ng bayan*, eastern part of the town.

—III. *v*. to be born in; be or become the birthplace of (someone).

silá-silá (si-lá + si-lá), *pron*. they themselves; themselves alone as in: *silá-silá lamang ang nakabábatíd niyón*. They themselves alone knew about it.

silát (si-lát), *n*.1. an open space or hole on bamboo flooring; break on the floor. Syn. *butas sa pagitan ng sahíg*. 2. a slipping of a floor or feet into this hole on the floor. Syn. *buslót*, *pagkábuslót*, *pagkápabuslót*.

silo (si-law), *n*. a dazzling or being dazzled, as by the glare of a strong light. Syn. *sulú*, *pagkasulú*. 2. a feeling of inferiority to another. Syn. *panganganino*.

silay (si-lay), *n*. 1. a brief appearance or showing up. Syn. *saglít na paglitáw o pagpapakita*. 2. glimpse; brief, quick look; passing look. Syn. *saglít na tingín o pagtingín*.

silbato (sil-ba-to), *n*. (*Sp*.) 1. whistle (device). Syn. *pito*. 2. the sound made by blowing a whistle or siren. Syn. *sipol*, *huni ng sirena*, *tunóg ng pito*. 3. the act of blowing a whistle or siren. Syn. *hihip o paghihip ng sirena*. 4. a signal, summon, etc. made by sounding a whistle or siren.

silbi (sil-bi; -bí), *n*. (*Sp. servir*) 1. use; function; utility. Syn. *gamit*, *kagamitán*. 2. worth; importance. Syn. *halagá*, *kahalágahan*, *importansiyá*. 3. act or manner of rendering service to (someone). Syn. *paglilingkód*. 4. (in volleyball, tennis, pingpong, etc.) the act, manner, or turn of serving; service. Syn. *serbisyo*, *pagserbisyo*.

sili (si-li), var. sile, *n*. (Sp. *chili*) a general term for various kinds or species of pepper (*Capsicum annuum Linn*.) commonly cultivated for their edible fruit.

silíd[1] (si-líd) *n*. 1. a closet or a small private room, esp. in a native house in the provinces. Cf. *sulambí*. 2. any room in a building. Syn. *kuwarto*.

silíd[2] (si-líd), *n*. act of putting (things) into a container. Syn. *lagáy*, *paglalagáy*.

silíd-aklatan (si-líd + ak-la-tan), *n*. 1. library room. 2. bookbinding room; bindery room. Syn. *silíd-pábalatang-aklát*.

silim (si-lim), n. 1. setting of sun; sunset. Syn. *lubóg o paglubóg ng araw*. 2. the beginning of darkness. Syn. *pagdidilím, pag-aagaw-dilím*.

silindro (si-lin-dro), n. (Sp. *cilindro*) 1. harmonica. 2. (*Mech.*), cylinder.

silip (si-lip), I. n. the act or manner of looking at someone or something through a hole or small opening; peep; peeping. Syn. *tingín o pagtingín sa butas*.
—II. adj. seen or can be seen through a hole or small opening.

siló (si-lò), n. 1. a rope or cord provided with a running loop or noose, used for catching animals; lariat; lasso. 2. the loop or noose at the end of a lariat. 3. act or manner of catching an animal or animals with a lariat. Also, *pagsilò*. 4. (*Fig.*) a trick or stratagem to catch an unsuspecting person or persons; trap or snare. Syn. *patibóng, umang*.

silong¹ (si-long), n. 1. the space or part under a house in a barrio where animals are kept. Syn. *ilalim ng bahay, lupà* (colloq.). 2. ground floor; downstairs; basement. Syn. *babâ, ibabâ, lapág*.

silong² (si-long), n. 1. act of taking shelter, as during a very hot day or during a heavy rain. Also, *pagsilong*. 2. act of taking things to shelter, as clothes, grains, etc. that are being dried under the sun, esp. when it is about to rain. Cf. *ligpít, pagliligpít*.

silóng (si-lóng), I. n. feeling of inferiority or inadequacy in the presence of another; inferiority complex. Syn. *panganganino*.
—II. adj. with or having a feeling of inferiority or inadequacy in the presence of someone. Syn. *nangánganino*.

silsíl (sil-síl), n. 1. act of pressing or pushing the end or point, as of a nose, cigarette, or the like, against a hard surface a hard surface to make it blunted, obtuse, or flattened. Syn. *dildíl, pagdidildíl*. 2. state or condition of being blunted, obtuse, or flattened at the end or point . Syn. *salsál, pagkasalsál; pudpód, pagkapudpód*.

silya (sil-ya; -yá), n. (Sp. *silla*) 1. chair. Cf. *úpuan, taburete, bangkô*. 2. (in traffic) left turn. Syn. *likô sa kaliwâ*.

silyár (sil-yár), n. (Sp. *cellar*) quarry stone. Also, *batóng-silyár*.

silyón (sil-yón), n. (Sp. *sillon*) armchair.

sim (sim), var. **siím**, n. (Eng. *zinc* ?) galvanized iron sheet. Syn.) galvanized iron sheet. Syn. *yero*.

sim- (sim-), pref. var. of sin- and sing-, used before words beginning with *b* and *p*, as in: *simbatà, simbuti, simpait*.

simana (si-ma-na), var. **semana**, n. (Sp.) week. Syn. *linggó*.

simangot (si-ma-ngot), n. scowl; frown or frowning. Syn. *pangungunót ng noó, samâ ng mukhâ*.

simarón (si-ma-rón), adj. (Sp. *cimarrón*) wild; untamed; savage; unruly; uncivilized. Syn. *mailáp; salbahe, mabangís*.

simba (sim-ba; -bá), n. act of attending or hearing Mass (in the church). Also, *pagsimba, pagsisimba*.

simbád (sim-bád), n. 1. a swooping down (of a bird of prey) to seize a victim. Syn. *dagit, pagdagit*. 2. plundering done in a very swift manner. Syn. *mábilisang pagnanakaw o pandarambóng*.

simbahan (sim-ba-han), n. church. Syn. *iglesya, simbahan*. Cf. *kapilya, tuklóng, bisita*.

simbaít (sim-ba-ít), adj. as good or as kind as (another). Also, *kasimbaít*. Cf. *simbuti, kasimbuti*.

simbang-gabí (sim-bang + ga-bí), n. 1. attending or hearing Mass, esp. in the early morning during the week before Christmas Eve. 2. an early morning Mass during the week before Christmas Eve.

simberguwensa (sim-ber-gu-wen-sa), var. **simbergwensa**, adj. (Sp. *sinverguenza*) shameless. Syn. *waláng-hiyâ, bastós*.

simbólikó (sim-bó-li-kó), adj. (Sp. *simbólico*) symbolic; meaningful. Syn. *may-sinaságisag, panagisag, makahalugán*.

simburyo (sim-bur-yo), n. (Sp. *simborrio*) 1. dome. Syn. *bóbedá*. 2. cockpit house. Syn. *sabungán*.

simì (si-mì), n. small particles or refuse of food, esp. fish, left on a plate or on the table after eating. Cf. *mismís, mumo*.

simod (si-mod), n. avariciousness; greed; greediness. Syn. *takaw, katakawan*.

simót

sinaing

simót (si-mót), I. *n.* 1. act of picking up things from the floor or ground. Syn. *pulot, pagpulot.* 2. act of consuming or using all, that is, without living anything. Syn. *ubos, pag-ubos; saíd, pagsaíd.* 3. state or condition of being entirely consumed or used up. Also, *pagkasimót.* Syn. *saíd, pagkasaíd.*

—II. *adj.* entirely consumed or used up; without anything left. Syn. *ubós na lahát, saíd, saíd na saíd, waláng naiwan kahit na kauntî.*

simoy (si-moy), *n.* breeze; soft wind or current of air. Syn. *mahinang hihip ng hangin, paláy-paláy na hangin.*

simpán (sim-pán), *n.* 1. act of saving for the future. Syn. *pagtatago, pagtitipon.* 2. thrift. Syn. *pagtitipíd.* 3. things saved for the future; savings.

simpátiká (sim-pá-ti-ká), *adj.* (Sp. *simpática*) winsome; charming; attractive. Syn. *kabighá-bighanî, kahalí-halina, kaakit-akit, maalindóg.*

simpátikó (sim-pá-ti-kó), *adj.* (Masc.; Sp. *simpático*) good-looking; handsome. See **simpátiká.**

simpatiyá (sim-pa-ti-yá), var. **simpatya,** *n.* (Sp. *simpatía*) 1. sympathy; sharing of another's sorrow or trouble. Syn. *pagdamay, pakikiramay, pakikidalamhatì.* 2. a kindly feeling toward a sufferer. Syn. *awà, pagkaawà; habág, pagkahabág.* 3. friendly feeling toward someone; liking. Syn. *gustó, pagkakagusto, kagustuhan.*

simple (sim-ple), *adj.* (Sp.) 1. simple; easy to do. Syn. *madalî o magaáng gawín.* 2. common; ordinary. Syn. *karaniwan, pangkaraniwan.* 3. easy to understand. Syn. *madalíng unawain.* 4. simple; plain. Syn. *payák.* 5. (Gram.). Syn. *payák.*

simsím (sim-sím), *n.* 1. act of tasting something sweet by sipping slowly or little by little. 2. slow enjoyment of something pleasant.

simulâ (si-mu-lâ), *n.* 1. beginning; start. Syn. *umpisá.* 2. the act or manner of starting something. Also, *pagsisimulâ.* Syn. *umpisá, pag-uumpisá.* 3. origin; source; cause. Syn. *dahilán, sanhî; pinanggalingan, pinag-umpisahán.*

simulain (si-mu-la-in), *n.* 1. motive; purpose; objective; aim. Syn. *layon, láyunin.* 2. principle; personal stand or belief. Syn. *paniwala, paninindigan.*

simunò (si-mu-nò), *n.* 1. (Gram.) subject (of a sentence). 2. cause. Syn. *sanhî, dahilán.* 3. start. Syn. *Simulâ, pinanggalingan, umpisá, pinág-umpisahán.* 4. same as *pasimunò.*

simungot (si-mu-ngot), *n.* sullen look of face due to one's failure to obtain something being asked, as from one's parents. Cf. *Simangot, pagsimangot.*

sin- (sin-), pref. var. of **sim-** and **sing-**, used before words beginning with *d, l, r, s,* and *t,* as in: *sindami, sinlaki, sinrunong, sinsamâ, sintibay,* etc. See **sim-** and **sing-**.

siná (si-ná), *art.* collective plural of *si*.

sinakop (si-na-kop), I. *adj.* 1. occupied, as by an invading army. Syn. *inakupahán.* 2. placed or included in one's jurisdiction. Syn. *sinakláw.*

—II. *v.* past tense of *sakupin,* which see.

sinadyâ (si-nad-yâ), I. *adj.* intentional; done intentionally.

sinag (si-nag), *n.* 1. ray or rays of light, as of the sun, moon, etc. Syn. *banaag.* 2. brightness or lucidity, as of a light. Syn. *liwanag.* 3. halo; symbolic ring or disk of light shown around the head of saints. 4. any representation of a ray or rays, as in a drawing, painting, etc.

sinag-araw (si-nag + a-raw), *n.* 1. sun rays. 2. sunshine.

sinag-buwán (si-nag + bu-wán), *n.* moonlight. Syn. *liwanag-buwán.*

sinagian (si-na-gi-an), I. *adj.* (Fig.) referring to a person who happened to be reminded of something.

—II. *v.* past tense of *sagian,* which see.

sinaglít (si-nag-lít), I. said of a person visited or fetched hurriedly from a certain place. Syn. *sinundóng madalî.*

—II. *v.* past tense of *saglitin.*

sinaing (si-na-ing), I. *n.* 1. rice that is being cooked or boiled over a fire or stove. 2. cooked or boiled rice that is still in the pot. 3. the amount of rice that someone cooked or boiled. 4. (Bats.) fish cooked or boiled in a little water with salt. Syn.

pangát o pinangát.

—II. *adj.* cooked or boiled, referring to rice.

sinalapî (si-na-la-pî), I. *adj.* turned into cash, as by selling. Syn. *Kinuwarta, ipinagbili.*

—II. *v.* past tense of *salapiin.*

sinalbahe (si-nal-ba-he), I. *adj.* 1. abused, referring to a girl or a woman. Syn. *ginahasà.* 2. made a victim of someone's cunning trickery. Syn. *naloko, niloko; nálinláng, nilinláng.*

—II. *v.* past tense of *salbahihin.*

sinamâ (si-na-mâ), I. *adj.* said of someone who met with a bad luck; unlucky. Syn. *minalas.*

—II. *v.* past tense of *samaín.*

sinamantala (si-na-man-ta-la; -lá), I. *adj.* said of a chance, opportunity, or an occasion that someone took advantage of.

—II. *v.* past tense of *samantalahín.*

sinamang-palad (si-na-mang + pa-lad), I. *adj.* said of someone who met with a bad luck; unlucky. Syn. *minalas.*

—II. *v.* past tense of *samaing-palad.*

sinamáy (si-na-máy), *n.* a kind of coarse cloth made from abacca fibers.

sinampaga (si-nam-pa-ga), *n.* (Bot.) 1. a high-class variety of rice plant. 2. the grains of this rice plant.

sinampál (si-nam-pál), I. *adj.* said of someone who was slapped (on the face) by another.

—II. *v.* past tense of *sampalin.*

sinangág (si-na-ngág), I. *n.* 1. fried rice. 2. roasted or toasted corn, coffee, etc.

—II. *adj.* 1. fried, referring esp. to left-over cooked rice. 2. roasted or toasted, as corn or coffee.

sinapupunan (si-na-pu-pu-nan), *n.* 1. (Anat.) in literary usage, womb. Syn. *matrís, bahay-batà.* 2. (Fig.) protection; aegis. Syn. *tangkilik, pangangalagà.*

sinariwà (si-na-ri-wà), I. *adj.* said of something that someone reminded another.

sinásamâ (si-ná-sa-mâ), *adj.* unlucky; unfortunate. Syn. *waláng-suwerte, malas, minamalas.*

sinásamba (si-ná-sam-ba; -bá), *adj.* said of someone who is being adored or worshipped.

sinásanto (si-na-san-to), *adj.* said of someone who is being looked upon with reverence or respect. Syn. *iginágalang, pinagpípitaganan.*

sinásangkalan (si-ná-sang-ka-lan), *adj.* 1. said of something that is being used as a chopping block. Syn. *ginágamit na sangkalan o tadtaran.* 2. said of a person or thing that is being utilized by someone as a reason or cause of his or her whim. Syn. *idinádahilán, ikinákatwiran, kiná-kasangkapan.*

sinásarili (si-ná-sa-ri-li), *adj.* said of something that a person appropriates exclusively for himself. Cf. *ináangkin.*

sinat (si-nat), var. **saynat**, *n.* slight fever. Syn. *bahagyáng lagnat.*

sinauna (si-na-u-na), *adj.* old-fashioned; out-of-date; antiquated.

sinawing-palad (si-na-wing + pa-lad), *adj.* 1. met failure; unsuccessful. Syn. *nabigó.* 2. met death. Syn. *namatáy.*

sinayà (si-na-yà), *n.* 1. first taste or experience of something. Syn. *unáng lasáp o karanasán.* 2. start or beginning of. Syn. *simulâ, umpisá.*

sindák (sin-dák), *n.* sudden fear or fright. Syn. *pagkabiglâ, kabiglaan.*

sindi (sin-di), *n.* (prob. Sp. *encender*) 1. act of lighting a candle, lamp, cigar, cigarette, etc. 2. the light or flame of a candle, lamp, etc. Syn. *ningas.*

sine (si-ne), *n.* (Sp. *cine*) 1. motion picture; cinema; movie. Syn. *pelikulá.* 2. (Colloq.) cinema house.

sinelas (si-ne-las), var. **sinilas, tsinelas**, *n.* (Sp. *chinelas*) slippers.

sinigáng (si-ni-gáng), *n.* a dish of fish or meat seasoned with tomatoes, tamarind, or other sour fruits, with condiments like raddish, kangkong leaves, etc., and provided with broth.

sinigwelas (si-nig-we-las), *n.* (Sp. Mex. *cirihuelas, ciruelas*) 1. a deciduous tree with a stout trunk and thick spreading branches (*Spondias furpurea* Linn.), cultivated for its edible fruit. 2. the fruit of this tree.

sinihán (si-ni-han), var. **sinehán**, *n.* movie

house; cinema house; motion-picture theater.

sining (si-ning), n. art; arts.

sinipì (si-ni-pì), adj. copied or quoted from.

sinisa (si-ni-sa), var. **senisa**, n. (Sp. ceniza) ash; ashes. Syn. abó, titis.

sino (si-no), pron. who, as in: Sino ka? Who are you?

sinók (si-nók), var. **sin-ok**, n. hiccup; hiccough.

sinop (si-nop), n. 1. the act or habit of being orderly and clean; neatness or cleanliness in one's work or habit. Syn. linis o kalinisan sa ugali at gáwain. 2. habit of saving for the future; thrift or thriftiness. Syn. tipíd, katipirán. 3. habit of collecting or gathering things for safekeeping. Syn. pagkamapágtipon.

sinsáy (sin-sáy), I. adj. 1. based on an error; erroneous; wrong; mistaken. Syn. malî; lisyâ. 2. deviating from the right path or direction. Syn. lihís, nalilihís. 3. contrary; against or opposed. Syn. labág, nálalabág; laban, nálalaban.
—II. n. 1. deviation from the right path or direction. Syn. lihís, paglihís. 2. violation, as of rules, regulation, etc. Syn. labág, paglabág. 3.* act of dropping at someone's place for a short time while on one's way to another place. Syn. pagdaáng sandalî.

sinseridád (sin-se-ri-dád), n. (Sp. sinceridad) sincerity; honesty. Syn. katápatan, pagkamatapát.

sinsilyo (sin-sil-yo), I. adj. (Sp. sencillo) 1. simple; plain. Syn. payák, simple. 2. composed of coins in small denominations, referring to someone's money.
—II. n. loose change; coins in small denominations. Syn. baryá, muláy.

sinsín (sin-sín), n. 1. fact, state, or condition of being set, placed, or arranged close together or to each other. Syn. limit, kalimitan, pagkamalimit. 2. density, as of growth of plants.

sinta¹ (sin-ta), I. n. love or affection for the opposite sex. Syn. pag-ibig, pagmamahal. 2. sweetheart; a dear one. Syn. mahál, kasintahan.
—II. adj. dear; beloved. Syn. mahál,

minámahál.

sinta² (sin-ta), n. act of standing on hind legs, as of dogs.

sintabì (sin-ta-bì), n. 1. a word of deference, courteous regard, or respect, esp. in begging excuse.

sinták (sin-ták), n. 1. jackstone, a kind of children's game. Syn. siklót. 2. act of tossing, catching, or picking (pebbles, small shells, or the like), as in playing jackstone. 3. a sudden pull or jerk, as on a fishing line. Syn. sintóg, bigláng haltak. 4. a kind of fishing gear composed of a pole and a line operated from a dugout. Cf. bingwít, pamingwít. 5. sudden throbbing or pulsation, as of the heart. Syn. sikdó.

sintahan (sin-ta-han), n. love affair. Syn. íbigan, pag-iibigan; mahalan, pagmamáhalan.

sintas (sin-tas), n. (Sp. cinta) 1. ribbon. Syn. laso. 2. lace or lacing, as of shoes; shoelace. Syn. talì ng sapatos.

sintesís (sin-te-sís), n. (Sp.) 1. synthesis; putting together of parts or elements to form a whole. 2. a whole made of parts or elements put together. Syn. kabuuán.

sintido (sin-ti-do), n. (Sp. sentido) 1. (Anat.) the temples of the head. Syn. pilipisan. 2. sense; meaning. Syn. diwà, kahulugán. 3. sound state of mind. Syn. isip, kaisipán, pag-iisip, baít.

sintido-komún (+ ko-mún), n. (Sp. sentido comun) common sense.

sintír (sin-tír), n. (Colloq.) resentment. Syn. pagdaramdám, hinanakit, paghihinanakít.

sintô (sin-tô), n. mental unsoundness. Syn. pagkasirá-sirâ, pagkamedyú-medyó.

sintomá (sin-to-má), var. **sintomás**, n. (Sp.) symptom; sign; indication. Syn. tandâ, palátandaan.

sinturera (sin-tu-re-ra), n. (Sp. cinturera) belt supports sewn on the waistline of pants, etc.

sinturón (sin-tu-rón), n. (Sp. cinturon) belt.

sintú-sintô (sin-tú + sin-tô), adj. mentally deranged. Syn. sirá-sirâ (ang'ulo), medyú-medyó.

sinubà (si-nu-bà), I. adj. said of a person who was swindled by someone, or of something obtained by swindling. Also, násubà.

—II. *v.* past tense of *subain.*.

sinuhin (si-nu-hin), *v.* to ask who a person is. Syn. *tanungín kung sino (ang isáng tao).*

sinulid (si-nu-lid), *n.* thread.

sinumán (si-nu-mán), *pron.* 1. whoever. 2. anyone; anybody. Syn. *kahit sino, kulób sino.*

sinumpâ (si-num-pâ), I. *adj.* under a curse; cursed. Also, *isinumpâ.*

—II. *v.* past tense of *sumpain.*

sinungalin (si-nu-nga-lin), *var.* **sinungaling,** I. *adj.* not telling the truth; lying; not truthful. Syn. *bulaán, nagbúbulaán.*

sinupan (si-nu-pan), *n.* 1. archives. Syn. *artsibo.* 2. filing cabinet.

sinusugan (si-nu-su-gan), I. *adj.* amended, said of a proposal, law, etc.

—II. *v.* past tense of susugan.

sing- (sing-), *pref.* used before roots beginning with *k, g, h, m, n, ng, w,* and *y* to denote similarity or likeness to another, as in: *sing-aga, singkahulugán, singhabà,* and the like. See *var. sin-* and *sim-.*

singá (si-ngá), *n.* 1. act of blowing the nose to expel mucus. 2. the mucus expelled in this manner. Syn. *uhog.*

singáp (si-ngáp), *n.* a gasping for breath, as in drowning, asphyxia, exhaustion, etc. Syn. *paghahaból ng hiningá.* Cf. *hingal, hingasing.*

singasing (si-nga-sing), *n.* 1. a puffing with anger, as of an enraged animal pursuing an enemy. 2. the sound produced in this manner. 3. sudden outburst of anger. Cf. *singhál.*

singáw[1] (si-ngáw), *n.* 1. vapor or steam from boiling water. 2. evaporation of vapor from the ground. Syn. *alimuóm.* 3. a leaking or slow loss of air or gas, as from an airtight container.

singaw[2] (si-ngaw), *n.* (*Med.*) 1. a kind of inflammation or sore on corners of lips. 2. skin eruptions, as rashes, prickly heat, and other skin diseases. Syn. *bukál.* 3. (*Bot.*) growth or appearance, as of plants like moss, some lichens, and fungus. 4. (*Bot.*) fungus and other similar plants. 5. (*Colloq.*) original traits, as in: *singaw sa mga kabataan,* original traits among the young generation.

singáw-buhay (si-ngáw + bu-hay), *n.* abiogenesis; spontaneous generation.

singkaban (sing-ka-ban), *n.* 1. a temporary arch built for Easter Sunday celebrations, commemorating the meeting of Jesus and Virgin Mary at Galilee. 2. fancy carved design or inlaid on canes and wood boards. Syn. *labór.*

singkád (sing-kád), I. *adj.* 1. whole; full; complete, as in: *isáng araw na singkád,* one whole day. 2. extreme; excessive, as in: *singkád na kahirapan,* extreme poverty.

—II. *adv.* extremely; exceedingly: as in *singkád hirap,* extremely hard.

—III. *n.* extreme; extreme degree, condition, or state, as in: *singkád ng kahirapan,* extreme degree of poverty.

singkahulugán (sing-ka-hù-lu-gán), I. *n.* synonym. Syn. *sinónimó.*

—II. *adj.* referring to a word of, with, or having the same or similar meaning. Also, *kasingkahulugán.*

singkamás (sing-ka-más), *n.* (*Bot.*) turnip, the plant or its fleshy root, usually eaten raw or used as vegetable.

singkaran (sing-ka-ran), *adv.* completely; fully; to the full extent. Syn. *lúbusan, gánapan, súkdulan.*

singkáw (sing-káw), *n.* 1. the act of hitching or harnessing a beast of burden. 2. harness; a trapping or gear used in hitching a work animal.

singkî (sing-kî), I. *adj.* inexperienced; unskilled; amateurish. Syn. *baguhan, walâ pang karanasán.*

—II. *n.* a beginner; novice; greenhorn.

singkíl (sing-kíl), *n.* a kind of Muslim folk dance using bamboo poles. Cf. *tiniklíng.*

singkit (sing-kit), *adj.* 1. slanting; with or having narrow slits; narrow-slit (s.o. eyes). Cf. *pingkit.* 2. with or having slanting or narrow-slit eyes, referring to a person.

singko (sing-ko), I. *adj.* & *n.* (*Sp. cinco*) five. Syn. *limá.*

—II. *n.* 1. a five centavo piece. 2. five pesos.

singkopá (sing-ko-pá), *n.* (*Gram.*; *Sp. cincopa*) syncope: dropping of sounds or letters from the middle of a word. Syn. *kaltás, pagkakaltás.*

singkuwenta (sing-ku-wen-ta), var. **singkwenta**, I. n. & adj. (Sp. cincuenta) fifty. Syn. limampû.

singgalíng (sing-ga-líng), adj. as good, proficient, skilled, adept, etc. as (another). Syn. singhusay, simbuti.

singgalong (sing-ga-long), n. 1. a small bamboo wine cup. 2. (S-) name of a district and of a street in Manila.

singgandá (sing-gan-dá), adj. as beautiful as (another). Also, kasinggandá.

singgulang (sing-gu-lang), adj. as old as (another). Also, kasinggulang. Syn. singedád, kasing-edád; sintandâ, kasintandâ.

singhál (sing-hál), n. 1. a sudden outburst of anger directed at someone, esp. by one in authority. Syn. burag. 2. a sudden growl or snarl, as of a dog.

singháp (sing-háp), n. gasp or gasping for breath, as of one being drowned or suffocated. Syn. singáp, pagsingáp.

singhót (sing-hót), n. the act or sound of sniffing; sniffle; drawing in air, mucus, vapor, etc. into the nose. Cf. langháp, paglangháp.

singíl (si-ngíl), n. 1. act of collecting payments of debts, back rentals, taxes, etc. Syn. kolekta, pangongolekta. 2. the amount charged, as for taxes, transportation, matriculation, medical fees, etc. Syn. bayad. 3. time or schedule for the collection of debts, payment of rentals, taxes, etc.

singit (si-ngit), n. 1. (Anat.) groin. 2. a slit or crack, as in a wall; chink; fissure. Syn. biták. 3. insertion of something into a slit, crack, etc., or between two close objects. 4. anything inserted or placed into a slit, crack, tight space, etc. Cf. pasak. 5. elbowing or forcing one's way, as into a thick crowd. Syn. siksík, pagsiksík. 6. act of doing something in between some other work being done.

singsing (sing-sing), n. (Ch.) finger ring.

sipà (si-pà), n. 1. kick; act or manner of kicking. Syn. tadyák, sikad. 2. a kind of Pilipino football game using a ball made of rattan splits; the game is played by two persons or in double, the ball being kicked from one player to another over a net, as in volleyball, or even without a net. 3. (Fig.) a kicking out, as of a worker from his place of employment. Syn. sisánte, pagsisante.

sipák (si-pák), I. n. act of splitting, e.g. a short piece of log, by hacking with or as with a hatchet. Syn. sibák, pagsibák. 2. a piece thus made by splitting. Syn. tipák. 3. state or condition of being cracked or split. 4. a big crack or split made by hacking. Syn. malakíng biták, biyák, etc. —II. adj. 1. with or having a big crack or split. 2. cleft or cracked.

sipag (si-pag), n. industry; constant diligence in work; assiduity. Cf. tiyagá, sikap.

sipat (si-pat), n. 1. act or manner of aiming (a gun) carefully at a target, usually with one of the eyes closed. Syn. puntiryá, pagpuntiryá. 2. act or manner of checking alignment, levelness of surface, etc. by looking over with one eye closed. Cf. silip, pagsilip.

siphayò (sip-ha-yò), n. disappointment; frustration; failure. Syn. kabiguán, pagkabigó.

sipì (si-pì), n. 1. act of copying or reproducing a new copy from an original. Syn. kopya, pagkopya. 2. a copy or reproduction from an original. Syn. kopya. 2. act of quoting something, as from a book. Syn. banggít, pagbanggít. 3. an issue or copy, as of a magazine, as in: unang sipì, first issue.

siping (si-ping), I. n. 1. act of sitting, lying, or sleeping close to another or together. Syn. abáy, pag-báy, pag-aabáy; tabí, pagtabí, pagtatabí; sigbáy; pagsigbáy, pagsisigbáy. 2. state or condition of being together in a bed or close together on a seat. 3. state or condition of being closely adjacent to each other. —II. adj. 1. sitting, lying, or sleeping close to another or together. Syn. tabí, magkatabí; sigbáy, magkasigbáy; abáy, magkaabáy. 2. adjoining or adjacent to each other. Syn. datig, magkaratig.

sipit (si-pit), n. 1. tongs. 2. a grasping claw or pinchers of a crab, lobster, and the like. 3. tweezers for plucking hair, handling or picking little objects, etc. Syn. tiyani. 4.

sipol

chopsticks. 5. forceps, esp. one used by a surgeon or dentist. 6. clip: specifically: paper clip, hair clip, or the like. Syn. *ipit*, *pang-ipit*. 7. clothespin or clip. 8. insertion of something, as between two leaves of a book. Syn. *ipit*, *pag-iipit*. 9. act of lifting, pulling, picking, pinching (something) with a pair of tongs, tweezers, pinchers, or the like.

sipol (si-pol) *n.* 1. act or manner of whistling. Also, *pagsipol*. 2. the sound thus produced. 3. the sound of a whistle or siren. Syn. *silbato*, *hihip o tunóg ng sinera o silbato*.

sipón (si-pón), colloq. var. **sip-on**, *n.* 1. cold; catarrh; coryza; acute nasal congestion. 2. the nasal discharge or mucus due to cold. Syn. *uhog*.

sipót (si-pót), *n.* 1. sudden appearance or coming out of someone, as from hiding or long absence. Syn. *litaw*, *paglitaw*, 2. an unexpected arrival or showing up, as of someone long lost or missing. Syn. *biglang dating*, *hindi inaasahang pagdating*.

sipsíp (sip-síp), *n.* 1. an absorbing or being absorbed; absorption. 2. act or manner of sipping or sucking in water or liquid through the mouth. Syn. *hitít*, *paghitít*; *hithít*, *paghithít*; *supsóp*, *pagsupsóp*.

sirà (si-rà), *n.* 1. act of tearing something. Syn. *punit*, *pagpunit*. 2. act of breaking something. Syn. *basag*, *pagbasag*. 3. act of destroying or damaging something. Syn. *gibâ*, *paggibâ*; *wasak*, *pagwasak*. 3. a tear; break; rupture. Syn. *punit*, *basag*, *lamat*. 4. a rotting or being rotten; decay; putrefaction. Syn. *bulók*, *pagkabulók*; *panis*, *pagkapanis*. 5. defamation; calumny; slander or libel. Syn. *pagpapasamá sa kapwà*, *paninirang-puri*. 6. misuse or malversation, as of funds. Syn. *lustáy*, *paglustáy*. 7. mental illness; insanity; lunacy. Syn. *pagkaloko*, *pagkasintú-sintô*, *pagkakuláng-kuláng*. 8. a breaking of or surpassing a record.

sirko (sir-ko), *n.* (Sp. *circo*) 1. circus; acrobatics. 2. act of doing somersaults and other acrobatic feats; tumbling or somersaulting. Also, *pagsisirko*.

sirkulár (sir-ku-lár), I. *n.* (Sp. *circular*)

sisid

circular; circular letter or memorandum. Syn. *palibot-sulat*, *palibot-liham*, *memorandum*.
—II. *adj.* round or shaped like a circle; circular. Syn. *bilóg*, *mabilog*.

sirkulasyón (sir-ku-las-yón), *n.* (Sp. *circulacion*) 1. the flow of blood throughout the body; circulation. Syn. *talaytáy*, *pananalaytáy*; *takbo*, *pagtakbó* (colloq.). 2. a circulating or moving around. Syn. *ikot*, *pag-ikot*. 3. circulation or number of copies sold or sent out, e.g. newspapers, magazines, etc. 4. the sending around of something; propagation. Syn. *pagpapalibot*, *pagpapakalat*, *pagpapalaganap*.

sírkuló (sír-ku-ló), *n.* (Sp. *circulo*) 1. circle. Syn. *bilog*. 2. a complete series, usually ending where it began; cycle. 3. a complete round, as in a circular field. Syn. *ligid*, *ikot*. 4. social group; coterie. Syn. *kalipunan*, *grupo*.

sirkúmperensiyá (sir-kúm-pe-ren-si-yá), *n.* (Sp. *circumferencia*) circumference; distance around. Syn. *kabilugan*, *paligid*.

sirena (si-re-na), *n.* (Sp.) 1. mermaid; siren. Cf. *nimpa*. 2. a warning device, as a foghorn, factory whistle; siren. Syn. *silbato*. 3. sound of a siren or whistle. Syn. *tunóg ng silbato*.

sirit (si-rit), *n.* 1. a hissing sound as that produced when a small amount of water is sprinkled into a hot frying pan. Cf. *sagitsit*. 2. a prolonged hissing sound caused by the jet or stream of water emitted from the tiny hole of a nozzle, leaking pipe, etc.

siruhano (si-ru-ha-no), *n.* (Sp. *cirujano*) surgeon. Syn. *tagatistis*, *máninistis*, *dalubtistis*.

siruhiya (si-ru-hi-ya), *n.* (Sp. *sirugia*) surgery; treatment of diseases, injuries, etc. by operation. Syn. *pag-operá*, *pag-ooperá*; *pagtistis*, *pagtitistís*.

sisi (si-si), *n.* 1. regret; repentance; remorse. Also, *pagsisisi*. 2. sense of loss. Syn. *hinayang*, *panghihinayang*. 3. act of blaming another for a mistake or fault done. Also, *pagsisi*. Cf. *pagpaparatang*.

sisid (si-sid), *n.* 1. act of swimming under water. 2. act of diving into water head first. Syn. *pagbulusok sa tubig*.

sisidlán (si-sid-lan), n. receptacle; container. Syn. *lalagyán*.

sisig (si-sig), n. pickled fruit. Cf. *atsara, buro*.

sisil (si-sil), n. a passionate kiss or kissing. Syn. *maapóy na halik o paghalik*.

sisiw (si-siw), n. chick; a young chicken. Cf. *inakáy*.

sisne (sis-ne), n. (Sp.) 1. (Ornith.) swan. 2. a great poet. Syn. *dakilang makatà*.

siste (sis-te), var. **sisti**, n. (Sp. *chiste*) joke, jest. Syn. *tuksó, panunuksó; birò, pagbibirò*.

sistema (sis-te-ma), n. (Sp.) 1. way of doing something; method; system. Syn. *paraán, pamamaraán, kaparaanán*. 2. regulation. Syn. *palakad, pamamalakad, pátakarán, tuntunin, pánuntunan*.

sistematik (sis-te-ma-tik), adj. (Eng.) systematic; according to a system or method. Syn. *nasa-paraán, nasa-pamamaraán*. 2. orderly in arranging or doing things. Syn. *maparaán, masistema*.

sitá (si-tá), n. act of questioning someone for a suspected violation, as of an ordinance, law, etc.

sitasyón (si-tas-yón), n. (Sp. *citacion*) 1. (Law) citation or summons to appear before the court of law. Syn. *patawag ng húkuman*. 2. a quoting or citing; mention. Syn. *banggít, pagbanggít*. 3. a passage cited; quotation. 4. citation of honor or merit. Syn. *parangál, pagkilala*.

sitaw (si-taw), n. (Bot.) variety of string beans.

sitio (si-ti-o), var. **sityo**, n. (Sp.) place; site; location.

sítsaró (sít-sa-ró), n. (Sp. *chicharo*) a variety of peas.

sitsarón (sit-sa-rón), var. **tsitsarón**, n. (Sp. *chicharron*) crispy fried pork rind; cracklings; cracknels.

sitsirika (sit-si-ri-ka), n. (Sp. *chichirica*) an erect, smooth or slightly hairy branched plant called "pink periwinkle" (*Gatharanthus roseus Linn.*).

sitsít (sit-sít), 1. n. 1. idle talk and rumors about others; gossip or chatter. Syn. *daldál, tsismis, bulúng-bulungan tungkól sa kapwà*. 2. a person fond of gossips or idle talks and rumors; a gossip. Syn. *taong tsismoso (daldalero)*.

—II. adj. fond of gossips or idle talk; gossipy. Syn. *madaldál, mapaghatíd-dumapit, daldalera (-ro)*.

siwalat (si-wa-lat), n. 1. revelation or disclosure, as of a secret, anomaly, etc. Syn. *bunyág, pagbubunyág*. 2. open declaration, as of one's plan, intention, or the like. Syn. *pagpapahayag, paghahayág, pagtatapát*.

siwang (si-wang), 1. n. 1. a small space or opening between two things or objects. Syn. *maliít na puwáng o awáng*. 2. crack; fissure. Syn. *biták*.

—II. adj. with or having a small space or opening between; not well closed. Syn. *awáng, nakaawáng, may-puwáng*.

siwî (si-wî), n. (Anat.) corners of the mouth.

síya (sí-ya), n. (Sp. *silla*) saddle.

siyá¹ (si-yá), pron. (personal, third person, singular, nominative) he; she.

siyá² (si-yá), n. satisfaction; pleasure; contentment. Also, *kasíyahan*. Syn. *lugód, kalúguran*.

siyaho (si-ya-ho), n. (Ch.) a term for one's elder sister's husband. Cf. *bayáw*.

siyám (si-yám), n. & adj. nine. Syn. *nuwebe*.

siyá nawâ, amen; so be it; may it be so. Syn. *amén*.

siyansi (si-yan-si; -sí), n. (Ch.) turner; a kitchen utensil used for turning food that is being fried.

siyangâ (si-ya-ngâ), 1. adv. of course; indeed; yes indeed. Syn. *talagá*.

—II. interj. Really. Syn. *Talagá*. (Distinguished from *siyá ngâ*).

siyá ngâ, he (she) is really the one. Syn. *talagáng siyá*.

siyáp (si-yáp), n. chirp or chirping of chicks or birdlings.

siyasat (si-ya-sat), n. 1. investigation; investigative inquiry. Also, *pagsisiyasat*. Syn. *imbestigasyón, pag-iimbestigá*. 2. examination or inspection. Syn. *surì, pagsusurì*.

siyempre (si-yem-pre), adv. (Sp. *siempre*) of course; naturally; certainly. Syn. *talagá, mangyari pa*.

siyénsiyá (si-yén-si-yá), n. (Sp. *ciencia*) science. Syn. *aghám*.

siyento (si-yen-to), n. & adj. (Sp. *ciento*) one

hundred. Syn. *sandaán, isáng daán.*

siyesta (si-yes-ta), n. (Sp. *siesta*) a brief nap or rest after the noon meal; siesta. Syn. *sandalíng pahingá o pamamahingá pagkapananghalì.*

siyete (si-ye-te), n. & adj. (Sp. *siete*) seven. Syn. *pitó.*

siyók (si-yók), n. (Ch.) 1. sudden cry of a frightened chicken. Syn. *piyák.* 2. the sound produced in an attempt to dislodge something that blocks the throat. Cf. *samíd.*

siyokè (si-yo-kè), var. **siyokì**, I. n. (Ch.) a womanish man; hermaphrodite. Syn. *binabaé, baklá.*

—II. adj. womanish; effeminate.

siyoktóng (si-yok-tóng), n. (Ch. sy hok tong) rice wine. Syn. *alak na bigás.*

siyomay (si-yo-may), var. **siyumay**, n. (Ch.) a kind of Chinese dish of ground meat with condiments and made into small balls and provided with thin broth.

siyopaw (si-yo-paw), n. (Ch.) steamed rice cake with meat and condiments inside. Cf. *putong may-palamán sa loób.*

siyukoy (si-yu-koy), n. (Ch.) merman.

siyudád (si-yu-dád), n. (Sp. *ciudad*) city. Syn. *lungsód (lunsód).*

siyuting (si-yu-ting), n. (Eng.) shooting; filming; act of taking pictures of a scene or scenes in movie or television show-making.

soberanya (so-be-ran-ya), n. (Sp. *soberanía*) 1. sovereignty; supreme power or authority. Syn. *kátaás-taasang kapang-yarihan, dakilang kapangyarihan.* 2. power and authority of a king. Syn. *pagkaharì.*

sobérbiyó (so-bér-bi-yó), adj. (Sp. *soberbio*) obstinate; hard-headed; stubborn. Syn. *matigás ang ulo, sutíl.*

sobra (so-bra), n. & adj. (Sp.) surplus; excess; extra. Syn. *labis, higít.*

sobre (so-bre), n. (Sp.) envelope.

sobrakama (so-bra-ka-ma), n. (Sp. *sobrecama*) bedspread; bedcover; coverlet. Syn. *kubrekama.*

sobresalyente (so-bre-sal-yen-te), adj. (Sp. *sobresaliente*) outstanding; excellent.

sokoro (so-ko-ro), n. (Sp. *socorro*) 1. succor; aid; help. Syn. *tulong, abuloy.* 2. persons

or things that succor. Syn. *daló, saklolo.* 3. act of answering a call for help or succor. Syn. *pagsokoro, pagsaklolo.*

soda (so-da), n. (Eng.) 1. soda; carbonated soft drink; soda water. 2. (Chem.) soda, Syn. *sosa.* 3. sodium carbonate. 4. sodium bicarbonate. 5. sodium oxide.

sol (sol), n. (Sp.) 1. sol, the fifth note of the musical scale. 2. sun. Syn. *araw.*

solár (so-lár), var. **sulár**, n. (Sp.) 1. lot; plot of ground. Syn. *lote.* 2. yard. Cf. *looban, bakuran.*

solemnidád (so-lem-ni-dád), n. (Sp.) 1. solemnity; impressiveness. Syn. *dingal, karingalán, kadakilaan.* 2. sincerity; seriousness. Syn. *katimtimán.*

soleras (so-le-ras), var. **suleras**, n. (Sp. *solera*) joist. Syn. *pámakuán ng sahíg o kisamé.*

solidaridád (so-li-da-ri-dád), n. (Sp.) solidarity; unity. Syn. *pagkakaisá, kabuuán.*

solitaryo (so-li-tar-yo), I. n. (Sp. *solitario*) 1. a single gem, esp. a diamond, set by itself in a ring solitaire. Also, *brilyanteng solitaryo.* 2. a kind of card game played by one person; solitaire. 3. solitary; solitary confinement.

—II. adj. 1. alone; only; single. Syn. *solo, íisá, nag-íisá, tangì, bugtóng.* 2. remote; distant. Syn. *malayò, liblíb.* 3. lonely; solitary. Syn. *malungkót, mapangláw.*

solo (so-lo), I. adj. (Sp.) 1. alone. Syn. *isá, íisá, nag-íisá.* 2. single; lone; only; one; solo; sole. Syn. *tangì, kaisá-isá, bugtóng.* 3. made, done, or performed by one person; solo.

—II. n. (Mus.) solo, a piece of music for one voice or instrument.

Solomón (So-lo-món), n. 1. a masculine name. 2. (Bib.) Solomon, the king of Israel. 3. (Fig.) a very wise man; sage.

solpeo (sol-pe-o), n. (Mus.; Sp. *solfeo*) 1. solfa; notes that represent the tones of a scale, regardless of its key. Syn. *nota sa músiká.* 2. solfeggio; solmization.

soltera (sol-te-ra), var. **sultera**, I. adj. (Sp.) 1. unmarried, referring to a woman. Syn. *dalaga.* 2. said of an old maid.

—II. n. spinster; old woman. Syn. *matandáng dalaga.*

soltero (sol-te-ro), var. **sultero**, I. *adj.* unmarried, referring to a man. Syn. *binatà, waláng-asawa*.

—II. *n.* an adult unmarried man; bachelor. Syn. *matandáng binatà*.

solusyón (so-lus-yón), *n.* (Sp. *solucíon*) 1. act, method, or process of solving a problem. 2. explanation or answer to a problem, mystery, etc.; solution; answer. Syn. *sagót, kasagutan, paliwanag*. 3. a liquid mixture formed by dissolving. Syn. *timplada*.

sombra (som-bra), *n.* (*Sp.*) 1. shade or shadow (in painting and drawing). 2. (*Colloq.*) adverse criticism or censure. Syn. *pintás, pamimintás*. 3. (*Colloq.*) banter; joke. Syn. *birò, pagbibirô; kantiyáw, pangangantiyáw; tuksó, panunuksó*.

sombrero (som-bre-ro), var. **sumbrero**, *n.* (*Sp.*) hat. Syn. *sambalilo*.

sona (so-na), *n.* (Sp. *zona*) 1. zone; section or district in a city, restricted by law for a certain purpose. 2. the division of a city, etc. into zones. 3. confinement of persons within a certain zone or district, as during war. Also, *pagsona, pagsosona*.

sonambulismo (so-nam-bu-lis-mo), *n.* (*Sp.*) somnambulism; sleep-walking. Syn. *paglalakád nang tulóg*.

sonda (son-da), var. **sunda**, *n.* (*Sp.*) 1. (*Surg.*) a probing instrument. 2. act of examining internal cavities with a probing instrument. Also, *pagsosonda*. 3. (*Med.*) catheter. 4. insertion of a catheter into the body cavity for the purpose of drawing liquid. 5. sounder; sounding instrument. Syn. *pang-arók*.

sopá (so-pá), *n.* (Sp. *sofá*) sofa.

sopas (so-pas), *n.* (*Sp.*) soup. Cf. *sabáw*.

sopera (so-pe-ra), *n.* (*Sp.*) soup bowl; tureen (a large, deep dish for serving soup).

sopero (so-pe-ro), *n.* (*Sp.*) soup plate. Syn. *plato o pinggáng pansopas*.

soplado (so-pla-do), var. **suplado**, *adj.* (*Sp.*) conceited; vain; having too high regard of oneself. Syn. *palalò, mapagmataás, hambóg*.

sor (sor), *n.* (*Sp.; Eccles.*) sister. Cf. *madre*.

sora (so-ra), *n.* (Sp. *zorra*) female fox; vixen.

See *soro*.

soro (so-ro), *n.* (Sp. *zorro*) fox; male fox.

sosa (so-sa), *n.* (*Sp.*) soda; sodium.

sosyál (sos-yál), *adj.* (Sp. *social*) 1. social; concerned with the social group. Syn. *panlipunán; ng, sa, o ukol sa lipunán*. 2. sociable; companionable. Syn. *mapágkapwà, mapâgkaibigan, magiliw, mabuting makisama*.

sosyedád (sos-ye-dád), *n.* (Sp. *sociedad*) society. Syn. *lipunán*.

sosyo (sos-yo), I. *n.* (Sp. *socio*) 1. share in a partnership or stock corporation. Syn. *sapì, saping-puhunan, bakas*. 2. state or condition of being partners in business or in a gambling investment. Syn. *pagkamágkabakas, pagkamágkasosyo*.

—II. *adj.* joined together in a business partnership, referring to share or stock holders. Syn. *bakas, magkabakas*.

sota (so-ta), *n.* (*Sp.*) 1. (in cards) jack. 2. stable boy.

sotana (so-ta-na), var. **sutana**, *n.* (*Sp.*) cassock; habit. Syn. *ábitó*.

sótanghón (só-tang-hón), var. **sútanghón, suwátanghón**, *n.* (*Ch.*) 1. a kind of small, white, crinkly rice noodle, opaque when raw but translucent when cooked. 2. a dish of this noodle.

soy (soy), *n.* (*Jap.*) 1. soy; a dark, salty sauce made from soybeans. 2. the soybean plant or its seeds.

su! (su), *interj.* an exclamation used in scaring away chickens and other animals; Shoo! Syn. *Hu!*

suang (su-ang), *n.* (*Ch.*) an earring with a pendant. Syn. *hikaw na may-palawít*.

subá (su-bá), *n.* 1. act of extinguishing or putting out (a small fire, firebrand, embers, and the like) by pouring or dousing with water. 2. sometimes used as a variant of *subó*, sense 2.

subà (su-bà), *n.* act of swindling someone, esp. by not paying one's debt.

subalì (su-ba-lì), *conj.* (usually followed by a coma) 1. but; on the contrary. Syn. *ngunì, nguni't (ngunit)*. 2. however; yet; still. Syn. *gayón man, gayón pa man*.

subali't (su-ba-li't), var. **subalit**, *conj.* (fr. *subalì* + *at*) 1. but. Syn. *ngunì, nguni't*,

ngunit. 2. however. Syn. *gayón man.*
(Note: The use of *subalit*, due to modern
tendency, has become more common).

subasob (su-ba-sob), n. 1. a violent fall or
falling with the face first. Also,
pagkásubsob, pagkápasubasob. 2. the
manner or position of a person after
falling down with the face under. Also,
pagkakásubasob. 3. (*Fig.*) an unexpected
defeat, esp. of a champion. Syn. *di-
inaasahang pagkatalo.*

subasta (su-bas-ta), n. (*Sp.*) auction; auction
sale. Cf. *almoneda.*

subaybáy (su-bay-báy), n. 1. act of following
a person or thing, as by a guard; a
convoying or escorting. Syn. *pagsunúd-
sunod ng tanod sa binábantayán.* 2. a secret
or watchful observation of someone; a
spying on (someone). Syn. *lihim na
pagmamasíd.* 3. a person acting or
appointed as a guard, convoy, or escort.
Cf. *tanod, guwardiyá.* 4. a following up, as
of events, serialized articles in a
newspaper, etc.

subdibisyon (sub-di-bis-yon), n. (*Eng.*)
subdivision; a large tract of land
subdivided into lots or into small parcels
for sale.

subenír (su-be-nír; sú-be-nír), n. (*Eng.*) 1.
a remembrance; souvenir. Cf. *alaala.* 2.
something kept as a remembrance. Syn.
tagapágpaalaala, tagapágpagunitâ.

suberbiyó (su-ber-bi-yó), var. **soberbiyó**, adj.
(*Masc.*; Sp. *soberbio*) obstinate,
hardheaded; stubborn. Syn. *matigás ang
ulo, sutíl.*

subérsiyón (su-bér-si-yón), var. **subersyón**,
n. (Sp. *subversión*) subversion; overthrow.
Syn. *pagbagsák.*

subida¹ (su-bi-da), n. (*Sp.*) 1. ascent, as of a
vehicle, on an upward slope. Syn. *ahon,
pag-ahon; akyát, pag-akyát.* 2. a rising or
ascending slope, as of a street or
thoroughfare. Syn. *akyát, ahon.*

subida² (su-bi-da), n. (*Sp.*) 1. a doctor's
professional call and treatment of a
patient. Syn. *dalaw o bisita ng doktór
(manggagamot).* 2. the fee charged by a
doctor on such a call.

sublî (sub-lî), n. a kind of folk dance popular

in the Tagalog provinces, esp. during and
immediately after the Spanish regime. Cf.
pandanggo.

subó (su-bó), n. 1. seething, as of boiling
water or liquid. Syn. *sulák, pagsulák.* 2.
tempering of metal by immersing in water
after having been made red hot by
heating. Also, *pagsusubó.* 3. violent
agitation or sudden fit of anger. Syn.
silakbó (ng galit).

subò (su-bò), n. 1. act or manner of putting
food into the mouth, esp. with a hand or
fingers. 2. the amount of food taken into
the mouth with or as with the hand at a
time. Cf. *sakól.* 3. reluctant involvement
into an affair or act of responsibility. Also,
pagsubò, pagkásubò. Syn. *lulóng, paglulóng,
pagkápalulóng.*

subok (su-bok), n. 1. secret observation or
watching; a spying on someone or
something. Syn. *lihim na pagbabantáy o
pagmamanmán.* 2. act of trying on shoes,
pants; tasting or sampling the taste of.
Syn. *tikím, pagtikím.* 4. trial or testing. Syn.
ato, pag-aton; purba, pagpurba.

subók (su-bók), adj. (usually with *na*)
already tried, tested, or proven.

subsístensiyá (sub-sís-ten-si-yá), n. (Sp.
subsistencia) 1. subsistence; means of
keeping alive. Syn. *pantawíd-buhay, pang-
agaw-buhay, ang ikinabúbuhay.* 2.
existence. Syn. *pananatili, pamamalagì,
pag-iral.* 3. living; being alive. Syn.
pagkabuháy.

subsób (sub-sób), I. n. 1. act of lowering or
drooping the face on the surface of
something. Also, *pagsubsób.* 2. the
downward position of the face on the
surface of something. Also,
pagkakásubsób. 3. (*Fig.*) defeat suffered
from an opponent. Syn. *talo, pagkatalo.*
—II. adj. 1. with or having the face fallen
on the surface of something. Also,
nakasubsób. 2. (*Fig.*) defeated. Syn. *talo,
natalo.*

substansiyá (subs-tan-si-yá), n. (Sp.
substancia) substance; matter; material.
Syn. *sangkáp, materyál.*

substantibo (subs-tan-ti-bo), I. n. (Sp.
substantivo) 1. (*Gram.*) noun. Syn.

pangngalan. 2. name of a person or thing.
Syn. *pangalan*.

—II. *adj*. substantive; real. Syn. *tunay*,
totoó.

subukan (su-bu-kan), *v*. 1. to spy on
someone; observe or watch someone
secretly. Syn. *bantayán nang palihím*. 2. to
taste; sample the taste of. Syn. *tikmán*. 3.
to try out; make a try. Syn. *atuhan*,
purbahán. 4. to try something for
appropriate size. Syn. *isukat*.

subukin (su-bu-kin), *v*. 1. to put to a test;
give someone a trial. Syn. *purbahán*. 2. to
make a try. Syn. *umato*, *pumurba*. 3. to
watch secretly what one is doing. Syn.
lihim na manmanán.

subyáng (sub-yáng), *n*. a sliver or splinter
left under the skin or flesh, esp. of the
feet. Cf. *salubsób*.

suka (su-ka), *n*. 1. vomit; act of vomiting.
2. the matter vomited. Cf. *lungád*.

sukà (su-kà), *n*. vinegar. 2. any sour fruit, as
tamarind, tomatoes, green mangoes, etc.
used for seasoning food, esp. *sinigáng*
(which see).

sukáb (su-káb), I. *adj*. traitorous; perfidious;
disloyal; treacherous. Syn. *lilo*, *taksíl*,
palamara, *sulupiká*, *kuhilá*.

—II. *n*. traitor; betrayer. Syn. *traidór*, *taong
taksíl o lilo*.

sukal (su-kal), *n*. 1. scattered weeds, rubbish,
etc.; useless things scattered around a
place. Syn. *kalat*, *basura*, *yagít*. 2. (with
ng loób) used figuratively: displeasure;
resentment. Syn. *hinanakít*, *pagdaramdám*,
sama-ng-loób.

sukat¹ (su-kat), I. *n*. 1. act of measuring
something; getting the measurement of.
Also, *pagsukat*. 2. size; the dimension or
measurement of. Syn. *lakí*. 3.
measurement of width. Syn. *lapad*,
luwáng. 5. act of trying the size of shoes,
pants, etc. Also, *pagsusukat*.

—II. *adj*. 1. made according to the size or
measure of. 2. enough; sufficient. Syn.
sapát, *tamà na*.

sukat² (su-kat), *adv*. just; merely; simply, as
in: *Hindî sukat magágawâ iyán*. That
cannot just be done.

sukbít (suk-bít), I. *n*. 1. act of inserting,

tucking or carrying something at the
waistband. 2. anything inserted, tucked,
or carried at the waistband.

—II. *adj*. inserted, tucked, or carried at
the waistband.

sukdán (suk-dán), *conj*. though; although;
even if. Syn. *kulubmán*, *kahiman*, *kahit na*,
maski.

sukdól (suk-dól), I. *n*. 1. termination; end;
finish; conclusion. Syn. *wakás*, *katapusán*.
2. limit; extreme degree, state, or
condition. Syn. *hangganan*, *hanggahan*.

—II. *adj*. extreme; excessive; too much.
Syn. *sobra*, *labis*, *labis-labis*, *lubhâ*.

sukdulan (suk-du-lan), I. *n*. 1. termination;
end; finish; conclusion. Syn. *wakás*,
katapusán. 2. limit; extremity. Syn.
duluhan, *hangganan*, *hanggahan*. 3.
terminal; either end, as of a transportation
line. Syn. *hanggahan*, *punduhan*. 4.
extreme degree, state, or condition.

—II. *conj*. although; though; even; even
if. Syn. *kulubmán*, *kahit na*, *maski*.

sukì (su-kì), *n*. (Ch.) a regular customer or
client; patron. Syn. *parokyano*, *pálagiáng
mámimili o kliyente*.

sukiyaki (su-ki-ya-ki), *n*. (Jap.) sukiyaki, a
dish of thinly sliced meat, onions, and
other vegetables cooked quickly with soy
sauce, sake, sugar, etc.

suklám (suk-lám), *n*. 1. annoyance; ennui;
boredom. Syn. *inís*, *pagkainís*; *yamót*,
pagkayamót; *suyà*, *pagkasuyà*. 2.
repugnance; extreme dislike or distaste;
antipathy; strong aversion. Syn. *diri*,
pandidiri, *pagkadiri*; *rimarim*, *pagkarimarim*,
panririmarim.

sukláy (suk-láy), *n*. 1. comb; hair comb. 2.
act or manner of combing the hair. Also,
pagsukláy, *pagsusukláy*. 3. the way hair is
combed. Also, *pagkakásuklay*.

suklî (suk-lî), *n*. 1. the amount of money
given to a buyer as a change of the bigger
amount paid for something bought by him
or her. Syn. *kambiyó*. 2. the act of giving
the change to a buyer in excess of her
payment. Also, *pagsusuklî*. 3. an
equivalent amount of money given to
someone in exchange of a bigger
denomination. Syn. *palít*.

suklô (suk-lô), I. *adj.* bent or pressed down by the force of weight or pressure, said esp. of a neck, finger, etc. Cf. *balikukô, nabalikukô.*
—II. *n.* 1. act of pressing down the neck with the force of the hand on the top of the head. Also, *pagsuklô.* 2. state or condition of being pressed down by the force of weight or pressure on the top. Also, *pagkasuklô.*

suklób (suk-lób), *n.* any movable cover with an encasing around its sides, as the lid of a pot. Syn. *taklób, saklob, tungtóng.* 2. act of putting a hat, cap, or the like on the head. Syn. *saklób, pagsasaklób.* 3. act of putting two things together face to face, as two plates, etc. 4. fact or state of being placed with one over the other face to face, as two plates, etc. 5. (in card games) fact or state of being partners in a capital investment by two bankers. Syn. *sosyuhán, bakasán.* 6. a metal cap or capping used to protect the point or end of something. Syn. *kalupkóp.*

sukmanì (suk-ma-nì), var. **sinukmanì**, *n.* glutinous rice cooked dry in coconut milk. Syn. *angít, inangít.*

sukó (su-kó), I. *adj.* 1. with the tip or top reaching up to the limit of a certain height. Syn. *sayad sa itaás o tuktók.* 2. said of something that has reached the maximum limit. Syn. *nasa sukdulan na.*
—II. *n.* fact, state, or condition of having reached the limit of a certain height or condition.

sukò (su-kò), I. *n.* 1. surrender; act of surrendering or giving up. Also, *pagsukò.* Syn. *kusang pagpapahuli.* 2. admission of defeat; surrender of an opponent. Syn. *pagpapatalo, pagtanggáp ng pagkatalo.*
—II. *adj.* (usually with *na*) referring to a fugitive or the like, who has surrendered or given up to the authorities, or to a fighter who has accepted defeat and refused to fight anymore.

sukób (su-kób), I. *n.* 1. act of sharing with another in an umbrella, blanket, etc. Also, *pagsukob, pakikisukob.* 2. act of sharing together (of two persons) in an umbrella, blanket, etc. Also, *pagsusukob.*

3. a person who shares with another in an umbrella, blanket, etc. Also, *kasukob.*
—II. *adj.* referring to two persons sharing together in an umbrella, blanket, etc. Also, *magkasukob.*

sukól (su-kól), I. *adj.* cornered; driven into a corner, hence, unable to escape. Syn. *piít, kulóng, gipít.*
—II. *n.* fact or state of being cornered or driven into a corner.

sukot (su-kot), *n.* a cowering or lowering of head in defeat, fear, shame, or humiliation. Also, *pagsukot.* Syn. *paguukô ng ulo sa hiyâ, takot, pagkatalo, atbp.*

suksók (suk-sók), *n.* 1. insertion of something into a slit, small hole or opening. Cf. *singít, pagsisingit.* 2. tucking, as of waistline of pants. Cf. *sukbít, pagsusukbít.* 3. act or manner of shuffling cards. Syn. *balasa, pagbalasa, pagbabalasa.* 4. the way or manner cards shuffled. Syn. *pagkábalasa, pagkakábalasa.* 5. turn of a card player to shuffle the cards. Syn. *pagbalasa.* 6. act or manner of repairing mats by changing the broken strips with new ones. Cf. *hayuma, paghahayuma.* 7. the new strips of buri leaves woven in place of the broken ones. 8. (*Fig.*) act of saving for the future. Syn. *pagtitipíd para sa kinábukasan.* 9. something saved for the future; savings. Also, *sinuksók.*

sudasob (su-da-sob), var. **sulasod**, *n.* 1. act of scraping or dislodging something on a surface with or as with a towel. 2. act of pushing something forward along a surface with or as with the toes of a foot. Cf. *talisod, pagtalisod.*

sudlóng (sud-lóng), *n.* 1. part added or joined to increase length or width. Syn. *dugtóng, hugpóng, sugpóng, datíg.* 2. point of intersection or juncture. Syn. *hugpungan, sugpungan, dugtungan, pinághugpungán, pinágsugpungán, pinágdugtungán.* 3. (*Construction*) an addition to a building; annex.

sudsód (sud-sód), *n.* 1. share; plowshare. 2. act of digging or dislodging something with or as with a trowel. See **sulasod.**

suga (su-ga), *n.* (Sp. *soga*) 1. tether. Also, *panuga.* 2. act of fastening an animal with a tether to keep it within certain bounds. Also, *pagsusuga*.

sugabang (su-ga-bang), I. *n.* 1. avarice; covetousness; greediness. Syn. *kaimbután, kasakimán, kakamkamán*. 2. an avaricious or covetous person. Syn. *taong masakím, makámkam, o maimbót*.

—II. *adj.* avaricious; covetous; greedy. Syn. *sakím, imbót*.

sugál (su-gál), *n.* (*Sp. jugar*) 1. any game in which players play for money; gambling. Syn. *huwego*. 2. act of gambling. Also, *pagsusugál*. Syn. *huwego, paghuhuwego*. 3. any act or undertaking involving risk. Syn. *sápalarán, pakikipágsápalarán*. 4 (*Fig.*) acceptance of a challenge. Syn. *laban, pakikipáglaban*.

sugapà (su-ga-pà), var. **sugapâ**, I. *n.* 1. addiction to liquor or to certain kind of drugs or narcotics. Also, *kasugapaan, pagkasugapà*. 2. an inveterate drunkard. Syn. *lasenggo*. 3. an addict (to some kind of drugs or narcotics).

—II. *adj.* 1. inveterate, referring to a drunkard. Syn. *maglalasing, lasenggo*. 2. addicted to a certain drug or narcotics.

sugaról (su-ga-ról), I. *n.* gambler. Syn. *hugadór, magsusugal, mánunugal*.

—II. *adj.* given to gambling.

sugasog (su-ga-sog), *n.* act of going or travelling around places in search of something badly needed; exploration. Syn. *galugad, paggalugad, paggagalugad*.

sugat (su-gat), *n.* 1. wound; any cut or open injury on the skin or flesh. Cf. *hiwà*. 2. any hurt or injury to a person's feeling, reputation, etc. Cf. *damdamin, pagdaramdám*.

sugatán (su-ga-tán), I. *adj.* 1. wounded; with or having many wounds; badly wounded.

—II. *n.* a wounded person.

sugbá (sug-bá), *n.* a rushing or dashing blindly into a fire or any danger. Cf. *sagasà, pagsagasà; subò, pagsubò* (*sa panganib*).

sugbo (sug-bo; -bó), *n.* 1. a headlong dive or plunging into water. Syn. *bigláng talón o sisid sa tubig*. 2. sudden dipping or immersing of something into water, as a burning object in order to put out the fire.

sugid (su-gid), *n.* 1. assiduity; diligence. Syn. *sikap, kasikapan; sigasig, kasigasigan; sipag, kasipagan*. 2. faithfulness, as of fans, followers, etc. Syn. *katápatán, pagkamatapát*.

sugnáy (sug-náy), *n.* 1. (*Gram.*) clause. Cf. *parirala*. 2. a part added or joined to the side or edge of something to make it bigger or wider. Syn. *datig, hugpóng, sugpóng*.

sugò (su-gò), *n.* 1. act of sending someone to a person or place for an errand. Syn. *utos, pag-uutos*. 2. messenger or emissary. Syn. *mensahero*. 3. envoy; delegate; ambassador. Syn. *kinatawán, delegado, embahadór*.

sugod (su-god), *n.* 1. a rushing forward, as in an attack. Syn. *bigláng daluhong o lusob*. 2. sudden departure or leaving for a certain place, as in answering an emergency call. Syn. *mádaliang alís o pagalís*.

sugpô¹ (sug-pô), *n.* lobster. Cf. *uláng, hipon*.

sugpô² (sug-pô), I. *n.* 1. suppression; prevention; nipping in the bud. Syn. *pigil, pagpigil; sawatâ, pagsawatâ; apulà, pagapulà*. 2. stopping, as of a bad habit.

—II. *adj.* (with *na*) already stopped, suppressed, or controlled. Syn. *pigíl na, apulà na*.

sugpóng (sug-póng), *n.* 1. part added or joined to another to increase length or width. Syn. *dugtóng, hugpóng, datig*. 2. the point of connection or juncture. Syn. *hugpungan, dugtungan*. 3. the way or manner a part was added or joined to another. Syn. *pagkakáhugpóng, pagkakádugtóng*. 4. an addition to a building, etc.; annex.

suhâ (su-hâ), *n.* (*Bot.*) a small tree with long, sharp, solitary spines called grapefruit, pomelo, or shaddock citrus (*Citrus grandis Osbeck*); also, the fruit of this tree. Syn. *lukbán*.

suhay (su-hay), *n.* 1. prop; an inclined support placed against a structure. Cf. *tukod*. 2. a person who is the main source of support, as of a family; mainstay. Syn. *tanging ináasahan o tagatustós*.

suhetado (su-he-ta-do), *adj.* (*Sp. sujetado*)

disciplined; controlled or trained.

suheto (su-he-to), n. (Sp. *sujeto*) discipline; treatment that corrects or punishes.

suhî (su-hî), I. adj. born or delivered with the feet first, said of a child.
—II. n. a child born or delivered with the feet first.

suhol (su-hol), n. 1. act of bribing; bribery. Also, *pagsuhol, pagsusuhol*. Syn. *pagpaparatíng, paglalagáy, pagpapabagsák*. 2. bribe; anything given as a bribe. Syn. *lagáy, paratíng, pabagsák, soborno*.

sulà (su-là), n. 1. a kind of deep-red gem, esp. a garnet with a smooth, convex surface; carbuncle. 2. glow at the tip of the tongue of a certain species of reptiles.

sulák (su-lák), n. 1. bubbling of water or liquid over a direct fire or heat. Syn. *bulák, pagbulák; kulô, pagkulô*. 2. the bubbles or foam produced by a boiling water or liquid.

sulapa (su-la-pa), n. (Sp. *solapa*) lapel (of a coat).

sulár (su-lár), n. (Sp. *solar*) a lot or small piece or parcel of land, usually residential and fenced. Syn. *lote, looban*.

sulasod (su-la-sod), n. 1. act of scraping or dislodging something on a surface by pushing it forward with or as with a trowel. Syn. *sudsód, pagsudsód*. 2. something used for scraping or dislodging something on a surface. Syn. *pansulasol, panulasod*. 3. act of pushing something on a surface with or as with the toes of the feet. Syn. *salisod, pagsalisod; tisod, pagtisod*.

sulasol (su-la-sol), n. act or manner of lightly pushing the teeth with the tip of the tongue or with the point of the finger.

sulat (su-lat), n. 1. act or manner of writing something on paper or on anything. Also, *pagsulat*. 2. writing; anything written on a surface. 3. handwriting; penmanship. Syn. *sulat-kamáy*. 4. a written or printed personal or business message, usually sent by mail in an envelope; letter. Syn. *liham*.

sulat-kamáy (su-lat + ka-máy), I. n. penmanship; handwriting.
—II. adj. hand-written.

suleras (su-ler-ras), var. **soleras**, n. (Sp. *solera*) joist. Syn. *pámakuán ng sahíg o kísamé*.

sulihiya (su-li-hi-ya), n. (Sp. *celosía*) wickerwork on seats or backs of chairs or on frames of beds.

suliling (su-li-ling), n. sudden turning or twisting of the neck due to over fatigue or to a kind of spasm.

sulimpát (su-lim-pát), I. n. a look through the corners of one's eyes; squint glance or look.
—II. adj. 1. squint; looking obliquely, askance, or sidelong, referring to eyes. 2. squint-eyed, referring to a person. Cf. *dulíng*.

suling (su-ling), n. 1. act of wandering or going around aimlessly. Syn. *galà, paggagalâ, pagpapagalá-galà; libot, paglilibót, pagpapalibut-libot*. 2. act of walking or going around with dazed feeling, in confusion or bewilderment. 3. act of going from one person to another or from one place to another in search for something badly needed.

súliranin (sú-li-ra-nin; sú-li-ra-nín), n. problem; matter of doubt or difficulty; something that poses a problem to someone. Syn. *problema, paláisipán*.

sulit (su-lit), I. n. 1. submission, as of a report or the like. Syn. *paghaharáp, pagbibigáy*. 2. return of something borrowed. Syn. *saulì, pagsasaulì*. 3. an examination or test. Syn. *iksamin*. 4. a.) act of giving a test or examination. Syn. *pagpapaiksamin, pagbibigáy ng iksamin o pagsusulit*. b) act of taking an examination or test. Syn. *pagiksamin, pagkuha ng iksamin o pagsusulit*. 5. remittance of money, as by a bill collector. Syn. *intrega, pag-iintrega; inggreso, pag-iinggreso*. 6. regain of capital in business or gambling. Syn. *bawì o pagkabawì (sa puhunan)*.
—II. adj. regained; with or having recovered one's capital in an investment. Syn. *bawì o nabawì na*.

suló (su-ló), I. n. 1. act of dazzling someone with or as with a strong light. Syn. *silaw, pasilaw*. 2. state or condition of being dazzled, as with a strong light. 3. colloq. var. of *sulô*, as used in some southern Tagalog provinces.

—II. adj. dazzled, as with a strong light. Syn. siláw, nasísilaw.

sulô (su-lô), n. torch. Syn. tangláw, panangláw, sigsíg.

sulok (su-lok), n. 1. corner, as of a room. 2. intersection, as of two streets. Syn. kanto, panulukan.

sulong (su-long), I. n. 1. act of moving forward; advance. Syn. abante, pag-abante; lakad, paglakad. 2. push; act of pushing something forward. Syn. tulak, pagtutulak. 3. something being pushed forward, as a pushcart. 4. progress, as of a country's culture or economy. Syn. unlád, pag-unlád; progreso, pagprogreso. 5. amount of money remitted, as by a bill collector. Syn. intrega, inggreso. 6. act or time of paying installment for something. Syn. hulog, paghuhulog. 7. installment; amount paid for such installment. Syn. hulog, halagá ng inihúhulog.
—II. interj. Go ahead! Go on! Syn. Sige! Lakad!
—III. v. (imper.) Go ahead; move forward.

sulót (su-lót), n. 1. act of inserting something into a hole, as in threading a needle. Also, pagsusulót. 2. act of poking or thrusting someone with or as with a stick passed through a hole or small opening, or between the slats of floors. Cf. sundót, pagsundót; ulos, pag-ulos. 3. act of discrediting a position holder in order to dislodge him and get his place. Cf. paninirà, pagpapasamâ.

sulpák (sul-pák), n. 1. act of forcing something into the hole of a cylinder or the like. Cf. saksák, pagsasaksák; siksík, pagsisiksík. 2. act of forcing something into someone's mouth. Syn. supalpál, pagsusupalpál; samuól, pagsasamuól. 3. indiscriminate use or wearing, as of one's shoes, hat, etc. Syn. pagsusuót o paggamit nang waláng-ingat. 4. a kind of toy popgun, made from an internode of a small bamboo and provided with a plunger to force out the fellets. Cf. sumpít.

sulpít (sul-pít), n. spurt or jet, as of liquid. Syn. puslít, tilandóy.

sulpót (sul-pót), n. 1. sudden appearance or sticking out, as of someone's head from

under the water. Syn. ultáw, pag-ultáw. 2. an unexpected appearance or showing up, as of a person, from a long absence or hiding. Syn. bigláng litáw o paglitáw.

sulsi (sul-si; -sí), var. sursi (sursí), n. (Sp. zurcir) 1. act or manner of mending clothes by stitching with the hands; darning. Also, pagsusulsi, panunursi. 2. the way or manner something was darned or mended with hand stitches. Also, pagkakásulsi, pagkakásursi. 3. the part darned or mended with hand stitches.

sulsól (sul-sól), n. instigation; incitement; act of urging on someone. Also, pagsulsol, panunulsól. Syn. pag-upat, pang-uupat; pag-udyók, pang-uudyók; pag-apoyo, pang-aapoyo. 2. something said to incite or instigate someone. Syn. upat, udyók, apoyo. 3. act of poking or pointing something at close range, as at someone's face. Syn. duldól, pagdududuldól. 4. act of thrusting something into, as plant cuttings into the soil. Syn. tundós, pagtutundós.

sultada (sul-ta-da), n. (Sp. soltada) a round or single game of cockfighting.

sultán (sul-tán), n. (Sp.) sultan; Moslem ruler.

sulukasok (su-lu-ka-sok), n. 1. annoyance; boredom; ennui. Syn. yamót, pagkayamót; inís, pagkainís. 2. disgust; sickening distance or dislike; repugnance. Syn. suyà, pagkasuyà.

sulupiká (su-lu-pi-ká), I. n. 1. a liar. Syn. taong sinungaling. 2. traitor; doublecrosser. Syn. taong taksíl o lilo, traidór.
—II. adj. 1. given to telling lies. Syn. sinungaling, bulaan. 2. traitorous. Syn. taksíl, lilo, palamara, sukáb.

sulyáp (sul-yáp), n. glance; brief, quick view; glimpse; passing look. 2. a look from the corner of one's eyes; side-glance. Syn. sulimpát.

suma (su-ma), n. 1. act of adding numbers. Also, pagsuma, pagsusuma. Syn. pagtutál, pagtututál. 2. sum; total. Syn. tutál, kabuuán. 3. totality; entirety. Syn. kabuuán, kalahatán.

sumakamáy (su-ma-ka-máy), v. (present and past form) to receive or be received by.

Syn. *mátanggáp, tanggapín.*

sumakop (su-ma-kop), *v.* (present and past form) 1. to put under one's jurisdiction. Syn. *saklawín ng kapangyarihan.* 2. to conquer or dominate. Syn. *ipailalim sa kapangyarihan.*

sumaganà (su-ma-ga-nà), *v.* (present and past form) 1. to become abundant; be plentiful. Syn. *sumaksâ.* 2. to become financially abundant. Syn. *yumaman.*

sumagì (su-ma-gì), *v.* (present and past form) to touch or collide tangently on or against something in passing or while in motion. Cf. *sumagid, dumagil.* 2. *(Fig.)* to come to one's mind; be reminded of. Syn. *máalaala, mágunitâ.*

sumagimsím (su-ma-gim-sím), *v.* (present and past form) to be suddenly reminded of; come into one's mind. Syn. *máalaala, mágunitâ.*

sumaglít (su-mag-lít), *v.* (present and past form) to go to someone or to a certain place for a moment. Syn. *pumunta o tumungong sandalî.*

sumamâ (su-ma-mâ), *v.* (present and past) 1. to get or become worse. Syn. *lumalâ, lumubhâ.* 2. to be (become) morally bad.

suman (su-man), *n.* a native delicacy made of glutinous rice or cassava flour, wrapped in banana or palm leaves.

sumandalî (su-man-da-lî), *adv.* for a moment; momentarily; as in: *Maghintáy kang sumandalî.* Wait for a moment.

sumáng (su-máng), *n.* act of contradicting or opposing someone in a reproachful manner. Also, *pagsumáng.* Syn. *pagkalaban, pagkontra.*

sumásainyó (su-má-sa-in-yó), *pron.* yours, as in a complimentary clause.

sumbát (sum-bát), *n.* 1. a flaunting reference to someone's debts of gratitude. Syn. *suat, pagsuát.* 2. an expression of blame or censure for an error or mistake done. Syn. *sisi, pagsisi.*

sumbóng (sum-bóng), *n.* 1. act of telling on somebody. Also, *pagsusumbóng.* 2. act of accusing or charging someone of wrong doing. Syn. *paratang, pagpaparatang.* 3. act of accusing or charging someone in court. Syn. *sakdál, pagsasakdál; hablá, paghahablá;*

demanda, pagdedemanda. 4. what a person is accused of; the charge of accusation against someone. Syn. *sakdál, demanda, hablá.*

sumbungan (sum-bu-ngan), *n.* 1. a person to whom another or others unbosom their hurt feelings or personal complaints. Syn. *hínakdalan, híngahan ng samâ ng loób.* 2. a person in authority or a court of justice where complaints or charges of wrongdoing are filed and investigated. Syn. *sakdalan, hablahan, demandahan.*

sumikat (su-mi-kat), *v.* (present and past form) 1. to rise or shine (s.o. sun, moon, stars, and the like). Syn. *sumilang.* 2. to become well known. Syn. *tumanyág, bumantóg.* 3. to become successful in life. Syn. *magtagumpáy.*

sumilang (su-mi-lang), *v.* (present and past form) 1. to rise or shine, as the sun, moon, stars, etc. Syn. *sumikat.* 2. to be born; come into being. Syn. *lumitáw sa maliwanag, ipanganák.*

sumilay (su-mi-lay), *v.* (present and past form) 1. to appear briefly; show oneself briefly. Syn. *magpakitang sandalî.* 2. to have a brief look or glance at. Syn. *tuminging sandalî.*

sumintá (su-min-tá), *v.* (present and past form) 1. to love; fall in love. Syn. *umibig, magmahál.* 2. to stand on one's hind legs, as dogs do.

sumiphayò (su-mip-ha-yò), *v.* (present and past form) to fail or disappoint (someone) by not giving in to his request, etc. Syn. *bumigô.*

sumpâ (sum-pâ), *n.* oath. Also, *panunumpâ.* 2. vow; solemn promise. Syn. *panata.* 3. curse; wishing evil. Also, *pagsumpâ.* Syn. *panalangin ng masamâ sa kapwà.*

sumpák (sum-pák), *n.* a kind of popgun. See *sumpít.*

sumpíng (sum-píng), I. *n.* 1. act or manner of combing one's hair backward without parting it. Syn. *pagsukláy na palikód.* 2. the way one's hair is combed backward without partition. Also, *pagkákásumpíng.* —II. *adj.* combed backward without partition, referring to one's hair.

sumpít (sum-pít), *n.* 1. blowgun. 2. popgun.

sumpóng

3. act or manner of shooting something with a blowgun or popgun.

sumpóng (sum-póng), n. 1. fit or attack, as of coughing, pain, disease, etc. Syn. *atake, pag-atake*. 2. caprice; freakish idea or notion; vagary; sudden change of mind without any reason. Syn. *kapritso*. 3. an accidental finding or discovery. Syn. *disinásadyáng pagkátagpô o pagkátuklás*.

sundalo (sun-da-lo), n. (Sp. *soldado*) 1. soldier. Syn. *kawal*. 2. (*Colloq.*) one's male child. 3. (*Colloq.*) follower. Syn. *tauhan*.

sundán (sun-dán), v. 1. to follow, e.g. someone who is being observed closely. Syn. *subaybayán, buntután*. 2. to be followed by another, as one's first child. 3. to pursue; run after. Syn. *habulin, tugisin*.

sundáng (sun-dáng), n. dagger; poniard. Syn. *daga, punyál, balaráw*.

sundín (sun-dín), v. 1. to follow or obey (an order or command). Syn. *tumalima, talimahin; tumupád, tuparín*. 2. to do what is being asked to perform. Syn. *gawín ang iniuutos*.

sundô (sun-dô), n. 1. act of fetching someone from a certain place. Syn. *kaón, pagkaón*. 2. time when someone is supposed to be fetched by another. Syn. *oras ng sundô o pagsundô*. 3. the person who fetches someone from a certain place. Syn. *kaón, tagakaón, ang kumákaón*.

sundót (sun-dót), n. 1. act of pricking or piercing something with the point of a pencil, stick, thorn, needle, or the like. Syn. *durò, pagdurò; tusok, pagtusok; turók, pagturók*. 2. hole or puncture made in this manner; prick. Syn. *durò, tusok, turók*.

sunò (su-nò), n. 1. act of sharing a ride with someone in his or her vehicle. Also, *pagsunò, pakikisunò*. 2. act of sharing a room, etc. with someone. 3. a person who shares a ride in someone's vehicle.

sunók (su-nók), n. loss of interest in some kind of food due to having too much of it. Syn. *suyà, pagkasuyà; sawà, pagsasawà*.

sunód (su-nód), I. n. 1. act of following orders, intructions, requirements, etc.; obedience. Syn. *talima, pagtalima*. 2. act of following or going after someone who

has just left. 3. one who follows another or others. Also, *kasunód*. 4. act of making something in accordance to a model or plan. Syn. *pagtulad, pagtutulad*.

—II. adj. 1. said of someone who follows another. 2. based from; done or made in accordance to a certain plan or requirement. Syn. *batay, ibinatay; salig, isinalig*.

sunog (su-nog), n. 1. act of burning something. Also, *pagsunog*. 2. fire; conflagration. Syn. *siláb*.

sunóg (su-nóg), adj. 1. reduced to ashes; completely burned. 2. (with *sa araw*) sunburned.

sunong (su-nong), I. n. 1. act or manner of carrying a load on the head. Also, *pagsunong, pagsusunong*. 2. a load carried on the head. Syn. *bagay na dalá sa ulo*.

—II. adj. referring to a load carried on the head. Syn. *dalá na nakapatong sa ulo*.

suntók (sun-tók), n. 1. a blow or strike with the fist. Syn. *sapók*. 2. act of giving someone a blow with one's fist. Also, *pagsuntók*.

sunúd-sunód (su-núd + su-nód), I. adj. consecutive; one after another; in succession. Syn. *magkakasunód*.

—II. adv. consecutively; in succession.

sunúd-súnuran (su-núd + sú-nu-ran), adj. 1. pliant; easily bent or twisted; pliable; flexible. Syn. *nabábaluktót, madalíng hutukin, malambót*. 2. obedient; docile; tractable; compliant. Syn. *masunurin*.

sungaw (su-ngaw), n. 1. act of looking or peeping out of a window. Syn. *dungaw, pagdungaw*. 2. appearance or showing of oneself through an opening. Syn. *litáw, paglitaw*.

sungay (su-ngay), I. n. horn (of an animal).
—II. adj. made of horn.

sungka (sung-ka), n. an old indoor game, usually played by two persons on a wood block shaped like a boat and provided with shallow holes along the sides where shells or pebbles are dropped by each player by turns.

sungkî (sung-kî), I. n. state or condition of being uneven or irregular in growth, referring esp. to teeth.
—II. adj. uneven or irregular in growth,

referring to teeth. Syn. *ungús-ungós, dipantáy-pantáy.*

sungkít (sung-kít), n. 1. act of picking (a fruit or fruits) with a long pole. Also, *pagsungkít, panunungkít.* 2. act of getting something by pulling with a pole provided with a hook at one end, for use in picking fruits or for getting or pulling something from a high place. Syn. *tikíng panungkít, kalawit, pangalawit.*

sunggáb (sung-gáb), n. 1. act of snatching or seizing something suddenly from someone. Syn. *daklót, biglang agaw o pagagaw.* 2. act of snatching something with the mouth. Syn. *sakmál, pagsakmál.* 3. sudden arrest, as of a long wanted man. Syn. *biglang paghuli o pag-aresto.* 4. sudden acceptance or grabbing, as of an offer or opportunity at hand. Syn. *biglâ o mádaliang pagtanggáp.*

sunggô (sung-gô), n. a light bumping. Syn. *marahang bunggô.*

sungì (su-ngì), n. harelip. Syn. *bingot, bungì.*

sungilngíl (su-ngil-ngíl), n. act of poking or forcing something into or against the face of someone. Syn. *duldól, pagduduldól.*

sungit (su-ngit; -ngít), n. 1. irascibility; irritableness; sulkiness. Syn. *init ng ulo; pagkamagagalitin.* 2. sternness; harshness. Syn. *lupít, kalupitán; balasik, kabalasikan.* 3. strictness. Syn. *higpít, kahigpitán.* 4. harshness or inclemency, as of the weather. Syn. *samâ o kasamaán.*

sungót (su-ngót), n. 1. feeler or antenna, as of an insect, spider, lobster, and the like. 2. the pointed end of a grain, pod, or the like.

sungsóng (sung-sóng), n. 1. act of going or sailing against the current or wind. Syn. *salunga, pagsalunga.* 2. (S-) an old term used in referring to China, as in: *galing sa Sungsóng,* from China.

suóng (su-óng), n. 1. a determined effort in undertaking something hard, risky, etc. Syn. *subò, pagsubò.* 2. (Bats.) wrestling. Syn. *bunô, pagbubunô.*

suób (su-ób), n. fumigation; act of fumigating; exposure to the action of smoke or fumes. Also, *pagsuób, pagsusuób.* Syn. *pausok, pagpapausok.*

suót (su-ót), I. n. 1. entry or getting into a hole, small opening, thick forest, etc. Syn. *pasok, pagpasok.* 2. putting or inserting something into a hole, as thread into the eye of a needle. Syn. *sulót, pagsusulót.* 3. act of wearing or putting on a hat, dress, trousers, stockings, shoes, etc. 4. clothing, or anything that someone is presently wearing.

—II. *adj.* said of something that one is presently wearing. Syn. *nakasuót, ginágamit, nasa-katawán.*

supalpál (su-pal-pál), n. 1. act of forcing something into someone's mouth. Syn. *samuól, pagsasamuól.* 2. something forced into someone's mouth.

superlatibo (su-per-la-ti-bo), I. *adj.* (Sp. *superlativo*) 1. superlative; of the highest kind. Syn. *sukdulan ng, ubod ng, pinaka-.*
—II. n. superlative of adjective and adverb. Syn. *sukdulan, pasukdól, pánukdulan.*

superyór (su-per-yór), I. n. (Sp. *superior*) superior; chief; boss. Syn. *hepe, punò, pinunò.*
—II. *adj.* superior; excellent; very good. Syn. *nápakagalíng, nápakahusay, nápakabuti.*

supí (su-pí), I. *interj.* used or said in driving a cat away.
—II. *v.* (usually use in the imperative, to drive away cats) scat; go away.

supiho (su-pi-ho), n. (Gram.; Sp. *sufijo*) suffix. Syn. *hulapì.*

supil (su-pil), n. 1. act of overpowering another; subjugation; domination. Syn. *lupig, paglupig.* 2. act of controlling or stopping from being wild or stubborn. Syn. *sugpô, pagsugpô; suheto, pagsuheto.*

suplá (sup-lá), n. (Sp. *soplar*) 1. blowpipe; blowgun. Cf. *sumpít, sumpák.* 2. act of hitting something with or as with a blowpipe. Cf. *sumpitín, sumpakín.* 3. a kind of children's game whereby the players hit the target with a cue piece blown out of their mouths. Syn. *bugá.* 4. act of whispering the answer to someone reciting in class. 5. act of contradicting someone on his or her opinion or argument. Syn. *kontra, pagkontra;*

suplado   **Susmaryosep**

salungát, pagsalungát; pagkalaban.

suplado (su-pla-do), *adj.* (*Masc.*; Sp. *soplado*) conceited; vain. Syn. *mapágmataás, palalò, hambóg, mayabang.*

suplíng (su-plíng), n. 1. development of a new growth, as from a branch or cutting. Also, *pagsuplíng.* 2. a new growth; bud; sprout. Syn. *suloy, supang, tubò.* 3. one's child or children; offspring; progeny; scion. Syn. *anák, mga anák.*

suplóng (su-plóng), n. 1. act of reporting or denouncing an anomaly or irregularity to the authorities. Syn. *sumbóng, pagsusumbóng; denunsiyá, pagdidenunsiyá.* 2. the anomaly or irregularity that is reported or denounced. Syn. *sumbóng, denunsiyá.*

supók (su-pók), I. n. state or condition of being completely burned or carbonized. —II. *adj.* carbonized; completely burned. Syn. *sunóg na sunóg.*

suporta (su-por-ta), n. (Sp. *soporte*) 1. support; prop. Syn. *suhay, tukod, talukod.* 2. financial support. Syn. *sustento; pagsustento; tustós, pagtustós.* 3. upholding or supporting, as of someone's stand or proposition. Syn. *taguyod, pagtataguyod; katig, pagkatig.* 4. help or aid given to someone. Syn. *tulong, abuloy.*

supot (su-pot), n. 1. paper or cloth bag. 2. small money bag. Syn. *bulsito; lukbutan.*

supót (su-pót), I. *adj.* uncircumcized. Syn. *di-tulí.* —II. n. 1. fact, state, or condition of a male person being uncircumcized. Syn. *lalakíng di-tulí.*

supráhiyó (su-prá-hi-yó), n. (Sp. *sufragio*) right to vote; suffrage. Syn. *karapatán sa pagboto, karapatáng bumoto.*

supremo (su-pre-mo), n. (Sp.) supreme or highest ruler or officer. Syn. *pinakamataás na punò.*

supsóp (sup-sóp), n. act of sucking something by means of the mouth. Also, *pagsupsóp.* Cf. *sipsíp, pagsipsíp.*

sur (sur), n. (Sp.) south. Syn. *timog.*

sura (su-ra), n. (Sp. *zurra*) making someone angry by trifles; act of vexation or annoyance. Syn. *yamót, pagyamót; inís, pag-inís, pang-iinís.*

suray (su-ray), n. a reeling or staggering, as of one who is extremely drunk or dazed by a blow. Syn. *pagpapahapay-hapay sa pagkalasíng o pagkatuliró.*

surì (su-rì), n. 1. analysis of qualities; evaluation or examination of comparative worth or value of something. Syn. *analisá, pag-analisá, pag-aanalisá.* 2. physical examination, as of a patient by a doctor. Syn. *iksamin, pag-iksamin.* 3. scientific investigation, as of old, literary document. Also, *pagsurì, pagsusurì.*

surián (su-ri-án), n. 1. place where analysis or scientific investigations are being done. Syn. *ánalisahan, iksaminán.* 2. institute, as in: *Surián ng Wikang Pambansá,* Institute of National Language. 3. place where gold ore and other metals are assayed. Syn. *urián.*

súring-aklát (sú-ring + ak-lát), n. book review.

suriso (su-ri-so), var. **tsuriso,** n. (Sp. *chorizo*) sausage; pork sausage. Cf. *longganisa, batutay.*

surot[1] (su-rot), n. bedbug. Cf. *kuto, katô, garapata.*

surot[2] (su-rot), n. 1. act of poking a finger at the eyes of someone. Also, *pagsurot (sa matá).* 2. act of shoving a thing at the face of someone to make him believe there is such a thing. 3. act of making a flaunting remark at someone about a debt of gratitude. Syn. *pagsuwát, sumbát, pagsumbát.*

surtido (sur-ti-do), *adj.* (Sp.) assorted; of various or different kinds. Syn. *sari-sarì, ibá-ibáng urì (klase), halu-halò.*

Sus (Sus), *interj.* an exclamation of surprise, disapproval, dislike, etc. Cf. *Naku!*

suskribí (sus-kri-bí), n. (Sp. *subscribir*) subscription for a periodical, etc. Syn. *pagpapahatíd o pagpaparasyón ng peryódikó o páhayagán.*

susì (su-sì), n. (Ch.) 1. key. Syn. *yawe.* 2. (*Colloq.*) answer or solution to a puzzle or problem. Syn. *sagót, kasagutan.*

Susmaryosep (Sus-mar-yo-sep), *interj.* (Sp. *Jesus, Maria, Josef*) used as an exclamation expressing surprise, dislike, or disapproval.

suso (su-so), n. (*Anat.*) 1. breast. Syn. *dibdíb*. 2. nipple; teat; udder. Syn. *utóng*. 3. act of sucking milk or feeding from the breast of one's mother. Also, *pagsuso*. 4. any of the four projections at the bottom corners of a sack, basket, and the like. Cf. *pusod*.

susô (su-sô), n. name for various species of snails.

susog (su-sog), n. 1. a revision or change proposed or made in a law, agreement, etc.; amendment. Syn. *enmyenda*; *panukalà o karagdagang pagbabago*. 2. act of proposing an amendment or amendments to a law, agreement, etc. Also, *pagsususog*.

susón (su-són), n. 1. underlayer. Syn. *sapín*. 2. lining, as of a dress, etc. Syn. *aporo*. 3. undergarment. Syn. *kasuutáng panloób*.

suspendido (sus-pen-di-do), adj. (*Sp.*) 1. under suspension; suspended. Syn. *pinigil* (*sa tungkulin*). 2. stopped; made to stop indefinitely. Syn. *pinatigil, pinahintô*.

sustánsiyá (sus-tán-si-yá), n. (*Sp. sustancia*) 1. substance; matter; material. Syn. *sangkáp, materyál*. 2. nutrient; nutriment; food substance.

sustantibo (sus-tan-ti-bo), I. n. (*Gram; Sp. sustantivo*) substantive; noun; name of person or thing. Syn. *pangngalan; pangalan ng tao o bagay*.
—II. adj. substantive; real; actual. Syn. *tunay, totoó*.

sustento (sus-ten-to), n. (*Sp.*) 1. act of providing sustenance or support to someone. Also, *pagsustento, pagsusustento*. 2. support or sustenance given to someone.

sustiné (sus-ti-né), n. (*Sp. sostiner*) 1. support; sustenance. Syn. *sustento, panggugol*. 2. a maintaining or upholding, as of one's belief, etc. Syn. *paninindigan*. 3. prop; support. Syn. *tukod, talukod, suhay*.

sustitusyón (sus-ti-tus-yón), n. (*Sp. sustitución*) a substituting or being substituted; substitution; replacing. Syn. *paghahalili, pagpapalít*. 2. a substitute; replacement; alternate. Syn. *kapalít, kahalili*.

sutíl (su-tíl), adj. stubborn; hardheaded. Syn. *matigás ang ulo*.

sutlâ (sut-lâ), I. n. 1. the soft, fine, shiny fiber made by silkworms; silk. 2. the thread or fabric made from this material. 3. a garment made of this fabric.
—II. adj. of or made of silk.

sutsót (sut-sót), n. 1. act of calling someone or the attention of someone by making a hissing or whistling sound. Also, *pagsutsót*. Syn. *baswít, pagbaswít*. 2. a whistling or hissing sound calling someone or the attention of someone. Syn. *baswít*.

suwabe (su-wa-be), adj. (*Sp. suave*) 1. soft; slow. Syn. *mahinà, dahan-dahan*. 2. smooth; soft. Syn. *banayad*. 3. gentle. Syn. *mayumì, mahinhín*.

suwág (su-wág), n. 1. a groping or butting with the horns. Also, *pagsuwág, panunuwág*. 2. wound made by goring or by the butt of horns. 3. (*Colloq.*) act of fighting back, esp. against a benefactor. Syn. *laban, paglaban*.

suwahe (su-wa-he), n. a species of freshwater shrimps.

suwaíl (su-wa-íl), adj. 1. disobedient; stubborn; hardheaded. Syn. *matigás ang ulo, sutíl*. 2. rebellious; insolent. Syn. *mapanlabán, rebelde*. 3. traitorous; disloyal. Syn. *taksíl, traidór*. 4. ungrateful. Syn. *waláng utang na loób*.

suwám (su-wám), var. **suám**, n. (*Ch.*) a sautéed dish of eggs, fish, or meat with garlic and ginger, provided with broth.

suwapang (su-wa-pang), adj. (*Ch.*) avaricious; covetous. Syn. *sakím, masakím; maimbót, mapág-imbót; matakaw; mukháng-pera; mukháng-salapî*.

suwáy (su-wáy), n. disobedience or refusal to obey an order or command. Syn. *di-pagsunód*. 2. act of violating an ordinance or law. Syn. *labág, paglabág*.

suwelas (su-we-las), n. (*Sp. suelas*) sole of a footwear.

suweldo (su-wel-do), n. (*Sp. sueldo*) salary. Syn. *sahod*.

suwelo (su-we-lo), n. (*Sp. suelo*) floor. Syn. *sahíg*.

suwero (su-we-ro), n. (*Sp. suero*) 1. serum; blood serum. 2. a long, large hypodermic needle.

suwerte (su-wer-te), n. (Sp. *suwerte*) 1. luck;
good luck. Syn. *buwenas*, *magandáng
kapalaran*. 2. fate; fortune. Syn. *kapalaran*.

suwí¹ (su-wí), n. (*Bot.*) a subordinate shoot
that grows from a bud on the root or stem
of a plant; sucker. Cf. *suplíng*, *supang*.

suwí² (su-wí), var. **suwî**, n. & adj. referring
to a baby born with the feet first.

suwitik (su-wi-tik), I. adj. (*Ch.*) cunning;
sly; tricky. Syn. *tuso*, *madayà*,
mapanlinláng.
—II. n. swindler; cheat. Syn. *manlilinláng*,
manggagantso, *mandaráyà*.

suyà (su-yà), n. (*Ch.*) 1. surfeit. Syn. *sawà*,
pagsasawà; *tusing*, *pagkatusing*. 2.
annoyance; dislike or disgust. Syn. *yamót*,
pagkayamót; *inís*, *pagkainís*.

suyò (su-yò), n. 1. act of bringing oneself
into another's favor or good graces;
ingratiation. Syn. *pagmamapurí*,
pagmamabutí, *pagsisipsíp* (*slang*). 2. act of
trying to win the affection or love of a
girl by giving gifts and doing all kinds of
favor. Also, *panunuyò*, *ligaw*.

suyod (su-yod), n. 1. fine-toothed comb used
for nits and catching lice. 2. act or method
of catching lice by using a fine-toothed
comb. Also, *pagsusuyod*. 3. (in farming)
farmer's harrow. Cf. *kalmót*. 4. act or
manner of harrowing a plowed or
cultivated field. Also, *pagsuyod*,
pagsusuyod. 5. a device on a loom that
serves as a comb that separates the threads
or yarns of the warp. 6. (*Fig.*) act of
combing or searching (a place)
thoroughly, as in searching for something.
Syn. *saliksík*, *pagsaliksík*, *pagsasaliksík*.

suysóy (suy-sóy), n. act of urging someone
to action by constantly reminding him of
what he neglects to do.

súyuan (sú-yu-an), n. 1. love affair. Syn.
íbigan, *pag-íibigan*; *máhalan*,
pagmamáhalan. 2. act of trying to please
each other, as by being kind,
accommodating, etc. to each other. Also,
pagsusuyuán.

T

T, t (ta; te), n. 1. the seventeenth letter of
the *abakada* (Pilipino alphabet). 2. a type
or impression representing this letter. 3.
a symbol for the seventeenth in a group
or series.

't (contracted form of *at*) used as a suffix, as
in: *bawa't*, *datapwa't*, *nguni't*, *subali't*, etc.

ta (ta), pron. (dual, prepositive, ablative) 1.
used as an apocope of *katá* ; we, as in *wala
tang magagawá sa bagay na iyán*, we can
do nothing about that matter. 2. short for
nata us, as in: *Gawín ta iyán*. Let us make
that. b) our, as in: *Ang anák ta'y may sakit*.
Our child is sick.

taab (ta-ab), n. 1. a tapering cut, as on one
end of a tenon for easier insertion. Cf.
tapyás. 2. act or manner of making a
tapering cut, as on one end of a tenon,
with a bolo or hatchet. Also, *pagtaáb*,
pagtataád. Cf. *tapyás*, *pagtapyás*,
pagtatapyás.

taad (ta-ad; -ád) n. a sugar cane cutting for
planting.

taal (ta-ál), adj. 1. native; aboriginal;
indigenous. Syn. *katutubò*, *lehitimó*. 2.
natural; inborn. Syn. *likás*, *natural*,
katutubò. 3. (T-) a first class town in the
province of Batangas.

taan¹ (ta-an), n. 1. reserve; something set
aside for a certain purpose. Syn. *laán*,
reserba. 2. reservation or setting aside
something for the future. Also, *pagtataan*.
Syn. *paglalaán*, *pagrereserba*.

taan² (ta-an), n. 1. act or manner of setting
up a trap or snare for (a person or
animal). Also, *pagtataán* (*ng silò o
patibóng*). 2. such a trap or snare. Syn.
silo, *patibóng*, *bitag*.

taás (ta-ás), I. n. 1. distance from the bottom
to the top; height. Syn. *tayog*, *layog*. 2.
the elevation or distance above a given
level; altitude. 3. height of the body in
the natural standing position; stature.
Syn. *hagwáy*, *tangkád*. 4. aloftness or
highness, as of person's habit in dealing
with others. Syn. *kataasán*, *kahambugán*,
kapalaluán. 5. eminence; nobility. Syn.

tabâ   **takal**

kadákilaán, kabunyián, kamahalan. 6.
excessiveness, as of prices. Syn.
kamahalán, kataasán (ng presyo o halagá).
7. promotion, as in position or office. Syn.
asenso, pag-asenso.

—II. *v. (imperative)* to put up; raise up, as
in: *itaás ang kamáy,* raise your hands.

tabâ (ta-bâ), n. 1. fat; the white or yellow
oily substance in the body of animals. 2.
fatness, as of persons or animals. Also,
katabaán. 3. lard; the inner fat of hogs. 4.
richness or fertility, as of soil. 5. a name
often attributed to someone who is very
fat.

tabák (ta-bák), n. 1. a kind of cutlass or bolo.
Syn. *iták, gulok.* 2. the act of hacking
(someone) with a cutlass or bolo. Also,
pagtabák. Syn. *tagâ, pagtagâ.* 3. a big cut
or wound, made by hacking with a cutlass
or bolo. Syn. *tagâ.*

tabakalera (ta-ba-ka-le-ra), n. (Sp.
tabacalera) tobacco dealer.

tabako (ta-ba-ko), n. 1. (Bot.) the tobacco
plant (*Nicotiana tobacus).* 2. the leaves of
this plant which are made into cigars and
cigarettes. 3. cigar. Syn. *sigaro, abano,
ubano.*

tabal (ta-bal), I. n. excessive growth of
foliage, resulting in fruitlessness or
sterility of plants.

—II. *adj.* with or having excessive growth
of foliage, referring to plants.

tabáng (ta-báng), n. 1. tastelessness;
insipidity. Syn *kawaláng-lasa, kakulangán
sa lasa.* 2. loss or lack of appetite (for
food). Syn. *kawaláng-gana, pagkawaláng-
gana sa pagkain.* 3. loss of interest in. Syn.
kawaláng-gusto, kawaláng- interes. 4.
insufficiency or lack of salt, sugar, vinegar,
etc. in food. Syn. *kakulangán ng asin,
asukal, sukà, atbp.*

tabas (ta-bas) n. 1. act of cutting (cloth,
paper, etc.) according to a pattern or
design. Also, *pagtabas.* 2. style of cut, esp.
of dresses. Syn. *korte.* 3. general feature,
as of one's face. Syn. *korte, hugis.*

tabás (ta-bás), I. n. act of cutting down
excessive growth of grass, weeds, and the
like, with or as with a cutlass. 2. act of
harvesting sugar cane, corn, etc.by cutting

them down with or as with a bolo.
—II. *adj.* already cut down or harvested
and ready for milling, referring to sugar
cane.

tabatsóy (ta-bat-sòy), var. **tabatsúy**, I. *adj.*
fat; very fat, referring to a person.
—II. n. (Colloq.) a fat person; fatty.

taberna (ta-ber-na), n. (Sp.) tavern; bar. Syn.
bar, inuman ng alak.

tabernákulo (ta-ber-ná-ku-lò), n. (Sp.
tabernáculo) 1. tabernacle; container for
something holy. Syn. *sagraryo.* 2. place for
worship; church; temple. Syn. *sambahan,
dàlanginàn, simbahan, templo.*

tabí[1] (ta-bí), I. n. 1. the space, place, or
position beside or near a person or thing.
Syn. *piling.* 2. act of taking a position near
or beside another. Syn. *pagtabí, pagpiling,
pagsiping, pagsigbáy.* 3. act of staying or
passing along the side or border of (a
road, river, etc.). Syn. *gilid.* 5. edge;
border. Syn. *gilid.* 5. fact or state of being
close together side by side. Syn.
*pagkamagkatabí, pagkamagkapiling,
pagkamagkasiping, pagkamagkasigbáy.*

—II. *v. (imperative)* Get out of the way.

tabí[2] (ta-bí), n. 1. act of keeping something
in a safe place. Syn. *tagò, pagtatagò; ligpít,
pagliligpít.* 2. act of saving or keeping
something for the future. Syn. *impók, pag-
iimpók.* 3. anything saved for the future;
savings. Syn. *ang inimpók o naimpók.*

tabì (ta-bì) *v. & interj.* used in telling or
ordering people to get out of one's way.

tabiké (ta-bi-ké) , var. **tabikì**, n. light
partition wall. Syn. *dingdíng.*

tabig (ta-big) n. a hard backward push or
strike with the elbow. Syn. *sikó, pagsikó.*

tabíl (ta-bíl) n. talkativeness; garrulity;
glibness of tongue. Also, *katabilán.* Syn.
daldál, kadaldalán; satsát, kasatsatán.

tabing (ta-bing), n. 1. temporary screen or
curtain to hide or cover something in the
other side. Syn. *tabil.* 2. curtain; screen.
Syn. *kurtina, kansél, talon, biyumbo.* 3. the
way or manner a curtain or screen was put.
Also, *pagkakátabing.*

takal (ta-kal) n. 1. act of measuring liquid,
grains, or the like by volume, that is by
the liter, gallon, etc. Also, *pagtatakal.* 2.

the volume of liquids, grains, etc. measured or contained in a liter, gallon, or the like. 3. measure of capacity.

takám (ta-kám) n. a hankering or craving for something very tasty, usually manifested by the secretion of saliva in the mouth and the smacking of the lips and tongue. Cf. *labis na pananabík o pag-asám*.

takáp (ta-káp) n. 1. long, tireless talk or babbling. Syn. *daldál, kadadaldál*. 2. a seemingly endless bawling or vociferation. Syn. *waláng-tigil na pagmumurá*. 3. act of smacking the lips and tongue noisily in anticipation of something very tasty. 4. the sound thus made in this manner.

takas (ta-kas) I. n. 1. a fleeing; escape; flight; running away. Syn. *tanan, pagtanan, pagtatanan; puga, pagpuga*. 2. a runaway prisoner; escapee. Syn. *pugante*. 3. a person or persons who flee for refuge or safety. Syn. *likás, mga nagsilikás*.
—II. adj. referring to a person who escaped from confinement or prison.

takaták (ta-ka-ták) n. 1. sound or noise created by heavy raindrops on galvanized iron roofing. 2. rapid sound like the burst of fires from a machine gun.

takáw (ta-kaw) n. greed; greediness; voracity. Also, *katakawan*. Syn. *sibà, kasibaan; kasakimán*.

takáw (ta-káw), adj. 1. very eager. Syn. *sabík na sabík* 2. with or having a feeling of intense desire, esp. for sleep.

takaw-matá (ta-kaw + ma-tá). n. passing fancy for something new and tasty which one happens to see.

takbó (tak-bó) n. 1. run; act or manner of running. Also, *pagtakbó*. 2. operation or working condition, as of a machine, motor, etc. Syn. *andár, pag-andár*. 3. progress or condition, as of business. Syn. *lakad, lagáy, kalagayan, kondisyón*. 4. trend, as of times. Syn. *lakad, kalakaran*. 5. in racing, turn of a horse or runner to run. Also, *pagtakbó*. 6. flow, as of water in a river. Syn. *agos, pag-agos*. 7. flow, as blood in the body, electric current in the wire, etc. Syn. *talaytáy, pananalaytáy*. 8.

participation or entry, as of a candidate in an election. Syn. *lahók, paglahók; sali, pagsali*. 9. a running away, as from a fight. Syn. *pag-ayáw sa laban*. 10. a running away; escape. Syn. *takas, pagtakas*.

takdâ (tak-dâ) n. 1. limit; limitation. Syn. *limité, limitasyón*. 2. fixing of time. Syn. *taning*. 3. quota. Syn. *kota, limitasyón*. 4. condition or provision, as in a contract or agreement. Syn. *kondisyón, tadhaná, probisyón*.

takdáng-aralín (tak-dáng + a-ra-lín), n. lesson or assignment (in class).

takdáng-araw (tak-dáng + a-raw) n. 1. assigned or scheduled date; fixed time or date. Syn. *kaarawán*. 2. (Colloq.) death; time of one's death. Syn. *kamatayan, araw ng kamatayan*.

takigrapiya (ta-ki-gra-pi-ya). var. **takigrapya,** n. (Sp. *taquigrafia*) stenography. Syn. *iklilat*.

takilya (ta-kil-ya) n. (Sp. *taquilla*) 1. ticket window or booth. 2. box office.

takíp (ta-kíp) n. (general term) 1. cover. Also, *pantakíp*. 2. act of covering something. Also, *pagtatakíp*. 3. the way a thing is covered. Also, *pagkakatakíp*.

takíp-butas (ta-kíp + bu-tas) n. 1. something inserted to close up a hole or small opening; plug. Syn. *pasak, pamasak*. 2. stopper. Syn. *tapón, panapón*. 3. (Colloq.) substitution or replacement of someone who fails to come. Syn. *paglalagáy ng kapalít sa isáng di-dumatíng*. 4. (Colloq.) a person asked to take the place of someone who is absent. Also, *panakíp-butas*.

takíp-matá (ta-kíp + ma-tá) var. **takipmatá,** n. 1. (Anat.) eyelid. Syn. *talukap-mata*. 2. a blindfold; eye cover. Syn. *piríng*. 3. blinder. Syn. *sa-matá* (colloq.) ; *piríng*.

takíp-silim (ta-kíp + si-lim) var. **takípsilim,** n. twilight; nightfall. Syn. *ágaw-dilím, dapit-hapon*.

taklâ (tak-lâ), n. (Slang) 1. excretion of waste matter from the bowels; defecation. Syn. *pagtae, pagdumí, pananabi (colloq.)* 2. feces; excrement. Syn. *tae, dumí*.

taklób (tak-lób) n. 1. act of putting two things, as two plates, face to face. Also, *pagtataklób*. 2. act of covering something fully from the top. 3. anything used as a top cover. Syn. *takíp, panakíp; takob, panakob.*

tako (ta-ko) n. (Sp. *taco*) 1. billiard cue. Syn. *panumbók ng bola (sa bilyar)*. 2. plug; wad; wadding. Syn. *pasak, pamasak.*

takóng (ta-kóng) n. (Sp. *tacon*) the heel or heelpiece of a shoe.

takot (ta-kot) n. fear; fright; dread. Also, *pagkatakot.* Syn. *pangambá, sindák, pagkasindák.*

taksán (tak-san) adj. (Jap.), (commonly used during Japanese occupation of the Philippines; usually repeated: *taksátaksán,* very many).

taksíl (tak-síl) I. adj. disloyal; unfaithful; traitorous; treacherous. Syn. *lilo, palamara, sukáb, mapagkánulô.*

—II. n. a traitor. Syn. *taong palamara o lilo.*

takták (ta-ták), n. act of shaking out the contents of a container, e.g. a bottle, by holding it upside down and pounding the open mouth lightly on something.

taktiká (tak-ti-ká) n. (Sp. *tactica*) 1. tactic or tactics. Syn. *paraán, pamámaraán, sístema.* 2. plot or scheme. Syn. *pakanâ.*

takurî (ta-ku-rî) n. tea kettle.

takwíl (tak-wíl) n. a disowning or being disowned; repudiation. Also, *pagtatakwíl.* Syn. *tatwâ, pagtatatwâ.*

takyád (tak-yád) n. act or manner of walking on stilts. Also, *pagtatakyád.* Syn. *pagtatayakád.* 2. stilt or pair of stilts. Syn. *tayakád.*

tadhanà (tad-ha-nà), n. 1. nature. Syn. *kalikasan.* 2. fate; destiny. Syn. *kapalaran, suwerte, destino.* 3. provision or condition, as provided in an agreement or contract. Syn. *takdâ, probisyón, kondisyón.* 4. time limit. Syn. *taning, takdâ.*

tadtád[1] (tad-tád), I. n. act of mincing or chopping up (meat, etc.) into small bits. 2. state or condition of being minced or chopped into small bits.

—II. adj. minced or chopped up into small bits.

tadtád[2] (tad-tád), I. n. state or condition of being full of or thickly covered with pockmarks, etc.

—II. adj. full of or thickly covered with (pockmarks, etc,) Syn. *punúng-punô.*

tádtarin (tád-ta-rin) n. a kind of dance participated in by old devotees who parade around during a certain season.

tadyák (tadyák) n 1. a strong kick. Syn. *malakás na sipá, sikad.* 2. recoil, as of a gun when fired. Syn. *sikad, pagsikad.*

tadyáng (tad-yáng) n. 1. (Anat.) rib or ribs (in man). 2 a cut of meat with or having one or more ribs. Syn. *kustilyás.* 3. any one of the metal supports used to form, strengthen, or shape an umbrella in opening it. 4. any of the main veins in a leaf.

tae (ta-e), var. tai, n. 1. act of moving one's bowels; excretion of waste matter from the bowels; defecation. Also, *pagtae.* Syn. *pagdumí, pananabí (colloq.).* 2. feces; excreta; excrement. Syn. *dumí.* 3. dung; manure. Syn. *taing-hayop.* 4. droppings (of fowls). Syn. *ipot.*

taeb (ta-eb). n. rise of tide; high tide. Syn. *taog, pagtaog.*

tag- (tag-); prefix used in the formation of nouns denoting time or season, as in: *tag-ani,* harvest season; *tag-ulán,* rainy season, etc.

tagâ (tagâ) n. 1. act or manner of hacking a person or thing with a cutlass or bolo. Also, *pagtagâ, pananagâ.* 2. a big cut or wound inflicted by hacking with a cutlass or bolo. Syn. *sugat ng iták o tabák.*

tagá- (ta-gá-) prefix used to denote: (a) place of origin, birth or residence of a person, as in: *tagabukid, tagabundók, tagabayan,* etc. (b) duty or occupation assigned to someone, as in: *tagahatíd, tagasiyasat, tagasurí,* etc.

tagaakò (ta-ga-a-kò) n. & adj. said of a person who serves as a guarantor for someone. Syn. *tagapanagót, tagagarantiyá.*

tagaadyá (ta-ga-ad-yá) n. & adj. said of a savior or liberator. Syn. *tagaligtás, tagapagligtás.*

tagaalíw (ta-ga-a-líw) n. & adj. referring to someone whose duty is to entertain people. Syn. *tagalibáng, tagapáglibáng.*

taga-amin (ta-ga + a-min), n. & adj. referring to someone who is from our place.

tagaaregio (ta-ga-a-leg-lo), n. & adj. 1. said
of someone who makes repairs. Also,
tagapág-aregló. Syn. *tagakumpuní,
tagapagkumpuní*. 2. said of someone who
is assigned as an arbiter or intermediary
in the amicable settlement of disputes or
conflicts. Syn. *tagapamagitan, tagaayos,
tagapág-ayos*.

tagabalitá (ta-ga-ba-li-tá) n. reporter;
newspaper reporter or correspondent.
Also, *tagapágbalita*. Syn. *reporter*.

tagabayan (ta-ga-ba-yan) I. n. town resident;
town folk.
—II. adj. of or from the town, referring
to a person..

tagabukid (ta-ga-bu-kid) I. n. 1. barrio
resident; barrio folk. Syn. *tagabaryo,
taganayon*. 2. a farmer; farm worker. Syn.
magsasaká, mag-aararo.
—II. adj. of or from the barrio (said of a
person). Syn. *taganayon, mulâ o tubò sa
bukid (nayon)*.

tagabulag (ta-ga-bu-lag), var. **tagibulag**, n.
power of invisibility.

tagabundók (ta-ga-bun-dók) I. n. a
mountain dweller; mountaineer. Syn.
taong-bundók.
—II. adj. 1. of or from the mountains,
referring to a person; living in the
mountains.

tagaták (ta-ga-ták) n. 1. downpour or
downpouring, as of rain. Syn. *malakás na
buhos*. 2. the sound or noise created by
this. Cf. *lagaslás, laguslós*. 3. (Colloq.)
copious flow, as of tears, perspiration, etc.

tagagubat (ta-ga-gu-bat), I. n. forest dweller.
—II adj. of, from, or living in the forest,
referring to a person or persons; wild or
uncivilized.

tagaibáng-bansá (ta-ga-i-báng + ban-sá; +
ban-sâ) 1. n. foreigner.
—II. adj. of or from a foreign country. Syn.
tagaibáng-bayan, tagaibáng-lupá (for both
senses).

tagailog (ta-ga-i-log), n. & adj. said of a river
dweller.

tagál (ta-gál) n. 1. long duration of time.
Syn. *luwát, laon, habà ng panahon*. 2.
ability or capacity to endure. Syn.
kakayaháng magbatá. 3. long time. Also,

katagalán.

Tagala (Ta-ga-la) n. a female native of the
Tagalog region.

Tagalista (Ta-ga-lis-ta) n. & adj. said of
someone who is proficient in Tagalog.
Syn. *mánanagalóg*.

tagalitis (ta-ga-li-tis) I. n. 1. investigator.
Also, *tagapaglitis*. Syn. *imbestigador,
tagasiyasat, tagapagsiyasat*. 2. prosecutor.
Syn. *tagausig, tagapág-usig*.
—II. adj. said of someone assigned to
conduct an investigation of a case in
court.

Tagalog (Ta-ga-log) , I. n. 1. a native of the
Southern Luzon provinces, comprising
the provinces of Rizal, Laguna, Tayabas
(now Quezon), Batangas, Cavite,
Mindoro and Palawan. 2. the common
language used in this region.
—II. adj. of, from, or native of this region.

tagalupà (ta-ga-lu-pà). i. n. 1. earth
inhabitant; earth man. 2. (Colloq.)
anyone living on the ground or building.
Cf. *tagasilong*.
—II. adj. 1. living on the ground floor,
referring to a person. 2. from the earth,
said of a person.

tagapágkawanggawâ (-ka-wang-ga-wâ) n.
said of someone from whom others
received help or charity.

tagapágpaganáp (-pa-ga-nap). I. adj. 1.
executive; having to do with
management. Syn *pampangasiwaán*. 2.
with the power to put something into
effect. Syn *tagapágpatupád*.
—II. n. 1. executive; manager. Syn.
tagapangasiwà, tagapamahalà, punò. 2. the
executive department .

tagapágpahayag (-pa-ha-yag) n. & adj.
referring to a person whose duty is to make
announcements or declarations.

tagapágpanayám (-pa-na-yám; -yam) var.
tagapanayám, n. & adj. referring to
someone who is invited as a guest lecturer.

tagapágpasinaya (-pa-si-na-yà) n. & adj.
referring to someone who is lucky enough
to have the first chance to use a certain
place or to be given the first taste of
something.

tagapágpatibay (-pa-ti-bay), n. & adj. 1.

referring to a person who has the power or authority to approve appointments, recommendations, etc. Syn. *tagapágpatotoó, tagapágpatunay.*

tagapágrekisa (-re-ki-sa), var. **tagarekisa**, *n. & adj.* said of a person whose duty is to inspect or search a place or containers for things illegally hidden. Syn. *tagapághalughóg, tagahalughóg; tagapágsaliksík, tagasaliksík.*

tagapágsalin (-sa-lin), var. **tagasalin**, *n. & adj.* 1. said of one whose duty is to transfer or pour the contents from one container to another. Syn. *tagaliwat, tagapagliwat.* 2. referring to someone whose duty is to make translation from one language to another.

tagapágsalitâ (-sa-li-tâ), *n. & adj.* 1. said of someone who is invited as guest speaker. Cf. *tagapágpanayám, tagapágtalumpatì.* 2. referring to someone who represents another or others in voicing or expressing their requests, views, or opinions. Syn. *tagapágsabi, tagapágpahayag, tagapágsaád.*

tagapágsimpán (-sim-pán), var. **tagasimpán**, *n. & adj.* referring to a person on whom the burden of saving for the family is dependent. Syn. *taga-impók, tagapág-impók.*

tagapágsiyasat (-si-ya-sat), var. **tagasiyasat**, *n. & adj.* said of someone who is assigned or given the duty of investigating or conducting an inquiry about something. Syn. *tagaimbestigá, tagapág-imbestigá.*

tagapágtaguyod (-ta-gu-yod), var. **tagata-guyod**, *n. & adj.* referring to someone who acts as sponsor or supporter of a project, movement, etc. Syn. *tagatangkilik.*

tagapágtanggól (-tang-gol), var. **tagatanggól**, *n. & adj.* said of a person who acts as a defender of someone or of something. Syn. *tagasanggaláng, tagapágsanggaláng; tagadepensa, tagapágdepensa.*

tagapágturò (-tu-rò) var. **tagaturò**, *n. & adj.* 1. referring to someone who works as a teacher or as an instructor. 2. said of a person who directs or guides someone to a certain place.

tagapamahalá (ta-ga-pa-ma-ha-lá), *n & adj.* 1. referring to a manager or administrator.

Syn. *tagapangasiwá, mánedyér.* 2. said of a caretaker or keeper. Syn. *tagaalagá, tagapangalagá, kátiwalá.*

tagapamagitan (ta-ga-pa-ma-gi-tan), *n. & adj.* 1. referring to someone who acts as a mediator or moderator. Syn. *tagapama-yapá.* 2. said of a go-between, intermediary, or contact man. Syn. *tuláy* (*fig.*) 3. referring to someone who acts as a liaison officer.

tagasilangan (ta-ga-si-la-ngan), I. *n.* a native or citizen of the Orient; an oriental; easterner.

—II. *adj.* of, from, or native of the east (Orient), referring to a person.

tagasusog (ta-ga-su-sog), var. **tagapágsusog**, *n. & adj.* said of someone who is assigned or given the duty to propose or introduce amendments. Syn. *tagaenmyenda, tagapág-enmyenda.*

tagatakíp-butas (ta-ga-ta-kíp + bu-tas) *n. & adj.* said of a person who substitutes or acts as a replacement for someone who fails to come.

tag-á-tag-aráw (tag + á + tag + a-ráw), *adv.* every summer; every hot season. Syn. *tuwíng tag-aráw* (*tag-init*).

tagatangkilik (ta-ga-tang-ki-lik) *n. & adj.* said of someone who patronizes or supports a program, project, etc. Syn. *tagataguyod, tagapágtaguyod.*

tagatimog (ta-ga-ti-mog), *n. & adj.* said of a person who lives in or hails from the south.

tagatramo (ta-ga-tra-mo), *n. & adj.* said of a person who lives along a railway line.

tagaugit (ta-ga-u-git), *n. & adj.* 1. said of someone who steers a ship. Syn. *tagatimón.* 2. said of someone who is at the helm of an office, etc.; said of one who acts as an administrator or manager. Syn. *tagapamahalà, tagapangasiwà.*

tagaulo (ta-ga-u-lo), var. **tagapàg-ulo**, *n. & adj.* referring to someone whose duty is to provide articles, stories, etc. with titles or headings. Syn. *tagatítuló, tagapágtítuló.*

tagay (ta-gay), *n.* 1. drinking of wine. Syn. *barik, pagbarik.* 2. a drink in honor of someone; toast. 3. (in Taal, Batangas) young girl. Syn. *nenè, inéng* (*ining*).

tagaytáy (ta-gay-táy), n. 1. mountain range; ridge. 2. flow, as of current, water, or liquid on a line, wire, etc. 3. (T-) a city in the province of Cavite. Syn. *talaytáy, pagtalaytáy.*

tagbagyó (tag-bag-yó), n. typhoon season. Syn. *panahón ng bagyó.*

taggutom (tag-gu-tom; -tóm), n. period of starvation; famine. Syn. *panahón ng gutom o pagkakagutom.*

taghóy (tag-hóy), n. violent lament; lamentation. Also, *panaghóy, pananaghóy.* Syn. *daíng, pagdaíng.*

tagiktík (ta-gik-tík), n. (echoic) light, but sharp sound caused by the drop of tiny, hard objects on a hard surface. Cf. *tagistis.*

tagihawat (ta-gi-ha-wat) n. 1. pimple. 2. blackheads; comedo.

tagilid (ta-gi-lid), adj. 1. with the body turned to a side, said of a person lying on a bed. 2. leaning; inclined or tilted to a side. Syn. *hilíg, nakahilig, kilíng, nakakiling.* 3. (Colloq.) in danger of. Syn. *namímiligro.*

tagiliran (ta-gi-li-ran), n. 1. (Anat.) either side of the human or animal body; side. 2. the position or space near the side of a person or thing. Syn. *tabí, gilid.*

tagiló (ta-gi-ló), I. n. pyramid. Syn. *piramide.*
—II. adj. shaped like a pyramid; pyramidal. Syn. *hugis-piramide.*

tag-iló (tag + i-ló), n. (Bats.) sugar cane milling season. Syn. *tagkabyáw, panahon ng kabyawan.*

tagilóg (ta-gi-lóg), I. n. cone. Syn. *kono.*
—II. adj. shaped like a cone; conical. Syn. *hugis-kono.*

tagimtim (ta-gim-tim), I. n. refreshing feeling or satisfaction after one has done an act of charity or kindness to someone. Syn. *kasiyahang-loób.*
—II. adj. heartfelt; sincere; genuine. Syn. *taimtim, tapát, matapát, taós-pusò.*

tag-init (tag + i-nit; + i-nít), n. hot season; summer. Syn. *tag-araw (tag-aráw).*

tagintíng (ta-gin-tíng) n. tinkling or jingling sound as that of hard metal beaten with another hard metal. Cf. *kalansíng.* 2. high pitch; resonance, as of one's voice. Syn. *tinís, katinisán.*

tagís (ta-gís) n. act of sharpening lightly (a razor, knife, or the like) on a hone or whetstone. Syn. *lagís, paglalagís.* 2. a sharp disagreement or opposition; clash; conflict. Syn. *laban, paglalaban.*

tagistís (ta-gis-tís), n. 1. rapid flow or drip of water or liquid from a small hole, or the like. Syn. *malakás na tulò.* 2. the noise or sound created by this.

taglagás (tag-la-gás) n. autumn; fall.

taglamíg (tag-la-míg) n. winter; cold season.

tagláy (tag-láy) I. n. 1. carrying or keeping something in one's possession. Also, *pagtatagláy.* Syn. *dalá, pagdadalá.* 2. possessing or owning, as certain characteristics. Syn. *angkín, pag-aangkín.* 3. anything carried or kept in one's possession. Syn. *dalá.* 4. something that someone owns or possesses. Syn. *bagay na angkín.*
—II. adj. 1. carried or kept in one's possession. Syn. *dalá.* 2. being possessed or owned. Syn. *angkín.*

tagnî (tag-nî) n. a small patch covering a small hole or tear. Syn. *patse, tagpî.* 2. a small piece added or sewn to the side of another. Syn. *datig.*

tagò (ta-gò) n. 1. act of hiding or keeping oneself out of sight. Also, *pagtagò, pagtatagò.* Syn. *kublí, pagkublí, pagkukublí.* 2. act of keeping a secret to oneself. Syn. *paglilihim.* 3. act of keeping or storing something for the future. Syn. *impók, pag-iimpók.* 4. act of keeping something in a safe place. Syn. *ligpít, pagliligpít.*

tagô (ta-gô), I. adj. 1. hidden; not seen, said esp. of a place. Syn. *kublí, nakakublí; hindí kita.* 2. secret; clandestine. Syn. *lihim, sekreto, lingíd.* 3. not obvious; not easily seen or noticeable. Syn. *hindî hálatain.*
—II. n. the fact or condition of being hidden or secret.

tagós (ta-gós), I. n. 1. a permeating or being permeated. Syn. *siníp, pagsiníp; taós, pagtaós.* 2. a penetrating or being penetrated; piercing or being pierced through and through. Syn. *lagós, paglagós, paglalagós; lampas, paglampás; lusót, paglusót.*
—II. adj. 1. having permeated, as with water, etc. Syn. *siníp, nasiníp; taós, nataós.*

2. penetrated or pierced through and
through. Syn. *lampás, lámpasan; lagós,
lágusan; lusót, lúsutan.*

tagpî (tag-pî), n. 1. act of covering a hole or
tear by patching. Also, *pagtatagpî.* Cf.
tapal, pagtatapal; patse, pagpapatse. 2. the
patch thus made.

tagpô (tag-po), n. 1. meeting or seeing each
other in a certain place. Also, *pagtatagpô.*
Syn. *pagkikita, pagpapangita.* 2. a finding
or discovery, as of a means or way of doing
something. Syn. *tuklás, pagkátuklás,
pagkákita.* 3. (*Theat.*) scene, as in a play
or drama. Syn. *eksena.*

tagsabog (tag-sa-bog) n. (*Agri.*) sowing
season. Syn. *taghasík, hásikan.*

tagsibol (tag-si-bol; -ból) n. spring;
springtime.

tagtág[1] (tag-tág) I. n. 1. an unfastening or
being unfastened; a detaching or being
detached. Syn. *tanggal, pagtanggál; alís,
pag-aalís; bakbák, pagbakbák, pagbabakbák;
pigtás, pagpigtás; tukláp, pagtukláp.* 2. a
dismantling or being dismantled; taking
apart. Syn. *kalás, pagkalás; tanggál,
pagtanggál, pagtatanggál.* 3. (*Colloq.*)
dismissal or removal, as from
employment. Syn. *sisante, pagkásisante;
tiwalág, pagtitiwalág, pagkatiwalág.*

tagtág[2] (tag-tág), n. a shaking or being
shaken, as of passengers in vehicle passing
through a bumpy road. Syn. *alóg,
pagkaalóg; tigtíg, pagkatigtíg.*

taguán (ta-gu-án) , n. place for keeping or
hiding things, as a safe, cabinet, drawer,
etc. Syn. *ligpitan.* 2. hideout; hiding place,
esp. of criminals. 3. the game of hide-and-
seek.

tagubilin (ta-gu-bi-lin), n. 1. advice;
counsel. Syn. *payo.* 2. instruction;
direction. Syn. *direksiyon, paliwanag.* 3.
recommendation; endorsement. Syn.
rekomendasyón. 4. parting instruction or
order. Syn. *bilin, utos na iniwan.*

tagudtód (ta-gud-tód), n. 1. promontory;
headland. Syn. *lungos.* 2. the prominent
part of a highland. Syn. *gulód.*

tagulabáy (ta-gu-la-báy), n. (*Med.*) a kind
of skin eruption, characterized by itching,
burning sensation and the formation of

red, smooth patches or wheals; urticaria;
hives.

tagulamín (ta-gu-la-mín), n. mildew. Cf.
amag.

tag-ulán (tag + u-lán), n. rainy days; rainy
season. Also, *úlanan, pag-uúlanan.*

tagulayláy (ta-gulay-láy), n. 1. a
monotonous style or manner of singing,
as in Passion reading. 2. any song or *awit*
rendered in this manner or style. 3. love
song with sweet, sad melody.

tagumpáy (ta-gum-páy), n. 1. victory;
triumph. Syn. *pagwawagí, panalo,
pananalo.* 2. success; gaining or
attainment of wealth, fame, etc. Also,
pagtatagumpáy, pananagumpáy.

tag-unós (tag + u-nós), n. season during
which squalls are prevalent; also, typhoon
season. Syn. *tagsirá, tagsigwada.*

taguntón[1] (ta-gun-tón)́, n. a species of small
shrimp. Also, *hipong taguntón.*

taguntón[2] (ta-gun-tón), n. 1. tracing or
retracing, as of a path or route of someone.
Syn. *taluntón, pagtaluntón; tuntón,
pagtuntón; sagunsón, pagsagunsón.* 2. an
inquiry about or finding out the source
or origin of. Syn. *pagtuntón, pagtaluntón.*

tagurî (ta-gu-rî), n. an appellation; term of
endearment; pet name, as in: *bunsô,
mahál, giliw, irog,* etc. 2. nickname. Syn.
palayaw, banság. 3. the common name or
term for something. Syn. *tawag,
katawagán; ngalan, pangalan.*

taguyod (ta-gu-yod) , n. 1. patronage or
support given to a project, program, etc.
Also, *pagtataguyod.* Syn. *tangkilik,
pagtangkilik; suporta, pagsuporta.* 2. a
carrying out or bringing to completion.
Syn. *tapos, pagtapos.*

tahak (ta-hak), n. 1. a passing or walking
through, on, along, or over a new or
unusual place or path, esp. a difficult one.
Also, *pagtahak.* 2. an attempt to engage
oneself in something new or unusual. Cf.
pakikipagsápalarán.

tahák (ta-hák), *adj.* 1. said of a place, esp.
an open field, that has already been used
for passing along. 2. explored; not new;
old, as a certain field of research.

tahán (ta-hán), I. n. 1. a ceasing or stopping,

táhanan   **talaán**

as of rain, crying, running, etc. Syn. *tigil, pagtigil; hintô, paghintô; humpáy, paghumpáy; tugot, pagtugot; likat, paglikát.* 2. a residing or living in (a house, etc.). Syn. *tirá, pagtirá, paninirahan.* 3. temporary stay or sojourn. Syn. *tulóy, pagtuloy, panunuluyan.* 4. stay, as water in a low place or area, as after a rain. Syn. *pamamahay (colloq.).* 5. temporary suspension, as of work. Syn. *pagkátigil, pagkápatigil; pagkáhintô, pagkápahintô.*

—II. *adj.* 1. no longer crying, said of a baby. Syn. *hindî (na) umíiyák.* 2. not moving; resting; at rest. Syn. *tigil, nakatigil, hintô, nakahintô.* 3. not working; resting. Syn. *namámahingá, nagpápahingá.*

táhanan (tá-ha-nan), *n.* 1. home; residence; dwelling place. Syn. *tírahan.* 2. simultaneous stopping or ceasing. Syn. *tígilan, pagtitígilan; híntuan, paghihíntuan.*

tahás (ta-hás), I. *adj.* 1. clear and direct; definite; without fear of contradiction; in unmistakable term. Syn. *túwiran, hántaran (lántaran), tiyák.* 2. (*Gram.*) active (said of voice).

—II. *adv.* clearly and directly; definitely.

táhasan (tá-ha-san), I. *adj.* 1. (*Gram.*) active, as in: *tinig na táhasan,* active voice. 2. open; clear and direct; definite. Syn. *tiyák, tíyakan, lántaran, háyagan.*

—II. *adv.* definitely; clearly and directly. Syn. *nang túwiran o lántaran, díretsahan.*

taháw (ta-háw) , *adj.* 1. wide-open. Syn. *malawák at aliwalas.* 2. in the open air; exposed to view. Syn. *hantád, lantád, hayág.*

tahî (ta-hî) I. *n.* 1. act or manner of sewing or stitching. Also, *pagtahî, pananahî.* 2. the way or manner something is sewn. Also, *pagkakatahî.* 3. (*Surg.*) stitches. 4. clothing materials that a tailor is supposed to sew. Also, *tinahî.*

—II. *adj.* 1. sewn; provided with stitches. 2. made by sewing or stitching. Also, *tinahî.*

tahik (ta-hik) *n.* a dry or barren region.

tahíd (ta-híd), *n.* spur of a rooster; cockspur.

tahimik (ta-hi-mik), *adj.* 1. silent; quiet. Syn. *waláng kibô, waláng-imík, waláng-ingay, silénsiyó.* 2. calm; quiet; serene;

peaceful; tranquil. Syn. *payapà, panatag, tiwasáy.*

tahíp (ta-híp), *n.* act or manner of winnowing grains by tossing them up and down in flat basket called *bilao.* 2. rapid beating or palpitation (of the heart). Syn. *malakás na tibók (ng pusò), sikdó, pagsikdó.*

tahuré (ta-hu-ré) var. **táhurí,** *n.* (*Ch.*) fermented cakes of salted soybean curd preparation.

taimtím (ta-im-tím) I. *adj.* sincere; heartfelt; fervent. Syn. *tapát, matapát; taós; taóspusò.*

—II. *adv.* sincerely; fervently; deeply.

tainga (ta-i-nga), var. **taynga,** *n.* (*Anat.*) 1. ear. 2. anything shaped or placed like an ear, as the handle of a box, pitcher, and the like. Cf. *hawakán, tatanghán.* 3. hangnail. Also called *taingang-dagâ.*

taingang-kawalì (ta-i-ngang + ka-wa-lì), I. *n.* 1. the handle or ear of a frying pan. Syn. *mango o hawakán ng kawalì.* 2. (*Fig.*) a person who turns a deaf ear to any suggestion. Syn. *taong ayaw makiníg.*

—II. *adj.* said of someone who pretends to be deaf or who is unwilling to hear or heed.

taingang-dagâ (ta-i-ngang + da-gâ), *n.* 1. ear of a mouse. 2. (*Bot.*) an edible parasitic fungus (*Auricularia affinis*) that looks like a mouse ear and found growing on rotting wood. 3. (*Bot.*) Indian sorrel prostrate herd (*Oxalis repens Thund.*) with creeping stems that grow at the nodes.

taing-bituín (ta-ing + bi-tu-ín) *n.* (*Colloq.*) meteor.

talà (ta-là) *n.* 1. bright star; planet. Syn. *planeta, bituin, estrelya.* 2. (*Fig.*) a beautiful woman. 3. popular star or artist. Syn. *bituin (fig.)*

talâ (ta-lâ), *n.* notes; record. Also, *tálaan.* Syn. *lista, listahan, nota.* 2. act of listing or jotting down in a list. Also, *pagtatalâ.*

tala- (ta-la; -lá), pref. meaning "list or record of," as in: *taláaklatan, taláarawán, taláhuluganan,* etc.

talaan (ta-la-an; tá-la-an), *n.* list; register; record. Syn. *listahan.*

talaán (ta-la-án) *v.* to write on, referring to a chart, graph, etc. Syn. *listahán.*

talaarawan (ta-la-a-ra-wan; ta-lá-a-ra-wán), n. diary; journal.

taláb (ta-láb), I. n. 1. the act or action of cutting tools, like knife, plane, saw, chisel, plowshare, etc. Syn. *kagát* (*colloq.*). 2. the efficacy or effective action, as of an advice, medicine, etc. Syn. *bias, epekto.* —II. adj. 1. that can effectively cut, said of cutting tools or instruments. Also, *tumátaláb.* 2. that proved effective. Syn. *mabisá, may-bisá, nagkabisá*

talabá (ta-la-bá), n. (*Zool.*) oyster.

talababaan (ta-la-ba-ba-an; ta-lá-ba-ba-an), n. footnotes.

talabís (ta-la-bís), var. **talibís**, n. a very steep slope or declivity; cliff. Syn. *dalisdís.*

talák (ta-lák), n. loud and long outcry or vociferation. Syn. *pagbubungangâ.*

tálakayan (tá-la-ka-yan; tá-la-ka-yán) n. discussion or exchange of opinions about a certain subject. Syn. *diskusyón, pálitang-kurò.*

talaksán (ta-lak-sán), n. an orderly pile, as of cut firewood, sacks of grains, etc. Syn. *salansán, patas.*

talád (ta-lád), n. fight or conflict now becoming obsolescent, except in derivatives like *pakikitaláá, pagtataláá,* etc.

talagá (ta-la-gá) I. n. 1. will or disposition, as of God. Syn. *loób, kaloobán.* 2. induction or installation, as of officers of an association. Syn. *pagpapanumpâ o pagpapaluklok (sa tungkulin).* 3. act of assigning an employee to a certain place. Syn. *destino, pagdidestino.* 4. setting aside of something for a certain purpose. Syn. *laán, paglalaán; taán, pagtataán.*

taláhanayan (ta-lá-ha-na-yan; -ha-na-yán), n. 1. list; register. Syn. *talaan, listahan.* 2 table; table of contents. Syn. *talaan ng nilalamán.*

talahib (ta-la-hib), n. (*Bot.*) a species of coarse, erect perennial tufted grass (*Anthisteria gegantea*) growing in open field from underground rootstocks.

talahuluganan (ta-la-hu-lu-ga-nan; ta-lá-hu-lu-ga-nan), n. list of words with explanations; glossary. 2. vocabulary; dictionary. Syn. *bokabularyo, diksiyunaryo.*

talamák (ta-la-mák) adj. 1. serious; critical.

Syn. *malubhâ, lalâ, malalâ, mabigát, maselan (maselang).* 2. addicted or given to a certain bad habit. Syn. *sugapà.* 3. infused with much liquid. Syn. *tigmák, babád.*

talámbuhay (ta-lám-bu-hay), n. biography. Syn. *biograpiya (biograpya, biyograpiya).*

talamitam (ta-la-mi-tam), n. intimate or close association with another or others. Also, *pakikitalamitam.* Syn. *salamuhà, pakikisalamuhà; halubilo, pakikihalubilo.*

talampák (ta-lam-pák), I. n. 1. act of telling something openly to someone without fear or reservation. Syn. *pagtatapát, pagsasabi nang hárapan o lántaran.* —II. adj. frank; open; direct; face to face; unreserved. Syn. *tápatan, hárapan, túwiran, lántaran.* —III. adv. frankly; directly; openly; unreservedly. Syn. *tápatan, nang tápatan; hárapan, nang hárapan; lántaran, nang lántaran.*

talampakan (ta-lam-pa-kan; ta-lám-pa-kan), n. 1. sole of a foot. Syn. *ilalim ng paá.* 2. the sole or bottom of a shoe, slipper, etc. Syn. *suwelas.* 3. foot (as a measure of length, equal to 12 inches). Syn. *piyé.*

talampás (ta-lam-pás) n. (*Geol.*) mesa; tableland; plateau. Cf. *patag na kataasan.* 2. stiff cliff. Syn. *matarík na dalisdís.*

talandî (ta-lan-dî) I. n. coquette; flirt. —II. adj. flirty; coquettish. Syn. *hitád, kirí.*

talangkâ (ta-lang-kâ), n. a species of small crabs. Cf. *katáng (Bats.).*

talangkás (ta-lang-kás), n. a wad or bundle, as of paper money, betel leaves, etc.

talas (ta-las) n. 1. sharpness or keenness, as of blades, points, etc. Syn. *talím, katalimán; hayap, kahayapan.* 2. perceptiveness or keenness, as of eyes, hearing, etc. Syn. *husay (ng paningin, pandinig, atbp.).* 2. sharp-wittedness. Syn. *talisik, katalisikan.*

talásalitaan (ta-lá-sa-li-ta-an), n. vocabulary. Syn. *bokabularyo.*

talastás (ta-las-tás) I. n. 1. something that one knows. Syn. *alam, kaalaman.* 2. knowledge or understanding about something. Syn. *unawà, pagkáunawà; batíd, pagkabatíd.*

—II. *adj.* known to; understood by. Syn. *alám, nálalaman; batíd, nabábatíd; talós, natátalós; tantô, natatantô.*

talatà (ta-la-tà), *n.* a written or printed line. Syn. *taludtòd.*

tálataan (tá-la-ta-an), *n.* paragraph. Syn. *párapó, saknóng, saklóng.*

talátinigan (ta-lá-ti-ni-gan), var. **talátingigan**, *n.* pronouncing vocabulary or dictionary.

talbóg (tal-bóg) I. *n.* rebound; bounce; springing back, as of a rubber ball after striking a surface. 2. non-acceptance by a bank of a payee's rubber check.
—II. *adj.* 1. unsuccessful. Syn. *bigô.* 2. not accepted; returned, referring to a check which has no sufficient fund in the drawer's account.

talbós (tal-bós), *n.* 1. the tender growth of shoot at the tip of branches of trees and plants. Cf. *usbóng, suloy, supang.* 2. the green, tender tops or shoots of vegetables that are used for food.

talento (ta-len-to), I. *n.* (*Sp.*) talent; special or superior ability. Syn. *dunong, talino.*
—II. *adj.* (*Colloq.*) talented; gifted. Syn. *marunong, matalino.*

talì (ta-lì), *n.* 1. string; twine; cord; anything used for tying. Syn. *pisì, lubid, leteng.* 2. act or manner of tying something. Also, *pagtatalì.* 3. the way or manner a thing is tied. Also, *pagkakátalì.* 4. act of tying an animal to prevent it from roaming around. Syn. *pugal, pagpupugal.* 5. act of tying the hands and feet of a person or of the feet of an animal. Syn. *gapos, paggapos.* 6. act of tying something into a knot. Syn. *buhól, pagbubuhól.* 7. act of tying things into bundles. Syn. *bigkís, pagbibigkís.* 8. (*Colloq.*) long confinement in the house, as of a person, due to being bed-ridden, having too much work, etc. 9. in family planning act of tying the fallopian tube as a means of birth control.

talibà (ta-li-bà), *n.* guard; vanguard; sentinel. Syn. *guwardiyá, tanod, sentinela, bantay.* 2. act of or one's turn of guarding. Also, *pagtalibá.* Syn. *guwardiyá, pagguwardiyá; tanod, pagtatanod.*

talik (ta-lik), *n.* intimacy or closeness, as in:

talik ng kanilang pagkakaibigan, intimacy of their friendship. 2. friendly talk or conversation. Also, *pagtatalik.* Syn. *magiliw na pag-uusap o pag-uulayaw.*

talikdán (ta-lik-dán), *v.* 1. to turn one's back on. Syn. *talikurán.* 2. to leave or abandon. Syn. *iwan, pabayaan, layasan.* 3. to renounce; repudiate; disown. Syn. *itakwíl, itatuwâ (itatwâ).*

talikód (ta-li-kód), *n.* 1. act of turning one's back. Also, *pagtalikód.* 2. the position of the body with the back turned to someone or something. 3. repudiation; renunciation; disowning. Syn. *takwíl, pagtatakwíl; tatuwâ, pagtatatwâ.*

talikop (ta-li-kop), *n.* closing, as of two curtains being pulled towards each other from opposite directions. Syn. *sará, pagsará, pagsasará; pinid, pagpinid, pagpipinid; tikom, pagtikom, pagtitikom.* 2. a hemming in, around, or about; surrounding or encircling, as by two groups of soldiers meeting together at a certain point from opposite directions. Syn. *salikop, pagsalikop; kubkòb, pagkubkòb; paligid, pagpaligid.*

talikwás (ta-lik-wás), I. *n.* 1. act of tilting or raising a side (of something) slightly. Syn. *tikwás, pagtikwás.* 2. state or condition of being tilted or tipped. 3. act of turning over (something) or putting it upside-down. Syn. *baligtád, pagbaliktád.* 4. the position of a thing that is turned over, that is, with the bottom up.
—II. *adj.* 1. with or having the bottom up. Syn. *baligtád, nakabaligtád; tuwarík, nakatuwarík.*

talím (ta-lím), *n.* 1. sharpness or keenness, as of blades. Syn. *talas, katalasan.* 2. the cutting edge of a tool, instrument, etc.; blade. 3. the cutting point, as of an auger; bit. 4. the point, as of an arrow, spear, etc. Syn. *tulis.* 5. severity or sharpness, as of one's word or language. Syn. *sakít, kasakitán (colloq.); hayap, kahayapan (colloq.).* 6. piercing quality, as of someone's look or eyes. Syn. *lisik, panlilisik.*

talimáng (ta-li-máng), *n.* 1. a misleading or being misled. Syn. *pagliligáw o*

talimusák   **talós**

pagkápaligaw. 2. loss of one's order of counting. Syn. *pagkalimang o pagkahirá sa pagbilang.*

talimusák (ta-li-mu-sak), *n.* long-finned goby (*Oxyurichtys microlepis*), also called mud-skipper.

talindáw (ta-lin-dáw), *n.* an ancient boat song.

talino (ta-li-no), *n.* talent; intelligence; intellect. Syn. *dunong, talento, intelihénsiyá.*

taling (ta-ling), *n.* mole; a small congenital spot on the human skin. Syn. *nunál.*

talinghabâ (ta-ling-ha-bâ), *var.* **taluhabâ**, *adj.* oblong; oval; elliptical; elongate. Cf. *hugis-itlóg.*

talinghagà (ta-ling-ha-gà), *n.* 1. allegory; metaphor. Syn. *alegorya, metáporá.* 2. figure of speech. Syn. *tayutay.* 3. mystery; secret. Syn. *lihim, hiwagà.* 4. something that cannot be explained; mystery. Syn. *hiwagà, himalâ, kababalaghán.*

talipandás (ta-li-pan-dás), I. *adj.* impudent; shamelessly bold; insolent; brazen; disrespectful. Syn. *pusóng, bastós, waláng-galang, pangahás.* 2. hypocritical. Syn. *mapágkunwarî.*
—II. *n.* hypocrite. Syn. *ipókritá.*

talipapâ (ta-li-pa-pâ), *n.* a temporary or makeshift market.

talisay (ta-li-say), *n.* 1. (*Bot.*) a large, deciduous, shade tree (*Terminaliacatappa Linn.*). 2. (T-) a town in the province of Batangas.

talisayin (ta-li-sa-yin), I. *n.* 1. the whitish-green color of the feathers of a rooster. 2. a rooster having this color. Cf. *bulik, alimbuyugin, mayahin.*
—II. *adj.* referring to a rooster with or having whitish-green feathers.

talisod (ta-li-sod), *n.* 1. an accidental or intentional tripping of one's toes on something. Also, *pagtalisod, pagkátalisod.* Cf. *patid, pagpatid, pagkápatid, pagkápapatid.* 2. act of pushing something forward on a surface with the tip of the foot. 3. (*Fig.*) an accidental finding or discovery. Syn. *di-sinásadyáng pagkakitagpo o pagkátuklás.*

talisuyò (ta-li-su-yò), *n.* 1. doing favors for someone with the expectation of being rewarded or praised; ingratiation. Also, *pagsuyò, panunuyò.* 2. suitor. Syn *manunuyò, tagasuyò, mangingibíg.*

talistís (ta-lis-tís), *n.* (*Anat.*) small intestines.

taliwás (ta-li-wás). I. *n.* 1. state or condition of being opposed or contrary to the usual procedure or rule. Syn. *salungát, pagkasalungát; labág, pagkalabág.* 2. anything that deviates from the usual pattern or course; exception. Also, *pagkataliwás, kataliwasán.* 3. reversal, as of a decision. Syn. *pagsaliwâ, pagbaliktád.*
—II. *adj.* 1. opposed or contrary to. Syn. *laban, kontra, labág.* 2. deviating from the usual pattern or course. Syn. *saliwâ, lihís.*

talo (ta-lo), I. *n.* 1. defeat; loss in a contest, game, fight, etc. Also, *pagkatalo.* 2. number of losses or defeats. 3. the amount of money that someone lost in gambling. 4. act of defeating an opponent, as in boxing, basketball, chess, etc. Also, *pagtalo.* 5. loser; a player, boxer, candidate, etc. who suffered loss or defeat. Syn. *ang talunan.* 6. debate; verbal dispute or controversy. Also, *pagtatalo.* Syn. *debate, diskusyón, balitaktakan.* 7. (*Colloq.*) loss in sales or business. Syn. *lugí, pagkalugí, kalugihan.*
—II. *adj.* 1. defeated; vanquished; subdued. Syn. *supíl, nasupíl; lupíg nalupig.* 2. said of someone who lost his bet in gambling. Also, *natalo.*

talón (ta-lón) *n.* 1. act or manner of jumping down (from a height). 2. act or manner of jumping over a height. Syn. *lundág, paglundág; igpáw, pag-igpáw.* 3. sudden jump due to fright. Syn. *igtád, pag-igtád, pagkapaigtád.* 2. act of jumping to get something high over or above. Syn. *lundág, luksó.* 5. a skip or omission, as in typing. Syn. *salto, pagsalto.* 6.waterfall.

talóng (ta-lóng), *n.* (*Bot.*) eggplant (the plant or its fruit).

talóp (ta-lóp), *adj.* removed of the skin or peeling; pared off; peeled off. Syn. *walâ nang balát.* 2. decorticated, referring to a person's skin. Syn. *lapnós, tukláp.*

talós (ta-lós), I. *n.* 1. knowledge or understanding about something. Syn.

unawà, pagkáunawà; intindí, pagkaíntindí. 2. something that someone knows about. Syn. *alam, nálalaman.*
—II. *adj.* 1. understood. Syn. *náuunawaan, náiintindihán* 2. known to or by. Syn. *nálalaman, hindî lingíd sa.*

tálpakan (tál-pa-kan), I. *adv.* openly; frankly; directly; unreservedly; without fear or reservation. Syn. *lántaran, hárapan, déretsahan.*
—II. *n.* act of accusing each other openly.

talsík (tal-sík), n. 1. sudden flight or a being thrown asunder, as of small pieces or chips of wood, stone, etc. in the process of chopping or hewing. Syn. *tilapon, pagtilapon* 2. splash of water, mud, etc. Syn. *tilamsík, pilansík.* 3. (*Fig.*) dismissal or suspension from office. Syn. *sesante, pagkásesante, pagkaalís o pagkápaalís sa trabaho.*

talubatâ (ta-lu-ba-tâ), *adj.* of medium age; medium-aged. Syn. *medyo batà pa.*

talukab (ta-lu-kab), n. 1. carapace; the upper shell of crabs and other crustaceans. Syn. *bahay (colloq.).* 2. loose or detached scab (scabs) of old wounds. Syn. *tukláp o tangál nang langib.* 3. also used as a synonym of *talukap.*

talukap (ta-lu-kap), n. 1. sheath of palm leaves or banana stalks. Syn. *upak, talupak.* 2. lid of an eye; eyelid.

talukbóng (ta-luk-bóng), n. 1. veil. Syn. *belo.* 2. any piece of light cloth, handkerchief, etc. used to cover the head or something, including the face. Syn. *pandóng, pindóng, kulubóng.*

taluktók (ta-lol-tók), n. summit (of a hill, mountain, etc.); apex; highest point of. Syn. *káitaasan, tuktók.*

taludtód (ta-lud-tód), n. 1. row, line; file. Syn. *hanay, hilera, linya.* 2. line of poetry or verse. Syn. *talatà.*

táludturan (tá-lud-tu-ran), n. stanza; paragraph. Syn. *párapó, istansa, saknóng.*

talulot (ta-lu-lot), n. (*Bot.*) petal (of a flower).

talumpatì (ta-lum-pa-tì), n. 1. public talk or speech; oration; address. Syn. *diskurso.* 2. act or manner of delivering a speech in. Also, *pagtatalumpatian.*

taluntón (ta-lun-tón), n. 1. act of following or tracing a line, path, or the like. Syn. *tuntón, pagtuntón; salugsóg, pagsalugsóg.* 2. obedience or adherence, as to certain rules, regulations, etc. Syn. *sunód, pagsunód; talima, pagtalima.* 3. tracing, as of one's ancestry or lineage. Syn. *tuntón, pagtuntón.*

talungkô (ta-lung-kô), n. 1. act or manner of sitting flat on the floor in a relaxed manner. Syn. *pag-upô nang patalungkô o pasalampák.* 2. the position of a person seated flat on the floor doing nothing.

talurok (ta-lu-rok), n. 1. precipe. Syn. *matarík na dahilig.* 2. precipitousness. Syn. *tarík, katarikán.*

talusaling (ta-lu-sa-líng), *adj.* easily offended. Syn. *maramdamin.*

talusirà (ta-lu-si-rà), n. breach of promise or agreement. Syn. *pagsirà sa pangakò o kàsunduan.*

talusok (ta-lu-sok), n. 1. a peg. Syn. *barál.* 2. latch. Syn. *aldaba, tarengka (trangka).*

talyasì (tal-ya-sì), n. (*Ch.*) medium-sized iron vat, usually used for cooking rice during parties or celebration. Cf. *kawa.*

talyér (tal-yér), n. (Sp. *taller*) 1. workshop. Syn. *gáwaan, tárabahuhán.* 2. factory. Syn. *pábriká, págawaan.* 3. workroom of a painter, sculptor, etc. Syn. *istudyo.*

tama (ta-mà), I. n. 1. a right or correct answer. Syn. *tumpàk o wastóng sagót (tugón).* 2. a successful hit or strike; a shot that hits the mark. 3. a wound caused by a bullet. Syn. *sugat ng punlô.* 4. a winning number or numbers. 5. a right fit or adjustment. Syn. *lapat; ayos na pagkakàlapat o pagkákakabit.* 6. fact or state of being right or correct, as one's answer to a question. 7. that which is right, lawful, morally good, or proper, etc.
—II. *adj.* 1. right; correct. Syn. *tumpák, wastô.* 2. fit or proper, as one's action, decision, etc. Syn. *akmâ, tugmâ, angkóp, bagay, nábabagay.* 3. winning, as a bet. Syn. *nanalo, panalo.* 4. that which hits the mark.

tamák (ta-mák), *adj.* 1. impregnated with water or liquid; thoroughly soaked or drenched. Syn. *babád, tigmák.* 2.

aggravated; already serious. Syn. *malalâ, talamák.*

tamád (ta-mád), I. *adj.* lazy; indolent; slothful. Syn. *batugan, matigás ang katawán.*

—II. *n.* state or fact of being lazy. Syn. *katámaran, pagkatamád, pagkabatugan.* 2. an indolent person.

tamaraw (ta-ma-raw; -ráw), *n.* (*Zool.*) a small, wild carabao specially found in the highland of Mindoro.

tamarindo ta-ma-rin-do) *n.* (*Sp.*) 1. a drink preparation made from the ripe tamarind fruit. 2. tamarind jam.

tamasa (ta-ma-sa), *n.* enjoyment, as of wealth, good health, abundance, etc. Syn. *pananaganà; pagtatamó ng kasaganaan, kayamanan, kalusugan, atbp.*

tambák (tam-bák), *n.* 1. act of filling up a low area or place. Also, *pagtatambák.* 2. a heap or pile, as of garbage, etc. Syn. *buntón.* 3. accumulation, as of official papers not acted upon.

tambakán (tam-ba-kán), *v.* 1. to fill up (a low place), as with earth, garbage, etc. Syn. *tabunan.* 2. to give, provide, supply, etc. with too much of. Syn. *buntunán ng maraming trabaho, pagkain, atbp.; bigyán nang labis-labis.*

tambakol (tam-ba-kol), *n.* 1. (*Ichth.*) yellowfin tuna (*Neothunnus macropterus*). 2. (by extension) a big, fat person. Syn. *tabatsóy.*

tambàd (tam-bád), I. *adj.* exposed to view; in the open. Syn. *hantád, nakahantád; lantád, nakalantád; kita, nákikita; litáw, nakalitáw; hayág, nakahayág.*

—II. *n.* 1. state or condition of being exposed to view. Syn. *pagkahantád, pagkalantád, paghayág.* 2. an open or exposed place.

tambál (tam-bál), I. *n.* 1. a pair, as of dancers. Syn. *pares, pareha.* 2. partners, as of two players playing doubles. Syn. *sanggá, ang magkasanggá.* 3. act of acting as a partner or a pair of another in dancing. Syn. *pagtambál, pagpareha.* 4. act of playing with another as his partner. Syn. *pagsanggá, pakikisanggá.* 5. act of joining together, as in a business partnership. Syn.

sosyo, pagsososyo. 6. something attached to the surface of another to reinforce it. Syn. *sapí.*

—II. *adj.* 1. dancing as a pair, referring to two dancers, Also, *magkatambál.* 2. playing together as partners, as in tennis doubles. Syn. *sanggá, magkasanggá.* 3. (*Gram.*) compound, said of a sentence.

tambáng (tam-báng), *n.* 1. an ambushing; ambush; ambuscade; waylaying. Also, *pagtambáng, pananambáng.* Syn. *harang, pagharang, panghaharang; abat, pag-abat, pang-aabat.* 2. a person or persons lying in wait in order to attack. Syn. *abat, tagaabat.*

tambilang (tam-bi-lang), *n.* any numeral from 0 to 9; digit.

tambíng[1] (tam-bíng), *adv.* at once; immediately, as in: *Hindî tambíng na magágawâ iyón.* That cannot be done at once.

tambíng[2] (tam-bíng), *n.* 1. act of putting or providing an equal amount, share. etc. to what another has given. Syn. *pagbibigáy ng katumbás.* 2. an equal amount or share thus put up or given. Syn. *tumbás, katumbás.*

tambís (tam-bís), *n.* an indirect statement. Syn. *pahiwatig, paramdám.* 2. innuendo; insinuation. Syn. *pasaríng, pariníg, parunggít.*

tambiyolo (tam-byo-lo, *n.* (Sp. *tambiolo*) lottery drum where numbered tickets or balls are deposited and drawn to get the winning numbers.

tambók (tam-bók), *n.* 1. bulge; protuberance. Syn. *umbók.* 2. swelling; swollen part. Syn. *magâ, pamamagâ.* 3. bulk; bulkiness. Syn. *lakì* (*colloq.*) . 4. convexity. Syn. *umbók, kaumbukán.*

tamból (tamból), *n.* (Sp. *tambór*) 1. drum. Syn. *bombo.* 2. the act or manner of beating a drum. Also, *pagtamból.*

tambulì (tam-bu-lì) *n.* 1. bugle made of horn; hornpipe. 2. the sound of a hornpipe.

tambutso (tam-but-so), *n.* (Sp.) exhaust pipe.

tamilmíl (ta-mil-míl), var. *tumilmíl,* *adj.* without appetite; eating just a little due to lack of appetite. Syn. *waláng ganáng kumain; mahinang kumain dahil sa kawaláng gana*.

tamís (ta-mís), n. 1. sweet taste, as of sugar; sweetness. Also, *katamisàn*. 2. pleasure; pleasurable experience.

tamláy (tam-láy), n. 1. indisposition; downheartedness; debility; lassitude; languor. Syn. *panlalambót o panghihiná ng katawán*. 2. coolness; lack of interest or liking. Syn. *kawalán ng gana o interés*. 3. dullness or sluggishness, as of business. Syn. *hinà ng negosyo*.

tamó (ta-mó), n. 1. acquisition, as of a prize, honor, etc. Syn. *tanggáp, pagtanggaáp; kamít, pagkakamít*. 2. benefit. Syn. *pakinabang, kapakinabangán*.

taód (ta-mód) , var. **tamúd**, n. semen.

tampák (tam-pák), I. n. act of accusing someone openly. Syn. *talampák, pagtalampák*.

—II. adj. open; frank. Syn. *hárapan, tápatan, prangka*. 2. evident; obvious. Syn. *hayág, lantád, di-lihim*.

—III adv. 1. openly; frankly. Syn. *háyagan, lántaran*. 2. obviously; evidently.

tampál (tam-pál), n. a slap or blow with the palm of the hand, as in killing a mosquito while biting the skin; distinguished from *sampál*.

tampalasan (tam-pa-la-san), adj. 1. destructive; vandalistic. Syn. *mapanirá, mapagwasák*. 2. (Colloq.) wasteful. Syn. *mapág-aksayá, mapagtapón*. 3. said of an embezzler. Syn. *mapáglustáy*.

tampipì (tam-pi-pì), n. a small clothes chest or trunk made of palm leaves, split rattan, bamboo, etc. Cf. *takbá, maleta, malitín*.

tampisák (tam-pi-sák), n. act of walking or wading through water and mud. Also, *pagtatampisák*.

tampisáw (tam-pi-sáw), n. act of wading playfully in water, as by splashing with one's feet.

tampó (tam-pó), n. 1. resentment; ill humor shown by a sullen, withdrawn behaviour. Syn. *hinanakít, paghihinanakít, samâ ng loob*. 2. act of sulking. Syn. *maktól, pagmamaktól*.

tampók (tam-pók), n. 1. (Bot.) the short

stem of a fruit or flower. Syn. *tangkáy*. 2. gem or precious stone set, esp. on a ring. Syn. *bató, pabató (colloq.)*. 3. main feature in a program or celebration. Syn. *pinakamahalagáng bahagi*. 4. the leading actor or actress in a certain production; star. Syn. *pangunahíng artista o bituín*. 5. the presentation or featuring of a person or thing as the main event in the celebration. Also, *pagtatampók*.

tampól (tam-pól), n. dashing or surging of water against the shore. Syn. *salpók ng alon sa baybaying-dagat*. 2. act of casting one's eyes on someone or something attractive.

tampóy (tam-póy) n. (Bot.) a small tree (*Syzygium jambos*) cultivated as a shade tree and for its fruit, which is rather dry, somewhat sweet, with faint odor of rose, and with a flavor similar to but better than *makopa*.

tamtám (tam-tám) adj. (obsolescent) sufficient; good enough.

taná (ta-ná). v. (Colloq.) short for *katâ na*, let us go.

tanaga (ta-na-ga), n. the Pilipino version of the Japanese haiku.

tanan (ta-nan), I. n. escape; act or manner of escaping. Syn. *takas, pagtakas*. 2. act of running away secretly, as two lovers, in order to get married; elopement. Also, *pagtatanan ng magkasintahan*. 3. escapee; fugitive; deserter. Syn. *takas, puga*. 4. refugee. Syn. *likas, ang lumikas o nagsilikas*. 5. lovers who eloped.

—II.. adj. 1. said of an escapee, fugitive, or deserter; having escaped or run away. Syn. *takas, tumakas, nakatakas*. 2. said of lovers who have eloped together.

tanàn (ta-nàn), pron. all; everyone; everybody. Syn. *lahát*.

tanáng (ta-náng), adj. all; without exception. Syn. *lahát, lahát-lahát, waláng hindî (kasama)*.

tanáw (ta-náw), I. n. 1. act of looking at someone or something from a distance. Syn. *tingín o pagtingín sa tao o bagay na nasa malayò*. 2.distant observation or assessment of, as in: *Sa tanáw ko'y magandá ang babaing iyón*. That woman is beautiful according to my distant

observation. 3. distant focus of one's eyes.
Syn. *malayóng tingín*.

—II. *adj.* visible or seen from a distance;
can be seen from afar. Syn. *kita o nakikita
sa malayò, abót ng matá (paningín)*.

tánawin (tá-na-win), n. scene; scenery; view;
panorama. Syn. *bista*.

tandâ¹ (tan-dâ), n. 1. age; the time that a
person or thing has existed since birth or
from the beginning. Syn. *edâd, gulang*. 2.
old age; oldness. Also, *katandaán*. Syn.
gulang, kagulangan, kaedarán 3. an old
person.

tandâ² (tan-dâ), n. 1. sign; indication. Syn.
palátandaan. 2. mark indicating a place,
time, etc. Syn. *marka, palátandaan*. 3.
marker; anything used to mark a place.
Syn. *panandâ*.

tandâ³ (tan-dâ), n. 1. remembering; retention in one's mind. Syn. *pagtatandâ,
pagsasaulo*. 2. memory; recollection. Syn.
alaala, gunitâ, memorya. 3. remembrance;
memorial. Syn. *alaala, pag-alaala*.

tandáng (tan-dáng) , n. 1. rooster; cock;
adult male of fowls. 2. a gamecock. Syn.
sasabungin, manók na panabong.

tandís (tan-dís), I. *adj.* 1. sure; definite;
certain. Syn. *tiyák, tahás, sigurado*. 2.
frank; open. Syn. *tapát, tápatan; hayág,
háyagan; lantád, lántaran*.

—II. *adj.* surely, definitely; certainly. 2.
frankly; openly.

tanikalâ (ta-ni-ka-lâ), n. 1. metal chain.
Syn. *kadena*. 2. act of fastening someone
or an animal with a chain or chains. Also,
pagtatanikalâ. Syn. *pagkakadena*. 3. the
manner a person, animal, or thing is
chained. Syn. *pagkakákadena*. 4. bonds;
shackles; anything that binds or ties. Syn.
kadena, posas, gapos.

tanigì (ta-ni-gì), n. (*Ichth.*) Spanish
mackerel (*Scomberomorus commerson*).

taním (ta-ním), I. n. plant. Syn. *halaman*. 2.
act or manner of planting. Also,
pagtataním. 3. the manner by which plants
were planted. Also, *pagkakátaním*. 4.
(*Fig.*) act or instance of harboring a
grudge or ill feeling against someone.
Also, *pagtataním*.

—II. *adj.* said of plants that are purposely

planted; planted, as distinguished from
wild or those not planted. Syn. *itinaním*.

taning (ta-ning), n. time limit; fixed time
or date. Syn. *takdâ, takdáng oras*. 2.
provision or term, as in a contract. Syn.
tadhanà, probisyón.

tanod (ta-nod), n. 1. guard; sentinel;
watcher; watchman. Syn. *guwardiyá,
talibà, sentinela, bantáy*. 2. the act, turn,
or time of guarding. Syn. *pagguwardiyá,
pagtalibà, pagsentinela*.

tanóng (ta-nóng), n. 1. question or problem
in an examination or test. 2. that which
someone is asking about. Also,
katanungan. 3. act of asking someone
about something interrogation. Also,
pagtatanóng. 4. act of inquiring from
someone what he knows about a certain
thing. Syn. *usisà, pag-uusisà*.

tansàn (tan-sàn), n. 1. bottle cap, esp. of
bottled soft drinks. 2. (*Colloq.*) soda water.

tansô (tan-sô), n. 1. (*Min.*) copper; brass
(alloy of two parts copper and one part
zinc); bronze (alloy of copper and tin). 2.
(*Colloq.*) a swindling or being swindled.
Syn. *gantso, paggantso, pagkágantso*.

tantán (tan-tán), n. cessation, as of
someone's continuous babbling or
chattering. Syn. *tigil, pagtigil; hintô,
paghintô; likát, paglikát*.

tantáng¹ (tan-táng), var. **tangtáng**, I. n. 1.
long exposure to heat, resulting in
excessive dryness. Syn. *matagál o labis na
pagkadaráng*. 2. fact or condition of being
excessively dry due to long exposure to
heat. Syn. *tigang, pagkatigang (nang labis)*.

—II. *adj.* exposed too long to heat; very
dry. Syn. *tuyúng-tuyô sa pagkadaráng,
tigáng*.

tantáng² (tan-táng), var. **tangtáng**, n. light
but continuous or repeated pull or jerk.

tantiyá (tan-ti-yá), var. **tantyá**, n. (*Sp.
tantear*) 1. estimate; calculation; result
found by reckoning. Syn. *taya, kalkulá*.
2. act of estimating; calculation. Syn.
pagtaya, pagkalkulá.

tanto (tan-to), *adv.* (*Sp.*) 1. so; too; very, as
in: *Hindî tantong mahirap intindihín*, not
so hard to understand. Syn. *lubhâ,
masyado*. 2. the more, as in: *Tanto mong*

pinàgbubuti, lalo pang nagkakámali. The more you do your best, the more you make mistakes.

tantô (tan-tô), I. *n.* 1. knowledge or understanding about something. Syn. *unawà, pagkaunawà; intindí, pagkáintindí; alam, pagkaalam.* 2. act of understanding or realizing, e.g. the consequences of. Syn. *pag-unawá, pag-intindí.*
—II. *adj.* having come to realize or understand; aware about. Syn. *alám, nálalaman; batíd, nabábatíd; intindido, naiintindihan; náuunawaan.*

tanyág (tan-yág), I. *adj.* popular; well-known; famous; prominent. Syn. *bantóg, kilaláng-kilalá, litáw, balitá.* 2. open; exposed to view. Syn. *lantád, hayág, kita.*
—II. *n.* an open place where everybody can be seen.

tangá (ta-ngá), *adj.* 1. stupid; ignorant; slow-witted. Syn. *ungás, hangál, gunggóng, bangág, tunggák.* 2. uneducated. Syn. *mangmáng, waláng-pinág-aralan, gago.*
—II. *n.* 1. a stupid person. Syn. *taong gago o mangmáng.* 2. act of gazing at something absent-mindedly. Also, *pagtangá.* 3. (by extension) act of wasting one's time by watching something, unmindful of his duty.

tangà (ta-ngà), *n.* 1. bookworm. 2. clothes moth. 3. potato or sweet potato bug or worm with a certain peculiar odor or taste.

tangab (ta-ngab), *n.* 1. a slanting cut at the end of a tenon, or the like, to make easier insertion. Syn. *tapyás.* 2. the slight indentation on the mouth of cups, pitchers, glasses to make pouring of contents easier.

tangan (ta-ngan), I. *n.* 1. act of holding something in or with one's hand. Syn. *hawak, paghawak, paghahawak.* 2. anything held in or with one's hand. 3. the right to own or possess something, or to occupy a position.
—II. *adj.* 1. held in, with, or by the hand. Syn. *hawak, pigil, nasa kamáy.* 2. occupied or held in one's possession.

tangas (ta-ngas), *n.* scornful or disdainful attitude towards others, esp. in one's language. Also, *katangasan, pagkamatangas.* Syn. *kasupladuhan, kapalaluan, o kataasan*

sa pagsasalitâ.

tangáy (ta-ngáy), I. *n.* 1. a carrying away or being carried away, as by running, kidnapping, by the current, wind, etc. Also, *pagtangáy, pagkatangáy.* Syn. *dalá, pagkadalá.* 2. act of holding tightly in the mouth, as bone by a dog. Syn. *pagkagát nang mahigpít.* 3. a person carried by a kidnapper, or anything carried by the current or wind. 4. anything held tightly in the mouth.
—II. *adj.* 1. carried away. Syn. *dalá, dinalá, nadalá.* 2. held tightly in the mouth. Syn. *kagát, kagat-kagát.*

tangkâ (tang-kâ), *n.* 1. a try or endeavour; attempt. Syn. *subok, pagsubok; ato, pag-ato.* 2. intent, intention; plan; purpose. Syn. *balak, pagbabalak; layon, láyunin; hangád, hangarin; pakay na tamuhin.*

tangkád (tang-kád), *n.* slenderness and tallness of structure. Syn. *hagwáy, kahagwayán, taás o kataasán ng tindig.*

tangkál (tang-kál), I. *n.* chicken coop or cage. Syn. *kúlungan ng manók.*
—II. *adj.* (Colloq.) kept or confined in a coop, referring to fowls. Syn. *nakatangkál, kulóng o nakakulóng sa tangkál.*

tangke (tang-ke; -ké), *n.* 1. (Mil.) tank (a heavily armoured combat vehicle). 2 tank (big container of water, gasoline, gas, etc.)

tangkilik (tang-ki-lik), *n.* 1. patronage; support. Also, *pagtangkilik.* Syn. *taguyod, pagtataguyod.* 2. help, aid. Syn. *tulong, pagtulong.*

tanggál (tang-gál), I. *n.* 1. a detaching or being detached. Also, *pagtanggál.* Syn. *bakbák, pagbakbák; tukláp, pagtukláp; puknát, pagpuknát.* 2. a disconnecting or being disconnected. Syn. *pag-alís o pag-aalís sa pagkakakábít.* 3. removal or dismissal, as from work. Syn. *sisante, pagsisante, pagtitiwalág.*
—II. *adj.* 1. detached; unfastened. Syn. *bakbák, nabakbák, binakbák; tukláp, natukláp, tinukláp.* 2. disconnected; removed. Syn. *inalís, naalís.* 3. dismissed or removed from employment. Syn. *inalís sa trabaho, sinisante, itiniwalág.*

tanggáp (tang-gáp), I. *n.* 1. act of accepting something offered or being given. Syn.

pagkuha o pag-abót sa ibiníbigáy. 2. act of receiving something sent by someone, as a *letter*, telegram, etc. 3. acceptance or recognition, as of an evidence or testimony in court. Cf. *pagkilala*, *pagpapahalagá.* 4. admission or confession of a crime or guilt by an accused. Syn. *pag-amin*, *pagtatapát.* 5. admission or approval, as of one's application for employment, enrollment, etc.
—II. *adj.* 1. admitted, referring to a crime or guilt levelled at an accused. Syn. *inamin.* 2. accepted; admitted; recognized. Syn. *kinilala.* 3. received. Also, *tinanggáp*, *natanggáp.*

tanggapan (tang-ga-pan), n. 1. office. Syn. *opisina (upisina).* 2. receiving or reception room; visitors' room. Syn. *sala o bulwagan ng mga panauhin.* 3. time or place of admission (as of workers) or enrolment (as of students).

tanggí (tang-gí), n. 1. refusal to grant or give. Syn. *pahindî*, *pagpapahindî.* 2. denial; refusal to tell the truth. Syn. *kailâ*, *pagkakailâ.* 3. a disowning; repudiation. Syn. *takwil*, *pagtatakwíl; tatwâ*, *pagtatwâ.*

tanggigì (tang-gi-gì), var. **tangginggì**, n. (*Ichth.*) Spanish mackerel.

tanggól (tang-gól), n. 1. guarding against attack; defense; protection. Syn. *sanggaláng*, *pagsasanggaláng; depensa*, *pagdedepensa.* 2. act of defending an accused in court.

tanggulan (tang-gu-lan), n. 1. defense, as in: *Tanggulang bansá*, national defense. 2. fort; fortification. Syn. *muóg*, *kutá.* 3. act of defending each other from attacks. Also, *pagtatánggulan.* Syn. *sánggalangan*, *pagsasánggalangan.*

tanghál (tang-hál), I. n. 1. an exhibit or exhibition; display. Syn. *eksibisyón.* 2. act of showing or exhibiting (things) to the public. Also, *pagtatanghál.* 3. showing or presentation, as of a play or drama. Syn. *palabás*, *pagpapalabás.* 4. an open place where everybody can be seen. Syn. *hantád na lugár o poók.*
—II. *adj.* 1. exposed to the view; in the open. Syn. *hantád*, *lantád*, *hayág*, *bukás*, *kita.* 2. popular; prominent. Syn. *tanyág*,

kilalá, *populár.*

tanghalan (tang-ha-lan), n. 1. exposition; fair. Syn. *perya.* 2. showhouse, as a theatre, cinemahouse, etc. Syn. *bahay-pálabasan.* 3. stage. Syn. *entablado.*

tanghalí (tang-ha-lí), I. n. noon; noonday; noontime; midday.
—II. *adj.* (*Colloq.*) late (in the morning); with the sun already high in the morning, as in: *Tanghalí ka na.* You are already late.

tanghalian (tang-ha-li-an), n. 1. the regular midday meal; luncheon. Syn. *pananghalí; pagkain ng pananghalian.* 2. the food eaten during a noontime meal. Syn. *pagkain sa tanghalí.*

tanghód (tang-hód), n. 1. act of watching or looking at something patiently. Syn. *matiyagáng panonoód o pagbabantáy.* 2. act of waiting around hopefully or patiently with the expectation that someone would give him something. Also, *pananaghód.* 3. a patient expectator or onlooker. Syn. *matiyagáng mirón.*

tangì (ta-ngì), I. n. 1. lone; alone; only; only one; single, as in: *tanging anák*, a lone child. Syn. *íisá,nag-íisá*, *bugtóng*, *kaisá-isá.* 2. special; different from all others. Syn. *ibá*, *náiiba.* 3. special; particular; exceptional, as in: *Tanging karapatán*, special right.
—II. n. 1. taking exception. 2. special regard for. Also, *pagtatangí* (for both senses).

tangilì (ta-ngi-lì), I. n. 1. (*Bot.*) a species of red mahogany (*Shores polysperma*), the wood or lumber of which is popularly used for furniture making. 2. the wood or lumber of this tree.
—II. *adj.* of or made of *tangilì.*

tangis (ta-ngis), n. 1. act of weeping or crying. Syn. *iyák*, *pag-iyák.* 2. mourning; wailing or lamentation. Also, *pagtangis*, *pananangis.* Syn. *pagtaghóy*, *pananaghóy.* 3. continuous subdued crying or weeping. Syn. *nguyngóy*, *pagnguyngóy.*

tanglád (tang-lád), var. **tanlád**, n. (*Bot.*) lemon grass; sweetgrass; gingergrass (*Andropogon citratus DC.*).

tangláw (tang-láw), var. **tanláw**, n. 1. light. Syn. *ilaw.* 2. any source of light, as a lamp, candle, moon, sun, etc. 3. anyone who participates in a night procession carrying a lighted candle. 4. anything that gives mental illumination.

tangnán (tang-nán), var. **tangnan**, v. 1. to hold in or with one's hand. Syn. *hawakan*. 2. to take over or hold, as an office or position. Syn. *tuparín, panungkulán, hawakan gampanán*.

tango (ta-ngô), n. 1. nod or nodding of head, as in assent or agreement. Also, *pagtangô*. 2. consent; agreement. Syn. *pagpayag, pagsang-ayon, pag-oo*.

tangos (ta-ngos), n. 1. prominence or sharpness, as of a nose; opposed to *pangô, kapanguán; sarát, kasaratán*. 2. (Geog.) cape; headland; promontory. Syn. *punta, tangwáy, lungos*.

tangwá (tang-wá), n. (Ch.) 1. the edge of a steep height, as of cliff or precipice. Syn. *bingit, gilid ng mataás at matarík na bangín*. 2. precipice; steep cliff. Syn. *matarík na dalisdís*.

tangwáy (tang-wáy), n. (Geog.) peninsula. Cf. *tangos, lungos*.

tao (ta-o), n. 1. human being; person; man, as distinguished from animal. 2. (Colloq.) people; persons, as in: *Sampúng tao lamang ang dumaló*. Only ten people attended. 3. (Colloq.) husband, as in: *Walâ rito ang tao ko*. My husband is not here. 4. a person left alone in the house, office, etc. as guard or caretaker when others are away. Cf. *bantáy, tanod*.

taób (ta-ób), I. n. 1. act of lying down with the stomach and face under. Syn. *dapâ, pagdapâ*. 2. act of placing a cup, plate, drinking glass, or the like with the bottom up. Syn. *tuwarik, pagtutuwarik*. 3. the position of something with the bottom up; upside down position of anything. 4. bankruptcy of a banker (in gambling). 5. (Fig.) loss or defeat, esp. of a champion, to an unknown opponent.

—II. adj. (nakataób) 1. lying flat with the stomach and face under. Syn. *nakadapâ*. 2. with the bottom or back up; placed upside down. Syn. *tuwarík, nakatuwarík*. 3. bankrupt, said of a banker in gambling. Syn. *bagsák, bumagsák*. 4. defeated, said

of a champion. Syn. *talo, natalo*.

taog (ta-og), I. n. 1. rise of tide; high tide. Syn. *lakí o taás ng tubig sa dagat*. Ant. *kati*. —II. adj. with or having high tide. Syn. *mataás ang tubig sa dagat*.

taón (ta-ón), n. 1. year; a period of 12 months. 2. (Med.) same as *taól*. 3. (Med.) infantile beriberi. 4. chance happening; coincidence. Syn. *pagkakátaón, disinásadyáng pangyayari*. 5. doing something to coincide with another. Also, *pagtataón*.

taong-bahay (ta-ong + ba-hay), n. a person left in the house, office, etc. to serve the absence of others.

taós (ta-ós), I. adj. 1. reaching or penetrating up to the bottom or from one side to the other. Syn. *lagós, lágusan; tagós, tágusan; abót sa ilalim o pusod*. 2. true; sincere; genuine; real; hearthfelt. Syn. *tapát, matapát; taimtím, mataimtím; tapát-pusó*. —II. n. 1. state or condition of being penetrated through and through. 2. fact or state of being true or sincere.

taós-pusò (ta-ós + pu-sò), I. adj. heartfelt; sincere; from the bottom of one's heart. Syn. *tapát, matapát; taimtím, mataimtím*. —II. adv. sincerely; truly; genuinely.

tapa (ta-pa), I. n. 1. jerk; jerky; jerked meat, esp. beef or pork. —II. adj. jerked; preserved by slicing and drying under the sun. Also, *tinapa*.

tapá (ta-pá), n. 1. curing or preserving of fish or meat by smoking. Also, *pagtatapá*. 2. the act of drying wet things by exposing near a fire. Syn. *daráng, pagdadaráng*.

tapak (ta-pak), n. 1. act of stepping on something; putting one's foot or feet on. Also, *pagtapak*. Syn *tuntóng, pagtuntóng*. 2. footmark; footprint; footstep. Syn. *bakás ng paá o talampakan*.

tapák (ta-pák), adj. & adv. barefoot. Syn. *waláng suót o sapín sa paá; nakatapák, nakaapák, nakayapák*.

tapal (ta-pal), n. 1. medical plaster or poultice. Syn. *patse, pamatse; implasto, pang-implasto*. 2. the act or method of applying this. Also, *pagtatapal*. Syn. *pagpapatse, pag-iinplasto*. 3. a patch or piece of material used to cover or mend a

hole or tear. Syn. *tagpî*. 4. act or manner
of patching a hole or a tear. Syn. *tagpî*,
pagtatagpî. 5. the way a patch is made on
a hole or tear. Syn. *pagkakátapal*,
pagkakátagpî.

tapang (ta-pang), n. 1. bravery; valor;
courage; boldness. Syn. *giting, kagitingan,
lakás o kalakasán ng loób*. 2. strength or
potency, as of wine, coffee, vinegar, etc.

tapas (ta-pas), n. 1. act of cutting off or
lopping evenly the top, as of a tree. Syn.
pálas, pagpalas. 2. act or manner of cutting
off the husk of a coconut fruit with a sharp
bolo. Cf. *tapyás, pagtapyás*.

tapát (ta-pát), I. n. 1. the side opposite or
fronting another. Also, *katapát*. Syn.
ibayo, kaibayo, kabilâ. 2. act of stopping
or staying in front of. Also, *pagtapát*. Syn.
paghintô o pagtigil sa haráp o harapán. 3.
act of going to a certain place by taking
the direct or shortest distance. Also,
pagtatapát. 4. the direct route from one
place to another. Syn. *tápatan, tápatang
daán*. 5. act of telling the truth. Syn.
pagsasabi ng katotohanan. 6. admission or
confession, as of one's guilt or crime. Syn.
pag-amin. 7. fact or quality of being
sincere, honest, etc. Syn. *katapatan*.
—II. adj. 1. direct; straight, as a route to
a certain place. Syn. *tuwíd, túwiran;
deretso, déretsuhan*. 2. facing the front.
Syn. *kaharáp, nasa haráp*. 3. sincere; true;
real; genuine; loyal. Syn. *tunay*. 4. frank;
outspoken; candid. Syn. *prangko, tahás*.

tapát-loób (tapát + lo-ób), var. **tapát-na-
loób**, n. & adj. referring to a person who
is frank or sincere.

tapay (ta-pay), n. 1. dough. Syn. *masa*. 2.
(in child's talk) bread; short for *tinapay*.

tapayan (ta-pa-yan), n. a large earthen jar,
usually used as water or vinegar container.

tapayán (ta-pa-yán), n. (Colloq.) bakery.
Syn. *tinapayán, panaderiyá (panaderya)*.

tapeta (ta-pe-ta) n. (Eng.) taffeta; thin silk.
Syn. *manipís na seda o sutlâ*.

tapete (ta-pe-te), n. (Sp.) cloth cover for a
table or chest; tablecloth. Syn. *mantel*.

taphán (tap-hán), v. (fr. *tahíp*) to winnow
grains by tossing them up and down in a
bilao (a shallow winnowing basket).

tapî (ta-pî), n. apron. Syn. *delantál (dilantál)*.
2. any piece of cloth used by women to
cover the body in bathing, or to protect
their clothes when working, washing, etc.
Cf. *tapis*.

tapík (ta-pík), n. 1. pat; gentle or light tap
with the hand. 2. (*Fig.*) a tap on the back;
praise. Syn. *puri, papuri*.

tapilók (ta-pi-lók), n. an accidental twisting
of the ankle due to a bad step or
misstepping. Syn. *tapiyók*.

tapis (ta-pis), n. 1. a wrap or an apron-like
garment worn by women over skirts. 2.
(*Bot*.) husk covering of an ear of corn.
Syn. *takupis*.

tapók (ta-pók), n. act or manner of beating
clothes, esp. *sinamáy*, between the palms
of the hands, as in applying starch evenly.

tapon (ta-pon), I. n. 1. act of throwing away
something. Also, *pagtatapon*. 2. anything
wasted or thrown away; wasted material.
Syn. *bagay o mga bagay na naaksayá*. 3. a
spilling or being spilled, as of liquid from
a container. Syn. *pagligwák,
pagkápaligwák, pagkáligwák*. 4. spilt liquid.
5. banishment or deportation. Syn.
distiyero, pagdidistiyero. 6. a deportee. Syn.
taong itinapon o nasa tapunán, desterado.
—II. adj. 1. thrown or cast away, as useless;
wasted. 2. spilt, as from a container. 3.
deported or banished, referring to a
person. Syn. *itinapon, idinestiyero*.

tapón (ta-pón), n. 1. a bottle stopper; cork.
2. plug. Syn. *pasak, pamasak*.

tapos (ta-pos), n. 1. completion or finishing
of something being done. Also, *pagtapos*.
2. a coming to an end, as of a program,
meeting, etc. Syn. *wakas, pagwawakás*. 3.
graduation, as of a student. Also,
pagtatapós. 4. complete cessation or stop,
as of rain, typhoon, etc. Syn. *hintô,
paghintô; tigil, pagtigil*.

tapós (ta-pós), I. adj. 1. completed; finished.
Syn. *yarî, nayarî na; gawâ o nagawâ na*. 2.
concluded; ended. Syn. *tigil na, nagwakás
na*. 3. graduated, as student. Syn.
graduwado, nagtapós.
—II. n. 1. last day of a novena. Syn. *huling
araw ng novena*. 2. end of a mourning
period for a departed relative. Syn. *laglág-*

luksâ, paglalaglág-luksâ.

tapyás (tap-yás), I. *n.* the slanting cut on the tip or end of a tenon, etc. 2. the act or manner of making this cut. Also, *pagtapyás.* 3. the sloping part or surface, as of an angled plate of glass; bevel. 4. any of the small, polished plain surfaces of a cut gem; facet.
—II. *adj.* chipped or cut off obliquely; with or having a sloping or bevelled surface.

tarak (ta-rak), n. 1. a stabbing or thrust with a knife, dagger, etc., leaving it embedded in the flesh. Cf. *saksák, pagsaksák; iwà, pag-iwà.* 2. a knife, dagger, or the like sticking out with the point embedded in the flesh. 3. act of driving a stake, wooden peg, or pin, etc. into the ground to mark a place or the boundary of.

tarantá (ta-ran-tá), I. *n.* 1. confused state or condition of the mind. Syn. *litó o pagkalitó ng isip, guló o pagkaguló ng isip.*
—II. *adj.* confused; in a confused state of mind. Syn. *litó o guló ang isip, hindî málaman ang gágawín, tuliró.*

tarantado (ta-ran-ta-do), I. *adj.* (Sp. *tarantado*) 1. foolish; silly. Syn. *lokó-lokó, sirâ ang ulo.* 2. imprudent; rash. Syn. *pabiglá-biglá, mapusok, waláng-pagpipigil.* 3. imprudent; without shame or modesty. Syn. *bastós, waláng-hiyâ, pangahás.* 4. disrespectful. Syn. *waláng-galang; waláng-pítagan, pusóng, barumbado.*
—II. *n.* 1. a fool; simpleton. Syn. *taong sirâ ang ulo, loko.* 2. dupe. Syn. *bobo, taong tangá.*

taráng (ta-ráng), *n.* rapid stamping of feet, as in anger, tantrum, pain etc.

tarangká (ta-rang-ká), var. **trangká,** *n.* (Sp. *tranca)* latch or bar for fastening a door or gate. Syn. *tarugo, barál.*

taras (ta-ras), *n.* arrogance or contemptuousness in speech.

tarát (ta-rát), *n.* (*Ornith.*) a long-tailed, sparrow-like bird. Syn. *kabisote, pakiskís.*

taray (ta-ray), *n.* arrogance or contemptuousness in speech, esp. of a woman.

tarheta (tar-he-ta), n. (Sp. *tarjeta)* 1. calling or visiting card. 3. label. Syn. *etiketa.*

tarì (ta-rì), *n.* 1. metal cockspur. 2. act or manner of attaching a metal spur to the leg of a gamecock. Also, *pagtatarì.* 3. the manner a metal spur is attached to the leg of a gamecock. Also, *pagkakátarì.*

tarík (ta-rík), *n.* steepness of a slope or incline. Also. *katarikán.*

tarima (ta-ri-ma), *n.* (*Sp.*) a low, movable platform placed on floors or pavements to support piles of sacks, etc.

taríng (ta-ríng), *adj.* elegant; elegantly dressed, referring esp. to a young man or bachelor.

taripa (ta-ri-pa), *n.* (Sp. *tarifa)* 1. system of taxes on imports and exports; tariff. Syn. *buwís sa luwás at angkát.* 2. the rate or scale of prices, charges, etc. Syn. *singíl.*

taro¹ (ta-ro), *n.* (*Bot.*) 1. tropical Asiatic plant (*Colocasia esculenta*) cultivated for its edible tubers. 2. the tuber of this plant. Syn. *gabi.*

taro² (ta-ro), *n.* (Sp. *tarro)* 1. can or jar, as in: *isáng tarong pomada,* a jar of pomade. 2. pail; bucket. Syn. *timbá, taóng.*

tarók (ta-rók), I. *n.* 1. sounding the depth, as of water in the sea, river, etc. Syn. *arók, pagsukat ng lalim (ng tubig).* 2. sounding the depth of water by swimming or diving. Syn. *pagsisid sa lalím (ng tubig).* 3. understanding or knowing the meaning of. Syn. *pag-unawà o pag-intindí sa kahulugán.*
—II. *adj.* 1. having been sounded, referring to the depth of water. 2. understood or known, referring to the meaning of.

tarós (ta-rós), *n.* regard or consideration for regulations, restrictions, etc. usually used in combination, as in: *waláng taros.* Syn. *alang-alang, pag-aálang-alang, pagsasáalang-alang.*

tasa¹ (ta-sa), n. (Sp. *taza)* 1. cup, usually with a holder. 2. cupful, as in: *dalawáng tasang tubig,* two cupfuls of water.

tasa² (ta-sa), *n.* (*Sp.*) 1. an assessing or determining the value of a property for taxation purposes; assessment; appraisal. Also, *pagtasa, pagtatasa.* Syn. *pagtaya sa halagá ng arí-arian.* 2. the assessed value of property; assessment. Syn. *tasasyón.* 3. limiting to the minimum, as of expenses,

tasá

tátiyáw

supply, etc. Syn. *tipíd, pagtitipíd*. 4. dieting; self-control in eating. Syn. *diyeta, pagdidiyeta*. 5. fixing of the price of. Syn. *paghahalagá*. 6. the price fixed for a certain commodity. Syn. *presyo, halagá*.

tasá (ta-sá), n. (Sp. *tasar, tajar*) 1. act or manner of sharpening a pencil. Also, *pagtatasá*. 2. the point or sharpened end of a pencil.

tasak (ta-sak), n. 1. something struck deeply into the flesh, as a splinter or sliver. Syn. *subyáng, tiník, salubsób*. 2. the deep wound caused by this. 3. act of piercing someone with anything pointed. Syn. *saksák, pagsaksák; tarak, pagtarak, pagtatarak; tusok, pagtusok*.

Tasaday (Ta-da-say), n. (*Anthrop.*) a tribe of cave dwellers in Southern Cotobato in Mindanao.

tasado (ta-sa-do), adj. 1. limited or controlled, as expenses, food, supplies, etc. Syn. *limitado, kontrolado*. 2. having been assessed or appraised, referring to a property. 3. under diet; observing a diet. Syn. *dinídiyeta, nagdídiyeta*.

tasadór (ta-sa-dór), n. (Sp.) assessor; tax assessor. Syn. *tagataya ng buwís o halagá ng arí-arian*.

tasik (ta-sik), n. salt water; brine.

tasita (ta-si-ta), n. (Sp. *tazita*) small cup. Syn. *maliít na tasa*.

tasón (ta-són), n. 1. a large cup; bowl. Syn. *mangkók, tagayán, sulyáw*. 2. bowlful, as in: *dalawáng tasóng sopas*, two bowlfuls of soup.

tastás (tas-tás), I. n. 1. unstitching or removing the stitches. Also. *pagtastás, pagtatastás*. Syn. *kalás, pagkalás, o pagkakalás sa tahî*. 2. the part of a seam that has been removed of the stitches. 3. unfastening or detaching the parts of a framework. Syn. *tanggál, pagtanggál; kalás, pagkalás, pagkakalás*.

—II. adj. 1. unstitched; with or having the stitches removed. Syn. *kalás ang tahî*. 2. detached or unfastened, referring to parts of a structure. Syn. *bakbák, binakbák; tanggál, tinanggál*.

tata (ta-ta), n. 1. an appellation for father. Syn *tatay, tatang , papa, dadi*. 2. (in some region) term for an uncle. Syn. *tiyó*. 3. (also in some region) a term of respect used before the name of an adult male, as in Tata Juan. Syn. *mang, mama*.

taták (ta-ták), n. 1. stamp; seal. Syn. *timbre, selyo*. 2. mark; imprint; print; impression, as in: *taták ng dalirí*, finger print or mark. 3. sign; identifying mark. Syn. *tandâ, palátandaan*. 4. trademark; brand. Also, *taták-pangkalakal*. Syn. *marka*. 5. brand, as on the skin of animals. Syn. *hero*.

tatag (ta-tag), var. **tatág**, I. n. 1. an organizing or founding; establishment. Syn. *pagtatayô, pagpupundár, pag-oorganisá*. 2. stability; firmness; security. Syn. *tibay, katibayan*.

—II. adj. founded, organized, or established by. Syn. *itinatag (itinatág), itinayô*.

tatagukán (ta-ta-gu-kán), var. **tatágukan**, n. (*Anat.*) 1. Adam's apple. Syn. *gulúnggulungan*. 2. throat. Syn. *lalamunan*.

tatal (ta-tal), n. wood chips or small fragments of wood, usually used for fuel or firewood. Syn. *malilíit na piraso ng kahoy na panggatong*.

tatang (ta-tang), n. appellation for father. Syn. *tata, dadi, itáy, tatay*.

tatangnán (ta-tang-nán), n. 1. handle. Syn. *manggo, puluhan, hawakán, tangkáy, bitbitan*. 2. something to hold on or upon. Syn. *hawakán, kapitán*.

tatap (ta-tap), I. n. understanding or coming to know or realize what a thing is all about. Syn. *tantô, pagkatantô; alam, pagkaalam; unawá, pagkáunawa; intindí, pag-káintindí*.

—II. adj. having come to realize or understand; aware of. Syn. *alám, nálalaman; batíd, nabábatíd; tantô, natátantô*.

tatás (ta-tás), n. 1. ability to speak intelligently and fluently. Syn. *husay o kahusayang magsalitâ*. 2. fluency of speech; clearness of diction or pronunciation. 3. glibness of tongue. Syn. *tamís ng dilá (fig.)*.

tatay (ta-tay), n. one's male parent; father. Syn. *amá*.

tátiyáw (tá-ti-yáw), var. **tátyaw**, n. 1. cockerel. 2. breeding cock. Syn. *ganadór*.

tatló (tat-ló), n. & adj. three. Syn. tres.

tatlóng- (tat-lóng-), a combining form, meaning "three."

tatlóng-kapat (tat-lóng + ka-pat), n. & adj. three fourths; ¾. Syn. treskuwarto.

Tatlóng-Harì (Tat-lóng +Ha-rí), n. the feast of the Epiphany; distinguished from Tatlóng Harì, Three Kings.

tatlumpû (tat-lum-pû), n. & adj. thirty. Syn. treinta.

tatso (tat-so, -só, tsó) n. (Sp. tacho) a deep pan or casserole made of copper or brass and usually used for cooking sweet preserves.

tatsulok (tat-su-lok), n. triangle. Syn. triánggguló (triyángguló).

tatsulók (tat-su-lók), adj. 1. triangular; three-cornered. Syn. hugis-triangguló, may-tatlóng-sulok. 2. involving three persons, factions, parts, etc.; three-cornered: as in: tatsulók na labanán, three-cornered fight.

tatwâ (tat-wâ), n. 1. denial; refusal to tell the truth. Syn. kailâ, pagkakailâ; lihim, paglilihim; tanggí, pagtanggí. 2. repudiation; disclaim; disowning. Syn. takwíl, pagtatakwíl.

tauhan (ta-u-han), I. n. 1. followers. Syn. mga tagasunód, alagád, disípuló. 2. workers or employees in an office; personnel. Syn. empleado (empleyado).
—II. v. 1. to remain in the house, office, etc. and act as the watcher or guard when others are all out. Cf. bantayán. 2. to furnish with personnel, as an office. Syn. lagyán ng mga empleyado o mga trabahadór. 3. to fill up, as a vacant position in an office. Syn. lagyán ng taong manúnungkulan.

tauhin (ta-u-hin), n. (Colloq.) gender (of a newly-born baby, as in: Anóng tauhín ang kanyáng bagong silang na anák? What is the sex of her newly-born baby? Syn. kasarian.

táumbayan (ta-um-ba-yan), var. taong-bayan, n. people; persons in general; public. Syn. mga tao, bayan (colloq.), públikó.

táunan (tá-u-nan), I. adj. annual; yearly; every year; once a year. Syn. taún-taón, bawa't taón, minsán sa isang taón.
—II. adv. annually; yearly.

taún-taón (ta-ún + ta-ón), I. adj. annual; yearly; once a year; every year.

táupû (tá-u-pû), var. tao po, tawpû, interj. greeting of someone calling or knocking at a door.

tawa (ta-wa), n. laugh; laughing; laughter. Cf. ngitî, halakhák.

tawád (ta-wád), n. act of asking for pardon or forgiveness. Syn. paghingî ng tawad. 2. pardon or forgiveness. Also, patawad. Syn. paumanhín. 3. request for a discount in buying. Also pagtawad. 4. the discount given to a buyer. Syn. patawad, diskuwento. 5. a bid or price offered for something being sold at auction. Syn. alók o tawad na halagá. 6. belittling or underrating someone's ability, etc. Syn. paghamak, pagmaliít.

tawag (ta-wag), n. 1. act of calling a person by his name or by signaling. 2. a call or summons, as by a court. Syn. patawág; pasundô. 3. act of calling someone by telephone, telegram, etc. Syn. pagteléponó, pagtelegrama. 4. a telephone call to or from someone. Syn. telépono (colloq.): tawag sa telépono o sa telegrama. 5. roll call. Syn. pásalista. 6. proclamation made in the church on three consecutive Sundays of an intended marriage; banns. 7. announcement, as by a loud crier. Syn. bando, pagbabando. 8. medical call or visit of a physician, esp. on request of someone. Syn. dalaw, pagdalaw; bisita, pagbisita. 9. fee for a doctor's call or visit. Syn. subida. 10. an identifying name; term; terminology. Syn. ngalan, pangalan, katawagán, terminolohiyá. 11. (in cockfights) announcement of the rate of betting, as by a tahór or a kristo.

tawang-aso (ta-wang + a-so), n. a derisive, boisterous laugh; mocking or ridiculing laughter. Syn. tawang mâpanuyâ o mápanuksó.

tawas (ta-was), n. 1. alum; the commonest form of potash alum. 2. in quackery, the practice of determining or discovering the cause of a person's disease or sickness by burning alum crystals accompanied by praying. Also, pagtawas, pagtatawas.

tawíd (ta-wíd) I. n. 1. act or manner of

crossing to the other side, as of a street, river, etc. Syn. *bagtás, pagbagtás, libán.* 2. transportation of passengers or cargoes across a river, canal, etc. Also, *pagtatawíd.* 3. the fee charged for this. Syn. *bayad o halagá sa pagtatawíd.* 4. passing a critical stage, as of a person hovering between life and death. Syn. *ligtás, pagkáligtás.* 5. any person or thing not native to a certain place but from across a river, sea, etc.

—II. *adj.* 1. referring to a person or thing from the other side of a river, sea, etc. 2. saved or having passed the critical state. Syn. *ligtás na.*

tawíd-dagat (ta-wíd + da-gat), *n.* act of sailing across the sea. Also, *pagtawíd-dagat, pagtatawíd-dagat.*

tawilis (ta-wi-lis; -lís), *n.* (*Ichth.*) adult freshwater sardine (*Harengula tawalis*)

táwiran (tá-wi-ran), *n.* 1. the part of a river, canal, etc. where people pass in crossing to the other side. 2. pedestrian lane used by people in crossing a street. Syn. *bágtasan.* 3. a bridge, footbridge, overpass, or underpass where people can pass through in crossing a place. 4. simultaneous crossing or passing across a street, etc. by a number of persons, animals, or vehicles. Also, *pagtatáwiran.*

tawsî (taw-sî), *n.* (*Ch.*) soya beans preserved in salt sauce. Cf. *táhurí.*

taya (ta-ya), *n.* calculation or estimate. Syn. *kalkulá, pagkalkulá; tantiyá, pagtantiyá.*

tayâ (ta-yâ), *n.* 1. act of betting or putting a bet on. Also, *pagtayâ, pananayâ.* Syn. *pusta, pagpusta, pamumusta.* 2. a stake in gambling; bet; wager. Syn. *pusta; halagá o tayá*

tayabas (ta-ya-bas), *n.* 1. obsolescent var. of *bayabas,* guava. 2. (T-) former name of Quezon province.

tayangtáng (ta-yang-táng), var. **tayantáng** I. *n.* 1. state or condition of being exposed too long to heat. Syn. *pagkadaráng nang matagál o labis.* 2. state or condition of being over-dried due to heat. Syn. *tigang, pagkatigang.* 3. (*Fig.*) fact or state of being used or accustomed to something undesirable. Syn. *hirati, pagkahirati; sanay, pagkasanay.*

—II. *adj.* 1. too dry. Syn. *tuyúng-tuyô, tigáng.* 2. used or accustomed to something not so good. Syn. *sanáy na, hiratí na.*

tayka (tay-ka), *v.* (fr. *hintáy ka*) wait a minute; wait for a while. Syn. *sandalî lamang.*

tayná (tay-ná), *v.* (short for *tayo na*) let us go.

tayo (ta-yo), *pron.* 1. (inclusive) we, as in: *Hulí na tayo.* We are already late. 2. (inclusive) us, as in: *Umalís na tayo.* Let us go. Let us leave now.

tayô (ta-yô), I. *n.* 1. act of standing or rising on one's feet. Also, *pagtayô.* Syn. *tindíg, pagtindig.* 2. standing position, as of a person. Also, *pagkakátayô.* 3. act of erecting or constructing an edifice, etc. Also, *pagtatayô.* 4. an organizing; founding. Syn. *tatag (tatág), pagtatatag (pagtatatág).* 5. state or condition, as of one's health. Syn. *lagáy, kalagayan.* 6. position or duty, as in an office. Syn. *tungkulin, trabaho.*

tayog (ta-yog), *n.* 1. loftiness, as the flight of a kite; highness, as the top of tall tree. Syn. *taás, kataasan.* 2. haughtiness; boastfulness. Syn. *kapalaluán, kahambugán.*

tayong (ta-yong), *n.* temporary suspension or delay of something being done. Syn. *bimbin, pagkabimbin.*

taypa (tay-pa), I. *adj.* (Slang; fr. the reversed syllable of *patáy*) dead.

—II. *n.* a dead person, esp. one lying in state. Syn. *bangkáy, patáy.*

taytáy (tay-táy), *n.* 1. a bamboo or wooden footbridge. Syn. *tuláy na kawayan o kahoy.* 2. flow, as of electric current on a wire. Syn. *talaytáy, pananalaytáy.* 3. low mountain range. Syn. *tagaytáy.*

tayumán (ta-yu-mán), *n.* place where fabrics are dyed; dyeing plant. Syn. *tinaán.*

tayungkô (ta-yung-kô), *n.* act or manner of sitting lazily with the body and head bent forward. Cf. *talungkô.*

tayung-tayong (ta-yung + ta-yong), *n.* act of doing one's work lazily or delayingly. Also, *pagpapatayung-tayong.*

tayutay (ta-yu-tay), *n.* 1. figure of speech. Syn. *talinghagá, pananalinghagá.* 2. an allegorical chant in verse. Syn. *awit, korido.*

tayu-tayo (ta-yu + ta-yo), var. **tayo-tayo**, *pron.* (usually with *lamang*) we only (exclusive of others).

teatro (te-a-tro), *n.* (*Sp.*) theater. Syn. *dúlaan*.

teka (te-ka), *interj.* (Short for *hintáy ka*) Wait!

tekas (te-kas), *n.* 1. swindler; cheater; defrauder. Syn. *mánunubà, manggagantsó, manánansô; mánunuwitik*. 2. stealer. Syn. *magnanakaw*. 3. pickpocket. Syn. *mandurukot*.

teklada (tek-la-da), var. **teklado**, *n.* (*Sp. teclada*) keyboard of a piano, typewriter, linotype machine, etc.

teknik (tek-nik; -ník) , *n.* (*Eng.*) 1. technique. Syn. *paraán, pamaraán, pamamaraán*. 2. the study or principle of an art or of the arts, esp. the practical arts.

tehada (te-ha-da), var. **tihada**, *n.* bar, as of soap.

tela (te-la), *n.* (*Sp.*) cloth; fabric; textile. Syn. *kayo, damít*.

telebong (te-le-bong), *n.* drumbeat.

telelíng (te-le-líng), var. **tililingín**, *v.* to ring, referring to a small bell, as an electric bell.

telembang (te-lem-bang) , *n.* 1. toll or sound of a big bell, esp. the church bell. 2. act or manner of ringing a church bell. Also, *pagtelembáng*.

tema (te-ma), *n.* (*Sp.*) 1. theme; subject. Syn. *paksâ*. 2. (*Colloq.*) resentment, often expressed indirectly in one's words or utterance. Syn. *hinanakít, samâ ng loób, pagdaramdám*.

temó (te-mó), *interj.* (Fr. *tingnán mo*) See that! Cf. *Nákita mo!*

temperamento (tem-pe-ra-men-to), *n.* (*Sp.*) temperament; a person's nature or disposition. Syn. *ugalì, kaugalián, pag-uugalì*.

temperatura (tem-pe-ra-tu-ra), *n.* (*Sp.*) degree of heat or cold; temperature. Syn. *antás ng init o lamíg*.

templo (tem-plo), *n.* (*Sp.*) temple; church. Syn. *sambahan, simbahan*.

tendénsiyá (ten-dén-si-yá), *n.* (*Sp. tendencia*) 1. tendency; inclination; leaning. Syn. *hilig, ugalì, kaugalián*. 2. definite purpose or object. Syn. *layon, láyunin*.

tenor (te-nór), *n.* (*Sp.*) 1. highest adult male voice; tenor. 2. an adult male singer with a tenor voice; tenor. 3. underlying meaning; purport. Syn. *himig, tono, tunóg*.

tenoryo (te-nor-yo), *n.* (Sp. *tenorio*) libertine; philanderer; rake; ladies' man; romantic swain. Syn. *palikero, babaero*.

tensiyón (ten-si-yón), var. **tensyón**, *n.*(*Sp.* *tensión*) 1. a tension; tightness or tautness, as of a rope, cord, or line. Syn. *bagtíng, higpít, igtíng, hapit*. 2. state or condition of nervousness or anxiety; tension. Syn. *bagabag, balino, di-pagkápalagáy*. 3. strained relations; tensity. Syn. *hidwaan, di-pagkakáunawaán*.

tenyente (ten-yen-te), var. **tenente, tininte**, *n.* (Sp. *teniente*) lieutenant.

teoría (te-o-rí-a), var. **teoriya, teorya**, *n.* (*Sp.*) 1. theory; principle or methods, as used in science. 2. explanation; idea or opinion about something. Syn. *kurú-kuró, paliwanag, palagáy*.

terible (te-ri-ble), *adj.* (*Sp.*) 1. causing terror; dreadful; fearsome; frightful; terrible. Syn. *nakatátakot; nakasísindák, kasindák-sindák; nakahihilakbót, kahilá-hilákbót*. 2. intense; extreme; awfully great; terrible. Syn. *masyado, labis, lubhá, katakut-takot*. 3. very hard; involving great hardship. Syn. *nápakahirap*. 4. very bad, unpleasant, etc. Syn. *nápakasamâ*.

teritoryo (te-ri-tor-yo), *n.* (Sp. *teritorio*) 1. territory; land under the jurisdiction of a nation, state, ruler, etc. Syn. *lupang sakóp (nasásakupan)*. 2. a vast tract of land, region, territory. Syn. *lupaín, rehiyón*. 3. an assigned area, as of a traveling salesman. Syn. *sakláw na poók*.

terminal (ter-mi-nál), *n.* (*Sp.*) 1. terminal; end; extremity; limit. Syn. *dulo, duluhan; hanggahan, hanggana*. 2. station at either end of a transportation line; terminal. Syn. *istasyón, himpilan*.

terminó (ter-mi-nó), *n.* 1. word or term. Syn. *salitâ, tawag, katawagán*. 2. condition or term, as in a contract. Syn. *tadhanâ; probisyón*.

terminolóhiyá (ter-mi-no-ló-hi-yá) *n.* (Sp. *terminologia*) terminology. Syn. *katawagán*.

terno (ter-no), *n.* (*Sp.*) 1. suit; set of clothes.

2. set of things used together, as a pair of earrings and a ring of similar design or color. Syn. *huwego*.

tesauro (te-sa-u-ro), n. *(Sp.)* thesaurus; book of synonyms and antonyms.

testamento (tes-ta-men-to), n. *(Sp.)* 1. *(Bib.)* testament, as in: *Bagong (o Lumang) Testamento*, New (or Old) Testament. Syn. *kasulatan, dokumento*. 3. will. Syn. *hulíng-habilin*.

testigo (tes-ti-go), n. *(Sp.)* 1. witness. Syn. *saksí*. 2. testifying, as of a witness. Also, *pagtestigo*. Syn. *pagsaksí*. 3. proof; evidence. Syn. *pruweba, patunay, katunayan, ebidensiyá*.

tibâ (ti-bâ), I. n. 1. act of harvesting banana fruits by cutting the plant and getting the whole bunch. Also, *pagtibâ*. 2. acquiring of a big gain, as from a business transaction. Syn. *pagtubó ng malakíng halagá*.
—II. adj. 1. (with *na*) already harvested, referring to a bunch of bananas. 2. having acquired or gained a big amount. Syn. *tumubó (nagtubó) ng malakíng halagá*.

tibág[1] (ti-bág), I. n. 1. a demolishing or tearing down, as of a stone wall; demolition. Syn. *paggibâ, pagwasák*. 2. a crumbling down, as of rocks, soil, etc., from a mountain side; landslide. Syn. *guhò, pagguhò*. 3. erosion, as of soil from a river bank. Syn. *bagbág, pagkabagbág*. 4. act of excavating stones or slates from a quarry.
—II. adj. 1. demolished, as a stone wall. 2. eroded, as a river bank, mountain side, etc. Syn. *bagbág, nabagbág; agnás, naagnás*.

Tibag[2] (Ti-bág), n. a kind of stage play or presentation with the search and finding of the main theme.

tibaw (ti-baw), n. a celebration in memory of a deceased, usually held on the ninth day of his or her death. Syn. *pasiyám, síyamang araw, tapós, patapós*.

tibay (ti-bay), n. 1. strength, as of materials. Ant. *dupók, karupukán; hunâ, kahunaan*. 2. firmness or stability, as of structures. Syn. *tatag, katatagan*. 3. quality or ability to endure physical stress, as of one's body; durability. Syn. *lakás, kalakasán*. Ant. *hina, kahinaan*. 4. resoluteness or firmness,

as of one's stand or decision. Syn. *tigás, katigasán; tatag, katatagan; pagkadisidido, kadisididuhan*. 5. rigidity or firmness. Syn. *higpít, kahigpitán*.

tibí (ti-bi) , n. 1. constipation. Syn. *dipagkádumí*. 2. hard excrement or feces. Syn. *matigás na tae o dumí*.

tibók (ti-bók), n. 1. beat or throb, as of the heart. Syn. *pintíg, pagbintíg*. 2. (Fig.); with *ng pusó*) a person's interior disposition or feeling; inner feeling. Syn. *damdamin, loób, kaloobán, nilóloób*.

tibtib (tib-tib), n. act of cutting or chopping wood, etc. little by little or into small pieces with or as with an ax. Cf. *tabtáb, pagtabtáb*.

tibubos (ti-bu-bos), I. adj. 1. real; true. Syn. *tunay, totoó*. 2. complete. Syn. *lubós* 3. absolute; pure.
—II. adv. completely; fully. Syn. *lubós, lubusan*.

tibuhos (ti-bu-hos), n. 1. a becoming involved, unwittingly, in an act or affair. Syn. *panibulos, pagkapanibulos*.

tiburín (ti-bu-rín), n. *(Sp.)* tilbury; light, topless, two-wheeled carriage for two persons. Cf. *kalesín*.

tika (ti-ka), n. 1. resolution; decision or determination to do. Syn. *pasiyá, kapasyahan*. 2. a feeling of sorrow, etc., esp. for wrongdoing; repentance; remorse; contrition. Syn. *sisi, pagsisisi*. 3. a vow or promise. Syn. *panata*.

tikatík (ti-ka-tík), adj. light but continuous, referring to rain. Syn. *ambún-ambón nguni't matagál*.

tiket (ti-ket)), n. *(Sp.; Eng.)* 1. ticket, esp. one that gives a person a right or privilege. Syn. *bilyete*. 2. pass; free ticket. Syn. *pases*. 3. list of official candidates of a political party. Syn. *tálaan ng mga kandidato-opisyál ng isáng partido*.

tikím (ti-kím)), n. 1. tasting; savoring or sampling the taste of (food). Syn. *paglasa, timos, pagtimos* (for broth and other liquid food). 2. first experience of something. Syn. *unang danas o pagdanas*.

tikín (ti-kín), n. 1. a long pole, usually provided with a hook at one end for picking fruits and other things. Syn.

sungkít, panungkít. 2. a bamboo pole or the like used to propel punts or flat-bottomed boats. Also, *pantikin o panikin.*

tikís (ti-kís), I. *n.* 1. act of making someone suffer by not helping him or her intentionally. 2. act of doing something against someone intentionally. Syn. *sadyâ, pagsadyâ, pananadyâ.*
—II. *adj.* intentionally. Syn. *sadyâ, sinadyâ.*
—III. *adv.* intentionally; purposely.

tikitiki (ti-ki-ti-ki), *n. (Med.)* extract from rice bran, given to infants to supplement certain food deficiencies.

tiklóp (tik-lóp), *n.* 1. act or manner of folding a thing or things. Also, *pagtiklop, pagtitiklóp.* 2. the way or manner a thing was or things were folded. Syn. *pagkakátiklop.* 3. plait; pleat. Syn. *pileges, lupî, tupî.*

tiklóp-tuhod (tik-lóp + tu-hod), *adj. & adv.* on one's bended knees. Syn. *nang paluhód, nang nakaluhód.*

tikmán (tik-mán), *v.* 1. to taste; savor or sample the taste of. 2. to try for experience. Syn. *subukan, atuhan.*

tikom (ti-kom), *n.* 1. closing, as of wings, umbrella, eyes, mouth, etc. Syn. *sarâ, pagsarâ; piníd, pagpiníd; ikom, pag-ikom.* 2. act of closing one's eyes, mouth, etc. Syn. *pag-iikom.* 3. act of gathering things together and putting them in a safe place. Syn. *likom, paglikom, paglilikom.*

tikoy (ti-koy), *n. (Ch.)* a sweet, sticky Chinese cake made from glutinous rice flour, usually fried or steamed before eating.

tiktak (tik-tak ; -ták), *n.* a recurring sound like the ticking of a clock; ticktack (tictac).

tiktík (tik-tík), *n.* 1. a spying on someone or something. Syn. *manmán, pagmamanmán.* 2. a detective. Syn. *sekreta.* 3. spy. Syn. *ispiyá, batyáw.* 4. a folkloric nocturnal bird whose song or cry is supposed to announce the presence of *aswáng.* 5. an echoic, recurring sound similar to the ticking of a clock. Cf. *tikták.*

tikwád (tik-wád)), I. *n.* 1. a slight tilt of something to one side; state or condition

of being slightly tilted to a side. Syn. *bahagyáng tikwás.*
—II. *adj.* slightly tilted to a side. Syn. *tikwás o nakatikwás nang bahagyâ.*

tikwás (tik-wás), *n.* 1. act of tilting or raising one side of something. Also, *pagtikwás.* Syn. *tiwás, pagtiwás.* 2. state or condition of being tilted to a side. Also, *pagkatikwás.*

tig- (tig-), *pref.* used as distributive determinate particle, meaning "for each" as in: *tig-isa,* one for each; *tigalawá,* two for each.

tigíb (ti-gíb), I. *adj.* 1. filled up to full capacity; overcrowded; overloaded. Syn. *punúng-punó, siksikan.* 2. overwhelmed or overburdened, as with sorrow, difficulties, etc. Syn. *lipós, puspós.*
—II. *n.* state or condition of being filled up to full capacity. Syn. *pagkapunúng-punô, pagkasíksikan.*

tigil (ti-gil), I. *n.* 1. cessation; stop, stopping. Syn. *hintô, paghintô; tahán, pagtahán; para, pagpara; humpáy, paghumpáy; tugot, pagtugot.* 2. rest; resting; temporary suspension of activity. Syn. *pahingá, pagpapahingá, pamamahingá.*
—II. *interj.* (T-) Stop! Halt! Syn. *Hintô! Para!*
—III. *adj.* not working or moving; at rest; resting. Syn. *hintô, nakahintô, waláng ginágawâ, namámahingá.*

tigíl (ti-gíl), *adj.* 1. unnaturally silent, as if sick or lonely. Syn. *waláng-kibô, di-nagkíkikibô.* 2. with or having the habit of stopping or resting very often during time of work. Syn. *palátigíl, mapágtigíl, patigil-tigil.*

tigis (ti-gis), *n.* 1. a slow drip or trickling of water or liquid that is being emptied to the last drop from a container. Also, *pagtigis.* 2. act or manner of pouring out water or liquid from a container up to the last drop. Also, *pagpapatigis.*

tigmák (tig-mák), I. *adj.* soaked, thoroughly drenched, or saturated with blood, water, etc. Syn. *basang-basâ, puyóg, pigtâ.*
—II. *n.* state or condition of being soaked, thoroughly drenched, or saturated with blood, etc. Also, *katigmakán, pagkatigmák.*

tigók (ti-gók), *n.* 1. the muscular movement

of the throat, esp. in swallowing something big. Syn. *tagók.* 2. the sound produced by this movement of the throat.

tigpás (tig-pás), var. **tagpás,** I. n. 1. act or manner of cutting something with one blow or stroke of a sharp cutting instrument. Syn. *pagputol sa isáng tagâ.* 2. state or condition of being cut off in such a manner.
—II. adj. cut off or severed with one blow of a sharp instrument. Syn. *putól o napatid sa isáng tagâ.*

tigre (ti-gre; -gré), n. *(Sp.)* 1. tiger. 2. a fierce, belligerent person. Syn. *taong malupít; taong halimaw.*

tigtíg (tig-tíg), n. 1. a jerking or shaking up and down, as of a vehicle passing along a bumpy road. Syn. *liglíg, pagkaliglíg.* 2. light, repeated pulls or jerks on something. Syn. *paghalták-halták nang mahina o marahan.* 3. act of shaking a container up and down lightly to make the contents more compact.

tihayá (ti-ha-yá), n. 1. act or manner of lying down flat on one's back. Also, *pagtihayá.* 2. such a position. Also, *pagkakátihayá.* 3. the position of a receptacle or container with the top or mouth up; opposed to *taób, pagkakátaób.*

tigagal (ti-ga-gal), n. state or condition of being suddenly astonished or surprised. Also, *pagkátigagal, pagkápatigagal.*

tigalawá (ti-ga-la-wá). adj. two for each one of.

tigáng (ti-gáng), adj. 1. dehydrated, referring to the body of a consumptive person. Syn. *nangángalirang sa tuyô.* 2. arid; extremely dry (s.o. land).

tigás (ti-gás), n. 1. hardness, as of a solid. 2. rigidity; firmness, as of a joint. Syn. *tibay, katibayan; higpít, kahigpitán.* 3. stiffness, as of a neck, etc. Also, *paninigás.* 4. firmness, as in one's decision. Syn. *tatag, katatagan.* 5. erection, as of a penis. Syn. *tayô, pagtayô; tingarô, pagtingarô.* 6. (with *ng ulo*) stubbornness. Syn. *kasutilan.* 7. (with *ng katawán*) laziness. Syn. *katámaran.* 8. the hard core of wood; heartwood.

tigatig (ti-ga-tig), n. 1. worried state of mind; uneasiness of feeling. Syn. *hindî pagkápalagay; kaguluhán ng isip; balino,*

pagkabalino; balisa, pagkabalisa; bahalà, pagkabahalà. 2. act of making someone feel worried or uneasy. Also, *pagtigatig.* Syn. *pagligalig, pagbibigáy-ligalig.*

tigdás (tig-dás), var. **tikdás,** n. *measles.* Syn. *bulutong-tubig.*

tigháw (tig-háw), I. n. cessation or mitigation, as of strong winds, typhoon, etc. 2. alleviation or temporary relief, as from pain, difficulties, and the like. Syn. *hulaw, paghulaw; hipâ, paghipâ.*
—II. adj. 1. reduced in intensity. 2. in a state of temporary relief.

tiím (ti-ím), I. n. 1. tight pressure, as of the teeth in suppressing anger, suffering pain, etc. Cf. *gitil, panggigitil.* Syn. *igtíng o higpít ng kagát.* 2. full saturation or soaking with brine or salt.
—II. adj. 1. pressed or closed tighly, referring esp. to one's teeth. 2. fully saturated or soaked with brine or salt.

tiím-bagáng (ti-ím + ba-gáng), adj. & adv. with the jaws pressed tightly, as in controlling anger or suffering from pain.

tiín (ti-ín), n. 1. act of pressing down one's hand on something, as in supporting one's body in getting up. Syn. *diín o tuón ng kamáy.* 2. such a pressure or weight. Syn. *tindí o bigát ng diín.*

tiís (ti-ís), n. 1. patient toleration of something hard, painful, etc.; suffering or endurance of pain, hardship, or the like. Syn. *batá, pagbabatá; agwanta, pag-agwanta.* 2. unconcerned attitude for the suffering of others. Syn. *pagwawaláng bahalá sa paghihirap ng ibá.*

tila (ti-la), adv. it seems; perhaps; it appears that. Syn. *warì, para.*

tilá (ti-lá), I. n. 1. momentary cessation or stopping of rain. Syn. *hintô o paghintô ng ulán.* 2. the time or period during which rain has stopped momentarily.
—II. adj. 1. not raining momentarily. Syn. *tigil ang ulán.* 2. not falling at the moment (referring to rain).

tilád (ti-lád), I. n. 1. act of cutting or splitting wood, bamboo, etc. horizontally into small pieces. Also, *pagtilád.* 2. a small piece of wood, bamboo, etc. cut or split horizontally.

—II. *adj*. cut or split horizontally into small pieces, referring to wood, bamboo, etc.

tilamsík (ti-lam-sík), var. **tilansík**, *n*. 1. splash, as of soft mud, water, or liquid. Syn. *tilabsik, tilapon*. 2. particles or mass of flying soft mud, liquid, water, etc. 3. the mark or spots caused by this splash. 4. sparks, as of fire while welding with a torch.

tilaó (ti-la-ó), *n*. *(Anat.)* the fleshy projection hanging from the soft palate above the back part of the tongue; uvula.

tilaok (ti-la-ok), var. of **talaok**, *n*. crow or crowing of a rooster.

tilapon (ti-la-pon), *n*. sudden flight, as of something thrown by accident. Cf. *hagis, pagkápahagis; itsá, pagkápaitsá*.

tilî (ti-lî), *n*. scream; shriek; sharp, piercing cry. Cf. *palatak, malakas na hiyaw*.

tililing (ti-li-ling), *n*. the continuous sound or ringing of a small bell, an alarm clock or a door bell. Syn. *kuliling*.

tilin (ti-lin), *n*. *(Anat.)* clitoris. Syn. *tinggíl, manî (colloq.)*.

tilos (ti-los), var. **tulis**, *n*. the sharp end or point of something.

timawà (ti-ma-wà), *n*. 1. a mean or despicable person. Syn. *hamak na tao*. 2. freeman; emancipated slave.

timbâ (tim-bâ), *n*. 1. a pail or bucket, esp. one used for fetching water from an open well. Cf. *balde*. 2. act or manner of fetching water from an open well by using a pail or bucket. Also, *pagtimbâ*. 3. *(Fig.)* acquisition, as of a big amount of money from a small investment. Syn. *tipák, pagtipák (colloq.)*.

timbáng (tim-báng) I. *n*. 1. weight. Syn. *bigát*. 2. act or manner of weighing something. Also, *pagkátimbang, pagkakátimbáng*.
—II. *adj*. 1. equal in weight; balanced; with or having the same weight. Syn. *magkatimbáng, pareho ng timbáng, magkasimbigát*. 2. symmetrical.

timbre (tim-bre), *n .(Sp.)* 1. stamping tool or machine; stamp; seal. Syn. *selyo, panaták, pantaták*. 2. the impression or mark made by a seal or stamping machine.

Syn. *taták*. 3. the push button of a buzzer or a call bell. Syn. *pindutan*. 4. buzzer; doorbell; electric bell. 5. volume or timbre of one's voice. Syn. *tunóg*.

timbulan (tim-bu-lan), *n*. 1. a piece of lumber, bamboo, or any light object that may be used by a person to keep himself afloat by holding on it; specifically, a life preserver. Syn. *salbabida*. 2. *(Fig.)* a person or thing that serves as one's source of guidance or inspiration. Cf. *patnubay*.

timbuwáng (tim-bu-wáng), I. *n*. 1. a falling flat helplessly on one's back. Also, *pagtimbuwáng*. 2. fallen position of the body with the back flat on the ground or floor, and the arms and legs stretched out.
—II. *adj*. fallen flat helplessly on one's back. Syn. *tihayâ, nakatihayâ*.

timo (ti-mo), *interj*. short colloq. form of *tingnán mo*: See! See what happened! See that!

timò (ti-mò), *n*. 1. penetration or piercing deeply into the flesh and remaining there stuck. 2. *(Fig.)* an affecting or being affected; affection. Syn. *taláb, pagtaláb*.

timog (ti-mog), I. *n*. south. Syn. *sur*.
—II. *adj*. southern.

timòn (ti-mòn), *n*. *(Sp.)* steering wheel; rudder. Syn. *ugit*. 2. helm; control or leadership, as of an organization, business enterprise, etc. Syn. *pamamahalà*.

timpalák (tim-pa-lák), *n*. contest or competition. Syn. *páligsahan*.

timpî (tim-pî), *n*. control of one's emotion or temper; self-control; temperance; moderation. Syn. *pigil, pagpipigil; hinahon, pagmamahinahon*.

timpla (tim-pla; -plá), *n*. (Sp. *templar*) 1. proportionate mixture of ingredients, as in preparing a doctor's prescription or in cooking food. 2. a prepared blend of various ingredients; mixture. 3. act of preparing a dish into a proper savor, as by adding salt. Also, *pagtimplá, pagtitimplá*. 4. any seasoning or ingredient added to food. 5. *(Colloq.)* assessment or opinion, as of someone's ability, etc. Syn. *taya, tantiyá, palagáy*. 6. *(Colloq.)* feeling, as of being sick or indisposed. Syn. *pakiramdám (sa katawán)*.

timsím (tim-sím), n. (Ch.) wick, esp. of an oil lamp. Syn. *mitsa ng tinghóy*.

timtím (tim-tím), n. 1. act of tasting or savoring something by just touching it with the tip of the tongue. Syn. *tikím, pagtikím; simsím, pagsimsím*. 2. prudent modesty in behavior or character, esp. of a lady.

timyás (tim-yás), n. sweetness, sincerity, or purity, esp. of one's love or devotion to another. Syn. *tamís, katapatan, kadalisayan, kawagasán*.

tinà (ti-nà), n. (Sp. *tinte*) 1. dye. Also, *paninà, pantinà*. Syn. *kolór, pangulór, pangkulór; tayum, panayum, pantayum*. 2. act of dyeing fabrics. Also, *pagtinà, pagtitinà*. Syn. *pagkukulór, pagkukulay*. 3. the way or manner a fabric was dyed. Also, *pagkakátinà*. Syn. *pagkakákulór, pagkakakulay*.

tinagin (ti-na-gin; -gín), v. 1. move or loosen, as a tight screw. Syn. *paluwagín*. 2. to move or change the place or position of a thing. Syn. *baguhin ang lagáy o puwesto; galawín*. 3. to arouse or stir (the emotion, passion, or sympathy of); touch the feeling of.

tinahanán (ti-na-ha-nán), I. adj. 1. said of a house or any place formerly occupied as residence or living quarters. Syn. *tinirahán*. 2. referring to something that a person decided to stop doing. Syn. *tinigilan, hinintuán*. 3. referring to a woman who has ceased to have menses. —II. v. past tense of *tahanán*.

tinalakay (ti-na-la-kay), I. adj. taken up or discussed, as in someone's speech, referring to a subject matter. —II. v. past tense of *talakayin*.

tinalî (ti-na-lî), I. n. 1. a rooster kept for cockfighting; gamecock. Syn. *sasabungin*. 2. bachelor, as in: *matandáng tinalí*, an old bachelor. —II. adj. referring to a cock or rooster kept for cockfighting.

tinamó (ti-na-mó), I. adj. referring to something that a person received or have gotten as a result or effect of. —II. v. past tense of *tamuhín*.

tinapa (ti-na-pa), I. adj. jerked, referring to meat; preserved by jerking. Syn. *pinindáng, binislád*. —II. v. past tense of *tapahin*.

tinapá (ti-na-pá), n. smoked fish.

tinapay (ti-na-pay), n. bread.

tinda (tin-da ; -dá), n. (Sp. *tienda*) 1. goods or merchandise for sale. Also called *panindá*. 2. sale of goods or articles, as in a store, esp. by retail. Also, *pagtitindá*.

tindi (tin-di), n. 1. amount of pressure caused by a heavy object placed on a surface. Syn. *bigát*. 2. intensity, as of one's anger. Syn. *sidhî, lakí* (colloq.). 3. gravity; seriousness. Syn. *lubhâ, kalubhaán; grabe, kagrabehan, grabedád*.

tindíg (tin-díg), n. 1. act or manner of standing or rising from a sitting position. Syn. *tayô, pagtayô*. 2. posture; standing position. Syn. *tayô, pagkakátayô*. 3. erection or hardening, as of a penis. Syn. *tigás, paninigás; tayô, pananayô*. 4. setting up or construction, as of a house, building, etc. Syn. *tayô, pagtatayô; gawâ, paggawâ; tirik, pagtitirik*. 5. firm stand or support for one's opinion or belief. Also, *paninindigan*.

tiník (ti-ník), n. 1. thorn or spine (of plants). 2. fish bone. 3. fish bone stuck in the throat. Syn. *bikíg, bitíg, tiník sa lalamunan*. 4. splinter or sliver stuck in the flesh. Syn. *subyáng, salubsób*.

tinidór (ti-ni-dór), n. (Sp. *tenedor*) 1. fork; table fork. 2. pitchfork.

tinig (ti-nig), var. **tingig**, n. 1. voice; human voice. Syn. *boses*. 2. (Gram.) voice, as in: *tinig na táhasan*, active voice. 3. intonation or pitch of the voice; tone. 4. mouthpiece, as in: *tinig ng pámahalaán*, mouthpiece of the government. 5. right to express one's opinion; voice, as in: *May tinig siyá sa pagpapasiyá*. He has voice in deciding.

tining (ti-ning), I. n. 1. settling down, as of dregs or sediment. Also, *pagtining*. 2. sediment; dregs; lees. Syn. *latak*. 3. the smooth, almost unnoticeable spin or gyration of a top. 4. placidity; calmness; tranquility (said of the sea). Syn. *katahimikan, kapatanagan*. —II. adj. with the dregs or lees having settled down (said of wine, vinegar, and other liquids). 2. quite; calm; tranquil (said of the sea). Syn. *payapá, tahimik, kalmado*.

tinis (ti-nis), var. **tin-is**, n. sonority or high-pitchedness, as of voice. Syn. *tagintíng*.

tinô (ti-nô), n. sensibleness; intelligence; reasonableness; moral integrity; good sense of judgement.

tinola (ti-no-la), n. stewed chicken meat with *upo* (bottle gourd).

tinta (tin-ta; -tá), n. (*Sp.*) 1. writing or drawing ink. 2. printer's ink. 3. the dark brown, ink-like fluid ejected by cuttlefish when in danger.

tinukoy (ti-nu-koy), I. *adj.* mentioned or said in passing by someone. Syn. *binanggít, nábanggít*.
—II. *v.* past tense of *tukuyin*.

tinuksó (ti-nuk-só), I. *adj.* 1. referring to someone who was tempted to do something wrong. 2. made the object of someone's joke. Syn. *biniró, sinister*.
—II. *v.* past tense of *tuksuhín*.

tinularan (ti-nu-la-ran), I. *adj* copied; imitated. Syn. *ginaya, kinopya, ginagád, pinarisan*.
—II. *v.* past tense of *tularan*.

tinungkól (ti-nung-kól), I. *adj.* referring to a certain job or assignment that someone performed. Syn. *ginampanán*.
—II. *v.* past tense of *tungkulin*.

tinupok (ti-nu-pok), I. *adj.* intentionally burned to ashes.
—II. *v.* past tense of *tupukin*.

tingá (ti-ngá), n. particles of food left between teeth.

tingalâ (ti-nga-lâ), I. n. 1. act or manner of looking upward. Also, *pagtingalâ*. 2. the position of the head with the face turned upward. Also, *pagkakátingalâ*. 3. the upward tilt of one end, as of a seesaw. Syn. *tikwás*.
—II. *adj.* 1. with or having the face turned upward. Also, *nakatingalâ*. 2. tilted upward; with one end, side, or edge raised or higher than the opposite. Syn. *tikwás, nakatikwás*.

tingalaín (ti-nga-la-ín), *v.* 1. to look up at something. Syn. *tingnán sa itaás*. 2. (*Fig.*) to look up to as something worthy of respect or veneration.

tingkád (ting-kád) n. 1. brightness of color. Also, *katingkarán*. 2. colorfulness, as of one's career. Syn. *kakulayan*.

tingkayád (ting-ka-yád), n. 1. act or manner of sitting on one's heels or in a squatting position. Also, *pagtingkayád, paniningkayád*. 2. squatting position; the manner a person is seated on his heels. Also, *pagkakátingkayád*.

tinggâ (ting-gâ), n. 1. lead (metal). 2. (*Colloq.*) soft solder. Syn. *istanyo*. 3. (*Colloq.*) bullets. Syn. *bala, punlô*.

tinggál (tin-gál), I. n. 1. act of storing up goods for future use or in waiting for better prices, as in hoarding. Also, *pagtitinggál*. Syn. *imbák, pag-iimbák*. 2. goods stored up, as in hoarding. Syn. *kalakal na nakatinggál (nakaimbák)*.
—II. *adj.* stored up; kept (s.o. goods) for future use or in anticipation for better prices. Also, *nakatinggál*. Syn. *imbák, nakaimbák*.

Tinggián (Ting-gi-án), var. **Tinggiyán**, n. (*Anthrop.*) a non-Christian ethnic group inhabiting the western side of the Central Cordillera.

tinggíl (ting-gíl) n. (*Anat.*) clitoris. Syn. *tilin, manî*.

tinghóy (ting-hóy) n. (*Ch.*) an oil lamp with a wick that burns with a small steady flame.

tingî (ti-ngî), I. n. sale of goods at retail prices; retail selling. Also, *pagtitingî*.
—II. *adj.* sold or bought at retail price.

tingín (ti-ngín) n. 1. act of looking at or viewing something. Also, *pagtingín*. Cf. *panoód, panonoód; tanáw, pagtanáw*. 2. diagnosis; observation; examination; investigation. Syn. *surì, pagsusurì; iksamin, pag-iksamin*. 3. personal opinion about something; viewpoint. Syn. *palagáy, palá-palagáy; opinyon; kurò, kuru-kurò*. 4. sight; faculty of sight. Syn. *matá, paningín* 5. respect; regard; appreciation; esteem. Syn. *galang, paggalang; pítagan, pamimítagan; alang-alang, pag-aálang-alang*. 6. estimate; calculation; assessment. Syn. *taya, kalkulá, tantiyá*. 7. taking care, as of a patient. Syn. *alagá, pag-aalagá*.

tingní (ting-ní), I. *v.* (imperative) See. Look.

—II. interj. (Poetic) See! Look!

tingtíng (ting-tíng), var. **ting-ting**, n. 1. act of beating (repeatedly) something that produces high-pitched metallic sound. Also, pagtingtíng. 2. high-pitched metallic sound thus produced.

tip (tip), n. (Eng.) 1. tip; a small present of money given to a waiter, etc. Syn. pabuyà. 2. a piece of secret or confidential information; tip.

tipâ (ti-pâ), var. **tupâ**, n. act or manner of striking lightly the keys of a typewriter, piano, etc. with the fingers.

tipák (ti-pák), I. n. 1. act of chopping off a lump or fragment with or as with an ax, from something solid, like a rock. Also, pagtipák. 2. a piece, fragment, or lump of hard matter chopped off from a big solid object. 3. the part or portion from which a solid piece or fragment was chopped off. 4. (Colloq.) killing; sudden big profit or success.

—II. adj. 1. cut or chopped off, referring to a piece or fragment of solid material. 2. having made a big profit or success. Also, nakátipák.

típaklóng (tí-pak-lóng), n.(Entom.) a species of small grasshopper. Cf. baling, luktón.

tipán (ti-pán), n. 1. act of making or arranging an appointment with someone. Also, pagtipán, pakikipagtipán. 2. an appointment to meet with someone at a certain time and place; tryst. Also, típanan, pagtitipán. Syn. pagtatagpô, pagkikita sa isáng poók at oras. 3. (T-) one of the two parts of the Bible; Testament, as in: Bagong Tipan, New Testament; Lumang (Matandang) Tipán, Old Testament.

tipî (ti-pî), I. adj. pressed flat; compressed. Syn. pipí.

—II. n. fact or condition of being pressed flat or compressed. Also, pagkatipî, katipián.

tipík (ti-pík), n. 1. tiny solid matter; particle; molecule. Syn. maliít na butil, bigí. 2. (Gram.) particle. Syn. katagâ. 3. (Gram.) an affix (prefix, infix, and suffix). Syn. panlapí. 4. a contracted word, phrase, etc. Syn. dinaglát na salitâ, pariralà, atb. 5.

(Ling.) morpheme. Syn. morpima, tipíl.

tipíd (ti-píd), n. economical use of money, materials, time, etc.; economy; thrift; frugality.

tipo (ti-po), n. (Sp.) 1. type; printing type. 2. (Print.) a specific kind of type. 3. kind; class; type; style. Syn. urí, klase, istilo. 4. feature; physical appearance; shape or form. Syn. anyô, hugis, hitsura.

tipong- (ti-pong-), a combining form (fr. tipo), meaning "of", "having", "belonging to", "a certain type", as in: tipong-Kastilá, of Spanish type.

tipunò (ti-pu-nò), n. strong physical feature or form of the body of a person. Syn. siksík at bilugáng pangangatawán.

tipyás (tip-yás), I. n. 1. a small, thin chip cut off slantingly from the edge or tip of something. 2. the slanting cut thus made on the edge or tip.

—II. adj. with or having a slanting cut on the edge or tip. Also, maytipyás. Cf. tapyás.

tira (ti-ra), n. 1. a player's turn in playing a game, as in billiards and other pool games. Also, pagtira. 2. act or manner of hitting or striking (a ball, etc.) with or as with a cue. Syn. tumbók, pagtumbók. 3. physical or verbal attack against someone. Syn. banat, atake, batikos, tuligsâ, bugbóg, gulpi, birá, buntál.

tirá[1] (ti-rá), n. act of staying, living, or residing in a certain place; dwelling or taking residence in. Syn. tahán, pagtahán, pananahanan.

tirá[2] (ti-rá), I. n. 1. setting aside something for someone who is absent. Also, pagtitirá. 2. something set aside for someone who is not present. 3. leftover. Syn. labis; labí, nálabí; sobra, násobra.

—II. adj. 1. set aside for someone (s.o.food). Syn. reserba para sa (kay). 2. remaining unused, uneaten, etc. Syn. sobra, sumobra; labis, lumabis; labi, nálabi.

tirada (ti-ra-da), n. (Sp.) 1. throw. Syn. hagis, paghagis; itsá, pag-itsá; pukól, pagpukól. 2. act or manner of hitting a ball with the cue. Syn. tira, pagtira. 3. (Colloq.) uncalled-for utterance or statement. 4. printing. Syn. limbág, paglimbág. 5. issue;

edition. Syn. *labás, edisyón*.

tiradór (ti-ra-dór), *n*. (*Sp*.) slingshot. Syn. *paltik* (*Bats*.).

tírahan (ti-ra-hán), *n*. 1. dwelling place; residence; abode. Syn. *táhanan*. 2. address. 3. boarding house. Syn. *túluyan, pánuluyan*. 4. a low place usually filled or covered with water, esp. after a strong rain. Syn. *tigilán, pámahayán*.

tirapâ (ti-ra-pâ), *n*. (fr. *dapâ*) a falling on one's knees, as in supplication. Syn. *pagpapakumbabá, pagmamakaawá, paninikluhód*.

tirik (ti-rik), *n*. 1. setting up, as of a post. Syn. *tayô, pagtatayô*. 2. act of lighting up a candle. Syn. *pagsisindí ng kandilà*. 3. erection or construction, as of a house. Syn. *tayô, pagtatayô; gawâ, paggawâ; tindíg, pagtitindíg*. 4. the position of the pupils of the eyes directed upward, as when a person is in the throes of death. 5. (*Colloq*.) a stalling or becoming stalled, as of a vehicle during a big flood. 6. erection or hardening, esp. of male child's penis. Syn. *tayô, pagtayô, paninigás*.

tirintás (ti-rin-tás), var. **trintás**, *n*. (*Sp*. *trenzas*) 1. pigtail; quee; braid of hair hanging at the back of the head. Syn. *salapíd* (*Bats*.). 2. a woven band, as of cloth, tape, ribbon, etc.; braid.

tirís (ti-rís) *n*. act or manner of crushing or killing lice, or the like, by pressing down with a thumbnail or between one's thumbnails.

tirya (tir-ya), *n*. 1. attack, physical or verbal. Syn. *atake, tuligsâ, batikos*. 2. vengeance; revenge. Syn. *benggansa, higantí, paghihigantí*.

tisà[1] (ti-sa) *n*. (*Sp*. *teja*) chalk (for writing on blackboards). Syn. *yeso, tsók*.

tisà[2] (ti-sà) *n*. (*Sp*. *tiza*) roof tile.

tisáy (ti-sáy), *n*. (*Colloq*.) a woman of mixed parentage; mestiza, esp. a Spanish mestiza. Syn. *mestisa*.

tisis (ti-sis), *n*. (*Med*.; *Sp*.) tuberculosis; consumption. Syn. *tuberculosis; sakít sa bagà; pagkatuyô*.

tisod (ti-sod), *n*. 1. a stubbing or tripping of the toes of one's foot against something, accidental or intentional. Also,

pagkátisod, pagtisod. Syn. *talisod, pagkátalisod, pagtalisod; takid, pagkátakid, pagtakid*. 2. act of pushing or shoving something on the ground or floor with the toes of one's foot.

tisóy (ti-sóy), *n*. (*Colloq*.) a male of mixed parentage; mestizo, esp. a Spanish mestizo. Syn. *mestiso*.

tistís (tis-tís), I. *n*. 1. surgical operation. Also, *pagtistís*. Syn. *opera, pag-operá, operasyon,*. 2. (*Med*.) cutting or opening, as of boil or the like. Syn. *busbós, pagbusbós, pagbubusbós*. 3. act of cutting or sewing (lumber) along the grains or longitudinally. Syn. *paglagarì nang paayón*. 4. a narrow strip, as of lumber; lath. —II. *adj*. 1. operated on (surgically). Syn. *operado, inoperá*. 2. sawn longitudinally, referring to lumber.

tita (ti-ta), *n*. auntie; aunt. Syn. *tiyá, tiyáng*.

titatita (ti-ta-ti-ta), *n*. pimp; procurer. Syn. *bugaw, alkagwete*.

titi (ti-ti), *n*. (*Anat*.) penis. Syn. *utin, bebot*.

titik (ti-tik), *n*. 1. any one of the letters that compose the alphabet of a language. Syn. *letra*. 2. any writing or inscription. Syn. *sulat*. 3. handwriting; penmanship. Syn. *sulat-kamáy*. 4. the words of a song, distinguished from music; lyrics.

titig (ti-tig), *n*. stare; steady, intent look or gaze. Syn. *matagál at waláng-kuráp na tingín*.

titigukan (ti-ti-gu-kan), var. **titígukan**, *n*. (*Anat*.) the part of the throat that contracts as one swallows something; also called *tatagukan*. Cf. *gulúnggulungan*.

titíng (ti-tíng), *n*. a tiny particle of anything; atom. Syn. *atomo*.

titis (ti-tis), *n*. 1. cigar or cigarette ash. Syn. *sinisa, abo ng sigarilyo o tabako*. 2. (*Fig*.) main or immediate cause of something devastating, as in: *titis ng digmaan*, the main cause of war.

tito (ti-to), *n*. a familiar or affectionate term for an uncle. Syn. *tiyó*.

titulado (ti-tu-la-do), I. *adj*. (*Sp*.) 1. with or having academic degree. Syn. *may-títuló*. 2. with or having been granted a title (torrens title), referring to a real estate property. Syn. *may-títuló torens*.

—II. n. a person with or having an academic degree.

título (tí-tu-ló) n. (Sp.) 1. title or head, as of an article in a newspaper. Syn. *ulo*. 2. title, as of a story, poem, book, etc. Syn. *pamagát*. 3. academic degree granted to someone. Syn. *digrí*. 4. a claim or right to the ownership of something. Syn. *karapatán sa pagkamay-arì*. 5. evidence of the right to the ownership, esp. of a real estate. Syn. *katibayan sa pagkamáy-arì*.

tiwakál (ti-kal-kál), n. suicide; self-destruction (now, obsolescent, except in derivative formation), as in *magpatiwakál* and *pagpapatiwakál*.

tiwalà (ti-wa-là), n. 1. trust or faith in someone. Syn. *kumpiyansa, pagtitiwalà*. 2. reliance; confidence; belief. Syn. *pananalig, paniniwalà*. 3. leaving something in the care or custody of someone. Also, *pagtitiwalà, pagkakátiwalà*. 4. a person or thing left under the care or custody of someone.

tiwalág (ti-wa-lág), I. n. 1. separation or being separated, as a member from a group, association, etc. Syn. *pagkápahiwalày*. 2. act of resigning, as of a person from his work or office. Syn. *pagbibitíw sa tungkulin*. 3. suspension or dismissal, as from one's employment. Syn. *pagkásisante o pagkápaalís sa trabaho*. 4. state or condition of being separated as a member of a group.
—II. adj. 1. separated. Syn. *hiwaláy, nakahiwaláy*. 2. no longer connected; removed or dismissed, as from one's work. Syn. *sisante, násisante; naalís o natanggál sa trabaho*.

tiwalwál (ti-wal-wál), I. n. state or condition of being neglected or unattended. Also, *pagkatiwalál*.
—II. adj. left unattended or neglected.

tiwangwáng (ti-wang-wáng), n. state or condition of being exposed or left in the open, esp. through neglect or inattention.

tiwarik (ti-wa-rik), var. **tuwarik**, n. 1. act or manner of turning one's body upside-down or heels over head. Syn. *tumbalík, pagtumbalík*. 2. act of setting up a thing upside-down or with the top under. Syn.

taób, pagkakátaób.

tiwasay (ti-wa-say), n. state or condition of being calm or quite; freedom from agitation; tranquility; calmness; quietude. Syn. *katahimikan, pananahimik; hinahon, kahinahunan; kapayapaan*.

tiyá (ti-yá) n. (Sp. *tia*) 1. aunt. 2. stepmother.

tiyák (ti-yák), I. adj. sure; certain; without doubt. Syn. *sigurado, waláng-duda, waláng-alinlangan, waláng-mintís*.
—II. adv. surely; certainly.

tiyád (ti-yád), n. 1. act of standing or walking on one's tiptoes. Syn. *pagtayô o paglakad nang patiyád*. 2. the position of the feet with the heels up and the toes upright.

tiyagà (tiya-gâ), n. diligence; constant, careful effort; perseverance. Also, *katiyagaán, pagtitiyagâ*. Syn. *tamán, katamanán; siyasig, kasiyasigan*. Cf. *sipag, kasipagan, sigasig, kasigasigan; sikap, kasikapan*.

tiyán (ti-yán), n. (Anat.) abdomen; belly. Syn. *sikmurà, pusón*.

tiyanak (ti-ya-nak), n. (Folklore) a goblin or mischievous sprite, which, according to tradition, is the spirit of a young child who died unbaptized. Syn. *patiyanak (patianak, patyanak)*.

tiyanì (ti-ya-nì) n. (Ch.) small pincers for plucking hair, handling or picking little objects, etc.; tweezers. Cf. *sipit, panipit*.

tiyangge (ti-yang-ge) n. (Ch.) 1. market; market place. Syn. *palengke, pámilihan, merkado, baraka*. 2. market day. Syn. *araw ng palengke (pámilihan)*.

tiyáp (ti-yáp), n. act of making an agreement to meet another at a certain time and place. Also, *pakikipágtiyáp*.

tiyara (ti-ya-ra), n. (Sp.; Eng.) 1. the Pope's triple crown; tiara. 2. a women's crownlike headdress of jewels or flowers; coronet.

tiyempo (ti-yem-po), n. (Sp. *tiempo*) 1. (Mus.) timing; cadence; rhythm. Syn. *ritmo, indayog, kumpás, kadénsiyá*. 2. doing something at precise moment of advantage; use of proper timing in acts or deed.

tiyenda (ti-yen-da), n. (Sp. *tienda*) 1. store;

shop. Syn. *tindahan*. 2. merchandise;
goods for sale in a store. Syn. *paninda*.

tiyó (ti-yó), n. (Sp. *tio*), 1. uncle. Syn. *tiyóng*,
amaín. 2. one's stepfather. Syn. *amáng*
pangumán.

toka (to-ka), n. (Sp. *tocar*) 1. turn or shift
of a worker to be on the job as per
schedule. Syn. *turno, pagturno*. 2. act of
assigning a certain kind of work to
someone. Also, *pagtotoka*. 3. the work or
duty that someone is assigned to do.

tokadór (to-ka-dór), n. (Sp. *tocador*) ladies'
table dresser with a big mirror.

tokayo (to-ka-yo), var. **tukayo**, n. (Sp.
tocayo) a man who has the same Christian
name as another; a man's namesake. Syn
kapangalan.

tokwa (tok-wa), n. (Ch.) 1. soybean curd.
2. a dish of fried soybean curd with
condiments.

todas (to-das), I. adj. (Sp.) 1. without
anything left; with everything consumed
or used up. Syn. *ubós, ubós na lahát,*
waláng-natirá, said (na lahát). 2.
exterminated; all killed. Syn. *lipól (na*
lahát), patáy na lahát, puksâ, napuksâ. 3.
without any exception; including all. Syn.
lahát, lahát-lahát, todos.

—II. n. 1. (in some kind of card games)
the coming out of the wanted card in
order to win. Also, *pagtodas*. 2. state or
condition of being all consumed or used
up. Syn. *pagkaubos ng lahát*. 3. death of
everyone in a group. Syn. *pagkapuksâ,*
pagkamatáy ng lahát.

todos (to-dos), adj. (Sp.) all; all of; the whole
of. Syn. *lahát, lahát-lahát, láhatan*.

todos los santos, (Sp.) All Saints' Day.

todo-todo (to-do + to-do), adj. (used an an
intensive) 1. all; without any exception.
Syn. *lahát-lahát*. 2. without control; giving
all what one has, knows, etc. Syn. *buhos,*
buhos na lahát.

toga (to-ga), n. (Sp.) academic gown or robe;
judicial robe; toga.

toge (to-ge), var. **togi**, n. 1. bean sprouts,
usually used as vegetable.

tolda (tol-da), n. (Sp.) 1. canvas tent. 2.
canvas. Syn. *lona, kambás*.

toma (to-ma), n. (Sp.) (Colloq.) drinking of

wine. Syn. *barik, tunggâ, pag-inóm ng alak*.

tomboy (tom-boy), n. (Eng.) a girl who acts
like a boy; tomboy. Syn. *binalaki*.

tomo (to-mo), n. (Sp.) tome; volume. Cf.
aklát.

tonelada (to-ne-la-da), n. (Sp.) ton (a unit
of weight).

tono (to-no), n. (Sp.) 1. tone; quality of
sound. Syn. *tunóg*. 2. tone or accent in
speech or dialect. Syn. *punto, estilo*. 3.
tune; an air of melody. Syn. *tugtugin*. 4.
proper pitch. Syn. *himig*. 5. (Colloq.) effort
in trying to be compatible with someone.
Syn. *pakikibagay*.

tonsura (ton-su-ra), n. (Sp.) 1. act of shaving
the crown of the head; tonsure. Syn. *pag-*
ahit sa tuktók, pag-anit. 2. the shaven part
of the head of a monk or priest; tonsure.
Syn. *anit, satsat, panot*.

tonto (ton-to), I. adj. (Masc.; Sp.) 1. silly;
stupid. Syn. *tangá*. 2. foolish. Syn. *sirâ ang*
ulo, ulól, loko, lokó-lokó.

—II. n. fool ; silly or foolish man. Syn.
lalaking tangá o sirâ ang ulo.

topasyo (to-pas-yo), n. (Sp. *topacio*) topaz
(a yellow variety of sapphire).

topo (to-po), n. (Sp.) act of winning the
first and second prizes or all of the prizes
in a contest or game.

tore (to-re), n. (Sp. *torre*) tower.

torero (to-re-ro), n. (Sp.) bullfighter, esp. a
matador.

torno (tor-no), n. (Sp.) 1. lathe; lathe
machine. Syn. *lalik, lalikán, panlalik*. 2. act
or manner of sharping an article of wood,
metal, etc. with a lathe . Also, *pagtorno,*
pagtotorno. Syn. *lalik, paglalik, paglalalik*.
3. the manner such an article was shaped
with a lathe. Also, *pagkakátorno*. Syn.
lalik, pagkakálalik.

toro (to-ro), n. (Sp.) bull.

torotot¹ (to-ro-tot), n. 1. trumpet; bugle.
Syn. *trumpeta*. 2. a native or home-made
trumpet or bugle. Syn. *pakakak*. 3. horn
trumpet or bugle. Syn. *tambuli*.

torotot² (to-ro-tot), I. n. (Colloq.)
unfaithfulness of a woman to her husband.
Syn. *pagtataksíl ng babae sa kanyáng asawa*.
—II. adj. referring to the husband of an
adulterous or unfaithful woman. Syn.

nilóloko o pinagtátaksilán ng asawa.

torpe (tor-pe), *adj. (Sp.)* 1. stupid. Syn. *tangá.* 2. timid, shy. Syn. *mahíyain.*

torta (tor-ta), n. *(Sp.)* omelet (omelette).

tosino (to-si-no), n. *(Sp. tocino)* bacon; salted and smoked meat.

tosperina (tos-pe-ri-na), var. **tospirina, tuspirina,** n. (Sp. *tosferina)* whooping cough.

tosta (tos-ta), n. (Sp. *tostar)* toasting; roasting or frying until deliciously brown.

total (to-tál), I. n. *(Sp.)* total; sum. Syn. *kabuuán.*

—II. *adv. (Colloq.)* as a matter of fact; actually. Syn. *gayón din lamang, kung sa bagay.*

toto (to-to), n. 1. discipline (in general); education. Syn. *turò, pinag-aralan.* 2. respect. Syn. *galang, paggalang; pítagan, pagpipítagan.*

totò (to-tò), n. an appellation for a small boy. Syn. *totoy, otóy.*

totohanan (to-to-ha-nan), I. *adj.* true; serious; not joking; sincere. Syn. *totoó, tunay, talagá, waláng halong biro.*

—II. *adv.* seriously; sincerely; truly. Syn. *tapát, tápatan.*

totoó (to-to-ó), I. *adj.* 1. true; real; genuine; authentic. Syn. *tunay.* 2. sincere. Syn. *tapát, matapát.*

—II. *adv.* (usually *totoóng)* really. Syn. *talagá.*

—III. *n.* truth, as in: *Magsabi ka ng totoó.* Tell the truth. Syn. *katotohanan.*

totoy (to-toy), var. **tutoy,** n. appellation for a small boy. Syn. *totò, otóy.*

totso (tot-so), n. *(Ch.)* a dish of sautéed fish with *táhuré* (which see) and other condiments.

toyò (to-yò), n. soy; salty soybean sauce.

trabahadór (tra-ba-ha-dór), n. (Sp. *trabajador)* worker; laborer. Syn. *manggagawà; obrero.*

trabaho (tra-ba-ho), n. (Sp. *trabajo)* 1. work; labor; job. Syn. *gawâ, gáwain, obra.* 2. task; duty. Syn. *tungkulin.* 3. employment; occupation. Syn. *hanapbuhay.* 4. workmanship; quality or manner of work. Syn. *pagkágawâ, pagkakágawâ; pagkáyarì, pagkakáyarì.*

traduksiyón (tra-duk-si-yón), n. (Sp. *traduccion)* 1. act of translating one language to another. Syn. *pagsasalin-wikà.* 2. translation; the result of translating. Syn. *salin.* 3. the manner a language was translated into another language. Syn. *pagkakásalin.*

trahe (tra-he), n. (Sp. *traje)* suit (of clothes).

trahe-de-boda (tra-he + de + bo-da), n. (Sp. *traje de boda)* wedding dress. Syn. *damít-pangkasál.*

trahedya (tra-hed-ya), n. (Sp. *tragedia)* tragedy; a play, drama, novel, or the like with an unhappy or disastrous ending. Syn. *drama o ano mang katháng may malungkót na wakas.* 2. a very sad or tragic event or events;. disaster. Syn. *malakíng kapahamakán.*

traidór (tra-i-dór), n. *(Sp.)* traitor; one guilty of treason or treachery. Syn. *taong taksíl, lilo, o sukáb.*

trambiyá (tram-bi-yá), n. (Sp. *tranvia)* streetcar.

tramo (tra-mo), n. *(Sp.)* stretch of land along a railway line.

transaksiyón (tran-sak-si-yón), n. (Sp. *transaccion*) 1. transaction; business deal or agreement. Syn. *únawaán (pag-uúnawaán o pakikipag-únawaán) sa negosyo.* 2. record of the proceedings of a society, convention, etc. Syn. *katitikan ng pagpupulong.*

transkrito (trans-kri-to), n. (Sp. *transcrito*) transcript; copy; written copy. Syn. *salin, kopya, sipì.*

transitibo (tran-si-ti-bo), n. (Sp. *transitivo*) in Gram., transitive. Syn. *palipát.*

transitoryo (tran-si-tor-yo), *adj.* (Sp. *transitorio*) transitory; transient; temporary; passing. Syn. *pansamantala, lumílipas, nawáwalâ, napáparam.*

transpigurasyón (trans-pi-gu-ras-yón), n. (Sp. *transfiguracion*) change in form or appearance; transfiguration. Syn. *pagbabagong-anyô, pag-iibáng-hitsura.*

trangka (trang-ka), var. **tarangka,** n. (Sp. *tranca*) bolt or bar used for fastening a door or gate. Syn. *tarugo, barál, aldaba.*

trangkaso (trang-ka-so), n. (Sp. *trancazo*) influenza; grippe. Syn. *plu (colloq.).*

trapál **tuba**

trapál (tra-pál), n. thick oilcloth, usually made of canvas.

trapo (tra-po), var. **tarapo**, n. (Sp.) rag; piece of torn or waste cloth used for cleaning or wiping dirt. Syn. *basahan, pamunas*.

tratado (tra-ta-do), n. (Sp.) treaty; an agreement between nations. Syn. *kásunduan*.

trato (tra-to), n. (Sp.) 1. treatment or regard for someone, esp. for a person of lower rank. Syn. *pakikitungo*. 2. agreement; deal; contract. Syn. *kásunduan; kontrata*. 3. (Colloq.) making an offer to buy something. Syn. *tawad, pagtawad*.

trauma (tra-u-ma), n. (Sp.; Eng.) trauma; injury; shock. Syn. *pinsalà, takot*.

treinta (tre-in-ta), n. & adj. (Sp.) thirty. Syn. *tatlumpû*.

tren (tren), n. (Sp.) train.

tres (tres), n. & adj. (Sp.) three. Syn. *tatló*.

tribulasyón (tri-bu-las-yón), n. (Sp. *tribulación*) tribulation; affliction. Syn. *malakíng hirap o paghihirap, tíisin, pagtitiís*.

tribuna (tri-bu-na), n. (Sp.) 1. dais; rostrum. Syn. *plataporma*. 2. grandstand; stage. Syn. *entablado, tanghalan*. 3. tribunal; court. Syn. *húkuman, korte*. 4. board of judges. Syn. *hurado, inampalán*.

trigo (tri-go), n. (Sp.) the wheat plant or its grains.

Trinidad (Tri-ni-dad), n. (Sp.; Eccl.) 1. Trinity. 2. feminine name.

tripulante (tri-pu-lan-te), n. (Sp.) crew member. Syn. *tauhan ng bapór*.

trono (tro-no), n. (Sp.) throne.

tropa (tro-pa), n. (Sp.) 1. (Mil.) troop. 2. group; band. Syn. *pangkát, pangkatin, grupo*. 3. herd; flock. Syn. *kawan*. 4. gang. Syn. *gang*. 5. troupe, as of singers.

tsa (tsa), var. **tsaá**, n. (Ch.) 1. the tea plant (*Thea sinensis*). 2. the dried and prepared leaves of this plant from which an aromatic beverage is prepared. 3. the beverage thus prepared.

tsampaka (tsam-pa-ka), var. **sampaka**, n. (Sp. *champaca*) 1. (Bot.) a shrub or small tree (*Michelia champaca Linn.*) usually cultivated for ornamental purposes and for its fragrant flowers which are made into necklaces. 2. the fragrant flowers of this plant.

tsampoy (tsam-poy; -póy), n. (Ch.) an evergreen tree known as box myrtle, bay berry, or Chinese strawberry (*Merica rubra*). 2. the cured fruit of this tree, usually sweetened or salted.

tsansa (tsan-sa), n. (Colloq.; Hispanized Eng.) chance. Syn. *pagkakátaón*.

tsapa (tsa-pa), n. (Sp. *chapa*) badge, esp. one worn on the breast.

tsata (tsa-ta), n. (Sp. *chata*.) bedpan.

tsato (tsa-to), I. adj. 1. flat; flattened. Syn. *sapád*. 2. flat-nosed. Syn. *pangô*.

tseke (tse-ke), n. (Sp. *cheque*) check; bank draft. Syn. *tsek*.

tsika (tsi-ka), n. (Sp. *chica*) 1. a small girl. 2. (Colloq.) one's female friend. Syn. *amiga*.

tsikita (tsi-ki-ta), n. (Sp. *chiquita*) a little girl, esp. a Chinese girl.

tsikitíng (tsi-ki-tíng), I. adj. (Colloq.) small, referring esp. to child. Syn. *bulilit*.
—II. n. (Colloq.) a small child.

tsimenea (tsi-me-ne-a), var. **tsiminiya**, n. (Sp. *chimenia*) 1. chimney; smokestack. Syn. *páusukán*. 2. fireplace.

Tsina (Tsi-na), n. (Sp. *China*) 1. China, a country east of Asia. Syn. *Sungsóng*. 2. Chinese woman.

tsinelas (tsi-ne-las) var. **sinelas**, n. (Sp. *chinela*) slipper or slippers.

Tsinito (Tsi-n-to), n. (Sp. *Chinito*) 1. a mall Chinese boy. 2. a small boy who looks like Chinese.

tsismis (tsis-mis; -mís), n. (Sp. *chismes*) idle talk and rumors about others; gossip. Syn. *daldál, sitsít, satsát*.

tsítsaró (tsí-tsa-ró; tsít-sa-ró), var. **sítsaro**, n. (Bot.; Sp. *chicharo*) pea.

tsítsarón (tsí-tsa-rón; tsít-sa-rón), var. **sítsaron**, n. (Sp. *chicharrón*) crispy fried pork rind.

tsoriso (tso-ri-so), var. **soriso**, n. (Sp. *chorizo*) sausage Syn. *longganisa*.

tsupér (tsu-pér), n. (Sp. *chofer*) chauffeur; vehicle driver.

tsupón (tsu-pón), n. (Sp. *chupón*) rubber teat or sucker for milk bottle.

tuba (tu-bâ), n. 1. the fresh, sweet juice obtained from nipa or buri palms by cutting the top; this juice is usually drunk fresh, made into vinegar, wine, *panutsa*, and *pakaskás*. 2. the wine made from this juice.

tubal (tu-bal), I. *n.* 1. dirt on clothes mixed with perspiration. 2. dirty clothes ready for washing. Syn. *lábahing mga damít*. —II. *adj.* soiled; already dirty, referring to clothes. Syn. *marumí (na)*.

tubig (tu-big), *n.* 1. water (in general). 2. water, as distinguished from land; opposed to *katihan*. Cf. *ílog, dagat*.

tubig-alat (tu-big + a-lat), *n.* salt water; sea water.

tubig-tabáng (tu-big + ta-báng), *n.* fresh water.

tubo (tu-bo), *n. (Sp.)* 1. pipe or tube for conveying water, gas, oil, and other liquids. 2. a tube of toothpaste, water color, artist's paints, etc. 3. the glass bulb or tube used to protect the light of a lamp. Syn. *imbudo*.

tubó (tu-bó), *n. (Bot.)* sugar cane (*Saccharum officinarum*).

tubò[1] (tu-bò), *n. (Comm. & Banking)* 1. gain; interest. Syn. *gana, ganansiyá, interés*. 2. gain from the sale of something. Syn. *pakinabang, ganansiyá*.

tubò[2] (tu-bò), *n.* 1. germination; growth, as of a seed. Also, *pagtubò*. Syn. *siból, pagsiból; supang, pagsupang*. 2. a new growth. Syn. *supang, suloy*.

tubò[3] (tu-bò), *n. & adj.* said of a person who is a native of a certain place.

tubóg (tu-bóg), I. *n.* 1. immersion of something into some kind of treated liquid in order to cool, color, plate, etc. Also, *pagtutubóg*. 2. a muddy pool or watery pit in which carabaos wallow; wallow. Syn. *lubluban*. —II. *adj.* plated or coated, as with gold, silver, etc.

tubong-nilugaw (tu-bong + ni-lu-gaw), *n.* excessive profit or gain, esp. from a small investment.

tubós (tu-bós), *n.* 1. redemption, as of mortgaged property. Also, *pagtubós*. 2. payment of money for the release of a captive; ransom. 3. the price or amount (of money) paid as a ransom.

tukâ (tu-kâ), *n.* 1. beak or bill (of birds and fowls) 2. peck or stroke with the beak or bill. Syn. *tuktók, pagtuktók*. 3. a mark or marks made by pecking with the beak or bill. 4. act of picking grains, seed, etc. with the beak or bill, as when birds and fowls eat. Also, *pagtukâ*. 5. feeding time for fowls in a poultry. Also, *pagpapatukâ*. 6. sudden bite, as of snake. Syn. *tukláw*.

tukláp (tuk-láp), I. *n.* 1. act or manner of detaching something pasted, glued, or nailed on a surface. Syn. *bakbák, pagbakbák; paknít, pagpaknít*. 2. state or condition of being detached (s.o. something that has been detached forcibly). —II. *adj.* detached forcibly, referring to something pasted, glued, or nailed, etc.

tuklás (tuk-lás), I. *n.* 1. a discovering or being discovered. Also, *pagtuklás*. Syn. *diskubré, pagdiskubré*. 2. anything discovered; discovery. Syn. *bagay na nátuklás*. 3. a finding out or discovery, as of a secret, etc. —II. *adj.* discovered (by).

tukláw (tuk-láw), *n.* 1. sudden bite of a snake. Syn. *tukâ, pagtukâ*. 2. bite of a snake; wound made by the bite of a snake. Syn. *sugat o kagát ng ahas*.

tuklóng (tuk-lóng), *n.* a small, temporary shrine or chapel. Syn. *bisita, kapilya*.

tukô (tu-kô), *n.* 1. (*Zool.*) gecko. 2. (*Med.*) measles. Syn. *tigdás*. 3. (*Med.*) chicken pox. Syn. *bulutong-tubig*.

tukod (tu-kod), *n.* 1. a prop, brace, or support under or against the side of a structure to prevent from falling or leaning. Syn. *suhay, haligi*. 2. a pole used to support a clothesline to prevent it from sagging at the middle. Syn. *talukod*.

tukop (tu-kop), *n.* act of covering something, esp. one's private part, with the palm of the hand. Syn. *tuóp, sapó*. 2. the position of the palm of the hand in trying to cover something. 3. the thing thus covered with the palm of the hand.

tukoy (tu-koy), *n.* 1. mention or mentioning; reference or referring. Syn. *banggít, pagbanggít*. 2. expertise in marksmanship.

tukso (tuk-so; -só), n. 1. a tempting or being tempted. 2. a person or thing that tempts; temptation. Syn. *tentasyón.* 3. act of joking or teasing someone. Syn. *biro, pagbirò; kantiyáw, pagkantiyáw, pangangantiyáw.* 4. a jest, banter, or joke. Syn. *biro, kantiyáw.*

tuktók[1] (tuk-tók), n. 1. top or crown of the head. Cf. *bumbunan.* 2. summit; highest part; top, as of a mountain. Syn. *taluktók, tugatog, rurok.*

tuktók[2] (tuk-tók), n. 1. knock or knocking, as at a door, on top of a hard surface, etc. Syn. *katók, kalatok, kalatóg.* 3. repeated pecks or bites with or as with a beak (bill) of a bird or fowl. Syn. *tukâ, pagtukâ.* 4. the mark or marks made by pecking. 5. a game of eggs whereby the heads of the two eggs are knocked together and whichever becomes broken is considered the loser.

túkuyan (tú-ku-yan), adj. (*Gram.*) active; transitive. Syn. *táhasan, palipát.*

tudlâ (tud-lâ), n. act or manner of shooting or hitting a target (with a gun, arrow, spear, etc). Syn. *pagbaríl, pagpanà, pagsibát.*

tudlíng (tud-líng), n. 1. (*Lit.*) a printed line, esp. of poetry. Syn. *taludtód.* 2. (*Journalism*) newspaper column. Syn. *kolumna.*

tudyo (tud-yo; -yó), n. 1. act of teasing or joking someone. Also, *pagtudyó.* Syn. *pagtuksó, panunuksó; biro, pagbirò, pagbibirò; kantiyáw, pagkantiyáw, pangangantiyáw.* 2. something said as a joke; jest; tease; banter. Syn. *biro, tukso, kantiyáw.*

tugák (tu-gák), adj. stupid, gullible; thoughtless. Syn. *tangá, hangál, waláng isip, gaga o gago.*

tugatog (tu-gatog), n. top, summit; highest point. Syn. *tuktók, taluktók; tugatog; rurok kárurukan.*

tugaygáy (tu-gay-gáy), n. 1. keeping track of; watching closely or secretly; spying on (someone). Syn. *manmán, pagmamanmán; subaybáy, pagsubaybáy.* 2. a person keeping track of someone.

tugî (tu-gî), n. 1. wild yam; a slender, somewhat hairy, spiny vine reaching a height of several meters (*Dioscorea*

esculenta). 2. the tuber of this vine.

tugis (tu-gis), n. 1. chasing; running after; pursuit. Syn. *habol, paghabol; hagad, paghagad; pagat, pagpagat.* 2. a person, animal, or thing being chased. Syn. *tao, hayop, o bagay na hináhabol o tinútugis.*

tugmâ (tug-mâ), I. n. 1. rhyme. Syn. *rima.* 2. compatibility. Syn. *pagkakásundô, pagkakátugmâ, pagkakáwastô, pagkamágkabagay.*
—II. adj. 1. rhyming or in harmony, as two lines in poetry. Also, *magkatugmâ.* Syn. *rima, magkarima.* 2. compatible; in agreement. Syn. *suwatò, magkasuwatò, magkabagay, magkasundô, magkaugmâ.* 3. proper; fit. Syn. *bagay, kabagay, nábabagay.* 4. right; correct. Syn. *tama, tumpák, wastô.*

tugnaw (tug-naw), I. n. state or condition of being burned completely. Syn. *pugnáw, pagkapugnáw; tupok, pagkatupok.*
—II. adj. burned to ashes; completely burned. Syn. *pugnáw, napugnáw; supók, nàsupok; tupók, natupok.*

tugón (tu-gón), n. 1. act of answering a letter, question, argument, etc. Syn. *sagót, pagsagót.* 2. a written or verbal answer or reply; response. Syn. *sagót, kaságutan.* 3. a solution to a problem; answer. Syn. *solusyón, paraán.* 4. (*Law*) defense; rebuttal. Syn. *pagtatanggól.*

tugot (tu-got), n. 1. stopping or cessation, as of one's act or action being done in anger. Syn. *humpáy, paghumpáy; hintô, paghintô; tigil, pagtigil.* 2. state or condition of being pacified or stopped from continuing something harsh.

tugtóg (tug-tóg), n. 1. act or manner of playing a musical instrument. Also, *pagtugtóg.* 2. the music or sound made by a musical instrument, piano, phonograph, etc. Also, *tugtugin.* Syn. *músiká.* 3. act or manner of ringing a bell. 4. the sound of a bell or an alarm clock. Syn. *tunóg.*

tuhod (tu-hod), n. 1. (*Anat.*) knee; the front part of the joint between the lower leg and the thigh. 2. the part of a stocking, trouser leg, etc. covering the knee.

tuhog (tu-hog), n. 1. act of stringing together things like beads, pearls,

sampaguita flowers, etc. Also, *pagtuhog,
pagtutuhog.* 2. a string, as of beads, pearls,
etc. 3. act of fastening or piercing
(something) with or as with a skewer. Syn.
durò, pagdudurò; tindág, pagtitindág. 4.
anything fastened or pierced with a
skewer.

tulâ (tu-lâ), n. 1. poem. Syn. *berso.* 2. act
or manner of reciting a poem. Also,
pagtulâ. Syn. *pagbigkás ng tulâ.* 3. the way
or manner a poem was recited. Syn.
pagkátulâ, pagkakátulâ.

tulak (tu-lak), I. n. 1. push; shove; act of
pushing or shoving a person or thing.
Also, *pagtulak, pagtutulak.* 2. a sudden or
strong push or shove. Syn. *salyá,
pagsasalyá.* 3. leaving or departure, as of
boats, train, etc. Syn. *lisan, paglisan; alís,
pag-alís; lakad, paglakad; biyahe, pagbiyahe.*
4. anything being pushed or shoved by
someone. Syn. *anó mang bagay na
itinútulak.*
—II. adj. 1. referring to something being
pushed or shoved forward or backward.
Syn. *itinútulak.* 2. forced, as by
circumstances. Syn. *dalá (colloq.)*

tulak-kabig (tu-lak + ka-big), n. act of
pushing away something and then pulling
it again toward oneself. Cf. *tulak-batak.*
2. a push-and-pull movement.

tulad (tu-lad), I. n. 1. act of copying or
imitating someone or something, as by
aping, drawing, cutting, carving, typing,
etc. Syn. *gaya, paggaya; gagád, paggagád;
kopya, pagkopya.* 2. something similar or
alike to another. Syn. *bagay na katulad.*
3. a comparing; comparison. Syn. *hawig,
paghahawig; wangis, pagwawangis.*
—II. adj.& adv. like; similar to, as in:
Siya'y tulad mo. He is like you. Syn. *gaya,
kagaya; paris, kaparis.*

tulalá (tu-la-lá), n. 1. stupidity; mental
dullness or weakness. Syn. *katangahán,
kahangalán, katontohán.* 2. stupor. Syn.
pagkabaghán.

tulámbuhay (tu-lám-bu-hay), var. **tulángbuhay**, n. metrical tale or romance.

tulas (tu-las), n. 1. ooze or oozing, as of a
decaying matter. Syn. *hulas, paghulas.* 2.
slow melting, as of salt, sugar, and the like.

Syn. *tunaw, pagkatunaw; lusaw,
pagkalusaw.* 3. act or process of seeping;
seepage; leakage. Syn. *tagas, pagkatagas.*
4. the liquid that seeps or oozes.

tuláy (tu-láy), n. 1. bridge. 2. act of passing
through or walking on a tight rope or wire
or on a horizontal pole, top of a wall, or
the like by balancing self. Also, *pagtuláy,
panunuláy.* 3. flow or passage of water
through a stretched wire or line. Syn.
talaytáy, pananalaytáy. 4. (*Fig.*) a go-
between; intermediary. Syn.
tagapamagitan. 5. (*Colloq.*) pimp; procurer.
Syn. *bugaw.*

tuldík (tul-dík), n. (*Gram.*) accent
(represented in Pilipino by the marks (?)
for the acute, (') for the grave, and (^)
for the circumflex). Syn. *asento.*

tuldók (tul-dók), n. 1. period; orthographic
dot. Syn. *punto.* 2. the dot placed over
the small letter 'i'.

tuldók-kuwít (tul-dók + ku-wít), var.
tuldukuwít, n. semicolon, represented by
the sign (;).

tulì (tu-lì), n. circumcision. Also, *pagtuli,
pagtutulì.* Syn. *binyág, pagbibinyág
(colloq.).*

tulig (tu-lig), adj. stupefied; confused or
deafened due to too much noise.

tuligsâ (tu-lig-sâ), n. 1. act of criticizing or
attacking someone or his work in public.
Syn. *háyagang pag-atake o pagbatikos.* 2.
any verbal or published attack or criticism
directed against someone or his work.

tulin (tu-lin), n. speed; rate of movement
or motion; velocity; swiftness. Syn. *bilís,
kabilisán.*

tulingan (tu-li-ngan), n. (*Ichth.*) tuna fish
(*Family thunnidae*).

tuliró (tu-li-ró), adj. confused; mentally
puzzled. Syn. *tarantá, natatarantá.*

tulis (tu-lis), n. 1. sharp point or end of
something tapering. Syn. *tilos.* 2. (*Colloq.*)
severity or sharpness, as of one's words of
language. Syn. *talím, katalimán; hayap,
kahayapan.*

tulisán (tu-li-sán), n. brigand; bandit;
robber. Syn. *bandido, manloloób, magnanakaw.*

tulò (tu-lò), n. 1. drip or slow flow, as of

water from a slightly open faucet. Syn. *daloy, paták*. 2. leak or leakage, as of rain water from a roof. 3. (*Colloq.*) discharge of mucus and pus from the genetourinary tract; gonorrhea. Syn. *sakít sa babae*.

tulóg (tu-lóg), *adj*. 1. asleep; sleeping; not awake. Syn. *natutulog*. Ant. *gisíng, ditulóg*. 2. not active; mentally dull or idle. Syn. *tigíl, waláng-siglá*. 3. not earning (said of capital). Syn. *hindî kumíkita*. 4. (in boxing) knocked out.

tulong (tu-long), *n*. 1. act or manner of helping another or others in any manner. Syn. *patulong*. 2. something given to help someone; aid; help; assistance; support. Syn. *abuloy, ambág*. 3. a person who runs to give succor to someone in danger. Syn. *saklolo, sukoro*.

tulos (tu-los), *n*. a stake or pole with one end pointed for driving into the ground. Syn. *istaká, urang*.

tulot (tu-lot), *n*. 1. permission; consent. Syn. *pahintulot, permiso*. 2. the will or blessing, as of God. Syn. *kaloobán*.

tulóy (tu-lóy), I. *n*. 1. act of staying temporarily, usually overnight, in someone's place. 2. sojourner; temporary guest or visitor. 3. fact or state of being continuous, as a labor contract. Syn. *patuloy, pagpapatuloy*. 4. a going on as planned or scheduled.
—II. *adj*. 1. will go on as planned or scheduled; no postponement. Syn. *hindî máhihintô, waláng-paliban*. 2. not staying permanently; only sojourning, referring to a temporary guest or visitor. Syn. *nanúnuluyan*.
—III. *interj*. Come in! Syn. *Pasok! Pumasok ka (o kayó)!*
—IV. *v. imper.* go on; go ahead; continue.

tulóy-tulóy (tu-lóy + tu-lóy), I. *adj*. continuous; unbroken; without let-up; without interruption or break. Syn. *patuloy, waláng-tigil, waláng-hintô, waláng-pahingâ*.
—II. *adv*. continuously; in an unbroken manner.

tulyá (tul-yá), var. **tulyá**, *n*. (*Zool*.) a species of small bivalve. Cf. *paros, halaan*.

tulyapis (tul-ya-pis), *n*. 1. rice grains that

failed to grow or develop cereal flesh. Syn. *palay na waláng lamán, palay na di naglamán*. 2. chaff; rice bran. Syn. *ipá, darák*. 3. (*Colloq*.) anything worthless. Syn. *bagay na patapón*.

tumagál (tu-ma-gál), *v*. 1. to last long; be prolonged in time. Also, *magtagál*. Syn. *lumuwát, magluwát*. 2. to take a long time before wearing out. 3. to endure; be able to have the power of resistance to something hard or taxing. Syn. *umagwanta, makaagwanta; tumiís, makatiís*.

tumag-araw (tu-mag + a-ráw), *v*. to come or set in, referring to rainy days or season. Syn. *magtag-ulán, magtag-ulanan*.

tumahak (tu-ma-hak), *v*. to pass through or across a new or unchartered field, as in taking a short-cut passage to a certain place. Syn. *tumalakták*.

tumal (tu-mal), *n*. dullness or sluggishness of sales or market activity. Also, *katumalan, pagkamatumal*. Syn. *hinà ng benta, tamláy ng bílihan*.

tumalagá (tu-ma-la-gá), *v*. 1. to resign oneself to. 2. to be ready or prepared for. Syn. *humandâ*. 3. to dedicate oneself to a certain service or cause. Syn. *lumaán*.

tumalik (tu-ma-lik), *v*. to become intimate or close, referring to friendship. Syn. *magíng matalik*.

tumanà (tu-ma-nà), *n*. a cultivated land or field; farm land. Syn. *tániman, lináng*.

tumandâ (tu-man-dâ), *v*. to grow old; become old. Syn. *magíng matandâ, gumulang*.

tumangláw (tu-mang-láw), *v*. to give light or illumination to. Syn. *umilaw, magbigáy ng liwanag sa*. 2. to go with a religious procession as a candle bearer. Syn. *umilaw, sumama sa prosisyón bilang tagailaw*.

tumátalaga (tu-má-ta-la-ga), *adj*. referring to someone whose mind is set to whatever happens to himself. Syn. *nakahandâ na o nakalaán na sa anó mang máaaring mangyari sa sarili*.

tumba (tum-ba), *n*. (*Sp*.) tomb. Syn. *mauseleo, puntód*.

tumbá (tum-bá), I. *n*. (*Sp. tumbar*) 1. falling down from an upright position. Syn.

buwál, pagbuwál, pagkabuwál. 2. state or condition of being fallen down (from a standard position). 3. a being knocked out, as in boxing. Syn. *bagsák, pagbagsák.* —II. *adj.* 1. fallen down (from an upright position). Syn. *buwál, nabuwál.* 2. bankrupt, said of business. Syn. *tumbado, bagsák, bangkarote.*

tumbaga (tum-baga), I. *n.* alloy of gold and copper. Cf. *bronse.* —II. *adj.* made of an alloy of gold and copper. Syn. *yari sa tumbaga.*

tumbalík (tum-ba-lík), I. *adj.* 1. inverted; upside down; with the upper part underneath or turned over. Syn. *tuwarík, nakatuwarik; baligtád, nakabaligtád; taób, nakataób.* 2. reverse; contrary or opposite, as in position, direction, etc. Syn. *saliwâ, magkasaliwâ.* —II. *n.* 1. act of inverting or reversing the position of. Syn. *pagbaligtád o pagsaliwâ sa puwesto.* 2. state or condition of being inverted or reversed in position. Syn. *pagkatumbalík, pagkabaligtád, pagkasaliwâ.* 3. a somersaulting. Syn. *sirkó, pagsirkó.*

tumbalilong (tum-ba-li-long), *n* a rolling down in a series with the head over heels over head.

tumbás (tum-bás), I. *n.* act of giving an equivalent of something received. Syn. *pagbibigáy ng katumbás ng tinanggáp.* 2. any thing given or received in exchange for another of equivalent amount or quantity. Syn. *kapalít, katumbás.* 3. doing or making something to equal what another has done or made. —II. *adj.* sufficient; enough, as in: *Tumbás na iyán sa aking pagod.* That is already sufficient for my efforts.

tumbá-tumbá (tum-bá + tum-bá), var. **tumbatumbá**, *n.* rocking chair. Syn. *tunggá-tunggâ.*

tumbók (tum-bók), *n.* 1. a direct hit or strike, as in a collision. Syn. *banggâ, pagbanggâ; bunggô, pagbunggô; bundól, pagbundól.* 2. strike or hit with the end of an elongated object. 3. (in billiards and other pool games) act of striking a ball or a cue piece with the cue. Syn. *tira, pagtira.*

tumbóng (tum-bóng), *n.* 1. (*Anat.*) rectum.

2. (*Bot.*) the fleshy, apple-shaped growth inside a germinating coconut fruit. 3. (*Bot.*) a species of mushroom called puffball (*Lycoperdaceae*).

tumilmíl (tu-mil-míl), *adj.* referring to a person who eats very little due to lack of appetite. Syn. *mahinà o waláng-ganang kumain.*

tumimyás (tu-mim-yás), *v.* to become sweet or sweeter, referring to one's love or affection for another. Syn. *tumamís.* 2. to be more pure or genuine. Syn. *dumalisay, maging dalisay.*

tumiwasáy (tu-mi-wa-sáy), *v.* to become quite, calm, or peaceful. Syn. *tumahimik, pumayapà, huminahon.*

tumók (tu-mók), *n.* (*Bot.*) 1. bush; thicket of shrubs. Syn. *makapál na damuhán.*

tumor (tu-mór), *n.* (*Med.; Sp.*) 1. tumor. Syn. *bukol, magâ, pamamagâ.* 2. boil. Syn. *pigsá.*

tumulad (tu-mu-lad), *v.* 1. to take after; be like another. Syn. *maging katulad; sumunod sa (colloq.), kumuha sa (colloq.).* 2. to copy; make a copy of. Syn. *kumopya.* 3. to imitate. Syn. *gumaya, pumaris.* 4. to ape. Syn. *bumadyá, gumagad.*

tunaw (tu-naw), *n.* 1. act or process of melting or liquefying something. Also, *pagtunaw, pagtutunaw.* 2. a liquefying or being liquefied; liquefaction. Syn. *pagkatunaw, pagkalusaw.* 3. digestion, as of food in the stomach.

tunay (tu-nay), I. *adj.* 1. true; real; genuine; legitimate; actual. Syn. *totoó, talagá.* 2. certain; reliable. Syn. *tiyák.* 3. right; correct. Syn. *tamà, wastô, tumpák.* —II. *adj.* truly; really. Syn. *talagá, totoó.*

túniká (tú-ni-ká), *n.* (*Sp. tunica*) tunic; gown; robe. Syn. *bata.*

tunóg (tu-nóg), *n.* 1. sound (in general). 2. sonority; clear and strong sound; resonance. Also, *katunugân.* 3. (*Fig.*) popularity. Syn. *katanyagán, kabantugán.*

tunsóy (tun-sóy), *n.* (*Ichth.*) fimbriated sardine (*Sardinella fimbriata*). Cf. *silinyasí.*

tuntón (tun-tón), *n.* 1. act or maner of following or tracing the path or trail of. Syn. *bakás, pagbakás; taluntón; pagtaluntón; sunód, pagsunód.* 2. act of following or being in accordance with the law, regulation, etc. 3. act of tracing the source or origin, as of one's family lineage. 4. tracing or retracing, as of lines in a drawing. Syn. *sunsón, pagsunsón.*

tuntóng[1] (tun-tóng), var. **tungtóng**[1], n. cooking pot cover or lid.

tuntóng[2] (tun-tóng), var. **tungtóng**[2], n. 1. a stepping or treading on something. Syn. *apak, pag-apak; yapak, pagyapak; tapak, pagtapak.* 2. footprint. Syn. *apak, tapák, yapak, bakás ng paá.* 3. setting of one's feet, esp. on a new land or territory. Syn. *unang pagsampa sa isáng bagong lupaín.* 4. reaching, as of one's age, on a certain year Syn. *sapit, pagsapit; dating, pagdatíng.*

tungangà (tu-nga-ngà), n. 1. a gazing at something, as in wonder or amazement. 2. act of passing one's time idly by watching others while working. Also, *pagtungangà.* Syn. *tangá, pagtangá.*

tungayaw (tu-nga-yaw), n. 1. act of castigating someone with an insulting or profane language. Syn. *mura, pagmura, pagmumurá* 2. an insulting or profane language directed at someone. Syn. *mura.*

tungkáb (tung-káb), var. **tingkáb**, I. n. 1. a dislodging or being dislodged; forcing something out of its place. Also, *pagtungkáb, pagkatungkáb.* 2. act of detaching or opening forcibly (a lock), with or as with a lever.
—II. adj. 1. dislodge or forced out of place, as a big rock from a mountain side. 2. forced open, as a lock.

tungkî (tung-kî), n. tip or point, as of the nose. Syn. *dulo, tulis.*

tungkô (tung-kô), n. a kind of native stove with tripodal base or support; trivet. Cf. *kalán.*

tungkód (tung-kód), n. walking stick; cane. Syn. *bastón.*

tungkól (tung-kól), I. n. 1. duty; work; occupation. Syn. *trabaho, gáwain.* 2. appointment or position, as in one's place of work. Also, *tungkulin, katungkulan.* 3. responsibility; obligation. Syn. *ságutin, pananágutan.*
—II. adj. all; every; all, taken individually and separately; without any exception.

Syn. *lahát, lahát-lahát, bawa't isá.*
—III. prep. (followed with sa when referring to things, and with kay and kina when referring to the name of a person or persons) regarding; about; referring to. Syn. *bagay sa, kay,* or *kiná.*

tungkós (tung-kós), n. 1. bouquet (of flowers). Syn. *pumpón.* 2. a small bundle, as of clothes. Syn. *munting balutan.* 3. a small bundle, as of leaves, shoots, and the like. Syn. *talí, bigkís.*

tungkulin (tung-ku-lin), n. 1. duty; work; function. Syn. *trabaho; gawâ, gáwain.* 2. position or appointment, as an office. Also, *katungkulan.* 3. responsibility; obligation. Syn. *ságutin, pananágutan.*

tunggâ[1] (tung-gâ), n. 1. act or manner of drinking in gulps. Syn. *langáp, paglangáp.* 2. act or habit of drinking wine. Syn. *barik, pagbarik.*

tunggâ[2] (tung-gâ), n. 1. act of rocking self on or a rocking chair. Also, *pagtunggá-tunggá.* 2. the rocking movement thus produced.

tunggák (tung-gák), v. doltish; slowwitted, referring to a woman. Syn. *ungás, tangá, bangág, tugá.*

tunggá-tunggá (tung-gá + tung-gá), n. rocking chair. Syn. *tumbá-tumbá.*

tungháy (tung-háy), I. n. 1. act or manner of raising one's head, as in assuming an erect position. Also, *pagtungháy.* 2. the erect or slightly raised position of the head. 3. act of looking at or reading something, as in a newspaper. Syn. *basa, pagbasa.*

tungo (tu-ngo), n. 1. act of going to a certain place; leaving for a certain destination. Syn. *punta, pagpunta; tumpa, pagtumpa.* 2. direction, as of the wind. 3. (Colloq.) aim; purpose; objective. Syn. *layon, layunin.*

tungó (tu-ngó), I. n. 1. act of lowering or bending the head forward. Also, *pagtungó.* Syn. *ukô o pag-ukô ng ulo.* 2. the bent or bowed position of the head, as in shame or defeat.
—II. adj. with or having the head bowed or bent forward. Also, *nakatungó.* Syn. *ukô o naka-ukô ang ulo.*

tuód (tu-ód), n. stump, as of a tree, tooth, or the like. Syn. *pungól.*

tuóp (tu-óp), I. n. 1. act of covering something with the hallow of one's palm. Cf. *sapó, kupkáp.* 2. something covered with the hallow of someone's palm. —II. *adj.* covered or protected by the hallow of someone's palm.

tuós (tu-ós), adj 1. computed; already computed. Syn. *kuwentado, tapós nang makuwenta.* 2. settled; already settled, referring to a dispute. Syn. *ayos na; naayos na.*

tupa (tu-pa), n. 1. sheep. 2. a young sheep; lamb. Syn. *batang tupa, bisiro ng tupa, kordero.* 3. the meat of sheep; mutton. Syn. *karne ng tupa.* 4. a weak or stupid person. Syn. *maamomg tao.*

tupád (tu-pád), I. n. 1. accomplishment or performance, as of a task, promise, or responsibility. Also, *pagsasaganáp, pagsasagawà.* Syn. *pagsasaganáp, pagsasagawà.* 2. fulfillment, as of an order. Syn. *talima, pagtalima; sunód, pagsunód.* 3. realization, as of a prediction, prophesy, or the like. Syn. *pagkatupád, pagkaganáp.* —II. *adj.* (usually with *na*) done; accomplished; finished; realized.

tupada (tu-pa-da), n. (*Sp.*) illegal cockfighting. Syn. *sabong na waláng pahintulot.*

tupî (tu-pî), n. 1. fold. Syn. *lupî, tiklóp* 2. plait; pleat. Syn. *pileges.*

tupok (tu-pok), n. a burning or being burned to ashes. Syn. *pagsunog o pagkasunog na lubós.*

tupukán (tu-pu-kán), n. 1. a furnace for cremating dead bodies; crematory. 2. incinerator for garbage, trash, etc. Syn. *sunugán.*

turan (tu-ran), v. 1. to name; mention. Syn. *banggitín, sabihin.* 2. to give or guess the answer to a riddle. Syn. *turingan, sabihin o hulaan ang sagót.*

turing (tu-ring), n. 1. a guess or answer to a riddle. Syn. *tuód, sagót.* 2. the selling price (of goods) given or set by the seller. 3. price offered (for goods) by a buyer. Syn. *tawad.* 4. name commonly used for something. Syn. *tawag, ngalan.* 5. making

mention of something. Syn. *banggít, pagbanggít.* 6. (*Colloq.*) respect; regard; consideration, as in: *waláng turing na anák,* a child without respect.

turnilyo (tur-nil-yo), n. (*Sp. tornillo*) 1. screw. 2. bolt.

turno (tur-no), n. (*Sp.*) 1. act of taking one's turn of duty in a rotation work. Also, *pagturno.* Syn. *halili, paghalili.* 2. one's turn in a rotation work.

turò[1] (tu-rò), n. 1. act of teaching or giving instructions or lessons to a student. Also, *pagtuturò.* 2. act of teaching or instructing someone the method of doing something 3. instructions; method of teaching. Syn. *paraán ng pagtuturò.* 4. education, as in: *batang kulang sa turò,* a child lacking in education.

turò[2] (tu-rò), n. 1. act of pointing to a person or thing with or as with a finger. 2. act of guiding someone to the place he wants to go to.

turók (tu-rók), n. 1. act or manner of piercing or pricking something with or as with a pin. Syn. *durò, pagdurò; tusok, pagtusok; sundót, pagsundót.* 2. act or manner of giving someone an injection. Syn. *iniksiyón, pag-iiniksiyón.* 3. a small puncture or hole made by a pin, needle, or the like. Syn. *duro, tusok, sundót.*

turól (tu-ról), n. direct mention or reference to something; direct statement about something. Syn. *túwirang banggít o pagbanggít, pagsasabi ng tíyakan.*

turón (tu-rón), n. (*Sp. turron*) a kind of fritters in *lumpiyâ* wrappers.

turulín (tu-ru-lín), v. to mention specifically; refer to direcly. Syn. *banggitín o sabihin nang tíyakan.*

turu-turò (tu-ru + tu-rò), var. **turo-turò**, n. a practice in some local restaurants or eateries in which customers usually point to what they want in ordering cooked food from the display at the counter.

tusino (tu-si-no), n. (*Sp. tocino*) bacon; salted and smoked pork.

tuso (tu-so). *adj.* 1. sly; deceitful. Syn. *madayà, mapanlinláng.* 2. astute; clever; cunning. Syn. *matalino.*

tusta (tus-ta), n. (*Sp. tostar*) act of frying,

roasting, or toasting (food) till crispy and brown.

utà (tu-tà), n. 1. a young dog; puppy. Syn. *bilót, kuwâ*. 2. doggy (a child's term for a puppy). 3. (*Colloq.*) blind follower. Syn. *alipuris*.

uto (tu-to), n. 1. learning; gaining knowledge or skill. Also, *pagkatuto*. Syn. *pagdunong*. 2. something learned; knowledge. Syn. *kábatiran, kaalaman*.

utok (tu-tok), n. act of pointing a gun closely or at close range at someone.

utsáng (tut-sáng), n. 1. pigtail. Syn. *tirintás, salapid*. 2. mustache. Syn. *bigote, misáy*.

utuldók (tu-tul-dók), n. (*Gram.*) colon.

utulì (tu-tu-lì), n. dry earwax in the inner earwalls.

uwâ (tu-wâ), n. joy; happiness; gladness; excitement. Syn. *galák, kagálakan; lugód, kalúguran; ligaya, kaligayahan*.

uwád (tu-wád), n. 1. act or manner of bending down the body forward with the buttocks raised higher than the head. Also, *pagtuwád*. 2. such position of the body with the head lower than the buttocks. 3. (*Colloq.*) complete defeat in a game or contest. Syn. *dapâ, pagdapâ (colloq.)*.

uwáng (tu-wáng), I. n. 1. act of carrying a load with another as partners. Syn. *usong, pag-uusong*. 2. act of dancing with another as partners. Syn. *pareha, pagpareha*. 3. act of being a co-sponsor with another, as in the baptism, confirmation, or marriage of someone.

—II. adj. acting as partners in doing or performing something. Syn. *pareha, magkapareha*.

uwerka (tu-wer-ka), n. (Sp. *tuerca*) nut (for screwing onto a bolt, etc.).

uwî (tu-wî), I. adj. every; each, individually and separately, as in: *tuwíng umaga*, every morning. Syn. *bawa't (bawat)*.

—II. adv. every time, each time; any time.
—III. conj. whenever.

uwíd (tu-wíd), I. adj. 1. straight, as a line; not bend or crooked. Syn. *deretso, matuwíd, di-baluktót*. 2. straight; not wavy or curly. Syn. *unát*. 3. upright; erect, as one's standing position. 4. direct;

continuous; unswerving. Syn. *tuluy-tulóy, di-maligoy*.

—II. adv. 1. in a straight line. Syn. *nang deretso o matuwíd*. 2. erect; upright; straight, as in: *Tumayô ka nang tuwíd*. stand erect.

—III. n. fact, state, or condition of being straight, erect, or upright.

tuwina (tu-wi-na), adv. (fr. *tuwí + na*) every time; always. Syn. *lagí, palagí, parati*

túwirang layon, (*Gram.*) direct object.

tuyâ (tu-yâ), n. a sarcastic remark or praise; mockery; sarcasm. Syn. *uyám, pag-uyám, pang-uuyám; kutyâ, pagkutyâ, pangungutyâ; aglahí, pag-aglahí, pang-aaglahí*.

tuyô (tu-yô), I. adj. 1. dried or withered, as leaves, flowers, or the like. Ant. *sariwà*. 2. dry; not wet, as clothes, soil, or the like. Ant. *basâ*. 3. waterless; dry, as a well, tank, pool, etc. Syn. *waláng-tubig, igá*. 4. lacking rain; rainless. Syn. *waláng-ulán*. Ant. *maulán*. 5. dried; preserved by salting and drying, said of fish.

—II. n. fact, state, or condition of being dry or dried. 2. salted dry fish, esp. *tunsóy*. Syn. *hawot* (in some Southern Tagalog provinces). 3. (*Med.*) tuberculosis. Syn. *tisis, tuberkolosis*.

tuyót (tu-yót). adj. 1. extremely dry. Syn. *tigáng, tuyúng-tuyô*. 2. insipid, dull, or boring. Syn. *waláng-latóy, nakaáantók*. 3. insipid; tasteless. Syn. *mayapá, waláng-lasa*.

U

U, u (pronounced like the Sp. "u" and the Eng. Short "u" in *push*), n. 1. the eighteenth letter of the *abakada* (Pilipino alphabet). 2. the type or impression representing this letter. 3. a symbol for the eighteenth in a group or series.

uban (u-ban), n. white hair; gray hair. Syn. *puting buhók*.

ubas (u-bas), n. (*Bot.*; Sp. *uvas*) 1. grapevine. 2. grape; grape fruit.

ubayà (u-ba-yà), n. an obsolescent root from which *paubayà, ipagpaubayà, ipaubayà*, *magpaubayà, pagpapaubayà,* etc. are traceable.

ubi (u-bi), I. *n.* 1. (*Bot.*) a species of yam (*Discorea alata*). 2. the rootstock of this plant. 3. violet (color). Syn. *kulay-ubi, biyoleta.*

ubó (u-bó), *n.* (*Med.*) cough.

ubod[1] (u-bod), *n.* (*Bot.*) pith, the soft, spongy tissue in the center of certain plants; core, as in fruits.

ubod[2] (u-bod), I. *n.* the essential part; core; gist. Syn. *diwà, buód.* 2. extreme limit or degree; utmost. Syn. *sukdulan, kásukdulan.*

—II. *adj.* of the highest or greatest degree. Syn. *pinaká-.*

ubós (u-bós), I. *adj.* all used up; totally eaten, consumed, or used up; without anything left. Syn. *saíd, walâ na, simót, waláng nátirá.*

—II. *n.* fact, state or condition of being totally eaten, consumed, or used up.

ubrá[1] (u-brá), *n.* (Sp. *obrar*) loose bowel movement after taking purgative or laxative, or after having been given enema. Syn. *pagdumí, pagtae.*

ubrá[2] (u-brá), I. *adj.* referring to something acceptable or usable; can be; possible. Syn. *puwede, máaarì.*

—II. *n.* state or condition of being acceptable, useable, or possible. Syn. *pagkamáaarì, pagkaposible.*

ubus-kaya (u-bus + ka-ya), var of **ubos-kaya**, I. *n.* all one's might or ability

—II. *adj. & adv.* with all one's might or ability.

ubús-ubós-biyayà (u-bús + u-bós + bi-ya-yà), *adj.* wasteful; extravagant. Sn. *mapágaksayá, bulagsák.*

ukà (u-kà), *n.* 1. act of hollowing out (something) with or as with a chisel. Also, *pag-ukà, pag-uukà.* 2. a small hollow or cavity thus made. Syn. *ukit, kutab.* 2. a shallow pit or hole on the surface of the ground. Syn. *hukay, lubák.* 3. a cavity made by biting, as on a guava fruit. Syn. *ukab.*

ukab (u-kab), *n.* 1. act of giving a fruit, esp. guava or apple, a big bite, leaving a hollow or cavity in it. 2. a big hollow or cavity made by a bite on a fruit like guava or apple. Syn. *malakíng kagát.*

ukalkál (u-kal-kál), *n.* persistent inquiry about the status of something. Syn. *masusing pag-uusisà o pagsisiyasat.*

ukbót (uk-bót), I. *n.* act or habit of sitting lazily or idly when one is supposed to be working. Syn. *ungkót, pag-ungkót.*

—II. *adj.* given to the habit of sitting lazily or idly during time of work. Syn. *ungkót, nakaungkót, paláungkót.*

ukilkíl (u-kil-kíl), I. *n.* persistent or repetitious request, offer, inquiry, etc. Syn. *mapilit na pakikiusap, pag-aalók, pagtatanóng, atb.*

—II. *adj.* persistent or repetitious referring to a person. Syn. *mapilit, magiít.*

ukit (u-kit), I. *n.* 1. groove or hollow cut on a surface with a tool. Syn. *ukà.* 2. act of cutting groove or hollow on a surface. Also, *pag-ukit.* Syn. *ukà, pag-ukà.* 3. any carved or engraven work, as a design statue, etc.; carving; engraving.

—II. *adj.* 1. carved or engraven by or as by a sculptor. Also, *inukit.* 2. done by carving or engraving.

ukô (u-kô), I. *n.* 1. bending of the head or body, as in saluting, greeting or respect; bow, bowing. Syn. *ukód, pag-ukód; yukô, pagyukô; yukód, pagyukód; saludo, pagsaludo.* 2. act of bending or stooping the head or body, as in avoiding a blow or in passing a low clearance. Syn. *yukód, pagyukód.* 3. (*Colloq.*) respect for or admission of someone's opinion. Syn. *pagkilala, pagtanggáp.*

—II. *adj.* with the head bowed, as in humility, shame, defeat, etc.

ukód (u-kód), *n.* 1. slight stoop or bow of the head, as in greeting or showing respect. 2. bending of the body or lowering of the head, as in passing a low clearance. Syn. *ukô, pag-ukô, pagyukód.*

ukol (u-kol), I. *prep.* (with *sa, kay,* or *kina*) regarding; in or with regard to; concerning; about. Syn. *tungkól sa, hinggíl sa.*

—II. *adj.* destined or intended for (someone or something). Syn. *para sa, kay, o kiná.*

—III. *n.* 1. a destining or being destined for (someone or something). Also, *pag-uukol.* Syn. *laán, paglalaán.* 2. that which is destined or intended for someone or something.

ukót (u-kót), *adj.* slightly bent or stooped, referring to a person or his body. Syn. *hukót, nakahukót.*

ukyabit (uk-ya-bit), *n.* act or manner of climbing on something by using both hands and feet or simply by hanging and pulling up oneself laboriously.

udlót (ud-lót), *n.* sudden stop or drawing back, as in fear of or avoiding something. Syn. *bigláng urong o hintô.*

udyók (ud-yók), *n.* 1. an inciting; instigation. Syn. *sulsól, pagsusulsól.* 2. something said or done to instigate or incite someone to do something undesirable. Syn. *sulsól, hibò, ulok.*

ugà (u-gà), *n.* 1. act of causing something to shake or move unsteadily. Also, *pag-ugà.* 2. shaking movement or motion of something loosely set, as teeth, chairs, tables, posts, etc., or of something being shaken or rocked, as by earthquake.

ugák (u-gák), *adj.* stupid; mentally dull. Syn. *tangá, gago, gaga, hangál, bangág.*

ugagà (u-ga-gà), *n.* an obsolescent root, meaning ability to cope up with one's work or responsibility: now usually used in the phrase "*di-makaugagà,*" (unable to cope up with one's work or responsibility).

ugalì (u-ga-lì), *n.* 1. personal behavior or conduct; habit; custom. Syn. *kustumbre.* 2. character or nature (of a person). Syn. *asal, kaasalán.* 3. inclination; propensity. Syn. *hilig, kahiligan, pagkáhilig.* 4. tradition; long-established custom or practice. Syn. *kaugalián, pag-uugalì.*

ugaog (u-ga-og), *n.* strong shaking, as of a tree or its branches, to cause the fruits, dried leaves, etc. to fall. Syn. *ugóg, pag-ugóg, pagkáugóg.*

ugát (u-gát), *n.* 1. (*Bot.*) root (of a plant or a tree). 2. (*Ling.*) root (of a word); root word. Also, *salitáng-ugát.* 3. (*Anat.*) artery or vein. 4. (*Fig.*) origin; source. Syn. *pinagmulán, pinanggalingan, pinagbuhatan.* 5. (*Colloq.*) cause. Syn. *dahilán, sanhî.*

ugit (u-git), *n.* 1. helm; rudder. Syn. *timón.* 2. (*Farming*) the part of a plow serving to guide or control its course. 3. the position of control or guidance. Syn. *kapang-yarihan.* 4. management or administration, as of an organization. Syn. *pama-mahalà, pangangasiwà.*

ugmâ (ug-mâ), I. *n.* 1. fitting of one thing to another, as of a tenon into a corresponding hole (mortise). Syn. *pagla-lapat, pagkakabít.* 2. fact or condition of being fit or proper. Syn. *pagkatumpák, katumpakán.* 3. compatibility; harmony; agreement. Syn. *pagkakásundô, pagka-kásuwatò.*

—II. *adj.* 1. fit; proper. Syn. *tamà, wastô, suwatò, bagay.* 2. well-adjusted; well-set, as a joint, etc. Syn. *lapat.*

ugnáy (ug-náy), *n.* 1. point of connection or attachment; joint. Syn. *hugpóng, húgpungan, pinaghugpungán.* 2. state or condition of being connected or related to each other. Also, *kaugnayan, pagkakáugnay.* Syn. *koneksiyón, relasyón.*

úgnayan (úg-na-yan), *n.* 1. understanding about certain matters. Syn. *únawaán, pagkakáunawaán; intindihan, pagkakáindihan.* 2. relation; relationship; connection. Syn. *relasyón, koneksiyón, kinalaman.*

ugók (u-gók), *adj.* stupid. Syn. *tangá, hangál, gago, torpe, bangág, tunggák.*

ugód (u-gód), *n.* act or manner of walking slowly and laboriously, as of a weak, old man.

ugong (u-gong), *n.* 1. deep, roaring sound, as of strong wind, gale, flying aeroplane, etc. Syn. *hugong.* 2. echoic sound, as of a distant firing of cannons. Syn. *dagundóng.*

ugoy (u-goy), *n.* (*rare*) a very slow movement, as in dancing.

ugóy (u-góy), *n.* 1. act or manner of causing a swing or cradle to sway or move to and from. Also, *pag-ugóy, pag-uugóy.* 2. the rocking or swaying motion of a swing or cradle. Syn. *undayon, tabyón.*

uguy-uguy (u-guy + u-guy), *n.* 1. a very slow movement, as in dancing the slow drag. 2. (*Colloq.*) a taxi-dancer. Syn. *bailerina.* 3. (*Colloq.*) harlot. Syn. *masamáng babae; puta, patutot, burikák.*

ugwák (ug-wák), *n*. 1. sudden, strong gush of water, as from a broken pipe, or of blood, from a cut-off artery. Syn. *bulwák, bugalwák*. 2. bubbling, as of boiling liquid. Syn. *bulwák, pagbulwák; sulák, pagsulák*.

uhâ (u-hâ), *n*. cry of a newly born baby. Syn. *iyák ng bagong silang na sanggól*.

uhales (u-ha-les), *n*. (Sp. *ojales*) 1. buttonhole. 2. act or manner of making buttonholes. Also, *pag-uuhales*. 3. the way buttonholes were made. Syn. *pagkakáuhales*.

uhaw (u-haw), *n*. 1. thirst (for water); desire for something to drink. Also, *kauhawan, pagkauhaw*. 2. strong desire or craving. Syn. *pananabík, kasabikán, masidhíng paghahangád o pagnanasâ*.

uhay (u-hay), *n*. (*Bot.*) 1. an ear of grain; spike. 2. growth or appearance of spikes. Also, *pag-uhay*.

uhetes (u-he-tes), *n*. (Sp. *ojetes*) eyelet or eyelets.

uhog (u-hog), *n*. mucus. Syn. *sipón* (*colloq.*).

uhugin (u-hu-gin), I. *adj*. 1. with or having a runny nose. Syn. *sinísipón, may-sipón*. 2. (*Colloq.*) very young; still very young, referring to a child. Syn. *musmós*.
—II. *v*. to have a runny nose; have much secretion of mucus from the nose.

ulalò (u-la-lò), *n*. grub or worm-like larva that commonly infest tubers, esp. sweet potatoes. Syn. *tangà*.

ulam (u-lam), *n*. 1. viand; victuals, like fish, meat, etc. eaten with boiled rice. Syn. *pang-ulam*. 2. eating of viands or choice dishes with boiled rice. Also, *pag-uulam*.

ulán (u-lán), *n*. 1. drops of water from the moisture in the atmosphere; rain. 2. fall of rain. Also, *pag-ulán*. 3. rapid falling of small objects, like bullets, and the like.

ulandés (u-lan-dés), *adj*. (Sp. *holandez*) blonde; with or having blonde hair.

uláng (u-láng), *n*. (*Zool.*) lobster; prawn. Syn. *sugpô*.

ulap (u-lap), *n*. 1. general term for cloud. Syn. *alapaap*. 2. rain cloud. Syn. *dagím*. 3. fog. Syn. *ulap*. 4. mist. Syn. *abuado*. 5. anything that darkens, obscures, or makes gloomy or dark. Syn. *lambóng*.

ulapíd (u-la-píd), var. **ulapír**, *adj*. 1. broke;

penniless. 2. bankrupt. Syn. *bangkarote, bagsák, tumbado* (*colloq.*).

ulat (u-lat), *n*. 1. an account or report about something. Syn. *report*. 2. news; news account; information, as in a newspaper. Syn. *balità*.

ulayaw (u-la-yaw), *n*. teta-a-tete; private or intimate conversation between two persons. Syn. *niíg, pagniniíg; talik, pagtatalik*.

ulbók (ul-bók), I. *n*. bulge; outward swelling; protuberance. Syn. *tambók, umbók*.
—II. *adj*. bulging. Syn. *matambók, maumbók*.

ulì (u-lì), *n*. act of wandering about; vagabondage. Syn. *libot, paglilibót; lagalag, paglalagalág; galà, paggagalâ*.

ulî (u-lî), I. *adv*. again; once more; once over again. Syn. *mulî, minsán pa, isá pa*.
—II. *n*. return of something borrowed or taken from a certain place. Syn. *saulì, pagsasaulì*.

ulian (u-li-an), I. *n*. state or condition of being mentally weak or queer; senility; dotage. Also, *kaulianan, pagkaulian*. 2. a person in his or her dotage; dotard.
—II. *adj*. senile; mentally weak and queer. Also, *ulianim*. 2. forgetful (due to old age). Syn. *malimutín, malilimutín*.

úlianin (ú-li-a-nin), *adj*. senile; mentally weak or queer. 2. forgetful (due to old age). Syn. *malimutín, malilimutín (dahil sa tandâ)*.

ulik (u-lik), *n*. hesitation; indecision; vacillation. Syn. *atubilì, pag-aatubilì, úrong-sulong, pag-uúrong-sulong*.

ulikbá (u-lik-bá), I. *adj*. (Ch.) with or having dark skin and meat, referring esp. to fowls. Syn. *may maitím na balát at lamán*.
—II. *n*. a fowl having dark skin and meat.

ulila (u-li-la), I. *n*. 1. a child whose parents are already dead; orphan. 2. fact or state of being without living parents. Also, *pagkaulila*. 3. a being alone in loneliness. Also, *pangungulila*.
—II. *adj*. 1. referring to an orphan; being an orphan. Syn. *patáy na ang mga magulang*. 2. alone, hence, lonely.

ulilang-lubós (u-li-lang + lu-bós), *adj*. referring to a person whose father and mother are already dead; also applied to a person who is survived by no other relatives.

ulinig (u-li-nig), *n.* 1. sense of hearing. Also, *pang-ulinig.* Syn. *pandiníg.* 2. hearing something in passing; getting wind of. Also, *pagkáulinig.* Syn. *pagkádiníg, pagkáriníg.*

uling (u-ling), *n.* 1. charcoal. 2. charcoal mark or dirt on the skin or on any surface. Syn. *dumí o marka ng uling.*

ulirán (u-li-rán), I. *adj.* worthy of imitation; serving as a model or standard of excellence.
—II. *n.* 1. something worthy of imitation; model. Syn. *húwaran, modelo.* 2. an example or standard of excellence. Syn. *mabuting halimbawà.*

ulirat (u-li-rat), *n.* 1. consciousness; awareness. Syn. *malay, kamalayan; malaytao, pagkamalay-tao.* 2. persistent asking. Syn. *pagkamaulít.*

ulit (u-lit), *n.* 1. saying again; doing again; repetition. Also, *pag-ulit, pag-uulit.* 2. time, as in: *limáng ulit,* five times.

ulí-ulî (u-lí + u-lî), *adv.* next time; again; once more. Syn. *sa ulit.*

uliuli (u-li-u-li), *n.* eddy; small whirlpool. Syn. *alimpuyó o puyó ng tubig.*

ulo (u-lo), *n.* 1. (*Anat.*) head. 2. (*Fig.*) talent; brains; intelligence. Syn. *talino, dunong, utak* (*fig.*). 3. common sense. Syn. *isip, sintido-kumún.* 4. head, as in a unit, used in counting herd. 5. chief; boss; head, as of an office. Syn. *hepe, punò, pinunò.* 6. leader, as of a gang of thieves. Syn. *lider, punò, pinunò.* 7. title or heading, as of a story, news, etc. Syn. *títuló, pamagát.* 8. top or summit, as of a mountain. Syn. *tuktók, taluktók, tugatog.* 9. front part or position, as of a column of marching soldiers. Syn. *dulo, harapán, unahán.* 10. part designed for striking, holding, or pushing, as that of a pin, tail, etc.; head. 11. head or bulb, as of garlic. 12. the top side or head, as of a bed. Syn. *ulunán.* 13. beginning; start. Syn. *simulâ, umpisá.* 14. topic, as one's speech. Syn. *paksâ.* 15. either of the two ends or heads of a dining table. Syn. *kabisera.* 16. the projecting point or head, as of a boiled egg, etc. Syn.

tingí, matá (*colloq.*). 17. source; origin. Syn. *mulâ, pinagmúmulán, pinanggágalingan.* 18. (*Colloq.*) cause. Syn. *sanhî, dahilán.* 19. (usually used with *ng,* thus becoming an adjectival phrase, expressing superlative degree) as in *ulo ng yaman,* richest of all.

ulok (u-lok), *n.* 1. act of inducing, cajoling, or coaxing. Syn. *himok, paghimok; hikayat, paghikayat.* 2. instigation. Syn. *sulsól, pagsulsól.*

ulól (u-lól), I. *adj.* crazy; demented; lunatic; insane; foolish. Syn. *loko, loko-loko, sirâ ang ulo, sintu-sintô, balíw.*
—II. *n.* 1. a fool; simpleton; silly person. Syn. *loko, taong lokó-lokó, taong sirâ ang ulo.* 2. state or condition of being crazy. Syn. *kaululán, kabaliwán.* 3. act of fooling someone. Syn. *linláng, panlinlang; dayà, pandayà.*

ulop (u-lop), *n.* 1. fog. Syn. *mababang ulap.* 2. mist. Syn. *abuado.*

ulos (u-los), *n.* 1. act of stabbing or piercing with any long, pointed instrument. Cf. *saksák, pagsaksák; sibát, pagsibát.* 2. any long, pointed instrument used as such. Also, *pang-ulos.*

ulpót (ul-pót), I. *n.* 1. sudden, partial appearance or sticking out (of something) on the surface, or from a hole or opening. Syn. *sulpót, pagsulpót, bigláng ultáw o pag-ultáw.* 2. the extent by which (a thing) has partially appeared or stuck out on the surface, from a hole or opening. Syn. *ultáw, litáw, uslî.*
—II. *adj.* partially seen or sticking out. Syn. *litáw, nakalitáw; ultáw, nakaultaw; uslî, nakauslî.*

ultimatum (ul-ti-ma-tum), *n.* (*Eng.; Sp.*) ultimatum; final proposal or statement of conditions. Syn. *hulíng-pasiyá.*

últimó (úl-ti-mó), I. *adj.* (*Sp.*) 1. last; final, as in: *últimó biyahe,* last trip. 2. even; including, as in: *ultimóng mga batà,* even children.
—II. *n.* (*Mil.*) private; lowest military rank.

ulumbayan (u-lum-ba-yan), var. **ulungbayan,** *n.* 1. capital town; provincial capital. Syn. *kabisera.* 2. town president;

town mayor. Syn. *alkalde, presidente*.

ulunán (u-lu- nán), *n.* the head or upper end, as of a bed.

ulupóng (u-lu-póng), *n.* 1. (*Zool.*) a Philippine species of cobra. Syn. *kobra*. 2. (*Fig.*) a treacherous person.

ulwâ (ul-wâ), I. *n.* 1. a sticking out or bulging, as of one's eye from its socket. Syn. *uslî, pag-uslî*. 2. belching out, as of food in vomiting. Syn. *luwâ, pagluwâ*.

um- (um-), prefix used to form simple verbs from roots beginning with vowels, as in: *umasa* (fr. *asa*), *umalis* (fr. *alís*), *umibig* (fr. *ibig*), *umulán* (fr. *ulán*), etc.

-um- (-um), infix used to form simple verbs from roots beginning with consonants, as in: *bumasa* (fr. *basa*), *kumain* (fr. *kain*), *lumakad* (fr. *lakad*), *sumulat* (fr. *sulat*), *tumawa* (fr. *tawa*), etc.

umabá (u-ma-bá), *v.* to greet (someone), as in meeting in the street. Syn. *bumatì, batiin*.

umabâ (u-ma-bâ), *v.* 1. to treat someone lowly; humble. Syn. *humamak, hamakin; dustâ, dustaín*. 2. to oppress; maltreat.

umablá (u-ma-blá), *v.* 1. to speak or talk out of turn. Syn. *magsalitâ nang hindî kinákausap*. 2. to talk without sense; babble. Syn. *dumaldál*.

umakdâ (u-mak-dâ), *v.* 1. to write (a story, novel, essay, etc); be a writer. Syn. *sumulat, magsulát*. 2. to compose (music); make musical composition; be a composer. Syn. *kumathá*.

umakó (u-ma-kó), *v.* 1. to admit (a crime, etc.) as one's own. Syn. *umamin*. 2. to admit responsibility of.

umakò (u-ma-kò), *v.* to act or stand as a guarantor for another's obligation. Syn. *sumagót, managót*.

umaktó (u-mak-tó), *v.* 1. to act as; hold office as (a mayor, etc.) Syn. *manungkulan, gumanáp ng tungkulin*. 2. to take action; make a decision. Syn. *magpasiyá, umaksiyón, kumilos*.

umaga (u-ma-ga), I. *n.* morning.
—II. *v.* (*Colloq.*) to be early, as in going to school the next morning. Also, *agahan*.

umagang-umaga (u-ma-gang + u-ma-ga), *adv.* in the early morning; very early in the morning.

umagwanta (u-mag-wan-ta; -tá), *v.* to try to endure (pain, suffering, misfortune, etc.); suffer fortitude. Syn. *tumiís, magtiís; bumatá, magbatá*.

umalí (u-ma-lí), *v.* to have a periodic manifestation of a diabolic urge or influence. Syn. *sumumpóng*.

umalumana (u-ma-lu-ma-na), *v.* to mind; think about; pay attention to.

umanó (u-ma-nó), I. *v.* (*Colloq.*) usually used interrogatively, as in: *Umanó ka ba roon?* What did you do there.
—II. *adv.* same as *di-umanó*, according to (someone); it is said.

umang (u-mang), *n.* 1. act of putting someone or something at the threshold of danger, etc. Syn. *subò, pagsusubò* (*fig.*); *buyò, pagbubuyò*. 2. snare; trap. Syn. *patibóng, silò, bitag*. 3. act of pointing (a gun) closely at someone. Syn. *tutok, pagtutok*.

umaraw (u-ma-raw), *v.* 1. to appear or show up, referring to the sun. Syn. *sumikat ang araw*. 2. to become sunny, referring to a certain day.

umasa (u-ma-sa), *v.* 1. to hope; have hope; feel confident about. Cf. *magtiwalà*. 2. to rely or depend (for support from someone).

umasám (u-ma-sám), *v.* to anticipate or expect something good from. Syn. *manabík*.

umat (u-mat), *n.* slowness; sluggishness. Syn. *bagal, kabagalan; kupad, kakuparan; sagal, kasagalan*.

umá-umaga (u-má +u-ma-ga), *adv.* every morning. Syn. *tuwíng umaga*.

umay (u-may), *n.* surfeit from overindulgence in sweets or fatty food. Cf. *suyà, pagkasuyà*.

umayáw (u-ma-yáw), *v.* 1. to refuse or turn down an offer, request, etc. Syn. *tumanggí*. 2. to back out; turn one's back on. Syn. *tumalikód, umurong*. 2. to refuse to fight anymore; accept defeat; surrender. Syn. *sumukó; umurong sa laban*.

umbáy (um-báy), *n.* (*OTag.*) mournful song. Syn. *malungkót na awit*.

umbayi (um-ba-yi; -yí; -yî), *n.* an old Tagalog funeral song or tune; dirge.

umbók (um-bók), n. convex surface; bulge; swelling; protuberance. Syn. *tambók, bukol.*

umedád (u-me-dád), n. (Sp. *humedad*) humidity; moistness in the air. Syn. *kahalumigmigan, pagkahalumigmíg; kaúmiduhán, pagkaúmidó.*

umibig (u-mi-big), v. 1. to love; fall in love; have affection for the opposite sex. Syn. *tubuan ng pag-ibig.* 2. to like; have a liking for. Syn. *gumustó, magkagustó.*

umid (u-mid), n. speechlessness due to shame, fear, embarrassment, etc.; state or condition of being speechless because of shame, fear, etc. Also, *kaumirán, pagkaumíd.*

umimporta (u-mim-por-ta), v. to request or ask for something (from someone) as a favor. Syn. *umutang na loób.*

uminó (u-mi-nó), v. 1. to call the attention of someone about something. Syn. *bumatì.* 2. to take notice of something. Syn. *pumansín.*

uminút-inót (u-mi-nút + i-nót), v. 1. to move little by little. Also, *magpainút-inót.* 2. to go or make something little by little. Syn. *umutáy-utáy, magpautáy-utáy.*

umisip (u-mi-sip), v. to think, as of a way or means of doing something; find a way or means of doing. Syn. *humanap ng paraán.*

umít (u-mít), I. n. 1. act of committing petty thievery; pilfering or filching. Also, *pag-umit, pangungumít, pang-uumít.* 2. anything pilfered or stolen. Syn. *bagay na nakaw o inumít.*

—II. *adj.* referring to anything pilfered or stolen. Syn. *nakaw, ninakaw.*

umok (u-mok), n. *(Entom.)* tiny worm or bug having certain peculiar odor and taste, usually found in rice, bread, etc. Cf. *bukbók.*

umog (u-mog), n. 1. simultaneous attack or assault on someone by a group of persons. Syn. *sabáy-sabáy na paglusob sa isáng tao* 2. a rushing together in eagerness to see, buy, etc. something.

umpís (um-pís), n. 1. state or condition of being flat or deflated, as of a punctured rubber tire or ball. 2. state or condition of being thin and haggard, as of the cheek

of a person. Syn. *hapís, pagkahapís.*

umpisá (um-pi-sá), n. (Sp. *empezar*) start; beginning; commencement. Syn. *simulâ, pagsisimulâ.*

umpók (um-pók), n. a huddle; small group of persons gathered in a huddle. Syn. *lipon; grupo, pangkát.*

umpóg (um-póg), n. 1. collision or bumping of the head against something hard. Syn. *untóg, pagkáuntóg, pagkápauntóg.* 2. act of striking together two hard objects.

umugin (u-mu-gin), v. 1. to attack or be attacked helplessly by or as by a group of persons. Syn. *pagtulúng-tulungan, salakayin ng marami.* 2. to rush or crowd around someone or something. Syn. *dumugin, pagkalipumpunán ng maraming tao.*

umumaga (u-mu-ma-ga), v. to dawn; begin to be day. Syn. *mag-umaga.*

umuna (u-mu-na), v. 1. to go, leave, or start ahead of another or others. Also, *magpáuná.* 2. to place oneself at the front. Syn. *lumagáy sa unahán.* 3. to be the first to do or make something.

umuntós (u-mun-tós), v. to wane; become less intense; subside. Syn. *humupâ, humulaw, lumubág.*

umutás (u-mu-tás), v. 1. to finish; complete; finalize. Syn. *tumapos.* 2. to kill; commit murder. Syn. *pumatáy.*

un- (un-), prefix derived from *una*, meaning "first" or "pre-", as in: *unlapì,* prefix.

una (u-na), I. *adj.* 1. first; ahead of another or others; before any other, as in: *unang araw,* first day. 2. earliest. Syn. *pinakauna, káuná-unahan.* 3. foremost in rank, quality, etc.; ranking before others. Syn. *primera, pángunahín.*

—II. *adv.* 1. for the first time. 2. before any other thing or person; at the beginning. Syn. *sa simulâ, sa umpisá.*

—III. *n.* 1. the one before the second; the first in a series. 2. any person, thing, kind, or rank that is first.

unab (u-nab), n. act or manner of scooping out the fatty substance on the surface of broth or any liquid food. Syn. *sagap, pagsagap; halagap, paghalagap.* 2. such fatty substance.

unan (u-nan), n. 1. pillow. 2. anything used for resting one's head in sleeping or lying.

unanaw (u-na-naw), n. an understanding of one's previous mistakes, etc. Syn. *pagkáunawá, pagkáintindí.*

unano (u-na-no), n. (Sp. *enano*) dwarf. Syn. *taong bulilít.*

unang- (u-nang-), used as a combining form, meaning "first."

unang-una (u-nang + u-na), I. *adj.* first among others; very first. Syn. *káuná-unahan.*
   —II. *adv.* firstly; in the first place. Syn. *una sa lahát.*
   —III. *n.* the very first; the first among many others.

unat (u-nat), n. 1. act of stretching or straightening one's arm, legs, or body. Syn. *tuwíd, pagtuwíd; deretso, pagderetso.* 2. act of stretching something by pulling. Syn. *banat, pagbanat.* 3. act of pressing something to make it flat or even, as in wrinkled clothes by ironing. 4. (Colloq.) act of giving someone a blow or strike. Syn. *tira, pagtira; banat, pagbanat.*

una-una (u-na + u-na), I. *adv.* 1. firstly; in the first place.
   —II. *adj. & adv.* one by one; one after another. Syn. *sunúd-sunód, isá-isá.*

unawà (u-na-wà), n. understanding; comprehension. Syn. *intindí, pag-intindí, pagkáintindí.*

unda (un-da; -dá), n. (Sp. *onda*) one of a series of curls of waves.

undás (un-dás), var. **undrás**, n. (Sp.) All Saints' Day. Syn. *Todos Los Santos, Araw ng mga Banál.*

undáy (un-dáy), n. a threatening gesture of the hand, as in trying to strike someone. Syn. *ambâ, yambâ.*

undayon (un-da-yon), n. swaying motion of a swing or any hanging object. Syn. *ugóy, pag-ugóy; tabyón, pagtabyón.*

únikó (ú-ni-kó), adj .(Sp. *único; Masc.*) 1. sole; only; single. Syn. *iisá, nag-íisá, solo.* 2. unique. Syn. *tangì, nátatangì.*

unlák (un-lák), n. a giving in to someone's wish or request. Also, *paunlák, pagpapaunlák.* Syn. *bigáy-loób, pagbibigáy-loób.*

unlád (un-lád), n. progress; advancement or improvement. Also, *kaunlarán, pag-unlád.* Syn. *progreso, sulong, pagsulong.*

unlapì (un-la-pì), n. (Gram.) prefix. Syn. *prepiho.*

uno (u-no), n. & adj. (Sp.) one. Syn. *isá.*

unós (u-nós), n. squall. Syn. *sigwá, sigwada.*

unsí (un-sí), n. (Sp. *uncir*) 1. act of harnessing (an animal) for work. Syn. *singkáw, pagsisingkáw.* 2. (Fig.) act of swindling another or others. Syn. *subà, pagsubà, panunubà.*

unsiyamì (un-si-ya-mì), n. a disappointing or being disappointed; frustration. Also, *pag-unsiyamì, pagkaunsiyamì.* Syn. *pagbigô, pagkabigô.*

unsiyón (un-si-yón), n. (Sp. *uncion*) unction; anointing with oil, as in a religious rite. Syn. *pagpapahid ng ungguwento o santo óleo.*

untág (un-tág), n. mention about something forgotten or neglected; reminding someone about something forgotten or neglected. Syn. *banggít, pagbanggít; ungkát, pag-ungkát.*

untî (un-tî), n. 1. smallness; littleness. Syn. *liít, kaliitan.* 2. meagerness. Syn. *kakauntián.* 3. lack. Syn. *kakulangán, kakapusán.*

untík (un-tík), n. closeness to realization or actual happening. Syn. *kamuntikanan.*

untóg (un-tóg), n. 1. collision or bumping of the head against something hard. Syn. *umpóg, pagkáumpóg, pagkápaumpóg.* 2. act of bumping someone with one's head. Also, *pag-untóg.* 3. a swelling or bump on the head caused in this manner. Syn. *bukol sa ulo dahil sa pagkáuntóg.*

untól (un-tól), n. 1. sudden stop or falling back. Syn. *bigláng hintô o paghintô, udlót, pag-udlót.* 2. temporary cessation or discontinuance. Syn. *pansamantaláng pagkápahintô o pagkápatigil.* 3. (Poetry) caesura; break or pause in a line of verse.

unyón (un-yón), n. (Sp. *union*) 1. union; association. Syn. *samahán, kapisanan, asosasyón.* 2. unity. Syn. *kaisahán, pagkakáisá.*

ungâ (u-ngâ), n. 1. low or lowing of cattle. 2. bleat of a sheep. Cf. *ungal.*

ungab (u-ngab), n. 1. a big hollow or cavity. Syn. *malaking ukà*. 2. a big bite, as on a fruit like apple. Syn. *ukab*.

ungal (u-ngal), n. 1. loud and continuous lowing of a cow or carabao. 2. loud crying of a child, esp. when hungry or in tantrum. Syn. *atungal, malakás na iyák*.

ungás (u-ngás), adj. stupid; ignorant. Syn. *tangá, hangál*.

ungkát (ung-kát), n. mention of something forgotten or neglected. Syn. *untág, paguntág*.

unggóy (ung-góy), n. (Zool.) monkey. Syn. *tsonggo*.

ungguwento (ung-gu-wen-to), n. (Sp. *unguento*) ointment. Syn. *pamahid, panghaplós*.

ungol (u-ngol), n. 1. moan; groan. 2. grumble; growl.

ungós (u-ngós), n. 1. protrusion or slight sticking out from alignment. Syn. *unsód, pagkaunsód*. 2. the part that juts or sticks out from alignment. 3. slight advantage over another or others. Syn. *bahagyáng lamáng o kalámangan*. 4. snout, as of a pig. Syn. *ngusò*. 5. proboscis. Syn. *sungót*.
—II. adj. jutting or sticking out of alignment. Syn. *nakaunsód, nakauslî, nakaungós*. 2. with or having a slight advantage. Syn. *lamáng o nakahíhigít nang bahagyâ*.

ungót (u-ngót), n. a mumbling complaint or request. Syn. *pabulóng na reklamo o pakiusap*.

uód (u-ód), n. worm; popularly, an insect larva, as caterpillar, grub, or maggot; also called *uhod* in some areas.

uóm (u-óm), var. uúm, n. 1. frightening dream; nightmare. Syn. *nakatátakot na panaginip, bangungot*. 2. suffocation in sleep; death in sleep, due esp. to a nightmare.

upa (u-pa), n. 1. act of hiring the services of a person or persons. Also, *pag-upa*. 2. the payment or compensation for such services. Syn. *bayad, kabayarán*. 3. act of hiring or renting something for one's own use. Syn. *arkilá, pag-arkilá*. 4. the rent or payment for something hired. Syn. *bayad, arkilá*.

upak[1] (u-pak), n. (*Bot.*) leaf base that envelopes a stem or trunk of plants like banana, palm tree, etc.; sheath. Syn. *talupak, takupis, balakbák*.

upak[2] (u-pak), n. 1. act of eating something with relish. Syn. *sabak, pagsabak*. 2. merciless attack on someone. Syn. *banat, pagbanat; tira, pagtira*.

upang (u-pang; u-páng), conj. so that; in order that. Syn. *nang, para, nang sa gayó'y*.

upás (u-pás), I. adj. removed or devoid of all the leaves, referring to a plant or tree. Syn. *waláng kadahún-dahon*.
—II. n. state or condition of being removed of all the leaves.

upasalà (u-pa-sa-là), n. 1. act or manner of berating another or others. Syn. *pagmura, pagdustâ, paghamak, pag-alipustâ, pagalimurà, pagdustâ*. 2. bitter, abusive language; vituperation. Syn. *mura, alipustâ, alimurà*.

upat (u-pat), n. 1. act of inciting someone to do an undesirable act; instigation. Syn. *pagsulsól, panunulsól, pagbubuyó, paguudyók*. 2. something said to instigate or incite someone to do an undesirable act. Syn. *sulsól, udyók*.

upisina (u-pi-si-na), var. opisina, n. (Sp. *oficina*) 1. office; place where one works. Syn. *tanggapan*. 2. official time of work in an office. Syn. *oras ng trabaho sa tanggapan*.

upo (u-po), n. (*Bot.*) 1. a species of trailing or climbing plant (*Lagenaria siceraria*) belonging to the gourd family that bears bottle-shaped fruits eaten as vegetable. 2. the fruit of this plant called bottle gourd. Syn. *tabayag* (*Bats.*).

upô (u-pô) I. n. 1. act or manner of sitting on a chair, etc. Also, *pag-upô*. Syn. *luklók, pagluklók*. 2. sitting position of a person. Syn. *pagkakáupô, pagkakáluklók*. 3. act or time of assuming the function of an office, as of a newly elected official. Syn. *simulâ ng panunungkól o pagtupád ng tungkulin*.
—II. v. imper. Sit down.

upód (u-pód), I. adj. worn-out or made blunt and short by friction or constant use. Syn. *upód, pulpól, gastado*.
—II. n. state or condition of being worn-

out at the business end.

upós¹ (u-pós), I. *n.* 1. cigarette or cigar stub; butt. Syn. *beha.* 2. the remaining short piece of a burnt candle. 3. state or condition of being reduced to a stub or butt, referring esp. to cigars, cigarettes, or candles.

—II. *adj.* burnt or reduced to a stub or butt, said of cigarettes, cigars, or candles.

upós² (u-pós), I. *n.* state or condition of being sunk or emerged fully into a certain depth; also, a being sunk up to the hilt.

—II. *adj.* sunk or emerged fully into a certain depth; sunk up to the hilt. Syn. *supák, sampák, sagád.*

urak (u-rak), *n.* act or manner of killing a person or animal by stabbing in the front of the neck.

urada (u-ra-da), *n.* (prob. Sp. *hora*) undue haste or hurry due to pressure of time or lack of preparation.

uralì (u-ra-lì), *n.* 1. instigation; deceptive incitement. Syn. *sulsól, panunulsól; upat, pang-uupat; udyók, pang-uudyók.* 2. intrigue; underhand plotting. Syn. *intriga; sábuwatan.* 3. compatibility. Syn. *pagkakásundô, pagkakáwastô, pagkakásuwatò.* 4. tete-a-tete. Syn. *pagniniíg, pag-uulayaw, pagsasarilinan.*

urbanidád (ur-ba-ni-dád), *n.* (*Sp.*) 1. urbanity; civility; good manners. Syn. *mabuting asal, kabutihang-asal; mabuting ugalì, kabutihang-ugalì.* 2. courtesy. Syn. *galang, kagalangan; pitagan, kapitagan.*

urbanismo (ur-ba-nis-mo), *n.* (*Sp.*) 1. city life, its organization, problems, etc. Syn. *buhay-lunsód.* 2. city planning. 3. urbanism; concentration of population in the city.

urì (u-rì), *n.* 1. sort; kind; class; quality. Syn. *klase.* 2. species or variety. 3. classification.

urirat (u-ri-rat), *n.* persistent asking or inquiry. Syn. *mapilit na pagtatanóng o pag-usisà.*

uriya (u-ri-ya; -yá), *n.* (Sp. *orilla, orillo*) selvage; selvedge.

urna (ur-na), *n.* (*Sp.*) ballot box.

urong (u-rong), *n.* 1. act of moving backward. Syn. *balík, pagbalík; atrás, pag-atrás.* 2. retreat, as of soldiers being pursued by the enemy. Syn. *atrás, pag-atras.* 3. a backing

out, as from one's promise. Syn. *talusirà, pagtatalusirà, pakikipágtalusirà.* 4. revocation, as of a permit. Syn. *bawí, pagbawí.* 5. shrinkage, as of fabrics. Syn. *pag-iklî, pangingiklî.* 6. postponement, as of a scheduled activity, to a latter date. Syn. *pagpapaliban.* 7. retraction, as of one's statement. Syn. *bawì, pagbawì.* 8. clearing of the table after eating. Syn. *imis, pag-iimis; ligpít, pagliligpít.* 9. dismissal or time of dismissal from work. Syn. *lábasan, paglalábasan.* 10. return of workers to their homes after dismissal from work. Syn. *úwian, pag-uúwian.* 11. retreat from a fight or contest; refusal to fight anymore. Syn. *ayáw, pag-ayáw.*

urung-sulong (u-rung + su-long), *adj.* irresolute; vacillating; undecided. Syn. *salawahan, nagsásalawahan; atubilî, nagáatubilî.*

usá (u-sá), *n.* (prob. Mal. *rusa*) 1. (*Zool.*) deer. 2. venison; flesh or meat of deer. Syn. *karne ng usá, karnéng usá.*

usád (u-sád), *n.* 1. slow movement, as of a child learning to crawl. Syn. *mahinang gapang o paggapang.* 2. act of moving slowly on one's buttocks, as a child. Syn. *alipod, pag-alipod.*

usál (u-sál), *n.* act or manner of saying something repeatedly and continuously, usually in whispers, as in praying.

usap (u-sap), *n.* 1. conversation; act of talking to each other. Also, *úsapan, pag-uusap.* 2. verbal dispute or quarrel. Syn. *pagtatalo.* 3. request for a favor. Also, *pakiúsap.* Syn. *suyò, pakikisuyò.*

usapín (u-sa-pín), I. *n.* case in court; lawsuit; litigation. Syn. *asunto, kaso.*

—II. *adj.* said of someone who is often invited or requested to help others. Syn. *malimit máanyayahan sa pagtulong.*

usap-úsapan (u-sap + ú-sa-pan), *n.* 1. news or report circulating around; subject of conversation among a number of persons. Syn. *balità, balí-balità.* 2. gossip or rumors. Syn. *bulúng-bulungan.*

usbóng (us-bóng), *n.* 1. bulge or swelling on a surface. Syn. *umbók, tambók.* 2. (*Bot.*) bud, as of a flower. Syn. *buko.* 2. a new growth; sprout. Syn. *supang, suloy.* 3.

(Fig.) progress; development. Syn. *unlád, pag-unlád; progreso; lagô, paglagô (fig.).* 4. *(Bot.)* the sprout of a mushroom. Syn. *butóng.*

usig (u-sig), n. 1. investigation or inquiry about something. Syn. *siyasat, pagsisiyasat.* 2. persecution. Syn. *pagpapahirap, pagpaparusa.* 3. prosecution. Syn. *litis, paglilitis, pag-uusig.*

usisà (u-si-saà), n. 1. act of asking or inquiring from someone about something; reminding someone about something previously promised. Syn. *pagpapaalaala sa isang tao tungkol sa kanyáng pangakò at ibá pa.* 2. an inquiry about the status of something. Syn. *ungkát, pag-ungkát.*

uslák (us-lák), adj. foolish; silly; stupid. Syn. *tangá, hangál, bangág, tunggák.*

uslî (us-lî), I. n. 1. protrusion or sticking out from a hole or socket. Also, *pag-uslî.* Syn. *luwâ, pagluwâ; ulwâ, pag-ulwâ.* 2. the part or portion that juts or sticks out. Syn. *bahaging nakauslî o nakaluwâ.* 3. state or condition of having a part jutting or sticking out. Also, *pagkauslî, kauslián.*

—II. *adj.* with or having a part sticking or jutting out. Syn. *luwâ, nakaluwâ; ulwâ, nakaulwâ.*

uso (u-so), n. current style or mode; fashion; vogue. Syn. *moda.*

usok (u-sok), n. smoke; black or dark smoke. Syn. *asó, asap.*

usod (u-sod), n. act of moving over a little, as in giving way or space to someone. Syn. *isod, pag-isod.*

usog (u-sog), n. *(Med.)* gas in the stomach or intestines; flatus or flatulence. Syn. *kabag.*

usóg (u-sóg), n. sickness of a child supposed to have been gotten from someone who had taken fancy on him.

usong (u-song), n. 1. act of helping another or each other in carrying a load cooperatively. Also, *pag-usong, pag-uusong.* 2. the act or manner by which a load is carried by two or more persons cooperatively.

usós (u-sós), var. **us-ós**, n. a slipping or sliding down, as on a slope or incline. Syn. *dausós (daus-os).*

usura (u-su-ra), n. *(Sp.)* 1. lending money

at extremely high rate of interest; usury. Syn. *labis na pagpapatubò.* 2. unlawful or extremely high rate of interest. Syn. *labis na tubò o patubò.*

utak (u-tak), n. 1. *(Anat.)* brains. 2. bone marrow; medulla. 3. *(Fig.)* mental ability; talent; intelligence; brains. Syn. *talino.*

utál (u-tál), I. *adj.* with or having a defective speech; stammering; stuttering. Syn. *humál.*

—II. n. a person who stammers or shutters in his speech.

utang (u-tang), I. n. 1. act of borrowing money or contracting a loan, as from a bank. Also, *pag-utang, pangungutang.* 2. debt; account; liability or obligation to pay; indebtedness. Also, *pagkakautang.* Syn. *bayarín, ságutin.* 3. loan; money loaned by a bank. Also, *pautang.* 4. act of buying something on credit.

—II. *adj.* 1. borrowed; obtained as a loan or obligation to pay. Also, *inutang.* 2. bought on credit.

utang-na-loób (u-tang + na + lo-ób), n. favor; debt of gratitude.

utás (u-tás), I. n. 1. completion or termination, as of a project or undertaking. Syn. *tapos, pagtapos, pagkatapos.* 2. a coming to an end. Syn. *wakás, pagwawakás.* 3. act of killing or causing the death of. Syn. *patáy, pagpatáy.*

—II. *adj.* 1. completed or finished, referring to a project, work, or undertaking. Syn. *tapos, pagtapos (na).* 2. dead or killed. Syn. *patáy (na).*

utaw (u-taw), n. *(Ch.)* soybean.

utáy (u-táy), n. act of trying or making efforts to do something little by little.

utin (u-tin), n. 1. *(Anat.; colloq.)* penis. Syn. *titì, punong katawán (fig.), arì ng lalaki.* 2. *(Colloq.)* an inconsequential person.

utô (u-tô), I. n. 1. a silly person; simpleton; fool. Syn. *taong lukú-luko o sirâ ang ulo.* 2. act of making a fool of someone. Also, *pag-utô.* Syn. *pagluko.*

—II. *adj.* silly; stupid; foolish; easily deceived or fooled. Syn. *lukú-lukó, sirá-sirâ ang ulo, hangál, tangá.*

utog (u-tog), n. sexual urge; libido. Syn. *libog.*

utol (u-tol), n. (Colloq.) one's brother or sister. Syn. kapatíd.

utóng (u-tóng), n. 1. (Anat.) nipple; teat; pap. 2. an artificial teat-like part in the cap of a baby's nursing bottle.

utos (u-tos), n. 1. order; command. Syn. mando, ordén, atas. 2. an official order, edict, or decision. Syn. dekreto, batás.

utót (u-tót), n. 1. expulsion of flatus or gas from the stomach or intestines; breaking wind. Also, pag-utót. 2. the foul smell (odor) of the flatus or gas expelled from the stomach or intestines.

ut-ot (ut + ot), n. act or manner of sucking the teat or nipple of the breast or udder. Cf. supsóp, pag-supsóp.

utusán (u-tu-sán), n. 1. messenger; errand boy. Syn. mensahero. 2. servant. Syn. alilà. 3. houseboy; housegirl; housemaid. Syn. katulong sa bahay.

uugúd-ugód (u-u-gúd + u-gód), adj. said of a person who walks slowly and laboriously due to weakness or old age.

uwák (u-wák), (Zool.) n. 1. crow; any of the crow family, like the raven, rook, and jackdaw. 2. the harsh cry of this bird.

uwáng (u-wáng), n. (Entom.) a species of horned beetle that usually infests coconut trees.

uwáy (u-wáy), n. 1. (Bot.) rattan, a climbing palm (Genera Calamus and Daemonorops) with long, tough stems. 2. a stem of this palm, commonly used in making wickerwork, etc. Syn. yantók. 3. a cane made from this.

uwî (u-wî), n. 1. act of going home or to one's place of abode; return to one's home town, province, or country. Syn. pagbalík sa sarili. 2. anything brought home by someone, esp. from a trip. Syn. dalá sa pag-uwî, pasalubong.

Uy (Uy), interj. an expression used to call the attention of someone, and to express surprise, admiration, joke, etc.

uyad (u-yad), n. act of walking with difficulty, as big-bellied persons do; slow, awkward movement of obese persons. Cf. ampáng, pag-ampáng-ampáng.

uyám (u-yám), n. 1. act of making fun of a person by using sarcasm. Syn. kutyâ, pagkutyâ; tuyâ, pagtuyâ. 2. any sarcastic remark directed at someone; mockery; sarcasm.

uyayi (u-ya-yi), var. **oyayi**, n. 1. lullaby; cradle song. 2. cradle. Syn. duyan.

W

W, w (wa), n. 1. the nineteenth letter of the abakada (Pilipino alphabet). 2. a type or impression representing this letter. 3. a symbol for the nineteenth in a group or series.

Wa! (Wa), interj. an exclamation expressing surprise, dismay, or sometimes a joke.

Wâ (Wâ), inter. an ejaculation usually made to make a child laugh; this is done by covering the eyes with both hands and uncovering them again suddenly.

waak (wa-ak), n. 1. act of tearing or ripping (a thing) apart roughly or vigorously. 2. a big, long rip or tear. Syn. wahak, gahak, walat.

waag (wa-ag), n. 1. a wide, open field or space. Syn. maluwáng at aliwalas na poók o lugár. 2. state or condition of being wide-open and clear to viewing.

wakás (wa-kás), n. 1. end or ending; finish; conclusion. Syn. katapusán. 2. a ceasing to exist; death. Syn. kamatayan. 3. final result; consequence; outcome. Syn. resulta, bunga, kinálabasán, kináuwian.

wakawak (wa-ka-wak), n. a falling into disrepute, etc. Syn. wakaak, pagkáwakaak; riwarà, pagkariwarà; pagkapahamak; roól, pagkaparoól; panganyayà, pagkapanganyayà.

waklás (wak-lás), I. n. 1. act or manner of ripping something in order to open. Also, pagwaklás. Syn. wiklás, pagwiklás. 2. the part of something that is ripped open. — II. adj. ripped open. Syn. wiklás, nawiklás.

waksi (wak-si; -sí), n. 1. act or manner of shaking off something that clings or hangs, esp. on one's hand. Syn. pagpág, pagpapagpág; wisík, pagwiwisík. 2. getting rid of something, as by forgetting, renouncing, etc. Syn. paglimot, pagtatapon, (colloq.), pagwawaglít sa alaala, *pagtatakwíl.*

wakwák (wak-wák), I. *n.* 1. act of tearing or ripping something wide-open. Also, *pagwakwak.* 2. a long, wide rip or tear. Syn. *gahak, wasak.* 3. state or condition of being ripped or torn violently.

—II. *adj.* ripped or torn violently; with or having a long, wide rip or tear. Syn. *wasák, gahák.*

wadwád (wad-wád), *n.* act of shaking something vigorously or angrily while being held with the mouth with the intention of tearing it to pieces. Syn. *wilwíl, pagwiwilwíl.*

wagás (wa-gás), *adj.* pure; genuine; sincere; true. Syn. *dalisay, tapát, tunay.*

wagawag (wa-ga-wag), *n.* act of shaking one's hands, or even the body, in order to get rid of something clinging on it. Syn. *pagpág, pagpapagpág; wagwág, pagwawagwág.*

wagaywáy (wa-gay-wáy), *n.* 1. waving, as of a flag in the air. Also, *pagwagaywáy.* 2. waving motion of the hand or something held by the hand, as in signaling to someone. Syn. *wasiwas, pagwawasiwas.*

wagí (wa-gí), *n.* triumph; victory; success. Syn. *tagumpáy, pananagumpáy.*

waglít (wag-lít), *n.* a misplacing or being misplaced. Cf. *walâ, pagkawalâ.*

wagwág[1] (wag-wág), *n.* (*Bot.*) a variety of first-class rice.

wagwág[2] (wag-wág), *n.* act of shaking a thing to rid it of things that cling on it, esp. water, dust, etc. Syn. *pagpág, pagpapagpág.*

wahak (wa-hak), *n.* a long rip, tear, or rent. Syn. *gahak, wakwák.*

walâ (wa-lâ), I. *adj.* absent; not present; did not come; did not attend. Syn. *di-pumasok, di-dumating, liban, di-dumaló.* 2. out; away; not in. Syn. *umalís, lumabás.* 3. without; lacking; not with. 4. free from. Syn. *ligtás.*

—II. *pron.* none; no one; not anyone; not any.

—III. *n.* none; no one; not any (of); nothing.

walám- (wa-lám-), var. **waláng-,** *pref.* used before roots beginning with *b* or *p.*

walámbahalà (wa-lám-ba-ha-là), var.

waláng-bahalà, *adj.* 1. unconcerned; disinterested or indifferent. Syn.*waláng-malasakit.* 2. irresponsible. Syn. *waláng-pananagutan, iresponsable.* 3. unaware; unmindful.

walán- (wa-lán), var. of **waláng-,** *pref.* used before roots beginning with *d* or *t.* See also **walám-.**

waláng- (wa-láng-), *pref.* used as a combining form equivalent to the suffix "–less" in forming adjectives, and to "without" in the formation of adjective phrases, as in: *waláng-abala, waláng-amóy,* etc.

waláng-abóg (wa-láng + a-bóg), I. *adj.* 1. noiseless; without noise. Syn. *waláng-ingay.* 2. without notice. Syn. *waláng-babalâ, waláng-sabí-sabí.*

—II. *adv.* suddenly; without notice.

waláng-alam (wa-láng + a-lam), *adj.* 1. ignorant; uninformed. Syn. *ignorante; tangá.* 2. innocent, as a child. Syn. *inosente, waláng-malay.*

waláng-alan (wa-láng + a-lan), *adj.* 1. without a name; nameless. Also, *waláng-pangalan.* 2. anonymous; left unnamed. 3. not publicly known; obscure. Syn. *di-kilalá.*

waláng-alang-alang (wa-láng + a-lang + a-lang), *adj.* 1. without consideration; inconsiderate. Syn. *waláng-konsiderasyón, waláng-pagbibigáy.* 2. unrespectful. Syn. *waláng-galang, waláng-pítagan, waláng pusóng.*

waláng-alinlangan (wa-láng + a-lin-la-ngan), I. *adj.* feeling no doubt about; sure; certain. Syn. *tiyák, nakatítiyák, waláng-duda, sigurado.*

—II. *adv.* surely; certainly; without doubt. Syn. *tiyák, sigurado.*

waláng-anumán (wa-láng + a-nu-mán), I. *adj.* 1. nothing at all. Syn. *walâ kahit anó.* 2. unmindful; unattentive to. Syn. *balewalâ, di-alintana.*

—II. *interj.* That's all right! Don't mention it.

—III. *n.* nothing; not anything.

waláng-angal (wa-láng + a-ngal), *adj.* without complaint or opposition. Syn. *waláng-reklamo, waláng-tutol.*

waláng-aral (wa-láng + a-ral), *adj.* 1.

uneducated; mannerless. Syn. *waláng-pinág-aralan*, *bastós*. 2. on vacation, referring to a student. Syn. *bakasyón, nagbábakasyón, waláng-pasok.* 3. without moral lesson; giving no moral lesson.

walâng-atindí (wa-láng + a-tin-dí), *adj.* 1. negligent. Syn. *waláng-asikaso, pabayâ.* 2. lazy. Syn. *tamád, batugan, matigás ang katawán.* 3. with or having nothing to attend to. Syn. *waláng-ináasikaso.*

walâng-atrás (wa-láng + a-trás), *adj.* no turning back. Syn. *waláng-urong.*

walâng-atraso (wa-láng + a-tra-so), *adj.* 1. without arrears, as in the payment of one's obligation; regular in paying one's account. 2. *(Colloq.)* sinless; innocent. Syn. *waláng-kasalanan.*

walâng-atubilî (wa-láng + a-tu-bi-lî), I. *adj.* without hesitation; without reluctance. Syn. *waláng-pag-uurung-sulong.*
—II. *adv.* unhesitatingly.

walâng-awà (wa-láng + a-wà), *adj.* without pity or mercy; merciless; cruel. Syn. *waláng-habág, malupít.*

walâng-bahalà (wa-láng + ba-ha-là), *adj.* 1. unconcerned; indifferent. 2. irresponsible. Syn. *waláng-pananagutan, iresponsable.*

walâng-baít (wa-láng + ba-ít), *adj.* senseless; thoughtless. Syn. *waláng-isip.*

walâng-balak (wa-láng + ba-lak), *adj.* without intention or plan to do something.

walâng-balino (wa-láng + ba-li-no), *adj.* unperturbed; not disturbed by worries or anxiety; unworried. Syn. *waláng-balisa, waláng-bagabag (-tigatig).*

walâng-batián (wa-láng + ba-ti-án), *adj.* not talking or speaking to each other; not on a speaking term with each other. Syn. *waláng-kíbuan, di-nag-úusap, di-nagbábatián.*

walâng-bibíg (wa-láng + bi-bíg), *adj.* 1. without a mouth. Syn. *waláng-bungangà.* 2. *(Fig.)* without power or authority. Syn. *waláng-kapangyarihan.*

walâng-bukas (wa-láng + bu-kas), var. **walâng-kinabukasan**, *adj. (Fig.)* without future.

walâng-budhî (wa-láng + bud-hî), *adj.* 1. without conscience. Syn. *waláng-*

konsiyénsiyá. 2. heartless; cruel. Syn. *malupít, waláng-awà, waláng-pusò.*

walâng-buhay (wa-láng + bu-hay), *adj.* 1. dead; lifeless. Syn. *patáy, hindî na humíhingá, walâ nang hiningá.* 2. inanimate. 3. dull; lacking spirit; not lively. Syn. *waláng-siglá.*

walâng-bunga (wa-láng + bu-nga), *adj.* 1. without fruits; fruitless. Syn. *di-namunga.* 2. without result. Syn. *waláng-resulta.* 3. *(Fig.)* childless. Syn. *waláng-anák, waláng-suplíng.*

walâng-butó (wa-láng + bu-tó), *adj.* 1. without bones; boneless. 2. without seeds; seedless. 3. *(Fig.)* weak; physically incapable.

walâng-kabuluhán (wa-láng + ka-bu-lu-hán), *adj.* 1. useless; unimportant; of no importance. Syn. *waláng-saysáy, waláng-kasaysayan, waláng-halagá.* 2. meaningless. Syn. *waláng-kahulugán.*

walâng-kahulilip (wa-láng + ka-hu-li-lip), *adj.* unequalled; unsurpassed; unparalleled; unmatched; matchless. Syn. *waláng-katulad, waláng-kapantáy, waláng-kaparis.*

walâng-kailangan (wa-láng + ka-i-la-ngan), I. *adj.* 1. said of a person who has nothing to ask for; without anything to ask for. 2. useless; unnecessary. Syn. *di-mahalagà, waláng-halagá.*
—II. *adv.* needlessly; unnecessarily.

walâng-káluluwá (wa-láng + ká-lu-lu-wá), *adj.* 1. lacking soul; without spirit. 2. heartless; without mercy; cruel. Syn. *waláng-pusò, malupít, waláng-awà.*

walâng-kamatayan (wa-láng + ka-ma-ta-yan), *adj.* deathless; living forever; immortal.

walâng-kapara (wa-láng + ka-pa-ra), *adj.* matchless; incomparable. Syn. *waláng-katulad, waláng-kaparis.*

walâng-kapararakan (wa-láng + ka-pa-ra-ra-kan), *adj.* of no value; useless; worthless. Syn. *waláng-halagá, waláng-saysáy.*

walâng-kapwà (wa-láng + kap-wà), *adj.* lacking public relations; unfriendly to others; without friends.

walâng-katulad (wa-láng + ka-tu-lad), *adj.* incomparable; without equal or peer. Syn. *waláng-kaparis.*

waláng-katuturán (wa-láng + ka-tu-tu-rán), *adj*. meaningless; senseless; useless; insignificant. Syn. *waláng-kabuluhán, waláng-kasaysayan, di-mahalagá*.

waláng-kawawaan (wa-láng + ka-wa-wa-an), *adj*. 1. useless. Syn. *waláng-halagá*. 2. without definite result. Syn. *waláng maliwanag na resulta*.

waláng-kiling (wa-láng + ki-ling), *adj*. 1. without inclination; not leaning; erect or upright. Syn. *waláng-lado*. 2. impartial; unprejudiced; not siding with anyone. Syn. *waláng-kinákampihán*.

waláng-kiyáw-kiyáw (wa-láng + ki-yáw + ki-yáw), *adj*. 1. without much ado. Syn. *waláng maraming kuskús-balungos*. 2. without useless fretting. Syn. *waláng-reklá-reklamo*.

waláng-kuntíl-butil (wa-láng + kun-tíl + bu-til), *adj*. without much ado or too many unnecessary details. Syn. *waláng-maraming-rekubeko*.

waláng-kupas (wa-láng + ku-pas), *adj*. 1. unfading; never fading; permanent, referring to colors. 2. never ceasing or ending; unfailing. Syn. *waláng-lipás*.

waláng-kusà (wa-láng + ku-sà), *adj*. without initíative. Syn. *waláng-sariling-palò* (*colloq.*).

waláng-kuwenta (wa-láng + ku-wen-ta), *adj*. not important; of no value or importance; useless. Syn. *waláng-halagá, di-mahalagá, balewalâ*.

waláng-dagím (wa-láng + da-gím), *adj*. cloudless; clear, referring to the sky. Syn. *waláng-ulap, maliwanag o aliwalas ang langit*.

waláng-dahilán (wa-láng + da-hi-lán), *adj*. 1. without cause. Syn. *waláng-sanhî*. 2. without reason or excuse. Syn. *waláng-katwiran*.

waláng-dalâ (wa-láng + da-lâ), *adj*. never scared off by previous unfortunate experience. Also, *waláng-pagkadalà*.

waláng-dangál (wa-láng + da-ngál), *adj*. without honor; undignified; dishonest. Also, *waláng-karángalan*.

waláng-dilà (wa-láng + di-là), *adj*. 1. without tongue; tongueless. 2. dumb; unable to speak. Syn. *pipi, di-makapágsalitâ*.

waláng-direksiyón (wa-láng + di-rek-si-yón), *adj*. 1. without instruction. Syn. *waláng-tagubilin; waláng-panuto*. 2. without definite course or direction. Syn. *waláng-tiyák na túnguhin, láyunin, atbp*. 3. without address or indication of one's place of residence, etc.

waláng-diwà (wa-láng + di-wà), *adj*.1. unconscious. Syn. *waláng-malay, waláng-malay-tao*. 2. without meaning; without sense; senseless; meaningless. Syn. *waláng-kahulugán, waláng-ibig-sabihin*.

waláng-duda (wa-láng + du-da), I. *adj*. feeling no doubt; sure; certain. Syn. *waláng-alinlangan, sigurado, tiyák*.
—II. *adv*. without doubt; certainly; surely.

waláng-gaanó (wa-láng + ga-a-nó), *adj*. not much; only a few. Syn. *di-gaanó*.

waláng-galang (wa-láng + ga-lang), *adj*. 1. without respect; disrespectful; discourteous. Syn. *waláng-pitagan, waláng-respeto*. 2. irreverent. Syn. *pusóng*.

waláng-habág (wa-láng + ha-bág), *adj*. 1. without pity or compassion. Syn. *waláng-awà, waláng-pusò*. 2. cruel. Syn. *malupít*.

waláng-habas (wa-láng + ha-bas), *adj*. without control, esp. in one's words; harsh in one's language.

waláng-halagá (wa-láng + ha-la-gá), *adj*. 1. without a price tag. Syn. *waláng-presyo*. 2. of no importance, value, or worth; useless; valueless. Syn. *waláng-saysáy, di-mahalagá, waláng-kabuluhán*.

waláng-hanggá (wa-láng + hang-gá), *adj*. without end; endless. Syn. *waláng-wakás; waláng-katapusán*.

waláng-hinawà (wa-láng + hi-na-wà), *adj*. said of a person who never loses appetite or interest in something. Syn. *waláng-sawà, waláng-pagsasawà*.

waláng-hinayang (wa-láng + hi-na-yang), *adj*. wasteful, esp. in spending money, etc. Syn. *bulagsák, mapág-aksayá*.

waláng-hirap (wa-láng + hi-rap), I. *adj*. 1. said of a person who has not contributed anything to the completion of something. Syn. *waláng-naitulong*. 2. effortless; with no effort.
—II. *adv*. easily; without difficulty or effort.

waláng-hiyâ (wa-láng + hi-yâ), var.
walanghiyâ, adj. shameless; without
shame; brazen. Syn. *hindî nahíhiyâ,
makapál ang mukhâ (fig.).*

waláng-lamat (wa-láng + la-mat), adj.
flawless, referring to glassware,
earthenware, etc. Syn. *waláng-basag,
waláng-putók.*

waláng-latóy (wa-láng + la-tóy), adj. 1.
uninteresting. Syn. *di-kawili-wili.* 2.
tasteless. Syn. *waláng-lasa.*

waláng-likát (wa-láng + li-kát), adj. 1.
without mitigation; without waning. Syn.
waláng-hupâ, waláng-hignáw. 2.
continuous; ceaseless; without
interruption. Syn. *waláng-tigil, waláng-
tahán, waláng-hintó, waláng-humpáy,
tulúy-tulóy.*

waláng-lipas (wa-láng + li-pas), adj. 1. never
losing potency or efficacy. Syn. *di-
lumílipas, di-nawáwalán ng bisà.* 2. that
never wanes or mitigates. Syn. *waláng-
hulaw, waláng-hignáw.* 3. that never lapse.
Syn. *waláng-pasó.*

waláng-liwag (wa-láng + li-wag), I. adj. easy
to do or make; not hard to make. Syn.
madalíng gawín, maalwáng gawín.
—II. adv. easily. Syn. *madalî, maalwán.* 2.
at once. Syn. *agád, agád-agád.*

waláng-loób (wa-láng + lo-ób), adj. without
affection or warm liking for; cool;
indiferrent. Syn. *matabáng ang loób,
waláng-gusto, malamíg ang loób.*

waláng-lubáy (wa-láng + lu-báy), adj.
without stopping or cessation. Syn.
waláng-humpáy, waláng-hintô, waláng-tigil.

waláng-lusót (wa-láng + lu-sót), adj. without
chance of being approved; sure of
disapproval or rejection.

waláng-malák (wa-láng + ma-lák), adj. 1.
without knowledge or idea about
something. Syn. *waláng-nálalaman.* 2.
innocent; ignorant about something. Syn.
waláng-malay, inosente sa.

waláng-malay (wa-láng + ma-lay), adj. 1.
unconscious. 2. innocent; too young to
understand. Syn. *inosente, musmós pa.*

waláng-maliw (wa-láng + ma-liw), adj. 1.
unending; endless. Syn. *waláng-katapusan,
waláng-wakás, waláng-hanggán.* 2.

unfading. Syn. *waláng-kupas.*

waláng-mayaw (wa-láng + ma-yaw), adj.
without let-up (s.o. loud noise, applause,
clapping of hands, etc.). Syn. *waláng-tigil.*

waláng-mukhâ (wa-láng + muk-hâ), I. adj.
without face; faceless.
—II. adv. not bold enough to see or face
someone due to shame.

waláng-pakiramdám (wa-láng + pa-ki-ram-
dám), adj. 1. without feeling; insensible.
2. numb; having lost the sense of feeling.
Syn. *manhíd, namámanhíd.*

waláng-pakundangan (wa-láng + pa-kun-da-
ngan), adj. irreverent; without respect;
unrespectful. Syn. *waláng-galang, waláng-
pítagan, pusóng.*

waláng-pag-asa (wa-láng + pag + a-sa), adj.
without hope; hopeless. Syn. *waláng-
esperansa, waláng-pagkakátaón.*

waláng-palad (wa-láng + pa-lad), adj.
unfortunate; unlucky. Syn. *waláng-
suwerte, sinásamâ, malas.*

waláng-panalo (wa-láng + pa-na-lo), adj. 1.
winless. Syn. *hindî pa nanánalo, laging talo.*
2. (Colloq.) incomparable to; not a match
for.

waláng-pangalawá (wa-láng + pa-nga-la-
wá), adj. 1. the best; without peer. Syn.
waláng-kaparis, pinakamahusay. 2. without
assistant or helper. Syn. *waláng-katulong.*

waláng-pangambá (wa-láng + pa-ngam-bá),
adj. unperturbed with fear, doubt, or
misgiving. Syn. *waláng-agam-agam,
waláng-pag-aalinlangan.* 2. without danger.
Syn. *waláng-peligró.*

waláng-pasintabì (wa-láng + pa-sin-ta-bì),
adj. 1. without taking exception. Syn.
waláng-pasubalì. 2. without begging
apology. Syn. *waláng-paghingî ng
paumanhín.*

waláng-patawad (wa-láng + pa-ta-wad), adj.
1. unforgiving; unmerciful. Syn. *waláng-
awà.* 2. not selective. Syn. *waláng-pilì-pilì,
waláng-delikadesa.*

waláng-pátumanggâ (wa-láng + pá-tu-mang-
gâ), adj. & adv. without regard for success
or failure; in a haphazard or aimless way.
Syn. *waláng-tarós, pikít-matá (colloq.).*

waláng-pinág-aralan (wa-láng + pi-nág + a-
ra-lan), adj. 1. uneducated. Syn.

mangmáng, di-nag-aral. 2. ill-bred;
impolite. Syn. *bastós, waláng-galang.*

waláng-piták (wa-láng + pi-ták), *adj.*
(Colloq.) without a place, as in one's
heart.

waláng-pitagan (wa-láng + pi-ta-gan), *adj.*
without respect; irreverent. Syn. *waláng-
galang, waláng-respeto, pusóng.*

waláng-puknát (wa-láng + puk-nát), *adj.*
always attached; inseparable.

waláng-pusò (wa-láng + pu-sò), *adj.*
heartless; cruel. Syn. *waláng-awà, waláng-
habág, malupít.*

waláng-puwáng (wa-láng + pu-wáng), *adj.*
1. without space between; without gap.
Syn. *waláng-pagitan, waláng-awáng.* 2.
without vacancy; no vacant position. Syn.
waláng-bakante.

waláng-sagabal (wa-láng + sa-ga-bal), *adj.*
1. without any impediment or obstacle.
Syn. *waláng-hadláng.* 2. without any
problem. Syn. *waláng-súliranín.*

waláng-sagwíl (wa-láng + sagwíl), *adj.*
without impediment or obstacle; with or
having nothing to hinder. Syn. *waláng-
sagabal, waláng-hadláng.*

waláng-sawà (wa-láng + sa-wà), *adj.* never
satisfied; never satiated, surfeited, or
cloyed. Syn. *di-nagsásawà.*

waláng-saysáy (wa-láng + say-sáy), *adj.*
useless; of no value or importance. Syn.
waláng-halagâ, patapón.

waláng-sikmurà (wa-láng + sik-mu-rà), *adj.*
(Colloq.) never ashamed; shameless. Syn.
*waláng-hiyâ, matapang ang mukhâ (fig.),
makapál ang mukhâ (fig.).*

waláng-suplíng (wa-láng + sup-líng), *adj.* 1.
without shoots or buds. 2. childless. Syn.
waláng-anák.

waláng-tawad (wa-láng + ta-wad), *adj.* 1. no
discount; without discount; with or
having fixed price. Syn. *waláng-bawas,
waláng-diskuwento.* 2. that cannot be
forgiven; unpardonable.

waláng-tigatig (wa-láng + ti-ga-tig), *adj.*
unperturbed; unalarmed. Syn. *di-
nabábalisa, di-nabábahalà.*

waláng-tinig (wa-láng + ti-nig), *adj.* 1.
without voice; voiceless. Syn. *waláng-
boses.* 2. *(Fig.)* without any say, power, etc.

waláng-tugot (wa-láng + tu-got), *adj.*
without stop; continuous. Syn. *waláng-
tigil, waláng-hintô, waláng-humpáy, tulúy-
tulóy.*

waláng-turing (wa-láng + tu-ring), *adj.* 1.
without answer; unanswered, referring esp.
to a riddle. Syn. *waláng-sagót.* 2. *(Colloq.)*
ungrateful. Syn. *waláng-utang-na-loób.* 3.
without respect; unrespectful. Syn. *waláng-
galang, waláng-pitagan, pusóng.*

waláng-ulo (wa-láng + u-lo), *adj.* 1. without
a head; headless. 2. without a title or
heading; untitled. Syn. *waláng-pamagát,
waláng-tituló.* 3. without a chief, head, or
leader. Syn. *waláng-punò, waláng-lider.* 4.
(Colloq.) without brains; lacking talents.
Syn. *mahinà ang ulo, waláng-utak, waláng-
talino.*

waláng-utang-na-loób (wa-láng + u-tang +
na + lo-ób), *adj.* ungrateful; not thankful.
Syn. *di-kumíkilala ng utang-na-loób.*

waláng-walâ (wa-láng + wa-lâ), *adj.* without
anything; truly broke or bankrupt.

waláng-wawà (wa-láng + wa-wà), *adj.*
useless; pointless; meaningless. Syn.
waláng-kabuluhán, waláng-kasaysayan.

walâ pa, 1. still out; not yet in. Syn. *di pa
dumárating.* 2. not yet available.

walas (wa-las), *n.* 1. an open, clear place or
space. Syn. *waag, tahaw.* 2. state or
condition of being wide-open and clear.
Syn. *kawaagan, katahawan.*

walat (wa-lat), *n.* 1. demolition or
destruction of structure, esp. of light
materials. Syn. *wasak, pagwasak.* 2. what
remains after the destruction or
demolition. Syn. *wasak, pagkakawasak.*

walay (wa-lay), *n.* 1. act of separating or
living separately from another or others,
esp. of a member of one's family. Syn.
*pagbukód ng tirahan, pamumuhay na mag-
isá.* 2. act of weaning a child from its
mother's breast. Syn. *awat o pag-awat sa
suso.*

waldás (wal-dás), I. *n.* a squandering;
wasteful or extravagant expenditure;
malversation or misappropriation of
funds. Syn. *lustáy, paglustáy.*
—II. *adj.* squandered; spent wastefully or
extravagantly; misappropriated, said of

waligwig   **wiklás**

funds. Syn. *lustáy, nilustáy, nalustáy.*

waligwíg (wa-lig-wíg), n. 1. shaking of the hands, head, or the body to get rid of clinging dust, water, etc. Syn. *wagwág, pagwawagwág.* 2. act of spraying or sprinkling water on clothes to be ironed. Syn. *wilíg, pagwiwilíg.*

walíng-bahalà (wa-líng + ba-ha-là), var. **walaíng-bahalà,** v. to disregard; pay no attention to; forget all about. Syn. *huwág intindihín, huwág pansinín.*

waling-waling (wa-ling + wa-ling), var. **walingwaling,** n. (Bot.) a species of Philippine orchid (*Vanda sanderiana*), said to be a native of the island of Mindanao.

walís (wa-lís), n. 1. broom. 2. sweeping stroke, as of a broom. 3. act of sweeping with a broom. Also, *pagwalís, pagwawalís.* 4. the manner a place was swept with a broom. Also, *pagkáwalís, pagkakáwalís.*

waliswís (wa-lis-wís), n. the fast, swishing movement of the tops of bamboos, small branches of trees, etc. when being blown by the wind. See **lawiswís.** 2. the swishing sound thus produced.

waló (wa-ló), n. & adv. eight. Syn. *otso.*

wansoy (wan-soy; -sóy), var. **wansúy,** n. (Ch.; Bot.) coriander (*Coriandrum sativum Linn.*).

wangkî (wang-kî), n. state or quality of being almost like or similar to another. Also, *pagkakáwangkî.* Syn. *wangis, pagkakáwangis; tulad, pagkakatulad.*

wangis (wa-ngis), n. state or condition of being identical or similar to someone or something.

waráy[1] (wa-ráy), adj. dilapidated; fallen into disrepair. Syn. *wasák.*

Waráy[2] (Wa-ráy), n. (Bis.) the familiar language of the Samar-Leyte area; the natives speaking this language. Same as *Waráy-waráy.*

wardi (war-di) n. act or manner of doing a thing carelessly. Syn. *daskól na paggawâ, pagdaskúl-daskól.*

warì (wa-rì), I. n. 1. opinion; personal view; way of thinking and feeling. Syn. *kurukuró, palagáy.* 2. careful deliberation in one's mind; reflection. Syn. *muni-muni, pagmumuni-muni; dili-dili, pagdidili-dili.*

wasak (wa-sak), n. 1. act or manner of destroying something completely. Also, *pagwasak, pagwawasak.* Syn. *walat, pagwalat, pagwawalat; gibâ, paggibâ, paggigibâ.* 2. the remains of something destroyed completely; ruins. Syn. *guhò, gibâ.*

wasiwas (wa-si-was), n. 1. act or manner of flourishing or waving, for example, a handkerchief, as in making a signal to someone. 2. a waving or flaunting motion, as of a flag in the air. Syn. *wagaywáy, pagwagaywáy.*

wastô (was-tô), I. adj. right; correct; in order; proper. Syn. *tamà, tumpák, ayos, nasaayos.*

—II. n. that which is right, correct, just, lawful, or morally good.

waták (wa-tak), n. state or condition of being disunited or widely separated from one another.

watas (wa-tas), n. understanding or comprehension of what someone heard. Syn. *unawà, pagkaunawà; intindi, pagkaintindi.*

watawat (wa-ta-wat), n. flag; standard or banner. Syn. *bandilà, bandera, estandarte.*

watíng (wa-tíng), n. temporary dimness or blurness of sight, as when a person is dizzy or his eyes is hurt.

wawà[1] (wa-wà), n. mouth of a river; estuary.

wawà[2] (wa-wà), n. 1. meaning; sense. Syn. *saysay, kahulugán.* 2. understanding. Syn. *unawà, pagkaunawà.*

welga (wel-ga), n. (Sp. *huelga*) strike or general walkout (of workers). Syn. *aklás, aklasan.*

wikà (wi-kà), n. 1. language. Syn. *lengguwahe.* 2. that which is said or expressed by someone; statement. Syn. *sabi, sinabi.*

wikaan (wi-ka-an), v. to reprimand; revoke severely. Syn. *kagalitan, pagsalitaan; pagwikaan.*

wiklás (wik-lás), I. n. 1. act of pulling apart something by force, as in tearing off a pocket, or opening a lock. 2. state or condition of being forcibly torn off or opened by force.

—II. adj. torn off or opened forcibly, as a

wiklát

pocket, lock, etc.

wiklát (wik-lát), I. *n.* 1. act of dilating a hole, cavity, or opening by pulling or tearing. Syn. *hiklát, paghiklát.* 2. state or condition of being dilated or enlarged forcibly.
—II. *adj.* dilated or enlarged by pulling or tearing apart. Syn. *hiklát, nahiklát.*

wigwíg (wig-wíg), *n.* sprinkling of water on clothes to be ironed. Syn. *wilíg, waligwíg.*

wili (wi-li), *n.* continuous enjoyment or interest in something; engrossment or absorption of one's interest in something.

wilíg (wi-líg), I. *n.* act or manner of sprinkling water on clothes to be ironed. Syn. *waligwíg, pagwawaligwíg.*
—II. *adj.* moistened by sprinkling with water, referring to clothes to be ironed.

wilwíl (wil-wíl), *n.* act of violently or angrily shaking something held tightly with the mouth, as when a dog caught a big mouse.

windáng (win-dáng), I. *n.* 1. act of tearing something to pieces. Syn. *wasak, pagwasak; luray, pagluray.* 2. state or condition of being torn to pieces.
—II. *adj.* torn to pieces. Syn. *wasák, luráy, gutáy.*

wisík (wi-sík), *n.* 1. act or manner of sprinkling water or liquid with or as with the fingers. Syn. *wilíg, waligwíg.* 2. tiny drops of water or liquid sprinkled with or as with the fingers.

wumagaywáy (wu-ma-gay-wáy), *v.* (present and past) to wave, flaunt, or flutter in the air. Cf. *wumasiwas.*

Y

Y, y (ya), *n.* 1. the twentieth and last letter of the *abakada* (Pilipino alphabet). 2. the type or impression representing this letter. 3. the symbol for the twentieth in a group or series.

'y, the contracted form of *ay,* suffixed to a word ending in a vowel, as in *ako'y* (fr. *ako ay*); or in *w* and *n,* as in *ika'y* (fr. *ikaw ay*) and in *baya'y* (fr. *bayan ay*). Note that in *bayan, n* is omitted.

yakap

yaan (ya-an), *v.* (used as an aphaeresis of *bayaan* and *hayaan,* usually written **'yaan**) to let or leave (someone) alone; allow (one) to continue what he or she is doing.

yaán (ya-án), *pron.* of prov. of *iyan* that: (referring to something near the person addressed).

yabág (ya-bág), *n.* 1. sound of a footstep or footsteps. Syn. *bagsák ng paá.* 2. any similar sound.

yabang (ya-bang), *n.* 1. a bragging or boasting; arrogance; boastfulness. Syn. *kahambugán, paghahambóg.* 2. falsehood; telling lies. Syn. *kasinungalingan, pagsisinungalíng.*

yabó (ya-bó), *n.* 1. sponginess, as of boiled tubers and other root crops. Syn. *labo.* 2. looseness, as of soil. Syn. *kabuhaghagán.*

yabong (ya-bong), *n.* 1. luxuriant growth; dense foliage; state or condition of being leafy. Syn. *kadahunan, pagkamadahon; labay, kalabayan.* 2. prosperity, as of someone's business. Syn. *unlád, pag-unlád.*

yabyáb (yab-yáb), *n.* 1. pounding of rice grains with a pestle in a mortar for the purpose of breaking the husks or shells. Cf. *luba, pagluba.* 2. *(Colloq.)* babble; empty, foolish talk. Syn. *yapyáp, ngawâ, ablá.*

yakag (ya-kag), I. *n.* 1. act of inviting another or others (personally) to go with oneself to a certain place, or to help do something, esp. for free. Syn. *yayà, pagyayà, pagyayayâ.* 2. a person or persons invited in this manner. Syn. *kumbidado.*
—II. *adj.* referring to a person or persons invited personally by someone to help perform a certain work for free.

yakál (ya-kál), I. *n.* 1. *(Bot.)* a kind of timber tree *(Hopea flagta),* the hard wood of which is classified as timber of the "first group" among Philippine lumber. 2. the hard wood or lumber obtained from this tree.
—II. *adj.* of or made of *yakál.*

yakap (ya-kap), *n.* 1. enclosing someone within one's arms; embrace; hug. Syn. *akap, pag-akap; yapós, pagyapós.* 2. someone embraced by another. 3. *(Colloq.)* ready acceptance or taking in, as of certain principles or doctrines, by someone. Syn. *tanggáp, pagtanggáp*. 4. attachment of something to the side surface of another, as a support or reinforcement, by nailing together. Syn. *tapal, pagtatapal (colloq.); sapì, pagsasapì*.

yakis (ya-kis), *n*. 1. a grazing or rubbing of a body or surface against another, as in passing or moving along. Syn. *kiyakis, pagkiyakis, pagkakiyakis; hilahid, paghilahid, pagkáhilahid*. 2. rubbing of one thing against another; friction. Syn. *kiskís, pagkiskís, pagkápakiskís; pingkî, pagpingkî, pagkápingkî*.

yakos (ya-kos), *n*. (*Colloq.*) a great number; pack, as in: *isáng yakos na kasinungalingan*, a pack of lies.

yakyák (yak-yák), I. *n*. 1. foolish or meaningless talk; babble; chatter. Syn. *daldál, ablá, satsát, yapyáp*. 2. (*OTag.*) envy; jealousy. Syn. *inggít, pagkainggít; hilì, pagkahilì, panaghilì*.

—II. *adj*. given to foolish and meaningless talk; fond of chatting or babbling. Syn. *madaldál, masatsát, maablá*.

yagít (ya-gít), *n*. 1. fallen dried twigs or small branches scattered around. Cf. *yabat*. 2. rubbish of flotsam and jetsam carried by the current and left in banks of rivers. Syn. *layák, sukal*. 3. a tramp; vagrant; beggar; any useless individual.

yamâ (ya-mâ), *n*. (*OTag.*) touch; sense of touch. Syn. *hipò*.

yaman[1] (ya-man), *n*. 1. valuable possessions; riches; wealth. Also, *kayamanan*. 2. a becoming rich or wealthy. Also, *pagyaman*. 3. state or condition of being rich or wealthy; richness; wealthiness. Also, *kayamanan, pagkamayaman*. 4. plentifulness; abundance; opulence. Syn. *kasaganaan*.

yaman[2] (ya-man), *adv. & conj.* (usually followed by *din lamang*) since; inasmuch; because. Syn. *gayón din lamang*.

yamang (ya-mang), *adv. & conj.* since; inasmuch as; whereas. Syn. *gayón din lamang*.

yambâ (yam-bâ), *n*. a threatening act or gesture with the hand or with anything held by the hand. Syn. *ambâ, yaang*.

yamo (ya-mo), *v*. (*Colloq.*) short of '*yaan mo* or *bayaan mo*, meaning "to let alone"; let one do what he wants.

yamót (ya-mót), *n*. 1. disgust; exasperation. Syn. *suyà, pagkasuyà; inís, pagkainís; galit, pagkagalit*. 2. boredom; impatience; loss of patience; tiredness, esp. in waiting; ennui. Syn. *iníp, pagkainíp*.

yamungmóng (ya-mung-móng), *n*. 1. luxuriant growth, esp. of leaves or foliage; frondescence. Syn. *yabong, kayabungan; kadahuhan, pagkamadahon; labay o kalabayan ng mga dahon*. 2. shade; shady place, esp. under the luxuriant growth of foliage of trees. Syn. *lilim (lilom)*. 3. (*Poetic*) protective care. Syn. *tangkilik, pagtangkilik; kandili, pagkandili*.

yamutmót (ya-mut-mót), *n*. 1. loose ends of fibers or thread, esp. those frayed or ravelled due to overuse. Syn. *mulmól, himulmól*. 2. fibrous part of husks or the like. Syn. *yanot*. 3. shavings or scrapings scattered all around.

yaníg (ya-níg), I. *n*. 1. shaking or tremor, as of buildings, mountains, earth, etc. 2. shock; a violent shake, as in collision. Syn. *malakás na alóg o pagkaalóg*. 3. any sudden disturbance or agitation of the mind or emotions, as a result of loss or surprise. Syn. *matindíng dagok*.

—II. *adj*. strongly shaken, as the earth during an earthquake.

yanot (ya-not), *n*. 1. coarse fibers, as of coconut husks. Syn. *yamutmót*, sense 2. 2. loose ends of fibers or treads, esp. of ravelled or frayed clothes. Syn. *mulmól, himulmól*.

yantók (yan-tók), I. *n*. 1. (*Bot.*) the rattan palm. Syn. *uwáy, bihuko, palasan*. 2. the long stem of this plant, usually made into canes, sticks, and furniture, like chairs, tables, etc. 3. strips of this plant, usually used for tying and for wickerworks.

—II. *adj*. of or made of rattan.

yangít (ya-ngít), *n*. fallen dried twigs or small branches of trees. See **yagít**.

yangyáng (yang-yáng), *n*. act or manner of exposing something in the air, esp. by hanging on a line, in order to dry. Also, *pagyayangyáng*. Syn. *pagbibilad o* *pagsasampáy sa hanginan upang matuyô.*

yao (ya-o), *n.* 1. act of leaving or going away; departure. Also, *pagyao.* Syn. *yaon, pagyaon; alís, pag-alís; lisan, paglisan.* 2. passing way of a person; death; demise. Syn. *pagkamatáy, kamatayan, pagpanaw.*

yaón (ya-ón), *pron. & adj.* that which is understood and mentioned before and also far from both the speaker and the one addressed. Syn. *iyón.*

yapá (ya-pá), *n.* insipidity or tastelessness of solid food due to dryness or juicelessness. Syn. *tabáng o kawaláng-lasa dahil sa katuyután.*

yapak (ya-pak), var. **apak, tapak,** *n.* 1. act of stepping or putting down one's foot on something. Also, *pag-apak, pagyapak, pagtapak.* Syn. *tuntóng, pagtuntóng.* 2. footstep; footprint; step. Syn. *apak, tapak, bakás ng paá.* 3. footfall. Syn. *bagsák ng paá, yabág.*

yapák (ya-pák), var. **apák, tapák,** *adj.* not wearing anything on one's feet; barefoot; barefooted. Syn. *waláng-suót sa paá.*

yapós (ya-pós), I. *n.* 1. a close, affectionate embrace or hug. Syn. *magiliw at mahigpít na yakap.* 2. a tight clasp or hold with the arms, as in wrestling or in a fight.
—II. *adj.* held or clasped tightly in one's arms.

yapyáp (yap-yáp), *n.* 1. idle or meaningless talking; chatter. Syn. *satsát, daldál.* 2. a person given to such kind of talking.

yarda (yar-da), *n.* (*Sp.*) 1. a measure of length equal to 3 feet or 36 inches; yard. 2. act or manner of measuring something in yards. Also, *pagyarda, pagyayarda.* 3. the manner a thing was measured in yards. Also, *pagkakáyarda.*

yari (ya-ri), *n.* an obsolescent root still traceable in some derivatives like *mangyari, pangyayari, kapangyarihan, etc.*

yarí (ya-rí), *pron.* this (referring to something close to the speaker's self). Syn. *irí, itó.*

yarì (ya-rì), I. *n.* 1. act of making or manufacturing something. Also, *pagyarì.* Syn. *gawâ, paggawâ.* 2. the manner a thing was made or manufactured. Syn. *pagkágawâ, pagkáyarì.* 3. completion or

finishing of something being done, manufactured, or built. Syn. *tapos, pagtapos.* 4. the things made or completed. Syn. *mga bagay na natapos o nayari.* 5. output; amount produced. Syn. *dami ng produkto o nagawâ.* 6. style; make; build. Syn. *kayarian, modelo.*
—II. *adj.* 1. made or manufactured by. Syn. *gawâ ni, gawâ ng.* 2. ready-made.

yatà (ya-tà), *adv.* perhaps; maybe; possibly; probably. Syn. *tila, marahil, warì.*

yate (ya-te), *n.* (*Sp.*) yacht.

yawà (ya-wà), I. *n.* (*Bis.*) Satan; the Devil.
—II. *interj.* exclamation expressing impatience or emotional distrust.

yaya (ya-ya), *n.* (*Mex.*) wet nurse. Syn. *sisiwa, mamáy, ama.*

yayà (ya-yà), I. *n.* 1. act of inviting (another or others) personally to come along to a certain place to help do something. Syn. *yakag, pagyakag.* 2. a person or persons invited in this manner.
—II. *adj.* said of a person or persons invited personally to help do a certain work. Syn. *yakag, niyakag.*

yayao (ya-ya-o), *v.* (fut. tense) & *adj.* set to leave or depart. Syn. *áalís, lílisan.*

yayat (ya-yat), *n.* emaciation; wasting away of body; abnormal leanness caused by lack of food, by disease, etc. Syn. *payat, pagpayat, pangangayayat.*

Yeba (Ye-ba), *interj.* (prob. a coined word fr. Sp. *Viva!*) Long live! Hurrah! Syn. *Mabuhay!* Note: The word was popularized by former Mayor Antonio J. Villegas during his incumbency.

yelo[1] (ye-lo), *n.* (Sp. *hielo*) 1. ice. 2. snow. Syn. *niyebe.*

yelo[2] (ye-lo), *n. & adj.* (*Eng.*) yellow (color). Syn. *diláw, amarilyo.*

yema (ye-ma), *n.* (*Sp.*) egg yolk. Syn. *pulá ng itlóg.*

yerbabuwena (yer-ba-bu-we-na), var. **herbabuwena,** *n.* (Bot.; Sp. *yerbabuena*) peppermint; marshmint (*Mentha arvensis Linn.*).

yero (ye-ro), *n.* (Sp. *hierro*) 1. galvanized iron sheet. Syn. *sim.* 2. (*Med.*) iron; a tonic or other preparations containing iron.

yeso (ye-so), n. (Sp.) 1. chalk, as that used in writing on blackboards. Syn. tsok, tisà. 2. plaster of paris; gypsum.

yirí (yi-rí), var. of yarí.

'yon ('yon), aphaeresis of "iyón."

yoyò (yo-yò), n. a kind of spool-like toy attached to a string upon which it may be made to spin up and down by manipulating the string; yo-yo.

yukayok (yu-ka-yok), n. 1. state or condition of being crestfallen, dejected, or disheartened. 2. complete exhaustion or weariness due to being heavily burdened with work, misfortunes, etc.

yukô (yu-kô), I. n. 1. act of bending the body or lowering the head forward, as in passing a low clearance. Syn. ukô, pag-ukô; ukód, pag-ukód; yukód, pagyukód. 2. the bent position of the head or body. 3. condescension. Syn. pagpapakumbabâ, paggalang.
—II. adj. 1. with the head or body bent forward. Syn. ukô, nakaukô; ukód, nakaukód; yukód, nakayukód. 2. bowing one's head in defeat. Syn. sukò.

yukód (yu-kód), n. bending of head or body in respect, greeting, or salute. Syn. yukô, pagyukô; ukô, pag-ukô; ukód, pag-ukód.

yukos (yu-kos), n. 1. act of crushing something into creases or wrinkles; crumpling something with one's hand or hands. Syn. kuyumos, pagkuyumos; lamukos, paglamukos. 2. creases or wrinkles, as in clothes, paper, etc. Syn. lukot, yukot.

yukyók (yuk-yók), I. n. 1. a squatting or crouching position, as of an animal cowering in fear. 2. gradual fall or sinking, as of loose pile of soil, garbage, etc. Syn. ukók, pag-ukók. 3. the sunken condition of a loose pile of soil, garbage, etc. Syn. pagkaukok, kaukukán.
—II. adj. sunken, referring to a loose pile of soil, garbage, etc. Syn. ukók, umukók.

yugayog (yu-ga-yog), n. 1. violent shaking, as of the branches of trees during a storm. 2. act or manner of shaking something violently, as in causing dried leaves or fruits to fall. Syn. yugyóg, pagyugyóg; ugaog, pag-ugaog.

yugtô (yug-tô), n. 1. division or act in a play or drama. Syn. akto. 2. part (in a series), as in: unang yugtô, first part.

yugyóg (yug-yóg), n. 1. act or manner of shaking (something) up and down. Cf. yugayog, ugóg. 2. state or condition of being shaken up and down.

yumamót (yu-ma-mót), v. to make someone annoyed or irritated. Also, magpayamót. Syn. uminís, magpainís.

yumaníg (yu-ma-níg), v. to shake or be shaken, as the earth. Syn. lumindól.

yumao (yu-ma-o), v. 1. to go or leave; depart. Syn. umalís, lumakad. 2. to die; pass away. Syn. mamatáy.

yumarì (yu-ma-rì), v. 1. to make or manufacture. Syn. gumawâ. 2. to build or construct. Syn. magtayô.

yumì (yu-mì), n. 1. refined manners or modest behavior, esp. of a young lady. Syn. hinhín, kahinhinán; binì, kabinian; kapinuhan (sa kilos). 2. softness or tenderness (of texture) to the touch. Syn. lambót at kapinuhan sa hipò.

yumukô (yu-mu-kô), v. 1. to stoop; bend one's head down, as in passing a low clearance. Syn. tumungó. 2. to bow one's head, as in respect or greeting. Syn. yumukód, umukód. 3. to respect (someone). Syn. gumalang.

yumurak (yu-mu-rak), v. 1. to crush something under one's feet; trample on or upon. Syn. tapakan. 2. to violate; make an infringement or breach of someone's right, etc. Syn. lumabág, labagín.

yunot (yu-not), n. coarse fibers like that of the coconut husk. Syn. bunót.

yungíb (yu-ngíb), n. cave; cavern. Syn. kuweba, lungaw.

yungyóng (yung-yóng), n. 1. overhanging or projection, as of a big branch over something. Cf. lukob, paglukob. 2. something that overhangs or projects over or beyond another; an overhanging part. 3. putting someone or something under one's protection or care. Syn. kandili, pagkandili. 4. act of looming over another or others; domination. Syn. sakop, pagsakop.

yupapà (yu-pa-pà), n. an obsolescent root, meaning "obeisance" or "gesture of respect, homage or deference," from which *mangayupapà, pangayupapaan, pangangayupapà,* etc. are derived.

yupì (yu-pì), n. 1. a small hollow or dent, as on the surface of a thin metal sheet, can, and the like. 2. a small fold on the edge of a metal plate. Syn. *lupî, tupí.*

yupyóp (yup-yóp), n. 1. act of sitting on eggs to hatch them; brooding. Syn. *limlím, paglimlím; halimlím, paghalimhim.* 2. act of protecting or covering (offspring, etc.) with the wings or by sitting on them. 3. (*Colloq.*) a delaying action, as in the approval of a written request, etc. Syn. *pagbimbín.*

yurak (yu-rak), n. 1. act of treading heavily on something in order to crush or destroy; trampling on something. Syn. *tapak, pagtapak; yasák, pagyasák.* 2. violation or infringement, as of someone's right, etc. Syn. *labág, paglabág.*

yutà (yu-tà), n. & adj. hundred thousand. Syn. *sandaanlibo.*

yutà-yutà (yu-tà + yu-tà), I. adj. hundreds and hundreds of thousand; very many; countless.

—II. adv. in countless number; by hundreds and hundreds of thousand.